Application Deadlines

You are encouraged to submit your materials by June 15 of your junior year. You may apply until November 1 of your senior year if you wish to enroll in graduate courses in your final undergraduate semester.

For more information, contact:

The Department of Economics
www.suffolk.edu/economics
econ@suffolk.edu
617.573.8259
 or
The Office of Graduate Admission
www.suffolk.edu/gradadm
grad.admission@suffolk.edu
617.573.8302

Earn a **Value-Added** Education

The Five-Year Joint Bachelor's and Master's Degree in Economics at Suffolk University

SUFFOLK
UNIVERSITY
COLLEGE OF ARTS & SCIENCES

Produced by OUC 111009

Four Undergraduate Years +
One Graduate Year =
Two Degrees

Looking for an economical way to accelerate your studies? **You can earn a master's degree at Suffolk University in one academic year upon completing your BA or BS in Economics or International Economics.** This program is ideal for economics majors seeking to further their knowledge of the field and strengthen their quantitative and analytical skills.

Graduate Degree Options

During your fourth year at Suffolk, you may choose to pursue one of these three graduate degrees:
- Master of Science in Economics
- Master of Science in Economic Policy
- Master of Science in International Economics

Talk to your faculty advisor to determine which degree is best suited to your career goals and interests.

Applicant Profile

You must complete your junior year with an overall GPA of 3.0 or higher, and a 3.3 GPA or higher in at least three economics major courses taken at Suffolk.

Application Process

While you will need to complete an official graduate admission application, you do not need to take the GRE. This requirement is waived for joint degree applicants.

Graduate Degree Curricula

Please note: Eight undergraduate credit hours are waived for joint degree candidates in all three graduate programs.

MASTER OF SCIENCE IN ECONOMICS

- Macroeconomics
- Applied Microeconomics
- Applied Econometrics
- Topics in Economics *or*
  Topics in International Economics
- Six Electives

MASTER OF SCIENCE IN ECONOMIC POLICY

- Macroeconomics
- Applied Microeconomics
- Public Economics: Tax and Budget Policy
- Economics of Regulation
- Cost-Benefit Analysis and Impact Evaluation
- Public Choice
- Applied Econometrics
- Applied Time Series Methods
- Topics in Economics
- One Elective

MASTER OF SCIENCE IN INTERNATIONAL ECONOMICS

- Macroeconomics
- Applied Microeconomics
- International Trade Theory and Policy
- International Monetary Economics
- International Financial Economics
- Applied Econometrics
- Global Data Analysis
- Applied Time Series Methods
- Topics in International Economics *or*
  Topics in Economics
- One Elective

Michael Parkin

Economics

Custom Edition for Suffolk University

Taken from:
Economics, Tenth Edition
by Michael Parkin

Pearson Learning Solutions, 501 Boylston Street, Suite 900, Boston, MA 02116
A Pearson Education Company
www.pearsoned.com

Printed in the United States of America

1 2 3 4 5 6 7 8 9 10 V011 16 15 14 13 12 11

000200010270765663

RH

ISBN 10: 1-256-13969-6
ISBN 13: 978-1-256-13969-0

TO ROBIN

Michael Parkin is Professor Emeritus in the Department of Economics at the University of Western Ontario, Canada. Professor Parkin has held faculty appointments at Brown University, the University of Manchester, the University of Essex, and Bond University. He is a past president of the Canadian Economics Association and has served on the editorial boards of the *American Economic Review* and the *Journal of Monetary Economics* and as managing editor of the *Canadian Journal of Economics*. Professor Parkin's research on macroeconomics, monetary economics, and international economics has resulted in over 160 publications in journals and edited volumes, including the *American Economic Review*, the *Journal of Political Economy*, the *Review of Economic Studies*, the *Journal of Monetary Economics*, and the *Journal of Money, Credit and Banking*. He became most visible to the public with his work on inflation that discredited the use of wage and price controls. Michael Parkin also spearheaded the movement toward European monetary union. Professor Parkin is an experienced and dedicated teacher of introductory economics.

PART ONE
INTRODUCTION 1
CHAPTER 1 What Is Economics? 1
CHAPTER 2 The Economic Problem 29

PART TWO
HOW MARKETS WORK 55
CHAPTER 3 Demand and Supply 55
CHAPTER 4 Elasticity 83
CHAPTER 5 Efficiency and Equity 105
CHAPTER 6 Government Actions in Markets 127
CHAPTER 7 Global Markets in Action 151

PART THREE
HOUSEHOLDS' CHOICES 179
CHAPTER 8 Utility and Demand 179
CHAPTER 9 Possibilities, Preferences, and Choices 203

PART FOUR
FIRMS AND MARKETS 227
CHAPTER 10 Organizing Production 227
CHAPTER 11 Output and Costs 251
CHAPTER 12 Perfect Competition 273
CHAPTER 13 Monopoly 299
CHAPTER 14 Monopolistic Competition 323
CHAPTER 15 Oligopoly 341

PART FIVE
MARKET FAILURE AND GOVERNMENT 371
CHAPTER 16 Public Choices and Public Goods 371
CHAPTER 17 Economics of the Environment 393

PART SIX
FACTOR MARKETS, INEQUALITY, AND UNCERTAINTY 417
CHAPTER 18 Markets for Factors of Production 417
CHAPTER 19 Economic Inequality 441
CHAPTER 20 Uncertainty and Information 465

PART SEVEN
MONITORING MACROECONOMIC PERFORMANCE 489
CHAPTER 21 Measuring GDP and Economic Growth 489
CHAPTER 22 Monitoring Jobs and Inflation 513

PART EIGHT
MACROECONOMIC TRENDS 539
CHAPTER 23 Economic Growth 539
CHAPTER 24 Finance, Saving, and Investment 565
CHAPTER 25 Money, the Price Level, and Inflation 589
CHAPTER 26 The Exchange Rate and the Balance of Payments 617

PART NINE
MACROECONOMIC FLUCTUATIONS 647
CHAPTER 27 Aggregate Supply and Aggregate Demand 647
CHAPTER 28 Expenditure Multipliers: The Keynesian Model 671
CHAPTER 29 U.S. Inflation, Unemployment, and Business Cycle 701

PART TEN
MACROECONOMIC POLICY 727
CHAPTER 30 Fiscal Policy 727
CHAPTER 31 Monetary Policy 753

Micro Flexibility

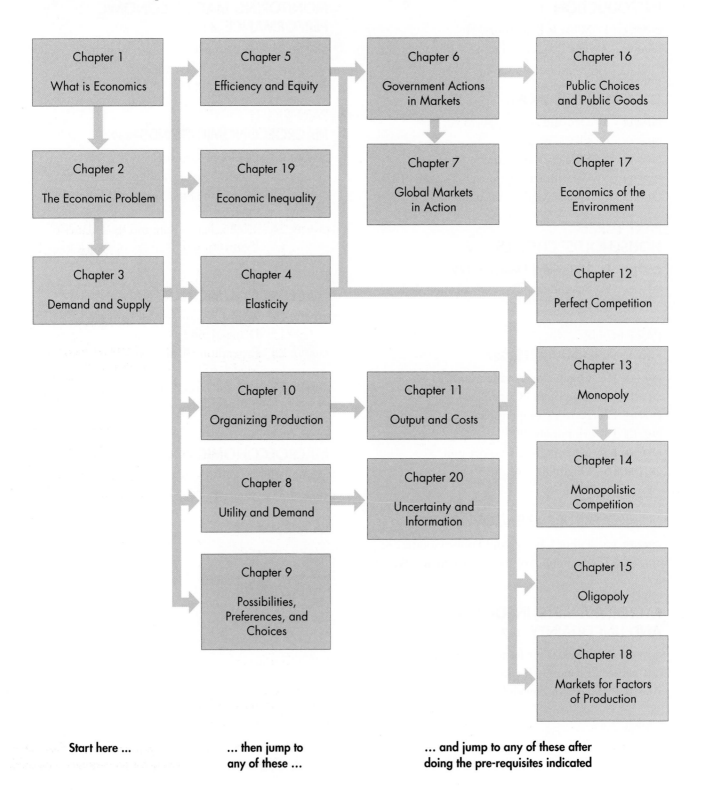

Macro Flexibility

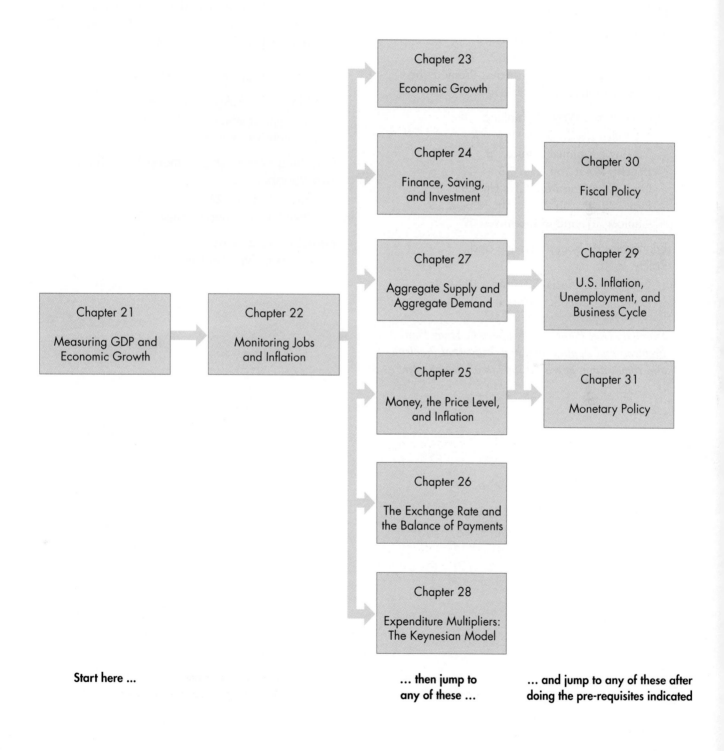

Start here ...   ... then jump to   ... and jump to any of these after
                                   any of these ...   doing the pre-requisites indicated

TABLE OF CONTENTS

PART ONE
INTRODUCTION 1

CHAPTER 1 ◆ WHAT IS ECONOMICS? 1

Definition of Economics 2

Two Big Economic Questions 3
What, How, and For Whom? 3
Can the Pursuit of Self-Interest Promote the
Social Interest? 5

The Economic Way of Thinking 8
A Choice Is a Tradeoff 8
Making a Rational Choice 8
Benefit: What You Gain 8
Cost: What You *Must* Give Up 8
How Much? Choosing at the Margin 9
Choices Respond to Incentives 9

Economics as Social Science and
Policy Tool 10
Economist as Social Scientist 10
Economist as Policy Adviser 10

*Summary (Key Points and Key Terms), Study Plan
Problems and Applications, and Additional Problems
and Applications appear at the end of each chapter.*

APPENDIX Graphs in Economics 13

Graphing Data 13
Scatter Diagrams 14

Graphs Used in Economic Models 16
Variables That Move in the Same Direction 16
Variables That Move in Opposite Directions 17
Variables That Have a Maximum or a
Minimum 18
Variables That Are Unrelated 19

The Slope of a Relationship 20
The Slope of a Straight Line 20
The Slope of a Curved Line 21

Graphing Relationships Among More Than
Two Variables 22
Ceteris Paribus 22
When Other Things Change 23

MATHEMATICAL NOTE
Equations of Straight Lines 24

CHAPTER 2 ◆ THE ECONOMIC PROBLEM   29

Production Possibilities and Opportunity Cost   30
Production Possibilities Frontier   30
Production Efficiency   31
Tradeoff Along the *PPF*   31
Opportunity Cost   31

Using Resources Efficiently   33
The *PPF* and Marginal Cost   33
Preferences and Marginal Benefit   34
Allocative Efficiency   35

Economic Growth   36
The Cost of Economic Growth   36
A Nation's Economic Growth   37

Gains from Trade   38
Comparative Advantage and Absolute Advantage   38
Achieving the Gains from Trade   39

Economic Coordination   41
Firms   41
Markets   42
Property Rights   42
Money   42
Circular Flows Through Markets   42
Coordinating Decisions   42

READING BETWEEN THE LINES
The Rising Opportunity Cost of Food   44

PART ONE **WRAP-UP** ◆

Understanding the Scope of Economics
Your Economic Revolution   51

Talking with
Jagdish Bhagwati   52

PART TWO
HOW MARKETS WORK   55

CHAPTER 3 ◆ DEMAND AND SUPPLY   55

Markets and Prices   56

Demand   57
The Law of Demand   57
Demand Curve and Demand Schedule   57
A Change in Demand   58
A Change in the Quantity Demanded Versus a Change in Demand   60

Supply   62
The Law of Supply   62
Supply Curve and Supply Schedule   62
A Change in Supply   63
A Change in the Quantity Supplied Versus a Change in Supply   64

Market Equilibrium   66
Price as a Regulator   66
Price Adjustments   67

Predicting Changes in Price and Quantity   68
An Increase in Demand   68
A Decrease in Demand   68
An Increase in Supply   70
A Decrease in Supply   70
All the Possible Changes in Demand and Supply   72

READING BETWEEN THE LINES
Demand and Supply: The Price of Coffee   74

MATHEMATICAL NOTE
Demand, Supply, and Equilibrium   76

CHAPTER 4 ◆ ELASTICITY 83

Price Elasticity of Demand 84
Calculating Price Elasticity of Demand 85
Inelastic and Elastic Demand 86
Elasticity Along a Linear Demand Curve 87
Total Revenue and Elasticity 88
Your Expenditure and Your Elasticity 89
The Factors That Influence the Elasticity of Demand 89

More Elasticities of Demand 91
Cross Elasticity of Demand 91
Income Elasticity of Demand 92

Elasticity of Supply 94
Calculating the Elasticity of Supply 94
The Factors That Influence the Elasticity of Supply 95

READING BETWEEN THE LINES
The Elasticities of Demand and Supply for Tomatoes 98

CHAPTER 5 ◆ EFFICIENCY AND EQUITY 105

Resource Allocation Methods 106
Market Price 106
Command 106
Majority Rule 106
Contest 106
First-Come, First-Served 106
Lottery 107
Personal Characteristics 107
Force 107

Benefit, Cost, and Surplus 108
Demand, Willingness to Pay, and Value 108
Individual Demand and Market Demand 108
Consumer Surplus 109
Supply and Marginal Cost 109
Supply, Cost, and Minimum Supply-Price 110
Individual Supply and Market Supply 110
Producer Surplus 111

Is the Competitive Market Efficient? 112
Efficiency of Competitive Equilibrium 112
Market Failure 113
Sources of Market Failure 114
Alternatives to the Market 115

Is the Competitive Market Fair? 116
It's Not Fair If the *Result* Isn't Fair 116
It's Not Fair If the *Rules* Aren't Fair 118
Case Study: A Water Shortage in a Natural Disaster 118

READING BETWEEN THE LINES
Is the Global Market for Roses Efficient? 120

CHAPTER 6 ◆ GOVERNMENT ACTIONS IN MARKETS   127

A Housing Market With a Rent Ceiling   128
A Housing Shortage   128
Increased Search Activity   128
A Black Market   128
Inefficiency of a Rent Ceiling   129
Are Rent Ceilings Fair?   130

A Labor Market With a Minimum Wage   131
Minimum Wage Brings Unemployment   131
Inefficiency of a Minimum Wage   131
Is the Minimum Wage Fair?   132

Taxes   133
Tax Incidence   133
A Tax on Sellers   133
A Tax on Buyers   134
Equivalence of Tax on Buyers and Sellers   134
Tax Incidence and Elasticity of Demand   135
Tax Incidence and Elasticity of Supply   136
Taxes and Efficiency   137
Taxes and Fairness   138

Production Quotas and Subsidies   139
Production Quotas   139
Subsidies   140

Markets for Illegal Goods   142
A Free Market for a Drug   142
A Market for an Illegal Drug   142
Legalizing and Taxing Drugs   143

READING BETWEEN THE LINES
Government Actions in Labor Markets   144

CHAPTER 7 ◆ GLOBAL MARKETS IN ACTION   151

How Global Markets Work   152
International Trade Today   152
What Drives International Trade?   152
Why the United States Imports T-Shirts   153
Why the United States Exports Airplanes   154

Winners, Losers, and the Net Gain from Trade   155
Gains and Losses from Imports   155
Gains and Losses from Exports   156
Gains for All   156

International Trade Restrictions   157
Tariffs   157
Import Quotas   160
Other Import Barriers   162
Export Subsidies   162

The Case Against Protection   163
The Infant-Industry Argument   163
The Dumping Argument   163
Saves Jobs   164
Allows Us to Compete with Cheap Foreign Labor   164
Penalizes Lax Environmental Standards   164
Prevents Rich Countries from Exploiting Developing Countries   165
Offshore Outsourcing   165
Avoiding Trade Wars   166
Why Is International Trade Restricted?   166
Compensating Losers   167

READING BETWEEN THE LINES
A Tarriff on Tires   168

PART TWO WRAP-UP ◆

Understanding How Markets Work
The Amazing Market   175

Talking with
Susan Athey   176

PART THREE
HOUSEHOLDS' CHOICES 179

CHAPTER 8 ◆ UTILITY AND DEMAND   179

Consumption Choices   180
Consumption Possibilities   180
Preferences   181

Utility-Maximizing Choice   183
A Spreadsheet Solution   183
Choosing at the Margin   184
The Power of Marginal Analysis   186
Revealing Preferences   186

Predictions of Marginal Utility Theory   187
A Fall in the Price of a Movie   187
A Rise in the Price of Soda   189
A Rise in Income   190
The Paradox of Value   191
Temperature: An Analogy   192

New Ways of Explaining Consumer
Choices   194
Behavioral Economics   194
Neuroeconomics   195
Controversy   195

READING BETWEEN THE LINES
A Paradox of Value: Paramedics and Hockey
Players   196

CHAPTER 9 ◆ POSSIBILITIES, PREFERENCES,
AND CHOICES   203

Consumption Possibilities   204
Budget Equation   205

Preferences and Indifference Curves   207
Marginal Rate of Substitution   208
Degree of Substitutability   209

Predicting Consumer Choices   210
Best Affordable Choice   210
A Change in Price   211
A Change in Income   213
Substitution Effect and Income Effect   214

READING BETWEEN THE LINES
Paper Books Versus e-Books   216

PART THREE WRAP-UP ◆

Understanding Households' Choices
Making the Most of Life 223

Talking with
Steven D. Levitt 224

PART FOUR
FIRMS AND MARKETS 227

CHAPTER 10 ◆ ORGANIZING
                PRODUCTION 227

The Firm and Its Economic Problem 228
The Firm's Goal 228
Accounting Profit 228
Economic Accounting 228
A Firm's Opportunity Cost of Production 228
Economic Accounting: A Summary 229
Decisions 229
The Firm's Constraints 230

Technological and Economic Efficiency 231
Technological Efficiency 231
Economic Efficiency 231

Information and Organization 233
Command Systems 233
Incentive Systems 233
Mixing the Systems 233
The Principal-Agent Problem 234
Coping with the Principal-Agent Problem 234
Types of Business Organization 234
Pros and Cons of Different Types of Firms 235

Markets and the Competitive Environment 237
Measures of Concentration 238
Limitations of a Concentration Measure 240

Produce or Outsource? Firms and Markets 242
Firm Coordination 242
Market Coordination 242
Why Firms? 242

READING BETWEEN THE LINES
Battling for Markets in Internet Advertising 244

CHAPTER 11 ◆ OUTPUT AND COSTS 251

Decision Time Frames 252
The Short Run 252
The Long Run 252

Short-Run Technology Constraint 253
Product Schedules 253
Product Curves 253
Total Product Curve 254
Marginal Product Curve 254
Average Product Curve 256

Short-Run Cost 257
Total Cost 257
Marginal Cost 258
Average Cost 258
Marginal Cost and Average Cost 258
Why the Average Total Cost Curve Is
  U-Shaped 258
Cost Curves and Product Curves 260
Shifts in the Cost Curves 260

Long-Run Cost 262
The Production Function 262
Short-Run Cost and Long-Run Cost 262
The Long-Run Average Cost Curve 264
Economies and Diseconomies of Scale 264

READING BETWEEN THE LINES
Cutting the Cost of Producing Electricity 266

CHAPTER 12 ◆ PERFECT COMPETITION 273

What Is Perfect Competition? 274
How Perfect Competition Arises 274
Price Takers 274
Economic Profit and Revenue 274
The Firm's Decisions 275

The Firm's Output Decision 276
Marginal Analysis and the Supply Decision 277
Temporary Shutdown Decision 278
The Firm's Supply Curve 279

Output, Price, and Profit in the Short Run 280
Market Supply in the Short Run 280
Short-Run Equilibrium 281
A Change in Demand 281
Profits and Losses in the Short Run 281
Three Possible Short-Run Outcomes 282

Output, Price, and Profit in the Long Run 283
Entry and Exit 283
A Closer Look at Entry 284
A Closer Look at Exit 284
Long-Run Equilibrium 285

Changing Tastes and Advancing Technology 286
A Permanent Change in Demand 286
External Economies and Diseconomies 287
Technological Change 289

Competition and Efficiency 290
Efficient Use of Resources 290
Choices, Equilibrium, and Efficiency 290

READING BETWEEN THE LINES
Perfect Competition in Corn 292

CHAPTER 13 ◆ MONOPOLY 299

Monopoly and How It Arises 300
How Monopoly Arises 300
Monopoly Price-Setting Strategies 301

A Single-Price Monopoly's Output and Price Decision 302
Price and Marginal Revenue 302
Marginal Revenue and Elasticity 303
Price and Output Decision 304

Single-Price Monopoly and Competition Compared 306
Comparing Price and Output 306
Efficiency Comparison 307
Redistribution of Surpluses 308
Rent Seeking 308
Rent-Seeking Equilibrium 308

Price Discrimination 309
Capturing Consumer Surplus 309
Profiting by Price Discriminating 310
Perfect Price Discrimination 311
Efficiency and Rent Seeking with Price Discrimination 312

Monopoly Regulation 313
Efficient Regulation of a Natural Monopoly 313
Second-Best Regulation of a Natural Monopoly 314

READING BETWEEN THE LINES
Is Google Misusing Monopoly Power? 316

CHAPTER 14 ◆ MONOPOLISTIC
                COMPETITION   323

What Is Monopolistic Competition?   324
    Large Number of Firms   324
    Product Differentiation   324
    Competing on Quality, Price, and Marketing
        324
    Entry and Exit   325
    Examples of Monopolistic Competition   325

Price and Output in Monopolistic
Competition   326
    The Firm's Short-Run Output and Price
        Decision   326
    Profit Maximizing Might Be Loss
        Minimizing   326
    Long-Run: Zero Economic Profit   327
    Monopolistic Competition and Perfect
        Competition   328
    Is Monopolistic Competition Efficient?   329

Product Development and Marketing   330
    Innovation and Product Development   330
    Advertising   330
    Using Advertising to Signal Quality   332
    Brand Names   333
    Efficiency of Advertising and Brand Names   333

READING BETWEEN THE LINES
    Product Differentiation and Entry in the Market
        for Smart Phones   334

CHAPTER 15 ◆ OLIGOPOLY   341

What Is Oligopoly?   342
    Barriers to Entry   342
    Small Number of Firms   343
    Examples of Oligopoly   343

Oligopoly Games   344
    What Is a Game?   344
    The Prisoners' Dilemma   344
    An Oligopoly Price-Fixing Game   346
    Other Oligopoly Games   350
    The Disappearing Invisible Hand   351
    A Game of Chicken   352

Repeated Games and Sequential
Games   353
    A Repeated Duopoly Game   353
    A Sequential Entry Game in a Contestable
        Market   354

Antitrust Law   356
    The Antitrust Laws   356
    Price Fixing Always Illegal   357
    Three Antitrust Policy Debates   357
    Mergers and Acquisitions   359

READING BETWEEN THE LINES
    Gillete and Schick in a Duopoly Game   360

PART FOUR WRAP-UP ◆

Understanding Firms and Markets
Managing Change and Limiting Market
Power   367

Talking with
Thomas Hubbard   368

PART FIVE
MARKET FAILURE AND GOVERNMENT 371

CHAPTER 16 ◆ PUBLIC CHOICES AND PUBLIC GOODS 371

Public Choices 372
Why Governments Exist 372
Public Choice and the Political Marketplace 372
Political Equilibrium 373
What is a Public Good? 374
A Fourfold Classification 374
Mixed Goods and Externalities 374
Inefficiencies that Require Public Choices 376

Providing Public Goods 377
The Free-Rider Problem 377
Marginal Social Benefit from a Public Good 377
Marginal Social Cost of a Public Good 378
Efficient Quantity of a Public Good 378
Inefficient Private Provision 378
Efficient Public Provision 378
Inefficient Public Overprovision 380

Providing Mixed Goods with External Benefits 381
Private Benefits and Social Benefits 381
Government Actions in the Market for a Mixed Good with External Benefits 382
Bureaucratic Inefficiency and Government Failure 383
Health-Care Services 384

READING BETWEEN THE LINES
Reforming Health Care 386

CHAPTER 17 ◆ ECONOMICS OF THE ENVIRONMENT 393

Negative Externalities: Pollution 394
Sources of Pollution 394
Effects of Pollution 394
Private Cost and Social Cost of Pollution 395
Production and Pollution: How Much? 396
Property Rights 396
The Coase Theorem 397
Government Actions in a Market with External Costs 398

The Tragedy of the Commons 400
Sustainable Use of a Renewable Resource 400
The Overuse of a Common Resource 402
Achieving an Efficient Outcome 403

READING BETWEEN THE LINES
Tax Versus Cap-and-Trade 406

PART FIVE WRAP-UP ◆

Understanding Market Failure and Government
We, the People, … 413

Talking with
Caroline M. Hoxby 414

PART SIX
FACTOR MARKETS, INEQUALITY, AND UNCERTAINTY 417

CHAPTER 18 ◆ MARKETS FOR FACTORS OF PRODUCTION 417

The Anatomy of Factor Markets 418
  Markets for Labor Services 418
  Markets for Capital Services 418
  Markets for Land Services and Natural Resources 418
  Entrepreneurship 418

The Demand for a Factor of Production 419
  Value of Marginal Product 419
  A Firm's Demand for Labor 419
  A Firm's Demand for Labor Curve 420
  Changes in a Firm's Demand for Labor 421

Labor Markets 422
  A Competitive Labor Market 422
  A Labor Market with a Union 424
  Scale of the Union–Nonunion Wage Gap 426
  Trends and Differences in Wage Rates 427

Capital and Natural Resource Markets 428
  Capital Rental Markets 428
  Land Rental Markets 428
  Nonrenewable Natural Resource Markets 429

READING BETWEEN THE LINES
  The Labor Market in Action 432

MATHEMATICAL NOTE
Present Value and Discounting 434

CHAPTER 19 ◆ ECONOMIC INEQUALITY 441

Economic Inequality in the United States 442
  The Distribution of Income 442
  The Income Lorenz Curve 443
  The Distribution of Wealth 444
  Wealth or Income? 444
  Annual or Lifetime Income and Wealth? 445
  Trends in Inequality 445
  Poverty 446

Inequality in the World Economy 448
  Income Distributions in Selected Countries 448
  Global Inequality and Its Trends 449

The Sources of Economic Inequality 450
  Human Capital 450
  Discrimination 452
  Contests Among Superstars 453
  Unequal Wealth 454

Income Redistribution 455
  Income Taxes 455
  Income Maintenance Programs 455
  Subsidized Services 455
  The Big Tradeoff 456

READING BETWEEN THE LINES
  Trends in Incomes of the Super Rich 458

CHAPTER 20 ◆ UNCERTAINTY AND INFORMATION   465

Decisions in the Face of Uncertainty   466
Expected Wealth   466
Risk Aversion   466
Utility of Wealth   466
Expected Utility   467
Making a Choice with Uncertainty   468

Buying and Selling Risk   469
Insurance Markets   469
A Graphical Analysis of Insurance   470
Risk That Can't Be Insured   471

Private Information   472
Asymmetric Information: Examples and Problems   472
The Market for Used Cars   472
The Market for Loans   475
The Market for Insurance   476

Uncertainty, Information, and the Invisible Hand   477
Information as a Good   477
Monopoly in Markets that Cope with Uncertainty   477

READING BETWEEN THE LINES
Grades as Signals   478

PART SIX **WRAP-UP** ◆

Understanding Factor Markets, Inequality, and Uncertainty
For Whom?   485

Talking with
David Card   486

**PART SEVEN
MONITORING MACROECONOMIC
PERFORMANCE   489**

CHAPTER 21 ◆ MEASURING GDP AND ECONOMIC GROWTH   489

Gross Domestic Product   490
GDP Defined   490
GDP and the Circular Flow of Expenditure and Income   491
Why Is Domestic Product "Gross"?   492

Measuring U.S. GDP   493
The Expenditure Approach   493
The Income Approach   493
Nominal GDP and Real GDP   495
Calculating Real GDP   495

The Uses and Limitations of Real GDP   496
The Standard of Living Over Time   496
The Standard of Living Across Countries   498
Limitations of Real GDP   499

READING BETWEEN THE LINES
Real GDP Forecasts in the Uncertain Economy of 2010   502

APPENDIX Graphs in Macroeconomics   504

MATHEMATICAL NOTE
Chained-Dollar Real GDP   506

CHAPTER 22 ◆ MONITORING JOBS AND INFLATION 513

Employment and Unemployment 514

Why Unemployment Is a Problem 514

Current Population Survey 515

Three Labor Market Indicators 515

Other Definitions of Unemployment 517

Most Costly Unemployment 518

Alternative Measure of Unemployment 518

Unemployment and Full Employment 519

Frictional Unemployment 519

Structural Unemployment 519

Cyclical Unemployment 519

"Natural" Unemployment 519

Real GDP and Unemployment Over the Cycle 520

The Price Level, Inflation, and Deflation 522

Why Inflation and Deflation are Problems 522

The Consumer Price Index 523

Reading the CPI Numbers 523

Constructing the CPI 523

Measuring the Inflation Rate 524

Distinguishing High Inflation from a High Price Level 525

The Biased CPI 525

The Magnitude of the Bias 526

Some Consequences of the Bias 526

Alternative Price Indexes 526

Core CPI Inflation 527

The Real Variables in Macroeconomics 527

READING BETWEEN THE LINES
Jobs Growth Lags Recovery 528

PART SEVEN WRAP-UP ◆

Monitoring Macroeconomic Performance
The Big Picture 535

Talking with
Richard Clarida 536

PART EIGHT
MACROECONOMIC TRENDS 539

CHAPTER 23 ◆ ECONOMIC GROWTH 539

The Basics of Economic Growth 540

Calculating Growth Rates 540

The Magic of Sustained Growth 540

Applying the Rule of 70 541

Economic Growth Trends 542

Growth in the U.S. Economy 542

Real GDP Growth in the World Economy 543

How Potential GDP Grows 545

What Determines Potential GDP? 545

What Makes Potential GDP Grow? 547

Why Labor Productivity Grows 550

Preconditions for Labor Productivity Growth 550

Physical Capital Growth 551

Human Capital Growth 551

Technological Advances 551

Growth Theories, Evidence, and Policies 553

Classical Growth Theory 553

Neoclassical Growth Theory 553

New Growth Theory 554

New Growth Theory Versus Malthusian Theory 556

Sorting Out the Theories 556

The Empirical Evidence on the Causes of Economic Growth 556

Policies for Achieving Faster Growth 556

READING BETWEEN THE LINES
Economic Growth in China 558

CHAPTER 24 ◆ FINANCE, SAVING, AND INVESTMENT 565

Financial Institutions and Financial Markets 566
Finance and Money 566
Physical Capital and Financial Capital 566
Capital and Investment 566
Wealth and Saving 566
Financial Capital Markets 567
Financial Institutions 568
Insolvency and Illiquidity 569
Interest Rates and Asset Prices 570

The Loanable Funds Market 570
Funds that Finance Investment 570
The Real Interest Rate 571
The Demand for Loanable Funds 572
The Supply of Loanable Funds 573
Equilibrium in the Loanable Funds Market 574
Changes in Demand and Supply 574

Government in the Loanable Funds Market 577
A Government Budget Surplus 577
A Government Budget Deficit 577

The Global Loanable Funds Market 579
International Capital Mobility 579
International Borrowing and Lending 579
Demand and Supply in the Global and National Markets 579

READING BETWEEN THE LINES
Crowding Out in the Global Recession 582

CHAPTER 25 ◆ MONEY, THE PRICE LEVEL, AND INFLATION 589

What Is Money? 590
Medium of Exchange 590
Unit of Account 590
Store of Value 591
Money in the United States Today 591

Depository Institutions 593
Types of Depository Institution 593
What Depository Institutions Do 593
Economic Benefits Provided by Depository Institutions 594
How Depository Institutions Are Regulated 594
Financial Innovation 595

The Federal Reserve System 596
The Structure of the Fed 596
The Fed's Balance Sheet 597
The Fed's Policy Tools 597

How Banks Create Money 599
Creating Deposits by Making Loans 599
The Money Creation Process 600
The Money Multiplier 601

The Money Market 602
The Influences on Money Holding 602
The Demand for Money 603
Shifts in the Demand for Money Curve 603
Money Market Equilibrium 604

The Quantity Theory of Money 606

READING BETWEEN THE LINES
Can More Money Keep the Recovery Going? 608

MATHEMATICAL NOTE
The Money Multiplier 610

CHAPTER 26 ◆ THE EXCHANGE RATE AND
THE BALANCE OF PAYMENTS
617

The Foreign Exchange Market   618
Trading Currencies   618
Exchange Rates   618
Questions About the U.S. Dollar Exchange
Rate   618
An Exchange Rate Is a Price   618
The Demand for One Money Is the Supply of
Another Money   619
Demand in the Foreign Exchange Market   619
Demand Curve for U.S. Dollars   620
Supply in the Foreign Exchange Market   621
Supply Curve for U.S. Dollars   621
Market Equilibrium   622

Exchange Rate Fluctuations   623
Changes in the Demand for U.S. Dollars   623
Changes in the Supply of U.S. Dollars   624
Changes in the Exchange Rate   624
Fundamentals, Expectations, and Arbitrage   626
The Real Exchange Rate   627

Exchange Rate Policy   628
Flexible Exchange Rate   628
Fixed Exchange Rate   628
Crawling Peg   629

Financing International Trade   631
Balance of Payments Accounts   631
Borrowers and Lenders   633
Debtors and Creditors   633
Is U.S. Borrowing for Consumption?   633
Current Account Balance   634
Net Exports   634
Where Is the Exchange Rate?   635

READING BETWEEN THE LINES
The Dollar and "Carry Trade"   636

PART EIGHT WRAP-UP ◆

Understanding Macroeconomic Trends
Expanding the Frontier   643

Talking with
Xavier Sala-i-Martin   644

PART NINE
MACROECONOMIC
FLUCTUATIONS 647

CHAPTER 27 ◆ AGGREGATE SUPPLY AND AGGREGATE DEMAND 647

Aggregate Supply 648
   Quantity Supplied and Supply 648
   Long-Run Aggregate Supply 648
   Short-Run Aggregate Supply 649
   Changes in Aggregate Supply 650

Aggregate Demand 652
   The Aggregate Demand Curve 652
   Changes in Aggregate Demand 653

Explaining Macroeconomic Trends and Fluctuations 656
   Short-Run Macroeconomic Equilibrium 656
   Long-Run Macroeconomic Equilibrium 657
   Economic Growth and Inflation in the *AS-AD* Model 657
   The Business Cycle in the *AS-AD* Model 658
   Fluctuations in Aggregate Demand 660
   Fluctuations in Aggregate Supply 661

Macroeconomic Schools of Thought 662
   The Classical View 662
   The Keynesian View 662
   The Monetarist View 663
   The Way Ahead 663

READING BETWEEN THE LINES
   Aggregate Supply and Aggregate Demand in Action 664

CHAPTER 28 ◆ EXPENDITURE MULTIPLIERS: THE KEYNESIAN MODEL 671

Fixed Prices and Expenditure Plans 672
   Expenditure Plans 672
   Consumption and Saving Plans 672
   Marginal Propensities to Consume and Save 674
   Slopes and Marginal Propensities 674
   Consumption as a Function of Real GDP 675
   Import Function 675

Real GDP with a Fixed Price Level 676
   Aggregate Planned Expenditure 676
   Actual Expenditure, Planned Expenditure, and Real GDP 677
   Equilibrium Expenditure 678
   Convergence to Equilibrium 679

The Multiplier 680
   The Basic Idea of the Multiplier 680
   The Multiplier Effect 680
   Why Is the Multiplier Greater than 1? 681
   The Size of the Multiplier 681
   The Multiplier and the Slope of the *AE* Curve 682
   Imports and Income Taxes 683
   The Multiplier Process 683
   Business Cycle Turning Points 684

The Multiplier and the Price Level 685
   Adjusting Quantities and Prices 685
   Aggregate Expenditure and Aggregate Demand 685
   Deriving the Aggregate Demand Curve 685
   Changes in Aggregate Expenditure and Aggregate Demand 686
   Equilibrium Real GDP and the Price Level 687

READING BETWEEN THE LINES
   Inventory Investment in the 2010 Expansion 690

MATHEMATICAL NOTE
The Algebra of the Keynesian Model 692

CHAPTER 29 ◆ U.S. INFLATION, UNEMPLOYMENT, AND BUSINESS CYCLE 701

Inflation Cycles 702
Demand-Pull Inflation 702
Cost-Push Inflation 704
Expected Inflation 706
Forecasting Inflation 707
Inflation and the Business Cycle 707

Inflation and Unemployment: The Phillips Curve 708
The Short-Run Phillips Curve 708
The Long-Run Phillips Curve 709
Changes in the Natural Unemployment Rate 709

The Business Cycle 711
Mainstream Business Cycle Theory 711
Real Business Cycle Theory 712

READING BETWEEN THE LINES
The Shifting Inflation–Unemployment Tradeoff 716

PART NINE **WRAP-UP** ◆

Understanding Macroeconomic Fluctuations
Boom and Bust 723

Talking with
Ricardo J. Cabellero 724

PART TEN
MACROECONOMIC POLICY 727

CHAPTER 30 ◆ FISCAL POLICY 727

The Federal Budget 728
The Institutions and Laws 728
Highlights of the 2011 Budget 729
The Budget in Historical Perspective 730
Budget Balance and Debt 732
State and Local Budgets 733

Supply-Side Effects of Fiscal Policy 734
Full Employment and Potential GDP 734
The Effects of the Income Tax 734
Taxes on Expenditure and the Tax Wedge 735
Taxes and the Incentive to Save and Invest 736
Tax Revenues and the Laffer Curve 737
The Supply-Side Debate 737

Generational Effects of Fiscal Policy 738
Generational Accounting and Present Value 738
The Social Security Time Bomb 738
Generational Imbalance 739
International Debt 739

Fiscal Stimulus 740
Automatic Fiscal Policy and Cyclical and Structural Budget Balances 740
Discretionary Fiscal Stimulus 743

READING BETWEEN THE LINES
Obama Fiscal Policy 746

CHAPTER 31 ◆ MONETARY POLICY 753

Monetary Policy Objectives and
Framework 754
  Monetary Policy Objectives 754
  Operational "Stable Prices" Goal 755
  Operational "Maximum Employment" Goal
    755
  Responsibility for Monetary Policy 756

The Conduct of Monetary Policy 756
  The Monetary Policy Instrument 756
  The Fed's Decision-Making Strategy 757

Monetary Policy Transmission 759
  Quick Overview 759
  Interest Rate Changes 759
  Exchange Rate Fluctuations 760
  Money and Bank Loans 761
  The Long-Term Real Interest Rate 761
  Expenditure Plans 761
  The Change in Aggregate Demand, Real GDP,
    and the Price Level 762
  The Fed Fights Recession 762
  The Fed Fights Inflation 764
  Loose Links and Long and Variable Lags 765

Extraordinary Monetary Stimulus 767
  The Key Elements of the Crisis 767
  The Policy Actions 768
  Persistently Slow Recovery 768
  Policy Strategies and Clarity 769

READING BETWEEN THE LINES
  The Fed's Monetary Policy Dilemma 770

PART TEN WRAP-UP ◆

Understanding Macroeconomic Policy
Tradeoffs and Free Lunches 777

Talking with
Stephanie Schmitt-Grohé 778

Glossary G-1
Index I-1
Credits C-1

The future is always uncertain. But at some times, and now is one such time, the range of possible near-future events is enormous. The major source of this great uncertainty is economic policy. There is uncertainty about the way in which international trade policy will evolve as protectionism is returning to the political agenda. There is uncertainty about exchange rate policy as competitive devaluation rears its head. There is extraordinary uncertainty about monetary policy with the Fed having doubled the quantity of bank reserves and continuing to create more money in an attempt to stimulate a flagging economy. And there is uncertainty about fiscal policy as a trillion dollar deficit interacts with an aging population to create a national debt time bomb.

Since the subprime mortgage crisis of August 2007 moved economics from the business report to the front page, justified fear has gripped producers, consumers, financial institutions, and governments.

Even the *idea* that the market is an efficient mechanism for allocating scarce resources came into question as some political leaders trumpeted the end of capitalism and the dawn of a new economic order in which tighter regulation reigned in unfettered greed.

Rarely do teachers of economics have such a rich feast on which to draw. And rarely are the principles of economics more surely needed to provide the solid foundation on which to think about economic events and navigate the turbulence of economic life.

Although thinking like an economist can bring a clearer perspective to and deeper understanding of today's events, students don't find the economic way of thinking easy or natural. *Economics* seeks to put clarity and understanding in the grasp of the student through its careful and vivid exploration of the tension between self-interest and the social interest, the role and power of incentives—of opportunity cost and marginal benefit—and demonstrating the possibility that markets supplemented by other mechanisms might allocate resources efficiently.

Parkin students begin to think about issues the way real economists do and learn how to explore difficult policy problems and make more informed decisions in their own economic lives.

◆ The Tenth Edition Revision

Simpler where possible, stripped of some technical detail, more copiously illustrated with well-chosen photographs, reinforced with improved chapter sum-

maries and problem sets, and even more tightly integrated with MyEconLab: These are the hallmarks of this tenth edition of *Economics*.

This comprehensive revision also incorporates and responds to the detailed suggestions for improvements made by reviewers and users, both in the broad architecture of the text and each chapter.

The revision builds on the improvements achieved in previous editions and retains its thorough and detailed presentation of the principles of economics, its emphasis on real-world examples and applications, its development of critical thinking skills, its diagrams renowned for pedagogy and precision, and its path-breaking technology.

Most chapters have been fine-tuned to achieve even greater clarity and to present the material in a more straightforward, visual, and intuitive way. Some chapters have been thoroughly reworked to cover new issues, particularly those that involve current policy problems. These changes are aimed at better enabling students to learn how to use the economic toolkit to analyze their own decisions and understand the events and issues they are confronted with in the media and at the ballot box.

Current issues organize each chapter. News stories about today's major economic events tie each chapter together, from new chapter-opening vignettes to end-of-chapter problems and online practice. Each chapter includes a discussion of a critical issue of our time to demonstrate how economic theory can be applied to explore a particular debate or question. Among the many issues covered are

- The gains from trade, globalization, and protectionism in Chapters 2 and 8 and an updated conversation with Jagdish Bhagwati in the first part closer
- How ethanol competes with food and drives its price up in Chapter 2
- Health care in Chapter 16
- Climate change in Chapter 17
- The carbon tax debate in Chapter 17
- Increasing inequality in the United States and decreasing inequality across the nations in Chapter 18
- The Fed's extraordinary actions and their impact on the balance sheets of banks in Chapter 25
- Stubbornly high unemployment in Chapters 22, 27, and 29
- Currency fluctuations and the managed Chinese yuan in Chapter 26
- Fiscal stimulus and the debate about the fiscal stimulus multipliers in Chapter 30

- Monetary stimulus in Chapter 31 and the dangers of targeting unemployment in an updated conversation with Stephanie Schmitt-Grohé
- Real-world examples and applications appear in the body of each chapter and in the end-of-chapter problems and applications

A selection of questions that appear daily in MyEconLab in *Economics in the News* are also available for assignment as homework, quizzes, or tests.

Highpoints of the Micro Revision

In addition to being thoroughly updated and revised to include the topics and features just described, the microeconomics chapters feature the following seven notable changes:

1. **What Is Economics?** (Chapter 1): I have reworked the explanation of the economic way of thinking around six key ideas, all illustrated with student-relevant choices. The graphing appendix to this chapter has an increased focus on scatter diagrams and their interpretation and on understanding shifts of curves.

2. **Utility and Demand** (Chapter 8): This chapter has a revised explanation of the marginal utility model of consumer choice that now begins with the budget line and consumption possibilities. It then returns to the budget line to explain and illustrate the utility-maximizing rule—equalize the marginal utility per dollar for all goods. The dramatic changes in the market for recorded music illustrate the theory in action.

3. **Possibilities, Preferences, and Choices** (Chapter 9): Students find the analysis of the income effect and the substitution effect difficult and I have reworked this material to make the explanation clearer. I have omitted the work-leisure choice coverage of earlier editions and given the chapter a student-friendly application to choices about movies and DVDs.

4. **Reorganized and expanded coverage of externalities, public goods, and common resources** (Chapters 16 and 17). These topics have been reorganized to achieve an issues focus rather than a technical focus. Chapter 16 is about public provision of both public goods and mixed goods with positive externalities; and Chapter 17 is about overproduction of goods with negative externalities and overuse of common resources.

5. **Public Goods and Public Choices** (Chapter 16): This new chapter begins with an overview of public choice theory, a classification of goods and externalities, and an identification of the market failures that give rise to public choices. The chapter then goes on to explain the free-rider problem and the underprovision of public goods, the bureaucracy problem and overprovision, and the underprovision of mixed goods with external benefits, illustrated by education and health-care. The chapter explains how education and health care vouchers provide an effective way of achieving efficiency in the provision of these two vital services, a view reinforced in a box on Larry Kotlikoff's health-care plan and Caroline Hoxby's part closer interview.

6. **Economics and the Environment** (Chapter 17): This new chapter brings all the environmental damage issues together by combining material on negative externalities and common resources. Covering all this material in the same chapter (the previous editions split them between two chapters) enables their common solutions—property rights (Coase) or individual transferable quotas—to be explained and emphasized.

7. **Economic Inequality** (Chapter 19): This chapter now includes a section on inequality in the world economy and compares U.S. inequality with that in nations at the two extremes of equality and inequality. The new section also looks at the trend in global inequality. The discussion of the sources of inequality now includes an explanation of the superstar contest idea. This idea is used to explain Emmanuel Saez's remarkable data on the income share of the top one percent of Americans.

Highpoints of the Macro Revision

All the macro chapters have been updated to incorporate data through the second quarter of 2010 (later for some variables) and the news and policy situation through the fall of 2010. Beyond these general updates, the macro chapters feature the following seven notable revisions:

1. **Measuring GDP and Economic Growth** (Chapter 21): I have revised the section on cross-country comparisons and the limitations of GDP to make the material clearer and added photo illustrations of PPP and items omitted from GDP.

2. **Monitoring Jobs and Inflation** (Chapter 22): This chapter now includes a discussion and illustration of the alternative measures of unemployment reported by the BLS and the costs of different types of unemployment. I have rewritten the section on full employment and the influences on the natural unemployment rate and illustrated this discussion

with a box on structural unemployment in Michigan. The coverage of the price level has been expanded to define and explain the costs of deflation as well as inflation.

3. **Economic Growth** (Chapter 23): I have simplified this chapter by omitting the technical details on growth accounting and replacing them with an intuitive discussion of the crucial role of human capital and intellectual property rights. I illustrate the role played by these key factors in Britain's *Industrial Revolution*. I have made the chapter more relevant and empirical by including a summary of the correlations between the growth rate and the positive and negative influences on it.

4. **Money, the Price Level, and Inflation** (Chapter 25): This chapter records and explains the Fed's extraordinary injection of monetary base following the financial panic of 2008. In revising this chapter, I have redrawn the line between this chapter, the "money and banking" chapter, and the later "monetary policy" chapter by including in this chapter a complete explanation with of how an open-market operation works. I have also provided clearer and more thorough explanations of the money multiplier and money market equilibrium in the short and the long run and in the transition to the long run.

5. **The Exchange Rate and the Balance of Payments** (Chapter 26): I have revised this chapter to better explain the distinction between the fundamentals and the role of expectations. I have also included an explanation of how arbitrage works in the foreign exchange market and the temporary and risky nature of seeking to profit from the so-called "carry trade."

6. **Fiscal Policy** (Chapter 30): The topic of this chapter is front-page news almost every day and is likely to remain so. The revision describes the deficit and the accumulating debt and explains the consequences of the uncertainty they engender. An entirely new section examines the fiscal stimulus measures taken over the past year, channels through which stimulus works, its unwanted side-effects, its potentially limited power, and its short-comings. The controversy about and range of views on the magnitude of fiscal stimulus multiplier is examined.

7. **Monetary Policy** (Chapter 31): This chapter describes and explains the dramatic monetary policy responses to the 2008–2009 recession and the persistently high unemployment of 2010. It also contains an improved description of the

FOMC's decision-making process. Technical details about alternative monetary policy strategies have been replaced with a shorter and more focused discussion of inflation targeting as a tool for bringing clarity to monetary policy and anchoring inflation expectations.

◆ Features to Enhance Teaching and Learning

Reading Between the Lines

This Parkin hallmark helps students think like economists by connecting chapter tools and concepts to the world around them. In *Reading Between the Lines*, which appears at the end of each chapter, students apply the tools they have just learned by analyzing an article from a newspaper or news Web site. Each article sheds additional light on the questions first raised in the Chapter Opener. Questions about the article also appear with the end-of-chapter problems and applications.

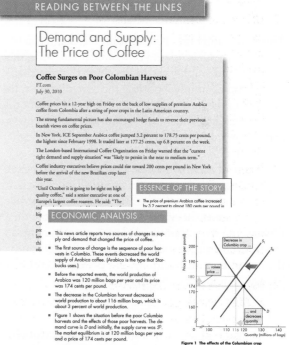

Economics in the News

31. After you have studied *Reading Between the Lines* on pp. 74–75 answer the following questions.
   a. What happened to the price of coffee in 2010?
   b. What substitutions do you expect might have been made to decrease the quantity of coffee demanded?
   c. What influenced the demand for coffee in 2010 and what influenced the quantity of coffee demanded?

Diagrams That Show the Action

Through the past nine editions, this book has set new standards of clarity in its diagrams; the tenth edition continues to uphold this tradition. My goal has always been to show "where the economic action is." The diagrams in this book continue to generate an enormously positive response, which confirms my view that graphical analysis is the most powerful tool available for teaching and learning economics.

Because many students find graphs hard to work with, I have developed the entire art program with the study and review needs of the student in mind.

The diagrams feature:

- Original curves consistently shown in blue
- Shifted curves, equilibrium points, and other important features highlighted in red
- Color-blended arrows to suggest movement
- Graphs paired with data tables
- Diagrams labeled with boxed notes
- Extended captions that make each diagram and its caption a self-contained object for study and review.

Economics in Action Boxes

This new feature uses boxes within the chapter to address current events and economic occurrences that highlight and amplify the topics covered in the chapter. Instead of simply reporting the current events, the material in the boxes applies the event to an economics lesson, enabling students to see how economics plays a part in the world around them as they read through the chapter.

Some of the many issues covered in these boxes include the global market for crude oil, the best affordable choice of movies and DVDs, the cost of selling a pair of shoes, how Apple doesn't make the iPhone, the structural unemployment in Michigan, how loanable funds fuel a home price bubble, and the size of the fiscal stimulus multipliers. A complete list can be found on the inside back cover.

Chapter Openers

Each chapter opens with a student-friendly vignette that raises questions to motivate the student and focus the chapter. This chapter-opening story is woven into the main body of the chapter and is explored in the *Reading Between the Lines* feature that ends each chapter.

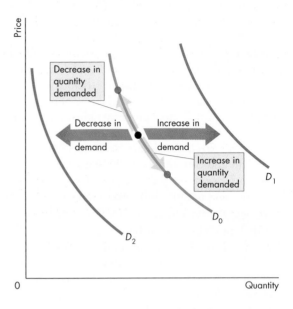

Economics in Action
The Global Market for Crude Oil

The demand and supply model provides insights into all competitive markets. Here, we'll apply what you've learned about the effects of an increase in demand to the global market for crude oil.

Crude oil is like the life-blood of the global economy. It is used to fuel our cars, airplanes, trains, and buses, to generate electricity, and to produce a wide range of plastics. When the price of crude oil rises, the cost of transportation, power, and materials all increase.

In 2001, the price of a barrel of oil was $20 (using the value of money in 2010). In 2008, before the global financial crisis ended a long period of economic expansion, the price peaked at $127 a barrel.

While the price of oil was rising, the quantity of oil produced and consumed also increased. In 2001, the world produced 65 million barrels of oil a day. By 2008, that quantity was 72 million barrels.

Who or what has been raising the price of oil? Is it the action of greedy oil producers? Oil producers might be greedy, and some of them might be big enough to withhold supply and raise the price, but it wouldn't be in their self-interest to do so. The higher price would bring forth a greater quantity supplied from other producers and the profit of the producer limiting supply would fall.

Oil producers could try to cooperate and jointly withhold supply. The Organization of Petroleum Exporting Countries, OPEC, is such a group of producers. But OPEC doesn't control the *world* supply and its members' self-interest is to produce the quantities that give them the maximum attainable profit.

So even though the global oil market has some big players, they don't fix the price. Instead, the actions of thousands of buyers and sellers and the forces of demand and supply determine the price of oil.

So how have demand and supply changed?

Because both the price and the quantity have increased, the demand for oil must have increased. Supply might have changed too, but here we'll suppose that supply has remained the same.

The global demand for oil has increased for one major reason: World income has increased. The increase has been particularly large in the emerging economies of Brazil, China, and India. Increased world income has increased the demand for oil-using goods such as electricity, gasoline, and plastics, which in turn has increased the demand for oil.

The figure illustrates the effects of the increase in demand on the global oil market. The supply of oil remained constant along supply curve S. The demand for oil in 2001 was D_{2001}, so in 2001 the price was $20 a barrel and the quantity was 65 million barrels per day. The demand for oil increased and by 2008 it had reached D_{2008}. The price of oil increased to $127 a barrel and the quantity increased to 72 million barrels a day. The increase in the quantity is an *increase in the quantity supplied*, not an increase in supply.

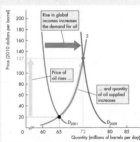

The Global Market for Crude Oil

Key Terms

Highlighted terms simplify the student's task of learning the vocabulary of economics. Each high-lighted term appears in an end-of-chapter list with its page number, in an end-of-book glossary with its page number, boldfaced in the index, in MyEconLab, in the interactive glossary, and in the Flash Cards.

In-Text Review Quizzes

A review quiz at the end of each major section enables students to determine whether a topic needs further study before moving on. This feature includes a reference to the appropriate MyEconLab study plan to help students further test their understanding.

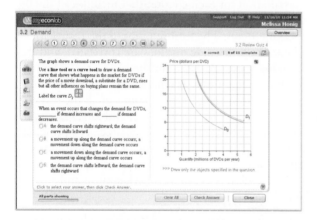

End-of-Chapter Study Material

Each chapter closes with a concise summary organized by major topics, lists of key terms with page references, and problems and applications. These learning tools provide students with a summary for review and exam preparation.

Interviews with Economists

Each major part of the text closes with a summary feature that includes an interview with a leading economist whose research and expertise correlates to what the student has just learned. These interviews explore the background, education, and research these prominent economists have conducted, as well as advice for those who want to continue the study of economics. New to this tenth edition is Thomas Hubbard of Northwestern University. I have also returned to Jagdish Bhagwati, Stephanie Schmitt-

Grohé, and Richard Clarida (all of Columbia University) and Ricardo Caballero (of the Massachusetts Institute of Technology) and included their more recent thoughts on our rapidly changing economic times.

For the Instructor

This book enables you to focus on the economic way of thinking and choose your own course structure in your principles course:

Focus on the Economic Way of Thinking

As an instructor, you know how hard it is to encourage a student to think like an economist. But that is your goal. Consistent with this goal, the text focuses on and repeatedly uses the central ideas: choice; tradeoff; opportunity cost; the margin; incentives; the gains from voluntary exchange; the forces of demand, supply, and equilibrium; the pursuit of economic rent; the tension between self-interest and the social interest; and the scope and limitations of government actions.

Flexible Structure

You have preferences for how you want to teach your course. I have organized this book to enable you to do so. The flexibility charts on pp. vi and vii illustrate the book's flexibility. By following the arrows through the charts you can select the path that best fits your preference for course structure. Whether you want to teach a traditional course that blends theory and policy, or one that takes a fast-track through either theory or policy issues, *Economics* gives you the choice.

Supplemental Resources

Instructor's Manuals We have streamlined and reorganized the Instructor's Manual to reflect the focus and intuition of the tenth edition. Two separate Instructor's Manuals—one for *Microeconomics* and one for *Macroeconomics*—written by Laura A. Wolff of Southern Illinois University Edwardsville and Russ McCullough at Iowa State University, respectively, integrate the teaching and learning package and serve as a guide to all the supplements.

Each chapter contains

- A chapter overview
- A list of what's new in the tenth edition
- Ready-to-use lecture notes from each chapter enable a new user of Parkin to walk into a classroom armed to deliver a polished lecture. The lecture notes provide an outline of the chapter; concise statements of key material; alternative tables and figures; key terms and definitions; and boxes that highlight key concepts; provide an interesting anecdote, or suggest how to handle a difficult idea; and additional discussion questions. The PowerPoint® lecture notes incorporate the chapter outlines and teaching suggestions.

Solutions Manual For ease of use and instructor reference, a comprehensive solutions manual provides instructors with solutions to the Review Quizzes and the end-of-chapter Problems and Applications as well as additional problems and the solutions to these problems. Written by Mark Rush of the University of Florida and reviewed for accuracy by Jeannie Gillmore of the University of Western Ontario, the Solutions Manual is available in hard copy and electronically on the Instructor's Resource Center CD-ROM, in the Instructor's Resources section of MyEconLab, and on the Instructor's Resource Center.

Test Item File Six separate Test Item Files—three for *Microeconomics* and three for *Macroeconomics*—with nearly 13,000 questions, provide multiple-choice, true/false, numerical, fill-in-the-blank, short-answer, and essay questions. Mark Rush reviewed and edited all existing questions to ensure their clarity and consistency with the tenth edition and incorporated new questions into the thousands of existing Test Bank questions. The new questions, written by Svitlana Maksymenko of the University of Pittsburgh, James K. Self at the University of Indiana, Bloomington, Gary Hoover at the University of Alabama, Barbara Moore at the University of Central Florida, and Luke Armstrong at Lee College, follow the style and format of the end-of-chapter text problems and provide the instructor with a whole new set of testing opportunities and/or homework assignments. Additionally, end-of-part tests contain questions that cover all the chapters in the part and feature integrative questions that span more than one chapter.

Computerized Testbanks Fully networkable, the test banks are available for Windows® and Macintosh®. TestGen's graphical interface enables instructors to view, edit, and add questions; transfer questions to tests; and print different forms of tests. Tests can be formatted with varying fonts and styles, margins, and headers and footers, as in any word-processing document. Search and sort features let the instructor quickly locate questions and arrange them in a preferred order. QuizMaster, working with your school's computer network, automatically grades the exams, stores the results, and allows the instructor to view or print a variety of reports.

PowerPoint Resources Robin Bade has developed a full-color Microsoft® PowerPoint Lecture Presentation for each chapter that includes all the figures and tables from the text, animated graphs, and speaking notes. The lecture notes in the Instructor's Manual and the slide outlines are correlated, and the speaking notes are based on the Instructor's Manual teaching suggestions. A separate set of PowerPoint files containing large-scale versions of all the text's figures (most of them animated) and tables (some of which are animated) are also available. The presentations can be used electronically in the classroom or can be printed to create hard copy transparency masters. This item is available for Macintosh and Windows.

Clicker-Ready PowerPoint Resources This edition features the addition of clicker-ready PowerPoint slides for the Personal Response System you use. Each chapter of the text includes ten multiple-choice questions that test important concepts. Instructors can assign these as in-class assignments or review quizzes.

Instructor's Resource Center CD-ROM Fully compatible with Windows and Macintosh, this CD-ROM contains electronic files of every instructor supplement for the tenth edition. Files included are: Microsoft® Word and Adobe® PDF files of the Instructor's Manual, Test Item Files and Solutions Manual; PowerPoint resources; and the Computerized TestGen® Test Bank. Add this useful resource to your exam copy bookbag, or locate your local Pearson Education sales representative at www.pearsonhighered.educator to request a copy.

Instructors can download supplements from a secure, instructor-only source via the Pearson Higher Education Instructor Resource Center Web page (www.pearsonhighered.com/irc).

BlackBoard and WebCT BlackBoard and WebCT Course Cartridges are available for download from www.pearsonhighered.com/irc. These standard course cartridges contain the Instructor's Manual, Solutions Manual, TestGen Test Item Files, Instructor PowerPoints, Student Powerpoints and Student Data Files.

Study Guide The tenth edition Study Guide by Mark Rush is carefully coordinated with the text, MyEconLab, and the Test Item Files. Each chapter of the Study Guide contains

- Key concepts
- Helpful hints
- True/false/uncertain questions
- Multiple-choice questions
- Short-answer questions
- Common questions or misconceptions that the student explains as if he or she were the teacher
- Each part allows students to test their cumulative understanding with questions that go across chapters and to work a sample midterm examination.

MYECONLAB

MyEconLab's powerful assessment and tutorial system works hand-in-hand with *Economics*. With comprehensive homework, quiz, test, and tutorial options, instructors can manage all assessment needs in one program.

- All of the Review Quiz questions and end-of-chapter Problems and Applications are assignable and automatically graded in MyEconLab.
- Students can work all the Review Quiz questions and end-of-chapter Study Plan Problems and Applications as part of the Study Plan in MyEconLab.
- Instructors can assign the end-of-chapter Additional Problems and Applications as auto-graded assignments. These Problems and Applications are not available to students in MyEconLab unless assigned by the instructor.
- Many of the problems and applications are algorithmic, draw-graph, and numerical exercises.
- Test Item File questions are available for assignment as homework.
- The Custom Exercise Builder allows instructors the flexibility of creating their own problems for assignment.

- The powerful Gradebook records each student's performance and time spent on Tests, the Study Plan, and homework and generates reports by student or by chapter.
- *Economics in the News* is a turn-key solution to bringing daily news into the classroom. Updated daily during the academic year, I upload two relevant articles (one micro, one macro) and provide links for further information and questions that may be assigned for homework or for classroom discussion.
- A comprehensive suite of ABC news videos, which address current topics such as education, energy, Federal Reserve policy, and business cycles, is available for classroom use. Video-specific exercises are available for instructor assignment.

Robin Bade and I, assisted by Jeannie Gillmore and Laurel Davies, author and oversee all of the MyEconLab content for *Economics*. Our peerless MyEconLab team has worked hard to ensure that it is tightly integrated with the book's content and vision. A more detailed walk-through of the student benefits and features of MyEconLab can be found on the inside front cover. Visit www.myeconlab.com for more information and an online demonstration of instructor and student features.

Experiments in MyEconLab

Experiments are a fun and engaging way to promote active learning and mastery of important economic concepts. Pearson's experiments program is flexible and easy for instructors and students to use.

- Single-player experiments allow your students to play against virtual players from anywhere at anytime with an Internet connection.
- Multiplayer experiments allow you to assign and manage a real-time experiment with your class.

Pre-and post-questions for each experiment are available for assignment in MyEconLab.

Economics Videos and Assignable Questions Featuring abcNEWS Economics videos featuring ABC news enliven your course with short news clips featuring real-world issues. These videos, available in MyEconLab, feature news footage and commentary by economists. Questions and problems for each video clip are available for assignment in MyEconLab.

◆ Acknowledgments

I thank my current and former colleagues and friends at the University of Western Ontario who have taught me so much. They are Jim Davies, Jeremy Greenwood, Ig Horstmann, Peter Howitt, Greg Huffman, David Laidler, Phil Reny, Chris Robinson, John Whalley, and Ron Wonnacott. I also thank Doug McTaggart and Christopher Findlay, co-authors of the Australian edition, and Melanie Powell and Kent Matthews, coauthors of the European edition. Suggestions arising from their adaptations of earlier editions have been helpful to me in preparing this edition.

I thank the several thousand students whom I have been privileged to teach. The instant response that comes from the look of puzzlement or enlightenment has taught me how to teach economics.

It is a special joy to thank the many outstanding editors, media specialists, and others at Addison-Wesley who contributed to the concerted publishing effort that brought this edition to completion. Denise Clinton, Publisher of MyEconLab has played a major role in the evolution of this text since its third edition, and her insights and ideas can still be found in this new edition. Donna Battista, Editor-in-Chief for Economics and Finance, is hugely inspiring and has provided overall direction to the project. As ever, Adrienne D'Ambrosio, Senior Acquisitions Editor for Economics and my sponsoring editor, played a major role in shaping this revision and the many outstanding supplements that accompany it. Adrienne brings intelligence and insight to her work and is the unchallengeable pre-eminent economics editor. Deepa Chungi, Development Editor, brought a fresh eye to the development process, obtained outstanding reviews from equally outstanding reviewers, digested and summarized the reviews, and made many solid suggestions as she diligently worked through the drafts of this edition. Deepa also provided outstanding photo research. Nancy Fenton, Managing Editor, managed the entire production and design effort with her usual skill, played a major role in envisioning and implementing the cover design, and coped fearlessly with a tight production schedule. Susan Schoenberg, Director of Media, directed the development of MyEconLab; Noel Lotz, Content Lead for MyEconLab, managed a complex and thorough reviewing process for the content of MyEconLab; and Melissa Honig, Senior Media Producer ensured that all our media assets were correctly assembled. Lori Deshazo, Executive Marketing Manager, provided inspired marketing strategy and direction. Catherine Baum provided a careful, consistent, and intelligent copy edit and accuracy check. Jonathan Boylan designed the cover and package and yet again surpassed the challenge of ensuring that we meet the highest design standards. Joe Vetere provided endless technical help with the text and art files. Jill Kolongowski and Alison Eusden managed our immense supplements program. And Heather Johnson with the other members of an outstanding editorial and production team at Integra-Chicago kept the project on track on an impossibly tight schedule. I thank all of these wonderful people. It has been inspiring to work with them and to share in creating what I believe is a truly outstanding educational tool.

I thank our talented tenth edition supplements authors and contributors—Luke Armstrong, Jeannie Gillmore, Laurel Davies, Gary Hoover, Svitlana Maksymenko, Russ McCullough, Barbara Moore, Jim Self, and Laurie Wolff.

I especially thank Mark Rush, who yet again played a crucial role in creating another edition of this text and package. Mark has been a constant source of good advice and good humor.

I thank the many exceptional reviewers who have shared their insights through the various editions of this book. Their contribution has been invaluable.

I thank the people who work directly with me. Jeannie Gillmore provided outstanding research assistance on many topics, including the *Reading Between the Lines* news articles. Richard Parkin created the electronic art files and offered many ideas that improved the figures in this book. And Laurel Davies managed an ever-growing and ever more complex MyEconLab database.

As with the previous editions, this one owes an enormous debt to Robin Bade. I dedicate this book to her and again thank her for her work. I could not have written this book without the tireless and unselfish help she has given me. My thanks to her are unbounded.

Classroom experience will test the value of this book. I would appreciate hearing from instructors and students about how I can continue to improve it in future editions.

Michael Parkin
London, Ontario, Canada
michael.parkin@uwo.ca

Reviewers

Eric Abrams, Hawaii Pacific University

Christopher Adams, Federal Trade Commission

Tajudeen Adenekan, Bronx Community College

Syed Ahmed, Cameron University

Frank Albritton, Seminole Community College

Milton Alderfer, Miami-Dade Community College

William Aldridge, Shelton State Community College

Donald L. Alexander, Western Michigan University

Terence Alexander, Iowa State University

Stuart Allen, University of North Carolina, Greensboro

Sam Allgood, University of Nebraska, Lincoln

Neil Alper, Northeastern University

Alan Anderson, Fordham University

Lisa R. Anderson, College of William and Mary

Jeff Ankrom, Wittenberg University

Fatma Antar, Manchester Community Technical College

Kofi Apraku, University of North Carolina, Asheville

John Atkins, University of West Florida

Moshen Bahmani-Oskooee, University of Wisconsin, Milwaukee

Donald Balch, University of South Carolina

Mehmet Balcilar, Wayne State University

Paul Ballantyne, University of Colorado

Sue Bartlett, University of South Florida

Jose Juan Bautista, Xavier University of Louisiana

Valerie R. Bencivenga, University of Texas, Austin

Ben Bernanke, Chairman of Federal Reserve

Radha Bhattacharya, California State University, Fullerton

Margot Biery, Tarrant County College, South

John Bittorowitz, Ball State University

David Black, University of Toledo

Kelly Blanchard, Purdue University

S. Brock Blomberg, Claremont McKenna College

William T. Bogart, Case Western Reserve University

Giacomo Bonanno, University of California, Davis

Tan Khay Boon, Nanyard Technological University

Sunne Brandmeyer, University of South Florida

Audie Brewton, Northeastern Illinois University

Baird Brock, Central Missouri State University

Byron Brown, Michigan State University

Jeffrey Buser, Columbus State Community College

Alison Butler, Florida International University

Colleen Callahan, American University

Tania Carbiener, Southern Methodist University

Kevin Carey, American University

Scott Carrell, University of California at Davis

Kathleen A. Carroll, University of Maryland, Baltimore County

Michael Carter, University of Massachusetts, Lowell

Edward Castronova, California State University, Fullerton

Francis Chan, Fullerton College

Ming Chang, Dartmouth College

Subir Chakrabarti, Indiana University-Purdue University

Joni Charles, Texas State University

Adhip Chaudhuri, Georgetown University

Gopal Chengalath, Texas Tech University

Daniel Christiansen, Albion College

Kenneth Christianson, Binghamton University

John J. Clark, Community College of Allegheny County, Allegheny Campus

Cindy Clement, University of Maryland

Meredith Clement, Dartmouth College

Michael B. Cohn, U. S. Merchant Marine Academy

Robert Collinge, University of Texas, San Antonio

Carol Condon, Kean University

Doug Conway, Mesa Community College

Larry Cook, University of Toledo

Bobby Corcoran, retired, Middle Tennessee State University

Kevin Cotter, Wayne State University

James Peery Cover, University of Alabama, Tuscaloosa

Erik Craft, University of Richmond

Eleanor D. Craig, University of Delaware

Jim Craven, Clark College

Jeremy Cripps, American University of Kuwait

Elizabeth Crowell, University of Michigan, Dearborn

Stephen Cullenberg, University of California, Riverside

David Culp, Slippery Rock University

Norman V. Cure, Macomb Community College

Dan Dabney, University of Texas, Austin

Andrew Dane, Angelo State University

Joseph Daniels, Marquette University

Gregory DeFreitas, Hofstra University

David Denslow, University of Florida

Shatakshee Dhongde, Rochester Institute of Technology

Mark Dickie, University of Central Florida

James Dietz, California State University, Fullerton

Carol Dole, State University of West Georgia

Ronald Dorf, Inver Hills Community College

John Dorsey, University of Maryland, College Park

Eric Drabkin, Hawaii Pacific University

Amrik Singh Dua, Mt. San Antonio College

Thomas Duchesneau, University of Maine, Orono

Lucia Dunn, Ohio State University

Donald Dutkowsky, Syracuse University

John Edgren, Eastern Michigan University

David J. Eger, Alpena Community College

Harry Ellis, Jr., University of North Texas

Ibrahim Elsaify, Goldey-Beacom College

Kenneth G. Elzinga, University of Virginia

Patrick Emerson, Oregon State University
Tisha Emerson, Baylor University
Monica Escaleras, Florida Atlantic University
Antonina Espiritu, Hawaii Pacific University
Gwen Eudey, University of Pennsylvania
Barry Falk, Iowa State University
M. Fazeli, Hofstra University
Philip Fincher, Louisiana Tech University
F. Firoozi, University of Texas, San Antonio
Nancy Folbre, University of Massachusetts, Amherst
Kenneth Fong, Temasek Polytechnic (Singapore)
Steven Francis, Holy Cross College
David Franck, University of North Carolina, Charlotte
Mark Frank, Sam Houston State University
Roger Frantz, San Diego State University
Mark Frascatore, Clarkson University
Alwyn Fraser, Atlantic Union College
Marc Fusaro, East Carolina University
James Gale, Michigan Technological University
Susan Gale, New York University
Roy Gardner, Indiana University
Eugene Gentzel, Pensacola Junior College
Kirk Gifford, Brigham Young University-Idaho
Scott Gilbert, Southern Illinois University, Carbondale
Andrew Gill, California State University, Fullerton
Robert Giller, Virginia Polytechnic Institute and State University
Robert Gillette, University of Kentucky
James N. Giordano, Villanova University
Maria Giuili, Diablo College
Susan Glanz, St. John's University
Robert Gordon, San Diego State University
Richard Gosselin, Houston Community College
John Graham, Rutgers University
John Griffen, Worcester Polytechnic Institute
Wayne Grove, Syracuse University
Robert Guell, Indiana State University
William Gunther, University of Southern Mississippi
Jamie Haag, Pacific University, Oregon
Gail Heyne Hafer, Lindenwood University
Rik W. Hafer, Southern Illinois University, Edwardsville
Daniel Hagen, Western Washington University
David R. Hakes, University of Northern Iowa
Craig Hakkio, Federal Reserve Bank, Kansas City
Bridget Gleeson Hanna, Rochester Institute of Technology
Ann Hansen, Westminster College
Seid Hassan, Murray State University
Jonathan Haughton, Suffolk University
Randall Haydon, Wichita State University
Denise Hazlett, Whitman College
Julia Heath, University of Memphis

Jac Heckelman, Wake Forest University
Jolien A. Helsel, Kent State University
James Henderson, Baylor University
Doug Herman, Georgetown University
Jill Boylston Herndon, University of Florida
Gus Herring, Brookhaven College
John Herrmann, Rutgers University
John M. Hill, Delgado Community College
Jonathan Hill, Florida International University
Lewis Hill, Texas Tech University
Steve Hoagland, University of Akron
Tom Hoerger, Fellow, Research Triangle Institute
Calvin Hoerneman, Delta College
George Hoffer, Virginia Commonwealth University
Dennis L. Hoffman, Arizona State University
Paul Hohenberg, Rensselaer Polytechnic Institute
Jim H. Holcomb, University of Texas, El Paso
Robert Holland, Purdue University
Harry Holzer, Georgetown University
Gary Hoover, University of Alabama
Linda Hooks, Washington and Lee University
Jim Horner, Cameron University
Djehane Hosni, University of Central Florida
Harold Hotelling, Jr., Lawrence Technical University
Calvin Hoy, County College of Morris
Ing-Wei Huang, Assumption University, Thailand
Julie Hunsaker, Wayne State University
Beth Ingram, University of Iowa
Jayvanth Ishwaran, Stephen F. Austin State University
Michael Jacobs, Lehman College
S. Hussain Ali Jafri, Tarleton State University
Dennis Jansen, Texas A&M University
Andrea Jao, University of Pennsylvania
Barbara John, University of Dayton
Barry Jones, Binghamton University
Garrett Jones, Southern Florida University
Frederick Jungman, Northwestern Oklahoma State University
Paul Junk, University of Minnesota, Duluth
Leo Kahane, California State University, Hayward
Veronica Kalich, Baldwin-Wallace College
John Kane, State University of New York, Oswego
Eungmin Kang, St. Cloud State University
Arthur Kartman, San Diego State University
Gurmit Kaur, Universiti Teknologi (Malaysia)
Louise Keely, University of Wisconsin, Madison
Manfred W. Keil, Claremont McKenna College
Elizabeth Sawyer Kelly, University of Wisconsin, Madison
Rose Kilburn, Modesto Junior College
Amanda King, Georgia Southern University
John King, Georgia Southern University

Robert Kirk, Indiana University-Purdue University, Indianapolis
Norman Kleinberg, City University of New York, Baruch College
Robert Kleinhenz, California State University, Fullerton
John Krantz, University of Utah
Joseph Kreitzer, University of St. Thomas
Patricia Kuzyk, Washington State University
David Lages, Southwest Missouri State University
W. J. Lane, University of New Orleans
Leonard Lardaro, University of Rhode Island
Kathryn Larson, Elon College
Luther D. Lawson, University of North Carolina, Wilmington
Elroy M. Leach, Chicago State University
Jim Lee, Texas A & M, Corpus Christi
Sang Lee, Southeastern Louisiana University
Robert Lemke, Florida International University
Mary Lesser, Iona College
Jay Levin, Wayne State University
Arik Levinson, University of Wisconsin, Madison
Tony Lima, California State University, Hayward
William Lord, University of Maryland, Baltimore County
Nancy Lutz, Virginia Polytechnic Institute and State University
Brian Lynch, Lakeland Community College
Murugappa Madhavan, San Diego State University
K. T. Magnusson, Salt Lake Community College
Svitlana Maksymenko, University of Pittsburgh
Mark Maier, Glendale Community College
Jean Mangan, Staffordshire University Business School
Denton Marks, University of Wisconsin, Whitewater
Michael Marlow, California Polytechnic State University
Akbar Marvasti, University of Houston
Wolfgang Mayer, University of Cincinnati
John McArthur, Wofford College
Amy McCormick, Mary Baldwin College
Russ McCullough, Iowa State University
Catherine McDevitt, Central Michigan University
Gerald McDougall, Wichita State University
Stephen McGary, Brigham Young University-Idaho
Richard D. McGrath, Armstrong Atlantic State University
Richard McIntyre, University of Rhode Island
John McLeod, Georgia Institute of Technology
Mark McLeod, Virginia Polytechnic Institute and State University
B. Starr McMullen, Oregon State University
Mary Ruth McRae, Appalachian State University
Kimberly Merritt, Cameron University
Charles Meyer, Iowa State University
Peter Mieszkowski, Rice University
John Mijares, University of North Carolina, Asheville
Richard A. Miller, Wesleyan University

Judith W. Mills, Southern Connecticut State University
Glen Mitchell, Nassau Community College
Jeannette C. Mitchell, Rochester Institute of Technology
Khan Mohabbat, Northern Illinois University
Bagher Modjtahedi, University of California, Davis
Shahruz Mohtadi, Suffolk University
W. Douglas Morgan, University of California, Santa Barbara
William Morgan, University of Wyoming
James Morley, Washington University in St. Louis
William Mosher, Clark University
Joanne Moss, San Francisco State University
Nivedita Mukherji, Oakland University
Francis Mummery, Fullerton College
Edward Murphy, Southwest Texas State University
Kevin J. Murphy, Oakland University
Kathryn Nantz, Fairfield University
William S. Neilson, Texas A&M University
Bart C. Nemmers, University of Nebraska, Lincoln
Melinda Nish, Orange Coast College
Anthony O'Brien, Lehigh University
Norman Obst, Michigan State University
Constantin Ogloblin, Georgia Southern University
Neal Olitsky, University of Massachusetts, Dartmouth
Mary Olson, Tulane University
Terry Olson, Truman State University
James B. O'Neill, University of Delaware
Farley Ordovensky, University of the Pacific
Z. Edward O'Relley, North Dakota State University
Donald Oswald, California State University, Bakersfield
Jan Palmer, Ohio University
Michael Palumbo, Chief, Federal Reserve Board
Chris Papageorgiou, Louisiana State University
G. Hossein Parandvash, Western Oregon State College
Randall Parker, East Carolina University
Robert Parks, Washington University
David Pate, St. John Fisher College
James E. Payne, Illinois State University
Donald Pearson, Eastern Michigan University
Steven Peterson, University of Idaho
Mary Anne Pettit, Southern Illinois University, Edwardsville
William A. Phillips, University of Southern Maine
Dennis Placone, Clemson University
Charles Plot, California Institute of Technology, Pasadena
Mannie Poen, Houston Community College
Kathleen Possai, Wayne State University
Ulrika Praski-Stahlgren, University College in Gavle-Sandviken, Sweden
Edward Price, Oklahoma State University
Rula Qalyoubi, University of Wisconsin, Eau Claire
K. A. Quartey, Talladega College

Herman Quirmbach, Iowa State University
Jeffrey R. Racine, University of South Florida
Ramkishen Rajan, George Mason University
Peter Rangazas, Indiana University-Purdue University, Indianapolis
Vaman Rao, Western Illinois University
Laura Razzolini, University of Mississippi
Rob Rebelein, University of Cincinnati
J. David Reed, Bowling Green State University
Robert H. Renshaw, Northern Illinois University
Javier Reyes, University of Arkansas
Jeff Reynolds, Northern Illinois University
Rupert Rhodd, Florida Atlantic University
W. Gregory Rhodus, Bentley College
Jennifer Rice, Indiana University, Bloomington
John Robertson, Paducah Community College
Malcolm Robinson, University of North Carolina, Greensboro
Richard Roehl, University of Michigan, Dearborn
Carol Rogers, Georgetown University
William Rogers, University of Northern Colorado
Thomas Romans, State University of New York, Buffalo
David R. Ross, Bryn Mawr College
Thomas Ross, Baldwin Wallace College
Robert J. Rossana, Wayne State University
Jeffrey Rous, University of North Texas
Rochelle Ruffer, Youngstown State University
Mark Rush, University of Florida
Allen R. Sanderson, University of Chicago
Gary Santoni, Ball State University
Jeffrey Sarbaum, University of North Carolina at Chapel Hill
John Saussy, Harrisburg Area Community College
Don Schlagenhauf, Florida State University
David Schlow, Pennsylvania State University
Paul Schmitt, St. Clair County Community College
Jeremy Schwartz, Hampden-Sydney College
Martin Sefton, University of Nottingham
James Self, Indiana University
Esther-Mirjam Sent, University of Notre Dame
Rod Shadbegian, University of Massachusetts, Dartmouth
Neil Sheflin, Rutgers University
Gerald Shilling, Eastfield College
Dorothy R. Siden, Salem State College
Mark Siegler, California State University at Sacramento
Scott Simkins, North Carolina Agricultural and Technical State University
Jacek Siry, University of Georgia
Chuck Skoro, Boise State University
Phil Smith, DeKalb College
William Doyle Smith, University of Texas, El Paso

Sarah Stafford, College of William and Mary
Rebecca Stein, University of Pennsylvania
Frank Steindl, Oklahoma State University
Jeffrey Stewart, New York University
Allan Stone, Southwest Missouri State University
Courtenay Stone, Ball State University
Paul Storer, Western Washington University
Richard W. Stratton, University of Akron
Mark Strazicich, Ohio State University, Newark
Michael Stroup, Stephen F. Austin State University
Robert Stuart, Rutgers University
Della Lee Sue, Marist College
Abdulhamid Sukar, Cameron University
Terry Sutton, Southeast Missouri State University
Gilbert Suzawa, University of Rhode Island
David Swaine, Andrews University
Jason Taylor, Central Michigan University
Mark Thoma, University of Oregon
Janet Thomas, Bentley College
Kiril Tochkov, SUNY at Binghamton
Kay Unger, University of Montana
Anthony Uremovic, Joliet Junior College
David Vaughn, City University, Washington
Don Waldman, Colgate University
Francis Wambalaba, Portland State University
Sasiwimon Warunsiri, University of Colorado at Boulder
Rob Wassmer, California State University, Sacramento
Paul A. Weinstein, University of Maryland, College Park
Lee Weissert, St. Vincent College
Robert Whaples, Wake Forest University
David Wharton, Washington College
Mark Wheeler, Western Michigan University
Charles H. Whiteman, University of Iowa
Sandra Williamson, University of Pittsburgh
Brenda Wilson, Brookhaven Community College
Larry Wimmer, Brigham Young University
Mark Witte, Northwestern University
Willard E. Witte, Indiana University
Mark Wohar, University of Nebraska, Omaha
Laura Wolff, Southern Illinois University, Edwardsville
Cheonsik Woo, Vice President, Korea Development Institute
Douglas Wooley, Radford University
Arthur G. Woolf, University of Vermont
John T. Young, Riverside Community College
Michael Youngblood, Rock Valley College
Peter Zaleski, Villanova University
Jason Zimmerman, South Dakota State University
David Zucker, Martha Stewart Living Omnimedia

Supplements Authors

Luke Armstrong, Lee College

Sue Bartlett, University of South Florida

Kelly Blanchard, Purdue University

James Cobbe, Florida State University

Carol Dole, Jacksonville University

Karen Gebhardt, Colorado State University

John Graham, Rutgers University

Jill Herndon, University of Florida

Gary Hoover, University of Alabama

Patricia Kuzyk, Washington State University

Sang Lee, Southeastern Louisiana University

Svitlana Maksymenko, University of Pittsburgh

Russ McCullough, Iowa State University

Barbara Moore, University of Central Florida

James Morley, Washington University in St. Louis

William Mosher, Clark University

Constantin Ogloblin, Georgia Southern University

Edward Price, Oklahoma State University

Mark Rush, University of Florida

James K. Self, University of Indiana, Bloomington

Michael Stroup, Stephen F. Austin State University

Della Lee Sue, Marist College

Nora Underwood, University of Central Florida

Laura A. Wolff, Southern Illinois University, Edwardsville

After studying this chapter,
you will be able to:

◆ Define economics and distinguish between microeconomics and macroeconomics

◆ Explain the two big questions of economics

◆ Explain the key ideas that define the economic way of thinking

◆ Explain how economists go about their work as social scientists and policy advisers

1

WHAT IS ECONOMICS?

You are studying economics at a time of extraordinary challenge and change. The United States, Europe, and Japan, the world's richest nations, are still not fully recovered from a deep recession in which incomes shrank and millions of jobs were lost. Brazil, China, India, and Russia, poorer nations with a combined population that dwarfs our own, are growing rapidly and playing ever-greater roles in an expanding global economy.

The economic events of the past few years stand as a stark reminder that we live in a changing and sometimes turbulent world. New businesses are born and old ones die. New jobs are created and old ones disappear. Nations, businesses, and individuals must find ways of coping with economic change.

Your life will be shaped by the challenges that *you* face and the opportunities that *you* create. But to face those challenges and seize the opportunities they present, you must understand the powerful forces at play. The economics that you're about to learn will become your most reliable guide. This chapter gets you started. It describes the questions that economists try to answer and the ways in which they think as they search for the answers.

1

◆ Definition of Economics

A fundamental fact dominates our lives: We want more than we can get. Our inability to get everything we want is called **scarcity**. Scarcity is universal. It confronts all living things. Even parrots face scarcity!

Not only do I want a cracker—we all want a cracker!

© The New Yorker Collection 1985
Frank Modell from cartoonbank.com. All Rights Reserved.

Think about the things that *you* want and the scarcity that *you* face. You want to live a long and healthy life. You want to go to a good school, college, or university. You want to live in a well-equipped, spacious, and comfortable home. You want the latest smart phone and a faster Internet connection for your laptop or iPad. You want some sports and recreational gear—perhaps some new running shoes, or a new bike. And you want more time, much more than is available, to go to class, do your homework, play sports and games, read novels, go to the movies, listen to music, travel, and hang out with your friends.

What you can afford to buy is limited by your income and by the prices you must pay. And your time is limited by the fact that your day has 24 hours.

You want some other things that only governments provide. You want to live in a peaceful and secure world and safe neighborhood and enjoy the benefits of clean air, lakes, and rivers.

What governments can afford is limited by the taxes they collect. Taxes lower people's incomes and compete with the other things they want to buy.

What everyone can get—what *society* can get—is limited by the productive resources available. These resources are the gifts of nature, human labor and ingenuity, and all the previously produced tools and equipment.

Because we can't get everything we want, we must make *choices*. You can't afford *both* a laptop *and* an iPhone, so you must *choose* which one to buy. You can't spend tonight *both* studying for your next test *and* going to the movies, so again, you must *choose* which one to do. Governments can't spend a tax dollar on *both* national defense *and* environmental protection, so they must *choose* how to spend that dollar.

Your choices must somehow be made consistent with the choices of others. If you choose to buy a laptop, someone else must choose to sell it. Incentives reconcile choices. An **incentive** is a reward that encourages an action or a penalty that discourages one. Prices act as incentives. If the price of a laptop is too high, more will be offered for sale than people want to buy. And if the price is too low, fewer will be offered for sale than people want to buy. But there is a price at which choices to buy and sell are consistent.

> **Economics** is the social science that studies the *choices* that individuals, businesses, governments, and entire societies make as they cope with *scarcity* and the *incentives* that influence and reconcile those choices.

The subject has two parts:

- Microeconomics
- Macroeconomics

Microeconomics is the study of the choices that individuals and businesses make, the way these choices interact in markets, and the influence of governments. Some examples of microeconomic questions are: Why are people downloading more movies? How would a tax on e-commerce affect eBay?

Macroeconomics is the study of the performance of the national economy and the global economy. Some examples of macroeconomic questions are: Why is the U.S. unemployment rate so high? Can the Federal Reserve make our economy expand by cutting interest rates?

◆ REVIEW QUIZ

1 List some examples of the scarcity that you face.
2 Find examples of scarcity in today's headlines.
3 Find an illustration of the distinction between microeconomics and macroeconomics in today's headlines.

You can work these questions in Study Plan 1.1 and get instant feedback.

◆ Two Big Economic Questions

Two big questions summarize the scope of economics:

- How do choices end up determining *what, how,* and *for whom* goods and services are produced?
- Can the choices that people make in the pursuit of their own *self-interest* also promote the broader *social interest?*

What, How, and For Whom?

Goods and services are the objects that people value and produce to satisfy human wants. *Goods* are physical objects such as cell phones and automobiles. *Services* are tasks performed for people such as cell-phone service and auto-repair service.

What? What we produce varies across countries and changes over time. In the United States today, agriculture accounts for 1 percent of total production, manufactured goods for 22 percent, and services (retail and wholesale trade, health care, and education are the biggest ones) for 77 percent. In contrast, in China today, agriculture accounts for 11 percent of total production, manufactured goods for 49 percent, and services for 40 percent. Figure 1.1 shows these numbers and also the percentages for Brazil, which fall between those for the United States and China.

What determines these patterns of production? How do choices end up determining the quantities of cell phones, automobiles, cell-phone service, auto-repair service, and the millions of other items that are produced in the United States and around the world?

How? Goods and services are produced by using productive resources that economists call **factors of production**. Factors of production are grouped into four categories:

- Land
- Labor
- Capital
- Entrepreneurship

Land The "gifts of nature" that we use to produce goods and services are called **land**. In economics, land is what in everyday language we call *natural resources*. It includes land in the everyday sense

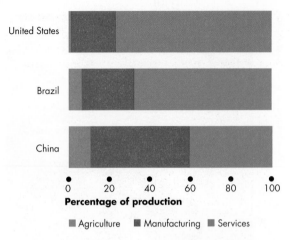

FIGURE 1.1   What Three Countries Produce

Percentage of production

■ Agriculture ■ Manufacturing ■ Services

Agriculture and manufacturing is a small percentage of production in rich countries such as the United States and a large percentage of production in poorer countries such as China. Most of what is produced in the United States is services.

Source of data: CIA Factbook 2010, Central Intelligence Agency.

myeconlab   animation

together with minerals, oil, gas, coal, water, air, forests, and fish.

Our land surface and water resources are renewable and some of our mineral resources can be recycled. But the resources that we use to create energy are nonrenewable—they can be used only once.

Labor The work time and work effort that people devote to producing goods and services is called **labor**. Labor includes the physical and mental efforts of all the people who work on farms and construction sites and in factories, shops, and offices.

The *quality* of labor depends on **human capital**, which is the knowledge and skill that people obtain from education, on-the-job training, and work experience. You are building your own human capital right now as you work on your economics course, and your human capital will continue to grow as you gain work experience.

Human capital expands over time. Today, 87 percent of the adult population of the United States have completed high school and 29 percent have a college or university degree. Figure 1.2 shows these measures of the growth of human capital in the United States over the past century.

FIGURE 1.2   A Measure of Human Capital

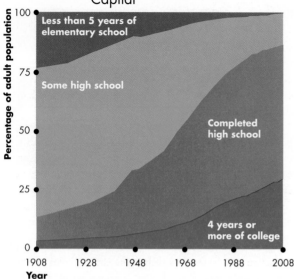

In 2008 (the most recent data), 29 percent of the population had 4 years or more of college, up from 2 percent in 1908. A further 58 percent had completed high school, up from 10 percent in 1908.

Source of data: U.S. Census Bureau, *Statistical Abstract of the United States*, 2010.

myeconlab animation

Capital The tools, instruments, machines, buildings, and other constructions that businesses use to produce goods and services are called **capital**.

In everyday language, we talk about money, stocks, and bonds as being "capital." These items are *financial* capital. Financial capital plays an important role in enabling businesses to borrow the funds that they use to buy physical capital. But because financial capital is not used to produce goods and services, it is not a productive resource.

Entrepreneurship The human resource that organizes labor, land, and capital is called **entrepreneurship**. Entrepreneurs come up with new ideas about what and how to produce, make business decisions, and bear the risks that arise from these decisions.

What determines the quantities of factors of production that are used to produce goods and services?

For Whom? Who consumes the goods and services that are produced depends on the incomes that people earn. People with large incomes can buy a wide

range of goods and services. People with small incomes have fewer options and can afford a smaller range of goods and services.

People earn their incomes by selling the services of the factors of production they own:

- Land earns **rent**.
- Labor earns **wages**.
- Capital earns **interest**.
- Entrepreneurship earns **profit**.

Which factor of production earns the most income? The answer is labor. Wages and fringe benefits are around 70 percent of total income. Land, capital, and entrepreneurship share the rest. These percentages have been remarkably constant over time.

Knowing how income is shared among the factors of production doesn't tell us how it is shared among individuals. And the distribution of income among individuals is extremely unequal. You know of some people who earn very large incomes: Angelina Jolie earns $10 million per movie; and the New York Yankees pays Alex Rodriguez $27.5 million a year.

You know of even more people who earn very small incomes. Servers at McDonald's average around $7.25 an hour; checkout clerks, cleaners, and textile and leather workers all earn less than $10 an hour.

You probably know about other persistent differences in incomes. Men, on average, earn more than women; whites earn more than minorities; college graduates earn more than high-school graduates.

We can get a good sense of who consumes the goods and services produced by looking at the percentages of total income earned by different groups of people. The 20 percent of people with the lowest incomes earn about 5 percent of total income, while the richest 20 percent earn close to 50 percent of total income. So on average, people in the richest 20 percent earn more than 10 times the incomes of those in the poorest 20 percent.

Why is the distribution of income so unequal? Why do women and minorities earn less than white males?

Economics provides some answers to all these questions about what, how, and for whom goods and services are produced and much of the rest of this book will help you to understand those answers.

We're now going to look at the second big question of economics: Can the pursuit of self-interest promote the social interest? This question is a difficult one both to appreciate and to answer.

Can the Pursuit of Self-Interest Promote the Social Interest?

Every day, you and 311 million other Americans, along with 6.9 billion people in the rest of the world, make economic choices that result in *what*, *how*, and *for whom* goods and services are produced.

Self-Interest A choice is in your **self-interest** if you think that choice is the best one available for you. You make most of your choices in your self-interest. You use your time and other resources in the ways that make the most sense to you, and you don't think too much about how your choices affect other people. You order a home delivery pizza because you're hungry and want to eat. You don't order it thinking that the delivery person needs an income. And when the pizza delivery person shows up at your door, he's not doing you a favor. He's pursuing his self-interest and hoping for a good tip.

Social Interest A choice is in the **social interest** if it leads to an outcome that is the best for society as a whole. The social interest has two dimensions: efficiency and equity (or fairness). What is best for society is an efficient and fair use of resources.

Economists say that **efficiency** is achieved when the available resources are used to produce goods and services at the lowest possible cost and in the quantities that give the greatest possible value or benefit. We will make the concept of efficiency precise and clear in Chapter 2. For now, just think of efficiency as a situation in which resources are put to their best possible use.

Equity or fairness doesn't have a crisp definition. Reasonable people, both economists and others, have a variety of views about what is fair. There is always room for disagreement and a need to be careful and clear about the notion of fairness being used.

The Big Question Can we organize our economic lives so that when each one of us makes choices that are in our self-interest, we promote the social interest? Can trading in free markets achieve the social interest? Do we need government action to achieve the social interest? Do we need international cooperation and treaties to achieve the global social interest?

Questions about the social interest are hard ones to answer and they generate discussion, debate, and disagreement. Let's put a bit of flesh on these questions with four examples.

The examples are:

- Globalization
- The information-age economy
- Climate change
- Economic instability

Globalization The term *globalization* means the expansion of international trade, borrowing and lending, and investment.

Globalization is in the self-interest of those consumers who buy low-cost goods and services produced in other countries; and it is in the self-interest of the multinational firms that produce in low-cost regions and sell in high-price regions. But is globalization in the self-interest of the low-wage worker in Malaysia who sews your new running shoes and the displaced shoemaker in Atlanta? Is it in the social interest?

Economics in Action
Life in a Small and Ever-Shrinking World

When Nike produces sports shoes, people in Malaysia get work; and when China Airlines buys new airplanes, Americans who work at Boeing in Seattle build them. While globalization brings expanded production and job opportunities for some workers, it destroys many American jobs. Workers across the manufacturing industries must learn new skills, take service jobs, which are often lower-paid, or retire earlier than previously planned.

The Information-Age Economy The technological change of the past forty years has been called the *Information Revolution*.

The information revolution has clearly served your self-interest: It has provided your cell phone, laptop, loads of handy applications, and the Internet. It has also served the self-interest of Bill Gates of Microsoft and Gordon Moore of Intel, both of whom have seen their wealth soar.

But did the information revolution best serve the social interest? Did Microsoft produce the best possible Windows operating system and sell it at a price that was in the social interest? Did Intel make the right quality of chips and sell them in the right quantities for the right prices? Or was the quality too low and the price too high? Would the social interest have been better served if Microsoft and Intel had faced competition from other firms?

Climate Change Climate change is a huge political issue today. Every serious political leader is acutely aware of the problem and of the popularity of having proposals that might lower carbon emissions.

Every day, when you make self-interested choices to use electricity and gasoline, you contribute to carbon emissions; you leave your carbon footprint. You can lessen your carbon footprint by walking, riding a bike, taking a cold shower, or planting a tree.

But can each one of us be relied upon to make decisions that affect the Earth's carbon-dioxide concentration in the social interest? Must governments change the incentives we face so that our self-interested choices are also in the social interest? How can governments change incentives? How can we encourage the use of wind and solar power to replace the burning of fossil fuels that brings climate change?

Economics in Action
Chips and Windows

Gordon Moore, who founded the chip-maker Intel, and Bill Gates, a co-founder of Microsoft, held privileged positions in the *Information Revolution*.

For many years, Intel chips were the only available chips and Windows was the only available operating system for the original IBM PC and its clones. The PC and Apple's Mac competed, but the PC had a huge market share.

An absence of competition gave Intel and Microsoft the power and ability to sell their products at prices far above the cost of production. If the prices of chips and Windows had been lower, many more people would have been able to afford a computer and would have chosen to buy one.

Economics in Action
Greenhouse Gas Emissions

Burning fossil fuels to generate electricity and to power airplanes, automobiles, and trucks pours a staggering 28 billions tons—4 tons per person—of carbon dioxide into the atmosphere each year.

Two thirds of the world's carbon emissions comes from the United States, China, the European Union, Russia, and India. The fastest growing emissions are coming from India and China.

The amount of global warming caused by economic activity and its effects are uncertain, but the emissions continue to grow and pose huge risks.

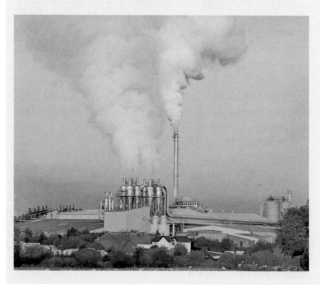

Economic Instability The years between 1993 and 2007 were a period of remarkable economic stability, so much so that they've been called the *Great Moderation*. During those years, the U.S. and global economies were on a roll. Incomes in the United States increased by 30 percent and incomes in China tripled. Even the economic shockwaves of 9/11

Economics in Action
A Credit Crunch

Flush with funds and offering record low interest rates, banks went on a lending spree to home buyers. Rapidly rising home prices made home owners feel well off and they were happy to borrow and spend. Home loans were bundled into securities that were sold and resold to banks around the world.

In 2006, as interest rates began to rise and the rate of rise in home prices slowed, borrowers defaulted on their loans. What started as a trickle became a flood. As more people defaulted, banks took losses that totaled billions of dollars by mid-2007.

Global credit markets stopped working, and people began to fear a prolonged slowdown in economic activity. Some even feared the return of the economic trauma of the *Great Depression* of the 1930s when more than 20 percent of the U.S. labor force was unemployed. The Federal Reserve, determined to avoid a catastrophe, started lending on a very large scale to the troubled banks.

brought only a small dip in the strong pace of U.S. and global economic growth.

But in August 2007, a period of financial stress began. A bank in France was the first to feel the pain that soon would grip the entire global financial system.

Banks take in people's deposits and get more funds by borrowing from each other and from other firms. Banks use these funds to make loans. All the banks' choices to borrow and lend and the choices of people and businesses to lend to and borrow from banks are made in self-interest. But does this lending and borrowing serve the social interest? Is there too much borrowing and lending that needs to be reined in, or is there too little and a need to stimulate more?

When the banks got into trouble, the Federal Reserve (the Fed) bailed them out with big loans backed by taxpayer dollars. Did the Fed's bailout of troubled banks serve the social interest? Or might the Fed's rescue action encourage banks to repeat their dangerous lending in the future?

Banks weren't the only recipients of public funds. General Motors was saved by a government bailout. GM makes its decisions in its self-interest. The government bailout of GM also served the firm's self-interest. Did the bailout also serve the social interest?

◢ REVIEW QUIZ

1. Describe the broad facts about *what*, *how*, and *for whom* goods and services are produced.
2. Use headlines from the recent news to illustrate the potential for conflict between self-interest and the social interest.

You can work these questions in Study Plan 1.2 and get instant feedback.

We've looked at four topics and asked many questions that illustrate the big question: Can choices made in the pursuit of self-interest also promote the social interest? We've asked questions but not answered them because we've not yet explained the economic principles needed to do so.

By working through this book, you will discover the economic principles that help economists figure out when the social interest is being served, when it is not, and what might be done when it is not being served. We will return to each of the unanswered questions in future chapters.

The Economic Way of Thinking

The questions that economics tries to answer tell us about the *scope of economics,* but they don't tell us how economists *think* and go about seeking answers to these questions. You're now going to see how economists go about their work.

We're going to look at six key ideas that define the *economic way of thinking.* These ideas are

- A choice is a *tradeoff.*
- People make *rational choices* by comparing *benefits* and *costs.*
- *Benefit* is what you gain from something.
- *Cost* is what you *must give up* to get something.
- Most choices are "*how-much*" choices made at the *margin.*
- Choices respond to *incentives.*

A Choice Is a Tradeoff

Because we face scarcity, we must make choices. And when we make a choice, we select from the available alternatives. For example, you can spend Saturday night studying for your next economics test or having fun with your friends, but you can't do both of these activities at the same time. You must choose how much time to devote to each. Whatever choice you make, you could have chosen something else.

You can think about your choices as tradeoffs. A **tradeoff** is an exchange—giving up one thing to get something else. When you choose how to spend your Saturday night, you face a tradeoff between studying and hanging out with your friends.

Making a Rational Choice

Economists view the choices that people make as rational. A **rational choice** is one that compares costs and benefits and achieves the greatest benefit over cost for the person making the choice.

Only the wants of the person making a choice are relevant to determine its rationality. For example, you might like your coffee black and strong but your friend prefers his milky and sweet. So it is rational for you to choose espresso and for your friend to choose cappuccino.

The idea of rational choice provides an answer to the first question: *What* goods and services will be produced and in what quantities? The answer is those that people rationally choose to buy!

But how do people choose rationally? Why do more people choose an iPod rather than a Zune? Why has the U.S. government chosen to build an interstate highway system and not an interstate high-speed railroad system? The answers turn on comparing benefits and costs.

Benefit: What You Gain

The **benefit** of something is the gain or pleasure that it brings and is determined by **preferences**—by what a person likes and dislikes and the intensity of those feelings. If you get a huge kick out of "Guitar Hero," that video game brings you a large benefit. And if you have little interest in listening to Yo Yo Ma playing a Vivaldi cello concerto, that activity brings you a small benefit.

Some benefits are large and easy to identify, such as the benefit that you get from being in school. A big piece of that benefit is the goods and services that you will be able to enjoy with the boost to your earning power when you graduate. Some benefits are small, such as the benefit you get from a slice of pizza.

Economists measure benefit as the most that a person is *willing to give up* to get something. You are willing to give up a lot to be in school. But you would give up only an iTunes download for a slice of pizza.

Cost: What You *Must* Give Up

The **opportunity cost** of something is the highest-valued alternative that must be given up to get it.

To make the idea of opportunity cost concrete, think about *your* opportunity cost of being in school. It has two components: the things you can't afford to buy and the things you can't do with your time.

Start with the things you can't afford to buy. You've spent all your income on tuition, residence fees, books, and a laptop. If you weren't in school, you would have spent this money on tickets to ball games and movies and all the other things that you enjoy. But that's only the start of your opportunity cost. You've also given up the opportunity to get a job. Suppose that the best job you could get if you weren't in school is working at Citibank as a teller earning $25,000 a year. Another part of your opportunity cost of being in school is all the things that you could buy with the extra $25,000 you would have.

As you well know, being a student eats up many hours in class time, doing homework assignments, preparing for tests, and so on. To do all these school activities, you must give up many hours of what would otherwise be leisure time spent with your friends.

So the opportunity cost of being in school is all the good things that you can't afford and don't have the spare time to enjoy. You might want to put a dollar value on that cost or you might just list all the items that make up the opportunity cost.

The examples of opportunity cost that we've just considered are all-or-nothing costs—you're either in school or not in school. Most situations are not like this one. They involve choosing _how much_ of an activity to do.

How Much? Choosing at the Margin

You can allocate the next hour between studying and instant messaging your friends, but the choice is not all or nothing. You must decide how many minutes to allocate to each activity. To make this decision, you compare the benefit of a little bit more study time with its cost—you make your choice at the **margin**.

The benefit that arises from an increase in an activity is called **marginal benefit**. For example, your marginal benefit from one more night of study before a test is the boost it gives to your grade. Your marginal benefit doesn't include the grade you're already achieving without that extra night of work.

The _opportunity cost_ of an _increase_ in an activity is called **marginal cost**. For you, the marginal cost of studying one more night is the cost of not spending that night on your favorite leisure activity.

To make your decisions, you compare marginal benefit and marginal cost. If the marginal benefit from an extra night of study exceeds its marginal cost, you study the extra night. If the marginal cost exceeds the marginal benefit, you don't study the extra night.

Choices Respond to Incentives

Economists take human nature as given and view people as acting in their self-interest. All people— you, other consumers, producers, politicians, and public servants—pursue their self-interest.

Self-interested actions are not necessarily _selfish_ actions. You might decide to use your resources in ways that bring pleasure to others as well as to yourself. But a self-interested act gets the most benefit for _you_ based on _your_ view about benefit.

The central idea of economics is that we can predict the self-interested choices that people make by looking at the _incentives_ they face. People undertake those activities for which marginal benefit exceeds marginal cost; and they reject options for which marginal cost exceeds marginal benefit.

For example, your economics instructor gives you a problem set and tells you these problems will be on the next test. Your marginal benefit from working these problems is large, so you diligently work them. In contrast, your math instructor gives you a problem set on a topic that she says will never be on a test. You get little marginal benefit from working these problems, so you decide to skip most of them.

Economists see incentives as the key to reconciling self-interest and social interest. When our choices are _not_ in the social interest, it is because of the incentives we face. One of the challenges for economists is to figure out the incentives that result in self-interested choices being in the social interest.

Economists emphasize the crucial role that institutions play in influencing the incentives that people face as they pursue their self-interest. Laws that protect private property and markets that enable voluntary exchange are the fundamental institutions. You will learn as you progress with your study of economics that where these institutions exist, self-interest can indeed promote the social interest.

REVIEW QUIZ

1 Explain the idea of a tradeoff and think of three tradeoffs that you have made today.
2 Explain what economists mean by rational choice and think of three choices that you've made today that are rational.
3 Explain why opportunity cost is the best forgone alternative and provide examples of some opportunity costs that you have faced today.
4 Explain what it means to choose at the margin and illustrate with three choices at the margin that you have made today.
5 Explain why choices respond to incentives and think of three incentives to which you have responded today.

You can work these questions in Study Plan 1.3 and get instant feedback.

Economics as Social Science and Policy Tool

Economics is both a social science and a toolkit for advising on policy decisions.

Economist as Social Scientist

As social scientists, economists seek to discover how the economic world works. In pursuit of this goal, like all scientists, economists distinguish between positive and normative statements.

Positive Statements A *positive* statement is about what *is*. It says what is currently believed about the way the world operates. A positive statement might be right or wrong, but we can test it by checking it against the facts. "Our planet is warming because of the amount of coal that we're burning" is a positive statement. We can test whether it is right or wrong.

A central task of economists is to test positive statements about how the economic world works and to weed out those that are wrong. Economics first got off the ground in the late 1700s, so it is a young science compared with, for example, physics, and much remains to be discovered.

Normative Statements A *normative* statement is about what *ought to be*. It depends on values and cannot be tested. Policy goals are normative statements. For example, "We ought to cut our use of coal by 50 percent" is a normative policy statement. You may agree or disagree with it, but you can't test it. It doesn't assert a fact that can be checked.

Unscrambling Cause and Effect Economists are particularly interested in positive statements about cause and effect. Are computers getting cheaper because people are buying them in greater quantities? Or are people buying computers in greater quantities because they are getting cheaper? Or is some third factor causing both the price of a computer to fall and the quantity of computers bought to increase?

To answer such questions, economists create and test economic models. An **economic model** is a description of some aspect of the economic world that includes only those features that are needed for the purpose at hand. For example, an economic model of a cell-phone network might include features such as the prices of calls, the number of cell-phone users, and the volume of calls. But the model would ignore cell-phone colors and ringtones.

A model is tested by comparing its predictions with the facts. But testing an economic model is difficult because we observe the outcomes of the simultaneous change of many factors. To cope with this problem, economists look for natural experiments (situations in the ordinary course of economic life in which the one factor of interest is different and other things are equal or similar); conduct statistical investigations to find correlations; and perform economic experiments by putting people in decision-making situations and varying the influence of one factor at a time to discover how they respond.

Economist as Policy Adviser

Economics is useful. It is a toolkit for advising governments and businesses and for making personal decisions. Some of the most famous economists work partly as policy advisers.

For example, Jagdish Bhagwati of Columbia University, whom you will meet on pp. 52–54, has advised governments and international organizations on trade and economic development issues.

Christina Romer of the University of California, Berkeley, is on leave and serving as the chief economic adviser to President Barack Obama and head of the President's Council of Economic Advisers.

All the policy questions on which economists provide advice involve a blend of the positive and the normative. Economics can't help with the normative part—the policy goal. But for a given goal, economics provides a method of evaluating alternative solutions—comparing marginal benefits and marginal costs and finding the solution that makes the best use of the available resources.

REVIEW QUIZ

1 Distinguish between a positive statement and a normative statement and provide examples.
2 What is a model? Can you think of a model that you might use in your everyday life?
3 How do economists try to disentangle cause and effect?
4 How is economics used as a policy tool?

You can work these questions in Study Plan 1.4 and get instant feedback.

SUMMARY

Key Points

Definition of Economics (p. 2)

- All economic questions arise from scarcity—from the fact that wants exceed the resources available to satisfy them.
- Economics is the social science that studies the choices that people make as they cope with scarcity.
- The subject divides into microeconomics and macroeconomics.

Working Problem 1 will give you a better understanding of the definition of economics.

Two Big Economic Questions (pp. 3–7)

- Two big questions summarize the scope of economics:

  1. How do choices end up determining *what*, *how*, and *for whom* goods and services are produced?

  2. When do choices made in the pursuit of *self-interest* also promote the *social interest*?

Working Problems 2 and 3 will give you a better understanding of the two big questions of economics.

The Economic Way of Thinking (pp. 8–9)

- Every choice is a tradeoff—exchanging more of something for less of something else.
- People make rational choices by comparing benefit and cost.
- Cost—*opportunity cost*—is what you must give up to get something.
- Most choices are "how much" choices made at the *margin* by comparing marginal benefit and marginal cost.
- Choices respond to incentives.

Working Problems 4 and 5 will give you a better understanding of the economic way of thinking.

Economics as Social Science and Policy Tool (p. 10)

- Economists distinguish between positive statements—what is—and normative statements—what ought to be.
- To explain the economic world, economists create and test economic models.
- Economics is a toolkit used to provide advice on government, business, and personal economic decisions.

Working Problem 6 will give you a better understanding of economics as social science and policy tool.

Key Terms

Benefit, 8
Capital, 4
Economic model, 10
Economics, 2
Efficiency, 5
Entrepreneurship, 4
Factors of production, 3
Goods and services, 3
Human capital, 3
Incentive, 2

Interest, 4
Labor, 3
Land, 3
Macroeconomics, 2
Margin, 9
Marginal benefit, 9
Marginal cost, 9
Microeconomics, 2
Opportunity cost, 8
Preferences, 8

Profit, 4
Rational choice, 8
Rent, 4
Scarcity, 2
Self-interest, 5
Social interest, 5
Tradeoff, 8
Wages, 4

STUDY PLAN PROBLEMS AND APPLICATIONS

myeconlab You can work Problems 1 to 6 in MyEconLab Chapter 1 Study Plan and get instant feedback.

Definition of Economics (Study Plan 1.1)

1. Apple Inc. decides to make iTunes freely available in unlimited quantities.
   a. Does Apple's decision change the incentives that people face?
   b. Is Apple's decision an example of a microeconomic or a macroeconomic issue?

Two Big Economic Questions (Study Plan 1.2)

2. Which of the following pairs does not match?
   a. Labor and wages
   b. Land and rent
   c. Entrepreneurship and profit
   d. Capital and profit

3. Explain how the following news headlines concern self-interest and the social interest.
   a. Starbucks Expands in China
   b. McDonald's Moves into Salads
   c. Food Must Be Labeled with Nutrition Data

The Economic Way of Thinking (Study Plan 1.3)

4. The night before an economics test, you decide to go to the movies instead of staying home and working your MyEconLab Study Plan. You get 50 percent on your test compared with the 70 percent that you normally score.
   a. Did you face a tradeoff?
   b. What was the opportunity cost of your evening at the movies?

5. **Costs Soar for London Olympics**
   The regeneration of East London, the site of the 2012 Olympic Games, is set to add extra £1.5 billion to taxpayers' bill.
   Source: *The Times*, London, July 6, 2006
   Is the cost of regenerating East London an opportunity cost of hosting the 2012 Olympic Games? Explain why or why not.

Economics as Social Science and Policy Tool

(Study Plan 1.4)

6. Which of the following statements is positive, which is normative, and which can be tested?
   a. The United States should cut its imports.
   b. China is the largest trading partner of the United States.
   c. If the price of antiretroviral drugs increases, HIV/AIDS sufferers will decrease their consumption of the drugs.

ADDITIONAL PROBLEMS AND APPLICATIONS

myeconlab You can work these problems in MyEconLab if assigned by your instructor.

Definition of Economics

7. **Hundreds Line up for 5 p.m. Ticket Giveaway**
   By noon, hundreds of Eminem fans had lined up for a chance to score free tickets to the concert.
   Source: *Detroit Free Press*, May 18, 2009
   When Eminem gave away tickets, what was free and what was scarce? Explain your answer.

Two Big Economic Questions

8. How does the creation of a successful movie influence *what*, *how*, and *for whom* goods and services are produced?

9. How does a successful movie illustrate self-interested choices that are also in the social interest?

The Economic Way of Thinking

10. Before starring in *Iron Man*, Robert Downey Jr. had appeared in 45 movies that grossed an average of $5 million on the opening weekend. In contrast, *Iron Man* grossed $102 million.
    a. How do you expect the success of *Iron Man* to influence the opportunity cost of hiring Robert Downey Jr.?
    b. How have the incentives for a movie producer to hire Robert Downey Jr. changed?

11. What might be an incentive for you to take a class in summer school? List some of the benefits and costs involved in your decision. Would your choice be rational?

Economics as Social Science and Policy Tool

12. Look at today's *Wall Street Journal*. What is the leading economic news story? With which of the big economic questions does it deal and what tradeoffs does it discuss or imply?

13. Provide two microeconomic statements and two macroeconomic statements. Classify your statements as positive or normative. Explain why.

APPENDIX

Graphs in Economics

After studying this appendix, you will be able to:

◆ Make and interpret a scatter diagram

◆ Identify linear and nonlinear relationships and relationships that have a maximum and a minimum

◆ Define and calculate the slope of a line

◆ Graph relationships among more than two variables

◆ Graphing Data

A graph represents a quantity as a distance on a line. In Fig. A1.1, a distance on the horizontal line represents temperature, measured in degrees Fahrenheit. A movement from left to right shows an increase in temperature. The point 0 represents zero degrees Fahrenheit. To the right of 0, the temperature is positive. To the left of 0 the temperature is negative (as indicated by the minus sign). A distance on the vertical line represents height, measured in thousands of feet. The point 0 represents sea level. Points above 0 represent feet above sea level. Points below 0 represent feet below sea level (indicated by a minus sign).

In Fig. A1.1, the two scale lines are perpendicular to each other and are called *axes*. The vertical line is the *y*-axis, and the horizontal line is the *x*-axis. Each axis has a zero point, which is shared by the two axes and called the *origin*.

To make a two-variable graph, we need two pieces of information: the value of the variable *x* and the value of the variable *y*. For example, off the coast of Alaska, the temperature is 32 degrees—the value of *x*. A fishing boat is located at 0 feet above sea level—the value of *y*. These two bits of information appear as point *A* in Fig. A1.1. A climber at the top of Mount McKinley on a cold day is 20,320 feet above sea level in a zero-degree gale. These two pieces of information appear as point *B*. On a warmer day, a climber might be at the peak of Mt. McKinley when the temperature is 32 degrees, at point *C*.

We can draw two lines, called *coordinates*, from point *C*. One, called the *x*-coordinate, runs from *C* to the vertical axis. This line is called "the *x*-coordinate"

FIGURE A1.1 Making a Graph

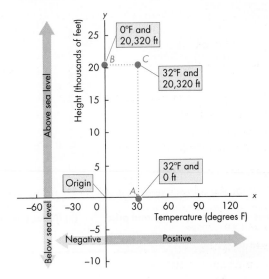

Graphs have axes that measure quantities as distances. Here, the horizontal axis (*x*-axis) measures temperature, and the vertical axis (*y*-axis) measures height. Point *A* represents a fishing boat at sea level (0 on the *y*-axis) on a day when the temperature is 32°F. Point *B* represents a climber at the top of Mt. McKinley, 20,320 feet above sea level at a temperature of 0°F. Point *C* represents a climber at the top of Mt. McKinley, 20,320 feet above sea level at a temperature of 32°F.

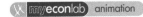

because its length is the same as the value marked off on the *x*-axis. The other, called the *y*-coordinate, runs from *C* to the horizontal axis. This line is called "the *y*-coordinate" because its length is the same as the value marked off on the *y*-axis.

We describe a point on a graph by the values of its *x*-coordinate and its *y*-coordinate. For example, at point *C*, *x* is 32 degrees and *y* is 20,320 feet.

A graph like that in Fig. A1.1 can be made using any quantitative data on two variables. The graph can show just a few points, like Fig. A1.1, or many points. Before we look at graphs with many points, let's reinforce what you've just learned by looking at two graphs made with economic data.

Economists measure variables that describe *what, how,* and *for whom* goods and services are produced. These variables are quantities produced and prices. Figure A1.2 shows two examples of economic graphs.

FIGURE A1.2   Two Graphs of Economic Data

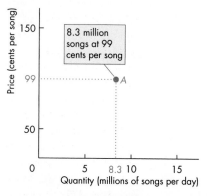

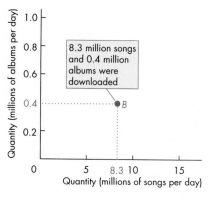

The graph in part (a) tells us that in January 2010, 8.3 million songs per day were downloaded from the iTunes store at a price of 99 cents a song.

The graph in part (b) tells us that in January 2010, 8.3 million songs per day and 0.4 million albums per day were downloaded from the iTunes store.

(a) iTunes downloads: quantity and price   **(b) iTunes downloads: songs and albums**

myeconlab animation

Figure A1.2(a) is a graph about iTunes song downloads in January 2010. The *x*-axis measures the quantity of songs downloaded per day and the *y*-axis measures the price of a song. Point *A* tells us what the quantity and price were. You can "read" this graph as telling you that in January 2010, 8.3 million songs a day were downloaded at a price of 99¢ per song.

Figure A1.2(b) is a graph about iTunes song and album downloads in January 2010. The *x*-axis measures the quantity of songs downloaded per day and the *y*-axis measures the quantity of albums downloaded per day. Point *B* tells us what these quantities were. You can "read" this graph as telling you that in January 2010, 8.3 million songs a day and 0.4 million albums were downloaded.

The three graphs that you've just seen tell you how to make a graph and how to read a data point on a graph, but they don't improve on the raw data. Graphs become interesting and revealing when they contain a number of data points because then you can visualize the data.

Economists create graphs based on the principles in Figs. A1.1 and A1.2 to reveal, describe, and visualize the relationships among variables. We're now going to look at some examples. These graphs are called scatter diagrams.

Scatter Diagrams

A **scatter diagram** is a graph that plots the value of one variable against the value of another variable for a number of different values of each variable. Such a graph reveals whether a relationship exists between

two variables and describes their relationship.

The table in Fig. A1.3 shows some data on two variables: the number of tickets sold at the box office and the number of DVDs sold for eight of the most popular movies in 2009.

What is the relationship between these two variables? Does a big box office success generate a large volume of DVD sales? Or does a box office success mean that fewer DVDs are sold?

We can answer these questions by making a scatter diagram. We do so by graphing the data in the table. In the graph in Fig. A1.3, each point shows the number of box office tickets sold (the *x* variable) and the number of DVDs sold (the *y* variable) of one of the movies. There are eight movies, so there are eight points "scattered" within the graph.

The point labeled *A* tells us that Star Trek sold 34 million tickets at the box office and 6 million DVDs. The points in the graph form a pattern, which reveals that larger box office sales are associated with larger DVD sales. But the points also tell us that this association is weak. You can't predict DVD sales with any confidence by knowing only the number of tickets sold at the box office.

Figure A1.4 shows two scatter diagrams of economic variables. Part (a) shows the relationship between income and expenditure, on average, during a ten-year period. Each point represents income and expenditure in a given year. For example, point *A* shows that in 2006, income was $31 thousand and expenditure was $30 thousand. This graph shows that as income increases, so does expenditure, and the relationship is a close one.

FIGURE A1.3   A Scatter Diagram

Movie	Tickets	DVDs
	(millions)	
Twilight	38	10
Transformers: Revenge of the Fallen	54	9
Up	39	8
Harry Potter and the Half-Blood Prince	40	7
Star Trek	34	6
The Hangover	37	6
Ice Age: Dawn of the Dinosaurs	26	5
The Proposal	22	5

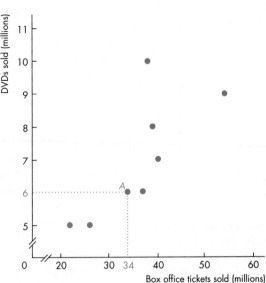

The table lists the number of tickets sold at the box office and the number of DVDs sold for eight popular movies. The scatter diagram reveals the relationship between these two variables. Each point shows the values of the two variables for a specific movie. For example, point *A* shows the point for *Star Trek*, which sold 34 million tickets at the box office and 6 million DVDs. The pattern formed by the points shows that there is a tendency for large box office sales to bring greater DVD sales. But you couldn't predict how many DVDs a movie would sell just by knowing its box office sales.

myeconlab animation

Figure A1.4(b) shows a scatter diagram of U.S. inflation and unemployment during the 2000s. Here, the points for 2000 to 2008 show no relationship between the two variables, but the high unemployment rate of 2009 brought a low inflation rate that year.

You can see that a scatter diagram conveys a wealth of information, and it does so in much less space than we have used to describe only some of its features. But you do have to "read" the graph to obtain all this information.

FIGURE A1.4   Two Economic Scatter Diagrams

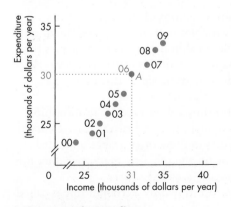

(a) Income and expenditure

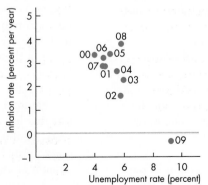

(b) Unemployment and inflation

The scatter diagram in part (a) shows the relationship between income and expenditure from 2000 to 2009. Point *A* shows that in 2006, income was $31 (thousand) on the *x*-axis and expenditure was $30 (thousand) on the *y*-axis. This graph shows that as income rises, so does expenditure and the relationship is a close one.

The scatter diagram in part (b) shows a weak relationship between unemployment and inflation in the United States during most of the 2000s.

myeconlab animation

Breaks in the Axes The graph in Fig. A1.4(a) has breaks in its axes, as shown by the small gaps. The breaks indicate that there are jumps from the origin, 0, to the first values recorded.

The breaks are used because the lowest values of income and expenditure exceed $20,000. If we made this graph with no breaks in its axes, there would be a lot of empty space, all the points would be crowded into the top right corner, and it would be difficult to see whether a relationship exists between these two variables. By breaking the axes, we are able to bring the relationship into view.

Putting a break in one or both axes is like using a zoom lens to bring the relationship into the center of the graph and magnify it so that the relationship fills the graph.

Misleading Graphs Breaks can be used to highlight a relationship, but they can also be used to mislead—to make a graph that lies. The most common way of making a graph lie is to put a break in the axis and either to stretch or compress the scale. For example, suppose that in Fig. A1.4(a), the *y*-axis that measures expenditure ran from zero to $35,000 while the *x*-axis was the same as the one shown. The graph would now create the impression that despite a huge increase in income, expenditure had barely changed.

To avoid being misled, it is a good idea to get into the habit of always looking closely at the values and the labels on the axes of a graph before you start to interpret it.

Correlation and Causation A scatter diagram that shows a clear relationship between two variables, such as Fig. A1.4(a), tells us that the two variables have a high correlation. When a high correlation is present, we can predict the value of one variable from the value of the other variable. But correlation does not imply causation.

Sometimes a high correlation is a coincidence, but sometimes it does arise from a causal relationship. It is likely, for example, that rising income causes rising expenditure (Fig. A1.4a) and that high unemployment makes for a slack economy in which prices don't rise quickly, so the inflation rate is low (Fig. A1.4b).

You've now seen how we can use graphs in economics to show economic data and to reveal relationships. Next, we'll learn how economists use graphs to construct and display economic models.

◆ Graphs Used in Economic Models

The graphs used in economics are not always designed to show real-world data. Often they are used to show general relationships among the variables in an economic model.

An *economic model* is a stripped-down, simplified description of an economy or of a component of an economy such as a business or a household. It consists of statements about economic behavior that can be expressed as equations or as curves in a graph. Economists use models to explore the effects of different policies or other influences on the economy in ways that are similar to the use of model airplanes in wind tunnels and models of the climate.

You will encounter many different kinds of graphs in economic models, but there are some repeating patterns. Once you've learned to recognize these patterns, you will instantly understand the meaning of a graph. Here, we'll look at the different types of curves that are used in economic models, and we'll see some everyday examples of each type of curve. The patterns to look for in graphs are the four cases in which

- Variables move in the same direction.
- Variables move in opposite directions.
- Variables have a maximum or a minimum.
- Variables are unrelated.

Let's look at these four cases.

Variables That Move in the Same Direction

Figure A1.5 shows graphs of the relationships between two variables that move up and down together. A relationship between two variables that move in the same direction is called a **positive relationship** or a **direct relationship**. A line that slopes upward shows such a relationship.

Figure A1.5 shows three types of relationships: one that has a straight line and two that have curved lines. All the lines in these three graphs are called curves. Any line on a graph—no matter whether it is straight or curved—is called a *curve*.

A relationship shown by a straight line is called a **linear relationship**. Figure A1.5(a) shows a linear relationship between the number of miles traveled in

FIGURE A1.5   Positive (Direct) Relationships

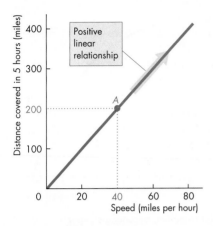

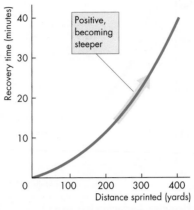

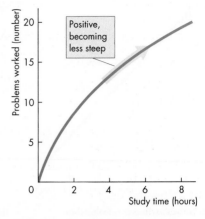

(a) Positive linear relationship   **(b) Positive, becoming steeper**   **(c) Positive, becoming less steep**

Each part shows a positive (direct) relationship between two variables. That is, as the value of the variable measured on the x-axis increases, so does the value of the variable measured on the y-axis. Part (a) shows a linear positive relationship—as the two variables increase together, we move along a straight line.

Part (b) shows a positive relationship such that as the two variables increase together, we move along a curve that becomes steeper.

Part (c) shows a positive relationship such that as the two variables increase together, we move along a curve that becomes flatter.

 animation

5 hours and speed. For example, point A shows that we will travel 200 miles in 5 hours if our speed is 40 miles an hour. If we double our speed to 80 miles an hour, we will travel 400 miles in 5 hours.

Figure A1.5(b) shows the relationship between distance sprinted and recovery time (the time it takes the heart rate to return to its normal resting rate). This relationship is an upward-sloping one that starts out quite flat but then becomes steeper as we move along the curve away from the origin. The reason this curve becomes steeper is that the additional recovery time needed from sprinting an additional 100 yards increases. It takes less than 5 minutes to recover from sprinting 100 yards but more than 10 minutes to recover from 200 yards.

Figure A1.5(c) shows the relationship between the number of problems worked by a student and the amount of study time. This relationship is an upward-sloping one that starts out quite steep and becomes flatter as we move along the curve away from the origin. Study time becomes less productive as the student spends more hours studying and becomes more tired.

Variables That Move in Opposite Directions

Figure A1.6 shows relationships between things that move in opposite directions. A relationship between variables that move in opposite directions is called a **negative relationship** or an **inverse relationship**.

Figure A1.6(a) shows the relationship between the hours spent playing squash and the hours spent playing tennis when the total time available is 5 hours. One extra hour spent playing tennis means one hour less spent playing squash and vice versa. This relationship is negative and linear.

Figure A1.6(b) shows the relationship between the cost per mile traveled and the length of a journey. The longer the journey, the lower is the cost per mile. But as the journey length increases, even though the cost per mile decreases, the fall in the cost is smaller the longer the journey. This feature of the relationship is shown by the fact that the curve slopes downward, starting out steep at a short journey length and then becoming flatter as the journey length increases. This relationship arises because some of the costs are fixed, such as auto insurance, and the fixed costs are spread over a longer journey.

FIGURE A1.6   Negative (Inverse) Relationships

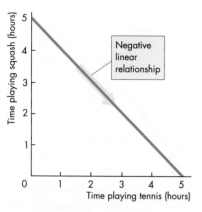

(a) Negative linear relationship

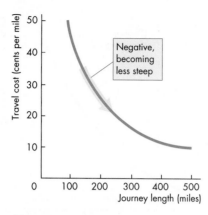

(b) Negative, becoming less steep

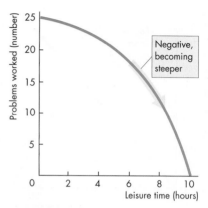

(c) Negative, becoming steeper

Each part shows a negative (inverse) relationship between two variables. Part (a) shows a linear negative relationship. The total time spent playing tennis and squash is 5 hours. As the time spent playing tennis increases, the time spent playing squash decreases, and we move along a straight line.

Part (b) shows a negative relationship such that as the journey length increases, the travel cost decreases as we move along a curve that becomes less steep.

Part (c) shows a negative relationship such that as leisure time increases, the number of problems worked decreases as we move along a curve that becomes steeper.

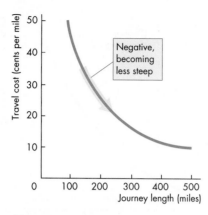 myeconlab animation

Figure A1.6(c) shows the relationship between the amount of leisure time and the number of problems worked by a student. Increasing leisure time produces an increasingly large reduction in the number of problems worked. This relationship is a negative one that starts out with a gentle slope at a small number of leisure hours and becomes steeper as the number of leisure hours increases. This relationship is a different view of the idea shown in Fig. A1.5(c).

Variables That Have a Maximum or a Minimum

Many relationships in economic models have a maximum or a minimum. For example, firms try to make the maximum possible profit and to produce at the lowest possible cost. Figure A1.7 shows relationships that have a maximum or a minimum.

Figure A1.7(a) shows the relationship between rainfall and wheat yield. When there is no rainfall, wheat will not grow, so the yield is zero. As the rainfall increases up to 10 days a month, the wheat yield

increases. With 10 rainy days each month, the wheat yield reaches its maximum at 40 bushels an acre (point *A*). Rain in excess of 10 days a month starts to lower the yield of wheat. If every day is rainy, the wheat suffers from a lack of sunshine and the yield decreases to zero. This relationship is one that starts out sloping upward, reaches a maximum, and then slopes downward.

Figure A1.7(b) shows the reverse case—a relationship that begins sloping downward, falls to a minimum, and then slopes upward. Most economic costs are like this relationship. An example is the relationship between the cost per mile and speed for a car trip. At low speeds, the car is creeping in a traffic snarl-up. The number of miles per gallon is low, so the cost per mile is high. At high speeds, the car is traveling faster than its efficient speed, using a large quantity of gasoline, and again the number of miles per gallon is low and the cost per mile is high. At a speed of 55 miles an hour, the cost per mile is at its minimum (point *B*). This relationship is one that starts out sloping downward, reaches a minimum, and then slopes upward.

FIGURE A1.7   Maximum and Minimum Points

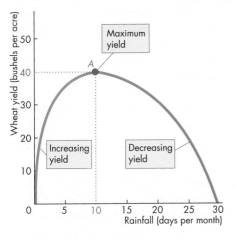

(a) Relationship with a maximum

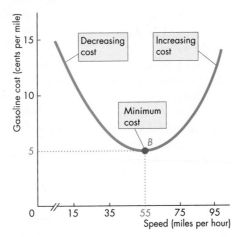

(b) Relationship with a minimum

Part (a) shows a relationship that has a maximum point, *A*. The curve slopes upward as it rises to its maximum point, is flat at its maximum, and then slopes downward.

Part (b) shows a relationship with a minimum point, *B*. The curve slopes downward as it falls to its minimum, is flat at its minimum, and then slopes upward.

Variables That Are Unrelated

There are many situations in which no matter what happens to the value of one variable, the other variable remains constant. Sometimes we want to show the independence between two variables in a graph, and Fig. A1.8 shows two ways of achieving this.

In describing the graphs in Fig. A1.5 through Fig. A1.7, we have talked about curves that slope upward or slope downward, and curves that become less steep or steeper. Let's spend a little time discussing exactly what we mean by *slope* and how we measure the slope of a curve.

FIGURE A1.8   Variables That Are Unrelated

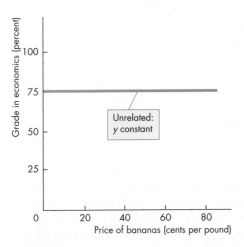

(a) Unrelated: *y* constant

(b) Unrelated: *x* constant

This figure shows how we can graph two variables that are unrelated. In part (a), a student's grade in economics is plotted at 75 percent on the *y*-axis regardless of the price of bananas on the *x*-axis. The curve is horizontal.

In part (b), the output of the vineyards of France on the *x*-axis does not vary with the rainfall in California on the *y*-axis. The curve is vertical.

◆ The Slope of a Relationship

We can measure the influence of one variable on another by the slope of the relationship. The **slope** of a relationship is the change in the value of the variable measured on the y-axis divided by the change in the value of the variable measured on the x-axis. We use the Greek letter Δ (*delta*) to represent "change in." Thus Δy means the change in the value of the variable measured on the y-axis, and Δx means the change in the value of the variable measured on the x-axis. Therefore the slope of the relationship is

$$\text{Slope} = \frac{\Delta y}{\Delta x}.$$

If a large change in the variable measured on the y-axis (Δy) is associated with a small change in the variable measured on the x-axis (Δx), the slope is large and the curve is steep. If a small change in the variable measured on the y-axis (Δy) is associated with a large change in the variable measured on the x-axis (Δx), the slope is small and the curve is flat.

We can make the idea of slope clearer by doing some calculations.

The Slope of a Straight Line

The slope of a straight line is the same regardless of where on the line you calculate it. The slope of a straight line is constant. Let's calculate the slope of the positive relationship in Fig. A1.9. In part (a),

---

FIGURE A1.9   The Slope of a Straight Line

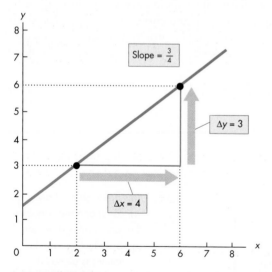

(a) Positive slope

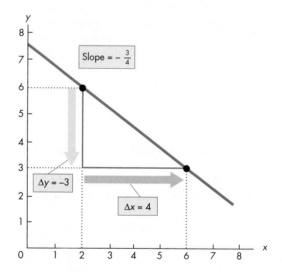

(b) Negative slope

To calculate the slope of a straight line, we divide the change in the value of the variable measured on the y-axis (Δy) by the change in the value of the variable measured on the x-axis (Δx) as we move along the line.

Part (a) shows the calculation of a positive slope. When x increases from 2 to 6, Δx equals 4. That change in x

brings about an increase in y from 3 to 6, so Δy equals 3. The slope (Δy/Δx) equals 3/4.

Part (b) shows the calculation of a negative slope. When x increases from 2 to 6, Δx equals 4. That increase in x brings about a decrease in y from 6 to 3, so Δy equals –3. The slope (Δy/Δx) equals –3/4.

when x increases from 2 to 6, y increases from 3 to 6. The change in x is +4—that is, Δx is 4. The change in y is +3—that is, Δy is 3. The slope of that line is

$$\frac{\Delta y}{\Delta x} = \frac{3}{4}.$$

In part (b), when x increases from 2 to 6, y decreases from 6 to 3. The change in y is *minus* 3—that is, Δy is –3. The change in x is *plus* 4—that is, Δx is 4. The slope of the curve is

$$\frac{\Delta y}{\Delta x} = \frac{-3}{4}.$$

Notice that the two slopes have the same magnitude (3/4), but the slope of the line in part (a) is positive (+3/+4 = 3/4) while that in part (b) is negative (–3/+4 = –3/4). The slope of a positive relationship is positive; the slope of a negative relationship is negative.

The Slope of a Curved Line

The slope of a curved line is trickier. The slope of a curved line is not constant, so the slope depends on where on the curved line we calculate it. There are two ways to calculate the slope of a curved line: You can calculate the slope at a point, or you can calculate the slope across an arc of the curve. Let's look at the two alternatives.

Slope at a Point To calculate the slope at a point on a curve, you need to construct a straight line that has the same slope as the curve at the point in question. Figure A1.10 shows how this is done. Suppose you want to calculate the slope of the curve at point A. Place a ruler on the graph so that the ruler touches point A and no other point on the curve, then draw a straight line along the edge of the ruler. The straight red line is this line, and it is the tangent to the curve at point A. If the ruler touches the curve only at point A, then the slope of the curve at point A must be the same as the slope of the edge of the ruler. If the curve and the ruler do not have the same slope, the line along the edge of the ruler will cut the curve instead of just touching it.

Now that you have found a straight line with the same slope as the curve at point A, you can calculate the slope of the curve at point A by calculating the slope of the straight line. Along the straight line, as x

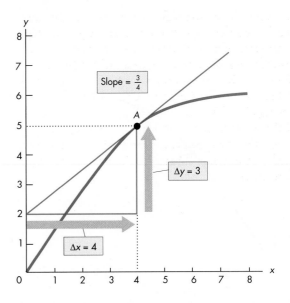

FIGURE A1.10   Slope at a Point

To calculate the slope of the curve at point A, draw the red line that just touches the curve at A—the tangent. The slope of this straight line is calculated by dividing the change in y by the change in x along the red line. When x increases from 0 to 4, Δx equals 4. That change in x is associated with an increase in y from 2 to 5, so Δy equals 3. The slope of the red line is 3/4, so the slope of the curve at point A is 3/4.

increases from 0 to 4 (Δx is 4) y increases from 2 to 5 (Δy is 3). Therefore the slope of the straight line is

$$\frac{\Delta y}{\Delta x} = \frac{3}{4}.$$

So the slope of the curve at point A is 3/4.

Slope Across an Arc An arc of a curve is a piece of a curve. Fig. A1.11 shows the same curve as in Fig. A1.10, but instead of calculating the slope at point A, we are now going to calculate the slope across the arc from point B to point C. You can see that the slope of the curve at point B is greater than at point C. When we calculate the slope across an arc, we are calculating the average slope between two points. As we move along the arc from B to C, x increases from 3 to 5 and y increases from 4.0 to 5.5. The change in x is 2 (Δx is 2), and the change in y is 1.5 (Δy is 1.5).

FIGURE A1.11   Slope Across an Arc

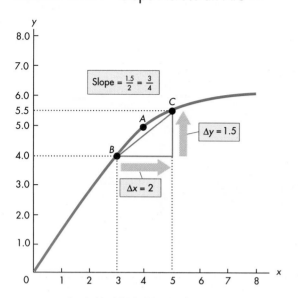

To calculate the average slope of the curve along the arc *BC*, draw a straight line from point *B* to point *C*. The slope of the line *BC* is calculated by dividing the change in *y* by the change in *x*. In moving from *B* to *C*, the increase in x is 2 (Δx equals 2) and the change in y is 1.5 (Δy equals 1.5). The slope of the line *BC* is 1.5 divided by 2, or 3/4. So the slope of the curve across the arc *BC* is 3/4.

 animation

Therefore the slope is

$$\frac{\Delta y}{\Delta x} = \frac{1.5}{2} = \frac{3}{4}.$$

So the slope of the curve across the arc *BC* is 3/4.

This calculation gives us the slope of the curve between points *B* and *C*. The actual slope calculated is the slope of the straight line from *B* to *C*. This slope approximates the average slope of the curve along the arc *BC*. In this particular example, the slope across the arc *BC* is identical to the slope of the curve at point *A*, but the calculation of the slope of a curve does not always work out so neatly. You might have fun constructing some more examples and a few counter examples.

You now know how to make and interpret a graph. So far, we've limited our attention to graphs of two variables. We're now going to learn how to graph more than two variables.

Graphing Relationships Among More Than Two Variables

We have seen that we can graph the relationship between two variables as a point formed by the *x*- and *y*-coordinates in a two-dimensional graph. You might be thinking that although a two-dimensional graph is informative, most of the things in which you are likely to be interested involve relationships among many variables, not just two. For example, the amount of ice cream consumed depends on the price of ice cream and the temperature. If ice cream is expensive and the temperature is low, people eat much less ice cream than when ice cream is inexpensive and the temperature is high. For any given price of ice cream, the quantity consumed varies with the temperature; and for any given temperature, the quantity of ice cream consumed varies with its price.

Figure A1.12 shows a relationship among three variables. The table shows the number of gallons of ice cream consumed each day at two different temperatures and at a number of different prices of ice cream. How can we graph these numbers?

To graph a relationship that involves more than two variables, we use the *ceteris paribus* assumption.

Ceteris Paribus

Ceteris paribus (often shortened to *cet par*) means "if all other relevant things remain the same." To isolate the relationship of interest in a laboratory experiment, a scientist holds everything constant except for the variable whose effect is being studied. Economists use the same method to graph a relationship that has more than two variables.

Figure A1.12 shows an example. There, you can see what happens to the quantity of ice cream consumed when the price of ice cream varies but the temperature is held constant.

The curve labeled 70°F shows the relationship between ice cream consumption and the price of ice cream if the temperature remains at 70°F. The numbers used to plot that curve are those in the first two columns of the table. For example, if the temperature is 70°F, 10 gallons are consumed when the price is $2.75 a scoop and 18 gallons are consumed when the price is $2.25 a scoop.

The curve labeled 90°F shows the relationship between ice cream consumption and the price of ice cream if the temperature remains at 90°F. The

FIGURE A1.12   Graphing a Relationship Among Three Variables

Price (dollars per scoop)	Ice cream consumption (gallons per day)	
	70°F	90°F
2.00	25	50
2.25	18	36
2.50	13	26
2.75	**10**	**20**
3.00	7	14
3.25	5	10
3.50	3	6

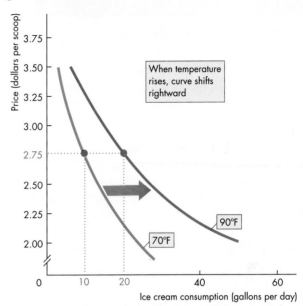

Ice cream consumption depends on its price and the temperature. The table tells us how many gallons of ice cream are consumed each day at different prices and two different temperatures. For example, if the price is $2.75 a scoop and the temperature is 70°F, 10 gallons of ice cream are consumed.

To graph a relationship among three variables, the value of one variable is held constant. The graph shows the relationship between price and consumption when temperature is held constant. One curve holds temperature at 70°F and the other holds it at 90°F.

A change in the price of ice cream brings a movement along one of the curves—along the blue curve at 70°F and along the red curve at 90°F.

When the temperature *rises* from 70°F to 90°F, the curve that shows the relationship between consumption and price *shifts* rightward from the blue curve to the red curve.

numbers used to plot that curve are those in the first and third columns of the table. For example, if the temperature is 90°F, 20 gallons are consumed when the price is $2.75 a scoop and 36 gallons are consumed when the price is $2.25 a scoop.

When the price of ice cream changes but the temperature is constant, you can think of what happens in the graph as a movement along one of the curves. At 70°F there is a movement along the blue curve and at 90°F there is a movement along the red curve.

When Other Things Change

The temperature is held constant along each of the curves in Fig. A1.12, but in reality the temperature

changes. When that event occurs, you can think of what happens in the graph as a shift of the curve. When the temperature rises from 70°F to 90°F, the curve that shows the relationship between ice cream consumption and the price of ice cream shifts rightward from the blue curve to the red curve.

You will encounter these ideas of movements along and shifts of curves at many points in your study of economics. Think carefully about what you've just learned and make up some examples (with assumed numbers) about other relationships.

With what you have learned about graphs, you can move forward with your study of economics. There are no graphs in this book that are more complicated than those that have been explained in this appendix.

MATHEMATICAL NOTE

Equations of Straight Lines

If a straight line in a graph describes the relationship between two variables, we call it a linear relationship. Figure 1 shows the *linear relationship* between a person's expenditure and income. This person spends $100 a week (by borrowing or spending previous savings) when income is zero. Out of each dollar earned, this person spends 50 cents (and saves 50 cents).

All linear relationships are described by the same general equation. We call the quantity that is measured on the horizontal axis (or x-axis) x, and we call the quantity that is measured on the vertical axis (or y-axis) y. In the case of Fig. 1, x is income and y is expenditure.

A Linear Equation

The equation that describes a straight-line relationship between x and y is

$$y = a + bx.$$

In this equation, a and b are fixed numbers and they are called *constants*. The values of x and y vary, so these numbers are called *variables*. Because the equation describes a straight line, the equation is called a *linear equation*.

The equation tells us that when the value of x is zero, the value of y is a. We call the constant a the y-axis intercept. The reason is that on the graph the straight line hits the y-axis at a value equal to a. Figure 1 illustrates the y-axis intercept.

For positive values of x, the value of y exceeds a. The constant b tells us by how much y increases above a as x increases. The constant b is the slope of the line.

Slope of Line

As we explain in the chapter, the *slope* of a relationship is the change in the value of y divided by the change in the value of x. We use the Greek letter Δ (delta) to represent "change in." So Δy means the change in the value of the variable measured on the y-axis, and Δx means the change in the value of the variable measured on the x-axis. Therefore the slope of the relationship is

$$\text{Slope} = \frac{\Delta y}{\Delta x}$$

To see why the slope is b, suppose that initially the value of x is x_1, or $200 in Fig. 2. The corresponding value of y is y_1, also $200 in Fig. 2. The equation of the line tells us that

$$y_1 = a + bx_1. \tag{1}$$

Now the value of x increases by Δx to $x_1 + \Delta x$ (or $400 in Fig. 2). And the value of y increases by Δy to $y_1 + \Delta y$ (or $300 in Fig. 2).

The equation of the line now tells us that

$$y_1 + \Delta y = a + b(x_1 + \Delta x). \tag{2}$$

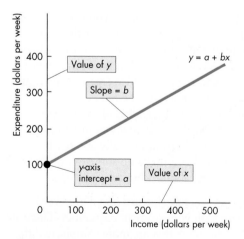

Figure 1 Linear relationship

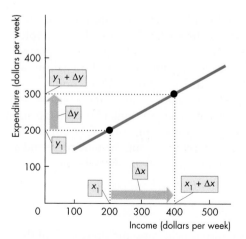

Figure 2 Calculating slope

To calculate the slope of the line, subtract equation (1) from equation (2) to obtain

$$\Delta y = b\Delta x \qquad (3)$$

and now divide equation (3) by Δx to obtain

$$\Delta y/\Delta x = b.$$

So the slope of the line is b.

Position of Line

The y-axis intercept determines the position of the line on the graph. Figure 3 illustrates the relationship between the y-axis intercept and the position of the line. In this graph, the y-axis measures saving and the x-axis measures income.

When the y-axis intercept, a, is positive, the line hits the y-axis at a positive value of y—as the blue line does. Its y-axis intercept is 100. When the y-axis intercept, a, is zero, the line hits the y-axis at the origin—as the purple line does. Its y-axis intercept is 0. When the y-axis intercept, a, is negative, the line hits the y-axis at a negative value of y—as the red line does. Its y-axis intercept is –100.

As the equations of the three lines show, the value of the y-axis intercept does not influence the slope of the line. All three lines have a slope equal to 0.5.

Positive Relationships

Figure 1 shows a positive relationship—the two variables x and y move in the same direction. All positive relationships have a slope that is positive. In the equation of the line, the constant b is positive. In this example, the y-axis intercept, a, is 100. The slope b equals $\Delta y/\Delta x$, which in Fig. 2 is 100/200 or 0.5. The equation of the line is

$$y = 100 + 0.5x.$$

Negative Relationships

Figure 4 shows a negative relationship—the two variables x and y move in the opposite direction. All negative relationships have a slope that is negative. In the equation of the line, the constant b is negative. In the example in Fig. 4, the y-axis intercept, a, is 30. The slope, b, equals $\Delta y/\Delta x$, which is –20/2 or –10. The equation of the line is

$$y = 30 + (-10)x$$

or

$$y = 30 - 10x.$$

Example

A straight line has a y-axis intercept of 50 and a slope of 2. What is the equation of this line?
The equation of a straight line is

$$y = a + bx$$

where a is the y-axis intercept and b is the slope. So the equation is

$$y = 50 + 2x.$$

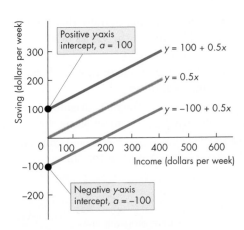

Figure 3 The y-axis intercept

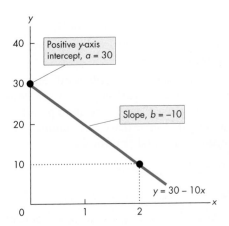

Figure 4 Negative relationship

REVIEW QUIZ

1 Explain how we "read" the three graphs in Figs A1.1 and A1.2.
2 Explain what scatter diagrams show and why we use them.
3 Explain how we "read" the three scatter diagrams in Figs A1.3 and A1.4.
4 Draw a graph to show the relationship between two variables that move in the same direction.
5 Draw a graph to show the relationship between two variables that move in opposite directions.
6 Draw a graph to show the relationship between two variables that have a maximum and a minimum.

7 Which of the relationships in Questions 4 and 5 is a positive relationship and which is a negative relationship?
8 What are the two ways of calculating the slope of a curved line?
9 How do we graph a relationship among more than two variables?
10 Explain what change will bring a *movement along* a curve.
11 Explain what change will bring a *shift* of a curve.

You can work these questions in Study Plan 1.A and get instant feedback.

SUMMARY

Key Points

Graphing Data (pp. 13–16)

- A graph is made by plotting the values of two variables x and y at a point that corresponds to their values measured along the x-axis and the y-axis.
- A scatter diagram is a graph that plots the values of two variables for a number of different values of each.
- A scatter diagram shows the relationship between the two variables. It shows whether they are positively related, negatively related, or unrelated.

Graphs Used in Economic Models (pp. 16–19)

- Graphs are used to show relationships among variables in economic models.
- Relationships can be positive (an upward-sloping curve), negative (a downward-sloping curve), positive and then negative (have a maximum point), negative and then positive (have a minimum point), or unrelated (a horizontal or vertical curve).

The Slope of a Relationship (pp. 20–22)

- The slope of a relationship is calculated as the change in the value of the variable measured on the y-axis divided by the change in the value of the variable measured on the x-axis—that is, $\Delta y/\Delta x$.
- A straight line has a constant slope.
- A curved line has a varying slope. To calculate the slope of a curved line, we calculate the slope at a point or across an arc.

Graphing Relationships Among More Than Two Variables (pp. 22–23)

- To graph a relationship among more than two variables, we hold constant the values of all the variables except two.
- We then plot the value of one of the variables against the value of another.
- A *cet par* change in the value of a variable on an axis of a graph brings a movement along the curve.
- A change in the value of a variable held constant along the curve brings a shift of the curve.

Key Terms

Ceteris paribus, 22
Direct relationship, 16
Inverse relationship, 17
Linear relationship, 16
Negative relationship, 17
Positive relationship, 16
Scatter diagram, 14
Slope, 20

STUDY PLAN PROBLEMS AND APPLICATIONS

myeconlab You can work Problems 1 to 11 in MyEconLab Chapter 1A Study Plan and get instant feedback.

Use the following spreadsheet to work Problems 1 to 3. The spreadsheet provides data on the U.S. economy: Column A is the year, column B is the inflation rate, column C is the interest rate, column D is the growth rate, and column E is the unemployment rate.

	A	B	C	D	E
1	1999	2.2	4.6	4.8	4.2
2	2000	3.4	5.8	4.1	4.0
3	2001	2.8	3.4	1.1	4.7
4	2002	1.6	1.6	1.8	5.8
5	2003	2.3	1.0	2.5	6.0
6	2004	2.7	1.4	3.6	5.5
7	2005	3.4	3.2	3.1	5.1
8	2006	3.2	4.7	2.7	4.6
9	2007	2.8	4.4	2.1	4.6
10	2008	3.8	1.4	0.4	5.8
11	2009	−0.4	0.2	−2.4	9.3

1. Draw a scatter diagram of the inflation rate and the interest rate. Describe the relationship.
2. Draw a scatter diagram of the growth rate and the unemployment rate. Describe the relationship.
3. Draw a scatter diagram of the interest rate and the unemployment rate. Describe the relationship.

Use the following news clip to work Problems 4 to 6.
***Clash of the Titans* Tops Box Office With Sales of $61.2 Million:**

Movie	Theaters (number)	Revenue (dollars per theater)
Clash of the Titans	3,777	16,213
Tyler Perry's Why Did I Get Married	2,155	13,591
How To Train Your Dragon	4,060	7,145
The Last Song	2,673	5,989

Source: Bloomberg.com, April 5, 2010

4. Draw a graph of the relationship between the revenue per theater on the y-axis and the number of theaters on the x-axis. Describe the relationship.
5. Calculate the slope of the relationship between 4,060 and 2,673 theaters.
6. Calculate the slope of the relationship between 2,155 and 4,060 theaters.

7. Calculate the slope of the following relationship.

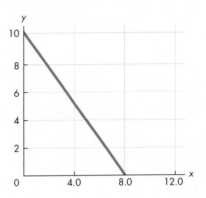

Use the following relationship to work Problems 8 and 9.

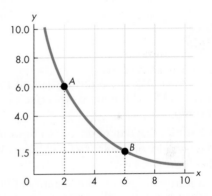

8. Calculate the slope of the relationship at point A and at point B.
9. Calculate the slope across the arc AB.

Use the following table to work Problems 10 and 11. The table gives the price of a balloon ride, the temperature, and the number of rides a day.

Price (dollars per ride)	Balloon rides (number per day)		
	50°F	70°F	90°F
5	32	40	50
10	27	32	40
15	18	27	32

10. Draw a graph to show the relationship between the price and the number of rides, when the temperature is 70°F. Describe this relationship.
11. What happens in the graph in Problem 10 if the temperature rises to 90°F?

ADDITIONAL ASSIGNABLE PROBLEMS AND APPLICATIONS

myeconlab You can work these problems in MyEconLab if assigned by your instructor.

Use the following spreadsheet to work Problems 12 to 14. The spreadsheet provides data on oil and gasoline: Column A is the year, column B is the price of oil (dollars per barrel), column C is the price of gasoline (cents per gallon), column D is U.S. oil production, and column E is the U.S. quantity of gasoline refined (both in millions of barrels per day).

	A	B	C	D	E
1	1999	24	118	5.9	8.1
2	2000	30	152	5.8	8.2
3	2001	17	146	5.8	8.3
4	2002	24	139	5.7	8.4
5	2003	27	160	5.7	8.5
6	2004	37	190	5.4	8.7
7	2005	49	231	5.2	8.7
8	2006	56	262	5.1	8.9
9	2007	86	284	5.1	9.0
10	2008	43	330	5.0	8.9
11	2009	76	241	4.9	8.9

12. Draw a scatter diagram of the price of oil and the quantity of U.S. oil produced. Describe the relationship.
13. Draw a scatter diagram of the price of gasoline and the quantity of gasoline refined. Describe the relationship.
14. Draw a scatter diagram of the quantity of U.S. oil produced and the quantity of gasoline refined. Describe the relationship.

Use the following data to work Problems 15 to 17. Draw a graph that shows the relationship between the two variables x and y:

x	0	1	2	3	4	5
y	25	24	22	18	12	0

15. a. Is the relationship positive or negative?
    b. Does the slope of the relationship become steeper or flatter as the value of x increases?
    c. Think of some economic relationships that might be similar to this one.
16. Calculate the slope of the relationship between x and y when x equals 3.
17. Calculate the slope of the relationship across the arc as x increases from 4 to 5.
18. Calculate the slope of the curve at point A.

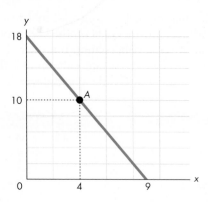

Use the following relationship to work Problems 19 and 20.

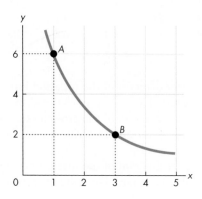

19. Calculate the slope at point A and at point B.
20. Calculate the slope across the arc AB.

Use the following table to work Problems 21 to 23. The table gives information about umbrellas: price, the number purchased, and rainfall in inches.

Price	Umbrellas (number purchased per day)		
(dollars per umbrella)	0 inches	1 inch	2 inches
20	4	7	8
30	2	4	7
40	1	2	4

21. Draw a graph to show the relationship between the price and the number of umbrellas purchased, holding the amount of rainfall constant at 1 inch. Describe this relationship.
22. What happens in the graph in Problem 21 if the price rises and rainfall is constant?
23. What happens in the graph in Problem 21 if the rainfall increases from 1 inch to 2 inches?

2

THE ECONOMIC PROBLEM

After studying this chapter, you will be able to:

◆ Define the production possibilities frontier and use it to calculate opportunity cost

◆ Distinguish between production possibilities and preferences and describe an efficient allocation of resources

◆ Explain how current production choices expand future production possibilities

◆ Explain how specialization and trade expand production possibilities

◆ Describe the economic institutions that coordinate decisions

Why does food cost much more today than it did a few years ago? One reason is that we now use part of our corn crop to produce ethanol, a clean biofuel substitute for gasoline. Another reason is that drought in some parts of the world has decreased global grain production. In this chapter, you will study an economic model—the production possibilities frontier—and you will learn why ethanol production and drought have increased the cost of producing food. You will also learn how to assess whether it is a good idea to increase corn production to produce fuel; how we can expand our production possibilities; and how we gain by trading with others.

At the end of the chapter, in *Reading Between the Lines*, we'll apply what you've learned to understanding why ethanol production is raising the cost of food.

◆ Production Possibilities and Opportunity Cost

Every working day, in mines, factories, shops, and offices and on farms and construction sites across the United States, 138 million people produce a vast variety of goods and services valued at $50 billion. But the quantities of goods and services that we can produce are limited both by our available resources and by technology. And if we want to increase our production of one good, we must decrease our production of something else—we face a tradeoff. You are going to learn about the production possibilities frontier, which describes the limit to what we can produce and provides a neat way of thinking about and illustrating the idea of a tradeoff.

The **production possibilities frontier** (*PPF*) is the boundary between those combinations of goods and services that can be produced and those that cannot. To illustrate the *PPF*, we focus on two goods at a time and hold the quantities produced of all the other goods and services constant. That is, we look at a *model* economy in which everything remains the same except for the production of the two goods we are considering.

Let's look at the production possibilities frontier for cola and pizza, which represent *any* pair of goods or services.

Production Possibilities Frontier

The *production possibilities frontier* for cola and pizza shows the limits to the production of these two goods, given the total resources and technology available to produce them. Figure 2.1 shows this production possibilities frontier. The table lists some combinations of the quantities of pizza and cola that can be produced in a month given the resources available. The figure graphs these combinations. The *x*-axis shows the quantity of pizzas produced, and the *y*-axis shows the quantity of cola produced.

The *PPF* illustrates *scarcity* because we cannot attain the points outside the frontier. These points describe wants that can't be satisfied. We can produce at any point *inside* the *PPF* or *on* the *PPF*. These points are attainable. Suppose that in a typical month, we produce 4 million pizzas and 5 million cans of cola. Figure 2.1 shows this combination as point *E* and as possibility *E* in the table. The figure

FIGURE 2.1   Production Possibilities Frontier

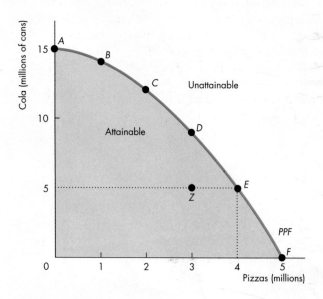

Possibility	Pizzas (millions)		Cola (millions of cans)
A	0	and	15
B	1	and	14
C	2	and	12
D	3	and	9
E	4	and	5
F	5	and	0

The table lists six production possibilities for cola and pizzas. Row *A* tells us that if we produce no pizzas, the maximum quantity of cola we can produce is 15 million cans. Points *A*, *B*, *C*, *D*, *E*, and *F* in the figure represent the rows of the table. The curve passing through these points is the production possibilities frontier (*PPF*).

The *PPF* separates the attainable from the unattainable. Production is possible at any point *inside* the orange area or *on* the frontier. Points outside the frontier are unattainable. Points inside the frontier, such as point *Z*, are inefficient because resources are wasted or misallocated. At such points, it is possible to use the available resources to produce more of either or both goods.

 animation

also shows other production possibilities. For example, we might stop producing pizza and move all the people who produce it into producing cola. Point *A* in the figure and possibility *A* in the table show this case. The quantity of cola produced increases to 15 million cans, and pizza production dries up. Alternatively, we might close the cola factories and switch all the resources into producing pizza. In this situation, we produce 5 million pizzas. Point *F* in the figure and possibility *F* in the table show this case.

Production Efficiency

We achieve **production efficiency** if we produce goods and services at the lowest possible cost. This outcome occurs at all the points *on* the *PPF*. At points *inside* the *PPF*, production is inefficient because we are giving up more than necessary of one good to produce a given quantity of the other good.

For example, at point *Z* in Fig. 2.1, we produce 3 million pizzas and 5 million cans of cola. But we have enough resources to produce 3 million pizzas and 9 million cans of cola. Our pizzas cost more cola than necessary. We can get them for a lower cost. Only when we produce *on* the *PPF* do we incur the lowest possible cost of production.

Production is *inefficient* inside the *PPF* because resources are either *unused* or *misallocated* or both.

Resources are *unused* when they are idle but could be working. For example, we might leave some of the factories idle or some workers unemployed.

Resources are *misallocated* when they are assigned to tasks for which they are not the best match. For example, we might assign skilled pizza chefs to work in a cola factory and skilled cola producers to work in a pizza shop. We could get more pizzas *and* more cola from these same workers if we reassigned them to the tasks that more closely match their skills.

Tradeoff Along the *PPF*

Every choice *along* the *PPF* involves a *tradeoff*. On the *PPF* in Fig. 2.1, we trade off cola for pizzas.

Tradeoffs arise in every imaginable real-world situation in which a choice must be made. At any given point in time, we have a fixed amount of labor, land, capital, and entrepreneurship. By using our available technologies, we can employ these resources to produce goods and services, but we are limited in what we can produce. This limit defines a boundary between what we can attain and what we cannot attain. This boundary is the real-world's production possibilities frontier, and it defines the tradeoffs that we must make. On our real-world *PPF*, we can produce more of any one good or service only if we produce less of some other goods or services.

When doctors want to spend more on AIDS and cancer research, they face a tradeoff: more medical research for less of some other things. When Congress wants to spend more on education and health care, it faces a tradeoff: more education and health care for less national defense or less homeland security. When an environmental group argues for less logging, it is suggesting a tradeoff: greater conservation of endangered wildlife for less paper. When you want to study more, you face a tradeoff: more study time for less leisure or sleep.

All tradeoffs involve a cost—an opportunity cost.

Opportunity Cost

The **opportunity cost** of an action is the highest-valued alternative forgone. The *PPF* makes this idea precise and enables us to calculate opportunity cost. Along the *PPF*, there are only two goods, so there is only one alternative forgone: some quantity of the other good. Given our current resources and technology, we can produce more pizzas only if we produce less cola. The opportunity cost of producing an additional pizza is the cola we *must* forgo. Similarly, the opportunity cost of producing an additional can of cola is the quantity of pizza we must forgo.

In Fig. 2.1, if we move from point *C* to point *D*, we get 1 million more pizzas but 3 million fewer cans of cola. The additional 1 million pizzas *cost* 3 million cans of cola. One pizza costs 3 cans of cola.

We can also work out the opportunity cost of moving in the opposite direction. In Fig. 2.1, if we move from point *D* to point *C*, the quantity of cola produced increases by 3 million cans and the quantity of pizzas produced decreases by 1 million. So if we choose point *C* over point *D*, the additional 3 million cans of cola *cost* 1 million pizzas. One can of cola costs 1/3 of a pizza.

Opportunity Cost Is a Ratio Opportunity cost is a ratio. It is the decrease in the quantity produced of one good divided by the increase in the quantity produced of another good as we move along the production possibilities frontier.

Because opportunity cost is a ratio, the opportunity cost of producing an additional can of cola is equal to the *inverse* of the opportunity cost of producing an additional pizza. Check this proposition by returning to the calculations we've just worked through. When we move along the *PPF* from *C* to *D*, the opportunity cost of a pizza is 3 cans of cola. The inverse of 3 is 1/3. If we decrease the production of pizza and increase the production of cola by moving from *D* to *C*, the opportunity cost of a can of cola must be 1/3 of a pizza. That is exactly the number that we calculated for the move from *D* to *C*.

Increasing Opportunity Cost The opportunity cost of a pizza increases as the quantity of pizzas produced increases. The outward-bowed shape of the *PPF* reflects increasing opportunity cost. When we produce a large quantity of cola and a small quantity of pizza—between points *A* and *B* in Fig. 2.1—the frontier has a gentle slope. An increase in the quantity of pizzas costs a small decrease in the quantity of cola—the opportunity cost of a pizza is a small quantity of cola.

When we produce a large quantity of pizzas and a small quantity of cola—between points *E* and *F* in Fig. 2.1—the frontier is steep. A given increase in the quantity of pizzas *costs* a large decrease in the quantity of cola, so the opportunity cost of a pizza is a large quantity of cola.

The *PPF* is bowed outward because resources are not all equally productive in all activities. People with many years of experience working for PepsiCo are good at producing cola but not very good at making pizzas. So if we move some of these people from PepsiCo to Domino's, we get a small increase in the quantity of pizzas but a large decrease in the quantity of cola.

Similarly, people who have spent years working at Domino's are good at producing pizzas, but they have no idea how to produce cola. So if we move some of these people from Domino's to PepsiCo, we get a small increase in the quantity of cola but a large decrease in the quantity of pizzas. The more of either good we try to produce, the less productive are the additional resources we use to produce that good and the larger is the opportunity cost of a unit of that good.

Economics in Action
Increasing Opportunity Cost on the Farm

Sanders Wright, a homesick Mississippi native, is growing cotton in Iowa. The growing season is short, so his commercial success is unlikely. Cotton does not grow well in Iowa, but corn does. A farm with irrigation can produce 300 bushels of corn per acre—twice the U.S. average.

Ronnie Gerik, a Texas cotton farmer, has started to grow corn. Ronnie doesn't have irrigation and instead relies on rainfall. That's not a problem for cotton, which just needs a few soakings a season. But it's a big problem for corn, which needs an inch of water a week. Also, corn can't take the heat like cotton, and if the temperature rises too much, Ronnie will be lucky to get 100 bushels an acre.

An Iowa corn farmer gives up almost no cotton to produce his 300 bushels of corn per acre—corn has a low opportunity cost. But Ronnie Gerick gives up a huge amount of cotton to produce his 100 bushels of corn per acre. By switching some land from cotton to corn, Ronnie has increased the production of corn, but the additional corn has a high opportunity cost.

"Deere worker makes 'cotton pickin' miracle happen," WCFCourier.com; and "Farmers stampede to corn," *USA Today*.

REVIEW QUIZ

1 How does the production possibilities frontier illustrate scarcity?
2 How does the production possibilities frontier illustrate production efficiency?
3 How does the production possibilities frontier show that every choice involves a tradeoff?
4 How does the production possibilities frontier illustrate opportunity cost?
5 Why is opportunity cost a ratio?
6 Why does the *PPF* bow outward and what does that imply about the relationship between opportunity cost and the quantity produced?

You can work these questions in Study Plan 2.1 and get instant feedback.

We've seen that what we can produce is limited by the production possibilities frontier. We've also seen that production on the *PPF* is efficient. But we can produce many different quantities on the *PPF*. How do we choose among them? How do we know which point on the *PPF* is the best one?

Using Resources Efficiently

We achieve *production efficiency* at every point on the *PPF*, but which point is best? The answer is the point on the *PPF* at which goods and services are produced in the quantities that provide the greatest possible benefit. When goods and services are produced at the lowest possible cost and in the quantities that provide the greatest possible benefit, we have achieved **allocative efficiency.**

The questions that we raised when we reviewed the four big issues in Chapter 1 are questions about allocative efficiency. To answer such questions, we must measure and compare costs and benefits.

The *PPF* and Marginal Cost

The **marginal cost** of a good is the opportunity cost of producing one more unit of it. We calculate marginal cost from the slope of the *PPF*. As the quantity of pizzas produced increases, the *PPF* gets steeper and the marginal cost of a pizza increases. Figure 2.2 illustrates the calculation of the marginal cost of a pizza.

Begin by finding the opportunity cost of pizza in blocks of 1 million pizzas. The cost of the first million pizzas is 1 million cans of cola; the cost of the second million pizzas is 2 million cans of cola; the cost of the third million pizzas is 3 million cans of cola, and so on. The bars in part (a) illustrate these calculations.

The bars in part (b) show the cost of an average pizza in each of the 1 million pizza blocks. Focus on the third million pizzas—the move from *C* to *D* in part (a). Over this range, because 1 million pizzas cost 3 million cans of cola, one of these pizzas, on average, costs 3 cans of cola—the height of the bar in part (b).

Next, find the opportunity cost of each additional pizza—the marginal cost of a pizza. The marginal cost of a pizza increases as the quantity of pizzas produced increases. The marginal cost at point *C* is less than it is at point *D*. On average over the range from *C* to *D*, the marginal cost of a pizza is 3 cans of cola. But it exactly equals 3 cans of cola only in the middle of the range between *C* and *D*.

The red dot in part (b) indicates that the marginal cost of a pizza is 3 cans of cola when 2.5 million pizzas are produced. Each black dot in part (b) is interpreted in the same way. The red curve that passes through these dots, labeled *MC*, is the marginal cost curve. It shows the marginal cost of a pizza at each quantity of pizzas as we move along the *PPF*.

FIGURE 2.2 The *PPF* and Marginal Cost

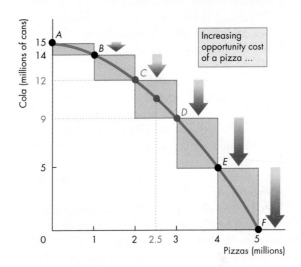

(a) *PPF* and opportunity cost

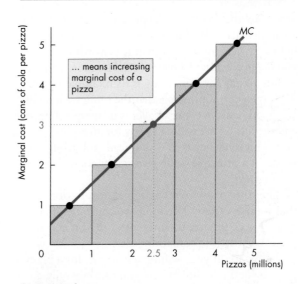

(b) Marginal cost

Marginal cost is calculated from the slope of the *PPF*. As the quantity of pizzas produced increases, the *PPF* gets steeper and the marginal cost of a pizza increases. The bars in part (a) show the opportunity cost of pizza in blocks of 1 million pizzas. The bars in part (b) show the cost of an average pizza in each of these 1 million blocks. The red curve, *MC*, shows the marginal cost of a pizza at each point along the *PPF*. This curve passes through the center of each of the bars in part (b).

Preferences and Marginal Benefit

The **marginal benefit** from a good or service is the benefit received from consuming one more unit of it. This benefit is subjective. It depends on people's **preferences**—people's likes and dislikes and the intensity of those feelings.

Marginal benefit and *preferences* stand in sharp contrast to *marginal cost* and *production possibilities.* Preferences describe what people like and want and the production possibilities describe the limits or constraints on what is feasible.

We need a concrete way of illustrating preferences that parallels the way we illustrate the limits to production using the *PPF.*

The device that we use to illustrate preferences is the **marginal benefit curve**, which is a curve that shows the relationship between the marginal benefit from a good and the quantity consumed of that good. Note that the *marginal benefit curve* is *unrelated* to the *PPF* and cannot be derived from it.

We measure the marginal benefit from a good or service by the most that people are *willing to pay* for an additional unit of it. The idea is that you are willing to pay less for a good than it is worth to you but you are not willing to pay more: The most you are willing to pay for something is its marginal benefit.

It is a general principle that the more we have of any good or service, the smaller is its marginal benefit and the less we are willing to pay for an additional unit of it. This tendency is so widespread and strong that we call it a principle—the *principle of decreasing marginal benefit.*

The basic reason why marginal benefit decreases is that we like variety. The more we consume of any one good or service, the more we tire of it and would prefer to switch to something else.

Think about your willingness to pay for a pizza. If pizza is hard to come by and you can buy only a few slices a year, you might be willing to pay a high price to get an additional slice. But if pizza is all you've eaten for the past few days, you are willing to pay almost nothing for another slice.

You've learned to think about cost as opportunity cost, not as a dollar cost. You can think about marginal benefit and willingness to pay in the same way. The marginal benefit, measured by what you are willing to pay for something, is the quantity of other goods and services that you are willing to forgo. Let's continue with the example of cola and pizza and illustrate preferences this way.

FIGURE 2.3   Preferences and the Marginal Benefit Curve

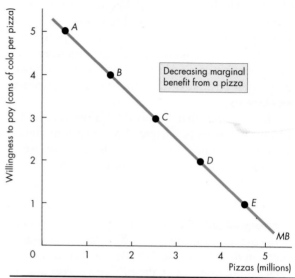

Possibility	Pizzas (millions)	Willingness to pay (cans of cola per pizza)
A	0.5	5
B	1.5	4
C	2.5	3
D	3.5	2
E	4.5	1

The smaller the quantity of pizzas available, the more cola people are willing to give up for an additional pizza. With 0.5 million pizzas available, people are willing to pay 5 cans of cola per pizza. But with 4.5 million pizzas, people are willing to pay only 1 can of cola per pizza. Willingness to pay measures marginal benefit. A universal feature of people's preferences is that marginal benefit decreases.

myeconlab   animation

Figure 2.3 illustrates preferences as the willingness to pay for pizza in terms of cola. In row *A*, with 0.5 million pizzas available, people are willing to pay 5 cans of cola per pizza. As the quantity of pizzas increases, the amount that people are willing to pay for a pizza falls. With 4.5 million pizzas available, people are willing to pay only 1 can of cola per pizza.

Let's now use the concepts of marginal cost and marginal benefit to describe allocative efficiency.

FIGURE 2.4   Efficient Use of Resources

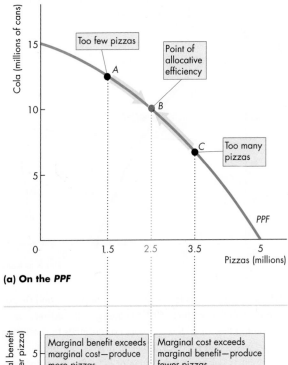

(a) On the PPF

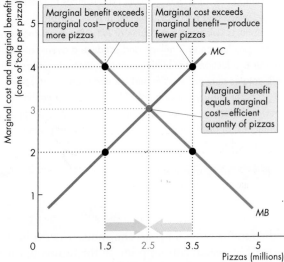

(b) Marginal benefit equals marginal cost

The greater the quantity of pizzas produced, the smaller is the marginal benefit (MB) from pizza—the less cola people are willing to give up to get an additional pizza. But the greater the quantity of pizzas produced, the greater is the marginal cost (MC) of a pizza—the more cola people must give up to get an additional pizza. When marginal benefit equals marginal cost, resources are being used efficiently.

 animation

Allocative Efficiency

At *any* point on the *PPF*, we cannot produce more of one good without giving up some other good. At the *best* point on the *PPF*, we cannot produce more of one good without giving up some other good that provides greater benefit. We are producing at the point of allocative efficiency—the point on the *PPF* that we prefer above all other points.

Suppose in Fig. 2.4, we produce 1.5 million pizzas. The marginal cost of a pizza is 2 cans of cola, and the marginal benefit from a pizza is 4 cans of cola. Because someone values an additional pizza more highly than it costs to produce, we can get more value from our resources by moving some of them out of producing cola and into producing pizza.

Now suppose we produce 3.5 million pizzas. The marginal cost of a pizza is now 4 cans of cola, but the marginal benefit from a pizza is only 2 cans of cola. Because the additional pizza costs more to produce than anyone thinks it is worth, we can get more value from our resources by moving some of them away from producing pizza and into producing cola.

Suppose we produce 2.5 million pizzas. Marginal cost and marginal benefit are now equal at 3 cans of cola. This allocation of resources between pizzas and cola is efficient. If more pizzas are produced, the forgone cola is worth more than the additional pizzas. If fewer pizzas are produced, the forgone pizzas are worth more than the additional cola.

REVIEW QUIZ

1   What is marginal cost? How is it measured?
2   What is marginal benefit? How is it measured?
3   How does the marginal benefit from a good change as the quantity produced of that good increases?
4   What is allocative efficiency and how does it relate to the production possibilities frontier?
5   What conditions must be satisfied if resources are used efficiently?

You can work these questions in Study Plan 2.2 and get instant feedback.

You now understand the limits to production and the conditions under which resources are used efficiently. Your next task is to study the expansion of production possibilities.

◆ Economic Growth

During the past 30 years, production per person in the United States has doubled. The expansion of production possibilities is called **economic growth**. Economic growth increases our *standard of living*, but it doesn't overcome scarcity and avoid opportunity cost. To make our economy grow, we face a trade-off—the faster we make production grow, the greater is the opportunity cost of economic growth.

The Cost of Economic Growth

Economic growth comes from technological change and capital accumulation. **Technological change** is the development of new goods and of better ways of producing goods and services. **Capital accumulation** is the growth of capital resources, including *human capital*.

Technological change and capital accumulation have vastly expanded our production possibilities. We can produce automobiles that provide us with more transportation than was available when we had only horses and carriages. We can produce satellites that provide global communications on a much larger scale than that available with the earlier cable technology. But if we use our resources to develop new technologies and produce capital, we must decrease our production of consumption goods and services. New technologies and new capital have an opportunity cost. Let's look at this opportunity cost.

Instead of studying the *PPF* of pizzas and cola, we'll hold the quantity of cola produced constant and examine the *PPF* for pizzas and pizza ovens. Figure 2.5 shows this *PPF* as the blue curve *PPF*$_0$. If we devote no resources to producing pizza ovens, we produce at point *A*. If we produce 3 million pizzas, we can produce 6 pizza ovens at point *B*. If we produce no pizza, we can produce 10 ovens at point *C*.

The amount by which our production possibilities expand depends on the resources we devote to technological change and capital accumulation. If we devote no resources to this activity (point *A*), our *PPF* remains the blue curve *PPF*$_0$ in Fig. 2.5. If we cut the current pizza production and produce 6 ovens (point *B*), then in the future, we'll have more capital and our *PPF* will rotate outward to the position shown by the red curve *PPF*$_1$. The fewer resources we use for producing pizza and the more resources we use for producing ovens, the greater is the expansion of our future production possibilities.

FIGURE 2.5   Economic Growth

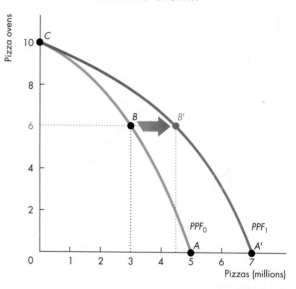

PPF$_0$ shows the limits to the production of pizzas and pizza ovens, with the production of all other goods and services remaining the same. If we devote no resources to producing pizza ovens and produce 5 million pizzas, our production possibilities will remain the same at *PPF*$_0$. But if we decrease pizza production to 3 million and produce 6 ovens, at point *B*, our production possibilities expand. After one period, the *PPF* rotates outward to *PPF*$_1$ and we can produce at point *B'*, a point outside the original *PPF*$_0$. We can rotate the *PPF* outward, but we cannot avoid opportunity cost. The opportunity cost of producing more pizzas in the future is fewer pizzas today.

⊗ myeconlab   animation

Economic growth brings enormous benefits in the form of increased consumption in the future, but it is not free and it doesn't abolish scarcity.

In Fig. 2.5, to make economic growth happen we must use some resources to produce new ovens, which leaves fewer resources to produce pizzas. To move to *B'* in the future, we must move from *A* to *B* today. The opportunity cost of more pizzas in the future is fewer pizzas today. Also, on the new *PPF*, we still face a tradeoff and opportunity cost.

The ideas about economic growth that we have explored in the setting of the pizza industry also apply to nations. Hong Kong and the United States provide a striking case study.

Economics in Action

Hong Kong Catching Up to the United States

In 1969, the production possibilities per person in the United States were more than four times those in Hong Kong (see the figure). The United States devotes one fifth of its resources to accumulating capital and in 1969 was at point *A* on its *PPF*. Hong Kong devotes one third of its resources to accumulating capital and in 1969, Hong Kong was at point *A* on its *PPF*.

Since 1969, both countries have experienced economic growth, but because Hong Kong devotes a bigger fraction of its resources to accumulating capital, its production possibilities have expanded more quickly.

By 2009, production possibilities per person in Hong Kong had reached 94 percent of those in the United States. If Hong Kong continues to devote more resources to accumulating capital than we do (at point *B* on its 2009 *PPF*), it will continue to grow more rapidly. But if Hong Kong decreases capital accumulation (moving to point *D* on its 2009 *PPF*), then its rate of economic growth will slow.

Hong Kong is typical of the fast-growing Asian economies, which include Taiwan, Thailand, South Korea, China, and India. Production possibilities expand in these countries by between 5 and almost 10 percent a year.

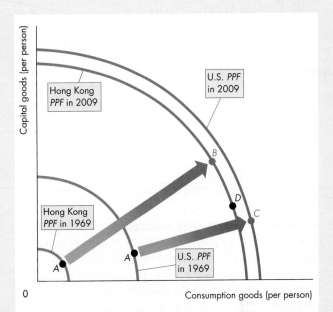

Economic Growth in the United States and Hong Kong

If such high economic growth rates are maintained, these other Asian countries will continue to close the gap between themselves and the United States, as Hong Kong is doing.

A Nation's Economic Growth

The experiences of the United States and Hong Kong make a striking example of the effects of our choices about consumption and capital goods on the rate of economic growth.

If a nation devotes all its factors of production to producing consumption goods and services and none to advancing technology and accumulating capital, its production possibilities in the future will be the same as they are today.

To expand production possibilities in the future, a nation must devote fewer resources to producing current consumption goods and services and some resources to accumulating capital and developing new technologies. As production possibilities expand, consumption in the future can increase. The decrease in today's consumption is the opportunity cost of tomorrow's increase in consumption.

REVIEW QUIZ

1 What generates economic growth?
2 How does economic growth influence the production possibilities frontier?
3 What is the opportunity cost of economic growth?
4 Why has Hong Kong experienced faster economic growth than the United States?
5 Does economic growth overcome scarcity?

You can work these questions in Study Plan 2.3 and get instant feedback.

Next, we're going to study another way in which we expand our production possibilities—the amazing fact that *both* buyers and sellers gain from specialization and trade.

◆ Gains from Trade

People can produce for themselves all the goods and services that they consume, or they can produce one good or a few goods and trade with others. Producing only one good or a few goods is called *specialization.* We are going to learn how people gain by specializing in the production of the good in which they have a *comparative advantage* and trading with others.

Comparative Advantage and Absolute Advantage

A person has a **comparative advantage** in an activity if that person can perform the activity at a lower opportunity cost than anyone else. Differences in opportunity costs arise from differences in individual abilities and from differences in the characteristics of other resources.

No one excels at everything. One person is an outstanding pitcher but a poor catcher; another person is a brilliant lawyer but a poor teacher. In almost all human endeavors, what one person does easily, someone else finds difficult. The same applies to land and capital. One plot of land is fertile but has no mineral deposits; another plot of land has outstanding views but is infertile. One machine has great precision but is difficult to operate; another is fast but often breaks down.

Although no one excels at everything, some people excel and can outperform others in a large number of activities—perhaps even in all activities. A person who is more productive than others has an **absolute advantage.**

Absolute advantage involves comparing productivities—production per hour—whereas comparative advantage involves comparing opportunity costs.

A person who has an absolute advantage does not have a *comparative* advantage in every activity. John Grisham is a better lawyer and a better author of fast-paced thrillers than most people. He has an absolute advantage in these two activities. But compared to others, he is a better writer than lawyer, so his *comparative* advantage is in writing.

Because ability and resources vary from one person to another, people have different opportunity costs of producing various goods. These differences in opportunity cost are the source of comparative advantage.

Let's explore the idea of comparative advantage by looking at two smoothie bars: one operated by Liz and the other operated by Joe.

Liz's Smoothie Bar Liz produces smoothies and salads. In Liz's high-tech bar, she can turn out either a smoothie or a salad every 2 minutes—see Table 2.1. If Liz spends all her time making smoothies, she can produce 30 an hour. And if she spends all her time making salads, she can also produce 30 an hour. If she splits her time equally between the two, she can produce 15 smoothies and 15 salads an hour. For each additional smoothie Liz produces, she must decrease her production of salads by one, and for each additional salad she produces, she must decrease her production of smoothies by one. So

> Liz's opportunity cost of producing 1 smoothie is 1 salad,

and

> Liz's opportunity cost of producing 1 salad is 1 smoothie.

Liz's customers buy smoothies and salads in equal quantities, so she splits her time equally between the two items and produces 15 smoothies and 15 salads an hour.

Joe's Smoothie Bar Joe also produces smoothies and salads, but his bar is smaller than Liz's. Also, Joe has only one blender, and it's a slow, old machine. Even if Joe uses all his resources to produce smoothies, he can produce only 6 an hour—see Table 2.2. But Joe is good at making salads. If he uses all his resources to make salads, he can produce 30 an hour.

Joe's ability to make smoothies and salads is the same regardless of how he splits an hour between the two tasks. He can make a salad in 2 minutes or a smoothie in 10 minutes. For each additional smoothie

---

TABLE 2.1   Liz's Production Possibilities

Item	Minutes to produce 1	Quantity per hour
Smoothies	2	30
Salads	2	30

TABLE 2.2   Joe's Production Possibilities

Item	Minutes to produce 1	Quantity per hour
Smoothies	10	6
Salads	2	30

Joe produces, he must decrease his production of salads by 5. And for each additional salad he produces, he must decrease his production of smoothies by 1/5 of a smoothie. So

Joe's opportunity cost of producing 1 smoothie is 5 salads,

and

Joe's opportunity cost of producing 1 salad is 1/5 of a smoothie.

Joe's customers, like Liz's, buy smoothies and salads in equal quantities. So Joe spends 50 minutes of each hour making smoothies and 10 minutes of each hour making salads. With this division of his time, Joe produces 5 smoothies and 5 salads an hour.

Liz's Comparative Advantage In which of the two activities does Liz have a comparative advantage? Recall that comparative advantage is a situation in which one person's opportunity cost of producing a good is lower than another person's opportunity cost of producing that same good. Liz has a comparative advantage in producing smoothies. Her opportunity cost of a smoothie is 1 salad, whereas Joe's opportunity cost of a smoothie is 5 salads.

Joe's Comparative Advantage If Liz has a comparative advantage in producing smoothies, Joe must have a comparative advantage in producing salads. Joe's opportunity cost of a salad is 1/5 of a smoothie, whereas Liz's opportunity cost of a salad is 1 smoothie.

Achieving the Gains from Trade

Liz and Joe run into each other one evening in a singles bar. After a few minutes of getting acquainted, Liz tells Joe about her amazing smoothie business. Her only problem, she tells Joe, is that she would like to produce more because potential customers leave when her lines get too long.

Joe is hesitant to risk spoiling his chances by telling Liz about his own struggling business, but he takes the risk. Joe explains to Liz that he spends 50 minutes of every hour making 5 smoothies and 10 minutes making 5 salads. Liz's eyes pop. "Have I got a deal for you!" she exclaims.

Here's the deal that Liz sketches on a paper napkin. Joe stops making smoothies and allocates all his time to producing salads; Liz stops making salads and allocates all her time to producing smoothies. That is, they both specialize in producing the good in which they have a comparative advantage. Together they produce 30 smoothies and 30 salads—see Table 2.3(b).

They then trade. Liz sells Joe 10 smoothies and Joe sells Liz 20 salads—the price of a smoothie is 2 salads—see Table 2.3(c).

After the trade, Joe has 10 salads—the 30 he produces minus the 20 he sells to Liz. He also has the 10 smoothies that he buys from Liz. So Joe now has increased the quantities of smoothies and salads that he can sell to his customers—see Table 2.3(d).

TABLE 2.3   Liz and Joe Gain from Trade

(a) Before trade	Liz	Joe
Smoothies	15	5
Salads	15	5

(b) Specialization	Liz	Joe
Smoothies	30	0
Salads	0	30

(c) Trade	Liz	Joe
Smoothies	sell 10	buy 10
Salads	buy 20	sell 20

(d) After trade	Liz	Joe
Smoothies	20	10
Salads	20	10

(e) Gains from trade	Liz	Joe
Smoothies	+5	+5
Salads	+5	+5

Liz has 20 smoothies—the 30 she produces minus the 10 she sells to Joe. She also has the 20 salads that she buys from Joe. Liz has increased the quantities of smoothies and salads that she can sell to her customers—see Table 2.3(d). Liz and Joe both gain 5 smoothies and 5 salads an hour—see Table 2.3(e).

To illustrate her idea, Liz grabs a fresh napkin and draws the graphs in Fig. 2.6. The blue *PPF* in part (a) shows Joe's production possibilities. Before trade, he is producing 5 smoothies and 5 salads an hour at point *A*. The blue *PPF* in part (b) shows Liz's production possibilities. Before trade, she is producing 15 smoothies and 15 salads an hour at point *A*.

Liz's proposal is that they each specialize in producing the good in which they have a comparative advantage. Joe produces 30 salads and no smoothies at point *B* on his *PPF*. Liz produces 30 smoothies and no salads at point *B* on her *PPF*.

Liz and Joe then trade smoothies and salads at a price of 2 salads per smoothie or 1/2 a smoothie per salad. Joe gets smoothies for 2 salads each, which is less than the 5 salads it costs him to produce a smoothie. Liz gets salads for 1/2 a smoothie each, which is less than the 1 smoothie that it costs her to produce a salad.

With trade, Joe has 10 smoothies and 10 salads at point *C*—a gain of 5 smoothies and 5 salads. Joe moves to a point *outside* his *PPF*.

With trade, Liz has 20 smoothies and 20 salads at point *C*—a gain of 5 smoothies and 5 salads. Liz moves to a point *outside* her *PPF*.

Despite Liz being more productive than Joe, both of them gain from specializing—producing the good in which they have a comparative advantage—and trading.

FIGURE 2.6   The Gains from Trade

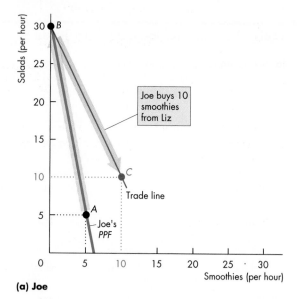

(a) Joe

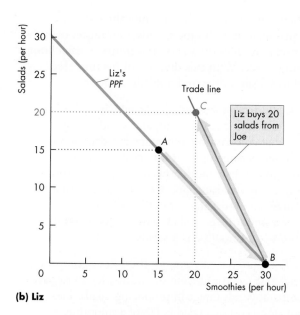

(b) Liz

Initially, Joe produces at point *A* on his *PPF* in part (a), and Liz produces at point *A* on her *PPF* in part (b). Joe's opportunity cost of producing a salad is less than Liz's, so Joe has a comparative advantage in producing salads. Liz's opportunity cost of producing a smoothie is less than Joe's, so Liz has a comparative advantage in producing smoothies.

If Joe specializes in making salads, he produces 30 salads and no smoothies at point *B* on his *PPF*. If Liz specializes

in making smoothies, she produces 30 smoothies and no salads at point *B* on her *PPF*. They exchange salads for smoothies along the red "Trade line." Liz buys salads from Joe for less than her opportunity cost of producing them. Joe buys smoothies from Liz for less than his opportunity cost of producing them. Each goes to point *C*—a point outside his or her *PPF*. With specialization and trade, Joe and Liz gain 5 smoothies and 5 salads each with no extra resources.

Economics in Action
The United States and China Gain From Trade

In Chapter 1 (see p. 5), we asked whether globalization is in the social interest. What you have just learned about the gains from trade provides a big part of the answer. We gain from specialization and trade.

The gains that we achieve from *international* trade are similar to those achieved by Joe and Liz. When Americans buy clothes that are manufactured in China and when China buys Boeing airplanes manufactured in the United States, the people of both countries gain.

We could slide along our *PPF* producing fewer airplanes and more jackets. Similarly, China could slide along its *PPF* producing more airplanes and fewer jackets. But everyone would lose. The opportunity cost of our jackets and China's opportunity cost of airplanes would rise.

By specializing in airplanes and trading with China, we get our jackets at a lower cost than that at which we can produce them, and China gets its aircraft at a lower cost than that at which it can produce them.

REVIEW QUIZ

1 What gives a person a comparative advantage?
2 Distinguish between comparative advantage and absolute advantage.
3 Why do people specialize and trade?
4 What are the gains from specialization and trade?
5 What is the source of the gains from trade?

You can work these questions in Study Plan 2.4 and get instant feedback.

Economic Coordination

People gain by specializing in the production of those goods and services in which they have a comparative advantage and then trading with each other. Liz and Joe, whose production of salads and smoothies we studied earlier in this chapter, can get together and make a deal that enables them to enjoy the gains from specialization and trade. But for billions of individuals to specialize and produce millions of different goods and services, their choices must somehow be coordinated.

Two competing economic coordination systems have been used: central economic planning and decentralized markets.

Central economic planning was tried in Russia and China and is still used in Cuba and North Korea. This system works badly because government economic planners don't know people's production possibilities and preferences. Resources get wasted, production ends up *inside* the *PPF,* and the wrong things get produced.

Decentralized coordination works best but to do so it needs four complementary social institutions. They are

■ Firms
■ Markets
■ Property rights
■ Money

Firms

A **firm** is an economic unit that hires factors of production and organizes those factors to produce and sell goods and services. Examples of firms are your local gas station, Wal-Mart, and General Motors.

Firms coordinate a huge amount of economic activity. For example, Wal-Mart buys or rents large buildings, equips them with storage shelves and checkout lanes, and hires labor. Wal-Mart directs the labor and decides what goods to buy and sell.

But Sam Walton would not have become one of the wealthiest people in the world if Wal-Mart produced all the goods that it sells. He became rich by specializing in providing retail services and buying from other firms that specialize in producing goods (just as Liz and Joe did). This trade between firms takes place in markets.

Markets

In ordinary speech, the word *market* means a place where people buy and sell goods such as fish, meat, fruits, and vegetables. In economics, a *market* has a more general meaning. A **market** is any arrangement that enables buyers and sellers to get information and to do business with each other. An example is the market in which oil is bought and sold—the world oil market. The world oil market is not a place. It is the network of oil producers, oil users, wholesalers, and brokers who buy and sell oil. In the world oil market, decision makers do not meet physically. They make deals by telephone, fax, and direct computer link.

Markets have evolved because they facilitate trade. Without organized markets, we would miss out on a substantial part of the potential gains from trade. Enterprising individuals and firms, each pursuing their own self-interest, have profited from making markets—standing ready to buy or sell the items in which they specialize. But markets can work only when property rights exist.

Property Rights

The social arrangements that govern the ownership, use, and disposal of anything that people value are called **property rights**. *Real property* includes land and buildings—the things we call property in ordinary speech—and durable goods such as plant and equipment. *Financial property* includes stocks and bonds and money in the bank. *Intellectual property* is the intangible product of creative effort. This type of property includes books, music, computer programs, and inventions of all kinds and is protected by copyrights and patents.

Where property rights are enforced, people have the incentive to specialize and produce the goods in which they have a comparative advantage. Where people can steal the production of others, resources are devoted not to production but to protecting possessions. Without property rights, we would still be hunting and gathering like our Stone Age ancestors.

Money

Money is any commodity or token that is generally acceptable as a means of payment. Liz and Joe didn't use money in the example above. They exchanged salads and smoothies. In principle, trade in markets can exchange any item for any other item. But you can perhaps imagine how complicated life would be if we exchanged goods for other goods. The "invention" of money makes trading in markets much more efficient.

Circular Flows Through Markets

Figure 2.7 shows the flows that result from the choices that households and firms make. Households specialize and choose the quantities of labor, land, capital, and entrepreneurial services to sell or rent to firms. Firms choose the quantities of factors of production to hire. These (red) flows go through the *factor markets*. Households choose the quantities of goods and services to buy, and firms choose the quantities to produce. These (red) flows go through the *goods markets*. Households receive incomes and make expenditures on goods and services (the green flows).

How do markets coordinate all these decisions?

Coordinating Decisions

Markets coordinate decisions through price adjustments. To see how, think about your local market for hamburgers. Suppose that too few hamburgers are available and some people who want to buy hamburgers are not able to do so. To make buying and selling plans the same, either more hamburgers must be offered for sale or buyers must scale down their appetites (or both). A rise in the price of a hamburger produces this outcome. A higher price encourages producers to offer more hamburgers for sale. It also encourages some people to change their lunch plans. Fewer people buy hamburgers, and more buy hot dogs. More hamburgers (and more hot dogs) are offered for sale.

Alternatively, suppose that more hamburgers are available than people want to buy. In this case, to make the choices of buyers and sellers compatible, more hamburgers must be bought or fewer hamburgers must be offered for sale (or both). A fall in the price of a hamburger achieves this outcome. A lower price encourages people to buy more hamburgers. It also encourages firms to produce a smaller quantity of hamburgers.

FIGURE 2.7   Circular Flows in the Market Economy

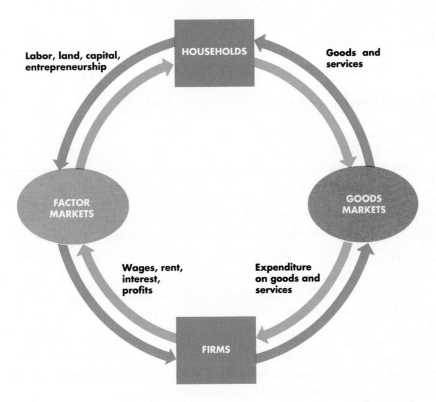

Households and firms make economic choices and markets coordinate these choices.

Households choose the quantities of labor, land, capital, and entrepreneurial services to sell or rent to firms in exchange for wages, rent, interest, and profits. Households also choose how to spend their incomes on the various types of goods and services available.

Firms choose the quantities of factors of production to hire and the quantities of goods and services to produce.

Goods markets and factor markets coordinate these choices of households and firms.

The counterclockwise red flows are real flows—the flow of factors of production from households to firms and the flow of goods and services from firms to households.

The clockwise green flows are the payments for the red flows. They are the flow of incomes from firms to households and the flow of expenditure on goods and services from households to firms.

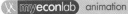 animation

REVIEW QUIZ

1   Why are social institutions such as firms, markets, property rights, and money necessary?
2   What are the main functions of markets?
3   What are the flows in the market economy that go from firms to households and the flows from households to firms?

You can work these questions in Study Plan 2.5 and get instant feedback.

◆ You have now begun to see how economists approach economic questions. Scarcity, choice, and divergent opportunity costs explain why we specialize and trade and why firms, markets, property rights, and money have developed. You can see all around you the lessons you've learned in this chapter. *Reading Between the Lines* on pp. 44–45 provides an opportunity to apply the *PPF* model to deepen your understanding of the reasons for the increase in the cost of food associated with the increase in corn production.

The Rising Opportunity Cost of Food

Fuel Choices, Food Crises, and Finger-Pointing

http://www.nytimes.com
April 15, 2008

The idea of turning farms into fuel plants seemed, for a time, like one of the answers to high global oil prices and supply worries. That strategy seemed to reach a high point last year when Congress mandated a fivefold increase in the use of biofuels.

But now a reaction is building against policies in the United States and Europe to promote ethanol and similar fuels, with political leaders from poor countries contending that these fuels are driving up food prices and starving poor people. …

In some countries, the higher prices are leading to riots, political instability, and growing worries about feeding the poorest people. …

Many specialists in food policy consider government mandates for biofuels to be ill advised, agreeing that the diversion of crops like corn into fuel production has contributed to the higher prices. But other factors have played big roles, including droughts that have limited output and rapid global economic growth that has created higher demand for food.

That growth, much faster over the last four years than the historical norm, is lifting millions of people out of destitution and giving them access to better diets. But farmers are having trouble keeping up with the surge in demand.

While there is agreement that the growth of biofuels has contributed to higher food prices, the amount is disputed. …

C. Ford Runge, an economist at the University of Minnesota, said it is "extremely difficult to disentangle" the effect of biofuels on food costs. Nevertheless, he said there was little that could be done to mitigate the effect of droughts and the growing appetite for protein in developing countries.

"Ethanol is the one thing we can do something about," he said. "It's about the only lever we have to pull, but none of the politicians have the courage to pull the lever." …

ESSENCE OF THE STORY

- In 2007, Congress mandated a fivefold increase in the use of biofuels.

- Political leaders in poor countries and specialists in food policy say the biofuel mandate is ill advised and the diversion of corn into fuel production has raised the cost of food.

- Drought that has limited corn production and global economic growth that has increased the demand for protein have also raised the cost of food.

- An economist at the University of Minnesota says that while it is difficult to determine the effect of biofuels on food costs, it is the only factor under our control.

ECONOMIC ANALYSIS

- Ethanol is made from corn in the United States, so biofuel and food compete to use the same resources.

- To produce more ethanol and meet the Congress's mandate, farmers increased the number of acres devoted to corn production.

- In 2008, the amount of land devoted to corn production increased by 20 percent in the United States and by 2 percent in the rest of the world.

- Figure 1 shows the U.S. production possibilities frontier, *PPF*, for corn and other goods and services.

- The increase in the production of corn is illustrated by a movement along the *PPF* in Fig. 1 from point *A* in 2007 to point *B* in 2008.

- In moving from point *A* to point *B*, the United States incurs a higher opportunity cost of producing corn, as the greater slope of the *PPF* at point *B* indicates.

- In other regions of the world, despite the fact that more land was devoted to corn production, the amount of corn produced didn't change.

- The reason is that droughts in South America and Eastern Europe lowered the crop yield per acre in those regions.

- Figure 2 shows the rest of the world's *PPF* for corn and other goods and services in 2007 and 2008.

- The increase in the amount of land devoted to producing corn is illustrated by a movement along PPF_{07}.

- With a decrease in the crop yield, production possibilities decreased and the *PPF* rotated inward.

- The rotation from PPF_{07} to PPF_{08} illustrates this decrease in production possibilities.

- The opportunity cost of producing corn in the rest of the world increased for two reasons: the movement along its *PPF* and the inward rotation of the *PPF*.

- With a higher opportunity cost of producing corn, the cost of both biofuel and food increases.

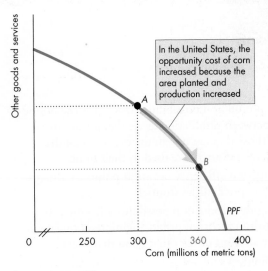

Figure 1 U.S. *PPF*

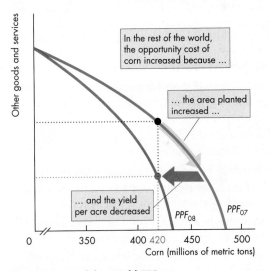

Figure 2 Rest of the World *PPF*

45

SUMMARY

Key Points

Production Possibilities and Opportunity Cost
(pp. 30–32)

- The production possibilities frontier is the boundary between production levels that are attainable and those that are not attainable when all the available resources are used to their limit.
- Production efficiency occurs at points on the production possibilities frontier.
- Along the production possibilities frontier, the opportunity cost of producing more of one good is the amount of the other good that must be given up.
- The opportunity cost of all goods increases as the production of the good increases.

Working Problems 1 to 3 will give you a better understanding of production possibilities and opportunity cost.

Using Resources Efficiently (pp. 33–35)

- Allocative efficiency occurs when goods and services are produced at the least possible cost and in the quantities that bring the greatest possible benefit.
- The marginal cost of a good is the opportunity cost of producing one more unit of it.
- The marginal benefit from a good is the benefit received from consuming one more unit of it and is measured by the willingness to pay for it.
- The marginal benefit of a good decreases as the amount of the good available increases.
- Resources are used efficiently when the marginal cost of each good is equal to its marginal benefit.

Working Problems 4 to 10 will give you a better understanding of the efficient use of resources.

Economic Growth (pp. 36–37)

- Economic growth, which is the expansion of production possibilities, results from capital accumulation and technological change.
- The opportunity cost of economic growth is forgone current consumption.
- The benefit of economic growth is increased future consumption.

Working Problem 11 will give you a better understanding of economic growth.

Gains from Trade (pp. 38–41)

- A person has a comparative advantage in producing a good if that person can produce the good at a lower opportunity cost than everyone else.
- People gain by specializing in the activity in which they have a comparative advantage and trading with others.

Working Problems 12 and 13 will give you a better understanding of the gains from trade.

Economic Coordination (pp. 41–43)

- Firms coordinate a large amount of economic activity, but there is a limit to the efficient size of a firm.
- Markets coordinate the economic choices of people and firms.
- Markets can work efficiently only when property rights exist.
- Money makes trading in markets more efficient.

Working Problem 14 will give you a better understanding of economic coordination.

Key Terms

Absolute advantage, 38
Allocative efficiency, 33
Capital accumulation, 36
Comparative advantage, 38
Economic growth, 36
Firm, 41

Marginal benefit, 34
Marginal benefit curve, 34
Marginal cost, 33
Market, 42
Money, 42
Opportunity cost, 31

Preferences, 34
Production efficiency, 31
Production possibilities frontier, 30
Property rights, 42
Technological change, 36

STUDY PLAN PROBLEMS AND APPLICATIONS

 You can work Problems 1 to 20 in MyEconLab Chapter 2 Study Plan and get instant feedback.

Production Possibilities and Opportunity Cost

(Study Plan 2.1)

Use the following information to work Problems 1 to 3. Brazil produces ethanol from sugar, and the land used to grow sugar can be used to grow food crops. Suppose that Brazil's production possibilities for ethanol and food crops are as follows

Ethanol (barrels per day)		Food crops (tons per day)
70	and	0
64	and	1
54	and	2
40	and	3
22	and	4
0	and	5

1. a. Draw a graph of Brazil's PPF and explain how your graph illustrates scarcity.
   b. If Brazil produces 40 barrels of ethanol a day, how much food must it produce to achieve production efficiency?
   c. Why does Brazil face a tradeoff on its *PPF*?

2. a. If Brazil increases its production of ethanol from 40 barrels per day to 54 barrels per day, what is the opportunity cost of the additional ethanol?
   b. If Brazil increases its production of food crops from 2 tons per day to 3 tons per day, what is the opportunity cost of the additional food?
   c. What is the relationship between your answers to parts (a) and (b)?

3. Does Brazil face an increasing opportunity cost of ethanol? What feature of Brazil's *PPF* illustrates increasing opportunity cost?

Using Resources Efficiently (Study Plan 2.2)

Use the above table to work Problems 4 and 5.

4. Define marginal cost and calculate Brazil's marginal cost of producing a ton of food when the quantity produced is 2.5 tons per day.

5. Define marginal benefit, explain how it is measured, and explain why the data in the table does not enable you to calculate Brazil's marginal benefit from food.

6. Distinguish between *production efficiency* and *allocative efficiency.* Explain why many production possibilities achieve production efficiency but only one achieves allocative efficiency.

Use the following graphs to work Problems 7 to 10. Harry enjoys tennis but wants a high grade in his economics course. The graphs show his *PPF* for these two "goods" and his *MB* curve from tennis.

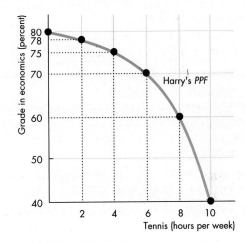

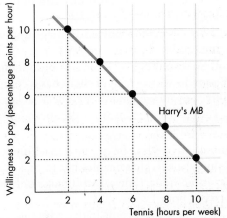

7. What is Harry's marginal cost of tennis if he plays for (i) 3 hours a week; (ii) 5 hours a week; and (iii) 7 hours a week?

8. a. If Harry uses his time to achieve allocative efficiency, what is his economics grade and how many hours of tennis does he play?
   b. Explain why Harry would be worse off getting a grade higher than your answer to part (a).

9. If Harry becomes a tennis superstar with big earnings from tennis, what happens to his *PPF*, *MB* curve, and his efficient time allocation?

10. If Harry suddenly finds high grades in economics easier to attain, what happens to his *PPF*, his *MB* curve, and his efficient time allocation?

Economic Growth (Study Plan 2.3)

11. A farm grows wheat and produces pork. The marginal cost of producing each of these products increases as more of it is produced.
    a. Make a graph that illustrates the farm's *PPF*.
    b. The farm adopts a new technology that allows it to use fewer resources to fatten pigs. Use your graph to illustrate the impact of the new technology on the farm's *PPF*.
    c. With the farm using the new technology described in part (b), has the opportunity cost of producing a ton of wheat increased, decreased, or remained the same? Explain and illustrate your answer.
    d. Is the farm more efficient with the new technology than it was with the old one? Why?

Gains from Trade (Study Plan 2.4)

12. In an hour, Sue can produce 40 caps or 4 jackets and Tessa can produce 80 caps or 4 jackets.
    a. Calculate Sue's opportunity cost of producing a cap.
    b. Calculate Tessa's opportunity cost of producing a cap.
    c. Who has a comparative advantage in producing caps?
    d. If Sue and Tessa specialize in producing the good in which each of them has a comparative advantage, and they trade 1 jacket for 15 caps, who gains from the specialization and trade?

13. Suppose that Tessa buys a new machine for making jackets that enables her to make 20 jackets an hour. (She can still make only 80 caps per hour.)
    a. Who now has a comparative advantage in producing jackets?
    b. Can Sue and Tessa still gain from trade?
    c. Would Sue and Tessa still be willing to trade 1 jacket for 15 caps? Explain your answer.

Economic Coordination (Study Plan 2.5)

14. For 50 years, Cuba has had a centrally planned economy in which the government makes the big decisions on how resources will be allocated.
    a. Why would you expect Cuba's production possibilities (per person) to be smaller than those of the United States?
    b. What are the social institutions that Cuba might lack that help the United States to achieve allocative efficiency?

Economics in the News (Study Plan 2.N)

Use the following data to work Problems 15 to 17. Brazil produces ethanol from sugar at a cost of 83 cents per gallon. The United States produces ethanol from corn at a cost of $1.14 per gallon. Sugar grown on one acre of land produces twice the quantity of ethanol as the corn grown on an acre. The United States imports 5 percent of the ethanol it uses and produces the rest itself. Since 2003, U.S. ethanol production has more than doubled and U.S. corn production has increased by 45 percent.

15. a. Does Brazil or the United States have a comparative advantage in producing ethanol?
    b. Sketch the *PPF* for ethanol and other goods and services for the United States.
    c. Sketch the *PPF* for ethanol and other goods and services for Brazil.

16. a. Do you expect the opportunity cost of producing ethanol in the United States to have increased since 2003? Explain why.
    b. Do you think the United States has achieved production efficiency in its manufacture of ethanol? Explain why or why not.
    c. Do you think the United States has achieved allocative efficiency in its manufacture of ethanol? Explain why or why not.

17. Sketch a figure similar to Fig. 2.6 on p. 40 to show how both the United States and Brazil can gain from specialization and trade.

Use this news clip to work Problems 18 to 20.

Time For Tea
Americans are switching to loose-leaf tea for its health benefits. Tea could be grown in the United States, but picking tea leaves would be costly because it can only be done by workers and not by machine.
Source: *The Economist*, July 8, 2005

18. a. Sketch *PPF*s for the production of tea and other goods and services in India and in the United States.
    b. Sketch marginal cost curves for the production of tea in India and in the United States.

19. a. Sketch the marginal benefit curves for tea in the United States before and after Americans began to appreciate the health benefits of loose tea.
    b. Explain how the quantity of loose tea that achieves allocative efficiency has changed.
    c. Does the change in preferences toward tea affect the opportunity cost of producing tea?

20. Explain why the United States does not produce tea and instead imports it from India.

ADDITIONAL PROBLEMS AND APPLICATIONS

 myeconlab You can work these problems in MyEconLab if assigned by your instructor.

Production Possibilities and Opportunity Cost

Use the following table to work Problems 21 to 22.
Suppose that Yucatan's production possibilities are

Food (pounds per month)		Sunscreen (gallons per month)
300	and	0
200	and	50
100	and	100
0	and	150

21. a. Draw a graph of Yucatan's *PPF* and explain how your graph illustrates a tradeoff.
    b. If Yucatan produces 150 pounds of food per month, how much sunscreen must it produce if it achieves production efficiency?
    c. What is Yucatan's opportunity cost of producing 1 pound of food?
    d. What is Yucatan's opportunity cost of producing 1 gallon of sunscreen?
    e. What is the relationship between your answers to parts (c) and (d)?

22. What feature of a *PPF* illustrates increasing opportunity cost? Explain why Yucatan's opportunity cost does or does not increase.

Using Resources Efficiently

23. In problem 21, what is the marginal cost of a pound of food in Yucatan when the quantity produced is 150 pounds per day? What is special about the marginal cost of food in Yucatan?

24. The table describes the preferences in Yucatan.

Sunscreen (gallons per month)	Willingness to pay (pounds of food per gallon)
25	3
75	2
125	1

    a. What is the marginal benefit from sunscreen and how is it measured?
    b. Draw a graph of Yucatan's marginal benefit from sunscreen.

Economic Growth

25. Capital accumulation and technological change bring economic growth, which means that the *PPF* keeps shifting outward: Production that was unattainable yesterday becomes attainable today; production that is unattainable today will become attainable tomorrow. Why doesn't this process of economic growth mean that scarcity is being defeated and will one day be gone?

Gains from Trade

Use the following data to work Problems 26 and 27.
Kim can produce 40 pies or 400 cakes an hour. Liam can produce 100 pies or 200 cakes an hour.

26. a. Calculate Kim's opportunity cost of a pie and Liam's opportunity cost of a pie.
    b. If each spends 30 minutes of each hour producing pies and 30 minutes producing cakes, how many pies and cakes does each produce?
    c. Who has a comparative advantage in producing pies? Who has a comparative advantage in producing cakes?

27. a. Draw a graph of Kim's *PPF* and Liam's *PPF*.
    b. On your graph, show the point at which each produces when they spend 30 minutes of each hour producing pies and 30 minutes producing cakes.
    c. On your graph, show what Kim produces and what does Liam produces when they specialize.
    d. When they specialize and trade, what are the total gains from trade?
    e. If Kim and Liam share the total gains equally, what trade takes place between them?

Economic Coordination

28. Indicate on a graph of the circular flows in the market economy, the real and money flows in which the following items belong:
    a. You buy an iPad from the Apple Store.
    b. Apple Inc. pays the designers of the iPad.
    c. Apple Inc. decides to expand and rents an adjacent building.
    d. You buy a new e-book from Amazon.
    e. Apple Inc. hires a student as an intern during the summer.

Economics in the News

29. After you have studied *Reading Between the Lines* on pp. 44–45, answer the following questions.
    a. How has an Act of the United States Congress increased U.S. production of corn?
    b. Why would you expect an increase in the quantity of corn produced to raise the opportunity cost of corn?

c. Why did the cost of producing corn increase in the rest of the world?

d. Is it possible that the increased quantity of corn produced, despite the higher cost of production, moves the United States closer to allocative efficiency?

30. **Malaria Eradication Back on the Table**

In response to the Gates Malaria Forum in October 2007, countries are debating the pros and cons of eradication. Dr. Arata Kochi of the World Health Organization believes that with enough money malaria cases could be cut by 90 percent, but he believes that it would be very expensive to eliminate the remaining 10 percent of cases. He concluded that countries should not strive to eradicate malaria.

Source: *The New York Times*, March 4, 2008

a. Is Dr. Kochi talking about *production efficiency* or *allocative efficiency* or both?

b. Make a graph with the percentage of malaria cases eliminated on the *x*-axis and the marginal cost and marginal benefit of driving down malaria cases on the *y*-axis. On your graph:

(i) Draw a marginal cost curve that is consistent with Dr. Kochi's opinion.

(ii) Draw a marginal benefit curve that is consistent with Dr. Kochi's opinion.

(iii) Identify the quantity of malaria eradicated that achieves allocative efficiency.

31. **Lots of Little Screens**

Inexpensive broadband access has created a generation of television producers for whom the Internet is their native medium. As they redirect the focus from TV to computers, cell phones, and iPods, the video market is developing into an open digital network.

Source: *The New York Times*, December 2, 2007

a. How has inexpensive broadband changed the production possibilities of video entertainment and other goods and services?

b. Sketch a *PPF* for video entertainment and other goods and services before broadband.

c. Show how the arrival of inexpensive broadband has changed the *PPF*.

d. Sketch a marginal benefit curve for video entertainment.

e. Show how the new generation of TV producers for whom the Internet is their native medium might have changed the marginal benefit from video entertainment.

f. Explain how the efficient quantity of video entertainment has changed.

Use the following information to work Problems 32 and 33.

Before the Civil War, the South traded with the North and with England. The South sold cotton and bought manufactured goods and food. During the war, one of President Lincoln's first actions was to blockade the ports and prevent this trade. The South increased its production of munitions and food.

32. In what did the South have a comparative advantage?

33. a. Draw a graph to illustrate production, consumption, and trade in the South before the Civil War.

b. Was the South consuming inside, on, or outside its *PPF*? Explain your answer.

c. Draw a graph to show the effects of the Civil War on consumption and production in the South.

d. Did the Civil War change any opportunity costs in the South? If so, did the opportunity cost of everything increase? Did the opportunity cost of any items decrease? Illustrate your answer with appropriate graphs.

Use the following information to work Problems 34 and 35.

He Shoots! He Scores! He Makes Movies!

NBA All-star Baron Davis and his school friend, Cash Warren, premiered their first movie *Made in America* at the Sundance Festival in January 2008. The movie, based on gang activity in South Central Los Angeles, received good reviews.

Source: *The New York Times*, February 24, 2008

34. a. Does Baron Davis have an absolute advantage in basketball and movie directing and is this the reason for his success in both activities?

b. Does Baron Davis have a comparative advantage in basketball or movie directing or both and is this the reason for his success in both activities?

35. a. Sketch a *PPF* between playing basketball and producing other goods and services for Baron Davis and for yourself.

b. How do you (and people like you) and Baron Davis (and people like him) gain from specialization and trade?

Your Economic Revolution

Three periods in human history stand out as ones of economic revolution. The first, the *Agricultural Revolution,* occurred 10,000 years ago. In what is today Iraq, people learned to domesticate animals and plant crops. People stopped roaming in search of food and settled in villages, towns, and cities where they specialized in the activities in which they had a comparative advantage and developed markets in which to exchange their products. Wealth increased enormously.

You are studying economics at a time that future historians will call the *Information Revolution.* Over the entire world, people are embracing new information technologies and prospering on an unprecedented scale.

Economics was born during the *Industrial Revolution,* which began in England during the 1760s. For the first time, people began to apply science and create new technologies for the manufacture of textiles and iron, to create steam engines, and to boost the output of farms.

During all three economic revolutions, many have prospered but many have been left behind. It is the range of human progress that poses the greatest question for economics and the one that Adam Smith addressed in the first work of economic science: What causes the differences in wealth among nations?

Many people had written about economics before **Adam Smith***, but he made economics a science. Born in 1723 in Kirkcaldy, a small fishing town near Edinburgh, Scotland, Smith was the only child of the town's customs officer. Lured from his professorship (he was a full professor at 28) by a wealthy Scottish duke who gave him a pension of £300 a year—ten times the average income at that time—Smith devoted ten years to writing his masterpiece:* An Inquiry into the Nature and Causes of the **Wealth of Nations***, published in 1776.*

Why, Adam Smith asked , are some nations wealthy while others are poor? He was pondering these questions at the height of the Industrial Revolution, and he answered by emphasizing the role of the division of labor and free markets.

To illustrate his argument, Adam Smith described two pin factories. In the first, one person, using the hand tools available in the 1770s, could make 20 pins a day. In the other, by using those same hand tools but breaking the process into a number of individually small operations in which people specialize—by the division of labor—*ten people could make a staggering 48,000 pins a day. One draws*

"It is not from the benevolence of the butcher, the brewer, or the baker that we expect our dinner, but from their regard to their own interest."

ADAM SMITH
The Wealth of Nations

out the wire, another straightens it, a third cuts it, a fourth points it, a fifth grinds it. Three specialists make the head, and a fourth attaches it. Finally, the pin is polished and packaged.

But a large market is needed to support the division of labor: One factory employing ten workers would need to sell more than 15 million pins a year to stay in business!

Professor Bhagwati, what attracted you to economics?

When you come from India, where poverty hits the eye, it is easy to be attracted to economics, which can be used to bring prosperity and create jobs to pull up the poor into gainful employment.

I learned later that there are two broad types of economist: those who treat the subject as an arid mathematical toy and those who see it as a serious social science.

If Cambridge, where I went as an undergraduate, had been interested in esoteric mathematical economics, I would have opted for something else. But the Cambridge economists from whom I learned—many among the greatest figures in the discipline—saw economics as a social science. I therefore saw the power of economics as a tool to address India's poverty and was immediately hooked.

Who had the greatest impact on you at Cambridge?

Most of all, it was Harry Johnson, a young Canadian of immense energy and profound analytical gifts. Quite unlike the shy and reserved British dons, Johnson was friendly, effusive, and supportive of students who flocked around him. He would later move to Chicago, where he became one of the most influential members of the market-oriented Chicago school. Another was Joan Robinson, arguably the world's most impressive female economist.

When I left Cambridge for MIT, going from one Cambridge to the other, I was lucky to transition from one phenomenal set of economists to another. At MIT, I learned much from future Nobel laureates Paul Samuelson and Robert Solow. Both would later become great friends and colleagues when I joined the MIT faculty in 1968.

After Cambridge and MIT, you went to Oxford and then back to India. What did you do in India?

I joined the Planning Commission in New Delhi, where my first big job was to find ways of raising the bottom 30 percent of India's population out of poverty to a "minimum income" level.

And what did you prescribe?

My main prescription was to "grow the pie." My research suggested that the share of the bottom 30 percent of the pie did not seem to vary dramatically with differences in economic and political systems.

So growth in the pie seemed to be the principal (but not the only) component of an anti-poverty strategy. To supplement growth's good effects on the poor, the Indian planners were also dedicated to education, health, social reforms, and land reforms. Also, the access of the lowest-income and socially disadvantaged groups to the growth process and its benefits was to be improved in many ways, such as extension of credit without collateral.

> My main prescription was to "grow the pie" ... Much empirical work shows that where growth has occurred, poverty has lessened.

Today, this strategy has no rivals. Much empirical work shows that where growth has occurred, poverty has lessened. It is nice to know that one's basic take on an issue of such central importance to humanity's well-being has been borne out by experience!

You left India in 1968 to come to the United States and an academic job at MIT. Why?

While the decision to emigrate often reflects personal factors—and they were present in my case—the offer of a professorship from MIT certainly helped me

JAGDISH BHAGWATI is University Professor at Columbia University. Born in India in 1934, he studied at Cambridge University in England, MIT, and Oxford University before returning to India. He returned to teach at MIT in 1968 and moved to Columbia in 1980. A prolific scholar, Professor Bhagwati also writes in leading newspapers and magazines throughout the world. He has been much honored for both his scientific work and his impact on public policy. His greatest contributions are in international trade but extend also to developmental problems and the study of political economy.

Michael Parkin talked with Jagdish Bhagwati about his work and the progress that economists have made in understanding the benefits of economic growth and international trade since the pioneering work of Adam Smith.

make up my mind. At the time, it was easily the world's most celebrated department. Serendipitously, the highest-ranked departments at MIT were not in engineering and the sciences but in linguistics (which had Noam Chomsky) and economics (which had Paul Samuelson). Joining the MIT faculty was a dramatic breakthrough: I felt stimulated each year by several fantastic students and by several of the world's most creative economists.

We hear a lot in the popular press about fair trade and level playing fields. What's the distinction between free trade and fair trade? How can the playing field be unlevel?

Free trade simply means allowing no trade barriers such as tariffs, subsidies, and quotas. Trade barriers make domestic prices different from world prices for traded goods. When this happens, resources are not being used efficiently. Basic economics from the time of Adam Smith tells us why free trade is good for us and why barriers to trade harm us, though our understanding of this doctrine today is far more nuanced and profound than it was at its creation.

Fair trade, on the other hand, is almost always a sneaky way of objecting to free trade. If your rivals are hard to compete with, you are not likely to get protection simply by saying that you cannot hack it. But if you say that your rival is an "unfair" trader, that is an easier sell! As international competition has grown fiercer, cries of "unfair trade" have therefore multiplied. The lesser rogues among the protectionists ask for "free and fair trade," whereas the worst ones ask for "fair, not free, trade."

> Fair trade ... is almost always a sneaky way of objecting to free trade.

At the end of World War II, the General Agreement on Tariffs and Trade (GATT) was established and there followed several rounds of multilateral trade negotiations and reductions in barriers to trade. How do you assess the contribution of GATT and its successor, the World Trade Organization (WTO)?

The GATT has made a huge contribution by overseeing massive trade liberalization in industrial goods among the developed countries. GATT rules, which "bind" tariffs to negotiated ceilings, prevent the raising of tariffs and have prevented tariff wars like those of the 1930s in which mutual and retaliatory tariff barriers were raised, to the detriment of everyone.

The GATT was folded into the WTO at the end of the Uruguay Round of trade negotiations, and the WTO is institutionally stronger. For instance, it has a binding dispute settlement mechanism, whereas the GATT had no such teeth. It is also more ambitious in its scope, extending to new areas such as the environment, intellectual property protection, and investment rules.

Running alongside the pursuit of multilateral free trade has been the emergence of bilateral trade agreements such as NAFTA and the European Union (EU). How do you view the bilateral free trade areas in today's world?

Unfortunately, there has been an explosion of bilateral free trade areas today. By some estimates, the ones in place and others being plotted approach 400! Each bilateral agreement gives preferential treatment to its trading partner over others. Because there are now so many bilateral agreements, such as those between the United States and Israel and between the United States and Jordan, the result is a chaotic pattern of different tariffs depending on where a product comes from. Also, "rules of origin" must be agreed upon to determine whether a product is, say, Jordanian or Taiwanese if Jordan qualifies for a preferential tariff but Taiwan does not and Taiwanese inputs enter the Jordanian manufacture of the product.

I have called the resulting crisscrossing of preferences and rules of origin the "spaghetti bowl" problem. The world trading system is choking under these proliferating bilateral deals. Contrast this complexity with the simplicity of a multilateral system with common tariffs for all WTO members.

We now have a world of uncoordinated and inefficient trade policies. The EU makes bilateral free trade agreements with different non-EU countries, so the United States follows with its own bilateral agreements; and with Europe and the United States doing it, the Asian countries, long wedded to multilateralism, have now succumbed to the mania.

> **We now have a world of uncoordinated and inefficient trade policies.**

Instead, if the United States had provided leadership by rewriting rules to make the signing of such bilateral agreements extremely difficult, this plague on the trading system today might well have been averted.

Is the "spaghetti bowl" problem getting better or worse?

Unquestionably it is getting worse. Multilateralism is retreating and bilateralism is advancing. The 2010 G-20 meeting in Canada was a disappointment. At the insistence of the United States, a definite date for completing the Doha Round was dropped and instead, unwittingly rubbing salt into the wound, President Barack Obama announced his administration's willingness to see the U.S.-South Korea free trade agreement through. There are distressing recent reports that the U.S. Commerce Department is exploring ways to strengthen the bite of anti-dumping actions, which are now generally agreed to be a form of discriminatory protectionism aimed selectively at successful exporting nations and firms. Equally distressing is Obama's decision to sign a bill that raises fees on some temporary work visas in order to pay for higher border-enforcement expenditures.Further, it was asserted that a tax on foreign workers would reduce the numbers coming in and "taking jobs away" from U.S. citizens. Many support-

ers of the proposal claimed, incoherently, that it would simultaneously discourage foreign workers from entering the United States and increase revenues.Obama's surrender exemplified the doctrine that one retreat often leads to another, with new lobbyists following in others' footsteps. Perhaps the chief mistake, as with recent "Buy American" provisions in U.S. legislation, was to allow the Employ American Workers Act (EAWA) to be folded into the stimulus bill. This act makes it harder for companies to get govern-mental support to hire skilled immigrants with H1(b) visas: They must first show that they have not laid off or plan to lay off U.S. workers in similar occupations. Whatever the shortcomings of such measures in economic-policy terms, the visa-fee-enhancement provision is de facto discriminatory, and thus violates WTO rules against discrimination between domestic and foreign firms, or between foreign firms from different WTO countries. While the visa-fee legislation is what lawyers call "facially" non-discriminatory, its design confers an advantage on U.S. firms vis-à-vis foreign firms.Such acts of discrimination in trade policies find succor in the media and in some of America's prominent think tanks. For example, in the wake of the vast misery brought by flooding to the people of Pakistan, the U.S. and other governments have risen to the occasion with emergency aid. But there have also been proposals to grant duty-free access to Pakistan's exports. But this would be discriminatory toward developing countries that do not have duty-free access, helping Pakistan at their expense.

What advice do you have for a student who is just starting to study economics? Is economics a good subject in which to major?

I would say: enormously so. In particular, we economists bring three unique insights to good policy making.

First, economists look for second- and subsequent-round effects of actions.

Second, we correctly emphasize that a policy cannot be judged without using a counterfactual. It is a witticism that an economist, when asked how her husband was, said, "compared to what?"

Third, we uniquely and systematically bring the principle of social cost and social benefit to our policy analysis.

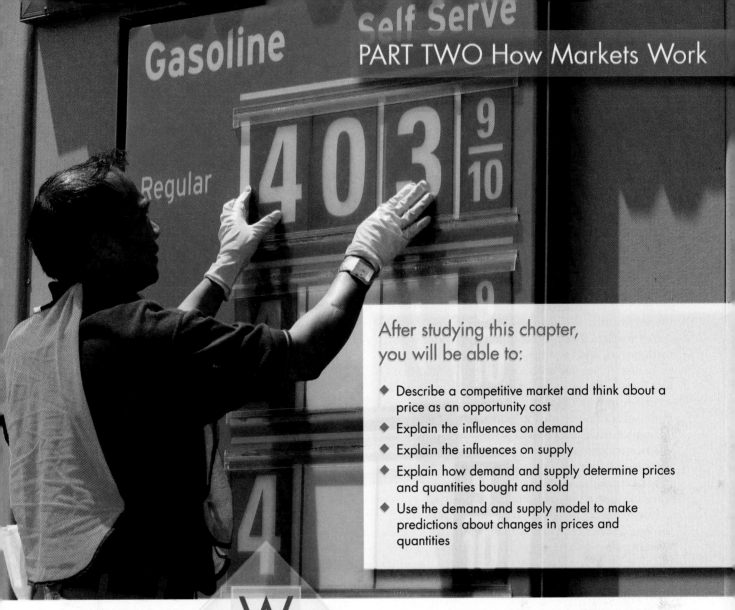

After studying this chapter,
you will be able to:

◆ Describe a competitive market and think about a
   price as an opportunity cost
◆ Explain the influences on demand
◆ Explain the influences on supply
◆ Explain how demand and supply determine prices
   and quantities bought and sold
◆ Use the demand and supply model to make
   predictions about changes in prices and
   quantities

3

DEMAND AND SUPPLY

What makes the price of oil double and the price of gasoline almost double in
just one year? Will these prices keep on rising? Are the oil companies taking
advantage of people? This chapter enables you to answer these and similar
questions about prices—prices that rise, prices that fall, and prices that
fluctuate.

You already know that economics is about the choices people make to cope
with scarcity and how those choices respond to incentives. Prices act as
incentives. You're going to see how people respond to prices and how prices
get determined by demand and supply. The demand and supply model that
you study in this chapter is the main tool of economics. It
helps us to answer the big economic question: What, how,
and for whom goods and services are produced?

At the end of the chapter, in *Reading Between the Lines*, we'll apply the
model to the market for coffee and explain why its price increased sharply in
2010 and why it was expected to rise again.

◆ Markets and Prices

When you need a new pair of running shoes, want a bagel and a latte, plan to upgrade your cell phone, or need to fly home for Thanksgiving, you must find a place where people sell those items or offer those services. The place in which you find them is a *market*. You learned in Chapter 2 (p. 42) that a market is any arrangement that enables buyers and sellers to get information and to do business with each other.

A market has two sides: buyers and sellers. There are markets for *goods* such as apples and hiking boots, for *services* such as haircuts and tennis lessons, for *factors of production* such as computer programmers and earthmovers, and for other manufactured *inputs* such as memory chips and auto parts. There are also markets for money such as Japanese yen and for financial securities such as Yahoo! stock. Only our imagination limits what can be traded in markets.

Some markets are physical places where buyers and sellers meet and where an auctioneer or a broker helps to determine the prices. Examples of this type of market are the New York Stock Exchange and the wholesale fish, meat, and produce markets.

Some markets are groups of people spread around the world who never meet and know little about each other but are connected through the Internet or by telephone and fax. Examples are the e-commerce markets and the currency markets.

But most markets are unorganized collections of buyers and sellers. You do most of your trading in this type of market. An example is the market for basketball shoes. The buyers in this $3 billion-a-year market are the 45 million Americans who play basketball (or who want to make a fashion statement). The sellers are the tens of thousands of retail sports equipment and footwear stores. Each buyer can visit several different stores, and each seller knows that the buyer has a choice of stores.

Markets vary in the intensity of competition that buyers and sellers face. In this chapter, we're going to study a **competitive market**—a market that has many buyers and many sellers, so no single buyer or seller can influence the price.

Producers offer items for sale only if the price is high enough to cover their opportunity cost. And consumers respond to changing opportunity cost by seeking cheaper alternatives to expensive items.

We are going to study how people respond to *prices* and the forces that determine prices. But to pursue these tasks, we need to understand the relationship between a price and an opportunity cost.

In everyday life, the *price* of an object is the number of dollars that must be given up in exchange for it. Economists refer to this price as the **money price**.

The *opportunity cost* of an action is the highest-valued alternative forgone. If, when you buy a cup of coffee, the highest-valued thing you forgo is some gum, then the opportunity cost of the coffee is the *quantity* of gum forgone. We can calculate the quantity of gum forgone from the money prices of the coffee and the gum.

If the money price of coffee is $1 a cup and the money price of gum is 50¢ a pack, then the opportunity cost of one cup of coffee is two packs of gum. To calculate this opportunity cost, we divide the price of a cup of coffee by the price of a pack of gum and find the *ratio* of one price to the other. The ratio of one price to another is called a **relative price**, and a *relative price is an opportunity cost.*

We can express the relative price of coffee in terms of gum or any other good. The normal way of expressing a relative price is in terms of a "basket" of all goods and services. To calculate this relative price, we divide the money price of a good by the money price of a "basket" of all goods (called a *price index*). The resulting relative price tells us the opportunity cost of the good in terms of how much of the "basket" we must give up to buy it.

The demand and supply model that we are about to study determines *relative prices,* and the word "price" means *relative* price. When we predict that a price will fall, we do not mean that its *money* price will fall—although it might. We mean that its *relative* price will fall. That is, its price will fall *relative* to the average price of other goods and services.

REVIEW QUIZ

1 What is the distinction between a money price and a relative price?
2 Explain why a relative price is an opportunity cost.
3 Think of examples of goods whose relative price has risen or fallen by a large amount.

You can work these questions in Study Plan 3.1 and get instant feedback.

Let's begin our study of demand and supply, starting with demand.

◆ Demand

If you demand something, then you

1. Want it,
2. Can afford it, and
3. Plan to buy it.

Wants are the unlimited desires or wishes that people have for goods and services. How many times have you thought that you would like something "if only you could afford it" or "if it weren't so expensive"? Scarcity guarantees that many—perhaps most—of our wants will never be satisfied. Demand reflects a decision about which wants to satisfy.

The **quantity demanded** of a good or service is the amount that consumers plan to buy during a given time period at a particular price. The quantity demanded is not necessarily the same as the quantity actually bought. Sometimes the quantity demanded exceeds the amount of goods available, so the quantity bought is less than the quantity demanded.

The quantity demanded is measured as an amount per unit of time. For example, suppose that you buy one cup of coffee a day. The quantity of coffee that you demand can be expressed as 1 cup per day, 7 cups per week, or 365 cups per year.

Many factors influence buying plans, and one of them is the price. We look first at the relationship between the quantity demanded of a good and its price. To study this relationship, we keep all other influences on buying plans the same and we ask: How, other things remaining the same, does the quantity demanded of a good change as its price changes?

The law of demand provides the answer.

The Law of Demand

The **law of demand** states

> Other things remaining the same, the higher the price of a good, the smaller is the quantity demanded; and the lower the price of a good, the greater is the quantity demanded.

Why does a higher price reduce the quantity demanded? For two reasons:

- Substitution effect
- Income effect

Substitution Effect When the price of a good rises, other things remaining the same, its *relative* price—its opportunity cost—rises. Although each good is unique, it has *substitutes*—other goods that can be used in its place. As the opportunity cost of a good rises, the incentive to economize on its use and switch to a substitute becomes stronger.

Income Effect When a price rises, other things remaining the same, the price rises *relative* to income. Faced with a higher price and an unchanged income, people cannot afford to buy all the things they previously bought. They must decrease the quantities demanded of at least some goods and services. Normally, the good whose price has increased will be one of the goods that people buy less of.

To see the substitution effect and the income effect at work, think about the effects of a change in the price of an energy bar. Several different goods are substitutes for an energy bar. For example, an energy drink could be consumed instead of an energy bar.

Suppose that an energy bar initially sells for $3 and then its price falls to $1.50. People now substitute energy bars for energy drinks—the substitution effect. And with a budget that now has some slack from the lower price of an energy bar, people buy even more energy bars—the income effect. The quantity of energy bars demanded increases for these two reasons.

Now suppose that an energy bar initially sells for $3 and then the price doubles to $6. People now buy fewer energy bars and more energy drinks—the substitution effect. And faced with a tighter budget, people buy even fewer energy bars—the income effect. The quantity of energy bars demanded decreases for these two reasons.

Demand Curve and Demand Schedule

You are now about to study one of the two most used curves in economics: the demand curve. You are also going to encounter one of the most critical distinctions: the distinction between *demand* and *quantity demanded*.

The term **demand** refers to the entire relationship between the price of a good and the quantity demanded of that good. Demand is illustrated by the demand curve and the demand schedule. The term *quantity demanded* refers to a point on a demand curve—the quantity demanded at a particular price.

Figure 3.1 shows the demand curve for energy bars. A **demand curve** shows the relationship between the quantity demanded of a good and its price when all other influences on consumers' planned purchases remain the same.

The table in Fig. 3.1 is the demand schedule for energy bars. A *demand schedule* lists the quantities demanded at each price when all the other influences on consumers' planned purchases remain the same. For example, if the price of a bar is 50¢, the quantity demanded is 22 million a week. If the price is $2.50, the quantity demanded is 5 million a week. The other rows of the table show the quantities demanded at prices of $1.00, $1.50, and $2.00.

We graph the demand schedule as a demand curve with the quantity demanded on the *x*-axis and the price on the *y*-axis. The points on the demand curve labeled *A* through *E* correspond to the rows of the demand schedule. For example, point *A* on the graph shows a quantity demanded of 22 million energy bars a week at a price of 50¢ a bar.

Willingness and Ability to Pay Another way of looking at the demand curve is as a willingness-and-ability-to-pay curve. The willingness and ability to pay is a measure of *marginal benefit*.

If a small quantity is available, the highest price that someone is willing and able to pay for one more unit is high. But as the quantity available increases, the marginal benefit of each additional unit falls and the highest price that someone is willing and able to pay also falls along the demand curve.

In Fig. 3.1, if only 5 million energy bars are available each week, the highest price that someone is willing to pay for the 5 millionth bar is $2.50. But if 22 million energy bars are available each week, someone is willing to pay 50¢ for the last bar bought.

A Change in Demand

When any factor that influences buying plans changes, other than the price of the good, there is a **change in demand**. Figure 3.2 illustrates an increase in demand. When demand increases, the demand curve shifts rightward and the quantity demanded at each price is greater. For example, at $2.50 a bar, the quantity demanded on the original (blue) demand curve is 5 million energy bars a week. On the new (red) demand curve, at $2.50 a bar, the quantity demanded is 15 million bars a week. Look closely at the numbers in the table and check that the quantity demanded at each price is greater.

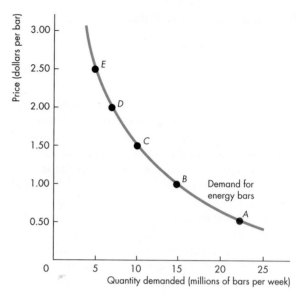

FIGURE 3.1   The Demand Curve

	Price (dollars per bar)	Quantity demanded (millions of bars per week)
A	0.50	22
B	1.00	15
C	1.50	10
D	2.00	7
E	2.50	5

The table shows a demand schedule for energy bars. At a price of 50¢ a bar, 22 million bars a week are demanded; at a price of $1.50 a bar, 10 million bars a week are demanded. The demand curve shows the relationship between quantity demanded and price, other things remaining the same. The demand curve slopes downward: As the price falls, the quantity demanded increases.

The demand curve can be read in two ways. For a given price, the demand curve tells us the quantity that people plan to buy. For example, at a price of $1.50 a bar, people plan to buy 10 million bars a week. For a given quantity, the demand curve tells us the maximum price that consumers are willing and able to pay for the last bar available. For example, the maximum price that consumers will pay for the 15 millionth bar is $1.00.

myeconlab animation

FIGURE 3.2   An Increase in Demand

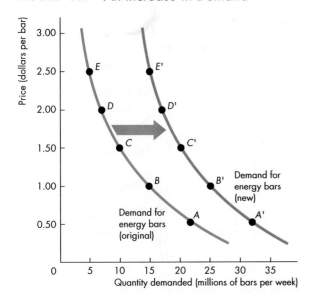

Original demand schedule Original income			New demand schedule New higher income		
	Price (dollars per bar)	Quantity demanded (millions of bars per week)		Price (dollars per bar)	Quantity demanded (millions of bars per week)
A	0.50	22	A'	0.50	32
B	1.00	15	B'	1.00	25
C	1.50	10	C'	1.50	20
D	2.00	7	D'	2.00	17
E	2.50	5	E'	2.50	15

A change in any influence on buying plans other than the price of the good itself results in a new demand schedule and a shift of the demand curve. A change in income changes the demand for energy bars. At a price of $1.50 a bar, 10 million bars a week are demanded at the original income (row C of the table) and 20 million bars a week are demanded at the new higher income (row C'). A rise in income increases the demand for energy bars. The demand curve shifts *rightward*, as shown by the shift arrow and the resulting red curve.

myeconlab animation

Six main factors bring changes in demand. They are changes in

- The prices of related goods
- Expected future prices
- Income
- Expected future income and credit
- Population
- Preferences

Prices of Related Goods The quantity of energy bars that consumers plan to buy depends in part on the prices of substitutes for energy bars. A **substitute** is a good that can be used in place of another good. For example, a bus ride is a substitute for a train ride; a hamburger is a substitute for a hot dog; and an energy drink is a substitute for an energy bar. If the price of a substitute for an energy bar rises, people buy less of the substitute and more energy bars. For example, if the price of an energy drink rises, people buy fewer energy drinks and more energy bars. The demand for energy bars increases.

The quantity of energy bars that people plan to buy also depends on the prices of complements with energy bars. A **complement** is a good that is used in conjunction with another good. Hamburgers and fries are complements, and so are energy bars and exercise. If the price of an hour at the gym falls, people buy more gym time *and more* energy bars.

Expected Future Prices If the expected future price of a good rises and if the good can be stored, the opportunity cost of obtaining the good for future use is lower today than it will be in the future when people expect the price to be higher. So people retime their purchases—they substitute over time. They buy more of the good now before its price is expected to rise (and less afterward), so the demand for the good today increases.

For example, suppose that a Florida frost damages the season's orange crop. You expect the price of orange juice to rise, so you fill your freezer with enough frozen juice to get you through the next six months. Your current demand for frozen orange juice has increased, and your future demand has decreased.

Similarly, if the expected future price of a good falls, the opportunity cost of buying the good today is high relative to what it is expected to be in the future. So again, people retime their purchases. They buy less of the good now before its price is expected to fall, so the demand for the good decreases today and increases in the future.

Computer prices are constantly falling, and this fact poses a dilemma. Will you buy a new computer now, in time for the start of the school year, or will you wait until the price has fallen some more? Because people expect computer prices to keep falling, the current demand for computers is less (and the future demand is greater) than it otherwise would be.

Income Consumers' income influences demand. When income increases, consumers buy more of most goods; and when income decreases, consumers buy less of most goods. Although an increase in income leads to an increase in the demand for *most* goods, it does not lead to an increase in the demand for *all* goods. A **normal good** is one for which demand increases as income increases. An **inferior good** is one for which demand decreases as income increases. As incomes increase, the demand for air travel (a normal good) increases and the demand for long-distance bus trips (an inferior good) decreases.

Expected Future Income and Credit When expected future income increases or credit becomes easier to get, demand for the good might increase now. For example, a salesperson gets the news that she will receive a big bonus at the end of the year, so she goes into debt and buys a new car right now, rather than wait until she receives the bonus.

Population Demand also depends on the size and the age structure of the population. The larger the population, the greater is the demand for all goods and services; the smaller the population, the smaller the demand for all goods and services.

For example, the demand for parking spaces or movies or just about anything that you can imagine is much greater in New York City (population 7.5 million) than it is in Boise, Idaho (population 150,000).

Also, the larger the proportion of the population in a given age group, the greater is the demand for the goods and services used by that age group.

For example, during the 1990s, a decrease in the college-age population decreased the demand for college places. During those same years, the number of Americans aged 85 years and over increased by more than 1 million. As a result, the demand for nursing home services increased.

TABLE 3.1   The Demand for Energy Bars

The Law of Demand

The quantity of energy bars demanded

Decreases if:	Increases if:
■ The price of an energy bar rises	■ The price of an energy bar falls

Changes in Demand

The demand for energy bars

Decreases if:	Increases if:
■ The price of a substitute falls	■ The price of a substitute rises
■ The price of a complement rises	■ The price of a complement falls
■ The expected future price of an energy bar falls	■ The expected future price of an energy bar rises
■ Income falls*	■ Income rises*
■ Expected future income falls or credit becomes harder to get*	■ Expected future income rises or credit becomes easier to get*
■ The population decreases	■ The population increases

*An energy bar is a normal good.

Preferences Demand depends on preferences. *Preferences* determine the value that people place on each good and service. Preferences depend on such things as the weather, information, and fashion. For example, greater health and fitness awareness has shifted preferences in favor of energy bars, so the demand for energy bars has increased.

Table 3.1 summarizes the influences on demand and the direction of those influences.

A Change in the Quantity Demanded Versus a Change in Demand

Changes in the influences on buying plans bring either a change in the quantity demanded or a change in demand. Equivalently, they bring either a movement along the demand curve or a shift of the demand curve. The distinction between a change in the quantity demanded and a change in demand is the same as that between a movement along the demand curve and a shift of the demand curve.

A point on the demand curve shows the quantity demanded at a given price, so a movement along the demand curve shows a **change in the quantity demanded**. The entire demand curve shows demand, so a shift of the demand curve shows a *change in demand*. Figure 3.3 illustrates these distinctions.

Movement Along the Demand Curve   If the price of the good changes but no other influence on buying plans changes, we illustrate the effect as a movement along the demand curve.

A fall in the price of a good increases the quantity demanded of it. In Fig. 3.3, we illustrate the effect of a fall in price as a movement down along the demand curve D_0.

A rise in the price of a good decreases the quantity demanded of it. In Fig. 3.3, we illustrate the effect of a rise in price as a movement up along the demand curve D_0.

A Shift of the Demand Curve   If the price of a good remains constant but some other influence on buying plans changes, there is a change in demand for that good. We illustrate a change in demand as a shift of the demand curve. For example, if more people work out at the gym, consumers buy more energy bars regardless of the price of a bar. That is what a rightward shift of the demand curve shows—more energy bars are demanded at each price.

In Fig. 3.3, there is a *change in demand* and the demand curve shifts when any influence on buying plans changes, other than the price of the good. Demand *increases* and the demand curve *shifts rightward* (to the red demand curve D_1) if the price of a substitute rises, the price of a complement falls, the expected future price of the good rises, income increases (for a normal good), expected future income or credit increases, or the population increases. Demand *decreases* and the demand curve *shifts leftward* (to the red demand curve D_2) if the price of a substitute falls, the price of a complement rises, the expected future price of the good falls, income decreases (for a normal good), expected future income or credit decreases, or the population decreases. (For an inferior good, the effects of changes in income are in the opposite direction to those described above.)

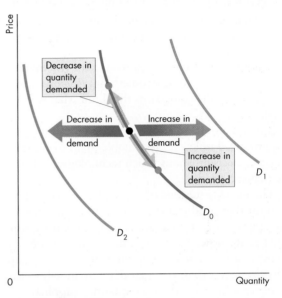

FIGURE 3.3   A Change in the Quantity Demanded Versus a Change in Demand

When the price of the good changes, there is a movement along the demand curve and a *change in the quantity demanded*, shown by the blue arrows on demand curve D_0. When any other influence on buying plans changes, there is a shift of the demand curve and a *change in demand*. An increase in demand shifts the demand curve rightward (from D_0 to D_1). A decrease in demand shifts the demand curve leftward (from D_0 to D_2).

 myeconlab animation

REVIEW QUIZ

1 Define the quantity demanded of a good or service.
2 What is the law of demand and how do we illustrate it?
3 What does the demand curve tell us about the price that consumers are willing to pay?
4 List all the influences on buying plans that change demand, and for each influence, say whether it increases or decreases demand.
5 Why does demand not change when the price of a good changes with no change in the other influences on buying plans?

You can work these questions in Study Plan 3.2 and get instant feedback.   myeconlab

◆ Supply

If a firm supplies a good or service, the firm

1. Has the resources and technology to produce it,
2. Can profit from producing it, and
3. Plans to produce it and sell it.

A supply is more than just having the *resources* and the *technology* to produce something. *Resources and technology* are the constraints that limit what is possible.

Many useful things can be produced, but they are not produced unless it is profitable to do so. Supply reflects a decision about which technologically feasible items to produce.

The **quantity supplied** of a good or service is the amount that producers plan to sell during a given time period at a particular price. The quantity supplied is not necessarily the same amount as the quantity actually sold. Sometimes the quantity supplied is greater than the quantity demanded, so the quantity sold is less than the quantity supplied.

Like the quantity demanded, the quantity supplied is measured as an amount per unit of time. For example, suppose that GM produces 1,000 cars a day. The quantity of cars supplied by GM can be expressed as 1,000 a day, 7,000 a week, or 365,000 a year. Without the time dimension, we cannot tell whether a particular quantity is large or small.

Many factors influence selling plans, and again one of them is the price of the good. We look first at the relationship between the quantity supplied of a good and its price. Just as we did when we studied demand, to isolate the relationship between the quantity supplied of a good and its price, we keep all other influences on selling plans the same and ask: How does the quantity supplied of a good change as its price changes when other things remain the same?

The law of supply provides the answer.

The Law of Supply

The **law of supply** states:

> Other things remaining the same, the higher the price of a good, the greater is the quantity supplied; and the lower the price of a good, the smaller is the quantity supplied.

Why does a higher price increase the quantity supplied? It is because *marginal cost increases.* As the quantity produced of any good increases, the marginal cost of producing the good increases. (See Chapter 2, p. 33 to review marginal cost.)

It is never worth producing a good if the price received for the good does not at least cover the marginal cost of producing it. When the price of a good rises, other things remaining the same, producers are willing to incur a higher marginal cost, so they increase production. The higher price brings forth an increase in the quantity supplied.

Let's now illustrate the law of supply with a supply curve and a supply schedule.

Supply Curve and Supply Schedule

You are now going to study the second of the two most used curves in economics: the supply curve. You're also going to learn about the critical distinction between *supply* and *quantity supplied*.

The term **supply** refers to the entire relationship between the price of a good and the quantity supplied of it. Supply is illustrated by the supply curve and the supply schedule. The term *quantity supplied* refers to a point on a supply curve—the quantity supplied at a particular price.

Figure 3.4 shows the supply curve of energy bars. A **supply curve** shows the relationship between the quantity supplied of a good and its price when all other influences on producers' planned sales remain the same. The supply curve is a graph of a supply schedule.

The table in Fig. 3.4 sets out the supply schedule for energy bars. A *supply schedule* lists the quantities supplied at each price when all the other influences on producers' planned sales remain the same. For example, if the price of an energy bar is 50¢, the quantity supplied is zero—in row *A* of the table. If the price of an energy bar is $1.00, the quantity supplied is 6 million energy bars a week—in row *B*. The other rows of the table show the quantities supplied at prices of $1.50, $2.00, and $2.50.

To make a supply curve, we graph the quantity supplied on the *x*-axis and the price on the *y*-axis. The points on the supply curve labeled *A* through *E* correspond to the rows of the supply schedule. For example, point *A* on the graph shows a quantity supplied of zero at a price of 50¢ an energy bar. Point *E* shows a quantity supplied of 15 million bars at $2.50 an energy bar.

FIGURE 3.4   The Supply Curve

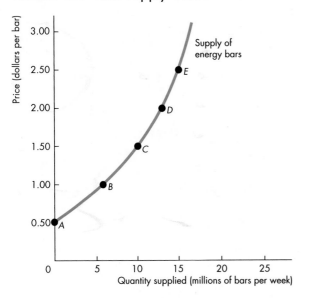

The table shows the supply schedule of energy bars. For example, at a price of $1.00, 6 million bars a week are supplied; at a price of $2.50, 15 million bars a week are supplied. The supply curve shows the relationship between the quantity supplied and the price, other things remaining the same. The supply curve slopes upward: As the price of a good increases, the quantity supplied increases.

A supply curve can be read in two ways. For a given price, the supply curve tells us the quantity that producers plan to sell at that price. For example, at a price of $1.50 a bar, producers are planning to sell 10 million bars a week. For a given quantity, the supply curve tells us the minimum price at which producers are willing to sell one more bar. For example, if 15 million bars are produced each week, the lowest price at which a producer is willing to sell the 15 millionth bar is $2.50.

Minimum Supply Price   The supply curve can be interpreted as a minimum-supply-price curve—a curve that shows the lowest price at which someone is willing to sell. This lowest price is the *marginal cost*.

If a small quantity is produced, the lowest price at which someone is willing to sell one more unit is low. But as the quantity produced increases, the marginal cost of each additional unit rises, so the lowest price at which someone is willing to sell an additional unit rises along the supply curve.

In Fig. 3.4, if 15 million bars are produced each week, the lowest price at which someone is willing to sell the 15 millionth bar is $2.50. But if 10 million bars are produced each week, someone is willing to accept $1.50 for the last bar produced.

A Change in Supply

When any factor that influences selling plans other than the price of the good changes, there is a **change in supply**. Six main factors bring changes in supply. They are changes in

- The prices of factors of production
- The prices of related goods produced
- Expected future prices
- The number of suppliers
- Technology
- The state of nature

Prices of Factors of Production   The prices of the factors of production used to produce a good influence its supply. To see this influence, think about the supply curve as a minimum-supply-price curve. If the price of a factor of production rises, the lowest price that a producer is willing to accept for that good rises, so supply decreases. For example, during 2008, as the price of jet fuel increased, the supply of air travel decreased. Similarly, a rise in the minimum wage decreases the supply of hamburgers.

Prices of Related Goods Produced   The prices of related goods that firms produce influence supply. For example, if the price of energy gel rises, firms switch production from bars to gel. The supply of energy bars decreases. Energy bars and energy gel are *substitutes in production*—goods that can be produced by using the same resources. If the price of beef rises, the supply of cowhide increases. Beef and cowhide are *complements in production*—goods that must be produced together.

Expected Future Prices If the expected future price of a good rises, the return from selling the good in the future increases and is higher than it is today. So supply decreases today and increases in the future.

The Number of Suppliers The larger the number of firms that produce a good, the greater is the supply of the good. As new firms enter an industry, the supply in that industry increases. As firms leave an industry, the supply in that industry decreases.

Technology The term "technology" is used broadly to mean the way that factors of production are used to produce a good. A technology change occurs when a new method is discovered that lowers the cost of producing a good. For example, new methods used in the factories that produce computer chips have lowered the cost and increased the supply of chips.

The State of Nature The state of nature includes all the natural forces that influence production. It includes the state of the weather and, more broadly, the natural environment. Good weather can increase the supply of many agricultural products and bad weather can decrease their supply. Extreme natural events such as earthquakes, tornadoes, and hurricanes can also influence supply.

Figure 3.5 illustrates an increase in supply. When supply increases, the supply curve shifts rightward and the quantity supplied at each price is larger. For example, at $1.00 per bar, on the original (blue) supply curve, the quantity supplied is 6 million bars a week. On the new (red) supply curve, the quantity supplied is 15 million bars a week. Look closely at the numbers in the table in Fig. 3.5 and check that the quantity supplied is larger at each price.

Table 3.2 summarizes the influences on supply and the directions of those influences.

A Change in the Quantity Supplied Versus a Change in Supply

Changes in the influences on selling plans bring either a change in the quantity supplied or a change in supply. Equivalently, they bring either a movement along the supply curve or a shift of the supply curve.

A point on the supply curve shows the quantity supplied at a given price. A movement along the supply curve shows a **change in the quantity supplied.** The entire supply curve shows supply. A shift of the supply curve shows a *change in supply.*

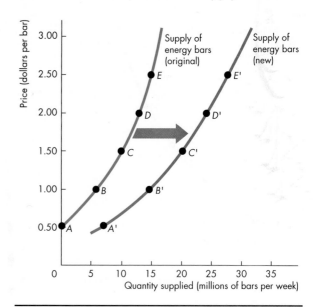

FIGURE 3.5   An Increase in Supply

Original supply schedule Old technology			New supply schedule New technology		
	Price (dollars per bar)	Quantity supplied (millions of bars per week)		Price (dollars per bar)	Quantity supplied (millions of bars per week)
A	0.50	0	A'	0.50	7
B	1.00	6	B'	1.00	15
C	1.50	10	C'	1.50	20
D	2.00	13	D'	2.00	25
E	2.50	15	E'	2.50	27

A change in any influence on selling plans other than the price of the good itself results in a new supply schedule and a shift of the supply curve. For example, a new, cost-saving technology for producing energy bars changes the supply of energy bars. At a price of $1.50 a bar, 10 million bars a week are supplied when producers use the old technology (row C of the table) and 20 million energy bars a week are supplied when producers use the new technology (row C'). An advance in technology *increases* the supply of energy bars. The supply curve shifts *rightward,* as shown by the shift arrow and the resulting red curve.

Figure 3.6 illustrates and summarizes these distinctions. If the price of the good changes and other things remain the same, there is a *change in the quantity supplied* of that good. If the price of the good falls, the quantity supplied decreases and there is a movement down along the supply curve S_0. If the price of the good rises, the quantity supplied increases and there is a movement up along the supply curve S_0. When any other influence on selling plans changes, the supply curve shifts and there is a *change in supply*. If supply increases, the supply curve shifts rightward to S_1. If supply decreases, the supply curve shifts leftward to S_2.

TABLE 3.2   The Supply of Energy Bars

The Law of Supply

The quantity of energy bars supplied

Decreases if:	*Increases if:*
■ The price of an energy bar falls	■ The price of an energy bar rises

Changes in Supply

The supply of energy bars

Decreases if:	*Increases if:*
■ The price of a factor of production used to produce energy bars rises	■ The price of a factor of production used to produce energy bars falls
■ The price of a substitute in production rises	■ The price of a substitute in production falls
■ The price of a complement in production falls	■ The price of a complement in production rises
■ The expected future price of an energy bar rises	■ The expected future price of an energy bar falls
■ The number of suppliers of bars decreases	■ The number of suppliers of bars increases
■ A technology change decreases energy bar production	■ A technology change increases energy bar production
■ A natural event decreases energy bar production	■ A natural event increases energy bar production

FIGURE 3.6   A Change in the Quantity Supplied Versus a Change in Supply

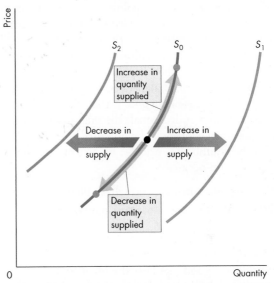

When the price of the good changes, there is a movement along the supply curve and *a change in the quantity supplied,* shown by the blue arrows on supply curve S_0. When any other influence on selling plans changes, there is a shift of the supply curve and a *change in supply*. An increase in supply shifts the supply curve rightward (from S_0 to S_1), and a decrease in supply shifts the supply curve leftward (from S_0 to S_2).

REVIEW QUIZ

1 Define the quantity supplied of a good or service.
2 What is the law of supply and how do we illustrate it?
3 What does the supply curve tell us about the producer's minimum supply price?
4 List all the influences on selling plans, and for each influence, say whether it changes supply.
5 What happens to the quantity of cell phones supplied and the supply of cell phones if the price of a cell phone falls?

You can work these questions in Study Plan 3.3 and get instant feedback.

Now we're going to combine demand and supply and see how prices and quantities are determined.

Market Equilibrium

We have seen that when the price of a good rises, the quantity demanded *decreases* and the quantity supplied *increases*. We are now going to see how the price adjusts to coordinate buying plans and selling plans and achieve an equilibrium in the market.

An *equilibrium* is a situation in which opposing forces balance each other. Equilibrium in a market occurs when the price balances buying plans and selling plans. The **equilibrium price** is the price at which the quantity demanded equals the quantity supplied. The **equilibrium quantity** is the quantity bought and sold at the equilibrium price. A market moves toward its equilibrium because

- Price regulates buying and selling plans.
- Price adjusts when plans don't match.

Price as a Regulator

The price of a good regulates the quantities demanded and supplied. If the price is too high, the quantity supplied exceeds the quantity demanded. If the price is too low, the quantity demanded exceeds the quantity supplied. There is one price at which the quantity demanded equals the quantity supplied. Let's work out what that price is.

Figure 3.7 shows the market for energy bars. The table shows the demand schedule (from Fig. 3.1) and the supply schedule (from Fig. 3.4). If the price is 50¢ a bar, the quantity demanded is 22 million bars a week but no bars are supplied. There is a shortage of 22 million bars a week. The final column of the table shows this shortage. At a price of $1.00 a bar, there is still a shortage but only of 9 million bars a week.

If the price is $2.50 a bar, the quantity supplied is 15 million bars a week but the quantity demanded is only 5 million. There is a surplus of 10 million bars a week.

The one price at which there is neither a shortage nor a surplus is $1.50 a bar. At that price, the quantity demanded equals the quantity supplied: 10 million bars a week. The equilibrium price is $1.50 a bar, and the equilibrium quantity is 10 million bars a week.

Figure 3.7 shows that the demand curve and the supply curve intersect at the equilibrium price of $1.50 a bar. At each price *above* $1.50 a bar, there is a surplus of bars. For example, at $2.00 a bar, the surplus is 6

FIGURE 3.7   Equilibrium

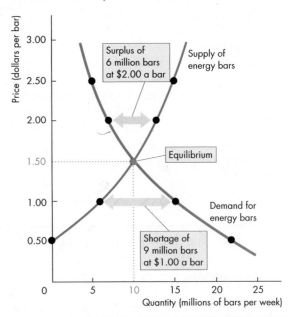

The table lists the quantity demanded and the quantity supplied as well as the shortage or surplus of bars at each price. If the price is $1.00 a bar, 15 million bars a week are demanded and 6 million bars are supplied. There is a shortage of 9 million bars a week, and the price rises.

If the price is $2.00 a bar, 7 million bars a week are demanded and 13 million bars are supplied. There is a surplus of 6 million bars a week, and the price falls.

If the price is $1.50 a bar, 10 million bars a week are demanded and 10 million bars are supplied. There is neither a shortage nor a surplus, and the price does not change. The price at which the quantity demanded equals the quantity supplied is the equilibrium price, and 10 million bars a week is the equilibrium quantity.

Price (dollars per bar)	Quantity demanded	Quantity supplied	Shortage (–) or surplus (+)
	(millions of bars per week)		
0.50	22	0	–22
1.00	15	6	–9
1.50	10	10	0
2.00	7	13	+6
2.50	5	15	+10

myeconlab   animation

million bars a week, as shown by the blue arrow. At each price *below* $1.50 a bar, there is a shortage of bars. For example, at $1.00 a bar, the shortage is 9 million bars a week, as shown by the red arrow.

Price Adjustments

You've seen that if the price is below equilibrium, there is a shortage and that if the price is above equilibrium, there is a surplus. But can we count on the price to change and eliminate a shortage or a surplus? We can, because such price changes are beneficial to both buyers and sellers. Let's see why the price changes when there is a shortage or a surplus.

A Shortage Forces the Price Up Suppose the price of an energy bar is $1. Consumers plan to buy 15 million bars a week, and producers plan to sell 6 million bars a week. Consumers can't force producers to sell more than they plan, so the quantity that is actually offered for sale is 6 million bars a week. In this situation, powerful forces operate to increase the price and move it toward the equilibrium price. Some producers, noticing lines of unsatisfied consumers, raise the price. Some producers increase their output. As producers push the price up, the price rises toward its equilibrium. The rising price reduces the shortage because it decreases the quantity demanded and increases the quantity supplied. When the price has increased to the point at which there is no longer a shortage, the forces moving the price stop operating and the price comes to rest at its equilibrium.

A Surplus Forces the Price Down Suppose the price of a bar is $2. Producers plan to sell 13 million bars a week, and consumers plan to buy 7 million bars a week. Producers cannot force consumers to buy more than they plan, so the quantity that is actually bought is 7 million bars a week. In this situation, powerful forces operate to lower the price and move it toward the equilibrium price. Some producers, unable to sell the quantities of energy bars they planned to sell, cut their prices. In addition, some producers scale back production. As producers cut the price, the price falls toward its equilibrium. The falling price decreases the surplus because it increases the quantity demanded and decreases the quantity supplied. When the price has fallen to the point at which there is no longer a surplus, the forces moving the price stop operating and the price comes to rest at its equilibrium.

The Best Deal Available for Buyers and Sellers

When the price is below equilibrium, it is forced upward. Why don't buyers resist the increase and refuse to buy at the higher price? The answer is because they value the good more highly than its current price and they can't satisfy their demand at the current price. In some markets—for example, the markets that operate on eBay—the buyers might even be the ones who force the price up by offering to pay a higher price.

When the price is above equilibrium, it is bid downward. Why don't sellers resist this decrease and refuse to sell at the lower price? The answer is because their minimum supply price is below the current price and they cannot sell all they would like to at the current price. Sellers willingly lower the price to gain market share.

At the price at which the quantity demanded and the quantity supplied are equal, neither buyers nor sellers can do business at a better price. Buyers pay the highest price they are willing to pay for the last unit bought, and sellers receive the lowest price at which they are willing to supply the last unit sold.

When people freely make offers to buy and sell and when demanders try to buy at the lowest possible price and suppliers try to sell at the highest possible price, the price at which trade takes place is the equilibrium price—the price at which the quantity demanded equals the quantity supplied. The price coordinates the plans of buyers and sellers, and no one has an incentive to change it.

REVIEW QUIZ

1   What is the equilibrium price of a good or service?
2   Over what range of prices does a shortage arise? What happens to the price when there is a shortage?
3   Over what range of prices does a surplus arise? What happens to the price when there is a surplus?
4   Why is the price at which the quantity demanded equals the quantity supplied the equilibrium price?
5   Why is the equilibrium price the best deal available for both buyers and sellers?

You can work these questions in Study Plan 3.4 and get instant feedback.

Predicting Changes in Price and Quantity

The demand and supply model that we have just studied provides us with a powerful way of analyzing influences on prices and the quantities bought and sold. According to the model, a change in price stems from a change in demand, a change in supply, or a change in both demand and supply. Let's look first at the effects of a change in demand.

An Increase in Demand

If more people join health clubs, the demand for energy bars increases. The table in Fig. 3.8 shows the original and new demand schedules for energy bars as well as the supply schedule of energy bars.

The increase in demand creates a shortage at the original price and to eliminate the shortage, the price must rise.

Figure 3.8 shows what happens. The figure shows the original demand for and supply of energy bars. The original equilibrium price is $1.50 an energy bar, and the equilibrium quantity is 10 million energy bars a week. When demand increases, the demand curve shifts rightward. The equilibrium price rises to $2.50 an energy bar, and the quantity supplied increases to 15 million energy bars a week, as highlighted in the figure. There is an *increase in the quantity supplied* but *no change in supply*—a movement along, but no shift of, the supply curve.

A Decrease in Demand

We can reverse this change in demand. Start at a price of $2.50 a bar with 15 million energy bars a week being bought and sold, and then work out what happens if demand decreases to its original level. Such a decrease in demand might arise if people switch to energy gel (a substitute for energy bars). The decrease in demand shifts the demand curve leftward. The equilibrium price falls to $1.50 a bar, the quantity supplied decreases, and the equilibrium quantity decreases to 10 million bars a week.

We can now make our first two predictions:

1. When demand increases, the price rises and the quantity increases.

2. When demand decreases, the price falls and the quantity decreases.

FIGURE 3.8 The Effects of a Change in Demand

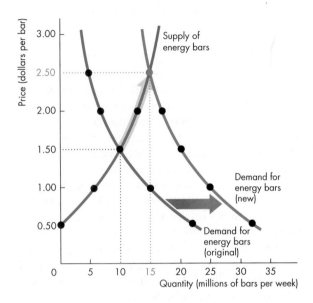

Price (dollars per bar)	Quantity demanded (millions of bars per week)		Quantity supplied (millions of bars per week)
	Original	New	
0.50	22	32	0
1.00	15	25	6
1.50	**10**	20	**10**
2.00	7	17	13
2.50	5	15	15

Initially, the demand for energy bars is the blue demand curve. The equilibrium price is $1.50 a bar, and the equilibrium quantity is 10 million bars a week. When more health-conscious people do more exercise, the demand for energy bars increases and the demand curve shifts rightward to become the red curve.

At $1.50 a bar, there is now a shortage of 10 million bars a week. The price of a bar rises to a new equilibrium of $2.50. As the price rises to $2.50, the quantity supplied increases—shown by the blue arrow on the supply curve—to the new equilibrium quantity of 15 million bars a week. Following an increase in demand, the quantity supplied increases but supply does not change—the supply curve does not shift.

myeconlab animation

Economics in Action
The Global Market for Crude Oil

The demand and supply model provides insights into all competitive markets. Here, we'll apply what you've learned about the effects of an increase in demand to the global market for crude oil.

Crude oil is like the life-blood of the global economy. It is used to fuel our cars, airplanes, trains, and buses, to generate electricity, and to produce a wide range of plastics. When the price of crude oil rises, the cost of transportation, power, and materials all increase.

In 2001, the price of a barrel of oil was $20 (using the value of money in 2010). In 2008, before the global financial crisis ended a long period of economic expansion, the price peaked at $127 a barrel.

While the price of oil was rising, the quantity of oil produced and consumed also increased. In 2001, the world produced 65 million barrels of oil a day. By 2008, that quantity was 72 million barrels.

Who or what has been raising the price of oil? Is it the action of greedy oil producers? Oil producers might be greedy, and some of them might be big enough to withhold supply and raise the price, but it wouldn't be in their self-interest to do so. The higher price would bring forth a greater quantity supplied from other producers and the profit of the producer limiting supply would fall.

Oil producers could try to cooperate and jointly withhold supply. The Organization of Petroleum Exporting Countries, OPEC, is such a group of producers. But OPEC doesn't control the *world* supply and its members' self-interest is to produce the quantities that give them the maximum attainable profit.

So even though the global oil market has some big players, they don't fix the price. Instead, the actions of thousands of buyers and sellers and the forces of demand and supply determine the price of oil.

So how have demand and supply changed?

Because both the price and the quantity have increased, the demand for oil must have increased. Supply might have changed too, but here we'll suppose that supply has remained the same.

The global demand for oil has increased for one major reason: World income has increased. The increase has been particularly large in the emerging economies of Brazil, China, and India. Increased world income has increased the demand for oil-using goods such as electricity, gasoline, and plastics, which in turn has increased the demand for oil.

The figure illustrates the effects of the increase in demand on the global oil market. The supply of oil remained constant along supply curve S. The demand for oil in 2001 was D_{2001}, so in 2001 the price was $20 a barrel and the quantity was 65 million barrels per day. The demand for oil increased and by 2008 it had reached D_{2008}. The price of oil increased to $127 a barrel and the quantity increased to 72 million barrels a day. The increase in the quantity is an *increase in the quantity supplied*, not an increase in supply.

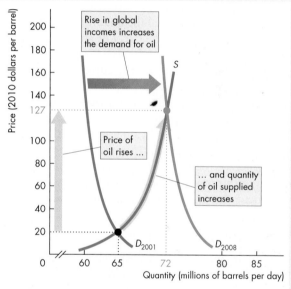

The Global Market for Crude Oil

An Increase in Supply

When Nestlé (the producer of PowerBar) and other energy bar producers switch to a new cost-saving technology, the supply of energy bars increases. Figure 3.9 shows the new supply schedule (the same one that was shown in Fig. 3.5). What are the new equilibrium price and quantity? The price falls to $1.00 a bar, and the quantity increases to 15 million bars a week. You can see why by looking at the quantities demanded and supplied at the old price of $1.50 a bar. The new quantity supplied at that price is 20 million bars a week, and there is a surplus. The price falls. Only when the price is $1.00 a bar does the quantity supplied equal the quantity demanded.

Figure 3.9 illustrates the effect of an increase in supply. It shows the demand curve for energy bars and the original and new supply curves. The initial equilibrium price is $1.50 a bar, and the equilibrium quantity is 10 million bars a week. When supply increases, the supply curve shifts rightward. The equilibrium price falls to $1.00 a bar, and the quantity demanded increases to 15 million bars a week, highlighted in the figure. There is an *increase in the quantity demanded* but *no change in demand*—a movement along, but no shift of, the demand curve.

A Decrease in Supply

Start out at a price of $1.00 a bar with 15 million bars a week being bought and sold. Then suppose that the cost of labor or raw materials rises and the supply of energy bars decreases. The decrease in supply shifts the supply curve leftward. The equilibrium price rises to $1.50 a bar, the quantity demanded decreases, and the equilibrium quantity decreases to 10 million bars a week.

We can now make two more predictions:

1. When supply increases, the price falls and the quantity increases.

2. When supply decreases, the price rises and the quantity decreases.

You've now seen what happens to the price and the quantity when either demand or supply changes while the other one remains unchanged. In real markets, both demand and supply can change together. When this happens, to predict the changes in price and quantity, we must combine the effects that you've just seen. That is your final task in this chapter.

FIGURE 3.9   The Effects of a Change in Supply

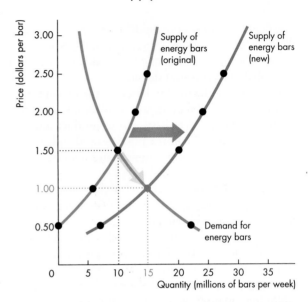

Price (dollars per bar)	Quantity demanded (millions of bars per week)	Quantity supplied (millions of bars per week)	
		Original	New
0.50	22	0	7
1.00	15	6	15
1.50	**10**	**10**	20
2.00	7	13	25
2.50	5	15	27

Initially, the supply of energy bars is shown by the blue supply curve. The equilibrium price is $1.50 a bar, and the equilibrium quantity is 10 million bars a week. When the new cost-saving technology is adopted, the supply of energy bars increases and the supply curve shifts rightward to become the red curve.

At $1.50 a bar, there is now a surplus of 10 million bars a week. The price of an energy bar falls to a new equilibrium of $1.00 a bar. As the price falls to $1.00, the quantity demanded increases—shown by the blue arrow on the demand curve—to the new equilibrium quantity of 15 million bars a week. Following an increase in supply, the quantity demanded increases but demand does not change—the demand curve does not shift.

myeconlab animation

Economics in Action

The Market for Strawberries

California produces 85 percent of the nation's strawberries and its crop, which starts to increase in March, is in top flight by April. During the winter months of January and February, Florida is the main strawberry producer.

In a normal year, the supplies from these two regions don't overlap much. As California's production steps up in March and April, Florida's production falls off. The result is a steady supply of strawberries and not much seasonal fluctuation in the price of strawberries.

But 2010 wasn't a normal year. Florida had exceptionally cold weather, which damaged the strawberry fields, lowered crop yields, and delayed the harvests. The result was unusually high strawberry prices.

With higher than normal prices, Florida farmers planted strawberry varieties that mature later than their normal crop and planned to harvest this fruit during the spring. Their plan worked perfectly and good growing conditions delivered a bumper crop by late March.

On the other side of the nation, while Florida was freezing, Southern California was drowning under unusually heavy rains. This wet weather put the strawberries to sleep and delayed their growth. But when the rains stopped and the temperature began to rise, California joined Florida with a super abundance of fruit.

With an abundance of strawberries, the price tumbled. Strawberry farmers in both regions couldn't hire enough labor to pick the super-sized crop, so some fruit was left in the fields to rot.

The figure explains what was happening in the market for strawberries.

Demand, shown by the demand curve, *D*, didn't change. In January, the failed Florida crop kept supply low and the supply curve was $S_{January}$. The price was high at $3.80 per pound and production was 5.0 million pounds per day.

In April, the bumper crops in both regions increased supply to S_{April}. This increase in supply lowered the price to $1.20 per pound and increased the quantity demanded—a movement along the demand curve—to 5.5 million pounds per day.

You can also see in the figure why farmers left fruit in the field to rot. At the January price of $3.80 a pound, farmers would have been paying top wages to

hire the workers needed to pick fruit at the rate of 6.0 million pounds per day. This is the quantity on supply curve S_{April} at $3.80 a pound.

But with the fall in price to $1.20 a pound, growers were not able to earn a profit by picking more than 5.5 million pounds.

For some growers the price wasn't high enough to cover the cost of hiring labor, so they opened their fields to anyone who wanted to pick their own strawberries for free.

The events we've described here in the market for strawberries illustrate the effects of a change in supply with no change in demand.

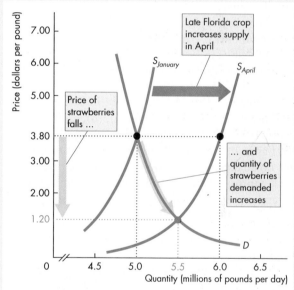

The Market for Strawberries

All the Possible Changes in Demand and Supply

Figure 3.10 brings together and summarizes the effects of all the possible changes in demand and supply. With what you've learned about the effects of a change in *either* demand or supply, you can predict what happens if *both* demand and supply change together. Let's begin by reviewing what you already know.

Change in Demand with No Change in Supply The first row of Fig. 3.10, parts (a), (b), and (c), summarizes the effects of a change in demand with no change in supply. In part (a), with no change in either demand or supply, neither the price nor the quantity changes. With an *increase* in demand and no change in supply in part (b), both the price and quantity increase. And with a *decrease* in demand and no change in supply in part (c), both the price and the quantity decrease.

Change in Supply with No Change in Demand The first column of Fig. 3.10, parts (a), (d), and (g), summarizes the effects of a change in supply with no change in demand. With an *increase* in supply and no change in demand in part (d), the price falls and quantity increases. And with a *decrease* in supply and no change in demand in part (g), the price rises and the quantity decreases.

Increase in Both Demand and Supply You've seen that an increase in demand raises the price and increases the quantity. And you've seen that an increase in supply lowers the price and increases the quantity. Fig. 3.10(e) combines these two changes. Because either an increase in demand or an increase in supply increases the quantity, the quantity also increases when both demand and supply increase. But the effect on the price is uncertain. An increase in demand raises the price and an increase in supply lowers the price, so we can't say whether the price will rise or fall when both demand and supply increase. We need to know the magnitudes of the changes in demand and supply to predict the effects on price. In the example in Fig. 3.10(e), the price does not change. But notice that if demand increases by slightly more than the amount shown in the figure, the price will rise. And if supply increases by slightly more than the amount shown in the figure, the price will fall.

Decrease in Both Demand and Supply Figure 3.10(i) shows the case in which demand and supply *both decrease*. For the same reasons as those we've just reviewed, when both demand and supply decrease, the quantity decreases, and again the direction of the price change is uncertain.

Decrease in Demand and Increase in Supply You've seen that a decrease in demand lowers the price and decreases the quantity. And you've seen that an increase in supply lowers the price and increases the quantity. Fig. 3.10(f) combines these two changes. Both the decrease in demand and the increase in supply lower the price, so the price falls. But a decrease in demand decreases the quantity and an increase in supply increases the quantity, so we can't predict the direction in which the quantity will change unless we know the magnitudes of the changes in demand and supply. In the example in Fig. 3.10(f), the quantity does not change. But notice that if demand decreases by slightly more than the amount shown in the figure, the quantity will decrease; if supply increases by slightly more than the amount shown in the figure, the quantity will increase.

Increase in Demand and Decrease in Supply Figure 3.10(h) shows the case in which demand increases and supply decreases. Now, the price rises, and again the direction of the quantity change is uncertain.

REVIEW QUIZ

What is the effect on the price and quantity of MP3 players (such as the iPod) if

1 The price of a PC falls or the price of an MP3 download rises? (Draw the diagrams!)
2 More firms produce MP3 players or electronics workers' wages rise? (Draw the diagrams!)
3 Any two of the events in questions 1 and 2 occur together? (Draw the diagrams!)

You can work these questions in Study Plan 3.5 and get instant feedback.

◆ To complete your study of demand and supply, take a look at *Reading Between the Lines* on pp. 74–75, which explains why the price of coffee increased in 2010. Try to get into the habit of using the demand and supply model to understand the movements in prices in your everyday life.

FIGURE 3.10   The Effects of All the Possible Changes in Demand and Supply

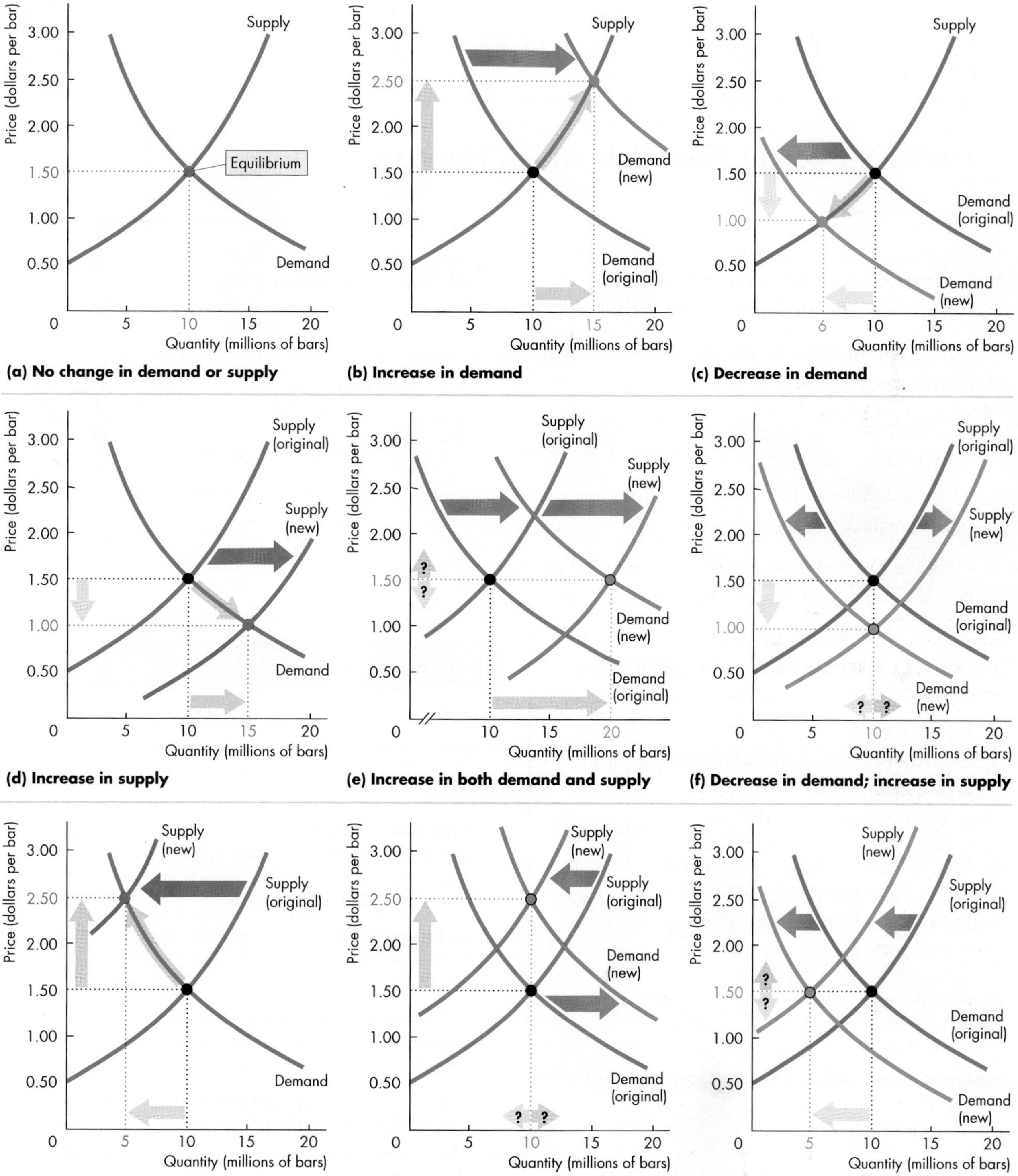

(a) No change in demand or supply

(b) Increase in demand

(c) Decrease in demand

(d) Increase in supply

(e) Increase in both demand and supply

(f) Decrease in demand; increase in supply

(g) Decrease in supply

(h) Increase in demand; decrease in supply

(i) Decrease in both demand and supply

myeconlab animation

nd and Supply:
ice of Coffee

Coffee Surges on Poor Colombian Harvests

FT.com
July 30, 2010

Coffee prices hit a 12-year high on Friday on the back of low supplies of premium Arabica coffee from Colombia after a string of poor crops in the Latin American country.

The strong fundamental picture has also encouraged hedge funds to reverse their previous bearish views on coffee prices.

In New York, ICE September Arabica coffee jumped 3.2 percent to 178.75 cents per pound, the highest since February 1998. It traded later at 177.25 cents, up 6.8 percent on the week.

The London-based International Coffee Organization on Friday warned that the "current tight demand and supply situation" was "likely to persist in the near to medium term."

Coffee industry executives believe prices could rise toward 200 cents per pound in New York before the arrival of the new Brazilian crop later this year.

"Until October it is going to be tight on high quality coffee," said a senior executive at one of Europe's largest coffee roasters. He said: "The industry has been surprised by the scarcity of high quality beans."

Colombia coffee production, key for supplies of premium beans, last year plunged to a 33-year low of 7.8m bags, each of 60kg, down nearly a third from 11.1m bags in 2008, tightening supplies worldwide. ...

Excerpted from "Coffee Surges on Poor Colombian Harvests" by Javier Blas. *Financial Times*, July 30, 2010. Reprinted with permission.

ESSENCE OF THE STORY

- The price of premium Arabica coffee increased by 3.2 percent to almost 180 cents per pound in July 2010, the highest price since February 1998.

- A sequence of poor crops in Columbia cut the production of premium Arabica coffee to a 33-year low of 7.8 million 60 kilogram bags, down from 11.1 million bags in 2008.

- The International Coffee Organization said that the "current tight demand and supply situation" was "likely to persist in the near to medium term."

- Coffee industry executives say prices might approach 200 cents per pound before the arrival of the new Brazilian crop later this year.

- Hedge funds previously expected the price of coffee to fall but now expect it to rise further.

ECONOMIC ANALYSIS

- This news article reports two sources of changes in supply and demand that changed the price of coffee.

- The first source of change is the sequence of poor harvests in Columbia. These events decreased the world supply of Arabica coffee. (Arabica is the type that Starbucks uses.)

- Before the reported events, the world production of Arabica was 120 million bags per year and its price was 174 cents per pound.

- The decrease in the Columbian harvest decreased world production to about 116 million bags, which is about 3 percent of world production.

- Figure 1 shows the situation before the poor Columbia harvests and the effects of those poor harvests. The demand curve is D and initially, the supply curve was S^0. The market equilibrium is at 120 million bags per year and a price of 174 cents per pound.

- The poor Columbian harvests decreased supply and the supply curve shifted leftward to S^1. The price increased to 180 cents per pound and the quantity decreased to 116 million bags.

- The second source of change influenced both supply and demand. It is a change in the expected future price of coffee.

- The hedge funds referred to in the news article are speculators that try to profit from buying at a low price and selling at a high price.

- With the supply of coffee expected to remain low, the price was expected to rise further—a rise in the expected future price of coffee.

- When the expected future price of coffee rises, some people want to buy more coffee (so they can sell it later)—an increase in the demand today. And some people offer less coffee for sale (so they can sell it later for a higher price)—a decrease in the supply today.

- Figure 2 shows the effects of these changes in the demand and supply today.

- Demand increased and the demand curve shifted from D^0 to D^1. Supply decreased and the supply curve shifted from S^1 to S^2.

- Because demand increases and supply decreases, the price rises. In this example, it rises to 200 cents per pound.

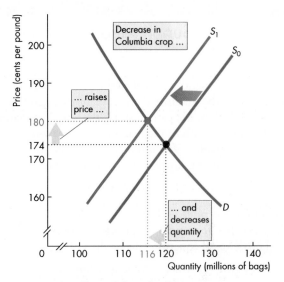

Figure 1 The effects of the Columbian crop

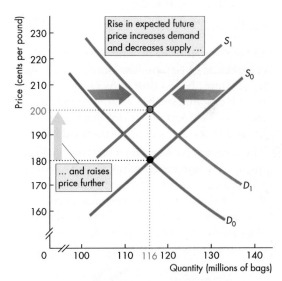

Figure 2 The effects of the expected future price

- Also, because demand increases and supply decreases, the change in the equilibrium quantity can go in either direction.

- In this example, the increase in demand equals the decrease in supply, so the equilibrium quantity remains constant at 116 million bags per year.

75

Demand Curve

The law of demand says that as the price of a good or service falls, the quantity demanded of that good or service increases. We can illustrate the law of demand by drawing a graph of the demand curve or writing down an equation. When the demand curve is a straight line, the following equation describes it:

$$P = a - bQ_D,$$

where P is the price and Q_D is the quantity demanded. The a and b are positive constants.

The demand equation tells us three things:

1. The price at which no one is willing to buy the good (Q_D is zero). That is, if the price is a, then the quantity demanded is zero. You can see the price a in Fig. 1. It is the price at which the demand curve hits the y-axis—what we call the demand curve's "y-intercept."

2. As the price falls, the quantity demanded increases. If Q_D is a positive number, then the price P must be less than a. As Q_D gets larger, the price P becomes smaller. That is, as the quantity increases, the maximum price that buyers are willing to pay for the last unit of the good falls.

3. The constant b tells us how fast the maximum price that someone is willing to pay for the good falls as the quantity increases. That is, the constant b tells us about the steepness of the demand curve. The equation tells us that the slope of the demand curve is $-b$.

Supply Curve

The law of supply says that as the price of a good or service rises, the quantity supplied of that good or service increases. We can illustrate the law of supply by drawing a graph of the supply curve or writing down an equation. When the supply curve is a straight line, the following equation describes it:

$$P = c + dQ_S,$$

where P is the price and Q_S is the quantity supplied. The c and d are positive constants.

The supply equation tells us three things:

1. The price at which sellers are not willing to supply the good (Q_S is zero). That is, if the price is c, then no one is willing to sell the good. You can see the price c in Fig. 2. It is the price at which the supply curve hits the y-axis—what we call the supply curve's "y-intercept."

2. As the price rises, the quantity supplied increases. If Q_S is a positive number, then the price P must be greater than c. As Q_S increases, the price P becomes larger. That is, as the quantity increases, the minimum price that sellers are willing to accept for the last unit rises.

3. The constant d tells us how fast the minimum price at which someone is willing to sell the good rises as the quantity increases. That is, the constant d tells us about the steepness of the supply curve. The equation tells us that the slope of the supply curve is d.

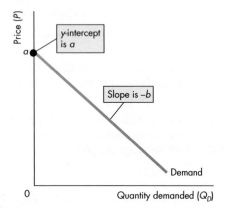

Figure 1 Demand curve

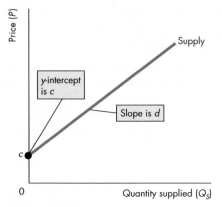

Figure 2 Supply curve

Market Equilibrium

Demand and supply determine market equilibrium. Figure 3 shows the equilibrium price (P^*) and equilibrium quantity (Q^*) at the intersection of the demand curve and the supply curve.

We can use the equations to find the equilibrium price and equilibrium quantity. The price of a good adjusts until the quantity demanded Q_D equals the quantity supplied Q_S. So at the equilibrium price (P^*) and equilibrium quantity (Q^*),

$$Q_D = Q_S = Q^*.$$

To find the equilibrium price and equilibrium quantity, substitute Q^* for Q_D in the demand equation and Q^* for Q_S in the supply equation. Then the price is the equilibrium price (P^*), which gives

$$P^* = a - bQ^*$$
$$P^* = c + dQ^*.$$

Notice that

$$a - bQ^* = c + dQ^*.$$

Now solve for Q^*:

$$a - c = bQ^* + dQ^*$$
$$a - c = (b + d)Q^*$$
$$Q^* = \frac{a - c}{b + d}.$$

To find the equilibrium price, (P^*), substitute for Q^* in either the demand equation or the supply equation.

Using the demand equation, we have

$$P^* = a - b\left(\frac{a - c}{b + d}\right)$$
$$P^* = \frac{a(b + d) - b(a - c)}{b + d}$$
$$P^* = \frac{ad + bc}{b + d}.$$

Alternatively, using the supply equation, we have

$$P^* = c + d\left(\frac{a - c}{b + d}\right)$$
$$P^* = \frac{c(b + d) + d(a - c)}{b + d}$$
$$P^* = \frac{ad + bc}{b + d}.$$

An Example

The demand for ice-cream cones is

$$P = 800 - 2Q_D.$$

The supply of ice-cream cones is

$$P = 200 + 1Q_S.$$

The price of a cone is expressed in cents, and the quantities are expressed in cones per day.

To find the equilibrium price (P^*) and equilibrium quantity (Q^*), substitute Q^* for Q_D and Q_S and P^* for P. That is,

$$P^* = 800 - 2Q^*$$
$$P^* = 200 + 1Q^*.$$

Now solve for Q^*:

$$800 - 2Q^* = 200 + 1Q^*$$
$$600 = 3Q^*$$
$$Q^* = 200.$$

And

$$P^* = 800 - 2(200)$$
$$= 400.$$

The equilibrium price is $4 a cone, and the equilibrium quantity is 200 cones per day.

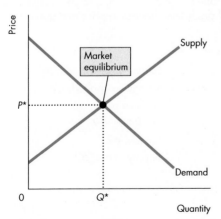

Price

Supply

Market equilibrium

P^*

Demand

0   Q^* Quantity

Figure 3 Market equilibrium

SUMMARY

Key Points

Markets and Prices (p. 56)

- A competitive market is one that has so many buyers and sellers that no single buyer or seller can influence the price.
- Opportunity cost is a relative price.
- Demand and supply determine relative prices.

Working Problem 1 will give you a better understanding of markets and prices.

Demand (pp. 57–61)

- Demand is the relationship between the quantity demanded of a good and its price when all other influences on buying plans remain the same.
- The higher the price of a good, other things remaining the same, the smaller is the quantity demanded—the law of demand.
- Demand depends on the prices of related goods (substitutes and complements), expected future prices, income, expected future income and credit, the population, and preferences.

Working Problems 2 to 5 will give you a better understanding of demand.

Supply (pp. 62–65)

- Supply is the relationship between the quantity supplied of a good and its price when all other influences on selling plans remain the same.
- The higher the price of a good, other things remaining the same, the greater is the quantity supplied—the law of supply.

- Supply depends on the prices of factors of production used to produce a good, the prices of related goods produced, expected future prices, the number of suppliers, technology, and the state of nature.

Working Problems 6 to 9 will give you a better understanding of supply.

Market Equilibrium (pp. 66–67)

- At the equilibrium price, the quantity demanded equals the quantity supplied.
- At any price above the equilibrium price, there is a surplus and the price falls.
- At any price below the equilibrium price, there is a shortage and the price rises.

Working Problems 10 and 11 will give you a better understanding of market equilibrium

Predicting Changes in Price and Quantity (pp. 68–73)

- An increase in demand brings a rise in the price and an increase in the quantity supplied. A decrease in demand brings a fall in the price and a decrease in the quantity supplied.
- An increase in supply brings a fall in the price and an increase in the quantity demanded. A decrease in supply brings a rise in the price and a decrease in the quantity demanded.
- An increase in demand and an increase in supply bring an increased quantity but an uncertain price change. An increase in demand and a decrease in supply bring a higher price but an uncertain change in quantity.

Working Problems 12 and 13 will give you a better understanding of predicting changes in price and quantity.

Key Terms

Change in demand, 58
Change in supply, 63
Change in the quantity
    demanded, 61
Change in the quantity supplied, 64
Competitive market, 56
Complement, 59
Demand, 57

Demand curve, 58
Equilibrium price, 66
Equilibrium quantity, 66
Inferior good, 60
Law of demand, 57
Law of supply, 62
Money price, 56
Normal good, 60

Quantity demanded, 57
Quantity supplied, 62
Relative price, 56
Substitute, 59
Supply, 62
Supply curve, 62

STUDY PLAN PROBLEMS AND APPLICATIONS

myeconlab You can work Problems 1 to 17 in MyEconLab Chapter 3 Study Plan and get instant feedback.

Markets and Prices (Study Plan 3.1)

1. William Gregg owned a mill in South Carolina. In December 1862, he placed a notice in the *Edgehill Advertiser* announcing his willingness to exchange cloth for food and other items. Here is an extract:

   1 yard of cloth for 1 pound of bacon
   2 yards of cloth for 1 pound of butter
   4 yards of cloth for 1 pound of wool
   8 yards of cloth for 1 bushel of salt

   a. What is the relative price of butter in terms of wool?

   b. If the money price of bacon was 20¢ a pound, what do you predict was the money price of butter?

   c. If the money price of bacon was 20¢ a pound and the money price of salt was $2.00 a bushel, do you think anyone would accept Mr. Gregg's offer of cloth for salt?

Demand (Study Plan 3.2)

2. The price of food increased during the past year.

   a. Explain why the law of demand applies to food just as it does to all other goods and services.

   b. Explain how the substitution effect influences food purchases and provide some examples of substitutions that people might make when the price of food rises and other things remain the same.

   c. Explain how the income effect influences food purchases and provide some examples of the income effect that might occur when the price of food rises and other things remain the same.

3. Place the following goods and services into pairs of likely substitutes and pairs of likely complements. (You may use an item in more than one pair.) The goods and services are

   coal, oil, natural gas, wheat, corn, rye, pasta, pizza, sausage, skateboard, roller blades, video game, laptop, iPod, cell phone, text message, email, phone call, voice mail

4. During 2010, the average income in China increased by 10 percent. Compared to 2009, how do you expect the following would change:

   a. The demand for beef? Explain your answer.

   b. The demand for rice? Explain your answer.

5. In January 2010, the price of gasoline was $2.70 a gallon. By spring 2010, the price had increased to $3.00 a gallon. Assume that there were no changes in average income, population, or any other influence on buying plans. Explain how the rise in the price of gasoline would affect

   a. The demand for gasoline.

   b. The quantity of gasoline demanded.

Supply (Study Plan 3.3)

6. In 2008, the price of corn increased by 35 percent and some cotton farmers in Texas stopped growing cotton and started to grow corn.

   a. Does this fact illustrate the law of demand or the law of supply? Explain your answer.

   b. Why would a cotton farmer grow corn?

Use the following information to work Problems 7 to 9.

Dairies make low-fat milk from full-cream milk. In the process of making low-fat milk, the dairies produce cream, which is made into ice cream. In the market for low-fat milk, the following events occur one at a time:

   (i)   The wage rate of dairy workers rises.

   (ii) The price of cream rises.

   (iii) The price of low-fat milk rises.

   (iv) With the period of low rainfall extending, dairies raise their expected price of low-fat milk next year.

   (v)   With advice from health-care experts, dairy farmers decide to switch from producing full-cream milk to growing vegetables.

   (vi) A new technology lowers the cost of producing ice cream.

7. Explain the effect of each event on the supply of low-fat milk.

8. Use a graph to illustrate the effect of each event.

9. Does any event (or events) illustrate the law of supply?

Market Equilibrium (Study Plan 3.4)

10. "As more people buy computers, the demand for Internet service increases and the price of Internet service decreases. The fall in the price of Internet service decreases the supply of Internet service." Explain what is wrong with this statement.

11. The demand and supply schedules for gum are

Price (cents per pack)	Quantity demanded (millions of packs a week)	Quantity supplied
20	180	60
40	140	100
60	100	140
80	60	180
100	20	220

a. Draw a graph of the market for gum and mark in the equilibrium price and quantity.

b. Suppose that the price of gum is 70¢ a pack. Describe the situation in the gum market and explain how the price adjusts.

c. Suppose that the price of gum is 30¢ a pack. Describe the situation in the gum market and explain how the price adjusts.

Predicting Changes in Price and Quantity

(Study Plan 3.5)

12. The following events occur one at a time:
    (i)   The price of crude oil rises.
    (ii) The price of a car rises.
    (iii) All speed limits on highways are abolished.
    (iv) Robots cut car production costs.

    Which of these events will increase or decrease (state which occurs)
    a. The demand for gasoline?
    b. The supply of gasoline?
    c. The quantity of gasoline demanded?
    d. The quantity of gasoline supplied?

13. In Problem 11, a fire destroys some factories that produce gum and the quantity of gum supplied decreases by 40 million packs a week at each price.

    a. Explain what happens in the market for gum and draw a graph to illustrate the changes.

    b. If at the time the fire occurs there is an increase in the teenage population, which increases the quantity of gum demanded by 40 million packs a week at each price, what are the new equilibrium price and quantity of gum? Illustrate these changes on your graph.

Economics in the News (Study Plan 3.N)

14. **American to Cut Flights, Charge for Luggage**
    American Airlines announced yesterday that it will begin charging passengers $15 for their first piece of checked luggage, in addition to raising other fees and cutting domestic flights as it grapples with record-high fuel prices.

    Source: *Boston Herald*, May 22, 2008

    a. According to the news clip, what is the influence on the supply of American Airlines flights?

    b. Explain how supply changes.

15. **Of Gambling, Grannies, and Good Sense**
    Nevada has plenty of jobs for the over 50s and its elderly population is growing faster than that in other states.

    Source: *The Economist*, July 26, 2006

    Explain how grannies have influenced:
    a. The demand in some Las Vegas markets.
    b. The supply in other Las Vegas markets.

16. **Frigid Florida Winter is Bad News for Tomato Lovers**
    An unusually cold January in Florida destroyed entire fields of tomatoes and forced many farmers to delay their harvest. Florida's growers are shipping only a quarter of their usual 5 million pounds a week. The price has risen from $6.50 for a 25-pound box a year ago to $30 now.

    Source: *USA Today*, March 3, 2010

    a. Make a graph to illustrate the market for tomatoes in January 2009 and January 2010.

    b. On the graph, show how the events in the news clip influence the market for tomatoes.

    c. Why is the news "bad for tomato lovers"?

17. **Pump Prices on Pace to Top 2009 High by Weekend**
    The cost of filling up the car is rising as the crude oil price soars and pump prices may exceed the peak price of 2009.

    Source: *USA Today*, January 7, 2010

    a. Does demand for gasoline or the supply of gasoline or both change when the price of oil soars?

    b. Use a demand-supply graph to illustrate what happens to the equilibrium price of gasoline and the equilibrium quantity of gasoline bought when the price of oil soars.

ADDITIONAL PROBLEMS AND APPLICATIONS

myeconlab You can work these problems in MyEconLab if assigned by your instructor.

Markets and Prices

18. What features of the world market for crude oil make it a competitive market?

19. The money price of a textbook is $90 and the money price of the Wii game *Super Mario Galaxy* is $45.
    a. What is the opportunity cost of a textbook in terms of the Wii game?
    b. What is the relative price of the Wii game in terms of textbooks?

Demand

20. The price of gasoline has increased during the past year.
    a. Explain why the law of demand applies to gasoline just as it does to all other goods and services.
    b. Explain how the substitution effect influences gasoline purchases and provide some examples of substitutions that people might make when the price of gasoline rises and other things remain the same.
    c. Explain how the income effect influences gasoline purchases and provide some examples of the income effects that might occur when the price of gasoline rises and other things remain the same.

21. Think about the demand for the three game consoles: Xbox, PS3, and Wii. Explain the effect of the following events on the demand for Xbox games and the quantity of Xbox games demanded, other things remaining the same.
    a. The price of an Xbox falls.
    b. The prices of a PS3 and a Wii fall.
    c. The number of people writing and producing Xbox games increases.
    d. Consumers' incomes increase.
    e. Programmers who write code for Xbox games become more costly to hire.
    f. The expected future price of an Xbox game falls.
    g. A new game console that is a close substitute for Xbox comes onto the market.

Supply

22. Classify the following pairs of goods and services as substitutes in production, complements in production, or neither.
    a. Bottled water and health club memberships
    b. French fries and baked potatoes
    c. Leather purses and leather shoes
    d. Hybrids and SUVs
    e. Diet coke and regular coke

23. As the prices of homes fell across the United States in 2008, the number of homes offered for sale decreased.
    a. Does this fact illustrate the law of demand or the law of supply? Explain your answer.
    b. Why would home owners decide not to sell?

24. **G.M. Cuts Production for Quarter**
    General Motors cut its fourth-quarter production schedule by 10 percent because Ford Motor, Chrysler, and Toyota sales declined in August.
    Source: *The New York Times*, September 5, 2007

    Explain whether this news clip illustrates a change in the supply of cars or a change in the quantity supplied of cars.

Market Equilibrium

Use the following figure to work Problems 25 and 26.

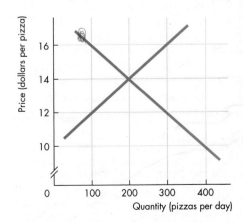

25. a. Label the curves. Which curve shows the willingness to pay for a pizza?
    b. If the price of a pizza is $16, is there a shortage or a surplus and does the price rise or fall?

c. Sellers want to receive the highest possible price, so why would they be willing to accept less than $16 a pizza?

26. a. If the price of a pizza is $12, is there a shortage or a surplus and does the price rise or fall?

   b. Buyers want to pay the lowest possible price, so why would they be willing to pay more than $12 for a pizza?

27. The demand and supply schedules for potato chips are

Price (cents per bag)	Quantity demanded (millions of bags per week)	Quantity supplied (millions of bags per week)
50	160	130
60	150	140
70	140	150
80	130	160
90	120	170
100	110	180

   a. Draw a graph of the potato chip market and mark in the equilibrium price and quantity.

   b. If the price is 60¢ a bag, is there a shortage or a surplus, and how does the price adjust?

Predicting Changes in Price and Quantity

28. In Problem 27, a new dip increases the quantity of potato chips that people want to buy by 30 million bags per week at each price.
   a. How does the demand and/or supply of chips change?
   b. How does the price and quantity of chips change?

29. In Problem 27, if a virus destroys potato crops and the quantity of potato chips produced decreases by 40 million bags a week at each price, how does the supply of chips change?

30. If the virus in Problem 29 hits just as the new dip in Problem 28 comes onto the market, how does the price and quantity of chips change?

Economics in the News

31. After you have studied *Reading Between the Lines* on pp. 74–75 answer the following questions.
   a. What happened to the price of coffee in 2010?
   b. What substitutions do you expect might have been made to decrease the quantity of coffee demanded?
   c. What influenced the demand for coffee in 2010 and what influenced the quantity of coffee demanded?
   d. What influenced the supply of coffee during 2010 and how did the supply of coffee change?
   e. How did the combination of the factors you have noted in parts (c) and (d) influence the price and quantity of coffee?
   f. Was the change in quantity of coffee a change in the quantity demanded or a change in the quantity supplied?

32. **Strawberry Prices Drop as Late Harvest Hits Market**

   Shoppers bought strawberries in March for $1.25 a pound rather than the $3.49 a pound they paid last year. With the price so low, some growers plowed over their strawberry plants to make way for spring melons; others froze their harvests and sold them to juice and jam makers.

   Source: *USA Today*, April 5, 2010

   a. Explain how the market for strawberries would have changed if growers had not plowed in their plants but offered locals "you pick for free."

   b. Describe the changes in demand and supply in the market for strawberry jam.

33. **"Popcorn Movie" Experience Gets Pricier**

   Cinemas are raising the price of popcorn. Demand for field corn, which is used for animal feed, corn syrup, and ethanol, has increased and its price has exploded. That's caused some farmers to shift from growing popcorn to easier-to-grow field corn.

   Source: *USA Today*, May 24, 2008

   Explain and illustrate graphically the events described in the news clip in the market for
   a. Popcorn
   b. Movie tickets

Use the following news clip to work Problems 34 and 35.

Sony's Blu-Ray Wins High-Definition War

Toshiba Corp. yesterday withdrew from the race to be the next-generation home movie format, leaving Sony Corp.'s Blu-ray technology the winner. The move could finally jump-start a high-definition home DVD market.

Source: *The Washington Times*, February 20, 2008

34. a. How would you expect the price of a used Toshiba player on eBay to change? Will the price change result from a change in demand, supply, or both, and in which directions?

   b. How would you expect the price of a Blu-ray player to change?

35. Explain how the market for Blu-ray format movies will change.

4

ELASTICITY

After studying this chapter,
you will be able to:

◆ Define, calculate, and explain the factors that influence
the price elasticity of demand

◆ Define, calculate, and explain the factors that influence
the cross elasticity of demand and the income elasticity
of demand

◆ Define, calculate, and explain the factors that influence
the elasticity of supply

What do you do when the price of gasoline soars to $3 a gallon? If you're
like most people, you complain a lot but keep on filling your tank and spending
more on gas. Would you react the same way to a rise in the price of tomatoes?
In the winter of 2010, a prolonged Florida frost wiped out most of the state's
tomato crop, driving the price of tomatoes to almost five times its normal level.
If faced with this price rise, do you keep buying the same quantity of tomatoes,
or do you find less costly substitutes?

How can we compare the effects of price changes on buying plans for
different goods such as gasoline and tomatoes?

This chapter introduces you to elasticity: a tool that addresses the
quantitative questions like the ones you've just considered and enables us to
compare the sensitivity of the quantity demanded to a change in price
regardless of the units in which the good is measured.

At the end of the chapter, in Reading Between the Lines, we'll use the
concepts of the elasticity of demand and the elasticity of supply to explain what
was happening in the market for fresh winter tomatoes from Florida during the
severe winter of 2010. But we'll begin by explaining elasticity in another
familiar setting: the market for pizza.

83

◆ Price Elasticity of Demand

You know that when supply increases, the equilibrium price falls and the equilibrium quantity increases. But does the price fall by a large amount and the quantity increase by a little? Or does the price barely fall and the quantity increase by a large amount?

The answer depends on the responsiveness of the quantity demanded to a change in price. You can see why by studying Fig. 4.1, which shows two possible scenarios in a local pizza market. Figure 4.1(a) shows one scenario, and Fig. 4.1(b) shows the other.

In both cases, supply is initially S_0. In part (a), the demand for pizza is shown by the demand curve D_A. In part (b), the demand for pizza is shown by the demand curve D_B. Initially, in both cases, the price is $20 a pizza and the equilibrium quantity is 10 pizzas an hour.

Now a large pizza franchise opens up, and the supply of pizza increases. The supply curve shifts rightward to S_1. In case (a), the price falls by an enormous $15 to $5 a pizza, and the quantity increases by only 3 to 13 pizzas an hour. In contrast, in case (b), the price falls by only $5 to $15 a pizza and the quantity increases by 7 to 17 pizzas an hour.

The different outcomes arise from differing degrees of responsiveness of the quantity demanded to a change in price. But what do we mean by responsiveness? One possible answer is slope. The slope of demand curve D_A is steeper than the slope of demand curve D_B.

In this example, we can compare the slopes of the two demand curves, but we can't always make such a comparison. The reason is that the slope of a demand curve depends on the units in which we measure the price and quantity. And we often must compare the demand for different goods and services that are measured in unrelated units. For example, a pizza producer might want to compare the demand for pizza with the demand for soft drinks. Which quantity demanded is more responsive to a price change? This question can't be answered by comparing the slopes of two demand curves. The units of measurement of pizza and soft drinks are unrelated. The question can be answered with a measure of responsiveness that is independent of units of measurement. Elasticity is such a measure.

The **price elasticity of demand** is a units-free measure of the responsiveness of the quantity demanded of a good to a change in its price when all other influences on buying plans remain the same.

FIGURE 4.1   How a Change in Supply Changes Price and Quantity

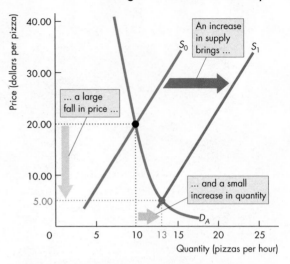

(a) Large price change and small quantity change

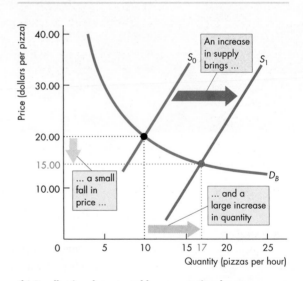

(b) Small price change and large quantity change

Initially, the price is $20 a pizza and the quantity sold is 10 pizzas an hour. Then supply increases from S_0 to S_1. In part (a), the price falls by $15 to $5 a pizza, and the quantity increases by 3 to 13 pizzas an hour. In part (b), the price falls by only $5 to $15 a pizza, and the quantity increases by 7 to 17 pizzas an hour. The price change is smaller and the quantity change is larger in case (b) than in case (a). The quantity demanded is more responsive to the change in the price in case (b) than in case (a).

◆ myeconlab animation ◆

Calculating Price Elasticity of Demand

We calculate the *price elasticity of demand* by using the formula:

$$\text{Price elasticity of demand} = \frac{\text{Percentage change in quantity demanded}}{\text{Percentage change in price}}.$$

To calculate the price elasticity of demand for pizza, we need to know the quantity demanded of pizza at two different prices, when all other influences on buying plans remain the same.

Figure 4.2 zooms in on the demand curve for pizza and shows how the quantity demanded responds to a small change in price. Initially, the price is $20.50 a pizza and 9 pizzas an hour are demanded—the original point. The price then falls to $19.50 a pizza, and the quantity demanded increases to 11 pizzas an hour—the new point. When the price falls by $1 a pizza, the quantity demanded increases by 2 pizzas an hour.

To calculate the price elasticity of demand, we express the change in price as a percentage of the *average price* and the change in the quantity demanded as a percentage of the *average quantity*. By using the average price and average quantity, we calculate the elasticity at a point on the demand curve midway between the original point and the new point.

The original price is $20.50 and the new price is $19.50, so the price change is $1 and the average price is $20 a pizza. Call the percentage change in the price $\%\Delta P$, then

$$\%\Delta P = \Delta P/P_{ave} \times 100 = (\$1/\$20) \times 100 = 5\%.$$

The original quantity demanded is 9 pizzas and the new quantity demanded is 11 pizzas, so the quantity change is 2 pizzas and the average quantity demanded is 10 pizzas. Call the percentage change in the quantity demanded $\%\Delta Q$, then

$$\%\Delta Q = \Delta Q/Q_{ave} \times 100 = (2/10) \times 100 = 20\%.$$

The price elasticity of demand equals the percentage change in the quantity demanded (20 percent) divided by the percentage change in price (5 percent) and is 4. That is,

$$\text{Price elasticity of demand} = \frac{\%\Delta Q}{\%\Delta P}$$
$$= \frac{20\%}{5\%} = 4.$$

FIGURE 4.2   Calculating the Elasticity of Demand

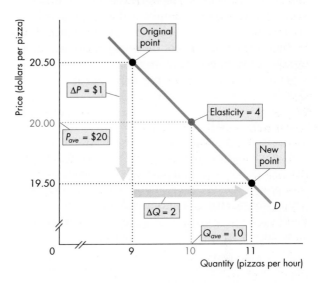

The elasticity of demand is calculated by using the formula:*

$$\text{Price elasticity of demand} = \frac{\text{Percentage change in quantity demanded}}{\text{Percentage change in price}}$$
$$= \frac{\%\Delta Q}{\%\Delta P}$$
$$= \frac{\Delta Q/Q_{ave}}{\Delta P/P_{ave}}$$
$$= \frac{2/10}{1/20} = 4.$$

This calculation measures the elasticity at an average price of $20 a pizza and an average quantity of 10 pizzas an hour.

* In the formula, the Greek letter delta (Δ) stands for "change in" and %Δ stands for "percentage change in."

myeconlab   animation

Average Price and Quantity   Notice that we use the *average* price and *average* quantity. We do this because it gives the most precise measurement of elasticity—at the midpoint between the original price and the new price. If the price falls from $20.50 to $19.50, the $1 price change is 4.9 percent of $20.50. The 2 pizza change in quantity is 22.2 percent of 9 pizzas, the original quantity. So if we use these numbers, the price elasticity of demand is 22.2 divided by 4.9, which equals 4.5. If the price rises from $19.50 to $20.50, the $1 price change is 5.1 percent of $19.50. The 2 pizza change in quantity is 18.2 percent of 11 pizzas, the original quantity. So if we use these numbers, the price elasticity of demand is 18.2 divided by 5.1, which equals 3.6.

By using percentages of the *average* price and *average* quantity, we get the same value for the elasticity regardless of whether the price falls from $20.50 to $19.50 or rises from $19.50 to $20.50.

Percentages and Proportions Elasticity is the ratio of two percentage changes, so when we divide one percentage change by another, the 100s cancel. A percentage change is a *proportionate* change multiplied by 100. The proportionate change in price is $\Delta P / P_{ave}$, and the proportionate change in quantity demanded is $\Delta Q / Q_{ave}$. So if we divide $\Delta Q / Q_{ave}$ by $\Delta P / P_{ave}$ we get the same answer as we get by using percentage changes.

A Units-Free Measure Now that you've calculated a price elasticity of demand, you can see why it is a *units-free measure*. Elasticity is a units-free measure because the percentage change in each variable is independent of the units in which the variable is measured. The ratio of the two percentages is a number without units.

Minus Sign and Elasticity When the price of a good *rises*, the quantity demanded *decreases*. Because a *positive* change in price brings a *negative* change in quantity demanded, the price elasticity of demand is a negative number. But it is the magnitude, or *absolute value*, of the price elasticity of demand that tells us how responsive the quantity demanded is. So to compare price elasticities of demand, we use the *magnitude* of the elasticity and ignore the minus sign.

Inelastic and Elastic Demand

Figure 4.3 shows three demand curves that cover the entire range of possible elasticities of demand. In Fig. 4.3(a), the quantity demanded is constant regardless of the price. If the quantity demanded remains constant when the price changes, then the price elasticity of demand is zero and the good is said to have a **perfectly inelastic demand**. One good that has a very low price elasticity of demand (perhaps zero over some price range) is insulin. Insulin is of such importance to some diabetics that if the price rises or falls, they do not change the quantity they buy.

If the percentage change in the quantity demanded equals the percentage change in the price, then the price elasticity equals 1 and the good is said to have a **unit elastic demand**. The demand in Fig. 4.3(b) is an example of a unit elastic demand.

Between the cases shown in Fig. 4.3(a) and Fig. 4.3(b) is the general case in which the percentage change in the quantity demanded is less than the percentage change in the price. In this case, the price elasticity of demand is between zero and 1 and the good is said to have an **inelastic demand**. Food and shelter are examples of goods with inelastic demand.

FIGURE 4.3   Inelastic and Elastic Demand

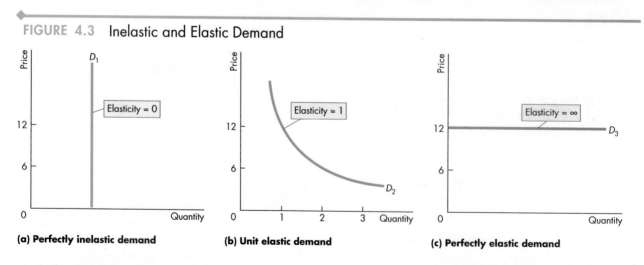

(a) Perfectly inelastic demand

(b) Unit elastic demand

(c) Perfectly elastic demand

Each demand illustrated here has a constant elasticity. The demand curve in part (a) illustrates the demand for a good that has a zero elasticity of demand. The demand curve in part (b) illustrates the demand for a good with a unit elasticity of demand. And the demand curve in part (c) illustrates the demand for a good with an infinite elasticity of demand.

myeconlab animation

If the quantity demanded changes by an infinitely large percentage in response to a tiny price change, then the price elasticity of demand is infinity and the good is said to have a **perfectly elastic demand**. Figure 4.3(c) shows a perfectly elastic demand. An example of a good that has a very high elasticity of demand (almost infinite) is a soft drink from two campus machines located side by side. If the two machines offer the same soft drinks for the same price, some people buy from one machine and some from the other. But if one machine's price is higher than the other's, by even a small amount, no one buys from the machine with the higher price. Drinks from the two machines are perfect substitutes. The demand for a good that has a perfect substitute is perfectly elastic.

Between the cases in Fig. 4.3(b) and Fig. 4.3(c) is the general case in which the percentage change in the quantity demanded exceeds the percentage change in price. In this case, the price elasticity of demand is greater than 1 and the good is said to have an **elastic demand**. Automobiles and furniture are examples of goods that have elastic demand.

Elasticity Along a Linear Demand Curve

Elasticity and slope are not the same. A linear demand curve has a constant slope but a varying elasticity. Let's see why.

The demand curve in Fig. 4.4 is linear. A $5 fall in the price brings an increase of 10 pizzas an hour no matter what the initial price and quantity.

Let's now calculate some elasticities along this demand curve.

At the midpoint of the demand curve, the price is $12.50 and the quantity is 25 pizzas per hour. When the price falls from $15 to $10 a pizza the quantity demanded increases from 20 to 30 pizzas an hour and the average price and average quantity are at the midpoint of the demand curve. So

$$\text{Price elasticity of demand} = \frac{10/25}{5/12.25}$$

$$= 1.$$

That is, at the midpoint of a linear demand curve, the price elasticity of demand is one.

At prices *above* the midpoint, demand is elastic. For example, when the price falls from $25 to $15 a pizza, the quantity demanded increases from zero to

20 pizzas an hour. The average price is $20 a pizza, and the average quantity is 10 pizzas. So

$$\text{Price elasticity of demand} = \frac{\Delta Q / Q_{ave}}{\Delta P / P_{ave}}$$

$$= \frac{20/10}{10/20}$$

$$= 4.$$

That is, the price elasticity of demand at an average price of $20 a pizza is 4.

At prices *below* the midpoint, demand is inelastic. For example, when the price falls from $10 a pizza to zero, the quantity demanded increases from 30 to 50 pizzas an hour. The average price is now $5 and the average quantity is 40 pizzas an hour. So

$$\text{Price elasticity of demand} = \frac{20/40}{10/5}$$

$$= 1/4.$$

That is, the price elasticity of demand at an average price of $5 a pizza is 1/4.

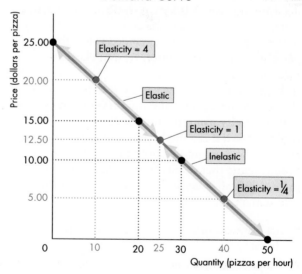

FIGURE 4.4   Elasticity Along a Linear Demand Curve

On a linear demand curve, demand is unit elastic at the midpoint (elasticity is 1), elastic above the midpoint, and inelastic below the midpoint.

Total Revenue and Elasticity

The **total revenue** from the sale of a good equals the price of the good multiplied by the quantity sold. When a price changes, total revenue also changes. But a cut in the price does not always decrease total revenue. The change in total revenue depends on the elasticity of demand in the following way:

- If demand is elastic, a 1 percent price cut increases the quantity sold by more than 1 percent and total revenue increases.

- If demand is inelastic, a 1 percent price cut increases the quantity sold by less than 1 percent and total revenue decreases.

- If demand is unit elastic, a 1 percent price cut increases the quantity sold by 1 percent and total revenue does not change.

In Fig. 4.5(a), over the price range from $25 to $12.50, demand is elastic. Over the price range from $12.50 to zero, demand is inelastic. At a price of $12.50, demand is unit elastic.

Figure 4.5(b) shows total revenue. At a price of $25, the quantity sold is zero, so total revenue is zero. At a price of zero, the quantity demanded is 50 pizzas an hour and total revenue is again zero. A price cut in the elastic range brings an increase in total revenue—the percentage increase in the quantity demanded is greater than the percentage decrease in price. A price cut in the inelastic range brings a decrease in total revenue—the percentage increase in the quantity demanded is less than the percentage decrease in price. At unit elasticity, total revenue is at a maximum.

Figure 4.5 shows how we can use this relationship between elasticity and total revenue to estimate elasticity using the total revenue test. The **total revenue test** is a method of estimating the price elasticity of demand by observing the change in total revenue that results from a change in the price, when all other influences on the quantity sold remain the same.

- If a price cut increases total revenue, demand is elastic.

- If a price cut decreases total revenue, demand is inelastic.

- If a price cut leaves total revenue unchanged, demand is unit elastic.

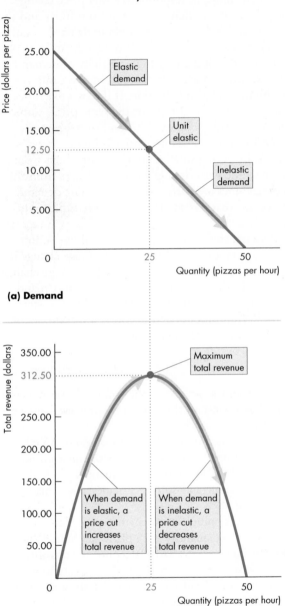

FIGURE 4.5   Elasticity and Total Revenue

(a) Demand

(b) Total revenue

When demand is elastic, in the price range from $25 to $12.50, a decrease in price (part a) brings an increase in total revenue (part b). When demand is inelastic, in the price range from $12.50 to zero, a decrease in price (part a) brings a decrease in total revenue (part b). When demand is unit elastic, at a price of $12.50 (part a), total revenue is at a maximum (part b).

myeconlab   animation

Your Expenditure and Your Elasticity

When a price changes, the change in your expenditure on the good depends on *your* elasticity of demand.

- If your demand is elastic, a 1 percent price cut increases the quantity you buy by more than 1 percent and your expenditure on the item increases.
- If your demand is inelastic, a 1 percent price cut increases the quantity you buy by less than 1 percent and your expenditure on the item decreases.
- If your demand is unit elastic, a 1 percent price cut increases the quantity you buy by 1 percent and your expenditure on the item does not change.

So if you spend more on an item when its price falls, your demand for that item is elastic; if you spend the same amount, your demand is unit elastic; and if you spend less, your demand is inelastic.

The Factors That Influence the Elasticity of Demand

The elasticity of demand for a good depends on

- The closeness of substitutes
- The proportion of income spent on the good
- The time elapsed since the price change

Closeness of Substitutes The closer the substitutes for a good or service, the more elastic is the demand for it. Oil from which we make gasoline has no close substitutes (imagine a steam-driven, coal-fueled car). So the demand for oil is inelastic. Plastics are close substitutes for metals, so the demand for metals is elastic.

The degree of substitutability depends on how narrowly (or broadly) we define a good. For example, a personal computer has no close substitutes, but a Dell PC is a close substitute for a Hewlett-Packard PC. So the elasticity of demand for personal computers is lower than the elasticity of demand for a Dell or a Hewlett-Packard.

In everyday language we call goods such as food and shelter *necessities* and goods such as exotic vacations *luxuries*. A necessity has poor substitutes and is crucial for our well-being. So a necessity generally has an inelastic demand. A luxury usually has many substitutes, one of which is not buying it. So a luxury generally has an elastic demand.

Proportion of Income Spent on the Good Other things remaining the same, the greater the proportion of income spent on a good, the more elastic (or less inelastic) is the demand for it.

Economics in Action
Elastic and Inelastic Demand

The real-world price elasticities of demand in the table range from 1.52 for metals, the item with the most elastic demand in the table, to 0.05 for oil, the item with the most inelastic demand in the table. The demand for food is also inelastic.

Oil and food, which have poor substitutes and inelastic demand, might be classified as necessities. Furniture and motor vehicles, which have good substitutes and elastic demand, might be classified as luxuries.

Price Elasticities of Demand

Good or Service	Elasticity
Elastic Demand	
Metals	1.52
Electrical engineering products	1.39
Mechanical engineering products	1.30
Furniture	1.26
Motor vehicles	1.14
Instrument engineering products	1.10
Professional services	1.09
Transportation services	1.03
Inelastic Demand	
Gas, electricity, and water	0.92
Chemicals	0.89
Drinks	0.78
Clothing	0.64
Tobacco	0.61
Banking and insurance services	0.56
Housing services	0.55
Agricultural and fish products	0.42
Books, magazines, and newspapers	0.34
Food	0.12
Oil	0.05

Sources of data: Ahsan Mansur and John Whalley, "Numerical Specification of Applied General Equilibrium Models: Estimation, Calibration, and Data," in *Applied General Equilibrium Analysis*, eds. Herbert E. Scarf and John B. Shoven (New York: Cambridge University Press, 1984), 109, and Henri Theil, Ching-Fan Chung, and James L. Seale, Jr., *Advances in Econometrics, Supplement I, 1989, International Evidence on Consumption Patterns* (Greenwich, Conn.: JAI Press Inc., 1989), and Geoffrey Heal, Columbia University, Web site.

Economics in Action
Price Elasticities of Demand for Food

The price elasticity of demand for food in the United States is estimated to be 0.12. This elasticity is an average over all types of food. The demand for most food items is inelastic, but there is a wide range of elasticities as the figure below shows for a range of fruits, vegetables, and meats.

The demand for grapes and beef is elastic. The demand for oranges is unit elastic. These food items have many good substitutes. Florida winter tomatoes have closer substitutes than tomatoes in general, so the demand for the Florida winter variety is more elastic (less inelastic) than the demand for tomatoes.

Carrots and cabbage, on which we spend a very small proportion of income, have an almost zero elastic demand.

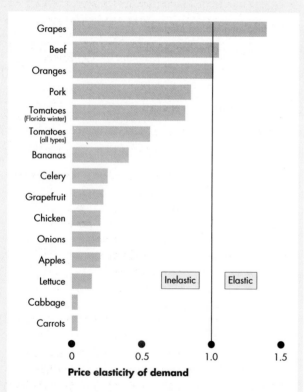

Price Elasticities of Demand for Food

Sources of data: Kuo S. Huang, *U.S. demand for food: A complete system of price and income effects* U.S. Dept. of Agriculture, Economic Research Service, Washington, DC, 1985 and J. Scott Shonkwiler and Robert D. Emerson, "Imports and the Supply of Winter Tomatoes: An Application of Rational Expectations", *American Journal of Agricultural Economics*, Vol. 64, No. 4 (Nov., 1982), pp. 634-641 and Kuo S. Huang, "A Further Look at Flexibilities and Elasticities", *American Journal of Agricultural Economics*, Vol. 76, No. 2 (May, 1994), pp. 313-317.

Think about your own elasticity of demand for chewing gum and housing. If the price of gum doubles, you consume almost as much as before. Your demand for gum is inelastic. If apartment rents double, you look for more students to share accommodation with you. Your demand for housing is not as inelastic as your demand for gum. Why the difference? Housing takes a large proportion of your budget, and gum takes only a tiny proportion. You don't like either price increase, but you hardly notice the higher price of gum, while the higher rent puts your budget under severe strain.

Time Elapsed Since Price Change The longer the time that has elapsed since a price change, the more elastic is demand. When the price of oil increased by 400 percent during the 1970s, people barely changed the quantity of oil and gasoline they bought. But gradually, as more efficient auto and airplane engines were developed, the quantity bought decreased. The demand for oil became more elastic as more time elapsed following the huge price hike.

◆ REVIEW QUIZ

1 Why do we need a units-free measure of the responsiveness of the quantity demanded of a good or service to a change in its price?

2 Define the price elasticity of demand and show how it is calculated.

3 What is the total revenue test? Explain how it works.

4 What are the main influences on the elasticity of demand that make the demand for some goods elastic and the demand for other goods inelastic?

5 Why is the demand for a luxury generally more elastic (or less inelastic) than the demand for a necessity?

You can work these questions in Study Plan 4.1 and get instant feedback.

You've now completed your study of the *price* elasticity of demand. Two other elasticity concepts tell us about the effects of other influences on demand. Let's look at these other elasticities of demand.

◆ More Elasticities of Demand

Back at the pizzeria, you are trying to work out how a price rise by the burger shop next door will affect the demand for your pizza. You know that pizzas and burgers are substitutes. You also know that when the price of a substitute for pizza rises, the demand for pizza increases. But by how much?

You also know that pizza and soft drinks are complements. And you know that if the price of a complement of pizza rises, the demand for pizza decreases. So you wonder, by how much will a rise in the price of a soft drink decrease the demand for your pizza?

To answer these questions, you need to calculate the cross elasticity of demand. Let's examine this elasticity measure.

Cross Elasticity of Demand

We measure the influence of a change in the price of a substitute or complement by using the concept of the cross elasticity of demand. The **cross elasticity of demand** is a measure of the responsiveness of the demand for a good to a change in the price of a substitute or complement, other things remaining the same. We calculate the *cross elasticity of demand* by using the formula:

$$\text{Cross elasticity of demand} = \frac{\text{Percentage change in quantity demanded}}{\text{Percentage change in price of a substitute or complement}}.$$

The cross elasticity of demand can be positive or negative. It is *positive* for a *substitute* and *negative* for a *complement*.

Substitutes Suppose that the price of pizza is constant and people buy 9 pizzas an hour. Then the price of a burger rises from $1.50 to $2.50. No other influence on buying plans changes and the quantity of pizzas bought increases to 11 an hour.

The change in the quantity demanded is +2 pizzas—the new quantity, 11 pizzas, minus the original quantity, 9 pizzas. The average quantity is 10 pizzas. So the quantity of pizzas demanded increases by 20 percent. That is,

$$\Delta Q/Q_{ave} \times 100 = (+2/10) \times 100 = +20\%.$$

The change in the price of a burger, a substitute for pizza, is +$1—the new price, $2.50, minus the original price, $1.50. The average price is $2 a burger. So the price of a burger rises by 50 percent. That is,

$$\Delta P/P_{ave} \times 100 = (+\$1/\$2) \times 100 = +50\%.$$

So the cross elasticity of demand for pizza with respect to the price of a burger is

$$\frac{+20\%}{+50\%} = 0.4.$$

Figure 4.6 illustrates the cross elasticity of demand. Pizza and burgers are substitutes. Because they are substitutes, when the price of a burger rises, the demand for pizza increases. The demand curve for pizza shifts rightward from D_0 to D_1. Because a *rise* in the price of a burger brings an *increase* in the demand for pizza, the cross elasticity of demand for pizza with respect to the price of a burger is *positive*. Both the price and the quantity change in the same direction.

FIGURE 4.6   Cross Elasticity of Demand

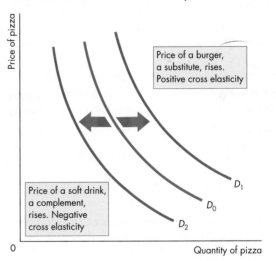

A burger is a *substitute* for pizza. When the price of a burger rises, the demand for pizza increases and the demand curve for pizza shifts rightward from D_0 to D_1. The cross elasticity of demand is *positive*.

A soft drink is a *complement* of pizza. When the price of a soft drink rises, the demand for pizza decreases and the demand curve for pizza shifts leftward from D_0 to D_2. The cross elasticity of demand is *negative*.

 animation

Complements Now suppose that the price of pizza is constant and 11 pizzas an hour are bought. Then the price of a soft drink rises from $1.50 to $2.50. No other influence on buying plans changes and the quantity of pizzas bought falls to 9 an hour.

The change in the quantity demanded is the opposite of what we've just calculated: The quantity of pizzas demanded decreases by 20 percent (–20%).

The change in the price of a soft drink, a complement of pizza, is the same as the percentage change in the price of a burger that we've just calculated. The price rises by 50 percent (+50%). So the cross elasticity of demand for pizza with respect to the price of a soft drink is

$$\frac{-20\%}{+50\%} = -0.4.$$

Because pizza and soft drinks are complements, when the price of a soft drink rises, the demand for pizza decreases. The demand curve for pizza shifts leftward from D_0 to D_2. Because a *rise* in the price of a soft drink brings a *decrease* in the demand for pizza, the cross elasticity of demand for pizza with respect to the price of a soft drink is *negative*. The price and quantity change in *opposite* directions.

The magnitude of the cross elasticity of demand determines how far the demand curve shifts. The larger the cross elasticity (absolute value), the greater is the change in demand and the larger is the shift in the demand curve.

If two items are close substitutes, such as two brands of spring water, the cross elasticity is large. If two items are close complements, such as movies and popcorn, the cross elasticity is large.

If two items are somewhat unrelated to each other, such as newspapers and orange juice, the cross elasticity is small—perhaps even zero.

Income Elasticity of Demand

Suppose the economy is expanding and people are enjoying rising incomes. This prosperity brings an increase in the demand for most types of goods and services. But by how much will the demand for pizza increase? The answer depends on the **income elasticity of demand**, which is a measure of the responsiveness of the demand for a good or service to a change in income, other things remaining the same.

The income elasticity of demand is calculated by using the formula:

$$\text{Income elasticity of demand} = \frac{\text{Percentage change in quantity demanded}}{\text{Percentage change in income}}.$$

Income elasticities of demand can be positive or negative and they fall into three interesting ranges:

- Greater than 1 (*normal* good, income elastic)
- Positive and less than 1 (*normal* good, income inelastic)
- Negative (*inferior* good)

Income Elastic Demand Suppose that the price of pizza is constant and 9 pizzas an hour are bought. Then incomes rise from $975 to $1,025 a week. No other influence on buying plans changes and the quantity of pizzas sold increases to 11 an hour.

The change in the quantity demanded is +2 pizzas. The average quantity is 10 pizzas, so the quantity demanded increases by 20 percent. The change in income is +$50 and the average income is $1,000, so incomes increase by 5 percent. The income elasticity of demand for pizza is

$$\frac{20\%}{5\%} = 4.$$

The demand for pizza is income elastic. The percentage increase in the quantity of pizza demanded exceeds the percentage increase in income. *When the demand for a good is income elastic, the percentage of income spent on that good increases as income increases.*

Income Inelastic Demand If the income elasticity of demand is positive but less than 1, demand is income inelastic. The percentage increase in the quantity demanded is positive but less than the percentage increase in income. *When the demand for a good is income inelastic, the percentage of income spent on that good decreases as income increases.*

Inferior Goods If the income elasticity of demand is negative, the good is an *inferior* good. The quantity demanded of an inferior good and the amount spent on it *decrease* when income increases. Goods in this category include small motorcycles, potatoes, and rice. Low-income consumers buy most of these goods.

Economics in Action
Necessities and Luxuries

The table shows estimates of some real-world income elasticities of demand. The demand for a necessity such as food or clothing is income inelastic, while the demand for a luxury such as transportation, which includes airline and foreign travel, is income elastic.

But what is a necessity and what is a luxury depends on the level of income. For people with a low income, food and clothing can be luxuries. So the level of income has a big effect on income elasticities of demand. The figure shows this effect on the income elasticity of demand for food in 10 countries. In countries with low incomes, such as Tanzania and India, the income elasticity of demand for food is high. In countries with high incomes, such as the United States, the income elasticity of

demand for food is low. That is, as income increases, the income elasticity of demand for food decreases. Low-income consumers spend a larger percentage of any increase in income on food than do high-income consumers.

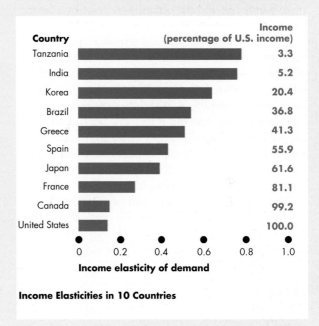

Income Elasticities in 10 Countries

Some Real-World Income Elasticities of Demand

Income Elastic Demand

Airline travel	5.82
Movies	3.41
Foreign travel	3.08
Electricity	1.94
Restaurant meals	1.61
Local buses and trains	1.38
Haircuts	1.36
Automobiles	1.07

Income Inelastic Demand

Tobacco	0.86
Alcoholic drinks	0.62
Furniture	0.53
Clothing	0.51
Newspapers and magazines	0.38
Telephone	0.32
Food	0.14

Sources of data: H.S. Houthakker and Lester D. Taylor, *Consumer Demand in the United States* (Cambridge, Mass.: Harvard University Press, 1970), and Henri Theil, Ching-Fan Chung, and James L. Seale, Jr., *Advances in Econometrics, Supplement 1, 1989, International Evidence on Consumption Patterns* (Greenwich, Conn.: JAI Press, Inc., 1989).

◆ REVIEW QUIZ

1 What does the cross elasticity of demand measure?
2 What does the sign (positive versus negative) of the cross elasticity of demand tell us about the relationship between two goods?
3 What does the income elasticity of demand measure?
4 What does the sign (positive versus negative) of the income elasticity of demand tell us about a good?
5 Why does the level of income influence the magnitude of the income elasticity of demand?

You can work these questions in Study Plan 4.2 and get instant feedback.

You've now completed your study of the *cross elasticity* of demand and the *income elasticity* of demand. Let's look at the other side of the market and examine the elasticity of supply.

◆ Elasticity of Supply

You know that when demand increases, the equilibrium price rises and the equilibrium quantity increases. But does the price rise by a large amount and the quantity increase by a little? Or does the price barely rise and the quantity increase by a large amount?

The answer depends on the responsiveness of the quantity supplied to a change in price. You can see why by studying Fig. 4.7, which shows two possible scenarios in a local pizza market. Figure 4.7(a) shows one scenario, and Fig. 4.7(b) shows the other.

In both cases, demand is initially D_0. In part (a), supply is shown by the supply curve S_A. In part (b), supply is shown by the supply curve S_B. Initially, in both cases, the price is $20 a pizza and the equilibrium quantity is 10 pizzas an hour.

Now increases in incomes and population increase the demand for pizza. The demand curve shifts rightward to D_1. In case (a), the price rises by $10 to $30 a pizza, and the quantity increases by only 3 to 13 pizzas an hour. In contrast, in case (b), the price rises by only $1 to $21 a pizza, and the quantity increases by 10 to 20 pizzas an hour.

The different outcomes arise from differing degrees of responsiveness of the quantity supplied to a change in price. We measure the degree of responsiveness by using the concept of the elasticity of supply.

Calculating the Elasticity of Supply

The **elasticity of supply** measures the responsiveness of the quantity supplied to a change in the price of a good when all other influences on selling plans remain the same. It is calculated by using the formula:

$$\text{Elasticity of supply} = \frac{\text{Percentage change in quantity supplied}}{\text{Percentage change in price}}.$$

We use the same method that you learned when you studied the elasticity of demand. (Refer back to p. 85 to check this method.) Let's calculate the elasticity of supply along the supply curves in Fig. 4.7.

In Fig. 4.7(a), when the price rises from $20 to $30, the price rise is $10 and the average price is $25, so the price rises by 40 percent of the average price. The quantity increases from 10 to 13 pizzas an hour,

FIGURE 4.7   How a Change in Demand Changes Price and Quantity

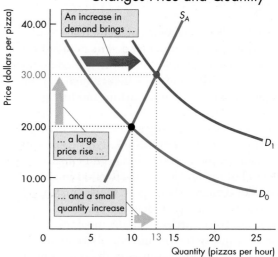

(a) Large price change and small quantity change

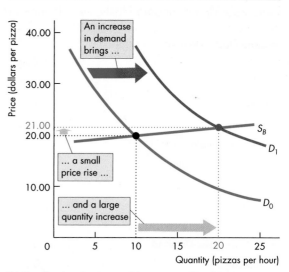

(b) Small price change and large quantity change

Initially, the price is $20 a pizza, and the quantity sold is 10 pizzas an hour. Then the demand for pizza increases. The demand curve shifts rightward to D_1. In part (a), the price rises by $10 to $30 a pizza, and the quantity increases by 3 to 13 pizzas an hour. In part (b), the price rises by only $1 to $21 a pizza, and the quantity increases by 10 to 20 pizzas an hour. The price change is smaller and the quantity change is larger in case (b) than in case (a). The quantity supplied is more responsive to a change in the price in case (b) than in case (a).

◆ myeconlab animation ◆

so the increase is 3 pizzas, the average quantity is 11.5 pizzas an hour, and the quantity increases by 26 percent. The elasticity of supply is equal to 26 percent divided by 40 percent, which equals 0.65.

In Fig. 4.7(b), when the price rises from $20 to $21, the price rise is $1 and the average price is $20.50, so the price rises by 4.9 percent of the average price. The quantity increases from 10 to 20 pizzas an hour, so the increase is 10 pizzas, the average quantity is 15 pizzas, and the quantity increases by 67 percent. The elasticity of supply is equal to 67 percent divided by 4.9 percent, which equals 13.67.

Figure 4.8 shows the range of elasticities of supply. If the quantity supplied is fixed regardless of the price, the supply curve is vertical and the elasticity of supply is zero. Supply is perfectly inelastic. This case is shown in Fig. 4.8(a). A special intermediate case occurs when the percentage change in price equals the percentage change in quantity. Supply is then unit elastic. This case is shown in Fig. 4.8(b). No matter how steep the supply curve is, if it is linear and passes through the origin, supply is unit elastic. If there is a price at which sellers are willing to offer any quantity for sale, the supply curve is horizontal and the elasticity of supply is infinite. Supply is perfectly elastic. This case is shown in Fig. 4.8(c).

The Factors That Influence the Elasticity of Supply

The elasticity of supply of a good depends on

- Resource substitution possibilities
- Time frame for the supply decision

Resource Substitution Possibilities Some goods and services can be produced only by using unique or rare productive resources. These items have a low, perhaps even a zero, elasticity of supply. Other goods and services can be produced by using commonly available resources that could be allocated to a wide variety of alternative tasks. Such items have a high elasticity of supply.

A Van Gogh painting is an example of a good with a vertical supply curve and a zero elasticity of supply. At the other extreme, wheat can be grown on land that is almost equally good for growing corn, so it is just as easy to grow wheat as corn. The opportunity cost of wheat in terms of forgone corn is almost constant. As a result, the supply curve of wheat is almost horizontal and its elasticity of supply is very large. Similarly, when a good is produced in many different countries (for example, sugar and beef), the supply of the good is highly elastic.

FIGURE 4.8   Inelastic and Elastic Supply

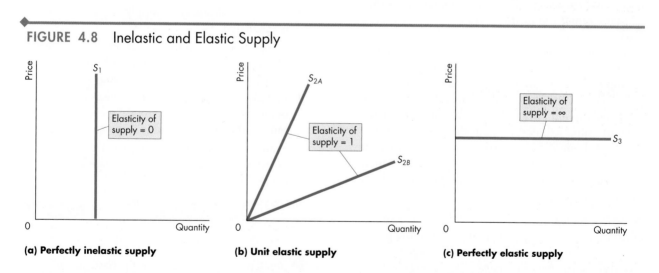

(a) Perfectly inelastic supply   **(b) Unit elastic supply**   **(c) Perfectly elastic supply**

Each supply illustrated here has a constant elasticity. The supply curve in part (a) illustrates the supply of a good that has a zero elasticity of supply. The supply curve in part (b) illustrates the supply of a good with a unit elasticity of supply. All linear supply curves that pass through the origin illustrate supplies that are unit elastic. The supply curve in part (c) illustrates the supply of a good with an infinite elasticity of supply.

The supply of most goods and services lies between these two extremes. The quantity produced can be increased but only by incurring a higher cost. If a higher price is offered, the quantity supplied increases. Such goods and services have an elasticity of supply between zero and infinity.

Time Frame for the Supply Decision To study the influence of the amount of time elapsed since a price change, we distinguish three time frames of supply:

- Momentary supply
- Short-run supply
- Long-run supply

Momentary Supply When the price of a good changes, the immediate response of the quantity supplied is determined by the *momentary supply* of that good.

Some goods, such as fruits and vegetables, have a perfectly inelastic momentary supply—a vertical supply curve. The quantities supplied depend on crop-planting decisions made earlier. In the case of oranges, for example, planting decisions have to be made many years in advance of the crop being available. Momentary supply is perfectly inelastic because, on a given day, no matter what the price of oranges, producers cannot change their output. They have picked, packed, and shipped their crop to market, and the quantity available for that day is fixed.

In contrast, some goods have a perfectly elastic momentary supply. Long-distance phone calls are an example. When many people simultaneously make a call, there is a big surge in the demand for telephone cables, computer switching, and satellite time. The quantity supplied increases, but the price remains constant. Long-distance carriers monitor fluctuations in demand and reroute calls to ensure that the quantity supplied equals the quantity demanded without changing the price.

Short-Run Supply The response of the quantity supplied to a price change when only *some* of the possible adjustments to production can be made is determined by *short-run supply*. Most goods have an inelastic short-run supply. To increase output in the short run, firms must work their labor force overtime and perhaps hire additional workers. To decrease their output in the short run, firms either lay off workers or reduce their hours of work. With the passage of time, firms can make more adjustments, per-

haps training additional workers or buying additional tools and other equipment.

For the orange grower, if the price of oranges falls, some pickers can be laid off and oranges left on the trees to rot. Or if the price of oranges rises, the grower can use more fertilizer and improved irrigation to increase the yields of their existing trees.

But an orange grower can't change the number of trees producing oranges in the short run.

Long-Run Supply The response of the quantity supplied to a price change after *all* the technologically possible ways of adjusting supply have been exploited is determined by *long-run supply*. For most goods and services, long-run supply is elastic and perhaps perfectly elastic.

For the orange grower, the long run is the time it takes new tree plantings to grow to full maturity—about 15 years. In some cases, the long-run adjustment occurs only after a completely new production plant has been built and workers have been trained to operate it—typically a process that might take several years.

REVIEW QUIZ

1 Why do we need a units-free measure of the responsiveness of the quantity supplied of a good or service to a change in its price?

2 Define the elasticity of supply and show how it is calculated.

3 What are the main influences on the elasticity of supply that make the supply of some goods elastic and the supply of other goods inelastic?

4 Provide examples of goods or services whose elasticities of supply are (a) zero, (b) greater than zero but less than infinity, and (c) infinity.

5 How does the time frame over which a supply decision is made influence the elasticity of supply? Explain your answer.

You can work these questions in Study Plan 4.3 and get instant feedback.

◆ You have now learned about the elasticities of demand and supply. Table 4.1 summarizes all the elasticities that you've met in this chapter. In the next chapter, we study the efficiency of competitive markets. But first study *Reading Between the Lines* on pp. 98–99, which puts the elasticity of demand to work and looks at the market for winter tomatoes.

TABLE 4.1 A Compact Glossary of Elasticities

Price Elasticities of Demand

A relationship is described as	When its magnitude is	Which means that
Perfectly elastic	Infinity	The smallest possible increase in price causes an infinitely large decrease in the quantity demanded*
Elastic	Less than infinity	The percentage decrease in the quantity demanded exceeds the percentage increase in price
Unit elastic	1	The percentage decrease in the quantity demanded equals the percentage increase in price
Inelastic	Less than 1 but greater than zero	The percentage decrease in the quantity demanded is less than the percentage increase in price
Perfectly inelastic	Zero	The quantity demanded is the same at all prices

Cross Elasticities of Demand

A relationship is described as	When its value is	Which means that
Close substitutes	Large	The smallest possible increase in the price of one good causes an infinitely large increase in the quantity demanded of the other good
Substitutes	Positive	If the price of one good increases, the quantity demanded of the other good also increases
Unrelated goods	Zero	If the price of one good increases, the quantity demanded of the other good remains the same
Complements	Negative	If the price of one good increases, the quantity demanded of the other good decreases

Income Elasticities of Demand

A relationship is described as	When its value is	Which means that
Income elastic (normal good)	Greater than 1	The percentage increase in the quantity demanded is greater than the percentage increase in income
Income inelastic (normal good)	Less than 1 but greater than zero	The percentage increase in the quantity demanded is greater than zero but less than the percentage increase in income
Negative (inferior good)	Less than zero	When income increases, quantity demanded decreases

Elasticities of Supply

A relationship is described as	When its magnitude is	Which means that
Perfectly elastic	Infinity	The smallest possible increase in price causes an infinitely large increase in the quantity supplied
Elastic	Less than infinity but greater than 1	The percentage increase in the quantity supplied exceeds the percentage increase in the price
Unit elastic	1	The percentage increase in the quantity supplied equals the percentage increase in the price
Inelastic	Greater than zero but less than 1	The percentage increase in the quantity supplied is less than the percentage increase in the price
Perfectly inelastic	Zero	The quantity supplied is the same at all prices

*In each description, the directions of change may be reversed. For example, in this case, the smallest possible *decrease* in price causes an infinitely large *increase* in the quantity demanded.

The Elasticities of Demand and Supply for Tomatoes

Frigid Florida Winter Is Bad News for Tomato Lovers

USA Today
March 5, 2010

ST. PETERSBURG, Fla. - A frigid Florida winter is taking its toll on your sandwich. The Sunshine State is the main U.S. source for fresh winter tomatoes, and its growers lost some 70 percent of their crop during January's prolonged cold snap. …

The average wholesale price for a 25-pound box of tomatoes is now $30, up from $6.50 a year ago. Florida's growers would normally ship about 25 million pounds of tomatoes a week; right now, they're shipping less than a quarter of that, according to Reggie Brown of the Florida Tomato Grower's Exchange, a tomato farmer cooperative in Maitland. …

And because high demand has driven up domestic prices, many wholesalers are buying from Mexico instead.

"We're obviously losing market share to Mexico, and there's always a price to pay to get the customer to get back into the Florida market," Brown said.

Florida is the only place where tomatoes are grown on a large scale in the United States during winter. California doesn't grow them until later in the year, and much of that state's crop is used for processed foods, such as ketchup, sauce, and juice. Other states grow tomatoes in greenhouses year-round, but Florida's winter tomato crop is by far the largest. …

Some Wendy's restaurants posted signs saying tomatoes would only be provided upon request because of limited availability. …

ESSENCE OF THE STORY

- Florida is the main U.S. source for fresh winter tomatoes.

- California tomatoes come to market later in the year and are mainly used for ketchup, sauce, and juice.

- Other states grow tomatoes in greenhouses year-round.

- In January 2010, a prolonged cold snap wiped out 70 percent of the Florida crop.

- The average wholesale price for a 25-pound box of tomatoes rose from $6.50 in January 2009 to $30 in January 2010.

- The quantity of tomatoes shipped decreased from a normal 25 million pounds per week to less than a quarter of that quantity.

- "High demand has driven up prices" and wholesalers are buying from Mexico.

- Some restaurants provided tomatoes only on request.

ECONOMIC ANALYSIS

- Using the information provided in this news article supplemented with an independent estimate of the price elasticity of demand, we can find the demand and supply curves in the market for winter tomatoes shown in Fig. 1.

- According to J. Scott Shonkwiler and Robert D. Emerson, two agricultural economists at the University of Florida, the price elasticity of demand for winter tomatoes is 0.8.

- A 1 percent rise in the price of these tomatoes brings a 0.8 percent decrease in the quantity demanded, other things remaining the same.

- According to the news article, in a normal period, the price of Florida winter tomatoes is $6.50 a box (25 pounds) and growers normally ship 25 million pounds a week.

- With the information just stated, we can determine the demand for winter tomatoes. It is the curve D in Figs. 1 and 2. This demand curve passes through the point that shows that 25 million pounds are demanded at a price of $6.50 a box. The elasticity of demand for winter tomatoes is 0.8.

- Figure 2 shows the calculation that confirms the price elasticity of demand is 0.8. When the price rises from $6.50 to $30 a box, as it did in January 2010, the quantity demanded decreases from 25 million to 8 million pounds. Use the numbers and the midpoint formula to confirm that the elasticity of demand is 0.8.

- Figures 1 and 3 show the supply of winter tomatoes. The news article says that Florida growers (the main producers of winter tomatoes) shipped less than a quarter of their normal 25 million pounds a week. So assume that they shipped 6 million pounds a week.

- Other growers (using greenhouses or in Mexico) make up the difference between what the Florida growers supply and the quantity demanded.

- The supply curve in normal times, S_0, must pass through the equilibrium point 25 million pounds and $6.50 a box.

- The supply curve in January 2010, S_1, must pass through the equilibrium point at that time of 8 million pounds and $30 a box. It also passes through the point 6 million pounds and $6.50 a box because that is the quantity that Florida growers would ship even if the price remained at $6.50 a box.

- We can calculate the elasticity of supply by using the numbers in Fig. 3 and the midpoint formula. The elasticity of supply is 0.22, which means that supply is inelastic.

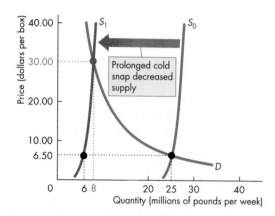

Figure 1 The market for winter tomatoes

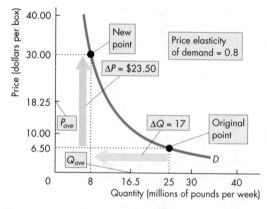

Figure 2 Price elasticity of demand for winter tomatoes

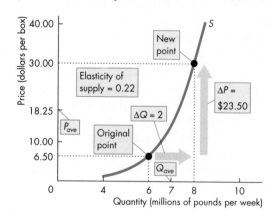

Figure 3 Price elasticity of supply of winter tomatoes

SUMMARY

Key Points

Price Elasticity of Demand (pp. 84–90)

- Elasticity is a measure of the responsiveness of the quantity demanded of a good to a change in its price, other things remaining the same.
- Price elasticity of demand equals the percentage change in the quantity demanded divided by the percentage change in the price.
- The larger the magnitude of the price elasticity of demand, the greater is the responsiveness of the quantity demanded to a given price change.
- If demand is elastic, a cut in price leads to an increase in total revenue. If demand is unit elastic, a cut in price leaves total revenue unchanged. And if demand is inelastic, a cut in price leads to a decrease in total revenue.
- Price elasticity of demand depends on how easily one good serves as a substitute for another, the proportion of income spent on the good, and the length of time elapsed since the price change.

Working Problems 1 to 8 will give you a better understanding of the price elasticity of demand.

More Elasticities of Demand (pp. 91–93)

- Cross elasticity of demand measures the responsiveness of the demand for one good to a change in the price of a substitute or a complement, other things remaining the same.
- The cross elasticity of demand with respect to the price of a substitute is positive. The cross elasticity of demand with respect to the price of a complement is negative.
- Income elasticity of demand measures the responsiveness of demand to a change in income, other things remaining the same. For a normal good, the income elasticity of demand is positive. For an inferior good, the income elasticity of demand is negative.
- When the income elasticity of demand is greater than 1 (income elastic), the percentage of income spent on the good increases as income increases.
- When the income elasticity of demand is less than 1 (income inelastic and inferior), the percentage of income spent on the good decreases as income increases.

Working Problems 9 to16 will give you a better understanding of cross and income elasticities of demand.

Elasticity of Supply (pp. 94–96)

- Elasticity of supply measures the responsiveness of the quantity supplied of a good to a change in its price, other things remaining the same.
- The elasticity of supply is usually positive and ranges between zero (vertical supply curve) and infinity (horizontal supply curve).
- Supply decisions have three time frames: momentary, short run, and long run.
- Momentary supply refers to the response of the quantity supplied to a price change at the instant that the price changes.
- Short-run supply refers to the response of the quantity supplied to a price change after some of the technologically feasible adjustments in production have been made.
- Long-run supply refers to the response of the quantity supplied to a price change when all the technologically feasible adjustments in production have been made.

Working Problems 17 and 18 will give you a better understanding of the elasticity of supply.

Key Terms

Cross elasticity of demand, 91
Elastic demand, 87
Elasticity of supply, 94
Income elasticity of demand, 92

Inelastic demand, 86
Perfectly elastic demand, 87
Perfectly inelastic demand, 86
Price elasticity of demand, 84

Total revenue, 88
Total revenue test, 88
Unit elastic demand, 86

STUDY PLAN PROBLEMS AND APPLICATIONS

 myeconlab You can work Problems 1 to 18 in MyEconLab Chapter 4 Study Plan and get instant feedback.

Price Elasticity of Demand (Study Plan 4.1)

1. Rain spoils the strawberry crop, the price rises from $4 to $6 a box, and the quantity demanded decreases from 1,000 to 600 boxes a week.
   a. Calculate the price elasticity of demand over this price range.
   b. Describe the demand for strawberries.

2. If the quantity of dental services demanded increases by 10 percent when the price of dental services falls by 10 percent, is the demand for dental services inelastic, elastic, or unit elastic?

3. The demand schedule for hotel rooms is

Price (dollars per night)	Quantity demanded (millions of rooms per night)
200	100
250	80
400	50
500	40
800	25

   a. What happens to total revenue when the price falls from $400 to $250 a night and from $250 to $200 a night?
   b. Is the demand for hotel rooms elastic, inelastic, or unit elastic?

4. The figure shows the demand for pens.

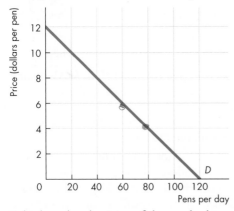

   Calculate the elasticity of demand when the price rises from $4 to $6 a pen. Over what price range is the demand for pens elastic?

5. In 2003, when music downloading first took off, Universal Music slashed the average price of a CD from $21 to $15. The company expected the price cut to boost the quantity of CDs sold by 30 percent, other things remaining the same.

   a. What was Universal Music's estimate of the price elasticity of demand for CDs?
   b. If you were making the pricing decision at Universal Music, what would be your pricing decision? Explain your decision.

6. The demand for illegal drugs is inelastic. Much of the expenditure on illegal drugs comes from crime. Assuming these statements to be correct,
   a. How will a successful campaign that decreases the supply of drugs influence the price of illegal drugs and the amount spent on them?
   b. What will happen to the amount of crime?
   c. What is the most effective way of decreasing the quantity of illegal drugs bought and decreasing the amount of drug-related crime?

7. **The Grip of Gas**
   U.S. drivers are ranked as the least sensitive to changes in the price of gasoline. For example, if the price rose from $3 to $4 per gallon and stayed there for a year U.S. purchases of gasoline would fall only about 5 percent.
   Source: *Slate*, September 27, 2005
   a. Calculate the price elasticity of demand for gasoline. Is the demand for gasoline elastic, unit elastic, or inelastic?
   b. Explain how the price rise from $3 to $4 a gallon changes the total revenue from gasoline sales.

8. **Spam Sales Rise as Food Costs Soar**
   Sales of Spam are rising as consumers realize that Spam and other lower-cost foods can be substituted for costlier cuts of meat as a way of controlling their already stretched food budgets.
   Source: *AOL Money & Finance*, May 28, 2008
   a. Is Spam a normal good or inferior good? Explain.
   b. Would the income elasticity of demand for Spam be negative or positive? Explain.

More Elasticities of Demand (Study Plan 4.2)

9. If a 12 percent rise in the price of orange juice decreases the quantity of orange juice demanded by 22 percent and increases the quantity of apple juice demanded by 14 percent, calculate the
   a. Price elasticity of demand for orange juice.
   b. Cross elasticity of demand for apple juice with respect to the price of orange juice.

10. When Judy's income increased from $130 to $170 a week, she increased her demand for concert tickets by 15 percent and decreased her demand for bus rides by 10 percent. Calculate Judy's income elasticity of demand for (a) concert tickets and (b) bus rides.

11. If a 5 percent rise in the price of sushi increases the quantity of soy sauce demanded by 2 percent and decreases the quantity of sushi demanded by 1 percent, calculate the
   a. Price elasticity of demand for sushi.
   b. Cross elasticity of demand for soy sauce with respect to the price of sushi.

12. **Swelling Textbook Costs Have College Students Saying "Pass"**
   Textbook prices have doubled and risen faster than average prices for the past two decades. Sixty percent of students do not buy textbooks. Some students hunt for used copies and sell them back at the end of the semester; some buy online, which is often cheaper than the campus store; some use the library copy and wait till it's free; some share the book with a classmate.
   Source: *Washington Post*, January 23, 2006
   Explain what this news clip implies about
   a. The price elasticity of demand for college textbooks.
   b. The income elasticity of demand for college textbooks.
   c. The cross elasticity of demand for college textbooks from the campus bookstore with respect to the online price of a textbook.

Use the following information to work Problems 13 to 15.

As Gas Costs Soar, Buyers Flock to Small Cars
Faced with high gas prices, Americans are substituting smaller cars for SUVs. In April 2008, Toyota Yaris sales increased 46 percent and Ford Focus sales increased 32 percent from a year earlier. Sales of SUVs decreased by more than 25 percent in 2008 and Chevrolet Tahoe sales fell 35 percent. Full-size pickup sales decreased more than 15 percent in 2008 and Ford F-Series pickup sales decreased by 27 percent in April 2008. The effect of a downsized vehicle fleet on fuel consumption is unknown. In California, gasoline consumption decreased by 4 percent in January 2008 from a year earlier. The price of gasoline in January 2008 increased by about 30 percent from a year earlier.
   Source: *The New York Times*, May 2, 2009

13. Calculate the price elasticity of demand for gasoline in California.

14. Calculate the cross elasticity of demand for
   a. Toyota Yaris with respect to the price of gasoline.
   b. Ford Focus with respect to the price of gasoline.

15. Calculate the cross elasticity of demand for
   a. Chevrolet Tahoe with respect to the price of gasoline.
   b. A full-size pickup with respect to the price of gasoline.

16. **Home Depot Earnings Hammered**
   As gas and food prices increased and home prices slumped, people had less extra income to spend on home improvements. And the improvements that they made were on small inexpensive types of repairs and not major big-ticket items.
   Source: CNN, May 20, 2008
   a. What does this news clip imply about the income elasticity of demand for big-ticket home-improvement items?
   b. Would the income elasticity of demand be greater or less than 1? Explain.

Elasticity of Supply (Study Plan 4.3)

17. The table sets out the supply schedule of jeans.

Price (dollars per pair)	Quantity supplied (millions of pairs per year)
120	24
125	28
130	32
135	36

Calculate the elasticity of supply when
   a. The price rises from $125 to $135 a pair.
   b. The average price is $125 a pair.

18. **Study Ranks Honolulu Third Highest for "Unaffordable Housing"**
   A study ranks Honolulu number 3 in the world for the most unaffordable housing market in urban locations, behind Los Angeles and San Diego and is deemed "severely unaffordable." With significant constraints on the supply of land for residential development, housing inflation has resulted.
   Source: *Hawaii Reporter*, September 11, 2007
   a. Would the supply of housing in Honolulu be elastic or inelastic?
   b. Explain how the elasticity of supply plays an important role in influencing how rapidly housing prices in Honolulu rise.

ADDITIONAL PROBLEMS AND APPLICATIONS

myeconlab You can work these problems in MyEconLab if assigned by your instructor.

Price Elasticity of Demand

19. With higher fuel costs, airlines raised their average fare from 75¢ to $1.25 per passenger mile and the number of passenger miles decreased from 2.5 million a day to 1.5 million a day.
    a. What is the price elasticity of demand for air travel over this price range?
    b. Describe the demand for air travel.

20. The figure shows the demand for DVD rentals.

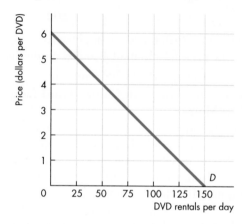

a. Calculate the elasticity of demand when the price of a DVD rental rises from $3 to $5.
b. At what price is the elasticity of demand for DVD rentals equal to 1?

Use the following table to work Problems 21 to 23. The demand schedule for computer chips is

Price (dollars per chip)	Quantity demanded (millions of chips per year)
200	50
250	45
300	40
350	35
400	30

21. a. What happens to total revenue if the price falls from $400 to $350 a chip and from $350 to $300 a chip?
    b. At what price is total revenue at a maximum?

22. At an average price of $350, is the demand for chips elastic, inelastic, or unit elastic? Use the total revenue test to answer this question.

23. At $250 a chip, is the demand for chips elastic or inelastic? Use the total revenue test to answer this question.

24. Your price elasticity of demand for bananas is 4. If the price of bananas rises by 5 percent, what is
    a. The percentage change in the quantity of bananas you buy?
    b. The change in your expenditure on bananas?

25. **As Gasoline Prices Soar, Americans Slowly Adapt**

    As gas prices rose in March 2008, Americans drove 11 billion fewer miles than in March 2007. Realizing that prices are not going down, Americans are adapting to higher energy costs. Americans spend 3.7 percent of their disposable income on transportation fuels. How much we spend on gasoline depends on the choices we make: what car we drive, where we live, how much time we spend driving, and where we choose to go. For many people, higher energy costs mean fewer restaurant meals, deferred weekend outings with the kids, less air travel, and more time closer to home.
    Source: *International Herald Tribune*, May 23, 2008
    a. List and explain the elasticities of demand that are implicitly referred to in the news clip.
    b. Why, according to the news clip, is the demand for gasoline inelastic?

More Elasticities of Demand

Use this information to work Problems 26 and 27.
Economy Forces Many to Shorten Summer Vacation Plans
This year Americans are taking fewer exotic holidays by air and instead are visiting local scenic places by car. The global financial crisis has encouraged many Americans to cut their holiday budgets.
Source: *USA Today*, May 22, 2009

26. Given the prices of the two holidays, is the income elasticity of demand for exotic holidays positive or negative? Are exotic holidays a normal good or an inferior good? Are local holidays a normal good or an inferior good?

27. Are exotic holidays and local holidays substitutes? Explain your answer.

28. When Alex's income was $3,000, he bought 4 bagels and 12 donuts a month. Now his income is $5,000 and he buys 8 bagels and 6 donuts a month.

Calculate Alex's income elasticity of demand for

a. Bagels.

b. Donuts.

29. **Wal-Mart's Recession-Time Pet Project**

During the recession, Wal-Mart moved its pet food and supplies to in front of its other fast-growing business, baby products. Retail experts point out that kids and pets tend to be fairly recession-resistant businesses—even in a recession, dogs will be fed and kids will get their toys.

Source: CNN, May 13, 2008

a. What does this news clip imply about the income elasticity of demand for pet food and baby products?

b. Would the income elasticity of demand be greater or less than 1? Explain.

30. If a 5 percent fall in the price of chocolate sauce increases the quantity of chocolate sauce demanded by 10 percent and increases the quantity of ice cream demanded by 15 percent, calculate the

a. Price elasticity of demand for chocolate sauce.

b. Cross elasticity of demand for ice cream with respect to the price of chocolate sauce.

31. **Netflix to Offer Online Movie Viewing**

Online movie rental service Netflix has introduced a new feature to allow customers to watch movies and television series on their personal computers. Netflix competes with video rental retailer Blockbuster, which added an online rental service to the in-store rental service.

Source: CNN, January 16, 2007

a. How will online movie viewing influence the price elasticity of demand for in-store movie rentals?

b. Would the cross elasticity of demand for online movies and in-store movie rentals be negative or positive? Explain.

c. Would the cross elasticity of demand for online movies with respect to high-speed Internet service be negative or positive? Explain.

32. **To Love, Honor, and Save Money**

In a survey of caterers and event planners, nearly half of them said that they were seeing declines in wedding spending in response to the economic slowdown; 12% even reported wedding cancellations because of financial concerns.

Source: Time, June 2, 2008

a. Based upon this news clip, are wedding events a normal good or inferior good? Explain.

b. Are wedding events more a necessity or a luxury? Would the income elasticity of demand be greater than 1, less than 1, or equal to 1? Explain.

Elasticity of Supply

33. The supply schedule of long-distance phone calls is

Price (cents per minute)	Quantity supplied (millions of minutes per day)
10	200
20	400
30	600
40	800

Calculate the elasticity of supply when

a. The price falls from 40¢ to 30¢ a minute.

b. The average price is 20¢ a minute.

34. **Weak Coal Prices Hit China's Third-Largest Coal Miner**

The chairman of Yanzhou Coal Mining reported that the recession had decreased the demand for coal, with its sales falling by 11.9 percent to 7.92 million tons from 8.99 million tons a year earlier, despite a 10.6 percent cut in the price.

Source: Dow Jones, April 27, 2009

Calculate the price elasticity of supply of coal. Is the supply of coal elastic or inelastic?

Economics in the News

35. After you have studied Reading Between the Lines on pp. 98–99 answer the following questions.

a. Which demand is more price elastic and why: tomatoes in general or Florida winter tomatoes?

b. When cold weather destroyed the Florida crop and more tomatoes came from Mexico and greenhouses, what happened to the supply of tomatoes and the quantity of tomatoes supplied?

c. The news article says the "High demand has driven up prices and wholesalers are buying from Mexico." What does this statement mean? Did demand increase? Did it decrease? Is the news article correct?

d. Reggie Brown says "We're obviously losing market share to Mexico, and there's always a price to pay to get the customer to get back into the Florida market." What does he mean and what does that imply about the elasticity of demand for Florida tomatoes when the price rises and when the price falls?

◆ Describe the alternative methods of allocating scarce resources

◆ Explain the connection between demand and marginal benefit and define consumer surplus; and explain the connection between supply and marginal cost and define producer surplus

◆ Explain the conditions under which markets are efficient and inefficient

◆ Explain the main ideas about fairness and evaluate claims that markets result in unfair outcomes

5

EFFICIENCY AND EQUITY

Every time you decide to buy something, whether it's an everyday pizza or a Valentine's Day rose, you express your view about how scarce resources should be used and you make choices in your *self-interest*. A pizza cook one block away and a Columbian rose grower 2,500 miles away make *their* self-interested choices about what to produce. Markets coordinate these self-interested choices. But do markets do a good job? Do they allocate resources between pizza and roses, and everything else, efficiently?

The market economy generates huge income inequality: *You* can afford to buy a pizza or give a rose, but they might be unaffordable luxuries for a pizza cook and a Columbian rose grower who supply them. Is this situation fair?

Efficiency and fairness (or equity) are the two dimensions of the *social interest*. So our central question in this chapter is: Do markets operate in the social interest?

You will learn how economists approach and answer this question by studying a model market for pizza. At the end of the chapter, in *Reading Between the Lines*, we return to the global market in which roses are traded and see whether this market allocates resources efficiently.

◆ Resource Allocation Methods

The goal of this chapter is to evaluate the ability of markets to allocate resources efficiently and fairly. But to see whether the market does a good job, we must compare it with its alternatives. Resources are scarce, so they must be allocated somehow. Trading in markets is just one of several alternative methods.

Resources might be allocated by

- Market price
- Command
- Majority rule
- Contest
- First-come, first-served
- Lottery
- Personal characteristics
- Force

Let's briefly examine each method.

Market Price

When a market price allocates a scarce resource, the people who are willing and able to pay that price get the resource. Two kinds of people decide not to pay the market price: those who can afford to pay but choose not to buy and those who are too poor and simply can't afford to buy.

For many goods and services, distinguishing between those who choose not to buy and those who can't afford to buy doesn't matter. But for a few items, it does matter. For example, poor people can't afford to pay school fees and doctors' fees. Because poor people can't afford items that most people consider to be essential, these items are usually allocated by one of the other methods.

Command

A **command system** allocates resources by the order (command) of someone in authority. In the U.S. economy, the command system is used extensively inside firms and government departments. For example, if you have a job, most likely someone tells you what to do. Your labor is allocated to specific tasks by a command.

A command system works well in organizations in which the lines of authority and responsibility are clear and it is easy to monitor the activities being per-formed. But a command system works badly when the range of activities to be monitored is large and when it is easy for people to fool those in authority. North Korea uses a command system and it works so badly that it even fails to deliver an adequate supply of food.

Majority Rule

Majority rule allocates resources in the way that a majority of voters choose. Societies use majority rule to elect representative governments that make some of the biggest decisions. For example, majority rule decides the tax rates that end up allocating scarce resources between private use and public use. And majority rule decides how tax dollars are allocated among competing uses such as education and health care.

Majority rule works well when the decisions being made affect large numbers of people and self-interest must be suppressed to use resources most effectively.

Contest

A contest allocates resources to a winner (or a group of winners). Sporting events use this method. Andy Roddick competes with other tennis professionals, and the winner gets the biggest payoff. But contests are more general than those in a sports arena, though we don't normally call them contests. For example, Bill Gates won a contest to provide the world's personal computer operating system.

Contests do a good job when the efforts of the "players" are hard to monitor and reward directly. When a manager offers everyone in the company the opportunity to win a big prize, people are motivated to work hard and try to become the winner. Only a few people end up with a big prize, but many people work harder in the process of trying to win. The total output produced by the workers is much greater than it would be without the contest.

First-Come, First-Served

A first-come, first-served method allocates resources to those who are first in line. Many casual restaurants won't accept reservations. They use first-come, first-served to allocate their scarce tables. Highway space is allocated in this way too: The first to arrive at the on-ramp gets the road space. If too many vehicles enter the highway, the speed slows and people wait in line for some space to become available.

First-come, first-served works best when, as in the above examples, a scarce resource can serve just one user at a time in a sequence. By serving the user who arrives first, this method minimizes the time spent waiting for the resource to become free.

Lottery

Lotteries allocate resources to those who pick the winning number, draw the lucky cards, or come up lucky on some other gaming system. State lotteries and casinos reallocate millions of dollars worth of goods and services every year.

But lotteries are more widespread than jackpots and roulette wheels in casinos. They are used to allocate landing slots to airlines at some airports, places in the New York and Boston marathons, and have been used to allocate fishing rights and the electromagnetic spectrum used by cell phones.

Lotteries work best when there is no effective way to distinguish among potential users of a scarce resource.

Personal Characteristics

When resources are allocated on the basis of personal characteristics, people with the "right" characteristics get the resources. Some of the resources that matter most to you are allocated in this way. For example, you will choose a marriage partner on the basis of personal characteristics. But this method can also be used in unacceptable ways. Allocating the best jobs to white, Anglo-Saxon males and discriminating against visible minorities and women is an example.

Force

Force plays a crucial role, for both good and ill, in allocating scarce resources. Let's start with the ill.

War, the use of military force by one nation against another, has played an enormous role historically in allocating resources. The economic supremacy of European settlers in the Americas and Australia owes much to the use of this method.

Theft, the taking of the property of others without their consent, also plays a large role. Both large-scale organized crime and small-scale petty crime collectively allocate billions of dollars worth of resources annually.

But force plays a crucial positive role in allocating resources. It provides the state with an effective method of transferring wealth from the rich to the poor, and it provides the legal framework in which voluntary exchange in markets takes place.

A legal system is the foundation on which our market economy functions. Without courts to enforce contracts, it would not be possible to do business. But the courts could not enforce contracts without the ability to apply force if necessary. The state provides the ultimate force that enables the courts to do their work.

More broadly, the force of the state is essential to uphold the principle of the rule of law. This principle is the bedrock of civilized economic (and social and political) life. With the rule of law upheld, people can go about their daily economic lives with the assurance that their property will be protected—that they can sue for violations against their property (and be sued if they violate the property of others).

Free from the burden of protecting their property and confident in the knowledge that those with whom they trade will honor their agreements, people can get on with focusing on the activity in which they have a comparative advantage and trading for mutual gain.

REVIEW QUIZ

1 Why do we need methods of allocating scarce resources?
2 Describe the alternative methods of allocating scarce resources.
3 Provide an example of each allocation method that illustrates when it works well.
4 Provide an example of each allocation method that illustrates when it works badly.

You can work these questions in Study Plan 5.1 and get instant feedback.

In the next sections, we're going to see how a market can achieve an efficient use of resources, examine the obstacles to efficiency, and see how sometimes an alternative method might improve on the market. After looking at efficiency, we'll turn our attention to the more difficult issue of fairness.

Benefit, Cost, and Surplus

Resources are allocated efficiently and in the *social interest* when they are used in the ways that people value most highly. You saw in Chapter 2 that this outcome occurs when the quantities produced are at the point on the *PPF* at which marginal benefit equals marginal cost (see pp. 33–35). We're now going to see whether competitive markets produce the efficient quantities.

We begin on the demand side of a market.

Demand, Willingness to Pay, and Value

In everyday life, we talk about "getting value for money." When we use this expression, we are distinguishing between *value* and *price*. Value is what we get, and price is what we pay.

The value of one more unit of a good or service is its marginal benefit. We measure marginal benefit by the maximum price that is willingly paid for another unit of the good or service. But willingness to pay determines demand. *A demand curve is a marginal benefit curve.*

In Fig. 5.1(a), Lisa is willing to pay $1 for the 30th slice of pizza and $1 is her marginal benefit from that slice. In Fig. 5.1(b), Nick is willing to pay $1 for the 10th slice of pizza and $1 is his marginal benefit from that slice. But at what quantity is the market willing to pay $1 for the marginal slice? The answer is provided by the *market demand curve*.

Individual Demand and Market Demand

The relationship between the price of a good and the quantity demanded by one person is called *individual demand*. And the relationship between the price of a good and the quantity demanded by all buyers is called *market demand*.

> The market demand curve is the horizontal sum of the individual demand curves and is formed by adding the quantities demanded by all the individuals at each price.

Figure 5.1(c) illustrates the market demand for pizza if Lisa and Nick are the only people in the market. Lisa's demand curve in part (a) and Nick's demand curve in part (b) sum horizontally to the market demand curve in part (c).

FIGURE 5.1 Individual Demand, Market Demand, and Marginal Social Benefit

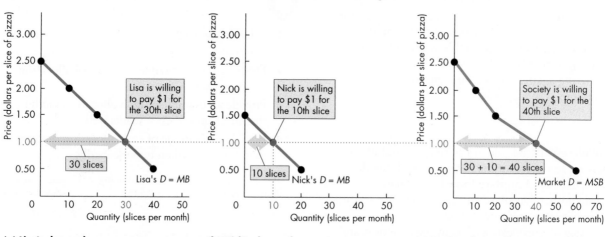

(a) Lisa's demand

(b) Nick's demand

(c) Market demand

At a price of $1 a slice, the quantity demanded by Lisa is 30 slices and the quantity demanded by Nick is 10 slices, so the quantity demanded by the market is 40 slices. Lisa's demand

curve in part (a) and Nick's demand curve in part (b) sum horizontally to the market demand curve in part (c). The market demand curve is the marginal social benefit (*MSB*) curve.

At a price of $1 a slice, Lisa demands 30 slices and Nick demands 10 slices, so the market quantity demanded at $1 a slice is 40 slices.

For Lisa and Nick, their demand curves are their marginal benefit curves. For society, the market demand curve is the marginal benefit curve. We call the marginal benefit to the entire society *marginal social benefit*. So the market demand curve is also the *marginal social benefit* (*MSB*) *curve*.

Consumer Surplus

We don't always have to pay as much as we are willing to pay. We get a bargain. When people buy something for less than it is worth to them, they receive a consumer surplus. **Consumer surplus** is the excess of the benefit received from a good over the amount paid for it. We can calculate consumer surplus as the marginal benefit (or value) of a good minus its price, summed over the quantity bought.

Figure 5.2(a) shows Lisa's consumer surplus from pizza when the price is $1 a slice. At this price, she buys 30 slices a month because the 30th slice is worth exactly $1 to her. But Lisa is willing to pay $2 for the 10th slice, so her marginal benefit from this slice is

$1 more than she pays for it—she receives a surplus of $1 on the 10th slice.

Lisa's consumer surplus is the sum of the surpluses on *all of the slices she buys*. This sum is the area of the green triangle—the area below the demand curve and above the market price line. The area of this triangle is equal to its base (30 slices) multiplied by its height ($1.50) divided by 2, which is $22.50. The area of the blue rectangle in Fig. 5.2(a) shows what Lisa pays for 30 slices of pizza.

Figure 5.2(b) shows Nick's consumer surplus, and part (c) shows the consumer surplus for the market. The consumer surplus for the market is the sum of the consumer surpluses of Lisa and Nick.

All goods and services have decreasing marginal benefit, so people receive more benefit from their consumption than the amount they pay.

Supply and Marginal Cost

Your next task is to see how market supply reflects marginal cost. The connection between supply and cost closely parallels the related ideas about demand and benefit that you've just studied. Firms are in business to make a profit. To do so, they must sell

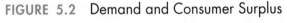

FIGURE 5.2 Demand and Consumer Surplus

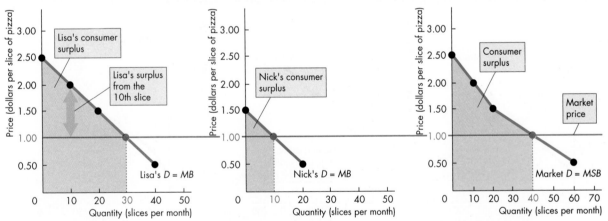

(a) Lisa's consumer surplus

(b) Nick's consumer surplus

(c) Market consumer surplus

Lisa is willing to pay $2.00 for her 10th slice of pizza in part (a). At a market price of $1 a slice, Lisa receives a surplus of $1 on the 10th slice. The green triangle shows her consumer surplus on the 30 slices she buys at $1 a slice.

The green triangle in part (b) shows Nick's consumer surplus on the 10 slices that he buys at $1 a slice. The green area in part (c) shows the consumer surplus for the market. The blue rectangles show the amounts spent on pizza.

myeconlab animation

their output for a price that exceeds the cost of production. Let's investigate the relationship between cost and price.

Supply, Cost, and Minimum Supply-Price

Firms make a profit when they receive more from the sale of a good or service than the cost of producing it. Just as consumers distinguish between value and price, so producers distinguish between *cost* and *price*. Cost is what a firm gives up when it produces a good or service and price is what a firm receives when it sells the good or service.

The cost of producing one more unit of a good or service is its marginal cost. Marginal cost is the minimum price that producers must receive to induce them to offer one more unit of a good or service for sale. But the minimum supply-price determines supply. *A supply curve is a marginal cost curve.*

In Fig. 5.3(a), Max is willing to produce the 100th pizza for $15, his marginal cost of that pizza. In Fig. 5.3(b), Mario is willing to produce the 50th pizza for $15, his marginal cost of that pizza.

What quantity is this market willing to produce for $15 a pizza? The answer is provided by the *market supply curve*.

Individual Supply and Market Supply

The relationship between the price of a good and the quantity supplied by one producer is called *individual supply*. And the relationship between the price of a good and the quantity supplied by all producers is called *market supply*.

> The market supply curve is the horizontal sum of the individual supply curves and is formed by adding the quantities supplied by all the producers at each price.

Figure 5.3(c) illustrates the market supply of pizzas if Max and Mario are the only producers. Max's supply curve in part (a) and Mario's supply curve in part (b) sum horizontally to the market supply curve in part (c).

At a price of $15 a pizza, Max supplies 100 pizzas and Mario supplies 50 pizzas, so the quantity supplied by the market at $15 a pizza is 150 pizzas.

For Max and Mario, their supply curves are their marginal cost curves. For society, the market supply curve is the marginal cost curve. We call the society's marginal cost *marginal social cost*. So the market supply curve is also the *marginal social cost (MSC) curve*.

FIGURE 5.3   Individual Supply, Market Supply, and Marginal Social Cost

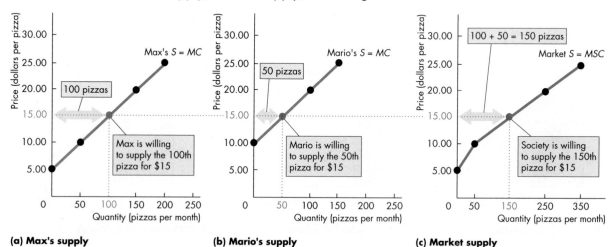

(a) Max's supply   **(b) Mario's supply**   **(c) Market supply**

At a price of $15 a pizza, the quantity supplied by Max is 100 pizzas and the quantity supplied by Mario is 50 pizzas, so the quantity supplied by the market is 150 pizzas. Max's

supply curve in part (a) and Mario's supply curve in part (b) sum horizontally to the market supply curve in part (c). The market supply curve is the marginal social cost (MSC) curve.

Producer Surplus

When price exceeds marginal cost, the firm receives a producer surplus. **Producer surplus** is the excess of the amount received from the sale of a good or service over the cost of producing it. It is calculated as the price received minus the marginal cost (or minimum supply-price), summed over the quantity sold.

Figure 5.4(a) shows Max's producer surplus from pizza when the price is $15 a pizza. At this price, he sells 100 pizzas a month because the 100th pizza costs him $15 to produce. But Max is willing to produce the 50th pizza for his marginal cost, which is $10, so he receives a surplus of $5 on this pizza.

Max's producer surplus is the sum of the surpluses on the pizzas he sells. This sum is the area of the blue triangle—the area below the market price and above the supply curve. The area of this triangle is equal to its base (100) multiplied by its height ($10) divided by 2, which is $500.

The red area below the supply curve in Fig. 5.4(a) shows what it costs Max to produce 100 pizzas.

The area of the blue triangle in Fig. 5.4(b) shows Mario's producer surplus and the blue area in Fig. 5.4(c) shows the producer surplus for the market.

The producer surplus for the market is the sum of the producer surpluses of Max and Mario.

Consumer surplus and producer surplus can be used to measure the efficiency of a market. Let's see how we can use these concepts to study the efficiency of a competitive market.

◆■ REVIEW QUIZ

1 What is the relationship between the marginal benefit, value, and demand?
2 What is the relationship between individual demand and market demand?
3 What is consumer surplus? How is it measured?
4 What is the relationship between the marginal cost, minimum supply-price, and supply?
5 What is the relationship between individual supply and market supply?
6 What is producer surplus? How is it measured?

You can work these questions in Study Plan 5.2 and get instant feedback.   ⓧ myeconlab

---

FIGURE 5.4   Supply and Producer Surplus

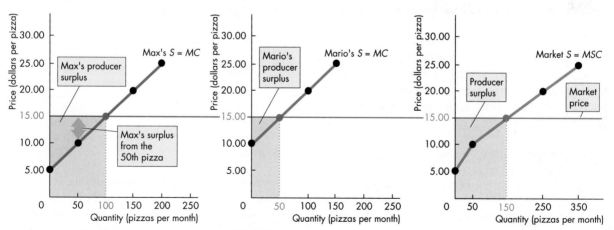

(a) Max's producer surplus   **(b) Mario's producer surplus**   **(c) Market producer surplus**

Max is willing to produce the 50th pizza for $10 in part (a). At a market price of $15 a pizza, Max gets a surplus of $5 on the 50th pizza. The blue triangle shows his producer surplus on the 100 he sells at $15 each. The

blue triangle in part (b) shows Mario's producer surplus on the 50 pizzas that he sells at $15 each. The blue area in part (c) shows producer surplus for the market. The red areas show the cost of producing the pizzas sold.

◆ Is the Competitive Market Efficient?

Figure 5.5(a) shows the market for pizza. The market forces that you studied in Chapter 3 (pp. 66–67) pull the pizza market to its equilibrium price of $15 a pizza and equilibrium quantity of 10,000 pizzas a day. Buyers enjoy a consumer surplus (green area) and sellers enjoy a producer surplus (blue area), but is this competitive equilibrium efficient?

Efficiency of Competitive Equilibrium

You've seen that the market demand curve for a good or service tells us the marginal social benefit from it. You've also seen that the market supply curve of a good or service tells us the marginal social cost of producing it.

Equilibrium in a competitive market occurs when the quantity demanded equals the quantity supplied at the intersection of the demand curve and the supply curve. At this intersection point, marginal social benefit on the demand curve equals marginal social cost on the supply curve. This equality is the condition for allocative efficiency. So in equilibrium, a competitive market achieves allocative efficiency.

Figure 5.5 illustrates the efficiency of competitive equilibrium. The demand curve and the supply curve intersect in part (a) and marginal social benefit equals marginal social cost in part (b).

If production is less than 10,000 pizzas a day, the marginal pizza is valued more highly than it costs to produce. If production exceeds 10,000 pizzas a day, the marginal pizza costs more to produce than the value that consumers place on it. Only when 10,000 pizzas a day are produced is the marginal pizza worth exactly what it costs.

The competitive market pushes the quantity of pizzas produced to its efficient level of 10,000 a day. If production is less than 10,000 pizzas a day, a shortage raises the price, which increases production. If production exceeds 10,000 pizzas a day, a surplus of pizzas lowers the price, which decreases production. So a competitive pizza market is efficient.

Figure 5.5(a) also shows the consumer surplus and producer surplus. The sum of consumer surplus and producer surplus is called **total surplus**. When the efficient quantity is produced, total surplus is maximized. Buyers and sellers acting in their self-interest end up promoting the social interest.

FIGURE 5.5　An Efficient Market for Pizza

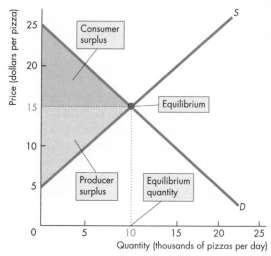

(a) Equilibrium and surpluses

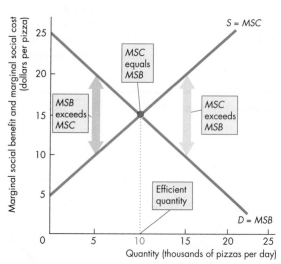

(b) Efficiency

Competitive equilibrium in part (a) occurs when the quantity demanded equals the quantity supplied. Resources are used efficiently in part (b) when marginal social benefit, *MSC*, equals marginal social cost, *MSC*. Total surplus, which is the sum of consumer surplus (the green triangle) and producer surplus (the blue triangle) is maximized.

The efficient quantity in part (b) is the same as the equilibrium quantity in part (a). The competitive pizza market produces the efficient quantity of pizzas.

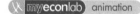 myeconlab animation

Economics in Action

The Invisible Hand

Writing in his *Wealth of Nations* in 1776, Adam Smith was the first to suggest that competitive markets send resources to the uses in which they have the highest value (see p. 51). Smith believed that each participant in a competitive market is "led by an invisible hand to promote an end [the efficient use of resources] which was no part of his intention."

You can see the invisible hand at work in the cartoon and in the world today.

Umbrella for Sale The cold drinks vendor has cold drinks and shade and he has a marginal cost and a minimum supply-price of each. The reader on the park bench has a marginal benefit and willingness to pay for each. The reader's marginal benefit from shade exceeds the vendor's marginal cost; but the vendor's marginal cost of a cold drink exceeds the reader's marginal benefit. They trade the umbrella. The vendor gets a producer surplus from selling the shade for more than its marginal cost, and the reader gets a consumer surplus from buying the shade for less than its marginal benefit. Both are better off and the umbrella has moved to its highest-valued use.

The Invisible Hand at Work Today The market economy relentlessly performs the activity illustrated in the cartoon to achieve an efficient allocation of resources.

A Florida frost cuts the supply of tomatoes. With fewer tomatoes available, the marginal social benefit increases. A shortage of tomatoes raises their price, so the market allocates the smaller quantity available to the people who value them most highly.

A new technology cuts the cost of producing a smart phone. With a lower production cost, the supply of smart phones increases and the price of a smart

© The New Yorker Collection 1985 Mike Twohy from cartoonbank.com. All Rights Reserved.

phone falls. The lower price encourages an increase in the quantity demanded of this now less-costly tool. The marginal social benefit from a smart phone is brought to equality with its marginal social cost.

Market Failure

Markets do not always achieve an efficient outcome. We call a situation in which a market delivers an inefficient outcome one of **market failure**. Market failure can occur because too little of an item is produced (underproduction) or too much is produced (overproduction). We'll describe these two market failure outcomes and then see why they arise.

Underproduction In Fig. 5.6(a), the quantity of pizzas produced is 5,000 a day. At this quantity, consumers are willing to pay $20 for a pizza that costs only $10 to produce. By producing only 5,000 pizzas a day, total surplus is smaller than its maximum possible level. The quantity produced is inefficient—there is underproduction.

We measure the scale of inefficiency by **deadweight loss**, which is the decrease in total surplus that results

FIGURE 5.6   Underproduction and Overproduction

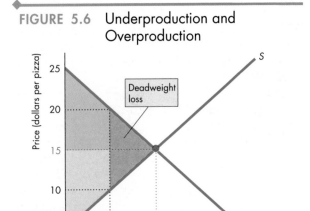

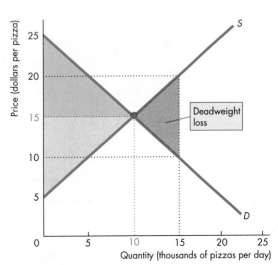

(a) Underproduction

(b) Overproduction

If 5,000 pizzas a day are produced, in part (a), total surplus (the sum of the green and blue areas) is smaller than its maximum by the amount of the deadweight loss (the gray triangle). At all quantities below 10,000 pizzas a day, the benefit from one more pizza exceeds its cost.

If 15,000 pizzas a day are produced, in part (b), total surplus is also smaller than its maximum by the amount of the deadweight loss. At all quantities in excess of 10,000 pizzas a day, the cost of one more pizza exceeds its benefit.

from an inefficient level of production. The gray triangle in Fig. 5.6(a) shows the deadweight loss.

Overproduction In Fig. 5.6(b), the quantity of pizzas produced is 15,000 a day. At this quantity, consumers are willing to pay only $10 for a pizza that costs $20 to produce. By producing the 15,000th pizza, $10 of resources are wasted. Again, the gray triangle shows the deadweight loss, which reduces the total surplus to less than its maximum.

Inefficient production creates a deadweight loss that is borne by the entire society: It is a social loss.

Sources of Market Failure

Obstacles to efficiency that bring market failure and create deadweight losses are

- Price and quantity regulations
- Taxes and subsidies
- Externalities
- Public goods and common resources
- Monopoly
- High transactions costs

Price and Quantity Regulations *Price regulations* that put a cap on the rent a landlord is permitted to charge and laws that require employers to pay a minimum wage sometimes block the price adjustments that balance the quantity demanded and the quantity supplied and lead to underproduction. *Quantity regulations* that limit the amount that a farm is permitted to produce also lead to underproduction.

Taxes and Subsidies *Taxes* increase the prices paid by buyers and lower the prices received by sellers. So taxes decrease the quantity produced and lead to underproduction. *Subsidies*, which are payments by the government to producers, decrease the prices paid by buyers and increase the prices received by sellers. So subsidies increase the quantity produced and lead to overproduction.

Externalities An *externality* is a cost or a benefit that affects someone other than the seller or the buyer. An *external cost* arises when an electric utility burns coal and emits carbon dioxide. The utility doesn't consider the cost of climate change when it decides how much power to produce. The result is overproduction. An *external benefit* arises when an apartment owner installs a smoke detector and decreases her neighbor's fire risk. She doesn't consider the benefit to her neighbor when she decides how many detectors to install. The result is underproduction.

Public Goods and Common Resources A *public good* is a good or service that is consumed simultaneously by everyone even if they don't pay for it. National defense is an example. Competitive markets would underproduce national defense because it is in each person's interest to free ride on everyone else and avoid paying for her or his share of such a good.

A *common resource* is owned by no one but is available to be used by everyone. Atlantic salmon is an example. It is in everyone's self-interest to ignore the costs they impose on others when they decide how much of a common resource to use. The result is that the resource is overused.

Monopoly A *monopoly* is a firm that is the sole provider of a good or service. Local water supply and cable television are supplied by firms that are monopolies. The monopoly's self-interest is to maximize its profit. Because the monopoly has no competitors, it can set the price to achieve its self-interested goal. To achieve its goal, a monopoly produces too little and charges too high a price. It leads to underproduction.

High Transactions Costs When you go to Starbucks, you pay for more than the coffee. You pay your share of the cost of the barrista's time, the espresso maker, and the decor. When you buy your first apartment, you will pay for more than the apartment. You will buy the services of a realtor and a lawyer. Economists call the costs of the services that enable a market to bring buyers and sellers together **transactions costs**.

It is costly to operate *any* market so to use market price to allocate resources, it must be worth bearing the transactions costs. Some markets are too costly to operate. For example, it is too costly to operate a market in time slots on a local tennis court. Instead of a market, the court uses first-come, first-served: You hang around until the court becomes vacant and "pay" with your waiting time. When transactions costs are high, the market might underproduce.

You now know the conditions under which resource allocation is efficient. You've seen how a competitive market can be efficient, and you've seen some obstacles to efficiency. Can alternative allocation methods improve on the market?

Alternatives to the Market

When a market is inefficient, can one of the alternative nonmarket methods that we described at the beginning of this chapter do a better job? Sometimes it can.

Often, majority rule might be used in an attempt to improve the allocation of resources. But majority rule has its own shortcomings. A group that pursues the self-interest of its members can become the majority. For example, a price or quantity regulation that creates inefficiency is almost always the result of a self-interested group becoming the majority and imposing costs on the minority. Also, with majority rule, votes must be translated into actions by bureaucrats who have their own agendas based on their self-interest.

Managers in firms issue commands and avoid the transactions costs that they would incur if they went to a market every time they needed a job done.

First-come, first-served works best in some situations. Think about the scene at a busy ATM. Instead of waiting in line people might trade places at a "market" price. But someone would need to ensure that trades were honored. At a busy ATM, first-come, first-served is the most efficient arrangement.

There is no one efficient mechanism that allocates all resources efficiently. But markets, when supplemented by other mechanisms such as majority rule, command systems, and first-come, first-served, do an amazingly good job.

REVIEW QUIZ

1   Do competitive markets use resources efficiently? Explain why or why not.
2   What is deadweight loss and under what conditions does it occur?
3   What are the obstacles to achieving an efficient allocation of resources in the market economy?

You can work these questions in Study Plan 5.3 and get instant feedback.

Is an efficient allocation of resources also a fair allocation? Does the competitive market provide people with fair incomes for their work? Do people always pay a fair price for the things they buy? Don't we need the government to step into some competitive markets to prevent the price from rising too high or falling too low? Let's now study these questions.

◆ Is the Competitive Market Fair?

When a natural disaster strikes, such as a severe winter storm or a hurricane, the prices of many essential items jump. The reason prices jump is that the demand and willingness to pay for these items has increased, but the supply has not changed. So the higher prices achieve an efficient allocation of scarce resources. News reports of these price hikes almost never talk about efficiency. Instead, they talk about equity or fairness. The claim that is often made is that it is unfair for profit-seeking dealers to cheat the victims of natural disaster.

Similarly, when low-skilled people work for a wage that is below what most would regard as a "living wage," the media and politicians talk of employers taking unfair advantage of their workers.

How do we decide whether something is fair or unfair? You know when you *think* something is unfair, but how do you *know*? What are the *principles* of fairness?

Philosophers have tried for centuries to answer this question. Economists have offered their answers too. But before we look at the proposed answers, you should know that there is no universally agreed upon answer.

Economists agree about efficiency. That is, they agree that it makes sense to make the economic pie as large as possible and to produce it at the lowest possible cost. But they do not agree about equity. That is, they do not agree about what are fair shares of the economic pie for all the people who make it. The reason is that ideas about fairness are not exclusively economic ideas. They touch on politics, ethics, and religion. Nevertheless, economists have thought about these issues and have a contribution to make. Let's examine the views of economists on this topic.

To think about fairness, think of economic life as a game—a serious game. All ideas about fairness can be divided into two broad groups. They are

- It's not fair if the *result* isn't fair.
- It's not fair if the *rules* aren't fair.

It's Not Fair If the *Result* Isn't Fair

The earliest efforts to establish a principle of fairness were based on the view that the result is what matters. The general idea was that it is unfair if people's incomes are too unequal. For example, it is unfair

that a bank president earns millions of dollars a year while a bank teller earns only thousands of dollars. It is unfair that a store owner makes a larger profit and her customers pay higher prices in the aftermath of a winter storm.

During the nineteenth century, economists thought they had made the incredible discovery: Efficiency requires equality of incomes. To make the economic pie as large as possible, it must be cut into equal pieces, one for each person. This idea turns out to be wrong. But there is a lesson in the reason that it is wrong, so this idea is worth a closer look.

Utilitarianism The nineteenth-century idea that only equality brings efficiency is called *utilitarianism*. **Utilitarianism** is a principle that states that we should strive to achieve "the greatest happiness for the greatest number." The people who developed this idea were known as utilitarians. They included the most eminent thinkers, such as Jeremy Bentham and John Stuart Mill.

Utilitarians argued that to achieve "the greatest happiness for the greatest number," income must be transferred from the rich to the poor up to the point of complete equality—to the point at which there are no rich and no poor.

They reasoned in the following way: First, everyone has the same basic wants and a similar capacity to enjoy life. Second, the greater a person's income, the smaller is the marginal benefit of a dollar. The millionth dollar spent by a rich person brings a smaller marginal benefit to that person than the marginal benefit that the thousandth dollar spent brings to a poorer person. So by transferring a dollar from the millionaire to the poorer person, more is gained than is lost. The two people added together are better off.

Figure 5.7 illustrates this utilitarian idea. Tom and Jerry have the same marginal benefit curve, *MB*. (Marginal benefit is measured on the same scale of 1 to 3 for both Tom and Jerry.) Tom is at point *A*. He earns $5,000 a year, and his marginal benefit from a dollar is 3 units. Jerry is at point *B*. He earns $45,000 a year, and his marginal benefit from a dollar is 1 unit. If a dollar is transferred from Jerry to Tom, Jerry loses 1 unit of marginal benefit and Tom gains 3 units. So together, Tom and Jerry are better off—they are sharing the economic pie more efficiently. If a second dollar is transferred, the same thing happens: Tom gains more than Jerry loses. And the same is true for every dollar transferred until they both reach point *C*. At point *C*, Tom and Jerry have $25,000

FIGURE 5.7   Utilitarian Fairness

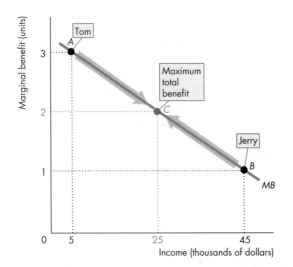

Tom earns $5,000 and has 3 units of marginal benefit at point A. Jerry earns $45,000 and has 1 unit of marginal benefit at point B. If income is transferred from Jerry to Tom, Jerry's loss is less than Tom's gain. Only when each of them has $25,000 and 2 units of marginal benefit (at point C) can the sum of their total benefit increase no further.

each and a marginal benefit of 2 units. Now they are sharing the economic pie in the most efficient way. It brings the greatest happiness to Tom and Jerry.

The Big Tradeoff One big problem with the utilitarian ideal of complete equality is that it ignores the costs of making income transfers. Recognizing the costs of making income transfers leads to what is called the **big tradeoff**, which is a tradeoff between efficiency and fairness.

The big tradeoff is based on the following facts. Income can be transferred from people with high incomes to people with low incomes only by taxing the high incomes. Taxing people's income from employment makes them work less. It results in the quantity of labor being less than the efficient quantity. Taxing people's income from capital makes them save less. It results in the quantity of capital being less than the efficient quantity. With smaller quantities of both labor and capital, the quantity of goods and services produced is less than the efficient quantity. The economic pie shrinks.

The tradeoff is between the size of the economic pie and the degree of equality with which it is shared. The greater the amount of income redistribution through income taxes, the greater is the inefficiency— the smaller is the economic pie.

There is a second source of inefficiency. A dollar taken from a rich person does not end up as a dollar in the hands of a poorer person. Some of the dollar is spent on administration of the tax and transfer system. The cost of tax-collecting agencies, such as the Internal Revenue Service (IRS), and welfare-administering agencies, such as the Centers for Medicare and Medicaid, must be paid with some of the taxes collected. Also, taxpayers hire accountants, auditors, and lawyers to help them ensure that they pay the correct amount of taxes. These activities use skilled labor and capital resources that could otherwise be used to produce goods and services that people value.

When all these costs are taken into account, taking a dollar from a rich person does not give a dollar to a poor person. It is possible that with high taxes, people with low incomes might end up being worse off. Suppose, for example, that highly taxed entrepreneurs decide to work less hard and shut down some of their businesses. Low-income workers get fired and must seek other, perhaps even lower-paid, work.

Today, because of the big tradeoff, no one says that fairness requires equality of incomes.

Make the Poorest as Well Off as Possible A new solution to the big-tradeoff problem was proposed by philosopher John Rawls in a classic book entitled *A Theory of Justice*, published in 1971. Rawls says that, taking all the costs of income transfers into account, the fair distribution of the economic pie is the one that makes the poorest person as well off as possible. The incomes of rich people should be taxed, and after paying the costs of administering the tax and transfer system, what is left should be transferred to the poor. But the taxes must not be so high that they make the economic pie shrink to the point at which the poorest person ends up with a smaller piece. A bigger share of a smaller pie can be less than a smaller share of a bigger pie. The goal is to make the piece enjoyed by the poorest person as big as possible. Most likely, this piece will not be an equal share.

The "fair results" idea requires a change in the results after the game is over. Some economists say that these changes are themselves unfair and propose a different way of thinking about fairness.

It's Not Fair If the *Rules* Aren't Fair

The idea that it's not fair if the rules aren't fair is based on a fundamental principle that seems to be hardwired into the human brain: the symmetry principle. The **symmetry principle** is the requirement that people in similar situations be treated similarly. It is the moral principle that lies at the center of all the big religions and that says, in some form or other, "Behave toward other people in the way you expect them to behave toward you."

In economic life, this principle translates into *equality of opportunity*. But equality of opportunity to do what? This question is answered by the philosopher Robert Nozick in a book entitled *Anarchy, State, and Utopia*, published in 1974.

Nozick argues that the idea of fairness as an outcome or result cannot work and that fairness must be based on the fairness of the rules. He suggests that fairness obeys two rules:

1. The state must enforce laws that establish and protect private property.
2. Private property may be transferred from one person to another only by voluntary exchange.

The first rule says that everything that is valuable must be owned by individuals and that the state must ensure that theft is prevented. The second rule says that the only legitimate way a person can acquire property is to buy it in exchange for something else that the person owns. If these rules, which are the only fair rules, are followed, then the result is fair. It doesn't matter how unequally the economic pie is shared, provided that the pie is made by people, each one of whom voluntarily provides services in exchange for the share of the pie offered in compensation.

These rules satisfy the symmetry principle. If these rules are not followed, the symmetry principle is broken. You can see these facts by imagining a world in which the laws are not followed.

First, suppose that some resources or goods are not owned. They are common property. Then everyone is free to participate in a grab to use them. The strongest will prevail. But when the strongest prevails, the strongest effectively *owns* the resources or goods in question and prevents others from enjoying them.

Second, suppose that we do not insist on voluntary exchange for transferring ownership of resources from one person to another. The alternative is *involuntary* transfer. In simple language, the alternative is theft.

Both of these situations violate the symmetry principle. Only the strong acquire what they want. The weak end up with only the resources and goods that the strong don't want.

In a majority-rule political system, the strong are those in the majority or those with enough resources to influence opinion and achieve a majority.

In contrast, if the two rules of fairness are followed, everyone, strong and weak, is treated in a similar way. All individuals are free to use their resources and human skills to create things that are valued by themselves and others and to exchange the fruits of their efforts with all others. This set of arrangements is the only one that obeys the symmetry principle.

Fairness and Efficiency If private property rights are enforced and if voluntary exchange takes place in a competitive market, resources will be allocated efficiently if there are no

1. Price and quantity regulations
2. Taxes and subsidies
3. Externalities
4. Public goods and common resources
5. Monopolies
6. High transactions costs

And according to the Nozick rules, the resulting distribution of income and wealth will be fair. Let's study an example to check the claim that if resources are allocated efficiently, they are also allocated fairly.

Case Study: A Water Shortage in a Natural Disaster

An earthquake has broken the pipes that deliver drinking water to a city. Bottled water is available, but there is no tap water. What is the fair way to allocate the bottled water?

Market Price Suppose that if the water is allocated by market price, the price jumps to $8 a bottle—five times its normal price. At this price, the people who own water can make a large profit by selling it. People who are willing and able to pay $8 a bottle get the water. And because most people can't afford the $8 price, they end up either without water or consuming just a few drops a day.

You can see that the water is being used efficiently. There is a fixed amount available, some people are willing to pay $8 to get a bottle, and the water goes to those people. The people who own and sell water receive a large producer surplus and total surplus is maximized.

In the rules view, the outcome is fair. No one is denied the water they are willing to pay for. In the results view, the outcome would most likely be regarded as unfair. The lucky owners of water make a killing, and the poorest end up the thirstiest.

Nonmarket Methods Suppose that by a majority vote, the citizens decide that the government will buy all the water, pay for it with a tax, and use one of the nonmarket methods to allocate the water to the citizens. The possibilities now are

Command Someone decides who is the most deserving and needy. Perhaps everyone is given an equal share. Or perhaps government officials and their families end up with most of the water.

Contest Bottles of water are prizes that go to those who are best at a particular contest.

First-come, first-served Water goes to the first off the mark or to those who place the lowest value on their time and can afford to wait in line.

Lottery Water goes to those in luck.

Personal characteristics Water goes to those with the "right" characteristics. Perhaps the old, the young, or pregnant women get the water.

Except by chance, none of these methods delivers an allocation of water that is either fair or efficient. It is unfair in the rules view because the distribution involves involuntary transfers of resources among citizens. It is unfair in the results view because the poorest don't end up being made as well off as possible.

The allocation is inefficient for two reasons. First, resources have been used to operate the allocation scheme. Second, some people are willing to pay for more water than the quantity they have been allocated and others have been allocated more water than they are willing to pay for.

The second source of inefficiency can be overcome if, after the nonmarket allocation, people are permitted to trade water at its market price. Those who value the water they have at less than the market price sell, and people who are willing to pay the market price to obtain more water buy. Those who value the water most highly are the ones who consume it.

Market Price with Taxes Another approach is to allocate the scarce water using the market price but then to alter the redistribution of buying power by taxing the sellers and providing benefits to the poor.

Suppose water owners are taxed on each bottle sold and the revenue from these taxes is given to the poorest people. People are then free, starting from this new distribution of buying power, to trade water at the market price.

Because the owners of water are taxed on what they sell, they have a weaker incentive to offer water for sale and the supply decreases. The equilibrium price rises to more than $8 a bottle. There is now a deadweight loss in the market for water—similar to the loss that arises from underproduction on pp. 113–114. (We study the effects of a tax and show its inefficiency in Chapter 6 on pp. 133–138.)

So the tax is inefficient. In the rules view, the tax is also unfair because it forces the owners of water to make a transfer to others. In the results view, the outcome might be regarded as being fair.

This brief case study illustrates the complexity of ideas about fairness. Economists have a clear criterion of efficiency but no comparably clear criterion of fairness. Most economists regard Nozick as being too extreme and want a fair tax system, but there is no consensus about what a fair tax system looks like.

 REVIEW QUIZ

1 What are the two big approaches to thinking about fairness?
2 What is the utilitarian idea of fairness and what is wrong with it?
3 Explain the big tradeoff. What idea of fairness has been developed to deal with it?
4 What is the idea of fairness based on fair rules?

You can work these questions in Study Plan 5.4 and get instant feedback.

◆ You've now studied efficiency and equity (fairness), the two biggest issues that run through the whole of economics. *Reading Between the Lines* on pp. 120–121 looks at an example of an efficient market in our economy today. At many points throughout this book—and in your life—you will return to and use the ideas you've learned in this chapter. We start in the next chapter where we study some sources of *in*efficiency and *un*fairness.

Is the Global Market for Roses Efficient?

More Ash Fallout: 10 Million Roses Ruined

http://www.cbsnews.com
April 19, 2010

NAIROBI, Kenya—Daniel Oyier has been eating only once a day since an ash-belching volcano more than 5,000 miles away caused him to be laid off from his $4-a-day job packing red roses and white lilies for export to Paris and Amsterdam.

Some 5,000 day laborers in Kenya have been without work since the ash cloud from Iceland shut down air traffic across Europe, showing how one event can have drastic consequences in distant lands in today's global economy. ...

Kenya has thrown away 10 million flowers—mostly roses—since the volcano eruption. ...

The world's biggest flower auction in the Dutch town of Aalsmeer saw a drop of 15 percent in flowers sold on Monday as a result of flight disruptions from the volcanic ash cloud. ...

Farmers have been forced to find alternative routes to get their products to market—even at a loss. They flew 1,000 metric tons of flowers to Spain on Monday, from where it would be transported by road to Paris and Amsterdam. ...

Other flower-growing regions have seen sales fall because of the eruption. ...

Willem Verhoogt [a South African exporter said his firm was] ... supposed to export 11,000 pounds of fresh cut flowers mainly to Europe, and to the United States via flights through Europe.

"All together, it could be between 10 to 15 tons that won't go in the end," he said. "We've advised farmers not to pick flowers anymore."

ESSENCE OF THE STORY

- In April 2010, the global fresh flower market was disrupted by the ash cloud from an erupting volcano in Iceland that shut down Europe's air traffic.

- Many of the world's flowers are traded at auction in the Dutch town of Aalsmeer, which saw a drop of 15 percent in the quantity of flowers sold.

- 5,000 workers in Kenya who pick and pack flowers were without work.

- Kenya's flower growers threw away 10 million flowers—mostly roses.

- South African flower growers were prevented from shipping as much as 15 tons of fresh cut flowers to Europe and the United States.

- Some farmers found alternative but more costly routes to get their flowers to market.

ECONOMIC ANALYSIS

- Roses are traded in a global market.

- Most of the roses sold in the United States come from Columbia and Ecuador, but the world's largest cut flower market is in Aalsmeer, Holland, where 75 percent of the world's flowers are traded every day.

- On a normal day, flowers arrive by air from Africa, Central and South America, the Middle East, and Asia and are traded at auction, and then delivered by air to the United States, Canada, and other destinations.

- Figure 1 illustrates the market on a normal day. The demand and marginal benefit curve is $D_0 = MSB_0$; the supply and marginal cost curve is $S_0 = MSC_0$; and the auction finds the equilibrium and efficient outcome.

- April 19, 2010, was not a normal day. The eruption of a volcano in Iceland closed northern Europe's air transportation. Flowers could not be transported either in or out of Holland by air.

- Alternative but more costly arrangements were quickly made to fly flowers in and out of Athens (Greece) and Madrid (Spain) and transport them by truck from these cities to Aalsmeer.

- Figure 2 shows the situation on April 19. Supply decreased because the cost of inbound transportation increased. Demand decreased because the cost of outbound transportation increased.

- The demand and marginal benefit curve is $D_1 = MSB_1$; the supply and marginal cost curve is $S_1 = MSC_1$; and the auction finds the new equilibrium and efficient outcome.

Traders in the flower auction at Aalsmeer, Holland, find the equilibrium prices.

- It turned out that the quantity decreased by 20 percent (from 20 million to 16 million), but the price was unchanged. Both demand and supply were influenced by the loss of air transportation and decreased by the same amount.

- Consumer surplus (the green triangle) and producer surplus (the blue triangle) shrank on April 19, but the total surplus was at its maximum given the circumstances.

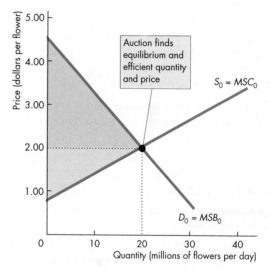

Figure 1 Aalsmeer flower market: Normal day

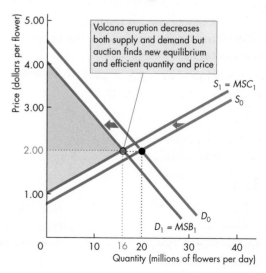

Figure 2 Aalsmeer flower market: April 19, 2010

121

SUMMARY

Key Points

Resource Allocation Methods (pp. 106–107)

- Because resources are scarce, some mechanism must allocate them.
- The alternative allocation methods are market price; command; majority rule; contest; first-come, first-served; lottery; personal characteristics; and force.

Working Study Plan Problems 1 and 2 will give you a better understanding of resource allocation methods.

Benefit, Cost, and Surplus (pp. 108–111)

- The maximum price willingly paid is marginal benefit, so a demand curve is also a marginal benefit curve.
- The market demand curve is the horizontal sum of the individual demand curves and is the marginal social benefit curve.
- Value is what people are *willing to* pay; price is what people *must* pay.
- Consumer surplus is the excess of the benefit received from a good or service over the amount paid for it.
- The minimum supply-price is marginal cost, so a supply curve is also a marginal cost curve.
- The market supply curve is the horizontal sum of the individual supply curves and is the marginal social cost curve.
- Cost is what producers pay; price is what producers receive.

- Producer surplus is the excess of the amount received from the sale of a good or service over the cost of producing it.

Working Study Plan Problems 3 to 10 will give you a better understanding of benefit, cost, and surplus.

Is the Competitive Market Efficient? (pp. 112–115)

- In a competitive equilibrium, marginal social benefit equals marginal social cost and resource allocation is efficient.
- Buyers and sellers acting in their self-interest end up promoting the social interest.
- Total surplus, consumer surplus plus producer surplus, is maximized.
- Producing less than or more than the efficient quantity creates deadweight loss.
- Price and quantity regulations; taxes and subsidies; externalities; public goods and common resources; monopoly; and high transactions costs can lead to market failure.

Working Study Plan Problems 11 to 13 will give you a better understanding of the efficiency of competitive markets.

Is the Competitive Market Fair? (pp. 116–119)

- Ideas about fairness can be divided into two groups: fair *results* and fair *rules*.
- Fair-results ideas require income transfers from the rich to the poor.
- Fair-rules ideas require property rights and voluntary exchange.

Working Study Plan Problems 14 and 15 will give you a better understanding of the fairness of competitive markets.

Key Terms

Big tradeoff, 117
Command system, 106
Consumer surplus, 109
Deadweight loss, 113

Market failure, 113
Producer surplus, 111
Symmetry principle, 118
Total surplus, 112

Transactions costs, 115
Utilitarianism, 116

STUDY PLAN PROBLEMS AND APPLICATIONS

myeconlab You can work Problems 1 to 17 in MyEconLab Chapter 5 Study Plan and get instant feedback.

Resource Allocation Methods (Study Plan 5.1)

Use the following information to work Problems 1 and 2.

At Chez Panisse, the restaurant in Berkeley that is credited with having created California cuisine, reservations are essential. At Mandarin Dynasty, a restaurant near the University of California San Diego, reservations are recommended. At Eli Cannon's, a restaurant in Middletown, Connecticut, reservations are not accepted.

1. a. Describe the method of allocating scarce table resources at these three restaurants.
   b. Why do you think restaurants have different reservations policies?

2. Why do you think restaurants don't use the market price to allocate their tables?

Benefit, Cost, and Surplus (Study Plan 5.2)

Use the following table to work Problems 3 to 5.
The table gives the demand schedules for train travel for the only buyers in the market, Ann, Beth, and Cy.

Price (dollars per mile)	Quantity demanded (miles)		
	Ann	Beth	Cy
3	30	25	20
4	25	20	15
5	20	15	10
6	15	10	5
7	10	5	0
8	5	0	0
9	0	0	0

3. a. Construct the market demand schedule.
   b. What are the maximum price that Ann, Beth, and Cy are willing to pay to travel 20 miles? Why?

4. a. What is the marginal social benefit when the total distance travelled is 60 miles?
   b. What is the marginal private benefit for each person when they travel a total distance of 60 miles and how many miles does each of the people travel?

5. a. What is each traveler's consumer surplus when the price is $4 a mile?

   b. What is the market consumer surplus when the price is $4 a mile?

Use the following table to work Problems 6 to 8.
The table gives the supply schedules of hot air balloon rides for the only sellers in the market, Xavier, Yasmin, and Zack.

Price (dollars per ride)	Quantity supplied (rides per week)		
	Xavier	Yasmin	Zack
100	30	25	20
90	25	20	15
80	20	15	10
70	15	10	5
60	10	5	0
50	5	0	0
40	0	0	0

6. a. Construct the market supply schedule.
   b. What are the minimum prices that Xavier, Yasmin, and Zack are willing to accept to supply 20 rides? Why?

7. a. What is the marginal social cost when the total number of rides is 30?
   b. What is the marginal cost for each supplier when the total number of rides is 30 and how many rides does each of the firms supply?

8. When the price is $70 a ride,
   a. What is each firm's producer surplus?
   b. What is the market producer surplus?

Use the following news clip to work Problems 9 and 10.

eBay Saves Billions for Bidders

If you think you would save money by bidding on eBay auctions, you would likely be right. Two Maryland researchers calculated the difference between the actual purchase price paid for auction items and the top price bidders stated they were willing to pay. They found that the difference averaged at least $4 per auction.

Source: *InformationWeek*, January 28, 2008

9. What method is used to allocate goods on eBay? How does the allocation method used by eBay auctions influence consumer surplus?

10. a. Can an eBay auction give the seller a surplus?

b. On a graph show the consumer surplus and producer surplus from an eBay auction.

Is the Competitive Market Efficient? (Study Plan 5.3)

11. The figure illustrates the competitive market for cell phones.

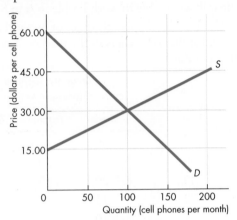

a. What are the equilibrium price and equilibrium quantity of cell phones?
b. Shade in and label the consumer surplus at the competitive equilibrium.
c. Shade in and label the producer surplus at the competitive equilibrium.
d. Calculate total surplus at the competitive equilibrium.
e. Is the competitive market for cell phones efficient?

12. The table gives the demand and supply schedules for sunscreen.

Price	Quantity demanded	Quantity supplied
(dollars per bottle)	(bottles per day)	
0	400	0
5	300	100
10	200	200
15	100	300
20	0	400

Sunscreen factories are required to limit production to 100 bottles a day.

a. What is the maximum price that consumers are willing to pay for the 100th bottle?
b. What is the minimum price that producers are willing to accept for the 100th bottle?
c. Describe the situation in this market.

13. Explain why each restaurant in Problem 1 might be using an efficient allocation method.

Is the Competitive Market Fair? (Study Plan 5.4)

14. Explain why the allocation method used by each restaurant in Problem 1 is fair or not fair.
15. In Problem 12, how can the 100 bottles available be allocated to beach-goers? Which possible methods would be fair and which would be unfair?

Economics in the News (Study Plan 5.N)

16. **The World's Largest Tulip and Flower Market**

   Every day 20 million tulips, roses, and other cut flowers are auctioned at the Dutch market called *The Bloemenveiling*. Each day 55,000 Dutch auctions take place, matching buyers and sellers.

   Source: Tulip-Bulbs.com

   A Dutch auction is one in which the auctioneer starts by announcing the highest price. If no one offers to buy the flowers, the auctioneer lowers the price until a buyer is found.

   a. What method is used to allocate flowers at the Bloemenveiling?
   b. How does a Dutch flower auction influence consumer surplus and producer surplus?
   c. Are the flower auctions at the Bloemenveiling efficient?

17. **Wii Sells Out Across Japan**

   After a two-month TV-ad blitz for Wii in Japan, demand was expected to be much higher than supply. Yodobashi Camera was selling Wii games on a first-come, first-served basis. Eager customers showed up early and those who tried to join the line after 6 or 7 a.m. were turned away—many rushed off to the smaller stores that were holding raffles to decide who got a Wii.

   Source: *Gamespot News*, December 1, 2006

   a. Why was the quantity demanded of Wii expected to exceed the quantity supplied?
   b. Did Nintendo produce the efficient quantity of Wii? Explain.
   c. Can you think of reasons why Nintendo might want to underproduce and leave the market with fewer Wii than people want to buy?
   d. What are the two methods of resource allocation described in the news clip? Is either method of allocating Wii efficient?
   e. What do you think some of the people who managed to buy a Wii did with it?
   f. Explain which is the fairer method of allocating the Wii: the market price or the two methods described in the news clip.

ADDITIONAL PROBLEMS AND APPLICATIONS

myeconlab You can work these problems in MyEconLab if assigned by your instructor.

Resource Allocation Methods

18. At McDonald's, no reservations are accepted; at Puck's at St. Louis Art Museum, reservations are accepted; at the Bissell Mansion restaurant, reservations are essential. Describe the method of allocating table resources in these three restaurants. Why do you think restaurants have different reservations policies?

Benefit, Cost, and Surplus

Use the following table to work Problems 19 to 22. The table gives the supply schedules for jet-ski rides by the only suppliers: Rick, Sam, and Tom.

Price (dollars per ride)	Quantity supplied (rides per day)		
	Rick	Sam	Tom
10.00	0	0	0
12.50	5	0	0
15.00	10	5	0
17.50	15	10	5
20.00	20	15	10

19. What is each owner's minimum supply-price of 10 rides a day?
20. Which owner has the largest producer surplus when the price of a ride is $17.50? Explain.
21. What is the marginal social cost of 45 rides a day?
22. Construct the market supply schedule of jet-ski rides.

Use the following table to work Problems 23 and 24.

The table gives the demand and supply schedules for sandwiches.

Price (dollars per sandwich)	Quantity demanded	Quantity supplied
	(sandwiches per hour)	
0	300	0
1	250	50
2	200	100
3	150	150
4	100	200
5	50	250
6	0	300

23. a. What is the maximum price that consumers are willing to pay for the 200th sandwich?

b. What is the minimum price that producers are willing to accept for the 200th sandwich?
c. If 200 sandwiches a day are available, what is the total surplus?

Is the Competitive Market Efficient?

24. a. If the sandwich market is efficient, what is the consumer surplus, what is the producer surplus, and what is the total surplus?
b. If the demand for sandwiches increases and sandwich makers produce the efficient quantity, what happens to producer surplus and deadweight loss?

Use the following news clip to work Problems 25 to 27.

The Right Price for Digital Music

Apple's $1.29-for-the-latest-songs model isn't perfect and isn't it too much to pay for music that appeals to just a few people? What we need is a system that will be profitable but fair to music lovers. The solution: Price song downloads according to demand. The more people who download a particular song, the higher will be the price of that song; The fewer people who buy a particular song, the lower will be the price of that song. That is a free-market solution—the market would determine the price.

Source: *Slate*, December 5, 2005

Assume that the marginal social cost of downloading a song from the iTunes Store is zero. (This assumption means that the cost of operating the iTunes Store doesn't change if people download more songs.)

25. a. Draw a graph of the market for downloadable music with a price of $1.29 for all the latest songs. On your graph, show consumer surplus and producer surplus.
b. With a price of $1.29 for all the latest songs, is the market efficient or inefficient? If it is inefficient, show the deadweight loss on your graph.

26. If the pricing scheme described in the news clip were adopted, how would consumer surplus, producer surplus, and the deadweight loss change?

27. a. If the pricing scheme described in the news clip were adopted, would the market be efficient or inefficient? Explain.

b. Is the pricing scheme described in the news clip a "free-market solution"? Explain.

Is the Competitive Market Fair?

28. The winner of the men's and women's tennis singles at the U.S. Open is paid twice as much as the runner-up, but it takes two players to have a singles final. Is the compensation arrangement fair?

Economics in the News

29. After you have studied *Reading Between the Lines* on pp. 120–121 answer the following questions.
    a. What is the method used to allocate the world's cut flowers?
    b. Who benefits from this method of resource allocation: buyers, sellers, or both? Explain your answer using the ideas of marginal social benefit, marginal social cost, consumer surplus, and producer surplus.
    c. On April 19, 2010, when the equilibrium quantity of cut flowers decreased by 20 percent, why was the outcome still efficient? Why was there not underproduction and a deadweight loss?
    d. If the government of Holland placed a limit of 15 million a day on the quantity of flowers traded at Aalsmeer, would there be underproduction and a deadweight loss created? Explain your answer.

Use the following news clip to work Problems 30 and 31.

Fight over Water Rates; Escondido Farmers Say Increase would Put Them out of Business

Agricultural users of water pay less than residential and business users. Since 1993, water rates have increased by more than 90 percent for residential customers and by only 50 percent for agricultural users.
Source: *The San Diego Union-Tribune*, June 14, 2006

30. a. Do you think that the allocation of water between agricultural and residential users is likely to be efficient? Explain your answer.
    b. If agricultural users paid a higher price, would the allocation of resources be more efficient?
    c. If agricultural users paid a higher price, what would happen to consumer surplus and producer surplus from water?

31. Is the difference in price paid by agricultural and residential users fair?

32. **MYTH: Price-Gouging Is Bad**
    Mississippi cracked down on gougers after Hurricane Katrina. John Shepperson was one of the "gougers" authorities arrested. Shepperson lives in Kentucky and he watched news reports about Katrina and learned that people desperately needed things. Shepperson thought he could help and make some money, too, so he bought 19 generators. He rented a U-Haul and drove 600 miles to an area of Mississippi that was left without power. He offered to sell his generators for twice what he had paid for them, and people were eager to buy. Police confiscated his generators, though, and Shepperson was jailed for four days for price-gouging.
    Source: *ABC News*, May 12, 2006
    a. Explain how the invisible hand (Shepperson) actually reduced deadweight loss in the market for generators following Katrina.
    b. Evaluate the "fairness" of Shepperson's actions.

Use the following information to work Problems 33 and 34.
Only 1 percent of the world supply of water is fit for human consumption. Some places have more water than they can use; some could use much more than they have. The 1 percent available would be sufficient if only it were in the right place.

33. a. What is the major problem in achieving an efficient use of the world's water?
    b. If there were a global market in water, like there is in oil, how do you think the market would be organized?
    c. Would a free world market in water achieve an efficient use of the world's water resources? Explain why or why not.

34. Would a free world market in water achieve a fair use of the world's water resources? Explain why or why not and be clear about the concept of fairness that you are using.

35. **"Two Buck Chuck" Wine Cult**
    "Two Buck Chuck," is a cheap, good wine. After a year flooding the West Coast market, it is still being sold by the case to wine lovers. An overabundance of grapes has made the wine cheap to bottle—about 5 million cases so far.
    Source: *CBS*, June 2, 2003
    How has "Two Buck Chuck" influenced the consumer surplus from wine, the producer surplus for its producer, and the producer surplus for the producers of other wines?

GOVERNMENT ACTIONS IN MARKETS

After studying this chapter, you will be able to:

◆ Explain how rent ceilings create housing shortages and inefficiency

◆ Explain how minimum wage laws create unemployment and inefficiency

◆ Explain the effects of a tax

◆ Explain the effects of production quotas and subsidies on production, costs, and prices

◆ Explain how markets for illegal goods work

In New York City, where the average weekly wage rate is $1,000, it costs $3,500 a month to rent an average two-bedroom apartment. Can governments cap rents to help renters live in affordable housing? Or instead, can governments make housing more affordable by raising incomes with minimum wage laws?

Taxes put the hand of government in almost every pocket and market. You probably think that you pay more than your fair share of taxes. But who actually pays and who benefits when a tax is cut: buyers or sellers?

In markets for farm products, governments intervene with the opposite of a tax: a subsidy. Sometimes, governments limit the quantities that farms may produce. Do subsidies and production limits help to make markets efficient?

Some people break the law to evade price and wage regulations and taxes and trade in an "underground" economy. How do markets work in the underground economy? In *Reading Between the Lines* at the end of this chapter, we apply what you've learned to the market for low-skilled labor in California and see how governments must be careful to avoid underground markets.

◆ A Housing Market with a Rent Ceiling

We spend more of our income on housing than on any other good or service, so it isn't surprising that rents can be a political issue. When rents are high, or when they jump by a large amount, renters might lobby the government for limits on rents.

A government regulation that makes it illegal to charge a price higher than a specified level is called a **price ceiling** or **price cap**.

The effects of a price ceiling on a market depend crucially on whether the ceiling is imposed at a level that is above or below the equilibrium price.

A price ceiling set *above the equilibrium price* has no effect. The reason is that the price ceiling does not constrain the market forces. The force of the law and the market forces are not in conflict. But a price ceiling *below the equilibrium price* has powerful effects on a market. The reason is that the price ceiling attempts to prevent the price from regulating the quantities demanded and supplied. The force of the law and the market forces are in conflict.

When a price ceiling is applied to a housing market, it is called a **rent ceiling**. A rent ceiling set below the equilibrium rent creates

- A housing shortage
- Increased search activity
- A black market

A Housing Shortage

At the equilibrium price, the quantity demanded equals the quantity supplied. In a housing market, when the rent is at the equilibrium level, the quantity of housing supplied equals the quantity of housing demanded and there is neither a shortage nor a surplus of housing.

But at a rent set below the equilibrium rent, the quantity of housing demanded exceeds the quantity of housing supplied—there is a shortage. So if a rent ceiling is set below the equilibrium rent, there will be a shortage of housing.

When there is a shortage, the quantity available is the quantity supplied and somehow, this quantity must be allocated among the frustrated demanders. One way in which this allocation occurs is through increased search activity.

Increased Search Activity

The time spent looking for someone with whom to do business is called **search activity**. We spend some time in search activity almost every time we make a purchase. When you're shopping for the latest hot new cell phone, and you know four stores that stock it, how do you find which store has the best deal? You spend a few minutes on the Internet, checking out the various prices. In some markets, such as the housing market, people spend a lot of time checking the alternatives available before making a choice.

When a price is regulated and there is a shortage, search activity increases. In the case of a rent-controlled housing market, frustrated would-be renters scan the newspapers, not only for housing ads but also for death notices! Any information about newly available housing is useful, and apartment seekers race to be first on the scene when news of a possible supplier breaks.

The *opportunity cost* of a good is equal not only to its price but also to the value of the search time spent finding the good. So the opportunity cost of housing is equal to the rent (a regulated price) plus the time and other resources spent searching for the restricted quantity available. Search activity is costly. It uses time and other resources, such as phone calls, automobiles, and gasoline that could have been used in other productive ways.

A rent ceiling controls only the rent portion of the cost of housing. The cost of increased search activity might end up making the full cost of housing *higher* than it would be without a rent ceiling.

A Black Market

A rent ceiling also encourages illegal trading in a **black market**, an illegal market in which the equilibrium price exceeds the price ceiling. Black markets occur in rent-controlled housing and many other markets. For example, scalpers run black markets in tickets for big sporting events and rock concerts.

When a rent ceiling is in force, frustrated renters and landlords constantly seek ways of increasing rents. One common way is for a new tenant to pay a high price for worthless fittings, such as charging $2,000 for threadbare drapes. Another is for the tenant to pay an exorbitant price for new locks and keys—called "key money."

The level of a black market rent depends on how tightly the rent ceiling is enforced. With loose enforcement, the black market rent is close to the unregulated rent. But with strict enforcement, the black market rent is equal to the maximum price that a renter is willing to pay.

Figure 6.1 illustrates the effects of a rent ceiling. The demand curve for housing is *D* and the supply curve is *S*. A rent ceiling is imposed at $800 a month. Rents that exceed $800 a month are in the gray-shaded illegal region in the figure. You can see that the equilibrium rent, where the demand and supply curves intersect, is in the illegal region.

At a rent of $800 a month, the quantity of housing supplied is 60,000 units and the quantity demanded is 100,000 units. So with a rent of $800 a month, there is a shortage of 40,000 units of housing.

To rent the 60,000th unit, someone is willing to pay $1,200 a month. They might pay this amount by incurring search costs that bring the total cost of housing to $1,200 a month, or they might pay a black market price of $1,200 a month. Either way, they end up incurring a cost that exceeds what the equilibrium rent would be in an unregulated market.

Inefficiency of a Rent Ceiling

A rent ceiling set below the equilibrium rent results in an inefficient underproduction of housing services. The *marginal social benefit* of housing exceeds its *marginal social cost* and a deadweight loss shrinks the producer surplus and consumer surplus (Chapter 5, pp. 112–114).

Figure 6.2 shows this inefficiency. The rent ceiling ($800 per month) is below the equilibrium rent ($1,000 per month) and the quantity of housing supplied (60,000 units) is less than the efficient quantity (80,000 units).

Because the quantity of housing supplied (the quantity available) is less than the efficient quantity, there is a deadweight loss, shown by the gray triangle. Producer surplus shrinks to the blue triangle and consumer surplus shrinks to the green triangle. The red rectangle represents the potential loss from increased search activity. This loss is borne by consumers and the full loss from the rent ceiling is the sum of the deadweight loss and the increased cost of search.

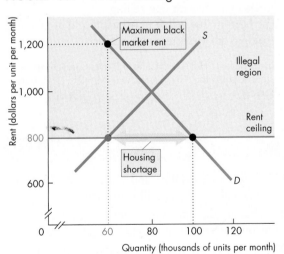

FIGURE 6.1   A Rent Ceiling

A rent above the rent ceiling of $800 a month is illegal (in the gray-shaded illegal region). At a rent of $800 a month, the quantity of housing supplied is 60,000 units. Frustrated renters spend time searching for housing and they make deals with landlords in a black market. Someone is willing to pay $1,200 a month for the 60,000th unit.

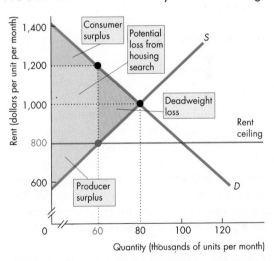

FIGURE 6.2   The Inefficiency of a Rent Ceiling

Without a rent ceiling, the market produces an efficient 80,000 units of housing at a rent of $1,000 a month. A rent ceiling of $800 a month decreases the quantity of housing supplied to 60,000 units. Producer surplus and consumer surplus shrink and a deadweight loss arises. The red rectangle represents the cost of resources used in increased search activity. The full loss from the rent ceiling equals the sum of the red rectangle and gray triangle.

Are Rent Ceilings Fair?

Rent ceilings might be inefficient, but don't they achieve a fairer allocation of scarce housing? Let's explore this question.

Chapter 5 (pp. 116–118) reviews two key ideas about fairness. According to the *fair rules* view, anything that blocks voluntary exchange is unfair, so rent ceilings are unfair. But according to the *fair result* view, a fair outcome is one that benefits the less well off. So according to this view, the fairest outcome is the one that allocates scarce housing to the poorest. To see whether rent ceilings help to achieve a fairer outcome in this sense, we need to consider how the market allocates scarce housing resources in the face of a rent ceiling.

Blocking rent adjustments doesn't eliminate scarcity. Rather, because it decreases the quantity of housing available, it creates an even bigger challenge for the housing market. Somehow, the market must ration a smaller quantity of housing and allocate that housing among the people who demand it.

When the rent is not permitted to allocate scarce housing, what other mechanisms are available, and are *they* fair? Some possible mechanisms are

- A lottery
- First-come, first-served
- Discrimination

A lottery allocates housing to those who are lucky, not to those who are poor. First-come, first-served (a method used to allocate housing in England after World War II) allocates housing to those who have the greatest foresight and who get their names on a list first, not to the poorest. Discrimination allocates scarce housing based on the views and self-interest of the owner of the housing. In the case of public housing, what counts is the self-interest of the bureaucracy that administers the allocation.

In principle, self-interested owners and bureaucrats could allocate housing to satisfy some criterion of fairness, but they are not likely to do so. Discrimination based on friendship, family ties, and criteria such as race, ethnicity, or sex is more likely to enter the equation. We might make such discrimination illegal, but we cannot prevent it from occurring.

It is hard, then, to make a case for rent ceilings on the basis of fairness. When rent adjustments are blocked, other methods of allocating scarce housing resources operate that do not produce a fair outcome.

Economics in Action

Rent Control Winners: The Rich and Famous

New York, San Francisco, London, and Paris, four of the world's great cities, have rent ceilings in some part of their housing markets. Boston had rent ceilings for many years but abolished them in 1997. Many other U.S. cities do not have, and have never had, rent ceilings. Among them are Atlanta, Baltimore, Chicago, Dallas, Philadelphia, Phoenix, and Seattle.

To see the effects of rent ceilings in practice we can compare the housing markets in cities with ceilings with those without ceilings. We learn two main lessons from such a comparison.

First, rent ceilings definitely create a housing shortage. Second, they do lower the rents for some but raise them for others.

A survey[*] conducted in 1997 showed that the rents of housing units *actually available for rent* were 2.5 times the average of all rents in New York, but equal to the average rent in Philadelphia. The winners from rent ceilings are the families that have lived in a city for a long time. In New York, these families include some rich and famous ones. The voting power of the winners keeps the rent ceilings in place. Mobile newcomers are the losers in a city with rent ceilings.

The bottom line is that in principle and in practice, rent ceilings are inefficient and unfair.

---

[*] William Tucker, "How Rent Control Drives Out Affordable Housing," Cato Policy Analysis No. 274, May 21, 1997, Cato Institute.

REVIEW QUIZ

1 What is a rent ceiling and what are its effects if it is set above the equilibrium rent?

2 What are the effects of a rent ceiling that is set below the equilibrium rent?

3 How are scarce housing resources allocated when a rent ceiling is in place?

4 Why does a rent ceiling create an inefficient and unfair outcome in the housing market?

You can work these questions in Study Plan 6.1 and get instant feedback.

You now know how a price ceiling (rent ceiling) works. Next, we'll learn about the effects of a price floor by studying a minimum wage in a labor market.

A Labor Market with a Minimum Wage

For each one of us, the labor market is the market that influences the jobs we get and the wages we earn. Firms decide how much labor to demand, and the lower the wage rate, the greater is the quantity of labor demanded. Households decide how much labor to supply, and the higher the wage rate, the greater is the quantity of labor supplied. The wage rate adjusts to make the quantity of labor demanded equal to the quantity supplied.

When wage rates are low, or when they fail to keep up with rising prices, labor unions might turn to governments and lobby for a higher wage rate.

A government imposed regulation that makes it illegal to charge a price lower than a specified level is called a **price floor**.

The effects of a price floor on a market depend crucially on whether the floor is imposed at a level that is above or below the equilibrium price.

A price floor set *below the equilibrium price* has no effect. The reason is that the price floor does not constrain the market forces. The force of the law and the market forces are not in conflict. But a price floor *above the equilibrium price* has powerful effects on a market. The reason is that the price floor attempts to prevent the price from regulating the quantities demanded and supplied. The force of the law and the market forces are in conflict.

When a price floor is applied to a labor market, it is called a **minimum wage**. A minimum wage imposed at a level that is above the equilibrium wage creates unemployment. Let's look at the effects of a minimum wage.

Minimum Wage Brings Unemployment

At the equilibrium price, the quantity demanded equals the quantity supplied. In a labor market, when the wage rate is at the equilibrium level, the quantity of labor supplied equals the quantity of labor demanded: There is neither a shortage of labor nor a surplus of labor.

But at a wage rate above the equilibrium wage, the quantity of labor supplied exceeds the quantity of labor demanded—there is a surplus of labor. So when a minimum wage is set above the equilibrium wage, there is a surplus of labor. The demand for labor determines the level of employment, and the surplus of labor is unemployed.

FIGURE 6.3 Minimum Wage and Unemployment

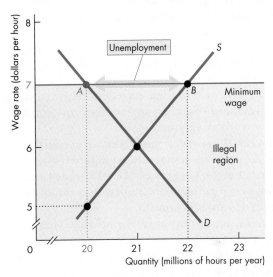

The minimum wage rate is set at $7 an hour. Any wage rate below $7 an hour is illegal (in the gray-shaded illegal region). At the minimum wage of $7 an hour, 20 million hours are hired but 22 million hours are available. Unemployment—AB—of 2 million hours a year is created. With only 20 million hours demanded, someone is willing to supply the 20 millionth hour for $5.

myeconlab   animation

Figure 6.3 illustrates the effect of the minimum wage on unemployment. The demand for labor curve is D and the supply of labor curve is S. The horizontal red line shows the minimum wage set at $7 an hour. A wage rate below this level is illegal, in the gray-shaded illegal region of the figure. At the minimum wage rate, 20 million hours of labor are demanded (point A) and 22 million hours of labor are supplied (point B), so 2 million hours of available labor are unemployed.

With only 20 million hours demanded, someone is willing to supply that 20 millionth hour for $5. Frustrated unemployed workers spend time and other resources searching for hard-to-find jobs.

Inefficiency of a Minimum Wage

In the labor market, the supply curve measures the marginal social cost of labor to workers. This cost is leisure forgone. The demand curve measures the marginal social benefit from labor. This benefit is the value of the goods and services produced. An unregulated labor market allocates the economy's scarce labor resources to the jobs in which they are valued most highly. The market is efficient.

The minimum wage frustrates the market mechanism and results in unemployment and increased job search. At the quantity of labor employed, the marginal social benefit of labor exceeds its marginal social cost and a deadweight loss shrinks the firms' surplus and the workers' surplus.

Figure 6.4 shows this inefficiency. The minimum wage ($7 an hour) is above the equilibrium wage ($6 an hour) and the quantity of labor demanded and employed (20 million hours) is less than the efficient quantity (21 million hours).

Because the quantity of labor employed is less than the efficient quantity, there is a deadweight loss, shown by the gray triangle. The firms' surplus shrinks to the blue triangle and the workers' surplus shrinks to the green triangle. The red rectangle shows the potential loss from increased job search, which is borne by workers. The full loss from the minimum wage is the sum of the deadweight loss and the increased cost of job search.

FIGURE 6.4   The Inefficiency of a Minimum Wage

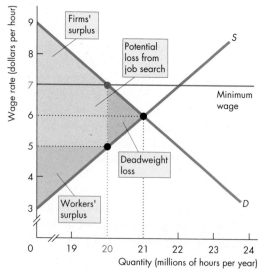

A minimum wage decreases employment. Firms' surplus (blue area) and workers' surplus (green area) shrink and a deadweight loss (gray area) arises. Job search increases and the red area shows the loss from this activity.

myeconlab   animation

Is the Minimum Wage Fair?

The minimum wage is unfair on both views of fairness: It delivers an unfair *result* and imposes an unfair *rule*.

The *result* is unfair because only those people who have jobs and keep them benefit from the minimum wage. The unemployed end up worse off than they would be with no minimum wage. Some of those who search for jobs and find them end up worse off because of the increased cost of job search they incur. Also those who find jobs aren't always the least well off. When the wage rate doesn't allocate labor, other mechanisms determine who finds a job. One such mechanism is discrimination, which is yet another source of unfairness.

The minimum wage imposes an unfair *rule* because it blocks voluntary exchange. Firms are willing to hire more labor and people are willing to work more, but they are not permitted by the minimum wage law to do so.

and less likely to quit, which lowers unproductive labor turnover. They also argue that a higher wage rate makes managers seek ways to increase labor productivity.

Most economists are skeptical about Card and Krueger's argument. Why, economists ask, don't firms freely pay wage rates above the equilibrium wage to encourage more productive work habits? Also, they point to other explanations for the employment responses that Card and Krueger found.

According to Daniel Hamermesh of the University of Texas at Austin, Card and Krueger got the timing wrong. Hamermesh says that firms cut employment *before* the minimum wage is increased in anticipation of the increase. If he is correct, looking for the effects of an increase *after* it has occurred misses its main effects.

Finis Welch of Texas A&M University and Kevin Murphy of the University of Chicago say the employment effects that Card and Krueger found are caused by regional differences in economic growth, not by changes in the minimum wage.

One effect of the minimum wage is an increase in the quantity of labor supplied. If this effect occurs, it might show up as an increase in the number of people who quit school to look for work before completing high school. Some economists say that this response does occur.

REVIEW QUIZ

1 What is a minimum wage and what are its effects if it is set above the equilibrium wage?

2 What are the effects of a minimum wage set below the equilibrium wage?

3 Explain how scarce jobs are allocated when a minimum wage is in place.

4 Explain why a minimum wage creates an inefficient allocation of labor resources.

5 Explain why a minimum wage is unfair.

You can work these questions in Study Plan 6.2 and get instant feedback.

Next we're going to study a more widespread government action in markets: taxes. We'll see how taxes change prices and quantities. You will discover the surprising fact that while the government can impose a tax, it can't decide who will pay the tax! You will also see that a tax creates a deadweight loss.

Taxes

Everything you earn and almost everything you buy is taxed. Income taxes and Social Security taxes are deducted from your earnings and sales taxes are added to the bill when you buy something. Employers also pay a Social Security tax for their workers, and producers of tobacco products, alcoholic drinks, and gasoline pay a tax every time they sell something.

Who *really* pays these taxes? Because the income tax and Social Security tax are deducted from your pay, and the sales tax is added to the prices that you pay, isn't it obvious that *you* pay these taxes? And isn't it equally obvious that your employer pays the employer's contribution to the Social Security tax and that tobacco producers pay the tax on cigarettes?

You're going to discover that it isn't obvious who *really* pays a tax and that lawmakers don't make that decision. We begin with a definition of tax incidence.

Tax Incidence

Tax incidence is the division of the burden of a tax between buyers and sellers. When the government imposes a tax on the sale of a good[*], the price paid by buyers might rise by the full amount of the tax, by a lesser amount, or not at all. If the price paid by buyers rises by the full amount of the tax, then the burden of the tax falls entirely on buyers—the buyers pay the tax. If the price paid by buyers rises by a lesser amount than the tax, then the burden of the tax falls partly on buyers and partly on sellers. And if the price paid by buyers doesn't change at all, then the burden of the tax falls entirely on sellers.

Tax incidence does not depend on the tax law. The law might impose a tax on sellers or on buyers, but the outcome is the same in either case. To see why, let's look at the tax on cigarettes in New York City.

A Tax on Sellers

On July 1, 2002, Mayor Bloomberg put a tax of $1.50 a pack on cigarettes sold in New York City. To work out the effects of this tax on the sellers of cigarettes, we begin by examining the effects on demand and supply in the market for cigarettes.

---

[*] These propositions also apply to services and factors of production (land, labor, capital).

In Fig. 6.5, the demand curve is *D*, and the supply curve is *S*. With no tax, the equilibrium price is $3 per pack and 350 million packs a year are bought and sold.

A tax on sellers is like an increase in cost, so it decreases supply. To determine the position of the new supply curve, we add the tax to the minimum price that sellers are willing to accept for each quantity sold. You can see that without the tax, sellers are willing to offer 350 million packs a year for $3 a pack. So with a $1.50 tax, they will offer 350 million packs a year only if the price is $4.50 a pack. The supply curve shifts to the red curve labeled *S + tax on sellers*.

Equilibrium occurs where the new supply curve intersects the demand curve at 325 million packs a year. The price paid by buyers rises by $1 to $4 a pack. And the price received by sellers falls by 50¢ to $2.50 a pack. So buyers pay $1 of the tax and sellers pay the other 50¢.

A Tax on Buyers

Suppose that instead of taxing sellers, New York City taxes cigarette buyers $1.50 a pack.

A tax on buyers lowers the amount they are willing to pay sellers, so it decreases demand and shifts the demand curve leftward. To determine the position of this new demand curve, we subtract the tax from the maximum price that buyers are willing to pay for each quantity bought. You can see, in Fig. 6.6, that without the tax, buyers are willing to buy 350 million packs a year for $3 a pack. So with a $1.50 tax, they are willing to buy 350 million packs a year only if the price including the tax is $3 a pack, which means that they're willing to pay sellers only $1.50 a pack. The demand curve shifts to become the red curve labeled *D – tax on buyers*.

Equilibrium occurs where the new demand curve intersects the supply curve at a quantity of 325 million packs a year. The price received by sellers is $2.50 a pack, and the price paid by buyers is $4.

Equivalence of Tax on Buyers and Sellers

You can see that the tax on buyers in Fig. 6.6 has the same effects as the tax on sellers in Fig. 6.5. In both cases, the equilibrium quantity decreases to 325 million packs a year, the price paid by buyers rises to $4 a pack, and the price received by sellers falls to $2.50 a pack. Buyers pay $1 of the $1.50 tax, and sellers pay the other 50¢ of the tax.

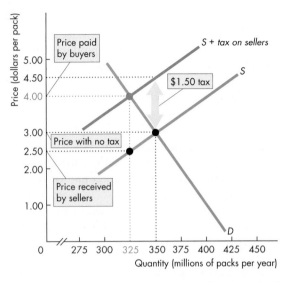

FIGURE 6.5   A Tax on Sellers

With no tax, 350 million packs a year are bought and sold at $3 a pack. A tax on sellers of $1.50 a pack shifts the supply curve from *S* to *S + tax on sellers*. The equilibrium quantity decreases to 325 million packs a year, the price paid by buyers rises to $4 a pack, and the price received by sellers falls to $2.50 a pack. The tax raises the price paid by buyers by less than the tax and lowers the price received by sellers, so buyers and sellers share the burden of the tax.

myeconlab   animation

Can We Share the Burden Equally? Suppose that Mayor Bloomberg wants the burden of the cigarette tax to fall equally on buyers and sellers and declares that a 75¢ tax be imposed on each. Is the burden of the tax then shared equally?

You can see that it is not. The tax is still $1.50 a pack. You've seen that the tax has the same effect regardless of whether it is imposed on sellers or buyers. So imposing half the tax on sellers and half on buyers is like an average of the two cases you've just examined. (Draw the demand-supply graph and work out what happens in this case. The demand curve shifts downward by 75¢ and the supply curve shifts upward by 75¢. The new equilibrium quantity is still 325 million packs a year. Buyers pay $4 a pack, of which 75¢ is tax. Sellers receive $3.25 from buyers, but pay a 75¢ tax, so sellers net $2.50 a pack.)

When a transaction is taxed, there are two prices: the price paid by buyers, which includes the tax; and the price received by sellers, which excludes the tax.

FIGURE 6.6   A Tax on Buyers

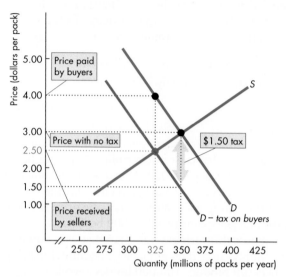

With no tax, 350 million packs a year are bought and sold at $3 a pack. A tax on buyers of $1.50 a pack shifts the demand curve from D to D – tax on buyers. The equilibrium quantity decreases to 325 million packs a year, the price paid by buyers rises to $4 a pack, and the price received by sellers falls to $2.50 a pack. The tax raises the price paid by buyers by less than the tax and lowers the price received by sellers, so buyers and sellers share the burden of the tax.

myeconlab animation

Buyers respond to the price that *includes* the tax and sellers respond to the price that *excludes* the tax.

A tax is like a wedge between the price buyers pay and the price sellers receive. The size of the wedge determines the effects of the tax, not the side of the market on which the government imposes the tax.

The Social Security Tax The Social Security tax is an example of a tax that Congress imposes equally on both buyers and sellers. But the principles you've just learned apply to this tax too. The market for labor, not Congress, decides how the burden of the Social Security tax is divided between firms and workers.

In the New York City cigarette tax example, buyers bear twice the burden of the tax borne by sellers. In special cases, either buyers or sellers bear the entire burden. The division of the burden of a tax between buyers and sellers depends on the elasticities of demand and supply, as you will now see.

Tax Incidence and Elasticity of Demand

The division of the tax between buyers and sellers depends in part on the elasticity of demand. There are two extreme cases:

- Perfectly inelastic demand—buyers pay.
- Perfectly elastic demand—sellers pay.

Perfectly Inelastic Demand Figure 6.7 shows the market for insulin, a vital daily medication for those with diabetes. Demand is perfectly inelastic at 100,000 doses a day, regardless of the price, as shown by the vertical demand curve D. That is, a diabetic would sacrifice all other goods and services rather than not consume the insulin dose that provides good health. The supply curve of insulin is S. With no tax, the price is $2 a dose and the quantity is 100,000 doses a day.

If insulin is taxed at 20¢ a dose, we must add the tax to the minimum price at which drug companies are willing to sell insulin. The result is the new supply curve S + tax. The price rises to $2.20 a dose, but the quantity does not change. Buyers pay the entire tax of 20¢ a dose.

FIGURE 6.7   Tax with Perfectly Inelastic Demand

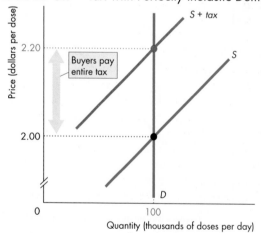

In this market for insulin, demand is perfectly inelastic. With no tax, the price is $2 a dose and the quantity is 100,000 doses a day. A tax of 20¢ a dose shifts the supply curve to S + tax. The price rises to $2.20 a dose, but the quantity bought does not change. Buyers pay the entire tax.

myeconlab animation

Perfectly Elastic Demand Figure 6.8 shows the market for pink marker pens. Demand is perfectly elastic at $1 a pen, as shown by the horizontal demand curve *D*. If pink pens are less expensive than the other colors, everyone uses pink. If pink pens are more expensive than other colors, no one uses pink. The supply curve is *S*. With no tax, the price of a pink pen is $1 and the quantity is 4,000 pens a week.

Suppose that the government imposes a tax of 10¢ a pen on pink marker pens but not on other colors. The new supply curve is *S* + *tax*. The price remains at $1 a pen, and the quantity decreases to 1,000 pink pens a week. The 10¢ tax leaves the price paid by buyers unchanged but lowers the amount received by sellers by the full amount of the tax. Sellers pay the entire tax of 10¢ a pink pen.

We've seen that when demand is perfectly inelastic, buyers pay the entire tax and when demand is perfectly elastic, sellers pay the entire tax. In the usual case, demand is neither perfectly inelastic nor perfectly elastic and the tax is split between buyers and sellers. But the division depends on the elasticity of demand: The more inelastic the demand, the larger is the amount of the tax paid by buyers.

FIGURE 6.8 Tax with Perfectly Elastic Demand

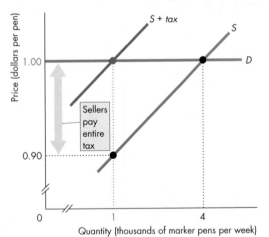

In this market for pink pens, demand is perfectly elastic. With no tax, the price of a pen is $1 and the quantity is 4,000 pens a week. A tax of 10¢ a pink pen shifts the supply curve to *S* + *tax*. The price remains at $1 a pen, and the quantity of pink pens sold decreases to 1,000 a week. Sellers pay the entire tax.

myeconlab animation

Tax Incidence and Elasticity of Supply

The division of the tax between buyers and sellers also depends, in part, on the elasticity of supply. Again, there are two extreme cases:

- Perfectly inelastic supply—sellers pay.
- Perfectly elastic supply—buyers pay.

Perfectly Inelastic Supply Figure 6.9(a) shows the market for water from a mineral spring that flows at a constant rate that can't be controlled. Supply is perfectly inelastic at 100,000 bottles a week, as shown by the supply curve *S*. The demand curve for the water from this spring is *D*. With no tax, the price is 50¢ a bottle and the quantity is 100,000 bottles.

Suppose this spring water is taxed at 5¢ a bottle. The supply curve does not change because the spring owners still produce 100,000 bottles a week, even though the price they receive falls. But buyers are willing to buy the 100,000 bottles only if the price is 50¢ a bottle, so the price remains at 50¢ a bottle. The tax reduces the price received by sellers to 45¢ a bottle, and sellers pay the entire tax.

Perfectly Elastic Supply Figure 6.9(b) shows the market for sand from which computer-chip makers extract silicon. Supply of this sand is perfectly elastic at a price of 10¢ a pound, as shown by the supply curve *S*. The demand curve for sand is *D*. With no tax, the price is 10¢ a pound and 5,000 pounds a week are bought.

If this sand is taxed at 1¢ a pound, we must add the tax to the minimum supply-price. Sellers are now willing to offer any quantity at 11¢ a pound along the curve *S* + *tax*. A new equilibrium is determined where the new supply curve intersects the demand curve: at a price of 11¢ a pound and a quantity of 3,000 pounds a week. The tax has increased the price buyers pay by the full amount of the tax—1¢ a pound—and has decreased the quantity sold. Buyers pay the entire tax.

We've seen that when supply is perfectly inelastic, sellers pay the entire tax, and when supply is perfectly elastic, buyers pay the entire tax. In the usual case, supply is neither perfectly inelastic nor perfectly elastic and the tax is split between buyers and sellers. But how the tax is split depends on the elasticity of supply: The more elastic the supply, the larger is the amount of the tax paid by buyers.

FIGURE 6.9   Tax and the Elasticity of Supply

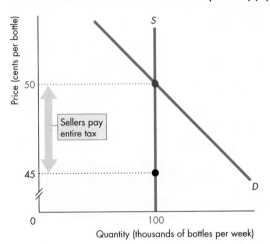

(a) Perfectly inelastic supply

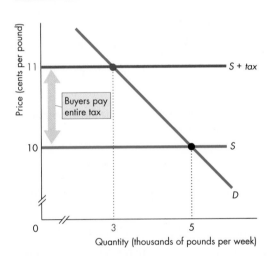

(b) Perfectly elastic supply

Part (a) shows the market for water from a mineral spring. Supply is perfectly inelastic. With no tax, the price is 50¢ a bottle. With a tax of 5¢ a bottle, the price remains at 50¢ a bottle. The number of bottles bought remains the same, but the price received by sellers decreases to 45¢ a bottle. Sellers pay the entire tax.

Part (b) shows the market for sand. Supply is perfectly elastic. With no tax, the price is 10¢ a pound. A tax of 1¢ a pound increases the minimum supply-price to 11¢ a pound. The supply curve shifts to S + tax. The price increases to 11¢ a pound. Buyers pay the entire tax.

myeconlab animation

Taxes and Efficiency

A tax drives a wedge between the buying price and the selling price and results in inefficient underproduction. The price buyers pay is also the buyers' willingness to pay, which measures *marginal social benefit*. The price sellers receive is also the sellers' minimum supply-price, which equals *marginal social cost*.

A tax makes marginal social benefit exceed marginal social cost, shrinks the producer surplus and consumer surplus, and creates a deadweight loss.

Figure 6.10 shows the inefficiency of a tax on MP3 players. The demand curve, *D*, shows marginal social benefit, and the supply curve, *S*, shows marginal social cost. Without a tax, the market produces the efficient quantity (5,000 players a week).

With a tax, the sellers' minimum supply-price rises by the amount of the tax and the supply curve shifts to *S + tax*. This supply curve does *not* show marginal social cost. The tax component isn't a *social* cost of

FIGURE 6.10   Taxes and Efficiency

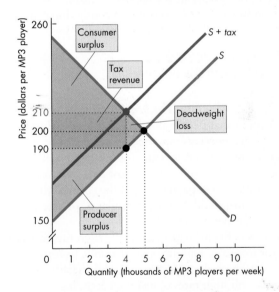

With no tax, 5,000 players a week are produced. With a $20 tax, the buyers' price rises to $210, the sellers' price falls to $190, and the quantity decreases to 4,000 players a week. Consumer surplus shrinks to the green area, and the producer surplus shrinks to the blue area. Part of the loss of consumer surplus and producer surplus goes to the government as tax revenue (the purple area) and part becomes a deadweight loss (the gray area).

myeconlab animation

production. It is a transfer of resources to the government. At the new equilibrium quantity (4,000 players a week), both consumer surplus and producer surplus shrink. Part of each surplus goes to the government in tax revenue—the purple area; part becomes a deadweight loss—the gray area.

Only in the extreme cases of perfectly inelastic demand and perfectly inelastic supply does a tax not change the quantity bought and sold so that no deadweight loss arises.

Taxes and Fairness

We've examined the incidence and the efficiency of taxes. But when political leaders debate tax issues, it is fairness, not incidence and efficiency, that gets the most attention. Democrats complain that Republican tax cuts are unfair because they give the benefits of lower taxes to the rich. Republicans counter that it is fair that the rich get most of the tax cuts because they pay most of the taxes. No easy answers are available to the questions about the fairness of taxes.

Economists have proposed two conflicting principles of fairness to apply to a tax system:

- The benefits principle
- The ability-to-pay principle

The Benefits Principle The *benefits principle* is the proposition that people should pay taxes equal to the benefits they receive from the services provided by government. This arrangement is fair because it means that those who benefit most pay the most taxes. It makes tax payments and the consumption of government-provided services similar to private consumption expenditures.

The benefits principle can justify high fuel taxes to pay for freeways, high taxes on alcoholic beverages and tobacco products to pay for public health-care services, and high rates of income tax on high incomes to pay for the benefits from law and order and from living in a secure environment, from which the rich might benefit more than the poor.

The Ability-to-Pay Principle The *ability-to-pay principle* is the proposition that people should pay taxes according to how easily they can bear the burden of the tax. A rich person can more easily bear the burden than a poor person can, so the ability-to-pay principle can reinforce the benefits principle to justify high rates of income tax on high incomes.

Economics in Action
Workers and Consumers Pay the Most Tax

Because the elasticity of the supply of labor is low and the elasticity of demand for labor is high, workers pay most of the personal income taxes and most of the Social Security taxes. Because the elasticities of demand for alcohol, tobacco, and gasoline are low and the elasticities of supply are high, the burden of these taxes (excise taxes) falls more heavily on buyers than on sellers.

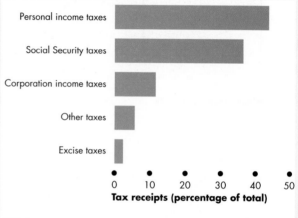

U.S. Taxes

Source of data: Budget of the United States Government, Fiscal Year 2011, Historical Tables, Table 2.2.

◆ REVIEW QUIZ

1 How does the elasticity of demand influence the incidence of a tax, the tax revenue, and the deadweight loss?
2 How does the elasticity of supply influence the incidence of a tax, the quantity bought, the tax revenue, and the deadweight loss?
3 Why is a tax inefficient?
4 When would a tax be efficient?
5 What are the two principles of fairness that are applied to tax systems?

You can work these questions in Study Plan 6.3 and get instant feedback.

Your next task is to study production quotas and subsidies, tools that are used to influence the markets for farm products.

Production Quotas and Subsidies

An early or late frost, a hot dry summer, and a wet spring present just a few of the challenges that fill the lives of farmers with uncertainty and sometimes with economic hardship. Fluctuations in the weather bring fluctuations in farm output and prices and sometimes leave farmers with low incomes. To help farmers avoid low prices and low incomes, governments intervene in the markets for farm products.

Price floors that work a bit like the minimum wage that you've already studied might be used. But as you've seen, this type of government action creates a surplus and is inefficient. These same conclusions apply to the effects of a price floor for farm products.

Governments often use two other methods of intervention in the markets for farm products:

- Production quotas
- Subsidies

Production Quotas

In the markets for sugarbeets, tobacco leaf, and cotton (among others), governments have, from time to time, imposed production quotas. A **production quota** is an upper limit to the quantity of a good that may be produced in a specified period. To discover the effects of a production quota, let's look at what a quota does to the market for sugarbeets.

Suppose that the growers of sugarbeets want to limit total production to get a higher price. They persuade the government to introduce a production quota on sugarbeets.

The effect of the production quota depends on whether it is set below or above the equilibrium quantity. If the government introduced a production quota above the equilibrium quantity, nothing would change because sugarbeet growers would already be producing less than the quota. But a production quota set *below the equilibrium quantity* has big effects, which are

- A decrease in supply
- A rise in price
- A decrease in marginal cost
- Inefficient underproduction
- An incentive to cheat and overproduce
  Figure 6.11 illustrates these effects.

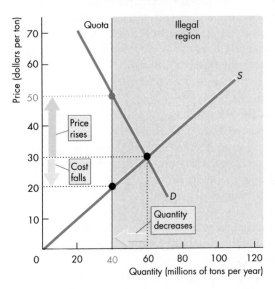

FIGURE 6.11   The Effects of a
Production Quota

With no quota, growers produce 60 million tons a year and the price is $30 a ton. A production quota of 40 million tons a year restricts total production to that amount. The quantity produced decreases to 40 million tons a year, the price rises to $50 a ton, and the farmers' marginal cost falls to $20 a ton. Because marginal social cost (on the supply curve) is less than marginal social benefit (on the demand curve), a deadweight loss arises from the underproduction.

[myeconlab animation]

A Decrease in Supply A production quota on sugarbeets decreases the supply of sugarbeets. Each grower is assigned a production limit that is less than the amount that would be produced—and supplied—without the quota. The total of the growers' limits equals the quota, and any production in excess of the quota is illegal.

The quantity supplied becomes the amount permitted by the production quota, and this quantity is fixed. The supply of sugarbeets becomes perfectly inelastic at the quantity permitted under the quota.

In Fig. 6.11, with no quota, growers would produce 60 million tons of sugarbeets a year—the market equilibrium quantity. With a production quota set at 40 million tons a year, the gray-shaded area shows the illegal region. As in the case of price ceilings and price floors, market forces and political forces are in conflict in this illegal region.

The vertical red line labeled "Quota" becomes the supply curve of sugarbeets at prices above $20 a ton.

A Rise in Price The production quota raises the price of sugarbeets. When the government sets a production quota, it leaves market forces free to determine the price. Because the quota decreases the supply of sugarbeets, it raises the price. In Fig. 6.11, with no quota, the price is $30 a ton. With a quota of 40 million tons, the price rises to $50 a ton.

A Decrease in Marginal Cost The production quota lowers the marginal cost of growing sugarbeets. Marginal cost decreases because growers produce less and stop using the resources with the highest marginal cost. Sugarbeet growers slide down their supply (and marginal cost) curves. In Fig. 6.11, marginal cost decreases to $20 a ton.

Inefficiency The production quota results in inefficient underproduction. Marginal social benefit at the quantity produced is equal to the market price, which has increased. Marginal social cost at the quantity produced has decreased and is less than the market price. So marginal social benefit exceeds marginal social cost and a deadweight loss arises.

An Incentive to Cheat and Overproduce The production quota creates an incentive for growers to cheat and produce more than their individual production limit. With the quota, the price exceeds marginal cost, so the grower can get a larger profit by producing one more unit. Of course, if all growers produce more than their assigned limit, the production quota becomes ineffective, and the price falls to the equilibrium (no quota) price.

To make the production quota effective, growers must set up a monitoring system to ensure that no one cheats and overproduces. But it is costly to set up and operate a monitoring system and it is difficult to detect and punish producers who violate their quotas.

Because of the difficulty of operating a quota, producers often lobby governments to establish a quota and provide the monitoring and punishment systems that make it work.

Subsidies

In the United States, the producers of peanuts, sugarbeets, milk, wheat, and many other farm products receive subsidies. A **subsidy** is a payment made by the government to a producer. A large and controversial Farm Bill passed by Congress in 2008 renewed and extended a wide range of subsidies.

The effects of a subsidy are similar to the effects of a tax but they go in the opposite directions. These effects are

- An increase in supply
- A fall in price and increase in quantity produced
- An increase in marginal cost
- Payments by government to farmers
- Inefficient overproduction

Figure 6.12 illustrates the effects of a subsidy to peanut farmers.

An Increase in Supply In Fig. 6.12, with no subsidy, the demand curve D and the supply curve S determine the price of peanuts at $40 a ton and the quantity of peanuts at 40 million tons a year.

Suppose that the government introduces a subsidy of $20 a ton to peanut farmers. A subsidy is like a negative tax. A tax is equivalent to an increase in cost, so a subsidy is equivalent to a decrease in cost. The subsidy brings an increase in supply.

To determine the position of the new supply curve, we subtract the subsidy from the farmers' minimum supply-price. In Fig. 6.12, with no subsidy, farmers are willing to offer 40 million tons a year at a price of $40 a ton. With a subsidy of $20 a ton, they will offer 40 million tons a year if the price is as low as $20 a ton. The supply curve shifts to the red curve labeled $S - subsidy$.

A Fall in Price and Increase in Quantity Produced The subsidy lowers the price of peanuts and increases the quantity produced. In Fig. 6.12, equilibrium occurs where the new supply curve intersects the demand curve at a price of $30 a ton and a quantity of 60 million tons a year.

An Increase in Marginal Cost The subsidy lowers the price paid by consumers but increases the marginal cost of producing peanuts. Marginal cost increases because farmers grow more peanuts, which means that they must begin to use some resources that are less ideal for growing peanuts. Peanut farmers slide up their supply (and marginal cost) curves. In Fig. 6.12, marginal cost increases to $50 a ton.

Payments by Government to Farmers The government pays a subsidy to peanut farmers on each ton of peanuts produced. In this example, farmers increase production to 60 million tons a year and receive a

FIGURE 6.12   The Effects of a Subsidy

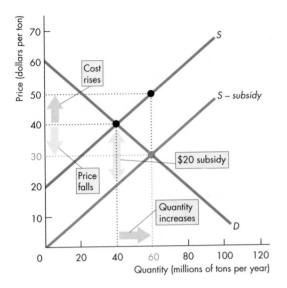

With no subsidy, farmers produce 40 million tons a year at $40 a ton. A subsidy of $20 a ton shifts the supply curve rightward to *S – subsidy*. The equilibrium quantity increases to 60 million tons a year, the price falls to $30 a ton, and the price plus the subsidy received by farmers rises to $50 a ton. In the new equilibrium, marginal social cost (on the supply curve) exceeds marginal social benefit (on the demand curve) and the subsidy results in inefficient overproduction.

 animation

subsidy of $20 a ton. So peanut farmers receive payments from the government that total $1,200 million a year.

Inefficient Overproduction The subsidy results in inefficient overproduction. At the quantity produced with the subsidy, marginal social benefit is equal to the market price, which has fallen. Marginal social cost has increased and it exceeds the market price. Because marginal social cost exceeds marginal social benefit, the increased production brings inefficiency.

Subsidies spill over to the rest of the world. Because a subsidy lowers the domestic market price, subsidized farmers will offer some of their output for sale on the world market. The increase in supply on the world market lowers the price in the rest of the world. Faced with lower prices, farmers in other countries decrease production and receive smaller revenues.

Economics in Action
Rich High-Cost Farmers the Winners

Farm subsidies are a major obstacle to achieving an efficient use of resources in the global markets for farm products and are a source of tension between the United States, Europe, and developing nations.

The United States and the European Union are the world's two largest and richest economies. They also pay their farmers the biggest subsidies, which create inefficient overproduction of food in these rich economies.

At the same time, U.S. and European subsidies make it more difficult for farmers in the developing nations of Africa, Asia, and Central and South America to compete in global food markets. Farmers in these countries can often produce at a lower opportunity cost than the U.S. and European farmers.

Two rich countries, Australia and New Zealand, have stopped subsidizing farmers. The result has been an improvement in the efficiency of farming in these countries. New Zealand is so efficient at producing lamb and dairy products that it has been called the Saudi Arabia of milk (an analogy with Saudi Arabia's huge oil reserve and production.)

International opposition to U.S. and European farm subsidies is strong. Opposition to farm subsidies inside the United States and Europe is growing, but it isn't as strong as the pro-farm lobby, so don't expect an early end to these subsidies.

◆ REVIEW QUIZ

1 Summarize the effects of a production quota on the market price and the quantity produced.
2 Explain why a production quota is inefficient.
3 Explain why a voluntary production quota is difficult to operate.
4 Summarize the effects of a subsidy on the market price and the quantity produced.
5 Explain why a subsidy is inefficient.

You can work these questions in Study Plan 6.4 and get instant feedback.

Governments intervene in some markets by making it illegal to trade in a good. Let's now see how these markets work.

Markets for Illegal Goods

The markets for many goods and services are regulated, and buying and selling some goods is illegal. The best-known examples of such goods are drugs, such as marijuana, cocaine, ecstasy, and heroin.

Despite the fact that these drugs are illegal, trade in them is a multibillion-dollar business. This trade can be understood by using the same economic model and principles that explain trade in legal goods. To study the market for illegal goods, we're first going to examine the prices and quantities that would prevail if these goods were not illegal. Next, we'll see how prohibition works. Then we'll see how a tax might be used to limit the consumption of these goods.

A Free Market for a Drug

Figure 6.13 shows the market for a drug. The demand curve, D, shows that, other things remaining the same, the lower the price of the drug, the larger is the quantity of the drug demanded. The supply curve, S, shows that, other things remaining the same, the lower the price of the drug, the smaller is the quantity supplied. If the drug were not illegal, the quantity bought and sold would be Q_C and the price would be P_C.

A Market for an Illegal Drug

When a good is illegal, the cost of trading in the good increases. By how much the cost increases and who bears the cost depend on the penalties for violating the law and the degree to which the law is enforced. The larger the penalties and the better the policing, the higher are the costs. Penalties might be imposed on sellers, buyers, or both.

Penalties on Sellers Drug dealers in the United States face large penalties if their activities are detected. For example, a marijuana dealer could pay a $200,000 fine and serve a 15-year prison term. A heroin dealer could pay a $500,000 fine and serve a 20-year prison term. These penalties are part of the cost of supplying illegal drugs, and they bring a decrease in supply—a leftward shift in the supply curve. To determine the new supply curve, we add the cost of breaking the law to the minimum price that drug dealers are willing to accept. In Fig. 6.13, the cost of breaking the law by selling drugs (CBL) is added to the minimum price that

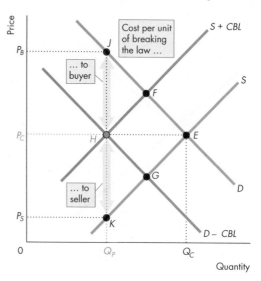

FIGURE 6.13   A Market for an Illegal Good

The demand curve for drugs is D, and the supply curve is S. If drugs are not illegal, the quantity bought and sold is Q_C at a price of P_C—point E. If selling drugs is illegal, the cost of breaking the law by selling drugs (CBL) is added to the minimum supply-price and supply decreases to $S + CBL$. The market moves to point F. If buying drugs is illegal, the cost of breaking the law is subtracted from the maximum price that buyers are willing to pay, and demand decreases to $D - CBL$. The market moves to point G. With both buying and selling illegal, the supply curve and the demand curve shift and the market moves to point H. The market price remains at P_C, but the market price plus the penalty for buying rises—point J—and the market price minus the penalty for selling falls—point K.

dealers will accept and the supply curve shifts leftward to $S + CBL$. If penalties were imposed only on sellers, the market equilibrium would move from point E to point F.

Penalties on Buyers In the United States, it is illegal to *possess* drugs such as marijuana, cocaine, ecstasy, and heroin. Possession of marijuana can bring a prison term of 1 year, and possession of heroin can bring a prison term of 2 years. Penalties fall on buyers, and the cost of breaking the law must be subtracted from the value of the good to determine the maximum price buyers are willing to pay for the drugs. Demand decreases, and the demand curve shifts leftward. In Fig. 6.13, the demand curve shifts to $D - CBL$. If penalties were imposed only on buyers, the market equilibrium would move from point E to point G.

Penalties on Both Sellers and Buyers If penalties are imposed on both sellers *and* buyers, both supply and demand decrease and both the supply curve and the demand curve shift. In Fig. 6.13, the costs of breaking the law are the same for both buyers and sellers, so both curves shift leftward by the same amount. The market equilibrium moves to point H. The market price remains at the competitive market price P_C, but the quantity bought decreases to Q_P. Buyers pay P_C plus the cost of breaking the law, which equals P_B. Sellers receive P_C minus the cost of breaking the law, which equals P_S.

The larger the penalties and the greater the degree of law enforcement, the larger is the decrease in demand and/or supply. If the penalties are heavier on sellers, the supply curve shifts farther than the demand curve and the market price rises above P_C. If the penalties are heavier on buyers, the demand curve shifts farther than the supply curve and the market price falls below P_C. In the United States, the penalties on sellers are larger than those on buyers, so the quantity of drugs traded decreases and the market price increases compared with a free market.

With high enough penalties and effective law enforcement, it is possible to decrease demand and/or supply to the point at which the quantity bought is zero. But in reality, such an outcome is unusual. It does not happen in the United States in the case of illegal drugs. The key reason is the high cost of law enforcement and insufficient resources for the police to achieve effective enforcement. Because of this situation, some people suggest that drugs (and other illegal goods) should be legalized and sold openly but also taxed at a high rate in the same way that legal drugs such as alcohol are taxed. How would such an arrangement work?

Legalizing and Taxing Drugs

From your study of the effects of taxes, it is easy to see that the quantity bought of a drug could be decreased if the drug was legalized and taxed. Imposing a sufficiently high tax could decrease the supply, raise the price, and achieve the same decrease in the quantity bought as does a prohibition on drugs. The government would collect a large tax revenue.

Illegal Trading to Evade the Tax It is likely that an extremely high tax rate would be needed to cut the quantity of drugs bought to the level prevailing with a prohibition. It is also likely that many drug dealers and consumers would try to cover up their activities to evade the tax. If they did act in this way, they would face the cost of breaking the law—the tax law. If the penalty for tax law violation is as severe and as effectively policed as drug-dealing laws, the analysis we've already conducted applies also to this case. The quantity of drugs bought would depend on the penalties for law breaking and on the way in which the penalties are assigned to buyers and sellers.

Taxes Versus Prohibition: Some Pros and Cons
Which is more effective: prohibition or taxes? In favor of taxes and against prohibition is the fact that the tax revenue can be used to make law enforcement more effective. It can also be used to run a more effective education campaign against illegal drug use. In favor of prohibition and against taxes is the fact that prohibition sends a signal that might influence preferences, decreasing the demand for illegal drugs. Also, some people intensely dislike the idea of the government profiting from trade in harmful substances.

REVIEW QUIZ

1 How does the imposition of a penalty for selling an illegal drug influence demand, supply, price, and the quantity of the drug consumed?
2 How does the imposition of a penalty for possessing an illegal drug influence demand, supply, price, and the quantity of the drug consumed?
3 How does the imposition of a penalty for selling *or* possessing an illegal drug influence demand, supply, price, and the quantity of the drug consumed?
4 Is there any case for legalizing drugs?

You can work these questions in Study Plan 6.5 and get instant feedback.

◆ You now know how to use the demand and supply model to predict prices, to study government actions in markets, and to study the sources and costs of inefficiency. In *Reading Between the Lines* on pp. 144–145, you will see how to apply what you've learned to the market for low-skilled labor in California and see some pitfalls of government intervention in this market.

Government Actions in Labor Markets

Bipartisan Plan to Crack Down on California's Underground Economy

The Mercury News
May 3, 2010

California has an underground economy that has been estimated to generate between $60 billion and $140 billion a year. This represents a tax loss to California of between $3 billion and $6 billion. ...

The underground economy in construction and other industries includes employers who pay cash under the table (often under the minimum wage); do not withhold payroll or other taxes; do not provide workers' compensation protection; and often do not maintain safe working conditions. ...

Consider an unscrupulous building contractor who is not playing by the rules and who underbids law-abiding competitors to win a home remodeling or other construction contract. The low bid wins because the violator is not paying the minimum wage, pays no overtime, pays no payroll tax, and does not provide workers' compensation insurance coverage. A worker who is injured operating an unsafe piece of equipment may be lucky to be dropped at a local emergency room, with implicit instructions not to identify the rogue employer.

Some workers actually gravitate toward a rule-breaking employer to avoid garnishment of wages for child support. As a result, these employers have provided a haven for some.

The underground economy represents a lose-lose-lose for California: Employees get cheated of wages, benefits, and other protections; law-abiding employers are forced to compete against scofflaws who gain an economic advantage; the state loses billions in tax revenue that could be keeping schools open and reducing the deficit.

[State legislators Bill Monning and Bill Berryhill] have ...[an] action plan to take on the underground economy. ...

ESSENCE OF THE STORY

- California's underground economy generates an estimated $60 billion to $140 billion a year.

- California loses $3 billion to $6 billion a year in tax revenues from underground production that could be used to keep schools open and to reduce the deficit.

- Employers in the underground economy pay cash wages at rates below the minimum wage.

- Employers in the underground economy don't withhold taxes.

- A builder in the underground economy underbids law-abiding competitors to win contracts.

- Some workers seek a rule-breaking employer to avoid garnishment of wages for child support.

- State legislators are working on a bipartisan bill to limit the underground economy.

ECONOMIC ANALYSIS

- The news article touches on three topics covered in this chapter: the minimum wage, taxes, and trading illegally.

- Trading illegally to avoid a minimum wage regulation or to avoid paying taxes is called "underground" activity and it takes place in the "underground economy."

- A minimum wage set above the competitive equilibrium wage creates incentives for law-breaking on both sides of the market: Employers can find unemployed workers willing to work for much less than the minimum wage and workers can find employers offering to pay a wage above the minimum they are willing to accept.

- Once the line is crossed into illegal activity, other laws get broken, in particular tax laws and health and safety laws.

- Thorough policing of regulations and stiff penalties for law-breaking are needed to achieve the intended regulated outcome.

- Figure 1 illustrates the situation that lawmakers want to achieve in a market for low-skilled labor in California.

- The demand for labor curve is D and the supply of labor curve is S. A tax on employment (income tax and payroll tax) shifts the supply curve to S + tax. A minimum wage regulation sets the minimum legal wage at $8 per hour.

- Employers obey the law and hire 300 million hours of labor at the minimum wage rate of $8 per hour.

- Workers want to supply 700 million hours of labor at the minimum wage rate, so 400 million hours of labor are unemployed.

- The law is enforced, but the outcome is inefficient. A deadweight loss arises from the tax on employment (dark gray) and the minimum wage (light gray).

- Figure 2 shows what happens when employers and workers break the law and trade in the underground economy.

- The demand curve, D, tells us the wage that employers are willing to pay and the supply curve, S, tells us the wage that workers are willing to accept. The minimum wage law and tax laws are broken.

- The underground market finds an equilibrium at a wage rate of $5 an hour and 600 million hours of labor are employed. There is no unemployment.

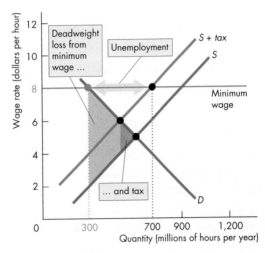

Figure 1 A regulated market with law enforcement

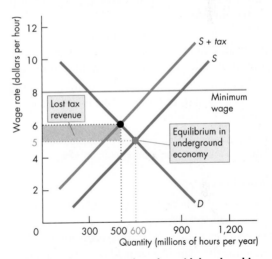

Figure 2 An underground market with law-breaking

- The outcome in the underground market is efficient—the deadweight loss is eliminated.

- The state loses tax revenues (the purple rectangle in Fig. 2). The loss of tax revenues means either that public services must be cut or taxes on other activities must be increased.

- The cost of lost public services and higher taxes is greater than the efficiency gain in the underground labor market, which is why lawmakers are attacking the underground economy.

SUMMARY

Key Points

A Housing Market with a Rent Ceiling (pp. 128–130)

■ A rent ceiling that is set above the equilibrium rent has no effect.

■ A rent ceiling that is set below the equilibrium rent creates a housing shortage, increased search activity, and a black market.

■ A rent ceiling that is set below the equilibrium rent is inefficient and unfair.

Working Problems 1 to 6 will give you a better understanding of a housing market with a rent ceiling.

A Labor Market with a Minimum Wage (pp. 131–133)

■ A minimum wage set below the equilibrium wage rate has no effect.

■ A minimum wage set above the equilibrium wage rate creates unemployment and increases the amount of time people spend searching for a job.

■ A minimum wage set above the equilibrium wage rate is inefficient, unfair, and hits low-skilled young people hardest.

Working Problems 7 to 12 will give you a better understanding of a labor market with a minimum wage.

Taxes (pp. 133–138)

■ A tax raises the price paid by buyers, but usually by less than the tax.

■ The elasticity of demand and the elasticity of supply determine the share of a tax paid by buyers and sellers.

■ The less elastic the demand or the more elastic the supply, the larger is the share of the tax paid by buyers.

■ If demand is perfectly elastic or supply is perfectly inelastic, sellers pay the entire tax. And if demand is perfectly inelastic or supply is perfectly elastic, buyers pay the entire tax.

Working Problems 13 to 15 will give you a better understanding of taxes.

Production Quotas and Subsidies (pp. 139–141)

■ A production quota leads to inefficient underproduction, which raises the price.

■ A subsidy is like a negative tax. It lowers the price, increases the cost of production, and leads to inefficient overproduction.

Working Problems 16 and 17 will give you a better understanding of production quotas and subsidies.

Markets for Illegal Goods (pp. 142–143)

■ Penalties on sellers increase the cost of selling the good and decrease the supply of the good.

■ Penalties on buyers decrease their willingness to pay and decrease the demand for the good.

■ Penalties on buyers and sellers decrease the quantity of the good, raise the price buyers pay, and lower the price sellers receive.

■ Legalizing and taxing can achieve the same outcome as penalties on buyers and sellers.

Working Problem 18 will give you a better understanding of markets for illegal goods.

Key Terms

Black market, 128
Minimum wage, 131
Price cap, 128
Price ceiling, 128

Price floor, 131
Production quota, 139
Rent ceiling, 128
Search activity, 128

Subsidy, 140
Tax incidence, 133

STUDY PLAN PROBLEMS AND APPLICATIONS

myeconlab You can work Problems 1 to 18 in MyEconLab Chapter 6 Study Plan and get instant feedback.

A Housing Market with a Rent Ceiling (Study Plan 6.1)

Use the following graph of the market for rental housing in Townsville to work Problems 1 and 2.

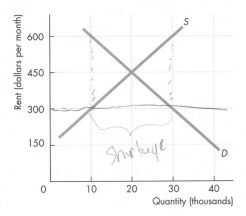

1. a. What are the equilibrium rent and equilibrium quantity of rental housing?

    b. If a rent ceiling is set at $600 a month, what is the quantity of housing rented and what is the shortage of housing?

2. If a rent ceiling is set at $300 a month, what is the quantity of housing rented, the shortage of housing, and the maximum price that someone is willing to pay for the last unit of housing available?

Use the following news clip to work Problems 3 to 6.

Capping Gasoline Prices

As gasoline prices rise, many people are calling for price caps, but price caps generate a distorted reflection of reality, which leads buyers and suppliers to act in ways inconsistent with the price cap. By masking reality, price caps only make matters worse.

Source: *Pittsburgh Tribune-Review*,
September 12, 2005

Suppose that a price ceiling is set below the equilibrium price of gasoline.

3. How does the price cap influence the quantity of gasoline supplied and the quantity demanded?

4. How does the price cap influence

    a. The quantity of gasoline sold and the shortage or surplus of gasoline?

    b. The maximum price that someone is willing to pay for the last gallon of gasoline available on a black market?

5. Draw a graph to illustrate the effects of a price ceiling set below the equilibrium price in the market for gasoline.

6. Explain the various ways in which a price ceiling on gasoline that is set below the equilibrium price would make buyers and sellers of gasoline better off or worse off. What would happen to total surplus and deadweight loss in this market?

A Labor Market with a Minimum Wage

(Study Plan 6.2)

Use the following data to work Problems 7 to 9.

The table gives the demand and supply schedules of teenage labor.

Wage rate (dollars per hour)	Quantity demanded	Quantity supplied
	(hours per month)	
4	3,000	1,000
5	2,500	1,500
6	2,000	2,000
7	1,500	2,500
8	1,000	3,000

7. Calculate the equilibrium wage rate, the number of hours worked, and the quantity of unemployment.

8. If a minimum wage for teenagers is set at $5 an hour, how many hours do they work and how many hours of teenage labor are unemployed?

9. If a minimum wage for teenagers is set at $7 an hour,

    a. How many hours do teenagers work and how many hours are unemployed?

    b. Demand for teenage labor increases by 500 hours a month. What is the wage rate paid to teenagers and how many hours of teenage labor are unemployed?

Use the following news clip to work Problems 10 to 12.

India Steps Up Pressure for Minimum Wage for Its Workers in the Gulf

Oil-rich countries in the [Persian] Gulf, already confronted by strong labor protests, are facing renewed pressure from India to pay minimum wages for unskilled workers. With five million immigrant workers in the region, India is trying to win better conditions for their citizens.

Source: *International Herald Tribune*,
March 27, 2008

Suppose that the Gulf countries paid a minimum wage above the equilibrium wage to Indian workers.

10. How would the market for labor be affected in the Gulf countries? Draw a supply and demand graph to illustrate your answer.

11. How would the market for labor be affected in India? Draw a supply and demand graph to illustrate your answer. [Be careful: the minimum wage is in the Gulf countries, not in India.]

12. Would migrant Indian workers be better off or worse off or unaffected by this minimum wage?

Taxes (Study Plan 6.3)

13. The table gives the demand and supply schedules for chocolate brownies.

Price (cents per brownie)	Quantity demanded	Quantity supplied
	(millions per day)	
50	5	3
60	4	4
70	3	5
80	2	6
90	1	7

a. If brownies are not taxed, what is the price of a brownie and how many are bought?

b. If sellers are taxed 20¢ a brownie, what is the price? How many are sold? Who pays the tax?

c. If buyers are taxed 20¢ a brownie, what is the price? How many are bought? Who pays the tax?

14. **Luxury Tax Heavier Burden on Working Class, it Would Seem**

The Omnibus Budget Reconciliation Act of 1990 included a stern tax on "luxury items." In 1990 the Joint Committee on Taxation projected that the 1991 revenue yield from the luxury taxes would be $31 million. The actual yield was $16.6 million. Why? Because —surprise!—the taxation changed behavior.

Source: *The Topeka Capital-Journal*, October 29, 1999

a. Would buyers or sellers of "luxury items" pay more of the luxury tax?

b. Explain why the luxury tax generated far less tax revenue than was originally anticipated.

15. **How to Take a Gas Holiday**

High fuel prices will probably keep Americans closer to home this summer, despite the gas-tax "holiday" that would shave 18¢ off every gallon.

Source: *Time*, May 19, 2008

Would the price of gasoline that consumers pay fall by 18¢ a gallon? How would consumer surplus change? Explain your answers.

Production Quotas and Subsidies (Study Plan 6.4)

Use the following data to work Problems 16 and 17.

The demand and supply schedules for rice are

Price (dollars per box)	Quantity demanded	Quantity supplied
	(boxes per week)	
1.20	3,000	1,500
1.30	2,750	2,000
1.40	2,500	2,500
1.50	2,250	3,000
1.60	2,000	3,500

16. Calculate the price, the marginal cost of rice, and the quantity produced if the government sets a production quota of 2,000 boxes a week.

17. Calculate the price, the marginal cost of rice, and the quantity produced if the government introduces a subsidy of $0.30 a box.

Markets for Illegal Goods (Study Plan 6.5)

18. The figure illustrates the market for a banned substance.

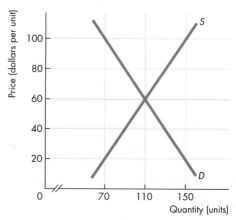

Calculate the market price and the quantity consumed if a penalty of $20 a unit is imposed on

a. Sellers only.

b. Buyers only.

c. Both sellers and buyers.

ADDITIONAL PROBLEMS AND APPLICATIONS

 myeconlab You can work these problems in MyEconLab if assigned by your instructor.

A Housing Market with a Rent Ceiling

Use this news clip to work Problems 19 and 20.

Despite Protests, Rent Board Sets 7.25% Increase

New York's Rent Guidelines Board voted for a rent increase of up to 7.25 percent over the next two years on rent-stabilized apartments. A survey reported that last year costs for the owners of rent-stabilized buildings rose by 7.8 percent. In addition there is growing concern about the ability of the middle class to afford to live in New York City.

Source: *The New York Times*, June 28, 2006

19. a. If rents for rent-stabilized apartments do not increase, how do you think the market for rental units in New York City will develop?

   b. Are rent ceilings in New York City helpful to the middle class? Why or why not?

20. a. Explain the effect of the increase in the rent ceiling on the quantity of rent-stabilized apartments.

   b. Why is rent stabilization a source of conflict between renters and owners of apartments?

A Labor Market with a Minimum Wage

Use the following news clip to work Problems 21 and 22.

House Passes Increase in Minimum Wage to $7.25

The rise in the federal minimum wage will boost the wages of the lowest-paid U.S. workers from $5.15 to $7.25 an hour. Republican leaders, backed by small-business and restaurant groups, argued that the higher minimum wage would cripple the economy, so it must be accompanied by tax cuts for small businesses.

Source: *The Washington Post*, January 11, 2007

21. On a graph of the market for low-skilled labor, show the effect of the increase in the minimum wage on the quantity of labor employed.

22. Explain the effects of the higher minimum wage on the workers' surplus and the firms' surplus. Does the labor market become more efficient or less efficient? Explain.

Taxes

23. Use the news clip in Problem 21.

   a. Would a cut in the tax on small business profits offset the effect of the higher minimum wage on employment? Explain.

   b. Would a cut in the Social Security tax that small businesses pay offset the effect of the higher minimum wage on employment? Explain.

24. The demand and supply schedules for tulips are

Price (dollars per bunch)	Quantity demanded	Quantity supplied
	(bunches per week)	
10	100	40
12	90	60
14	80	80
16	70	100
18	60	120

   a. If tulips are not taxed, what is the price and how many bunches are bought?

   b. If tulips are taxed $6 a bunch, what are the price and quantity bought? Who pays the tax?

25. **Cigarette Taxes, Black Markets, and Crime: Lessons from New York's 50-Year Losing Battle**

New York City has the highest cigarette taxes in the country. During the four months following the recent tax hike, sales of taxed cigarettes in the city fell by more than 50 percent as consumers turned to the city's bustling black market. The thriving illegal market for cigarettes has diverted billions of dollars from legitimate businesses and governments to criminals.

Source: Cato Institute, February 6, 2003

   a. How has the market for cigarettes in New York City responded to the high cigarette taxes?

   b. How does the emergence of a black market impact the elasticity of demand in a legal market?

   c. Why might an increase in the tax rate actually cause a decrease in the tax revenue?

Production Quotas and Subsidies

Use the following news clip to work Problems 26 to 28.

Congress Passes Farm Bill, Defies Bush

Congress sent the White House a huge $290 billion-election-year farm bill which contained $40 billion for farm subsidies and almost $30 billion to farmers to idle their land. Bush has threatened to veto the bill, saying it is irresponsible and too generous to wealthy corporate farmers in a time of record crop prices.

Source: CNN, May 15, 2008

26. a. Why does the federal government subsidize farmers?

  b. Explain how a subsidy paid to cotton farmers affects the price of cotton and the marginal cost of producing it.

27. Explain how a subsidy paid to cotton farmers affects the consumer surplus and the producer surplus from cotton. Does the subsidy make the cotton market more efficient or less efficient? Explain.

28. a. How would a payment to cotton farmers to idle their land influence the supply of cotton?

  b. How would a payment to cotton farmers to idle their land affect the consumer surplus and the producer surplus from cotton? Explain.

Markets for Illegal Goods

29. The table gives the demand and supply schedules for an illegal drug.

Price (dollars per unit)	Quantity demanded	Quantity supplied
	(units per day)	
50	500	300
60	400	400
70	300	500
80	200	600
90	100	700

  a. If there are no penalties on buying or selling the drug, what is the price and how many units are consumed?

  b. If the penalty on sellers is $20 a unit, what are the price and quantity consumed?

  c. If the penalty on buyers is $20 a unit, what are the price and quantity consumed?

Economics in the News

30. After you have studied *Reading Between the Lines* on pp. 144–145 answer the following questions.

  a. In what ways do employers break laws in the underground labor market described in the news article?

  b. How does a tax on labor change the equilibrium level of employment and the wage rate paid by employers?

  c. How does a minimum wage law make tax evasion more likely to occur?

  d. How can the minimum wage law and tax law be enforced more effectively?

  e. Use the analysis of a market for an illegal good (on pp. 142–143) to explain how stiffer penalties would change the quantity of labor traded and change the wage rate in the underground economy.

Use the following news clip to work Problems 31 to 33.

Coal Shortage at China Plants

Chinese power plants have run short of coal, an unintended effect of government-mandated price controls designed to shield the public from rising global energy costs. Beijing has also frozen retail prices of gasoline and diesel. That helped farmers and the urban poor, but it has spurred sales of gas-guzzling luxury cars and propelled double-digit annual growth in fuel consumption. At the same time, oil refiners are suffering heavy losses and some have begun cutting production, causing fuel shortages.

Source: CNN, May 20, 2008

31. a. Are China's price controls described in the news clip price floors or price ceilings?

  b. Explain how China's price controls have created shortages or surpluses in the markets for coal, gasoline, and diesel.

  c. Illustrate your answer to part (b) graphically by using the supply and demand model.

32. Explain how China's price controls have changed consumer surplus, producer surplus, total surplus, and the deadweight loss in the markets for coal, gasoline, and diesel.

33. Show on a graph the change in consumer surplus, producer surplus, total surplus, and the deadweight loss in the markets for coal, gasoline, and diesel.

34. On December 31, 1776, Rhode Island established wage controls to limit wages to 70¢ a day for carpenters and 42¢ a day for tailors.

  a. Are these wage controls a price ceiling or a price floor? Why might they have been introduced?

  b. If these wage controls are effective, would you expect to see a surplus or a shortage of carpenters and tailors?

35. **Drivers Feel the Pinch as Diesel Hits $4 a Gallon**

  "The high price of gasoline is hurting our economy," said Mark Kirsch, a trucker, who organized a rally in Washington. "It's hurting middle-class people."

  Source: *The Washington Post*, April 29, 2008

  Explain to truck drivers why a cap on the price of gasoline would hurt middle-class people more than the high price of gasoline hurts.

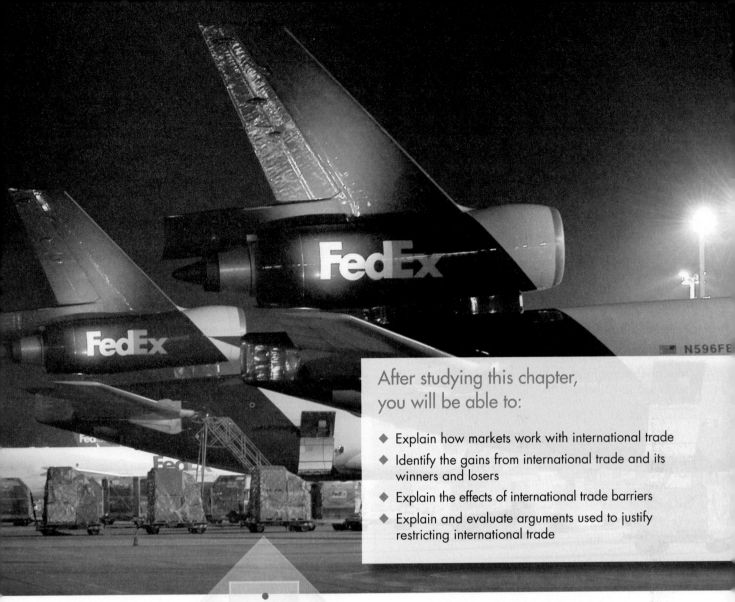

After studying this chapter,
you will be able to:

◆ Explain how markets work with international trade

◆ Identify the gains from international trade and its winners and losers

◆ Explain the effects of international trade barriers

◆ Explain and evaluate arguments used to justify restricting international trade

7

GLOBAL MARKETS IN ACTION

Pods, Wii games, and Nike shoes are just three of the items you might buy that are not produced in the United States. In fact, most of the goods that you buy are produced abroad, often in Asia, and transported here in container ships and FedEx cargo jets. And it's not just *goods* produced abroad that you buy—it is *services* too. When you make a technical support call, most likely you'll be talking with someone in India, or to a voice recognition system that was programmed in India. Satellites or fiber cables will carry your conversation along with huge amounts of other voice messages, video images, and data.

All these activities are part of the globalization process that is having a profound effect on our lives. Globalization is controversial and generates heated debate. Many Americans want to know how we can compete with people whose wages are a fraction of our own.

Why do we go to such lengths to trade and communicate with others in faraway places? You will find some answers in this chapter. And in *Reading Between the Lines* at the end of the chapter, you can apply what you've learned and examine the effects of a tariff that the Obama government has put on tires imported from China.

◆ How Global Markets Work

Because we trade with people in other countries, the goods and services that we can buy and consume are not limited by what we can produce. The goods and services that we buy from other countries are our **imports**; and the goods and services that we sell to people in other countries are our **exports**.

International Trade Today

Global trade today is enormous. In 2009, global exports and imports were $31 trillion, which is one half of the value of global production. The United States is the world's largest international trader and accounts for 10 percent of world exports and 13 percent of world imports. Germany and China, which rank 2 and 3 behind the United States, lag by a large margin.

In 2009, total U.S. exports were $1.6 trillion, which is about 11 percent of the value of U.S. production. Total U.S. imports were $2 trillion, which is about 14 percent of total expenditure in the United States.

We trade both goods and services. In 2009, exports of services were about 33 percent of total exports and imports of services were about 19 percent of total imports.

What Drives International Trade?

Comparative advantage is the fundamental force that drives international trade. Comparative advantage (see Chapter 2, p. 38) is a situation in which a person can perform an activity or produce a good or service at a lower opportunity cost than anyone else. This same idea applies to nations. We can define *national comparative advantage* as a situation in which a nation can perform an activity or produce a good or service at a lower opportunity cost than any other nation.

The opportunity cost of producing a T-shirt is lower in China than in the United States, so China has a comparative advantage in producing T-shirts. The opportunity cost of producing an airplane is lower in the United States than in China, so the United States has a comparative advantage in producing airplanes.

You saw in Chapter 2 how Liz and Joe reap gains from trade by specializing in the production of the good at which they have a comparative advantage and then trading with each other. Both are better off.

Economics in Action
Trading Services for Oil

Services top the list of U.S. exports and oil is the nation's largest import by a large margin.

The services that we export are business, professional, and technical services and transportation services. Chemicals were the largest category of goods that we exported in 2009.

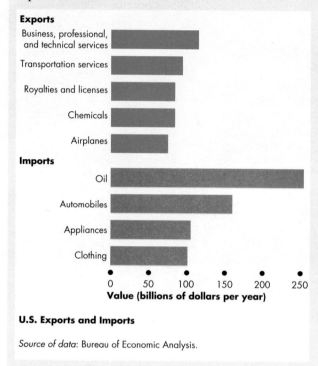

U.S. Exports and Imports

Source of data: Bureau of Economic Analysis.

This same principle applies to trade among nations. Because China has a comparative advantage at producing T-shirts and the United States has a comparative advantage at producing airplanes, the people of both countries can gain from specialization and trade. China can buy airplanes from the United States at a lower opportunity cost than that at which Chinese firms can produce them. And Americans can buy T-shirts from China for a lower opportunity cost than that at which U.S. firms can produce them. Also, through international trade, Chinese producers can get higher prices for their T-shirts and Boeing can sell airplanes for a higher price. Both countries gain from international trade.

Let's now illustrate the gains from trade that we've just described by studying demand and supply in the global markets for T-shirts and airplanes.

Why the United States Imports T-Shirts

The United States imports T-shirts because the rest of the world has a comparative advantage in producing T-shirts. Figure 7.1 illustrates how this comparative advantage generates international trade and how trade affects the price of a T-shirt and the quantities produced and bought.

The demand curve D_{US} and the supply curve S_{US} show the demand and supply in the U.S. domestic market only. The demand curve tells us the quantity of T-shirts that Americans are willing to buy at various prices. The supply curve tells us the quantity of T-shirts that U.S. garment makers are willing to sell at various prices—that is, the quantity supplied at each price when all T-shirts sold in the United States are produced in the United States.

Figure 7.1(a) shows what the U.S. T-shirt market would be like with no international trade. The price of a shirt would be $8 and 40 million shirts a year would be produced by U.S. garment makers and bought by U.S. consumers.

Figure 7.1(b) shows the market for T-shirts with international trade. Now the price of a T-shirt is determined in the world market, not the U.S. domestic market. The world price is less than $8 a T-shirt, which means that the rest of the world has a comparative advantage in producing T-shirts. The world price line shows the world price at $5 a shirt.

The U.S. demand curve, D_{US}, tells us that at $5 a shirt, Americans buy 60 million shirts a year. The U.S. supply curve, S_{US}, tells us that at $5 a shirt, U.S. garment makers produce 20 million T-shirts a year. To buy 60 million T-shirts when only 20 million are produced in the United States, we must import T-shirts from the rest of the world. The quantity of T-shirts imported is 40 million a year.

FIGURE 7.1   A Market with Imports

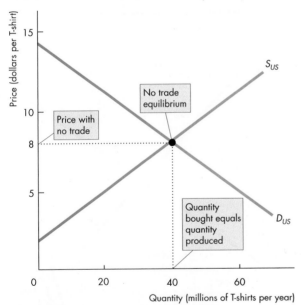

(a) Equilibrium with no international trade

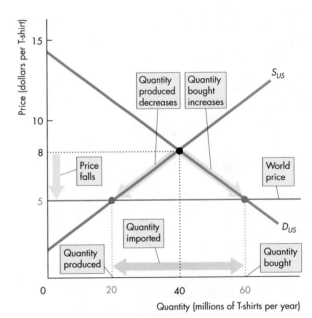

(b) Equilibrium in a market with imports

Part (a) shows the U.S. market for T-shirts with no international trade. The U.S. domestic demand curve D_{US} and U.S. domestic supply curve S_{US} determine the price of a T-shirt at $8 and the quantity of T- shirts produced and bought in the United States at 40 million a year.

Part (b) shows the U.S. market for T-shirts with interna-

tional trade. World demand and world supply determine the world price, which is $5 per T-shirt. The price in the U.S. market falls to $5 a shirt. U.S. purchases of T-shirts increase to 60 million a year, and U.S. production of T-shirts decreases to 20 million a year. The United States imports 40 million T-shirts a year.

Why the United States Exports Airplanes

Figure 7.2 illustrates international trade in airplanes. The demand curve D_{US} and the supply curve S_{US} show the demand and supply in the U.S. domestic market only. The demand curve tells us the quantity of airplanes that U.S. airlines are willing to buy at various prices. The supply curve tells us the quantity of airplanes that U.S. aircraft makers are willing to sell at various prices.

Figure 7.2(a) shows what the U.S. airplane market would be like with no international trade. The price of an airplane would be $100 million and 400 airplanes a year would be produced by U.S. aircraft makers and bought by U.S. airlines.

Figure 7.2(b) shows the U.S. airplane market with international trade. Now the price of an airplane is determined in the world market and the world price is higher than $100 million, which means that the United States has a comparative advantage in produc-

ing airplanes. The world price line shows the world price at $150 million.

The U.S. demand curve, D_{US}, tells us that at $150 million an airplane, U.S. airlines buy 200 airplanes a year. The U.S. supply curve, S_{US}, tells us that at $150 million an airplane, U.S. aircraft makers produce 700 airplanes a year. The quantity produced in the United States (700 a year) minus the quantity purchased by U.S. airlines (200 a year) is the quantity of airplanes exported, which is 500 airplanes a year.

REVIEW QUIZ

1 Describe the situation in the market for a good or service that the United States imports.
2 Describe the situation in the market for a good or service that the United States exports.

You can work these questions in Study Plan 7.1 and get instant feedback.

FIGURE 7.2 A Market with Exports

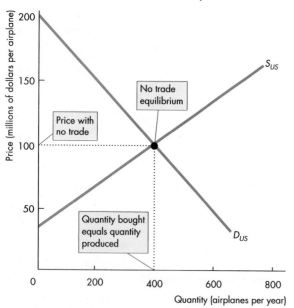

(a) Equilibrium without international trade

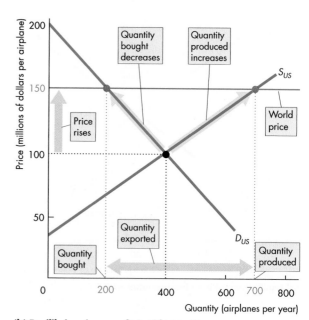

(b) Equilibrium in a market with exports

In part (a), the U.S. market with no international trade, the U.S. domestic demand curve D_{US} and the U.S. domestic supply curve S_{US} determine the price of an airplane at $100 million and 400 airplanes are produced and bought each year.

In part (b), the U.S. market with international trade,

world demand and world supply determine the world price, which is $150 million per airplane. The price in the U.S. market rises. U.S. airplane production increases to 700 a year, and U.S. purchases of airplanes decrease to 200 a year. The United States exports 500 airplanes a year.

◆ Winners, Losers, and the Net Gain from Trade

In Chapter 1 (see p. 5), we asked whether globalization is in the self-interest of the low-wage worker in Malaysia who sews your new running shoes and the shoemaker in Atlanta—whether it is in the social interest. We're now going to answer these questions. You will learn why producers complain about cheap foreign imports, but consumers of imports never complain.

Gains and Losses from Imports

We measure the gains and losses from imports by examining their effect on consumer surplus, producer surplus, and total surplus. In the importing country the winners are those whose surplus increases and the losers are those whose surplus decreases.

Figure 7.3(a) shows what consumer surplus and producer surplus would be with no international

trade in T-shirts. U.S. domestic demand, D_{US}, and U.S. domestic supply, S_{US}, determine the price and quantity. The green area shows consumer surplus and the blue area shows producer surplus. Total surplus is the sum of consumer surplus and producer surplus.

Figure 7.3(b) shows how these surpluses change when the U.S. market opens to imports. The U.S. price falls to the world price. The quantity bought increases to the quantity demanded at the world price and consumer surplus expands from A to the larger green area $A + B + D$. The quantity produced in the United States decreases to the quantity supplied at the world price and producer surplus shrinks to the smaller blue area C.

Part of the gain in consumer surplus, the area B, is a loss of producer surplus—a redistribution of total surplus. But the other part of the increase in consumer surplus, the area D, is a net gain. This increase in total surplus results from the lower price and increased purchases and is the gain from imports.

FIGURE 7.3   Gains and Losses in a Market with Imports

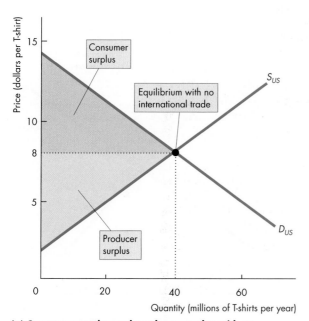

(a) Consumer surplus and producer surplus with no international trade

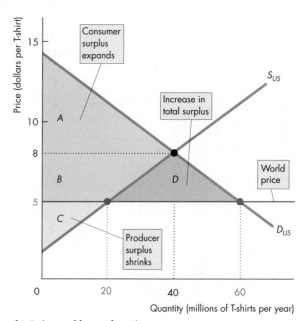

(b) Gains and losses from imports

In part (a), with no international trade, the green area shows the consumer surplus and the blue area shows the producer surplus.

In part (b), with international trade, the price falls to the

world price of $5 a shirt. Consumer surplus expands from area A to the area A + B + D. Producer surplus shrinks to area C. Area B is a transfer of surplus from producers to consumers. Area D is an increase in total surplus—the gain from imports.

Gains and Losses from Exports

We measure the gains and losses from exports just like we measured those from imports, by their effect on consumer surplus, producer surplus, and total surplus.

Figure 7.4(a) shows the situation with no international trade. Domestic demand, D_{US}, and domestic supply, S_{US}, determine the price and quantity, the consumer surplus, and the producer surplus.

Figure 7.4(b) shows how the consumer surplus and producer surplus change when the good is exported. The price rises to the world price. The quantity bought decreases to the quantity demanded at the world price and the consumer surplus shrinks to the green area A. The quantity produced increases to the quantity supplied at the world price and the producer surplus expands to the blue area $B + C + D$.

Part of the gain in producer surplus, the area B, is a loss in consumer surplus—a redistribution of the total surplus. But the other part of the increase in producer surplus, the area D, is a net gain. This increase in total

surplus results from the higher price and increased production and is the gain from exports.

Gains for All

You've seen that both imports and exports bring gains. Because one country's exports are other countries' imports, international trade brings gain for all countries. International trade is a win-win game.

REVIEW QUIZ

1 How is the gain from imports distributed between consumers and domestic producers?
2 How is the gain from exports distributed between consumers and domestic producers?
3 Why is the net gain from international trade positive?

You can work these questions in Study Plan 7.2 and get instant feedback.

FIGURE 7.4   Gains and Losses in a Market with Exports

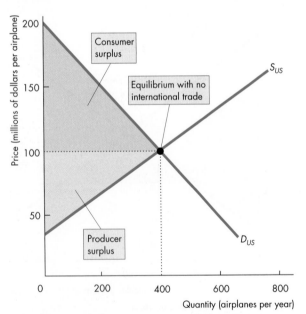

(a) Consumer surplus and producer surplus with no international trade

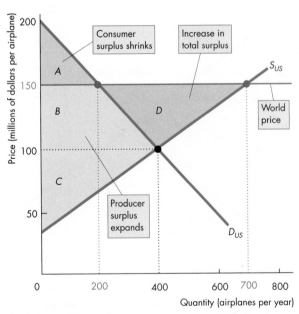

(b) Gains and losses from exports

In part (a), the U.S. market with no international trade, the green area shows the consumer surplus and the blue area shows the producer surplus. In part (b), the U.S. market with international trade, the price rises to the world price.

Consumer surplus shrinks to area A. Producer surplus expands from area C to the area B + C + D. Area B is a transfer of surplus from consumers to producers. Area D is an increase in total surplus—the gain from exports.

  animation

◆ International Trade Restrictions

Governments use four sets of tools to influence international trade and protect domestic industries from foreign competition. They are

- Tariffs
- Import quotas
- Other import barriers
- Export subsidies

Tariffs

A **tariff** is a tax on a good that is imposed by the importing country when an imported good crosses its international boundary. For example, the government of India imposes a 100 percent tariff on wine imported from California. So when an Indian imports a $10 bottle of Californian wine, he pays the Indian government a $10 import duty.

Tariffs raise revenue for governments and serve the self-interest of people who earn their incomes in import-competing industries. But as you will see, restrictions on free international trade decrease the gains from trade and are not in the social interest.

The Effects of a Tariff To see the effects of a tariff, let's return to the example in which the United States imports T-shirts. With free trade, the T-shirts are imported and sold at the world price. Then, under pressure from U.S. garment makers, the U.S. government imposes a tariff on imported T-shirts. Buyers of T-shirts must now pay the world price plus the tariff. Several consequences follow and Fig. 7.5 illustrates them.

Figure 7.5(a) shows the situation with free international trade. The United States produces 20 million T-shirts a year and imports 40 million a year at the world price of $5 a shirt. Figure 7.5(b) shows what happens with a tariff set at $2 per T-shirt.

FIGURE 7.5   The Effects of a Tariff

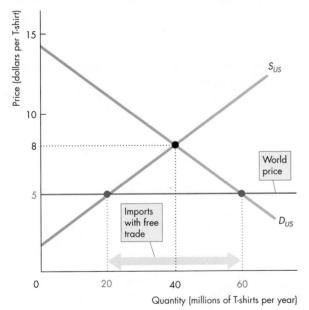

(a) Free trade

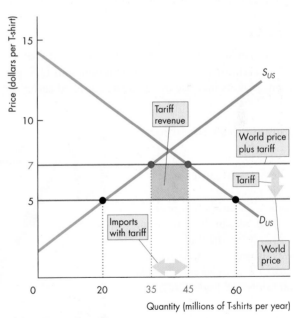

(b) Market with tariff

The world price of a T-shirt is $5. With free trade in part (a), Americans buy 60 million T-shirts a year. U.S. garment makers produce 20 million T-shirts a year and the United States imports 40 million a year.

With a tariff of $2 per T-shirt in part (b), the price in

the U.S. market rises to $7 a T-shirt. U.S. production increases, U.S. purchases decrease, and the quantity imported decreases. The U.S. government collects a tariff revenue of $2 on each T-shirt imported, which is shown by the purple rectangle.

The following changes occur in the market for T-shirts:

- The price of a T-shirt in the United States rises by $2.
- The quantity of T-shirts bought in the United States decreases.
- The quantity of T-shirts produced in the United States increases.
- The quantity of T-shirts imported into the United States decreases.
- The U.S. government collects a tariff revenue.

Rise in Price of a T-Shirt To buy a T-shirt, Americans must pay the world price plus the tariff, so the price of a T-shirt rises by the $2 tariff to $7. Figure 7.5(b) shows the new domestic price line, which lies $2 above the world price line. The price rises by the full amount of the tariff. The buyer pays the entire tariff because supply from the rest of the world is perfectly elastic (see Chapter 6, p. 137).

Decrease in Purchases The higher price of a T-shirt brings a decrease in the quantity demanded along the demand curve. Figure 7.5(b) shows the decrease from 60 million T-shirts a year at $5 a shirt to 45 million a year at $7 a shirt.

Increase in Domestic Production The higher price of a T-shirt stimulates domestic production, and U.S. garment makers increase the quantity supplied along the supply curve. Figure 7.5(b) shows the increase from 20 million T-shirts at $5 a shirt to 35 million a year at $7 a shirt.

Decrease in Imports T-shirt imports decrease by 30 million, from 40 million to 10 million a year. Both the decrease in purchases and the increase in domestic production contribute to this decrease in imports.

Tariff Revenue The government's tariff revenue is $20 million—$2 per shirt on 10 million imported shirts—shown by the purple rectangle.

Winners, Losers, and the Social Loss from a Tariff A tariff on an imported good creates winners and losers and a social loss. When the U.S. government imposes a tariff on an imported good,

- U.S. consumers of the good lose.
- U.S. producers of the good gain.
- U.S. consumers lose more than U.S. producers gain.
- Society loses: a deadweight loss arises.

U.S. Consumers of the Good Lose Because the price of a T-shirt in the United States rises, the quantity of T-shirts demanded decreases. The combination of a higher price and smaller quantity bought decreases consumer surplus—the loss to U.S. consumers that arises from a tariff.

Economics in Action
U.S. Tariffs Almost Gone

The Smoot-Hawley Act, which was passed in 1930, took U.S. tariffs to a peak average rate of 20 percent in 1933. (One third of imports was subject to a 60 percent tariff.) The **General Agreement on Tariffs and Trade (GATT)** was established in 1947. Since then tariffs have fallen in a series of negotiating rounds, the most significant of which are identified in the figure. Tariffs are now as low as they have ever been but import quotas and other trade barriers persist.

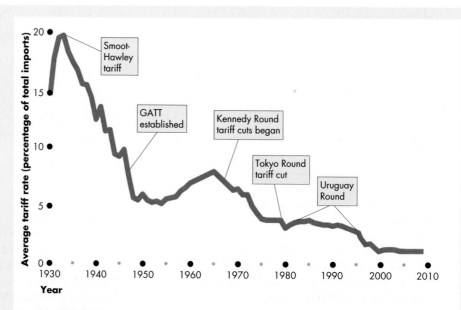

Tariffs: 1930–2009

Sources of data: U.S. Bureau of the Census, *Historical Statistics of the United States, Colonial Times to 1970,* Bicentennial Edition, Part 1 (Washington, D.C., 1975); Series U-212: updated from *Statistical Abstract of the United States:* various editions.

U.S. Producers of the Good Gain

Because the price of an imported T-shirt rises by the amount of the tariff, U.S. T-shirt producers are now able to sell their T-shirts for the world price plus the tariff. At the higher price, the quantity of T-shirts supplied by U.S. producers increases. The combination of a higher price and larger quantity produced increases producer surplus—the gain to U.S. producers from the tariff.

U.S. Consumers Lose More Than U.S. Producers Gain

Consumer surplus decreases for four reasons: Some becomes producer surplus, some is lost in a higher cost of production (domestic producers have higher costs than foreign producers), some is lost because imports decrease, and some goes to the government as tariff revenue. Figure 7.6 shows these sources of lost consumer surplus.

Figure 7.6(a) shows the consumer surplus and producer surplus with free international trade in T-shirts. Figure 7.6(b) shows the consumer surplus and producer surplus with a $2 tariff on imported T-shirts. By comparing Fig. 7.6(b) with Fig. 7.6(a), you can see how a tariff changes these surpluses.

Consumer surplus—the green area—shrinks for four reasons. First, the higher price transfers surplus from consumers to producers. The blue area *B* represents this loss (and gain of producer surplus). Second, domestic production costs more than imports. The supply curve S_{US} shows the higher cost of production and the gray area *C* shows this loss of consumer surplus. Third, some of the consumer surplus is transferred to the government. The purple area *D* shows this loss (and gain of government revenue). Fourth, some of the consumer surplus is lost because imports decrease. The gray area *E* shows this loss.

Society Loses: A Deadweight Loss Arises

Some of the loss of consumer surplus is transferred to producers and some is transferred to the government and spent on government programs that people value. But the increase in production cost and the loss from decreased imports is transferred to no one: It is a social loss—a deadweight loss. The gray areas labeled *C* and *E* represent this deadweight loss. Total surplus decreases by the area *C* + *E*.

FIGURE 7.6   The Winners and Losers from a Tariff

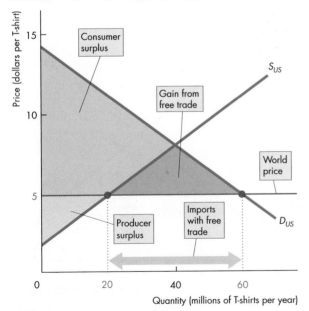

(a) Free trade

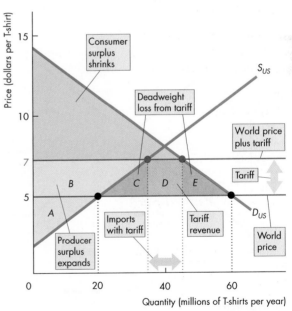

(b) Market with tariff

The world price of a T-shirt is $5. In part (a), with free trade, the United States imports 40 million T-shirts. Consumer surplus, producer surplus, and the gains from free trade are as large as possible.

In part (b), a tariff of $2 per T-shirt raises the U.S. price

of a T-shirt to $7. The quantity imported decreases. Consumer surplus shrinks by the areas *B*, *C*, *D*, and *E*. Producer surplus expands by area *B*. The government's tariff revenue is area *D*, and the tariff creates a deadweight loss equal to the area *C* + *E*.

Import Quotas

We now look at the second tool for restricting trade: import quotas. An **import quota** is a restriction that limits the maximum quantity of a good that may be imported in a given period.

Most countries impose import quotas on a wide range of items. The United States imposes them on food products such as sugar and bananas and manufactured goods such as textiles and paper.

Import quotas enable the government to satisfy the self-interest of the people who earn their incomes in the import-competing industries. But you will discover that like a tariff, an import quota decreases the gains from trade and is not in the social interest.

The Effects of an Import Quota The effects of an import quota are similar to those of a tariff. The price rises, the quantity bought decreases, and the quantity produced in the United States increases. Figure 7.7 illustrates the effects.

Figure 7.7(a) shows the situation with free international trade. Figure 7.7(b) shows what happens with an import quota of 10 million T-shirts a year. The U.S. supply curve of T-shirts becomes the domestic supply curve, S_{US}, plus the quantity that the import quota permits. So the supply curve becomes $S_{US} + quota$. The price of a T-shirt rises to $7, the quantity of T-shirts bought in the United States decreases to 45 million a year, the quantity of T-shirts produced in the United States increases to 35 million a year, and the quantity of T-shirts imported into the United States decreases to the quota quantity of 10 million a year. All the effects of this quota are identical to the effects of a $2 per shirt tariff, as you can check in Fig. 7.5(b).

Winners, Losers, and the Social Loss from an Import Quota An import quota creates winners and losers that are similar to those of a tariff but with an interesting difference.

FIGURE 7.7   The Effects of an Import Quota

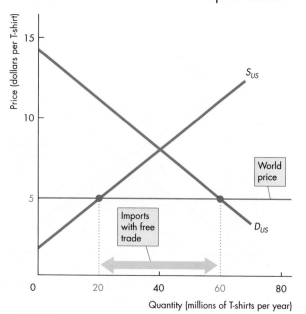

(a) Free trade

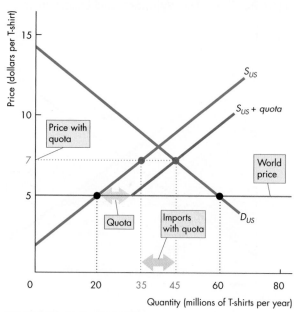

(b) Market with import quota

With free international trade, in part (a), Americans buy 60 million T-shirts at the world price. The United States produces 20 million T-shirts and imports 40 million a year. With an import quota of 10 million T-shirts a year, in part (b),

the supply of T-shirts in the United States is shown by the curve $S_{US} + quota$. The price in the United States rises to $7 a T-shirt. U.S. production increases, U.S. purchases decrease, and the quantity of T-shirts imported decreases.

When the government imposes an import quota,

- U.S. consumers of the good lose.
- U.S. producers of the good gain.
- Importers of the good gain.
- Society loses: a deadweight loss arises.

Figure 7.8 shows these gains and losses from a quota. By comparing Fig. 7.8(b) with a quota and Fig. 7.8(a) with free trade, you can see how an import quota of 10 million T-shirts a year changes the consumer and producer surpluses.

Consumer surplus—the green area—shrinks. This decrease is the loss to consumers from the import quota. The decrease in consumer surplus is made up of four parts. First, some of the consumer surplus is transferred to producers. The blue area B represents this loss of consumer surplus (and gain of producer surplus). Second, part of the consumer surplus is lost because the domestic cost of production is higher

than the world price. The gray area C represents this loss. Third, part of the consumer surplus is transferred to importers who buy T-shirts for $5 (the world price) and sell them for $7 (the U.S. domestic price). The two blue areas D represent this loss of consumer surplus and profit for importers. Fourth, part of the consumer surplus is lost because imports decrease. The gray area E represents this loss.

The losses of consumer surplus from the higher cost of production and the decrease in imports is a social loss—a deadweight loss. The gray areas labeled C and E represent this deadweight loss. Total surplus decreases by the area C + E.

You can now see the one difference between a quota and a tariff. A tariff brings in revenue for the government while a quota brings a profit for the importers. All the other effects are the same, provided the quota is set at the same quantity of imports that results from the tariff.

FIGURE 7.8 The Winners and Losers from an Import Quota

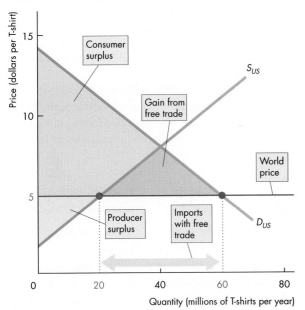

(a) Free trade

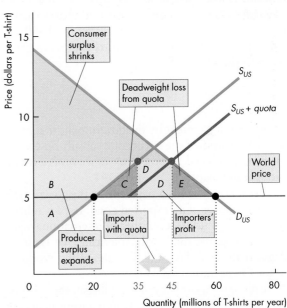

(b) Market with import quota

The world price of a T-shirt is $5. In part (a), with free trade, the United States produces 20 million T-shirts a year and imports 40 million T-shirts. Consumer surplus, producer surplus, and the gain from free international trade (darker green area) are as large as possible.

In part (b), the import quota raises the price of a T-shirt to $7. The quantity imported decreases. Consumer surplus shrinks by the areas B, C, D, and E. Producer surplus expands by area B. Importers' profit is the two areas D, and the quota creates a deadweight loss equal to C + E.

Other Import Barriers

Two sets of policies that influence imports are

- Health, safety, and regulation barriers
- Voluntary export restraints

Health, Safety, and Regulation Barriers Thousands of detailed health, safety, and other regulations restrict international trade. For example, U.S. food imports are examined by the Food and Drug Administration to determine whether the food is "pure, wholesome, safe to eat, and produced under sanitary conditions." The discovery of BSE (mad cow disease) in just one U.S. cow in 2003 was enough to close down international trade in U.S. beef. The European Union bans imports of most genetically modified foods, such as U.S.-produced soybeans. Although regulations of the type we've just described are not designed to limit international trade, they have that effect.

Voluntary Export Restraints A *voluntary export restraint* is like a quota allocated to a foreign exporter of a good. This type of trade barrier isn't common. It was initially used during the 1980s when Japan voluntarily limited its exports of car parts to the United States.

Export Subsidies

A *subsidy* is a payment by the government to a producer. You studied the effects of a subsidy on the quantity produced and the price of a subsidized farm product in Chapter 6, pp. 140–141.

An *export subsidy* is a payment by the government to the producer of an exported good. Export subsidies are illegal under a number of international agreements, including the North American Free Trade Agreement (NAFTA), and the rules of the World Trade Organization (WTO).

Although export subsidies are illegal, the subsidies that the U.S. and European Union governments pay to farmers end up increasing domestic production, some of which gets exported. These exports of subsidized farm products make it harder for producers in other countries, notably in Africa and Central and South America, to compete in global markets. Export subsidies bring gains to domestic producers, but they result in inefficient underproduction in the rest of the world and create a deadweight loss.

Economics in Action
Self-Interest Beats the Social Interest

The **World Trade Organization (WTO)** is an international body established by the world's major trading nations for the purpose of supervising international trade and lowering the barriers to trade.

In 2001, at a meeting of trade ministers from all the WTO member-countries held in Doha, Qatar, an agreement was made to begin negotiations to lower tariff barriers and quotas that restrict international trade in farm products and services. These negotiations are called the **Doha Development Agenda** or the **Doha Round**.

In the period since 2001, thousands of hours of conferences in Cancún in 2003, Geneva in 2004, and Hong Kong in 2005, and ongoing meetings at WTO headquarters in Geneva, costing millions of taxpayers' dollars, have made disappointing progress.

Rich nations, led by the United States, the European Union, and Japan, want greater access to the markets of developing nations in exchange for allowing those nations greater access to the markets of the rich world, especially those for farm products.

Developing nations, led by Brazil, China, India, and South Africa, want access to the markets of farm products of the rich world, but they also want to protect their infant industries.

With two incompatible positions, these negotiations are stalled and show no signs of a breakthrough. The self-interests of rich nations and developing nations are preventing the achievement of the social interest.

 REVIEW QUIZ

1   What are the tools that a country can use to restrict international trade?
2   Explain the effects of a tariff on domestic production, the quantity bought, and the price.
3   Explain who gains and who loses from a tariff and why the losses exceed the gains.
4   Explain the effects of an import quota on domestic production, consumption, and price.
5   Explain who gains and who loses from an import quota and why the losses exceed the gains.

You can work these questions in Study Plan 7.3 and get instant feedback.

◆ The Case Against Protection

For as long as nations and international trade have existed, people have debated whether a country is better off with free international trade or with protection from foreign competition. The debate continues, but for most economists, a verdict has been delivered and is the one you have just seen. Free trade promotes prosperity for all countries; protection is inefficient. We've seen the most powerful case for free trade—it brings gains for consumers that exceed any losses incurred by producers, so there is a net gain for society.

But there is a broader range of issues in the free trade versus protection debate. Let's review these issues.

Two classical arguments for restricting international trade are

- The infant-industry argument
- The dumping argument

The Infant-Industry Argument

The **infant-industry argument** for protection is that it is necessary to protect a new industry to enable it to grow into a mature industry that can compete in world markets. The argument is based on the idea that comparative advantage changes or is dynamic and that on-the-job experience—*learning-by-doing*—is an important source of changes in comparative advantage. The fact that learning-by-doing can change comparative advantage doesn't justify protecting an infant industry.

First, the infant-industry argument is not valid if the benefits of learning-by-doing accrue *only* to the firms in the infant industry. The reason is that these firms will anticipate and reap the benefits of learning-by-doing without the additional incentive of protection from foreign competition.

For example, there are huge productivity gains from learning-by-doing in the manufacture of aircraft, but these gains benefit Boeing and other aircraft producers. Because the people making the decisions are the ones who benefit, they take the future gains into account when they decide on the scale of their activities. No benefits accrue to firms in other industries or other parts of the economy, so there is no need for government assistance to achieve an efficient outcome.

Second, even if the case is made for protecting an infant industry, it is more efficient to do so by giving the firms in the industry a subsidy, which is financed out of taxes. Such a subsidy would encourage the industry to mature and to compete with efficient world producers and keep the price faced by consumers at the world price.

The Dumping Argument

Dumping occurs when a foreign firm sells its exports at a lower price than its cost of production. Dumping might be used by a firm that wants to gain a global monopoly. In this case, the foreign firm sells its output at a price below its cost to drive domestic firms out of business. When the domestic firms have gone, the foreign firm takes advantage of its monopoly position and charges a higher price for its product. Dumping is illegal under the rules of the WTO and is usually regarded as a justification for temporary tariffs, which are called *countervailing duties*.

But there are powerful reasons to resist the dumping argument for protection. First, it is virtually impossible to detect dumping because it is hard to determine a firm's costs. As a result, the test for dumping is whether a firm's export price is below its domestic price. But this test is a weak one because it can be rational for a firm to charge a low price in a market in which the quantity demanded is highly sensitive to price and a higher price in a market in which demand is less price-sensitive.

Second, it is hard to think of a good that is produced by a *global* monopoly. So even if all the domestic firms in some industry were driven out of business, it would always be possible to find alternative foreign sources of supply and to buy the good at a price determined in a competitive market.

Third, if a good or service were a truly global monopoly, the best way of dealing with it would be by regulation—just as in the case of domestic monopolies (see Chapter 13, pp. 313–315). Such regulation would require international cooperation.

The two arguments for protection that we've just examined have an element of credibility. The counterarguments are in general stronger, however, so these arguments do not make the case for protection. But they are not the only arguments that you might encounter. There are many other new arguments against globalization and for protection.

The most common ones are that protection

- Saves jobs
- Allows us to compete with cheap foreign labor
- Penalizes lax environmental standards
- Prevents rich countries from exploiting developing countries

Saves Jobs

First, free trade does cost some jobs, but it also creates other jobs. It brings about a global rationalization of labor and allocates labor resources to their highest-valued activities. International trade in textiles has cost tens of thousands of jobs in the United States as textile mills and other factories closed. But tens of thousands of jobs have been created in other countries as textile mills opened. And tens of thousands of U.S. workers got better-paying jobs than as textile workers because U.S. export industries expanded and created new jobs. More jobs have been created than destroyed.

Although protection does save particular jobs, it does so at a high cost. For example, until 2005, U.S. textile jobs were protected by an international agreement called the Multifiber Arrangement. The U.S. International Trade Commission (ITC) has estimated that because of import quotas, 72,000 jobs existed in the textile industry that would otherwise have disappeared and that the annual clothing expenditure in the United States was $15.9 billion ($160 per family) higher than it would have been with free trade. Equivalently, the ITC estimated that each textile job saved cost $221,000 a year.

Imports don't only destroy jobs. They create jobs for retailers that sell imported goods and for firms that service those goods. Imports also create jobs by creating income in the rest of the world, some of which is spent on U.S.-made goods and services.

Allows Us to Compete with Cheap Foreign Labor

With the removal of tariffs on trade between the United States and Mexico, people said we would hear a "giant sucking sound" as jobs rushed to Mexico. Let's see what's wrong with this view.

The labor cost of a unit of output equals the wage rate divided by labor productivity. For example, if a U.S. autoworker earns $30 an hour and produces 15 units of output an hour, the average labor cost of a

unit of output is $2. If a Mexican auto assembly worker earns $3 an hour and produces 1 unit of output an hour, the average labor cost of a unit of output is $3. Other things remaining the same, the higher a worker's productivity, the higher is the worker's wage rate. High-wage workers have high productivity; low-wage workers have low productivity.

Although high-wage U.S. workers are more productive, on average, than low-wage Mexican workers, there are differences across industries. U.S. labor is relatively more productive in some activities than in others. For example, the productivity of U.S. workers in producing movies, financial services, and customized computer chips is relatively higher than their productivity in the production of metals and some standardized machine parts. The activities in which U.S. workers are relatively more productive than their Mexican counterparts are those in which the United States has a *comparative advantage*. By engaging in free trade, increasing our production and exports of the goods and services in which we have a comparative advantage, and decreasing our production and increasing our imports of the goods and services in which our trading partners have a comparative advantage, we can make ourselves and the citizens of other countries better off.

Penalizes Lax Environmental Standards

Another argument for protection is that many poorer countries, such as China and Mexico, do not have the same environmental policies that we have and, because they are willing to pollute and we are not, we cannot compete with them without tariffs. So if poorer countries want free trade with the richer and "greener" countries, they must raise their environmental standards.

This argument for protection is weak. First, a poor country cannot afford to be as concerned about its environmental standard as a rich country can. Today, some of the worst pollution of air and water is found in China, Mexico, and the former communist countries of Eastern Europe. But only a few decades ago, London and Los Angeles topped the pollution league chart. The best hope for cleaner air in Beijing and Mexico City is rapid income growth. And free trade contributes to that growth. As incomes in developing countries grow, they will have the *means* to match their desires to improve their environment. Second, a poor country may have a comparative advantage at doing "dirty" work, which helps it to raise its income and at the same time enables the global economy to achieve higher environmental standards than would otherwise be possible.

Prevents Rich Countries from Exploiting Developing Countries

Another argument for protection is that international trade must be restricted to prevent the people of the rich industrial world from exploiting the poorer people of the developing countries and forcing them to work for slave wages.

Child labor and near-slave labor are serious problems that are rightly condemned. But by trading with poor countries, we increase the demand for the goods that these countries produce and, more significantly, we increase the demand for their labor. When the demand for labor in developing countries increases, the wage rate also increases. So, rather than exploiting people in developing countries, trade can improve their opportunities and increase their incomes.

The arguments for protection that we've reviewed leave free-trade unscathed. But a new phenomenon is at work in our economy: *offshore outsourcing*. Surely we need protection from this new source of foreign competition. Let's investigate.

Offshore Outsourcing

Citibank, the Bank of America, Apple, Nike, Wal-Mart: What do these U.S. icons have in common? They all send jobs that could be done in America to China, India, Thailand, or even Canada—they are offshoring. What exactly is offshoring?

What Is Offshoring? A firm in the United States can obtain the goods and services that it sells in any of four ways:

1. Hire American labor and produce in America.
2. Hire foreign labor and produce in other countries.
3. Buy finished goods, components, or services from other firms in the United States.
4. Buy finished goods, components, or services from other firms in other countries.

Activities 3 and 4 are **outsourcing**, and activities 2 and 4 are **offshoring**. Activity 4 is **offshore outsourcing**. Notice that offshoring includes activities that take place inside U.S. firms. If a U.S. firm opens its own facilities in another country, then it is offshoring.

Offshoring has been going on for hundreds of years, but it expanded rapidly and became a source of concern during the 1990s as many U.S. firms moved information technology services and general office services such as finance, accounting, and human resources management overseas.

Why Did Offshoring of Services Boom During the 1990s? The gains from specialization and trade that you saw in the previous section must be large enough to make it worth incurring the costs of communication and transportation. If the cost of producing a T-shirt in China isn't lower than the cost of producing the T-shirt in the United States by more than the cost of transporting the shirt from China to America, then it is more efficient to produce shirts in the United States and avoid the transportation costs.

The same considerations apply to trade in services. If services are to be produced offshore, then the cost of delivering those services must be low enough to leave the buyer with an overall lower cost. Before the 1990s, the cost of communicating across large distances was too high to make the offshoring of business services efficient. But during the 1990s, when satellites, fiber-optic cables, and computers cut the cost of a phone call between America and India to less than a dollar an hour, a huge base of offshore resources became competitive with similar resources in the United States.

What Are the Benefits of Offshoring? Offshoring brings gains from trade identical to those of any other type of trade. We could easily change the names of the items traded from T-shirts and airplanes (the examples in the previous sections of this chapter) to banking services and call center services (or any other pair of services). An American bank might export banking services to Indian firms, and Indians might provide call center services to U.S. firms. This type of trade would benefit both Americans and Indians provided the United States has a comparative advantage in banking services and India has a comparative advantage in call center services.

Comparative advantages like these emerged during the 1990s. India has the world's largest educated English-speaking population and is located in a time zone half a day ahead of the U.S. east coast and midway between Asia and Europe, which facilitates 24/7 operations. When the cost of communicating with a worker in India was several dollars a minute, as it was before the 1990s, tapping these vast resources was just too costly. But at today's cost of a long-distance telephone call or Internet connection, resources in India can be used to produce services in the United States at a lower cost than those services can be produced by using resources located in the United States. And with the incomes that Indians earn from exporting services, some of the services (and goods) that Indians buy are produced in the United States.

Why Is Offshoring a Concern? Despite the gain from specialization and trade that offshoring brings, many people believe that it also brings costs that eat up the gains. Why?

A major reason is that offshoring is taking jobs in services. The loss of manufacturing jobs to other countries has been going on for decades, but the U.S. service sector has always expanded by enough to create new jobs to replace the lost manufacturing jobs. Now that service jobs are also going overseas, the fear is that there will not be enough jobs for Americans. This fear is misplaced.

Some service jobs are going overseas, while others are expanding at home. The United States imports call center services, but it exports education, health care, legal, financial, and a host of other types of services. Jobs in these sectors are expanding and will continue to expand.

The exact number of jobs that have moved to lower-cost offshore locations is not known, and estimates vary. But even the highest estimate is a tiny number compared to the normal rate of job creation.

Winners and Losers Gains from trade do not bring gains for every single person. Americans, on average, gain from offshore outsourcing, but some people lose. The losers are those who have invested in the human capital to do a specific job that has now gone offshore.

Unemployment benefits provide short-term temporary relief for these displaced workers. But the long-term solution requires retraining and the acquisition of new skills.

Beyond providing short-term relief through unemployment benefits, there is a large role for government in the provision of education and training to enable the labor force of the twenty-first century to be capable of ongoing learning and rapid retooling to take on new jobs that today we can't foresee.

Schools, colleges, and universities will expand and get better at doing their jobs of producing a highly educated and flexible labor force.

Avoiding Trade Wars

We have reviewed the arguments commonly heard in favor of protection and the counterarguments against it. There is one counterargument to protection that is general and quite overwhelming: Protection invites retaliation and can trigger a trade war.

The best example of a trade war occurred during the Great Depression of the 1930s when the United States introduced the Smoot-Hawley tariff. Country after country retaliated with its own tariff, and in a short period, world trade had almost disappeared. The costs to all countries were large and led to a renewed international resolve to avoid such self-defeating moves in the future. The costs also led to the creation of GATT and are the impetus behind current attempts to liberalize trade.

Why Is International Trade Restricted?

Why, despite all the arguments against protection, is trade restricted? There are two key reasons:

- Tariff revenue
- Rent seeking

Tariff Revenue Government revenue is costly to collect. In developed countries such as the United States, a well-organized tax collection system is in place that can generate billions of dollars of income tax and sales tax revenues. This tax collection system is made possible by the fact that most economic transactions are done by firms that must keep properly audited financial records. Without such records, revenue collection agencies (the Internal Revenue Service in the United States) would be severely hampered in their work. Even with audited financial accounts, some potential tax revenue is lost. Nonetheless, for industrialized countries, the income tax and sales taxes are the major sources of revenue and tariffs play a very small role.

But governments in developing countries have a difficult time collecting taxes from their citizens. Much economic activity takes place in an informal economy with few financial records, so only a small amount of revenue is collected from income taxes and sales taxes. The one area in which economic transactions are well recorded and audited is international trade. So this activity is an attractive base for tax collection in these countries and is used much more extensively than it is in developed countries.

Rent Seeking Rent seeking is the major reason why international trade is restricted. **Rent seeking** is lobbying for special treatment by the government to create economic profit or to divert consumer surplus or producer surplus away from others. Free trade increases consumption possibilities *on average*, but not everyone shares in the gain and some people even lose. Free trade brings benefits to some and imposes costs on others, with total benefits exceeding total costs. The uneven distribution of costs and benefits is the principal obstacle to achieving more liberal international trade.

Returning to the example of trade in T-shirts and airplanes, the benefits from free trade accrue to all the producers of airplanes and to those producers of T-shirts that do not bear the costs of adjusting to a smaller garment industry. These costs are transition costs, not permanent costs. The costs of moving to free trade are borne by the garment producers and their employees who must become producers of other goods and services in which the United States has a comparative advantage.

The number of winners from free trade is large, but because the gains are spread thinly over a large number of people, the gain per person is small. The winners could organize and become a political force lobbying for free trade. But political activity is costly. It uses time and other scarce resources and the gains per person are too small to make the cost of political activity worth bearing.

In contrast, the number of losers from free trade is small, but the loss per person is large. Because the loss per person is large, the people who lose *are* willing to incur considerable expense to lobby against free trade.

Both the winners and losers weigh benefits and costs. Those who gain from free trade weigh the benefits it brings against the cost of achieving it. Those who lose from free trade and gain from protection weigh the benefit of protection against the cost of maintaining it. The protectionists undertake a larger quantity of political lobbying than the free traders.

Compensating Losers

If, in total, the gains from free international trade exceed the losses, why don't those who gain compensate those who lose so that everyone is in favor of free trade?

Some compensation does take place. When Congress approved the North American Free Trade Agreement (NAFTA) with Canada and Mexico, it set up a $56 million fund to support and retrain workers who lost their jobs as a result of the new trade agreement. During NAFTA's first six months, only 5,000 workers applied for benefits under this scheme. The losers from international trade are also compensated indirectly through the normal unemployment compensation arrangements. But only limited attempts are made to compensate those who lose.

The main reason why full compensation is not attempted is that the costs of identifying all the losers and estimating the value of their losses would be enormous. Also, it would never be clear whether a person who has fallen on hard times is suffering because of free trade or for other reasons that might be largely under her or his control. Furthermore, some people who look like losers at one point in time might, in fact, end up gaining. The young autoworker who loses his job in Michigan and becomes a computer assembly worker in Minneapolis might resent the loss of work and the need to move. But a year later, looking back on events, he counts himself fortunate.

Because we do not, in general, compensate the losers from free international trade, protectionism is a popular and permanent feature of our national economic and political life.

REVIEW QUIZ

1 What are the infant industry and dumping arguments for protection? Are they correct?

2 Can protection save jobs and the environment and prevent workers in developing countries from being exploited?

3 What is offshore outsourcing? Who benefits from it and who loses?

4 What are the main reasons for imposing a tariff?

5 Why don't the winners from free trade win the political argument?

You can work these questions in Study Plan 7.4 and get instant feedback.

We end this chapter on global markets in action in *Reading Between the Lines* on pp. 168–169, where we apply what you've learned by looking at the effects of a U.S. tariff on imports of tires from China.

A Tariff on Tires

China: Tire Trade Penalties Will Hurt Relations with U.S.

USAToday
September 12, 2009

WASHINGTON—President Obama's decision to impose trade penalties on Chinese tires has infuriated Beijing. …

The federal trade panel recommended a 55% tariff in the first year, 45% in the second year, and 35% in the third year. Obama settled on 35% the first year, 30% in the second, and 25% in the third, [White House Press Secretary Robert] Gibbs said.

"For trade to work for everybody, it has to be based on fairness and rules. We're simply enforcing those rules and would expect the Chinese to understand those rules," Gibbs said. …

The steelworkers union … says more than 5,000 tire workers have lost jobs since 2004, as Chinese tires overwhelmed the U.S. market.

The U.S. trade representative's office said four tire plants closed in 2006 and 2007 and three more are closing this year. During that time, just one new plant opened. U.S. imports of Chinese tires more than tripled from 2004 to 2008 and China's market share in the United States went from 4.7% of tires purchased in 2004 to 16.7% in 2008, the office said. …

China said the tariffs do not square with the facts, … citing a 2.2% increase in 2008 from 2007, and a 16% fall in exports in the first half of 2009 compared with the first half of 2008.

The new tariffs, on top of an existing 4% tariff on all tire imports, take effect Sept. 26. …

ESSENCE OF THE STORY

- The United States is imposing a tariff on tires imported from China of 35 percent in 2009 and falling after two years to 25 percent.

- The steelworkers union says that more than 5,000 U.S. tire workers have lost jobs since 2004.

- Four U.S. tire plants closed in 2006 and 2007 and three were closing in 2009.

- Between 2004 and 2008, U.S. imports of Chinese tires more than tripled and China's share of the U.S. tire market increased from 4.7 percent of tires purchased in 2004 to 16.7 percent in 2008.

- China said that the rate of increase in 2008 was 2.2 percent and in the first half of 2009 its tire exports to the United States fell by 16 percent compared with the first half of 2008.

ECONOMIC ANALYSIS

- In the global economy, 450 firms produce more than 1 billion tires a year.

- The United States produces tires and imports tires from other countries.

- In 2004, the wholesale price of a tire, on average, was $40. The United States produced 235 million tires and imported 15 million.

- Figure 1 shows this situation. The demand curve is D_{US} and the supply curve is S_{US04}. The world price is $40 a tire and the gap between the quantity demanded and quantity supplied was filled by tire imports.

- Between 2004 and 2008, the price of rubber, one of the main inputs into a tire, doubled. With this rise in the price of a resource used to produce tires, the supply of tires in the United States decreased and the supply curve shifted leftward to S_{US08}.

- Tire producers in China felt the same rise in the price of rubber, but by installing the latest technology machines and with low-cost labor, they were able to prevent the cost of producing a tire from rising. The world price didn't rise.

- The decrease in U.S. supply with no change in the world price brought a surge of tire imports, especially from China.

- U.S. tire producers scaled back production and fired workers. In Fig. 1, U.S. production fell to 200 million tires a year and tire imports rose to 50 million a year.

- In this situation, the United States imposed a 35 percent tariff on Chinese-made tires. Figure 2 illustrates. The world price plus tariff raised the wholesale price in the United States to $55 a tire.

- U.S. supply is S_{US09} and at the higher price, U.S. firms increase the quantity of tires supplied to 215 million a year. The quantity demanded decreases to 240 million a year and U.S. imports shrink.

- The U.S. government collects tariff revenue (the purple rectangle) and a deadweight loss arises (the sum of the two gray triangles).

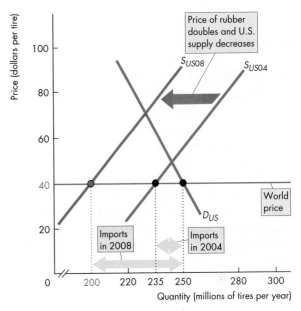

Figure 1 The surge in tire imports

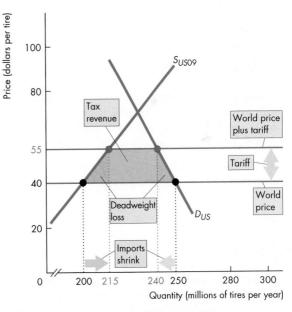

Figure 2 The effects of the tariff on tire imports

SUMMARY

Key Points

How Global Markets Work (pp. 152–154)

- Comparative advantage drives international trade.
- If the world price of a good is lower than the domestic price, the rest of the world has a comparative advantage in producing that good and the domestic country gains by producing less, consuming more, and importing the good.
- If the world price of a good is higher than the domestic price, the domestic country has a comparative advantage in producing that good and gains by producing more, consuming less, and exporting the good.

Working Problems 1 to 6 will give you a better understanding of how global markets work.

Winners, Losers, and the Net Gain from Trade
(pp. 155–156)

- Compared to a no-trade situation, in a market with imports, consumer surplus is larger, producer surplus is smaller, and total surplus is larger with free international trade.
- Compared to a no-trade situation, in a market with exports, consumer surplus is smaller, producer surplus is larger, and total surplus is larger with free international trade.

Working Problems 7 and 8 will give you a better understanding of winners, losers, and the net gains from trade.

International Trade Restrictions (pp. 157–162)

- Countries restrict international trade by imposing tariffs, import quotas, and other import barriers.
- Trade restrictions raise the domestic price of imported goods, lower the quantity imported, decrease consumer surplus, increase producer surplus, and create a deadweight loss.

Working Problems 9 to 20 will give you a better understanding of international trade restrictions.

The Case Against Protection (pp. 163–167)

- Arguments that protection is necessary for infant industries and to prevent dumping are weak.
- Arguments that protection saves jobs, allows us to compete with cheap foreign labor, is needed to penalize lax environmental standards, and prevents exploitation of developing countries are flawed.
- Offshore outsourcing is just a new way of reaping gains from trade and does not justify protection.
- Trade restrictions are popular because protection brings a small loss per person to a large number of people and a large gain per person to a small number of people. Those who gain have a stronger political voice than those who lose and it is too costly to identify and compensate losers.

Working Problem 21 will give you a better understanding of the case against protection.

Key Terms

Doha Development Agenda
   (Doha Round), 162
Dumping, 163
Exports, 152
General Agreement on Tariffs and
   Trade (GATT), 159

Import quota, 160
Imports, 152
Infant-industry argument, 163
Offshore outsourcing, 165
Offshoring, 165
Outsourcing, 165

Rent seeking, 167
Tariff, 157
World Trade Organization
   (WTO), 162

STUDY PLAN PROBLEMS AND APPLICATIONS

myeconlab You can work Problems 1 to 21 in MyEconLab Chapter 7 Study Plan and get instant feedback.

How Global Markets Work (Study Plan 7.1)

Use the following information to work Problems 1 to 3.

Wholesalers of roses (the firms that supply your local flower shop with roses for Valentine's Day) buy and sell roses in containers that hold 120 stems. The table provides information about the wholesale market for roses in the United States. The demand schedule is the wholesalers' demand and the supply schedule is the U.S. rose growers' supply.

Price (dollars per container)	Quantity demanded	Quantity supplied
	(millions of containers per year)	
100	15	0
125	12	2
150	9	4
175	6	6
200	3	8
225	0	10

Wholesalers can buy roses at auction in Aalsmeer, Holland, for $125 per container.

1. a. Without international trade, what would be the price of a container of roses and how many containers of roses a year would be bought and sold in the United States?

   b. At the price in your answer to part (a), does the United States or the rest of the world have a comparative advantage in producing roses?

2. If U.S. wholesalers buy roses at the lowest possible price, how many do they buy from U.S. growers and how many do they import?

3. Draw a graph to illustrate the U.S. wholesale market for roses. Show the equilibrium in that market with no international trade and the equilibrium with free trade. Mark the quantity of roses produced in the United States, the quantity imported, and the total quantity bought.

Use the following news clip to work Problems 4 and 5.

Underwater Oil Discovery to Transform Brazil into a Major Exporter

A huge underwater oil field discovered late last year has the potential to transform Brazil into a sizable exporter. Fifty years ago, Petrobras was formed as a trading company to import oil to support Brazil's growing economy. Two years ago, Brazil reached its long-sought goal of energy self-sufficiency.

Source: *International Herald Tribune*, January 11, 2008

4. Describe Brazil's comparative advantage in producing oil and explain why its comparative advantage has changed.

5. a. Draw a graph to illustrate the Brazilian market for oil and explain why Brazil was an importer of oil until a few years ago.

   b. Draw a graph to illustrate the Brazilian market for oil and explain why Brazil may become an exporter of oil in the near future.

6. **Postcard: Bangalore. Hearts Set on Joining the Global Economy, Indian IT Workers are Brushing Up on Their Interpersonal Skills**

   The huge number of Indian workers staffing the world's tech firms and call centers possess cutting-edge technical knowledge, but their interpersonal and communication skills lag far behind. Enter Bangalore's finishing schools.

   Source: *Time*, May 5, 2008

   a. What comparative advantages does this news clip identify?

   b. Using the information in this news clip, what services do you predict Bangalore (India) exports and what services do you predict it imports?

Winners, Losers, and the Net Gain from Trade

(Study Plan 7.2)

7. In the news clip in Problem 6, who will gain and who will lose from the trade in services that the news clip predicts?

8. Use the information on the U.S. wholesale market for roses in Problem 1 to

   a. Explain who gains and who loses from free international trade in roses compared to a situation in which Americans buy only roses grown in the United States.

   b. Draw a graph to illustrate the gains and losses from free trade.

   c. Calculate the gain from international trade.

International Trade Restrictions (Study Plan 7.3)

Use the following news clip to work Problems 9 and 10.

Steel Tariffs Appear to Have Backfired on Bush

President Bush set aside his free-trade principles last year and imposed heavy tariffs on imported steel to help out struggling mills in Pennsylvania and West Virginia. Some economists say the tariffs may have cost more jobs than they saved, by driving up costs for automakers and other steel users.

Source: *The Washington Post*, September 19, 2003

9. a. Explain how a high tariff on steel imports can help domestic steel producers.

    b. Explain how a high tariff on steel imports can harm steel users.

10. Draw a graph of the U.S. market for steel to show how a high tariff on steel imports
    i. Helps U.S. steel producers.
    ii. Harms U.S. steel users.
    iii. Creates a deadweight loss.

Use the information on the U.S. wholesale market for roses in Problem 1 to work Problems 11 to 16.

11. If the United States puts a tariff of $25 per container on imports of roses, what happens to the U.S. price of roses, the quantity of roses bought, the quantity produced in the United States, and the quantity imported?

12. Who gains and who loses from this tariff?

13. Draw a graph to illustrate the gains and losses from the tariff and on the graph identify the gains and losses, the tariff revenue, and the deadweight loss.

14. If the United States puts an import quota on roses of 5 million containers, what happens to the U.S. price of roses, the quantity of roses bought, the quantity produced in the United States, and the quantity imported?

15. Who gains and who loses from this quota?

16. Draw a graph to illustrate the gains and losses from the import quota and on the graph identify the gains and losses, the importers' profit, and the deadweight loss.

Use the following news clip to work Problems 17 and 18.

Car Sales Go Up as Prices Tumble

Car affordability in Australia is now at its best in 20 years, fueling a surge in sales as prices tumble. In 2000, Australia cut the tariff to 15 percent and on January 1, 2005, it cut the tariff to 10 percent.

Source: *Courier Mail*, February 26, 2005

17. Explain who gains and who loses from the lower tariff on imported cars.

18. Draw a graph to show how the price of a car, the quantity of cars bought, the quantity of cars produced in Australia, and the quantity of cars imported into Australia changed.

Use the following news clip to work Problems 19 and 20.

Why the World Can't Afford Food

As [food] stocks dwindled, some countries placed export restrictions on food to protect their own supplies. This in turn drove up prices, punishing countries—especially poor ones—that depend on imports for much of their food.

Time, May 19, 2008

19. a. What are the benefits to a country from importing food?

    b. What costs might arise from relying on imported food?

20. If a country restricts food exports, what effect does this restriction have in that country on the price of food, the quantity of food it produces, the quantity of food it consumes, and the quantity of food it exports?

The Case Against Protection (Study Plan 7.4)

21. **Chinese Tire Maker Rejects U.S. Charge of Defects**

    U.S. regulators ordered the recall of more than 450,000 faulty tires. The Chinese producer of the tires disputed the allegations and hinted that the recall might be an effort by foreign competitors to hamper Chinese exports to the United States. Mounting scrutiny of Chinese-made goods has become a source of new trade frictions between the United States and China and fueled worries among regulators, corporations, and consumers about the risks associated with many products imported from China.

    Source: *International Herald Tribune*, June 26, 2007

    a. What does the information in the news clip imply about the comparative advantage of producing tires in the United States and China?

    b. Could product quality be a valid argument against free trade?

    c. How would the product-quality argument against free trade be open to abuse by domestic producers of the imported good?

ADDITIONAL PROBLEMS AND APPLICATIONS

 These problems can be worked in MyEconLab if assigned by your instructor.

How Global Markets Work

22. Suppose that the world price of sugar is 10 cents a pound, the United States does not trade internationally, and the equilibrium price of sugar in the United States is 20 cents a pound. The United States then begins to trade internationally.
    a. How does the price of sugar in the United States change?
    b. Do U.S. consumers buy more or less sugar?
    c. Do U.S. sugar growers produce more or less sugar?
    d. Does the United States export or import sugar and why?

23. Suppose that the world price of steel is $100 a ton, India does not trade internationally, and the equilibrium price of steel in India is $60 a ton. India then begins to trade internationally.
    a. How does the price of steel in India change?
    b. How does the quantity of steel produced in India change?
    c. How does the quantity of steel bought by India change?
    d. Does India export or import steel and why?

24. A semiconductor is a key component in your laptop, cell phone, and iPod. The table provides information about the market for semiconductors in the United States.

Price (dollars per unit)	Quantity demanded	Quantity supplied
	(billions of units per year)	
10	25	0
12	20	20
14	15	40
16	10	60
18	5	80
20	0	100

Producers of semiconductors can get $18 a unit on the world market.
    a. With no international trade, what would be the price of a semiconductor and how many semiconductors a year would be bought and sold in the United States?
    b. Does the United States have a comparative advantage in producing semiconductors?

25. Act Now, Eat Later

The hunger crisis in poor countries has its roots in U.S. and European policies of subsidizing the diversion of food crops to produce biofuels like corn-based ethanol. That is, doling out subsidies to put the world's dinner into the gas tank.

Source: *Time*, May 5, 2008

    a. What is the effect on the world price of corn of the increased use of corn to produce ethanol in the United States and Europe?
    b. How does the change in the world price of corn affect the quantity of corn produced in a poor developing country with a comparative advantage in producing corn, the quantity it consumes, and the quantity that it either exports or imports?

Winners, Losers, and the Net Gain from Trade

26. Use the news clip in Problem 25. Draw a graph of the market for corn in a poor developing country to show the changes in consumer surplus, producer surplus, and deadweight loss.

Use the following news clip to work Problems 27 and 28.

South Korea to Resume U.S. Beef Imports

South Korea will reopen its market to most U.S. beef. South Korea banned imports of U.S. beef in 2003 amid concerns over a case of mad cow disease in the United States. The ban closed what was then the third-largest market for U.S. beef exporters.

Source: CNN, May 29, 2008

27. a. Explain how South Korea's import ban on U.S. beef affected beef producers and consumers in South Korea.
    b. Draw a graph of the market for beef in South Korea to illustrate your answer to part (a). Identify the changes in consumer surplus, producer surplus, and deadweight loss.

28. a. Assuming that South Korea is the only importer of U.S. beef, explain how South Korea's import ban on U.S. beef affected beef producers and consumers in the United States.
    b. Draw a graph of the market for beef in the United States to illustrate your answer to part (a). Identify the changes in consumer surplus, producer surplus, and deadweight loss.

International Trade Restrictions

Use the following information to work Problems 29 to 31.

Before 1995, trade between the United States and Mexico was subject to tariffs. In 1995, Mexico joined NAFTA and all U.S. and Mexican tariffs have gradually been removed.

29. Explain how the price that U.S. consumers pay for goods from Mexico and the quantity of U.S. imports from Mexico have changed. Who are the winners and who are the losers from this free trade?

30. Explain how the quantity of U.S. exports to Mexico and the U.S. government's tariff revenue from trade with Mexico have changed.

31. Suppose that in 2008, tomato growers in Florida lobby the U.S. government to impose an import quota on Mexican tomatoes. Explain who in the United States would gain and who would lose from such a quota.

Use the following information to work Problems 32 and 33.

Suppose that in response to huge job losses in the U.S. textile industry, Congress imposes a 100 percent tariff on imports of textiles from China.

32. Explain how the tariff on textiles will change the price that U.S. buyers pay for textiles, the quantity of textiles imported, and the quantity of textiles produced in the United States.

33. Explain how the U.S. and Chinese gains from trade will change. Who in the United States will lose and who will gain?

Use the following information to work Problems 34 and 35.

With free trade between Australia and the United States, Australia would export beef to the United States. But the United States imposes an import quota on Australian beef.

34. Explain how this quota influences the price that U.S. consumers pay for beef, the quantity of beef produced in the United States, and the U.S. and the Australian gains from trade.

35. Explain who in the United States gains from the quota on beef imports and who loses.

The Case Against Protection

36. **Trading Up**

The cost of protecting jobs in uncompetitive sectors through tariffs is high: Saving a job in the sugar industry costs American consumers $826,000 in higher prices a year; saving a dairy industry job costs $685,000 per year; and saving a job in the manufacturing of women's handbags costs $263,000.

Source: *The New York Times*, June 26, 2006
a. What are the arguments for saving the jobs mentioned in this news clip?
b. Explain why these arguments are faulty.
c. Is there any merit to saving these jobs?

Economics in the News

37. After you have studied *Reading Between the Lines* on pp. 168–169, answer the following questions.
a. What events put U.S. tire producers under pressure and caused some to go out of business?
b. Explain how a tariff on tire imports changes domestic production, consumption, and imports of tires.
c. Illustrate your answer to part (b) with an appropriate graphical analysis.
d. Explain how a tariff on tire imports changes consumer surplus and producer surplus.
e. Explain the four sources of loss of consumer surplus that result from a tariff on tire imports.
f. Illustrate your answer to part (e) with an appropriate graphical analysis.

38. **Aid May Grow for Laid-Off Workers**

Expansion of the Trade Adjustment Assistance (TAA) program would improve the social safety net for the 21st century, as advances permit more industries to take advantage of cheap foreign labor—even for skilled, white-collar work. By providing special compensation to more of globalization's losers and retraining them for stable jobs at home, an expanded program could begin to ease the resentment and insecurity arising from the new economy.

Source: *The Washington Post*, July 23, 2007
a. Why does the United States engage in international trade if it causes U.S. workers to lose their jobs?
b. Explain how an expansion of the TAA program will make it easier for the United States to move toward freer international trade.

The Amazing Market

The five chapters that you've just studied explain how markets work. The market is an amazing instrument. It enables people who have never met and who know nothing about each other to interact and do business. It also enables us to allocate our scarce resources to the uses that we value most highly. Markets can be very simple or highly organized. Markets are ancient and they are modern.

A simple and ancient market is one that the American historian Daniel J. Boorstin describes in *The Discoverers* (p. 161). In the late fourteenth century,

> *The Muslim caravans that went southward from Morocco across the Atlas Mountains arrived after twenty days at the shores of the Senegal River. There the Moroccan traders laid out separate piles of salt, of beads from Ceutan coral, and cheap manufactured goods. Then they retreated out of sight. The local tribesmen, who lived in the strip mines where they dug their gold, came to the shore and put a heap of gold beside each pile of Moroccan goods. Then they, in turn, went out of view, leaving the Moroccan traders either to take the gold offered for a particular pile or to reduce the pile of their merchandise to suit the offered price in gold. Once again the Moroccan traders withdrew, and the process went on. By this system of commercial etiquette, the Moroccans collected their gold.*

An organized and modern market is an auction at which the U.S. government sells rights to cell phone companies for the use of the airwaves.

Everything and anything that can be exchanged is traded in markets to the benefit of both buyers and sellers.

Alfred Marshall *(1842–1924) grew up in an England that was being transformed by the railroad and by the expansion of manufacturing. Mary Paley was one of Marshall's students at Cambridge, and when Alfred and Mary married, in 1877, celibacy rules barred Alfred from continuing to teach at Cambridge. By 1884, with more liberal rules, the Marshalls returned to Cambridge, where Alfred became Professor of Political Economy.*

Many economists had a hand in refining the demand and supply model, but the first thorough and complete statement of the model as we know it today was set out by Alfred Marshall, with the help of Mary Paley Marshall. Published in 1890, this monumental treatise, The Principles of Economics, *became the textbook on economics on both sides of the Atlantic for almost half a century.*

"The forces to be dealt with are ... so numerous, that it is best to take a few at a time .... Thus we begin by isolating the primary relations of supply, demand, and price."

ALFRED MARSHALL
The Principles of Economics

What sparked your interest in economics?

I was studying mathematics and computer science, but I felt that the subjects were not as relevant as I would like.

I discovered economics through a research assistantship with a professor who was working on auctions. I had a summer job working for a firm that sold computers to the government through auctions. Eventually my professor, Bob Marshall, wrote two articles on the topic and testified before Congress to help reform the system for government procurement of computers. That really inspired me and showed me the power of economic ideas to change the world and to make things work more efficiently.

This original inspiration has remained and continues to drive much of your research. Can you explain how economists study auctions?

The study of the design of markets and auction-based marketplaces requires you to use all of the different tools that economics offers.

An auction is a well-defined game. You can write down the rules of the game and a formal theoretical model does a great job capturing the real problem that the players face. And theories do an excellent job predicting behavior.

Buyers have a valuation for an object that is private information. They do not know the valuations of other bidders, and sometimes they don't even know their own valuation. For example, if they're buying oil rights, there may be uncertainty about how much oil there is in the ground. In that case, information about the amount of oil available is dispersed among the bidders, because each bidder has done their own survey. The bidders face a strategic problem of bidding, and they face an informational problem of trying to draw inferences about how valuable the object will be if they win.

Bidders need to recognize that their bid only matters when they win the auction, and they only win when they bid the most. The knowledge that they were the most optimistic of all the competitors should cause them to revise their beliefs.

From the seller's perspective, there are choices about how an auction is designed—auctions can use sealed bidding, where the seller receives bids and then opens them at a pre-determined time, or alternatively bidding may be interactive, where each bidder has an

opportunity to outbid the previous high bidder. There are also different ways to use bids received by the auctioneer to determine the price. Create an new screamer: Both revenue and efficiency are affected by auction design. The seller may consider revenue, though governments are often most concerned about efficient allocation.

Both revenue and efficiency are affected by auction design. One key question the seller must consider is how the design will affect the participation of bidders, as this will determine how competitive bidding will be as well as whether the object gets to the potential bidder who values the item the most.

What must the designer of an auction-based marketplace take into account?

An example of an auction-based marketplace is eBay, where the market designer sets the rules for buyers and sellers to interact.

When you design an auction-based marketplace, you have a whole new set of concerns. The buyers and sellers themselves are independent agents, each

SUSAN ATHEY is Professor of Economics at Harvard University. Born in 1970 in Boston and growing up in Rockville, Maryland, she completed high school in three years, wrapped up three majors—in economics, mathematics, and computer science—at Duke University at 20, completed her Ph.D. at Stanford University at 24, and was voted tenure at MIT and Stanford at 29. After teaching at MIT for six years and Stanford for five years, she moved to Harvard in 2006. Among her many honors and awards, the most prestigious is the John Bates Clark Medal given to the best economist under 40. She is the first woman to receive this award.

Professor Athey's research is broad both in scope and style. A government that wants to auction natural resources will turn to her fundamental discoveries (and possibly consult with her) before deciding how to organize the auction. An economist who wants to test a theory using a large data set will use her work on statistics and econometrics.

Michael Parkin talked with Susan Athey about her research, the progress that economists have made in understanding and designing markets, and her advice to students.

acting in their own interest. The design is a two-step process: you need to design an auction that is going to achieve an efficient allocation; and you need to design both the auction and the overall structure of the marketplace to attract participation.

In the case of eBay, the platform itself chooses the possible auction formats: auctions take place over time and bidders have the opportunity to outbid the standing high bidder during that time. The platform also allows sellers to use the "buy it now" option. The platform also makes certain tools and services available, such as the ability to search for items in various ways, track auctions, provide feedback, and monitor reputation. The sellers can select the level of the reserve price, whether they want to have a secret reserve price, how long the auction will last, whether to use "buy it now," what time of day the auction closes, how much information to provide, how many pictures they post.

These are all factors that impact participation of bidders and the revenue the seller will receive. The success of the platform hinges on both buyers and sellers choosing to participate.

Does auction theory enable us to predict the differences in the outcomes of an open ascending-bid English auction and a sealed-bid auction?

Sure. In some of my research, I compared open ascending auctions and pay-your-bid, sealed-bid auctions. I showed how the choice of auction format can make a big difference when you have small bidders bidding against larger, stronger bidders who usually (but not always) have higher valuations.

In an open ascending auction, it is hard for a small weaker bidder to ever win, because a stronger bidder can see their bids, respond to them, and outbid them.

> Sealed-bid auctions can do a better job of deterring collusion ... and generate larger revenue

But in a pay-your-bid, sealed-bid auction, bidders shade their bids—they bid less than their value, assuring themselves of some profit if they win—and a large bidder doesn't have the opportunity to see and respond to an unusually high bid from a weak bidder. Strong bidders realize that their competition is weak, and they shade their bids a lot—they bid a lot less than their value. That gives a small bidder the opportunity to be aggressive and outbid a larger bidder, even if it has a lower value. So what that does is encourage entry of small bidders. I found empirically that this entry effect was important and it helps sealed-bid auctions generate larger revenue than open ascending-bid auctions.

Does a sealed-bid auction always generate more revenue, other things equal, than an open ascending-bid auction?

Only if you have asymmetric bidders—strong large bidders and weaker small bidders—and even then the effect is ambiguous. It's an empirical question, but it tends to be true. We also showed that sealed-bid auctions can do a better job of deterring collusion. There are theoretical reasons to suggest that sealed bid auctions are more difficult to collude at than open ascending auctions, since at open ascending auctions, bidders can detect an opponent who is bidding higher than an agreement specifies and then respond to that. We found empirically in U.S. Forest Service timber auctions that the gap between sealed-bid auctions and ascending auctions was even greater than what a competitive model would predict, suggesting that some collusion may be at work.

What is the connection between auctions and the supply and demand model?

The basic laws of supply and demand can be seen in evidence in a market like eBay. The more sellers that are selling similar products, the lower the prices they can expect to achieve. Similarly the more buyers there are demanding those objects, the higher the prices the sellers can achieve.

An important thing for an auction marketplace is to attract a good balance of buyers and sellers so that both the buyers and the sellers find it more profitable to transact in that marketplace rather than using some other mechanism. From a seller's perspective, the more bidders there are on the platform, the greater the demand and the higher the prices. And from the buyer's perspective, the more sellers there are on the platform, the greater the supply and the lower the prices.

> The basic laws of supply and demand can be seen in evidence in a market like eBay.

Can we think of this thought experiment you just described as discovering demand and supply curves?

Exactly. When you study supply and demand curves, you wave your hands about how the prices actually get set. In different kinds of market settings, the actual mechanisms for setting prices are different. One way of setting prices is through auctions. But we tend to use auctions in settings where there are unique objects, so there isn't just one market price for the thing you are selling. If you were selling something that had lots of market substitutes, you can think of there being a market price in which this object can transact. An auction is a way to find a market price for something where there might not be a fixed market.

Can we think of an auction as a mechanism for finding the equilibrium price and quantity?

Exactly. We can think of the whole collection of auctions on eBay as being a mechanism to discover a market clearing price, and individual items might sell a little higher or a little lower but over all we believe that the prices on eBay auctions will represent market-clearing (equilibrium) prices.

Is economics a good subject in which to major? What subjects work well as complements with economics?

Of course I think economics is a fabulous major and I am passionate about it. I think it's a discipline that trains you to think rigorously. And if you apply yourself you'll finish an economics major with a more disciplined mind than when you started. Whether you go into the business world or academics, you'll be able to confront and think in a logical and structured way about whether a policy makes sense, a business model makes sense, or an industry structure is likely to be sustainable. You should look for that in an undergraduate major. You should not be looking to just absorb facts, but you should be looking to train your mind and to think in a way that you will be able to apply to the rest of your career. I think that economics combines well with statistics and mathematics or with more policy-oriented disciplines.

Do you have anything special to say to women who might be making a career choice? Why is economics a good field for a woman?

On the academic side, economics is a fairly objective field, where the best ideas win, so it's a level playing field. Academics is not very family friendly before you get tenured and extremely family friendly after. Within academics or outside of it, there are a wide range of fairly high-paying jobs that still allow some autonomy over your schedule and that have a deeper and more compelling meaning. For both men and women, if you choose to have a family, you reevaluate your career choices, and the tradeoff between time and money changes. And you're more likely to stick with and excel in a career if you find some meaning in it. So economics combines some of the advantages of having a strong job market and opportunities to have a large enough salary to pay for child care, and makes it economically worthwhile to stay in the work force, without sacrificing the sense of the greater good.

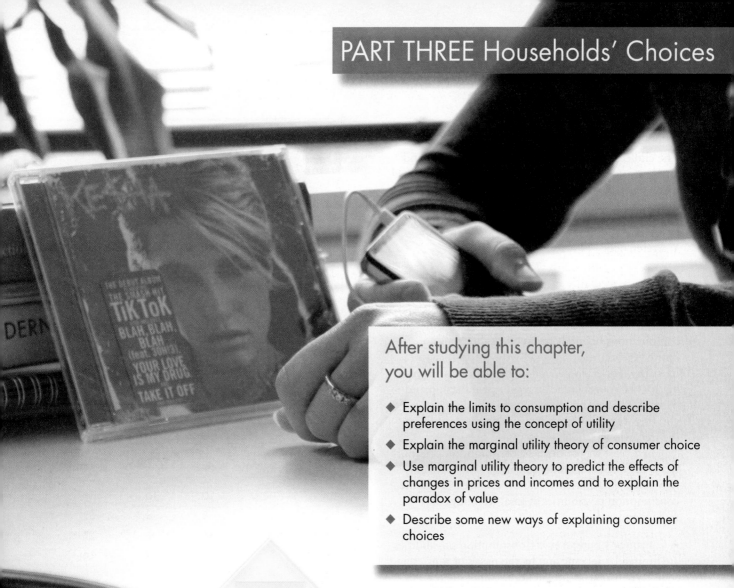

After studying this chapter,
you will be able to:

◆ Explain the limits to consumption and describe
preferences using the concept of utility

◆ Explain the marginal utility theory of consumer choice

◆ Use marginal utility theory to predict the effects of
changes in prices and incomes and to explain the
paradox of value

◆ Describe some new ways of explaining consumer
choices

8

UTILITY AND DEMAND

You want Ke$ha's album *Animal*. Will you buy the CD version from Amazon
for $11.88, or will you download it from the iTunes store for $7.99? Some
people choose a physical CD, others a download. What determines our choices
as buyers of recorded music? Also, how much better off are we because we can
download an album for less than $10 and some songs for less than $1?

You know that diamonds are expensive and water is cheap. Doesn't that
seem odd? Why do we place a higher value on useless diamonds than on
essential-to-life water? You can think of many other examples of this paradox.
For example, paramedics who save peoples lives get paid a tiny fraction of
what a National Hockey League player earns. Do we really
place less value on the people who take care of the injured
and the sick than we place on those who provide us with
entertaining hockey games?

The theory of consumer choice that you're going to study in this chapter
answers questions like the ones we've just posed and *Reading Between the
Lines* at the end of the chapter looks at the paramedic and hockey player
paradox of value.

Consumption Choices

The choices that you make as a buyer of goods and services—your consumption choices—are influenced by many factors. We can summarize them under two broad headings:

- Consumption possibilities
- Preferences

Consumption Possibilities

Your consumption possibilities are all the things that you can afford to buy. You can afford many different combinations of goods and services, but they are all limited by your income and by the prices that you must pay. For example, you might decide to spend a big part of your income on a gym membership and personal trainer and little on movies and music, or you might spend lots on movies and music and use the free gym at school.

The easiest way to describe consumption possibilities is to consider a model consumer who buys only two items. That's what we'll now do. We'll study the consumption possibilities of Lisa, who buys only movies and soda.

A Consumer's Budget Line Consumption possibilities are limited by income and by the prices of movies and soda. When Lisa spends all her income, she reaches the limits to her consumption possibilities. We describe this limit with a **budget line**, which marks the boundary between those combinations of goods and services that a household can afford to buy and those that it cannot afford.

Figure 8.1 illustrates Lisa's consumption possibilities of movies and soda and her budget line. Lisa has an income of $40 a month, the price of a movie is $8, and the price of soda is $4 a case. Rows A through F in the table show six possible ways of allocating $40 to these two goods. For example, in row A Lisa buys 10 cases of soda and sees no movies; in row F she sees 5 movies and buys no soda; and in row C she sees 2 movies and buys 6 cases of soda.

Points A through F in the graph illustrate the possibilities presented in the table, and the line passing through these points is Lisa's budget line.

The budget line constrains choices: It marks the boundary between what is affordable and unafford-able. Lisa can afford all the points on the budget line and inside it. Points outside the line are unaffordable.

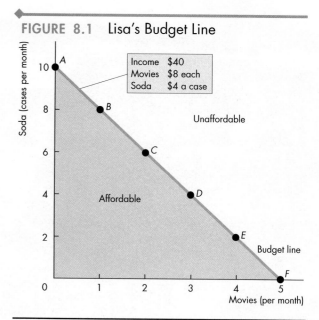

FIGURE 8.1   Lisa's Budget Line

Income $40
Movies $8 each
Soda $4 a case

Possibility	Movies		Soda	
	Quantity	Expenditure (dollars)	Cases	Expenditure (dollars)
A	0	0	10	40
B	1	8	8	32
C	**2**	**16**	**6**	**24**
D	3	24	4	16
E	4	32	2	8
F	5	40	0	0

The graph and the table show six possible ways in which Lisa can allocate $40 to movies and soda. In row C and at point C, she sees 2 movies and buys 6 cases of soda. The line AF is Lisa's budget line and is a boundary between what she can afford and what she cannot afford. Her choices must lie along the line AF or inside the orange area.

myeconlab   animation

Changes in Consumption Possibilities Consumption possibilities change when income or prices change. A rise in income shifts the budget line outward but leaves its slope unchanged. A change in a price changes the slope of the line[1]. Our goal is to predict the effects of such changes on consumption choices. To do so, we must determine the choice a consumer makes. The budget line shows what is possible; preferences determine which possibility is chosen. We'll now describe a consumer's preferences.

[1] Chapter 9 explains an alternative model of consumer choice and pp. 203–204 provides some detail on how changes in income and prices change the budget line.

Preferences

Lisa's income and the prices that she faces limit her consumption choices, but she still has lots of choice. The choice that she makes depends on her **preferences**—a description of her likes and dislikes.

You saw one way that economists use to describe preferences in Chapter 2 (p. 34), the concept of *marginal benefit* and the *marginal benefit curve*. But you also saw in Chapter 5 (p. 108) that a marginal benefit curve is also a demand curve. The goal of a theory of consumer choice is to derive the demand curve from a deeper account of how consumers make their buying plans. That is, we want to *explain what determines demand and marginal benefit.*

To achieve this goal, we need a deeper way of describing preferences. One approach to this problem uses the idea of utility, and defines **utility** as the benefit or satisfaction that a person gets from the consumption of goods and services. We distinguish two utility concepts:

- Total utility
- Marginal utility

Total Utility The total benefit that a person gets from the consumption of all the different goods and services is called **total utility**. Total utility depends on the level of consumption—more consumption generally gives more total utility.

To illustrate the concept of total utility, think about Lisa's choices. We tell Lisa that we want to measure her utility from movies and soda. We can use any scale that we wish to measure her total utility and we give her two starting points: (1) We will call the total utility from no movies and no soda zero utility; and (2) We will call the total utility she gets from seeing 1 movie a month 50 units.

We then ask Lisa to tell us, using the same scale, how much she would like 2 movies, and more, up to 10 movies a month. We also ask her to tell us, on the same scale, how much she would like 1 case of soda a month, 2 cases, and more, up to 10 cases a month.

In Table 8.1, the columns headed "Total utility" show Lisa's answers. Looking at those numbers, you can say a lot about how much Lisa likes soda and movies. She says that 1 case of soda gives her 75 units of utility—50 percent more than the utility that she gets from seeing 1 movie. You can also see that her total utility from soda climbs more slowly than her total utility from movies. This difference turns on the second utility concept: *marginal utility*.

TABLE 8.1   Lisa's Utility from Movies and Soda

Movies			Soda		
Quantity (per month)	Total utility	Marginal utility	Cases (per month)	Total utility	Marginal utility
0	0		0	0	
		 50			 75
1	50		1	75	
		 40			 48
2	90		2	123	
		 32			 36
3	122		3	159	
		 28			 24
4	150		4	183	
		 26			 22
5	176		5	205	
		 24			 20
6	200		6	225	
		 22			 13
7	222		7	238	
		 20			 10
8	242		8	248	
		 17			 7
9	259		9	255	
		 16			 5
10	275		10	260	

Marginal Utility We define **marginal utility** as the *change* in total utility that results from a one-unit increase in the quantity of a good consumed.

In Table 8.1, the columns headed "Marginal utility" show Lisa's marginal utility from movies and soda. You can see that if Lisa increases the soda she buys from 1 to 2 cases a month, her total utility from soda increases from 75 units to 123 units. For Lisa, the marginal utility from the second case each month is 48 units (123 − 75).

The marginal utility numbers appear midway between the quantities of soda because it is the *change* in the quantity she buys from 1 to 2 cases that produces the marginal utility of 48 units.

Marginal utility is *positive*, but it *diminishes* as the quantity of a good consumed increases.

Positive Marginal Utility All the things that people enjoy and want more of have a positive marginal utility. Some objects and activities can generate negative marginal utility—and lower total utility. Two examples are hard labor and polluted air. But all the goods and services that people value and that we are thinking about here have positive marginal utility: Total utility increases as the quantity consumed increases.

Diminishing Marginal Utility As Lisa sees more movies, her total utility from movies increases but her marginal utility from movies decreases. Similarly, as she

FIGURE 8.2   Total Utility and Marginal Utility

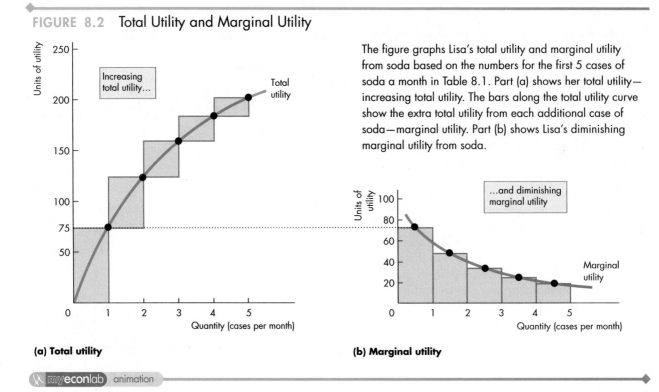

The figure graphs Lisa's total utility and marginal utility from soda based on the numbers for the first 5 cases of soda a month in Table 8.1. Part (a) shows her total utility—increasing total utility. The bars along the total utility curve show the extra total utility from each additional case of soda—marginal utility. Part (b) shows Lisa's diminishing marginal utility from soda.

(a) Total utility

(b) Marginal utility

 animation

consumes more soda, her total utility from soda increases but her marginal utility from soda decreases.

The tendency for marginal utility to decrease as the consumption of a good increases is so general and universal that we give it the status of a *principle*—the principle of **diminishing marginal utility**.

You can see Lisa's diminishing marginal utility by calculating a few numbers. Her marginal utility from soda decreases from 75 units from the first case to 48 units from the second case and to 36 units from the third. Her marginal utility from movies decreases from 50 units for the first movie to 40 units for the second and 32 units for the third. Lisa's marginal utility diminishes as she buys more of each good.

Your Diminishing Marginal Utility You've been studying all day and into the evening, and you've been too busy finishing an assignment to shop for soda. A friend drops by with a can of soda. The utility you get from that soda is the marginal utility from your first soda of the day—from *one* can. On another day you've been on a soda binge. You've been working on an assignment, but you've guzzled 10 cans of soda while doing so, and are now totally wired. You are happy enough to have one more can, but the thrill that you get from it is not very large. It is the marginal utility from the *eleventh* can in a day.

Graphing Lisa's Utility Schedules Figure 8.2(a) illustrates Lisa's total utility from soda. The more soda Lisa consumes in a month, the more total utility she gets. Her total utility curve slopes upward.

Figure 8.2(b) illustrates Lisa's marginal utility from soda. It is a graph of the marginal utility numbers in Table 8.1. This graph shows Lisa's diminishing marginal utility from soda. Her marginal utility curve slopes downward as she consumes more soda.

We've described Lisa's consumption possibilities and preferences. Your next task is to see how Lisa chooses what to consume.

REVIEW QUIZ

1 Explain how a consumer's income and the prices of goods limit consumption possibilities.
2 What is utility and how do we use the concept of utility to describe a consumer's preferences?
3 What is the distinction between total utility and marginal utility?
4 What is the key assumption about marginal utility?

You can work these questions in Study Plan 8.1 and get instant feedback.

◆ Utility-Maximizing Choice

Consumers want to get the most utility possible from their limited resources. They make the choice that maximizes utility. To discover this choice, we combine the constraint imposed by the budget and the consumer's preferences and find the point on the budget line that gives the consumer the maximum attainable utility. Let's find Lisa's utility-maximizing choice.

A Spreadsheet Solution

Lisa's most direct way of finding the quantities of movies and soda that maximize her utility is to make a table in a spreadsheet with the information and calculations shown in Table 8.2. Let's see what that table tells us.

Find the Just-Affordable Combinations Table 8.2 shows the combinations of movies and soda that Lisa can afford and that exhaust her $40 income. For example, in row *A*, Lisa buys only soda and at $4 a case she can buy 10 cases. In row *B*, Lisa sees 1 movie and buys 8 cases of soda. She spends $8 on the movie. At $4 a case, she spends $32 on soda and can buy 8 cases. The combination in row *B* just exhausts her $40. The combinations shown in the table are the same as those plotted on her budget line in Fig. 8.1.

We noted that the budget line shows that Lisa can also afford any combination *inside* the budget line. The quantities in those combinations would be smaller than the ones shown in Table 8.2 and they do not exhaust her $40. But smaller quantities don't maximize her utility. Why? The marginal utilities of movies and soda are positive, so the more of each that Lisa buys, the more total utility she gets.

Find the Total Utility for Each Just-Affordable Combination Table 8.2 shows the total utility that Lisa gets from the just-affordable quantities of movies and soda. The second and third columns show the numbers for movies and fourth and fifth columns show those for soda. The center column adds the total utility from movies to the total utility from soda. This number, the total utility from movies *and* soda, is what Lisa wants to maximize.

In row A of the table, Lisa sees no movies and buys 10 cases of soda. She gets no utility from movies and 260 units of utility from soda. Her total utility from movies and soda (the center column) is 260 units.

TABLE 8.2   Lisa's Utility-Maximizing Choice

	Movies $8		Total utility from movies and soda	Soda $4	
	Quantity (per month)	Total utility		Total utility	Cases (per month)
A	0	0	260	260	10
B	1	50	298	248	8
C	2	90	315	225	6
D	3	122	305	183	4
E	4	150	273	123	2
F	5	176	176	0	0

In row C of the table, Lisa sees 2 movies and buys 6 cases of soda. She gets 90 units of utility from movies and 225 units of utility from soda. Her total utility from movies and soda is 315 units. This combination of movies and soda maximizes Lisa's total utility. That is, given the prices of movies and soda, Lisa's best choice when she has $40 to spend is to see 2 movies and buy 6 cases of soda.

If Lisa sees 1 movie, she can buy 8 cases of soda, but she gets only 298 units of total utility—17 units less than the maximum attainable. If she sees 3 movies, she can buy only 4 cases of soda. She gets 305 units of total utility—10 units less than the maximum attainable.

Consumer Equilibrium We've just described Lisa's consumer equilibrium. A **consumer equilibrium** is a situation in which a consumer has allocated all of his or her available income in the way that maximizes his or her total utility, given the prices of goods and services. Lisa's consumer equilibrium is 2 movies and 6 cases of soda.

To find Lisa's consumer equilibrium, we did something that an economist might do but that a consumer is not likely to do: We measured her total utility from all the affordable combinations of movies and soda and then, by inspection of the numbers, selected the combination that gives the highest total utility. There is a more natural way of finding a consumer's equilibrium—a way that uses the idea that choices are made at the margin, as you first met in Chapter 1. Let's look at this approach.

Choosing at the Margin

When you go shopping you don't do utility calculations. But you do decide how to allocate your budget, and you do so in a way that you think is best for you. If you could make yourself better off by spending a few more dollars on an extra unit of one item and the same number of dollars less on something else, you would make that change. So, when you've allocated your budget in the best possible way, you can't make yourself better off by spending more on one item and less on others.

Marginal Utility per Dollar Economists interpret your best possible choice by using the idea of marginal utility per dollar. *Marginal utility* is the increase in total utility that results from consuming *one more unit* of a good. **Marginal utility per dollar** is the *marginal utility* from a good that results from spending *one more dollar* on it.

The distinction between these two marginal concepts is clearest for a good that is infinitely divisible, such as gasoline. You can buy gasoline by the smallest fraction of a gallon and literally choose to spend one more or one less dollar at the pump. The increase in total utility that results from spending one more dollar at the pump is the marginal utility per dollar from gasoline. When you buy a movie ticket or a case of soda, you must spend your dollars in bigger lumps. To buy our marginal movie ticket or case of soda, you must spend the price of one unit and your total utility increases by the marginal utility from that item. So to calculate the marginal utility per dollar for movies (or soda), we must divide marginal utility from the good by its price.

Call the marginal utility from movies MU_M and the price of a movie P_M. Then the *marginal utility per dollar from movies* is

$$MU_M/P_M.$$

Call the marginal utility from soda MU_S and the price of a case of soda P_S. Then the *marginal utility per dollar from soda* is

$$MU_S/P_S.$$

By comparing the marginal utility per dollar from all the goods that a person buys, we can determine whether the budget has been allocated in the way that maximizes total utility.

Let's see how we use the marginal utility per dollar to define a utility-maximizing rule.

Utility-Maximizing Rule A consumer's total utility is maximized by following the rule:

- Spend all the available income
- Equalize the marginal utility per dollar for all goods

Spend All the Available Income Because more consumption brings more utility, only those choices that exhaust income can maximize utility. For Lisa, combinations of movies and soda that leave her with money to spend don't give her as much total utility as those that exhaust her $40 per month income.

Equalize the Marginal Utility per Dollar The basic idea behind this rule is to move dollars from good *A* to good *B* if doing so increases the utility from good *A* by more than it decreases the utility from good *B*. Such a utility-increasing move is possible if the marginal utility per dollar from good *A* exceeds that from good *B*.

But buying more of good *A* decreases its marginal utility. And buying less of good *B* increases its marginal utility. So by moving dollars from good *A* to good *B*, total utility rises, but the gap between the marginal utilities per dollar gets smaller.

As long as the gap exists—as long as the marginal utility per dollar from good *A* exceeds that from good *B*—total utility can be increased by spending more on *A* and less on *B*. But when enough dollars have been moved from *B* to *A* to make the two marginal utilities per dollar equal, total utility cannot be increased further. Total utility is maximized.

Lisa's Marginal Calculation Let's apply the basic idea to Lisa. To calculate Lisa's marginal utility per dollar, we divide her marginal utility numbers for each quantity of each good by the price of the good. The table in Fig. 8.3 shows these calculations for Lisa, and the graph illustrates the situation on Lisa's budget line. The rows of the table are three of her affordable combinations of movies and soda.

Too Much Soda and Too Few Movies In row *B*, Lisa sees 1 movie a month and consumes 8 cases of soda a month. Her marginal utility from seeing 1 movie a month is 50 units. Because the price of a movie is $8, Lisa's marginal utility per dollar from movies is 50 units divided by $8, or 6.25 units of utility per dollar.

Lisa's marginal utility from soda when she consumes 8 cases of soda a month is 10 units. Because the price of soda is $4 a case, Lisa's marginal utility per dollar from soda is 10 units divided by $4, or 2.50 units of utility per dollar.

When Lisa sees 1 movie and consumes 8 cases of soda a month, her marginal utility per dollar from soda is *less than* her marginal utility per dollar from movies. That is,

$$MU_S/P_S < MU_M/P_M.$$

If Lisa spent an extra dollar on movies and a dollar less on soda, her total utility would increase. She would get 6.25 units from the extra dollar spent on movies and lose 2.50 units from the dollar less spent on soda. Her total utility would increase by 3.75 units (6.25 − 2.50).

Too Little Soda and Too Many Movies In row *D*, Lisa sees 3 movies a month and consumes 4 cases of soda. Her marginal utility from seeing the third movie a month is 32 units. At a price of $8 a movie, Lisa's marginal utility per dollar from movies is 32 units divided by $8, or 4 units of utility per dollar.

Lisa's marginal utility from soda when she buys 4 cases a month is 24 units. At a price of $4 a case, Lisa's marginal utility per dollar from soda is 24 units divided by $4, or 6 units of utility per dollar.

When Lisa sees 3 movies and consumes 4 cases of soda a month, her marginal utility from soda *exceeds* her marginal utility from movies. That is,

$$MU_S/P_S > MU_M/P_M.$$

If Lisa spent an extra dollar on soda and a dollar less on movies, her total utility would increase. She would get 6 units from the extra dollar spent on soda and she would lose 4 units from the dollar less spent on movies. Her total utility would increase by 2 units (6 − 4).

Utility-Maximizing Movies and Soda In Fig. 8.3, if Lisa moves from row *B* to row *C*, she increases the movies she sees from 1 to 2 a month and decreases the soda she consumes from 8 to 6 cases a month. Her marginal utility per dollar from movies falls to 5 and her marginal utility per dollar from soda rises to 5.

Similarly, if Lisa moves from row *D* to row *C*, she decreases the movies she sees from 3 to 2 a month and increases the soda she consumes from 4 to 6 cases a month. Her marginal utility per dollar from movies rises to 5 and her marginal utility per dollar from soda falls to 5.

When Lisa sees 2 movies and consumes 6 cases of soda a month, her marginal utility per dollar from soda *equals* her marginal utility per dollar from

movies. That is,

$$MU_S/P_S = MU_M/P_M.$$

Lisa can't move from this allocation of her budget without making herself worse off.

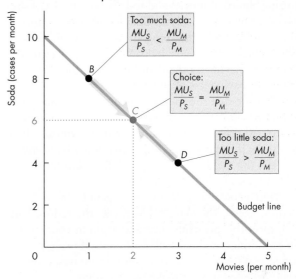

FIGURE 8.3 Equalizing Marginal Utilities per Dollar

	Movies ($8 each)			Soda ($4 per case)		
	Quantity	Marginal utility	Marginal utility per dollar	Cases	Marginal utility	Marginal utility per dollar
B	1	50	6.25	8	10	2.50
C	2	40	5.00	6	20	5.00
D	3	32	4.00	4	24	6.00

The graph shows Lisa's budget line and identifies three points on it. The rows of the table describe these points.

At point *B* (row *B*), with 1 movie and 8 cases of soda, Lisa's marginal utility per dollar from soda is less than that from movies: Buy less soda and see more movies.

At point *D* (row *D*), with 3 movies and 4 cases of soda, Lisa's marginal utility per dollar from soda is greater than that from movies: Buy more soda and see fewer movies.

At point *C* (row *C*), with 2 movies and 6 cases of soda, Lisa's marginal utility per dollar from soda is equal to that from movies: Lisa's utility is maximized.

The Power of Marginal Analysis

The method we've just used to find Lisa's utility-maximizing choice of movies and soda is an example of the power of marginal analysis. Lisa doesn't need a computer and a spreadsheet program to maximize utility. She can achieve this goal by comparing the marginal gain from having more of one good with the marginal loss from having less of another good.

The rule that she follows is simple: If the marginal utility per dollar from movies exceeds the marginal utility per dollar from soda, see more movies and buy less soda; if the marginal utility per dollar from soda exceeds the marginal utility per dollar from movies, buy more soda and see fewer movies.

More generally, if the marginal gain from an action exceeds the marginal loss, take the action. You will meet this principle time and again in your study of economics, and you will find yourself using it when you make your own economic choices, especially when you must make big decisions.

Revealing Preferences

When we introduced the idea of utility, we arbitrarily chose 50 units as Lisa's total utility from 1 movie, and we pretended that we asked Lisa to tell us how many units of utility she got from different quantities of soda and movies.

You're now about to discover that we don't need to ask Lisa to tell us her preferences. We can figure them out for ourselves by observing what she buys at various prices.

Also, the units in which we measure Lisa's preferences don't matter. Any arbitrary units will work. In this respect, utility is like temperature. Predictions about the freezing point of water don't depend on the temperature scale; and predictions about a household's consumption choice don't depend on the units of utility.

Lisa's Preferences In maximizing total utility by making the marginal utility per dollar equal for all goods, the units in which utility is measured do not matter.

You've seen that when Lisa maximizes her total utility, her marginal utility per dollar from soda, MU_S/P_S, equals her marginal utility per dollar from movies, MU_M/P_M. That is,

$$MU_S/P_S = MU_M/P_M.$$

Multiply both sides of this equation by the price of soda, P_S, to obtain

$$MU_S = MU_M \times (P_S/P_M).$$

This equation says that the marginal utility from soda, MU_S, is equal to the marginal utility from movies, MU_M, multiplied by the ratio of the price of soda, P_S, to the price of a movie, P_M.

The ratio P_S/P_M is the relative price of soda in terms of movies: It is the number of movies that must be forgone to get 1 case of soda. It is also the opportunity cost of soda. (See Chapter 2, p. 31 and Chapter 3, p. 56.)

For Lisa, when $P_M = \$8$ and $P_S = \$4$ we observe that in a month she goes to the movies twice and buys 6 cases of soda. So we know that her MU_S from 6 cases of soda equals her MU_M from 2 movies multiplied by $\$4/\$8$ or 0.5. That is, for Lisa, the marginal utility from 6 cases of soda equals one-half of the marginal utility from 2 movies.

If we observe the choices that Lisa makes at more prices, we can find more rows in her utility schedule. By her choices, Lisa reveals her preferences.

Units of Utility Don't Matter Lisa's marginal utility from 2 movies is a half of her marginal utility from 6 cases of soda. So if the marginal utility from the second movie is 40 units, then the marginal utility from the sixth case of soda is 20 units. But if we call the marginal utility from the second movie 50 units, then the marginal utility from the sixth case of soda is 25 units. The units of utility are arbitrary.

 REVIEW QUIZ

1   Why does a consumer spend the entire budget?
2   What is the marginal utility per dollar and how is it calculated?
3   What two conditions are met when a consumer is maximizing utility?
4   Explain why equalizing the marginal utility per dollar for all goods maximizes utility.

You can work these questions in Study Plan 8.2 and get instant feedback.

You now understand the marginal utility theory of consumer choices. Your next task is to see what the theory predicts.

Predictions of Marginal Utility Theory

We're now going to use marginal utility theory to make some predictions. You will see that marginal utility theory predicts the law of demand. The theory also predicts that a fall in the price of a substitute of a good decreases the demand for the good and that for a normal good, a rise in income increases demand. All these effects, which in Chapter 3 we simply assumed, are predictions of marginal utility theory.

To derive these predictions, we will study the effects of three events:

- A fall in the price of a movie
- A rise in the price of soda
- A rise in income

A Fall in the Price of a Movie

With the price of a movie at $8 and the price of soda at $4, Lisa is maximizing utility by seeing 2 movies and buying 6 cases of soda each month. Then, with no change in her $40 income and no change in the price of soda, the price of a movie falls from $8 to $4. How does Lisa change her buying plans?

Finding the New Quantities of Movies and Soda
You can find the effect of a fall in the price of a movie on the quantities of movies and soda that Lisa buys in a three-step calculation.

1. Determine the just-affordable combinations of movies and soda at the new prices.

2. Calculate the new marginal utilities per dollar from the good whose price has changed.

3. Determine the quantities of movies and soda that make their marginal utilities per dollar equal.

Affordable Combinations The lower price of a movie means that Lisa can afford more movies or more soda. Table 8.3 shows her new affordable combinations. In row *A*, if she continues to see 2 movies a month, she can now afford 8 cases of soda and in row *B*, if she continues to buy 6 cases of soda, she can now afford 4 movies. Lisa can afford any of the combinations shown in the rows of Table 8.3.

The next step is to find her new marginal utilities per dollar from movies.

New Marginal Utilities per Dollar from Movies A person's preferences don't change just because a price has changed. With no change in her preferences, Lisa's marginal utilities in Table 8.3 are the same as those in Table 8.1. But because the price of a movie has changed, the marginal utility *per dollar* from movies changes. In fact, with a halving of the price of a movie from $8 to $4, the marginal utility per dollar from movies has doubled.

The numbers in Table 8.3 show Lisa's new marginal utility per dollar from movies for each quantity of movies. The table also shows Lisa's marginal utility per dollar from soda for each quantity.

Equalizing the Marginal Utilities per Dollar You can see that if Lisa continues to see 2 movies a month and buy 6 cases of soda, her marginal utility per dollar from movies (row *A*) is 10 units and her marginal utility per dollar from soda (row *B*) is 5 units. Lisa is buying too much soda and too few movies. If she spends a dollar more on movies and a dollar less on soda, her total utility increases by 5 units (10 – 5).

If Lisa continues to buy 6 cases of soda and decreases the number of movies to 4 (row *B*), her

TABLE 8.3   How a Change in the Price of Movies Affects Lisa's Choices

	Movies ($4 each)			Soda ($4 per case)		
	Quantity	Marginal utility	Marginal utility per dollar	Cases	Marginal utility	Marginal utility per dollar
	0	0		10	5	1.25
	1	50	12.50	9	7	1.75
A	2	40	10.00	8	10	2.50
	3	32	8.00	7	13	3.25
B	4	28	7.00	6	20	5.00
	5	26	6.50	5	22	5.50
C	6	24	6.00	4	24	6.00
	7	22	5.50	3	36	9.00
	8	20	5.00	2	48	12.00
	9	17	4.25	1	75	18.75
	10	16	4.00	0	0	

marginal utility per dollar from movies falls to 7 units, but her marginal utility per dollar from soda is 5 units. Lisa is still buying too much soda and seeing too few movies. If she spends a dollar more on movies and a dollar less on soda, her total utility increases by 2 units (7 − 5).

But if Lisa sees 6 movies and buys 4 cases of soda a month (row C), her marginal utility per dollar from movies (6 units) equals her marginal utility per dollar from soda and she is maximizing utility. If Lisa moves from this allocation of her budget in either direction, her total utility decreases.

Lisa's increased purchases of movies results from a substitution effect—she substitutes the now lower-priced movies for soda—and an income effect—she can afford more movies.

A Change in the Quantity Demanded Lisa's increase in the quantity of movies that she sees is a change in the quantity demanded. It is the change in the quantity of movies that she plans to see each month when the price of a movie changes and all other influences on buying plans remain the same. We illustrate a change in the quantity demanded by a movement along a demand curve.

Figure 8.4(a) shows Lisa's demand curve for movies. When the price of a movie is $8, Lisa sees 2 movies a month. When the price of a movie falls to $4, she sees 6 movies a month. Lisa moves downward along her demand curve for movies.

The demand curve traces the quantities that maximize utility at each price, with all other influences remaining the same. You can also see that utility-maximizing choices generate a downward-sloping demand curve. Utility maximization with diminishing marginal utility implies the law of demand.

A Change in Demand The decrease in the quantity of soda that Lisa buys is the change in the quantity of soda that she plans to buy at a given price of soda when the price of a movie changes. It is a change in her demand for soda. We illustrate a change in demand by a shift of a demand curve.

Figure 8.4(b) shows Lisa's demand curve for soda. The price of soda is fixed at $4 a case. When the price of a movie is $8, Lisa buys 6 cases of soda on demand curve D_0. When the price of a movie falls to $4, Lisa buys 4 cases of soda on demand curve D_1. The fall in the price of a movie decreases Lisa's demand for soda. Her demand curve for soda shifts leftward. For Lisa, soda and movies are substitutes.

FIGURE 8.4   A Fall in the Price of a Movie

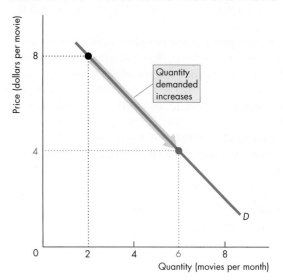

(a) Demand for movies

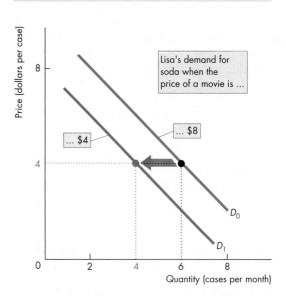

(b) Demand for soda

When the price of a movie falls and the price of soda remains the same, the quantity of movies demanded by Lisa increases, and in part (a), Lisa moves along her demand curve for movies. Also, when the price of a movie falls, Lisa's demand for soda decreases, and in part (b), her demand curve for soda shifts leftward. For Lisa, soda and movies are substitutes.

A Rise in the Price of Soda

Now suppose that with the price of a movie at $4, the price of soda rises from $4 to $8 a case. How does this price change influence Lisa's buying plans? We find the answer by repeating the three-step calculation with the new price of soda.

Table 8.4 shows Lisa's new affordable combinations. In row *A*, if she continues to buy 4 cases of soda a month she can afford to see only 2 movies; and in row *B*, if she continues to see 6 movies a month, she can afford only 2 cases of soda.

Table 8.4 show Lisa's marginal utility per dollar from soda for each quantity of soda when the price is $8 a case. The table also shows Lisa's marginal utility per dollar from movies for each quantity.

If Lisa continues to buy 4 cases of soda (row *A*), her marginal utility per dollar from soda is 3. But she must cut the movies she sees to 2, which increases her marginal utility per dollar from movies to 10. Lisa is buying too much soda and too few movies. If she spends a dollar less on soda and a dollar more on movies, her utility increases by 7 units (10 – 3) .

But if Lisa sees 6 movies a month and cuts her soda to 2 cases (row *B*), her marginal utility per dollar from movies (6 units) equals her marginal utility per dollar from soda. She is maximizing utility.

Lisa's decreased purchases of soda results from an income effect—she can afford fewer cases and she buys fewer cases. But she continues to buy the same quantity of movies.

Lisa's Demand for Soda Now that we've calculated the effect of a change in the price of soda on Lisa's buying plans when income and the price of movies remain the same, we have found two points on her demand curve for soda: When the price of soda is $4 a case, Lisa buys 4 cases a month; and when the price of soda is $8 a case, she buys 2 cases a month.

Figure 8.5 shows these points on Lisa's demand curve for soda. It also shows the change in the quantity of soda demanded when the price of soda rises and all other influences on Lisa's buying plans remain the same.

In this example, Lisa continues to buy the same quantity of movies, but this outcome does not always occur. It is a consequence of Lisa's preferences. With different marginal utilities, she might have decreased or increased the quantity of movies that she sees when the price of soda changes.

You've seen that marginal utility theory predicts the law of demand—the way in which the quantity demanded of a good changes when its price changes. Next, we'll see how marginal utility theory predicts the effect of a change in income on demand.

TABLE 8.4   How a Change in the Price of Soda Affects Lisa's Choices

	Movies ($4 each)			Soda ($8 per case)		
	Quantity	Marginal utility	Marginal utility per dollar	Cases	Marginal utility	Marginal utility per dollar
	0	0		5	22	2.75
A	2	40	10.00	**4**	24	**3.00**
	4	28	7.00	3	36	4.50
B	6	24	6.00	2	48	6.00
	8	20	5.00	1	75	9.38
	10	16	4.00	0	0	

FIGURE 8.5   A Rise in the Price of Soda

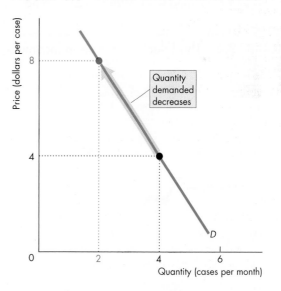

When the price of soda rises and the price of a movie and Lisa's income remain the same, the quantity of soda demanded by Lisa decreases. Lisa moves along her demand curve for soda.

A Rise in Income

Suppose that Lisa's income increases from $40 to $56 a month and that the price of a movie is $4 and the price of soda is $4 a case. With these prices and with an income of $40 a month, Lisa sees 6 movies and buys 4 cases of soda a month (Table 8.3). How does the increase in Lisa's income from $40 to $56 change her buying plans?

Table 8.5 shows the calculations needed to answer this question. If Lisa continues to see 6 movies a month, she can now afford to buy 8 cases of soda (row *A*); if she continues to buy 4 cases of soda, she can now afford to see 10 movies (row *C*).

In row *A*, Lisa's marginal utility per dollar from movies is greater than her marginal utility per dollar from soda. She is buying too much soda and too few movies. In row *C*, Lisa's marginal utility per dollar from movies is less than her marginal utility per dollar from soda. She is buying too little soda and too many movies. But in row *B*, when Lisa sees 8 movies a month and buys 6 cases of soda, her marginal utility per dollar from movies equals that from soda. She is maximizing utility.

Figure 8.6 shows the effects of the rise in Lisa's income on her demand curves for movies and soda. The price of each good is $4. When Lisa's income

TABLE 8.5   Lisa's Choices with an Income of $56 a Month

	Movies ($4 each)			Soda ($4 per case)		
	Quantity	Marginal utility	Marginal utility per dollar	Cases	Marginal utility	Marginal utility per dollar
	4	28	7.00	10	5	1.25
	5	26	6.50	9	7	1.75
A	**6**	24	**6.00**	8	10	2.50
	7	22	5.50	7	13	3.25
B	8	20	5.00	6	20	5.00
	9	17	4.25	5	22	5.50
C	10	16	4.00	**4**	24	**6.00**

rises to $56 a month, she sees 2 more movies and buys 2 more cases of soda. Her demand curves for both movies and soda shift rightward—her demand for both movies and soda increases. With a larger income, the consumer always buys more of a *normal* good. For Lisa, movies and soda are normal goods.

FIGURE 8.6   The Effects of a Rise in Income

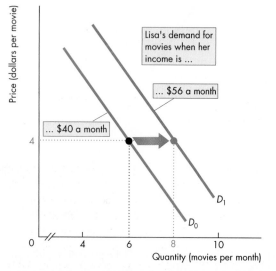

(a) Demand for movies

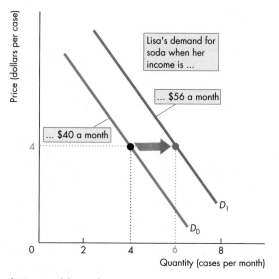

(b) Demand for soda

When Lisa's income increases, her demand for movies and her demand for soda increase. Lisa's demand curves for movies, in part (a), and for soda, in part (b), shift rightward. For Lisa, movies and soda are normal goods.

myeconlab   animation

The Paradox of Value

The price of water is low and the price of a diamond is high, but water is essential to life while diamonds are used mostly for decoration. How can valuable water be so cheap while a relatively useless diamond is so expensive? This so-called *paradox of value* has puzzled philosophers for centuries. Not until the theory of marginal utility had been developed could anyone give a satisfactory answer.

The Paradox Resolved The paradox is resolved by distinguishing between *total* utility and *marginal* utility. The total utility that we get from water is enormous. But remember, the more we consume of something, the smaller is its marginal utility.

We use so much water that its marginal utility—the benefit we get from one more glass of water or another 30 seconds in the shower—diminishes to a small value.

Diamonds, on the other hand, have a small total utility relative to water, but because we buy few diamonds, they have a high marginal utility.

When a household has maximized its total utility, it has allocated its income in the way that makes the marginal utility per dollar equal for all goods. That is, the marginal utility from a good divided by the price of the good is equal for all goods.

This equality of marginal utilities per dollar holds true for diamonds and water: Diamonds have a high price and a high marginal utility. Water has a low price and a low marginal utility. When the high marginal utility from diamonds is divided by the high price of a diamond, the result is a number that equals the low marginal utility from water divided by the low price of water. The marginal utility per dollar is the same for diamonds and water.

Value and Consumer Surplus Another way to think about the paradox of value and illustrate how it is resolved uses *consumer surplus*. Figure 8.7 explains the paradox of value by using this idea. The supply of water in part (a) is perfectly elastic at price P_W, so the quantity of water consumed is Q_W and the large green area shows the consumer surplus from water. The supply of diamonds in part (b) is perfectly inelastic at the quantity Q_D, so the price of a diamond is P_D and the small green area shows the consumer surplus from diamonds. Water is cheap, but brings a large consumer surplus; diamonds are expensive, but bring a small consumer surplus.

FIGURE 8.7   The Paradox of Value

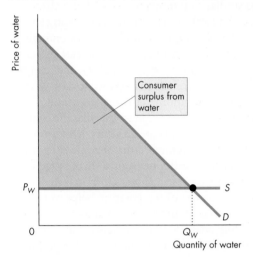

(a) Water

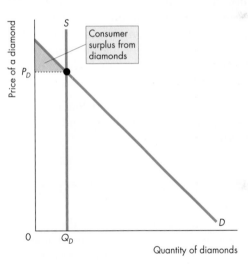

(b) Diamonds

Part (a) shows the demand for and supply of water. Supply is perfectly elastic at the price P_W. At this price, the quantity of water consumed is Q_W and the large green triangle shows consumer surplus. Part (b) shows the demand for and supply of diamonds. Supply is perfectly inelastic at the quantity Q_D. At this quantity, the price of a diamond is P_D and the small green triangle shows consumer surplus. Water is valuable—has a large consumer surplus—but cheap. Diamonds are less valuable than water—have a smaller consumer surplus—but are expensive.

 animation

Temperature: An Analogy

Utility is similar to temperature—both are abstract concepts. You can't *observe* temperature. You can observe water turning to steam if it is hot enough or turning to ice if it is cold enough. You can also construct an instrument—a thermometer—that can help you to predict when such changes will occur. We call the scale on the thermometer *temperature* and we call the units of temperature *degrees*. But like the units of utility, these degree units are arbitrary. We can use Celsius units or Fahrenheit units or some other units.

The concept of utility helps us to make predictions about consumption choices in much the same way that the concept of temperature helps us to make predictions about physical phenomena.

Admittedly, marginal utility theory does not enable us to predict how buying plans change with the same precision that a thermometer enables us to predict when water will turn to ice or steam. But the theory provides important insights into buying plans and has some powerful implications. It helps us to understand why people buy more of a good or service when its price falls and why people buy more of most goods when their incomes increase. It also resolves the paradox of value.

We're going to end this chapter by looking at some new ways of studying individual economic choices and consumer behavior.

REVIEW QUIZ

1 When the price of a good falls and the prices of other goods and a consumer's income remain the same, explain what happens to the consumption of the good whose price has fallen and to the consumption of other goods.

2 Elaborate on your answer to the previous question by using demand curves. For which good does demand change and for which good does the quantity demanded change?

3 If a consumer's income increases and if all goods are normal goods, explain how the quantity bought of each good changes.

4 What is the paradox of value and how is the paradox resolved?

5 What are the similarities between utility and temperature?

You can work these questions in Study Plan 8.3 and get instant feedback.

Economics in Action
Maximizing Utility from Recorded Music

In 2007, Americans spent $10 billion on recorded music, down from $14 billion in 2000. But the combined quantity of discs and downloads bought increased from 1 billion in 2000 to 1.8 billion in 2007 and the average price of a unit of recorded music fell from $14 to $5.50.

The average price fell because the mix of formats bought changed dramatically. In 2000, we bought 940 million CDs; in 2007, we bought only 500 million CDs and downloaded 1.2 billion music files.

Figure 1 shows the longer history of the changing formats of recorded music.

The music that we buy isn't just one good—it is several goods. Singles and albums are different goods; downloads and discs are different goods; and downloads to a computer and downloads to a cell phone are different goods. There are five major categories and the table shows the quantities of each that we bought in 2007 (excluding DVDs and cassettes).

Format	Singles	Albums
	(millions in 2007)	
Disc	3	500
Download	800	40
Mobile	400	–

Source of data: Recording Industry Association of America.

Most people buy all their music in digital form, but many still buy physical CDs and some people buy both downloads and CDs.

We get utility from the singles and albums that we buy, and the more songs and albums we have, the more utility we get. But our marginal utility from songs and albums decreases as the quantity that we own increases.

We also get utility from convenience. A song that we can buy with a mouse click and play with the spin of a wheel is more convenient both to buy and to use than a song on a CD. The convenience of songs downloaded over the Internet means that, song for song, we get more utility from a song downloaded than we get from a song on a physical CD.

But most albums are still played at home on a CD player. So for most people, a physical CD is a more convenient medium for delivering an album. Album for album, people on average get more utility from a CD than from a download.

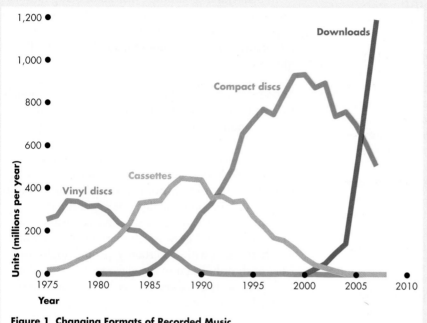

Figure 1 Changing Formats of Recorded Music
Graph from www.swivel.com.

In the 1970s, recorded music came on vinyl discs. Cassettes gradually replaced vinyl, then compact discs (CDs) gradually replaced cassettes, and today, digital files downloaded to computers and mobile devices are replacing physical CDs.

When we decide how many singles and albums to download and how many to buy on CD, we compare the marginal utility per dollar from each type of music in each format. We make the marginal utility per dollar from each type of music in each format equal, as the equations below show.

The market for single downloads has created an enormous consumer surplus. The table shows that the quantity of single downloads demanded at 99 cents each was 800 million in 2007, and the quantity of singles on a disc demanded at $4.75 a disc was 3 million in 2007. If we assume that $4.75 is the most that anyone would pay for a single download (probably an underestimate), the demand curve for single downloads is that shown in Fig. 2.

With the price of a single download at $0.99, consumer surplus (the area of the green triangle in Fig. 2) is $1.5 billion.

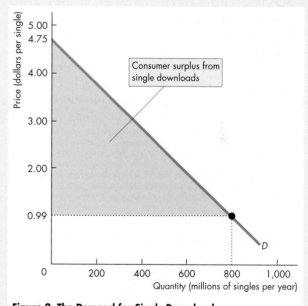

Figure 2 The Demand for Single Downloads

$$\frac{MU_{single\ downloads}}{P_{single\ downloads}} = \frac{MU_{album\ downloads}}{P_{album\ downloads}} = \frac{MU_{physical\ singles}}{P_{physical\ singles}} = \frac{MU_{physical\ albums}}{P_{physical\ albums}} = \frac{MU_{mobile}}{P_{mobile}}$$

$$\frac{MU_{single\ downloads}}{\$0.99} = \frac{MU_{album\ downloads}}{\$10} = \frac{MU_{physical\ singles}}{\$4.75} = \frac{MU_{physical\ albums}}{\$15} = \frac{MU_{mobile}}{\$2.50}$$

◆ New Ways of Explaining Consumer Choices

When William Stanley Jevons developed marginal utility theory in the 1860s, he would have loved to look inside people's brains and "see" their utility. But he believed that the human brain was the ultimate black box that could never be observed directly. For Jevons, and for most economists today, the purpose of marginal utility theory is to explain our *actions*, not what goes on inside our brains.

Economics has developed over the past 150 years with little help from and paying little attention to advances being made in psychology. Both economics and psychology seek to explain human behavior, but they have developed different ways of attacking the challenge.

A few researchers *have* paid attention to the potential payoff from exploring economic problems by using the tools of psychology. These researchers, some economists and some psychologists, think that marginal utility theory is based on a view of how people make choices that attributes too much to reason and rationality. They propose an alternative approach based on the methods of psychology.

Other researchers, some economists and some neuroscientists, are using new tools to look inside the human brain and open up Jevons' "black box."

This section provides a very brief introduction to these new and exciting areas of economics. We'll explore the two related research agendas:

- Behavioral economics
- Neuroeconomics

Behavioral Economics

Behavioral economics studies the ways in which limits on the human brain's ability to compute and implement rational decisions influences economic behavior—both the decisions that people make and the consequences of those decisions for the way markets work.

Behavioral economics starts with observed behavior. It looks for anomalies—choices that do not seem to be rational. It then tries to account for the anomalies by using ideas developed by psychologists that emphasize features of the human brain that limit rational choice.

In behavioral economics, instead of being rational utility maximizers, people are assumed to have three impediments that prevent rational choice: bounded rationality, bounded willpower, and bounded self-interest.

Bounded Rationality Bounded rationality is rationality that is limited by the computing power of the human brain. We can't always work out the rational choice.

For Lisa, choosing between movies and soda, it seems unlikely that she would have much trouble figuring out what to buy. But toss Lisa some uncertainty and the task becomes harder. She's read the reviews of "Ironman 2" on Fandango, but does she really want to see that movie? How much marginal utility will it give her? Faced with uncertainty, people might use rules of thumb, listen to the views of others, and make decisions based on gut instinct rather than on rational calculation.

Bounded Willpower Bounded willpower is the less-than-perfect willpower that prevents us from making a decision that we know, at the time of implementing the decision, we will later regret.

Lisa might be feeling particularly thirsty when she passes a soda vending machine. Under Lisa's rational utility-maximizing plan, she buys her soda at the discount store, where she gets it for the lowest possible price. Lisa has already bought her soda for this month, but it is at home. Spending $1 on a can now means giving up a movie later this month.

Lisa's rational choice is to ignore the temporary thirst and stick to her plan. But she might not possess the willpower to do so—sometimes she will and sometimes she won't.

Bounded Self-Interest Bounded self-interest is the limited self-interest that results in sometimes suppressing our own interests to help others.

A hurricane hits the Florida coast and Lisa, feeling sorry for the victims, donates $10 to a fund-raiser. She now has only $30 to spend on movies and soda this month. The quantities that she buys are not, according to her utility schedule, the ones that maximize her utility.

The main applications of behavioral economics are in two areas: finance, where uncertainty is a key factor in decision making, and savings, where the future is a key factor. But one behavior observed by behavioral economists is more general and might affect your choices. It is called the endowment effect.

The Endowment Effect The endowment effect is the tendency for people to value something more highly simply because they own it. If you have allocated your income to maximize utility, then the price you would be willing to accept to give up something that you own (for example, your coffee mug) should be the same as the price you are willing to pay for an identical one.

In experiments, students seem to display the endowment effect: The price they are willing to pay for a coffee mug that is identical to the one they own is less than the price they would be willing to accept to give up the coffee mug that they own. Behavioral economists say that this behavior contradicts marginal utility theory.

Neuroeconomics

Neuroeconomics is the study of the activity of the human brain when a person makes an economic decision. The discipline uses the observational tools and ideas of neuroscience to obtain a better understanding of economic decisions.

Neuroeconomics is an experimental discipline. In an experiment, a person makes an economic decision and the electrical or chemical activity of the person's brain is observed and recorded using the same type of equipment that neurosurgeons use to diagnose brain disorders.

The observations provide information about which regions of the brain are active at different points in the process of making an economic decision.

Observations show that some economic decisions generate activity in the area of the brain (called the prefrontal cortex) where we store memories, analyze data, and anticipate the consequences of our actions. If people make rational utility-maximizing decisions, it is in this region of the brain that the decision occurs.

But observations also show that some economic decisions generate activity in the region of the brain (called the hippocampus) where we store memories of anxiety and fear. Decisions that are influenced by activity in this part of the brain might not be rational and be driven by fear or panic.

Neuroeconomists are also able to observe the amount of a brain hormone (called dopamine), the quantity of which increases in response to pleasurable events and decreases in response to disappointing events. These observations might one day enable neuroeconomists to actually measure utility and shine a bright light inside what was once believed to be the ultimate black box.

Controversy

The new ways of studying consumer choice that we've briefly described here are being used more widely to study business decisions and decisions in financial markets, and this type of research is surely going to become more popular.

But behavioral economics and neuroeconomics generate controversy. Most economists hold the view of Jevons that the goal of economics is to explain the decisions that we observe people making and not to explain what goes on inside people's heads.

Most economists would prefer to probe apparent anomalies more deeply and figure out why they are not anomalies after all.

Economists also point to the power of marginal utility theory and its ability to explain consumer choice and demand as well as resolve the paradox of value.

REVIEW QUIZ

1 Define behavioral economics.
2 What are the three limitations on human rationality that behavioral economics emphasizes?
3 Define neuroeconomics.
4 What do behavioral economics and neuroeconomics seek to achieve?

You can work these questions in Study Plan 8.4 and get instant feedback.

◆ You have now completed your study of the marginal utility theory and some new ideas about how people make economic choices. You can see marginal utility theory in action once again in *Reading Between the Lines* on pp. 196–197, where it is used to explain why paramedics who save people's lives earn so much less than hockey players who merely provide entertainment.

A Paradox of Value: Paramedics and Hockey Players

Salaries, Strong Recruitment Ease Area Paramedic Shortage

The Washington Post
April 4, 2008

To curb a critical shortage, fire departments across the Washington region have pursued paramedics like star athletes in recent years, enticing them with signing bonuses, handsome salaries and the promise of fast-track career paths.

Montgomery County hired a marketing expert and launched a national recruiting drive, reaching out in particular to women and minorities. Fairfax County offered top starting salaries, now totaling about $57,000—as much as 50 percent higher than some other local jurisdictions, though Fairfax paramedics generally work longer hours. ...

Excerpted from "Salaries, Strong Recruitment Ease Area Paramedic Shortage" by William McCaffrey. *The Washington Post*, April 4, 2008.

Ducks Give Perry $26.6 Million Deal

The Daily News of Los Angeles
July 2, 2008

The Ducks' first free-agent signing might also be their last, their biggest and their most expected.

Within the first hour of the NHL's free agency period, Corey Perry signed a five-year, $26.625 million contract that will keep the 23-year-old in Anaheim until 2013. Both parties had expressed an interest in completing the deal for several months but it wasn't possible until Tuesday, when the Ducks had enough room for long-term contracts under the salary cap.

"I really wanted to stay in Anaheim," Perry said. "It's home now and I didn't want to leave here. It's a great place to play hockey and it just shows how well the organization is run."

Including an $8 million signing bonus spread over its duration, the contract will pay Perry $4.5 million in 2008–09, then $6.5 million, $5.375 million, $5.375 million, and $4.875 million, respectively, over the final four years. ...

Reprinted with permission from the San Bernadino Sun.

ESSENCE OF THE STORIES

- In Washington, the starting salary for a paramedic is $57,000 per year.

- Corey Perry has a 5-year contract with the Anaheim Ducks that will earn him $26.6 million.

ECONOMIC ANALYSIS

- If resources are used efficiently, the marginal utility per dollar from the services of a paramedic, MU_P/P_P, equals the marginal utility per dollar from the services of a hockey player, MU_H/P_H. That is,

$$\frac{MU_P}{P_P} = \frac{MU_H}{P_H}.$$

- A paramedic in Washington earns $57,000 a year, but the national average paramedic wage is $27,000 a year.

- Corey Perry earns $26.6 million over 5 years, or $5.32 million a year on average.

- If we put these numbers into the above formula, we get

$$\frac{MU_P}{\$27,000} = \frac{MU_H}{\$5,320,000}.$$

Equivalently,

$$\frac{MU_H}{MU_P} = 197.$$

- Is the marginal utility from Corey Perry's services really 197 times that from the paramedic's services?

- The answer is no. A paramedic might serve about 8 people a day, or perhaps 2,000 in a year; a hockey player like Corey Perry serves millions of people a year.

- If a paramedic serves 2,000 people a year, then the price of a paramedic's service per customer served is $27,000/2,000, which equals $13.50.

- If Corey Perry serves 1,000,000 people a year, then the price of Corey Perry's service per customer served is $5,320,000/1,000,000, which equals $5.32.

- Using these prices of the services per customer, a paramedic is worth 2.5 times as much as a hockey player—the marginal utility from the services of a paramedic is 2.5 times that from a hockey player.

- Figure 1 shows the market for paramedics. The equilibrium quantity is 200,000 workers, and the average wage rate is $27,000 a year.

- Figure 2 shows the market for professional hockey players. The equilibrium quantity is 750 players and the average wage rate is $2,000,000 a year. (Corey Perry earns more than the average player.)

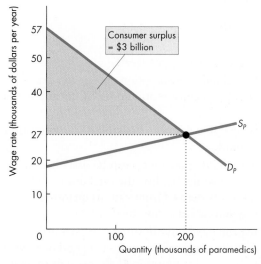

Figure 1 The value of paramedics

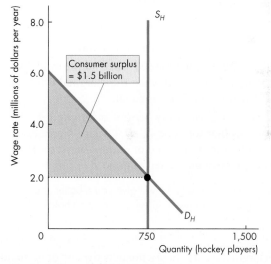

Figure 2 The value of hockey players

- Not only is the marginal utility from a paramedic greater than that from a hockey player, but paramedics also create a greater consumer surplus.

197

SUMMARY

Key Points

Consumption Choices (pp. 180–182)

- A household's consumption choices are determined by its consumption possibilities and preferences.
- A budget line defines a household's consumption possibilities.
- A household's preferences can be described by a utility schedule that lists the total utility and marginal utility derived from various quantities of goods and services consumed.
- The principle of diminishing marginal utility is that the marginal utility from a good or service decreases as consumption of the good or service increases.

Working Problems 1 to 5 will give you a better understanding of consumption choices.

Utility-Maximizing Choice (pp. 183–186)

- A consumer's objective is to maximize total utility.
- Total utility is maximized when all the available income is spent and when the marginal utility per dollar from all goods is equal.
- If the marginal utility per dollar for good *A* exceeds that for good *B*, total utility increases if the quantity purchased of good *A* increases and the quantity purchased of good *B* decreases.

Working Problems 6 to 11 will give you a better understanding of a consumer's utility-maximizing choice.

Predictions of Marginal Utility Theory (pp. 187–193)

- Marginal utility theory predicts the law of demand. That is, other things remaining the same, the higher the price of a good, the smaller is the quantity demanded of that good.
- Marginal utility theory also predicts that, other things remaining the same, an increase in the consumer's income increases the demand for a normal good.
- Marginal utility theory resolves the paradox of value.
- Total value is *total* utility or consumer surplus. But price is related to *marginal* utility.
- Water, which we consume in large amounts, has a high total utility and a large consumer surplus, but the price of water is low and the marginal utility from water is low.
- Diamonds, which we buy in small quantities, have a low total utility and a small consumer surplus, but the price of a diamond is high and the marginal utility from diamonds is high.

Working Problems 12 to 21 will give you a better understanding of the predictions of marginal utility theory.

New Ways of Explaining Consumer Choices
(pp. 194–195)

- Behavioral economics studies limits on the ability of the human brain to compute and implement rational decisions.
- Bounded rationality, bounded willpower, and bounded self-interest are believed to explain some choices.
- Neuroeconomics uses the ideas and tools of neuroscience to study the effects of economic events and choices inside the human brain.

Working Problems 22 and 23 will give you a better understanding of the new ways of explaining consumer choices.

Key Terms

Behavioral economics, 194
Budget line, 180
Consumer equilibrium, 183
Diminishing marginal utility, 182

Marginal utility, 181
Marginal utility per dollar, 184
Neuroeconomics, 195
Preferences, 181

Total utility, 181
Utility, 181

STUDY PLAN PROBLEMS AND APPLICATIONS

 myeconlab You can work Problems 1 to 23 in MyEconLab Chapter 8 Study Plan and get instant feedback.

Consumption Choices (Study Plan 8.1)

Jerry has $12 a week to spend on yogurt and magazines. The price of yogurt is $2, and the price of a magazine is $4.

1. List the combinations of yogurt and magazines that Jerry can afford. Draw a graph of Jerry's budget line with the quantity of magazines plotted on the *x*-axis.

2. Describe how Jerry's consumption possibilities change if, other things remaining the same, (i) the price of a magazine falls and (ii) Jerry's income increases.

Use the following data to work Problems 3 to 9.

Max enjoys windsurfing and snorkeling. Max has $35 a day to spend, and he can spend as much time as he likes on his leisure pursuits. The price of renting equipment for windsurfing is $10 an hour and for snorkeling is $5 an hour. The table shows the total utility Max gets from each activity.

Hours per day	Total utility from windsurfing	Total utility from snorkeling
1	120	40
2	220	76
3	300	106
4	360	128
5	396	140
6	412	150
7	422	158

3. Calculate Max's marginal utility from windsurfing at each number of hours per day. Does Max's marginal utility from windsurfing obey the principle of diminishing marginal utility?

4. Calculate Max's marginal utility from snorkeling at each number of hours per day. Does Max's marginal utility from snorkeling obey the principle of diminishing marginal utility?

5. Which does Max enjoy more: his 6th hour of windsurfing or his 6th hour of snorkeling?

Utility-Maximizing Choice (Study Plan 8.2)

6. Make a table that shows the various combinations of hours spent windsurfing and snorkeling that Max can afford.

7. In your table in Problem 6, add two columns and list Max's marginal utility per dollar from windsurfing and from snorkeling.

8. a. How many hours does Max windsurf and how many hours does he snorkel to maximize his utility?

   b. If Max spent a dollar more on windsurfing and a dollar less on snorkeling than in part (a), by how much would his total utility change?

   c. If Max spent a dollar less on windsurfing and a dollar more on snorkeling than in part (a), by how much would his total utility change?

9. Explain why, if Max equalized the marginal utility per hour from windsurfing and from snorkeling, he would *not* maximize his utility.

10. **Schools Get a Lesson in Lunch Line Economics**

    Sharp rises in the cost of milk, grain, and fresh fruits and vegetables are hitting cafeterias across the country, forcing cash-strapped schools to raise prices or serve more economical dishes. For example, Fairfax schools serve oranges —14¢ each—instead of grapes, which are 25¢ a serving.

    Source: *The Washington Post*, April 14, 2008

    Assume that a Fairfax school has a $14 daily fruit budget.

    a. How many oranges a day can the school afford to serve if it serves no grapes? How many servings of grapes can the school afford each day if it serves no oranges?

    b. If the school provides 50 oranges a day and maximizes utility, how many servings of grapes does it provide? If the marginal utility from an orange is 14 units, what is the marginal utility from a serving of grapes?

11. **Can Money Buy Happiness?**

    Whoever said money can't buy happiness isn't spending it right. There must be some connection, but once your basic human needs are met, does more money buy more happiness? An increase in income from $20,000 a year to $50,000 makes you twice as likely to be happy, but the payoff from more than $90,000 is slight.

    Source: CNN, July 18, 2006

a. What does the fundamental assumption of marginal utility theory suggest about the connection between money and happiness?

b. Explain why this news clip is consistent with marginal utility theory.

Predictions of Marginal Utility Theory
(Study Plan 8.3)

Use the data in Problem 3 to work Problems 12 to 16.

12. Max is offered a special deal: The price of renting windsurfing equipment is cut to $5 an hour. How many hours does Max spend windsurfing and how many hours does he spend snorkeling?

13. Draw Max's demand curve for rented windsurfing equipment. Over the price range from $5 to $10 an hour, is Max's demand for windsurfing equipment elastic or inelastic?

14. How does Max's demand for snorkeling equipment change when the price of windsurfing equipment falls? What is Max's cross elasticity of demand for snorkeling with respect to the price of windsurfing? Are windsurfing and snorkeling substitutes or complements for Max?

15. If Max's income increases from $35 to $55 a day, how does his demand for rented windsurfing equipment change? Is windsurfing a normal good or an inferior good for Max? Explain.

16. If Max's income increases from $35 to $55 a day, how does his demand for rented snorkeling equipment change? Is snorkeling a normal good or an inferior good for Max? Explain.

Use the following news clip to work Problems 17 and 18.

Compared to Other Liquids, Gasoline is Cheap

In 2008, when gasoline hit $4 a gallon, motorists complained, but they didn't complain about $1.59 for a 20-oz Gatorade and $18 for 16 mL of HP ink.

Source: *The New York Times*, May 27, 2008

The prices per gallon are $10.17 for Gatorade and $4,294.58 for printer ink.

17. a. What does marginal utility theory predict about the marginal utility per dollar from gasoline, Gatorade, and printer ink?

b. What do the prices per gallon tell you about the marginal utility from a gallon of gasoline, Gatorade, and printer ink?

18. a. What do the prices per unit reported in the news clip tell you about the marginal utility from a gallon of gasoline, a 20-oz bottle of Gatorade, and a cartridge of printer ink?

b. How can the paradox of value be used to explain why the fluids listed in the news clip might be less valuable than gasoline, yet far more expensive?

Use the following news clip to work Problems 19 to 21.

Exclusive Status: It's in The Bag; $52,500 Purses. 24 Worldwide. 1 in Washington.

Forget your Coach purse. Put away your Kate Spade. Even Hermes's famous Birkin bag seems positively discount. The Louis Vuitton Tribute Patchwork is this summer's ultimate status bag, ringing in at $52,500, and the company is offering only five for sale in North America and 24 worldwide.

Source: *The Washington Post*, August 21, 2007

19. Use marginal utility theory to explain the facts reported in the news clip.

20. If Louis Vuitton offered 500 Tribute Patchwork bags in North America and 2,400 worldwide, what do you predict would happen to the price that buyers would be willing to pay and what would happen to the consumer surplus?

21. If the Tribute Patchwork bag is copied and thousands are sold illegally, what do you predict would happen to the price that buyers would be willing to pay for a genuine bag and what would happen to the consumer surplus?

New Ways of Explaining Consumer Choices
(Study Plan 8.4)

Use the following news clip to work Problems 22 and 23.

Eating Away the Innings in Baseball's Cheap Seats

Baseball and gluttony, two of America's favorite pastimes, are merging and taking hold at Major League Baseball stadiums: all-you-can-eat seats. Some fans try to "set personal records" during their first game in the section, but by their second or third time in such seats they eat normally, just as they would at a game.

Source: *USA Today*, March 6, 2008

22. a. What conflict might exist between utility-maximization and setting "personal records" for eating?

b. What does the fact that fans eat less at subsequent games indicate about the marginal utility from ballpark food as the quantity consumed increases?

23. a. How can setting personal records for eating be reconciled with marginal utility theory?

b. Which ideas of behavioral economics are consistent with the information in the news clip?

ADDITIONAL PROBLEMS AND APPLICATIONS

Consumption Choices

24. Tim buys 2 pizzas and sees 1 movie a week when he has $16 to spend. The price of a movie ticket is $8, and the price of a pizza is $4. Draw Tim's budget line. If the price of a movie ticket falls to $4, describe how Tim's consumption possibilities change.

Use the following information to work Problems 25 to 32.

Cindy has $70 a month to spend, and she can spend as much time as she likes playing golf and tennis. The price of an hour of golf is $10, and the price of an hour of tennis is $5. The table shows Cindy's marginal utility from each sport.

Hours per month	Marginal utility from golf	Marginal utility from tennis
1	80	40
2	60	36
3	40	30
4	30	10
5	20	5
6	10	2
7	6	1

25. Make a table that shows Cindy's affordable combinations of hours playing golf and tennis. If Cindy increases her expenditure to $100, describe how her consumption possibilities change.

Utility-Maximizing Choice

26. a. When Cindy has $70 to spend on golf and tennis, how many hours of golf and how many hours of tennis does she play to maximize her utility?
   b. Compared to part (a), if Cindy spent a dollar more on golf and a dollar less on tennis, by how much would her total utility change?
   c. Compared to part (a), if Cindy spent a dollar less on golf and a dollar more on tennis, by how much would her total utility change?

27. Explain why, if Cindy equalized the marginal utility per hour of golf and tennis, she would *not* maximize her utility.

Predictions of Marginal Utility Theory

28. Cindy's tennis club raises its price of an hour of tennis to $10. The price of golf remains at $10

an hour and Cindy continues to spend $70 on tennis and golf.
   a. List the combinations of hours spent playing golf and tennis that Cindy can now afford.
   b. Along with the combinations in part (a), list Cindy's marginal utility per dollar from golf and from tennis.
   c. How many hours does Cindy now spend playing golf and how many hours does she spend playing tennis?

29. Use your answers to Problems 26a and 28 to draw Cindy's demand curve for tennis. Over the price range of $5 to $10 an hour of tennis, is Cindy's demand for tennis elastic or inelastic?

30. Use your answers to Problems 26a and 28 to explain how Cindy's demand for golf changed when the price of an hour of tennis increased. What is Cindy's cross elasticity of demand for golf with respect to the price of tennis? Are tennis and golf substitutes or complements for Cindy?

31. Cindy loses her math tutoring job and the amount she has to spend on golf and tennis falls to $35 a month. How does Cindy's demand for golf change? For Cindy, is golf a normal good or an inferior good? Is tennis a normal good or an inferior good?

32. Cindy takes a Club Med vacation, the cost of which includes unlimited sports activities. With no extra charge for golf and tennis, Cindy allocates a total of 4 hours a day to these activities.
   a. How many hours does Cindy play golf and how many hours does she play tennis?
   b. What is Cindy's marginal utility from golf and from tennis?
   c. Why does Cindy equalize the marginal utilities rather than the marginal utility per dollar from golf and from tennis?

33. **Blu-Ray Format Expected to Dominate, but When?**

Blu-ray stomped HD DVD to become the standard format for high-definition movie discs, but years may pass before it can claim victory over the good old DVD. The people who bought $2,000, 40-inch TVs are the ones that will lead the charge. Everyone else will come along when the price falls. Blu-ray machine prices are now starting to drop and Wal-Mart Stores Inc. began stocking a $298 Magnavox model. That's cheaper than most alternatives, but a hefty price hike from a typical $50 DVD player.

Source: CNN, June 2, 2008

a. What does marginal utility theory predict about the marginal utility from a Magnavox Blu-ray machine compared to the marginal utility from a typical DVD player?

b. What will have to happen to the marginal utility from a Blu-ray machine before it is able to "claim victory over the good old DVD"?

34. Ben spends $50 a year on 2 bunches of flowers and $50 a year on 10,000 gallons of tap water. Ben is maximizing utility and his marginal utility from water is 0.5 unit per gallon.

a. Are flowers or water more valuable to Ben?

b. Explain how Ben's expenditure on flowers and water illustrates the paradox of value.

New Ways of Explaining Consumer Choices

Use the following news clip to work Problems 35 to 37.

Putting a Price on Human Life

Researchers at Stanford and the University of Pennsylvania estimated that a healthy human life is worth about $129,000. Using Medicare records on treatment costs for kidney dialysis as a benchmark, the authors tried to pinpoint the threshold beyond which ensuring another "quality" year of life was no longer financially worthwhile. The study comes amid debate over whether Medicare should start rationing health care on the basis of cost effectiveness.

Source: *Time*, June 9, 2008

35. Why might Medicare ration health care according to treatment that is "financially worthwhile" as opposed to providing as much treatment as is needed by a patient, regardless of costs?

36. What conflict might exist between a person's valuation of his or her own life and the rest of society's valuation of that person's life?

37. How does the potential conflict between self-interest and the social interest complicate setting a financial threshold for Medicare treatments?

Economics in the News

38. After you have studied *Reading Between the Lines* (pp. 196–197) answer the following questions.

a. If a wave of natural disasters put paramedics in the news and a large number of people decide to try to get jobs as paramedics, how does

(i) The marginal utility of the services of a paramedic change?

(ii) Consumer surplus in the market for the services of paramedics change?

b. If television advertising revenues during hockey games double, how does

(i) The marginal utility of the services of a hockey player change?

(ii) Consumer surplus in the market for the services of hockey players change?

39. **Five Signs You Have Too Much Money**

When a bottle of water costs $38, it's hard not to agree that bottled water is a fool's drink. The drink of choice among image-conscious status seekers and high-end tee-totalers in L.A. is Bling H2O. It's not the water that accounts for the cost of the $38, but the "limited edition" bottle decked out in Swarovski crystals.

Source: CNN, January 17, 2006

a. Assuming that the price of a bottle of Bling H2O is $38 in all the major U.S. cities, what might its popularity in Los Angeles reveal about consumers' incomes or preferences in Los Angeles relative to other U.S. cities?

b. Why might the marginal utility from a bottle of Bling H2O decrease more rapidly than the marginal utility from ordinary bottled water?

Use the following news clip to work Problems 40 and 41.

How to Buy Happiness. Cheap

At any given point in time, the rich tend to be a bit happier than the poor, but across-the-board increases in living standards don't seem to make people happier. The average American's income has grown about 80% since 1972, but the percentage describing themselves as "very happy" (roughly a third) has barely changed over the years. As living standards increase, most of us respond by raising our own standards: Things that once seemed luxuries now are necessities. As a result, we're working harder than ever to buy stuff that satisfies us less and less.

Source: CNN, October 1, 2004

40. According to the news clip, how do widespread increases in living standards influence total utility?

41. a. What does the news clip imply about how the total utility from consumption changes over time?

b. What does the news clip imply about how the marginal utility from consumption changes over time?

◆ Describe a household's budget line and show how it changes when prices or income change

◆ Use indifference curves to map preferences and explain the principle of diminishing marginal rate of substitution

◆ Predict the effects of changes in prices and income on consumption choices

9

POSSIBILITIES, PREFERENCES, AND CHOICES

You buy your music online and play it on an iPod. And as the prices of a music download and an iPod have tumbled, the volume of downloads and sales of iPods have skyrocketed.

The price of a DVD rental has also fallen and we're renting ever more of them. But we're also going to movie theaters in ever-greater numbers. Why are we going to the movies more when it is so cheap and easy to rent a DVD?

The price of electronic books—e-books—and electronic readers such as Amazon's Kindle are also falling. But most students continue to buy printed textbooks and in the entire $24-billion book market, e-books contribute only 1.3 percent of the total revenue.

Why have downloading music and watching movies on DVD become so popular while downloading e-books has made only a tiny inroad into the overall market for books?

In this chapter, we're going to study a model of choice that answers questions like the ones just posed. We'll use this model to explain the choices we make about movies, and at the end of the chapter in *Reading Between the Lines*, to explain why e-books are only slowly replacing printed books.

◆ Consumption Possibilities

Consumption choices are limited by income and by prices. A household has a given amount of income to spend and cannot influence the prices of the goods and services it buys. A household's **budget line** describes the limits to its consumption choices.

Let's look at Lisa's budget line.* Lisa has an income of $40 a month to spend. She buys two goods: movies and soda. The price of a movie is $8, and the price of soda is $4 a case.

Figure 9.1 shows alternative combinations of movies and soda that Lisa can afford. In row A, she sees no movies and buys 10 cases of soda. In row F, she sees 5 movies and buys no soda. Both of these combinations of movies and soda exhaust the $40 available. Check that the combination of movies and soda in each of the other rows also exhausts Lisa's $40 of income. The numbers in the table and the points A through F in the graph describe Lisa's consumption possibilities.

Divisible and Indivisible Goods Some goods— called divisible goods—can be bought in any quantity desired. Examples are gasoline and electricity. We can best understand household choice if we suppose that all goods and services are divisible. For example, Lisa can see half a movie a month on average by seeing one movie every two months. When we think of goods as being divisible, the consumption possibilities are not only the points A through F shown in Fig. 9.1, but also all the intermediate points that form the line running from A to F. This line is Lisa's budget line.

Affordable and Unaffordable Quantities Lisa's budget line is a constraint on her choices. It marks the boundary between what is affordable and what is unaffordable. She can afford any point on the line and inside it. She cannot afford any point outside the line. The constraint on her consumption depends on the prices and her income, and the constraint changes when the price of a good or her income changes. To see how, we use a budget equation.

---

* If you have studied Chapter 8 on marginal utility theory, you have already met Lisa. This tale of her thirst for soda and zeal for movies will sound familiar to you—up to a point. In this chapter, we're going to explore her budget line in more detail and use a different method for representing preferences—one that does not require the idea of utility.

FIGURE 9.1   The Budget Line

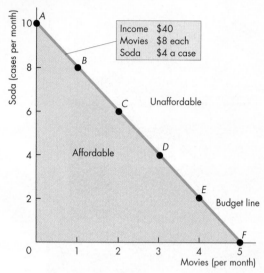

Consumption possibility	Movies (per month)	Soda (cases per month)
A	0	10
B	1	8
C	2	6
D	3	4
E	4	2
F	5	0

Lisa's budget line shows the boundary between what she can and cannot afford. The rows of the table list Lisa's affordable combinations of movies and soda when her income is $40, the price of soda is $4 a case, and the price of a movie is $8. For example, row A tells us that Lisa spends all of her $40 income when she buys 10 cases of soda and sees no movies. The figure graphs Lisa's budget line. Points A through F in the graph represent the rows of the table. For divisible goods, the budget line is the continuous line AF. To calculate the equation for Lisa's budget line, start with expenditure equal to income:

$$\$4Q_S + \$8Q_M = \$40.$$

Divide by $4 to obtain

$$Q_S + 2Q_M = 10.$$

Subtract $2Q_M$ from both sides to obtain

$$Q_S = 10 - 2Q_M.$$

 animation

Budget Equation

We can describe the budget line by using a *budget equation.* The budget equation starts with the fact that

$$\text{Expenditure} = \text{Income}.$$

Expenditure is equal to the sum of the price of each good multiplied by the quantity bought. For Lisa,

$$\text{Expenditure} = (\text{Price of soda} \times \text{Quantity of soda})$$
$$+ (\text{Price of movie} \times \text{Quantity of movies}).$$

Call the price of soda P_S, the quantity of soda Q_S, the price of a movie P_M, the quantity of movies Q_M, and income Y. We can now write Lisa's budget equation as

$$P_S Q_S + P_M Q_M = Y.$$

Or, using the prices Lisa faces, $4 a case of soda and $8 a movie, and Lisa's income, $40, we get

$$\$4 Q_S + \$8 Q_M = \$40.$$

Lisa can choose any quantities of soda (Q_S) and movies (Q_M) that satisfy this equation. To find the relationship between these quantities, divide both sides of the equation by the price of soda (P_S) to get

$$Q_S + \frac{P_M}{P_S} \times Q_M = \frac{Y}{P_S}.$$

Now subtract the term $(P_M/P_S) \times Q_M$ from both sides of this equation to get

$$Q_S = \frac{Y}{P_S} - \frac{P_M}{P_S} \times Q_M.$$

For Lisa, income (Y) is $40, the price of a movie (P_M) is $8, and the price of soda (P_S) is $4 a case. So Lisa must choose the quantities of movies and soda to satisfy the equation

$$Q_S = \frac{\$40}{\$4} - \frac{\$8}{\$4} \times Q_M,$$

or

$$Q_S = 10 - 2Q_M.$$

To interpret the equation, look at the budget line in Fig. 9.1 and check that the equation delivers that budget line. First, set Q_M equal to zero. The budget equation tells us that Q_S, the quantity of soda, is Y/P_S, which is 10 cases. This combination of Q_M and Q_S is the one shown in row A of the table in Fig. 9.1. Next set Q_M equal to 5. Q_S now equals zero (row F of the table). Check that you can derive the other rows.

The budget equation contains two variables chosen by the household (Q_M and Q_S) and two variables that the household takes as given (Y/P_S and P_M/P_S). Let's look more closely at these variables.

Real Income A household's **real income** is its income expressed as a quantity of goods that the household can afford to buy. Expressed in terms of soda, Lisa's real income is Y/P_S. This quantity is the maximum quantity of soda that she can buy. It is equal to her money income divided by the price of soda. Lisa's money income is $40 and the price of soda is $4 a case, so her real income in terms of soda is 10 cases, which is shown in Fig. 9.1 as the point at which the budget line intersects the y-axis.

Relative Price A **relative price** is the price of one good divided by the price of another good. In Lisa's budget equation, the variable P_M/P_S is the relative price of a movie in terms of soda. For Lisa, P_M is $8 a movie and P_S is $4 a case, so P_M/P_S is equal to 2 cases of soda per movie. That is, to see 1 movie, Lisa must give up 2 cases of soda.

You've just calculated Lisa's opportunity cost of seeing a movie. Recall that the opportunity cost of an action is the best alternative forgone. For Lisa to see 1 more movie a month, she must forgo 2 cases of soda. You've also calculated Lisa's opportunity cost of soda. For Lisa to buy 2 more cases of soda a month, she must forgo seeing 1 movie. So her opportunity cost of 2 cases of soda is 1 movie.

The relative price of a movie in terms of soda is the magnitude of the slope of Lisa's budget line. To calculate the slope of the budget line, recall the formula for slope (see the Chapter 1 Appendix): Slope equals the change in the variable measured on the y-axis divided by the change in the variable measured on the x-axis as we move along the line. In Lisa's case (Fig. 9.1), the variable measured on the y-axis is the quantity of soda and the variable measured on the x-axis is the quantity of movies. Along Lisa's budget line, as soda decreases from 10 to 0 cases, movies increase from 0 to 5. So the magnitude of the slope of the budget line is 10 cases divided by 5 movies, or 2 cases of soda per movie. The magnitude of this slope is exactly the same as the relative price we've just calculated. It is also the opportunity cost of a movie.

A Change in Prices When prices change, so does the budget line. The lower the price of the good measured on the x-axis, other things remaining the same, the flatter is the budget line. For example, if the price of a movie falls from $8 to $4, real income

FIGURE 9.2   Changes in Prices and Income

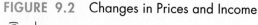

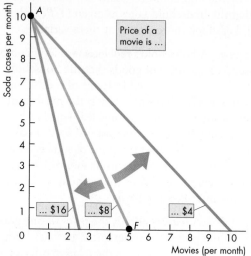

(a) A change in price

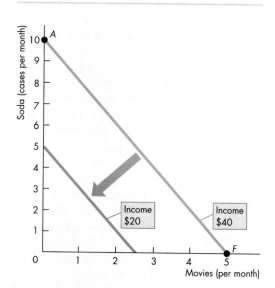

(b) A change in income

In part (a), the price of a movie changes. A fall in the price from $8 to $4 rotates the budget line outward and makes it flatter. A rise in the price from $8 to $16 rotates the budget line inward and makes it steeper.

In part (b), income falls from $40 to $20 while the prices of movies and soda remain the same. The budget line shifts leftward, but its slope does not change.

in terms of soda does not change but the relative price of a movie falls. The budget line rotates outward and becomes flatter, as Fig. 9.2(a) illustrates. The higher the price of the good measured on the *x*-axis, other things remaining the same, the steeper is the budget line. For example, if the price of a movie rises from $8 to $16, the relative price of a movie increases. The budget line rotates inward and becomes steeper, as Fig. 9.2(a) illustrates.

A Change in Income A change in money income changes real income but does not change the relative price. The budget line shifts, but its slope does not change. An increase in money income increases real income and shifts the budget line rightward. A decrease in money income decreases real income and shifts the budget line leftward.

Figure 9.2(b) shows the effect of a change in money income on Lisa's budget line. The initial budget line when Lisa's income is $40 is the same as in Fig. 9.1. The new budget line shows how much Lisa can buy if her income falls to $20 a month. The two budget lines have the same slope because the relative price is the same. The new budget line is closer to the origin because Lisa's real income has decreased.

REVIEW QUIZ

1 What does a household's budget line show?
2 How does the relative price and a household's real income influence its budget line?
3 If a household has an income of $40 and buys only bus rides at $2 each and magazines at $4 each, what is the equation of the household's budget line?
4 If the price of one good changes, what happens to the relative price and the slope of the household's budget line?
5 If a household's money income changes and prices do not change, what happens to the household's real income and budget line?

You can work these questions in Study Plan 9.1 and get instant feedback.

We've studied the limits to what a household can consume. Let's now learn how we can describe preferences and make a map that contains a lot of information about a household's preferences.

Preferences and Indifference Curves

You are going to discover a very cool idea: that of drawing a map of a person's preferences. A preference map is based on the intuitively appealing idea that people can sort all the possible combinations of goods into three groups: preferred, not preferred, and indifferent. To make this idea more concrete, let's ask Lisa to tell us how she ranks various combinations of movies and soda.

Figure 9.3 shows part of Lisa's answer. She tells us that she currently sees 2 movies and buys 6 cases of soda a month at point *C*. She then lists all the combinations of movies and soda that she says are just as acceptable to her as her current situation. When we plot these combinations of movies and soda, we get the green curve in Fig. 9.3(a). This curve is the key element in a preference map and is called an indifference curve.

An **indifference curve** is a line that shows combinations of goods among which a consumer is *indifferent*. The indifference curve in Fig. 9.3(a) tells us that Lisa is just as happy to see 2 movies and buy 6 cases of soda a month at point *C* as she is to have the combination of movies and soda at point *G* or at any other point along the curve.

Lisa also says that she prefers all the combinations of movies and soda above the indifference curve in Fig. 9.3(a)—the yellow area—to those on the indifference curve. And she prefers any combination on the indifference curve to any combination in the gray area below the indifference curve.

The indifference curve in Fig. 9.3(a) is just one of a whole family of such curves. This indifference curve appears again in Fig. 9.3(b), labeled I_1. The curves labeled I_0 and I_2 are two other indifference curves. Lisa prefers any point on indifference curve I_2 to any point on indifference curve I_1, and she prefers any point on I_1 to any point on I_0. We refer to I_2 as being a higher indifference curve than I_1 and I_1 as being higher than I_0.

A preference map is a series of indifference curves that resemble the contour lines on a map. By looking at the shape of the contour lines on a map, we can draw conclusions about the terrain. Similarly, by looking at the shape of the indifference curves, we can draw conclusions about a person's preferences.

Let's learn how to "read" a preference map.

FIGURE 9.3   A Preference Map

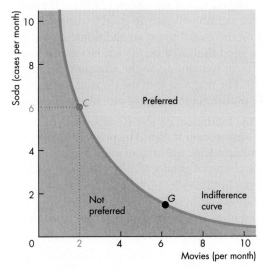

(a) An indifference curve

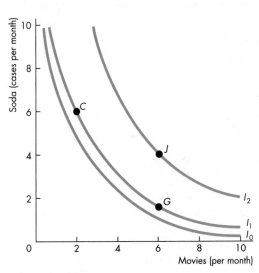

(b) Lisa's preference map

Part (a) shows one of Lisa's indifference curves. She is indifferent between point *C* (with 2 movies and 6 cases of soda) and all other points on the green indifference curve, such as *G*. She prefers points above the indifference curve (in the yellow area) to points on it, and she prefers points on the indifference curve to points below it (in the gray area).
Part (b) shows three of the indifference curves—I_0, I_1, and I_2—in Lisa's preference map. She prefers point *J* to point *C* or *G*, and she prefers all the points on I_2 to those on I_1.

 myeconlab animation

Marginal Rate of Substitution

The **marginal rate of substitution** (*MRS*) is the rate at which a person will give up good *y* (the good measured on the *y*-axis) to get an additional unit of good *x* (the good measured on the *x*-axis) while remaining indifferent (remaining on the same indifference curve). The magnitude of the slope of an indifference curve measures the marginal rate of substitution.

- If the indifference curve is *steep*, the marginal rate of substitution is *high*. The person is willing to give up a large quantity of good *y* to get an additional unit of good *x* while remaining indifferent.
- If the indifference curve is *flat*, the marginal rate of substitution is *low*. The person is willing to give up a small amount of good *y* to get an additional unit of good *x* while remaining indifferent.

Figure 9.4 shows you how to calculate the marginal rate of substitution.

At point *C* on indifference curve I_1, Lisa buys 6 cases of soda and sees 2 movies. Her marginal rate of substitution is the magnitude of the slope of the indifference curve at point *C*. To measure this magnitude, place a straight line against, or tangent to, the indifference curve at point *C*. Along that line, as the quantity of soda decreases by 10 cases, the number of movies increases by 5—or 2 cases per movie. At point *C*, Lisa is willing to give up soda for movies at the rate of 2 cases per movie—a marginal rate of substitution of 2.

At point *G* on indifference curve I_1, Lisa buys 1.5 cases of soda and sees 6 movies. Her marginal rate of substitution is measured by the slope of the indifference curve at point *G*. That slope is the same as the slope of the tangent to the indifference curve at point *G*. Now, as the quantity of soda decreases by 4.5 cases, the number of movies increases by 9—or 1/2 case per movie. At point *G*, Lisa is willing to give up soda for movies at the rate of 1/2 case per movie—a marginal rate of substitution of 1/2.

As Lisa sees more movies and buys less soda, her marginal rate of substitution diminishes. Diminishing marginal rate of substitution is the key assumption about preferences. A **diminishing marginal rate of substitution** is a general tendency for a person to be willing to give up less of good *y* to get one more unit of good *x*, while at the same time remaining indifferent as the quantity of *x* increases. In Lisa's case, she is less willing to give up soda to see one more movie as the number of movies she sees increases.

FIGURE 9.4   The Marginal Rate of Substitution

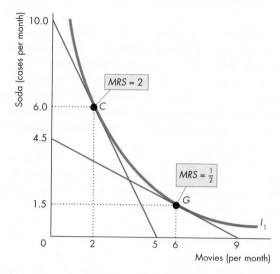

The magnitude of the slope of an indifference curve is called the marginal rate of substitution (*MRS*). The red line at point *C* tells us that Lisa is willing to give up 10 cases of soda to see 5 movies. Her marginal rate of substitution at point *C* is 10 divided by 5, which equals 2. The red line at point *G* tells us that Lisa is willing to give up 4.5 cases of soda to see 9 movies. Her marginal rate of substitution at point *G* is 4.5 divided by 9, which equals 1/2.

Your Diminishing Marginal Rate of Substitution

Think about your own diminishing marginal rate of substitution. Imagine that in a week, you drink 10 cases of soda and see no movies. Most likely, you are willing to give up a lot of soda so that you can see just 1 movie. But now imagine that in a week, you buy 1 case of soda and see 6 movies. Most likely, you will now not be willing to give up much soda to see a seventh movie. As a general rule, the greater the number of movies you see, the smaller is the quantity of soda you are willing to give up to see one additional movie.

The shape of a person's indifference curves incorporates the principle of the diminishing marginal rate of substitution because the curves are bowed toward the origin. The tightness of the bend of an indifference curve tells us how willing a person is to substitute one good for another while remaining indifferent. Let's look at some examples that make this point clear.

Degree of Substitutability

Most of us would not regard movies and soda as being *close* substitutes, but they are substitutes. No matter how much you love soda, some increase in the number of movies you see will compensate you for being deprived of a can of soda. Similarly, no matter how much you love going to the movies, some number of cans of soda will compensate you for being deprived of seeing one movie. A person's indifference curves for movies and soda might look something like those for most ordinary goods and services shown in Fig. 9.5(a).

Close Substitutes Some goods substitute so easily for each other that most of us do not even notice which we are consuming. The different brands of marker pens and pencils are examples. Most people don't care which brand of these items they use or where they buy them. A marker pen from the campus bookstore is just as good as one from the local grocery store. You would be willing to forgo a pen from the campus store if you could get one more pen from

the local grocery store. When two goods are perfect substitutes, their indifference curves are straight lines that slope downward, as Fig. 9.5(b) illustrates. The marginal rate of substitution is constant.

Complements Some goods do not substitute for each other at all. Instead, they are complements. The complements in Fig. 9.5(c) are left and right running shoes. Indifference curves of perfect complements are L-shaped. One left running shoe and one right running shoe are as good as one left shoe and two right shoes. Having two of each is preferred to having one of each, but having two of one and one of the other is no better than having one of each.

The extreme cases of perfect substitutes and perfect complements shown here don't often happen in reality, but they do illustrate that the shape of the indifference curve shows the degree of substitutability between two goods. The closer the two goods are to perfect substitutes, the closer the marginal rate of substitution is to being constant (a straight line), rather than diminishing (a curved line). Indifference

FIGURE 9.5   The Degree of Substitutability

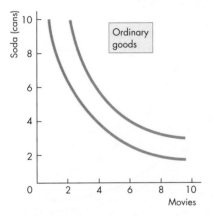

(a) Ordinary goods

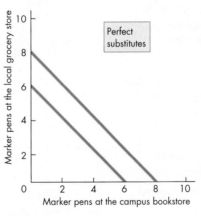

(b) Perfect substitutes

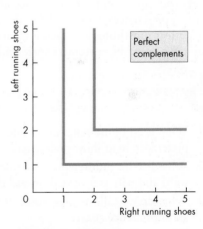

(c) Perfect complements

The shape of the indifference curves reveals the degree of substitutability between two goods. Part (a) shows the indifference curves for two ordinary goods: movies and soda. To drink less soda and remain indifferent, one must see more movies. The number of movies that compensates for a reduction in soda increases as less soda is consumed. Part (b) shows the indifference curves for two perfect substitutes. For

the consumer to remain indifferent, one fewer marker pen from the local grocery store must be replaced by one extra marker pen from the campus bookstore. Part (c) shows two perfect complements—goods that cannot be substituted for each other at all. Having two left running shoes with one right running shoe is no better than having one of each. But having two of each is preferred to having one of each.

myeconlab   animation

"With the pork I'd recommend an Alsatian white or a Coke."

© The New Yorker Collection 1988
Robert Weber from cartoonbank.com. All Rights Reserved.

curves for poor substitutes are tightly curved and lie between the shapes of those shown in Figs. 9.5(a) and 9.5(c).

As you can see in the cartoon, according to the waiter's preferences, Coke and Alsatian white wine are perfect substitutes and each is a complement of pork. We hope the customers agree with him.

REVIEW QUIZ

1 What is an indifference curve and how does a preference map show preferences?

2 Why does an indifference curve slope downward and why is it bowed toward the origin?

3 What do we call the magnitude of the slope of an indifference curve?

4 What is the key assumption about a consumer's marginal rate of substitution?

You can work these questions in Study Plan 9.2 and get instant feedback.

The two components of the model of household choice are now in place: the budget line and the preference map. We will now use these components to work out a household's choice and to predict how choices change when prices and income change.

◆ Predicting Consumer Choices

We are now going to predict the quantities of movies and soda that Lisa chooses to buy. We're also going to see how these quantities change when a price changes or when Lisa's income changes. Finally, we're going to see how the *substitution effect* and the *income effect*, two ideas that you met in Chapter 3 (see p. 57), guarantee that for a normal good, the demand curve slopes downward.

Best Affordable Choice

When Lisa makes her best affordable choice of movies and soda, she spends all her income and is on her highest attainable indifference curve. Figure 9.6 illustrates this choice: The budget line is from Fig. 9.1 and the indifference curves are from Fig. 9.3(b). Lisa's best affordable choice is 2 movies and 6 cases of soda at point *C*—the *best affordable point*.

FIGURE 9.6   The Best Affordable Choice

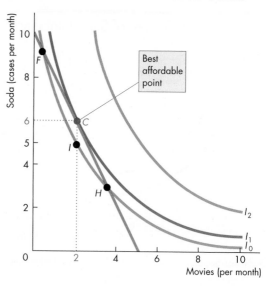

Lisa's best affordable choice is at point *C*, the point on her budget line and on her highest attainable indifference curve. At point *C*, Lisa's marginal rate of substitution between movies and soda (the magnitude of the slope of the indifference curve I_1) equals the relative price of movies and soda (the slope of the budget line).

 animation

On the Budget Line The best affordable point is on the budget line. For every point inside the budget line, such as point *I*, there are points on the budget line that Lisa prefers. For example, she prefers all the points on the budget line between *F* and *H* to point *I*, so she chooses a point on the budget line.

On the Highest Attainable Indifference Curve Every point on the budget line lies on an indifference curve. For example, points *F* and *H* lie on the indifference curve I_0. By moving along her budget line from either *F* or *H* toward *C*, Lisa reaches points on ever-higher indifference curves that she prefers to points *F* or *H*. When Lisa gets to point *C*, she is on the highest attainable indifference curve.

Marginal Rate of Substitution Equals Relative Price At point *C*, Lisa's marginal rate of substitution between movies and soda (the magnitude of the slope of the indifference curve) is equal to the relative price of movies and soda (the magnitude of the slope of the budget line). Lisa's willingness to pay for a movie equals her opportunity cost of a movie.

Let's now see how Lisa's choices change when a price changes.

A Change in Price

The effect of a change in the price of a good on the quantity of the good consumed is called the **price effect**. We will use Fig. 9.7(a) to work out the price effect of a fall in the price of a movie. We start with the price of a movie at $8, the price of soda at $4 a case, and Lisa's income at $40 a month. In this situation, she buys 6 cases of soda and sees 2 movies a month at point *C*.

Now suppose that the price of a movie falls to $4. With a lower price of a movie, the budget line rotates outward and becomes flatter. The new budget line is the darker orange one in Fig. 9.7(a). For a refresher on how a price change affects the budget line, check back to Fig. 9.2(a).

Lisa's best affordable point is now point *J*, where she sees 6 movies and drinks 4 cases of soda. Lisa drinks less soda and watches more movies now that movies are cheaper. She cuts her soda purchases from 6 to 4 cases and increases the number of movies she sees from 2 to 6 a month. When the price of a movie falls and the price of soda and her income remain constant, Lisa substitutes movies for soda.

FIGURE 9.7   Price Effect and Demand Curve

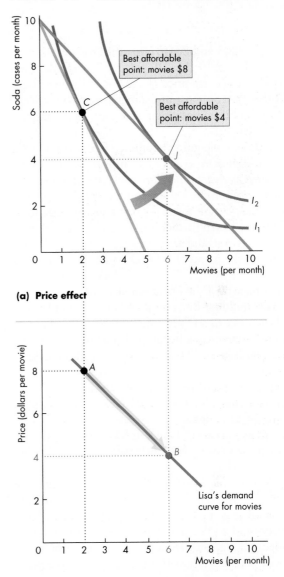

(a) Price effect

(b) Demand curve

Initially, Lisa's best affordable point is *C* in part (a). If the price of a movie falls from $8 to $4, Lisa's best affordable point is *J*. The move from *C* to *J* is the price effect.

At a price of $8 a movie, Lisa sees 2 movies a month, at point *A* in part (b). At a price of $4 a movie, she sees 6 movies a month, at point *B*. Lisa's demand curve for movies traces out her best affordable quantity of movies as the price of a movie varies.

Economics in Action

Best Affordable Choice of Movies and DVDs

Between 2005 and 2010, box-office receipts increased by more than 20 percent. During that same period, the average price of a movie ticket increased by 6 percent. So most of the increase in box-office receipts occurred because people went to the movies more often.

Why is movie-going booming? One answer is that the consumer's experience has improved. Movies in 3-D such as *Avatar* and *Alice in Wonderland* play much better on the big screen than at home. Also, movie theaters are able to charge a higher price for 3-D films, which further boosts receipts. But there is another answer, and at first thought an unlikely one: Events in the market for DVD rentals have impacted going to the movies. To see why, let's look at the recent history of the DVD rentals market.

Back in 2005, Blockbuster was the main player and the price of a DVD rental was around $4 a night. Redbox was a fledgling. It had started a year earlier with just 140 kiosks in selected McDonald's restaurants. But Redbox expanded rapidly and by 2007 had as many outlets as Blockbuster. In February 2008, Redbox rented 100 million DVDs at a price of $1 a night.

The easy access to DVDs at $1 a night transformed the markets for movie watching and the figure shows why.

A student has a budget of $40 a month to allocate to movies. To keep the story clear, we'll suppose that it cost $8 to go to a movie in both 2005 and 2010. The price of a DVD rental in 2005 was $4, so the student's budget line is the one that runs from 5 movies on the *y*-axis to 10 DVD rentals on the *x*-axis.

The student's best affordable point is 2 movies and 6 rentals a month.

In 2010, the price of a rental falls to $1 a night but the price of a movie ticket remains at $8. So the budget line rotates outward. The student's best affordable point is now at 3 movies and 16 rentals a month. (This student loves movies!)

Many other things changed between 2005 and 2010 that influenced the markets for movies and DVD rentals, but the fall in the price of a DVD rental was the biggest influence.

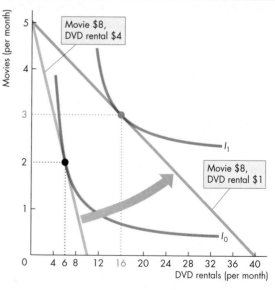

Best Affordable Movies and DVD Rentals

The Demand Curve In Chapter 3, we asserted that the demand curve slopes downward. We can now derive a demand curve from a consumer's budget line and indifference curves. By doing so, we can see that the law of demand and the downward-sloping demand curve are consequences of a consumer's choosing her or his best affordable combination of goods.

To derive Lisa's demand curve for movies, lower the price of a movie and find her best affordable point at different prices. We've just done this for two movie prices in Fig. 9.7(a). Figure 9.7(b) highlights these two prices and two points that lie on Lisa's demand curve for movies. When the price of a movie is $8, Lisa sees 2 movies a month at point A. When the price falls to $4, she increases the number of movies she sees to 6 a month at point B. The demand curve is made up of these two points plus all the other points that tell us Lisa's best affordable quantity of movies at each movie price, with the price of soda and Lisa's income remaining the same. As you can see, Lisa's demand curve for movies slopes downward—the lower the price of a movie, the more movies she sees. This is the law of demand.

Next, let's see how Lisa changes her purchases of movies and soda when her income changes.

A Change in Income

The effect of a change in income on buying plans is called the **income effect**. Let's work out the income effect by examining how buying plans change when income changes and prices remain constant. Figure 9.8 shows the income effect when Lisa's income falls. With an income of $40, the price of a movie at $4, and the price of soda at $4 a case, Lisa's best affordable point is J—she buys 6 movies and 4 cases of soda. If her income falls to $28, her best affordable point is K—she sees 4 movies and buys 3 cases of soda. When Lisa's income falls, she buys less of both goods. Movies and soda are normal goods.

The Demand Curve and the Income Effect A change in income leads to a shift in the demand curve, as shown in Fig. 9.8(b). With an income of $40, Lisa's demand curve for movies is D_0, the same as in Fig. 9.7(b). But when her income falls to $28, she plans to see fewer movies at each price, so her demand curve shifts leftward to D_1.

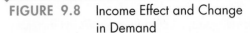

FIGURE 9.8   Income Effect and Change in Demand

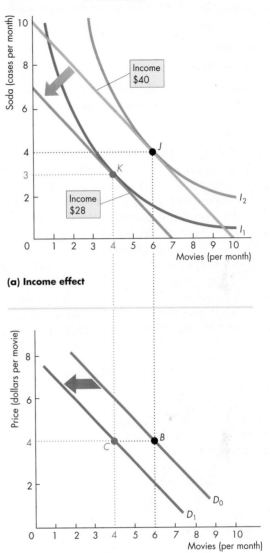

(a) Income effect

(b) Demand curve for movies

A change in income shifts the budget line, changes the best affordable point, and changes demand.

In part (a), when Lisa's income decreases from $40 to $28, she sees fewer movies and buys less soda.

In part (b), when Lisa's income is $40, her demand curve for movies is D_0. When Lisa's income falls to $28, her demand curve for movies shifts leftward to D_1. For Lisa, going to the movies is a normal good. Her demand for movies decreases because she now sees fewer movies at each price.

myeconlab animation

Substitution Effect and Income Effect

For a normal good, a fall in its price *always* increases the quantity bought. We can prove this assertion by dividing the price effect into two parts:

- Substitution effect
- Income effect

Figure 9.9(a) shows the price effect and Figs. 9.9(b) and 9.9(c) show the two parts into which we separate the price effect.

Substitution Effect The **substitution effect** is the effect of a change in price on the quantity bought when the consumer (hypothetically) remains indifferent between the original situation and the new one. To work out Lisa's substitution effect when the price of a movie falls, we must lower her income by enough to keep her on the same indifference curve as before.

Figure 9.9(a) shows the price effect of a fall in the price of a movie from $8 to $4. The number of movies increases from 2 to 6 a month. When the price falls, suppose (hypothetically) that we cut Lisa's income to $28. What's special about $28? It is the

income that is just enough, at the new price of a movie, to keep Lisa's best affordable point on the same indifference curve (I_1) as her original point C. Lisa's budget line is now the medium orange line in Fig. 9.9(b). With the lower price of a movie and a smaller income, Lisa's best affordable point is K. The move from C to K along indifference curve I_1 is the substitution effect of the price change. The substitution effect of the fall in the price of a movie is an increase in the quantity of movies from 2 to 4. The direction of the substitution effect never varies: When the relative price of a good falls, the consumer substitutes more of that good for the other good.

Income Effect To calculate the substitution effect, we gave Lisa a $12 pay cut. To calculate the income effect, we give Lisa back her $12. The $12 increase in income shifts Lisa's budget line outward, as shown in Fig. 9.9(c). The slope of the budget line does not change because both prices remain the same. This change in Lisa's budget line is similar to the one illustrated in Fig. 9.8. As Lisa's budget line shifts outward, her consumption possibilities expand and her best affordable

---

FIGURE 9.9   Substitution Effect and Income Effect

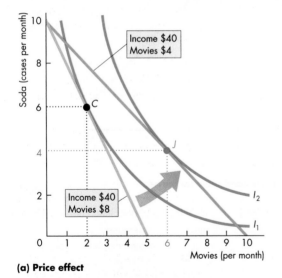

(a) Price effect

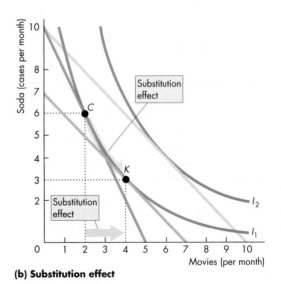

(b) Substitution effect

When the price of a movie falls from $8 to $4, Lisa moves from point C to point J in part (a). The price effect is an increase in the number of movies from 2 to 6 a month. This price effect is separated into a substitution effect in part (b) and an income effect in part (c).

To isolate the substitution effect, we confront Lisa with the new price but keep her on her original indifference curve, I_1. The substitution effect is the move from C to K along indifference curve I_1—an increase from 2 to 4 movies a month.

point becomes J on indifference curve I_2. The move from K to J is the income effect of the price change.

As Lisa's income increases, she sees more movies. For Lisa, a movie is a normal good. For a normal good, the income effect *reinforces* the substitution effect. Because the two effects work in the same direction, we can be sure that the demand curve slopes downward. But some goods are inferior goods. What can we say about the demand for an inferior good?

Inferior Goods Recall that an *inferior good* is a good for which *demand decreases* when *income increases*. For an inferior good, the income effect is negative, which means that a lower price does not inevitably lead to an increase in the quantity demanded. The substitution effect of a fall in the price increases the quantity demanded, but the negative income effect works in the opposite direction and offsets the substitution effect to some degree. The key question is to what degree.

If the negative income effect *equals* the positive substitution effect, a fall in price leaves the quantity bought the same. When a fall in price leaves the quantity demanded unchanged, the demand curve is vertical and demand is perfectly inelastic.

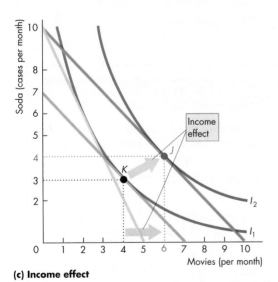

(c) Income effect

To isolate the income effect, we confront Lisa with the new price of movies but increase her income so that she can move from the original indifference curve, I_1, to the new one, I_2. The income effect is the move from K to J—an increase from 4 to 6 movies a month.

If the negative income effect *is smaller than* the positive substitution effect, a fall in price increases the quantity bought and the demand curve still slopes downward like that for a normal good. But the demand for an inferior good might be less elastic than that for a normal good.

If the negative income effect *exceeds* the positive substitution effect, a fall in the price *decreases* the quantity bought and the demand curve *slopes upward*. This case does not appear to occur in the real world.

You can apply the indifference curve model that you've studied in this chapter to explain the changes in the way we buy recorded music, see movies, and make all our other consumption choices. We allocate our budgets to make our best affordable choices. Changes in prices and incomes change our best affordable choices and change consumption patterns.

REVIEW QUIZ

1   When a consumer chooses the combination of goods and services to buy, what is she or he trying to achieve?
2   Explain the conditions that are met when a consumer has found the best affordable combination of goods to buy. (Use the terms budget line, marginal rate of substitution, and relative price in your explanation.)
3   If the price of a normal good falls, what happens to the quantity demanded of that good?
4   Into what two effects can we divide the effect of a price change?
5   For a normal good, does the income effect reinforce the substitution effect or does it partly offset the substitution effect?

You can work these questions in Study Plan 9.3 and get instant feedback.

◆ *Reading Between the Lines* on pp. 216–217 shows you how the theory of household choice explains why e-books are taking off, and how people chose whether to buy their books in electronic or paper format.

In the chapters that follow, we study the choices that firms make in their pursuit of profit and how those choices determine the supply of goods and services and the demand for productive resources.

Paper Books Versus e-Books

Amazon.com E-Book Sales Exceed Hardcovers for First Time

http://www.bloomberg.com
July 19, 2010

Amazon.com Inc., the largest Internet retailer, said growth in sales of its Kindle digAmazon.com Inc., the largest Internet retailer, said growth in sales of its Kindle digital reader accelerated every month in the second quarter and that it's selling more electronic books than hardcover editions.

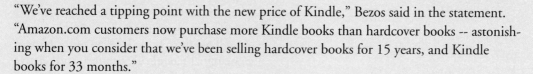

The pace of Kindle sales also has tripled since the company cut the price to $189 from $259, Amazon.com Chief Executive Officer Jeff Bezos said in a statement. ...Amazon.com sold more than triple the number of Kindle books in the first half of the year as it did in the same period last year, Seattle-based Amazon.com said. More than 81 percent of its 630,000 electronic books are $9.99 or less.

"We've reached a tipping point with the new price of Kindle," Bezos said in the statement. "Amazon.com customers now purchase more Kindle books than hardcover books -- astonishing when you consider that we've been selling hardcover books for 15 years, and Kindle books for 33 months."

...In the past three months, Amazon.com has sold 143 Kindle books for every 100 hardcover books, the company said. In July, sales of e-books accelerated to 180 sold for every 100 hardcover versions. Kindle book sales this year have also exceeded broader e-book sales growth, pegged by the Association of American Publishers at 207 percent through May, Amazon.com said.

ESSENCE OF THE STORY

- During the three months ended June 30, 2010, Amazon sold 143 Kindle e-books for every 100 hardcover paper books.

- The Kindle store lists 630,000 eBooks, and 80 percent of them are priced at less than $10.

- Amazon has cut the price of its Kindle reader from $259 to $189 and the quantity sold has tripled.

- The quantity sold might explode if the Kindle was cheaper still.

ECONOMIC ANALYSIS

- Print books and e-books are substitutes.

- For most people, though, e-books and print books are extremely poor substitutes.

- For a committed print-book lover, no quantity of e-books can compensate for a print book—the marginal rate of substitution between print books and e-books is zero.

- Beth is a print-book lover and Fig. 1 shows her indifference curves for print books and e-books.

- With print books on the x-axis, Beth's indifference curves are steep. They tell us that Beth is willing to forgo a large number of e-books to get one more print book.

- Beth's annual book budget is $340. The price of an e-book reader is $190 (the current price of the Kindle reader is $189). The price of an e-book is $10 and the price of a print book is $20.

- We'll assume that an e-book reader has only a one-year life. (Buyers know they will want the next-generation, improved reader next year.)

- The orange line is Beth's budget line if she buys a reader. She can afford 15 e-books if she buys no print books [$190 + (15 × $10) = $340] and along this line, by forgoing 2 e-books she can buy 1 print book.

- If Beth doesn't buy an e-book reader, she buys no e-books and can afford 17 print books ($340 ÷ $20 = 17). The red dot shows this affordable point.

- The red dot is also the best affordable choice because this choice gets her onto her highest attainable indifference curve, I_2.

- Andy differs from Beth: He thinks that print books and e-books are perfect substitutes. But he also likes music and buys albums. Figure 2 shows Andy's indifference curves for books (all types) and albums.

- Andy's annual budget for albums and books is $550. The price of an album is $10 and the prices of an e-book reader, an e-book, and a print book are the same as those that Beth faces.

- Figure 2 shows Andy's two budget lines: one if he buys only e-books and albums and another if he buys only print books and albums.

- If Andy buys e-books, he must spend $190 on a reader, which leaves him with $360 for albums and e-books. If he buys 10 e-books, he can afford 25 albums [(10 x $10) + (26 x $10) = $360].

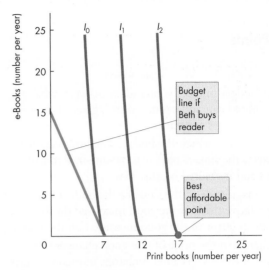

Figure 1 Print books versus e-books for a print-book lover

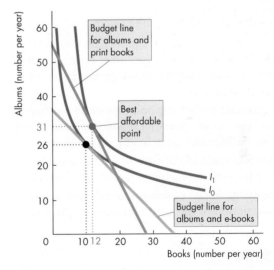

Figure 2 Books versus albums

- If Andy buys print books and albums, he can afford 12 print books and 22 albums [(12 × $20) + (31 × $10) = $550].

- Andy's best affordable choice is 12 print books and 31 albums.

- So even Andy, who thinks that e-books and print books are perfect substitutes, doesn't buy e-books. But he probably would if he had a larger budget.

SUMMARY

Key Points

Consumption Possibilities (pp. 204–206)

- The budget line is the boundary between what a household can and cannot afford, given its income and the prices of goods.
- The point at which the budget line intersects the y-axis is the household's real income in terms of the good measured on that axis.
- The magnitude of the slope of the budget line is the relative price of the good measured on the x-axis in terms of the good measured on the y-axis.
- A change in the price of one good changes the slope of the budget line. A change in income shifts the budget line but does not change its slope.

Working Problems 1 to 10 will give you a better understanding of consumption possibilities.

Preferences and Indifference Curves (pp. 207–210)

- A consumer's preferences can be represented by indifference curves. The consumer is indifferent among all the combinations of goods that lie on an indifference curve.
- A consumer prefers any point above an indifference curve to any point on it and prefers any point on an indifference curve to any point below it.
- The magnitude of the slope of an indifference curve is called the marginal rate of substitution.
- The marginal rate of substitution diminishes as consumption of the good measured on the y-axis

decreases and consumption of the good measured on the x-axis increases.

Working Problems 11 to 15 will give you a better understanding of preferences and indifference curves.

Predicting Consumer Choices (pp. 210–215)

- A household consumes at its best affordable point. This point is on the budget line and on the highest attainable indifference curve and has a marginal rate of substitution equal to relative price.
- The effect of a price change (the price effect) can be divided into a substitution effect and an income effect.
- The substitution effect is the effect of a change in price on the quantity bought when the consumer (hypothetically) remains indifferent between the original choice and the new choice.
- The substitution effect always results in an increase in consumption of the good whose relative price has fallen.
- The income effect is the effect of a change in income on consumption.
- For a normal good, the income effect reinforces the substitution effect. For an inferior good, the income effect works in the opposite direction to the substitution effect.

Working Problems 16 to 20 will give you a better understanding of predicting consumer choices.

Key Terms

Budget line, 204
Diminishing marginal rate of
  substitution, 208
Income effect, 213

Indifference curve, 207
Marginal rate of substitution, 208
Price effect, 211
Real income, 205

Relative price, 205
Substitution effect, 214

STUDY PLAN PROBLEMS AND APPLICATIONS

 myeconlab You can work Problems 1 to 22 in MyEconLab Chapter 9 Study Plan and get instant feedback.

Consumption Possibilities (Study Plan 9.1)

Use the following information to work Problems 1 to 4.

Sara's income is $12 a week. The price of popcorn is $3 a bag, and the price of a smoothie is $3.

1. Calculate Sara's real income in terms of smoothies. Calculate her real income in terms of popcorn.

2. What is the relative price of smoothies in terms of popcorn? What is the opportunity cost of a smoothie?

3. Calculate the equation for Sara's budget line (with bags of popcorn on the left side).

4. Draw a graph of Sara's budget line with the quantity of smoothies on the x-axis. What is the slope of Sara's budget line? What determines its value?

Use the following information to work Problems 5 to 8.

Sara's income falls from $12 to $9 a week, while the price of popcorn is unchanged at $3 a bag and the price of a smoothie is unchanged at $3.

5. What is the effect of the fall in Sara's income on her real income in terms of smoothies?

6. What is the effect of the fall in Sara's income on her real income in terms of popcorn?

7. What is the effect of the fall in Sara's income on the relative price of a smoothie in terms of popcorn?

8. What is the slope of Sara's new budget line if it is drawn with smoothies on the x-axis?

Use the following information to work Problems 9 and 10.

Sara's income is $12 a week. The price of popcorn rises from $3 to $6 a bag, and the price of a smoothie is unchanged at $3.

9. What is the effect of the rise in the price of popcorn on Sara's real income in terms of smoothies and her real income in terms of popcorn?

10. What is the effect of the rise in the price of popcorn on the relative price of a smoothie in terms of popcorn? What is the slope of Sara's new budget line if it is drawn with smoothies on the x-axis?

Preferences and Indifference Curves (Study Plan 9.2)

11. Draw figures that show your indifference curves for the following pairs of goods:
    - Right gloves and left gloves
    - Coca-Cola and Pepsi
    - Tylenol and acetaminophen (the generic form of Tylenol)
    - Desktop computers and laptop computers
    - Strawberries and ice cream

For each pair, are the goods perfect substitutes, perfect complements, substitutes, complements, or unrelated?

12. Discuss the shape of the indifference curve for each of the following pairs of goods:
    - Orange juice and smoothies
    - Baseballs and baseball bats
    - Left running shoe and right running shoe
    - Eyeglasses and contact lenses

Explain the relationship between the shape of the indifference curve and the marginal rate of substitution as the quantities of the two goods change.

Use the following news clip to work Problems 13 and 14.

The Year in Medicine

Sudafed, used by allergy sufferers, contains as the active ingredient pseudoephedrine, which is widely used to make home-made methamphetamine. Allergy sufferers looking to buy Sudafed, must now show photo ID, and sign a logbook. The most common alternative, phenylephrine, isn't as effective as pseudoephedrine.

Source: *Time*, December 4, 2006

13. Sketch an indifference curve for Sudafed and phenylephrine that is consistent with this news clip. On your graph, identify combinations that allergy sufferers prefer, do not prefer, and are indifferent among.

14. Explain how the marginal rate of substitution changes as an allergy sufferer increases the consumption of Sudafed.

Use the following news clip to work Problems 15 and 16.

Gas Prices to Stunt Memorial Day Travel

With high gas prices, 12% of the people surveyed say that they have cancelled their Memorial Day road trip and 11% will take a shorter trip near home. That may save consumers some money, but it will also likely hurt service stations, which will sell less gas and fewer snacks and hurt roadside hotels, which will have fewer rooms used and serve fewer casual meals.

Source: *MarketWatch*, May 22, 2008

15. Describe the degree of substitutability between Memorial Day trips and other trip-related goods and services and sketch a consumer's preference map that illustrates your description.

Predicting Consumer Choices (Study Plan 9.3)

16. a. Sketch a consumer's preference map between Memorial Day trips and other goods and services. Draw a consumer's budget line prior to the rise in the price of gasoline and mark the consumer's best affordable point.
   b. On your graph, show how the best affordable point changes when the price of gasoline rises.

Use the following information to work Problems 17 and 18.

Pam has chosen her best affordable combination of cookies and granola bars. She spends all of her weekly income on 30 cookies at $1 each and 5 granola bars at $2 each. Next week, people expect the price of a cookie to fall to 50¢ and the price of a granola bar to rise to $5.

17. a. Will Pam be able to buy and want to buy 30 cookies and 5 granola bars next week?
   b. Which situation does Pam prefer: cookies at $1 and granola bars at $2 or cookies at 50¢ and granola bars at $5?

18. a. If Pam changes how she spends her weekly income, will she buy more or fewer cookies and more or fewer granola bars?
   b. When the prices change next week, will there be an income effect, a substitution effect, or both at work?

Use the following information to work Problems 19 and 20.

Boom Time For "Gently Used" Clothes

Most retailers are blaming the economy for their poor sales, but one store chain that sells used name-brand children's clothes, toys, and furniture is boldly declaring that an economic downturn can actually be a boon for its business. Last year, the company took in $20 million in sales, up 5% from the previous year. Sales are already up 5% this year.

Source: CNN, April 17, 2008

19. a. According to the news clip, is used clothing a normal good or an inferior good?
   b. If the price of used clothing falls and income remains the same, explain how the quantity of used clothing bought changes.
   c. If the price of used clothing falls and income remains the same, describe the substitution effect and the income effect that occur.

20. a. Use a graph to illustrate a family's indifference curves for used clothing and other goods and services.
   b. In your graph in part (a), draw two budget lines to show the effect of a fall in income on the quantity of used clothing purchased.

Economics in the News (Study Plan 9.N)

Use the following information to work Problems 21 and 22.

Gas Prices Send Surge of Travelers to Mass Transit

With the price of gas approaching $4 a gallon, more commuters are abandoning their cars and taking the train or bus. It's very clear that a significant portion of the increase in transit use is directly caused by people who are looking for alternatives to paying $3.50 a gallon for gas. Some cities with long-established public transit systems, like New York and Boston, have seen increases in ridership of 5 percent, but the biggest surges—of 10 to 15 percent over last year—are occurring in many metropolitan areas in the Southwest where the driving culture is strongest and bus and rail lines are more limited.

Source: *The New York Times*, May 10, 2008

21. a. Sketch a graph of a preference map and a budget line to illustrate the best affordable combination of gasoline and public transit.
   b. On your graph in part (a), show the effect of a rise in the price of gasoline on the quantities of gasoline and public transit services purchased.

22. If the gas price rise has been similar in all regions, compare the marginal rates of substitution in the Northeast and the Southwest. Explain how you have inferred the different marginal rates of substitution from the information in the news clip.

ADDITIONAL PROBLEMS AND APPLICATIONS

 These problems are available in MyEconLab if assigned by your instructor.

Consumption Possibilities

Use the following information to work Problems 23 to 26.

Marc has a budget of $20 a month to spend on root beer and DVDs. The price of root beer is $5 a bottle, and the price of a DVD is $10.

23. What is the relative price of root beer in terms of DVDs and what is the opportunity cost of a bottle of root beer?

24. Calculate Marc's real income in terms of root beer. Calculate his real income in terms of DVDs.

25. Calculate the equation for Marc's budget line (with the quantity of root beer on the left side).

26. Draw a graph of Marc's budget line with the quantity of DVDs on the x-axis. What is the slope of Marc's budget line? What determines its value?

Use the following information to work Problems 27 to 30.

Amy has $20 a week to spend on coffee and cake. The price of coffee is $4 a cup, and the price of cake is $2 a slice.

27. Calculate Amy's real income in terms of cake. Calculate the relative price of cake in terms of coffee.

28. Calculate the equation for Amy's budget line (with cups of coffee on the left side).

29. If Amy's income increases to $24 a week and the prices of coffee and cake remain unchanged, describe the change in her budget line.

30. If the price of cake doubles while the price of coffee remains at $4 a cup and Amy's income remains at $20, describe the change in her budget line.

Use the following news clip to work Problems 31 and 32.

Gas Prices Straining Budgets

With gas prices rising, many people say they are staying in and scaling back spending to try to keep within their budget. They are driving as little as possible, cutting back on shopping and eating out, and reducing other discretionary spending.

Source: CNN, February 29, 2008

31. a. Sketch a budget line for a household that spends its income on only two goods: gasoline and restaurant meals. Identify the combinations of gasoline and restaurant meals that are affordable and those that are unaffordable.
    b. Sketch a second budget line to show how a rise in the price of gasoline changes the affordable and unaffordable combinations of gasoline and restaurant meals. Describe how the household's consumption possibilities change.

32. How does a rise in the price of gasoline change the relative price of a restaurant meal? How does a rise in the price of gasoline change real income in terms of restaurant meals?

Preferences and Indifference Curves

Use the following information to work Problems 33 and 34.

Rashid buys only books and CDs and the figure shows his preference map.

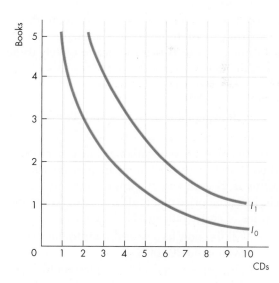

33. a. If Rashid chooses 3 books and 2 CDs, what is his marginal rate of substitution?
    b. If Rashid chooses 2 books and 6 CDs, what is his marginal rate of substitution?

34. Do Rashid's indifference curves display diminishing marginal rate of substitution? Explain why or why not.

35. You May Be Paid More (or Less) Than You Think

It's so hard to put a price on happiness, isn't it? But if you've ever had to choose between a job you like and a better-paying one that you like less, you probably wished some economist would tell you how much job satisfaction is worth. Trust in management is by far the biggest component to consider. Say you get a new boss and your trust in management goes up a bit (say, up 1 point on a 10-point scale). That's like getting a 36 percent pay raise. In other words, that increased level of trust will boost your level of overall satisfaction in life by about the same amount as a 36 percent raise would.

Source: CNN, March 29, 2006

a. Measure trust in management on a 10-point scale, measure pay on the same 10-point scale, and think of them as two goods. Sketch an indifference curve (with trust on the *x*-axis) that is consistent with the news clip.

b. What is the marginal rate of substitution between trust in management and pay according to this news clip?

c. What does the news clip imply about the principle of diminishing marginal rate of substitution? Is that implication likely to be correct?

Predicting Consumer Choices

Use the following information to work Problems 36 and 37.

Jim has made his best affordable choice of muffins and coffee. He spends all of his income on 10 muffins at $1 each and 20 cups of coffee at $2 each. Now the price of a muffin rises to $1.50 and the price of coffee falls to $1.75 a cup.

36. a. Will Jim now be able and want to buy 10 muffins and 20 coffees?

b. Which situation does Jim prefer: muffins at $1 and coffee at $2 a cup or muffins at $1.50 and coffee at $1.75 a cup?

37. a. If Jim changes the quantities that he buys, will he buy more or fewer muffins and more or less coffee?

b. When the prices change, will there be an income effect, a substitution effect, or both at work?

Use the following information to work Problems 38 to 40.

Sara's income is $12 a week. The price of popcorn is $3 a bag, and the price of cola is $1.50 a can. The figure shows Sara's preference map for popcorn and cola.

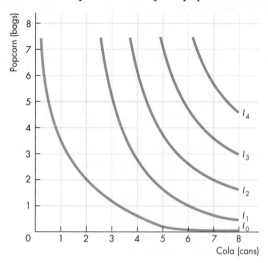

38. What quantities of popcorn and cola does Sara buy? What is Sara's marginal rate of substitution at the point at which she consumes?

39. Suppose that the price of cola rises to $3.00 a can and the price of popcorn and Sara's income remain the same. What quantities of cola and popcorn does Sara now buy? What are two points on Sara's demand curve for cola? Draw Sara's demand curve.

40. Suppose that the price of cola rises to $3.00 a can and the price of popcorn and Sara's income remain the same.

a. What is the substitution effect of this price change and what is the income effect of the price change?

b. Is cola a normal good or an inferior good? Explain.

Economics in the News

41. After you have studied *Reading Between the Lines* on pp. 216–217 answer the following questions.

a. How do you buy books?

b. Sketch your budget line for books and other goods.

c. Sketch your indifference curves for books and other goods.

d. Explain why Andy would buy e-books if the price of a reader fell to $100.

Making the Most of Life

The powerful forces of demand and supply shape the fortunes of families, businesses, nations, and empires in the same unrelenting way that the tides and winds shape rocks and coastlines. You saw in Chapters 3 through 7 how these forces raise and lower prices, increase and decrease quantities bought and sold, cause revenues to fluctuate, and send resources to their most valuable uses.

These powerful forces begin quietly and privately with the choices that each one of us makes. Chapters 8 and 9 probe these individual choices, offering two alternative approaches to explaining both consumption plans and the allocation of time. These explanations of consumption plans can also explain "non-economic" choices, such as whether to marry and how many children to have. In a sense, there are no non-economic choices. If there is scarcity, there must be choice, and economics studies all choices.

The earliest economists (Adam Smith and his contemporaries) did not have a very deep understanding of households' choices. It was not until the nineteenth century that progress was made in this area when Jeremy Bentham (below) introduced the concept of utility and applied it to the study of human choices. Today, Steven Levitt of the University of Chicago, whom you will meet on the following pages, is one of the most influential students of human behavior.

Jeremy Bentham *(1748–1832), who lived in London, was the son and grandson of lawyers and was himself trained as a barrister. But Bentham rejected the opportunity to maintain the family tradition and, instead, spent his life as a writer, activist, and Member of Parliament in the pursuit of rational laws that would bring the greatest happiness to the greatest number of people.*

Bentham, whose embalmed body is preserved to this day in a glass cabinet in the University of London, was the first person to use the concept of utility to explain human choices. But in Bentham's day, the distinction between explaining and prescribing was not a sharp one, and Bentham was ready to use his ideas to tell people how they ought to behave. He was one of the first to propose pensions for the retired, guaranteed employment, minimum wages, and social benefits such as free education and free medical care.

"... It is the greatest happiness of the greatest number that is the measure of right and wrong."

JEREMY BENTHAM
Fragment on Government

Why did you become an economist?

As a freshman in college, I took introductory economics. All the ideas made perfect sense to me—it was the way I naturally thought. My friends were befuddled. I thought, "This is the field for me!"

The idea of rational choice made at the margin lies at the heart of economics. Would you say that your work generally supports that idea or challenges it? Can you provide some examples?

I don't like the word "rational" in this context. I think economists model agents as being rational just for convenience. What really matters is whether people respond to incentives. My work very much supports the idea that humans in all types of circumstances respond strongly to incentives. I've seen it with drug dealers, auto thieves, sumo wrestlers, real estate agents, and elementary school teachers, just to name a few examples.

Can you elaborate? What are the incentives to which drug dealers respond? And does an understanding of these responses tell us anything about how public policy might influence drug use?

The incentives people face differ depending on their particular circumstances. Drug dealers, for instance, want to make money, but they also want to avoid being arrested or even killed. In the data we have on drug sellers, we see that when the drug trade is more lucrative, dealers are willing to take greater risks of arrest to carve out a share of the market. On the other hand, they also do their best to minimize their risks. For example, crack sellers used to carry the crack with them. When laws were passed imposing stiff penalties on anyone caught with anything more than a minimal amount of crack, drug dealers responded by storing the crack somewhere else, and retrieving only the amount being sold to the current client. Sumo wrestlers, on the other hand, care mostly about their official ranking. Sometimes matches occur where one wrestler has more to lose or gain than the other wrestler. We find that sumo wrestlers make corrupt deals to make sure the wrestler who needs the win is the one who actually wins.

Why is an economist interested in crime and cheating?

I think of economics as being primarily about a way of looking at the world and a set of tools for thinking

clearly. The topics you apply these tools to are unlimited. That is why I think economics has been so powerful. If you understand economics and use the tools wisely, you will be a better business person, doctor, public servant, parent.

> I think of economics as being primarily about a way of looking at the world and a set of tools for thinking clearly.

What is the economic model of crime, and how does it help to design better ways of dealing with criminal activity? Can you illustrate by talking a bit about your work on the behavior of auto thieves?

The economic model of crime argues that people have a choice of either working for a wage in the legal sector or earning money from illegal activity. The model carefully lays out the set of costs associated with being a criminal (e.g., forgone wages and being punished) and benefits (e.g., the loot) associated with crime and ana-

STEVEN D. LEVITT is Alvin H. Baum Professor of Economics at the University of Chicago. Born in Minneapolis, he was an undergraduate at Harvard and a graduate student at MIT. Among his many honors, he was recently awarded the John Bates Clark Medal, given to the best economist under 40.

Professor Levitt has studied an astonishingly wide range of human choices and their outcomes. He has examined the effects of policing on crime, shown that real estate agents get a higher price when they sell their own homes than when they sell other people's, devised a test to detect cheating teachers, and studied the choices of drug dealers and gang members. Much of this research has been popularized in *Freakonomics* (Steven D. Levitt and Stephen J. Dubner, HarperCollins, 2005). What unifies this apparently diverse body of research is the use of natural experiments. Professor Levitt has an incredible ability to find just the right set of events and the data the events have generated to enable him to isolate the effect he's looking for.

Michael Parkin talked with Steven Levitt about his career and the progress that economists have made in understanding how people respond to incentives in all aspects of life.

police. If you just look at different cities, the places with the most police also have the most crime, but it is not because police cause crime, it is because crime causes police to be hired.

To figure out a causal impact of police on crime, you would like to do a randomized experiment where you added a lot of police at random to some cities and took them away in other cities. That is something you cannot really do in real life. So instead, the economist has to look for "natural experiments" to answer the question.

> If you just look at different cities, the places with the most police also have the most crime, but it is not because police cause crime, it is because crime causes police to be hired.

I used the timing of mayoral elections. It turns out that mayors hire a lot of police before elections to "look tough on crime." If elections do not otherwise affect crime, then the election is kind of like a randomizing device that puts more police in some cities every once in a while. Indeed, I found that crime goes down in the year following elections once the police hired are up and running. It is indirect evidence, but it is an example of how economists use their toolbox to handle difficult questions.

lyzes how a maximizing individual will choose whether to commit crimes and how much crime to commit. One reason the model is useful is because it lays out the various ways in which public policy might influence crime rates. For instance, we can increase the probability of a criminal getting caught or make the prison sentence longer for those who are caught. The government might also try to intervene in the labor market to make legal work more attractive—for instance, with a minimum wage.

What is the problem in figuring out whether more police leads to less crime? How did you find the answer?

We think that when you add more police, crime will fall because the cost of being a criminal goes up because of increased detection. From a public policy perspective, understanding how much crime falls in response to police is an important question. In practice, it is hard to answer this question because we don't randomly hire police. Rather, where crime is bad, there is greater demand for police and thus more

Your work shows that legalized abortion leads to less crime. Can you explain how you reach that conclusion? Can you also explain its implications for the pro-life, pro-choice debate?

The theory is simple: Unwanted children have hard lives (including being much more likely to be criminals); after legalized abortion, there are fewer unwanted children. Therefore, there should be less crime (with a 15–20 year lag while the babies grow up and reach high-crime ages).

We looked at what happened to crime 15–20 years after *Roe v. Wade*, in states with high and low abortion rates and in states that legalized abortion a few years earlier than the rest of the country. We could even look at people born immediately before or after abortion became legal.

All the evidence pointed the same way: Crime fell a lot because abortion was legalized.

Our results, however, don't have large implications for the abortion debate. If abortion is murder, as pro-life advocates argue, then the changes in crime we see are trivial in comparison. If a woman simply has the right to control her body, as pro-choice advocates argue, then our estimates about crime are likewise irrelevant.

Our results have more to say about unwantedness: There are big benefits to making sure that children who are brought into the world are wanted and well cared for, through either birth control, adoption, abortion, or parental education.

> ... every time I observed anything in the world I asked myself, "Is that a natural experiment?"

Terrorism is on everyone's minds these days. And presumably, terrorists respond to incentives. Have you thought about how we might be able to use the insights of economics to better understand and perhaps even combat terrorism?

Terrorism is an unusually difficult question to tackle through incentives. The religious terrorists we are most worried about are willing to give up their lives to carry out terrorist acts. So the only punishment we can really offer is preventing them from committing the act by catching them beforehand or maybe

minimizing the damage they can do. Unlike typical criminals, the threat of punishing them after the fact will not help deter the crime. Luckily, even among extremists, there are not many people willing to give their lives for a cause.

Can a student learn how to use natural experiments or do you have a gift that is hard to teach?

I don't think I have such a gift. Most people who are good at something are good because they have worked hard and practiced. That is certainly true with me.

For a while, I just walked around and every time I observed anything in the world I asked myself, "Is that a natural experiment?" Every once in a while I stumbled onto one because I was on the lookout.

What else can a student who wants to become a natural experimenting economist or broader social scientist do to better prepare for that career?

I would say that the best thing students can do is to try to really apply what they are learning to their lives, rather than just memorizing for an exam and quickly forgetting. If you are passionate about economics (or anything else for that matter), you are way ahead of others who are just trying to get by.

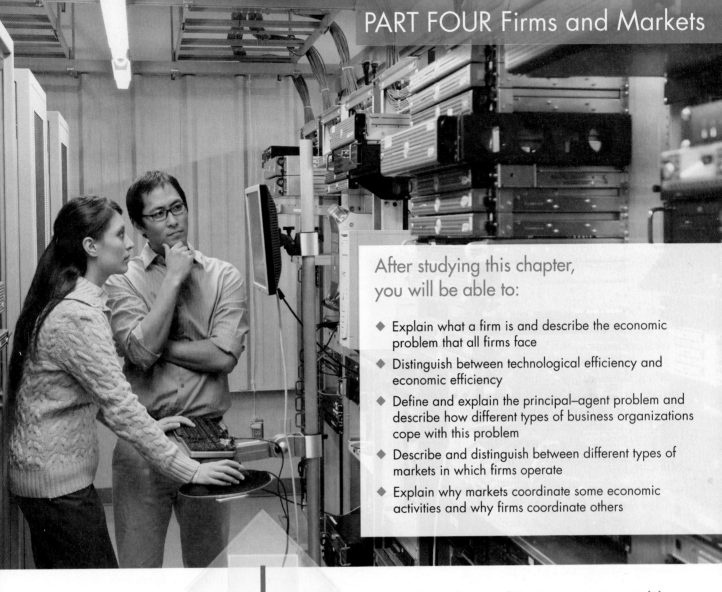

After studying this chapter, you will be able to:

◆ Explain what a firm is and describe the economic problem that all firms face

◆ Distinguish between technological efficiency and economic efficiency

◆ Define and explain the principal–agent problem and describe how different types of business organizations cope with this problem

◆ Describe and distinguish between different types of markets in which firms operate

◆ Explain why markets coordinate some economic activities and why firms coordinate others

10

ORGANIZING PRODUCTION

In the fall of 1990, a British scientist named Tim Berners-Lee invented the World Wide Web. This remarkable idea paved the way for the creation of thousands of profitable businesses that include Facebook and Twitter, Apple, Microsoft, Google, and Yahoo!.

Some of these successful dot.com firms sell goods and others sell services. But many firms, especially those that you can name, don't *make* the things they sell: They *buy* them from other firms. For example, Apple doesn't make the iPhone. Intel makes its memory chip and Foxconn, a firm in Taiwan, assembles its components. Why doesn't Apple make the iPhone? How do firms decide what to make themselves and what to buy from other firms?

How do Facebook, Twitter, Apple, Microsoft, Google, Intel, Foxconn, and the millions of other firms make their business decisions?

In this chapter, you are going to learn about firms and the choices they make. In *Reading Between the Lines* at the end of the chapter, we'll apply some of what you've learned and look at some of the choices made by Facebook and Yahoo in the Internet advertising game.

◆ The Firm and Its Economic Problem

The 20 million firms in the United States differ in size and in the scope of what they do, but they all perform the same basic economic functions. Each **firm** is an institution that hires factors of production and organizes those factors to produce and sell goods and services. Our goal is to predict firms' behavior. To do so, we need to know a firm's goal and the constraints it faces. We start with the goal.

The Firm's Goal

When economists ask entrepreneurs what they are trying to achieve, they get many different answers. Some talk about making a high-quality product, others about business growth, others about market share, others about the job satisfaction of their workforce, and an increasing number today talk about social and environmental responsibility. All of these goals are pursued by firms, but they are not the fundamental goal: They are the means to that goal.

A firm's goal is to maximize profit. A firm that does not seek to maximize profit is either eliminated or taken over by a firm that does seek that goal.

What is the profit that a firm seeks to maximize? To answer this question, we'll look at Campus Sweaters, Inc., a small producer of knitted sweaters owned and operated by Cindy.

Accounting Profit

In 2010, Campus Sweaters received $400,000 for the sweaters it sold and paid out $80,000 for wool, $20,000 for utilities, $120,000 for wages, $5,000 for the lease of a computer, and $5,000 in interest on a bank loan. These expenses total $230,000, so the firm had a cash surplus of $170,000.

To measure the profit of Campus Sweaters, Cindy's accountant subtracted $20,000 for the depreciation of buildings and knitting machines from the $170,000 cash surplus. *Depreciation* is the fall in the value of a firm's capital. To calculate depreciation, accountants use Internal Revenue Service rules based on standards established by the Financial Accounting Standards Board. Using these rules, Cindy's accountant calculated that Campus Sweaters made a profit of $150,000 in 2010.

Economic Accounting

Accountants measure a firm's profit to ensure that the firm pays the correct amount of income tax and to show its investors how their funds are being used.

Economists measure a firm's profit to enable them to predict the firm's decisions, and the goal of these decisions is to maximize *economic profit*. **Economic profit** is equal to total revenue minus total cost, with total cost measured as the *opportunity cost of production*.

A Firm's Opportunity Cost of Production

The *opportunity cost* of any action is the highest-valued alternative forgone. The *opportunity cost of production* is the value of the best alternative use of the resources that a firm uses in production.

A firm's opportunity cost of production is the value of real alternatives forgone. We express opportunity cost in money units so that we can compare and add up the value of the alternatives forgone.

A firm's opportunity cost of production is the sum of the cost of using resources

- Bought in the market
- Owned by the firm
- Supplied by the firm's owner

Resources Bought in the Market A firm incurs an opportunity cost when it buys resources in the market. The amount spent on these resources is an opportunity cost of production because the firm could have bought different resources to produce some other good or service. For Campus Sweaters, the resources bought in the market are wool, utilities, labor, a leased computer, and a bank loan. The $230,000 spent on these items in 2010 could have been spent on something else, so it is an opportunity cost of producing sweaters.

Resources Owned by the Firm A firm incurs an opportunity cost when it uses its own capital. The cost of using capital owned by the firm is an opportunity cost of production because the firm could sell the capital that it owns and rent capital from another firm. When a firm uses its own capital, it implicitly rents it from itself. In this case, the firm's opportunity cost of using the capital it owns is called the **implicit rental rate** of capital. The implicit rental rate of capital has two components: economic depreciation and forgone interest.

Economic Depreciation Accountants measure *depreciation*, the fall in the value of a firm's capital, using formulas that are unrelated to the change in the market value of capital. **Economic depreciation** is the fall in the *market value* of a firm's capital over a given period. It equals the market price of the capital at the beginning of the period minus the market price of the capital at the end of the period.

Suppose that Campus Sweaters could have sold its buildings and knitting machines on January 1, 2010, for $400,000 and that it can sell the same capital on December 31, 2010, for $375,000. The firm's economic depreciation during 2010 is $25,000 ($400,000 − $375,000). This forgone $25,000 is an opportunity cost of production.

Forgone Interest The funds used to buy capital could have been used for some other purpose, and in their next best use, they would have earned interest. This forgone interest is an opportunity cost of production.

Suppose that Campus Sweaters used $300,000 of its own funds to buy capital. If the firm invested its $300,000 in bonds instead of a knitting factory (and rented the capital it needs to produce sweaters), it would have earned $15,000 a year in interest. This forgone interest is an opportunity cost of production.

Resources Supplied by the Firm's Owner A firm's owner might supply *both* entrepreneurship and labor.

Entrepreneurship The factor of production that organizes a firm and makes its decisions might be supplied by the firm's owner or by a hired entrepreneur. The return to entrepreneurship is profit, and the profit that an entrepreneur earns *on average* is called **normal profit**. Normal profit is the cost of entrepreneurship and is an opportunity cost of production.

If Cindy supplies entrepreneurial services herself, and if the normal profit she can earn on these services is $45,000 a year, this amount is an opportunity cost of production at Campus Sweaters.

Owner's Labor Services *In addition* to supplying entrepreneurship, the owner of a firm might supply labor but not take a wage. The opportunity cost of the owner's labor is the wage income forgone by not taking the best alternative job.

If Cindy supplies labor to Campus Sweaters, and if the wage she can earn on this labor at another firm is $55,000 a year, this amount of wages forgone is an opportunity cost of production at Campus Sweaters.

Economic Accounting: A Summary

Table 10.1 summarizes the economic accounting. Campus Sweaters' total revenue is $400,000; its opportunity cost of production is $370,000; and its economic profit is $30,000.

Cindy's personal income is the $30,000 of economic profit plus the $100,000 that she earns by supplying resources to Campus Sweaters.

Decisions

To achieve the objective of maximum economic profit, a firm must make five decisions:

1. What to produce and in what quantities
2. How to produce
3. How to organize and compensate its managers and workers
4. How to market and price its products
5. What to produce itself and buy from others

In all these decisions, a firm's actions are limited by the constraints that it faces. Your next task is to learn about these constraints.

TABLE 10.1   Economic Accounting

Item		Amount
Total Revenue		**$400,000**
Cost of Resources Bought in Market		
Wool	$80,000	
Utilities	20,000	
Wages	120,000	
Computer lease	5,000	
Bank interest	5,000	$230,000
Cost of Resources Owned by Firm		
Economic depreciation	$25,000	
Forgone interest	15,000	$40,000
Cost of Resources Supplied by Owner		
Cindy's normal profit	$45,000	
Cindy's forgone wages	55,000	$100,000
Opportunity Cost of Production		**$370,000**
Economic Profit		**$30,000**

The Firm's Constraints

Three features of a firm's environment limit the maximum economic profit it can make. They are

- Technology constraints
- Information constraints
- Market constraints

Technology Constraints Economists define technology broadly. A **technology** is any method of producing a good or service. Technology includes the detailed designs of machines and the layout of the workplace. It includes the organization of the firm. For example, the shopping mall is one technology for producing retail services. It is a different technology from the catalog store, which in turn is different from the downtown store.

It might seem surprising that a firm's profit is limited by technology because it seems that technological advances are constantly increasing profit opportunities. Almost every day, we learn about some new technological advance that amazes us. With computers that speak and recognize our own speech and cars that can find the address we need in a city we've never visited, we can accomplish more than ever.

Technology advances over time. But at each point in time, to produce more output and gain more revenue, a firm must hire more resources and incur greater costs. The increase in profit that a firm can achieve is limited by the technology available. For example, by using its current plant and workforce, Ford can produce some maximum number of cars per day. To produce more cars per day, Ford must hire more resources, which increases its costs and limits the increase in profit that it can make by selling the additional cars.

Information Constraints We never possess all the information we would like to have to make decisions. We lack information about both the future and the present. For example, suppose you plan to buy a new computer. When should you buy it? The answer depends on how the price is going to change in the future. Where should you buy it? The answer depends on the prices at hundreds of different computer stores. To get the best deal, you must compare the quality and prices in every store. But the opportunity cost of this comparison exceeds the cost of the computer!

A firm is constrained by limited information about the quality and efforts of its workforce, the current and future buying plans of its customers, and the plans of its competitors. Workers might make too little effort, customers might switch to competing suppliers, and a competitor might enter the market and take some of the firm's business.

To address these problems, firms create incentives to boost workers' efforts even when no one is monitoring them; conduct market research to lower uncertainty about customers' buying plans, and "spy" on each other to anticipate competitive challenges. But these efforts don't eliminate incomplete information and uncertainty, which limit the economic profit that a firm can make.

Market Constraints The quantity each firm can sell and the price it can obtain are constrained by its customers' willingness to pay and by the prices and marketing efforts of other firms. Similarly, the resources that a firm can buy and the prices it must pay for them are limited by the willingness of people to work for and invest in the firm. Firms spend billions of dollars a year marketing and selling their products. Some of the most creative minds strive to find the right message that will produce a knockout television advertisement. Market constraints and the expenditures firms make to overcome them limit the profit a firm can make.

REVIEW QUIZ

1 What is a firm's fundamental goal and what happens if the firm doesn't pursue this goal?
2 Why do accountants and economists calculate a firm's cost and profit in different ways?
3 What are the items that make opportunity cost differ from the accountant's measure of cost?
4 Why is normal profit an opportunity cost?
5 What are the constraints that a firm faces? How does each constraint limit the firm's profit?

You can work these questions in Study Plan 10.1 and get instant feedback.

In the rest of this chapter and in Chapters 11 through 14, we study the choices that firms make. You're going to learn how we can predict a firm's decisions as those that maximize profit given the constraints the firm faces. We begin by taking a closer look at a firm's technology constraints.

◆ Technological and Economic Efficiency

Microsoft employs a large workforce, and most Microsoft workers possess a large amount of human capital. But the firm uses a small amount of physical capital. In contrast, a coal-mining company employs a huge amount of mining equipment (physical capital) and almost no labor. Why? The answer lies in the concept of efficiency. There are two concepts of production efficiency: technological efficiency and economic efficiency. **Technological efficiency** occurs when the firm produces a given output by using the least amount of inputs. **Economic efficiency** occurs when the firm produces a given output at the least cost. Let's explore the two concepts of efficiency by studying an example.

Suppose that there are four alternative techniques for making TVs:

A. *Robot production.* One person monitors the entire computer-driven process.
B. *Production line.* Workers specialize in a small part of the job as the emerging TV passes them on a production line.
C. *Hand-tool production.* A single worker uses a few hand tools to make a TV.
D. *Bench production.* Workers specialize in a small part of the job but walk from bench to bench to perform their tasks.

Table 10.2 sets out the amounts of labor and capital required by each of these four methods to make 10 TVs a day.

Which of these alternative methods are technologically efficient?

Technological Efficiency

Recall that *technological efficiency* occurs when the firm produces a given output by using the least amount of inputs. Look at the numbers in the table and notice that method *A* uses the most capital and the least labor. Method *C* uses the most labor and the least capital. Method *B* and method *D* lie between the two extremes. They use less capital and more labor than method *A* and less labor but more capital than method *C*.

Compare methods *B* and *D*. Method *D* requires 100 workers and 10 units of capital to produce 10

TABLE 10.2 Four Ways of Making 10 TVs a Day

		Quantities of inputs	
	Method	Labor	Capital
A	Robot production	1	1,000
B	Production line	10	10
C	Hand-tool production	1,000	1
D	Bench production	100	10

TVs. Those same 10 TVs can be produced by method *B* with 10 workers and the same 10 units of capital. Because method *D* uses the same amount of capital and more labor than method *B*, method *D* is not technologically efficient.

Are any of the other methods not technologically efficient? The answer is no. Each of the other methods is technologically efficient. Method *A* uses more capital but less labor than method *B*, and method *C* uses more labor but less capital than method *B*.

Which of the methods are economically efficient?

Economic Efficiency

Recall that *economic efficiency* occurs when the firm produces a given output at the least cost.

Method *D*, which is technologically inefficient, is also economically inefficient. It uses the same amount of capital as method *B* but 10 times as much labor, so it costs more. A technologically inefficient method is never economically efficient.

One of the three technologically efficient methods is economically efficient. The other two are economically inefficient. But which method is economically efficient depends on factor prices.

In Table 10.3(a), the wage rate is $75 per day and the rental rate of capital is $250 per day. By studying Table 10.3(a), you can see that method *B* has the lowest cost and is the economically efficient method.

In Table 10.3(b), the wage rate is $150 a day and the rental rate of capital is $1 a day. Looking at Table 10.3(b), you can see that method *A* has the lowest cost and is the economically efficient method. In this case, capital is so cheap relative to labor that the

TABLE 10.3   The Costs of Different Ways of Making 10 TVs a Day

(a) Wage rate $75 per day; Capital rental rate $250 per day

Method	Inputs Labor	Inputs Capital	Labor cost ($75 per day)		Capital cost ($250 per day)		Total cost
A	1	1,000	$75	+	$250,000	=	$250,075
B	10	10	750	+	2,500	=	3,250
C	1,000	1	75,000	+	250	=	75,250

(b) Wage rate $150 per day; Capital rental rate $1 per day

Method	Inputs Labor	Inputs Capital	Labor cost ($150 per day)		Capital cost ($1 per day)		Total cost
A	1	1,000	$150	+	$1,000	=	$1,150
B	10	10	1,500	+	10	=	1,510
C	1,000	1	150,000	+	1	=	150,001

(c) Wage rate $1 per day; Capital rental rate $1,000 per day

Method	Inputs Labor	Inputs Capital	Labor cost ($1 per day)		Capital cost ($1,000 per day)		Total cost
A	1	1,000	$1	+	$1,000,000	=	$1,000,001
B	10	10	10	+	10,000	=	10,010
C	1,000	1	1,000	+	1,000	=	2,000

method that uses the most capital is the economically efficient method.

In Table 10.3(c), the wage rate is $1 a day and the rental rate of capital is $1,000 a day. You can see that method *C* has the lowest cost and is the economically efficient method. In this case, labor is so cheap relative to capital that the method that uses the most labor is the economically efficient method.

Economic efficiency depends on the relative costs of resources. The economically efficient method is the one that uses a smaller amount of the more expensive resource and a larger amount of the less expensive resource.

A firm that is not economically efficient does not maximize profit. Natural selection favors efficient firms and inefficient firms disappear. Inefficient firms go out of business or are taken over by firms that produce at lower costs.

REVIEW QUIZ

1   Is a firm technologically efficient if it uses the latest technology? Why or why not?

2   Is a firm economically inefficient if it can cut its costs by producing less? Why or why not?

3   Explain the key distinction between technological efficiency and economic efficiency.

4   Why do some firms use large amounts of capital and small amounts of labor while others use small amounts of capital and large amounts of labor?

You can work these questions in Study Plan 10.2 and get instant feedback.

Next we study the information constraints that firms face and the wide array of organization structures these constraints generate.

◆ Information and Organization

Each firm organizes the production of goods and services by combining and coordinating the productive resources it hires. But there is variety across firms in how they organize production. Firms use a mixture of two systems:

- Command systems
- Incentive systems

Command Systems

A **command system** is a method of organizing production that uses a managerial hierarchy. Commands pass downward through the hierarchy, and information passes upward. Managers spend most of their time collecting and processing information about the performance of the people under their control and making decisions about what commands to issue and how best to get those commands implemented.

The military uses the purest form of command system. A commander-in-chief (in the United States, the President) makes the big decisions about strategic goals. Beneath this highest level, generals organize their military resources. Beneath the generals, successively lower ranks organize smaller and smaller units but pay attention to ever-increasing degrees of detail. At the bottom of the managerial hierarchy are the people who operate weapons systems.

Command systems in firms are not as rigid as those in the military, but they share some similar features. A chief executive officer (CEO) sits at the top of a firm's command system. Senior executives who report to and receive commands from the CEO specialize in managing production, marketing, finance, personnel, and perhaps other aspects of the firm's operations. Beneath these senior managers might be several tiers of middle management ranks that stretch downward to the managers who supervise the day-to-day operations of the business. Beneath these managers are the people who operate the firm's machines and who make and sell the firm's goods and services.

Small firms have one or two layers of managers, while large firms have several layers. As production processes have become ever more complex, management ranks have swollen. Today, more people have management jobs than ever before, even though the information revolution of the 1990s slowed the growth of management. In some industries, the information revolution reduced the number of layers of managers and brought a shakeout of middle managers.

Managers make enormous efforts to be well informed. They try hard to make good decisions and issue commands that end up using resources efficiently. But managers always have incomplete information about what is happening in the divisions of the firm for which they are responsible. For this reason, firms use incentive systems as well as command systems to organize production.

Incentive Systems

An **incentive system** is a method of organizing production that uses a market-like mechanism inside the firm. Instead of issuing commands, senior managers create compensation schemes to induce workers to perform in ways that maximize the firm's profit.

Selling organizations use incentive systems most extensively. Sales representatives who spend most of their working time alone and unsupervised are induced to work hard by being paid a small salary and a large performance-related bonus.

But incentive systems operate at all levels in a firm. The compensation plan of a CEO includes a share in the firm's profit, and factory floor workers sometimes receive compensation based on the quantity they produce.

Mixing the Systems

Firms use a mixture of commands and incentives, and they choose the mixture that maximizes profit. Firms use commands when it is easy to monitor performance or when a small deviation from an ideal performance is very costly. They use incentives when it is either not possible to monitor performance or too costly to be worth doing.

For example, PepsiCo can easily monitor the performance of workers on a production line. If one person works too slowly, the entire line slows, so a production line is organized with a command system.

In contrast, it is costly to monitor a CEO. For example, what does Steve Jobs, the CEO of Apple Inc., contribute to Apple's success? This question can't be answered with certainty, yet Apple's stockholders have to put someone in charge of the business and provide that person with an incentive to maximize stockholders' returns. The performance of Apple illustrates a general problem, known as the principal–agent problem.

The Principal–Agent Problem

The **principal–agent problem** is the problem of devising compensation rules that induce an *agent* to act in the best interest of a *principal*. For example, the stockholders of Texaco are *principals*, and the firm's managers are *agents*. The stockholders (the principals) must induce the managers (agents) to act in the stockholders' best interest. Similarly, Steve Jobs (a principal) must induce the designers who are working on the next generation iPhone (agents) to work efficiently.

Agents, whether they are managers or workers, pursue their own goals and often impose costs on a principal. For example, the goal of stockholders of Citicorp (principals) is to maximize the firm's profit—its true profit, not some fictitious paper profit. But the firm's profit depends on the actions of its managers (agents), and they have their own goals. Perhaps a bank manager takes a customer to a ball game on the pretense that she is building customer loyalty, when in fact she is simply enjoying on-the-job leisure. This same manager is also a principal, and her tellers are agents. The manager wants the tellers to work hard and attract new customers so that she can meet her operating targets. But the workers enjoy conversations with each other and take on-the-job leisure. Nonetheless, the firm constantly strives to find ways of improving performance and increasing profits.

Coping with the Principal–Agent Problem

Issuing commands does not address the principal–agent problem. In most firms, the shareholders can't monitor the managers and often the managers can't monitor the workers. Each principal must create incentives that induce each agent to work in the interests of the principal. Three ways of attempting to cope with the principal–agent problem are

- Ownership
- Incentive pay
- Long-term contracts

Ownership By assigning ownership (or part-ownership) of a business to managers or workers, it is sometimes possible to induce a job performance that increases a firm's profits. Part-ownership is quite common for senior managers but less common for workers. When United Airlines was running into problems a few years ago, it made most of its employees owners of the company.

Incentive Pay Incentive pay—pay related to performance—is very common. Incentives are based on a variety of performance criteria such as profits, production, or sales targets. Promoting an employee for good performance is another example of the use of incentive pay.

Long-Term Contracts Long-term contracts tie the long-term fortunes of managers and workers (agents) to the success of the principal(s)—the owner(s) of the firm. For example, a multiyear employment contract for a CEO encourages that person to take a long-term view and devise strategies that achieve maximum profit over a sustained period.

These three ways of coping with the principal–agent problem give rise to different types of business organization. Each type of business organization is a different response to the principal–agent problem. Each type uses a different combination of ownership, incentives, and long-term contracts. Let's look at the main types of business organization.

Types of Business Organization

The three main types of business organization are

- Proprietorship
- Partnership
- Corporation

Proprietorship A *proprietorship* is a firm with a single owner—a proprietor—who has unlimited liability. *Unlimited liability* is the legal responsibility for all the debts of a firm up to an amount equal to the entire wealth of the owner. If a proprietorship cannot pay its debts, those to whom the firm owes money can claim the personal property of the owner. Businesses of some farmers, computer programmers, and artists are examples of proprietorships.

The proprietor makes management decisions, receives the firm's profits, and is responsible for its losses. Profits from a proprietorship are taxed at the same rate as other sources of the proprietor's personal income.

Partnership A *partnership* is a firm with two or more owners who have unlimited liability. Partners must agree on an appropriate management structure and on how to divide the firm's profits among themselves. The profits of a partnership are taxed as the personal income of the owners, but each partner is legally liable for all the debts of the partnership (limited only by the wealth of that individual partner). Liability for the full debts of the partnership is called *joint unlimited liability*. Most law firms are partnerships.

Corporation A *corporation* is a firm owned by one or more limited liability stockholders. *Limited liability* means that the owners have legal liability only for the value of their initial investment. This limitation of liability means that if the corporation becomes bankrupt, its owners are not required to use their personal wealth to pay the corporation's debts.

Corporations' profits are taxed independently of stockholders' incomes. Stockholders pay a capital gains tax on the profit they earn when they sell a stock for a higher price than they paid for it. Corporate stocks generate capital gains when a corporation retains some of its profit and reinvests it in profitable activities. So retained earnings are taxed twice because the capital gains they generate are taxed. Dividend payments are also taxed but at a lower rate than other sources of income.

Pros and Cons of Different Types of Firms

The different types of business organization arise from firms trying to cope with the principal–agent problem. Each type has advantages in particular situations and because of its special advantages, each type continues to exist. Each type of business organization also has disadvantages.

Table 10.4 summarizes these and other pros and cons of the different types of firms.

TABLE 10.4   The Pros and Cons of Different Types of Firms

Type of Firm	Pros	Cons
Proprietorship	■ Easy to set up ■ Simple decision making ■ Profits taxed only once as owner's income	■ Bad decisions not checked; no need for consensus ■ Owner's entire wealth at risk ■ Firm dies with owner ■ Cost of capital and labor is high relative to that of a corporation
Partnership	■ Easy to set up ■ Diversified decision making ■ Can survive withdrawal of partner ■ Profits taxed only once as owners' incomes	■ Achieving consensus may be slow and expensive ■ Owners' entire wealth at risk ■ Withdrawal of partner may create capital shortage ■ Cost of capital and labor is high relative to that of a corporation
Corporation	■ Owners have limited liability ■ Large-scale, low-cost capital available ■ Professional management not restricted by ability of owners ■ Perpetual life ■ Long-term labor contracts cut labor costs	■ Complex management structure can make decisions slow and expensive ■ Retained profits taxed twice: as company profit and as stockholders' capital gains

Economics in Action
Types of Firms in the Economy

Proprietorships, partnerships, and corporations: These are the three types of firms that operate in the United States. Which type of firm dominates? Which produces most of the output of the U.S. economy?

Proprietorships Most Common Three quarters of the firms in the United States are proprietorships and they are mainly small businesses. Almost one fifth of the firms are corporations, and only a twentieth are partnerships (see Fig. 1).

Corporations Produce Most Corporations generate almost 90 percent of business revenue. Revenue is a measure of the value of production, so corporations produce most of the output in the U.S. economy.

Variety Across Industries In agriculture, forestry, and fishing, proprietorships generate about 40 percent of the total revenue. Proprietorships also generate a significant percentage of the revenue in services, construction, and retail trades. Partnerships account for a small percentage of revenue in all sectors and feature most in agriculture, forestry, and fishing, services, and mining. Corporations dominate all sectors and have the manufacturing industries almost to themselves.

Why do corporations dominate the business scene? Why do the other types of businesses survive? And why are proprietorships and partnerships more prominent in some sectors? The answers lie in the pros and cons of the different types of business organization. Corporations dominate where a large amount of capital is used; proprietorships dominate where flexibility in decision making is critical.

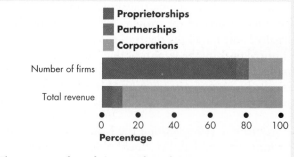

Figure 1 Number of Firms and Total Revenue

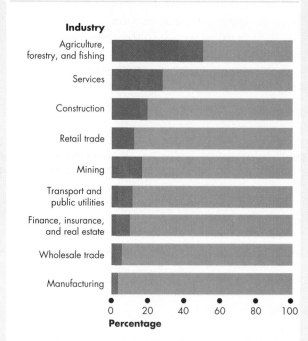

Figure 2 Total Revenue in Various Industries

Source of data: U.S. Bureau of the Census, *Statistical Abstract of the United States, 2001.*

REVIEW QUIZ

1 Explain the distinction between a command system and an incentive system.
2 What is the principal–agent problem? What are three ways in which firms try to cope with it?
3 What are the three types of firms? Explain the major advantages and disadvantages of each.
4 Why do all three types of firms survive and in which sectors is each type most prominent?

You can work these questions in Study Plan 10.3 and get instant feedback.

You've now seen how technology constraints and information constraints influence the way firms operate. You've seen why some firms operate with a large amount of labor and human capital and a small amount of physical capital. You've also seen how firms use a mixture of command and incentive systems and employ different types of business organization to cope with the principle–agent problem.

Your next task is to look at the variety of market situations in which firms operate and classify the different market environments in which firms do business.

Markets and the Competitive Environment

The markets in which firms operate vary a great deal. Some are highly competitive, and profits in these markets are hard to come by. Some appear to be almost free from competition, and firms in these markets earn large profits. Some markets are dominated by fierce advertising campaigns in which each firm seeks to persuade buyers that it has the best products. And some markets display the character of a strategic game.

Economists identify four market types:

1. Perfect competition
2. Monopolistic competition
3. Oligopoly
4. Monopoly

Perfect competition arises when there are many firms, each selling an identical product, many buyers, and no restrictions on the entry of new firms into the industry. The many firms and buyers are all well informed about the prices of the products of each firm in the industry. The worldwide markets for corn, rice, and other grain crops are examples of perfect competition.

Monopolistic competition is a market structure in which a large number of firms compete by making similar but slightly different products. Making a product slightly different from the product of a competing firm is called **product differentiation**. Product differentiation gives a firm in monopolistic competition an element of market power. The firm is the sole producer of the particular version of the good in question. For example, in the market for pizzas, hundreds of firms make their own version of the perfect pizza. Each of these firms is the sole producer of a particular brand. Differentiated products are not necessarily different products. What matters is that consumers perceive them to be different. For example, different brands of potato chips and ketchup might be almost identical but be perceived by consumers to be different.

Oligopoly is a market structure in which a small number of firms compete. Computer software, airplane manufacture, and international air transportation are examples of oligopolistic industries. Oligopolies might produce almost identical products, such as the colas produced by Coke and Pepsi. Or they might produce differentiated products such as Boeing and Airbus aircraft.

Monopoly arises when there is one firm, which produces a good or service that has no close substitutes and in which the firm is protected by a barrier preventing the entry of new firms. In some places, the phone, gas, electricity, cable television, and water suppliers are local monopolies—monopolies restricted to a given location. Microsoft Corporation, the software developer that created Windows and Vista, is an example of a global monopoly.

Perfect competition is the most extreme form of competition. Monopoly is the most extreme absence of competition. The other two market types fall between these extremes.

Many factors must be taken into account to determine which market structure describes a particular real-world market. One of these factors is the extent to which a small number of firms dominates the market. To measure this feature of markets, economists use indexes called measures of concentration. Let's look at these measures.

Measures of Concentration

Economists use two measures of concentration:

- The four-firm concentration ratio
- The Herfindahl-Hirschman Index

The Four-Firm Concentration Ratio The **four-firm concentration ratio** is the percentage of the value of sales accounted for by the four largest firms in an industry. The range of the concentration ratio is from almost zero for perfect competition to 100 percent for monopoly. This ratio is the main measure used to assess market structure.

Table 10.5 shows two calculations of the four-firm concentration ratio: one for tire makers and one for printers. In this example, 14 firms produce tires. The largest four have 80 percent of the sales, so the four-firm concentration ratio is 80 percent. In the printing industry, with 1,004 firms, the largest four firms have only 0.5 percent of the sales, so the four-firm concentration ratio is 0.5 percent.

A low concentration ratio indicates a high degree of competition, and a high concentration ratio indicates an absence of competition. A monopoly has a concentration ratio of 100 percent—the largest (and only) firm has 100 percent of the sales. A four-firm concentration ratio that exceeds 60 percent is regarded as an indication of a market that is highly concentrated and dominated by a few firms in an oligopoly. A ratio of less than 60 percent is regarded as an indication of a competitive market.

The Herfindahl-Hirschman Index The **Herfindahl-Hirschman Index**—also called the HHI—is the square of the percentage market share of each firm summed over the largest 50 firms (or summed over all the firms if there are fewer than 50) in a market. For example, if there are four firms in a market and the market shares of the firms are 50 percent, 25 percent, 15 percent, and 10 percent, the Herfindahl-Hirschman Index is

$$HHI = 50^2 + 25^2 + 15^2 + 10^2 = 3,450.$$

TABLE 10.5   Calculating the Four-Firm Concentration Ratio

Tire makers		Printers	
Firm	**Sales** (millions of dollars)	**Firm**	**Sales** (millions of dollars)
Top, Inc.	200	Fran's	2.5
ABC, Inc.	250	Ned's	2.0
Big, Inc.	150	Tom's	1.8
XYZ, Inc.	100	Jill's	1.7
Largest 4 firms	700	Largest 4 firms	8.0
Other 10 firms	175	Other 1,000 firms	1,592.0
Industry	875	Industry	1,600.0

Four-firm concentration ratios:

Tire makers: $\dfrac{700}{875} \times 100 = 80$ percent

Printers: $\dfrac{8}{1,600} \times 100 = 0.5$ percent

Economics in Action

Concentration in the U.S. Economy

The U.S. Department of Commerce calculates and publishes data showing concentration ratios and the HHI for each industry in the United States. The bars in the figure show the four-firm concentration ratio and the number at the end of each bar is the HHI.

Chewing gum is one of the most concentrated industries. William Wrigley Jr. Company of Chicago employs 16,000 people and sells $5 billion worth of gum a year. It does have some competitors but they have a very small market share.

Household laundry equipment, light bulbs, breakfast cereal, and motor vehicles are highly concentrated industries. They are oligopolies.

Pet food, cookies and crackers, computers, and soft drinks are moderately concentrated industries. They are examples of monopolistic competition.

Ice cream, milk, clothing, concrete blocks and bricks, and commercial printing industries have low concentration measures and are highly competitive.

Concentration measures are useful indicators of the degree of competition in a market, but they must be supplemented by other information to determine the structure of the market.

Newspapers and automobiles are examples of how the concentration measures give a misleading reading of the degree of competition. Most newspapers are local. They serve a single city or even smaller area. So despite the low concentration measure, newspapers are concentrated in their own local areas. Automobiles are traded internationally and foreign cars are freely imported into the United States. Despite the high U.S. concentration measure, the automobile industry is competitive.

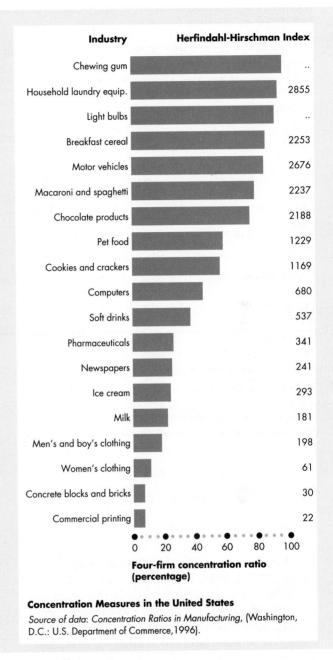

Concentration Measures in the United States

Source of data: Concentration Ratios in Manufacturing, (Washington, D.C.: U.S. Department of Commerce, 1996).

In perfect competition, the HHI is small. For example, if each of the largest 50 firms in an industry has a market share of 0.1 percent, then the HHI is $0.1^2 \times 50 = 0.5$. In a monopoly, the HHI is 10,000. The firm has 100 percent of the market: $100^2 = 10,000$.

The HHI became a popular measure of the degree of competition during the 1980s, when the Justice Department used it to classify markets. A market in which the HHI is less than 1,000 is regarded as being competitive. A market in which the HHI lies between 1,000 and 1,800 is regarded as being moderately competitive. But a market in which the HHI exceeds 1,800 is regarded as being uncompetitive. The Justice Department scrutinizes any merger of firms in a market in which the HHI exceeds 1,000 and is likely to challenge a merger if the HHI exceeds 1,800.

TABLE 10.6 Market Structure

Characteristics	Perfect competition	Monopolistic competition	Oligopoly	Monopoly
Number of firms in industry	Many	Many	Few	One
Product	Identical	Differentiated	Either identical or differentiated	No close substitutes
Barriers to entry	None	None	Moderate	High
Firm's control over price	None	Some	Considerable	Considerable or regulated
Concentration ratio	0	Low	High	100
HHI (approx. ranges)	Less than 100	101 to 999	More than 1,000	10,000
Examples	Wheat, corn	Food, clothing	Computer chips	Local water supply

Limitations of a Concentration Measure

The three main limitations of using only concentration measures as determinants of market structure are their failure to take proper account of

- The geographical scope of the market
- Barriers to entry and firm turnover
- The correspondence between a market and an industry

Geographical Scope of Market Concentration measures take a national view of the market. Many goods are sold in a *national* market, but some are sold in a *regional* market and some in a *global* one. The concentration measures for newspapers are low, indicating competition, but in most cities the newspaper industry is highly concentrated. The concentration measures for automobiles is high, indicating little competition, but the biggest three U.S. car makers compete with foreign car makers in a highly competitive global market.

Barriers to Entry and Firm Turnover Some markets are highly concentrated but entry is easy and the turnover of firms is large. For example, small towns have few restaurants, but no restrictions hinder a new restaurant from opening and many attempt to do so.

Also, a market with only a few firms might be competitive because of *potential entry*. The few firms in a market face competition from the many potential firms that will enter the market if economic profit opportunities arise.

Market and Industry Correspondence To calculate concentration ratios, the Department of Commerce classifies each firm as being in a particular industry. But markets do not always correspond closely to industries for three reasons.

First, markets are often narrower than industries. For example, the pharmaceutical industry, which has a low concentration ratio, operates in many separate markets for individual products—for example, measles vaccine and AIDS-fighting drugs. These drugs do not compete with each other, so this industry, which looks competitive, includes firms that are monopolies (or near monopolies) in markets for individual drugs.

Second, most firms make several products. For example, Westinghouse makes electrical equipment and, among other things, gas-fired incinerators and plywood. So this one firm operates in at least three separate markets, but the Department of Commerce classifies Westinghouse as being in the electrical goods and equipment industry. The fact that Westinghouse competes with other producers of plywood does not

Economics in Action

A Competitive Environment

How competitive are markets in the United States? Do most U.S. firms operate in competitive markets, in monopolistic competition, in oligopoly, or in monopoly markets?

The data needed to answer these questions are hard to get. The last attempt to answer the questions, in a study by William G. Shepherd, an economics professor at the University of Massachusetts at Amherst, covered the years from 1939 to 1980. The figure shows what he discovered.

In 1980, three quarters of the value of goods and services bought and sold in the United States was traded in markets that are essentially competitive—markets that have almost perfect competition or monopolistic competition. Monopoly and the dominance of a single firm accounted for about 5 percent of sales. Oligopoly, which is found mainly in manufacturing, accounted for about 18 percent of sales.

Over the period studied, the U.S. economy became increasingly competitive. The percentage of output sold by firms operating in competitive markets (blue bars) has expanded most, and has shrunk most in oligopoly markets (red bars).

The Market Structure of the U.S. Economy

William G. Shepherd, "Causes of Increased Competition in the U.S. Economy, 1939–1980," *Review of Economics and Statistics*, 64:4 (November, 1982), pp. 613–626. © 1982 by the President and Fellows of Harvard College. Reprinted with permission.

But also during the past decades, the U.S. economy has become much more exposed to competition from the rest of the world. The data used by William G. Shepherd don't capture this international competition, so the data probably understate the degree of true competition in the U.S. economy.

show up in the concentration numbers for the plywood market.

Third, firms switch from one market to another depending on profit opportunities. For example, Motorola, which today produces cellular telephones and other communications products, has diversified from being a TV and computer chip maker. Motorola no longer produces TVs. Publishers of newspapers, magazines, and textbooks are today rapidly diversifying into Internet and multimedia products. These switches among markets show that there is much scope for entering and exiting a market, and so measures of concentration have limited usefulness.

Despite their limitations, concentration measures do provide a basis for determining the degree of competition in a market when they are combined with information about the geographical scope of the market, barriers to entry, and the extent to which large, multiproduct firms straddle a variety of markets.

REVIEW QUIZ

1 What are the four market types? Explain the distinguishing characteristics of each.

2 What are the two measures of concentration? Explain how each measure is calculated.

3 Under what conditions do the measures of concentration give a good indication of the degree of competition in a market?

4 Is our economy competitive? Is it becoming more competitive or less competitive?

You can work these questions in Study Plan 10.4 and get instant feedback.

You now know the variety of market types and how we identify them. Our final question in this chapter is: What determines the things that firms decide to buy from other firms rather than produce for themselves?

◆ Produce or Outsource? Firms and Markets

To produce a good or service, even a simple one such as a shirt, factors of production must be hired and their activities coordinated. To produce a good as complicated as an iPhone, an enormous range of specialist factors of production must be coordinated.

Factors of production can be coordinated either by firms or markets. We'll describe these two ways of organizing production and then see why firms play a crucial role in achieving an efficient use of resources.

Firm Coordination

Firms hire labor, capital, and land, and by using a mixture of command systems and incentive systems (see p. 233) organize and coordinate their activities to produce goods and services.

Firm coordination occurs when you take your car to the garage for an oil change, brake check, and service. The garage owner hires a mechanic and tools and coordinates all the activities that get your car serviced. Firms also coordinate the production of cornflakes, golf clubs, and a host of other items.

Market Coordination

Markets coordinate production by adjusting prices and making the decisions of buyers and sellers of factors of production and components consistent. Markets can coordinate production.

Market coordination occurs to produce a rock concert. A promoter books a stadium, rents some stage equipment, hires some audio and video recording engineers and technicians, engages some rock groups, a superstar, a publicity agent, and a ticket agent. The promoter sells tickets to thousands of rock fans, audio rights to a recording company, and video and broadcasting rights to a television network. All these transactions take place in markets that coordinate this huge variety of factors of production.

Outsourcing, buying parts or products from other firms, is another example of market coordination. Dell outsources the production of all the components of its computers. Automakers outsource the production of windshields, windows, transmission systems, engines, tires, and many other auto parts. Apple outsources the entire production of iPods and iPhones.

Why Firms?

What determines whether a firm or a market coordinates a particular set of activities? How does a firm decide whether to buy an item from another firm or manufacture it itself? The answer is cost. Taking account of the opportunity cost of time as well as the costs of the other inputs, a firm uses the method that costs least. In other words, it uses the economically efficient method.

If a task can be performed at a lower cost by markets than by a firm, markets will do the job, and any attempt to set up a firm to replace such market activity will be doomed to failure.

Firms coordinate economic activity when a task can be performed more efficiently by a firm than by markets. In such a situation, it is profitable to set up a firm. Firms are often more efficient than markets as coordinators of economic activity because they can achieve

- Lower transactions costs
- Economies of scale
- Economies of scope
- Economies of team production

Transactions Costs Firms eliminate transactions costs. **Transactions costs** are the costs that arise from finding someone with whom to do business, of reaching an agreement about the price and other aspects of the exchange, and of ensuring that the terms of the agreement are fulfilled. Market transactions require buyers and sellers to get together and to negotiate the terms and conditions of their trading. Sometimes, lawyers have to be hired to draw up contracts. A broken contract leads to still more expense. A firm can lower such transactions costs by reducing the number of individual transactions undertaken.

Imagine getting your car fixed using market coordination. You hire a mechanic to diagnose the problems and make a list of the parts and tools needed to fix them. You buy the parts from several dealers, rent the tools from ABC Rentals, hire an auto mechanic, return the tools, and pay your bills. You can avoid all these transactions and the time they cost you by letting your local garage fix the car.

Economies of Scale When the cost of producing a unit of a good falls as its output rate increases, **economies of scale** exist. An automaker experiences economies of scale because as the scale of production increases, the firm can use cost-saving equipment and

Economics in Action

Apple Doesn't Make the iPhone!

Apple designed the iPhone and markets it, but Apple doesn't manufacture it. Why? Apple wants to produce the iPhone at the lowest possible cost. Apple achieves its goal by assigning the production task to more than 30 firms, some of which are listed in the table opposite. These 30 firms produce the components in Asia, Europe, and North America and then the components are assembled in the familiar case by Foxconn and Quanta in Taiwan.

Most electronic products—TVs, DVD players, iPods and iPads, and personal computers—are produced in a similar way to the iPhone with a combination of firm and market coordination. Hundreds of little-known firms compete fiercely to get their components into well-known consumer products.

Altus-Tech	Taiwan
Balda	Germany
Broadcom	United States
Cambridge Silicon Radio	UK
Catcher	Taiwan
Cyntec	Taiwan
Delta Electronics	Taiwan
Epson	Japan
Foxconn	Taiwan
Infineon Technology	Germany
Intel	United States
Largan Precision	Taiwan
Lite On	Taiwan
Marvell	United States
Micron	United States
National Semiconductor	United States
Novatek	Taiwan
Primax	Taiwan
Quanta	Taiwan
Samsung	Korea
Sanyo	Japan
Sharp	Japan
Taiwan Semiconductor	Taiwan
TMD	Japan

highly specialized labor. An automaker that produces only a few cars a year must use hand-tool methods that are costly. Economies of scale arise from specialization and the division of labor that can be reaped more effectively by firm coordination rather than market coordination.

Economies of Scope A firm experiences **economies of scope** when it uses specialized (and often expensive) resources to produce a *range of goods and services.* For example, Toshiba uses its designers and specialized equipment to make the hard drive for the iPod. But it makes many different types of hard drives and other related products. As a result, Toshiba produces the iPod hard drive at a lower cost than a firm making only the iPod hard drive could achieve.

Economies of Team Production A production process in which the individuals in a group specialize in mutually supportive tasks is *team production.* Sports provide the best examples of team activity. In baseball, some team members specialize in pitching and others in fielding. In basketball, some team members specialize in defense and some in offense. The production of goods and services offers many examples of team activity. For example, production lines in a TV manufacturing plant work most efficiently when individual activity is organized in teams, each worker specializing in a few tasks. You can also think of an entire firm as being a team. The team has buyers of raw materials and other inputs, production workers, and salespeople. Each individual member of the team

specializes, but the value of the output of the team and the profit that it earns depend on the coordinated activities of all the team's members.

Because firms can economize on transactions costs, reap economies of scale and economies of scope, and organize efficient team production, it is firms rather than markets that coordinate most of our economic activity.

REVIEW QUIZ

1 What are the two ways in which economic activity can be coordinated?

2 What determines whether a firm or markets coordinate production?

3 What are the main reasons why firms can often coordinate production at a lower cost than markets can?

You can work these questions in Study Plan 10.5 and get instant feedback.

◆ *Reading Between the Lines* on pp. 244–245 explores the market for Internet advertising. In the next four chapters, we continue to study firms and their decisions. In Chapter 11, we learn about the relationships between cost and output at different output levels. These relationships are common to all types of firms in all types of markets. We then turn to problems that are specific to firms in different types of markets.

Battling for Markets in Internet Advertising

Facebook Makes Gains in Web Ads

http://online.wsj.com
May 12, 2010

Facebook Inc. is catching up to rivals Yahoo Inc. and Microsoft Corp. in selling display ads.

In the first quarter, Facebook pulled ahead of Yahoo for the first time and delivered more banner ads to its U.S. users than any other Web publisher, according to market-research firm comScore Inc. ...

By revenue, Facebook has a long way to go to catch up to its more established rivals. The social-networking site earned more than $500 million in revenue in 2009 and is forecasting revenue of more than $1 billion in 2010, according to people familiar with the matter. Yahoo earned $6.5 billion in revenue in 2009, mostly from advertising. ...

Nielsen Co., another measurement firm, found that Facebook's share of the U.S. display-ad market grew to 20% in April 2010, up from 2% in April 2009. Nielsen still shows Yahoo in the lead, with 34% of all display ads in April 2010, compared with 35% in April 2009. ...

Facebook's rise could help fuel an already rebounding online-advertising market, which shrank during the recession. Display ads have recently shown strong growth as budgets have returned and technology companies have developed new ways to measure the effectiveness of graphical ads. Overall display impressions grew to 1.1 trillion in the first quarter of 2010, up from 944 billion in the first quarter of 2009, according to comScore.

Wall Street Journal, excerpted from "Facebook Makes Gains in Web Ads" by Jessica E. Vascellaro. Copyright 2010 by *Dow Jones & Company, Inc.* Reproduced with permission of *Dow Jones & Company, Inc.* via Copyright Clearance Center.

ESSENCE OF THE STORY

- Facebook is catching up to rivals in selling display ads and according to comScore Facebook sold more ads than Yahoo in the first quarter of 2010.

- Facebook's total revenue was more than $500 million in 2009 and is forecast to exceed $1 billion in 2010.

- Yahoo's total revenue, mostly from advertising, was $6.5 billion in 2009.

- Nielsen says that Facebook's share of U.S. display-ads grew from 2 percent to 20 percent in the year to April 2010 while Yahoo's shrank slightly from 35 percent to 34 percent in the same period.

- Display ads are growing because technology companies have developed new ways to measure the effectiveness of graphical ads.

ECONOMIC ANALYSIS

- Like all firms, Facebook and Yahoo aim to maximize profit.

- Facebook provides social networking services and Yahoo provides an Internet search service.

- Facebook and Yahoo face constraints imposed by the market and technology.

- People who use social networks and search engines demand these services, and Facebook and Yahoo supply them.

- MySpace is Facebook's biggest competitor and Wikipedia lists 189 other social networking sites.

- Google is Yahoo's largest competitor but another 58 search engines compete for attention.

- The equilibrium price of social-networking services and search engine services to their users is zero.

- But social networks and Internet search providers enjoy economies of scope: They produce advertising services as well as their other service.

- To generate revenue and profit, social networks and Internet search providers sell advertising services.

- To attract advertising revenue, a social network or search site must be able to offer the advertiser access to a large potential customer base and target the people most likely to buy the advertised product or service.

- Facebook and Yahoo are attractive to advertisers because they are able to deliver both of these features: hundreds of millions of users, identified by their interests and likely buying patterns.

- To maximize the use of their services, Facebook and Yahoo offer a variety of enticements to users.

- One enticement is the quality of the primary service: social networking or search. Facebook innovates to make its social networking services better than those of MySpace; and Yahoo tries to make its search technology as good as those of Google.

- Another enticement is a variety of related attractions. Yahoo's photo-sharing service is an example.

- Facebook aims to attract even more users and to offer advertisers the most effective return on the marketing dollar.

- Although Facebook has seen explosive growth in users, Fig. 1 shows that it is not generating revenues

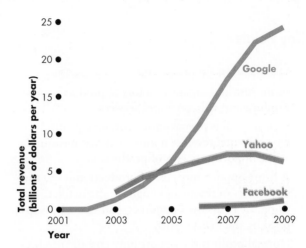

Figure 1 Total revenue comparison

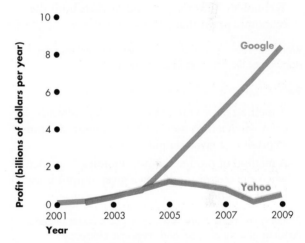

Figure 2 Profit comparison

on the scale of the leading search engines. (No data are available for Facebook profit.)

- Figures 1 and 2 show that Yahoo is not maintaining its position in the market for Internet search.

- The data shown in Figs 1 and 2 suggest that Internet search is a more effective tool for generating revenue and profit than social networking.

- The data also suggest that Google's expansion is tightening the market constraint that Yahoo faces.

SUMMARY

Key Points

The Firm and Its Economic Problem (pp. 228–230)

- Firms hire and organize factors of production to produce and sell goods and services.
- A firm's goal is to maximize economic profit, which is total revenue minus total cost measured as the opportunity cost of production.
- A firm's opportunity cost of production is the sum of the cost of resources bought in the market, using the firm's own resources, and resources supplied by the firm's owner.
- Normal profit is the opportunity cost of entrepreneurship and is part of the firm's opportunity cost.
- Technology, information, and markets limit the economic profit that a firm can make.

Working Problems 1 and 2 will give you a better understanding of the firm and its economic problem.

Technological and Economic Efficiency (pp. 231–232)

- A method of production is technologically efficient when a firm uses the least amount of inputs to produce a given output.
- A method of production is economically efficient when the cost of producing a given output is as low as possible.

Working Problems 3 and 4 will give you a better understanding of technological and economic efficiency.

Information and Organization (pp. 233–236)

- Firms use a combination of command systems and incentive systems to organize production.
- Faced with incomplete information and uncertainty, firms induce managers and workers to perform in ways that are consistent with the firms' goals.
- Proprietorships, partnerships, and corporations use ownership, incentive pay, and long-term contracts to cope with the principal–agent problem.

Working Problems 5 to 8 will give you a better understanding of information and organization.

Markets and the Competitive Environment (pp. 237–241)

- In perfect competition, many sellers offer an identical product to many buyers and entry is free.
- In monopolistic competition, many sellers offer slightly different products to many buyers and entry is free.
- In oligopoly, a small number of sellers compete and barriers to entry limit the number of firms.
- In monopoly, one firm produces an item that has no close substitutes and the firm is protected by a barrier to entry that prevents the entry of competitors.

Working Problems 9 and 10 will give you a better understanding of markets and the competitive environment.

Produce or Outsource? Firms and Markets (pp. 242–243)

- Firms coordinate economic activities when they can perform a task more efficiently—at lower cost—than markets can.
- Firms economize on transactions costs and achieve the benefits of economies of scale, economies of scope, and economies of team production.

Working Problems 11 and 12 will give you a better understanding of firms and markets.

Key Terms

Command system, 233
Economic depreciation, 229
Economic efficiency, 231
Economic profit, 228
Economies of scale, 242
Economies of scope, 243
Firm, 228

Four-firm concentration ratio, 238
Herfindahl-Hirschman Index, 238
Implicit rental rate, 228
Incentive system, 233
Monopolistic competition, 237
Monopoly, 237
Normal profit, 229

Oligopoly, 237
Perfect competition, 237
Principal–agent problem, 234
Product differentiation, 237
Technological efficiency, 231
Technology, 230
Transactions costs, 242

STUDY PLAN PROBLEMS AND APPLICATIONS

 myeconlab You can work Problems 1 to 13 in MyEconLab Chapter 10 Study Plan and get instant feedback.

The Firm and Its Economic Problem (Study Plan 10.1)

1. One year ago, Jack and Jill set up a vinegar-bottling firm (called JJVB). Use the following information to calculate JJVB's opportunity cost of production during its first year of operation:
   - Jack and Jill put $50,000 of their own money into the firm.
   - They bought equipment for $30,000.
   - They hired one employee to help them for an annual wage of $20,000.
   - Jack gave up his previous job, at which he earned $30,000, and spent all his time working for JJVB.
   - Jill kept her old job, which paid $30 an hour, but gave up 10 hours of leisure each week (for 50 weeks) to work for JJVB.
   - JJVB bought $10,000 of goods and services from other firms.
   - The market value of the equipment at the end of the year was $28,000.
   - Jack and Jill have a $100,000 home loan on which they pay interest of 6 percent a year.

2. Joe, who has no skills, no job experience, and no alternative employment, runs a shoeshine stand at the airport. Operators of other shoeshine stands earn $10,000 a year. Joe pays rent to the airport of $2,000 a year, and his total revenue from shining shoes is $15,000 a year. Joe spent $1,000 on a chair, polish, and brushes, using his credit card to buy them. The interest on a credit card balance is 20 percent a year. At the end of the year, Joe was offered $500 for his business and all its equipment. Calculate Joe's opportunity cost of production and his economic profit.

Technological and Economic Efficiency (Study Plan 10.2)

3. Alternative ways of laundering 100 shirts are

Method	Labor (hours)	Capital (machines)
A	1	10
B	5	8
C	20	4
D	50	1

a. Which methods are technologically efficient?

b. Which method is economically efficient if the hourly wage rate and the implicit rental rate of capital are as follows:
   (i) Wage rate $1, rental rate $100?
   (ii) Wage rate $5, rental rate $50?
   (iii) Wage rate $50, rental rate $5?

4. **John Deere's Farm Team**

Deere opened up the Pune [India] center in 2001. Deere's move was unexpected: Deere is known for its heavy-duty farm equipment and big construction gear whereas many of India's 300 million farmers still use oxen-pulled plows.

Source: *Fortune*, April 14, 2008

a. Why do many Indian farmers still use oxen-pulled plows? Are they efficient or inefficient? Explain.

b. How might making John Deere farm equipment available to Indian farmers change the technology constraint they face?

Information and Organization (Study Plan 10.3)

5. **Here It Is. Now, You Design It!**

The idea is that the most successful companies no longer invent new products and services on their own. They create them along with their customers, and they do it in a way that produces a unique experience for each customer. The important corollary is that no company owns enough resources—or can possibly own enough—to furnish unique experiences for each customer, so companies must organize a constantly shifting global web of suppliers and partners to do the job.

Source: *Fortune*, May 26, 2008

a. Describe this method of organizing and coordinating production: Does it use a command system or incentive system?

b. How does this method of organizing and coordinating production help firms achieve lower costs?

6. **Rewarding Failure**

Over the past 25 years CEO pay has risen faster than corporate profits, economic growth, or average wages. A more sensible alternative to the current compensation system would require CEOs to own a lot of company stock. If the stock is given to the boss, his salary and bonus should be docked to reflect its value. As for bonuses, they should be based on improving a company's cash earnings relative to its cost of capital, not to more easily manipulated measures like earnings per share. Bonuses should not be capped, but they should be unavailable to the CEO for some period of years.

Source: *Fortune*, April 28, 2008

a. What is the economic problem that CEO compensation schemes are designed to solve?

b. How do the proposed changes to CEO compensation outlined in the news clip address the problem you described in part (a)?

Use the following news clip to work Problems 7 and 8.

Steps to Creating a Super Startup

Starting a business is a complicated and risky task. Just two-thirds of new small businesses survive at least two years, and only 44 percent survive at least four years. Most entrepreneurs start their businesses by dipping into their savings, borrowing from the family, and using the founder's credit cards. Getting a bank loan is tough unless you have assets—and that often means using your home as collateral.

Source: CNN, October 18, 2007

7. When starting a business, what are the risks and potential rewards identified in the news clip that are associated with a proprietorship?

8. How might (i) a partnership and (ii) a corporation help to overcome the risks identified in the news clip?

Markets and the Competitive Environment
(Study Plan 10.4)

9. Sales of the firms in the tattoo industry are

Firm	Sales (dollars per year)
Bright Spots	450
Freckles	325
Love Galore	250
Native Birds	200
Other 15 firms	800

Calculate the four-firm concentration ratio. What is the structure of the tattoo industry?

10. **GameStop Racks Up the Points**

No retailer has more cachet among gamers than GameStop. For now, only Wal-Mart has a larger market share—21.3% last year. GameStop's share was 21.1% last year, and may well overtake Wal-Mart this year. But if new women gamers prefer shopping at Target to GameStop, Wal-Mart and Target might erode GameStop's market share.

Source: *Fortune*, June 9, 2008

a. According to the news clip, what is the structure of the U.S. retail video-game market?

b. Estimate a range for the four-firm concentration ratio and the HHI for the game market in the United States based on the information provided in this news clip.

Produce or Outsource? Firms and Markets
(Study Plan 10.5)

11. American automakers buy auto parts from independent suppliers rather than produce the parts themselves. In the 1980s, Chrysler got about 70 percent of its auto parts from independent suppliers, while Ford got about 60 percent and General Motors got 25 percent. A decade earlier, the proportions were 50 percent at Chrysler, 5 percent at Ford, and 20 percent at General Motors.

Source: The Cato Institute Policy Analysis, 1987

a. Why did American automakers decide to outsource most of their parts production?

b. Explain why independent producers of auto parts are more efficient than the automakers.

12. Federal Express enters into contracts with independent truck operators who offer FedEx service and who are rewarded by the volume of packages they carry. Why doesn't FedEx buy more trucks and hire more drivers? What incentive problems might arise from this arrangement?

Economics in the News (Study Plan 10.N)

13. Lego, the Danish toymaker, incurred economic losses in 2003 and 2004. Lego faced competition from low-cost copiers of its products and a fall in demand. In 2004, to restore profits, Lego fired 3,500 of its 8,000 workers; closed factories in Switzerland and the United States; opened factories in Eastern Europe and Mexico; and introduced performance-based pay for its managers. Lego returned to profit in 2005.

Based on **Picking Up the Pieces**, *The Economist*, October 28, 2006

a. Describe the problems that Lego faced in 2003 and 2004, using the concepts of the three types of constraints that all firms face.

b. Which of the actions that Lego took to restore profits addressed an inefficiency? How did Lego seek to achieve economic efficiency?

c. Which of Lego's actions addressed an information and organization problem? How did Lego change the way in which it coped with the principal–agent problem?

d. In what type of market does Lego operate?

ADDITIONAL PROBLEMS AND APPLICATIONS

myeconlab These problems are available in MyEconLab if assigned by your instructor.

The Firm and Its Economic Problem

Use the following information to work Problems 14 and 15.

Lee is a computer programmer who earned $35,000 in 2009. But on January 1, 2010, Lee opened a body board manufacturing business. At the end of the first year of operation, he submitted the following information to his accountant:

■ He stopped renting out his cottage for $3,500 a year and used it as his factory. The market value of the cottage increased from $70,000 to $71,000.

■ He spent $50,000 on materials, phone, etc.

■ He leased machines for $10,000 a year.

■ He paid $15,000 in wages.

■ He used $10,000 from his savings account, which earns 5 percent a year interest.

■ He borrowed $40,000 at 10 percent a year.

■ He sold $160,000 worth of body boards.

■ Normal profit is $25,000 a year.

14. Calculate Lee's opportunity cost of production and his economic profit.

15. Lee's accountant recorded the depreciation on his cottage during 2010 as $7,000. According to the accountant, what profit did Lee make?

16. In 2009, Toni taught music and earned $20,000. She also earned $4,000 by renting out her basement. On January 1, 2010, she quit teaching, stopped renting out her basement, and began to use it as the office for her new Web site design business. She took $2,000 from her savings account to buy a computer. During 2010, she paid $1,500 for the lease of a Web server and $1,750 for high-speed Internet service. She received a total revenue from Web site designing of $45,000 and earned interest at 5 percent a year on her savings account balance. Normal profit is $55,000 a year. At the end of 2010, Toni could have sold her computer for $500. Calculate Toni's opportunity cost of production and her economic profit in 2010.

17. **The Colvin Interview: Chrysler**

The key driver of profitability will be that the focus of the company isn't on profitability. Our focus is on the customer. If we can find a way to give customers what they want better than anybody else, then what can stop us?

Source: *Fortune*, April 14, 2008

a. In spite of what Chrysler's vice chairman and co-president claims, why is Chrysler's focus actually on profitability?

b. What would happen to Chrysler if it didn't focus on maximizing profit, but instead focused its production and pricing decisions to "give customers what they want"?

18. **Must Watches**

Stocks too volatile? Bonds too boring? Then try an alternative investment—one you can wear on your wrist. ... [The] typical return on a watch over five to ten years is roughly 10%. [One could] do better in an index fund, but ... what other investment is so wearable?

Source: *Fortune*, April 14, 2008

a. What is the cost of buying a watch?

b. What is the opportunity cost of owning a watch?

c. Does owning a watch create an economic profit opportunity?

Technological and Economic Efficiency

Use the following information to work Problems 19 and 20.

Four methods of completing a tax return and the time taken by each method are: with a PC, 1 hour; with a pocket calculator, 12 hours; with a pocket calculator and paper and pencil, 12 hours; and with a pencil and paper, 16 hours. The PC and its software cost $1,000, the pocket calculator costs $10, and the pencil and paper cost $1.

19. Which, if any, of the methods is technologically efficient?

20. Which method is economically efficient if the wage rate is

(i) $5 an hour?

(ii) $50 an hour?

(iii) $500 an hour?

21. **A Medical Sensation**

Hospitals are buying da Vinci surgical robots. Surgeons, sitting comfortably at a da Vinci console, can use various robotic attachments to perform even the most complex procedures.

Source: *Fortune*, April 28, 2008

a. Assume that performing a surgery with a surgical robot requires fewer surgeons and nurses.

Is using the surgical robot technologically efficient?

b. What additional information would you need to be able to say that switching to surgical robots is economically efficient for a hospital?

Information and Organization

22. Wal-Mart has more than 3,700 stores, more than one million employees, and total revenues of close to a quarter of a trillion dollars in the United States alone. Sarah Frey-Talley runs the family-owned Frey Farms in Illinois and supplies Wal-Mart with pumpkins and other fresh produce.

a. How does Wal-Mart coordinate its activities? Is it likely to use mainly a command system or also to use incentive systems? Explain.

b. How do you think Sarah Frey-Talley coordinates the activities of Frey Farms? Is she likely to use mainly a command system or also to use incentive systems? Explain.

c. Describe, compare, and contrast the principal–agent problems faced by Wal-Mart and Frey Farms. How might these firms cope with their principal–agent problems?

23. **Where Does Google Go Next?**

Google gives its engineers one day a week to work on whatever project they want. A couple of colleagues did what many of the young geniuses do at Google: They came up with a cool idea. At Google, you often end up with a laissez-faire mess instead of resource allocation.

Source: *Fortune*, May 26, 2008

a. Describe Google's method of organizing production with their software engineers.

b. What are the potential gains and opportunity costs associated with this method?

Markets and the Competitive Environment

24. Market shares of chocolate makers are

Firm	Market share (percent)
Mayfair, Inc.	15
Bond, Inc.	10
Magic, Inc.	20
All Natural, Inc.	15
Truffles, Inc.	25
Gold, Inc.	15

a. Calculate the Herfindahl-Hirschman Index.

b. What is the structure of the chocolate industry?

Produce or Outsource? Firms and Markets

Use the following information to work Problems 25 to 27.

Two leading design firms, Astro Studios of San Francisco and Hers Experimental Design Laboratory, Inc. of Osaka, Japan, worked with Microsoft to design the Xbox 360 video game console. IBM, ATI, and SiS designed the Xbox 360's hardware. Three firms—Flextronics, Wistron, and Celestica—manufacture the Xbox 360 at their plants in China and Taiwan.

25. Describe the roles of market coordination and coordination by firms in the design, manufacture, and marketing of the Xbox 360.

26. a. Why do you think Microsoft works with a large number of other firms, rather than performing all the required tasks itself?

b. What are the roles of transactions costs, economies of scale, economies of scope, and economies of team production in the design, manufacture, and marketing of the Xbox?

27. Why do you think the Xbox is designed in the United States and Japan but built in China?

Economics in the News

28. After you have studied *Reading Between the Lines* on pp. 244–245 answer the following questions.

a. What products do Facebook and Yahoo sell?

b. In what types of markets do Facebook and Yahoo compete?

c. How do social networks and Internet search providers generate revenue?

d. What is special about social networking sites that make them attractive to advertisers?

e. What is special about Internet search providers that make them attractive to advertisers?

f. What technological changes might increase the profitability of social networks and Internet search providers?

29. **Long Reviled, Merit Pay Gains Among Teachers**

School districts in many states experiment with plans that compensate teachers partly based on classroom performance, rather than their years on the job and coursework completed. Working with mentors to improve their instruction and getting bonuses for raising student achievement encourages efforts to raise teaching quality.

Source: *The New York Times*, June 18, 2007

How does "merit pay" attempt to cope with the principal–agent problem in public education?

11

OUTPUT AND COSTS

After studying this chapter,
you will be able to:

◆ Distinguish between the short run and the long run

◆ Explain the relationship between a firm's output and labor employed in the short run

◆ Explain the relationship between a firm's output and costs in the short run and derive a firm's short-run cost curves

◆ Explain the relationship between a firm's output and costs in the long run and derive a firm's long-run average cost curve

What does a big electricity supplier in Pennsylvania, PennPower, and Campus Sweaters, a small (fictional) producer of knitwear have in common? Like every firm, they must decide how much to produce, how many people to employ, and how much and what type of capital equipment to use. How do firms make these decisions?

PennPower and the other electric utilities in the United States face a demand for electricity that fluctuates across the day and that fluctuates from day to day depending on the temperature. How do electric utilities cope with these demand fluctuations?

We are going to answer these questions in this chapter. To explain the basic ideas as clearly as possible, we focus on the economic decisions of Campus Sweaters, Inc. Studying the way this firm copes with its economic problems will give us a clear view of the problems faced by all firms. We'll then apply what we learn in this chapter to the real-world costs of producing cars and electricity. In *Reading Between the Lines*, we'll look at the effects of a new generation of 'smart' meters that encourage users to even out electricity consumption across the day.

◆ Decision Time Frames

People who operate firms make many decisions, and all of their decisions are aimed at achieving one overriding goal: maximum attainable profit. But not all decisions are equally critical. Some decisions are big ones. Once made, they are costly (or impossible) to reverse. If such a decision turns out to be incorrect, it might lead to the failure of the firm. Other decisions are small. They are easily changed. If one of these decisions turns out to be incorrect, the firm can change its actions and survive.

The biggest decision that an entrepreneur makes is in what industry to establish a firm. For most entrepreneurs, their background knowledge and interests drive this decision. But the decision also depends on profit prospects—on the expectation that total revenue will exceed total cost.

Cindy has already decided to set up Campus Sweaters. She has also decided the most effective method of organizing the firm. But she has not decided the quantity to produce, the factors of production to hire, or the price to charge for sweaters.

Decisions about the quantity to produce and the price to charge depend on the type of market in which the firm operates. Perfect competition, monopolistic competition, oligopoly, and monopoly all confront the firm with their own special problems. Decisions about *how* to produce a given output do not depend on the type of market in which the firm operates. *All* types of firms in *all* types of markets make similar decisions about how to produce.

The actions that a firm can take to influence the relationship between output and cost depend on how soon the firm wants to act. A firm that plans to change its output rate tomorrow has fewer options than one that plans to change its output rate six months or six years from now.

To study the relationship between a firm's output decision and its costs, we distinguish between two decision time frames:

- The short run
- The long run

The Short Run

The **short run** is a time frame in which the quantity of at least one factor of production is fixed. For most firms, capital, land, and entrepreneurship are fixed factors of production and labor is the variable factor of production. We call the fixed factors of production the firm's *plant*: In the short run, a firm's plant is fixed.

For Campus Sweaters, the fixed plant is its factory building and its knitting machines. For an electric power utility, the fixed plant is its buildings, generators, computers, and control systems.

To increase output in the short run, a firm must increase the quantity of a variable factor of production, which is usually labor. So to produce more output, Campus Sweaters must hire more labor and operate its knitting machines for more hours a day. Similarly, an electric power utility must hire more labor and operate its generators for more hours a day.

Short-run decisions are easily reversed. The firm can increase or decrease its output in the short run by increasing or decreasing the amount of labor it hires.

The Long Run

The **long run** is a time frame in which the quantities of *all* factors of production can be varied. That is, the long run is a period in which the firm can change its *plant*.

To increase output in the long run, a firm can change its plant as well as the quantity of labor it hires. Campus Sweaters can decide whether to install more knitting machines, use a new type of machine, reorganize its management, or hire more labor. Long-run decisions are *not* easily reversed. Once a plant decision is made, the firm usually must live with it for some time. To emphasize this fact, we call the past expenditure on a plant that has no resale value a **sunk cost**. A sunk cost is irrelevant to the firm's current decisions. The only costs that influence its current decisions are the short-run cost of changing its labor inputs and the long-run cost of changing its plant.

REVIEW QUIZ

1 Distinguish between the short run and the long run.
2 Why is a sunk cost irrelevant to a firm's current decisions?

You can work these questions in Study Plan 11.1 and get instant feedback.

We're going to study costs in the short run and the long run. We begin with the short run and describe a firm's technology constraint.

Short-Run Technology Constraint

To increase output in the short run, a firm must increase the quantity of labor employed. We describe the relationship between output and the quantity of labor employed by using three related concepts:

1. Total product
2. Marginal product
3. Average product

These product concepts can be illustrated either by product schedules or by product curves. Let's look first at the product schedules.

Product Schedules

Table 11.1 shows some data that describe Campus Sweaters' total product, marginal product, and average product. The numbers tell us how the quantity of sweaters produced increases as Campus Sweaters employs more workers. The numbers also tell us about the productivity of the labor that Campus Sweaters employs.

Focus first on the columns headed "Labor" and "Total product." **Total product** is the maximum output that a given quantity of labor can produce. You can see from the numbers in these columns that as Campus Sweaters employs more labor, total product increases. For example, when 1 worker is employed, total product is 4 sweaters a day, and when 2 workers are employed, total product is 10 sweaters a day. Each increase in employment increases total product.

The **marginal product** of labor is the increase in total product that results from a one-unit increase in the quantity of labor employed, with all other inputs remaining the same. For example, in Table 11.1, when Campus Sweaters increases employment from 2 to 3 workers and does not change its capital, the marginal product of the third worker is 3 sweaters—total product increases from 10 to 13 sweaters.

Average product tells how productive workers are on average. The **average product** of labor is equal to total product divided by the quantity of labor employed. For example, in Table 11.1, the average product of 3 workers is 4.33 sweaters per worker—13 sweaters a day divided by 3 workers.

If you look closely at the numbers in Table 11.1, you can see some patterns. As Campus Sweaters hires more labor, marginal product increases initially, and

TABLE 11.1 Total Product, Marginal Product, and Average Product

	Labor (workers per day)	Total product (sweaters per day)	Marginal product (sweaters per additional worker)	Average product (sweaters per worker)
A	0	0		
			4	
B	1	4		4.00
			6	
C	2	10		5.00
			3	
D	3	13		4.33
			2	
E	4	15		3.75
			1	
F	5	16		3.20

Total product is the total amount produced. Marginal product is the change in total product that results from a one-unit increase in labor. For example, when labor increases from 2 to 3 workers a day (row C to row D), total product increases from 10 to 13 sweaters a day. The marginal product of going from 2 to 3 workers is 3 sweaters. Average product is total product divided by the quantity of labor employed. For example, the average product of 3 workers is 4.33 sweaters per worker (13 sweaters a day divided by 3 workers).

then begins to decrease. For example, marginal product increases from 4 sweaters a day for the first worker to 6 sweaters a day for the second worker and then decreases to 3 sweaters a day for the third worker. Average product also increases at first and then decreases. You can see the relationships between the quantity of labor hired and the three product concepts more clearly by looking at the product curves.

Product Curves

The product curves are graphs of the relationships between employment and the three product concepts you've just studied. They show how total product, marginal product, and average product change as employment changes. They also show the relationships among the three concepts. Let's look at the product curves.

Total Product Curve

Figure 11.1 shows Campus Sweaters' total product curve, *TP*, which is a graph of the total product schedule. Points *A* through *F* correspond to rows *A* through *F* in Table 11.1. To graph the entire total product curve, we vary labor by hours rather than whole days.

Notice the shape of the total product curve. As employment increases from zero to 1 worker a day, the curve becomes steeper. Then, as employment increases to 3, 4, and 5 workers a day, the curve becomes less steep.

The total product curve is similar to the *production possibilities frontier* (explained in Chapter 2). It separates the attainable output levels from those that are unattainable. All the points that lie above the curve are unattainable. Points that lie below the curve, in the orange area, are attainable, but they are inefficient—they use more labor than is necessary to produce a given output. Only the points *on* the total product curve are technologically efficient.

FIGURE 11.1   Total Product Curve

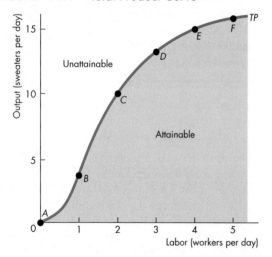

The total product curve, *TP*, is based on the data in Table 11.1. The total product curve shows how the quantity of sweaters produced changes as the quantity of labor employed changes. For example, 2 workers can produce 10 sweaters a day (point *C*). Points *A* through *F* on the curve correspond to the rows of Table 11.1. The total product curve separates attainable outputs from unattainable outputs. Points below the *TP* curve are inefficient.

myeconlab animation

Marginal Product Curve

Figure 11.2 shows Campus Sweaters' marginal product of labor. Part (a) reproduces the total product curve from Fig. 11.1 and part (b) shows the marginal product curve, *MP*.

In part (a), the orange bars illustrate the marginal product of labor. The height of a bar measures marginal product. Marginal product is also measured by the slope of the total product curve. Recall that the slope of a curve is the change in the value of the variable measured on the *y*-axis—output—divided by the change in the variable measured on the *x*-axis—labor—as we move along the curve. A one-unit increase in labor, from 2 to 3 workers, increases output from 10 to 13 sweaters, so the slope from point *C* to point *D* is 3 sweaters per additional worker, the same as the marginal product we've just calculated.

Again varying the amount of labor in the smallest units possible, we can draw the marginal product curve shown in Fig. 11.2(b). The *height* of this curve measures the *slope* of the total product curve at a point. Part (a) shows that an increase in employment from 2 to 3 workers increases output from 10 to 13 sweaters (an increase of 3). The increase in output of 3 sweaters appears on the *y*-axis of part (b) as the marginal product of going from 2 to 3 workers. We plot that marginal product at the midpoint between 2 and 3 workers. Notice that the marginal product shown in Fig. 11.2(b) reaches a peak at 1.5 workers, and at that point, marginal product is 6 sweaters per additional worker. The peak occurs at 1.5 workers because the total product curve is steepest when employment increases from 1 worker to 2 workers.

The total product and marginal product curves differ across firms and types of goods. GM's product curves are different from those of PennPower, whose curves in turn are different from those of Campus Sweaters. But the shapes of the product curves are similar because almost every production process has two features:

- Increasing marginal returns initially
- Diminishing marginal returns eventually

Increasing Marginal Returns Increasing marginal returns occur when the marginal product of an additional worker exceeds the marginal product of the previous worker. Increasing marginal returns arise from increased specialization and division of labor in the production process.

FIGURE 11.2   Total Product and Marginal Product

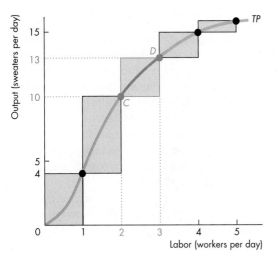

(a) Total product

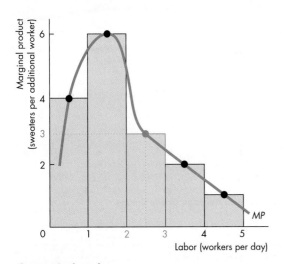

(b) Marginal product

Marginal product is illustrated by the orange bars. For example, when labor increases from 2 to 3 workers a day, marginal product is the orange bar whose height is 3 sweaters. (Marginal product is shown midway between the quantities of labor to emphasize that marginal product results from *changing* the quantity of labor.) The steeper the slope of the total product curve (*TP*) in part (a), the larger is marginal product (*MP*) in part (b). Marginal product increases to a maximum (in this example when 1.5 workers a day are employed) and then declines—diminishing marginal product.

myeconlab   animation

For example, if Campus Sweaters employs one worker, that person must learn all the aspects of sweater production: running the knitting machines, fixing breakdowns, packaging and mailing sweaters, buying and checking the type and color of the wool. All these tasks must be performed by that one person.

If Campus Sweaters hires a second person, the two workers can specialize in different parts of the production process and can produce more than twice as much as one worker. The marginal product of the second worker is greater than the marginal product of the first worker. Marginal returns are increasing.

Diminishing Marginal Returns Most production processes experience increasing marginal returns initially, but all production processes eventually reach a point of *diminishing* marginal returns. **Diminishing marginal returns** occur when the marginal product of an additional worker is less than the marginal product of the previous worker.

Diminishing marginal returns arise from the fact that more and more workers are using the same capital and working in the same space. As more workers are added, there is less and less for the additional workers to do that is productive. For example, if Campus Sweaters hires a third worker, output increases but not by as much as it did when it hired the second worker. In this case, after two workers are hired, all the gains from specialization and the division of labor have been exhausted. By hiring a third worker, the factory produces more sweaters, but the equipment is being operated closer to its limits. There are even times when the third worker has nothing to do because the machines are running without the need for further attention. Hiring more and more workers continues to increase output but by successively smaller amounts. Marginal returns are diminishing. This phenomenon is such a pervasive one that it is called a "law"—the law of diminishing returns. The **law of diminishing returns** states that

As a firm uses more of a variable factor of production with a given quantity of the fixed factor of production, the marginal product of the variable factor eventually diminishes.

You are going to return to the law of diminishing returns when we study a firm's costs, but before we do that, let's look at the average product of labor and the average product curve.

Average Product Curve

Figure 11.3 illustrates Campus Sweaters' average product of labor and shows the relationship between average product and marginal product. Points *B* through *F* on the average product curve *AP* correspond to those same rows in Table 11.1. Average product increases from 1 to 2 workers (its maximum value at point *C*) but then decreases as yet more workers are employed. Notice also that average product is largest when average product and marginal product are equal. That is, the marginal product curve cuts the average product curve at the point of maximum average product. For the number of workers at which marginal product exceeds average product, average product is *increasing*. For the number of workers at which marginal product is less than average product, average product is *decreasing*.

The relationship between the average product and marginal product is a general feature of the relationship between the average and marginal values of any variable—even your grades.

FIGURE 11.3   Average Product

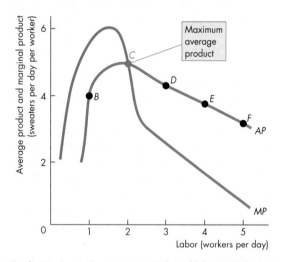

The figure shows the average product of labor and the connection between average product and marginal product. With 1 worker, marginal product exceeds average product, so average product is increasing. With 2 workers, marginal product equals average product, so average product is at its maximum. With more than 2 workers, marginal product is less than average product, so average product is decreasing.

myeconlab   animation

Economics in Action
How to Pull Up Your Average

Do you want to pull up your average grade? Then make sure that your grade this semester is better than your current average! This semester is your marginal semester. If your marginal grade exceeds your average grade (like the second semester in the figure), your average will rise. If your marginal grade equals your average grade (like the third semester in the figure), your average won't change. If your marginal grade is below your average grade (like the fourth semester in the figure), your average will fall.

The relationship between your marginal and average grades is exactly the same as that between marginal product and average product.

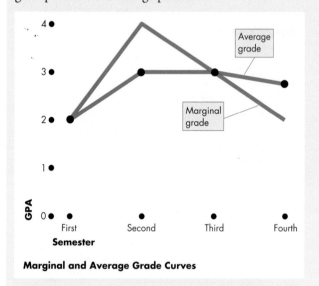

Marginal and Average Grade Curves

◆ REVIEW QUIZ

1   Explain how the marginal product and average product of labor change as the labor employed increases (a) initially and (b) eventually.
2   What is the law of diminishing returns? Why does marginal product eventually diminish?
3   Explain the relationship between marginal product and average product.

You can work these questions in Study Plan 11.2 and get instant feedback.

Campus Sweaters' product curves influence its costs, as you are now going to see.

Short-Run Cost

To produce more output in the short run, a firm must employ more labor, which means that it must increase its costs. We describe the relationship between output and cost by using three cost concepts:

- Total cost
- Marginal cost
- Average cost

Total Cost

A firm's **total cost** (*TC*) is the cost of *all* the factors of production it uses. We separate total cost into total *fixed* cost and total *variable* cost.

Total fixed cost (*TFC*) is the cost of the firm's fixed factors. For Campus Sweaters, total fixed cost includes the cost of renting knitting machines and *normal profit*, which is the opportunity cost of Cindy's entrepreneurship (see Chapter 10, p. 229). The quantities of fixed factors don't change as output changes, so total fixed cost is the same at all outputs.

Total variable cost (*TVC*) is the cost of the firm's variable factors. For Campus Sweaters, labor is the variable factor, so this component of cost is its wage bill. Total variable cost changes as output changes.

Total cost is the sum of total fixed cost and total variable cost. That is,

$$TC = TFC + TVC.$$

The table in Fig. 11.4 shows total costs. Campus Sweaters rents one knitting machine for $25 a day, so its *TFC* is $25. To produce sweaters, the firm hires labor, which costs $25 a day. *TVC* is the number of workers multiplied by $25. For example, to produce 13 sweaters a day, in row *D*, the firm hires 3 workers and *TVC* is $75. *TC* is the sum of *TFC* and *TVC*, so to produce 13 sweaters a day, *TC* is $100. Check the calculations in the other rows of the table.

Figure 11.4 shows Campus Sweaters' total cost curves, which graph total cost against output. The green *TFC* curve is horizontal because total fixed cost ($25 a day) does not change when output changes. The purple *TVC* curve and the blue *TC* curve both slope upward because to increase output, more labor must be employed, which increases total variable cost. Total fixed cost equals the vertical distance between the *TVC* and *TC* curves.

Let's now look at a firm's marginal cost.

FIGURE 11.4   Total Cost Curves

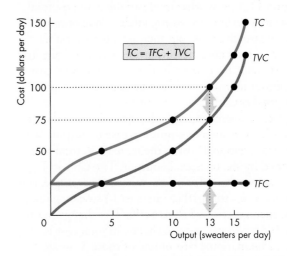

Labor (workers per day)	Output (sweaters per day)	Total fixed cost (*TFC*)	Total variable cost (*TVC*)	Total cost (*TC*)
		(dollars per day)		
A 0	0	25	0	25
B 1	4	25	25	50
C 2	10	25	50	75
D 3	**13**	**25**	**75**	**100**
E 4	15	25	100	125
F 5	16	25	125	150

Campus Sweaters rents a knitting machine for $25 a day, so this cost is the firm's total fixed cost. The firm hires workers at a wage rate of $25 a day, and this cost is its total variable cost. For example, in row *D*, Campus Sweaters employs 3 workers and its total variable cost is 3 × $25, which equals $75. Total cost is the sum of total fixed cost and total variable cost. For example, when Campus Sweaters employs 3 workers, total cost is $100—total fixed cost of $25 plus total variable cost of $75.

The graph shows Campus Sweaters' total cost curves. Total fixed cost is constant—the *TFC* curve is a horizontal line. Total variable cost increases as output increases, so the *TVC* curve and the *TC* curve increase as output increases. The vertical distance between the *TC* curve and the *TVC* curve equals total fixed cost, as illustrated by the two arrows.

Marginal Cost

Figure 11.4 shows that total variable cost and total cost increase at a decreasing rate at small outputs but eventually, as output increases, total variable cost and total cost increase at an increasing rate. To understand this pattern in the change in total cost as output increases, we need to use the concept of *marginal cost*.

A firm's **marginal cost** is the increase in total cost that results from a one-unit increase in output. We calculate marginal cost as the increase in total cost divided by the increase in output. The table in Fig. 11.5 shows this calculation. When, for example, output increases from 10 sweaters to 13 sweaters, total cost increases from $75 to $100. The change in output is 3 sweaters, and the change in total cost is $25. The marginal cost of one of those 3 sweaters is ($25 ÷ 3), which equals $8.33.

Figure 11.5 graphs the marginal cost data in the table as the red marginal cost curve, *MC*. This curve is U-shaped because when Campus Sweaters hires a second worker, marginal cost decreases, but when it hires a third, a fourth, and a fifth worker, marginal cost successively increases.

At small outputs, marginal cost decreases as output increases because of greater specialization and the division of labor. But as output increases further, marginal cost eventually increases because of the *law of diminishing returns*. The law of diminishing returns means that the output produced by each additional worker is successively smaller. To produce an additional unit of output, ever more workers are required, and the cost of producing the additional unit of output—marginal cost—must eventually increase.

Marginal cost tells us how total cost changes as output increases. The final cost concept tells us what it costs, on average, to produce a unit of output. Let's now look at Campus Sweaters' average costs.

Average Cost

Three average costs of production are

1. Average fixed cost
2. Average variable cost
3. Average total cost

Average fixed cost (*AFC*) is total fixed cost per unit of output. **Average variable cost** (*AVC*) is total variable cost per unit of output. **Average total cost** (*ATC*) is total cost per unit of output. The average cost con-

cepts are calculated from the total cost concepts as follows:

$$TC = TFV + TVC.$$

Divide each total cost term by the quantity produced, *Q*, to get

$$\frac{TC}{Q} = \frac{TFC}{Q} + \frac{TVC}{Q},$$

or

$$ATC = AFC + AVC.$$

The table in Fig. 11.5 shows the calculation of average total cost. For example, in row *C*, output is 10 sweaters. Average fixed cost is ($25 ÷ 10), which equals $2.50, average variable cost is ($50 ÷ 10), which equals $5.00, and average total cost is ($75 ÷ 10), which equals $7.50. Note that average total cost is equal to average fixed cost ($2.50) plus average variable cost ($5.00).

Figure 11.5 shows the average cost curves. The green average fixed cost curve (*AFC*) slopes downward. As output increases, the same constant total fixed cost is spread over a larger output. The blue average total cost curve (*ATC*) and the purple average variable cost curve (*AVC*) are U-shaped. The vertical distance between the average total cost and average variable cost curves is equal to average fixed cost—as indicated by the two arrows. That distance shrinks as output increases because average fixed cost declines with increasing output.

Marginal Cost and Average Cost

The marginal cost curve (*MC*) intersects the average variable cost curve and the average total cost curve *at their minimum points*. When marginal cost is less than average cost, average cost is decreasing, and when marginal cost exceeds average cost, average cost is increasing. This relationship holds for both the *ATC* curve and the *AVC* curve. It is another example of the relationship you saw in Fig. 11.3 for average product and marginal product and in your average and marginal grades.

Why the Average Total Cost Curve Is U-Shaped

Average total cost is the sum of average fixed cost and average variable cost, so the shape of the *ATC* curve

FIGURE 11.5   Marginal Cost and Average Costs

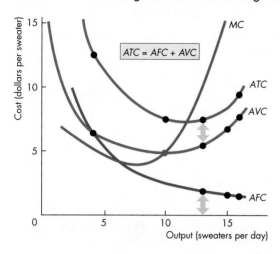

Marginal cost is calculated as the change in total cost divided by the change in output. When output increases from 4 to 10 sweaters, an increase of 6 sweaters, total cost increases by $25. Marginal cost is $25 ÷ 6, which is $4.17.

Each average cost concept is calculated by dividing the related total cost by output. When 10 sweaters are produced, AFC is $2.50 ($25 ÷ 10), AVC is $5 ($50 ÷ 10), and ATC is $7.50 ($75 ÷ 10).

The graph shows that the MC curve is U-shaped and intersects the AVC curve and the ATC curve at their minimum points. The average fixed cost curve (AFC) is downward sloping. The ATC curve and AVC curve are U-shaped. The vertical distance between the ATC curve and the AVC curve is equal to average fixed cost, as illustrated by the two arrows.

	Labor (workers per day)	Output (sweaters per day)	Total fixed cost (TFC)	Total variable cost (TVC)	Total cost (TC)	Marginal cost (MC) (dollars per additional sweater)	Average fixed cost (AFC)	Average variable cost (AVC)	Average total cost (ATC)
			(dollars per day)				(dollars per sweater)		
A	0	0	25	0	25		—	—	—
						.... 6.25			
B	1	4	25	25	50		6.25	6.25	12.50
						.... 4.17			
C	2	10	25	50	75		2.50	5.00	7.50
						.... 8.33			
D	3	13	25	75	100		1.92	5.77	7.69
						.......12.50			
E	4	15	25	100	125		1.67	6.67	8.33
						.......25.00			
F	5	16	25	125	150		1.56	7.81	9.38

myeconlab   animation

combines the shapes of the *AFC* and *AVC* curves. The U shape of the *ATC* curve arises from the influence of two opposing forces:

1. Spreading total fixed cost over a larger output
2. Eventually diminishing returns

When output increases, the firm spreads its total fixed cost over a larger output and so its average fixed cost decreases—its *AFC* curve slopes downward.

Diminishing returns means that as output increases, ever-larger amounts of labor are needed to produce an additional unit of output. So as output increases, average variable cost decreases initially but

eventually increases, and the *AVC* curve slopes upward. The *AVC* curve is U shaped.

The shape of the *ATC* curve combines these two effects. Initially, as output increases, both average fixed cost and average variable cost decrease, so average total cost decreases. The *ATC* curve slopes downward.

But as output increases further and diminishing returns set in, average variable cost starts to increase. With average fixed cost decreasing more quickly than average variable cost is increasing, the *ATC* curve continues to slope downward. Eventually, average variable cost starts to increase more quickly than average fixed cost decreases, so average total cost starts to increase. The *ATC* curve slopes upward.

Cost Curves and Product Curves

The technology that a firm uses determines its costs. Figure 11.6 shows the links between the firm's product curves and its cost curves. The upper graph shows the average product curve, *AP*, and the marginal product curve, *MP*—like those in Fig. 11.3. The lower graph shows the average variable cost curve, *AVC*, and the marginal cost curve, *MC*—like those in Fig. 11.5.

As labor increases up to 1.5 workers a day (upper graph), output increases to 6.5 sweaters a day (lower graph). Marginal product and average product rise and marginal cost and average variable cost fall. At the point of maximum marginal product, marginal cost is at a minimum.

As labor increases from 1.5 workers to 2 workers a day, (upper graph) output increases from 6.5 sweaters to 10 sweaters a day (lower graph). Marginal product falls and marginal cost rises, but average product continues to rise and average variable cost continues to fall. At the point of maximum average product, average variable cost is at a minimum. As labor increases further, output increases. Average product diminishes and average variable cost increases.

Shifts in the Cost Curves

The position of a firm's short-run cost curves depends on two factors:

- Technology
- Prices of factors of production

Technology A technological change that increases productivity increases the marginal product and average product of labor. With a better technology, the same factors of production can produce more output, so the technological advance lowers the costs of production and shifts the cost curves downward.

For example, advances in robot production techniques have increased productivity in the automobile industry. As a result, the product curves of Chrysler, Ford, and GM have shifted upward and their cost curves have shifted downward. But the relationships between their product curves and cost curves have not changed. The curves are still linked in the way shown in Fig. 11.6.

Often, as in the case of robots producing cars, a technological advance results in a firm using more capital, a fixed factor, and less labor, a variable factor.

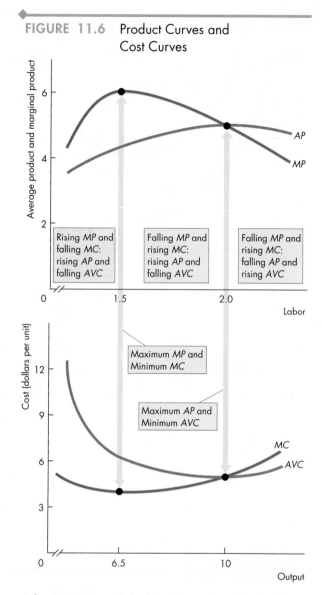

FIGURE 11.6   Product Curves and Cost Curves

A firm's *MP* curve is linked to its *MC* curve. If, as the firm increases its labor from 0 to 1.5 workers a day, the firm's marginal product rises, its marginal cost falls. If marginal product is at a maximum, marginal cost is at a minimum. If, as the firm hires more labor, its marginal product diminishes, its marginal cost rises.

A firm's *AP* curve is linked to its *AVC* curve. If, as the firm increases its labor to 2 workers a day, its average product rises, its average variable cost falls. If average product is at a maximum, average variable cost is at a minimum. If, as the firm hires more labor, its average product diminishes, its average variable cost rises.

TABLE 11.2   A Compact Glossary of Costs

Term	Symbol	Definition	Equation
Fixed cost		Cost that is independent of the output level; cost of a fixed factor of production	
Variable cost		Cost that varies with the output level; cost of a variable factor of production	
Total fixed cost	TFC	Cost of the fixed factors of production	
Total variable cost	TVC	Cost of the variable factors of production	
Total cost	TC	Cost of all factors of production	$TC = TFC + TVC$
Output (total product)	TP	Total quantity produced (output Q)	
Marginal cost	MC	Change in total cost resulting from a one-unit increase in total product	$MC = \Delta TC \div \Delta Q$
Average fixed cost	AFC	Total fixed cost per unit of output	$AFC = TFC \div Q$
Average variable cost	AVC	Total variable cost per unit of output	$AVC = TVC \div Q$
Average total cost	ATC	Total cost per unit of output	$ATC = AFC + AVC$

Another example is the use of ATMs by banks to dispense cash. ATMs, which are fixed capital, have replaced tellers, which are variable labor. Such a technological change decreases total cost but increases fixed costs and decreases variable cost. This change in the mix of fixed cost and variable cost means that at small outputs, average total cost might increase, while at large outputs, average total cost decreases.

Prices of Factors of Production   An increase in the price of a factor of production increases the firm's costs and shifts its cost curves. How the curves shift depends on which factor price changes.

An increase in rent or some other component of *fixed* cost shifts the *TFC* and *AFC* curves upward and shifts the *TC* curve upward but leaves the *AVC* and *TVC* curves and the *MC* curve unchanged. For example, if the interest expense paid by a trucking company increases, the fixed cost of transportation services increases.

An increase in wages, gasoline, or another component of *variable* cost shifts the *TVC* and *AVC* curves upward and shifts the *MC* curve upward but leaves the *AFC* and *TFC* curves unchanged. For example, if

truck drivers' wages or the price of gasoline increases, the variable cost and marginal cost of transportation services increase.

You've now completed your study of short-run costs. All the concepts that you've met are summarized in a compact glossary in Table 11.2.

 REVIEW QUIZ

1   What relationships do a firm's short-run cost curves show?
2   How does marginal cost change as output increases (a) initially and (b) eventually?
3   What does the law of diminishing returns imply for the shape of the marginal cost curve?
4   What is the shape of the *AFC* curve and why does it have this shape?
5   What are the shapes of the *AVC* curve and the *ATC* curve and why do they have these shapes?

You can work these questions in Study Plan 11.3 and get instant feedback.   myeconlab

Long-Run Cost

We are now going to study the firm's long-run costs. In the long run, a firm can vary both the quantity of labor and the quantity of capital, so in the long run, all the firm's costs are variable.

The behavior of long-run cost depends on the firm's *production function*, which is the relationship between the maximum output attainable and the quantities of both labor and capital.

The Production Function

Table 11.3 shows Campus Sweaters' production function. The table lists total product schedules for four different quantities of capital. The quantity of capital identifies the plant size. The numbers for plant 1 are for a factory with 1 knitting machine—the case we've just studied. The other three plants have 2, 3, and 4 machines. If Campus Sweaters uses plant 2 with 2 knitting machines, the various amounts of labor can produce the outputs shown in the second column of the table. The other two columns show the outputs of yet larger quantities of capital. Each column of the table could be graphed as a total product curve for each plant.

Diminishing Returns Diminishing returns occur with each of the four plant sizes as the quantity of labor increases. You can check that fact by calculating the marginal product of labor in each of the plants with 2, 3, and 4 machines. With each plant size, as the firm increases the quantity of labor employed, the marginal product of labor (eventually) diminishes.

Diminishing Marginal Product of Capital
Diminishing returns also occur with each quantity of labor as the quantity of capital increases. You can check that fact by calculating the marginal product of capital at a given quantity of labor. The *marginal product of capital* is the change in total product divided by the change in capital when the quantity of labor is constant—equivalently, the change in output resulting from a one-unit increase in the quantity of capital. For example, if Campus Sweaters has 3 workers and increases its capital from 1 machine to 2 machines, output increases from 13 to 18 sweaters a day. The marginal product of the second machine is 5 sweaters a day. If Campus Sweaters continues to employ 3 workers

TABLE 11.3 The Production Function

Labor (workers per day)	Output (sweaters per day)			
	Plant 1	Plant 2	Plant 3	Plant 4
1	4	10	13	15
2	10	15	18	20
3	13	18	22	24
4	15	20	24	26
5	16	21	25	27
Knitting machines (number)	1	2	3	4

The table shows the total product data for four quantities of capital (plant sizes). The greater the plant size, the larger is the output produced by any given quantity of labor. For a given plant size, the marginal product of labor diminishes as more labor is employed. For a given quantity of labor, the marginal product of capital diminishes as the quantity of capital used increases.

and increases the number of machines from 2 to 3, output increases from 18 to 22 sweaters a day. The marginal product of the third machine is 4 sweaters a day, down from 5 sweaters a day for the second machine.

Let's now see what the production function implies for long-run costs.

Short-Run Cost and Long-Run Cost

As before, Campus Sweaters can hire workers for $25 a day and rent knitting machines for $25 a day. Using these factor prices and the data in Table 11.3, we can calculate the average total cost and graph the *ATC* curves for factories with 1, 2, 3, and 4 knitting machines. We've already studied the costs of a factory with 1 machine in Figs. 11.4 and 11.5. In Fig. 11.7, the average total cost curve for that case is ATC_1. Figure 11.7 also shows the average total cost curve for a factory with 2 machines, ATC_2, with 3 machines, ATC_3, and with 4 machines, ATC_4.

You can see, in Fig. 11.7, that the plant size has a big effect on the firm's average total cost.

FIGURE 11.7   Short-Run Costs of Four Different Plants

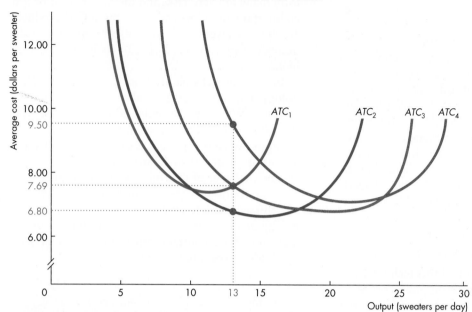

The figure shows short-run average total cost curves for four different quantities of capital at Campus Sweaters. The firm can produce 13 sweaters a day with 1 knitting machine on ATC_1 or with 3 knitting machines on ATC_3 for an average cost of $7.69 a sweater. The firm can produce 13 sweaters a day by using 2 machines on ATC_2 for $6.80 a sweater or by using 4 machines on ATC_4 for $9.50 a sweater.

If the firm produces 13 sweaters a day, the least-cost method of production, *the long-run method*, is with 2 machines on ATC_2.

 animation

In Fig. 11.7, two things stand out:

1. Each short-run ATC curve is U-shaped.
2. For each short-run ATC curve, the larger the plant, the greater is the output at which average total cost is at a minimum.

Each short-run ATC curve is U-shaped because, as the quantity of labor increases, its marginal product initially increases and then diminishes. This pattern in the marginal product of labor, which we examined in some detail for the plant with 1 knitting machine on pp. 254–255, occurs at all plant sizes.

The minimum average total cost for a larger plant occurs at a greater output than it does for a smaller plant because the larger plant has a higher total fixed cost and therefore, for any given output, a higher average fixed cost.

Which short-run ATC curve a firm operates on depends on the plant it has. In the long run, the firm can choose its plant and the plant it chooses is the one that enables it to produce its planned output at the lowest average total cost.

To see why, suppose that Campus Sweaters plans to produce 13 sweaters a day. In Fig. 11.7, with 1 machine, the average total cost curve is ATC_1 and the

average total cost of 13 sweaters a day is $7.69 a sweater. With 2 machines, on ATC_2, average total cost is $6.80 a sweater. With 3 machines, on ATC_3, average total cost is $7.69 a sweater, the same as with 1 machine. Finally, with 4 machines, on ATC_4, average total cost is $9.50 a sweater.

The economically efficient plant for producing a given output is the one that has the lowest average total cost. For Campus Sweaters, the economically efficient plant to use to produce 13 sweaters a day is the one with 2 machines.

In the long run, Cindy chooses the plant that minimizes average total cost. When a firm is producing a given output at the least possible cost, it is operating on its *long-run average cost curve*.

The **long-run average cost curve** is the relationship between the lowest attainable average total cost and output when the firm can change both the plant it uses and the quantity of labor it employs.

The long-run average cost curve is a planning curve. It tells the firm the plant and the quantity of labor to use at each output to minimize average cost. Once the firm chooses a plant, the firm operates on the short-run cost curves that apply to that plant.

The Long-Run Average Cost Curve

Figure 11.8 shows how a long-run average cost curve is derived. The long-run average cost curve *LRAC* consists of pieces of the four short-run *ATC* curves. For outputs up to 10 sweaters a day, average total cost is the lowest on ATC_1. For outputs between 10 and 18 sweaters a day, average total cost is the lowest on ATC_2. For outputs between 18 and 24 sweaters a day, average total cost is the lowest on ATC_3. And for outputs in excess of 24 sweaters a day, average total cost is the lowest on ATC_4. The piece of each *ATC* curve with the lowest average total cost is highlighted in dark blue in Fig. 11.8. This dark blue scallop-shaped curve made up of the pieces of the four *ATC* curves is the *LRAC* curve.

Economies and Diseconomies of Scale

Economies of scale are features of a firm's technology that make average total cost *fall* as output increases. When economies of scale are present, the *LRAC* curve slopes downward. In Fig. 11.8, Campus Sweaters has economies of scale for outputs up to 15 sweaters a day.

Greater specialization of both labor and capital is the main source of economies of scale. For example, if

GM produces 100 cars a week, each worker must perform many different tasks and the capital must be general-purpose machines and tools. But if GM produces 10,000 cars a week, each worker specializes in a small number of tasks, uses task-specific tools, and becomes highly proficient.

Diseconomies of scale are features of a firm's technology that make average total cost *rise* as output increases. When diseconomies of scale are present, the *LRAC* curve slopes upward. In Fig. 11.8, Campus Sweaters experiences diseconomies of scale at outputs greater than 15 sweaters a day.

The challenge of managing a large enterprise is the main source of diseconomies of scale.

Constant returns to scale are features of a firm's technology that keep average total cost constant as output increases. When constant returns to scale are present, the *LRAC* curve is horizontal.

Economies of Scale at Campus Sweaters The economies of scale and diseconomies of scale at Campus Sweaters arise from the firm's production function in Table 11.3. With 1 machine and 1 worker, the firm produces 4 sweaters a day. With 2 machines and 2 workers, total cost doubles but out-

FIGURE 11.8 Long-Run Average Cost Curve

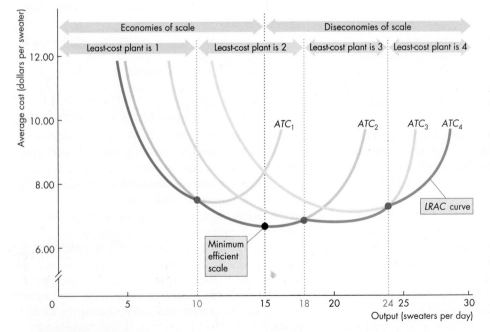

The long-run average cost curve traces the lowest attainable *ATC* when both labor and capital change. The green arrows highlight the output range over which each plant achieves the lowest *ATC*. Within each range, to change the quantity produced, the firm changes the quantity of labor it employs.

Along the *LRAC* curve, economies of scale occur if average cost falls as output increases; diseconomies of scale occur if average cost rises as output increases. Minimum efficient scale is the output at which average cost is lowest, 15 sweaters a day.

Economics in Action
Produce More to Cut Cost

Why do GM, Ford, and the other automakers have expensive equipment lying around that isn't fully used? You can answer this question with what you've learned in this chapter.

The basic answer is that auto production enjoys economies of scale. A larger output rate brings a lower long-run average cost—the firm's *LRAC* curve slopes downward.

An auto producer's average total cost curves look like those in the figure. To produce 20 vehicles an hour, the firm installs the plant with the short-run average total cost curve ATC_1. The average cost of producing a vehicle is $20,000.

Producing 20 vehicles an hour doesn't use the plant at its lowest possible average total cost. If the firm could sell enough cars for it to produce 40 vehicles an hour, the firm could use its current plant and produce at an average cost of $15,000 a vehicle.

But if the firm planned to produce 40 vehicles an hour, it would not stick with its current plant. The firm would install a bigger plant with the short-run average total cost curve ATC_2, and produce 40 vehicles an hour for $10,000 a car.

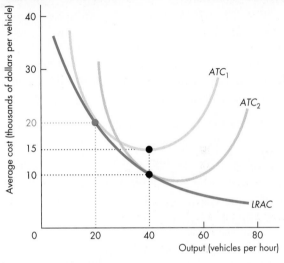

Automobile Plant Average Cost Curves

---

put more than doubles to 15 sweaters a day, so average cost decreases and Campus Sweaters experiences economies of scale. With 4 machines and 4 workers, total cost doubles again but output less than doubles to 26 sweaters a day, so average cost increases and the firm experiences diseconomies of scale.

Minimum Efficient Scale A firm's **minimum efficient scale** is the *smallest* output at which long-run average cost reaches its lowest level. At Campus Sweaters, the minimum efficient scale is 15 sweaters a day.

The minimum efficient scale plays a role in determining market structure. In a market in which the minimum efficient scale is small relative to market demand, the market has room for many firms, and the market is competitive. In a market in which the minimum efficient scale is large relative to market demand, only a small number of firms, and possibly only one firm, can make a profit and the market is either an oligopoly or monopoly. We will return to this idea in the next three chapters.

REVIEW QUIZ

1 What does a firm's production function show and how is it related to a total product curve?
2 Does the law of diminishing returns apply to capital as well as labor? Explain why or why not.
3 What does a firm's *LRAC* curve show? How is it related to the firm's short-run *ATC* curves?
4 What are economies of scale and diseconomies of scale? How do they arise? What do they imply for the shape of the *LRAC* curve?
5 What is a firm's minimum efficient scale?

You can work these questions in Study Plan 11.4 and get instant feedback.

◆ *Reading Between the Lines* on pp. 266–267 applies what you've learned about a firm's cost curves. It looks at the cost of producing electricity and explains how the use of smart meters can lower average variable cost.

Cutting the Cost of Producing Electricity

Here Come the "Smart" Meters

http://www.wsj.com
May 21, 2010

One of modern life's most durable features—fixed-price electricity—is slowly being pushed to the sidelines, a creeping change that will influence such things as what time millions of Americans cook dinner and what appliances they buy.

Driving the change is the rollout of so-called smart meters, which can transmit data on how much power is being used at any given time. That gives utilities the ability to charge more for electricity at peak times and less during lulls. Spreading out electricity consumption more evenly across the day leads to more efficient use of power plants and lower emissions. ...

The new system uses digital meters to charge prices that vary during the day.

Though fewer than 10 percent of U.S. homes have smart meters now, the Department of Energy is funding efforts that will boost that number to nearly a third by 2015. The majority of homes in California and Texas, the two most populous states, will have smart meters by 2013.

Smart meters lie at the heart of efforts to get Americans to use less electricity. Power generation accounts for about 40 percent of greenhouse-gas emissions in the United States. A 2009 federal study found that smart meters could help cut peak electricity use by 20 percent.

In California, power plants totaling 30,000 to 35,000 megawatts of capacity are needed on a typical day. But 50,000 megawatts or more are needed on hot days. That forces generators to turn on their least efficient and most polluting plants to meet demand. In New York, average demand is 42 percent less than peak-time demand. Flatten peak use, experts say, and system costs drop, as does pollution. ...

ESSENCE OF THE STORY

- Fixed-price electricity is being replaced by time-of-day pricing.

- Smart meters make it possible for utilities to charge more for electricity at peak times and less at off-peak times.

- Fewer than 10 percent of U.S. homes had smart meters in 2010, but the majority of homes in California and Texas will have them by 2013 and almost a third of all U.S. homes will have them by 2015.

- Time-of-day pricing makes electricity consumption more even across the day.

- A 2009 federal study found that smart meters could help cut peak electricity use by 20 percent.

- Making electricity consumption more even across the day lowers the cost of electricity generation.

- In California, power plants produce 30,000 to 35,000 megawatts on a typical day and 50,000 megawatts or more on a hot day.

- In New York, average production is 42 percent less than peak-time production.

ECONOMIC ANALYSIS

- The average variable cost of producing electricity depends on the technology used and on the quantity of electricity produced.

- Figure 1 shows some of the cost differences that arise from using different technologies.

- The variable cost of using wind power is zero; nuclear is the next least costly; and a turbine has the highest cost.

- Electric power utilities use the lowest-cost technologies to meet normal demand and where possible to meet peak demand. At very high peak demand, they also use turbines that burn a high-cost gasoline fuel.

- For a given technology, average variable cost depends on the quantity produced, and Fig. 2 illustrates this relationship.

- In the example in Fig. 2 the plant is designed to have minimum *AVC* when it produces 60 percent of its physical maximum output.

- If production could be held steady at 60 percent of the plant's physical maximum output, the cost of producing electricity is minimized.

- But if production increases to meet peak demand at the physical limit of the plant, the cost of production increases along the rising *AVC* curve and *MC* curve.

- When electricity is sold for a single price, consumers have no incentive to limit their peak-hour usage.

A smart meter being installed

- By introducing smart meters that enable time-of-day pricing of electricity, consumers can be confronted with the marginal cost of their choices.

- By raising the price during the peak hours and lowering the price during off-peak hours, electricity consumption can be kept more even over the day and closer to the quantity at minimum average variable cost.

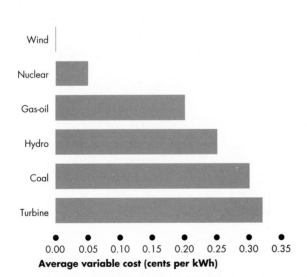

Figure 1 Average variable costs of alternative technologies

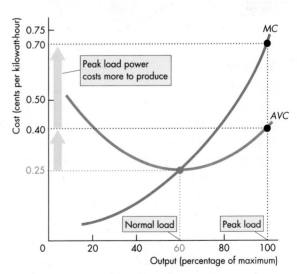

Figure 2 Cost curves for generating electricity

SUMMARY

Key Points

Decision Time Frames (p. 252)

- In the short run, the quantity of at least one factor of production is fixed and the quantities of the other factors of production can be varied.
- In the long run, the quantities of all factors of production can be varied.

Working Problems 1 and 2 will give you a better understanding of a firm's decision time frames.

Short-Run Technology Constraint (pp. 253–256)

- A total product curve shows the quantity a firm can produce with a given quantity of capital and different quantities of labor.
- Initially, the marginal product of labor increases as the quantity of labor increases, because of increased specialization and the division of labor.
- Eventually, marginal product diminishes because an increasing quantity of labor must share a fixed quantity of capital—the law of diminishing returns.
- Initially, average product increases as the quantity of labor increases, but eventually average product diminishes.

Working Problems 3 to 8 will give you a better understanding of a firm's short-run technology constraint.

Short-Run Cost (pp. 257–261)

- As output increases, total fixed cost is constant, and total variable cost and total cost increase.
- As output increases, average fixed cost decreases and average variable cost, average total cost, and marginal cost decrease at low outputs and increase at high outputs. These cost curves are U-shaped.

Working Problems 9 to 14 will give you a better understanding of a firm's short-run cost.

Long-Run Cost (pp. 262–265)

- A firm has a set of short-run cost curves for each different plant. For each output, the firm has one least-cost plant. The larger the output, the larger is the plant that will minimize average total cost.
- The long-run average cost curve traces out the lowest attainable average total cost at each output when both capital and labor inputs can be varied.
- With economies of scale, the long-run average cost curve slopes downward. With diseconomies of scale, the long-run average cost curve slopes upward.

Working Problems 15 to 20 will give you a better understanding of a firm's long-run cost.

Key Terms

Average fixed cost, 258
Average product, 253
Average total cost, 258
Average variable cost, 258
Constant returns to scale, 264
Diminishing marginal returns, 255
Diseconomies of scale, 264

Economies of scale, 264
Law of diminishing returns, 255
Long run, 252
Long-run average cost curve, 263
Marginal cost, 258
Marginal product, 253
Minimum efficient scale, 265

Short run, 252
Sunk cost, 252
Total cost, 257
Total fixed cost, 257
Total product, 253
Total variable cost, 257

STUDY PLAN PROBLEMS AND APPLICATIONS

myeconlab You can work Problems 1 to 21 in MyEconLab Chapter 11 Study Plan and get instant feedback.

Decision Time Frames (Study Plan 11.1)

1. Which of the following news items involves a short-run decision and which involves a long-run decision? Explain.
   January 31, 2008: Starbucks will open 75 more stores abroad than originally predicted, for a total of 975.
   February 25, 2008: For three hours on Tuesday, Starbucks will shut down every single one of its 7,100 stores so that baristas can receive a refresher course.
   June 2, 2008: Starbucks replaces baristas with vending machines.
   July 18, 2008: Starbucks is closing 616 stores by the end of March.

2. **Maryland Farmers Turn from Tobacco to Flowers**
   Maryland tobacco farmers will be subsidized if they switch from growing tobacco to growing crops such as flowers and organic vegetables.
   Source: *The New York Times*, February 25, 2001
   a. How does offering farmers a payment to exit tobacco growing influence the opportunity cost of growing tobacco?
   b. What is the opportunity cost of using the equipment owned by a tobacco farmer?

Short-Run Technology Constraint (Study Plan 11.2)

Use the following table to work Problems 3 to 7. The table sets out Sue's Surfboards' total product schedule.

Labor (workers per week)	Output (surfboards per week)
1	30
2	70
3	120
4	160
5	190
6	210
7	220

3. Draw the total product curve.
4. Calculate the average product of labor and draw the average product curve.
5. Calculate the marginal product of labor and draw the marginal product curve.

6. a. Over what output range does Sue's Surfboards enjoy the benefits of increased specialization and division of labor?
   b. Over what output range does the firm experience diminishing marginal product of labor?
   c. Over what output range does the firm experience an increasing average product of labor but a diminishing marginal product of labor?

7. Explain how it is possible for a firm to experience simultaneously an increasing *average* product but a diminishing *marginal* product.

8. **Business Boot Camp**
   At a footwear company called Caboots, sales rose from $160,000 in 2000 to $2.3 million in 2006, but in 2007 sales dipped to $1.5 million. Joey and Priscilla Sanchez, who run Caboots, blame the decline partly on a flood that damaged the firm's office and sapped morale.
   Source: CNN, April 23, 2008
   If the Sanchezes are correct in their assumptions and the prices of footwear didn't change
   a. Explain the effect of the flood on the total product curve and marginal product curve at Caboots.
   b. Draw a graph to show the effect of the flood on the total product curve and marginal product curve at Caboots.

Short-Run Cost (Study Plan 11.3)

Use the following data to work Problems 9 to 13.

Sue's Surfboards, in Problem 3, hires workers at $500 a week and its total fixed cost is $1,000 a week.

9. Calculate total cost, total variable cost, and total fixed cost of each output in the table. Plot these points and sketch the short-run total cost curves passing through them.
10. Calculate average total cost, average fixed cost, average variable cost, and marginal cost of each output in the table. Plot these points and sketch the short-run average and marginal cost curves passing through them.
11. Illustrate the connection between Sue's *AP*, *MP*, *AVC*, and *MC* curves in graphs like those in Fig. 11.6.

12. Sue's Surfboards rents a factory building. If the rent is increased by $200 a week and other things remain the same, how do Sue's Surfboards' short-run average cost curves and marginal cost curve change?

13. Workers at Sue's Surfboards negotiate a wage increase of $100 a week for each worker. If other things remain the same, explain how Sue's Surfboards' short-run average cost curves and marginal cost curve change.

14. **Grain Prices Go the Way of the Oil Price**

Every morning millions of Americans confront the latest trend in commodities markets at their kitchen table. Rising prices for crops have begun to drive up the cost of breakfast.

Source: *The Economist*, July 21, 2007

Explain how the rising price of crops affects the average total cost and marginal cost of producing breakfast cereals.

Long-Run Cost (Study Plan 11.4)

Use the table in Problem 3 and the following information to work Problems 15 and 16.

Sue's Surfboards buys a second plant and the output produced by each worker increases by 50 percent. The total fixed cost of operating each plant is $1,000 a week. Each worker is paid $500 a week.

15. Calculate the average total cost of producing 180 and 240 surfboards a week when Sue's Surfboards operates two plants. Graph these points and sketch the *ATC* curve.

16. a. To produce 180 surfboards a week, is it efficient to operate one or two plants?

    b. To produce 160 surfboards a week, is it efficient for Sue's to operate one or two plants?

Use the following table to work Problems 17 to 20. The table shows the production function of Jackie's Canoe Rides.

Labor (workers per day)	Output (rides per day)			
	Plant 1	Plant 2	Plant 3	Plant 4
10	20	40	55	65
20	40	60	75	85
30	65	75	90	100
40	75	85	100	110
Canoes	10	20	30	40

Jackie's pays $100 a day for each canoe it rents and $50 a day for each canoe operator it hires.

17. Graph the *ATC* curves for Plant 1 and Plant 2. Explain why these *ATC* curves differ.

18. Graph the *ATC* curves for Plant 3 and Plant 4. Explain why these *ATC* curves differ.

19. a. On Jackie's *LRAC* curve, what is the average cost of producing 40, 75, and 85 rides a week?

    b. What is Jackie's minimum efficient scale?

20. a. Explain how Jackie's uses its *LRAC* curve to decide how many canoes to rent.

    b. Does Jackie's production function feature economies of scale or diseconomies of scale?

Economics in the News (Study Plan 11.N)

21. **Airlines Seek Out New Ways to Save on Fuel as Costs Soar**

The financial pain of higher fuel prices is particularly acute for airlines because it is their single biggest expense. Airlines pump about 7,000 gallons into a Boeing 737 and about 60,000 gallons into the bigger 747 jet. Each generation of aircraft is more efficient: An Airbus A330 long-range jet uses 38 percent less fuel than the DC-10 it replaced, while the Airbus A319 medium-range jet is 27 percent more efficient than the DC-9 it replaced.

Source: *The New York Times*, June 11, 2008

a. Is the price of fuel a fixed cost or a variable cost for an airline?

b. Explain how an increase in the price of fuel changes an airline's total costs, average costs, and marginal cost.

c. Draw a graph to show the effects of an increase in the price of fuel on an airline's *TFC*, *TVC*, *AFC*, *AVC*, and *MC* curves.

d. Explain how a technological advance that makes an airplane engine more fuel efficient changes an airline's total product, marginal product, and average product.

e. Draw a graph to illustrate the effects of a more fuel-efficient aircraft on an airline's *TP*, *MP*, and *AP* curves.

f. Explain how a technological advance that makes an airplane engine more fuel efficient changes an airline's average variable cost, marginal cost, and average total cost.

g. Draw a graph to illustrate how a technological advance that makes an airplane engine more fuel efficient changes an airline's *AVC*, *MC*, and *ATC* curves.

ADDITIONAL PROBLEMS AND APPLICATIONS

 These problems are available in MyEconLab if assigned by your instructor.

Decision Time Frames

22. A Bakery on the Rise

Some 500 customers a day line up to buy Avalon's breads, scones, muffins, and coffee. Staffing and management are worries. Avalon now employs 35 and plans to hire 15 more. Its payroll will climb by 30 percent to 40 percent. The new CEO has executed an ambitious agenda that includes the move to a larger space, which will increase the rent from $3,500 to $10,000 a month.

Source: CNN, March 24, 2008

a. Which of Avalon's decisions described in the news clip is a short-run decision and which is a long-run decision?

b. Why is Avalon's long-run decision riskier than its short-run decision?

23. The Sunk-Cost Fallacy

You have good tickets to a basketball game an hour's drive away. There's a blizzard raging outside, and the game is being televised. You can sit warm and safe at home and watch it on TV, or you can bundle up, dig out your car, and go to the game. What do you do?

Source: *Slate*, September 9, 2005

a. What type of cost is your expenditure on tickets?

b. Why is the cost of the ticket irrelevant to your current decision about whether to stay at home or go to the game?

Short-Run Technology Constraint

24. Terri runs a rose farm. One worker produces 1,000 roses a week; hiring a second worker doubles her total product; hiring a third worker doubles her output again; hiring a fourth worker increased her total product but by only 1,000 roses. Construct Terri's marginal product and average product schedules. Over what range of workers do marginal returns increase?

Short-Run Cost

25. Use the events described in the news clip in Problem 22. By how much will Avalon's short-run decision increase its total variable cost? By how much will Avalon's long-run decision increase its monthly total fixed cost? Sketch Avalon's short-run *ATC* curve before and after the events described in the news clip.

26. Coffee King Starbucks Raises Its Prices

Starbucks is raising its prices because the wholesale price of milk has risen 70 percent and there's a lot of milk in Starbucks lattes.

Source: *USA Today*, July 24, 2007

Is milk a fixed factor of production or a variable factor of production? Describe how the increase in the price of milk changes Starbucks' short-run cost curves.

27. Bill's Bakery has a fire and Bill loses some of his cost data. The bits of paper that he recovers after the fire provide the information in the following table (all the cost numbers are dollars).

TP	AFC	AVC	ATC	MC
10	120	100	220	
				80
20	*A*	*B*	150	
				90
30	40	90	130	
				130
40	30	*C*	*D*	
				E
50	24	108	132	

Bill asks you to come to his rescue and provide the missing data in the five spaces identified as *A, B, C, D,* and *E*.

Use the following table to work Problems 28 and 29.
ProPainters hires students at $250 a week to paint houses. It leases equipment at $500 a week. The table sets out its total product schedule.

Labor (students)	Output (houses painted per week)
1	2
2	5
3	9
4	12
5	14
6	15

28. If ProPainters paints 12 houses a week, calculate its total cost, average total cost, and marginal cost. At what output is average total cost a minimum?

29. Explain why the gap between ProPainters' total cost and total variable cost is the same no matter how many houses are painted.

Long-Run Cost

Use the table in Problem 28 and the following information to work Problems 30 and 31.

If ProPainters doubles the number of students it hires and doubles the amount of equipment it leases, it experiences diseconomies of scale.

30. Explain how the *ATC* curve with one unit of equipment differs from that when ProPainters uses double the amount of equipment.

31. Explain what might be the source of the diseconomies of scale that ProPainters experiences.

Use the following information to work Problems 32 and 33.

The table shows the production function of Bonnie's Balloon Rides. Bonnie's pays $500 a day for each balloon it rents and $25 a day for each balloon operator it hires.

Labor (workers per day)	Output (rides per day)			
	Plant 1	Plant 2	Plant 3	Plant 4
10	6	10	13	15
20	10	15	18	20
30	13	18	22	24
40	15	20	24	26
50	16	21	25	27
Balloons (number)	1	2	3	4

32. Graph the *ATC* curves for Plant 1 and Plant 2. Explain why these *ATC* curves differ.

33. Graph the *ATC* curves for Plant 3 and Plant 4 Explain why these *ATC* curves differ.

34. a. On Bonnie's *LRAC* curve, what is the average cost of producing 18 rides and 15 rides a day?
    b. Explain how Bonnie's uses its long-run average cost curve to decide how many balloons to rent.

Use the following news clip to work Problems 35 and 36.

Gap Will Focus on Smaller Scale Stores

Gap has too many stores that are 12,500 square feet. The target store size is 6,000 square feet to 10,000 square feet, so Gap plans to combine previously separate concept stores. Some Gap body, adult, maternity, baby and kids stores will be combined in one store.

Source: CNN, June 10, 2008

35. Thinking of a Gap store as a production plant, explain why Gap is making a decision to reduce the size of its stores. Is Gap's decision a long-run decision or a short-run decision?

36. How might combining Gap's concept stores into one store help better take advantage of economies of scale?

Economics in the News

37. After you have studied *Reading Between the Lines* on pp. 266–267 answer the following questions.
    a. Sketch the *AFC*, *AVC*, *ATC*, and *MC* curves for electricity production using the six technologies shown in Fig. 1 on p. 267.
    b. Given the cost differences among the different methods of generating electricity, why do you think we use more than one method? If we could use only one method, which would it be?
    c. Explain how time-of-day pricing that succeeds in smoothing out fluctuations in production across the day lowers the average variable cost and marginal cost of generating electricity.
    d. Draw a graph to illustrate your answer to part (c).

38. **Starbucks Unit Brews Up Self-Serve Espresso Bars**
    Automated, self-serve espresso kiosks have appeared in many grocery stores. The machines, which grind their own beans, crank out lattes, and drip coffees take credit and debit cards, and cash. Coinstar buys the kiosks for just under $40,000 per unit, installs them, and provides maintenance. The self-serve kiosks remove the labor costs of having a barista. The kiosks use Starbucks' Seattle's Best Coffee and store personnel handle refills of coffee beans and milk.

    Source: MSNBC, June 1, 2008

    a. What is Coinstar's total fixed cost of operating one self-serve kiosk?
    b. What are Coinstar's variable costs of providing coffee at a self-serve kiosk?
    c. Assume that a coffee machine operated by a barista costs less than $40,000. Explain how the fixed costs, variable costs, and total costs of barista-served and self-served coffee differ.
    d. Sketch the marginal cost and average cost curves implied by your answer to part (c).

After studying this chapter, you will be able to:

◆ Define perfect competition

◆ Explain how a firm makes its output decision and why it sometimes shuts down temporarily and lays off its workers

◆ Explain how price and output are determined in a perfectly competitive market

◆ Explain why firms enter and leave a competitive market and the consequences of entry and exit

◆ Predict the effects of a change in demand and of a technological advance

◆ Explain why perfect competition is efficient

12

PERFECT COMPETITION

An Iowa corn farmer must make many decisions, but figuring out the price to charge for his corn is not one of them. Corn farmers must accept the price determined by supply and demand. The producers of most crops—among them wheat, rice, soybean, sugarbeet, and coffee—must also accept the prices that markets determine.

During the booming economic conditions of 2006 and 2007, crop prices and production soared. Then, following the global financial crisis of 2008 prices sagged, but for many crops production kept rising.

What are the forces that brought these changes in prices and production in the world's markets for farm products?

We're going to answer this question by studying competitive markets and building a model of a market in which competition is as fierce and extreme as possible. We call this situation *perfect* competition.

In *Reading Between the Lines* at the end of the chapter, we'll apply the model to the global market for corn and see how changes in demand and fortunate weather bring changes in prices and quantities produced in this key global agricultural market.

◆ What Is Perfect Competition?

The firms that you study in this chapter face the force of raw competition. We call this extreme form of competition perfect competition. **Perfect competition** is a market in which

- Many firms sell identical products to many buyers.
- There are no restrictions on entry into the market.
- Established firms have no advantage over new ones.
- Sellers and buyers are well informed about prices.

Farming, fishing, wood pulping and paper milling, the manufacture of paper cups and shopping bags, grocery and fresh flower retailing, photo finishing, lawn services, plumbing, painting, dry cleaning, and laundry services are all examples of highly competitive industries.

How Perfect Competition Arises

Perfect competition arises if the minimum efficient scale of a single producer is small relative to the market demand for the good or service. In this situation, there is room in the market for many firms. A firm's *minimum efficient scale* is the smallest output at which long-run average cost reaches its lowest level. (See Chapter 11, p. 265.)

In perfect competition, each firm produces a good that has no unique characteristics, so consumers don't care which firm's good they buy.

Price Takers

Firms in perfect competition are price takers. A **price taker** is a firm that cannot influence the market price because its production is an insignificant part of the total market.

Imagine that you are a wheat farmer in Kansas. You have a thousand acres planted—which sounds like a lot. But compared to the millions of acres in Colorado, Oklahoma, Texas, Nebraska, and the Dakotas, as well as the millions more in Canada, Argentina, Australia, and Ukraine, your thousand acres are a drop in the ocean. Nothing makes your wheat any better than any other farmer's, and all the buyers of wheat know the price at which they can do business.

If the market price of wheat is $4 a bushel, then that is the highest price you can get for your wheat. Ask for $4.10 and no one will buy from you. Offer it for $3.90 and you'll be sold out in a flash and have given away 10¢ a bushel. You take the market price.

Economic Profit and Revenue

A firm's goal is to maximize *economic profit*, which is equal to total revenue minus total cost. Total cost is the *opportunity cost* of production, which includes *normal profit*. (See Chapter 10, p. 228.)

A firm's **total revenue** equals the price of its output multiplied by the number of units of output sold (price × quantity). **Marginal revenue** is the change in total revenue that results from a one-unit increase in the quantity sold. Marginal revenue is calculated by dividing the change in total revenue by the change in the quantity sold.

Figure 12.1 illustrates these revenue concepts. In part (a), the market demand curve, D, and market supply curve, S, determine the market price. The market price is $25 a sweater. Campus Sweaters is just one of many producers of sweaters, so the best it can do is to sell its sweaters for $25 each.

Total Revenue Total revenue is equal to the price multiplied by the quantity sold. In the table in Fig. 12.1, if Campus Sweaters sells 9 sweaters, its total revenue is $225 (9 × $25).

Figure 12.1(b) shows the firm's total revenue curve (*TR*), which graphs the relationship between total revenue and the quantity sold. At point A on the *TR* curve, the firm sells 9 sweaters and has a total revenue of $225. Because each additional sweater sold brings in a constant amount—$25—the total revenue curve is an upward-sloping straight line.

Marginal Revenue Marginal revenue is the change in total revenue that results from a one-unit increase in quantity sold. In the table in Fig. 12.1, when the quantity sold increases from 8 to 9 sweaters, total revenue increases from $200 to $225, so marginal revenue is $25 a sweater.

Because the firm in perfect competition is a price taker, the change in total revenue that results from a one-unit increase in the quantity sold equals the market price. *In perfect competition, the firm's marginal revenue equals the market price.* Figure 12.1(c) shows the firm's marginal revenue curve (*MR*) as the horizontal line at the market price.

Demand for the Firm's Product The firm can sell any quantity it chooses at the market price. So the demand curve for the firm's product is a horizontal line at the market price, the same as the firm's marginal revenue curve.

FIGURE 12.1   Demand, Price, and Revenue in Perfect Competition

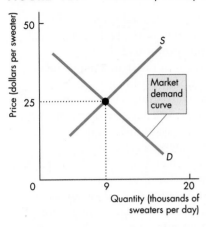

(a) Sweater market

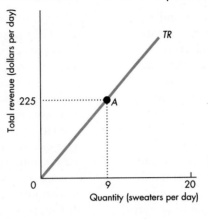

(b) Campus Sweaters' total revenue

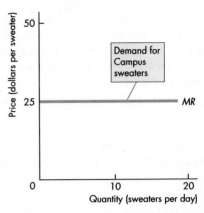

(c) Campus Sweaters' marginal revenue

Quantity sold (Q) (sweaters per day)	Price (P) (dollars per sweater)	Total revenue (TR = P × Q) (dollars)	Marginal revenue (MR = ΔTR/ΔQ) (dollars per additional sweater)
8	25	200	
			 25
9	25	225	
			 25
10	25	250	

In part (a), market demand and market supply determine the market price (and quantity). Part (b) shows the firm's total revenue curve (*TR*). Point *A* corresponds to the second row of the table—Campus Sweaters sells 9 sweaters at $25 a sweater, so total revenue is $225. Part (c) shows the firm's marginal revenue curve (*MR*). This curve is also the demand curve for the firm's sweaters. The demand for sweaters from Campus Sweaters is perfectly elastic at the market price of $25 a sweater.

 myeconlab animation

A horizontal demand curve illustrates a perfectly elastic demand, so the demand for the firm's product is perfectly elastic. A sweater from Campus Sweaters is a *perfect substitute* for a sweater from any other factory. But the *market* demand for sweaters is *not* perfectly elastic: Its elasticity depends on the substitutability of sweaters for other goods and services.

The Firm's Decisions

The goal of the competitive firm is to maximize economic profit, given the constraints it faces. To achieve its goal, a firm must decide

1. How to produce at minimum cost
2. What quantity to produce
3. Whether to enter or exit a market

You've already seen how a firm makes the first decision. It does so by operating with the plant that minimizes long-run average cost—by being on its long-run average cost curve. We'll now see how the firm makes the other two decisions. We start by looking at the firm's output decision.

REVIEW QUIZ

1 Why is a firm in perfect competition a price taker?
2 In perfect competition, what is the relationship between the demand for the firm's output and the market demand?
3 In perfect competition, why is a firm's marginal revenue curve also the demand curve for the firm's output?
4 What decisions must a firm make to maximize profit?

You can work these questions in Study Plan 12.1 and get instant feedback.   myeconlab

◆ The Firm's Output Decision

A firm's cost curves (total cost, average cost, and marginal cost) describe the relationship between its output and costs (see pp. 257–261). And a firm's revenue curves (total revenue and marginal revenue) describe the relationship between its output and revenue (p. 275). From the firm's cost curves and revenue curves, we can find the output that maximizes the firm's economic profit.

Figure 12.2 shows how to do this for Campus Sweaters. The table lists the firm's total revenue and total cost at different outputs, and part (a) of the figure shows the firm's total revenue curve, *TR*, and total cost curve, *TC*. These curves are graphs of numbers in the first three columns of the table.

Economic profit equals total revenue minus total cost. The fourth column of the table in Fig. 12.2 shows the economic profit made by Campus Sweaters, and part (b) of the figure graphs these numbers as its economic profit curve, *EP*.

Campus Sweaters maximizes its economic profit by producing 9 sweaters a day: Total revenue is $225, total cost is $183, and economic profit is $42. No other output rate achieves a larger profit.

At outputs of less than 4 sweaters and more than 12 sweaters a day, the Campus Sweaters would incur an economic loss. At either 4 or 12 sweaters a day, the Campus Sweaters would make zero economic profit, called a *break-even point*.

FIGURE 12.2   Total Revenue, Total Cost, and Economic Profit

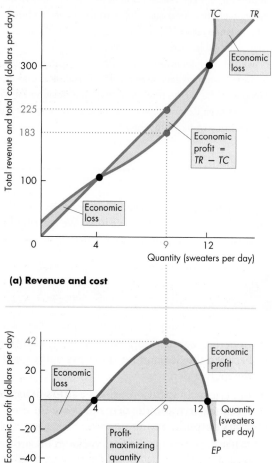

(a) Revenue and cost

(b) Economic profit and loss

Quantity (Q) (sweaters per day)	Total revenue (TR) (dollars)	Total cost (TC) (dollars)	Economic profit (TR – TC) (dollars)
0	0	22	–22
1	25	45	–20
2	50	66	–16
3	75	85	–10
4	100	100	0
5	125	114	11
6	150	126	24
7	175	141	34
8	200	160	40
9	**225**	**183**	**42**
10	250	210	40
11	275	245	30
12	300	300	0
13	325	360	–35

The table lists Campus Sweaters' total revenue, total cost, and economic profit. Part (a) graphs the total revenue and total cost curves and part (b) graphs economic profit.

Campus Sweaters makes maximum economic profit, $42 a day ($225 – $183), when it produces 9 sweaters a day. At outputs of 4 sweaters and 12 sweaters a day, Campus Sweaters makes zero economic profit—these are break-even points. At outputs less than 4 sweaters and greater than 12 sweaters a day, Campus Sweaters incurs an economic loss.

Marginal Analysis and the Supply Decision

Another way to find the profit-maximizing output is to use marginal analysis, which compares marginal revenue, *MR*, with marginal cost, *MC*. As output increases, the firm's marginal revenue is constant but its marginal cost eventually increases.

If marginal revenue exceeds marginal cost (*MR* > *MC*), then the revenue from selling one more unit exceeds the cost of producing it and an increase in output increases economic profit. If marginal revenue is less than marginal cost (*MR* < *MC*), then the revenue from selling one more unit is less than the cost of producing that unit and a *decrease* in output *increases* economic profit. If marginal revenue equals marginal cost (*MR* = *MC*), then the revenue from selling one more unit equals the cost incurred to produce that unit. Economic profit is maximized and either an increase or a decrease in output decreases economic profit.

Figure 12.3 illustrates these propositions. If Campus Sweaters increases its output from 8 sweaters to 9 sweaters a day, marginal revenue ($25) exceeds marginal cost ($23), so by producing the 9th sweater economic profit increases by $2 from $40 to $42 a day. The blue area in the figure shows the increase in economic profit when the firm increases production from 8 to 9 sweaters per day.

If Campus Sweaters increases its output from 9 sweaters to 10 sweaters a day, marginal revenue ($25) is less than marginal cost ($27), so by producing the 10th sweater, economic profit decreases. The last column of the table shows that economic profit decreases from $42 to $40 a day. The red area in the figure shows the economic loss that arises from increasing production from 9 to 10 sweaters a day.

Campus Sweaters maximizes economic profit by producing 9 sweaters a day, the quantity at which marginal revenue equals marginal cost.

A firm's profit-maximizing output is its quantity supplied at the market price. The quantity supplied at a price of $25 a sweater is 9 sweaters a day. If the price were higher than $25 a sweater, the firm would increase production. If the price were lower than $25 a sweater, the firm would decrease production. These profit-maximizing responses to different market prices are the foundation of the law of supply:

> Other things remaining the same, the higher the market price of a good, the greater is the quantity supplied of that good.

FIGURE 12.3   Profit-Maximizing Output

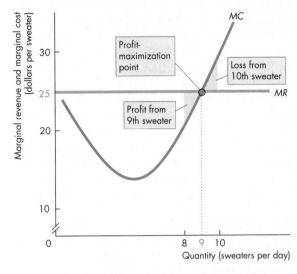

Quantity (Q) (sweaters per day)	Total revenue (TR) (dollars)	Marginal revenue (MR) (dollars per additional sweater)	Total cost (TC) (dollars)	Marginal cost (MC) (dollars per additional sweater)	Economic profit (TR − TC) (dollars)
7	175		141		34
		25		19	
8	200		160		40
		25		23	
9	225		183		42
		25		27	
10	250		210		40
		25		35	
11	275		245		30

The firm maximizes profit by producing the output at which marginal revenue equals marginal cost and marginal cost is increasing. The table and figure show that marginal cost equals marginal revenue and economic profit is maximized when Campus Sweaters produces 9 sweaters a day.

The table shows that if Campus Sweaters increases output from 8 to 9 sweaters, marginal cost is $23, which is less than the marginal revenue of $25. If output increases from 9 to 10 sweaters, marginal cost is $27, which exceeds the marginal revenue of $25. If marginal revenue exceeds marginal cost, an increase in output increases economic profit. If marginal revenue is less than marginal cost, an increase in output decreases economic profit. If marginal revenue equals marginal cost, economic profit is maximized.

Temporary Shutdown Decision

You've seen that a firm maximizes profit by producing the quantity at which marginal revenue (price) equals marginal cost. But suppose that at this quantity, price is less than average total cost. In this case, the firm incurs an economic loss. Maximum profit is a loss (a minimum loss). What does the firm do?

If the firm expects the loss to be permanent, it goes out of business. But if it expects the loss to be temporary, the firm must decide whether to shut down temporarily and produce no output, or to keep producing. To make this decision, the firm compares the loss from shutting down with the loss from producing and takes the action that minimizes its loss.

Loss Comparisons A firm's economic loss equals total fixed cost, TFC, plus total variable cost minus total revenue. Total variable cost equals average variable cost, AVC, multiplied by the quantity produced, Q, and total revenue equals price, P, multiplied by the quantity Q. So

$$\text{Economic loss} = TFC + (AVC - P) \times Q.$$

If the firm shuts down, it produces no output ($Q = 0$). The firm has no variable costs and no revenue but it must pay its fixed costs, so its economic loss equals total fixed cost.

If the firm produces, then in addition to its fixed costs, it incurs variable costs. But it also receives revenue. Its economic loss equals total fixed cost—the loss when shut down—plus total variable cost minus total revenue. If total variable cost exceeds total revenue, this loss exceeds total fixed cost and the firm shuts down. Equivalently, if average variable cost *exceeds* price, this loss exceeds total fixed cost and the firm *shuts down*.

The Shutdown Point A firm's **shutdown point** is the price and quantity at which it is indifferent between producing and shutting down. The shutdown point occurs at the price and the quantity at which average variable cost is a minimum. At the shutdown point, the firm is minimizing its loss and its loss equals total fixed cost. If the price falls below minimum average variable cost, the firm shuts down temporarily and continues to incur a loss equal to total fixed cost. At prices above minimum average variable cost but below average total cost, the firm produces the loss-minimizing output and incurs a loss, but a loss that is less than total fixed cost.

Figure 12.4 illustrates the firm's shutdown decision and the shutdown point that we've just described for Campus Sweaters.

The firm's average variable cost curve is AVC and the marginal cost curve is MC. Average variable cost has a minimum of $17 a sweater when output is 7 sweaters a day. The MC curve intersects the AVC curve at its minimum. (We explained this relationship between marginal cost and average cost in Chapter 11; see pp. 258–259.)

The figure shows the marginal revenue curve MR when the price is $17 a sweater, a price equal to minimum average variable cost.

Marginal revenue equals marginal cost at 7 sweaters a day, so this quantity maximizes economic profit (minimizes economic loss). The ATC curve shows that the firm's average total cost of producing 7 sweaters a day is $20.14 a sweater. The firm incurs a loss equal to $3.14 a sweater on 7 sweaters a day, so its loss is $22 a day, which equals total fixed cost.

FIGURE 12.4   The Shutdown Decision

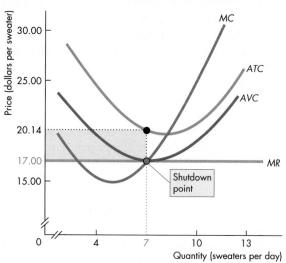

The shutdown point is at minimum average variable cost. At a price below minimum average variable cost, the firm shuts down and produces no output. At a price equal to minimum average variable cost, the firm is indifferent between shutting down and producing no output or producing the output at minimum average variable cost. Either way, the firm minimizes its economic loss and incurs a loss equal to total fixed cost.

The Firm's Supply Curve

A perfectly competitive firm's supply curve shows how its profit-maximizing output varies as the market price varies, other things remaining the same. The supply curve is derived from the firm's marginal cost curve and average variable cost curves. Figure 12.5 illustrates the derivation of the supply curve.

When the price *exceeds* minimum average variable cost (more than $17), the firm maximizes profit by producing the output at which marginal cost equals price. If the price rises, the firm increases its output—it moves up along its marginal cost curve.

When the price is *less than* minimum average variable cost (less than $17 a sweater), the firm maximizes profit by temporarily shutting down and producing no output. The firm produces zero output at all prices below minimum average variable cost.

When the price *equals* minimum average variable cost, the firm maximizes profit *either* by temporarily shutting down and producing no output *or* by producing the output at which average variable cost is a minimum—the shutdown point, *T*. The firm never produces a quantity between zero and the quantity at the shutdown point *T* (a quantity greater than zero and less than 7 sweaters a day).

The firm's supply curve in Fig. 12.5(b) runs along the *y*-axis from a price of zero to a price equal to minimum average variable cost, jumps to point *T*, and then, as the price rises above minimum average variable cost, follows the marginal cost curve.

FIGURE 12.5   A Firm's Supply Curve

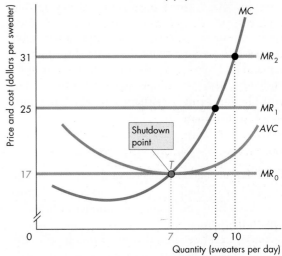

(a) Marginal cost and average variable cost

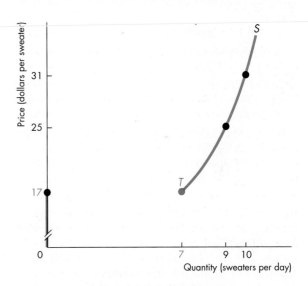

(b) Campus Sweaters' short-run supply curve

Part (a) shows the firm's profit-maximizing output at various market prices. At $25 a sweater, it produces 9 sweaters, and at $17 a sweater, it produces 7 sweaters. At all prices below $17 a sweater, Campus Sweaters produces nothing. Its shutdown point is *T*. Part (b) shows the firm's supply curve—the quantity of sweaters it produces at each price. Its supply curve is made up of the marginal cost curve at all prices above minimum average variable cost and the vertical axis at all prices below minimum average variable cost.

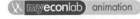 animation

◤ REVIEW QUIZ

1   Why does a firm in perfect competition produce the quantity at which marginal cost equals price?

2   What is the lowest price at which a firm produces an output? Explain why.

3   What is the relationship between a firm's supply curve, its marginal cost curve, and its average variable cost curve?

You can work these questions in Study Plan 12.2 and get instant feedback.

So far, we've studied a single firm in isolation. We've seen that the firm's profit-maximizing decision depends on the market price, which it takes as given. How is the market price determined? Let's find out.

Output, Price, and Profit in the Short Run

To determine the price and quantity in a perfectly competitive market, we need to know how market demand and market supply interact. We start by studying a perfectly competitive market in the short run. The short run is a situation in which the number of firms is fixed.

Market Supply in the Short Run

The **short-run market supply curve** shows the quantity supplied by all the firms in the market at each price when each firm's plant and the number of firms remain the same.

You've seen how an individual firm's supply curve is determined. The market supply curve is derived from the individual supply curves. The quantity supplied by the market at a given price is the sum of the quantities supplied by all the firms in the market at that price.

Figure 12.6 shows the supply curve for the competitive sweater market. In this example, the market consists of 1,000 firms exactly like Campus Sweaters. At each price, the quantity supplied by the market is 1,000 times the quantity supplied by a single firm.

The table in Fig. 12.6 shows the firm's and the market's supply schedules and how the market supply curve is constructed. At prices below $17 a sweater, every firm in the market shuts down; the quantity supplied by the market is zero. At $17 a sweater, each firm is indifferent between shutting down and producing nothing or operating and producing 7 sweaters a day. Some firms will shut down, and others will supply 7 sweaters a day. The quantity supplied by each firm is *either* 0 or 7 sweaters, and the quantity supplied by the market is *between* 0 (all firms shut down) and 7,000 (all firms produce 7 sweaters a day each).

The market supply curve is a graph of the market supply schedules and the points on the supply curve *A* through *D* represent the rows of the table.

To construct the market supply curve, we sum the quantities supplied by all the firms at each price. Each of the 1,000 firms in the market has a supply schedule like Campus Sweaters. At prices below $17 a sweater, the market supply curve runs along the *y*-axis. At $17 a sweater, the market supply curve is horizontal—supply is perfectly elastic. As the price

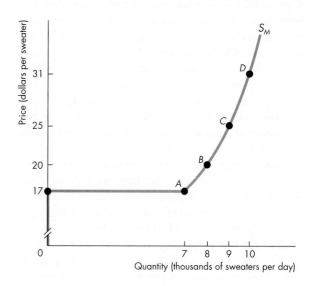

FIGURE 12.6   Short-Run Market Supply Curve

	Price (dollars per sweater)	Quantity supplied by Campus Sweaters (sweaters per day)	Quantity supplied by market (sweaters per day)
A	17	0 or 7	0 to 7,000
B	20	8	8,000
C	25	9	9,000
D	31	10	10,000

The market supply schedule is the sum of the supply schedules of all the individual firms. A market that consists of 1,000 identical firms has a supply schedule similar to that of one firm, but the quantity supplied by the market is 1,000 times as large as that of the one firm (see the table). The market supply curve is S_M. Points *A*, *B*, *C*, and *D* correspond to the rows of the table. At the shutdown price of $17 a sweater, each firm produces either 0 or 7 sweaters a day and the quantity supplied by the market is between 0 and 7,000 sweaters a day. The market supply is perfectly elastic at the shutdown price.

myeconlab animation

rises above $17 a sweater, each firm increases its quantity supplied and the quantity supplied by the market increases by 1,000 times that of one firm.

Short-Run Equilibrium

Market demand and short-run market supply determine the market price and market output. Figure 12.7(a) shows a short-run equilibrium. The short-run supply curve, S, is the same as S_M in Fig. 12.6. If the market demand curve is D_1, the market price is $20 a sweater. Each firm takes this price as given and produces its profit-maximizing output, which is 8 sweaters a day. Because the market has 1,000 identical firms, the market output is 8,000 sweaters a day.

A Change in Demand

Changes in demand bring changes to short-run market equilibrium. Figure 12.7 shows these changes.

If demand increases and the demand curve shifts rightward to D_2, the market price rises to $25 a sweater. At this price, each firm maximizes profit by increasing its output to 9 sweaters a day. The market output increases to 9,000 sweaters a day.

If demand decreases and the demand curve shifts leftward to D_3, the market price falls to $17. At this price, each firm maximizes profit by decreasing its output. If each firm produces 7 sweaters a day, the market output decreases to 7,000 sweaters a day.

If the demand curve shifts farther leftward than D_3, the market price remains at $17 a sweater because the market supply curve is horizontal at that price. Some firms continue to produce 7 sweaters a day, and others temporarily shut down. Firms are indifferent between these two activities, and whichever they choose, they incur an economic loss equal to total fixed cost. The number of firms continuing to produce is just enough to satisfy the market demand at a price of $17 a sweater.

Profits and Losses in the Short Run

In short-run equilibrium, although the firm produces the profit-maximizing output, it does not necessarily end up making an economic profit. It might do so, but it might alternatively break even or incur an economic loss. Economic profit (or loss) per sweater is price, P, minus average total cost, ATC. So economic profit (or loss) is $(P - ATC) \times Q$. If price

---

FIGURE 12.7   Short-Run Equilibrium

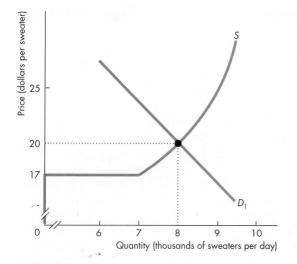

(a) Equilibrium

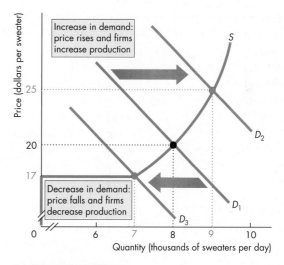

(b) Change in equilibrium

In part (a), the market supply curve is S and the market demand curve is D_1. The market price is $20 a sweater. At this price, each firm produces 8 sweaters a day and the market produces 8,000 sweaters a day.

In part (b), if the market demand increases to D_2, the price rises to $25 a sweater. Each firm produces 9 sweaters a day and market output is 9,000 sweaters. If market demand decreases to D_3, the price falls to $17 a sweater and each firm decreases its output. If each firm produces 7 sweaters a day, the market output is 7,000 sweaters a day.

equals average total cost, a firm breaks even—the entrepreneur makes normal profit. If price exceeds average total cost, a firm makes an economic profit. If price is less than average total cost, a firm incurs an economic loss. Figure 12.8 shows these three possible short-run profit outcomes for Campus Sweaters. These outcomes correspond to the three different levels of market demand that we've just examined.

Three Possible Short-Run Outcomes

Figure 12.8(a) corresponds to the situation in Fig. 12.7(a) where the market demand is D_1. The equilibrium price of a sweater is $20 and the firm produces 8 sweaters a day. Average total cost is $20 a sweater. Price equals average total cost (ATC), so the firm breaks even (makes zero economic profit).

Figure 12.8(b) corresponds to the situation in Fig. 12.7(b) where the market demand is D_2. The equilibrium price of a sweater is $25 and the firm produces 9 sweaters a day. Here, price exceeds average total cost, so the firm makes an economic profit. Its economic profit is $42 a day, which equals $4.67 per sweater ($25.00 – $20.33) multiplied by 9, the

profit-maximizing number of sweaters produced. The blue rectangle shows this economic profit. The height of that rectangle is profit per sweater, $4.67, and the length is the quantity of sweaters produced, 9 a day. So the area of the rectangle is economic profit of $42 a day.

Figure 12.8(c) corresponds to the situation in Fig. 12.7(b) where the market demand is D_3. The equilibrium price of a sweater is $17. Here, the price is less than average total cost, so the firm incurs an economic loss. Price and marginal revenue are $17 a sweater, and the profit-maximizing (in this case, loss-minimizing) output is 7 sweaters a day. Total revenue is $119 a day (7 × $17). Average total cost is $20.14 a sweater, so the economic loss is $3.14 per sweater ($20.14 – $17.00). This loss per sweater multiplied by the number of sweaters is $22. The red rectangle shows this economic loss. The height of that rectangle is economic loss per sweater, $3.14, and the length is the quantity of sweaters produced, 7 a day. So the area of the rectangle is the firm's economic loss of $22 a day. If the price dips below $17 a sweater, the firm temporarily shuts down and incurs an economic loss equal to total fixed cost.

FIGURE 12.8   Three Short-Run Outcomes for the Firm

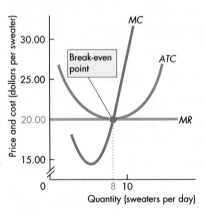

(a) Break even

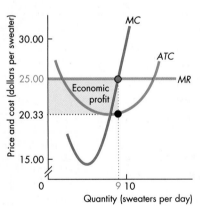

(b) Economic profit

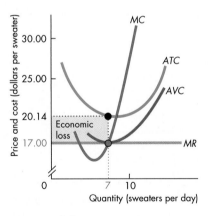

(c) Economic loss

In the short run, the firm might break even (make zero economic profit), make an economic profit, or incur an economic loss. In part (a), the price equals minimum average total cost. At the profit-maximizing output, the firm breaks even and makes zero economic profit. In part (b), the market price is $25 a sweater. At the profit-maximizing output,

the price exceeds average total cost and the firm makes an economic profit equal to the area of the blue rectangle. In part (c), the market price is $17 a sweater. At the profit-maximizing output, the price is below minimum average total cost and the firm incurs an economic loss equal to the area of the red rectangle.

Economics in Action
Production Cutback and Temporary Shutdown

The high price of gasoline and anxiety about unemployment and future incomes brought a decrease in the demand for luxury goods including high-end motorcycles such as Harley-Davidsons.

Harley-Davidson's profit-maximizing response to the decrease in demand was to cut production and lay off workers. Some of the production cuts and lay-offs were temporary and some were permanent.

Harley-Davidson's bike production plant in York County, Pennsylvania, was temporarily shut down in the summer of 2008 because total revenue was insufficient to cover total variable cost.

The firm also permanently cut its workforce by 300 people. This permanent cut was like that at Campus Sweaters when the market demand for sweaters decreased from D_1 to D_3 in Fig. 12.7(b).

◆ REVIEW QUIZ

1 How do we derive the short-run market supply curve in perfect competition?
2 In perfect competition, when market demand increases, explain how the price of the good and the output and profit of each firm changes in the short run.
3 In perfect competition, when market demand decreases, explain how the price of the good and the output and profit of each firm changes in the short run.

You can work these questions in Study Plan 12.3 and get instant feedback.

◆ Output, Price, and Profit in the Long Run

In short-run equilibrium, a firm might make an economic profit, incur an economic loss, or break even. Although each of these three situations is a short-run equilibrium, only one of them is a long-run equilibrium. The reason is that in the long run, firms can enter or exit the market.

Entry and Exit

Entry occurs in a market when new firms come into the market and the number of firms increases. Exit occurs when existing firms leave a market and the number of firms decreases.

Firms respond to economic profit and economic loss by either entering or exiting a market. New firms enter a market in which existing firms are making an economic profit. Firms exit a market in which they are incurring an economic loss. Temporary economic profit and temporary economic loss don't trigger entry and exit. It's the prospect of persistent economic profit or loss that triggers entry and exit.

Entry and exit change the market supply, which influences the market price, the quantity produced by each firm, and its economic profit (or loss).

If firms enter a market, supply increases and the market supply curve shifts rightward. The increase in supply lowers the market price and eventually eliminates economic profit. When economic profit reaches zero, entry stops.

If firms exit a market, supply decreases and the market supply curve shifts leftward. The market price rises and economic loss decreases. Eventually, economic loss is eliminated and exit stops.

To summarize:

■ New firms enter a market in which existing firms are making an economic profit.
■ As new firms enter a market, the market price falls and the economic profit of each firm decreases.
■ Firms exit a market in which they are incurring an economic loss.
■ As firms leave a market, the market price rises and the economic loss incurred by the remaining firms decreases.
■ Entry and exit stop when firms make zero economic profit.

A Closer Look at Entry

The sweater market has 800 firms with cost curves like those in Fig. 12.9(a). The market demand curve is D, the market supply curve is S_1, and the price is $25 a sweater in Fig. 12.9(b). Each firm produces 9 sweaters a day and makes an economic profit.

This economic profit is a signal for new firms to enter the market. As entry takes place, supply increases and the market supply curve shifts rightward toward S^*. As supply increases with no change in demand, the market price gradually falls from $25 to $20 a sweater. At this lower price, each firm makes zero economic profit and entry stops.

Entry results in an increase in market output, but each firm's output *decreases*. Because the price falls, each firm moves down its supply curve and produces less. Because the number of firms increases, the market produces more.

A Closer Look at Exit

The sweater market has 1,200 firms with cost curves like those in Fig. 12.9(a). The market demand curve is D, the market supply curve is S_2, and the price is $17 a sweater in Fig. 12.9(b). Each firm produces 7 sweaters a day and incurs an economic loss.

This economic loss is a signal for firms to exit the market. As exit takes place, supply decreases and the market supply curve shifts leftward toward S^*. As supply decreases with no change in demand, the market price gradually rises from $17 to $20 a sweater. At this higher price, losses are eliminated, each firm makes zero economic profit, and exit stops.

Exit results in a decrease in market output, but each firm's output *increases*. Because the price rises, each firm moves up its supply curve and produces more. Because the number of firms decreases, the market produces less.

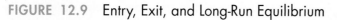

FIGURE 12.9   Entry, Exit, and Long-Run Equilibrium

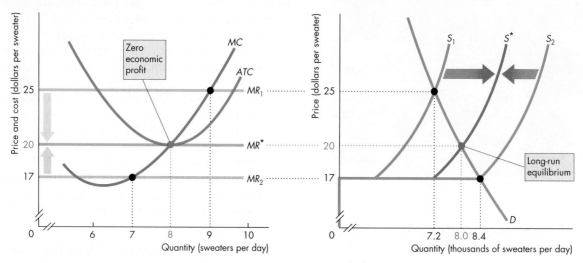

(a) Campus Sweaters

(b) The sweater market

Each firm has cost curves like those of Campus Sweaters in part (a). The market demand curve is D in part (b).

When the market supply curve in part (b) is S_1, the price is $25 a sweater. In part (a), each firm produces 9 sweaters a day and makes an economic profit. Profit triggers the entry of new firms and as new firms enter, the market supply curve shifts rightward, from S_1 toward S^*. The price falls from $25 to $20 a sweater, and the quantity produced increases from 7,200 to 8,000 sweaters. Each firm's output decreases to 8

sweaters a day and economic profit falls to zero.

When the market supply curve is S_2, the price is $17 a sweater. In part (a), each firm produces 7 sweaters a day and incurs an economic loss. Loss triggers exit and as firms exit, the market supply curve shifts leftward, from S_2 toward S^*. The price rises from $17 to $20 a sweater, and the quantity produced decreases from 8,400 to 8,000 sweaters. Each firm's output increases from 7 to 8 sweaters a day and economic profit rises to zero.

myeconlab   animation

Economics in Action
Entry and Exit

An example of entry and falling prices occurred during the 1980s and 1990s in the personal computer market. When IBM introduced its first PC in 1981, IBM had little competition. The price was $7,000 (about $16,850 in today's money) and IBM made a large economic profit selling the new machine.

Observing IBM's huge success, new firms such as Gateway, NEC, Dell, and a host of others entered the market with machines that were technologically identical to IBM's. In fact, they were so similar that they came to be called "clones." The massive wave of entry into the personal computer market increased the market supply and lowered the price. The economic profit for all firms decreased.

Today, a $400 computer is vastly more powerful than its 1981 ancestor that cost 42 times as much.

The same PC market that saw entry during the 1980s and 1990s has seen some exit more recently. In 2001, IBM, the firm that first launched the PC, announced that it was exiting the market. The intense competition from Gateway, NEC, Dell, and others that entered the market following IBM's lead has lowered the price and eliminated the economic profit. So IBM now concentrates on servers and other parts of the computer market.

IBM exited the PC market because it was incurring economic losses. Its exit decreased market supply and made it possible for the remaining firms in the market to make zero economic profit.

International Harvester, a manufacturer of farm equipment, provides another example of exit. For decades, people associated the name "International Harvester" with tractors, combines, and other farm machines. But International Harvester wasn't the only maker of farm equipment. The market became intensely competitive, and the firm began to incur economic losses. Now the firm has a new name, Navistar International, and it doesn't make tractors any more. After years of economic losses and shrinking revenues, it got out of the farm-machine business in 1985 and started to make trucks.

International Harvester exited because it was incurring an economic loss. Its exit decreased supply and made it possible for the remaining firms in the market to break even.

Long-Run Equilibrium

You've now seen how economic profit induces entry, which in turn eliminates the profit. You've also seen how economic loss induces exit, which in turn eliminates the loss.

When economic profit and economic loss have been eliminated and entry and exit have stopped, a competitive market is in *long-run equilibrium.*

You've seen how a competitive market adjusts toward its long-run equilibrium. But a competitive market is rarely *in* a state of long-run equilibrium. Instead, it is constantly and restlessly evolving toward long-run equilibrium. The reason is that the market is constantly bombarded with events that change the constraints that firms face.

Markets are constantly adjusting to keep up with changes in tastes, which change demand, and changes in technology, which change costs.

In the next sections, we're going to see how a competitive market reacts to changing tastes and technology and how it guides resources to their highest-valued use.

 REVIEW QUIZ

1 What triggers entry in a competitive market? Describe the process that ends further entry.

2 What triggers exit in a competitive market? Describe the process that ends further exit.

You can work these questions in Study Plan 12.4 and get instant feedback.

◆ Changing Tastes and Advancing Technology

Increased awareness of the health hazards of smoking has decreased the demand for tobacco products. The development of inexpensive automobile and air transportation during the 1990s decreased the demand for long-distance trains and buses. Solid-state electronics has decreased the demand for TV and radio repair. The development of good-quality inexpensive clothing has decreased the demand for sewing machines. What happens in a competitive market when there is a permanent decrease in the demand for its product?

Microwave food preparation has increased the demand for paper, glass, and plastic cooking utensils and for plastic wrap. The Internet has increased the demand for personal computers and the widespread use of computers has increased the demand for high-speed connections and music downloads. What happens in a competitive market when the demand for its output increases?

Advances in technology are constantly lowering the costs of production. New biotechnologies have dramatically lowered the costs of producing many food and pharmaceutical products. New electronic technologies have lowered the cost of producing just about every good and service. What happens in a competitive market for a good when technological change lowers its production costs?

Let's use the theory of perfect competition to answer these questions.

A Permanent Change in Demand

Figure 12.10(a) shows a competitive market that initially is in long-run equilibrium. The demand curve is D_0, the supply curve is S_0, the market price is P_0, and market output is Q_0. Figure 12.10(b) shows a single firm in this initial long-run equilibrium. The firm produces q_0 and makes zero economic profit.

Now suppose that demand decreases and the demand curve shifts leftward to D_1, as shown in Fig. 12.10(a). The market price falls to P_1, and the quantity supplied by the market decreases from Q_0 to Q_1 as the market moves down along its short-run supply curve S_0. Figure 12.10(b) shows the situation facing a firm. The market price is now below the firm's minimum average total cost, so the firm incurs an eco-

nomic loss. But to minimize its loss, the firm adjusts its output to keep marginal cost equal to price. At a price of P_1, each firm produces an output of q_1.

The market is now in short-run equilibrium but not long-run equilibrium. It is in short-run equilibrium because each firm is maximizing profit; it is not in long-run equilibrium because each firm is incurring an economic loss—its average total cost exceeds the price.

The economic loss is a signal for some firms to exit the market. As they do so, short-run market supply decreases and the market supply curve gradually shifts leftward. As market supply decreases, the price rises. At each higher price, a firm's profit-maximizing output is greater, so the firms remaining in the market increase their output as the price rises. Each firm moves up along its marginal cost or supply curve in Fig. 12.10(b). That is, as some firms exit the market, market output decreases but the output of the firms that remain in the market increases.

Eventually, enough firms have exited the market for the market supply curve to have shifted to S_1 in Fig. 12.10(a). The market price has returned to its original level, P_0. At this price, the firms remaining in the market produce q_0, the same quantity that they produced before the decrease in demand. Because firms are now making zero economic profit, no firm has an incentive to enter or exit the market. The market supply curve remains at S_1, and market output is Q_2. The market is again in long-run equilibrium.

The difference between the initial long-run equilibrium and the final long-run equilibrium is the number of firms in the market. A permanent decrease in demand has decreased the number of firms. Each firm remaining in the market produces the same output in the new long-run equilibrium as it did initially and makes zero economic profit. In the process of moving from the initial equilibrium to the new one, firms incur economic losses.

We've just worked out how a competitive market responds to a permanent *decrease* in demand. A permanent increase in demand triggers a similar response, except in the opposite direction. The increase in demand brings a higher price, economic profit, and entry. Entry increases market supply and eventually lowers the price to its original level and economic profit to zero.

The demand for Internet service increased permanently during the 1990s and huge profit opportunities arose in this market. The result was a massive rate

FIGURE 12.10   A Decrease in Demand

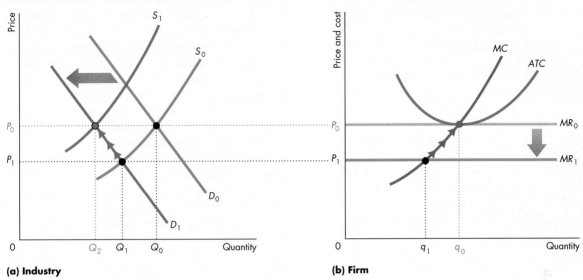

(a) Industry

(b) Firm

A market starts out in long-run competitive equilibrium. Part (a) shows the market demand curve D_0, the market supply curve S_0, the market price P_0, and the equilibrium quantity Q_0. Each firm sells its output at the price P_0, so its marginal revenue curve is MR_0 in part (b). Each firm produces q_0 and makes zero economic profit.

Market demand decreases permanently from D_0 to D_1 in part (a) and the market price falls to P_1. Each firm decreases its output to q_1 in part (b), and the market output

decreases to Q_1 in part (a). Firms now incur economic losses. Some firms exit the market, and as they do so, the market supply curve gradually shifts leftward, from S_0 toward S_1. This shift gradually raises the market price from P_1 back to P_0. While the price is below P_0, firms incur economic losses and some firms exit the market. Once the price has returned to P_0, each firm makes zero economic profit and has no incentive to exit. Each firm produces q_0, and the market output is Q_2.

 animation

of entry of Internet service providers. The process of competition and change in the Internet service market is similar to what we have just studied but with an increase in demand rather than a decrease in demand.

We've now studied the effects of a permanent change in demand for a good. In doing so, we began and ended in a long-run equilibrium and examined the process that takes a market from one equilibrium to another. It is this process, not the equilibrium points, that describes the real world.

One feature of the predictions that we have just generated seems odd: In the long run, regardless of whether demand increases or decreases, the market price returns to its original level. Is this outcome inevitable? In fact, it is not. It is possible for the equilibrium market price in the long run to remain the same, rise, or fall.

External Economies and Diseconomies

The change in the long-run equilibrium price depends on external economies and external diseconomies. **External economies** are factors beyond the control of an individual firm that lower the firm's costs as the *market* output increases. **External diseconomies** are factors outside the control of a firm that raise the firm's costs as the *market* output increases. With no external economies or external diseconomies, a firm's costs remain constant as the market output changes.

Figure 12.11 illustrates these three cases and introduces a new supply concept: the long-run market supply curve.

A **long-run market supply curve** shows how the quantity supplied in a market varies as the market price varies after all the possible adjustments have been made, including changes in each firm's plant and the number of firms in the market.

Figure 12.11(a) shows the case we have just studied—no external economies or diseconomies. The long-run market supply curve (LS_A) is perfectly elastic. In this case, a permanent increase in demand from D_0 to D_1 has no effect on the price in the long run. The increase in demand brings a temporary increase in price to P_S and in the short run the quantity increases from Q_0 to Q_S. Entry increases short-run supply from S_0 to S_1, which lowers the price from P_S back to P_0 and increases the quantity to Q_1.

Figure 12.11(b) shows the case of external diseconomies. The long-run market supply curve (LS_B) slopes upward. A permanent increase in demand from D_0 to D_1 increases the price in both the short run and the long run. The increase in demand brings a temporary increase in price to P_S and in the short run the quantity increases from Q_0 to Q_S. Entry increases short-run supply from S_0 to S_2, which lowers the price from P_S to P_2 and increases the quantity to Q_2.

One source of external diseconomies is congestion. The airline market provides a good example. With bigger airline market output, congestion at both airports and in the air increases, resulting in longer delays and extra waiting time for passengers and airplanes. These external diseconomies mean that as the output of air transportation services increases (in the absence of technological advances), average cost increases. As a result, the long-run market supply curve is upward sloping. A permanent increase in demand brings an increase in quantity and a rise in the price. (Markets with external diseconomies might nonetheless have a falling price because technological advances shift the long-run supply curve downward.)

Figure 12.11(c) shows the case of external economies. The long-run market supply curve (LS_C) slopes downward. A permanent increase in demand from D_0 to D_1 increases the price in the short run and lowers it in the long run. Again, the increase in demand brings a temporary increase in price to P_S and in the short run the quantity increases from Q_0 to Q_S. Entry increases short-run supply from S_0 to S_3, which lowers the price to P_3 and increases the quantity to Q_3.

An example of external economies is the growth of specialist support services for a market as it expands.

FIGURE 12.11   Long-Run Changes in Price and Quantity

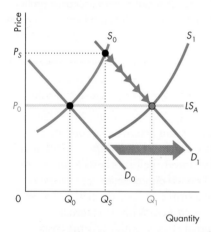

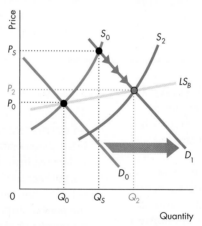

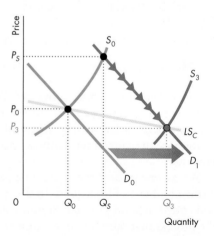

(a) Constant-cost industry   **(b) Increasing-cost industry**   **(c) Decreasing-cost industry**

Three possible changes in price and quantity occur in the long run. When demand increases from D_0 to D_1, entry occurs and the market supply curve shifts rightward from S_0 to S_1. In part (a), the long-run market supply curve, LS_A, is horizontal. The quantity increases from Q_0 to Q_1, and the price remains constant at P_0.

In part (b), the long-run market supply curve is LS_B; the price rises to P_2, and the quantity increases to Q_2. This case occurs in industries with external diseconomies. In part (c), the long-run market supply curve is LS_C; the price falls to P_3, and the quantity increases to Q_3. This case occurs in a market with external economies.

As farm output increased in the nineteenth and early twentieth centuries, the services available to farmers expanded. New firms specialized in the development and marketing of farm machinery and fertilizers. As a result, average farm costs decreased. Farms enjoyed the benefits of external economies. As a consequence, as the demand for farm products increased, the output increased but the price fell.

Over the long term, the prices of many goods and services have fallen, not because of external economies but because of technological change. Let's now study this influence on a competitive market.

Technological Change

Industries are constantly discovering lower-cost techniques of production. Most cost-saving production techniques cannot be implemented, however, without investing in new plant and equipment. As a consequence, it takes time for a technological advance to spread through a market. Some firms whose plants are on the verge of being replaced will be quick to adopt the new technology, while other firms whose plants have recently been replaced will continue to operate with an old technology until they can no longer cover their average variable cost. Once average variable cost cannot be covered, a firm will scrap even a relatively new plant (embodying an old technology) in favor of a plant with a new technology.

New technology allows firms to produce at a lower cost. As a result, as firms adopt a new technology, their cost curves shift downward. With lower costs, firms are willing to supply a given quantity at a lower price or, equivalently, they are willing to supply a larger quantity at a given price. In other words, market supply increases, and the market supply curve shifts rightward. With a given demand, the quantity produced increases and the price falls.

Two forces are at work in a market undergoing technological change. Firms that adopt the new technology make an economic profit, so there is entry by new-technology firms. Firms that stick with the old technology incur economic losses. They either exit the market or switch to the new technology.

As old-technology firms disappear and new-technology firms enter, the price falls and the quantity produced increases. Eventually, the market arrives at a long-run equilibrium in which all the firms use the new technology and make a zero economic profit. Because in the long run competition eliminates economic profit, technological change brings only temporary gains to producers. But the lower prices and better products that technological advances bring are permanent gains for consumers.

The process that we've just described is one in which some firms experience economic profits and others experience economic losses. It is a period of dynamic change in a market. Some firms do well, and others do badly. Often, the process has a geographical dimension—the expanding new-technology firms bring prosperity to what was once the boondocks, and traditional industrial regions decline. Sometimes, the new-technology firms are in a foreign country, while the old-technology firms are in the domestic economy. The information revolution of the 1990s produced many examples of changes like these. Commercial banking, which was traditionally concentrated in New York, San Francisco, and other large cities now flourishes in Charlotte, North Carolina, which has become the nation's number three commercial banking city. Television shows and movies, traditionally made in Los Angeles and New York, are now made in large numbers in Orlando.

Technological advances are not confined to the information and entertainment industries. Even food production is undergoing a major technological change because of genetic engineering.

REVIEW QUIZ

1   Describe the course of events in a competitive market following a permanent decrease in demand. What happens to output, price, and economic profit in the short run and in the long run?

2   Describe the course of events in a competitive market following a permanent increase in demand. What happens to output, price, and economic profit in the short run and in the long run?

3   Describe the course of events in a competitive market following the adoption of a new technology. What happens to output, price, and economic profit in the short run and in the long run?

You can work these questions in Study Plan 12.5 and get instant feedback.

We've seen how a competitive market operates in the short run and the long run, but is a competitive market efficient?

◆ Competition and Efficiency

A competitive market can achieve an efficient use of resources. You first studied efficiency in Chapter 2. Then in Chapter 5, using only the concepts of demand, supply, consumer surplus, and producer surplus, you saw how a competitive market achieves efficiency. Now that you have learned what lies behind the demand and supply curves of a competitive market, you can gain a deeper understanding of the efficiency of a competitive market.

Efficient Use of Resources

Recall that resource use is efficient when we produce the goods and services that people value most highly (see Chapter 2, pp. 33–35, and Chapter 5, p. 108). If someone can become better off without anyone else becoming worse off, resources are *not* being used efficiently. For example, suppose we produce a computer that no one wants and no one will ever use and, at the same time, some people are clamoring for more video games. If we produce fewer computers and reallocate the unused resources to produce more video games, some people will become better off and no one will be worse off. So the initial resource allocation was inefficient.

In the more technical language that you have learned, resource use is efficient when marginal social benefit equals marginal social cost. In the computer and video games example, the marginal social benefit of a video game exceeds its marginal social cost; the marginal social cost of a computer exceeds its marginal social benefit. So by producing fewer computers and more video games, we move resources toward a higher-valued use.

Choices, Equilibrium, and Efficiency

We can use what you have learned about the decisions made by consumers and competitive firms and market equilibrium to describe an efficient use of resources.

Choices Consumers allocate their budgets to get the most value possible out of them. We derive a consumer's demand curve by finding how the best budget allocation changes as the price of a good changes. So consumers get the most value out of their resources at all points along their demand curves. If the people who consume a good or service are the only ones who benefit from it, then the market demand curve measures the benefit to the entire society and is the marginal social benefit curve.

Competitive firms produce the quantity that maximizes profit. We derive the firm's supply curve by finding the profit-maximizing quantity at each price. So firms get the most value out of their resources at all points along their supply curves. If the firms that produce a good or service bear all the costs of producing it, then the market supply curve measures the marginal cost to the entire society and the market supply curve is the marginal social cost curve.

Equilibrium and Efficiency Resources are used efficiently when marginal social benefit equals marginal social cost. Competitive equilibrium achieves this efficient outcome because, with no externalities, price equals marginal social benefit for consumers, and price equals marginal social cost for producers.

The gains from trade are the sum of consumer surplus and producer surplus. The gains from trade for consumers are measured by *consumer surplus*, which is the area below the demand curve and above the price paid. (See Chapter 5, p. 109.) The gains from trade for producers are measured by *producer surplus*, which is the area above the supply curve and below the price received. (See Chapter 5, p. 111.) The total gains from trade equals total surplus —the sum of consumer surplus and producer surplus. When the market for a good or service is in equilibrium, the gains from trade are maximized.

Illustrating an Efficient Allocation Figure 12.12 illustrates the efficiency of perfect competition in long-run equilibrium. Part (a) shows the individual firm, and part (b) shows the market. The equilibrium market price is P^*. At that price, each firm makes zero economic profit and each firm has the plant that enables it to produce at the lowest possible average total cost. Consumers are as well off as possible because the good cannot be produced at a lower cost and the price equals that least possible cost.

In part (b), consumers get the most out of their resources at all points on the market demand curve, $D = MSB$. Consumer surplus is the green area. Producers get the most out of their resources at all points on the market supply curve, $S = MSC$. Producer surplus is the blue area. Resources are used efficiently at the quantity Q^* and price P^*. At this point, marginal social benefit equals marginal social

FIGURE 12.12   Efficiency of Perfect Competition

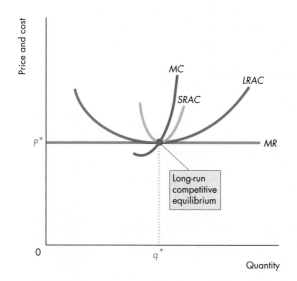

(a) A single firm

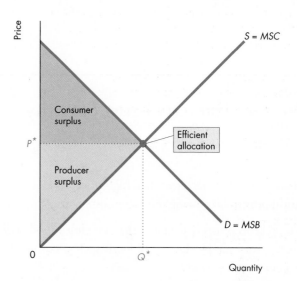

(b) A market

Demand, *D*, and supply, *S*, determine the equilibrium price, *P**. A firm in perfect competition in part (a) produces *q** at the lowest possible long-run average total cost. In part (b), consumers have made the best available choices and are

on the market demand curve, and firms are producing at least cost and are on the market supply curve. With no externalities, marginal social benefit equals marginal social cost, so resources are used efficiently at the quantity *Q**.

cost, and total surplus (the sum of producer surplus and consumer surplus) is maximized.

When firms in perfect competition are away from long-run equilibrium, either entry or exit is taking place and the market is moving toward the situation depicted in Fig. 12.12. But the market is still efficient. As long as marginal social benefit (on the market demand curve) equals marginal social cost (on the market supply curve), the market is efficient. But it is only in long-run equilibrium that consumers pay the lowest possible price.

◆ You've now completed your study of perfect competition. *Reading Between the Lines* on pp. 292–293 gives you an opportunity to use what you have learned to understand events in the global market for corn during the past few years.

Although many markets approximate the model of perfect competition, many do not. In Chapter 13, we study markets at the opposite extreme of market power: monopoly. Then we'll study markets that lie between perfect competition and monopoly. In

◆ REVIEW QUIZ

1 State the conditions that must be met for resources to be allocated efficiently.
2 Describe the choices that consumers make and explain why consumers are efficient on the market demand curve.
3 Describe the choices that producers make and explain why producers are efficient on the market supply curve.
4 Explain why resources are used efficiently in a competitive market.

You can work these questions in Study Plan 12.6 and get instant feedback.   myeconlab

Chapter 14 we study monopolistic competition and in Chapter 15 we study oligopoly. When you have completed this study, you'll have a tool kit that will enable you to understand the variety of real-world markets.

Perfect Competition in Corn

Bumper Harvests Bring Stability

http://www.ft.com

June 1, 2010

There is no better fertilizer than high prices, the old farming adage goes. Trends in agriculture appear to be proving this resoundingly true.

The spike in prices that caused the first global food crisis in 30 years in 2007–08 has led to large increases in production of foods such as corn and wheat. Farmers have responded to higher prices. ...

The U.S. Department of Agriculture said ..."Higher prices, and thus expanded acreage, in combination with favorable weather, have helped production expand sharply."

Global corn production will hit 835m metric tons in the 2010–11 season, its highest ever level, the USDA forecasts. ... That is likely to lead to a period of relatively stable prices. ...

While prices for the main food and feed grain crops—corn, wheat, and soybeans—are likely to remain steady and low in the next year or so, that does not mean a repeat of the food crisis is impossible. ...

One argument against that view holds that technological gains in response to the crisis have boosted productivity, making farmers more able to deal with increasing consumption.

Some crops, such as corn, saw record yields in the 2009–10 season and the USDA is predicting high yields for next year as well.

But analysts ascribe the gains in productivity more to fortunate weather conditions than a revolution in farming technology. ...

ESSENCE OF THE STORY

- In 2010–11, global corn production will reach its highest ever level at 835 million metric tons.

- High prices in 2007–08 led to large increases in the acreage of corn and wheat.

- Favorable weather also helped to increase production of these crops.

- Prices for corn, wheat, and soybeans will likely remain low next year, but a future price rise might occur.

- A revolution in farming technology would increase production without raising costs and prices.

- The current gain in productivity is most likely the result of fortunate weather and likely to be temporary.

ECONOMIC ANALYSIS

- The global market for corn is competitive and the model of perfect competition shows how that market works.

- During 2006 through 2008, increases in demand brought a rising price and an increase in the quantity of corn supplied.

- In 2009 and 2010, good weather conditions brought an increase in the supply of corn and the quantity of corn increased further but its price fell.

- Figure 1 illustrates these events in the market for corn and Fig. 2 their effects on an individual farm.

- From 2006 through 2008, the supply curve of corn was S_0 in Fig. 1. The demand for corn increased and by 2008, the demand curve was D. The price of corn in 2008 was $310 per metric ton and 800 million metric tons were produced.

- In 2008, the farm faced a marginal revenue curve MR_0 and had average total cost curve ATC_0 and marginal cost curve MC_0 in Fig. 2.

- The farm maximized profit by producing 8,000 metric tons and (we will assume) made zero economic profit.

- In 2009 and 2010, good weather conditions increased the supply of corn. By 2010–11, the supply curve had shifted rightward to S_1. The price fell to $230 per metric ton and production increased to 835 million metric tons.

- Back on the farm in Fig. 2, the lower price decreased marginal revenue and the MR curve shifted downward to MR_1.

- But the fortunate weather increased farm productivity and lowered the cost of producing corn. The average total cost curve shifted downward to ATC_1 and the marginal cost curve shifted downward to MC_1.

- The combination of the lower price and lower costs might leave the farm with an economic profit. In Fig. 2 we're assuming that the farm again made zero economic profit.

- If farms did make a positive (or negative) economic profit, entry (or exit) would eventually return them to a zero economic profit position like that shown in Fig. 2.

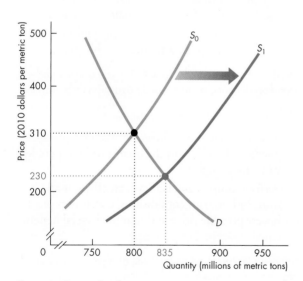

Figure 1 The market for corn

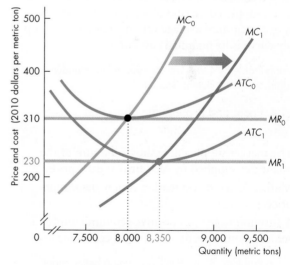

Figure 2 A corn farmer

SUMMARY

Key Points

What Is Perfect Competition? (pp. 274–275)

- In perfect competition, many firms sell identical products to many buyers; there are no restrictions on entry; sellers and buyers are well informed about prices.
- A perfectly competitive firm is a price taker.
- A perfectly competitive firm's marginal revenue always equals the market price.

Working Problems 1 to 3 will give you a better understanding of perfect competition.

The Firm's Output Decision (pp. 276–279)

- The firm produces the output at which marginal revenue (price) equals marginal cost.
- In short-run equilibrium, a firm can make an economic profit, incur an economic loss, or break even.
- If price is less than minimum average variable cost, the firm temporarily shuts down.
- At prices below minimum average variable cost, a firm's supply curve runs along the y-axis; at prices above minimum average variable cost, a firm's supply curve is its marginal cost curve.

Working Problems 4 to 7 will give you a better understanding of a firm's output decision.

Output, Price, and Profit in the Short Run (pp. 280–283)

- The market supply curve shows the sum of the quantities supplied by each firm at each price.
- Market demand and market supply determine price.
- A firm might make a positive economic profit, a zero economic profit, or incur an economic loss.

Working Problems 8 and 9 will give you a better understanding of output, price, and profit in the short run.

Output, Price, and Profit in the Long Run (pp. 283–285)

- Economic profit induces entry and economic loss induces exit.
- Entry increases supply and lowers price and profit. Exit decreases supply and raises price and profit.
- In long-run equilibrium, economic profit is zero. There is no entry or exit.

Working Problems 10 and 11 will give you a better understanding of output, price, and profit in the long run.

Changing Tastes and Advancing Technology (pp. 286–289)

- A permanent decrease in demand leads to a smaller market output and a smaller number of firms. A permanent increase in demand leads to a larger market output and a larger number of firms.
- The long-run effect of a change in demand on price depends on whether there are external economies (the price falls) or external diseconomies (the price rises) or neither (the price remains constant).
- New technologies increase supply and in the long run lower the price and increase the quantity.

Working Problems 12 to 16 will give you a better understanding of changing tastes and advancing technologies.

Competition and Efficiency (pp. 290–291)

- Resources are used efficiently when we produce goods and services in the quantities that people value most highly.
- Perfect competition achieves an efficient allocation. In long-run equilibrium, consumers pay the lowest possible price and marginal social benefit equals marginal social cost.

Working Problems 17 and 18 will give you a better understanding of competition and efficiency.

Key Terms

External diseconomies, 287
External economies, 287
Long-run market supply curve, 287
Marginal revenue, 274
Perfect competition, 274
Price taker, 274
Short-run market supply curve, 280
Shutdown point, 278
Total revenue, 274

STUDY PLAN PROBLEMS AND APPLICATIONS

 You can work Problems 1 to 18 in MyEconLab Chapter 12 Study Plan and get instant feedback.

What Is Perfect Competition? (Study Plan 12.1)

Use the following information to work Problems 1 to 3.

Lin's makes fortune cookies that are identical to those made by dozens of other firms, and there is free entry in the fortune cookie market. Buyers and sellers are well informed about prices.

1. In what type of market does Lin's operate? What determines the price of fortune cookies and what determines Lin's marginal revenue from fortune cookies?

2. a. If fortune cookies sell for $10 a box and Lin's offers its cookies for sale at $10.50 a box, how many boxes does it sell?

   b. If fortune cookies sell for $10 a box and Lin's offers its cookies for sale at $9.50 a box, how many boxes does it sell?

3. What is the elasticity of demand for Lin's fortune cookies and how does it differ from the elasticity of the market demand for fortune cookies?

The Firm's Output Decision (Study Plan 12.2)

Use the following table to work Problems 4 to 6. Pat's Pizza Kitchen is a price taker. Its costs are

Output (pizzas per hour)	Total cost (dollars per hour)
0	10
1	21
2	30
3	41
4	54
5	69

4. Calculate Pat's profit-maximizing output and economic profit if the market price is
   (i) $14 a pizza.
   (ii) $12 a pizza.
   (iii) $10 a pizza.

5. What is Pat's shutdown point and what is Pat's economic profit if it shuts down temporarily?

6. Derive Pat's supply curve.

7. The market for paper is perfectly competitive and there are 1,000 firms that produce paper. The table sets out the market demand schedule for paper.

Price (dollars per box)	Quantity demanded (thousands of boxes per week)
3.65	500
5.20	450
6.80	400
8.40	350
10.00	300
11.60	250
13.20	200

Each producer of paper has the following costs when it uses its least-cost plant:

Output (boxes per week)	Marginal cost (dollars per additional box)	Average variable cost	Average total cost
		(dollars per box)	
200	6.40	7.80	12.80
250	7.00	7.00	11.00
300	7.65	7.10	10.43
350	8.40	7.20	10.06
400	10.00	7.50	10.00
450	12.40	8.00	10.22
500	20.70	9.00	11.00

   a. What is the market price of paper?
   b. What is the market's output?
   c. What is the output produced by each firm?
   d. What is the economic profit made or economic loss incurred by each firm?

Output, Price, and Profit in the Short Run
(Study Plan 12.3)

8. In Problem 7, as more and more computer users read documents online rather than print them, the market demand for paper decreases and in the short run the demand schedule becomes

Price (dollars per box)	Quantity demanded (thousands of boxes per week)
2.95	500
4.13	450
5.30	400
6.48	350
7.65	300
8.83	250
10.00	200
11.18	150

If each firm producing paper has the costs set out in Problem 7, what is the market price and the economic profit or loss of each firm in the short run?

9. **Fuel Prices Could Squeeze Cheap Flights**

Airlines are having difficulty keeping prices low, especially as fuel prices keep rising. Airlines have raised fares to make up for the fuel costs. American Airlines increased its fuel surcharge by $20 a roundtrip, which Delta, United Airlines, and Continental matched.

Source: *CNN*, June 12, 2008

a. Explain how an increase in fuel prices might cause an airline to change its output (number of flights) in the short run.

b. Draw a graph to show the increase in fuel prices on an airline's output in the short run.

c. Explain why an airline might incur an economic loss in the short run as fuel prices rise.

Output, Price, and Profit in the Long Run

(Study Plan 12.4)

10. The pizza market is perfectly competitive, and all pizza producers have the same costs as Pat's Pizza Kitchen in Problem 4.
    a. At what price will some firms exit the pizza market in the long run?
    b. At what price will firms enter the pizza market in the long run?

11. In Problem 7, in the long run,
    a. Do firms have an incentive to enter or exit the paper market?
    b. If firms do enter or exit the market, explain how the economic profit or loss of the remaining paper producers will change.
    c. What is the long-run equilibrium market price and the quantity of paper produced? What is the number of firms in the market?

Changing Tastes and Advancing Technology

(Study Plan 12.5)

12. If in the long run, the market demand for paper remains the same as in Problem 8,
    a. What is the long-run equilibrium price of paper, the market output, and the economic profit or loss of each firm?
    b. Does this market experience external economies, external diseconomies, or constant cost? Illustrate by drawing the long-run supply curve.

Use the following news clip to work Problems 13 and 14.

Coors Brewing Expanding Plant

Coors Brewing Co. of Golden will expand its Virginia packaging plant at a cost of $24 million. The addition will accommodate a new production line, which will bottle beer faster. Coors Brewing employs 470 people at its Virginia plant. The expanded packaging line will add another eight jobs.

Source: *Denver Business Journal*, January 6, 2006

13. a. How will Coors' expansion change its marginal cost curve and short-run supply curve?
    b. What does this expansion decision imply about the point on Coors' *LRAC* curve at which the firm was before the expansion?

14. a. If other breweries follow the lead of Coors, what will happen to the market price of beer?
    b. How will the adjustment that you have described in part (a) influence the economic profit of Coors and other beer producers?

15. Explain and illustrate graphically how the growing world population is influencing the world market for wheat and a representative individual wheat farmer.

16. Explain and illustrate graphically how the diaper service market has been affected by the decrease in the North American birth rate and the development of disposable diapers.

Competition and Efficiency (Study Plan 12.6)

17. In a perfectly competitive market in long-run equilibrium, can consumer surplus be increased? Can producer surplus be increased? Can a consumer become better off by making a substitution away from this market?

18. **Never Pay Retail Again**

Not only has scouring the Web for the best possible price become standard protocol before buying a big-ticket item, but more consumers are employing creative strategies for scoring hot deals. Comparison shopping, haggling and swapping discount codes are all becoming mainstream marks of savvy shoppers. Online shoppers can check a comparison service like Price Grabber before making a purchase.

Source: *CNN*, May 30, 2008

a. Explain the effect of the Internet on the degree of competition in the market.

b. Explain how the Internet influences market efficiency.

ADDITIONAL PROBLEMS AND APPLICATIONS

myeconlab You can work these problems in MyEconLab if assigned by your instructor.

What Is Perfect Competition?

Use the following news clip to work Problems 19 to 21.

Money in the Tank

Two gas stations stand on opposite sides of the road: Rutter's Farm Store and Sheetz gas station. Rutter's doesn't even have to look across the highway to know when Sheetz changes its price for a gallon of gas. When Sheetz raises the price, Rutter's pumps are busy. When Sheetz lowers prices, there's not a car in sight. Both gas stations survive but each has no control over the price.

Source: *The Mining Journal*, May 24, 2008

19. In what type of market do these gas stations operate? What determines the price of gasoline and the marginal revenue from gasoline?

20. Describe the elasticity of demand that each of these gas stations faces.

21. Why does each of these gas stations have so little control over the price of the gasoline it sells?

The Firm's Output Decision

22. The figure shows the costs of Quick Copy, one of many copy shops near campus.

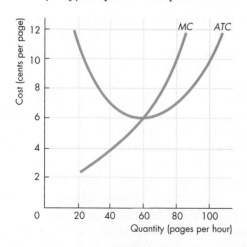

If the market price of copying is 10¢ a page, calculate Quick Copy's

a. Profit-maximizing output.

b. Economic profit.

23. The market for smoothies is perfectly competitive. The following table sets out the market demand schedule.

Price (dollars per smoothie)	Quantity demanded (smoothies per hour)
1.90	1,000
2.00	950
2.20	800
2.91	700
4.25	550
5.25	400
5.50	300

Each of the 100 producers of smoothies has the following costs when it uses its least-cost plant:

Output (smoothies per hour)	Marginal cost (dollars per additional smoothie)	Average variable cost	Average total cost
		(dollars per smoothie)	
3	2.50	4.00	7.33
4	2.20	3.53	6.03
5	1.90	3.24	5.24
6	2.00	3.00	4.67
7	2.91	2.91	4.34
8	4.25	3.00	4.25
9	8.00	3.33	4.44

a. What is the market price of a smoothie?

b. What is the market quantity of smoothies?

c. How many smoothies does each firm sell?

d. What is the economic profit made or economic loss incurred by each firm?

24. **Cadillac Plant Shuts Down Temporarily, Future Uncertain**

Delta Truss in Cadillac [Michigan] is shutting down and temporarily discontinuing truss production. Workers fear this temporary shutdown will become permanent, but the firm announced that it anticipates that production will resume when the spring business begins.

Source: *9&10 News*, February 18, 2008

a. Explain how the shutdown decision will affect Delta Truss' *TFC*, *TVC*, and *TC*.

b. Under what conditions would this shutdown decision maximize Delta Truss' economic profit (or minimize its loss)?

c. Under what conditions will Delta Truss start producing again?

Output, Price, and Profit in the Short Run

25. **Big Drops in Prices for Crops Make It Tough Down on the Farm**

    Grain prices have fallen roughly 50 percent from earlier this year. With better-than-expected crop yields, world grain production this year will rise 5 percent from 2007 to a record high.

    Source: *USA Today*, October 23, 2008

    Why did grain prices fall in 2008? Draw a graph to show that short-run effect on an individual farmer's economic profit.

Output, Price, and Profit in the Long Run

26. In Problem 23, do firms enter or exit the market in the long run? What is the market price and the equilibrium quantity in the long run?

27. In Problem 24, under what conditions will Delta Truss exit the market?

28. **Exxon Mobil Selling All Its Retail Gas Stations**

    Exxon Mobil is not alone among Big Oil exiting the retail gas business, a market where profits have gotten tougher as crude oil prices have risen. Gas station owners say they're struggling to turn a profit because while wholesale gasoline prices have risen sharply, they've been unable to raise pump prices fast enough to keep pace.

    Source: *Houston Chronicle*, June 12, 2008

    a. Is Exxon Mobil making a shutdown or exit decision in the retail gasoline market?

    b. Under what conditions will this decision maximize Exxon Mobil's economic profit?

    c. How might Exxon Mobil's decision affect the economic profit of other gasoline retailers?

Changing Tastes and Advancing Technology

29. **Another DVD Format, but It's Cheaper**

    New Medium Enterprises claims the quality of its new system, HD VMD, is equal to Blu-ray's but it costs only $199—cheaper than the $300 cost of a Blu-ray player. Chairman of the Blu-ray Disc Association says New Medium will fail because it believes that Blu-ray technology will always be more expensive. But mass production will cut the cost of a Blu-ray player to $90.

    Source: *The New York Times*, March 10, 2008

    a. Explain how technological change in Blu-ray production might support the prediction of lower prices in the long run. Illustrate your explanation with a graph.

    b. Even if Blu-ray prices do drop to $90 in the long run, why might the HD VMD still end up being less expensive at that time?

Competition and Efficiency

30. In a perfectly competitive market, each firm maximizes its profit by choosing only the quantity to produce. Regardless of whether the firm makes an economic profit or incurs an economic loss, the short-run equilibrium is efficient. Is the statement true? Explain why or why not.

Economics in the News

31. After you have studied *Reading Between the Lines* on pp. 292–293 answer the following questions.

    a. What are the features of the global market for corn that make it competitive?

    b. If the increase in production during 2009 and 2010 was due entirely to good weather, what will happen to the price and quantity produced when normal weather returns?

    c. What will happen to an individual farmer's marginal revenue, marginal cost, average total cost, and economic profit if the events in part (b) occur?

    d. If the increase in production during 2009 and 2010 was due mainly to a revolution in farm technology, what will happen to the price and quantity produced when normal weather returns?

32. **Cell Phone Sales Hit 1 Billion Mark**

    More than 1.15 billion mobile phones were sold worldwide in 2007, a 16 percent increase in a year. Emerging markets, especially China and India, provided much of the growth as many people bought their first phone. Carolina Milanesi, research director for mobile devices at Gartner, reported that in mature markets, such as Japan and Western Europe, consumers' appetite for feature-laden phones was met with new models packed with TV tuners, global positioning satellite functions, touch screens, and cameras.

    Source: CNET News, February 27, 2008

    a. Explain the effects of the increase in global demand for cell phones on the market for cell phones and on an individual cell-phone producer in the short run.

    b. Draw a graph to illustrate your explanation in part (a).

    c. Explain the long-run effects of the increase in global demand for cell phones on the market for cell phones.

    d. What factors will determine whether the price of cell phones will rise, fall, or stay the same in the new long-run equilibrium?

After studying this chapter, you will be able to:

◆ Explain how monopoly arises and distinguish between single-price monopoly and price-discriminating monopoly

◆ Explain how a single-price monopoly determines its output and price

◆ Compare the performance and efficiency of single-price monopoly and competition

◆ Explain how price discrimination increases profit

◆ Explain how monopoly regulation influences output, price, economic profit, and efficiency

Microsoft, Google, and eBay are dominant players in the markets they serve. Because most PCs use Windows, programmers write most applications for this operating system, which attracts more users. Because most Web searchers use Google, most advertisers use it too, which attracts more searchers. Because most online auction buyers use eBay, most online sellers do too, which attracts more buyers. Each of these firms benefits from a phenomenon called a network externality, which makes it hard for other firms to break into their markets.

Microsoft, Google, and eBay are obviously not like firms in perfect competition. How does their behavior compare with perfectly competitive firms? Do they charge prices that are too high and that damage the interests of consumers? What benefits do they bring?

In this chapter, we study markets in which the firm can influence the price. We also compare the performance of the firm in such a market with that in a competitive market and examine whether monopoly is as efficient as competition. In *Reading Between the Lines* at the end of the chapter, we'll look at a claim by Consumer Watchdog, a California consumer protection organization, that Google abuses its market power and should be scrutinized by the Justice Department using the antitrust laws.

◆ Monopoly and How It Arises

A **monopoly** is a market with a single firm that produces a good or service for which no close substitute exists and that is protected by a barrier that prevents other firms from selling that good or service.

How Monopoly Arises

Monopoly arises for two key reasons:

- No close substitute
- Barrier to entry

No Close Substitute If a good has a close substitute, even though only one firm produces it, that firm effectively faces competition from the producers of the substitute. A monopoly sells a good or service that has no good substitute. Tap water and bottled water are close substitutes for drinking, but tap water has no effective substitute for showering or washing a car and a local public utility that supplies tap water is a monopoly.

Barrier to Entry A constraint that protects a firm from potential competitors is called a **barrier to entry**. The three types of barrier to entry are

- Natural
- Ownership
- Legal

Natural Barrier to Entry A natural barrier to entry creates a **natural monopoly**: a market in which economies of scale enable one firm to supply the entire market at the lowest possible cost. The firms that deliver gas, water, and electricity to our homes are examples of natural monopoly.

In Fig. 13.1 the market demand curve for electric power is *D*, and the long-run average cost curve is *LRAC*. Economies of scale prevail over the entire length of the *LRAC* curve.

One firm can produce 4 million kilowatt-hours at 5 cents a kilowatt-hour. At this price, the quantity demanded is 4 million kilowatt-hours. So if the price was 5 cents, one firm could supply the entire market.

If two firms shared the market equally, it would cost each of them 10 cents a kilowatt-hour to produce a total of 4 million kilowatt-hours.

In conditions like those shown in Fig. 13.1, one firm can supply the entire market at a lower cost than

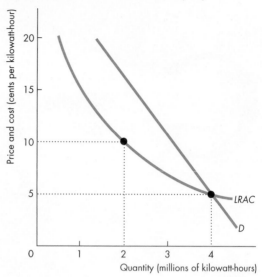

FIGURE 13.1   Natural Monopoly

The market demand curve for electric power is *D*, and the long-run average cost curve is *LRAC*. Economies of scale exist over the entire *LRAC* curve. One firm can distribute 4 million kilowatt-hours at a cost of 5 cents a kilowatt-hour. This same total output costs 10 cents a kilowatt-hour with two firms. One firm can meet the market demand at a lower cost than two or more firms can. The market is a natural monopoly.

myeconlab   animation

two or more firms can. The market is a natural monopoly.

Ownership Barrier to Entry An ownership barrier to entry occurs if one firm owns a significant portion of a key resource. An example of this type of monopoly occurred during the last century when De Beers controlled up to 90 percent of the world's supply of diamonds. (Today, its share is only 65 percent.)

Legal Barrier to Entry A legal barrier to entry creates a **legal monopoly**: a market in which competition and entry are restricted by the granting of a public franchise, government license, patent, or copyright.

A *public franchise* is an exclusive right granted to a firm to supply a good or service. An example is the U.S. Postal Service, which has the exclusive right to carry first-class mail. A *government license* controls entry into particular occupations, professions, and industries. Examples of this type of barrier to entry occur in medicine, law, dentistry, schoolteaching, architecture, and many other professional services. Licensing does not always create a monopoly, but it does restrict competition.

A *patent* is an exclusive right granted to the inventor of a product or service. A *copyright* is an exclusive right granted to the author or composer of a literary, musical, dramatic, or artistic work. Patents and copyrights are valid for a limited time period that varies from country to country. In the United States, a patent is valid for 20 years. Patents encourage the *invention* of new products and production methods. They also stimulate *innovation*—the use of new inventions—by encouraging inventors to publicize their discoveries and offer them for use under license. Patents have stimulated innovations in areas as diverse as soybean seeds, pharmaceuticals, memory chips, and video games.

Economics in Action
Information-Age Monopolies

Information-age technologies have created four big natural monopolies. These firms have large plant costs but almost zero marginal cost, so they experience economies of scale.

Microsoft has captured 90 percent of the personal computer operating system market with Windows and 73 percent of the Web browser market with Internet Explorer. eBay has captured 85 percent of the consumer-to-consumer Internet auction market and Google has 78 percent of the search engine market.

New technologies also destroy monopoly. FedEx, UPS, the fax machine, and e-mail have weakened the monopoly of the U.S. Postal Service; and the satellite dish has weakened the monopoly of cable television companies.

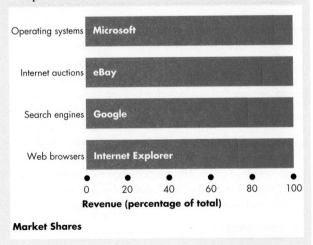

Market Shares

Monopoly Price-Setting Strategies

A major difference between monopoly and competition is that a monopoly sets its own price. In doing so, the monopoly faces a market constraint: To sell a larger quantity, the monopoly must set a lower price. There are two monopoly situations that create two pricing strategies:

- Single price
- Price discrimination

Single Price A **single-price monopoly** is a firm that must sell each unit of its output for the same price to all its customers. De Beers sells diamonds (of a given size and quality) for the same price to all its customers. If it tried to sell at a low price to some customers and at a higher price to others, only the low-price customers would buy from De Beers. Others would buy from De Beers' low-price customers. De Beers is a *single-price* monopoly.

Price Discrimination When a firm practices **price discrimination**, it sells different units of a good or service for different prices. Many firms price discriminate. Microsoft sells its Windows and Office software at different prices to different buyers. Computer manufacturers who install the software on new machines, students and teachers, governments, and businesses all pay different prices. Pizza producers offer a second pizza for a lower price than the first one. These are examples of *price discrimination*.

When a firm price discriminates, it looks as though it is doing its customers a favor. In fact, it is charging the highest possible price for each unit sold and making the largest possible profit.

 REVIEW QUIZ

1 How does monopoly arise?
2 How does a natural monopoly differ from a legal monopoly?
3 Distinguish between a price-discriminating monopoly and a single-price monopoly.

You can work these questions in Study Plan 13.1 and get instant feedback.

We start with a single-price monopoly and see how it makes its decisions about the quantity to produce and the price to charge to maximize its profit.

A Single-Price Monopoly's Output and Price Decision

To understand how a single-price monopoly makes its output and price decision, we must first study the link between price and marginal revenue.

Price and Marginal Revenue

Because in a monopoly there is only one firm, the demand curve facing the firm is the market demand curve. Let's look at Bobbie's Barbershop, the sole supplier of haircuts in Cairo, Nebraska. The table in Fig. 13.2 shows the market demand schedule. At a price of $20, Bobbie sells no haircuts. The lower the price, the more haircuts per hour she can sell. For example, at $12, consumers demand 4 haircuts per hour (row *E*).

Total revenue (*TR*) is the price (*P*) multiplied by the quantity sold (*Q*). For example, in row *D*, Bobbie sells 3 haircuts at $14 each, so total revenue is $42. *Marginal revenue* (*MR*) is the change in total revenue (ΔTR) resulting from a one-unit increase in the quantity sold. For example, if the price falls from $16 (row *C*) to $14 (row *D*), the quantity sold increases from 2 to 3 haircuts. Total revenue increases from $32 to $42, so the change in total revenue is $10. Because the quantity sold increases by 1 haircut, marginal revenue equals the change in total revenue and is $10. Marginal revenue is placed between the two rows to emphasize that marginal revenue relates to the *change* in the quantity sold.

Figure 13.2 shows the market demand curve and marginal revenue curve (*MR*) and also illustrates the calculation we've just made. Notice that at each level of output, marginal revenue is less than price—the marginal revenue curve lies below the demand curve. Why is marginal revenue *less* than price? It is because when the price is lowered to sell one more unit, two opposing forces affect total revenue. The lower price results in a revenue loss, and the increased quantity sold results in a revenue gain. For example, at a price of $16, Bobbie sells 2 haircuts (point *C*). If she lowers the price to $14, she sells 3 haircuts and has a revenue gain of $14 on the third haircut. But she now receives only $14 on the first two haircuts—$2 less than before. As a result, she loses $4 of revenue on the first 2 haircuts. To calculate marginal revenue, she must deduct this amount from the revenue gain of $14. So her marginal revenue is $10, which is less than the price.

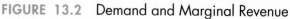

FIGURE 13.2   Demand and Marginal Revenue

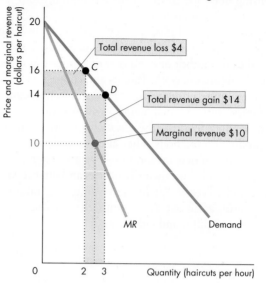

	Price (P) (dollars per haircut)	Quantity demanded (Q) (haircuts per hour)	Total revenue (TR = P × Q) (dollars)	Marginal revenue (MR = ΔTR/ΔQ) (dollars per haircut)
A	20	0	0	
				18
B	18	1	18	
				14
C	16	2	32	
				10
D	14	3	42	
				6
E	12	4	48	
				2
F	10	5	50	

The table shows the demand schedule. Total revenue (*TR*) is price multiplied by quantity sold. For example, in row *C*, the price is $16 a haircut, Bobbie sells 2 haircuts, and total revenue is $32. Marginal revenue (*MR*) is the change in total revenue that results from a one-unit increase in the quantity sold. For example, when the price falls from $16 to $14 a haircut, the quantity sold increases from 2 to 3, an increase of 1 haircut, and total revenue increases by $10. Marginal revenue is $10. The demand curve and the marginal revenue curve, *MR*, are based on the numbers in the table and illustrate the calculation of marginal revenue when the price falls from $16 to $14 a haircut.

myeconlab animation

Marginal Revenue and Elasticity

A single-price monopoly's marginal revenue is related to the *elasticity of demand* for its good. The demand for a good can be *elastic* (the elasticity is greater than 1), *inelastic* (the elasticity is less than 1), or *unit elastic* (the elasticity is equal to 1). Demand is *elastic* if a 1 percent fall in the price brings a greater than 1 percent increase in the quantity demanded. Demand is *inelastic* if a 1 percent fall in the price brings a less than 1 percent increase in the quantity demanded. Demand is *unit elastic* if a 1 percent fall in the price brings a 1 percent increase in the quantity demanded. (See Chapter 4, pp. 84–86.)

If demand is elastic, a fall in the price brings an increase in total revenue—the revenue gain from the increase in quantity sold outweighs the revenue loss from the lower price—and marginal revenue is *positive*. If demand is inelastic, a fall in the price brings a decrease in total revenue—the revenue gain from the increase in quantity sold is outweighed by the revenue loss from the lower price—and marginal revenue is *negative*. If demand is unit elastic, total revenue does not change—the revenue gain from the increase in the quantity sold offsets the revenue loss from the lower price—and marginal revenue is *zero*. (See Chapter 4, p. 88.)

Figure 13.3 illustrates the relationship between marginal revenue, total revenue, and elasticity. As the price gradually falls from $20 to $10 a haircut, the quantity demanded increases from 0 to 5 haircuts an hour. Over this output range, marginal revenue is positive in part (a), total revenue increases in part (b), and the demand for haircuts is elastic. As the price falls from $10 to $0 a haircut, the quantity of haircuts demanded increases from 5 to 10 an hour. Over this output range, marginal revenue is negative in part (a), total revenue decreases in part (b), and the demand for haircuts is inelastic. When the price is $10 a haircut, marginal revenue is zero in part (a), total revenue is at a maximum in part (b), and the demand for haircuts is unit elastic.

In Monopoly, Demand Is Always Elastic The relationship between marginal revenue and elasticity of demand that you've just discovered implies that a profit-maximizing monopoly never produces an output in the inelastic range of the market demand curve. If it did so, it could charge a higher price, produce a smaller quantity, and increase its profit. Let's now look at a monopoly's price and output decision.

FIGURE 13.3 Marginal Revenue and Elasticity

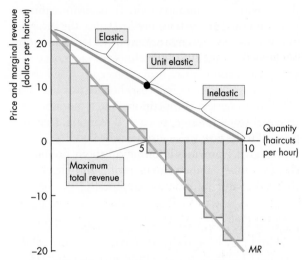

(a) Demand and marginal revenue curves

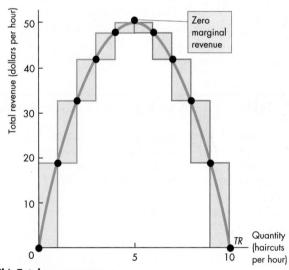

(b) Total revenue curve

In part (a), the demand curve is *D* and the marginal revenue curve is *MR*. In part (b), the total revenue curve is *TR*. Over the range 0 to 5 haircuts an hour, a price cut increases total revenue, so marginal revenue is positive—as shown by the blue bars. Demand is elastic. Over the range 5 to 10 haircuts an hour, a price cut decreases total revenue, so marginal revenue is negative—as shown by the red bars. Demand is inelastic. At 5 haircuts an hour, total revenue is maximized and marginal revenue is zero. Demand is unit elastic.

myeconlab animation

Price and Output Decision

A monopoly sets its price and output at the levels that maximize economic profit. To determine this price and output level, we need to study the behavior of both cost and revenue as output varies. A monopoly faces the same types of technology and cost constraints as a competitive firm, so its costs (total cost, average cost, and marginal cost) behave just like those of a firm in perfect competition. And a monopoly's revenues (total revenue, price, and marginal revenue) behave in the way we've just described.

Table 13.1 provides information about Bobbie's costs, revenues, and economic profit, and Fig. 13.4 shows the same information graphically.

Maximizing Economic Profit You can see in Table 13.1 and Fig. 13.4(a) that total cost (*TC*) and total revenue (*TR*) both rise as output increases, but *TC* rises at an increasing rate and *TR* rises at a decreasing rate. Economic profit, which equals *TR* minus *TC*, increases at small output levels, reaches a maximum, and then decreases. The maximum profit ($12) occurs when Bobbie sells 3 haircuts for $14 each. If she sells 2 haircuts for $16 each or 4 haircuts for $12 each, her economic profit will be only $8.

Marginal Revenue Equals Marginal Cost You can see Bobbie's marginal revenue (*MR*) and marginal cost (*MC*) in Table 13.1 and Fig. 13.4(b).

When Bobbie increases output from 2 to 3 haircuts, *MR* is $10 and *MC* is $6. *MR* exceeds *MC* by $4 and Bobbie's profit increases by that amount. If Bobbie increases output yet further, from 3 to 4 haircuts, *MR* is $6 and *MC* is $10. In this case, *MC* exceeds *MR* by $4, so profit decreases by that amount. When *MR* exceeds *MC*, profit increases if output increases. When *MC* exceeds *MR*, profit increases if output *decreases*. When *MC* equals *MR*, profit is maximized.

Figure 13.4(b) shows the maximum profit as price (on the demand curve *D*) minus average total cost (on the *ATC* curve) multiplied by the quantity produced—the blue rectangle.

Maximum Price the Market Will Bear Unlike a firm in perfect competition, a monopoly influences the price of what it sells. But a monopoly doesn't set the price at the maximum *possible* price. At the maximum possible price, the firm would be able to sell only one unit of output, which in general is less than the profit-maximizing quantity. Rather, a monopoly produces the profit-maximizing quantity and sells that quantity for the highest price it can get.

TABLE 13.1   A Monopoly's Output and Price Decision

Price (P) (dollars per haircut)	Quantity demanded (Q) (haircuts per hour)	Total revenue (TR = P × Q) (dollars)	Marginal revenue (MR = ΔTR/ΔQ) (dollars per haircut)	Total cost (TC) (dollars)	Marginal cost (MC = ΔTC/ΔQ) (dollars per haircut)	Profit (TR − TC) (dollars)
20	0	0		20		−20
			18		1	
18	1	18		21		−3
			14		3	
16	2	32		24		+8
			10		6	
14	3	42		30		+12
			6		10	
12	4	48		40		+8
			2		15	
10	5	50		55		−5

This table gives the information needed to find the profit-maximizing output and price. Total revenue (*TR*) equals price multiplied by the quantity sold. Profit equals total revenue minus total cost (*TC*). Profit is maximized when 3 haircuts are sold at a price of $14 each. Total revenue is $42, total cost is $30, and economic profit is $12 ($42 − $30).

FIGURE 13.4   A Monopoly's Output and Price

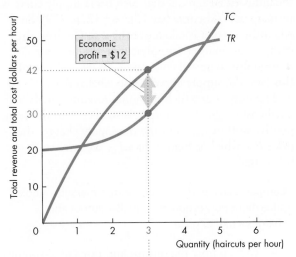

(a) Total revenue and total cost curves

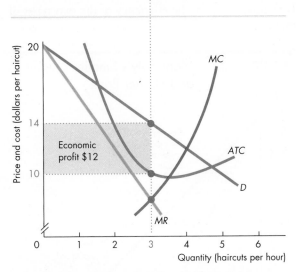

(b) Demand and marginal revenue and cost curves

In part (a), economic profit is the vertical distance equal to total revenue (*TR*) minus total cost (*TC*) and it is maximized at 3 haircuts an hour. In part (b), economic profit is maximized when marginal cost (*MC*) equals marginal revenue (*MR*). The profit-maximizing output is 3 haircuts an hour. The price is determined by the demand curve (*D*) and is $14 a haircut. The average total cost of a haircut is $10, so economic profit, the blue rectangle, is $12—the profit per haircut ($4) multiplied by 3 haircuts.

myeconlab animation

All firms maximize profit by producing the output at which marginal revenue equals marginal cost. For a competitive firm, price equals marginal revenue, so price also equals marginal cost. For a monopoly, price exceeds marginal revenue, so price also exceeds marginal cost.

A monopoly charges a price that exceeds marginal cost, but does it always make an economic profit? In Fig. 13.4(b), Bobbie produces 3 haircuts an hour. Her average total cost is $10 (on the *ATC* curve) and her price is $14 (on the *D* curve), so her profit per haircut is $4 ($14 minus $10). Bobbie's economic profit is shown by the area of the blue rectangle, which equals the profit per haircut ($4) multiplied by the number of haircuts (3), for a total of $12.

If firms in a perfectly competitive market make a positive economic profit, new firms enter. That does *not* happen in monopoly. Barriers to entry prevent new firms from entering the market, so a monopoly can make a positive economic profit and might continue to do so indefinitely. Sometimes that economic profit is large, as in the international diamond business.

Bobbie makes a positive economic profit. But suppose that Bobbie's landlord increases the rent on her salon. If Bobbie pays an additional $12 an hour for rent, her fixed cost increases by $12 an hour. Her marginal cost and marginal revenue don't change, so her profit-maximizing output remains at 3 haircuts an hour. Her profit decreases by $12 an hour to zero. If Bobbie's salon rent increases by more than $12 an hour, she incurs an economic loss. If this situation were permanent, Bobbie would go out of business.

◢■ REVIEW QUIZ

1 What is the relationship between marginal cost and marginal revenue when a single-price monopoly maximizes profit?

2 How does a single-price monopoly determine the price it will charge its customers?

3 What is the relationship between price, marginal revenue, and marginal cost when a single-price monopoly is maximizing profit?

4 Why can a monopoly make a positive economic profit even in the long run?

You can work these questions in Study Plan 13.2 and get instant feedback.

Single-Price Monopoly and Competition Compared

Imagine a market that is made up of many small firms operating in perfect competition. Then imagine that a single firm buys out all these small firms and creates a monopoly.

What will happen in this market? Will the price rise or fall? Will the quantity produced increase or decrease? Will economic profit increase or decrease? Will either the original competitive situation or the new monopoly situation be efficient?

These are the questions we're now going to answer. First, we look at the effects of monopoly on the price and quantity produced. Then we turn to the questions about efficiency.

Comparing Price and Output

Figure 13.5 shows the market we'll study. The market demand curve is D. The demand curve is the same regardless of how the industry is organized. But the supply side and the equilibrium are different in monopoly and competition. First, let's look at the case of perfect competition.

Perfect Competition Initially, with many small perfectly competitive firms in the market, the market supply curve is S. This supply curve is obtained by summing the supply curves of all the individual firms in the market.

In perfect competition, equilibrium occurs where the supply curve and the demand curve intersect. The price is P_C, and the quantity produced by the industry is Q_C. Each firm takes the price P_C and maximizes its profit by producing the output at which its own marginal cost equals the price. Because each firm is a small part of the total industry, there is no incentive for any firm to try to manipulate the price by varying its output.

Monopoly Now suppose that this industry is taken over by a single firm. Consumers do not change, so the market demand curve remains the same as in the case of perfect competition. But now the monopoly recognizes this demand curve as a constraint on the price at which it can sell its output. The monopoly's marginal revenue curve is MR.

The monopoly maximizes profit by producing the quantity at which marginal revenue equals marginal cost. To find the monopoly's marginal cost curve, first

recall that in perfect competition, the market supply curve is the sum of the supply curves of the firms in the industry. Also recall that each firm's supply curve is its marginal cost curve (see Chapter 12, p. 279). So when the market is taken over by a single firm, the competitive market's supply curve becomes the monopoly's marginal cost curve. To remind you of this fact, the supply curve is also labeled MC.

The output at which marginal revenue equals marginal cost is Q_M. This output is smaller than the competitive output Q_C. And the monopoly charges the price P_M, which is higher than P_C. We have established that

Compared to a perfectly competitive market, a single-price monopoly produces a smaller output and charges a higher price.

We've seen how the output and price of a monopoly compare with those in a competitive market. Let's now compare the efficiency of the two types of market.

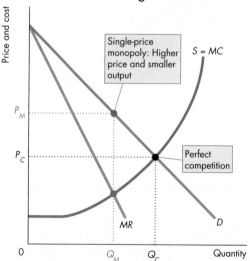

FIGURE 13.5   Monopoly's Smaller Output and Higher Price

A competitive market produces the quantity Q_C at price P_C. A single-price monopoly produces the quantity Q_M at which marginal revenue equals marginal cost and sells that quantity for the price P_M. Compared to perfect competition, a single-price monopoly produces a smaller output and charges a higher price.

myeconlab   animation

Efficiency Comparison

Perfect competition (with no externalities) is efficient. Figure 13.6(a) illustrates the efficiency of perfect competition and serves as a benchmark against which to measure the inefficiency of monopoly. Along the demand curve and marginal social benefit curve ($D = MSB$), consumers are efficient. Along the supply curve and marginal social cost curve ($S = MSC$), producers are efficient. In competitive equilibrium, the price is P_C, the quantity is Q_C, and marginal social benefit equals marginal social cost.

Consumer surplus is the green triangle under the demand curve and above the equilibrium price (see Chapter 5, p. 109). *Producer surplus* is the blue area above the supply curve and below the equilibrium price (see Chapter 5, p. 111). Total surplus (consumer surplus and producer surplus) is maximized.

Also, in long-run competitive equilibrium, entry and exit ensure that each firm produces its output at the minimum possible long-run average cost.

To summarize: At the competitive equilibrium, marginal social benefit equals marginal social cost; total surplus is maximized; firms produce at the lowest possible long-run average cost; and resource use is efficient.

Figure 13.6(b) illustrates the inefficiency of monopoly and the sources of that inefficiency. A monopoly produces Q_M and sells its output for P_M. The smaller output and higher price drive a wedge between marginal social benefit and marginal social cost and create a *deadweight loss*. The gray triangle shows the deadweight loss and its magnitude is a measure of the inefficiency of monopoly.

Consumer surplus shrinks for two reasons. First, consumers lose by having to pay more for the good. This loss to consumers is a gain for monopoly and increases the producer surplus. Second, consumers lose by getting less of the good, and this loss is part of the deadweight loss.

Although the monopoly gains from a higher price, it loses some producer surplus because it produces a smaller output. That loss is another part of the deadweight loss.

A monopoly produces a smaller output than perfect competition and faces no competition, so it does not produce at the lowest possible long-run average cost. As a result, monopoly damages the consumer interest in three ways: A monopoly produces less, increases the cost of production, and raises the price by more than the increased cost of production.

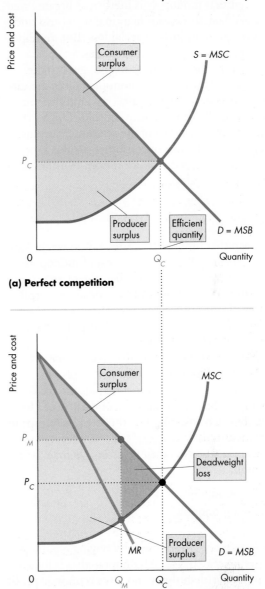

FIGURE 13.6   Inefficiency of Monopoly

(a) Perfect competition

(b) Monopoly

In perfect competition in part (a), output is Q_C and the price is P_C. Marginal social benefit (*MSB*) equals marginal social cost (*MSC*); total surplus, the sum of consumer surplus (the green triangle) and producer surplus (the blue area), is maximized; and in the long run, firms produce at the lowest possible average cost. Monopoly in part (b) produces Q_M and raises the price to P_M. Consumer surplus shrinks, the monopoly gains, and a deadweight loss (the gray triangle) arises.

Redistribution of Surpluses

You've seen that monopoly is inefficient because marginal social benefit exceeds marginal social cost and there is deadweight loss—a social loss. But monopoly also brings a *redistribution* of surpluses.

Some of the lost consumer surplus goes to the monopoly. In Fig. 13.6, the monopoly takes the difference between the higher price, P_M, and the competitive price, P_C, on the quantity sold, Q_M. So the monopoly takes that part of the consumer surplus. This portion of the loss of consumer surplus is not a loss to society. It is redistribution from consumers to the monopoly producer.

Rent Seeking

You've seen that monopoly creates a deadweight loss and is inefficient. But the social cost of monopoly can exceed the deadweight loss because of an activity called rent seeking. Any surplus—consumer surplus, producer surplus, or economic profit—is called **economic rent**. The pursuit of wealth by capturing economic rent is called **rent seeking**.

You've seen that a monopoly makes its economic profit by diverting part of consumer surplus to itself—by converting consumer surplus into economic profit. So the pursuit of economic profit by a monopoly is rent seeking. It is the attempt to capture consumer surplus.

Rent seekers pursue their goals in two main ways. They might

- Buy a monopoly
- Create a monopoly

Buy a Monopoly To rent seek by buying a monopoly, a person searches for a monopoly that is for sale at a lower price than the monopoly's economic profit. Trading of taxicab licenses is an example of this type of rent seeking. In some cities, taxicabs are regulated. The city restricts both the fares and the number of taxis that can operate so that operating a taxi results in economic profit. A person who wants to operate a taxi must buy a license from someone who already has one. People rationally devote time and effort to seeking out profitable monopoly businesses to buy. In the process, they use up scarce resources that could otherwise have been used to produce goods and services. The value of this lost production is part of the social cost of monopoly. The amount paid for a

monopoly is not a social cost because the payment is just a transfer of an existing producer surplus from the buyer to the seller.

Create a Monopoly Rent seeking by creating a monopoly is mainly a political activity. It takes the form of lobbying and trying to influence the political process. Such influence might be sought by making campaign contributions in exchange for legislative support or by indirectly seeking to influence political outcomes through publicity in the media or more direct contacts with politicians and bureaucrats. An example of a monopoly created in this way is the government-imposed restrictions on the quantities of textiles that may be imported into the United States. Another is a regulation that limits the number of oranges that may be sold in the United States. These are regulations that restrict output and increase price.

This type of rent seeking is a costly activity that uses up scarce resources. Taken together, firms spend billions of dollars lobbying Congress, state legislators, and local officials in the pursuit of licenses and laws that create barriers to entry and establish a monopoly.

Rent-Seeking Equilibrium

Barriers to entry create monopoly. But there is no barrier to entry into rent seeking. Rent seeking is like perfect competition. If an economic profit is available, a new rent seeker will try to get some of it. And competition among rent seekers pushes up the price that must be paid for a monopoly, to the point at which the rent seeker makes zero economic profit by operating the monopoly. For example, competition for the right to operate a taxi in New York City leads to a price of more than $100,000 for a taxi license, which is sufficiently high to eliminate the economic profit made by a taxi operator.

Figure 13.7 shows a rent-seeking equilibrium. The cost of rent seeking is a fixed cost that must be added to a monopoly's other costs. Rent seeking and rent-seeking costs increase to the point at which no economic profit is made. The average total cost curve, which includes the fixed cost of rent seeking, shifts upward until it just touches the demand curve. Economic profit is zero. It has been lost in rent seeking.

Consumer surplus is unaffected, but the deadweight loss from monopoly is larger. The deadweight loss now includes the original deadweight loss triangle plus the lost producer surplus, shown by the enlarged gray area in Fig. 13.7.

FIGURE 13.7   Rent-Seeking Equilibrium

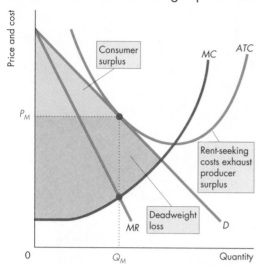

With competitive rent seeking, a monopoly uses all its economic profit to maintain its monopoly. The firm's rent-seeking costs are fixed costs. They add to total fixed cost and to average total cost. The *ATC* curve shifts upward until, at the profit-maximizing price, the firm breaks even.

 animation

REVIEW QUIZ

1 Why does a single-price monopoly produce a smaller output and charge more than the price that would prevail if the market were perfectly competitive?
2 How does a monopoly transfer consumer surplus to itself?
3 Why is a single-price monopoly inefficient?
4 What is rent seeking and how does it influence the inefficiency of monopoly?

You can work these questions in Study Plan 13.3 and get instant feedback.

So far, we've considered only a single-price monopoly. But many monopolies do not operate with a single price. Instead, they price discriminate. Let's now see how a price-discriminating monopoly works.

Price Discrimination

You encounter *price discrimination*—selling a good or service at a number of different prices—when you travel, go to the movies, get your hair cut, buy pizza, or visit an art museum or theme park. Many of the firms that price discriminate are not monopolies, but monopolies price discriminate when they can do so.

To be able to price discriminate, a firm must be able to identify and separate different buyer types and sell a product that cannot be resold.

Not all price *differences* are price *discrimination*. Some goods that are similar have different prices because they have different costs of production. For example, the price per ounce of cereal is lower if you buy your cereal in a big box than if you buy individual serving size boxes. This price difference reflects a cost difference and is not price discrimination.

At first sight, price discrimination appears to be inconsistent with profit maximization. Why would a movie theater allow children to see movies at a discount? Why would a hairdresser charge students and senior citizens less? Aren't these firms losing profit by being nice to their customers?

Capturing Consumer Surplus

Price discrimination captures consumer surplus and converts it into economic profit. It does so by getting buyers to pay a price as close as possible to the maximum willingness to pay.

Firms price discriminate in two broad ways. They discriminate:

- Among groups of buyers
- Among units of a good

Discriminating Among Groups of Buyers People differ in the value they place on a good—their marginal benefit and willingness to pay. Some of these differences are correlated with features such as age, employment status, and other easily distinguished characteristics. When such a correlation is present, firms can profit by price discriminating among the different groups of buyers.

For example, a face-to-face sales meeting with a customer might bring a large and profitable order. So for salespeople and other business travelers, the marginal benefit from a trip is large and the price that such a traveler is willing to pay for a trip is high. In contrast, for a vacation traveler, any of several different trips and even no vacation trip are options. So for vacation travelers, the marginal benefit of a trip is small and the price that such a traveler is willing to pay for a trip is low. Because business travelers are willing to pay more than vacation travelers are, it is possible for an airline to profit by price discriminating between these two groups.

Discriminating Among Units of a Good Everyone experiences diminishing marginal benefit and has a downward-sloping demand curve. For this reason, if all the units of the good are sold for a single price, buyers end up with a consumer surplus equal to the value they get from each unit of the good minus the price paid for it.

A firm that price discriminates by charging a buyer one price for a single item and a lower price for a second or third item can capture some of the consumer surplus. Buy one pizza and get a second one free (or for a low price) is an example of this type of price discrimination.

(Note that some discounts for bulk arise from lower costs of production for greater bulk. In these cases, such discounts are not price discrimination.)

Let's see how price discriminating increases economic profit.

Profiting by Price Discriminating

Global Airlines has a monopoly on an exotic route. Figure 13.8 shows the market demand curve (*D*) for travel on this route. It also shows Global Airline's marginal revenue curve (*MR*), marginal cost curve (*MC*), and average total cost curve (*ATC*).

As a single-price monopoly, Global maximizes profit by producing the quantity at which *MR* equals *MC*, which is 8,000 trips a year, and charging $1,200 per trip. At this quantity, average total cost is $600 per trip, economic profit is $600 a trip, and Global's economic profit is $4.8 million a year, shown by the blue rectangle. Global's customers enjoy a consumer surplus shown by the green triangle.

Global is struck by the fact that many of its customers are business travelers, and it suspects they are willing to pay more than $1,200 a trip. Global does some market research, which reveals that some business travelers are willing to pay as much as $1,800 a trip. Also, these customers frequently change their travel plans at the last minute. Another group of business travelers is willing to pay $1,600. These

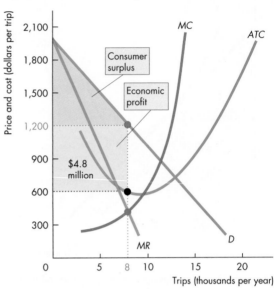

FIGURE 13.8   A Single Price of Air Travel

Global Airlines has a monopoly on an air route. The market demand curve is *D*. Global Airline's marginal revenue curve is *MR*, its marginal cost curve is *MC*, and its average total cost curve is *ATC*. As a single-price monopoly, Global maximizes profit by selling 8,000 trips a year at $1,200 a trip. Its profit is $4.8 million a year—the blue rectangle. Global's customers enjoy a consumer surplus—the green triangle.

myeconlab   animation

customers know a week ahead when they will travel, and they never want to stay over a weekend. Yet another group would pay up to $1,400. These travelers know two weeks ahead when they will travel and also don't want to stay away over a weekend.

Global announces a new fare schedule: no restrictions, $1,800; 7-day advance purchase, nonrefundable, $1,600; 14-day advance purchase, nonrefundable, $1,400; 14-day advance purchase, must stay over a weekend, $1,200.

Figure 13.9 shows the outcome with this new fare structure and also shows why Global is pleased with its new fares. It sells 2,000 seats at each of its four prices. Global's economic profit increases by the dark blue steps. Its economic profit is now its original $4.8 million a year plus an additional $2.4 million from its new higher fares. Consumer surplus shrinks to the sum of the smaller green areas.

FIGURE 13.9   Price Discrimination

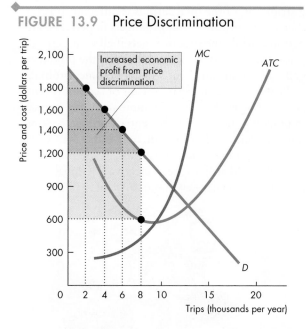

Global revises its fare structure: no restrictions at $1,800, 7-day advance purchase at $1,600, 14-day advance purchase at $1,400, and must stay over a weekend at $1,200. Global sells 2,000 trips at each of its four new fares. Its economic profit increases by $2.4 million a year to $7.2 million a year, which is shown by the original blue rectangle plus the dark blue steps. Global's customers' consumer surplus shrinks.

myeconlab animation

Perfect Price Discrimination

Perfect price discrimination occurs if a firm is able to sell each unit of output for the highest price anyone is willing to pay for it. In such a case, the entire consumer surplus is eliminated and captured by the producer. To practice perfect price discrimination, a firm must be creative and come up with a host of prices and special conditions, each one of which appeals to a tiny segment of the market.

With perfect price discrimination, something special happens to marginal revenue—the market demand curve becomes the marginal revenue curve. The reason is that when the price is cut to sell a larger quantity, the firm sells only the marginal unit at the lower price. All the other units continue to be sold for the highest price that each buyer is willing to pay. So for the perfect price discriminator, marginal revenue *equals* price and the demand curve becomes the marginal revenue curve.

With marginal revenue equal to price, Global can obtain even greater profit by increasing output up to the point at which price (and marginal revenue) is equal to marginal cost.

So Global seeks new travelers who will not pay as much as $1,200 a trip but who will pay more than marginal cost. Global offers a variety of vacation specials at different low fares that appeal only to new travelers. Existing customers continue to pay the higher fares. With all these fares and specials, Global increases sales, extracts the entire consumer surplus, and maximizes economic profit.

Figure 13.10 shows the outcome with perfect price discrimination. The fares paid by the original travelers extract the entire consumer surplus from this group. The new fares between $900 and $1,200 attract 3,000 additional travelers and take their entire consumer surplus also. Global now makes an economic profit of more than $9 million.

FIGURE 13.10   Perfect Price Discrimination

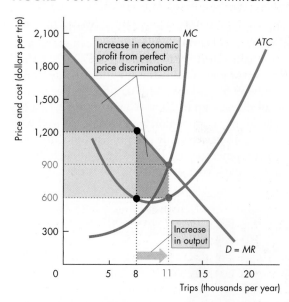

Dozens of fares discriminate among many different types of business traveler, and many new low fares with restrictions appeal to vacation travelers. With perfect price discrimination, the market demand curve becomes Global's marginal revenue curve. Economic profit is maximized when the lowest price equals marginal cost. Global sells 11,000 trips and makes an economic profit of more than $9 million a year.

myeconlab animation

Efficiency and Rent Seeking with Price Discrimination

With perfect price discrimination, output increases to the point at which price equals marginal cost—where the marginal cost curve intersects the market demand curve (see Fig. 13.10). This output is identical to that of perfect competition. Perfect price discrimination pushes consumer surplus to zero but increases the monopoly's producer surplus to equal the total surplus in perfect competition. With perfect price discrimination, deadweight loss is zero, so perfect price discrimination achieves efficiency.

The more perfectly the monopoly can price discriminate, the closer its output is to the competitive output and the more efficient is the outcome.

But there are two differences between perfect competition and perfect price discrimination. First, the distribution of the total surplus is different. It is shared by consumers and producers in perfect competition, while the producer gets it all with perfect price discrimination. Second, because the producer grabs all the surplus, rent seeking becomes profitable.

People use resources in pursuit of economic rent, and the bigger the rents, the more resources get used in pursuing them. With free entry into rent seeking, the long-run equilibrium outcome is that rent seekers use up the entire producer surplus.

Real-world airlines are as creative as Global Airlines, as you can see in the cartoon!

Would it bother you to hear how little I paid for this flight?

From William Hamilton, "Voodoo Economics," © 1992 by The Chronicle Publishing Company, p.3. Reprinted with permission of Chronicle Books.

Economics in Action

Attempting Perfect Price Discrimination

If you want to spend a day at Disney World in Orlando, it will cost you $75.62. You can spend a second (consecutive) day for an extra $72.42. A third day will cost you $68.17. But for a fourth day, you'll pay only $9.59 and for a fifth day, $3.20. For more days all the way up to 10, you'll pay only $2.12 a day.

The Disney Corporation hopes that it has read your willingness to pay correctly and not left you with too much consumer surplus. Disney figures though that after three days, your marginal benefit is crashing.

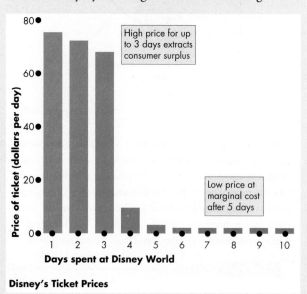

Disney's Ticket Prices

◆ REVIEW QUIZ

1 What is price discrimination and how is it used to increase a monopoly's profit?
2 Explain how consumer surplus changes when a monopoly price discriminates.
3 Explain how consumer surplus, economic profit, and output change when a monopoly perfectly price discriminates.
4 What are some of the ways that real-world airlines price discriminate?

You can work these questions in Study Plan 13.4 and get instant feedback.

You've seen that monopoly is profitable for the monopoly but costly for consumers. It results in inefficiency. Because of these features of monopoly, it is subject to policy debate and regulation. We'll now study the key monopoly policy issues.

◆ Monopoly Regulation

Natural monopoly presents a dilemma. With economies of scale, it produces at the lowest possible cost. But with market power, it has an incentive to raise the price above the competitive price and produce too little—to operate in the self-interest of the monopolist and not in the social interest.

Regulation—rules administered by a government agency to influence prices, quantities, entry, and other aspects of economic activity in a firm or industry—is a possible solution to this dilemma.

To implement regulation, the government establishes agencies to oversee and enforce the rules. For example, the Surface Transportation Board regulates prices on interstate railroads, some trucking and bus lines, and water and oil pipelines. By the 1970s, almost a quarter of the nation's output was produced by regulated industries (far more than just natural monopolies) and a process of deregulation began.

Deregulation is the process of removing regulation of prices, quantities, entry, and other aspects of economic activity in a firm or industry. During the past 30 years, deregulation has occurred in domestic air transportation, telephone service, interstate trucking, and banking and financial services. Cable TV was deregulated in 1984, re-regulated in 1992, and deregulated again in 1996.

Regulation is a possible solution to the dilemma presented by natural monopoly but not a guaranteed solution. There are two theories about how regulation actually works: *the social interest theory* and the *capture theory*.

The **social interest theory** is that the political and regulatory process relentlessly seeks out inefficiency and introduces regulation that eliminates deadweight loss and allocates resources efficiently.

The **capture theory** is that regulation serves the self-interest of the producer, who captures the regulator and maximizes economic profit. Regulation that benefits the producer but creates a deadweight loss gets adopted because the producer's gain is large and visible while each individual consumer's loss is small and invisible. No individual consumer has an incentive to oppose the regulation but the producer has a big incentive to lobby for it.

We're going to examine efficient regulation that serves the social interest and see why it is not a simple matter to design and implement such regulation.

Efficient Regulation of a Natural Monopoly

A cable TV company is a *natural monopoly*—it can supply the entire market at a lower price than two or more competing firms can. Cox Communications, based in Atlanta, provides cable TV to households in 20 states. The firm has invested heavily in satellite receiving dishes, cables, and control equipment and so has large fixed costs. These fixed costs are part of the firm's average total cost. Its average total cost decreases as the number of households served increases because the fixed cost is spread over a larger number of households.

Unregulated, Cox produces the quantity that maximizes profit. Like all single-price monopolies, the profit-maximizing quantity is less than the efficient quantity, and underproduction results in a deadweight loss.

How can Cox be regulated to produce the efficient quantity of cable TV service? The answer is by being regulated to set its price equal to marginal cost, known as the **marginal cost pricing rule**. The quantity demanded at a price equal to marginal cost is the efficient quantity—the quantity at which marginal benefit equals marginal cost.

Figure 13.11 illustrates the marginal cost pricing rule. The demand curve for cable TV is *D*. Cox's marginal cost curve is *MC*. That marginal cost curve is (assumed to be) horizontal at $10 per household per month—that is, the cost of providing each additional household with a month of cable programming is $10. The efficient outcome occurs if the price is regulated at $10 per household per month with 10 million households served.

But there is a problem: At the efficient output, average total cost exceeds marginal cost, so a firm that uses marginal cost pricing incurs an economic loss. A cable TV company that is required to use a marginal cost pricing rule will not stay in business for long. How can the firm cover its costs and, at the same time, obey a marginal cost pricing rule?

There are two possible ways of enabling the firm to cover its costs: price discrimination and a two-part price (called a *two-part tariff*).

For example, Verizon offers plans at a fixed monthly price that give access to the cell-phone network and unlimited free calls. The price of a call (zero) equals Verizon's marginal cost of a call. Similarly, a cable TV operator can charge a one-time connection fee that covers its fixed cost and then charge a monthly fee equal to marginal cost.

FIGURE 13.11   Regulating a Natural Monopoly

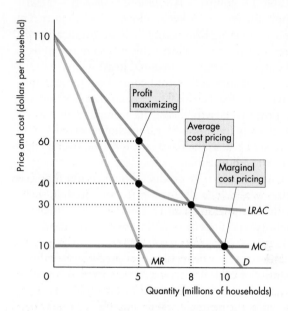

A natural monopoly cable TV supplier faces the demand curve *D*. The firm's marginal cost is constant at $10 per household per month, as shown by the curve labeled *MC*. The long-run average cost curve is *LRAC*.

Unregulated, as a profit-maximizer, the firm serves 5 million households at a price of $60 a month. An efficient marginal cost pricing rule sets the price at $10 a month. The monopoly serves 10 million households and incurs an economic loss. A second-best average cost pricing rule sets the price at $30 a month. The monopoly serves 8 million households and earns zero economic profit.

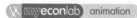

Second-Best Regulation of a Natural Monopoly

A natural monopoly cannot always be regulated to achieve an efficient outcome. Two possible ways of enabling a regulated monopoly to avoid an economic loss are

- Average cost pricing
- Government subsidy

Average Cost Pricing The **average cost pricing rule** ets price equal to average total cost. With this rule the firm produces the quantity at which the average

total cost curve cuts the demand curve. This rule results in the firm making zero economic profit—breaking even. But because for a natural monopoly average total cost exceeds marginal cost, the quantity produced is less than the efficient quantity and a deadweight loss arises.

Figure 13.11 illustrates the average cost pricing rule. The price is $30 a month and 8 million households get cable TV.

Government Subsidy A government subsidy is a direct payment to the firm equal to its economic loss. To pay a subsidy, the government must raise the revenue by taxing some other activity. You saw in Chapter 6 that taxes themselves generate deadweight loss.

And the Second-Best Is ... Which is the better option, average cost pricing or marginal cost pricing with a government subsidy? The answer depends on the relative magnitudes of the two deadweight losses. Average cost pricing generates a deadweight loss in the market served by the natural monopoly. A subsidy generates deadweight losses in the markets for the items that are taxed to pay for the subsidy. The smaller deadweight loss is the second-best solution to regulating a natural monopoly. Making this calculation in practice is too difficult and average cost pricing is generally preferred to a subsidy.

Implementing average cost pricing presents the regulator with a challenge because it is not possible to be sure what a firm's costs are. So regulators use one of two practical rules:

- Rate of return regulation
- Price cap regulation

Rate of Return Regulation Under **rate of return regulation**, a firm must justify its price by showing that its return on capital doesn't exceed a specified target rate. This type of regulation can end up serving the self-interest of the firm rather than the social interest. The firm's managers have an incentive to inflate costs by spending on items such as private jets, free baseball tickets (disguised as public relations expenses), and lavish entertainment. Managers also have an incentive to use more capital than the efficient amount. The rate of return on capital is regulated but not the total return on capital, and the greater the amount of capital, the greater is the total return.

Price Cap Regulation For the reason that we've just examined, rate of return regulation is increasingly being replaced by price cap regulation. A **price cap regulation** is a price ceiling—a rule that specifies the highest price the firm is permitted to set. This type of regulation gives a firm an incentive to operate efficiently and keep costs under control. Price cap regulation has become common for the electricity and telecommunications industries and is replacing rate of return regulation.

To see how a price cap works, let's suppose that the cable TV operator is subject to this type of regulation. Figure 13.12 shows that without regulation, the firm maximizes profit by serving 5 million households and charging a price of $60 a month. If a price cap is set at $30 a month, the firm is permitted to sell

any quantity it chooses at that price or at a lower price. At 5 million households, the firm now incurs an economic loss. It can decrease the loss by increasing output to 8 million households. To increase output above 8 million households, the firm would have to lower the price and again it would incur a loss. So the profit-maximizing quantity is 8 million households—the same as with average cost pricing.

Notice that a price cap lowers the price and increases output. This outcome is in sharp contrast to the effect of a price ceiling in a competitive market that you studied in Chapter 6 (pp. 128–130). The reason is that in a monopoly, the unregulated equilibrium output is less than the competitive equilibrium output, and the price cap regulation replicates the conditions of a competitive market.

In Fig. 13.12, the price cap delivers average cost pricing. In practice, the regulator might set the cap too high. For this reason, price cap regulation is often combined with *earnings sharing regulation*—a regulation that requires firms to make refunds to customers when profits rise above a target level.

FIGURE 13.12   Price Cap Regulation

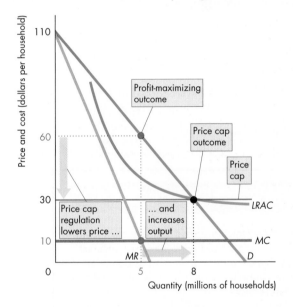

A natural monopoly cable TV supplier faces the demand curve *D*. The firm's marginal cost is constant at $10 per household per month, as shown by the curve labeled *MC*. The long-run average cost curve is *LRAC*.

Unregulated, the firm serves 5 million households at a price of $60 a month. A price cap sets the maximum price at $30 a month. The firm has an incentive to minimize cost and serve the quantity of households that demand service at the price cap. The price cap regulation lowers the price and increases the quantity.

myeconlab animation

REVIEW QUIZ

1 What is the pricing rule that achieves an efficient outcome for a regulated monopoly? What is the problem with this rule?

2 What is the average cost pricing rule? Why is it not an efficient way of regulating monopoly?

3 What is a price cap? Why might it be a more effective way of regulating monopoly than rate of return regulation?

4 Compare the consumer surplus, producer surplus, and deadweight loss that arise from average cost pricing with those that arise from profit-maximization pricing and marginal cost pricing.

You can work these questions in Study Plan 13.5 and get instant feedback.

You've now completed your study of monopoly. *Reading Between the Lines* on pp. 316–317 looks at Google's dominant position in the market for Internet search advertising.

In the next chapter, we study markets that lie between the extremes of perfect competition and monopoly and that blend elements of the two.

Is Google Missing Monopoly Power?

Data Show Google Abuses Search Role, Group Contends

http://www.sfgate.com

June 3, 2010

Consumer Watchdog continues to push its case that Google Inc.'s behavior necessitates antitrust scrutiny, releasing a report Wednesday that alleges that the company is abusing its dominance in online search to direct users to its own services.

The study, which will be sent to U.S. and European antitrust regulators, cites online traffic data that the Santa Monica group claims shows the Mountain View Internet giant seized large portions of market share in areas like online maps, video and comparison shopping after its search engine began highlighting links to its products in results.

Google called the report's methodology and premise flawed and said its practices are designed to benefit users.

"Our goal is to give users the info they're seeking as quickly as possible," a spokesman said in a statement. "Sometimes that means showing a map, a streaming audio link, or an answer to a question at the top of the page if we think that's what users want. We strive to deliver what we think is the most relevant result from a variety of content types, and if we're not giving users the information they want then other sources of information are always one click away."

Google doubled its market share in online video to nearly 80 percent since 2007, the year in which the company began returning high or prominent links to videos from its YouTube subsidiary in search results, according to the report by Consumer Watchdog's Inside Google project.

…

ESSENCE OF THE STORY

- Consumer Watchdog says that Google should be scrutinized by U.S. and European antitrust regulators because it is abusing its dominant position in online search by directing users to its own services.

- The claim is that Google has grown a large market share in online maps, video, and comparison shopping because its search engine highlights links to these products in search results.

- Google says its goal is to give users the information they are seeking, in the format required, as quickly as possible.

- Google's market share in online video has doubled to nearly 80 percent since 2007 when it began returning links to YouTube videos.

ECONOMIC ANALYSIS

- Google began selling advertisements associated with search keywords in 2000.

- Google sells keywords based on a combination of willingness-to-pay and the number of clicks an advertisement receives, with bids starting at 5 cents per click.

- Google has steadily improved its search engine and refined and simplified its interface with both searchers and advertisers to make searches more powerful and advertising more effective.

- Figure 1 shows Google's extraordinary success in terms of its revenue, cost, and profit.

- Google could have provided a basic search engine with none of the features of today's Google.

- If Google had followed this strategy, people seeking information would have used other search engines and advertisers would have been willing to pay low prices for Google ads.

- Google would have faced the market described in Fig. 2 and earned a small economic profit.

- Instead, Google improved its search and the effectiveness of advertising. The demand for Google ads increased.

- By selling keywords to the highest bidder, Google is able to achieve perfect price discrimination.

- Figure 3 shows the consequences of Google's successful strategy. With perfect price discrimination, Google's producer surplus is maximized. Google produces the efficient quantity of search and advertising by accepting ads as long as price exceeds marginal cost.

- Google does not appear to be acting against the social interest: There is no antitrust case to answer.

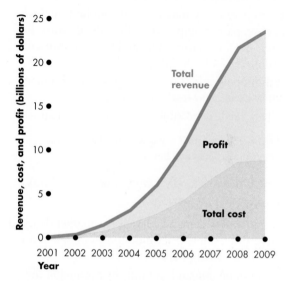

Figure 1 Google's revenue, cost, and profit

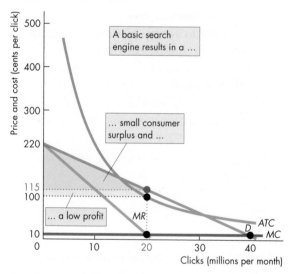

Figure 2 Basic search engine

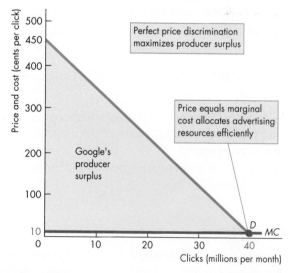

Figure 3 Google with AdWords and other features

317

SUMMARY

Key Points

Monopoly and How It Arises (pp. 300–301)

- A monopoly is a market with a single supplier of a good or service that has no close substitutes and in which barriers to entry prevent competition.
- Barriers to entry may be legal (public franchise, license, patent, copyright), firm owns control of a resource, or natural (created by economies of scale).
- A monopoly might be able to price discriminate when there is no resale possibility.
- Where resale is possible, a firm charges one price.

Working Problems 1 to 4 will give you a better understanding of monopoly and how it arises.

A Single-Price Monopoly's Output and Price Decision

(pp. 302–305)

- A monopoly's demand curve is the market demand curve and a single-price monopoly's marginal revenue is less than price.
- A monopoly maximizes profit by producing the output at which marginal revenue equals marginal cost and by charging the maximum price that consumers are willing to pay for that output.

Working Problems 5 to 9 will give you a better understanding of a single-price monopoly's output and price.

Single-Price Monopoly and Competition Compared

(pp. 306–309)

- A single-price monopoly charges a higher price and produces a smaller quantity than a perfectly competitive market.
- A single-price monopoly restricts output and creates a deadweight loss.

- The total loss that arises from monopoly equals the deadweight loss plus the cost of the resources devoted to rent seeking.

Working Problems 10 to 12 will give you a better understanding of the comparison of single-price monopoly and perfect competition.

Price Discrimination (pp. 309–312)

- Price discrimination converts consumer surplus into economic profit.
- Perfect price discrimination extracts the entire consumer surplus; each unit is sold for the maximum price that each consumer is willing to pay; the quantity produced is the efficient quantity.
- Rent seeking with perfect price discrimination might eliminate the entire consumer surplus and producer surplus.

Working Problems 13 to 16 will give you a better understanding of price discrimination.

Monopoly Regulation (pp. 313–315)

- Monopoly regulation might serve the social interest or the interest of the monopoly (the monopoly captures the regulator).
- Price equal to marginal cost achieves efficiency but results in economic loss.
- Price equal to average cost enables the firm to cover its cost but is inefficient.
- Rate of return regulation creates incentives for inefficient production and inflated cost.
- Price cap regulation with earnings sharing regulation can achieve a more efficient outcome than rate of return regulation.

Working Problems 17 to 19 will give you a better understanding of monopoly regulation.

Key Terms

Average cost pricing rule, 314
Barrier to entry, 300
Capture theory, 313
Deregulation, 313
Economic rent, 308
Legal monopoly, 300

Marginal cost pricing rule, 313
Monopoly, 300
Natural monopoly, 300
Perfect price discrimination, 311
Price cap regulation, 315
Price discrimination, 301

Rate of return regulation, 314
Regulation, 313
Rent seeking, 308
Single-price monopoly, 301
Social interest theory, 313

STUDY PLAN PROBLEMS AND APPLICATIONS

myeconlab You can work problems 1 to 19 in MyEconLab Chapter 13 Study Plan and get instant feedback.

Monopoly and How It Arises (Study Plan 13.1)

Use the following information to work Problems 1 to 3.

The United States Postal Service has a monopoly on non-urgent First Class Mail and the exclusive right to put mail in private mailboxes. Pfizer Inc. makes LIPITOR, a prescription drug that lowers cholesterol. Cox Communications is the sole provider of cable television service in some parts of San Diego.

1. a. What are the substitutes, if any, for the goods and services described above?
   b. What are the barriers to entry, if any, that protect these three firms from competition?

2. Which of these three firms, if any, is a natural monopoly? Explain your answer and draw a graph to illustrate it.

3. a. Which of these three firms, if any, is a legal monopoly? Explain your answer.
   b. Which of these three firms are most likely to be able to profit from price discrimination and which are most likely to sell their good or service for a single price?

4. **Barbie's Revenge: Brawl over Doll Is Heading to Trial**

   Four years ago, Mattel Inc. exhorted its executives to help save Barbie from a new doll clique called the Bratz. With its market share dropping at a "chilling rate," Barbie needed to be more "aggressive, revolutionary, and ruthless." Mattel has gone to court and is trying to seize ownership of the Bratz line, which Mattel accuses of stealing the idea for the pouty-lipped dolls with the big heads.

   Source: *The Wall Street Journal*, May 23, 2008

   a. Before Bratz entered the market, what type of monopoly did Mattel Inc. possess in the market for "the pouty-lipped dolls with the big heads"?

   b. What is the barrier to entry that Mattel might argue should protect it from competition in the market for Barbie dolls?

   c. Explain how the entry of Bratz dolls might be expected to change the demand for Barbie dolls.

A Single-Price Monopoly's Output and Price Decision

(Study Plan 13.2)

Use the following table to work Problems 5 to 8.
Minnie's Mineral Springs, a single-price monopoly, faces the market demand schedule:

Price (dollars per bottle)	Quantity demanded (bottles per hour)
10	0
8	1
6	2
4	3
2	4
0	5

5. a. Calculate Minnie's total revenue schedule.
   b. Calculate its marginal revenue schedule.

6. a. Draw a graph of the market demand curve and Minnie's marginal revenue curve.
   b. Why is Minnie's marginal revenue less than the price?

7. a. At what price is Minnie's total revenue maximized?
   b. Over what range of prices is the demand for water from Minnie's Mineral Springs elastic?

8. Why will Minnie not produce a quantity at which the market demand for water is inelastic?

9. Minnie's Mineral Springs faces the market demand schedule in Problem 5 and has the following total cost schedule:

Quantity produced (bottles per hour)	Total cost (dollars)
0	1
1	3
2	7
3	13
4	21
5	31

   a. Calculate Minnie's profit-maximizing output and price.
   b. Calculate the economic profit.

Single-Price Monopoly and Competition Compared
(Study Plan 13.3)

Use the following news clip to work Problems 10 to 12.

Zoloft Faces Patent Expiration

Pfizer's antidepressant Zoloft, with $3.3 billion in 2005 sales, loses patent protection on June 30. When a brand name drug loses its patent, both the price of the drug and the dollar value of its sales each tend to drop 80 percent over the next year, as competition opens to a host of generic drugmakers. The real winners are the patients and the insurers, who pay much lower prices. The Food and Drug Administration insists that generics work identically to brand-names.

Source: CNN, June 15, 2006

10. a. Assume that Pfizer has a monopoly in the antidepressant market and that Pfizer cannot price discriminate. Use a graph to illustrate the market price and quantity of Zoloft sold.

   b. On your graph, identify consumer surplus, producer surplus, and deadweight loss.

11. How might you justify protecting Pfizer from competition with a legal barrier to entry?

12. a. Explain how the market for an antidepressant drug changes when a patent expires.

   b. Draw a graph to illustrate how the expiration of the Zoloft patent will change the price and quantity in the market for antidepressants.

   c. Explain how consumer surplus, producer surplus, and deadweight loss change with the expiration of the Zoloft patent.

Price Discrimination (Study Plan 13.4)

Use the following news clip to work Problems 13 and 14.

The Saturday-Night Stay Requirement Is on Its Final Approach

The Saturday-night stay—the requirement that airlines instituted to ensure that business travelers pay an outrageous airfare if he or she wants to go home for the weekend—has gone the way of the dodo bird. Experts agree that low-fare carriers, such as Southwest, are the primary reason major airlines are adopting more consumer-friendly fare structures, which include the elimination of the Saturday-night stay, the introduction of one-way and walk-up fares, and the general restructuring of fares.

Source: *Los Angeles Times*, August 15, 2004

13. Explain why the opportunity for price discrimination exists for air travel. How does an airline profit from price discrimination?

14. Describe the change in price discrimination in the market for air travel when discount airlines entered the market and explain the effect of discount airlines on the price and the quantity of air travel.

Use the following information to work Problems 15 and 16.

La Bella Pizza can produce a pizza for a marginal cost of $2. Its standard price is $15 a pizza. It offers a second pizza for $5. It also distributes coupons that give a $5 rebate on a standard-priced pizza.

15. How can La Bella Pizza make a larger economic profit with this range of prices than it could if it sold every pizza for $15? Use a graph to illustrate your answer.

16. How might La Bella Pizza make even more economic profit? Would La Bella Pizza then be more efficient than it would be if it charged $15 for each pizza?

Monopoly Regulation (Study Plan 13.5)

Use the following information to work Problems 17 to 19.

The figure shows a situation similar to that of Calypso U.S. Pipeline, a firm that operates a natural gas distribution system in the United States. Calypso is a natural monopoly that cannot price discriminate.

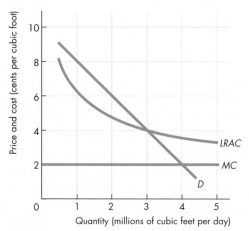

What quantity will Calypso produce, what price will it charge, what is the total surplus, and what is the deadweight loss if Calypso is

17. An unregulated profit-maximizing firm?

18. Regulated to make zero economic profit?

19. Regulated to be efficient?

ADDITIONAL PROBLEMS AND APPLICATIONS

myeconlab You can work these problems in MyEconLab if assigned by your instructor.

Monopoly and How It Arises

Use the following list, which gives some information about seven firms, to answer Problems 20 and 21.

- Coca-Cola cuts its price below that of Pepsi-Cola in an attempt to increase its market share.
- A single firm, protected by a barrier to entry, produces a personal service that has no close substitutes.
- A barrier to entry exists, but the good has some close substitutes.
- A firm offers discounts to students and seniors.
- A firm can sell any quantity it chooses at the going price.
- The government issues Nike an exclusive license to produce golf balls.
- A firm experiences economies of scale even when it produces the quantity that meets the entire market demand.

20. In which of the seven cases might monopoly arise?

21. Which of the seven cases are natural monopolies and which are legal monopolies? Which can price discriminate, which cannot, and why?

A Single-Price Monopoly's Output and Price Decision

Use the following information to work Problems 22 to 26.

Hot Air Balloon Rides is a single-price monopoly. Columns 1 and 2 of the table set out the market demand schedule and columns 2 and 3 set out the total cost schedule:

Price (dollars per ride)	Quantity demanded (rides per month)	Total cost (dollars per month)
220	0	80
200	1	160
180	2	260
160	3	380
140	4	520
120	5	680

22. Construct Hot Air's total revenue and marginal revenue schedules.

23. Draw a graph of the market demand curve and Hot Air's marginal revenue curve.

24. Find Hot Air's profit-maximizing output and price and calculate the firm's economic profit.

25. If the government imposes a tax on Hot Air's profit, how do its output and price change?

26. If instead of taxing Hot Air's profit, the government imposes a sales tax on balloon rides of $30 a ride, what are the new profit-maximizing quantity, price, and economic profit?

27. The figure illustrates the situation facing the publisher of the only newspaper containing local news in an isolated community.

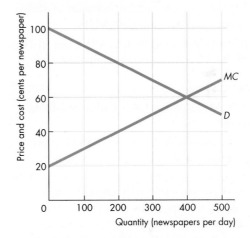

a. On the graph, mark the profit-maximizing quantity and price and the publisher's total revenue per day.

b. At the price charged, is the demand for this newspaper elastic or inelastic? Why?

Single-Price Monopoly and Competition Compared

28. Show on the graph in Problem 27 the consumer surplus from newspapers and the deadweight loss created by the monopoly. Explain why this market might encourage rent seeking.

29. If the newspaper market in Problem 27 were perfectly competitive, what would be the quantity, price, consumer surplus, and producer surplus? Mark each on the graph.

30. **Telecoms Look to Grow by Acquisition**

Multibillion-dollar telecommunications mergers show how global cellular powerhouses are scouting for growth in emerging economies while consolidating in their own, crowded backyards. France Télécom offered to buy TeliaSonera, a Swedish-Finnish telecommunications operator, but within hours, TeliaSonera rejected the offer as too low. Analysts said higher bids—either from France Télécom or others—could persuade TeliaSonera to accept a deal. In the United States, Verizon Wireless agreed to buy Alltel for $28.1 billion—a deal that would make the company the biggest mobile phone operator in the United States. A combination of France Télécom and TeliaSonera would create the world's fourth-largest mobile operator, smaller only than China Mobile, Vodafone, and Telefónica of Spain.

Source: *International Herald Tribune*,
June 5, 2008

a. Explain the rent-seeking behavior of global telecommunications companies.

b. Explain how mergers may affect the efficiency of the telecommunications market.

Price Discrimination

31. **AT&T Moves Away from Unlimited-Data Pricing**

AT&T said it will eliminate its $30 unlimited data plan as the crush of data use from the iPhone has hurt call quality. AT&T is introducing new plans costing $15 a month for 200 megabytes of data traffic or $25 a month for 2 gigabytes. AT&T says those who exceed 2 gigabytes of usage will pay $10 a month for each additional gigabyte. AT&T hopes that these plans will attract more customers.

Source: *The Wall Street Journal*, June 2, 2010

a. Explain why AT&T's new plans might be price discrimination.

b. Draw a graph to illustrate the original plan and the new plans.

Monopoly Regulation

32. **iSurrender**

Getting your hands on a new iPhone means signing a two-year AT&T contract. Some markets, because of the costs of being a player, tend toward either a single firm or a small number of firms. Everyone hoped the wireless market would be different. A telephone monopoly has been the norm for most of American telecommunication history, except for what may turn out to have been a brief experimental period from 1984 through 2012 or so. It may be that telephone monopolies in America are a national tradition.

Source: *Slate*, June 10, 2008

a. How does AT&T being the exclusive provider of wireless service for the iPhone influence the wireless telecommunication market?

b. Explain why the wireless market may "tend toward either a single firm or a small number of firms." Why might this justify allowing a regulated monopoly to exist in this market?

Economics in the News

33. After you have studied *Reading Between the Lines* on pp. 316 – 317 answer the following questions.

a. Why does Consumer Watchdog say that Google needs to be investigated? Do you agree? Explain why or why not.

b. Explain why it would be inefficient to regulate Google to make it charge the same price per keyword click to all advertisers.

c. Explain why selling keywords to the highest bidder can lead to an efficient allocation of advertising resources.

34. **F.C.C. Planning Rules to Open Cable Market**

The Federal Communications Commission (F.C.C.) is setting new regulations to open the cable television market to independent programmers and rival video services. The new rules will make it easier for small independent programmers to lease access to cable channels and the size of the nation's largest cable companies will be capped at 30 percent of the market.

Source: *The New York Times*,
November 10, 2007

a. What barriers to entry exist in the cable television market?

b. Are high cable prices evidence of monopoly power?

c. Draw a graph to illustrate the effects of the F.C.C.'s new regulations on the price, quantity, total surplus, and deadweight loss.

35. **Antitrust Inquiry Launched into Intel**

Intel, the world's largest chipmaker, holds 80 percent of the microprocessor market. Advanced Micro Devices complains that Intel stifles competition, but Intel says that the 42.4 percent fall in prices between 2000 and 2007 shows that this industry is fiercely competitive.

Source: *The Washington Post*, June 7, 2008

a. Is Intel a monopoly in the chip market?

b. Evaluate the argument made by Intel that the fall in prices "shows that this industry is fiercely competitive."

14

MONOPOLISTIC COMPETITION

After studying this chapter,
you will be able to:

◆ Define and identify monopolistic competition

◆ Explain how a firm in monopolistic competition determines its price and output in the short run and the long run

◆ Explain why advertising costs are high and why firms use brand names in a monopolistically competitive industry

The online shoe store shoebuy.com lists athletic shoes made by 56 different producers in 40 different categories and priced between $25 and $850. Shoebuy offers 1,401 different types of athletic shoes for women and 1,757 different types for men. Because there are many different types of athletic shoes, the market for them isn't perfectly competitive. Athletic shoe producers compete, but each has a monopoly on its own special kind of shoe.

Most of the things that you buy are like athletic shoes—they come in many different types. Pizza and cell phones are two more striking examples.

The model of monopolistic competition that is explained in this chapter helps us to understand the competition that we see every day in the markets for athletic shoes, pizza, cell phones, and for most other consumer goods and services.

This chapter blends the models in the two preceding chapters on perfect competition and monopoly sto create the model of monopolistic competition. To get the most out of this chapter, you will have studied the two preceding ones.

Reading Between the Lines, at the end of this chapter, applies the monopolistic competition model to the market for smart phones and the entry of other firms in that market following the success of the Apple iPhone.

◆ What Is Monopolistic Competition?

You have studied perfect competition, in which a large number of firms produce at the lowest possible cost, make zero economic profit, and are efficient. You've also studied monopoly, in which a single firm restricts output, produces at a higher cost and price than in perfect competition, and is inefficient.

Most real-world markets are competitive but not perfectly competitive, because firms in these markets have some power to set their prices, as monopolies do. We call this type of market *monopolistic competition*.

Monopolistic competition is a market structure in which

- A large number of firms compete.
- Each firm produces a differentiated product.
- Firms compete on product quality, price, and marketing.
- Firms are free to enter and exit the industry.

Large Number of Firms

In monopolistic competition, as in perfect competition, the industry consists of a large number of firms. The presence of a large number of firms has three implications for the firms in the industry.

Small Market Share In monopolistic competition, each firm supplies a small part of the total industry output. Consequently, each firm has only limited power to influence the price of its product. Each firm's price can deviate from the average price of other firms by only a relatively small amount.

Ignore Other Firms A firm in monopolistic competition must be sensitive to the average market price of the product, but the firm does not pay attention to any one individual competitor. Because all the firms are relatively small, no one firm can dictate market conditions, and so no one firm's actions directly affect the actions of the other firms.

Collusion Impossible Firms in monopolistic competition would like to be able to conspire to fix a higher price—called *collusion*. But because the number of firms in monopolistic competition is large, coordination is difficult and collusion is not possible.

Product Differentiation

A firm practices **product differentiation** if it makes a product that is slightly different from the products of competing firms. A differentiated product is one that is a close substitute but not a perfect substitute for the products of the other firms. Some people are willing to pay more for one variety of the product, so when its price rises, the quantity demanded of that variety decreases, but it does not (necessarily) decrease to zero. For example, Adidas, Asics, Diadora, Etonic, Fila, New Balance, Nike, Puma, and Reebok all make differentiated running shoes. If the price of Adidas running shoes rises and the prices of the other shoes remain constant, Adidas sells fewer shoes and the other producers sell more. But Adidas shoes don't disappear unless the price rises by a large enough amount.

Competing on Quality, Price, and Marketing

Product differentiation enables a firm to compete with other firms in three areas: product quality, price, and marketing.

Quality The quality of a product is the physical attributes that make it different from the products of other firms. Quality includes design, reliability, the service provided to the buyer, and the buyer's ease of access to the product. Quality lies on a spectrum that runs from high to low. Some firms—such as Dell Computer Corp.—offer high-quality products. They are well designed and reliable, and the customer receives quick and efficient service. Other firms offer a lower-quality product that is poorly designed, that might not work perfectly, and that is not supported by effective customer service.

Price Because of product differentiation, a firm in monopolistic competition faces a downward-sloping demand curve. So, like a monopoly, the firm can set both its price and its output. But there is a tradeoff between the product's quality and price. A firm that makes a high-quality product can charge a higher price than a firm that makes a low-quality product.

Marketing Because of product differentiation, a firm in monopolistic competition must market its product. Marketing takes two main forms: advertising and packaging. A firm that produces a high-quality product wants to sell it for a suitably high price. To be able to do so, it must advertise and package its product in a way that convinces buyers that they are getting the higher quality for which they are paying a higher price. For example, pharmaceutical companies advertise and package their brand-name drugs to persuade buyers that these items are superior to the lower-priced generic alternatives. Similarly, a low-quality producer uses advertising and packaging to persuade buyers that although the quality is low, the low price more than compensates for this fact.

Entry and Exit

Monopolistic competition has no barriers to prevent new firms from entering the industry in the long run. Consequently, a firm in monopolistic competition cannot make an economic profit in the long run. When existing firms make an economic profit, new firms enter the industry. This entry lowers prices and eventually eliminates economic profit. When firms incur economic losses, some firms leave the industry in the long run. This exit increases prices and eventually eliminates the economic loss.

In long-run equilibrium, firms neither enter nor leave the industry and the firms in the industry make zero economic profit.

Examples of Monopolistic Competition

The box below shows 10 industries that are good examples of monopolistic competition. These industries have a large number of firms (shown in parentheses after the name of the industry). In the market for audio and video equipment, the largest 4 firms produce only 30 percent of the industry's total sales and the largest 20 firms produce 75 percent of total sales. The number on the right is the Herfindahl-Hirschman Index. Producers of clothing, jewelry, computers, and sporting goods operate in monopolistic competition.

REVIEW QUIZ

1 What are the distinguishing characteristics of monopolistic competition?
2 How do firms in monopolistic competition compete?
3 Provide some examples of industries near your school that operate in monopolistic competition (excluding those in the figure below).

You can work these questions in Study Plan 14.1 and get instant feedback.

Economics in Action
Monopolistic Competition Today

These ten industries operate in monopolistic competition. The number of firms in the industry is shown in parentheses after the name of the industry. The red bars show the percentage of industry sales by the largest 4 firms. The green bars show the percentage of industry sales by the next 4 largest firms, and the blue bars show the percentage of industry sales by the next 12 largest firms. So the entire length of the combined red, green, and blue bars shows the percentage of industry sales by the largest 20 firms. The Herfindahl-Hirschman Index is shown on the right.

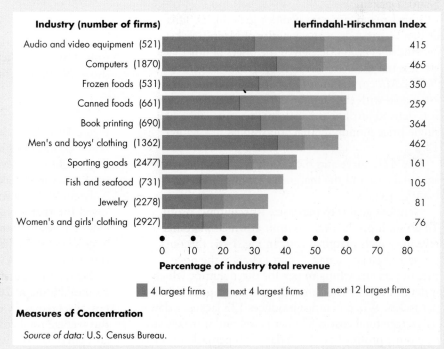

Measures of Concentration

Source of data: U.S. Census Bureau.

Price and Output in Monopolistic Competition

Suppose you've been hired by VF Corporation, the firm that owns Nautica Clothing Corporation, to manage the production and marketing of Nautica jackets. Think about the decisions that you must make at Nautica. First, you must decide on the design and quality of jackets and on your marketing program. Second, you must decide on the quantity of jackets to produce and the price at which to sell them.

We'll suppose that Nautica has already made its decisions about design, quality, and marketing and now we'll concentrate on the output and pricing decision. We'll study quality and marketing decisions in the next section.

For a given quality of jackets and marketing activity, Nautica faces given costs and market conditions. Given its costs and the demand for its jackets, how does Nautica decide the quantity of jackets to produce and the price at which to sell them?

The Firm's Short-Run Output and Price Decision

In the short run, a firm in monopolistic competition makes its output and price decision just like a monopoly firm does. Figure 14.1 illustrates this decision for Nautica jackets.

The demand curve for Nautica jackets is *D*. This demand curve tells us the quantity of Nautica jackets demanded at each price, given the prices of other jackets. It is not the demand curve for jackets in general.

The *MR* curve shows the marginal revenue curve associated with the demand curve for Nautica jackets. It is derived just like the marginal revenue curve of a single-price monopoly that you studied in Chapter 13.

The *ATC* curve and the *MC* curve show the average total cost and the marginal cost of producing Nautica jackets.

Nautica's goal is to maximize its economic profit. To do so, it produces the output at which marginal revenue equals marginal cost. In Fig. 14.1, this output is 125 jackets a day. Nautica charges the price that buyers are willing to pay for this quantity, which is determined by the demand curve. This price is $75 per jacket. When Nautica produces 125 jackets a day, its average total cost is $25 per jacket and it makes an economic profit of $6,250 a day ($50 per jacket mul-

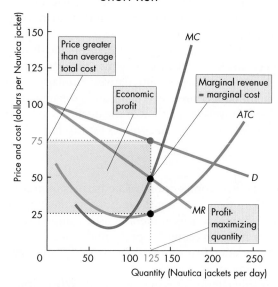

FIGURE 14.1 Economic Profit in the Short Run

Nautica maximizes profit by producing the quantity at which marginal revenue equals marginal cost, 125 jackets a day, and charging the price of $75 a jacket. This price exceeds the average total cost of $25 a jacket, so the firm makes an economic profit of $50 a jacket. The blue rectangle illustrates economic profit, which equals $6,250 a day ($50 a jacket multiplied by 125 jackets a day).

myeconlab animation

tiplied by 125 jackets a day). The blue rectangle shows Nautica's economic profit.

Profit Maximizing Might Be Loss Minimizing

Figure 14.1 shows that Nautica is making a large economic profit. But such an outcome is not inevitable. A firm might face a level of demand for its product that is too low for it to make an economic profit.

Excite@Home was such a firm. Offering high-speed Internet service over the same cable that provides television, Excite@Home hoped to capture a large share of the Internet portal market in competition with AOL, MSN, and a host of other providers.

Figure 14.2 illustrates the situation facing Excite@Home in 2001. The demand curve for its portal service is *D*, the marginal revenue curve is *MR*, the average total cost curve is *ATC*, and the marginal cost curve is *MC*. Excite@Home maximized profit—

FIGURE 14.2   Economic Loss in the Short Run

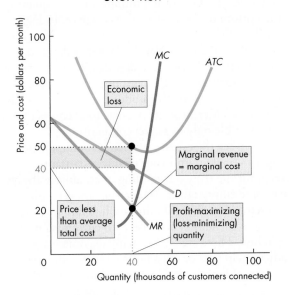

Profit is maximized where marginal revenue equals marginal cost. The loss-minimizing quantity is 40,000 customers. The price of $40 a month is less than the average total cost of $50 a month, so the firm incurs an economic loss of $10 a customer. The red rectangle illustrates economic loss, which equals $400,000 a month ($10 a customer multiplied by 40,000 customers).

(X) myeconlab animation

equivalently, it minimized its loss—by producing the output at which marginal revenue equals marginal cost. In Fig. 14.2, this output is 40,000 customers. Excite@Home charged the price that buyers were willing to pay for this quantity, which was determined by the demand curve and which was $40 a month. With 40,000 customers, Excite@Home's average total cost was $50 per customer, so it incurred an economic loss of $400,000 a month ($10 a customer multiplied by 40,000 customers). The red rectangle shows Excite@Home's economic loss.

So far, the firm in monopolistic competition looks like a single-price monopoly. It produces the quantity at which marginal revenue equals marginal cost and then charges the price that buyers are willing to pay for that quantity, as determined by the demand curve. The key difference between monopoly and monopolistic competition lies in what happens next when firms either make an economic profit or incur an economic loss.

Long Run: Zero Economic Profit

A firm like Excite@Home is not going to incur an economic loss for long. Eventually, it goes out of business. Also, there is no restriction on entry into monopolistic competition, so if firms in an industry are making economic profit, other firms have an incentive to enter that industry.

As the Gap and other firms start to make jackets similar to those made by Nautica, the demand for Nautica jackets decreases. The demand curve for Nautica jackets and the marginal revenue curve shift leftward. As these curves shift leftward, the profit-maximizing quantity and price fall.

Figure 14.3 shows the long-run equilibrium. The demand curve for Nautica jackets and the marginal revenue curve have shifted leftward. The firm produces 75 jackets a day and sells them for $25 each. At this output level, average total cost is also $25 per jacket.

FIGURE 14.3   Output and Price in the Long Run

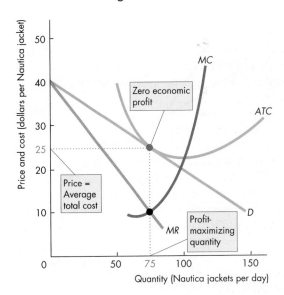

Economic profit encourages entry, which decreases the demand for each firm's product. When the demand curve touches the ATC curve at the quantity at which MR equals MC, the market is in long-run equilibrium. The output that maximizes profit is 75 jackets a day, and the price is $25 per jacket. Average total cost is also $25 per jacket, so economic profit is zero.

(X) myeconlab animation

So Nautica is making zero economic profit on its jackets. When all the firms in the industry are making zero economic profit, there is no incentive for new firms to enter.

If demand is so low relative to costs that firms incur economic losses, exit will occur. As firms leave an industry, the demand for the products of the remaining firms increases and their demand curves shift rightward. The exit process ends when all the firms in the industry are making zero economic profit.

Monopolistic Competition and Perfect Competition

Figure 14.4 compares monopolistic competition and perfect competition and highlights two key differences between them:

- Excess capacity
- Markup

Excess Capacity A firm has **excess capacity** if it produces below its **efficient scale**, which is the quantity at which average total cost is a minimum—the quantity at the bottom of the U-shaped *ATC* curve. In Fig. 14.4, the efficient scale is 100 jackets a day. Nautica in part (a) produces 75 Nautica jackets a day and has *excess capacity* of 25 jackets a day. But if all jackets are alike and are produced by firms in perfect competition, each firm in part (b) produces 100 jackets a day, which is the efficient scale. Average total cost is the lowest possible only in *perfect* competition.

You can see the excess capacity in monopolistic competition all around you. Family restaurants (except for the truly outstanding ones) almost always have some empty tables. You can always get a pizza delivered in less than 30 minutes. It is rare that every pump at a gas station is in use with customers waiting in line. There are always many real estate agents ready to help find or sell a home. These industries are examples of monopolistic competition. The firms

FIGURE 14.4 Excess Capacity and Markup

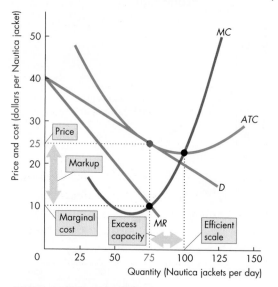

(a) Monopolistic competition

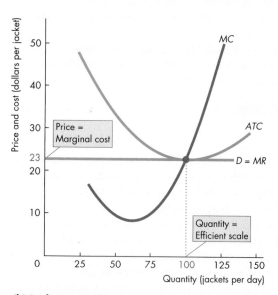

(b) Perfect competition

The efficient scale is 100 jackets a day. In monopolistic competition in the long run, because the firm faces a downward-sloping demand curve for its product, the quantity produced is less than the efficient scale and the firm has excess capacity. Price exceeds marginal cost by the amount of the markup.

In contrast, because in perfect competition the demand for each firm's product is perfectly elastic, the quantity produced in the long run equals the efficient scale and price equals marginal cost. The firm produces at the least possible cost and there is no markup.

have excess capacity. They could sell more by cutting their prices, but they would then incur losses.

Markup A firm's **markup** is the amount by which price exceeds marginal cost. Figure 14.4(a) shows Nautica's markup. In perfect competition, price always equals marginal cost and there is no markup. Figure 14.4(b) shows this case. In monopolistic competition, buyers pay a higher price than in perfect competition and also pay more than marginal cost.

Is Monopolistic Competition Efficient?

Resources are used efficiently when marginal social benefit equals marginal social cost. Price equals marginal social benefit and the firm's marginal cost equals marginal social cost (assuming there are no external benefits or costs). So if the price of a Nautica jacket exceeds the marginal cost of producing it, the quantity of Nautica jackets produced is less than the efficient quantity. And you've just seen that in long-run equilibrium in monopolistic competition, price *does* exceed marginal cost. So is the quantity produced in monopolistic competition less than the efficient quantity?

Making the Relevant Comparison Two economists meet in the street, and one asks the other, "How is your husband?" The quick reply is "Compared to what?" This bit of economic wit illustrates a key point: Before we can conclude that something needs fixing, we must check out the available alternatives.

The markup that drives a gap between price and marginal cost in monopolistic competition arises from product differentiation. It is because Nautica jackets are not quite the same as jackets from Banana Republic, CK, Diesel, DKNY, Earl Jackets, Gap, Levi's, Ralph Lauren, or any of the other dozens of producers of jackets that the demand for Nautica jackets is not perfectly elastic. The only way in which the demand for jackets from Nautica might be perfectly elastic is if there is only one kind of jacket and all firms make it. In this situation, Nautica jackets are indistinguishable from all other jackets. They don't even have identifying labels.

If there was only one kind of jacket, the total benefit of jackets would almost certainly be less than it is with variety. People value variety—not only because it enables each person to select what he or she likes best but also because it provides an external benefit. Most of us enjoy seeing variety in the choices of oth-

ers. Contrast a scene from the China of the 1960s, when everyone wore a Mao tunic, with the China of today, where everyone wears the clothes of their own choosing. Or contrast a scene from the Germany of the 1930s, when almost everyone who could afford a car owned a first-generation Volkswagen Beetle, with the world of today with its enormous variety of styles and types of automobiles.

If people value variety, why don't we see infinite variety? The answer is that variety is costly. Each different variety of any product must be designed, and then customers must be informed about it. These initial costs of design and marketing—called setup costs—mean that some varieties that are too close to others already available are just not worth creating.

The Bottom Line Product variety is both valued and costly. The efficient degree of product variety is the one for which the marginal social benefit of product variety equals its marginal social cost. The loss that arises because the quantity produced is less than the efficient quantity is offset by the gain that arises from having a greater degree of product variety. So compared to the alternative—product uniformity—monopolistic competition might be efficient.

REVIEW QUIZ

1 How does a firm in monopolistic competition decide how much to produce and at what price to offer its product for sale?

2 Why can a firm in monopolistic competition make an economic profit only in the short run?

3 Why do firms in monopolistic competition operate with excess capacity?

4 Why is there a price markup over marginal cost in monopolistic competition?

5 Is monopolistic competition efficient?

You can work these questions in Study Plan 14.2 and get instant feedback.

You've seen how the firm in monopolistic competition determines its output and price in both the short run and the long run when it produces a given product and undertakes a *given* marketing effort. But how does the firm choose its product quality and marketing effort? We'll now study these decisions.

◆ Product Development and Marketing

When Nautica made its price and output decision that we've just studied, it had already made its product quality and marketing decisions. We're now going to look at these decisions and see how they influence the firm's output, price, and economic profit.

Innovation and Product Development

The prospect of new firms entering the industry keeps firms in monopolistic competition on their toes! To enjoy economic profits, they must continually seek ways of keeping one step ahead of imitators—other firms who imitate the success of profitable firms.

One major way of trying to maintain economic profit is for a firm to seek out new products that will provide it with a competitive edge, even if only temporarily. A firm that introduces a new and differentiated product faces a demand that is less elastic and is able to increase its price and make an economic profit. Eventually, imitators will make close substitutes for the innovative product and compete away the economic profit arising from an initial advantage. So to restore economic profit, the firm must again innovate.

Profit-Maximizing Product Innovation The decision to innovate and develop a new or improved product is based on the same type of profit-maximizing calculation that you've already studied.

Innovation and product development are costly activities, but they also bring in additional revenues. The firm must balance the cost and revenue at the margin.

The marginal dollar spent on developing a new or improved product is the marginal cost of product development. The marginal dollar that the new or improved product earns for the firm is the marginal revenue of product development. At a low level of product development, the marginal revenue from a better product exceeds the marginal cost. At a high level of product development, the marginal cost of a better product exceeds the marginal revenue.

When the marginal cost and marginal revenue of product development are equal, the firm is undertaking the profit-maximizing amount of product development.

Efficiency and Product Innovation Is the profit-maximizing amount of product innovation also the efficient amount? Efficiency is achieved if the marginal social benefit of a new and improved product equals its marginal social cost.

The marginal social benefit of an innovation is the increase in price that consumers are willing to pay for it. The marginal social cost is the amount that the firm must pay to make the innovation. Profit is maximized when marginal *revenue* equals marginal cost. But in monopolistic competition, marginal revenue is less than price, so product innovation is probably not pushed to its efficient level.

Monopolistic competition brings many product innovations that cost little to implement and are purely cosmetic, such as new and improved packaging or a new scent in laundry powder. And even when there is a genuine improved product, it is never as good as what the consumer is willing to pay for. For example, "The Legend of Zelda: Twilight Princess" is regarded as an almost perfect and very cool game, but users complain that it isn't quite perfect. It is a game whose features generate a marginal revenue equal to the marginal cost of creating them.

Advertising

A firm with a differentiated product needs to ensure that its customers know how its product is different from the competition. A firm also might attempt to create a consumer perception that its product is different from its competitors, even when that difference is small. Firms use advertising and packaging to achieve this goal.

Advertising Expenditures Firms in monopolistic competition incur huge costs to ensure that buyers appreciate and value the differences between their own products and those of their competitors. So a large proportion of the price that we pay for a good covers the cost of selling it, and this proportion is increasing. Advertising in newspapers and magazines and on radio, television, and the Internet is the main selling cost. But it is not the only one. Selling costs include the cost of shopping malls that look like movie sets, glossy catalogs and brochures, and the salaries, airfares, and hotel bills of salespeople.

Advertising expenditures affect the profits of firms in two ways: They increase costs, and they change demand. Let's look at these effects.

Economics in Action

The Cost of Selling a Pair of Shoes

When you buy a pair of running shoes that cost you $70, you're paying $9 for the materials from which the shoes are made, $2.75 for the services of the Malaysian worker who made the shoes, and $5.25 for the production and transportation services of a manufacturing firm in Asia and a shipping company. These numbers total $17. You pay $3 to the U.S. government in import duty. So we've now accounted for a total of $20. Where did the other $50 go? It is the cost of advertising, retailing, and other sales and distribution services.

The selling costs associated with running shoes are not unusual. Almost everything that you buy includes a selling cost component that exceeds one half of the total cost. Your clothing, food, electronic items, DVDs, magazines, and even your textbooks cost more to sell than they cost to manufacture.

Advertising costs are only a part, and often a small part, of total selling costs. For example, Nike spends about $4 on advertising per pair of running shoes sold.

For the U.S. economy as a whole, there are some 20,000 advertising agencies, which employ more than 200,000 people and have sales of $45 billion. These numbers are only part of the total cost of advertising because firms have their own internal advertising departments, the costs of which we can only guess.

But the biggest part of selling costs is not the cost of advertising. It is the cost of retailing services. The retailer's selling costs (and economic profit) are often as much as 50 percent of the price you pay.

| Raw materials $9 | Production costs $8 | Import duty $3 | Selling costs $50 |

Selling Costs and Total Cost Selling costs are fixed costs and they increase the firm's total cost. So like the fixed cost of producing a good, advertising costs per unit decrease as the quantity produced increases.

Figure 14.5 shows how selling costs change a firm's average total cost. The blue curve shows the average total cost of production. The red curve shows the firm's average total cost of production plus advertising. The height of the red area between the two curves shows the average fixed cost of advertising. The *total* cost of advertising is fixed. But the *average* cost of advertising decreases as output increases.

Figure 14.5 shows that if advertising increases the quantity sold by a large enough amount, it can lower average total cost. For example, if the quantity sold increases from 25 jackets a day with no advertising to 100 jackets a day with advertising, average total cost falls from $60 to $40 a jacket. The reason is that although the *total* fixed cost has increased, the greater fixed cost is spread over a greater output, so average total cost decreases.

FIGURE 14.5   Selling Costs and Total Cost

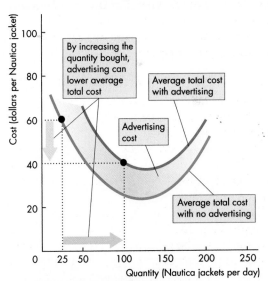

Selling costs such as the cost of advertising are fixed costs. When added to the average total cost of production, selling costs increase average total cost by a greater amount at small outputs than at large outputs. If advertising enables sales to increase from 25 jackets a day to 100 jackets a day, average total cost *falls* from $60 to $40 a jacket.

Selling Costs and Demand Advertising and other selling efforts change the demand for a firm's product. But how? Does demand increase or does it decrease? The most natural answer is that advertising increases demand. By informing people about the quality of its products or by persuading people to switch from the products of other firms, a firm might expect to increase the demand for its own products.

But all firms in monopolistic competition advertise, and all seek to persuade customers that they have the best deal. If advertising enables a firm to survive, the number of firms in the market might increase. And to the extent that the number of firms does increase, advertising *decreases* the demand faced by any one firm. It also makes the demand for any one firm's product more elastic. So advertising can end up not only lowering average total cost but also lowering the markup and the price.

Figure 14.6 illustrates this possible effect of advertising. In part (a), with no advertising, the demand for Nautica jackets is not very elastic. Profit is maxi-

mized at 75 jackets per day, and the markup is large. In part (b), advertising, which is a fixed cost, increases average total cost from ATC_0 to ATC_1 but leaves marginal cost unchanged at MC. Demand becomes much more elastic, the profit-maximizing quantity increases, and the markup shrinks.

Using Advertising to Signal Quality

Some advertising, like the Ashton Kutcher Nikon Coolpix ads on television or the huge number of dollars that Coke and Pepsi spend, seems hard to understand. There doesn't seem to be any concrete information about a camera in an actor's glistening smile. And surely everyone knows about Coke and Pepsi. What is the gain from pouring millions of dollars into advertising these well-known colas?

One answer is that advertising is a signal to the consumer of a high-quality product. A **signal** is an action taken by an informed person (or firm) to send a message to uninformed people. Think about two colas:

FIGURE 14.6   Advertising and the Markup

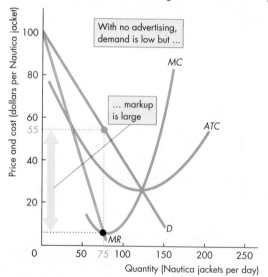

(a) No firms advertise

If no firms advertise, demand for each firm's product is low and not very elastic. The profit-maximizing output is small, the markup is large, and the price is high.

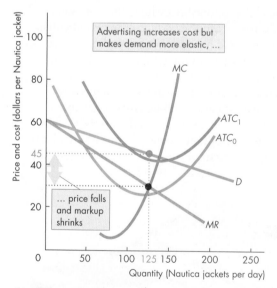

(b) All firms advertise

Advertising increases average total cost and shifts the *ATC* curve upward from ATC_0 to ATC_1. If all firms advertise, the demand for each firm's product becomes more elastic. Output increases, the price falls, and the markup shrinks.

Coke and Oke. Oke knows that its cola is not very good and that its taste varies a lot depending on which cheap batch of unsold cola it happens to buy each week. So Oke knows that while it could get a lot of people to try Oke by advertising, they would all quickly discover what a poor product it is and switch back to the cola they bought before. Coke, in contrast, knows that its product has a high-quality consistent taste and that once consumers have tried it, there is a good chance they'll never drink anything else. On the basis of this reasoning, Oke doesn't advertise but Coke does. And Coke spends a lot of money to make a big splash.

Cola drinkers who see Coke's splashy ads know that the firm would not spend so much money advertising if its product were not truly good. So consumers reason that Coke is indeed a really good product. The flashy expensive ad has signaled that Coke is really good without saying anything about Coke.

Notice that if advertising is a signal, it doesn't need any specific product information. It just needs to be expensive and hard to miss. That's what a lot of advertising looks like. So the signaling theory of advertising predicts much of the advertising that we see.

Brand Names

Many firms create and spend a lot of money promoting a brand name. Why? What benefit does a brand name bring to justify the sometimes high cost of establishing it?

The basic answer is that a brand name provides information to consumers about the quality of a product, and is an incentive to the producer to achieve a high and consistent quality standard.

To see how a brand name helps the consumer, think about how you use brand names to get information about quality. You're on a road trip, and it is time to find a place to spend the night. You see roadside advertisements for Holiday Inn, Joe's Motel, and Annie's Driver's Stop. You know about Holiday Inn because you've stayed in it before. You've also seen their advertisements and know what to expect. You have no information at all about Joe's and Annie's. They might be better than the lodgings you do know about, but without that knowledge, you're not going to try them. You use the brand name as information and stay at Holiday Inn.

This same story explains why a brand name provides an incentive to achieve high and consistent quality. Because no one would know whether Joe's and Annie's were offering a high standard of service, they

have no incentive to do so. But equally, because everyone expects a given standard of service from Holiday Inn, a failure to meet a customer's expectation would almost surely lose that customer to a competitor. So Holiday Inn has a strong incentive to deliver what it promises in the advertising that creates its brand name.

Efficiency of Advertising and Brand Names

To the extent that advertising and brand names provide consumers with information about the precise nature of product differences and about product quality, they benefit the consumer and enable a better product choice to be made. But the opportunity cost of the additional information must be weighed against the gain to the consumer.

The final verdict on the efficiency of monopolistic competition is ambiguous. In some cases, the gains from extra product variety unquestionably offset the selling costs and the extra cost arising from excess capacity. The tremendous varieties of books and magazines, clothing, food, and drinks are examples of such gains. It is less easy to see the gains from being able to buy a brand-name drug that has a chemical composition identical to that of a generic alternative, but many people do willingly pay more for the brand-name alternative.

REVIEW QUIZ

1 How, other than by adjusting price, do firms in monopolistic competition compete?
2 Why might product innovation and development be efficient and why might it be inefficient?
3 How do selling costs influence a firm's cost curves and its average total cost?
4 How does advertising influence demand?
5 Are advertising and brand names efficient?

You can work these questions in Study Plan 14.3 and get instant feedback.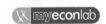

◆ Monopolistic competition is one of the most common market structures that you encounter in your daily life. *Reading Between the Lines* on pp. 334–335 applies the model of monopolistic competition to the market for smart phones and shows why you can expect continual innovation and the introduction of new phones from Apple and other producers of smart phones.

Product Differentiation and Entry in the Market for Smart Phones

Apple Sues Rival HTC as Phone Competition Rises

http://seattletimes.nwsource.com
March 2, 2010

As Apple Inc.'s iPhone faces stiffer competition in the lucrative market for smart phones, the company is going after one of its main rivals with patent lawsuits claiming theft of touch screen technology and other features.

The complaints, which Apple filed Tuesday, cover a slew of models made by Taiwanese phone maker HTC Corp., including the Nexus One, G1, and myTouch 3G—all using the free, rival Android mobile operating software from Google Inc. Non-Android phones include HTC's Touch series.

But consumers shouldn't worry about buying or using any of those phones. Patent cases can take months or years to resolve—sometimes longer than the life of these phones—and agreements over licensing and royalty payments often emerge.

Still, it shows Apple's get-tough strategy as significant competitors emerge.

"We can sit by and watch competitors steal our patented inventions, or we can do something about it," Apple CEO Steve Jobs said in a statement. "We've decided to do something about it."...

Since the iPhone's debut, Apple has had a lock on much of the smart phone market, alongside Research In Motion Ltd., which makes the popular BlackBerry devices.

However, over the last year or so, more competition has emerged from such phone makers as HTC and Motorola Inc., which are rolling out smart phones that use Google's Android software. Not only do these phones appeal to consumers, but they also work on numerous wireless networks, unlike the iPhone, which is still limited in the United States to AT&T Inc. ...

ESSENCE OF THE STORY

- The iPhone faces stiff competition in the market for smart phones.

- Apple is bringing patent lawsuits against HTC Corp., one of its main rivals, claiming theft of touch screen technology.

- The smart phones produced by HTC Corp. include the Nexus One, G1, and myTouch 3G.

- Resolving patent cases can take longer than the life of the product.

- Apple and Research In Motion Ltd., which makes the BlackBerry, have the largest share of the smart phone market.

- More competition is coming from phone makers HTC, Motorola Inc., and others.

ECONOMIC ANALYSIS

- Apple sold its first iPhone in 2007 and brought the more powerful 3G version to market in 2008.

- By creating a substantially differentiated product, Apple was able to generate a great deal of interest in smart phones throughout the world.

- In the first weekend, Apple sold 1 million of the 3G iPhone.

- But within a month of the launch of the 3G iPhone, many competing but differentiated devices were on the market.

- The monopolistic competition model explains what is happening in the smart phone market.

- Figure 1 shows the market for Apple's iPhone in its first month. (The numbers are assumptions.)

- Because Apple's iPhone differs from its competitors and has features that users value, the demand curve, *D*, and marginal revenue curve, *MR*, provide a large short-run profit opportunity.

- The marginal cost curve is *MC* and the average total cost curve is *ATC*. Apple maximizes its economic profit by producing the quantity at which marginal revenue equals marginal cost, which in this example is 3 million iPhones a month.

- This quantity of iPhones can be sold for $200 each.

- The blue rectangle shows Apple's economic profit.

- Because this market is profitable, entry takes place. HTC, Motorola, and others (such as Research in Motion, LG, Nokia, and Samsung) enter the smart phone market.

- Figure 2 shows the the consequences of entry.

- The demand for the iPhone decreases as the market is shared with the other phones.

- Apple's profit-maximizing price for the iPhone falls, and in the long run, economic profit is eliminated.

- With zero economic profit, Apple has an incentive to develop an even better differentiated phone and start the cycle described here again, making an economic profit in a new phone in the short run.

- The iPhone 4, announced in June 2010, was Apple's response to the entry described in the news article.

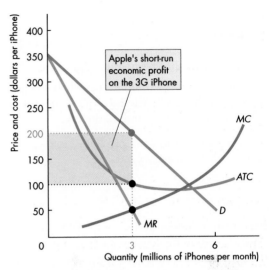

Figure 1 Economic profit in the short run

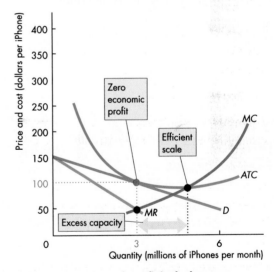

Figure 2 Zero economic profit in the long run

◆ **SUMMARY**

Key Points

What Is Monopolistic Competition? (pp. 324–325)

- Monopolistic competition occurs when a large number of firms compete with each other on product quality, price, and marketing.

Working Problems 1 and 2 will give you a better understanding of what monopolistic competition is.

Price and Output in Monopolistic Competition

(pp. 326–329)

- Each firm in monopolistic competition faces a downward-sloping demand curve and produces the profit-maximizing quantity.
- Entry and exit result in zero economic profit and excess capacity in long-run equilibrium.

Working Problems 3 to 12 will give you a better understanding of price and output in monopolistic competition.

Product Development and Marketing (pp. 330–333)

- Firms in monopolistic competition innovate and develop new products.
- Advertising expenditures increase total cost, but average total cost might fall if the quantity sold increases by enough.
- Advertising expenditures might increase demand, but demand might decrease if competition increases.
- Whether monopolistic competition is inefficient depends on the value we place on product variety.

Working Problems 13 to 18 will give you a better understanding of product development and marketing.

Key Terms

Efficient scale, 328	Markup, 329	Product differentiation, 324
Excess capacity, 328	Monopolistic competition, 324	Signal, 332

STUDY PLAN PROBLEMS AND APPLICATIONS

 myeconlab You can work Problems 1 to 19 in MyEconLab Chapter 14 Study Plan and get instant feedback.

What Is Monopolistic Competition? (Study Plan 14.1)

1. Which of the following items are sold by firms in monopolistic competition? Explain your selections.
   - Cable television service
   - Wheat
   - Athletic shoes
   - Soda
   - Toothbrushes
   - Ready-mix concrete

2. The four-firm concentration ratio for audio equipment makers is 30 and for electric lamp makers it is 89. The HHI for audio equipment makers it is 415 and for electric lamp makers it is 2,850. Which of these markets is an example of monopolistic competition?

Price and Output in Monopolistic Competition

(Study Plan 14.2)

Use the following information to work Problems 3 and 4.

Sara is a dot.com entrepreneur who has established a Web site at which people can design and buy sweatshirts. Sara pays $1,000 a week for her Web server and Internet connection. The sweatshirts that her customers design are made to order by another firm, and Sara pays this firm $20 a sweatshirt. Sara has no other costs. The table sets out the demand schedule for Sara's sweatshirts.

Price (dollars per sweatshirt)	Quantity demanded (sweatshirts per week)
0	100
20	80
40	60
60	40
80	20
100	0

3. Calculate Sara's profit-maximizing output, price, and economic profit.

4. a. Do you expect other firms to enter the Web sweatshirt business and compete with Sara?
   b. What happens to the demand for Sara's sweatshirts in the long run? What happens to Sara's economic profit in the long run?

Use the following figure, which shows the situation facing a producer of running shoes, to work Problems 5 to 10.

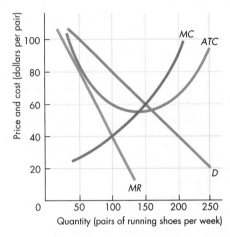

5. What quantity does the firm produce, what price does it charge, and what is its economic profit or economic loss?

6. In the long run, how does the number of firms producing running shoes change?

7. In the long run, how does the price of running shoes and the quantity the firm produces change? What happens to the market output?

8. Does the firm have excess capacity in the long run? If the firm has excess capacity in the long run, why doesn't it decrease its capacity?

9. In the long run, compare the price of a pair of running shoes and the marginal cost of producing the pair.

10. Is the market for running shoes efficient or inefficient in the long run? Explain your answer.

11. **Wake Up and Smell the Coffee**

    Every change that Starbucks made over the past few years—automated espresso machines, pre-ground coffee, drive-throughs, fewer soft chairs and less carpeting—was made for a reason: to smooth operations or boost sales. Those may have been the right choices at the time, but together they ultimately diluted the coffee-centric experience. By 2008, Starbucks experienced a drop in traffic as customers complained that in pursuing rapid growth, the company has strayed too far from its roots. Starbucks will once again grind beans in its stores for drip coffee, give free drip refills, and provide two hours of wi-fi. The company will roll out its new sleek, low-rise espresso machine that makes baristas more visible.

Source: *Time*, April 7, 2008

a. Explain how Starbucks' past attempts to maximize profits ended up eroding product differentiation.

b. Explain how Starbucks' new plan intends to increase economic profit.

12. **The Shoe That Won't Quit**

I finally decided to take the plunge and buy a pair of Uggs, but when I got around to shopping for my Uggs, the style that I wanted was sold out. The scarcity factor was not a glitch in the supply chain, but rather a carefully calibrated strategy by Ugg's parent Deckers Outdoor that is one of the big reasons behind the brand's success. Deckers tightly controls distribution to ensure that supply does not outstrip demand. If Deckers ever opened up the supply of Uggs to meet demand, sales would shoot up like a rocket, but they'd come back down just as fast.

Source: *Fortune*, June 5, 2008

a. Explain why Deckers intentionally restricts the quantity of Uggs that the firm sells.

b. Draw a graph to illustrate how Deckers maximizes the economic profit from Uggs.

Product Development and Marketing (Study Plan 14.3)

Use the following information to work Problems 13 to 16.

Suppose that Tommy Hilfiger's marginal cost of a jacket is a constant $100 and the total fixed cost at one of its stores is $2,000 a day. This store sells 20 jackets a day, which is its profit-maximizing number of jackets. Then the stores nearby start to advertise their jackets. The Tommy Hilfiger store now spends $2,000 a day advertising its jackets, and its profit-maximizing number of jackets sold jumps to 50 a day.

13. a. What is this store's average total cost of a jacket sold before the advertising begins?

b. What is this store's average total cost of a jacket sold after the advertising begins?

14. a. Can you say what happens to the price of a Tommy Hilfiger jacket? Why or why not?

b. Can you say what happens to Tommy's markup? Why or why not?

c. Can you say what happens to Tommy's economic profit? Why or why not?

15. How might Tommy Hilfiger use advertising as a signal? How is a signal sent and how does it work?

16. How does having a brand name help Tommy Hilfiger to increase its economic profit?

Use the following news clip to work Problems 17 and 18.

Food's Next Billion-Dollar Brand?

While it's not the biggest brand in margarine, Smart Balance has an edge on its rivals in that it's made with a patented blend of vegetable and fruit oils that has been shown to help improve consumers' cholesterol levels. Smart Balance sales have skyrocketed while overall sales for margarine have stagnated. It remains to be seen if Smart Balance's healthy message and high price will resound with consumers.

Source: *Fortune*, June 4, 2008

17. How do you expect advertising and the Smart Balance brand name will affect Smart Balance's ability to make a positive economic profit?

18. Are long-run economic profits a possibility for Smart Balance? In long-run equilibrium, will Smart Balance have excess capacity or a markup?

Economics in the News (Study Plan 14.N)

19. **Computer Makers Prepare to Stake Bigger Claim in Phones**

Emboldened by Apple's success with its iPhone, many PC makers and chip companies are charging into the mobile-phone business, promising new devices that can pack the horsepower of standard computers into palm-size packages—devices that handle the full glory of the Internet, power two-way video conferences, and stream high-definition movies to your TV. It is a development that spells serious competition for established cell-phone makers and phone companies.

Source: *The New York Times*, March 15, 2009

a. Draw a graph of the cost curves and revenue curves of a cell-phone company that makes a positive economic profit in the short run.

b. If cell-phone companies start to include the popular features introduced by PC makers, explain how this decision will affect their profit in the short run.

c. What do you expect to happen to the cell-phone company's economic profit in the long run, given the information in the news clip?

d. Draw a graph to illustrate your answer to part (c).

ADDITIONAL PROBLEMS AND APPLICATIONS

 myeconlab You can work these problems in MyEconLab if assigned by your instructor.

What Is Monopolistic Competition?

20. Which of the following items are sold by firms in monopolistic competition? Explain your selection.
    - Orange juice
    - Canned soup
    - PCs
    - Chewing gum
    - Breakfast cereals
    - Corn

21. The HHI for automobiles is 2,350, for sporting goods it is 161, for batteries it is 2,883, and for jewelry it is 81. Which of these markets is an example of monopolistic competition?

Price and Output in Monopolistic Competition

Use the following information to work Problems 22 and 23.

Lorie teaches singing. Her fixed costs are $1,000 a month, and it costs her $50 of labor to give one class. The table shows the demand schedule for Lorie's singing lessons.

Price (dollars per lesson)	Quantity demanded (lessons per month)
0	250
50	200
100	150
150	100
200	50
250	0

22. Calculate Lorie's profit-maximizing output, price, and economic profit.

23. a. Do you expect other firms to enter the singing lesson business and compete with Lorie?
    b. What happens to the demand for Lorie's lessons in the long run? What happens to Lorie's economic profit in the long run?

Use the following figure, which shows the situation facing Mike's Bikes, a producer of mountain bikes, to work Problems 24 to 28. The demand and costs of other mountain bike producers are similar to those of Mike's Bikes.

24. What quantity does the firm produce and what is its price? Calculate the firm's economic profit or economic loss.

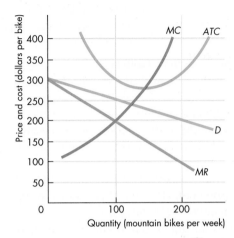

25. What will happen to the number of firms producing mountain bikes in the long run?

26. a. How will the price of a mountain bike and the number of bikes produced by Mike's Bikes change in the long run?
    b. How will the quantity of mountain bikes produced by all firms change in the long run?

27. Is there any way for Mike's Bikes to avoid having excess capacity in the long run?

28. Is the market for mountain bikes efficient or inefficient in the long run? Explain your answer.

Use the following news clip to work Problems 29 and 30.

Groceries for the Gourmet Palate

No food, it seems, is safe from being repackaged to look like an upscale product. Samuel Adams' $120 Utopias, in a ridiculous copper-covered 24-oz. bottle meant to resemble an old-fashioned brew kettle, is barely beer. It's not carbonated like a Bud, but aged in oak barrels like scotch. It has a vintage year, like a Bordeaux, is light, complex, and free of any alcohol sting, despite having six times as much alcohol content as a regular can of brew.

Source: *Time*, April 14, 2008

29. a. Explain how Samuel Adams has differentiated its Utopias to compete with other beer brands in terms of quality, price, and marketing.
    b. Predict whether Samuel Adams produces at, above, or below the efficient scale in the short run.

30. a. Predict whether the $120 price tag on the Utopias is at, above, or below marginal cost:

(i) In the short run.

(ii) In the long run.

b. Do you think that Samuel Adams Utopias makes the market for beer inefficient?

Use the following news clip to work Problems 31 and 32.

Swinging for Female Golfers

One of the hottest areas of innovation is in clubs for women, who now make up nearly a quarter of the 24 million golfers in the United States. Callaway and Nike, two of the leading golf-equipment manufacturers, recently released new clubs designed specifically for women.

Source: *Time*, April 21, 2008

31. a. How are Callaway and Nike attempting to maintain economic profit?

b. Draw a graph to illustrate the cost curves and revenue curves of Callaway or Nike in the market for golf clubs for women.

c. Show on your graph in part (b) the short-run economic profit.

32. a. Explain why the economic profit that Callaway and Nike make on golf clubs for women is likely to be temporary.

b. Draw a graph to illustrate the cost curves and revenue curves of Callaway or Nike in the market for golf clubs for women in the long run. Mark the firm's excess capacity.

Product Development and Marketing

Use the following information to work Problems 33 to 35.

Bianca bakes delicious cookies. Her total fixed cost is $40 a day, and her average variable cost is $1 a bag. Few people know about Bianca's Cookies, and she is maximizing her profit by selling 10 bags a day for $5 a bag. Bianca thinks that if she spends $50 a day on advertising, she can increase her market share and sell 25 bags a day for $5 a bag.

33. If Bianca's advertising works as she expects, can she increase her economic profit by advertising?

34. If Bianca advertises, will her average total cost increase or decrease at the quantity produced?

35. If Bianca advertises, will she continue to sell her cookies for $5 a bag or will she change her price?

Use the following news clip to work Problems 36 and 37.

A Thirst for More Champagne

Champagne exports have tripled in the past 20 years. That poses a problem for northern France, where the bubbly hails from—not enough grapes. So French authorities have unveiled a plan to extend the official Champagne grape-growing zone to cover 40 new villages. This revision has provoked debate. The change will take several years to become effective. In the meantime the vineyard owners whose land values will jump markedly if the changes are finalized certainly have reason to raise a glass.

Source: *Fortune*, May 12, 2008

36. a. Why is France so strict about designating the vineyards that can use the Champagne label?

b. Explain who most likely opposes this plan.

37. Assuming that vineyards in these 40 villages are producing the same quality of grapes with or without this plan, why will their land values "jump markedly" if this plan is approved?

38. **Under Armour's Big Step Up**

Under Armour, the red-hot athletic-apparel brand, has joined Nike, Adidas, and New Balance as a major player in the market for athletic footwear. Under Armour plans to revive the long-dead cross-training category. But will young athletes really spend $100 for a cross training shoe to lift weights in?

Source: *Time*, May 26, 2008

What factors influence Under Armour's ability to make an economic profit in the cross-training shoe market?

Economics in the News

39. After you have studied *Reading Between the Lines* on pp. 334–335 answer the following questions.

a. Describe the cost curves (*MC* and *ATC*) and the marginal revenue and demand curves for the iPhone when Apple first introduced it.

b. How do you think the creation of the iPhone influenced the demand for older generation cell phones?

c. Explain the effects of the introduction of the 3G iPhone on HTC and other firms in the market for smart phones.

d. Draw a graph to illustrate your answer to part (c).

e. Explain the effect on Apple of the decisions by BlackBerry and HTC to bring their own smart phones to market.

f. Draw a graph to illustrate your answer to part (e).

g. Do you think the smart phone market is efficient? Explain your answer.

h. Do you predict that producers of smart phones have excess capacity? Explain your answer.

15

OLIGOPOLY

After studying this chapter,
you will be able to:

◆ Define and identify oligopoly
◆ Use game theory to explain how price and output are
determined in oligopoly
◆ Use game theory to explain other strategic decisions
◆ Describe the antitrust laws that regulate oligopoly

The chip in your laptop was made by either Intel or Advanced Micro Devices;
the battery in your TV remote is most likely a Duracell or Energizer; if you use a
high-tech razor, it is either a Gillette or a Schick; and if you take a long-
distance trip by air, you will fly in an airplane made by either Boeing or the
European firm Airbus. In the markets for computer chips, batteries, high-tech
razors, and big airplanes, two producers compete for market share in the
pursuit of maximum profit. Many other markets have only a small number of
firms. Among them are the markets for light bulbs, breakfast cereals, and major
appliances.

How does a market work when only a handful of firms compete? Is the
market efficient like perfect competition with the firms operating in the social
interest? Or is the market inefficient like monopoly with the firms restricting
output to increase profit?

To answer these questions, we need to understand the models of oligopoly.
These models use game theory, which the chapter explains.

At the end of the chapter, in *Reading Between the Lines*, we'll look at the market
for high-tech razors and see the game that Gillette and Schick are playing in their
battle for market shares and maximum profit.

341

◆ What Is Oligopoly?

Oligopoly, like monopolistic competition, lies between perfect competition and monopoly. The firms in oligopoly might produce an identical product and compete only on price, or they might produce a differentiated product and compete on price, product quality, and marketing. **Oligopoly** is a market structure in which

- Natural or legal barriers prevent the entry of new firms.
- A small number of firms compete.

Barriers to Entry

Natural or legal barriers to entry can create oligopoly. You saw in Chapter 13 how economies of scale and demand form a natural barrier to entry that can create a *natural monopoly*. These same factors can create a *natural oligopoly*.

Figure 15.1 illustrates two natural oligopolies. The demand curve, *D* (in both parts of the figure), shows the demand for taxi rides in a town. If the average

total cost curve of a taxi company is ATC_1 in part (a), the market is a natural **duopoly**—an oligopoly market with two firms. You can probably see some examples of duopoly where you live. Some cities have only two taxi companies, two car rental firms, two copy centers, or two college bookstores.

The lowest price at which the firm would remain in business is $10 a ride. At that price, the quantity of rides demanded is 60 a day, the quantity that can be provided by just two firms. There is no room in this market for three firms. But if there were only one firm, it would make an economic profit and a second firm would enter to take some of the business and economic profit.

If the average total cost curve of a taxi company is ATC_2 in part (b), the efficient scale of one firm is 20 rides a day. This market is large enough for three firms.

A legal oligopoly arises when a legal barrier to entry protects the small number of firms in a market. A city might license two taxi firms or two bus companies, for example, even though the combination of demand and economies of scale leaves room for more than two firms.

FIGURE 15.1   Natural Oligopoly

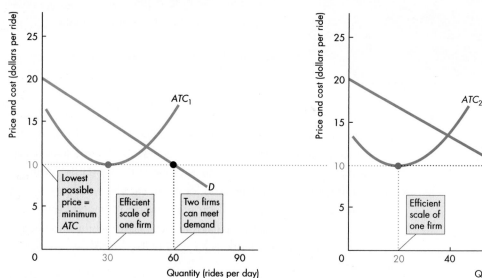

(a) Natural duopoly

(b) Natural oligopoly with three firms

The lowest possible price is $10 a ride, which is the minimum average total cost. When a firm produces 30 rides a day, the efficient scale, two firms can satisfy the market demand. This natural oligopoly has two firms—a natural duopoly.

When the efficient scale of one firm is 20 rides per day, three firms can satisfy the market demand at the lowest possible price. This natural oligopoly has three firms.

Small Number of Firms

Because barriers to entry exist, oligopoly consists of a small number of firms, each of which has a large share of the market. Such firms are interdependent, and they face a temptation to cooperate to increase their joint economic profit.

Interdependence With a small number of firms in a market, each firm's actions influence the profits of all the other firms. When Penny Stafford opened her coffee shop in Bellevue, Washington, a nearby Starbucks coffee shop took a hit. Within days, Starbucks began to attract Penny's customers with enticing offers and lower prices. Starbucks survived but Penny eventually went out of business. Penny Stafford and Starbucks were interdependent.

Temptation to Cooperate When a small number of firms share a market, they can increase their profits by forming a cartel and acting like a monopoly. A **cartel** is a group of firms acting together—colluding—to limit output, raise price, and increase economic profit. Cartels are illegal, but they do operate in some markets. But for reasons that you'll discover in this chapter, cartels tend to break down.

Examples of Oligopoly

The box below shows some examples of oligopoly. The dividing line between oligopoly and monopolistic competition is hard to pin down. As a practical matter, we identify oligopoly by looking at concentration ratios, the Herfindahl-Hirschman Index, and information about the geographical scope of the market and barriers to entry. The HHI that divides oligopoly from monopolistic competition is generally taken to be 1,000. An HHI below 1,000 is usually an example of monopolistic competition, and a market in which the HHI exceeds 1,000 is usually an example of oligopoly.

REVIEW QUIZ

1 What are the two distinguishing characteristics of oligopoly?
2 Why are firms in oligopoly interdependent?
3 Why do firms in oligopoly face a temptation to collude?
4 Can you think of some examples of oligopolies that you buy from?

You can work these questions in Study Plan 15.1 and get instant feedback.

Economics in Action
Oligopoly Today

These markets are oligopolies. Although in some of them, the number of firms (in parentheses) is large, the share of the market held by the 4 largest firms (the red bars) is close to 100 percent.

The most concentrated markets—cigarettes, glass bottles and jars, washing machines and dryers, and batteries, are dominated by just one or two firms.

If you want to buy a battery for your TV remote or toothbrush, you'll find it hard to avoid buying a Duracell or an Energizer.

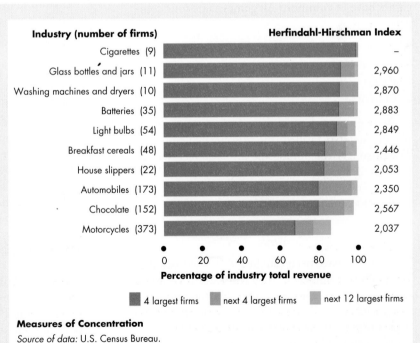

Measures of Concentration
Source of data: U.S. Census Bureau.

Oligopoly Games

Economists think about oligopoly as a game between two or a few players, and to study oligopoly markets they use game theory. **Game theory** is a set of tools for studying *strategic behavior*—behavior that takes into account the expected behavior of others and the recognition of mutual interdependence. Game theory was invented by John von Neumann in 1937 and extended by von Neumann and Oskar Morgenstern in 1944 (p. 367). Today, it is one of the major research fields in economics.

Game theory seeks to understand oligopoly as well as other forms of economic, political, social, and even biological rivalries by using a method of analysis specifically designed to understand games of all types, including the familiar games of everyday life (see Talking with Thomas Hubbard on pp. 368–370). To lay the foundation for studying oligopoly games, we first think about the features that all games share.

What Is a Game?

What is a game? At first thought, the question seems silly. After all, there are many different games. There are ball games and parlor games, games of chance and games of skill. But what is it about all these different activities that makes them games? What do all these games have in common? All games share four common features:

- Rules
- Strategies
- Payoffs
- Outcome

We're going to look at these features of games by playing at a game called "the prisoners' dilemma." The prisoners' dilemma game displays the essential features of many games, including oligopoly games, and it gives a good illustration of how game theory works and generates predictions.

The Prisoners' Dilemma

Art and Bob have been caught red-handed stealing a car. Facing airtight cases, they will receive a sentence of two years each for their crime. During his interviews with the two prisoners, the district attorney begins to suspect that he has stumbled on the two people who were responsible for a multimillion-dollar bank robbery some months earlier. But this is just a suspicion. He has no evidence on which he can convict them of the greater crime unless he can get them to confess. But how can he extract a confession? The answer is by making the prisoners play a game. The district attorney makes the prisoners play the following game.

Rules Each prisoner (player) is placed in a separate room and cannot communicate with the other prisoner. Each is told that he is suspected of having carried out the bank robbery and that

If both of them confess to the larger crime, each will receive a sentence of 3 years for both crimes.

If he alone confesses and his accomplice does not, he will receive only a 1-year sentence while his accomplice will receive a 10-year sentence.

Strategies In game theory, **strategies** are all the possible actions of each player. Art and Bob each have two possible actions:

1. Confess to the bank robbery.
2. Deny having committed the bank robbery.

Because there are two players, each with two strategies, there are four possible outcomes:

1. Both confess.
2. Both deny.
3. Art confesses and Bob denies.
4. Bob confesses and Art denies.

Payoffs Each prisoner can work out his *payoff* in each of these situations, and we can tabulate the four possible payoffs for each of the prisoners in what is called a payoff matrix for the game. A **payoff matrix** is a table that shows the payoffs for every possible action by each player for every possible action by each other player.

Table 15.1 shows a payoff matrix for Art and Bob. The squares show the payoffs for each prisoner—the red triangle in each square shows Art's and the blue triangle shows Bob's. If both prisoners confess (top left), each gets a prison term of 3 years. If Bob confesses but Art denies (top right), Art gets a 10-year sentence and Bob gets a 1-year sentence. If Art confesses and Bob denies (bottom left), Art gets a 1-year sentence and Bob gets a 10-year sentence. Finally, if both of them deny (bottom right), neither can be convicted of the bank robbery charge but both are sentenced for the car theft—a 2-year sentence.

Outcome The choices of both players determine the outcome of the game. To predict that outcome, we use an equilibrium idea proposed by John Nash of Princeton University (who received the Nobel Prize for Economic Science in 1994 and was the subject of the 2001 movie *A Beautiful Mind*). In **Nash equilibrium**, player *A* takes the best possible action given the action of player *B* and player *B* takes the best possible action given the action of player *A*.

In the case of the prisoners' dilemma, the Nash equilibrium occurs when Art makes his best choice given Bob's choice and when Bob makes his best choice given Art's choice.

To find the Nash equilibrium, we compare all the possible outcomes associated with each choice and eliminate those that are dominated—that are not as good as some other choice. Let's find the Nash equilibrium for the prisoners' dilemma game.

Finding the Nash Equilibrium Look at the situation from Art's point of view. If Bob confesses (top row), Art's best action is to confess because in that case, he is sentenced to 3 years rather than 10 years. If Bob denies (bottom row), Art's best action is still to confess because in that case he receives 1 year rather than 2 years. So Art's best action is to confess.

Now look at the situation from Bob's point of view. If Art confesses (left column), Bob's best action is to confess because in that case, he is sentenced to 3 years rather than 10 years. If Art denies (right column), Bob's best action is still to confess because in that case, he receives 1 year rather than 2 years. So Bob's best action is to confess.

Because each player's best action is to confess, each does confess, each goes to jail for 3 years, and the district attorney has solved the bank robbery. This is the Nash equilibrium of the game.

The Nash equilibrium for the prisoners' dilemma is called a **dominant-strategy equilibrium**, which is an equilibrium in which the best strategy of each player is to cheat (confess) *regardless of the strategy of the other player*.

The Dilemma The dilemma arises as each prisoner contemplates the consequences of his decision and puts himself in the place of his accomplice. Each knows that it would be best if both denied. But each also knows that if he denies it is in the best interest of the other to confess. So each considers whether to deny and rely on his accomplice to deny or to confess

TABLE 15.1   Prisoners' Dilemma Payoff Matrix

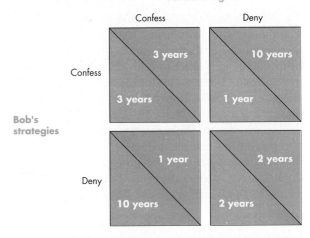

Each square shows the payoffs for the two players, Art and Bob, for each possible pair of actions. In each square, the red triangle shows Art's payoff and the blue triangle shows Bob's. For example, if both confess, the payoffs are in the top left square. The equilibrium of the game is for both players to confess and each gets a 3-year sentence.

hoping that his accomplice denies but expecting him to confess. The dilemma leads to the equilibrium of the game.

A Bad Outcome For the prisoners, the equilibrium of the game, with each confessing, is not the best outcome. If neither of them confesses, each gets only 2 years for the lesser crime. Isn't there some way in which this better outcome can be achieved? It seems that there is not, because the players cannot communicate with each other. Each player can put himself in the other player's place, and so each player can figure out that there is a best strategy for each of them. The prisoners are indeed in a dilemma. Each knows that he can serve 2 years *only* if he can trust the other to deny. But each prisoner also knows that it is *not* in the best interest of the other to deny. So each prisoner knows that he must confess, thereby delivering a bad outcome for both.

The firms in an oligopoly are in a similar situation to Art and Bob in the prisoners' dilemma game. Let's see how we can use this game to understand oligopoly.

An Oligopoly Price-Fixing Game

We can use game theory and a game like the prisoners' dilemma to understand price fixing, price wars, and other aspects of the behavior of firms in oligopoly. We'll begin with a price-fixing game.

To understand price fixing, we're going to study the special case of duopoly—an oligopoly with two firms. Duopoly is easier to study than oligopoly with three or more firms, and it captures the essence of all oligopoly situations. Somehow, the two firms must share the market. And how they share it depends on the actions of each. We're going to describe the costs of the two firms and the market demand for the item they produce. We're then going to see how game theory helps us to predict the prices charged and the quantities produced by the two firms in a duopoly.

Cost and Demand Conditions Two firms, Trick and Gear, produce switchgears. They have identical costs. Figure 15.2(a) shows their average total cost curve (*ATC*) and marginal cost curve (*MC*). Figure 15.2(b) shows the market demand curve for switchgears (*D*). The two firms produce identical switchgears, so one firm's switchgear is a perfect substitute for the other's, and the market price of each firm's product is identical. The quantity demanded depends on that price—the higher the price, the smaller is the quantity demanded.

This industry is a natural duopoly. Two firms can produce this good at a lower cost than either one firm or three firms can. For each firm, average total cost is at its minimum when production is 3,000 units a week. When price equals minimum average total cost, the total quantity demanded is 6,000 units a week, and two firms can just produce that quantity.

Collusion We'll suppose that Trick and Gear enter into a collusive agreement. A **collusive agreement** is an agreement between two (or more) producers to form a cartel to restrict output, raise the price, and increase profits. Such an agreement is illegal in the United States and is undertaken in secret. The strategies that firms in a cartel can pursue are to

- Comply
- Cheat

A firm that complies carries out the agreement. A firm that cheats breaks the agreement to its own benefit and to the cost of the other firm.

Because each firm has two strategies, there are four possible combinations of actions for the firms:

1. Both firms comply.
2. Both firms cheat.
3. Trick complies and Gear cheats.
4. Gear complies and Trick cheats.

FIGURE 15.2 Costs and Demand

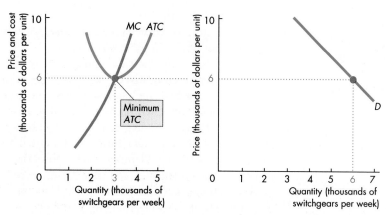

(a) Individual firm **(b) Industry**

The average total cost curve for each firm is *ATC*, and the marginal cost curve is *MC* (part a). Minimum average total cost is $6,000 a unit, and it occurs at a production of 3,000 units a week.

Part (b) shows the market demand curve. At a price of $6,000, the quantity demanded is 6,000 units per week. The two firms can produce this output at the lowest possible average cost. If the market had one firm, it would be profitable for another to enter. If the market had three firms, one would exit. There is room for only two firms in this industry. It is a natural duopoly.

Colluding to Maximize Profits Let's work out the payoffs to the two firms if they collude to make the maximum profit for the cartel by acting like a monopoly. The calculations that the two firms perform are the same calculations that a monopoly performs. (You can refresh your memory of these calculations by looking at Chapter 13, pp. 304–305.) The only thing that the firms in duopoly must do beyond what a monopoly does is to agree on how much of the total output each of them will produce.

Figure 15.3 shows the price and quantity that maximize industry profit for the duopoly. Part (a) shows the situation for each firm, and part (b) shows the situation for the industry as a whole. The curve labeled *MR* is the industry marginal revenue curve. This marginal revenue curve is like that of a single-price monopoly (Chapter 13, p. 302).The curve labeled MC_I is the industry marginal cost curve if each firm produces the same quantity of output. This curve is constructed by adding together the outputs of the two firms at each level of marginal cost. Because the two firms are the same size, at each level of marginal cost, the industry output is twice the output of one firm. The curve MC_I in part (b) is twice as far to the right as the curve *MC* in part (a).

To maximize industry profit, the firms in the duopoly agree to restrict output to the rate that makes the industry marginal cost and marginal revenue equal. That output rate, as shown in part (b), is 4,000 units a week. The demand curve shows that the highest price for which the 4,000 switchgears can be sold is $9,000 each. Trick and Gear agree to charge this price.

To hold the price at $9,000 a unit, production must be 4,000 units a week. So Trick and Gear must agree on output rates for each of them that total 4,000 units a week. Let's suppose that they agree to split the market equally so that each firm produces 2,000 switchgears a week. Because the firms are identical, this division is the most likely.

The average total cost (*ATC*) of producing 2,000 switchgears a week is $8,000, so the profit per unit is $1,000 and economic profit is $2 million (2,000 units × $1,000 per unit). The economic profit of each firm is represented by the blue rectangle in Fig. 15.3(a).

We have just described one possible outcome for a duopoly game: The two firms collude to produce the monopoly profit-maximizing output and divide that output equally between themselves. From the industry point of view, this solution is identical to a monopoly. A duopoly that operates in this way is indistinguishable from a monopoly. The economic profit that is made by a monopoly is the maximum total profit that can be made by the duopoly when the firms collude.

But with price greater than marginal cost, either firm might think of trying to increase profit by cheating on the agreement and producing more than the agreed amount. Let's see what happens if one of the firms does cheat in this way.

FIGURE 15.3   Colluding to Make Monopoly Profits

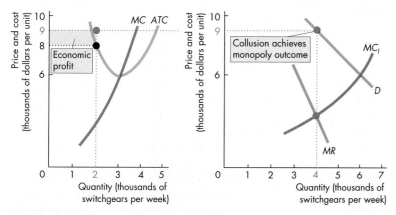

(a) Individual firm

(b) Industry

The industry marginal cost curve, MC_I in part (b), is the horizontal sum of the two firms' marginal cost curves, *MC* in part (a). The industry marginal revenue curve is *MR*. To maximize profit, the firms produce 4,000 units a week (the quantity at which marginal revenue equals marginal cost). They sell that output for $9,000 a unit. Each firm produces 2,000 units a week. Average total cost is $8,000 a unit, so each firm makes an economic profit of $2 million (blue rectangle)—2,000 units multiplied by $1,000 profit a unit.

myeconlab   animation

One Firm Cheats on a Collusive Agreement To set
the stage for cheating on their agreement, Trick convinces Gear that demand has decreased and that it
cannot sell 2,000 units a week. Trick tells Gear that it
plans to cut its price so that it can sell the agreed
2,000 units each week. Because the two firms produce an identical product, Gear matches Trick's price
cut but still produces only 2,000 units a week.

In fact, there has been no decrease in demand.
Trick plans to increase output, which it knows will
lower the price, and Trick wants to ensure that Gear's
output remains at the agreed level.

Figure 15.4 illustrates the consequences of Trick's
cheating. Part (a) shows Gear (the complier); part (b)
shows Trick (the cheat); and part (c) shows the industry as a whole. Suppose that Trick increases output to
3,000 units a week. If Gear sticks to the agreement to
produce only 2,000 units a week, total output is now
5,000 a week, and given demand in part (c), the price
falls to $7,500 a unit.

Gear continues to produce 2,000 units a week at a
cost of $8,000 a unit and incurs a loss of $500 a unit,
or $1 million a week. This economic loss is shown by
the red rectangle in part (a). Trick produces 3,000
units a week at a cost of $6,000 a unit. With a price

of $7,500, Trick makes a profit of $1,500 a unit and
therefore an economic profit of $4.5 million. This
economic profit is the blue rectangle in part (b).

We've now described a second possible outcome for
the duopoly game: One of the firms cheats on the collusive agreement. In this case, the industry output is
larger than the monopoly output and the industry
price is lower than the monopoly price. The total economic profit made by the industry is also smaller than
the monopoly's economic profit. Trick (the cheat)
makes an economic profit of $4.5 million, and Gear
(the complier) incurs an economic loss of $1 million.
The industry makes an economic profit of $3.5 mil-
lion. This industry profit is $0.5 million less than the
economic profit that a monopoly would make, but it
is distributed unevenly. Trick makes a bigger economic
profit than it would under the collusive agreement,
while Gear incurs an economic loss.

A similar outcome would arise if Gear cheated and
Trick complied with the agreement. The industry
profit and price would be the same, but in this case,
Gear (the cheat) would make an economic profit of
$4.5 million and Trick (the complier) would incur an
economic loss of $1 million.

Let's next see what happens if both firms cheat.

FIGURE 15.4   One Firm Cheats

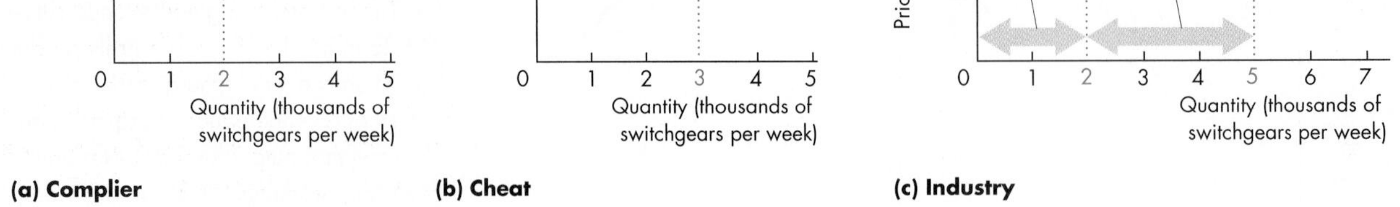

(a) Complier   **(b) Cheat**   **(c) Industry**

One firm, shown in part (a), complies with the agreement
and produces 2,000 units. The other firm, shown in part (b),
cheats on the agreement and increases its output to 3,000
units a week. Given the market demand curve, shown in
part (c), and with a total production of 5,000 units a week,

the price falls to $7,500 a unit. At this price, the complier in
part (a) incurs an economic loss of $1 million ($500 per unit
× 2,000 units), shown by the red rectangle. In part (b), the
cheat makes an economic profit of $4.5 million ($1,500 per
unit × 3,000 units), shown by the blue rectangle.

myeconlab animation

Both Firms Cheat Suppose that both firms cheat and that each firm behaves like the cheating firm that we have just analyzed. Each tells the other that it is unable to sell its output at the going price and that it plans to cut its price. But because both firms cheat, each will propose a successively lower price. As long as price exceeds marginal cost, each firm has an incentive to increase its production—to cheat. Only when price equals marginal cost is there no further incentive to cheat. This situation arises when the price has reached $6,000. At this price, marginal cost equals price. Also, price equals minimum average total cost. At a price less than $6,000, each firm incurs an economic loss. At a price of $6,000, each firm covers all its costs and makes zero economic profit. Also, at a price of $6,000, each firm wants to produce 3,000 units a week, so the industry output is 6,000 units a week. Given the demand conditions, 6,000 units can be sold at a price of $6,000 each.

Figure 15.5 illustrates the situation just described. Each firm, in part (a), produces 3,000 units a week, and its average total cost is a minimum ($6,000 per unit). The market as a whole, in part (b), operates at the point at which the market demand curve (D) intersects the industry marginal cost curve (MC_I). Each firm has lowered its price and increased its output to try to gain an advantage over the other firm. Each has pushed this process as far as it can without incurring an economic loss.

We have now described a third possible outcome of this duopoly game: Both firms cheat. If both firms cheat on the collusive agreement, the output of each firm is 3,000 units a week and the price is $6,000 a unit. Each firm makes zero economic profit.

The Payoff Matrix Now that we have described the strategies and payoffs in the duopoly game, we can summarize the strategies and the payoffs in the form of the game's payoff matrix. Then we can find the Nash equilibrium.

Table 15.2 sets out the payoff matrix for this game. It is constructed in the same way as the payoff matrix for the prisoners' dilemma in Table 15.1. The squares show the payoffs for the two firms—Gear and Trick. In this case, the payoffs are profits. (For the prisoners' dilemma, the payoffs were losses.)

The table shows that if both firms cheat (top left), they achieve the perfectly competitive outcome—each firm makes zero economic profit. If both firms comply (bottom right), the industry makes the monopoly profit and each firm makes an economic profit of $2 million. The top right and bottom left squares show the payoff if one firm cheats while the other complies. The firm that cheats makes an economic profit of $4.5 million, and the one that complies incurs a loss of $1 million.

Nash Equilibrium in the Duopolists' Dilemma The duopolists have a dilemma like the prisoners' dilemma. Do they comply or cheat? To answer this question, we must find the Nash equilibrium.

FIGURE 15.5 Both Firms Cheat

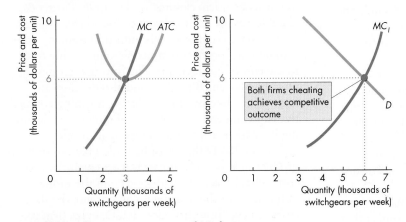

(a) Individual firm

(b) Industry

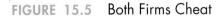
Both firms cheating achieves competitive outcome

If both firms cheat by increasing production, the collusive agreement collapses. The limit to the collapse is the competitive equilibrium. Neither firm will cut its price below $6,000 (minimum average total cost) because to do so will result in losses. In part (a), each firm produces 3,000 units a week at an average total cost of $6,000. In part (b), with a total production of 6,000 units, the price falls to $6,000. Each firm now makes zero economic profit. This output and price are the ones that would prevail in a competitive industry.

myeconlab animation

TABLE 15.2   Duopoly Payoff Matrix

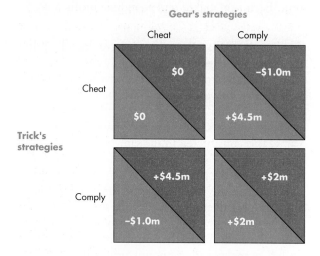

Each square shows the payoffs from a pair of actions. For example, if both firms comply with the collusive agreement, the payoffs are recorded in the bottom right square. The red triangle shows Gear's payoff, and the blue triangle shows Trick's. In Nash equilibrium, both firms cheat.

Look at things from Gear's point of view. Gear reasons as follows: Suppose that Trick cheats. If I comply, I will incur an economic loss of $1 million. If I also cheat, I will make zero economic profit. Zero is better than *minus* $1 million, so I'm better off if I cheat. Now suppose Trick complies. If I cheat, I will make an economic profit of $4.5 million, and if I comply, I will make an economic profit of $2 million. A $4.5 million profit is better than a $2 million profit, so I'm better off if I cheat. So regardless of whether Trick cheats or complies, it pays Gear to cheat. Cheating is Gear's best strategy.

Trick comes to the same conclusion as Gear because the two firms face an identical situation. So both firms cheat. The Nash equilibrium of the duopoly game is that both firms cheat. And although the industry has only two firms, they charge the same price and produce the same quantity as those in a competitive industry. Also, as in perfect competition, each firm makes zero economic profit.

This conclusion is not general and will not always arise. We'll see why not by looking first at some other games that are like the prisoners' dilemma. Then we'll broaden the types of games we consider.

Other Oligopoly Games

Firms in oligopoly must decide whether to mount expensive advertising campaigns; whether to modify their product; whether to make their product more reliable and more durable; whether to price discriminate and, if so, among which groups of customers and to what degree; whether to undertake a large research and development (R&D) effort aimed at lowering production costs; and whether to enter or leave an industry.

All of these choices can be analyzed as games that are similar to the one that we've just studied. Let's look at one example: an R&D game.

Economics in Action
An R&D Game in the Market for Diapers

Disposable diapers have been around for a bit more than 40 years. Procter & Gamble (which has a 40 percent market share with Pampers) and Kimberly-Clark (which has a 33 percent market share with Huggies) have always been the market leaders.

When the disposable diaper was first introduced, it had to be cost-effective in competition with reusable, laundered diapers. A costly research and development effort resulted in the development of machines that could make disposable diapers at a low enough cost to achieve that initial competitive edge. But new firms tried to get into the business and take market share away from the two industry leaders, and the industry leaders themselves battled each other to maintain or increase their own market shares.

During the early 1990s, Kimberly-Clark was the first to introduce Velcro closures. And in 1996, Procter & Gamble was the first to introduce "breathable" diapers.

The key to success in this industry (as in any other) is to design a product that people value highly relative to the cost of producing it. The firm that creates the most highly valued product and also develops the least-cost technology for producing it gains a competitive edge, undercutting the rest of the market, increasing its market share, and increasing its profit.

But the R&D that must be undertaken to improve product quality and cut cost is itself costly. So the cost of R&D must be deducted from the profit resulting from the increased market share that lower costs achieve. If no firm does R&D, every firm can be better off, but if one firm initiates the R&D activity, all must follow.

Table 15.3 illustrates the dilemma (with hypothetical numbers) for the R&D game that Kimberly-Clark and Procter & Gamble play. Each firm has two strategies: Spend $25 million a year on R&D or spend nothing on R&D. If neither firm spends on R&D, they make a joint profit of $100 million: $30 million for Kimberly-Clark and $70 million for Procter & Gamble (bottom right of the payoff matrix). If each firm conducts R&D, market shares are maintained but each firm's profit is lower by the amount spent on R&D (top left square of the payoff matrix). If Kimberly-Clark pays for R&D but Procter & Gamble does not, Kimberly-Clark gains a large part of Procter & Gamble's market. Kimberly-Clark profits, and Procter & Gamble loses (top right square of the payoff matrix). Finally, if Procter & Gamble conducts R&D and Kimberly-Clark does not, Procter & Gamble gains market share from Kimberly-Clark, increasing its profit, while Kimberly-Clark incurs a loss (bottom left square).

TABLE 15.3   Pampers Versus Huggies: An R&D Game

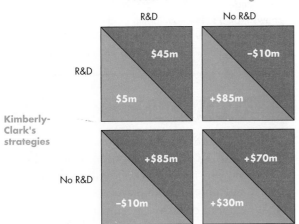

If both firms undertake R&D, their payoffs are those shown in the top left square. If neither firm undertakes R&D, their payoffs are in the bottom right square. When one firm undertakes R&D and the other one does not, their payoffs are in the top right and bottom left squares. The red triangle shows Procter & Gamble's payoff, and the blue triangle shows Kimberly-Clark's. The Nash equilibrium for this game is for both firms to undertake R&D. The structure of this game is the same as that of the prisoners' dilemma.

Confronted with the payoff matrix in Table 15.3, the two firms calculate their best strategies. Kimberly-Clark reasons as follows: If Procter & Gamble does not undertake R&D, we will make $85 million if we do and $30 million if we do not; so it pays us to conduct R&D. If Procter & Gamble conducts R&D, we will lose $10 million if we don't and make $5 million if we do. Again, R&D pays off. So conducting R&D is the best strategy for Kimberly-Clark. It pays, regardless of Procter & Gamble's decision.

Procter & Gamble reasons similarly: If Kimberly-Clark does not undertake R&D, we will make $70 million if we follow suit and $85 million if we conduct R&D. It therefore pays to conduct R&D. If Kimberly-Clark does undertake R&D, we will make $45 million by doing the same and lose $10 million by not doing R&D. Again, it pays us to conduct R&D. So for Procter & Gamble, R&D is also the best strategy.

Because R&D is the best strategy for both players, it is the Nash equilibrium. The outcome of this game is that both firms conduct R&D. They make less profit than they would if they could collude to achieve the cooperative outcome of no R&D.

The real-world situation has more players than Kimberly-Clark and Procter & Gamble. A large number of other firms share a small portion of the market, all of them ready to eat into the market share of Procter & Gamble and Kimberly-Clark. So the R&D efforts by these two firms not only serve the purpose of maintaining shares in their own battle but also help to keep barriers to entry high enough to preserve their joint market share.

The Disappearing Invisible Hand

All the games that we've studied are versions of the prisoners' dilemma. The essence of that game lies in the structure of its payoffs. The worst possible outcome for each player arises from cooperating when the other player cheats. The best possible outcome, for each player to cooperate, is not a Nash equilibrium because it is in neither player's *self-interest* to cooperate if the other one cooperates. It is this failure to achieve the best outcome for both players—the best social outcome if the two players are the entire economy—that led John Nash to claim (as he was portrayed as doing in the movie *A Beautiful Mind*) that he had challenged Adam Smith's idea that we are always guided, as if by an invisible hand, to promote the social interest when we are pursuing our self-interest.

A Game of Chicken

The Nash equilibrium for the prisoners' dilemma is unique: both players cheat (confess). Not all games have a unique equilibrium, and one that doesn't is a game called "chicken."

An Example of the Game of Chicken A graphic, if disturbing, version of "chicken" has two cars racing toward each other. The first driver to swerve and avoid a crash is the "chicken." The payoffs are a big loss for both if no one "chickens out;" zero for both if both "chicken out;" and zero for the chicken and a gain for the one who stays the course. If player 1 swerves, player 2's best strategy is to stay the course; and if player 1 stays the course, player 2's best strategy is to swerve.

An Economic Example of Chicken An economic game of chicken can arise when R&D creates a new technology that cannot be kept secret or patented, so both firms benefit from the R&D of either firm. The chicken in this case is the firm that does the R&D.

Suppose, for example, that either Apple or Nokia spends $9 million developing a new touch-screen technology that both would end up being able to use regardless of which of them developed it.

Table 15.4 illustrates a payoff matrix for the game that Apple and Nokia play. Each firm has two strategies: Do the R&D ("chicken out") or do not do the R&D. Each entry shows the additional profit (the profit from the new technology minus the cost of the research), given the strategies adopted.

If neither firm does the R&D, each makes zero additional profit. If both firms conduct the R&D, each firm makes an additional $5 million. If one of the firms does the R&D ("chickens out"), the chicken makes $1 million and the other firm makes $10 million. Confronted with these payoffs the two firms calculate their best strategies. Nokia is better off doing R&D if Apple does no R&D. Apple is better off doing R&D if Nokia does no R&D. There are two Nash equilibrium outcomes: Only one of them does the R&D, but we can't predict which one.

You can see that an outcome with no firm doing R&D isn't a Nash equilibrium because one firm would be better off doing it. Also both firms doing R&D isn't a Nash equilibrium because one firm would be better off *not* doing it. To decide *which* firm does the R&D, the firms might toss a coin, called a mixed strategy.

TABLE 15.4   An R&D Game of Chicken

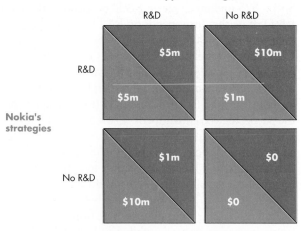

If neither firm does the R&D, their payoffs are in the bottom right square. When one firm "chickens out" and does the R&D while the other does no R&D, their payoffs are in the top right and bottom left squares. When both "chicken out" and do the R&D, the payoffs are in the top left square. The red triangle shows Apple's payoff, and the blue triangle shows Nokia's. The equilibrium for this R&D game of chicken is for only one firm to undertake the R&D. We cannot tell which firm will do the R&D and which will not.

REVIEW QUIZ

1 What are the common features of all games?
2 Describe the prisoners' dilemma game and explain why the Nash equilibrium delivers a bad outcome for both players.
3 Why does a collusive agreement to restrict output and raise price create a game like the prisoners' dilemma?
4 What creates an incentive for firms in a collusive agreement to cheat and increase production?
5 What is the equilibrium strategy for each firm in a duopolists' dilemma and why do the firms not succeed in colluding to raise the price and profits?
6 Describe two structures of payoffs for an R&D game and contrast the prisoners' dilemma and the chicken game.

You can work these questions in Study Plan 15.2 and get instant feedback.

Repeated Games and Sequential Games

The games that we've studied are played just once. In contrast, many real-world games are played repeatedly. This feature of games turns out to enable real-world duopolists to cooperate, collude, and make a monopoly profit.

Another feature of the games that we've studied is that the players move simultaneously. But in many real-world situations, one player moves first and then the other moves—the play is sequential rather than simultaneous. This feature of real-world games creates a large number of possible outcomes.

We're now going to examine these two aspects of strategic decision-making.

A Repeated Duopoly Game

If two firms play a game repeatedly, one firm has the opportunity to penalize the other for previous "bad" behavior. If Gear cheats this week, perhaps Trick will cheat next week. Before Gear cheats this week, won't it consider the possibility that Trick will cheat next week? What is the equilibrium of this game?

Actually, there is more than one possibility. One is the Nash equilibrium that we have just analyzed. Both players cheat, and each makes zero economic profit forever. In such a situation, it will never pay one of the players to start complying unilaterally because to do so would result in a loss for that player and a profit for the other. But a **cooperative equilibrium** in which the players make and share the monopoly profit is possible.

A cooperative equilibrium might occur if cheating is punished. There are two extremes of punishment. The smallest penalty is called "tit for tat." A *tit-for-tat strategy* is one in which a player cooperates in the current period if the other player cooperated in the previous period, but cheats in the current period if the other player cheated in the previous period. The most severe form of punishment is called a trigger strategy. A *trigger strategy* is one in which a player cooperates if the other player cooperates but plays the Nash equilibrium strategy forever thereafter if the other player cheats.

In the duopoly game between Gear and Trick, a tit-for-tat strategy keeps both players cooperating and making monopoly profits. Let's see why with an example.

Table 15.5 shows the economic profit that Trick and Gear will make over a number of periods under two alternative sequences of events: colluding and cheating with a tit-for-tat response by the other firm.

If both firms stick to the collusive agreement in period 1, each makes an economic profit of $2 million. Suppose that Trick contemplates cheating in period 1. The cheating produces a quick $4.5 million economic profit and inflicts a $1 million economic loss on Gear. But a cheat in period 1 produces a response from Gear in period 2. If Trick wants to get back into a profit-making situation, it must return to the agreement in period 2 even though it knows that Gear will punish it for cheating in period 1. So in period 2, Gear punishes Trick and Trick cooperates. Gear now makes an economic profit of $4.5 million, and Trick incurs an economic loss of $1 million. Adding up the profits over two periods of play, Trick would have made more profit by cooperating—$4 million compared with $3.5 million.

What is true for Trick is also true for Gear. Because each firm makes a larger profit by sticking with the collusive agreement, both firms do so and the monopoly price, quantity, and profit prevail.

In reality, whether a cartel works like a one-play game or a repeated game depends primarily on the

TABLE 15.5   Cheating with Punishment

Period of play	Collude		Cheat with tit-for-tat	
	Trick's profit	Gear's profit	Trick's profit	Gear's profit
	(millions of dollars)		(millions of dollars)	
1	2	2	4.5	–1.0
2	2	2	–1.0	4.5
3	2	2	2.0	2.0
4	.	.	.	.

If duopolists repeatedly collude, each makes a profit of $2 million per period of play. If one player cheats in period 1, the other player plays a tit-for-tat strategy and cheats in period 2. The profit from cheating can be made for only one period and must be paid for in the next period by incurring a loss. Over two periods of play, the best that a duopolist can achieve by cheating is a profit of $3.5 million, compared to an economic profit of $4 million by colluding.

number of players and the ease of detecting and punishing cheating. The larger the number of players, the harder it is to maintain a cartel.

Games and Price Wars A repeated duopoly game can help us understand real-world behavior and, in particular, price wars. Some price wars can be interpreted as the implementation of a tit-for-tat strategy. But the game is a bit more complicated than the one we've looked at because the players are uncertain about the demand for the product.

Playing a tit-for-tat strategy, firms have an incentive to stick to the monopoly price. But fluctuations in demand lead to fluctuations in the monopoly price, and sometimes, when the price changes, it might seem to one of the firms that the price has fallen because the other has cheated. In this case, a price war will break out. The price war will end only when each firm is satisfied that the other is ready to cooperate again. There will be cycles of price wars and the restoration of collusive agreements. Fluctuations in the world price of oil might be interpreted in this way.

Some price wars arise from the entry of a small number of firms into an industry that had previously been a monopoly. Although the industry has a small number of firms, the firms are in a prisoners' dilemma and they cannot impose effective penalties for price cutting. The behavior of prices and outputs in the computer chip industry during 1995 and 1996 can be explained in this way. Until 1995, the market for Pentium chips for IBM-compatible computers was dominated by one firm, Intel Corporation, which was able to make maximum economic profit by producing the quantity of chips at which marginal cost equaled marginal revenue. The price of Intel's chips was set to ensure that the quantity demanded equaled the quantity produced. Then in 1995 and 1996, with the entry of a small number of new firms, the industry became an oligopoly. If the firms had maintained Intel's price and shared the market, together they could have made economic profits equal to Intel's profit. But the firms were in a prisoners' dilemma, so prices fell toward the competitive level.

Let's now study a sequential game. There are many such games, and the one we'll examine is among the simplest. It has an interesting implication and it will give you the flavor of this type of game. The sequential game that we'll study is an entry game in a contestable market.

A Sequential Entry Game in a Contestable Market

If two firms play a sequential game, one firm makes a decision at the first stage of the game and the other makes a decision at the second stage.

We're going to study a sequential game in a **contestable market**—a market in which firms can enter and leave so easily that firms in the market face competition from *potential* entrants. Examples of contestable markets are routes served by airlines and by barge companies that operate on the major waterways. These markets are contestable because firms could enter if an opportunity for economic profit arose and could exit with no penalty if the opportunity for economic profit disappeared.

If the Herfindahl-Hirschman Index (p. 238) is used to determine the degree of competition, a contestable market appears to be uncompetitive. But a contestable market can behave as if it were perfectly competitive. To see why, let's look at an entry game for a contestable air route.

A Contestable Air Route Agile Air is the only firm operating on a particular route. Demand and cost conditions are such that there is room for only one airline to operate. Wanabe Inc. is another airline that could offer services on the route.

We describe the structure of a sequential game by using a *game tree* like that in Fig. 15.6. At the first stage, Agile Air must set a price. Once the price is set and advertised, Agile can't change it. That is, once set, Agile's price is fixed and Agile can't react to Wanabe's entry decision. Agile can set its price at either the monopoly level or the competitive level.

At the second stage, Wanabe must decide whether to enter or to stay out. Customers have no loyalty (there are no frequent-flyer programs) and they buy from the lowest-price firm. So if Wanabe enters, it sets a price just below Agile's and takes all the business.

Figure 15.6 shows the payoffs from the various decisions (Agile's in the red triangles and Wanabe's in the blue triangles).

To decide on its price, Agile's CEO reasons as follows: Suppose that Agile sets the monopoly price. If Wanabe enters, it earns 90 (think of all payoff numbers as thousands of dollars). If Wanabe stays out, it earns nothing. So Wanabe will enter. In this case Agile will lose 50.

Now suppose that Agile sets the competitive price. If Wanabe stays out, it earns nothing, and if it enters,

FIGURE 15.6   Agile Versus Wanabe: A Sequential Entry Game in a Contestable Market

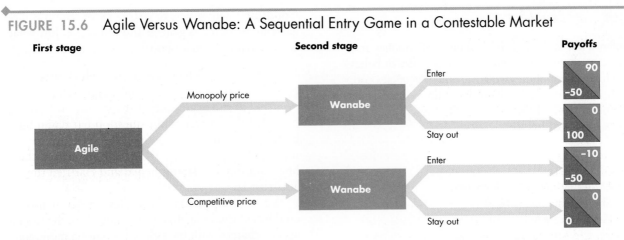

If Agile sets the monopoly price, Wanabe makes 90 (thousand dollars) by entering and earns nothing by staying out. So if Agile sets the monopoly price, Wanabe enters.

If Agile sets the competitive price, Wanabe earns nothing if it stays out and incurs a loss if it enters. So if Agile sets the competitive price, Wanabe stays out.

(X) **myeconlab** animation

it loses 10, so Wanabe will stay out. In this case, Agile will make zero economic profit.

Agile's best strategy is to set its price at the competitive level and make zero economic profit. The option of earning 100 by setting the monopoly price with Wanabe staying out is not available to Agile. If Agile sets the monopoly price, Wanabe enters, undercuts Agile, and takes all the business.

In this example, Agile sets its price at the competitive level and makes zero economic profit. A less costly strategy, called **limit pricing**, sets the price at the highest level that inflicts a loss on the entrant. Any loss is big enough to deter entry, so it is not always necessary to set the price as low as the competitive price. In the example of Agile and Wanabe, at the competitive price, Wanabe incurs a loss of 10 if it enters. A smaller loss would still keep Wanabe out.

This game is interesting because it points to the possibility of a monopoly behaving like a competitive industry and serving the social interest without regulation. But the result is not general and depends on one crucial feature of the setup of the game: At the second stage, Agile is locked in to the price set at the first stage.

If Agile could change its price in the second stage, it would want to set the monopoly price if Wanabe stayed out—100 with the monopoly price beats zero with the competitive price. But Wanabe can figure out what Agile would do, so the price set at the first stage

has no effect on Wanabe. Agile sets the monopoly price and Wanabe might either stay out or enter.

We've looked at two of the many possible repeated and sequential games, and you've seen how these types of games can provide insights into the complex forces that determine prices and profits.

REVIEW QUIZ

1 If a prisoners' dilemma game is played repeatedly, what punishment strategies might the players employ and how does playing the game repeatedly change the equilibrium?

2 If a market is contestable, how does the equilibrium differ from that of a monopoly?

You can work these questions in Study Plan 15.3 and get instant feedback.

So far, we've studied oligopoly with unregulated market power. Firms like Trick and Gear are free to collude to maximize their profit with no concern for the consumer or the law.

But when firms collude to achieve the monopoly outcome, they also have the same effects on efficiency and the social interest as monopoly. Profit is made at the expense of consumer surplus and a deadweight loss arises. Your next task is to see how U.S. antitrust law limits market power.

◆ Antitrust Law

Antitrust law is the law that regulates oligopolies and prevents them from becoming monopolies or behaving like monopolies. Two government agencies cooperate to enforce the antitrust laws: the Federal Trade Commission and the Antitrust Division of the U.S. Department of Justice.

The Antitrust Laws

The two main antitrust laws are

- The Sherman Act, 1890
- The Clayton Act, 1914

The Sherman Act The Sherman Act made it a felony to create or attempt to create a monopoly or a cartel.

During the 1880s, lawmakers and the general public were outraged and disgusted by the practices of some of the big-name leaders of American business. The actions of J.P. Morgan, John D. Rockefeller, and W.H. Vanderbilt led to them being called the "robber barons." It turns out that the most lurid stories of the actions of these great American capitalists were not of their creation of monopoly power to exploit consumers but of their actions to damage each other.

Nevertheless, monopolies that damaged the consumer interest did emerge. For example, John D. Rockefeller had a virtual monopoly in the market for oil.

Table 15.6 summarizes the two main provisions of the Sherman Act. Section 1 of the act is precise:

TABLE 15.6   The Sherman Act of 1890

Section 1:

Every contract, combination in the form of trust or otherwise, or conspiracy, in restraint of trade or commerce among the several States, or with foreign nations, is hereby declared to be illegal.

Section 2:

Every person who shall monopolize, or attempt to monopolize, or combine or conspire with any other person or persons, to monopolize any part of the trade or commerce among the several States, or with foreign nations, shall be deemed guilty of a felony.

Conspiring with others to restrict competition is illegal. But Section 2 is general and imprecise. Just what is an "attempt to monopolize"?

The Clayton Act The Clayton Act, which was passed in response to a wave of mergers that occurred at the beginning of the twentieth century, provided the answer to the question left dangling by the Sherman Act: It defined the "attempt to monopolize." The Clayton Act supplemented the Sherman Act and strengthened and clarified the antitrust law.

When Congress passed the Clayton Act, it also established the Federal Trade Commission, the federal agency charged with the task of preventing monopoly practices that damage the consumer interest.

Two amendments to the Clayton Act—the Robinson-Patman Act of 1936 and the Celler-Kefauver Act of 1950—outlaw specific practices and provide even greater precision to the antitrust law. Table 15.7 describes these practices and summarizes the main provisions of these three acts.

TABLE 15.7   The Clayton Act and Its Amendments

Clayton Act	1914
Robinson-Patman Act	1936
Celler-Kefauver Act	1950

These acts prohibit the following practices *only if* they substantially lessen competition or create monopoly:

1. Price discrimination
2. Contracts that require other goods to be bought from the same firm (called *tying arrangements*)
3. Contracts that require a firm to buy all its requirements of a particular item from a single firm (called *requirements contracts*)
4. Contracts that prevent a firm from selling competing items (called *exclusive dealing*)
5. Contracts that prevent a buyer from reselling a product outside a specified area (called *territorial confinement*)
6. Acquiring a competitor's shares or assets
7. Becoming a director of a competing firm

Price Fixing Always Illegal

Colluding with competitors to fix the price is *always* a violation of the antitrust law. If the Justice Department can prove the existence of a price fixing cartel, also called a *horizontal price fixing agreement*, defendants can offer no acceptable excuse.

The predictions of the effects of price fixing that you saw in the previous sections of this chapter provide the reasons for the unqualified attitude toward price fixing. A duopoly cartel can maximize profit and behave like a monopoly. To achieve the monopoly outcome, the cartel restricts production and fixes the price at the monopoly level. The consumer suffers because consumer surplus shrinks. And the outcome is inefficient because a deadweight loss arises.

It is for these reasons that the law declares that all price fixing is illegal. No excuse can justify the practice.

Other antitrust practices are more controversial and generate debate among lawyers and economists. We'll examine three of these practices.

Three Antitrust Policy Debates

The three practices that we'll examine are

- Resale price maintenance
- Tying arrangements
- Predatory pricing

Resale Price Maintenance Most manufacturers sell their products to the final consumer indirectly through a wholesale and retail distribution system. **Resale price maintenance** occurs when a distributor agrees with a manufacturer to resell a product *at or above a specified minimum price*.

A resale price maintenance agreement, also called a *vertical price fixing agreement*, is *not* illegal under the Sherman Act provided it is not anticompetitive. Nor is it illegal for a manufacturer to refuse to supply a retailer who doesn't accept guidance on what the minimum price should be.

In 2007, the Supreme Court ruled that a handbag manufacturer could impose a minimum retail price on a Dallas store, Kay's Kloset. Since that ruling, many manufacturers have imposed minimum retail prices. The practice is judged on a case-by-case basis.

Does resale price maintenance create an inefficient or efficient use of resources? Economists can be found on both sides of this question.

Inefficient Resale Price Maintenance Resale price maintenance is inefficient if it enables dealers to charge the monopoly price. By setting and enforcing the resale price, the manufacturer might be able to achieve the monopoly price.

Efficient Resale Price Maintenance Resale price maintenance might be efficient if it enables a manufacturer to induce dealers to provide the efficient standard of service. Suppose that SilkySkin wants shops to demonstrate the use of its new unbelievable moisturizing cream in an inviting space. With resale price maintenance, SilkySkin can offer all the retailers the same incentive and compensation. Without resale price maintenance, a cut-price drug store might offer SilkySkin products at a low price. Buyers would then have an incentive to visit a high-price shop for a product demonstration and then buy from the low-price shop. The low-price shop would be a free rider (like the consumer of a public good in Chapter 16, p. 377), and an inefficient level of service would be provided.

SilkySkin could pay a fee to retailers that provide good service and leave the resale price to be determined by the competitive forces of supply and demand. But it might be too costly for SilkySkin to monitor shops and ensure that they provide the desired level of service.

Tying Arrangements A **tying arrangement** is an agreement to sell one product only if the buyer agrees to buy another, different product. With tying, the only way the buyer can get the one product is to also buy the other product. Microsoft has been accused of tying Internet Explorer and Windows. Textbook publishers sometimes tie a Web site and a textbook and force students to buy both. (You can't buy the book you're now reading, new, without the Web site. But you can buy the Web site access without the book, so these products are not tied.)

Could textbook publishers make more money by tying a book and access to a Web site? The answer is sometimes but not always. Suppose that you and other students are willing to pay $80 for a book and $20 for access to a Web site. The publisher can sell these items separately for these prices or bundled for $100. The publisher does not gain from bundling.

But now suppose that you and only half of the students are willing to pay $80 for a book and $20 for a Web site and the other half of the students are willing to pay $80 for a Web site and $20 for a book. Now if the two items are sold separately, the publisher can charge $80 for the book and $80 for the Web site. Half the students buy the book but not the Web site, and the other half buy the Web site but not the book. But if the book and Web site are bundled for $100, everyone buys the bundle and the publisher makes an extra $20 per student. In this case, bundling has enabled the publisher to price discriminate.

There is no simple, clear-cut test of whether a firm is engaging in tying or whether, by doing so, it has increased its market power and profit and created inefficiency.

Predatory Pricing **Predatory pricing** is setting a low price to drive competitors out of business with the intention of setting a monopoly price when the com-petition has gone. John D. Rockefeller's Standard Oil Company was the first to be accused of this practice in the 1890s, and it has been claimed often in antitrust cases since then. Predatory pricing is an attempt to cre-ate a monopoly and as such it is illegal under Section 2 of the Sherman Act.

It is easy to see that predatory pricing is an idea, not a reality. Economists are skeptical that predatory pric-ing occurs. They point out that a firm that cuts its price below the profit-maximizing level loses during the low-price period. Even if it succeeds in driving its competitors out of business, new competitors will enter as soon as the price is increased, so any potential gain from a monopoly position is temporary. A high and certain loss is a poor exchange for a temporary and uncertain gain. No case of predatory pricing has been definitively found.

Economics in Action
The United States Versus Microsoft

In 1998, the Antitrust Division of the U.S. Depart-ment of Justice along with the Departments of Justice of a number of states charged Microsoft, the world's largest producer of software for personal computers, with violations of both sections of the Sherman Act.

A 78-day trial followed that pitched two promi-nent MIT economics professors against each other, Franklin Fisher for the government and Richard Schmalensee for Microsoft.

The Case Against Microsoft The claims against Microsoft were that it

- Possessed monopoly power
- Used predatory pricing and tying arrangements
- Used other anticompetitive practices

It was claimed that with 80 percent of the market for PC operating systems, Microsoft had excessive monopoly power. This monopoly power arose from two barriers to entry: economies of scale and network economies. Microsoft's average total cost falls as pro-duction increases (economies of scale) because the fixed cost of developing an operating system such as Windows is large while the marginal cost of produc-ing one copy of Windows is small. Further, as the number of Windows users increases, the range of Windows applications expands (network economies), so a potential competitor would need to produce not only a competing operating system but also an entire range of supporting applications as well.

When Microsoft entered the Web browser market with its Internet Explorer, it offered the browser for a zero price. This price was viewed as predatory pricing. Microsoft integrated Internet Explorer with Windows so that anyone who uses this operating system would not need a separate browser such as Netscape Navigator. Microsoft's competitors claimed that this practice was an illegal tying arrangement.

Microsoft's Response Microsoft challenged all these claims. It said that Windows was vulnerable to com-petition from other operating systems such as Linux and Apple's Mac OS and that there was a permanent threat of competition from new entrants.

Microsoft claimed that integrating Internet Explorer with Windows provided a single, unified product of greater consumer value like a refrigerator with a chilled water dispenser or an automobile with a CD player.

The Outcome The court agreed that Microsoft was in violation of the Sherman Act and ordered that it be broken into two firms: an operating systems producer and an applications producer. Microsoft successfully appealed this order. In the final judgment, though, Microsoft was ordered to disclose to other software developers details of how its operating system works, so that they could compete effectively against Microsoft. In the summer of 2002, Microsoft began to comply with this order.

Mergers and Acquisitions

Mergers, which occur when two or more firms agree to combine to create one larger firm, and *acquisitions*, which occur when one firm buys another firm, are common events. Mergers occurred when Chrysler and the German auto producer Daimler-Benz combined to form DaimlerChrysler and when the Belgian beer producer InBev bought the U.S. brewing giant Anheuser-Busch and created a new combined company, Anheuser-Busch InBev. An acquisition occurred when Rupert Murdoch's News Corp bought Myspace.

The mergers and acquisitions that occur don't create a monopoly. But two (or more) firms might be tempted to try to merge so that they can gain market power and operate like a monopoly. If such a situation arises, the Federal Trade Commission (FTC) takes an interest in the move and stands ready to block the merger.

To determine which mergers it will examine and possibly block, the FTC uses guidelines, one of which is the Herfindahl-Hirschman Index (HHI) (see Chapter 10, pp. 238–239).

A market in which the HHI is less than 1,000 is regarded as competitive. An index between 1,000 and 1,800 indicates a moderately concentrated market, and a merger in this market that would increase the index by 100 points is challenged by the FTC. An index above 1,800 indicates a concentrated market, and a merger in this market that would increase the index by 50 points is challenged. You can see an application of these guidelines in the box below.

REVIEW QUIZ

1 What are the two main antitrust laws and when were they enacted?

2 When is price fixing not a violation of the antitrust laws?

3 What is an attempt to monopolize an industry?

4 What are resale price maintenance, tying arrangements, and predatory pricing?

5 Under what circumstances is a merger unlikely to be approved?

You can work these questions in Study Plan 15.4 and get instant feedback.

Oligopoly is a market structure that you often encounter in your daily life. *Reading Between the Lines* on pp. 360–361 looks at a game played in the market for high-tech razors.

Economics in Action

FTC Takes the Fizz out of Soda Mergers

The FTC used its HHI guidelines to block proposed mergers in the market for soft drinks. PepsiCo wanted to buy 7-Up and Coca-Cola wanted to buy Dr Pepper. The market for carbonated soft drinks is highly concentrated. Coca-Cola had a 39 percent share, PepsiCo had 28 percent, Dr Pepper was next with 7 percent, followed by 7-Up with 6 percent. One other producer, RJR, had a 5 percent market share. So the five largest firms in this market had an 85 percent market share.

The PepsiCo and 7-Up merger would have increased the HHI by more than 300 points. The Coca-Cola and Dr Pepper merger would have increased it by more than 500 points, and both mergers together would have increased the index by almost 800 points.

The FTC decided that increases in the HHI of these magnitudes were not in the social interest and blocked the mergers. The figure summarizes the HHI guideline and HHIs in the soft drinks market.

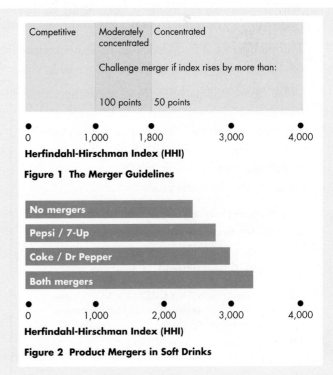

Figure 1 The Merger Guidelines

Figure 2 Product Mergers in Soft Drinks

Gillette and Schick in a Duopoly Game

Battle for Beards Heats Up

St. Louis Public Radio
June 4, 2010

The battle for the American beard is heating up. After months of hype, Gillette's latest razor finally hits store shelves this Sunday. This skirmish pits a consumer products behemoth against a much smaller, but formidable, challenger.

This latest version of Gillette's Fusion, the ProGlide, still has just six blades. But you wouldn't know it from the hundreds of millions of dollars Gillette pumped into the razor's design and its marketing.

The ProGlide features thinner blades and better lubrication. But Damon Jones, with Procter & Gamble, says even the loudest ads aren't enough to make men switch brands.

"It's one thing to watch a commercial, but when we put the razor in the hands of guys and they try it, they tell us wow," Jones said. "So we're really going to depend on the word of mouth."

Meanwhile Schick, owned by St. Louis-based Energizer, is pushing its new Hydro razor just as aggressively. Its selling point is a reservoir of water-activated gel. ...

"This product has a four-blade disposable on one end. It has a hair cutting tool on the other end. Its operated by a Triple-A battery."

Lindell Chew, ... a marketing professor at the University of Missouri, ... says Schick has always been more innovative ... But despite Schick's technical wizardry, Chew says "it'll have to fight hard for shelf space because Gillette's Procter & Gamble dominates the consumer products industry."

"They're going very aggressive with these billion dollar brands that they have, and carving out deals that will often wipe out the number two brand, not just the 3, 4, 5, and 6 brand," Chew says. ...

ESSENCE OF THE STORY

- Procter & Gamble (P&G) has developed a new razor, the Gillette Fusion ProGlide.

- P&G has spent "hundreds of millions of dollars" on the design and marketing of the new razor.

- The ProGlide has thinner blades and better lubrication than its predecessor.

- Energizer has also developed a new razor, the Schick Hydro.

- The Hydro has a reservoir of water-activated gel, a four-blade shaver, and a hair cutting tool.

- The Hydro is expected to have to fight hard for shelf space in stores because P&G dominates the market.

ECONOMIC ANALYSIS

- The global market in high-tech razors (razors with multiple blades, a battery, and other aids to comfort) is dominated by two brands and firms: Gillette, made by Procter & Gamble, and Schick, made by Energizer.

- Figure 1 shows the shares in this market. You can see that Gillette has 70 percent of the market, Schick 20 percent, and others only 10 percent.

- In 2010, P&G and Energizer increased the intensity of their competition by spending hundreds of millions of dollars developing and marketing more advanced razors: the Gillette ProGlide and the Schick Hydro.

- We can interpret this competition as a prisoners' dilemma game.

- Table 1 shows the payoff matrix (millions of dollars of profit) for the game played by P&G and Energizer. (The numbers are hypothetical.)

- This game is a prisoners' dilemma like that on p. 345 and has a dominant-strategy Nash equilibrium.

- If P&G develops and markets a new razor, Energizer makes a larger profit by also developing and marketing a new razor (+$30 million versus –$60 million); and if P&G *doesn't* develop and market a new razor, Energizer again makes a larger profit by developing and marketing a new razor (+$90 million versus +$50 million).

- So Energizer's best strategy is to develop and market a new razor.

- If Energizer develops and markets a new razor, P&G makes a larger profit by also developing and marketing a new razor (+$75 million versus –$40 million); and if Energizer *doesn't* develop and market a new razor, P&G again makes a larger profit by developing and marketing a new razor (+$275 million versus +$175 million).

- So P&G's best strategy is to develop and market a new razor.

- Because both firm's best strategy is to develop and market a new razor, that is the equilibrium of the game.

- The firms are in a prisoners' dilemma because each would be better off avoiding the costly development and marketing costs and continuing to sell large quantities of their older style razor.

- With neither firm bringing the new razor to market, P&G would gain $100 million ($175 million versus $75 million) and Energizer would gain $20 million ($50 million versus $30 million).

- But each firm can see that if it doesn't bring a new razor to market, the other firm will and the consequence for the one that doesn't have a new razor will be a large loss.

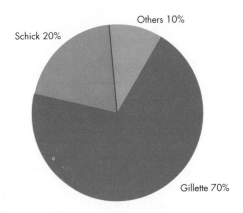

Figure 1 Market shares in the high-end razor market

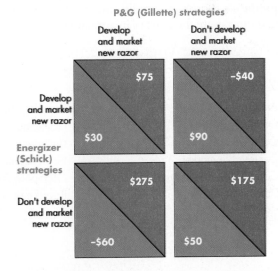

Table 1 P&G and Energizer in a prisoners' dilemma

SUMMARY

Key Points

What Is Oligopoly? (pp. 342–343)

■ Oligopoly is a market in which a small number of firms compete.

Working Problems 1 to 3 will give you a better understanding of what oligopoly is.

Oligopoly Games (pp. 344–352)

■ Oligopoly is studied by using game theory, which is a method of analyzing strategic behavior.

■ In a prisoners' dilemma game, two prisoners acting in their own self-interest harm their joint interest.

■ An oligopoly (duopoly) price-fixing game is a prisoners' dilemma in which the firms might collude or cheat.

■ In Nash equilibrium, both firms cheat and output and price are the same as in perfect competition.

■ Firms' decisions about advertising and R&D can be studied by using game theory.

Working Problems 4 to 7 will give you a better understanding of oligopoly games.

Repeated Games and Sequential Games (pp. 353–355)

■ In a repeated game, a punishment strategy can produce a cooperative equilibrium in which price and output are the same as in a monopoly.

■ In a sequential contestable market game, a small number of firms can behave like firms in perfect competition.

Working Problem 8 will give you a better understanding of repeated and sequential games.

Antitrust Law (pp. 356–359)

■ The first antitrust law, the Sherman Act, was passed in 1890, and the law was strengthened in 1914 when the Clayton Act was passed and the Federal Trade Commission was created.

■ All price-fixing agreements are violations of the Sherman Act, and no acceptable excuse exists.

■ Resale price maintenance might be efficient if it enables a producer to ensure the efficient level of service by distributors.

■ Tying arrangements can enable a monopoly to price discriminate and increase profit, but in many cases, tying would not increase profit.

■ Predatory pricing is unlikely to occur because it brings losses and only temporary potential gains.

■ The Federal Trade Commission uses guidelines such as the Herfindahl-Hirschman Index to determine which mergers to investigate and possibly block.

Working Problems 9 to 11 will give you a better understanding of antitrust law.

Key Terms

Antitrust law, 356
Cartel, 343
Collusive agreement, 346
Contestable market, 354
Cooperative equilibrium, 353
Dominant-strategy equilibrium, 345

Duopoly, 342
Game theory, 344
Limit pricing, 355
Nash equilibrium, 345
Oligopoly, 342
Payoff matrix, 344

Predatory pricing, 358
Resale price maintenance, 357
Strategies, 344
Tying arrangement, 357

STUDY PLAN PROBLEMS AND APPLICATIONS

 myeconlab You can work Problems 1 to 12 in MyEconLab Chapter 15 Study Plan and get instant feedback.

What Is Oligopoly? (Study Plan 15.1)

1. Two firms make most of the chips that power a PC: Intel and Advanced Micro Devices. What makes the market for PC chips a duopoly? Sketch the market demand curve and cost curves that describe the situation in this market and that prevent other firms from entering.

2. **Sparks Fly for Energizer**

   Energizer is gaining market share against competitor Duracell and its profit is rising despite the sharp rise in the price of zinc, a key battery ingredient.

   Source: www.businessweek.com, August 2007

   In what type of market are batteries sold? Explain your answer.

3. **Oil City**

   In the late 1990s, Reliance spent $6 billion to build a world-class oil refinery at Jamnagar, India. Now Reliance is more than doubling the size of the facility, which will make it the world's biggest producer of gasoline —1.2 million gallons of gasoline per day, or about 5% of global capacity. Reliance plans to sell the gasoline in the United States and Europe where it's too expensive and politically difficult to build new refineries. The bulked-up Jamnagar will be able to move the market and Singapore traders expect a drop in fuel prices as soon as it's going at full steam.

   Source: *Fortune*, April 28, 2008

   a. Explain why the news clip claims that the global market for gasoline is not perfectly competitive.

   b. What barriers to entry might limit competition in this market and give a firm such as Reliance power to influence the market price?

Oligopoly Games (Study Plan 15.2)

4. Consider a game with two players who cannot communicate, and in which each player is asked a question. The players can answer the question honestly or lie. If both answer honestly, each receives $100. If one player answers honestly and the other lies, the liar receives $500 and the honest player gets nothing. If both lie, then each receives $50.

   a. Describe the strategies and payoffs of this game.

   b. Construct the payoff matrix.

   c. What is the equilibrium of this game?

   d. Compare this game to the prisoners' dilemma. Are the two games similar or different? Explain.

Use the following information to work Problems 5 and 6.

Soapy Inc. and Suddies Inc. are the only producers of soap powder. They collude and agree to share the market equally. If neither firm cheats on the agreement, each makes $1 million profit. If either firm cheats, the cheat makes a profit of $1.5 million, while the complier incurs a loss of $0.5 million. If both cheat, they break even. Neither firm can monitor the other's actions.

5. a. What are the strategies in this game?

   b. Construct the payoff matrix for this game.

6. a. What is the equilibrium of this game if it is played only once?

   b. Is the equilibrium a dominant-strategy equilibrium? Explain.

7. **The World's Largest Airline**

   On May 3, 2010, United Airlines and Continental Airlines announced a $3 billion merger that would create the world's biggest airline. The deal was completed in a remarkably short three weeks, and would give the airlines the muscle to fend off low-cost rivals at home and to take on foreign carriers abroad. For consumers, the merger could eventually result in higher prices although the new company does not intend to raise fares. One of the rationales for airline mergers is to cut capacity.

   Source: *The New York Times*, June 7, 2010

   a. Explain how this airline merger might increase air travel prices.

   b. Explain how this airline merger might lower air travel production costs.

   c. Explain how cost savings arising from a cut in capacity might get passed on to travelers and might boost producers' profits. Which do you predict will happen from this airline merger and why?

Repeated Games and Sequential Games

(Study Plan 15.3)

8. If Soapy Inc. and Suddies Inc., repeatedly play the duopoly game that has the payoffs described in Problem 5, on each round of play:
   a. What now are the strategies that each firm might adopt?
   b. Can the firms adopt a strategy that gives the game a cooperative equilibrium?
   c. Would one firm still be tempted to cheat in a cooperative equilibrium? Explain your answer.

Antitrust Law (Study Plan 15.4)

9. **Price Cuts Seen for Apple's New iPhone**
   AT&T plans to sell the new iPhone for $200. The lower-priced phone would give AT&T an attractive weapon to win new subscribers.
   AT&T's revenue is an average of $95 a month from each iPhone customer, nearly twice the average of its conventional cell phone user. AT&T has a revenue-sharing agreement with Apple that requires it to give Apple 25% of its iPhone customers' monthly payments.
   AT&T offers a $200 subsidy to customers who lock into the carrier for two years. It's a small investment for AT&T for a large return. After giving Apple its cut of the revenue, AT&T receives between $70 and $75 a month per iPhone user, totaling more than $1,700 over the life of the two-year contract.

   Source: *Fortune*, June 2, 2008
   a. How does this arrangement between AT&T and Apple regarding the iPhone affect competition in the market for cell-phone service?
   b. Does the iPhone arrangement between AT&T and Apple violate U.S. antitrust laws? Explain.

10. **Congress Examines Giant Airline Merger**
    Congress examined a proposed merger between Delta Airlines and Northwest Airlines that would discourage competition, reduce service, and result in higher fares. Delta claims that the merger would not limit competition because the carriers primarily serve different geographic regions. Witnesses scheduled to testify before the House Subcommittee were likely to focus on whether the merger would result in lower airfares or reduced competition.

    Source: CNN, May 14, 2008

    Explain the guidelines that the Federal Trade Commission uses to evaluate mergers and why it might permit or block this merger.

11. **AT&T's New Pricing Takes Smartphones to the Masses**
    AT&T, the second largest U.S. wireless carrier and only operator offering the iPhone, plans to attract average consumers to sign up for data service by cutting its prices: A $15 a month plan for 200 megabytes of data; $25 a month plan for 2 gigabytes of data. Verizon Wireless, the largest U.S. wireless operator, wouldn't comment on AT&T's new pricing plans. But if history is any indication, it won't take long before Verizon, operator of the HTC Incredible, a smartphone that looks very similar to an iPhone, begins offering tiered data service.

    Source: Cnet News, June 3, 2010
    a. Describe the basis of the competition between AT&T and Verizon.
    b. Is AT&T likely to be using predatory pricing?
    c. If a price war develops in the market for data services, who benefits most?

Economics in the News (Study Plan 15.N)

12. **Starbucks Sued for Trying to Sink Competition**
    Penny Stafford, owner of the Seattle-based Belvi Coffee and Tea Exchange Inc. filed the lawsuit, which contends that Starbucks exploited its monopoly power. Starbucks used predatory practices such as offering to pay leases that exceeded market value if the building owner would refuse to allow competitors into the same building; having its employees offer free coffee samples in front of her store to lure away customers; and offering to buy out competitors at below-market prices and threatening to open nearby stores if the offer is rejected.

    Source: CNN, September 26, 2006
    a. Explain how Starbucks is alleged to have violated U.S. antitrust laws in Seattle.
    b. Explain why it is unlikely that Starbucks might use predatory pricing to permanently drive out competition.
    c. What information would you need that is not provided in the news clip to decide whether Starbucks had practiced predatory pricing?
    d. Sketch the situation facing Belvi Coffee and Tea Exchange Inc. when the firm closed.

ADDITIONAL PROBLEMS AND APPLICATIONS

myeconlab You can work these problems in MyEconLab if assigned by your instructor.

What Is Oligopoly?

13. **An Energy Drink with a Monster of a Stock**

    The $5.7 billion energy-drink category, in which Monster holds the No. 2 position behind industry leader Red Bull, has slowed down as copycat brands jostle for shelf space. Over the past five years Red Bull's market share in dollar terms has gone from 91 percent to well under 50 percent and much of that loss has been Monster's gain.

    Source: *Fortune*, December 25, 2006

    a. Describe the structure of the energy-drink market. How has that structure changed over the past few years?

    b. If Monster and Red Bull formed a cartel, how would the price charged for energy drinks and the profits made change?

Oligopoly Games

Use the following information to work Problems 14 and 15

Bud and Wise are the only two producers of aniseed beer, a New Age product designed to displace root beer. Bud and Wise are trying to figure out how much of this new beer to produce. They know:

(i) If they both limit production to 10,000 gallons a day, they will make the maximum attainable joint profit of $200,000 a day—$100,000 a day each.

(ii) If either firm produces 20,000 gallons a day while the other produces 10,000 a day, the one that produces 20,000 gallons will make an economic profit of $150,000 and the other one will incur an economic loss of $50,000.

(iii) If both increase production to 20,000 gallons a day, each firm will make zero economic profit.

14. Construct a payoff matrix for the game that Bud and Wise must play.

15. Find the Nash equilibrium of the game that Bud and Wise play.

16. **Asian Rice Exporters to Discuss Cartel**

    The rice-exporting nations Thailand, Cambodia, Laos, and Myanmar planned to discuss a proposal by Thailand, the world's largest rice exporter, that they form a cartel. Ahead of the meeting, the countries said that the purpose of the rice cartel would be to contribute to ensuring food stability, not just in an individual country but also to address food shortages in the region

    and the world. The cartel will not hoard rice and raise prices when there are shortages.

    The Philippines says that it is a bad idea. It will create an oligopoly, and the cartel could price the grain out of reach for millions of people.

    Source: CNN, May 6, 2008

    a. Assuming the rice-exporting nations become a profit-maximizing colluding oligopoly, explain how they would influence the global market for rice and the world price of rice.

    b. Assuming the rice-exporting nations become a profit-maximizing colluding oligopoly, draw a graph to illustrate their influence on the global market for rice.

    c. Even in the absence of international antitrust laws, why might it be difficult for this cartel to successfully collude? Use the ideas of game theory to explain.

17. Suppose that Mozilla and Microsoft each develop their own versions of an amazing new Web browser that allows advertisers to target consumers with great precision. Also, the new browser is easier and more fun to use than existing browsers. Each firm is trying to decide whether to sell the browser or to give it away. What are the likely benefits from each action? Which action is likely to occur?

18. Why do Coca-Cola and PepsiCo spend huge amounts on advertising? Do they benefit? Does the consumer benefit? Explain your answer by constructing a game to illustrate the choices Coca-Cola and PepsiCo make.

Use the following information to work Problems 19 and 20.

Microsoft with Xbox 360, Nintendo with Wii, and Sony with PlayStation 3 are slugging it out in the market for the latest generation of video game consoles. Xbox 360 was the first to market; Wii has the lowest price; PS3 uses the most advanced technology and has the highest price.

19. a. Thinking of the competition among these firms in the market for consoles as a game, describe the firms' strategies concerning design, marketing, and price.

    b. What, based on the information provided, turned out to be the equilibrium of the game?

20. Can you think of reasons why the three consoles are so different?

Repeated Games and Sequential Games

21. If Bud and Wise in Problem 15 play the game repeatedly, what is the equilibrium of the game?

22. Agile Airlines' profit on a route on which it has a monopoly is $10 million a year. Wanabe Airlines is considering entering the market and operating on this route. Agile warns Wanabe to stay out and threatens to cut the price so that if Wanabe enters it will make no profit. Wanabe determines that the payoff matrix for the game in which it is engaged with Agile is shown in the table.

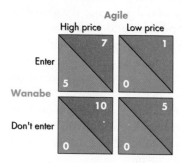

Does Wanabe believe Agile's assertion? Does Wanabe enter or not? Explain.

23. **Oil Trading Probe May Uncover Manipulation**

Amid soaring oil prices the Commodity Futures Trade Commission (CFTC) is looking into manipulation of the oil market—withholding oil in an attempt to drive prices higher. The CFTC has found such evidence in the past and it's likely it will find evidence again. But it is unlikely that a single player acting alone would be able to run the price up from $90 to $135.

Source: CNN, May 30, 2008

What type of market does the news clip imply best describes the U.S. oil market?

Antitrust Law

Use the following news clip to work Problems 24 and 25.

Gadgets for Sale … or Not

How come the prices of some gadgets, like the iPod, are the same no matter where you shop? No, the answer isn't that Apple illegally manages prices. In reality, Apple uses an accepted retail strategy called minimum advertised price to discourage resellers from discounting. The minimum advertised price (MAP) is the absolute lowest price of a product that resellers can advertise. MAP is usually enforced through marketing subsidies offered by a manufacturer to its resellers that keep the price at or above the MAP. Stable prices are important to the company that is both a manufacturer and a retailer. If Apple resellers advertised the iPod below cost, they could squeeze the Apple Stores out of their own markets. The downside to the price stability is that by limiting how low sellers can go, MAP keeps prices artificially high (or at least higher than they might otherwise be with unfettered price competition).

Source: *Slate*, December 22, 2006

24. a. Describe the practice of resale price maintenance that violates the Sherman Act.

    b. Describe the MAP strategy used by iPod and explain how it differs from a resale price maintenance agreement that would violate the Sherman Act.

25. Why might the MAP strategy be against the social interest and benefit only the producer?

Economics in the News

26. After you have studied *Reading Between the Lines* on pp. 360–361 answer the following questions.

    a. What are the strategies of P&G and Energizer in the market for high-tech razors?

    b. Why, according to the news article, would Energizer have a hard time competing with P&G?

    c. Why wouldn't Energizer stick with its old razor and leave P&G to incur the cost of developing and marketing a new one on its own?

    d. Could Energizer do something that would make the Schick Hydro the market leader? Would that action maximize Energizer's profit?

27. **Boeing and Airbus Predict Asian Sales Surge**

Airlines in the Asia-Pacific region are emerging as the biggest customers for aircraft makers Boeing and Airbus. The two firms predict that over the next 20 years, more than 8,000 planes worth up to $1.2 trillion will be sold there.

Source: BBC News, February 3, 2010

    a. In what type of market are big airplanes sold?

    b. Thinking of competition between Boeing and Airbus as a game, what are the strategies and the payoffs?

    c. Set out a hypothetical payoff matrix for the game you've described in part (b). What is the equilibrium of the game?

    d. Do you think the market for big airplanes is efficient? Explain and illustrate your answer.

Managing Change and Limiting Market Power

Our economy is constantly changing. Every year, new goods appear and old ones disappear. New firms are born, and old ones die. This process of change is initiated and managed by firms operating in markets.

When a new product appears, just one or two firms sell it: Apple and IBM were the only producers of personal computers; Microsoft was (and almost still is) the only producer of the PC operating system; Intel was the only producer of the PC chip. These firms had enormous power to determine the quantity to produce and the price of their products.

In many markets, entry eventually brings competition. Even with just two rivals, the industry changes its face in a dramatic way. *Strategic interdependence* is capable of leading to an outcome like perfect competition.

With the continued arrival of new firms in an industry, the market becomes competitive. But in most markets, the competition isn't perfect: it becomes *monopolistic competition* with each firm selling its own differentiated product.

Often, an industry that is competitive becomes less so as the bigger and more successful firms in the industry begin to swallow up the smaller firms, either by driving them out of business or by acquiring their assets. Through this process, an industry might return to oligopoly or even monopoly. You can see such a movement in the auto and banking industries today.

By studying firms and markets, we gain a deeper understanding of the forces that allocate resources and begin to see the invisible hand at work.

John von Neumann *was one of the great minds of the twentieth century. Born in Budapest, Hungary, in 1903, Johnny, as he was known, showed early mathematical brilliance. He was 25 when he published the article that changed the social sciences and began a flood of research on* **game theory**—*a flood that has not subsided. In that article, von Neumann proved that in a zero-sum game (such as sharing a pie), there exists a best strategy for each player.*

Von Neumann did more than invent game theory: He also invented and built the first practical computer, and he worked on the Manhattan Project, which developed the atomic bomb during World War II.

Von Neumann believed that the social sciences would progress only if they used their own mathematical tools, not those of the physical sciences.

"Real life consists of bluffing, of little tactics of deception, of asking yourself what is the other man going to think I mean to do."

JOHN VON NEUMANN,
told to Jacob Bronowski (in a London taxi) and reported in *The Ascent of Man*

Professor Hubbard, why did you decide to become an economist and what attracted you to the empirical study of firms and markets? And why your special interest in the role of information?

I became an economist a little bit by accident. My first job coming out of undergrad was in an economic consulting firm. I'd never considered doing a Ph.D. in economics before then. I didn't know any Ph.D.s growing up. I don't come from an academic background. But working with Ph.D. economists, I noticed that they were doing some pretty interesting things. They were looking at anti-competitive practices and regulatory stuff associated with the television and casino industries. What I saw when doing this work made me think that an academic job would be even better. I figured I'd go to graduate school to think about all of these interesting things.

When I went to graduate school I got interested in industrial organization. Now I did take a side trip. After doing my first year of graduate school, I took a year off. I spent it on the President's Council of Economic Advisers. That was loads of fun because it reminded me about what I like most about economics—applying it to understanding real world problems. A typical first-year Ph.D. program doesn't give you that sense. You are learning a lot of method and technique. But being thrust into a world where you have to skilfully use Econ concepts has you very quickly using them and applying them to real world policy discussions. I worked on the policy discussion surrounding environmental issues and that lead to my dissertation.

Some economists who specialize in the study of firms and markets focus on theory and in particular game theory. Others, like you, have an empirical, data-driven approach. How do you see these two ways of studying, and seeking to understand, how firms and markets work?

I don't think my approach is all that data driven. It's problem driven. I think the core of economics is theory, not data. I think what I try to do is to be a strong consumer of theory, at least the theory that is relevant to the problems that I'm interested in. What I try to do with respect to my research is to find a circumstance where the theory is a good fit for the data and the data are a good fit for the theory. Both are good fits for the general question at hand.

My dissertation was about the expert services market. Famous examples of these are doctors and lawyers, but I looked at auto repair guys. In these markets, doctors know more than their patients about the patient's condition; lawyers know more than their clients about the client's condition. A lot of people have tried to study these markets in these contexts—especially the medical context.

> The core of economics is theory, not data. I try to be a consumer ... of the theory that is relevant to the problems that I'm interested in

Well, coming out of my experience at the Council of Economic Advisers, I was exposed to a lower-brow expert service market—the market for auto emissions inspection.

The basic economic issues for auto repair are pretty similar to the set of issues that doctors face. But data on auto repairers are far superior to data on physicians' services. When you investigate a specific expert services question with lots of good data you can discover how the organizational structure of firms and

THOMAS HUBBARD is the John L. and Helen Kellogg Distinguished Professor of Management and Strategy at the Kellogg School of Management, Northwestern University and a research fellow at the National Bureau of Economic Research.

Professor Hubbard is an empirical economist. His work is driven by data. The central problems that unify much of his work are the limits to information and the fact that information is costly to obtain. Professor Hubbard studies the ways in which information problems influence the organization of firms; the extent to which firms make or buy what they sell; and the structure and performance of markets.

His work appears in the leading journals such as the *American Economic Review*, the *Quarterly Journal of Economics*, and the *Rand Journal of Economics*. He is a co-editor of the *Journal of Industrial Economics*.

Michael Parkin talked with Thomas Hubbard about his research and what we learn from it about the choices that firms make and their implications for market structure and performance.

the information environment affect the economic outcome. Doing things like that appeals to me.

Same way with trucking: I wrote a whole mass of papers about trucking. I was interested in the organization of firms and the organizational tradeoffs in the context of trucking happen to be manifested in very easy-to-understand and obvious ways. And you could get extremely good data, essentially close to the level of individual transactions.

Some people are good at creating theory and we need that work. But as I see it, good problem-driven economics needs three things: understanding the theory, understanding the institutional structure and evidence at hand, and integrating theory with institutional structure and data. It's fascinating when you can triangulate.

You have made important contributions to our understanding of the factors that determine whether a firm will make or buy. Can you summarize what you we know about this question?

If there is one thing that Coase (Ronald Coase, see p. 413) taught us about the boundaries of the firm, it is that thinking about whether to do something internally or to outsource it, a very useful starting point is to make the decision on a transaction-by-transaction basis.

Most firms probably don't think at that level of detail. But still it's the right starting point because it gets you to think about the useful fact that activities have to be performed and they have to be performed either internally or externally. The way I like to think about it is to boil it down to the theory of markets and incentives.

Markets provide strong incentives but not necessarily good incentives. So when you outsource something, you rely on a market mechanism rather than on something within a firm that is less than a market mechanism. By outsourcing, you expose people to a strong market incentive. Now that can be good, and it is good most of the time. Strong market incentives get people to do things that the market rewards. Market rewards are generally quite valuable, but in some circumstances what the market rewards isn't what the buyer would want to reward. So there's a tradeoff. Strong incentives are sometimes good and sometimes bad. Therefore, keeping things inside the firm provides a weaker incentive. Sometimes that is good.

> Markets provide strong incentives but not necessarily good incentives.

Can you provide an example?

Think about McDonald's. McDonald's is not one firm. It is many firms because a lot of the outlets are owned and managed by franchisees and some are owned and managed internally by McDonald's.

McDonald's thinks about whether to run one of its restaurants itself or franchise it out. One thing that it has in mind is if it franchises it out, then the franchisor is going to be exposed to very strong market incentives. Now under some circumstances this is great. The franchisee treats the business as if he owns it. So the good part about it is the franchisee works hard to try to develop his business.

But there is a flip side to the franchisee treating the business as his own that can be harmful for the chain. For example, a franchisee might want to install a menu item that is locally popular but not globally accepted. Or putting this item on the menu might cause logistical problems elsewhere. There could be externalities in other words. So a restaurant owned by a franchisee might not be the best option even though it provides good incentives in one dimension. Therefore, you might bring it inside and own the place yourself.

You've used the construction of the interstate highway system as a natural experiment through which to study the structure of the market for gasoline. Can you describe the question you posed and what you discovered?

The question is really pretty simple: How does an industry respond to an anticipated increase in demand? And how does this response differ depending on whether demand is in the same place—new demanders have the same preferences as older demanders did—or is in a different place—new demanders have different preferences than what the existing demanders have?

So I got thinking about this question and realized that the construction of the interstate highways provided a way of addressing it. The U.S. interstate highway system, an enormous public works project, was built slowly and steadily over the course of 20 years. Sometimes a new interstate highway would be close and parallel to an existing road and sometimes it would be several miles away from the road it replaced. So when a new highway was opened, it did either one or two things: When it was close by, it increased demand; when it was far away, it both increased demand and shifted demand spatially.

If the new highway was parallel to an existing road, it increased the volume of traffic along the route and increased the demand for gasoline in the corridor in which the highway was built. But when a new highway was some miles distant from the route it replaced, it shifted demand as well as increasing demand.

The unique thing about this research is we know exactly when a new highway opened, so we know the exact day that demand changed. We also know how many gas stations there were in that area and the time and the distribution of those gas stations. We can watch this over time. We can do this not just for one town. We can do this for hundreds of places as the highways developed over time.

So what we found is that the timing and the margin of the adjustment differed depending on whether the new highway was close to or far away from the old highway. When the highway was close, all the adjustment in demand was in larger firms, larger service stations. You didn't see any new service stations. You just

saw bigger service stations. And when the new highway was far away, you saw the adjustment to be in more service stations. So if you are a business person you're thinking about changes in demand and if entry opportunities occur when new demand comes, will they tend to occur when the new demanders have different demands than the existing ones?

As far as timing goes we saw something a little surprising. When the highway was opened near the existing route, you see that the adjustment takes place before the highway even opened. When I said that you saw larger gas stations once the highway is opened close to the old route, you saw this starting to happen two to three years before the highway actually opened. By the time the highway opened, most of the adjustments had already taken place.

But when the highway was opened far from the existing road, the opposite was true—all the action happened after the highway opened.

You've given us a wonderful glimpse into the fascinating research of a problem-driven economist who creatively finds rich data. Let's end with your advice to a student who is just starting to study economics. What makes it a good subject in which to major?

Watch what I do, not what I say! When I took my first economics course in my freshman year my reaction to it was "Wow, this explains everything." I took an undergraduate micro course. Just seeing supply curves and demand curves was wonderful. I thought economics explained things in ways that other disciplines didn't do. And the truth is although I'm a specialist in industrial organization and we've been talking about game theory and so on and so forth, the power of introductory micro is astounding. In

> ... understanding microeconomics is useful to anybody that works for a living.

most of the economic questions that I encounter outside of my role as a researcher, essentially I'm deploying undergraduate introductory microeconomics but at a real high level. So understanding microeconomics extremely deeply is going to be useful to anybody that works for a living. You always have to deal with your demanders. You always have to deal with prices and competition. You'll take your first course and you'll have some ability to use these tools. But understanding at some extraordinary deep level takes a career to do really well, but the returns are always positive.

After studying this chapter,
you will be able to:

◆ Explain why some choices are *public* choices and
how these choices are made in the political marketplace

◆ Explain how the free-rider problem arises and how
the quantity of public goods is determined

◆ Explain why mixed goods with external benefits lead
to inefficient underproduction and how public production, subsidies, and vouchers can achieve allocative
efficiency

16

PUBLIC CHOICES
AND PUBLIC GOODS

Fighting a California wildfire, screening passengers at an airport, providing
good schools and colleges, defending the nation's borders and interests
around the globe, policing neighborhoods and highways, operating courts and
a legal system: Governments are involved in all these activities. But why? Why
does government provide some goods and services and not others? Why don't
we leave it to private firms to provide and sell *all* goods and services? Do
governments overprovide or underprovide—provide too much or too little?
These are the questions we study in this chapter.

We begin by classifying goods and services and explaining the economic
theory of why and how governments intervene in markets, or
even replace them. We apply this theory to the provision of
public services. Two such public services are education and
health care. You will see how the political marketplace provides
these services.

In *Reading Between the Lines* at the end of the chapter, we
look at some of the strengths and weaknesses of the 2010 Affordable Care Act.

371

◆ Public Choices

All economic choices are made by individuals, but some choices are *private* and some are *public*. A *private choice* is a decision that has consequences for only the person making it. Decisions to buy (demand) or to sell (supply) goods and services in competitive markets are examples of private choices. At the market equilibrium price, these choices are consistent and one person's decision to buy or sell a little bit more or a little bit less has an imperceptible effect on the outcome.

A **public choice** is a decision that has consequences for many people and perhaps for an entire society. Decisions by political leaders and senior public servants about price and quantity regulations, taxes, international trade policy, and government spending are examples of public choices.

You studied the consequences of some public choices in Chapter 6 where you saw how price ceilings and price floors prevent voluntary exchanges even though marginal social benefit exceeds marginal social cost; you also saw how taxes drive a wedge between marginal social benefit and marginal social cost. In Chapter 7, you saw how tariffs and import quotas restrict international trade. All of these public choices result in scarce resources being used inefficiently—they create deadweight loss.

Why do governments do things that create inefficiency? Aren't they supposed to make things better? If governments make things worse, why do they exist? Why aren't the successful societies those that have no government? The economic theory of government explains both why governments exist and why they do a less-than-perfect job.

Why Governments Exist

Governments exist for three major reasons. First, they establish and maintain property rights. Second, they provide nonmarket mechanisms for allocating scarce resources. Third, they implement arrangements that redistribute income and wealth.

Property rights are the fundamental foundation of the market economy. By establishing property rights and the legal system that enforces them, governments enable markets to function. In many situations, markets function well and allocate scarce resources efficiently. But sometimes the market results in inefficiency—market failure (see Chapter 5, pp. 114–115).

When market failure occurs, too many of some things and too few of some other things are produced. Choices made in the pursuit of self-interest have not served the social interest. By reallocating resources, it is possible to make some people better off while making no one worse off.

The market economy also delivers a distribution of income and wealth that most people regard as unfair. Equity requires some redistribution.

Replacing markets with government resource-allocation decisions is no simple matter. Just as there can be market failure, there can also be government failure. **Government failure** is a situation in which government actions lead to inefficiency—to either underprovision or overprovision.

Government failure can arise because government is made up of many individuals, each with their own economic objectives. Public choices are the outcome of the choices made by these individuals. To analyse these choices, economists have developed a public choice theory of the political marketplace.

Public Choice and the Political Marketplace

Four groups of decision makers, shown in Fig. 16.1, interact in the political marketplace. They are

- Voters
- Firms
- Politicians
- Bureaucrats

Voters Voters evaluate politicians' policy proposals, benefit from public goods and services, and pay some of the taxes. In the economic model of public choice, voters support the politicians whose policy proposals make them better off and express their demand for public goods and services by voting, helping in political campaigns, lobbying, and making campaign contributions.

Firms Firms also evaluate politicians' policy proposals, benefit from public goods and services, and pay some of the taxes. Although firms don't vote, they do make campaign contributions and are a major source of funds for political parties. Firms also engage in lobbying activity to persuade politicians to propose policies that benefit them.

Politicians Politicians are the elected persons in the federal, state, and local governments—from the President of the United States to the Superintendent

FIGURE 16.1   The Political Marketplace

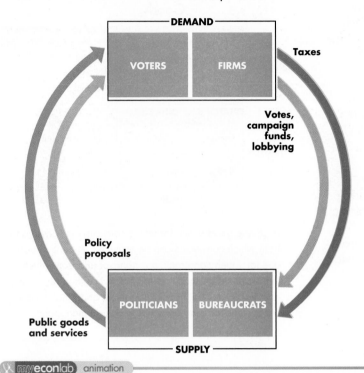

Voters express their demand for policies with their votes.

Voters and firms express their demand for policies with campaign contributions and by lobbying.

Politicians express their supply of policies with proposals that they hope will attract enough votes to get them elected and keep them in office. Politicians also set the taxes paid by voters and firms.

Bureaucrats provide public goods and services and try to get the largest possible budget for their departments.

A political equilibrium balances all these public choices.

myeconlab animation

of Yuma, Arizona, School District One. Federal and state politicians form coalitions—political parties—to develop policy proposals, which they present to voters in the hope of attracting majority support. Politicians also direct bureaucrats in the delivery of public goods and services and other policy actions. The goal of a politician is to get elected and to remain in office. Votes, to a politician, are like profit to a firm.

Bureaucrats Bureaucrats are the public servants who work in government departments. They administer tax collection, the delivery of public goods and services, and the administration of rules and regulations.

The self-interest of a bureaucrat is best served when the budget of her or his department is maximized. The bigger the budget of a department, the greater is the prestige of its chief and the greater are the opportunities for promotion for people further down the bureaucratic ladder. So all the members of a department have an interest in maximizing the department's budget. This economic assumption does not imply that bureaucrats do a poor job. Rather it implies that, in doing what they perceive to be a good job, they take care of their own self-interest too.

Political Equilibrium

Voters, firms, politicians, and bureaucrats make their economic choices to achieve their own self-interest. Public choices, like private choices, are constrained by what is feasible. Each person's public choices are also constrained by the public choices of others.

The balance of forces in the political marketplace determines the outcome of all the public choices that people make. In a **political equilibrium** the choices of voters, firms, politicians, and bureaucrats are all compatible and no group can see a way of improving its position by making a different choice.

Ideally, the political equilibrium will achieve allocative efficiency and serve the social interest, but such an outcome is not guaranteed, as you'll see later in this chapter.

We make public choices because some situations just don't permit private choices. The core of the reason we can't always make private choices is that some goods and services (and some factors of production) have a public nature—they are *public* goods and services.

Your next task is to see exactly what we mean by a *public* good or service.

What is a Public Good?

To see what makes a good a *public* good, we distinguish two features of all goods: the extent to which people can be *excluded* from consuming them and the extent to which one person's consumption *rivals* the consumption of others.

Excludable A good is **excludable** if it is possible to prevent someone from enjoying its benefits. Brink's security services, East Point Seafood's fish, and a U2 concert are examples. People must pay to benefit from them.

A good is **nonexcludable** if it is impossible (or extremely costly) to prevent anyone from benefiting from it. The services of the LAPD, fish in the Pacific Ocean, and a concert on network television are examples. When an LAPD cruiser enforces the speed limit, everyone on the highway benefits; anyone with a boat can fish in the ocean; and anyone with a TV can watch a network broadcast.

Rival A good is **rival** if one person's use of it decreases the quantity available for someone else. A Brink's truck can't deliver cash to two banks at the same time. A fish can be consumed only once.

A good is **nonrival** if one person's use of it does not decrease the quantity available for someone else. The services of the LAPD and a concert on network television are nonrival. One person's benefit doesn't lower the benefit of others.

A Fourfold Classification

Figure 16.2 classifies goods, services, and resources into four types.

Private Goods A **private good** is both rival and excludable. A can of Coke and a fish on East Point Seafood's farm are examples of private goods.

Public Goods A **public good** is both nonrival and nonexcludable. A public good simultaneously benefits everyone, and no one can be excluded from its benefits. National defense is the best example of a public good.

Common Resources A **common resource** is rival and nonexcludable. A unit of a common resource can be used only once, but no one can be prevented from using what is available. Ocean fish are a common resource. They are rival because a fish taken by one person isn't available for anyone else, and they are

FIGURE 16.2   Fourfold Classification of Goods

	Excludable	Nonexcludable
Rival	**Private goods** Food and drink Car House	**Common resources** Fish in ocean Atmosphere National parks
Nonrival	**Natural monopoly goods** Internet Cable television Bridge or tunnel	**Public goods** National defense The law Air traffic control

A private good is one for which consumption is rival and from which consumers can be excluded. A public good is one for which consumption is nonrival and from which it is impossible to exclude a consumer. A common resource is one that is rival but nonexcludable. A good that is nonrival but excludable is produced by a natural monopoly.

myeconlab   animation

nonexcludable because it is difficult to prevent people from catching them.

Natural Monopoly Goods A **natural monopoly good** is nonrival and excludable. When buyers can be excluded if they don't pay but the good is nonrival, marginal cost is zero. The fixed cost of producing such a good is usually high so economies of scale exist over the entire range of output for which there is a demand (see p. 300). An iTunes song and cable television are examples of natural monopoly goods.

Mixed Goods and Externalities

Some goods don't fit neatly into the four-fold classification of Fig. 16.2. They are mixed goods. A **mixed good** is a private good the production or consumption of which creates an externality. An **externality** is a cost (external cost) or a benefit (external benefit) that arises from the production or consumption of a private good and that falls on someone other than its producer or consumer. A **negative externality** imposes a cost and a **positive externality** provides a benefit.

We'll look at some examples of mixed goods with externalities and study those with positive externalities later in this chapter and those with negative externalities in Chapter 17.

Economics in Action
Is a Lighthouse a Public Good?

Built on Little Brewster Island in 1716 to guide ships into and out of the Boston Harbor, Boston Lighthouse was the first light station in North America.

For two centuries, economists used the lighthouse as an example of a public good. No one can be prevented from seeing its warning light—*nonexcludable*—and one person seeing its light doesn't prevent someone else from doing so too—*nonrival.*

Ronald Coase, who won the 1991 Nobel Prize for ideas he first developed when he was an undergraduate at the London School of Economics, discovered that before the nineteenth century, lighthouses in England were built and operated by private corporations that earned profits by charging tolls on ships docking at nearby ports. A ship that refused to pay the lighthouse toll was *excluded* from the port.

So the benefit arising from the services of a lighthouse is *excludable*. Because the services provided by a lighthouse are nonrival but excludable, a lighthouse is an example of a natural monopoly good and not a public good.

Mixed Goods with External Benefits Two of the things that have the greatest impact on your welfare, your education and health care, are mixed goods with external benefits.

Think about a flu vaccination. It is *excludable* because it would be possible to sell vaccinations and exclude those not willing to pay from benefiting from them. A flu vaccination is also *rival* because providing one person with a vaccination means one fewer available for everyone else. A flu vaccination is a private good, but it creates an externality.

If you decide to get a flu vaccination, you benefit from a lower risk of getting infected in the coming flu season. But if you avoid the flu, your neighbor who didn't get vaccinated has a better chance of avoiding it too. A flu vaccination brings a benefit to others, so it is a *mixed good* with an external benefit.

The external benefit of a flu vaccination is like a public good. It is nonexcludable because everyone with whom you come into contact benefits. You can't selectively benefit only your friends! And it is nonrival—protecting one person from the flu does not diminish the protection for others.

Your education is another example of a mixed good with external benefits. If all education was organized by private schools and universities, those not willing or able to pay would be excluded, and one person's place in a class would rival another's. So education is a private good.

But your being educated brings benefits to others. It brings benefits to your friends who enjoy your sharp, educated wit and it brings benefits to the community in which you live because well-educated people with a strong sense of fellowship and responsibility toward others make good neighbors. These external benefits are like a public good. You can't selectively decide who benefits from your good neighborliness and one person's enjoyment of your good behavior doesn't rival someone else's. So education is a mixed good with an external benefit.

Mixed Goods with External Costs Mixed goods with external costs have become a huge political issue in recent years. The main ones are electricity and transportation (road, rail, and air) produced by burning hydrocarbon fuels—coal, oil, and natural gas.

Electricity and transportation are excludable and rival—they are private goods. But when you use electricity or travel by car, bus, train, or airplane, carbon dioxide and other chemicals pour into the atmosphere. This consequence of consuming a private good creates an external cost and is a public bad. (A "bad" is the opposite of a good.) No one can be excluded from bearing the external cost and one person's discomfort doesn't rival another's. Electricity and transportation are mixed goods with external costs.

Other private goods that generate external costs include logging and the clearing of forests, which destroy the habitat of wildlife and influence the amount of carbon dioxide in the atmosphere; smoking cigarettes in a confined space, which imposes a health risk on others; and driving under the influence of alcohol, which increases the risk of accident and injury for others.

Inefficiencies that Require Public Choices

Public goods, mixed goods, common resources, and natural monopoly goods all create inefficiency problems that require public choices. Public choices must be made to

- Provide public goods and mixed goods
- Conserve common resources
- Regulate natural monopoly

Provide Public Goods and Mixed Goods Because no one can be excluded from enjoying the benefits of a public good, no one has an incentive to pay for their share of it. Even people with a social conscience have no incentive to pay because one person's enjoyment of a public good doesn't lower the enjoyment of others—it is nonrival.

If private firms tried to produce and sell public goods to consumers, they wouldn't remain in business for very long. The market economy would fail to deliver the efficient quantity of those goods. For example, there would be too little national defense, police services and law enforcement, courts and judges, storm-water and sewage disposal services.

Mixed goods pose a less extreme problem. The market economy would underprovide mixed goods with external benefits because their producers and consumers don't take the external benefits into account when they make their own choices. The market economy would overprovide mixed goods with

external costs because their producers and consumers don't take the external costs into account when they make their own choices.

Conserve Common Resources Because no one can be excluded from enjoying the benefits of a common resource, no one has an incentive to pay for their share of it or to conserve it for future enjoyment.

If boat owners are left to catch as much Southern Bluefin tuna as they wish, the stock will deplete and eventually the species will vanish. The market economy would overproduce tuna while stocks lasted and then underproduce as stocks ran out.

This problem, called the *tragedy of the commons*, requires public choices to limit the overuse and eventual destruction of common resources.

Regulate Natural Monopoly When people can be excluded from enjoying the benefits of a good if they don't pay for it, and when the good is nonrival, the marginal cost of producing it is zero. A natural monopoly can produce such a good at the lowest cost. But as Chapter 13 explains, when one firm serves a market, that firm maximizes profit by producing too little of the good.

You studied the regulation of natural monopoly in Chapter 13. This chapter and the next one study the other two public choices that must be made. In this chapter, we'll focus on the underprovision of public goods and mixed goods with external benefits. Chapter 17 studies mixed goods with external costs and conserving common resources.

REVIEW QUIZ

1 List three main reasons why governments exist.
2 Describe the political marketplace. Who demands, who supplies, and what is the political equilibrium?
3 Distinguish among public goods, private goods, common resources, natural monopoly goods, and mixed goods.
4 What are the problems that arise from public goods, common resources, natural monopoly goods, and mixed goods?

You can work these questions in Study Plan 16.1 and get instant feedback.

Providing Public Goods

Why do governments provide firefighting services? Why don't the people of California buy brush fire-fighting services from Firestorm, a private firm that competes for our dollars in the marketplace in the same way that McDonalds does? The answer is that firefighting is a public good. It is nonexcludable and nonrival and it has a free-rider problem.

The Free-Rider Problem

A free rider enjoys the benefits of a good or service without paying for it. Because a public good is provided for everyone to use and no one can be excluded from its benefits, no one has an incentive to pay his or her share of the cost. Everyone has an incentive to free ride. The **free-rider problem** is that the economy would provide an inefficiently small quantity of a public good. Marginal social benefit from the public good would exceed its marginal social cost and a deadweight loss would arise.

Let's look at the marginal social benefit and marginal social cost of a public good.

Marginal Social Benefit from a Public Good

Lisa and Max (the only people in a society) value fire-fighting airplanes. Figure 16.3(a) and 16.3(b) graph their marginal benefits from the airplanes as MB_L for Lisa and MB_M for Max. The marginal benefit from a public good (like that from a private good) diminishes as the quantity of the good increases.

Figure 16.3(c) shows the marginal *social* benefit curve, *MSB*. Because everyone gets the same quantity of a public good, its marginal social benefit curve is the sum of the marginal benefits of all the individuals at each *quantity*—it is the *vertical* sum of the individual marginal benefit curves. So the curve *MSB* is the marginal social benefit curve for the economy made up of Lisa and Max. For each airplane, Lisa's marginal benefit is added to Max's marginal benefit.

Contrast the *MSB* curve for a public good with that of a private good. To obtain the economy's *MSB* curve for a private good, we sum the *quantities demanded* by all the individuals at each *price*—we sum the individual marginal benefit curves *horizontally* (see Chapter 5, p. 108).

FIGURE 16.3 Benefits of a Public Good

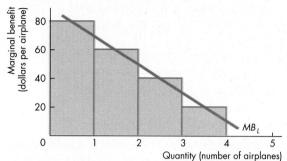

(a) Lisa's marginal benefit

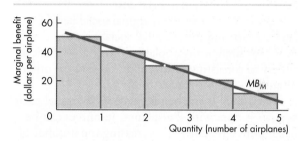

(b) Max's marginal benefit

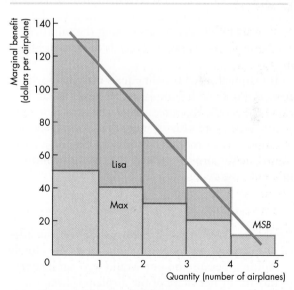

(c) Economy's marginal social benefit

The marginal social benefit at each quantity of the public good is the sum of the marginal benefits of all individuals. The marginal benefit curves are MB_L for Lisa and MB_M for Max. The economy's marginal social benefit curve is *MSB*.

 animation

Marginal Social Cost of a Public Good

The marginal social cost of a public good is determined in exactly the same way as that of a private good—see Chapter 5, p. 110. The principle of increasing marginal cost applies to the marginal cost of a public good, so the marginal social cost decreases as the quantity of the public good increases.

Efficient Quantity of a Public Good

To determine the efficient quantity of a public good, we use the principles that you learned in Chapter 5. The efficient quantity is that at which marginal social benefit equals marginal social cost.

Figure 16.4 shows the marginal social benefit curve, *MSB*, and the marginal social cost curve, *MSC*, for firefighting airplanes. (We'll now think of society as consisting of Lisa and Max and the other 39 million Californians.)

If marginal social benefit exceeds marginal social cost, as it does with 2 airplanes, resources can be used more efficiently by increasing the number of airplanes. The extra benefit exceeds the extra cost. If marginal social cost exceeds marginal social benefit, as it does with 4 airplanes, resources can be used more efficiently by decreasing the number of airplanes. The cost saving exceeds the loss of benefit.

If marginal social benefit equals marginal social cost, as it does with 3 airplanes, resources are allocated efficiently. Resources cannot be used more efficiently because to provide more than 3 airplanes increases cost by more than the extra benefit, and to provide fewer airplanes lowers the benefit by more than the cost saving.

Inefficient Private Provision

Could a private firm—Firestorm—deliver the efficient quantity of firefighting airplanes? Most likely it couldn't, because no one would have an incentive to buy his or her share of the airplanes. Everyone would reason as follows: The number of airplanes provided by Firestorm is not affected by my decision to pay my share or not. But my own private consumption will be greater if I free ride and do not pay my share of the cost of the airplanes. If I don't pay, I enjoy the same level of fire protection and I can buy more private goods. I will spend my money on private goods and free ride on fire protection. Such reasoning is the free-rider problem. If

FIGURE 16.4   The Efficient Quantity of a Public Good

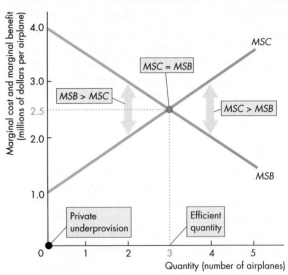

With fewer than 3 airplanes, marginal social benefit, *MSB*, exceeds marginal social cost, *MSC*. With more than 3 airplanes, *MSC* exceeds *MSB*. Only with 3 airplanes is *MSC* equal to *MSB* and the number of airplanes is efficient.

myeconlab animation

everyone reasons the same way, Firestorm has no revenue and so provides no airplanes. Because the efficient number of airplanes is 3, private provision is inefficient.

Efficient Public Provision

The outcome of the political process might be efficient or inefficient. We look first at an efficient outcome. There are two political parties: Fears and Hopes. They agree on all issues except the number of firefighting airplanes: The Fears want 4, and the Hopes want 2. Both parties want to get elected, so they run a voter survey and discover the marginal social benefit curve of Fig. 16.5. They also consult with airplane producers to establish the marginal cost curve. The parties then do a "what-if" analysis. If the Fears propose 4 airplanes and the Hopes propose 2, the voters will be equally unhappy with both parties. Compared to the efficient quantity, the Hopes want an underprovision of 1 airplaneand the Fears want an overprovision of 1 airplane. The deadweight losses are equal and the election would be too close to call.

Contemplating this outcome, the Fears realize that they are too fearful to get elected. They figure that, if they scale back to 3 airplanes, they will win the election if the Hopes stick with 2. The Hopes reason in a similar way and figure that, if they increase the number of airplanes to 3, they can win the election if the Fears propose 4.

So they both propose 3 airplanes. The voters are indifferent between the parties, and each party receives 50 percent of the vote. But regardless of which party wins the election, 3 airplanes are provided and this quantity is efficient. Competition in the political place results in the efficient provision of a public good.

The Principle of Minimum Differentiation The **principle of minimum differentiation** is the tendency for competitors (including political parties) to make themselves similar to appeal to the maximum number of clients or voters. This principle describes the behavior of political parties. It also explains why fast-food restaurants cluster in the same block. For example, if Dominoes opens a new pizza outlet, it is likely that Pizza Hut will soon open nearby.

FIGURE 16.5   An Efficient Political Outcome

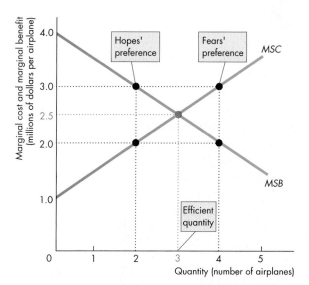

The Hopes would like to provide 2 airplanes and the Fears would like to provide 4 airplanes. The political outcome is 3 airplanes because unless each party proposes 3 airplanes, the other party will beat it in an election.

myeconlab animation

Economics in Action
Fighting California's Wildfires

During the 2009 wildfire season (July through November), 63 fires burned across more than 500 square miles of California. The two largest and deadliest fires, Station Fire north of Los Angeles and La Brea Fire in Santa Barbara County, together consumed almost 400 square miles of land.

Wildfires are natural and vital for the ecosystem, but some fires are started by human action, and some both human-made and naturally occurring fires burn close to where people live. So protection against wildfires is a vital public good.

Fighting wildfires is an example of a public good that is *provided* by government and paid for with tax revenues but *produced* by private firms.

Firestorm Wildfire Suppression Inc. is one such firm. Operating from Chico, CA, Firestorm hires and trains firefighters and produces firefighting services to maximize its profit. To achieve this goal, the firm must produce firefighting services at the lowest possible cost.

But if Firestorm (and its competitors) tried to sell their services to each individual home owner in the wildfire regions of California, they wouldn't get enough revenue to remain in business. There would be a free-rider problem. The free-rider problem is avoided because the state of California and federal emergency services agencies buy the services of Firestorm—government is the *provider* of this public good and Firestorm and others are the *producers*.

For the political process to deliver the efficient outcome, voters must be well informed, evaluate the alternatives, and vote in the election. Political parties must be well informed about voter preferences. As the next section shows, we can't expect to achieve this outcome.

Inefficient Public Overprovision

If competition between two political parties is to deliver the efficient quantity of a public good, bureaucrats must cooperate and help to achieve this outcome. But bureaucrats might have a different idea and end up frustrating rather than facilitating an efficient outcome. Their actions might bring *government failure*.

Objective of Bureaucrats Bureaucrats want to maximize their department's budget because a bigger budget brings greater status and more power. So the Emergency Services Department's objective is to maximize the budget for firefighting airplanes.

Figure 16.6 shows the outcome if the bureaucrats are successful in the pursuit of their goal. They might try to persuade the politicians that 3 airplanes cost more than the originally budgeted amount; or they might press their position more strongly and argue for more than 3 airplanes. In Fig. 16.6, the Emergency Services Department persuades the politicians to provide 4 airplanes.

Why don't the politicians block the bureaucrats? Won't overproviding airplanes cost future votes? It will if voters are well informed and know what is best for them. But voters might not be well informed, and well-informed interest groups might enable the bureaucrats to achieve their objective and overcome the objections of the politicians.

Rational Ignorance A principle of the economic analysis of public choices is that it is rational for a voter to be ignorant about an issue unless that issue has a perceptible effect on the voter's economic welfare. Each voter knows that he or she can make virtually no difference to the fire protection policy of the government of California and that it would take an enormous amount of time and effort to become even moderately well informed about alternative fire-protection technologies. Rationally uninformed voters enable bureaucrats and special interest groups to overprovide public goods.

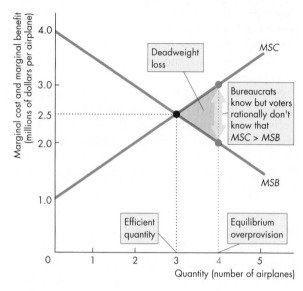

FIGURE 16.6   Bureaucratic Overprovision

Well-informed bureaucrats want to maximize their budget and rationally ignorant voters enable the bureaucrats to go some way toward achieving their goal. A public good might be inefficiently overprovided with a deadweight loss.

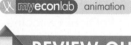 animation

REVIEW QUIZ

1 What is the free-rider problem? Why do free riders make the private provision of a public good inefficient?

2 Under what conditions will competition among politicians for votes result in an efficient provision of a public good?

3 How do rationally ignorant voters and budget-maximizing bureaucrats prevent the political marketplace from delivering the efficient quantity of a public good?

4 Explain why public choices might lead to the overprovision rather than the underprovision of a public good.

You can work these questions in Study Plan 16.2 and get instant feedback.

You've seen how the political marketplace provides public goods and why it might *over*provide them. Your next task is to see how the political marketplace provides mixed goods that bring external benefits.

Providing Mixed Goods with External Benefits

Most of the goods and services provided by governments are *mixed* goods, not *public* goods. Two of the largest mixed goods with external benefits are education and health care. We're going to look at how governments operate in such s. We're also going to look at possible improvements on the current arrangements in these markets.

To keep our explanation clear, we'll focus first on the market for college education. We'll then apply the lessons we learn to the market for health care.

We begin our study of the provision of mixed goods by distinguishing between private benefits and social benefits.

Private Benefits and Social Benefits

A *private benefit* is a benefit that the consumer of a good or service receives. For example, expanded job opportunities and a higher income are private benefits of a college education.

Marginal benefit is the benefit from an *additional unit* of a good or service. So **marginal private benefit** (*MB*) is the benefit that the consumer of a good or service receives from an additional unit of it. When one additional student attends college, the benefit that student receives is the marginal private benefit from college education.

The *external benefit* from a good or service is the benefit that someone other than the consumer of the good or service receives. College graduates generate many external benefits. On average, they are better citizens, have lower crime rates, and are more tolerant of the views of others. They enable the success of high quality newspapers and television channels, music, theater, and other organized social activities that bring benefits to many other people.

A **marginal external benefit** is the benefit from an additional unit of a good or service that people *other than its consumer* enjoy. The benefit that your friends and neighbors get from your college education is the marginal external benefit of your college education.

Marginal social benefit (*MSB*) is the marginal benefit enjoyed by society—by the consumer of a good or service (marginal private benefit) and by others (the marginal external benefit). That is,

$$MSB = MB + \text{Marginal external benefit.}$$

Figure 16.7 shows an example of the relationship between marginal private benefit, marginal external benefit, and marginal social benefit. The marginal benefit curve, *MB*, describes the marginal private benefit enjoyed by the people who receive a college education. Marginal private benefit decreases as the number of students enrolled in college increases.

In the example in Fig. 16.7, when 15 million students enroll in college, the marginal external benefit is $15,000 per student per year . The marginal social benefit curve, *MSB*, is the sum of marginal private benefit and marginal external benefit at each number of students. For example, when 15 million students a year enroll in college, the marginal private benefit is $10,000 per student and the marginal external benefit is $15,000 per student, so the marginal social benefit is $25,000 per student.

When people make schooling decisions, they ignore its external benefits and consider only its private benefits. So if education were provided by private schools

FIGURE 16.7   An External Benefit

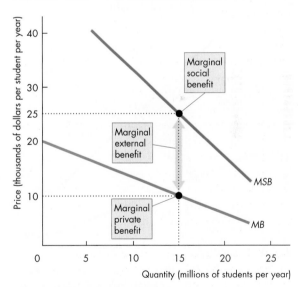

The *MB* curve shows the marginal private benefit enjoyed by the people who receive a college education. The *MSB* curve shows the sum of marginal private benefit and marginal external benefit. When 15 million students attend college, the marginal private benefit is $10,000 per student, the marginal external benefit is $15,000 per student, and the marginal social benefit is $25,000 per student.

myeconlab animation

that charged full-cost tuition, there would be too few college graduates.

Figure 16.8 illustrates this private underprovision. The supply curve is the marginal social cost curve, $S = MSC$. The demand curve is the marginal *private* benefit curve, $D = MB$. Market equilibrium occurs at a tuition of $15,000 per student per year and 7.5 million students per year. At this equilibrium, the marginal social benefit of $38,000 per student exceeds the marginal social cost by $23,000 per student. Too few students are enrolled in college. The efficient number is 15 million per year, where marginal social benefit equals marginal social cost. The gray triangle shows the deadweight loss created.

To get closer to producing the efficient quantity of a mixed good with an external benefit, we make public choices, through governments, to modify the market outcome.

Government Actions in the Market for a Mixed Good with External Benefits

To encourage more students to enroll in college —to achieve an efficient quantity of college education— students must be confronted with a lower market price and the taxpayer must somehow pay for the costs not covered by what the student pays.

Figure 16.9 illustrates an efficient outcome. With marginal social cost curve *MSC* and marginal social benefit curve *MSB*, the efficient number of college students is 15,000. The marginal *private* benefit curve *MB*, tells us that 15,000 students will enroll only if the tuition is $10,000 per year. But the marginal social cost of 15,000 students is $25,000 per year. To enable the marginal social cost to be paid, taxpayers must pay the balance of $15,000 per student per year.

FIGURE 16.8   Inefficiency with an External Benefit

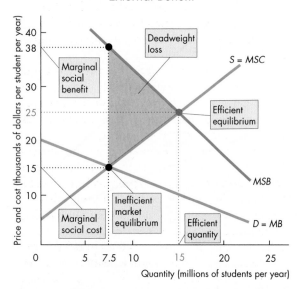

The market demand curve is the marginal private benefit curve, $D = MB$. The supply curve is the marginal social cost curve, $S = MSC$. Market equilibrium at a tuition of $15,000 a year and 7.5 million students is inefficient because marginal social benefit exceeds marginal social cost. The efficient quantity is 15 million students. A deadweight loss arises (gray triangle) because too few students enroll in college.

FIGURE 16.9   An Efficient Outcome with an External Benefit

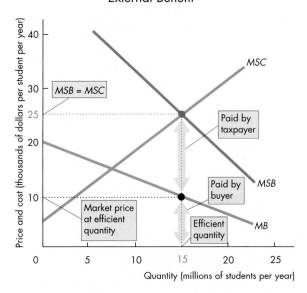

The efficient number of college students is 15 million, where marginal social benefit equals marginal social cost. With the demand and marginal private benefit curve, $D = MB$, the price at which the efficient number will enrol is $10,000 per year. If students pay this price, the taxpayer must somehow pay the rest, which equals the marginal external cost at the efficient quantity—$15,000 per student per year.

Four devices that governments can use to achieve a more efficient allocation of resources in the presence of external benefits are

- Public production
- Private subsidies
- Vouchers

Public Production With **public production,** a good or service is produced by a public authority that receives its revenue from the government. The education services produced by state universities and colleges and public schools are examples of public production.

In the example in Fig. 16.9, efficient public production occurs if public colleges receive funds from government equal to $15,000 per student per year, charge tuition of $10,000 per student per year, and enrol 15 million students.

Private Subsidies A **subsidy** is a payment that the government makes to private producers. By making the subsidy depend on the level of output, the government can induce private decision-makers to consider external benefits when they make their choices.

In the example in Fig. 16.9, efficient private provision would occur if private colleges received a government subsidy of $15,000 per student per year. This subsidy reduces the colleges' costs and would make their marginal cost equal to $10,000 per student at the efficient quantity. Tuition of $10,000 would cover this cost, and the subsidy of $15,000 per student would cover the balance of the cost.

Vouchers A **voucher** is a token that the government provides to households, which they can use to buy specified goods or services. Food stamps are examples of vouchers. The vouchers (food stamps) can be spent only on food and are designed to improve the diet and health of extremely poor families.

School vouchers have been advocated as a means of improving the quality of education and are used in Washington D.C. A school voucher allows parents to choose the school their children will attend and to use the voucher to pay part of the cost. The school cashes the vouchers to pay its bills. A voucher could be provided to a college student in a similar way, and although technically not a voucher, a federal Pell Grant has a similar effect.

Because vouchers can be spent only on a specified item, they increase the willingness to pay for that item and so increase the demand for it.

Efficient provision of college education occurs if the government provides a voucher to each student with a value equal to the marginal external benefit at the efficient number of students. In the example in Fig. 16.9, the efficient number of students is 15 million and the voucher is valued at $15,000 per student. Each student pays $10,000 tuition and gives the college a $15,000 voucher. The colleges receive $25,000 per student, which equals their marginal cost.

Bureaucratic Inefficiency and Government Failure

You've seen three government actions that achieve an efficient provision of a mixed good with an external benefit. In each case, if the government estimates the marginal external benefit correctly and makes marginal social benefit equal to marginal social cost, the outcome is efficient.

Does the comparison that we've just made mean that pubic provision, subsidized private provision, and vouchers are equivalent? It does not. And the reason lies in something that you've already encountered in your study of public goods earlier in this chapter—the behavior of bureaucrats combined with rational ignorance that leads to government failure.

The Problem with Public Production Public colleges (and schools) are operated by a bureaucracy and are subject to the same problems as the provision of public goods. If bureaucrats seek to maximize their budgets, the outcome might be inefficient.

But *overprovision* of colleges (and schools) doesn't seem to be a problem. Just the opposite: People complain about *underprovision*—about inadequate public colleges and schools. The probable reason is that there is another type of bureaucratic budget maximization: budget padding and waste.

Bureaucrats often incur costs that exceed the minimum efficient cost. They might hire more assistants than the number needed to do their work efficiently; give themselves sumptuous offices; get generous expense allowances; build schools in the wrong places where land costs are too high.

Economists have studied the possibility that education bureaucrats pad their budgets by comparing the production costs of private and public colleges and schools. They have found that the costs per student of public schools are of the order of *three times* the costs of comparable private schools (see Talking With Carolyn Hoxby on pp. 414– 416.)

Problems with Private Subsidies Subsidizing private producers might overcome some of the problems created by public production. A private producer has an incentive to produce at minimum cost and avoid the budget padding of a bureaucratic producer. But two problems arise with private subsidies.

First, the subsidy budget must be allocated by a bureau. A national, state, or local department of education must lobby for its own budget and allocate this budget between school subsidies and its own administration costs. To the extent that the bureaucrats succeed in maximizing their own adminstration budget, they siphon off resources from schools and a problem similar to that of public production arises.

Second, it is in the self-interest of subsidized producers to maximize their subsidy. These producers might even spend some of the subsidy they receive lobbying for an even bigger one.

So neither public production nor subsidized private provision are likely to achieve an efficient allocation of resources in the face of external benefits.

Are Vouchers the Solution? Vouchers have four advantages over the other two approaches:

1. Vouchers can be used with public production, private provision, or competition between the two.
2. Governments can set the value of vouchers and the total voucher budget to overcome bureaucratic overprovision and budget padding.
3. Vouchers spread the public contribution thinly across millions of consumers, so no one consumer has an interest in wasting part of the value received in lobbying for overprovision.
4. By giving the buying power to the final consumer, producers must compete for business and provide a high standard of service at the lowest attainable cost.

For these four reasons, vouchers are popular with economists. But they are controversial and opposed by most education administrators and teachers.

In *The Economics of School Choice*, a book edited by Caroline M. Hoxby, economists study the effect of school choice on student achievement and school productivity and show how vouchers can be designed to achieve their goals while avoiding their potential pitfalls. Caroline Hoxby is confident that she can design a voucher that best achieves any educational and school performance objective (see p. 416).

Economics in Action
Delivering Health Care Efficiently

Americans spend 17 percent of income—$8,000 per person per year—on health care, which is more than double the average of other rich countries. And the cost is projected to rise as the population ages and the "baby boom" generation retires. Despite this enormous expenditure, until the passage of the 2010 Affordable Care Act, 47 million people had no health insurance and a further 25 million had too little insurance.

Of those who do have health insurance nearly 40 million are covered by the government's Medicare and Medicaid programs. These programs are in effect an open-ended commitment of public funds to the health care of the aged (Medicare) and those too poor to buy private health care (Medicaid). In 2035, when those born in 1955 turn 80, benefits under these programs will cost an estimated $50,000 per person per year. Benefits on these programs alone will cost more than 18 percent of the value of the nation's total production.

You can see that health care in the United States faces two problems: *underprovision* because private choices don't value all the external benefits; and *over expenditure* because private health-care producers decide how much to produce and then collect fees for their services from the government.

Health-Care Services

Health care is another example of a mixed good with external benefits. The external benefits from health care include avoiding infectious diseases, living and working with healthy neighbors, and for many people, just living in a society in which poor, sick people have access to affordable health care.

An additional problem arises in the case of health care: People with the biggest health problems are the elderly and the poor, who are least able to afford health care.

Because of its special features, no country just leaves the delivery of health care to the private market economy. In almost all countries, health care is provided at a zero price, or very low price, and doctors and other health-care professionals and the hospitals in which they work receive most (and in some cases all) their incomes from government.

The Obama Affordable Care Act addresses the first of these problems by requiring everyone to be insured and by creating a new Pre-Existing Condition Insurance Plan financed partly by the government.

But the act does little to address the problem of over-expenditure, and this problem is extremely serious. It is so serious that without massive change, the present open-ended health-care programs will bankrupt the United States.

Other countries contain health-care costs by limiting the budget and the number of physicians and hospital beds and by rationing services with long wait-times for treatment. This "solution" is inefficient because some people would be willing to pay more than the cost (marginal benefit exceeds marginal cost) and it is unfair (some people are better at playing the system than others and are able to jump the line).

A more effective solution to both the problem of coverage and access and the problem of over-expenditure has been suggested by Laurence Kotlikoff, an economics professor at Boston University. His proposal uses health-care vouchers to ensure universal coverage and a cap on total expenditure. His *Medicare Part C for all* is summarized in the ten-point plan in the next column.

This solution can deliver health care efficiently, distribute public funds among individuals based on their health status, and cap total expenditure.

Professor Laurence J. Kotlikoff of Boston University; author of *The Healthcare Fix* and creator of *Medicare Part C for all*.

1. Everyone is covered.
2. Every American gets a health-plan voucher.
3. Those with higher expected health-care costs receive bigger vouchers.
4. Can change health plan annually.
5. Government defines basic policy each year.
6. Basic policy covers drugs, home health care, and nursing home care.
7. Plans must cover basic policy.
8. Plans compete for participants.
9. Annual voucher budget is fixed as a percentage of the value of total production.
10. Medicare and employer-based health insurance tax breaks are eliminated.

In the United States, most health-care services are produced by private doctors and hospitals that receive their incomes from both governments and private health insurance companies. The health insurance companies in turn receive their income from employers and individual contributors.

Economics in Action (above) describes some of the features of health-care delivery in the United States and explains why it faces two serious problems, only one of which has been addressed by the Affordable Care Act of 2010.

Again, vouchers—health-care vouchers—are a crucial component of a program capable of achieving an efficient quantity and distribution of health-care services across individuals.

 Reading Between the Lines on pp. 386–387 looks at the effects of the 2010 Act and some of the problems that it brings.

REVIEW QUIZ

1   What is special about education and health care that makes them mixed goods with external benefits?

2   Why would the market economy produce too little education and health care?

3   How might public production, private subsidies, and vouchers achieve an efficient provision of a mixed good with external benefits?

4   What are the key differences among public production, private subsidies, and vouchers?

5   Why do economists generally favor vouchers rather than public production or subsidies to achieve an efficient outcome?

You can work these questions in Study Plan 16.3 and get instant feedback.

Reforming Health Care

Protective Net for All Residents; Q&A Legislation Details

Financial Times
March 22, 2010

What would the U.S. health-care bill do?

Offer or subsidise health-care coverage for 32m people, a tenth of the population, who are uninsured; mandate that every U.S. and legal resident receive minimal coverage.

Beginning in 2014, people who are out of work, self-employed, or working for companies that do not offer insurance could buy coverage from "health exchanges" in which private insurers would offer different kinds of plans.

About 19m people would be eligible for financial subsidies to help pay for insurance. If individuals refused to buy insurance coverage, they would be subject to a tax penalty.

How much would it cost and who is paying for it?

The non-partisan Congressional Budget Office estimates the bill would cost $940 billion over 10 years. This is expected to be paid for through tax on the wealthy and health-related industries, including a tax on so-called "Cadillac" insurance plans that would raise $32 billion over 10 years. The bill would also create a Medicare (the healthcare scheme for the elderly) commission that would have power to impose steep cuts in payments. Individuals making more than $200,000 a year, or couples making more than $250,000 a year, would pay higher taxes on Medicare and face a new 3.8 percent tax on dividends, interest, and other unearned income. The tax would take effect in January 2013. The CBO estimates the health-care bill would reduce the U.S. deficit by $138 billion over 10 years. ...

ESSENCE OF THE STORY

- Over the first ten years, health-care reform will cost $940 billion.

- Coverage will expand to 32 million American who are currently uninsured.

- New taxes will pay for the plan and cut the budget deficit.

- Medicaid will expand to cover about 19 million low-income people.

- Insurance companies will not be able to deny coverage for preexisting conditions.

- Except for some low-income families, everyone will be required to buy health insurance and will face penalties if they refuse to do so.

- Health care in the United States faces two problems:
  1) *Underprovision* because private choices leave too many families and individuals without health insurance;
  2) *Over expenditure* on public programs because the government pays for the quantity that patients demand and doctors supply.

- The health-care reform of 2010 (the Patient Protection and Affordable Care Act of 2010) addresses the first problem. It expands the scope of government provision of health care by covering more families and individuals and by improving the health-care insurance of those already covered. (The news article describes some of the details of the Act.)

- The 2010 Act notes the problem of cost containment but does little to address the main source of over expenditure: Medicare and Medicaid.

- Medicare and Medicaid remain and Medicaid will be expanded to cover more people.

- Figure 1 shows how Medicare and Medicaid overprovide services to those covered by the programs. The quantity is the quantity demanded by patients and supplied by doctors at a zero (or almost zero) price.

- Because the price is zero, marginal benefit, *MB*, is also zero.

- Doctors and hospitals negotiate fees with the government that equal marginal cost, which also equals marginal social cost, *MSC*.

- Marginal social cost, shown by the *MSC* curve, exceeds the (zero) marginal benefit. In this example, *MSC* is $25 at the quantity provided.

- Medicare and Medicaid services would be provided efficiently if marginal social cost, *MSC* equalled marginal social benefit, *MSB*.

- With overprovision, a deadweight loss arises shown by the gray triangle.

- Expenditure on Medicare and Medicaid equals the fee per unit of service multiplied by the quantity provided, and Fig. 2 illustrates this expenditure.

- The white rectangle shows what expenditure would be on the efficient quantity. The purple area shows the over expenditure. Total expenditure is the sum of these areas and equals $25 × 30 million.

- As the population gets older and as treatment techniques become more sophisticated and more conditions can be treated, the *MB* curve shifts rightward.

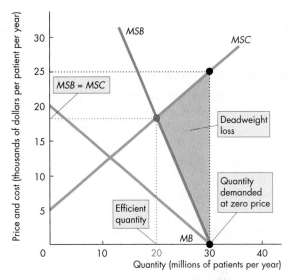

Figure 1 Overprovision of Medicare and Medicaid

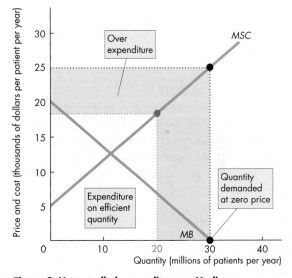

Figure 2 Uncontrolled expenditure on Medicare and Medicaid

- The quantity of health-care services provided by Medicare and Medicaid increases and the expenditure on these programs grows.

- A health-care voucher program like that explained on pp. 384–385 is one way (and possibly the only effective way) of achieving an efficient provision of Medicare and Medicaid and of containing their cost.

SUMMARY

Key Points

Public Choices (pp. 372–376)

- Governments establish and maintain property rights, provide nonmarket mechanisms for allocating scarce resources, and redistribute income and wealth.
- Public choice theory explains how voters, firms, politicians, and bureaucrats interact in the political marketplace and why government failure might occur.
- A private good is a good or service that is rival and excludable.
- A public good is a good or service that is nonrival and nonexcludable.
- A mixed good is a private good that creates an external benefit or external cost.

Working Problems 1 to 6 will give you a better understanding of public choices.

Providing Public Goods (pp. 377–380)

- Because a public good is a good or service that is *nonrival* and *nonexcludable*, it creates a *free-rider* problem: No one has an incentive to pay their share of the cost of providing a public good.
- The efficient level of provision of a public good is that at which marginal social benefit equals marginal social cost.

- Competition between political parties can lead to the efficient scale of provision of a public good.
- Bureaucrats who maximize their budgets and voters who are rationally ignorant can lead to the inefficient overprovision of a public good—government failure.

Working Problems 7 to 15 will give you a better understanding of providing public goods.

Providing Mixed Goods with External Benefits (pp. 381–385)

- Mixed goods provide external benefits—benefits that are received by people other than the consumer of a good or service.
- Marginal social benefit equals marginal private benefit plus marginal external benefit.
- External benefits arise from education and health care.
- Vouchers provided to households can achieve a more efficient provision of education and health care than public production or subsidies to private producers.

Working Problems 16 to 20 will give you a better understanding of providing mixed goods with external benefits.

Key Terms

Common resource, 374
Excludable, 374
Externality, 374
Free-rider problem, 377
Government failure, 372
Marginal external benefit, 381
Marginal private benefit, 381
Marginal social benefit, 381
Mixed good, 374

Natural monopoly good, 374
Negative externality, 374
Nonexcludable, 374
Nonrival, 374
Political equilibrium, 373
Postive externality, 374
Principle of minimum differentiation, 379
Private good, 374

Public choice, 372
Public good, 374
Public production, 383
Rival, 374
Subsidy, 383
Voucher, 383

STUDY PLAN PROBLEMS AND APPLICATIONS

myeconlab You can work Problems 1 to 20 in MyEconLab Chapter 16 Study Plan and get instant feedback.

Public Choices (Study Plan 16.1)

1. Classify each of the following items as excludable, nonexcludable, rival, or nonrival.
   - A Big Mac
   - Brooklyn Bridge
   - A view of the Statue of Liberty
   - A tsunami warning system

2. Classify each of the following items as a public good, a private good, a natural monopoly good, or a common resource.
   - Highway control services
   - City sidewalks
   - U.S. Postal Service
   - FedEx courier service

3. Classify the following services for computer owners with an Internet connection as rival, nonrival, excludable, or nonexcludable:
   - eBay
   - A mouse
   - A Twitter page
   - MyEconLab Web site

4. Classify each of the following items as a public good, a private good, a mixed good, or a common resource:
   - Firefighting services
   - A courtside seat at the U.S. Open (tennis)
   - A well-stocked buffet that promises the most bang for your buck
   - The Mississippi River

5. Explain which of the following events creates an external benefit or an external cost:
   - A huge noisy crowd gathers outside the lecture room
   - Your neighbor grows beautiful flowers on his apartment deck.
   - A fire alarm goes off accidently in the middle of a lecture.
   - Your instructor offers a free tutorial after class.

6. **Wind Farm Off Cape Cod Clears Hurdle**

   The nation's first offshore wind farm with 130 turbines will be built 5 miles off the coast. Wind turbines are noisy, stand 440 feet tall, can be seen from the coast, and will produce power for 75 percent of nearby homes.

   Source: *The New York Times*, January 16, 2009

   List the externalities created by this wind farm.

Providing Public Goods (Study Plan 16.2)

7. For each of the following goods, explain whether there is a free-rider problem. If there is no such problem, how is it avoided?
   - July 4th fireworks display
   - Interstate 81 in Virginia
   - Wireless Internet access in hotels
   - The public library in your city

8. The table sets out the marginal benefits that Terri and Sue receive from police officers on duty on the college campus:

Police officers on duty (number per night)	Marginal benefit	
	Terri	Sue
	(dollars per police officer)	
1	18	22
2	14	18
3	10	14
4	6	10
5	2	6

   a. If the police officers are provided by the city government, is the presence of the police on-campus a private good or a public good?

   b. Suppose that Terri and Sue are the only students on the campus at night. Draw a graph to show the marginal social benefit from on-campus police officers on duty at night.

9. For each of the following goods and services, explain whether there is a free-rider problem. If there is no such problem, how is it avoided?
   - National hurricane warning system
   - Ambulance service
   - Road safety signs
   - The U.S. Coast Guard

10. **Vaccination Dodgers**

    Doctors struggle to eradicate polio worldwide, but one of the biggest problems is persuading parents to vaccinate their children. Since the discovery of the vaccine, polio has been eliminated from Europe and the law requires everyone to be vaccinated. People who refuse to be vaccinated are "free riders."

    Source: *USA Today*, March 12, 2008

    Explain why someone who has not opted out on medical or religious grounds and refuses to be vaccinated is a "free rider."

Use the following figure to work Problems 11 to 13. The figure provides information about a waste disposal system that a city of 1 million people is considering installing.

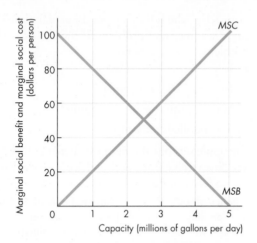

Capacity (millions of gallons per day)

11. What is the efficient capacity of the waste disposal system? How much will each person have to pay in taxes for the city to install the efficient capacity?
12. What is the political equilibrium if voters are well informed?
13. What is the political equilibrium if voters are rationally ignorant and bureaucrats achieve the highest attainable budget?

Use the data on a mosquito control program in the following table to work Problems 14 and 15.

Quantity (square miles sprayed per day)	Marginal social cost	Marginal social benefit
	(thousands of dollars per day)	
1	2	10
2	4	8
3	6	6
4	8	4
5	10	2

14. What quantity of spraying would a private mosquito control program provide? What is the efficient quantity of spraying? In a single-issue election on the quantity of spraying, what quantity would the winner of the election provide?
15. If the government sets up a Department of Mosquito Control and appoints a bureaucrat to run it, would mosquito spraying most likely be underprovided, overprovided, or provided at the efficient quantity?

Providing Mixed Goods with External Benefits

(Study Plan 16.3)

Use the following figure, which shows the marginal private benefit from college education, to work Problems 16 to 19. The marginal cost of a college education is a constant $6,000 per student per year. The marginal external benefit from a college education is a constant $4,000 per student per year.

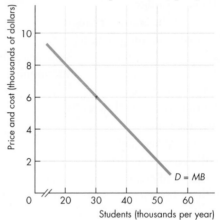

Students (thousands per year)

16. What is the efficient number of students? If all colleges are private, how many people enroll in college and what is the tuition?
17. If the government decides to provide public colleges, what tuition will these colleges charge to achieve the efficient number of students? How much will taxpayers have to pay?
18. If the government decides to subsidize private colleges, what subsidy will achieve the efficient number of college students?
19. If the government offers vouchers to those who enroll at a college and no subsidy, what is the value of the voucher that will achieve the efficient number of students?
20. **Tuition Hikes, not Loan Access, Should Frighten Students**

    The real danger during a recession is a hike in tuition, not a cut in student loans. In past recessions, states have cut funding for colleges and increased tuition. The Cato Institute says a better policy would be for states to maintain the subsidies to colleges and increase their deficits.

    Source: *USA Today*, October 22, 2008

    If government cuts the subsidy to colleges, why will tuition rise and the number of students enrolled decrease? Why is it a better policy for government to maintain the subsidy to colleges?

ADDITIONAL PROBLEMS AND APPLICATIONS

myeconlab You can work these problems in MyEconLab if assigned by your instructor.

Public Choices

21. Classify each of the following items as excludable, nonexcludable, rival, or nonrival.
    - Firefighting service
    - A Starbucks coffee
    - A view of the Liberty Bell
    - The Appalachian Trail
    - A google search

22. Classify each of the following items as a public good, a private good, a natural monopoly good, a common resource, or a mixed good.
    - Measles vaccinations
    - Tuna in the Pacific Ocean
    - Air service in the United States
    - Local storm-water system

23. Consider each of the following activities or events and say for each one whether it creates an externality. If so, say whether it creates an external benefit or external cost and whether the externality arises from production or consumption.
    - Airplanes take off from LaGuardia Airport during the U.S. Open tennis tournament, which is taking place nearby.
    - A sunset over the Pacific Ocean
    - An increase in the number of people who are studying for graduate degrees
    - A person wears strong perfume to class.

24. Classify each of the following goods as a private good, a public good, or a mixed good and say whether it creates an external benefit, external cost, or neither.
    - Chewing gum
    - The Santa Monica freeway at peak travel time
    - The New York City subway
    - A skateboard
    - The Santa Monica beach

Providing Public Goods

Use the following news clip to work Problems 25 and 26.

"Free Riders" Must be Part of Health Debate

President Obama insists that "the reason people don't have health insurance isn't because they don't want it, it's because they can't afford it." There are 47 million uninsured people in the United States. Of these, 16 percent earn more than $75,000 a year and 15 percent earn between $50,000 and $75,000 a year. About 16 percent of those who received "free" medical care in 2004 had incomes at least four times the federal poverty level.

Source: *Los Angeles Times*, March 4, 2008

25. Explain why government-subsidized health-care services can create a free-rider problem.

26. Explain the evidence the news clip presents to contradict the argument that "the reason people don't have health insurance isn't because they don't want it, it's because they can't afford it."

27. The table sets out the marginal benefits that Sam and Nick receive from the town's street lighting:

| Number of street lights | Marginal benefit | |
| | Sam | Nick |
	(dollars per street light)	
1	10	12
2	8	9
3	6	6
4	4	3
5	2	0

a. Is the town's street lighting a private good or a public good?

b. Suppose that Sam and Nick are the only residents of the town. Draw a graph to show the marginal social benefit from the town's street lighting.

28. What is the principle of diminishing marginal benefit? In Problem 27, does Sam's, Nick's or the society's marginal benefit diminish faster?

Use the following news clip to work Problems 29 and 30.

A Bridge Too Far Gone

The gas taxes paid for much of America's post-war freeway system. Now motorists pay about one-third in gas taxes to drive a mile as they did in the 1960s. Yet raising such taxes is politically tricky. This would matter less if private cash was flooding into infrastructure, or if new ways were being found to control demand. Neither is happening, and private companies building toll roads brings howls of outrage.

Source: *The Economist*, August 9, 2007

29. Why is it "politically tricky" to raise gas taxes to finance infrastructure?

30. What in this news clip points to a distinction between public *production* of a public good and

public *provision*? Give examples of three public goods that are *produced* by private firms but *provided* by government and paid for with taxes.

Providing Mixed Goods with External Benefits

Use the following information and figure to work Problems 31 and 34.

The marginal cost of educating a student is a costant $4,000 a year and the figure shows the students' marginal benefit curve. Suppose that college education creates an external benefit of a constant $2,000 per student per year.

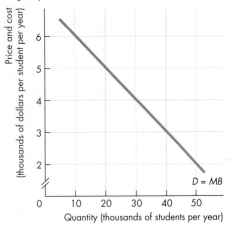

31. If all colleges are private and the market for education is competitive, how many students enroll, what is the tuition, and what is the deadweight loss created?

32. If the government decides to provide public colleges, what tuition will these colleges charge to achieve the efficient number of students? How much will taxpayers have to pay?

33. If the government decides to subsidize private colleges, what subsidy will achieve the efficient number of college students?

34. If the government offers vouchers to those who enroll at a college and no subsidy, what is the value of the voucher that will achieve the efficient number of students?

35. **My Child, My Choice**

Fully vaccinating all U.S. children born in a given year saves 33,000 lives, prevents 14 million infections and saves $10 billion in medical costs. Part of the reason is that vaccinations protect not only the kids that receive the shots but also those who can't receive them—such as newborns and cancer patients with suppressed immune systems.

Source: *Time*, June 2, 2008

a. Describe the private benefits and external benefits of vaccinations and explain why a private market for vaccinations would produce an inefficient outcome.

b. Draw a graph to illustrate a private market for vaccinations and show the deadweight loss.

c. Explain how government intervention could achieve an efficient quantity of vaccinations and draw a graph to illustrate this outcome.

Economics in the News

36. After you have studied *Reading Between the Lines* on pp. 386–387 answer the following questions:

a. What are the two major problems confronting the provision of health-care services in the United States?

b. How is it possible for the two problems you've identified to occur together?

c. Why might a voucher system be superior to the current method of providing health-care services?

d. Compare the main features of the 2010 health care reform with the plan suggested by Laurence Kotlikoff on p. 385.

e. Which plan would be better and why?

37. **Who's Hiding under Our Umbrella?**

Students of the Cold War learn that, to deter possible Soviet aggression, the United States placed a "strategic umbrella" over NATO Europe and Japan, with the United States providing most of their national security. Under President Ronald Reagan, the United States spent 6 percent of GDP on defense, whereas the Europeans spent only 2 to 3 percent and the Japanese spent only 1 percent, although all faced a common enemy. Thus the U.S. taxpayer paid a disproportionate share of the overall defense spending, whereas NATO Europe and Japan spent more on consumer goods or saved

Source: *International Herald Tribune*,
January 30, 2008

a. Explain the free-rider problem described in this news clip.

b. Does the free-rider problem in international defense mean that the world has too little defense against aggression?

c. How do nations try to overcome the free-rider problem among nations?

17
ECONOMICS OF THE ENVIRONMENT

After studying this chapter, you will be able to:

◆ Explain why external costs bring market failure and too much pollution and how property rights, pollution taxes, emission charges, and marketable permits might achieve an efficient outcome

◆ Explain the tragedy of the commons and its possible solutions

We burn huge quantities of fossil fuels—coal, natural gas, and oil—that cause acid rain and global warming. We dump toxic waste into rivers, lakes, and oceans. These environmental issues are simultaneously everybody's problem and nobody's problem. How can we take account of the damage that we cause others every time we turn on our heating or air-conditioning systems?

More and more people with ever-increasing incomes demand ever-greater quantities of most goods and services. One item that we demand more and more of is fish grown wild in the ocean. The fish stocks of the world's oceans are not owned by anyone. They are common resources and everyone is free to use them. But we are overusing our fish stocks and bringing some species to extinction. Must the price of fish inevitably keep rising? What can be done to conserve the world's fish stocks?

In this chapter, we study the problems that arise because many of our actions impose costs on other people in ways that we do not take into account when we make our own economic choices. We focus on two big issues—air pollution and overfishing. In *Reading Between the Lines* at the end of the chapter, we look at the effects of a carbon tax designed to lower carbon emissions and address global warming and climate change.

393

◆ Negative Externality: Pollution

Can each individual be relied upon to make decisions that influence the Earth's carbon-dioxide concentration in the social interest? Must governments change the incentives we face so that our self-interested choices are also in the social interest? How can governments change incentives? These questions about climate change that we posed in Chapter 1 (see p. 6) involve *external costs* and this chapter answers them.

This chapter also studies another environmental problem that requires public choices: the overuse and sometimes the depletion of renewable natural resources.

We first study the external costs of pollution and begin with a quick review of the production activities that pollute our environment.

Sources of Pollution

Economic activity pollutes air, water, and land, and these individual areas of pollution interact through the ecosystem. The three biggest sources of pollution are road transportation, electricity generation, and industrial processes.

A common belief is that our advanced industrial economy is creating ever more pollution. But for many pollutants, in the rich countries that include

the United States, pollution is less serious today that it was in earlier years (see *Economics in Action* below for a description of the trends in air pollution).

Effects of Pollution

While the facts about the sources and trends in air pollution are not in doubt, there is disagreement about the effects of air pollution. The least controversial is acid rain caused by sulphur dioxide and nitrogen oxide emissions from coal- and oil-fired generators of power stations. Acid rain begins with air pollution, and it leads to water pollution and damages vegetation.

More than 180 others airborne substances (suspended particulates) such as lead from leaded gasoline have been identified, which in sufficiently large concentrations, are believed to cause cancer and other life-threatening conditions.

Many scientists believe that carbon dioxide emissions are a major cause of global warming and climate change.

The effects of pollution mean that production and consumption decisions impose costs that are not taken fully into account when decisions are made. You are now going to see how economists analyse these decisions and solve the pollution problem.

Economics in Action
U.S. Air Pollution Trends: Cleaner and Safer

The figure shows the percentage changes in the concentrations of six air pollutants between 1990 and 2008 and their economic sources. All of these pollutants decreased.

These reductions in air pollution are more impressive when they are seen against the trends in economic activity. Between 1990 and 2008, total production in the United States increased by 66 percent, vehicle miles traveled increased by 40 percent, and the population increased by 20 percent.

The Clean Air Act has brought regulations that cut emissions of carbon monoxide, volatile organic compounds, oxides of nitrogen, sulfur dioxide and particulate matter to around a half of their 1990 levels. And economic actions that you will learn about in this chapter almost eliminated lead from highways and industrial processes.

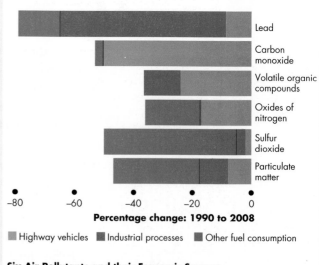

Six Air Pollutants and their Economic Sources

Source of data: Latest Findings on National Air Quality: Status and Trends through 2008, United States Environmental Protection Agency, http://www.epa.gov/air/airtrends/2010/report/airpollution.pdf

Private Cost and Social Cost of Pollution

To study the economics of the external costs that arise from pollution, we distinguish between the private cost and the social cost of production.

A *private cost* of production is a cost that is borne by the producer of a good or service. *Marginal cost* is the cost of producing an *additional unit* of a good or service. So **marginal private cost** (*MC*) is the cost of producing an additional unit of a good or service that is borne by its producer.

An *external cost* is a cost of producing a good or service that is *not* borne by the producer but borne by other people. A **marginal external cost** is the cost of producing an additional unit of a good or service that falls on people other than the producer.

Marginal social cost (*MSC*) is the marginal cost incurred by the producer and by everyone else on whom the cost falls—by society. It is the sum of marginal private cost and marginal external cost. That is,

$$MSC = MC + \text{Marginal external cost.}$$

We express costs in dollars, but we must always remember that a cost is an opportunity cost—something real, such as clean air or a clean river, is given up to get something.

Valuing an External Cost Economists use market prices to put a dollar value on the cost of pollution. For example, suppose that there are two similar rivers, one polluted and the other clean. Five hundred identical homes are built along the side of each river. The homes on the clean river rent for $2,500 a month, and those on the polluted river rent for $1,500 a month. If the pollution is the only detectable difference between the two rivers and the two locations, the rent decrease of $1,000 per month is the cost of the pollution. With 500 homes on the polluted river, the external cost of pollution is $500,000 a month.

External Cost and Output Figure 17.1 shows an example of the relationship between output and cost in a chemical industry that pollutes. The marginal cost curve, *MC*, describes the marginal private cost borne by the firms that produce the chemical. Marginal cost increases as the quantity of chemical produced increases.

If the firms dump waste into a river, they impose an external cost on other users of the river. We will assume that the marginal external cost increases with the amount of the chemical produced.

The marginal social cost curve, *MSC*, is found by adding the marginal external cost to the marginal private cost. So a point on the *MSC* curve shows the sum of the marginal private cost of producing a given output and marginal external cost created.

For example, when the chemical industry produces 4,000 tons of chemical a month, its marginal private cost is $100 a ton and the marginal external cost is $125 a ton, so the marginal social cost is $225 a ton.

In Fig. 17.1, when the quantity of chemical produced increases, the amount of pollution increases and the external cost of pollution increases.

Figure 17.1 shows the relationship between the quantity of chemical produced and the cost of the pollution it creates, but it doesn't tell us how much pollution the chemical industry creates. That quantity depends on the quantity of the chemical produced, which depends on supply and demand in the market for the chemical. We now look at that market.

FIGURE 17.1   An External Cost

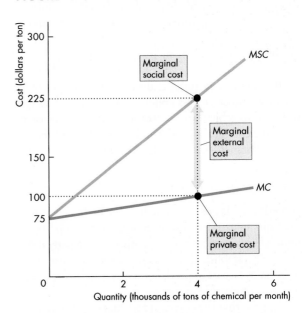

The *MC* curve shows the marginal private cost borne by the factories that produce a chemical. The *MSC* curve shows the sum of marginal private cost and marginal external cost. When output is 4,000 tons of chemical a month, marginal private cost is $100 a ton, marginal external cost is $125 a ton, and marginal social cost is $225 a ton.

Production and Pollution: How Much?

When an industry is unregulated and free to pollute, the amount of pollution it creates depends on the market equilibrium price and quantity of the good produced. In Fig. 17.2, the demand curve for a pollution-creating chemical is *D*. This curve also measures the marginal social benefit, *MSB*, from the chemical. The supply curve of the chemical is *S*. This curve also measures the producers' marginal private cost, *MC*. The supply curve is the marginal private cost curve because when firms make their production and supply decisions, they consider only the costs that they will bear. Market equilibrium occurs at a price of $100 a ton and 4,000 tons of chemical a month.

This equilibrium is inefficient. You learned in Chapter 5 that the allocation of resources is efficient when marginal social benefit equals marginal social cost. But we must count *all* the costs—private and external—when we compare marginal social benefit and marginal social cost. So with an external cost, the allocation is efficient when marginal social benefit equals marginal *social* cost. This outcome occurs when the quantity of chemical produced is 2,000 tons a month. The unregulated market overproduces by 2,000 tons of chemical a month and creates a deadweight loss shown by the gray triangle.

How can the people who live by the polluted river get the chemical factories to decrease their output of chemical and create less pollution? If some method can be found to achieve this outcome, everyone—the owners of the chemical factories and the residents of the riverside homes—can gain. Let's explore some solutions.

Property Rights

Sometimes it is possible to reduce the inefficiency arising from an external cost by establishing a property right where one does not currently exist. **Property rights** are legally established titles to the ownership, use, and disposal of factors of production and goods and services that are enforceable in the courts.

Suppose that the chemical factories own the river and the 500 homes alongside it. The rent that people are willing to pay depends on the amount of pollution. Using the earlier example, people are willing to pay $2,500 a month to live alongside a pollution-free river but only $1,500 a month to live with the pollution created by 4,000 tons of chemical a month. If the factories produce this quantity, they lose $1,000 a month for each home for a total of $500,000 a month. The chem-

FIGURE 17.2   Inefficiency with an External Cost

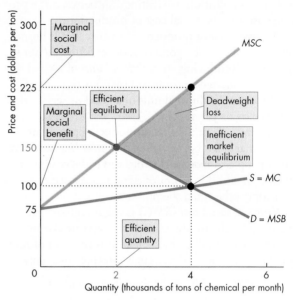

The market supply curve is the factories' marginal private cost curve, *S = MC*. The market demand curve is the marginal social benefit curve, *D = MSB*. The market equilibrium occurs at a price of $100 a ton and 4,000 tons of chemical a month This market outcome is inefficient because marginal social cost exceeds marginal social benefit. The efficient quantity of chemical is 2,000 tons a month. The gray triangle shows the deadweight loss created by the pollution.

ical factories are now confronted with the cost of their pollution—forgone rent from the people who live by the river.

Figure 17.3 illustrates the outcome by using the same example as in Fig. 17.2. With property rights in place, the *MC* curve no longer measures all the costs that the factories face in producing the chemical. It excludes the pollution costs that they must now bear. The *MSC* curve now becomes the factories' marginal private cost curve *MC*. The factories bear all the costs, so the market supply curve based on all the costs is the curve labeled *S = MC = MSC*.

Market equilibrium now occurs at a price of $150 a ton and 2,000 tons of chemical a month. This outcome is efficient. The factories still produce some pollution, but it is the efficient quantity.

FIGURE 17.3   Property Rights Achieve an
                Efficient Outcome

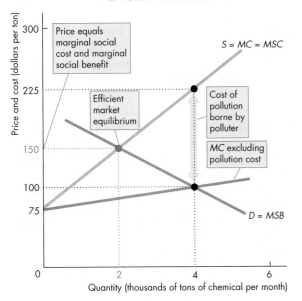

With property rights, the marginal cost curve that excludes pollution costs shows only part of the producers' marginal cost. The marginal cost of producing the chemical now includes the cost of pollution—the external cost. So the producers' supply curve is $S = MC = MSC$. The market equilibrium now occurs at a price of $150 a ton and 2,000 tons of chemical a month. This outcome is efficient because marginal social cost equals marginal social benefit. The pollution created is not zero, but it is the efficient quantity.

The Coase Theorem

Does it matter how property rights are assigned? Does it matter whether the polluter or the victim of the pollution owns the resource that might be polluted? Until 1960, everyone thought that it did matter. But in 1960, Ronald Coase (see p. 413) had a remarkable insight, now called the Coase theorem.

The **Coase theorem** is the proposition that if property rights exist, if only a small number of parties are involved, and if transactions costs are low, then private transactions are efficient. There are no externalities because the transacting parties take all the costs and benefits into account. Furthermore, it doesn't matter who has the property rights.

Application of the Coase Theorem In the example that we've just studied, the factories own the river and the homes. Suppose that instead, the residents own their homes and the river. Now the factories must pay a fee to the homeowners for the right to dump their waste. The greater the quantity of waste dumped into the river, the more the factories must pay. So again, the factories face the opportunity cost of the pollution they create. The quantity of chemical produced and the amount of waste dumped are the same whoever owns the homes and the river. If the factories own them, they bear the cost of pollution because they receive a lower income from home rents. If the residents own the homes and the river, the factories bear the cost of pollution because they must pay a fee to the homeowners. In both cases, the factories bear the cost of their pollution and dump the efficient amount of waste into the river.

The Coase solution works only when transactions costs are low. **Transactions costs** are the opportunity costs of conducting a transaction. For example, when you buy a house, you incur a series of transactions costs. You might pay a realtor to help you find the best place and a lawyer to run checks that assure you that the seller owns the property and that after you've paid for it, the ownership has been properly transferred to you.

In the example of the homes alongside a river, the transactions costs that are incurred by a small number of chemical factories and a few homeowners might be low enough to enable them to negotiate the deals that produce an efficient outcome. But in many situations, transactions costs are so high that it would be inefficient to incur them. In these situations, the Coase solution is not available.

Suppose, for example, that everyone owns the airspace above their homes up to, say, 10 miles. If someone pollutes your airspace, you can charge a fee. But to collect the fee, you must identify who is polluting your airspace and persuade them to pay you. Imagine the costs of negotiating and enforcing agreements with the 50 million people who live in your part of the United States (and perhaps in Canada or Mexico) and the several thousand factories that emit sulfur dioxide and create acid rain that falls on your property! In this situation, we use public choices to cope with external costs. But the transactions costs that block a market solution are real costs, so attempts by the government to deal with external costs offer no easy solution. Let's look at some of these attempts.

Government Actions in a Market with External Costs

The three main methods that governments use to cope with external costs are

- Taxes
- Emission charges
- Cap-and-trade

Taxes The government can use taxes as an incentive for producers to cut back the pollution they create. Taxes used in this way are called **Pigovian taxes**, in honor of Arthur Cecil Pigou, the British economist who first worked out this method of dealing with external costs during the 1920s.

By setting the tax equal to the marginal external cost, firms can be made to behave in the same way as they would if they bore the cost of the externality directly. To see how government actions can change the outcome in a market with external costs, let's

return to the example of the chemical factories and the river.

Assume that the government has assessed the marginal external cost accurately and imposes a tax on the factories that exactly equals this cost. Figure 17.4 illustrates the effects of this tax.

The demand curve and marginal social benefit curve, $D = MSB$, and the firms' marginal cost curve, MC, are the same as in Fig. 17.2. The pollution tax equals the marginal external cost of the pollution. We add this tax to the marginal private cost to find the market supply curve. This curve is the one labeled $S = MC + tax = MSC$. This curve is the market supply curve because it tells us the quantity supplied at each price given the firms' marginal cost and the tax they must pay. This curve is also the marginal social cost curve because the pollution tax has been set equal to the marginal external cost.

Demand and supply now determine the market equilibrium price at $150 a ton and a quantity of

Economics in Action

The Greatest Market Failure?

British economist Nicholas Stern reviewed the science and economics of global warming and climate change for the United Kingdom government and his report, the *Stern Review on the Economics of Climate Change* attracted much attention. Stern calls climate change "the greatest market failure the world has ever seen."

As the figure shows, global temperature and carbon dioxide (CO_2) trends are starkly upward. Stern says that to avoid the risk of catastrophic climate change, this upward trend must be stopped.

Scientists debate the contribution of human economic activity to these trends, but most say it is the major source. Although ice-core estimates show long swings in CO_2 concentration, the recent increase is the most rapid recorded.

The cost of achieving Stern's target is high, estimated at 1 percent of the value of global production. If this cost is to be met by the people who live in the rich countries, and realistically they are the only ones who can afford to pay, it will cost about $750 per person every year.

Some economists question Stern's assumptions and conclusions and argue that the cost of reducing emissions will be much lower if we go a bit more slowly and take advantage of future technological advances

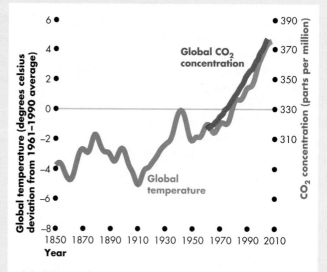

Global Warming Trends

Sources of data: Met Office Hadley Centre and Scripps Institution of Oceanography.

that will lower the cost of renewable energy sources—the sun, tide, and wind.

All economists agree that solving the global warming problem will require changes in the incentives that people face. The cost of carbon-emitting activities must rise and the cost of the search for new energy technologies must fall. A carbon tax or tradeable carbon permits are two possible ways of addressing this problem.

FIGURE 17.4   A Pollution Tax to Achieve an Efficient Outcome

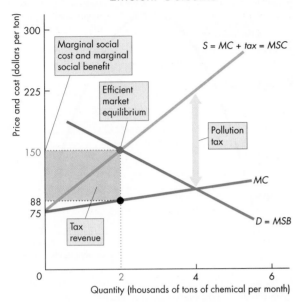

When the government imposes a pollution tax equal to the marginal external cost of pollution, the supply curve becomes the marginal private cost curve, *MC*, plus the tax—the curve *S = MC + tax*. Market equilibrium occurs at a price of $150 a ton and a quantity of 2,000 tons of chemical a month. This equilibrium is efficient because marginal social cost equals marginal social benefit. The purple rectangle shows the government's tax revenue.

 myeconlab animation

2,000 tons of chemical a month. At this quantity of chemical production, the marginal social cost is $150 and the marginal social benefit is $150, so the outcome is efficient. The firms incur a marginal private cost of $88 a ton and pay a tax of $62 a ton. The government collects tax revenue of $124,000 a month.

Emission Charges Emission charges are an alternative to a tax for confronting a polluter with the external cost of pollution. The government sets a price per unit of pollution. The more pollution a firm creates, the more it pays in emission charges. This method of dealing with pollution externalities has been used only modestly in the United States but is common in Europe where, for example, France, Germany, and the Netherlands make water polluters pay a waste disposal charge.

To work out the emission charge that achieves efficiency, the government needs information about the polluting industry that, in practice, is rarely available.

Cap-and-Trade Instead of taxing or imposing emission charges on polluters, each potential polluter might be assigned a permitted pollution limit. Each firm knows its own costs and its benefits from pollution, and making pollution limits marketable is a clever way of using this private information that is unknown to the government. The government issues each firm a permit to emit a certain amount of pollution, and firms can trade these permits. Firms that have a low marginal cost of reducing pollution sell their permits, and firms that have a high marginal cost of reducing pollution buy permits. The market in permits determines the price at which firms trade permits. Each firm buys or sells permits until its marginal cost of pollution equals the market price of a permit.

This method of dealing with pollution provides an even stronger incentive than emission charges to find lower-polluting technologies because the price of a pollution permit rises as the demand for permits increases.

Trading in lead pollution permits became common during the 1980s, and this marketable permit program enabled lead pollution to be virtually eliminated in the United States (see p. 394). But this success might not easily translate to other pollutant because most lead pollution came from gasoline, which was easy to monitor.

REVIEW QUIZ

1 What is the distinction between private cost and social cost?
2 How do external costs prevent a competitive market from allocating resources efficiently?
3 How can external costs be eliminated by assigning property rights?
4 How do taxes help us to cope with external costs? At what level must a pollution tax be set to be efficient?
5 How do emission charges and marketable pollution permits work?

You can work these questions in Study Plan 17.1 and get instant feedback.    **myeconlab**

Your next task is to study common resources and the government actions that can bring efficient use.

◆ The Tragedy of the Commons

Overgrazing the pastures around a village in Middle Ages England, and overfishing the cod stocks of the North Atlantic Ocean during the recent past are tragedies of the commons. The **tragedy of the commons** is the overuse of a common resource that arises when its users have no incentive to conserve it and use it sustainably.

To study the tragedy of the commons and its possible remedies, we'll focus on the recent and current tragedy—overfishing and depleting the stock of Atlantic cod. We begin by thinking about the sustainable use of a renewable resource.

Sustainable Use of a Renewable Resource

A *renewable natural resource* is one that replenishes itself by the birth and growth of new members of the population. Fish, trees, and the fertile soil are all examples of this type of resource.

Focusing on fish, the sustainable catch is the quantity that can be caught year after year without depleting the stock. This quantity depends on the stock and in the interesting way illustrated in Fig. 17.6.

If the stock of fish is small, the quantity of new fish born is also small, so the sustainable catch is small.

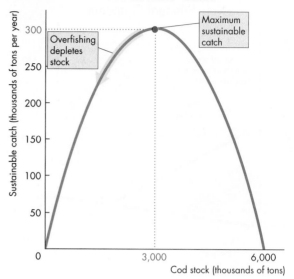

FIGURE 17.5   Sustainable Catch

As the stock of fish increases (on the *x*-axis), the sustainable catch (on the *y*-axis) increases to a maximum. Beyond that number, more fish must compete for food and the sustainable catch falls.

If the catch exceeds the sustainable catch, the fish stock diminishes.

myeconlab   animation

Economics in Action
The Original Tragedy of the Commons

The term "tragedy of the commons" comes from fourteenth-century England, where areas of rough grassland surrounded villages. The commons were open to all and used for grazing cows and sheep owned by the villagers.

Because the commons were open to all, no one had an incentive to ensure that the land was not overgrazed. The result was a severe overgrazing situation. Because the commons were overgrazed, the quantity of cows and sheep that they could feed kept falling, the longer the overgrazing continued.

During the sixteenth century, the price of wool increased and England became a wool exporter to the world. Sheep farming became profitable, and sheep owners wanted to gain more effective control of the land they used. So the commons were gradually privatized and enclosed. Overgrazing ended, and land use became more efficient.

Economics in Action
One of Today's Tragedies of the Commons

Before 1970, Atlantic cod was abundant. It was fished for many centuries and a major food source for the first European settlers in North America. During the sixteenth century, hundreds of European ships caught large quantities of cod in the northwest Atlantic off the coast of what is now New England and Newfoundland, Canada. By 1620, there were more than 1,000 fishing boats in the waters off Newfoundland, and in 1812 about 1,600 boats. During these years, cod were huge fish, typically weighing in at more than 220 pounds and measuring 3-6 feet in length.

Most of the fishing during these years was done using lines and productivity was low. But low productivity limited the catch and enabled cod to be caught sustainably over hundreds of years.

The situation changed dramatically during the 1960s with the introducton of high-efficiency nets (called trawls, seines, and gill nets), sonar technology to find fish concentrations, and large ships with efficient processing and storage facilities. These technological advances brought soaring cod harvests. In less than a decade, cod landings increased from less than 300,000 tons a year to 800,000 tons.

This volume of cod could not be taken without a serious collapse in the remaining stock and by the 1980s it became vital to regulate cod fishing. But regulation was of limited success and stocks continued to fall.

In 1992, a total ban on cod fishing in the North Atlantic stabilized the population but at a very low level. Two decades of ban have enabled the species to repopulate, and it is now hoped that one day cod fishing will return but at a low and sustainable rate.

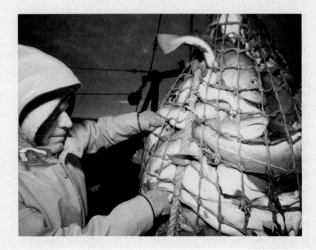

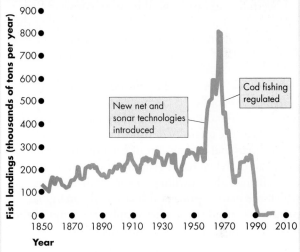

The Atlantic Cod Catch: 1850–2005

Source of data for graph: Millenium Ecosystem Assessment.
Source of information: Codfishes—Atlantic cod and its fishery, http://science.jrank.org/

If the fish stock is large, many fish are born, but they must compete with each other for food so only a small number survive to reproduce and to grow large enough to catch.

Between a small and a large stock is a quantity of fish stock that maximizes the sustainable catch. In Fig. 17.5, this fish stock is 3,000 thousand tons and the sustainable catch is 300 thousand tons a year. The maximum sustainable catch arises from a balancing of the birth of new fish from the stock and the availability of food to sustain the fish popuation.

If the quantity of fish caught is less than the sustainable catch, the fish stock grows; if the quantity caught exceeds the sustainable catch, the fish stock shrinks; and if the quantity caught equals the sustainable catch, the fish stock remains constant and is available for future generations of fishers in the same quantity that is available today.

If the fish stock exceeds the level that maximizes the sustainable catch, overfishing isn't a problem. But if the fish stock is less than the level that maximizes the sustainable catch, overfishing depletes the stock.

The Overuse of a Common Resource

Why might a fish stock be overused? Why might overfishing occur? The answer is that fishers face only their own private cost and don't face the cost they impose on others—external cost. The *social* cost of fishing combines the *private* cost and *external* cost. Let's examine the costs of catching fish to see how the presence of external cost brings overfishing.

Marginal Private Cost You can think of the *marginal private cost* of catching fish as the additional cost incurred by keeping a boat and crew at sea for long enough to increase the catch by one ton. Keeping a fishing boat at sea for an additional amount of time eventually runs into *diminishing marginal returns* (see p. 255). As the crew gets tired, the storage facilities get overfull, and boat's speed is cut to conserve fuel, the catch per hour decreases. The cost of keeping the boat at sea for an additional hour is constant so the marginal cost of catching fish increases as the quantity caught increases.

You've just seen that the *principle of increasing marginal cost* applies to catching fish just as it applies to other production activities: Marginal private cost increases as the quantity of fish caught increases.

The marginal private cost of catching fish determines an indiviual fisher's supply of fish. A profit-maximizing fisher is willing to supply the quantity at which the market price of fish covers the marginal private cost. And the market supply is the sum of the quantities supplied by each individual fisher.

Marginal External Cost The marginal exernal cost of catching fish is the cost per additional ton that one fisher's production imposes on all other fishers. This additional cost arises because one fisher's catch decreases the remaining stock, which in turn decreases the renewal rate of the stock and makes it harder for others to find and catch fish.

Marginal external cost also increases as the quantity of fish caught increases. If the quantity of fish caught is so large that it drives the species to near extinction, the marginal external cost becomes infinitely large.

Marginal Social Cost The *marginal social cost* of catching fish is the marginal private cost plus the marginal external cost. Because both of its components increase as the quantity caught increases, marginal social cost also increases with the quantity of fish caught.

Marginal Social Benefit and Demand The marginal social benefit from fish is the price that consumers are willing to pay for an additional pound of fish. Marginal social benefit decreases as the quantity of fish consumed increases, so the demand curve, which is also the marginal social benefit curve, slopes downward.

Overfishing Equilibrium Figure 17.6 illustrates overfishing and how it arises. The market demand curve for fish is the marginal social benefit curve, *MSB*. The market supply curve is the marginal *private* cost curve, *MC*. Market equilibrium occurs at the intersection point of these two curves. The equilibrium quantity is 800 thousand tons per year and the equilibrium price is $10 per pound.

At this market equilibrium, overfishing is running down the fish stock. Figure. 17.6 illustrates why

---

FIGURE 17.6   Why Overfishing Occurs

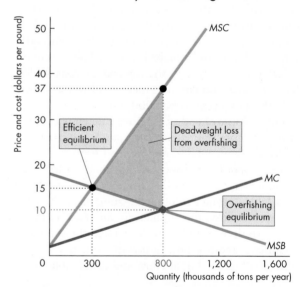

The supply curve is the marginal private cost curve, *MC*. The demand curve is the marginal social benefit curve *MSB*. Market equilibrium occurs at a quantity of 800 thousand tons and a price of $10 per pound.

The marginal social cost curve is *MSC* and at the market equilibrium there is overfishing—marginal social cost exceeds marginal social benefit.

The quantity at which *MSC* equals *MSB* is the efficient quantity, 300 thousand tons per year. The gray triangle shows the deadweight loss from overfishing.

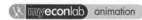 animation

overfishing occurs. At the market equilibrium quantity, marginal social benefit (and willingness to pay) is $10 per pound, but the marginal social cost exceeds this amount. The marginal external cost is the cost of running down the fish stock.

Efficient Equilibrium What is the efficient use of a common resource? It is the use of the resource that makes the marginal social benefit from the resource equal to the marginal social cost of using it.

In Fig. 17.6, the efficient quantity of fish is 300 thousand tons per year—the quantity that makes marginal social cost (on the *MSC* curve) equal to marginal social benefit (on the *MSB* curve). At this quantity, the marginal catch of each individual fisher costs society what people are willing to pay for it.

Deadweight Loss from Overfishing Deadweight loss measures the cost of overfishing. The gray triangle in Fig. 17.6 illustrates this loss. It is the marginal social cost minus the marginal social benefit from all the fish caught in excess of the efficient quantity.

Achieving an Efficient Outcome

Defining the conditions under which a common resource is used efficiently is easier than delivering those conditions. To use a common resource efficiently, it is necessary to design an incentive mechanism that confronts the users of the resource with the marginal *social* consequences of their actions. The same principles apply to common resources as those that you met earlier in this chapter when you studied the external cost of pollution.

The three main methods that might be used to achieve the efficient use of a common resource are

- Property rights
- Production quotas
- Individual transferable quotas (ITQs)

Property Rights A common resource that no one owns and that anyone is free to use contrasts with *private property*, which is a resource that *someone* owns and has an incentive to use in the way that maximizes its value. One way of overcoming the tragedy of the commons is to convert a common resource to private property. By assigning private property rights to what was previously a common resource, its owner faces the same conditions as society faces. It doesn't matter who owns the resource.

The users of the resource will be confronted with the full cost of using it because they either own it or pay a fee to the owner for permission to use it.

When private property rights over a resource are established and enforced, the *MSC* curve becomes the marginal *private* cost curve, and the use of the resource is efficient.

Figure 17.7 illustrate an efficient outcome with property rights. The supply curve $S = MC = MSC$ and the demand curve $D = MSB$ determine the equilibrium price and quantity. The price equals both marginal social benefit and marginal social cost and the quantity is efficient.

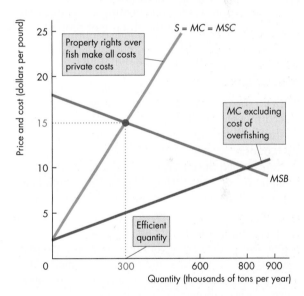

FIGURE 17.7   Property Rights Achieve an Efficient Outcome

With private property rights, fishers pay the owner of the fish stock for permission to fish and face the full social cost of their actions. The marginal cost curve includes the external cost, so the supply curve is the marginal private cost curve and the marginal social cost curve, $S = MC = MSC$.

Market equilibrium occurs at $15 per pound and at that price, the quantity is 300 thousand tons per year. At this quantity, marginal social cost equals marginal social benefit, and the quantity of fish caught is efficient.

The property rights convert the fish stock from a common resource to a private resource and it is used efficiently.

 animation

The private property solution to the tragedy of the commons *is* available in some cases. It was the solution to the original tragedy of the commons in England's Middle Ages. It is also a solution that has been used to prevent overuse of the airwaves that carry cell-phone services. The right to use this space (called the frequency spectrum) has been auctioned by governments to the highest bidders. The owner of each part of the spectrum is the only one permitted to use it (or to license someone else to use it).

But assigning private property rights is not always feasible. It would be difficult, for example, to assign private property rights to the oceans. It would not be impossible, but the cost of enforcing private property rights over thousands of square miles of ocean would be high. It would be even more difficult to assign and protect private property rights to the atmosphere.

In some cases, there is an emotional objection to assigning private property rights. Critics of it have a moral objection to someone owning a resource that they regard as public. In the absence of property rights, some form of government intervention is used, one of which is a production quota.

Production Quota A *production quota* is an upper limit to the quantity of a good that may be produced in a specified period. The quota is allocated to individual producers, so each producer has its own quota.

You studied the effects of a production quota in Chapter 6 (pp. 139–140) and learned that a quota can drive a wedge between marginal social benefit and marginal social cost and create deadweight loss. In that earlier example, the market was efficient without a quota. But in the case of common resources, the market overuses the resource and produces an inefficient quantity. A production quota in this market brings a move toward a more efficient outcome.

Figure 17.8 shows a quota that achieves an efficient outcome. The quota limits the catch (production) to 300 thousand tons, the efficient quantity at which marginal social benefit, *MSB*, equals marginal social cost, *MSC*. If everyone sticks to their own quota, the outcome is efficient. But implementing a production quota has two problems.

First, it is in every fisher's self-interest to catch more fish than the quantity permitted under the quota. The reason is that price exceeds marginal private cost, so by catching more fish, a fisher gets a higher income. If enough fishers break the quota, overfishing and the tragedy of the commons remain.

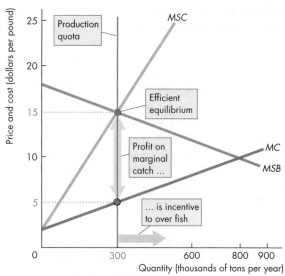

FIGURE 17.8   A Production Quota to Use a Common Resource Efficiently

A quota of 300 thousand tons that limits production to this quantity, raises the price to $15 per pound, and lowers marginal cost to $5 per pound. A fisher who cheats and produces more that the alloted quota increases his profit by $10 per pound. If all (or most) fishers cheat, production exceeds the quota and there is a return to overfishing.

myeconlab   animation

Second, marginal cost is not, in general, the same for all producers—as we're assuming here. Efficiency requires that the quota be allocated to the producers with the lowest marginal cost. But bureaucrats who allocate quotas do not have information about the marginal cost of individual producers. Even if they tried to get this information, producers would have an incentive to lie about their costs so as to get a bigger quota.

So where producers are difficult, or very costly, to monitor or where marginal cost varies across producers, a production quota cannot achieve an efficient outcome.

Individual Transferable Quotas Where producers are difficult to monitor or where marginal cost varies across producers, a more sophisticated quota system can be effective. It is an **individual transferable quota (ITQ)**, which is a production limit that is assigned to an individual who is then free to transfer (sell) the quota to someone else. A market in ITQs emerges and ITQs are traded at their market price.

The market price of an ITQ is the highest price that someone is willing to pay for one. That price is marginal social benefit minus marginal cost. The price of an ITQ will rise to this level because fishers who don't have a quota would be willing to pay this amount to get one.

A fisher with an ITQ could sell it for the market price, so by not selling the ITQ the fisher incurs an opportunity cost. The marginal cost of fishing, which now includes the opportunity cost of the ITQ, equals the marginal social benefit from the efficient quantity.

Figure 17.9 illustrates how ITQs work. Each fisher receives an allocation of ITQs and the total catch permited by the ITQs is 300 thousand tons per year. Fishers trade ITQs: Those with low marginal cost buy ITQs from those with high marginal cost and the market price of an ITQ settles at $10 per pound of fish. The marginal private cost of fishing now becomes the original marginal private cost, *MC* plus the cost of the ITQ. The marginal private cost curve shifts upward from *MC* to *MC + price of ITQ* and each fisher is confronted with the marginal *social* cost of fishing. No one has an incentive to exceed the quota because to do so would send marginal cost above price and result in a loss on the marginal catch. The outcome is efficient.

FIGURE 17.9   ITQs to Use a Common Resource Efficiently

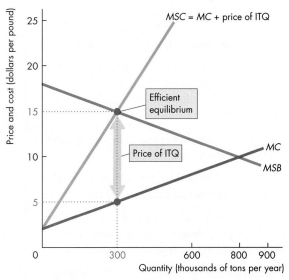

ITQs are issued on a scale that keeps output at the efficient level. The market price of an ITQ equals the marginal social benefit minus marginal cost. Because each user of the common resource faces the opportunity cost of using the resource, self-interest achieves the social interest.

myeconlab   animation

Economics in Action
ITQs Work

Iceland introduced the first ITQs in 1984 to conserve its stocks of lobster. In 1986, New Zealand and a bit later Australia introduced ITQs to conserve fish stocks in the South Pacific and Southern Oceans. The evidence from these countries suggests that ITQs work well.

ITQs help maintain fish stocks, but they also reduce the size of the fishing industry. This consequence of ITQs puts them against the self-interest of fishers. In all countries, the fishing industry opposes restrictions on its activities, but in Australia and New Zealand, the opposition is not strong enough to block ITQs.

In the United States the opposition has been harder to overcome and in 1996, Congress passed the Sustainable Fishing Act that put a moratorium on ITQs. This moratorium was lifted in 2004 and since then, ITQs have been applied to 28 fisheries from the Gulf of Alaska to the Gulf of Mexico. Economists have studied the effects of ITQs extensively and agree that they work. ITQs offer an effective tool for achieving an efficient use of the stock of ocean fish.

REVIEW QUIZ

1 What is the tragedy of the commons? Give two examples, including one from your state.
2 Describe the conditions under which a common resource is used efficiently.
3 Review three methods that might achieve the efficient use of a common resource and explain the obstacles to efficiency.

You can work these questions in Study Plan 17.2 and get instant feedback.

◆ *Reading Between the Lines* on pp. 406–407 looks at the use of a tax versus cap-and-trade to lower carbon emissions.

The next two chapters examine the third big question of economics: For whom are goods and services produced? We examine the markets for factors of production and discover how factor incomes and the distribution of income are determined.

Tax Versus Cap-and-Trade

Oil Spill Pushes Carbon Tax Back into Spotlight

http://www.SFGate.com

June 22, 2010

… Oil's true cost also includes the well-known litany of other hidden burdens: military spending to protect Middle East oil, the $1 billion of U.S. wealth and jobs sent overseas each day to buy oil, and pollution of all sorts, including carbon dioxide emissions. None of these costs is included in the price of the fossil fuels Americans use.

"There has to be a price, and a reward for moving to low-carbon fuels," said Rep. Pete Stark, D-Fremont. Stark may be the only one in Congress who has the temerity to propose a direct tax on carbon. …

Congress instead is considering cap-and-trade systems for carbon emissions that do the same thing as a carbon tax, …

The leading Senate plan … would set an increasingly stricter limit on carbon emissions and auction emissions permits. Revenue would go to alternative energy investments and utility rebates to help low-income consumers burdened by rising energy costs. …

Europeans pay $7 to $8 for a gallon of gas, mostly in taxes, and "they still drive," said Severin Borenstein, co-director of the UC Energy Institute. "They use much less oil per capita than we do, but they still use more than we need to get to." …

Borenstein called for a big increase in federal funding for basic research into alternatives. "When you take a realistic look at the economic side, without major technological breakthroughs at a much faster pace than we've seen over the last couple of decades, it doesn't look very doable," he said. …

ESSENCE OF THE STORY

- The cost of oil includes external costs that include military spending to protect Middle East oil, pollution, and carbon dioxide emissions.

- Representative Pete Stark, D-Fremont, says that there has to be a price, and a reward for moving to low-carbon fuels, so he proposes a tax on carbon.

- Congress is considering cap-and-trade systems for carbon emissions.

- The leading Senate plan puts a limit on carbon emissions and auctions emissions permits.

- Revenue from the sale of permits would be spent on developing clean alternative energy and utility rebates to help low-income consumers.

- Europeans pay $7 to $8 for a gallon of gasoline and use less than Americans but more than the required target.

- Without a technological breakthrough to make clean energy cheap, it will be hard to reach a low carbon emission target.

ECONOMIC ANALYSIS

- The news article lists some external costs of using oil. One of them, "sending jobs overseas," isn't such a cost. International trade brings gains for all, not external costs—see Chapter 7, pp. 155–156.

- The price of gasoline might be raised to incude marginal external cost with a carbon tax or a cap-and-trade carbon permit system.

- The news article says that using either of these measures would do little to curb gas consumption and Fig. 1 illustrates why.

- In the short run, the demand for gasoline, D_{SR}, is inelastic. If the U.S. gas price was raised to the European level, gas consumption would decrease by very little.

- In the long run, the demand for gasoline, D_{LR}, is elastic. Raising the U.S. gas price to the European level might eventually cut U.S. consumption to the European level.

- Figure 2 illustrates how a technological breakthrough that results in a low-cost clean fuel would work (suggests in the news article by Severin Borenstein).

- Figure 2(a) shows the short-run effects. Taxing carbon emissions or putting a price on them raises the marginal cost of gasoline to the marginal social cost, and the supply curve becomes the MSC curve. The price of gasoline rises, but the quantity consumed barely changes. The government collects the revenue shown by the purple rectangle.

- Figure 2(b) shows the long-run effect when a new technology is developed.

- The availablity of a low-cost clean fuel decreases the demand for gasoline from D_0 to D_1. The price of gasoline falls and the quantity consumed decreases.

- In the new equilibrium, the price of gasoline is lower, and so is the carbon tax or carbon price.

- Technological change is a crucial source of eventually curbing carbon emissions.

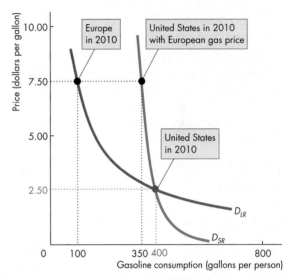

Figure 1 Inelastic demand for gasoline

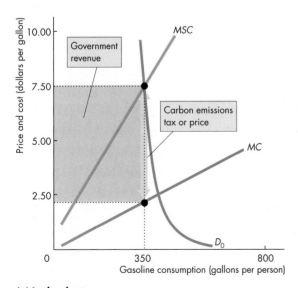

(a) In the short run

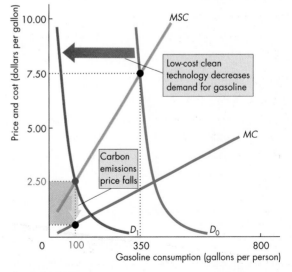

(b) In the long run

Figure 2 Short-run and long-run effects of tax and technological change

407

SUMMARY

Key Points

Negative Externality: Pollution (pp. 394–399)

- A competitive market would produce too much of a good that has external production costs.
- External costs are costs of production that fall on people other than the producer of a good or service. Marginal social cost equals marginal private cost plus marginal external cost.
- Producers take account only of marginal private cost and produce more than the efficient quantity when there is a marginal external cost.
- Sometimes it is possible to overcome a negative externality by assigning a property right.
- When property rights cannot be assigned, governments might overcome externalities by using taxes, emission charges, or marketable permits.

Working Problems 1 to 12 will give you a better understanding of the external costs of pollution.

The Tragedy of the Commons (pp. 400–405)

- Common resources create a problem that is called the tragedy of the commons—no one has a private incentive to conserve the resources and use them at an efficient rate.
- A common resource is used to the point at which the marginal private benefit equals the marginal cost.
- A common resource might be used efficiently by creating a private property right, setting a quota, or issuing individual transferable quotas.

Working Problems 13 to 19 will give you a better understanding of the tragedy of the commons.

Key Terms

Coase theorem, 397

Individual transferable quota (ITQ), 404

Marginal external cost, 395

Marginal private cost, 395

Marginal social cost, 395

Pigovian taxes, 398

Property rights, 396

Tragedy of the commons, 400

Transactions costs, 397

STUDY PLAN PROBLEMS AND APPLICATIONS

 myeconlab You can work Problems 1 to 19 in MyEconLab Chapter 17 Study Plan and get instant feedback.

Negative Externality: Pollution   (Study Plan 17.1)

Use the following figure to work Problems 1 to 5.

The figure illustrates the market for cotton. Consider a small town surrounded by a large cotton farm. Suppose that the cotton grower sprays the plants with chemicals to control insects and the chemical waste flows into the river passing through the town. The marginal external cost of the chemical waste is equal to the marginal private cost of producing the cotton (that is, the marginal social cost of producing the cotton is double the marginal private cost).

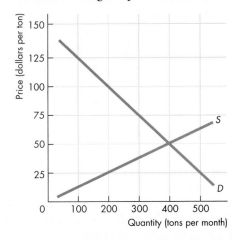

1. If no one owns the river and the town takes no action to control the waste, what is the quantity of cotton, and the deadweight loss created?

2. a. Suppose that the town owns the river and makes the cotton grower pay the cost of pollution. How much cotton is produced and what does the farmer pay the town per ton of cotton produced?

   b. Suppose that the cotton grower owns the river and rents it to the town. How much cotton is produced and how is the rent paid by the town to the grower (per ton of cotton produced) influenced by cotton growing?

   c. Compare the quantities of cotton produced in parts (a) and (b) and explain the relationship between these quantities.

3. Suppose that no one owns the river and that the city introduces a pollution tax. What is the tax per ton of cotton produced that achieves an efficient outcome?

4. Compare the outcomes when property rights exist and when the pollution tax achieves the efficient amount of waste.

5. Suppose that no one owns the river and that the government issues two marketable pollution permits: one to the cotton grower and one to the city. Each permit allows the same amount of pollution of the river, and the total pollution created is the efficient amount.

   What is the quantity of cotton produced and what is the market price of a pollution permit? Who buys and who sells a permit?

Use the following news clip to work Problems 6 to 8.

Bag Revolution

Thin plastic shopping bags aren't biodegradable and often end up in the ocean or in trees. Americans use about 110 billion bags a year. In 2007, San Francisco required all retailers with revenue over $2 million to offer only compostable or reusable bags. In all, 28 U.S. cities have proposed laws restricting the use of plastic bags.

Source: *Fortune*, May 12, 2008

6. a. Describe the externality that arises from plastic bags.

   b. Draw a graph to illustrate how plastic bags create deadweight loss.

7. a. With 70 percent of all plastic bags coming from grocery, drug and convenience stores, in July 2008, Seattle imposed a tax of 20¢ per bag from these outlets. Explain the effects of Seattle's policy on the use of plastic bags.

   b. Draw a graph to illustrate Seattle's policy and show the change in the deadweight loss that arises from this policy.

8. In 2010, the Governor of California supported a move to make California the first state in the nation to ban plastic shopping bags. He said that the bill "will be a great victory for our environment." Explain why a complete ban on plastic bags might be inefficient.

Use the following news clip to work Problems 9 to 11.

The Year in Medicine: Cell Phones

Talking on a hands-free cell phone while driving might seem safe, but think again. People who used hands-free cell phones in simulation trials exhibited slower reaction times and took longer to hit the brakes than drivers who weren't otherwise distracted. Data from real-life driving tests show that cell-phone use rivals drowsy driving as a major cause of accidents.

Source: *Time*, December 4, 2006

9. a. Explain the external costs that arise from using a cell phone while driving.
    b. Explain why the market for cell-phone service creates a deadweight loss.

10. Draw a graph to illustrate how a deadweight loss arises from the use of cell phones.

11. Explain how government intervention might improve the efficiency of cell-phone use.

12. **Pollution Rules Squeeze Strawberry Crop**

    Last year, Ventura County farmers harvested nearly 12,000 acres of strawberries valued at more than $323 million. To comply with the federal Clean Air Act, growers must use 50 percent less pesticide. It is estimated that strawberry output will fall by 60 percent.

    Source: *USA Today*, February 29, 2008

    Explain how a limit on pesticide will change the efficiency of the strawberry industry. Would a cap-and-trade scheme be more efficient?

Tragedy of the Commons (Study Plan 17.2)

Use the following figure to work Problems 13 to 15. The figure shows the market for North Atlantic tuna.

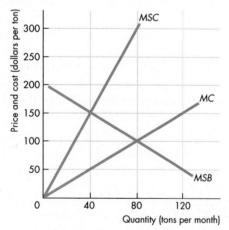

13. a. What is the quantity of tuna that fishers catch and the price of tuna? Is the tuna stock being used efficiently? Explain why or why not.
    b. What would be the price of tuna, if the stock of tuna is used efficiently?

14. a. With a quota of 40 tons a month for the tuna fishing industry, what is the equilibrium price of tuna and the quantity of tuna that fishers catch?
    b. Is the equilibrium an overfishing equilibrium?

15. If the government issues ITQs to individual fishers that limit the total catch to the efficient quantity, what is the market price of an ITQ?

16. **Whaling "Hurts Tourist Industry"**

    Leah Garces, the director of programs at the World Society for the Protection of Animals, reported that whale watching is more economically significant and sustainable to people and communities than whaling. The global whale-watching industry is estimated to be a $1.25 billion business enjoyed by over 10 million people in more than 90 countries each year.

    Source: BBC, June 2, 2009

    Describe the tradeoff facing communities that live near whaling areas. How might a thriving whale-watching industry avoid the tragedy of the commons?

Use the following information to work Problems 17 to 19.

A natural spring runs under land owned by ten people. Each person has the right to sink a well and can take water from the spring at a constant marginal cost of $5 a gallon. The table sets out the external cost and the social benefit of water.

Quantity of water (gallons per day)	Marginal external cost (dollars per gallon)	Marginal social benefits (dollars per gallon)
10	1	10
20	2	9
30	3	8
40	4	7
50	5	6
60	6	5
70	7	4

17. Draw a graph to illustrate the market equilibrium. On your graph, show the efficient quantity of water taken.

18. If the government sets a quota on the total amount of water such that the spring is used efficiently, what would that quota be?

19. If the government issues ITQs to land owners that limit the total amount of water taken to the efficient quantity, what is the market price of an ITQ?

ADDITIONAL PROBLEMS AND APPLICATIONS

 You can work these problems in MyEconLab if assigned by your instructor.

Negative Externality: Pollution

20. Betty and Anna work at the same office in Philadelphia. They both must attend a meeting in Pittsburgh, so they decide to drive to the meeting together. Betty is a cigarette smoker and her marginal benefit from smoking a package of cigarettes a day is $40. Cigarettes are $6 a pack. Anna dislikes cigarette smoke, and her marginal benefit from a smoke-free environment is $50 a day. What is the outcome if
    a. Betty drives her car with Anna as a passenger?
    b. Anna drives her car with Betty as a passenger?

Use the following information and the figure, which illustrates the market for a pesticide with no government intervention, to work Problems 21 to 24.

When factories produce pesticide, they also create waste, which they dump into a lake on the outskirts of the town. The marginal external cost of the waste is equal to the marginal private cost of producing the pesticide (that is, the marginal social cost of producing the pesticide is double the marginal private cost).

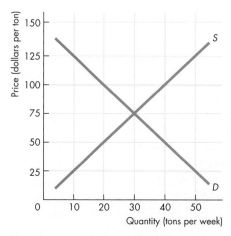

21. What is the quantity of pesticide produced if no one owns the lake and what is the efficient quantity of pesticide?

22. If the residents of the town own the lake, what is the quantity of pesticide produced and how much do residents of the town charge the factories to dump waste?

23. If the pesticide factories own the lake, how much pesticide is produced?

24. If no one owns the lake and the government levies a pollution tax, what is the tax that achieves the efficient outcome?

Use the following table to work Problems 25 to 27.

The first two columns of the table show the demand schedule for electricity from a coal burning utility; the second and third columns show the utility's cost of producing electricity. The marginal external cost of the pollution created is equal to the marginal cost.

Price (cents per kilowatt)	Quantity (kilowatts per day)	Marginal cost (cents per kilowatt)
4	500	10
8	400	8
12	300	6
16	200	4
20	100	2

25. With no government action to control pollution, what is the quantity of electricity produced, the price of electricity, and the marginal external cost of the pollution generated?

26. With no government action to control pollution, what is the marginal social cost of the electricity generated and the deadweight loss created?

27. Suppose that the government levies a pollution tax, such that the utility produces the efficient quantity. What is the price of electricity? What is the tax levied, and the government's tax revenue per day?

28. **EPA Pushes to have Companies Track Greenhouse Gases**

    Congress plans to make large polluters, such as oil refiners and automobile manufacturers, and makers of cement, aluminum, glass and paper, start tracking their emissions next year. The EPA's climate change division noted that this is an important step. A cap-and-trade scheme will be introduced for factories that emit 90 percent of U.S. greenhouse gases.

    Source: *USA Today*, March 11, 2009

    The monitoring cost of the scheme is expected to be about $127 million a year. Who will benefit from the scheme? Who will bear the burden of this scheme?

The Tragedy if the Commons

29. If hikers and other visitors were required to pay a fee to use the Appalachian Trail,
    a. Would the use of this common resource be more efficient?
    b. Would it be even more efficient if the most popular spots along the trail had the highest prices?
    c. Why do you think we don't see more market solutions to the tragedy of the commons?

Use the following figure to work Problems 30 to 32.

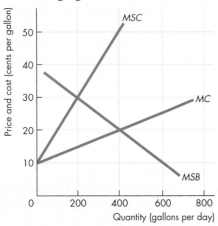

A spring runs under a village. Everyone can sink a well on her or his land and take water from the spring. The figure shows the marginal social benefit from and the marginal cost of taking water.

30. What is the quantity of water taken and what is the private cost of the water taken?
31. What is the efficient quantity of water taken and the marginal social cost at the efficient quantity?
32. If the village council sets a quota on the total amount of water such that the spring is used efficiently, what would be the quota and the market value of the water taken per day?

33. **Polar Ice Cap Shrinks Further and Thins**
    With the warming of the planet, the polar ice cap is shrinking and the Arctic Sea is expanding. As the ice cap shrinks further, more and more underwater mineral resources will become accessible. Many countries are staking out territorial claims to parts of the polar region.
    Source: *The Wall Street Journal*, April 7, 2009
    Explain how ownership of these mineral resources will influence the amount of damage done to the Arctic Sea and its wildlife.

Economics in the News

34. After you have studied *Reading Between the Lines* on pp. 406–407 answer the following questions:
    a. Why is it difficult to decrease carbon emissions in the short run?
    b. Which holds the greater promise as a method of lowering carbon emissions: actions that decrease the demand for gasoline or actions that decrease the supply of gasoline? Explain.
    c. Why might a carbon cap-and-trade program be preferred to a carbon tax?

Use the following information to work Problems 35 and 36.

Where the Tuna Roam

To the first settlers, the Great Plains posed the same problem as the oceans today: a vast, open area where there seemed to be no way to protect animals. But animals thrived once the settlers divvied up the land and devised ways to protect their livestock. Today, the ocean are much like an open range. Fishermen catch as much as they can this year, even if they are over-fishing. They figure any fish they don't take for themselves will just be taken by someone else.
    Source: *The New York Times*, November 4, 2006

35. a. What are the similarities between the problems faced by the earliest settlers in the West and today's fishers?
    b. Can the tragedy of the commons in the oceans be eliminated in the same manner used by the early settlers on the plains?

36. How can ITQs change the short-term outlook of fishers to a long-term outlook?

37. **Commuting More than Pain at Pump**
    Half of the respondents polled in 10 cities said that traffic congestion increased their stress levels and cut their productivity. IBM has been devising ways for cities to cut traffic congestion, such as automated tolling, congestion pricing plans and real-time traffic modeling. Commuters want more options to work from home and improved public transit.
    Source: CNN, May 30, 2008
    a. Explain the problem of congested city streets that results in inefficient usage. Draw a graph to illustrate the inefficient equilibrium.
    b. How could government policies be used to achieve an efficient use of city streets?

We, the People, …

Thomas Jefferson knew that creating a government of the people, by the people, and for the people was a huge enterprise and one that could easily go wrong. Creating a constitution that made despotic and tyrannical rule impossible was relatively easy. The founding fathers did their best to practice sound economics. They designed a sophisticated system of incentives—of carrots and sticks—to make the government responsive to public opinion and to limit the ability of individual self-interests to gain at the expense of the majority. But they were not able to create a constitution that effectively blocks the ability of special interest groups to capture the consumer and producer surpluses that result from specialization and exchange.

We have created a system of government to deal with four market failures: (1) monopoly; (2) externalities; (3) public goods; and (4) common resources.

Government might help cope with these market failures, but as the founding fathers knew well, government does not eliminate the pursuit of self-interest. Voters, politicians, and bureaucrats pursue their self-interest, sometimes at the expense of the social interest, and instead of market failure, we get government failure.

Many economists have thought long and hard about the problems discussed in this part. But none has had as profound an effect on our ideas in this area as Ronald Coase.

Ronald Coase *(1910–), was born in England and educated at the London School of Economics, where he was deeply influenced by his teacher, Arnold Plant, and by the issues of his youth: communist central planning versus free markets.*

Professor Coase has lived in the United States since 1951. He first visited America as a 20-year-old on a traveling scholarship during the depths of the Great Depression. It was on this visit, and before he had completed his bachelor's degree, that he conceived the ideas that 60 years later were to earn him the 1991 Nobel Prize for Economic Science.

Ronald Coase discovered and clarified the significance of transactions costs and property rights for the functioning of the economy. He has revolutionized the way we think about property rights and externalities and has opened up the growing field of law and economics.

"The question to be decided is: Is the value of fish lost greater or less than the value of the product which contamination of the stream makes possible?"

RONALD H. COASE
The Problem of Social Cost

Why did you decide to become an economist?

I've wanted to be an economist from about the age of 13. That was when I took my first class in economics (an interesting story in itself) and discovered that all of the thoughts swimming around in my head belonged to a "science" and there was an entire body of people who understood this science—a lot better than I did, anyway. I can still recall reading *The Wealth of Nations* for the first time; it was a revelation.

What drew you to study the economics of education?

We all care about education, perhaps because it is the key means by which opportunity is (or should be) extended to all in the United States. Also, nearly everyone now acknowledges that highly developed countries like the United States rely increasingly on education as the engine of economic growth. Thus, one reason I was drawn to education is its importance. However, what primarily drew me was that education issues were so clearly begging for economic analysis and that there was so little of it. I try hard to understand educational institutions and problems, but I insist on bringing economic logic to bear on educational issues.

Why is education different from fast food? Why don't we just let people buy it from private firms that are regulated to maintain quality standards analogous to the safety standards that the FDA imposes on fast-food producers?

The thing that makes education different from fast food is not that we cannot buy it from private institutions that are regulated to maintain quality standards. We do this all the time—think of private schools and colleges. What makes education different is that it is (a) an investment, not consumption, and (b) the capital markets for financing the investments work poorly when left on their own. Essentially, our country has an interest in every person investing optimally in his or her education. To make investments, however, people need funds that allow them to attend good schools and take time away from work. Children don't have these funds and cannot arrange for loans that they may or may not pay off decades later. Therefore, children depend on their families for funds, and families do not necessarily have the funds to invest optimally or

the right incentives to do so. Society has a role in filling the gaps in the capital market; it fills this role by public funding of elementary and secondary education, government guaranteed loans, college savings programs, and so on. There is no particular reason, however, why government needs to actually run schools; it can provide the funding without actually providing schooling.

In one of your papers, you posed the question: Does competition among public schools benefit students or taxpayers? What are the issues, what was your answer, and how did you arrive at it?

We are all familiar with the fact that families choose public schools when they choose where to live. This traditional form is by far the most pervasive form of school choice in the United States, and few parents who exercise it would be willing to give it up. Yet, until quite recently, we did not know whether having such traditional school choice was good for students (high achievement) or taxpayers (more efficient schools). It is important to know because some people in the United States, especially poor people who live in central cities, are unable to exercise this form

CAROLINE M. HOXBY is the Allie S. Freed Professor of Economics at Harvard University. Born in Cleveland, Ohio, she was an undergraduate at Harvard and a graduate student at Oxford and MIT.

Professor Hoxby is a leading student of the economics of education. She has written many articles on this topic and has published books entitled *The Economics of School Choice* and *College Choices* (both University of Chicago Press, 2003 and 2004, respectively). She is Program Director of the Economics of Education Program at the National Bureau of Economic Research, serves on several other national boards that study education issues, and has advised or provided testimony to several state legislatures and the United States Congress.

Michael Parkin talked with Caroline Hoxby about her work and the progress that economists have made in understanding how the financing and the provision of education influence the quality of education and the equality of access to it.

of school choice. Economists hypothesized that this lack of choice might be a reason why many children from poor, central city families receive such a deficient education, especially considering the dollars spent in their schools (which spend significantly more than the median school).

To investigate this hypothesis, I examined all of the metropolitan areas in the United States. They vary a great deal in the degree of traditional choice available to parents. On one extreme, there is a group of metropolitan areas with hundreds of school districts. On the other extreme, there is a group of metropolitan areas with only one school district. Most are somewhere in between. A family in a metropolitan area with one district may have no easy way of "escaping" a badly run district administration. A family in a metropolitan area with hundreds of districts can choose among several districts that match well with its job location, housing preferences, and so on.

Looking across metropolitan areas with many districts (lots of potential competition from traditional school choice) and few districts (little potential competition), I found that areas with greater competition had substantially higher student achievement for any given level of school spending. This suggests that schools are more efficient producers of achievement when they face competition.

What do we know about the relative productivity of public and private schools?

It is somewhat difficult to say whether achievement is higher at public or private schools in the United States. The best studies use randomly assigned private school scholarships, follow the same children over time, or use "natural experiments" in which some areas accidentally end up with more private schools than others. These studies tend to find that, for the same student, private schools produce achievement that is up to 10 percent higher. However, for understanding which type of school is more productive, we actually do not need private schools to have higher achievement. For the sake of argument, let's "call it a draw" on the achievement question.

In recent studies comparing achievement in public and private schools, the public schools spent an average of $9,662 per student and the private schools spent an average of $2,427 per student. These spending numbers, combined with achievement that we will call equal, suggest that the private schools were 298 percent more productive. I would not claim that this number is precisely correct; we could think of some minor adjustments. But it is difficult not to conclude that the private schools are significantly more productive. They produce equal achievement for a fraction of the cost.

> Economists should say to policy makers: "Tell me your goals; I'll design you a voucher."

What can economists say about the alternative methods of financing education? Is there a voucher solution that could work?

There is definitely a voucher solution that could work because vouchers are inherently an extremely flexible policy. People often see the word "voucher" and think of, say, a $2000 voucher being given to a small share of children. But this need not be so. Anything that we can do with public school financing we can do better with a voucher because vouchers can be specific to a student, whereas the government can never ensure that funds get to an individual student by giving those funds to his or her district.

Any well-designed voucher system will give schools an incentive to compete. However, when designing vouchers, we can also build in remedies for a variety of educational problems. Vouchers can be used to ensure that disabled children get the funding they need and the program choices they need. Compared to current school finance programs, vouchers can do a better job of ensuring that low-income families have sufficient funds to invest in the child's education. Well-designed vouchers can encourage schools to make their student bodies socio-economically diverse. Economists should say to policy makers: "Tell me your goals; I'll design you a voucher."

Is there a conflict between efficiency and equity in the provision of quality education?

To raise the public funds that allow all families to invest optimally in their children's education, we have to have taxes. Taxes always create some deadweight loss, so we always create some inefficiency when we raise the funds we need to provide equitable educational opportunities. However, if the funds are used successfully and actually induce people to make optimal investments in their education, we have eliminated much more inefficiency than the taxes created. Thus, in an ideal world, there need not be a conflict between efficiency and equity.

In the real world, public funds are often raised with taxes (creating deadweight loss) and then are not successfully used. If we spend twice as much on public schools and do not have higher achievement to show for it, then there are no efficiency gains to overwhelm the efficiency losses from taxation. In other words, to avoid a conflict between equity and efficiency, we must learn how to use public funds productively in education. This is what the economics of education is all about.

What advice do you have for a student who is just starting to study economics? Is economics a good subject in which to major? What other subjects go well alongside it? And do you have anything special to say to women who are making a career choice? What must we do to get more women involved in our subject?

Students who are just starting to study economics should do two things. First, learn the tools even if they seem abstruse. Once you have mastered the tools, you will be able to "see the forest for the trees." As long as you don't master the tools, you will be in the trees and will find it hard to think about economic problems. Second, think about economic problems! The real world is a great moving textbook of economics, once you have the tools to analyze it.

Economics is a great subject in which to major because it trains you for life, for many careers, and for the thinking that you would need in a leadership position. I think that it is the best training for a future career in business, the law, or policy making. Don't forget nonprofits: every year, nonprofit organizations try to hire people with economics skills who are also interested in charitable schemes.

Math and statistics courses are complementary to economics because they make it easier for a student to master the tools quickly. Economics goes well with many studies in the arts and sciences, too. It all depends on what you want to use economics for. If you want to do health policy making, take economics along with premedical courses. If you want to be a policy maker in the performing arts, take economics along with music.

I wish that there were more women in economics. Our field loses far too many talented minds. Also, women who need to understand economics for their careers are sometimes without it. To aspiring women economists, I can only say to hang in there. Mastering economics is empowering. You will never have to worry about your opinion not being taken seriously if you are a good economist.

416

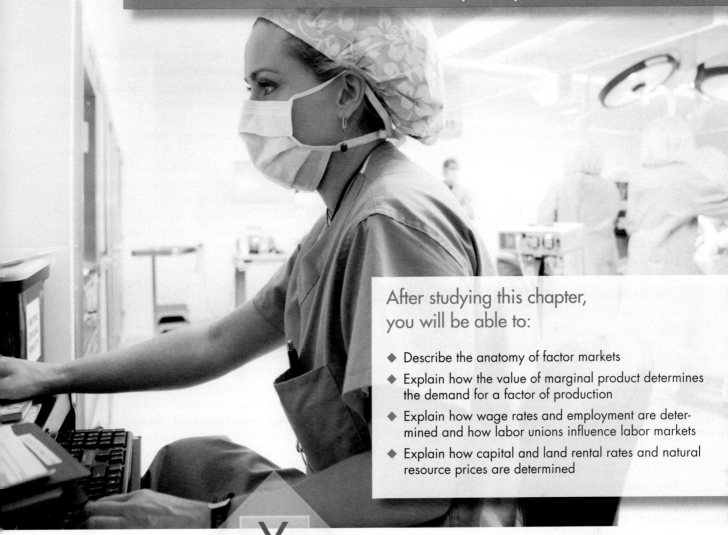

After studying this chapter,
you will be able to:

◆ Describe the anatomy of factor markets

◆ Explain how the value of marginal product determines
the demand for a factor of production

◆ Explain how wage rates and employment are determined and how labor unions influence labor markets

◆ Explain how capital and land rental rates and natural
resource prices are determined

18

MARKETS FOR FACTORS OF PRODUCTION

You know that wage rates vary a lot. A worker at McDonald's earns $8 an hour. Demetrio Luna, who spends his days in a small container suspended from the top of Houston's high-rise buildings cleaning windows, makes $12 an hour. Richard Seymour, who plays for the New England Patriots, collects a cool $25 million a year. Some differences in earnings might seem surprising. For example, your college football coach earns much more than your economics professor. What determines the wages that people earn?

Wages are important, but just finding a job is even more important, especially in today's tough labor markets. Factory jobs are vanishing as technological change and foreign competition shrink manufacturing production in the United States. But new job opportunities are opening in service industries, and especially in health care where, in the next 10 years, jobs for more than 500,000 nurses will be created.

In this chapter, we study labor markets as well as markets for capital and natural resources. You will learn how the prices and quantities of factors of production are determined. *In Reading Between the Lines* at the end of the chapter we look at the ever-changing labor markets and how they constantly reallocate labor resources.

417

◆ The Anatomy of Factor Markets

The four factors of production are

- Labor
- Capital
- Land (natural resources)
- Entrepreneurship

Let's take a brief look at the anatomy of the markets in which these factors of production are traded.

Markets for Labor Services

Labor services are the physical and mental work effort that people supply to produce goods and services. A labor market is a collection of people and firms who trade labor services. The price of labor services is the wage rate.

Some labor services are traded day by day. These services are called *casual labor*. People who pick fruit and vegetables often just show up at a farm and take whatever work is available that day. But most labor services are traded on a contract, called a **job**.

Most labor markets have many buyers and many sellers and are competitive. In these labor markets, the wage rate is determined by supply and demand, just like the price is determined in any other competitive market.

In some labor markets, a labor union organizes labor, which introduces an element of monopoly on the supply-side of the labor market. In this type of labor market, a bargaining process between the union and the employer determines the wage rate.

We'll study both competitive labor markets and labor unions in this chapter.

Markets for Capital Services

Capital consists of the tools, instruments, machines, buildings, and other constructions that have been produced in the past and that businesses now use to produce goods and services. These physical objects are themselves goods—capital goods. Capital goods are traded in goods markets, just as bottled water and toothpaste are. The price of a dump truck, a capital good, is determined by supply and demand in the market for dump trucks. This market is not a market for capital services.

A market for *capital services* is a *rental market*—a market in which the services of capital are hired.

An example of a market for capital services is the vehicle rental market in which Avis, Budget, Hertz, U-Haul, and many other firms offer automobiles and trucks for hire. The price in a capital services market is a *rental rate*.

Most capital services are not traded in a market. Instead, a firm buys capital and uses it itself. The services of the capital that a firm owns and operates have an implicit price that arises from depreciation and interest costs (see Chapter 10, pp. 228–229). You can think of this price as the implicit rental rate of capital. Firms that buy capital and use it themselves are *implicitly* renting the capital to themselves.

Markets for Land Services and Natural Resources

Land consists of all the gifts of nature—natural resources. The market for land as a factor of production is the market for the *services of land*—the use of land. The price of the services of land is a rental rate.

Most natural resources, such as farm land, can be used repeatedly. But a few natural resources are non-renewable. **Nonrenewable natural resources** are resources that can be used only once. Examples are oil, natural gas, and coal. The prices of nonrenewable natural resources are determined in global *commodity markets* and are called *commodity prices*.

Entrepreneurship

Entrepreneurial services are not traded in markets. Entrepreneurs receive the profit or bear the loss that results from their business decisions.

 REVIEW QUIZ

1 What are the factors of production and their prices?
2 What is the distinction between capital and the services of capital?
3 What is the distinction between the price of capital equipment and the rental rate of capital?

You can work these questions in Study Plan 18.1 and get instant feedback.

The rest of this chapter explores the influences on the demand and supply of factors of production. We begin by studying the demand for a factor of production.

The Demand for a Factor of Production

The demand for a factor of production is a **derived demand**—it is derived from the demand for the goods and services that the labor produces. You've seen, in Chapters 10 through 15, how a firm determines its profit-maximizing output. The quantities of factors of production demanded are a consequence of the firm's output decision. A firm hires the quantities of factors of production that produce the firm's profit-maximizing output.

To decide the quantity of a factor of production to hire, a firm compares the cost of hiring an additional unit of the factor with its value to the firm. The cost of hiring an additional unit of a factor of production is the factor price. The value to the firm of hiring one more unit of a factor of production is called the factor's **value of marginal product.** We calculate the value of marginal product as the price of a unit of output multiplied by the marginal product of the factor of production.

To study the demand for a factor of production, we'll use labor as the example. But what you learn here about the demand for labor applies to the demand for all factors of production.

Value of Marginal Product

Table 18.1 shows you how to calculate the value of the marginal product of labor at Angelo's Bakery. The first two columns show Angelo's total product schedule—the number of loaves per hour that each quantity of labor can produce. The third column shows the marginal product of labor—the change in total product that results from a one-unit increase in the quantity of labor employed. (See Chapter 11, pp. 253–256 for a refresher on product schedules.)

Angelo can sell bread at the going market price of $2 a loaf. Given this information, we can calculate the value of marginal product (fourth column). It equals price multiplied by marginal product. For example, the marginal product of hiring the second worker is 6 loaves. Each loaf sold brings in $2, so the value of the marginal product of the second worker is $12 (6 loaves at $2 each).

A Firm's Demand for Labor

The value of the marginal product of labor tells us what an additional worker is worth to a firm. It tells us the revenue that the firm earns by hiring one more worker. The wage rate tells us what an additional worker costs a firm.

The value of the marginal product of labor and the wage rate together determine the quantity of labor demanded by a firm. Because the value of marginal product decreases as the quantity of labor employed increases, there is a simple rule for maximizing profit: Hire the quantity of labor at which the value of marginal product equals the wage rate.

If the value of marginal product of labor exceeds the wage rate, a firm can increase its profit by hiring

TABLE 18.1   Value of Marginal Product at Angelo's Bakery

	Quantity of labor (L) (workers)	Total product (TP) (loaves per hour)	Marginal product (MP = ΔTP/ΔL) (loaves per worker)	Value of marginal product (VMP = MP × P) (dollars per worker)
A	0	0		
			7	14
B	1	7		
			6	**12**
C	**2**	13		
			5	10
D	3	18		
			4	8
E	4	22		
			3	6
F	5	25		

The value of the marginal product of labor equals the price of the product multiplied by marginal product of labor. If Angelo's hires 2 workers, the marginal product of the second worker is 6 loaves (in the third column). The price of a loaf is $2, so the value of the marginal product of the second worker is $2 a loaf multiplied by 6 loaves, which is $12 (in fourth column).

one more worker. If the wage rate exceeds the value of marginal product of labor, a firm can increase its profit by firing one worker. But if the wage rate equals the value of the marginal product of labor, the firm cannot increase its profit by changing the number of workers it employs. The firm is making the maximum possible profit. So

> The quantity of labor demanded by a firm is the quantity at which the value of the marginal product of labor equals the wage rate.

A Firm's Demand for Labor Curve

A firm's demand for labor curve is derived from its value of marginal product curve. Figure 18.1 shows these two curves. Figure 18.1(a) shows the value of marginal product curve at Angelo's Bakery. The blue bars graph the numbers in Table 18.1. The curve labeled *VMP* is Angelo's value of marginal product curve.

If the wage rate falls and other things remain the same, a firm hires more workers. Figure 18.1(b) shows Angelo's demand for labor curve.

Suppose the wage rate is $10 an hour. You can see in Fig.18.1(a) that if Angelo hires 2 workers, the value of the marginal product of labor is $12 an hour. At a wage rate of $10 an hour, Angelo makes a profit of $2 an hour on the second worker. If Angelo hires a third worker, the value of the marginal product of that worker is $10 an hour. So on this third worker, Angelo breaks even.

If Angelo hired 4 workers, his profit would fall. The fourth worker generates a value of marginal product of only $8 an hour but costs $10 an hour, so Angelo does not hire the fourth worker. When the wage rate is $10 an hour, the quantity of labor demanded by Angelo is 3 workers.

Figure 18.1(b) shows Angelo's demand for labor curve, *D*. At $10 an hour, the quantity of labor demanded by Angelo is 3 workers. If the wage rate increased to $12 an hour, Angelo would decrease the quantity of labor demanded to 2 workers. If the wage rate decreased to $8 an hour, Angelo would increase the quantity of labor demanded to 4 workers.

A change in the wage rate brings a change in the quantity of labor demanded and a movement along the demand for labor curve.

A change in any other influence on a firm's labor-hiring plans changes the demand for labor and shifts the demand for labor curve.

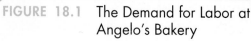

FIGURE 18.1 The Demand for Labor at Angelo's Bakery

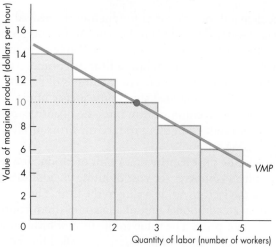

(a) Value of marginal product

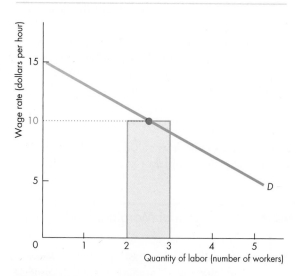

(b) Demand for labor

Angelo's Bakery can sell any quantity of bread at $2 a loaf. The blue bars in part (a) represent the firm's value of marginal product of labor (based on Table 18.1). The line labeled *VMP* is the firm's value of marginal product curve. Part (b) shows Angelo's demand for labor curve. Angelo hires the quantity of labor that makes the value of marginal product equal to the wage rate. The demand for labor curve slopes downward because the value of marginal product diminishes as the quantity of labor employed increases.

myeconlab   animation

Changes in a Firm's Demand for Labor

A firm's demand for labor depends on

- The price of the firm's output
- The prices of other factors of production
- Technology

The Price of the Firm's Output The higher the price of a firm's output, the greater is the firm's demand for labor. The price of output affects the demand for labor through its influence on the value of marginal product of labor. A higher price for the firm's output increases the value of the marginal product of labor. A change in the price of a firm's output leads to a shift in the firm's demand for labor curve. If the price of the firm's output increases, the demand for labor increases and the demand for labor curve shifts rightward.

For example, if the price of bread increased to $3 a loaf, the value of the marginal product of Angelo's fourth worker would increase from $8 an hour to $12 an hour. At a wage rate of $10 an hour, Angelo would now hire 4 workers instead of 3.

The Prices of Other Factors of Production If the price of using capital decreases relative to the wage rate, a firm substitutes capital for labor and increases the quantity of capital it uses. Usually, the demand for labor will decrease when the price of using capital falls. For example, if the price of a bread-making machine falls, Angelo might decide to install one machine and lay off a worker. But the demand for labor could increase if the lower price of capital led to a sufficiently large increase in the scale of production. For example, with cheaper machines available, Angelo might install a machine and hire more labor to operate it. This type of factor substitution occurs in the long run when the firm can change the size of its plant.

Technology New technologies decrease the demand for some types of labor and increase the demand for other types. For example, if a new automated bread-making machine becomes available, Angelo might install one of these machines and fire most of his workforce—a decrease in the demand for bakery workers. But the firms that manufacture and service automated bread-making machines hire more labor, so there is an increase in the demand for this type of labor. An event similar to this one occurred during the 1990s when the introduction of electronic telephone exchanges decreased the demand for telephone operators and increased the demand for computer programmers and electronics engineers.

Table 18.2 summarizes the influences on a firm's demand for labor.

TABLE 18.2   A Firm's Demand for Labor

The Law of Demand

(Movements along the demand curve for labor)

The quantity of labor demanded by a firm

Decreases if:	Increases if:
■ The wage rate increases	■ The wage rate decreases

Changes in Demand

(Shifts in the demand curve for labor)

A firm's demand for labor

Decreases if:	Increases if:
■ The price of the firm's output decreases	■ The price of the firm's output increases
■ The price of a substitute for labor falls	■ The price of a substitute for labor rises
■ The price of a complement of labor rises	■ The price of a complement of labor falls
■ A new technology or new capital decreases the marginal product of labor	■ A new technology or new capital increases the marginal product of labor

---

 REVIEW QUIZ

1 What is the value of marginal product of labor?
2 What is the relationship between the value of marginal product of labor and the marginal product of labor?
3 How is the demand for labor derived from the value of marginal product of labor?
4 What are the influences on the demand for labor?

You can work these questions in Study Plan 18.2 and get instant feedback.

◆ Labor Markets

Labor services are traded in many different labor markets. Examples are markets for bakery workers, van drivers, crane operators, computer support specialists, air traffic controllers, surgeons, and economists. Some of these markets, such as the market for bakery workers, are local. They operate in a given urban area. Some labor markets, such as the market for air traffic controllers, are national. Firms and workers search across the nation for the right match of worker and job. And some labor markets are global, such as the market for superstar hockey, basketball, and soccer players.

We'll look at a local market for bakery workers as an example. First, we'll look at a *competitive* labor market. Then, we'll see how monopoly elements can influence a labor market.

A Competitive Labor Market

A competitive labor market is one in which many firms demand labor and many households supply labor.

Market Demand for Labor Earlier in the chapter, you saw how an individual firm decides how much labor to hire. The market demand for labor is derived from the demand for labor by individual firms. We determine the market demand for labor by adding together the quantities of labor demanded by all the firms in the market at each wage rate. (The market demand for a good or service is derived in a similar way—see Chapter 5, p. 109.)

Because each firm's demand for labor curve slopes downward, the market demand for labor curve also slopes downward.

The Market Supply of Labor The market supply of labor is derived from the supply of labor decisions made by individual households.

Individual's Labor Supply Decision People can allocate their time to two broad activities: labor supply and leisure. (Leisure is a catch-all term. It includes all activities other than supplying labor.) For most people, leisure is more fun than work so to induce them to work they must be offered a wage.

Think about the labor supply decision of Jill, one of the workers at Angelo's Bakery. Let's see how the wage rate influences the quantity of labor she is willing to supply.

Reservation Wage Rate Jill enjoys her leisure time, and she would be pleased if she didn't have to spend her time working at Angelo's Bakery. But Jill wants to earn an income, and as long as she can earn a wage rate of at least $5 an hour, she's willing to work. This wage is called her *reservation wage*. At any wage rate above her reservation wage, Jill supplies some labor.

The wage rate at Angelo's is $10 an hour, and at that wage rate, Jill chooses to work 30 hours a week. At a wage rate of $10 an hour, Jill regards this use of her time as the best available. Figure 18.2 illustrates.

Backward-Bending Labor Supply Curve If Jill were offered a wage rate between $5 and $10 an hour, she would want to work fewer hours. If she were offered a wage rate above $10 an hour, she would want to work more hours, but only up to a point. If Jill could

---

◆

FIGURE 18.2   Jill's Labor Supply Curve

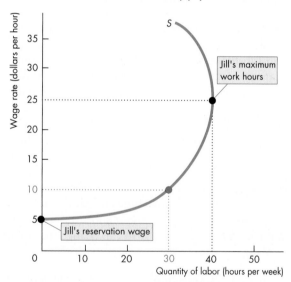

Jill's labor supply curve is S. Jill supplies no labor at wage rates below her reservation wage of $5 an hour. As the wage rate rises above $5 an hour, the quantity of labor that Jill supplies increases to a maximum of 40 hours a week at a wage rate of $25 an hour. As the wage rate rises above $25 an hour, Jill supplies a decreasing quantity of labor: her labor supply curve bends backward. The income effect on the demand for leisure dominates the substitution effect.

ⓧ myeconlab animation   ◆

earn $25 an hour, she would be willing to work 40 hours a week (and earn $1,000 a week). But at a wage rate above $25 an hour, with the goods and services that Jill can buy for $1,000, her priority would be a bit more leisure time. So if the wage rate increased above $25 an hour, Jill would cut back on her work hours and take more leisure. Jill's labor supply curve eventually bends backward.

Jill's labor supply decisions are influenced by a substitution effect and an income effect.

Substitution Effect At wage rates below $25 an hour, the higher the wage rate Jill is offered, the greater is the quantity of labor that she supplies. Jill's wage rate is her *opportunity cost of leisure*. If she quits work an hour early to catch a movie, the cost of that extra hour of leisure is the wage rate that Jill forgoes. The higher the wage rate, the less willing Jill is to forgo the income and take the extra leisure time. This tendency for a higher wage rate to induce Jill to work longer hours is a *substitution effect*.

Income Effect The higher Jill's wage rate, the higher is her income. A higher income, other things remaining the same, induces Jill to increase her demand for most goods and services. Leisure is one of those goods. Because an increase in income creates an increase in the demand for leisure, it also creates a decrease in the quantity of labor supplied.

Market Supply Curve Jill's supply curve shows the quantity of labor supplied by Jill as her wage rate changes. Most people behave like Jill and have a backward bending labor supply curve, but they have different reservation wage rates and wage rates at which their labor supply curves bend backward.

A market supply curve shows the quantity of labor supplied by all households in a particular job market. It is found by adding together the quantities of labor supplied by all households to a given job market at each wage rate.

Also, along a supply curve in a particular job market, the wage rates available in other job markets remain the same. For example, along the supply curve of car-wash workers, the wage rates of car salespeople, mechanics, and all other labor are constant.

Despite the fact that an individual's labor supply curve eventually bends backward, the market supply curve of labor slopes upward. The higher the wage rate for car-wash workers, the greater is the quantity of labor supplied in that labor market.

Let's now look at labor market equilibrium.

Competitive Labor Market Equilibrium Labor market equilibrium determines the wage rate and employment. In Fig. 18.3, the market demand curve for bakery workers is D and the market supply curve of bakery workers is S. The equilibrium wage rate is $10 an hour, and the equilibrium quantity is 300 bakery workers. If the wage rate exceeded $10 an hour, there would be a surplus of bakery workers. More people would be looking for jobs in bakeries than firms were willing to hire. In such a situation, the wage rate would fall as firms found it easy to hire people at a lower wage rate. If the wage rate were less than $10 an hour, there would be a shortage of bakery workers. Firms would not be able to fill all the positions they had available. In this situation, the wage rate would rise as firms found it necessary to offer higher wages to attract labor. Only at a wage rate of $10 an hour are there no forces operating to change the wage rate.

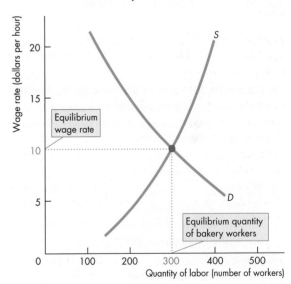

FIGURE 18.3   The Market for Bakery Workers

A competitive labor market coordinates firms' and households' plans. The market is in equilibrium—the quantity of labor demanded equals the quantity supplied at a wage rate of $10 an hour when 300 workers are employed. If the wage rate exceeds $10 an hour, the quantity supplied exceeds the quantity demanded and the wage rate will fall. If the wage rate is below $10 an hour, the quantity demanded exceeds the quantity supplied and the wage rate will rise.

myeconlab animation

A Labor Market with a Union

A **labor union** is an organized group of workers that aims to increase the wage rate and influence other job conditions. Let's see what happens when a union enters a competitive labor market.

Influences on Labor Supply One way of raising the wage rate is to decrease the supply of labor. In some labor markets, a union can restrict supply by controlling entry into apprenticeship programs or by influencing job qualification standards. Markets for skilled workers, doctors, dentists, and lawyers are the easiest ones to control in this way.

If there is an abundant supply of nonunion labor, a union can't decrease supply. For example, in the market for farm labor in southern California, the flow of nonunion labor from Mexico makes it difficult for a union to control the supply.

On the demand side of the labor market, the union faces a tradeoff: The demand for labor curve slopes downward, so restricting supply to raise the wage rate costs jobs. For this reason, unions also try to influence the demand for union labor.

Influences on Labor Demand A union tries to increase the demand for the labor of its members in four main ways:

1. Increasing the value of marginal product of its members by organizing and sponsoring training schemes and apprenticeship programs, and by professional certification.

2. Lobbying for import restrictions and encouraging people to buy goods made by unionized workers.

3. Supporting minimum wage laws, which increase the cost of employing low-skilled labor and lead firms to substitute high-skilled union labor for low-skilled nonunion labor.

4. Lobbying for restrictive immigration laws to decrease the supply of foreign workers.

Labor Market Equilibrium with a Union Figure 18.4 illustrates what happens to the wage rate and employment when a union successfully enters a competitive labor market. With no union, the demand curve is D_C, the supply curve is S_C, the wage rate is $10 an hour, and 300 workers have jobs.

Now a union enters this labor market. First, look at what happens if the union has sufficient control over the supply of labor to be able to restrict supply

FIGURE 18.4   A Union Enters a Competitive Labor Market

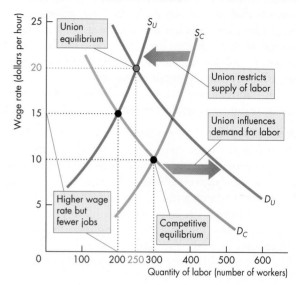

In a competitive labor market, the demand curve is D_C and the supply curve is S_C. The wage rate is $10 an hour and 300 workers are employed. If a union decreases the supply of labor and the supply of labor curve shifts to S_U, the wage rate rises to $15 an hour and employment decreases to 200 workers. If the union can also increase the demand for labor and shift the demand for labor curve to D_U, the wage rate rises to $20 an hour and 250 workers are employed.

myeconlab animation

below its competitive level—to S_U. If that is all the union is able to do, employment falls to 200 workers and the wage rate rises to $15 an hour.

Suppose now that the union is also able to increase the demand for labor to D_U. The union can get an even bigger increase in the wage rate and with a smaller fall in employment. By maintaining the restricted labor supply at S_U, the union increases the wage rate to $20 an hour and achieves an employment level of 250 workers.

Because a union restricts the supply of labor in the market in which it operates, the union's actions spill over into nonunion markets. Workers who can't get union jobs must look elsewhere for work. This action increases the supply of labor in nonunion markets and lowers the wage rate in those markets. This spillover effect further widens the gap between union and nonunion wages.

Monopsony in the Labor Market Not all labor markets in which unions operate are competitive. Rather, some are labor markets in which the employer possesses market power and the union enters to try to counteract that power.

A market in which there is a single buyer is called a **monopsony**. A monopsony labor market has one employer. In some parts of the country, managed health-care organizations are the major employer of health-care professionals. In some communities, Wal-Mart is the main employer of sales clerks. These firms have monopsony power.

A monopsony acts on the buying side of a market in a similar way to a monopoly on the selling side. The firm maximizes profit by hiring the quantity of labor that makes the marginal cost of labor equal to the value of marginal product of labor and by paying the lowest wage rate at which it can attract this quantity of labor.

Figure 18.5 illustrates a monopsony labor market. Like all firms, a monopsony faces a downward-sloping value of marginal product curve, *VMP*, which is its demand for labor curve, *D*—the curve labeled *VMP = D* in the figure.

What is special about monopsony is the marginal cost of labor. For a firm in a competitive labor market, the marginal cost of labor is the wage rate. For a monopsony, the marginal cost of labor exceeds the wage rate. The reason is that being the only buyer in the market, the firm faces an upward-sloping supply of labor curve—the curve *S* in the figure.

To attract one more worker, the monopsony must offer a higher wage rate. But it must pay this higher wage rate to all its workers, so the marginal cost of a worker is the wage rate plus the increased wage bill that arises from paying all the workers the higher wage rate.

The supply curve is now the average cost of labor curve and the relationship between the supply curve and the marginal cost of labor curve, *MCL*, is similar to that between a monopoly's demand curve and marginal revenue curve (see p. 302). The relationship between the supply curve and the *MCL* curve is also similar to that between a firm's average cost curve and marginal cost curve (see pp. 258–259).

To find the profit-maximizing quantity of labor to hire, the monopsony sets the marginal cost of labor equal to the value of marginal product of labor. In Fig. 18.5, this outcome occurs when the firm employs 100 workers.

To hire 100 workers, the firm must pay $10 an hour (on the supply of labor curve). Each worker is paid $10 an hour, but the value of marginal product of labor is $20 an hour, so the firm makes an economic profit of $10 an hour on the marginal worker.

If the labor market in Fig. 18.5 were competitive, the equilibrium wage rate and employment would be determined by the demand and supply curves. The wage rate would be $15 an hour, and 150 workers would be employed. So compared with a competitive labor market, a monopsony pays a lower wage rate and employs fewer workers.

A Union and a Monopsony A union is like a monopoly. If the union (monopoly seller) faces a monopsony buyer, the situation is called **bilateral monopoly**. An example of bilateral monopoly is the Writers Guild of America that represents film, television, and radio writers, and an employers' alliance that represents

FIGURE 18.5   A Monopsony Labor Market

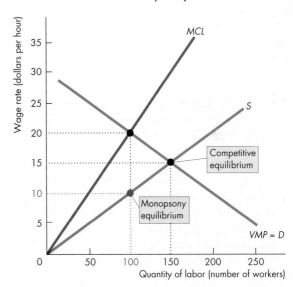

A monopsony is a market structure in which there is a single buyer. A monopsony in the labor market has a value of marginal product curve *VMP* and faces a labor supply curve *S*. The marginal cost of labor curve is *MCL*. Making the marginal cost of labor equal to the value of marginal product maximizes profit. The monopsony hires 100 hours of labor and pays the lowest wage rate for which that quantity of labor will work, which is $10 an hour.

CBS, MGM, NBC, and other entertainment companies. Every three years, the Writers Guild and the employers' alliance negotiate a pay deal.

In bilateral monopoly, the outcome is determined by bargaining, which depends on the costs that each party can inflict on the other. The firm can shut down temporarily and lock out its workers, and the workers can shut down the firm by striking. Each party estimates the other's strength and what it will lose if it does not agree to the other's demands.

Usually, an agreement is reached without a strike or a lockout. The threat is usually enough to bring the bargaining parties to an agreement. When a strike or lockout does occur, it is because one party has misjudged the costs each party can inflict on the other. Such an event occurred in November 2007 when the writers and entertainment producers failed to agree on a compensation deal. A 100-day strike followed that ended up costing the entertainment industry an estimated $2 billion.

In the example in Fig. 18.5, if the union and employer are equally strong, and each party knows the strength of the other, they will agree to split the gap between $10 (the wage rate on the supply curve) and $20 (the wage rate on the demand curve) and agree to a wage rate of $15 an hour.

You've now seen that in a monopsony, a union can bargain for a higher wage rate without sacrificing jobs. A similar outcome can arise in a monopsony labor market when a minimum wage law is enforced. Let's look at the effect of a minimum wage.

Monopsony and the Minimum Wage In a competitive labor market, a minimum wage that exceeds the equilibrium wage decreases employment (see Chapter 6, pp. 131–132). In a monopsony labor market, a minimum wage can increase both the wage rate and employment. Let's see how.

Figure 18.6 shows a monopsony labor market without a union. The wage rate is $10 an hour and 100 workers are employed.

A minimum wage law is passed that requires employers to pay at least $15 an hour. The monopsony now faces a perfectly elastic supply of labor at $15 an hour up to 150 workers (along the minimum wage line). To hire more than 150 workers, a wage rate above $15 an hour must be paid (along the supply curve). Because the wage rate is $15 an hour up to 150 workers, so is the marginal cost of labor $15 an hour up to 150 workers. To maximize profit, the monopsony sets the marginal cost of

FIGURE 18.6   Minimum Wage Law in Monopsony

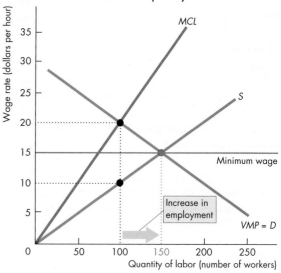

In a monopsony labor market, the wage rate is $10 an hour and 100 workers are hired. If a minimum wage law increases the wage rate to $15 an hour, the wage rate rises to this level and employment increases to 150 workers.

myeconlab   animation

labor equal to the value of marginal product of labor (on the demand curve). That is, the monopsony hires 150 workers and pays $15 an hour. The minimum wage law has succeeded in raising the wage rate and increasing the number of workers employed.

Scale of the Union–Nonunion Wage Gap

You've seen how a union can influence the wage rate, but how much of a difference to wage rates do unions actually make? This question is difficult to answer. To measure the difference in wages attributable to unions, economists have looked at the wages of unionized and nonunionized workers who do similar work and have similar skills.

The evidence based on these comparisons is that the union–nonunion wage gap lies between 10 and 25 percent of the wage. For example, unionized airline pilots earn about 25 percent more than nonunion pilots with the same level of skill. In markets that have only a union wage rate, we might presume that the wage rate is 10 to 25 percent higher than it would be in the absence of a union.

Economics in Action
Wage Rates in the United States

In 2007, the average wage rate in the United States was a bit less than $20 an hour. The figure shows the *average hourly wage rates* for twenty jobs selected from the more than 700 jobs for which the Bureau of Labor Statistics reports wage rate data.

You can see that a surgeon, on average, earns more than 11 times as much per hour as a fast-food worker and more than twice as much as an economist. Remember that these numbers are averages. Some surgeons earn much more and some earn much less than the average surgeon.

Many more occupations earn a wage rate below the national average than above it. Most of the occupations that earn more than the national average require a college degree and postgraduate training.

Earning differences are explained by differences in the value of the marginal product of the skills in the various occupations and in market power.

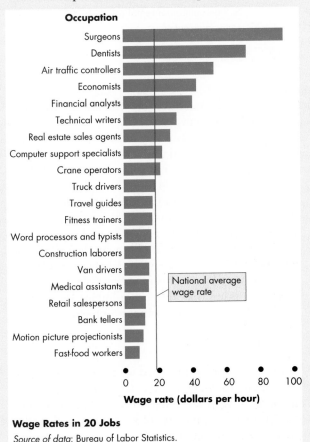

Wage Rates in 20 Jobs
Source of data: Bureau of Labor Statistics.

Trends and Differences in Wage Rates

You can use what you've learned about labor markets to explain the trend in wage rates and differences between wage rates.

Wage rates increase over time—trend upward. The reason is that the value of marginal product of labor trends upward. Technological change and the new types of capital that it brings make workers more productive. With greater labor productivity, the demand for labor increases and so does the average wage rate. Even jobs in which productivity doesn't increase experience an increase in the *value* of marginal product. Child care is an example. A child-care worker can't care for an increasing number of children, but an increasing number of parents who earn high wages are willing to hire child-care workers. The *value* of marginal product of these workers increases.

Wage rates are unequal, and in recent years they have become increasingly unequal. High wage rates have increased rapidly while low wage rates have stagnated or even fallen. The reasons are complex and not fully understood.

One reason is that the new technologies of the 1990s and 2000s made skilled workers more productive and destroyed some low-skilled jobs. An example is the ATM, which took the jobs and lowered the wage rate of bank tellers and created the jobs and increased the wage rates of computer programmers and electronic engineers. Another reason is that globalization has brought increased competition for low-skilled workers and opened global markets for high-skilled workers.

REVIEW QUIZ

1 What determines the amount of labor that households plan to supply?
2 How is the wage rate and employment determined in a competitive labor market?
3 How do labor unions influence wage rates?
4 What is a monopsony and why is a monopsony able to pay a lower wage rate than a firm in a competitive labor market?
5 How is the wage rate determined when a union faces a monopsony?
6 What is the effect of a minimum wage law in a monopsony labor market?

You can work these questions in Study Plan 18.3 and get instant feedback.

Capital and Natural Resource Markets

The markets for capital and land can be understood by using the same basic ideas that you've seen when studying a competitive labor market. But markets for nonrenewable natural resources are different. We'll now examine three groups of factor markets:

- Capital rental markets
- Land rental markets
- Nonrenewable natural resource markets

Capital Rental Markets

The demand for capital is derived from the *value of marginal product of capital*. Profit-maximizing firms hire the quantity of capital services that makes the value of marginal product of capital equal to the *rental rate of capital*. The *lower* the rental rate of capital, other things remaining the same, the *greater* is the quantity of capital demanded. The supply of capital responds in the opposite way to the rental rate. The *higher* the rental rate, other things remaining the same, the *greater* is the quantity of capital supplied. The equilibrium rental rate makes the quantity of capital demanded equal to the quantity of capital supplied.

Figure 18.7 illustrates the rental market for tower cranes—capital used to construct high-rise buildings. The value of marginal product and the demand curve is *VMP = D*. The supply curve is *S*. The equilibrium rental rate is $1,000 per day and 100 tower cranes are rented.

Rent-Versus-Buy Decision Some capital services are obtained in a rental market like the market for tower cranes. And like tower cranes, many of the world's large airlines rent their airplanes. But not all capital services are obtained in a rental market. Instead, firms buy the capital equipment that they use. You saw in Chapter 10 (pp. 228–229) that the cost of the services of the capital that a firm owns and operates itself is an implicit rental rate that arises from depreciation and interest costs. Firms that buy capital *implicitly* rent the capital to themselves.

The decision to obtain capital services in a rental market rather than buy capital and rent it implicitly is made to minimize cost. The firm compares the cost of explicitly renting the capital and the cost of buying and implicitly renting it. This decision is the same as

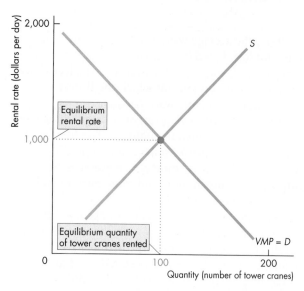

FIGURE 18.7 A Rental Market for Capital

The value of marginal product of tower cranes, *VMP*, determines the demand, *D*, for tower crane rentals. With the supply curve, *S*, the equilibrium rental rate is $1,000 a day and 100 cranes are rented.

myeconlab   animation

the one that a household makes in deciding whether to rent or buy a home.

To make a rent-versus-buy decision, a firm must compare a cost incurred in the *present* with a stream of rental costs incurred over some *future* period. The Mathematical Note (pp. 434–435) explains how to make this comparison by calculating the *present value* of a future amount of money. If the *present value* of the future rental payments of an item of capital equipment exceeds the cost of buying the capital, the firm will buy the equipment. If the *present value* of the future rental payments of an item of capital equipment is less than the cost of buying the capital, the firm will rent (or lease) the equipment.

Land Rental Markets

The demand for land is based on the same factors as the demand for labor and the demand for capital—the *value of marginal product of land*. Profit-maximizing firms rent the quantity of land at which the value of marginal product of land is equal to the *rental rate of land*. The *lower* the rental rate, other things remaining the same, the *greater* is the quantity of land demanded.

But the supply of land is special: Its quantity is fixed, so the quantity supplied cannot be changed by people's decisions. The supply of each particular block of land is perfectly inelastic.

The equilibrium rental rate makes the quantity of land demanded equal to the quantity available. Figure 18.8 illustrates the market for a 10-acre block of land on 42nd Street in New York City. The quantity supplied is fixed and the supply curve is S. The value of marginal product and the demand curve is VMP = D. The equilibrium rental rate is $1,000 an acre per day.

The rental rate of land is high in New York because the willingness to pay for the services produced by that land is high, which in turn makes the VMP of land high. A Big Mac costs more at McDonald's on 42nd Street, New York, than at McDonald's on Jefferson Avenue, St. Louis, but not because the rental rate of land is higher in New York. The rental rate of land is higher in New York because of the greater willingness to pay for a Big Mac (and other goods and services) in New York.

FIGURE 18.8   A Rental Market for Land

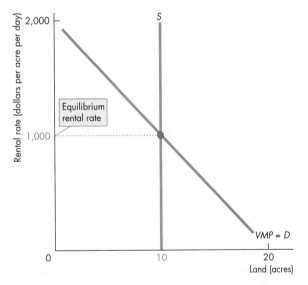

The value of marginal product of a 10-acre block, *VMP*, determines the rental demand, *D*, for this land. With the supply curve, *S*, the block rents for $10,000 a day.

myeconlab   animation

Nonrenewable Natural Resource Markets

The nonrenewable natural resources are oil, gas, and coal. Burning one of these fuels converts it to energy and other by-products, and the used resource cannot be re-used. The natural resources that we use to make metals are also nonrenewable, but they can be used again, at some cost, by recycling them.

Oil, gas, and coal are traded in global commodity markets. The price of a given grade of crude oil is the same in New York, London, and Singapore. Traders, linked by telephone and the Internet, operate these markets around the clock every day of the year.

Demand and supply determine the prices and the quantities traded in these commodity markets. We'll look at the influences on demand and supply by considering the global market for crude oil.

The Demand for Oil   The two key influences on the demand for oil are

1. The *value of marginal product* of oil
2. The expected future price of oil

The value of marginal product of oil is the *fundamental* influence on demand. It works in exactly the same way for a nonrenewable resource as it does for any other factor of production. The greater the quantity of oil used, the smaller is the value of marginal product of oil. Diminishing value of marginal product makes the demand curve slope downward. The lower the price, the greater is the quantity demanded.

The higher the expected future price of oil, the greater is the present demand for oil. The expected future price is a *speculative* influence on demand. Oil in the ground and oil in storage tanks are inventories that can be held or sold. A trader might plan to buy oil to hold now and to sell it later for a profit. Instead of buying oil to hold and sell later, the trader could buy a bond and earn interest. The interest forgone is the opportunity cost of holding the oil. If the price of oil is expected to rise by a bigger percentage than the interest rate, a trader will hold oil and incur the opportunity cost. In this case, the return from holding oil exceeds the return from holding bonds.

The Supply of Oil   The three key influences on the supply of oil are

1. The known oil reserves
2. The scale of current oil production facilities
3. The expected future price of oil

Known oil reserves are the oil that has been discovered and can be extracted with today's technology. This quantity increases over time because advances in technology enable ever-less accessible sources to be discovered. The greater the size of known reserves, the greater is the supply of oil. But this influence on supply is small and indirect. It operates by changing the expected distant future price of oil. Even a major new discovery of oil would have a negligible effect on current supply of oil.

The scale of current oil production facilities is the *fundamental* influence on the supply of oil. Producing oil is like any production activity: It is subject to increasing marginal cost. The increasing marginal cost of extracting oil means that the supply curve of oil slopes upward. The higher the price of oil, the greater is the quantity supplied. When new oil wells are sunk or when new faster pumps are installed, the supply of oil increases. When existing wells run dry, the supply of oil decreases. Over time, the factors that increase supply are more powerful than those that decrease supply, so changes in the fundamental influence increase the supply of oil.

Speculative forces based on expectations about the future price also influence the supply of oil. The *higher* the expected future price of oil, the *smaller* is the present supply of oil. A trader with an oil inventory might plan to sell now or to hold and sell later. You've seen that interest forgone is the opportunity cost of holding the oil. If the price of oil is expected to rise by a bigger percentage than the interest rate, it is profitable to incur the opportunity cost of holding oil rather than selling it immediately.

The Equilibrium Price of Oil The demand for oil and the supply of oil determine the equilibrium price and quantity traded. Figure 18.9 illustrates the market equilibrium.

The value of marginal product of oil, *VMP*, is the *fundamental determinant of demand*, and the marginal cost of extraction, *MC*, is the *fundamental determinant of supply*. Together, they determine the *market fundamentals price*.

If expectations about the future price are also based on fundamentals, the equilibrium price is the market fundamentals price. But if expectations about the future price of oil depart from what the market fundamentals imply, *speculation* can drive a wedge between the equilibrium price and the market fundamentals price.

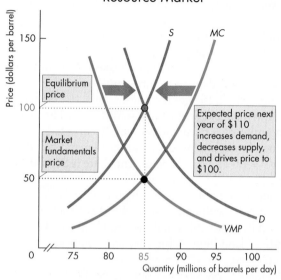

FIGURE 18.9   A Nonrenewable Natural Resource Market

The value of marginal product of a natural resource, *VMP*, and the marginal cost of extraction, *MC*, determine the *market fundamentals* price. Demand, *D*, and supply, *S*, which determine the equilibrium price, are influenced by the expected future price. Speculation can bring a gap between the market fundamentals price and the equilibrium price.

myecon**lab**   animation

The Hotelling Principle Harold Hotelling, an economist at Columbia University, had an incredible idea: Traders expect the price of a nonrenewable natural resource to rise at a rate equal to the interest rate. We call this idea the **Hotelling Principle.** Let's see why it is correct.

You've seen that the interest rate is the opportunity cost of holding an oil inventory. If the price of oil is expected to rise at a rate that exceeds the interest rate, it is profitable to hold a bigger inventory. Demand increases, supply decreases, and the price rises. If the interest rate exceeds the rate at which the price of oil is expected to rise, it is not profitable to hold an oil inventory. Demand decreases, supply increases, and the price falls. But if the price of oil is expected to rise at a rate equal to the interest rate, holding an inventory of oil is just as good as holding bonds. Demand and supply don't change and the price does not change. Only when the price of oil is expected to rise at a rate equal to the interest rate is the price at its equilibrium.

Economics in Action
The World and U.S. Markets for Oil

The world produced about 31 billion barrels of oil in 2008 and the price shot upward from $85 in January to $135 in June. The high price and foreign dependence became major political issues.

Although the United States imports almost three quarters of its oil from other countries, much of it comes from close to home. Figure 1 provides the details: Only 14 percent of the U.S. oil supply comes from the Middle East and more than one third comes from Canada, Mexico, and other Western Hemisphere nations.

Even if the United States produced all its own oil, it would still face a fluctuating global price. U.S. producers would not willingly sell to U.S. buyers for a price below the world price. So energy independence doesn't mean an independent oil price.

The Hotelling Principle tells us that we must expect the price of oil to rise at a rate equal to the interest rate. But expecting the price to rise at a rate equal to the interest rate doesn't mean that the price will rise at this rate. As you can see in Fig. 2, the price of oil over the past 50 or so years has not followed the path predicted by the Hotelling Principle.

The forces that influence expectations are not well understood. The expected future price of oil depends on its expected future rate of use and the rate of discovery of new sources of supply. One person's expectation about a future price also depends on guesses about other people's expectations. These guesses can

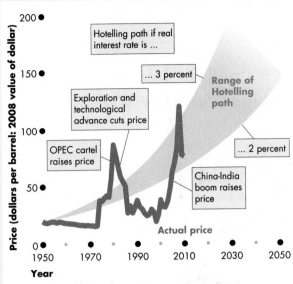

Figure 2 The Price of Oil and Its Hotelling Path
Source of data: U.S. Energy Information Administration.

change abruptly and become self-reinforcing. When the expected future price of oil changes for whatever reason, demand and supply change, and so does the price. Prices in speculative markets are always volatile.

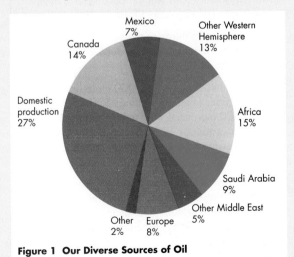

Figure 1 Our Diverse Sources of Oil
Source of data: U.S. Energy Information Administration.

REVIEW QUIZ

1 What determines demand and supply in rental markets for capital and land?
2 What determines the demand for a nonrenewable natural resource?
3 What determines the supply of a nonrenewable natural resource?
4 What is the market fundamentals price and how might it differ from the equilibrium price?
5 Explain the Hotelling Principle.

You can work these questions in Study Plan 18.4 and get instant feedback.

◆ *Reading Between the Lines* on pp. 432–433 focuses on the U.S. labor market and the tough conditions that workers are likely to face.

The next chapter looks at how the market economy distributes income and explains the trends in the distribution of income. The chapter also looks at the efforts by governments to redistribute income and modify the market outcome.

The Labor Market in Action

Outlook for Job Market Is Grim; When Jobs Do Return, Many Won't Pay Well

http://www.usatoday.com
January 8, 2010

… Foreign competition and automation will continue to kill manufacturing jobs: The government expects factories to cut 1.2 million manufacturing jobs by 2018. …

Still the government's Bureau of Labor Statistics expects the overall economy to generate 15.3 million new jobs (not counting replacements) from 2008 to 2018. … Where will the new jobs come from? …

Computer network and data analysts (median wage: $71,100) will see their ranks surge 53% from 2008 to 2018, the government predicts. And financial examiners, who ensure that companies are complying with financial laws and regulations, will grow in number by 41%. Their median earnings: $70,930. (The median wage figures—half earn more, half less—are from May 2008.) …

Measured by sheer numbers, the new jobs of the next decade don't look nearly as lucrative: The number of home health aides, for instance, is expected to expand by 461,000. But their median earnings come to just $20,460—well below the median U.S. wage of $32,390. …

The economy will also demand 400,000 new customer service representatives, an occupation with median earnings of $29,860 a year; and 394,000 workers who prepare and serve food, including fast food, earning $16,430. …

More than two thirds of new jobs won't require any education past high school. For several decades after World War II, high school graduates could find decent-paying manufacturing jobs. But factories are shedding workers or closing altogether. …

One bright spot: nursing. The country is expected to need 582,000 new registered nurses—a profession that pays a median $62,450 a year. …

From *USA Today*, a divison of Gannett Co., Inc. Reprinted with permission.

ESSENCE OF THE STORY

- The Bureau of Labor Statistics forecasts that 1.2 million factory jobs will be lost and 15.3 million new jobs will be created from 2008 to 2018.

- More than two thirds of the new jobs will require only a high school education and will be low paid.

- Among these will be 461,000 more home health aides (median earnings $20,460); 400,000 more customer service representatives (median earnings $29,860); and 394,000 more fast-food workers (median earnings $16,430).

- Job growth will be most rapid for computer network and data analysts (median earnings $71,100) and financial examiners (median earnings: $70,930), but the number of these jobs is small.

- There will be an additional 582,000 nurses (median earnings $62,450).

ECONOMIC ANALYSIS

- The labor markets are constantly in a state of change, reallocating the nation's labor resources to their highest-value employments.

- The value of marginal product (*VMP*) of workers in service industries is rising.

- The *VMP* of nurses is rising because an aging population is increasing the demand for health care and technological advances are making nurses more productive.

- With an increase in *VMP*, the demand for nurses increases.

- Anticipating good job prospects in nursing, more college students and other young workers train as nurses, which increases the supply of nurses.

- The combination of an increase in demand and an increase in supply increases employment and the increase is forecasted to be 582,000 nurses from 2008 to 2018.

- Nurses' wages might rise, fall, or remain unchanged, depending on whether supply or demand increases more.

- The figures illustrate the market for nurses in 2008 and 2018. The 2008 demand curve, D_{08}, and supply curve, S_{08}, determine the equilibrium number of nurses (2,760,000) and the equilibrium wage rate ($62,450 per year).

- By 2018, the demand for nurses will increase to D_{18}. With no change in supply in Fig. 1, the wage rate rises to $66,000 a year and employment increases to 2,900,000.

- But the anticipation of good job prospects increases supply to S_{18} in Fig. 2. Employment increases by 582,000 and the wage rate remains at its 2008 level (an assumption).

- As the *VMP* of nurses is rising, the *VMP* of workers in manufacturing industries is falling. Foreign competition is cutting the prices of manufactured goods and automation is making machines more productive than factory labor, decreasing their marginal product.

- With a decrease in *VMP*, the demand for factory workers decreases.

- Faced with the prospect of unemployment or working for a lower wage, young workers stop looking for factory jobs and undertake training for service jobs, which decreases the supply of factory workers.

- The combination of a decrease in demand and a decrease in supply decreases factory employment and

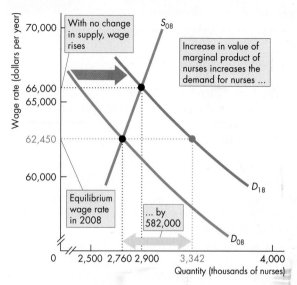

Figure 1 The market for nurses with no change in supply

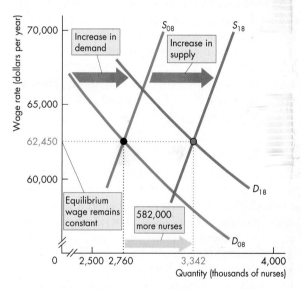

Figure 2 The market for nurses when supply increases

the decrease is forecasted to be 1.2 million workers from 2008 to 2018.

- The wages of factory workers might rise, fall, or remain unchanged, depending on whether supply or demand decreases more.

- Similar events are occurring in the markets for all types of labor, some expanding like nurses and some contracting like factory workers.

433

MATHEMATICAL NOTE

Present Value and Discounting

Rent-Versus-Buy Decision

To decide whether to rent an item of capital equipment or to buy the capital and implicitly rent it, a firm must compare the present expenditure on the capital with the future rental cost of the capital.

Comparing Current and Future Dollars

To compare a present expenditure with a future expenditure, we convert the future expenditure to its "present value."

The **present value** of a future amount of money is the amount that, if invested today, will grow to be as large as that future amount when the interest that it will earn is taken into account.

So the present value of a future amount of money is smaller than the future amount. The calculation that we use to convert a future amount of money to its present value is called **discounting**.

The easiest way to understand discounting and present value is to first consider its opposite: How a present value grows to a future amount of money because of *compound interest*.

Compound Interest

Compound interest is the interest on an initial investment plus the interest on the interest that the investment has previously earned. Because of compound interest, a present amount of money (a present value) grows into a larger future amount. The future amount is equal to the present amount (present value) plus the interest it will earn in the future. That is,

Future amount = Present value + Interest income.

The interest in the first year is equal to the present value multiplied by the interest rate, r, so

Amount after 1 year = Present value +
$$(r \times \text{Present value}).$$

or

Amount after 1 year = Present value $\times (1 + r)$.

If you invest \$100 today and the interest rate is 10 percent a year ($r = 0.1$), one year from today you will have \$110—the original \$100 plus \$10 interest. Check that the above formula delivers that answer:

$$\$100 \times 1.1 = \$110.$$

If you leave this \$110 invested to earn 10 percent during a second year, at the end of that year you will have

Amount after 2 years = Present value $\times (1 + r)^2$.

With the numbers of the previous example, you invest \$100 today at an interest rate of 10 percent a year ($r = 0.1$). After one year you will have \$110—the original \$100 plus \$10 interest. And after the second year, you will have \$121. In the second year, you earned \$10 on your initial \$100 plus \$1 on the \$10 interest that you earned in the first year. Check that the above formula delivers that answer:

$$\$100 \times (1.1)^2 = \$100 \times 1.21 = \$121.$$

If you leave your \$100 invested for n years, it will grow to

Amount after n years = Present value $\times (1 + r)^n$.

With an interest rate of 10 percent a year, your \$100 will grow to \$195 after 7 years ($n = 7$)—almost double the present value of \$100.

Discounting a Future Amount

We have just calculated future amounts one year, two years, and n years in the future, knowing the present value and the interest rate. To calculate the present value of these future amounts, we just work backward.

To find the present value of an amount one year in the future, we divide the future amount by $(1 + r)$. That is,

$$\text{Present value} = \frac{\text{Amount of money one year in future}}{(1 + r)}.$$

Let's check that we can use the present value formula by calculating the present value of \$110 one year from now when the interest rate is 10 percent a year. You'll be able to guess that the answer is $100 because we just calculated that $100 invested today at 10 percent a year becomes $110 in one year. So the present value of $110 one year from today is $100. But let's use the formula. Putting the numbers into the above formula, we have

$$\text{Present value} = \frac{\$110}{(1 + 0.1)}$$

$$= \frac{\$110}{1.1} = \$100.$$

To calculate the present value of an amount of money two years in the future, we use the formula:

$$\text{Present value} = \frac{\text{Amount of money two years in future}}{(1 + r)^2}.$$

Use this formula to calculate the present value of $121 two years from now at an interest rate of 10 percent a year. With these numbers, the formula gives

$$\text{Present value} = \frac{\$121}{(1 + 0.1)^2}$$

$$= \frac{\$121}{(1.1)^2}$$

$$= \frac{\$121}{1.21}$$

$$= \$100.$$

We can calculate the present value of an amount of money n years in the future by using the general formula

$$\text{Present value} = \frac{\text{Amount of money } n \text{ years in future}}{(1 + r)^n}.$$

For example, if the interest rate is 10 percent a year, $100 to be received 10 years from now has a present value of $38.55. That is, if $38.55 is invested today at 10 percent a year it will accumulate to $100 in 10 years.

Present Value of a Sequence of Future Amounts

You've seen how to calculate the present value of an amount of money one year, two years, and n years in the future. Most practical applications of present value calculate the present value of a sequence of future amounts of money that are spread over several years. An airline's payment of rent for the lease of airplanes is an example.

To calculate the present value of a sequence of amounts over several years, we use the formula you have learned and apply it to each year. We then sum the present values for all the years to find the present value of the sequence of amounts.

For example, suppose that a firm expects to pay $100 a year for each of the next five years and the interest rate is 10 percent a year ($r = 0.1$). The present value (PV) of these five payments of $100 each is calculated by using the following formula:

$$PV = \frac{\$100}{1.1} + \frac{\$100}{1.1^2} + \frac{\$100}{1.1^3} + \frac{\$100}{1.1^4} + \frac{\$100}{1.1^5},$$

which equals

$$PV = \$90.91 + \$82.64 + \$75.13 + \$68.30 + \$62.09$$
$$= \$379.07.$$

You can see that the firm pays $500 over five years. But because the money is paid in the future, it is not worth $500 today. Its present value is only $379.07. And the farther in the future the money is paid, the smaller is its present value. The $100 paid one year in the future is worth $90.91 today, but the $100 paid five years in the future is worth only $62.09 today.

The Decision

If this firm could lease a machine for five years at $100 a year or buy the machine for $500, it would jump at leasing. Only if the firm could buy the machine for less than $379.07 would it want to buy.

Many personal and business decisions turn on calculations like the one you've just made. A decision to buy or rent an apartment, to lease or rent a car, to pay off a student loan or let the loan run another year can all be made using the above calculation.

SUMMARY

Key Points

The Anatomy of Factor Markets (p. 418)

- The factor markets are: job markets for labor; rental markets (often implicit rental markets) for capital and land; and global commodity markets for nonrenewable natural resources.
- The services of entrepreneurs are not traded on a factor market.

Working Problem 1 will give you a better understanding of the anatomy of factor markets.

The Demand for a Factor of Production

(pp. 419–421)

- The value of marginal product determines the demand for a factor of production.
- The value of marginal product decreases as the quantity of the factor employed increases.
- The firm employs the quantity of each factor of production that makes the value of marginal product equal to the factor price.

Working Problems 2 to 8 will give you a better understanding of the demand for a factor of production.

Labor Markets (pp. 422–427)

- The value of marginal product of labor determines the demand for labor. A rise in the wage rate brings a decrease in the quantity demanded.
- The quantity of labor supplied depends on the wage rate. At low wage rates, a rise in the wage rate increases the quantity supplied. Beyond a high enough wage rate, a rise in the wage rate decreases the quantity supplied—the supply curve eventually bends backward.

- Demand and supply determine the wage rate in a competitive labor market.
- A labor union can raise the wage rate by restricting the supply or increasing the demand for labor.
- A monopsony can lower the wage rate below the competitive level.
- A union or a minimum wage in a monopsony labor market can raise the wage rate without a fall in employment.

Working Problems 9 to 11 will give you a better understanding of labor markets.

Capital and Natural Resource Markets (pp. 428–431)

- The value of marginal product of capital (and land) determines the demand for capital (and land).
- Firms make a rent-versus-buy decision by choosing the option that minimizes cost.
- The supply of land is inelastic and the demand for land determines the rental rate.
- The demand for a nonrenewable natural resource depends on the value of marginal product and on the expected future price.
- The supply of a nonrenewable natural resource depends on the known reserves, the cost of extraction, and the expected future price.
- The price of nonrenewable natural resources can differ from the market fundamentals price because of speculation based on expectations about the future price.
- The price of a nonrenewable natural resource is expected to rise at a rate equal to the interest rate.

Working Problems 12 to 17 will give you a better understanding of capital and natural resource markets.

Key Terms

Bilateral monopoly, 425
Compound interest, 434
Derived demand, 419
Discounting, 434

Hotelling Principle, 430
Job, 418
Labor union, 424
Monopsony, 425

Nonrenewable natural
    resources, 418
Present value, 434
Value of marginal product, 419

STUDY PLAN PROBLEMS AND APPLICATIONS

 myeconlab You can work Problems 1 to 18 in Chapter 18 Study Plan and get instant feedback.

The Anatomy of Factor Markets (Study Plan18.1)

1. Tim is opening a new online store. He plans to hire two people to key in the data at $10 an hour. Tim is also considering buying or leasing some new computers. The purchase price of a computer is $900 and after three years it is worthless. The annual cost of leasing a computer is $450.
   a. In which factor markets does Tim operate?
   b. What is the price of the capital equipment and the rental rate of capital?

The Demand for a Factor of Production

(Study Plan18.2)

Use the following data to work Problems 2 to 7.

Wanda owns a fish store. She employs students to sort and pack the fish. Students can pack the following amounts of fish:

Number of students	Quantity of fish (pounds)
1	20
2	50
3	90
4	120
5	145
6	165
7	180
8	190

The fish market is competitive and the price of fish is 50¢ a pound. The market for packers is competitive and their market wage rate is $7.50 an hour.

2. Calculate the marginal product of the students and draw the marginal product curve.
3. Calculate the value of marginal product of labor and draw the value of marginal product curve.
4. a. Find Wanda's demand for labor curve.
   b. How many students does Wanda employ?

Use the following additional information to work Problems 5 and 6.

The market price of fish falls to 33.33¢ a pound, but the packers' wage rate remains at $7.50 an hour.

5. a. How does the students' marginal product change?

b. How does the value of marginal product of labor change?
6. a. How does Wanda's demand for labor change?
   b. What happens to the number of students that Wanda employs?
7. At Wanda's fish store packers' wages increase to $10 an hour, but the price of fish remains at 50¢ a pound.
   a. What happens to the value of marginal product of labor?
   b. What happens to Wanda's demand for labor curve?
   c. How many students does Wanda employ?

8. **British Construction Activity Falls**
   Construction activity in Britain declined in June at the fastest rate in 11 years. A major home builder was unable to raise more capital—both signs of worsening conditions in the battered housing industry. Employment of construction labor declined in June after 23 months of growth. Average house prices fell 0.9 percent in June, the eighth consecutive month of declines, leaving the average 6.3 percent below June 2007.
   Source: *Forbes*, July 2, 2008
   a. Explain how a fall in house prices influences the market for construction labor.
   b. On a graph illustrate the effect of falling house prices in the market for construction labor.

Labor Markets (Study Plan18.3)

Use the following news clip to work Problems 9 to 11.

In Modern Rarity, Workers Form Union at Small Chain

In New York's low-income neighborhoods, labor unions have virtually no presence. But after a year-long struggle, 95 workers at a chain of 10 sneaker stores have formed a union. After months of negotiations, the two sides signed a three-year contract that sets the wage rate at $7.25 an hour.
   Source: *The New York Times*, February 5, 2006

9. Why are labor unions scarce in New York's low-income neighborhoods?
10. Who wins from this union contract? Who loses?
11. How can this union try to change the demand for labor?

Capital and Natural Resource Markets

(Study Plan 18.4)

12. Classify the following items as a nonrenewable natural resource, a renewable natural resource, or not a natural resource. Explain your answers.
    a. Trump Tower
    b. Lake Michigan
    c. Coal in a West Virginia coal mine
    d. The Internet
    e. Yosemite National Park
    f. Power generated by wind turbines

13. **Trump Group Selling Parcel For $1.8 Billion**

    A consortium of Hong Kong investors and Donald J. Trump are selling a stretch of river-front land and three buildings on the Upper West Side for about $1.8 billion in the largest residential sale in city history. Mr. Trump acquired the land for less than $100 million a decade ago during a real estate recession.

    Source: *The New York Times*, June 1, 2005

    a. Why has the price of land on New York City's Upper West Side increased over the last decade? In your answer include a discussion of the demand for and supply of land.
    b. Use a graph to show why the price of land on the Upper West Side increased over the last decade.
    c. Is the supply of land on the Upper West Side perfectly inelastic?

14. In the news clip in Problem 8,
    a. Explain how a fall in house prices influences the market for construction equipment leases.
    b. Draw a graph to illustrate the effect of a fall in house prices in the market for construction equipment leases.

Use the following news clip to work Problems 15 and 16.

Fixing Farming

Solutions to the global food crisis will come from genetically engineered crops and large-scale farms. Demand for farm products will keep growing as the population grows. But the supply of farmland is limited and farms already use 55 percent of the habitable land. The solution is for farmers to become more productive—generating more output from fewer inputs.

Source: *Fortune*, May 22, 2008

15. a. Is farmland a renewable or nonrenewable resource?
    b. Explain how the growing demand for farm products will affect the market for land and draw a graph to illustrate your answer.

16. How might farmers meet the growing demand for farm products without having to use a greater quantity of farmland?

17. **Copter Crisis**

    Helicopters are in short supply these days. You could blame a rise in military spending, a jump in disaster relief, even crowded airports pushing executives into private travel. But the fastest growth is coming from the offshore oil-and-gas industry, where helicopters are the only way to ferry crews to and from rigs and platforms. Hundred-dollar oil has pushed producers to work existing fields harder and to open new deep-sea wells in Brazil, India, and Alaska. The number of rigs and platforms has grown by 13% over the past decade. Oil companies are facing a two-year backlog in orders for the Sikorsky S92, a favorite of the oil industry, and a 40% rise in prices for used models.

    Source: *Fortune*, May 12, 2008

    a. Explain how high oil prices influence the market for helicopter leases and services (such as the Sikorsky S92).
    b. What happens to the value of marginal product of a helicopter as a firm leases or buys additional helicopters?

Mathematical Note (Study Plan 18.MN)

18. Keshia is opening a new bookkeeping service. She is considering buying or leasing some new laptop computers. The purchase price of a laptop is $1,500 and after three years it is worthless. The annual lease rate is $550 per laptop. The value of marginal product of one laptop is $700 a year. The value of marginal product of a second laptop is $625 a year. The value of marginal product of a third laptop is $575 a year. And the value of marginal product of a fourth laptop is $500 a year.
    a. How many laptops will Keshia lease or buy?
    b. If the interest rate is 4 percent a year, will Keshia lease or buy her laptops?
    c. If the interest rate is 6 percent a year, will Keshia lease or buy her laptops?

ADDITIONAL PROBLEMS AND APPLICATIONS

 myeconlab You can work these problems in MyEconLab if assigned by your instructor.

The Anatomy of Factor Markets

19. Venus is opening a tennis school. She plans to hire a marketing graduate to promote the school and an administrator at $20 an hour. Venus is also considering buying or leasing a new tennis ball machine. The purchase price of the machine is $1,000 and after three years it is worthless. The annual cost of leasing the machine is $500.
    a. In which factor markets does Venus operate?
    b. What is the price of the capital equipment and the rental rate of capital?

The Demand for a Factor of Production

Use the following data to work Problems 20 to 23. Kaiser's Ice Cream Parlor hires workers to produce smoothies. The market for smoothies is perfectly competitive, and the price of a smoothie is $4. The labor market is competitive, and the wage rate is $40 a day. The table shows the workers' total product schedule.

Number of workers	Quantity produced (smoothies per day)
1	7
2	21
3	33
4	43
5	51
6	55

20. Calculate the marginal product of hiring the fourth worker and the fourth worker's value of marginal product.
21. How many workers will Kaiser's hire to maximize its profit and how many smoothies a day will Kaiser's produce?
22. If the price rises to $5 a smoothie, how many workers will Kaiser's hire?
23. Kaiser's installs a new soda fountain that increases the productivity of workers by 50 percent. If the price of a smoothie remains at $4 and the wage rises to $48 a day, how many workers does Kaiser's hire?

24. **Detroit Oil Refinery Expansion Approved**
    Marathon Oil Saturday started work on a $1.9 billion expansion of its gasoline refinery in Detroit. Marathon will employ 800 construction workers and add 135 permanent jobs to the existing 480 workers at the refinery.
    Source: *United Press International*, June 21, 2008
    a. Explain how rising gasoline prices influence the market for refinery labor.
    b. Draw a graph to illustrate the effects of rising gasoline prices on the market for refinery labor.

Labor Markets

25. **You May be Paid More (or Less) than You Think**
    It's hard to put a price on happiness, but if you've ever had to choose between a job you like and a better-paying one that you like less, you'd like to know what job satisfaction is worth.
    John Helliwell and Haifang Huang (economists at the University of British Columbia) have estimated four key factors influencing job satisfaction: Trust in management is like a 36 percent pay raise; a job with lots of variety is like a 21 percent pay raise; a job that requires a high level of skill is like a 19 percent pay raise; and a job with enough time to finish your work is like an 11 percent pay raise.
    Source: CNN, March 29, 2006
    a. How might the job characteristics described here affect the supply of labor for different types of jobs?
    b. How might this influence on supply result in different wage rates that reflect the attractiveness of a job's characteristics?

Use the following news clip to work Problems 26 to 29.

The New War over Wal-Mart
Today, Wal-Mart employs more people—1.7 million—than any other private employer in the world. With size comes power: Wal-Mart's prices are lower and United Food and Commercial Workers International Union argues that Wal-Mart's wages are also lowers than its competitors. Last year, the workers at a Canadian outlet joined the union and Wal-Mart immediately closed the outlet. But does Wal-Mart behave

any worse than its competitors? When it comes to payroll, Wal-Mart's median hourly wage tracks the national median wage for general merchandise retail jobs.

Source: *The Atlantic*, June 2006

26. a. Assuming that Wal-Mart has market power in a labor market, explain how the firm could use that market power in setting wages.
    b. Draw a graph to illustrate how Wal-Mart might use labor market power to set wages.

27. a. Explain how a union of Wal-Mart's employees would attempt to counteract Wal-Mart's wage offers (a bilateral monopoly).
    b. Explain the response by the Canadian Wal-Mart to the unionization of employees.

28. Based upon evidence presented in this article, does Wal-Mart function as a monopsony in labor markets, or is the market for retail labor more competitive? Explain.

29. If the market for retail labor is competitive, explain the potential effect of a union on the wage rates. Draw a graph to illustrate your answer.

Capital and Natural Resource Markets

Use the following news clip to work Problems 30 and 31.

Gas Prices Create Land Rush

There is a land rush going on across Pennsylvania, but buyers aren't interested in the land itself. Buyers are interested in what lies beneath the earth's surface—mineral rights to natural gas deposits. Record high natural gas prices have already pushed up drilling activity across the state, but drilling companies have discovered a new technology that will enable deep gas-bearing shale to be exploited. Development companies, drilling companies and speculators have been crisscrossing the state, trying to lease mineral rights from landowners. The new drilling techniques might recover about 10 percent of those reserves, and that would ring up at a value of $1 trillion.

Source: *Erie Times-News*, June 15, 2008

30. a. Is natural gas a renewable or nonrenewable resource? Explain.
    b. Explain why the demand for land in Pennsylvania has increased.

31. a. If companies are responding to the higher prices for natural gas by drilling right now wherever they can, what does that imply about their assumptions about the future price of natural gas in relation to current interest rates?

    b. What could cause the price of natural gas to fall in the future?

32. New technology has allowed oil to be pumped from much deeper offshore oil fields than before. For example, 28 deep ocean rigs operate in the deep waters of the Gulf of Mexico.
    a. What effect do you think deep ocean sources have had on the world oil price?
    b. Who will benefit from drilling for oil in the Gulf of Mexico? Explain your answer.

33. Water is a natural resource that is plentiful in Canada but not plentiful in Arizona and southern California.
    a. If Canadians start to export bulk water to Arizona and southern California, what do you predict will be the effect on the price of bulk water?
    b. Will Canada eventually run out of water?
    c. Do you think the Hotelling Principle applies to Canada's water? Explain why or why not.

Economics in the News

34. After you have studied *Reading Between the Lines* on pp. 432–433 answer the following questions.
    a. Name some jobs for which future employment will expand and some for which it will shrink.
    b. What are the influences on the demand for labor that bring an increase in demand and what are the influences that bring a decrease in demand?
    c. Why is an increase in the demand for nurses likely to bring a similar increase in the supply of nurses?
    d. Draw a graph of the market for factory workers in 2008 and 2018. Show the effects of a decrease in the demand for factory workers with no change in the supply on the employment and wage rate of factory workers.
    e. If the outcome you've shown in part (d) occurred, explain how the incentives faced by young workers just entering the labor force would be affected.
    f. On your graph of the labor market in part (d), show how you would expect the supply of factory workers to change by 2018 and show your predicted level of employment and wage rate of factory workers in 2018.

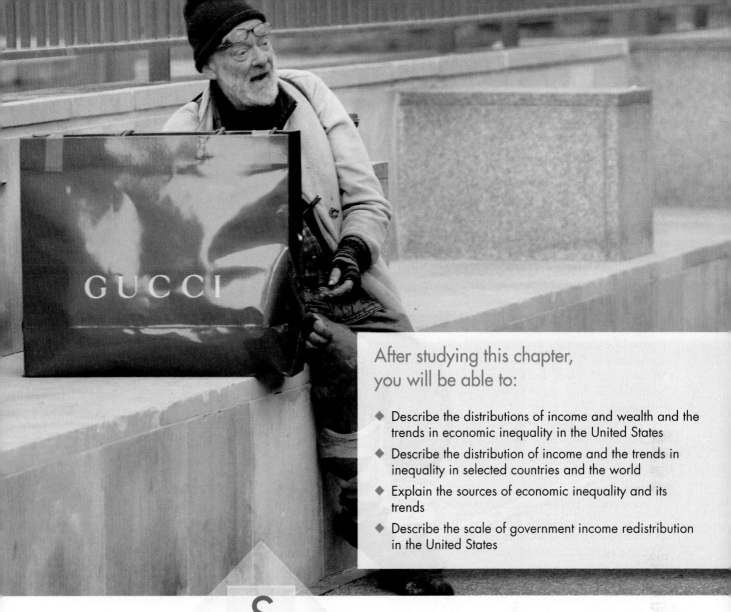

19
ECONOMIC INEQUALITY

After studying this chapter,
you will be able to:

- ◆ Describe the distributions of income and wealth and the trends in economic inequality in the United States
- ◆ Describe the distribution of income and the trends in inequality in selected countries and the world
- ◆ Explain the sources of economic inequality and its trends
- ◆ Describe the scale of government income redistribution in the United States

Six percent of adults in Los Angeles County, some 375,000 people, experienced homelessness during the past five years. In this same county is Beverly Hills, with its mansions that are home to some fabulously wealthy movie stars. Los Angeles is not unusual. In New York City, where Donald Trump has built a luxury apartment tower with a penthouse priced at $13 million, more than 20,000 people, 9,000 of whom are children, seek a bed every night in a shelter for the homeless. Extreme poverty and extreme wealth exist side by side in every major city in the United States and in most parts of the world.

How does the distribution of income in the United States compare with that in other countries? Is income distributed more unequally or less unequally in the United States than in other countries? Are the rich getting richer and the poor getting poorer? Or are incomes becoming more equal?

In this chapter, we study economic inequality—its extent, its sources, and the things governments do to make it less extreme. We begin by looking at some facts about economic inequality in the United States. We end, in *Reading Between the Lines*, by looking at the widening gap between the incomes of top CEOs and average wage rates.

◆ Economic Inequality in the United States

The most commonly used measure of economic inequality is the distribution of annual income. The Census Bureau defines income as **money income**, which equals *market income* plus cash payments to households by government. **Market income** equals wages, interest, rent, and profit earned in factor markets, before paying income taxes.

The Distribution of Income

Figure 19.1 shows the distribution of annual income across the 117.5 million households in the United States in 2009. Note that the *x*-axis measures household income and the *y*-axis is percentage of households.

The most common household income, called the *mode* income, was received by the 6 percent of the households whose incomes fell between $20,000 and $25,000. The value of $22,000 marked on the figure is an estimate.

The middle level of household income in 2009, called the *median* income, was $49,777. Fifty percent of households have an income that exceeds the median and fifty percent have an income below the median.

The average household money income in 2009, called the *mean* income, was $67,976. This number equals total household income, about $8 trillion, divided by the 117.5 million households. You can see in Fig. 19.1 that the mode is less than the median and that the median is less than the mean. This feature of the distribution of income tells us that there are more households with low incomes than with high incomes. It also tells us that some of the high incomes are very high.

The income distribution in Fig. 19.1 is called a *positively skewed* distribution, which means that it has a long tail of high values. This distribution contrasts with the bell that describes the distribution of people's heights. In a bell-shaped distribution, the mean, median, and mode are all equal.

Another way of looking at the distribution of income is to measure the percentage of total income received by each given percentage of households. Data are reported for five groups—called *quintiles* or fifth shares—each consisting of 20 percent of households.

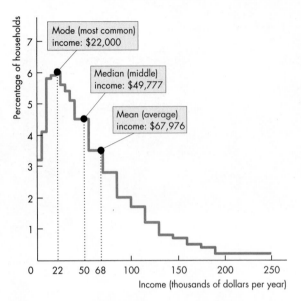

FIGURE 19.1   The Distribution of Income in the United States in 2009

The distribution of income is positively skewed. The mode (most common) income is less than the median (middle) income, which in turn is less than the mean (average) income. The distribution shown here ends at $250,000 because data above that level are not available, but the distribution goes up to several million dollars a year.

Source of data: U.S. Bureau of the Census, "Income, Poverty, and Health Insurance Coverage in the United States: 2007," *Current Population Reports*, P-60-235, (Washington, DC: U.S. Government Printing Office, 2008).

Figure 19.2 shows the distribution based on these shares in 2009. The poorest 20 percent of households received 3.4 percent of total income; the second poorest 20 percent received 8.6 percent of total income; the middle 20 percent received 14.6 percent of total income; the next highest 20 percent received 23.2 percent of total income; and the highest 20 percent received 50.2 percent of total income.

The distribution of income in Fig. 19.1 and the quintile shares in Fig. 19.2 tell us that income is distributed unequally. But we need a way of comparing the distribution of income in different periods and using different measures. A clever graphical tool called the *Lorenz curve* enables us to make such comparisons.

FIGURE 19.2   U.S. Quintile Shares in 2009

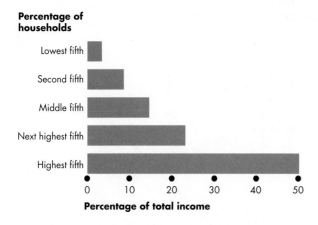

Percentage of households

Households (percentage)	Income (percentage of total income)
Lowest 20	3.4
Second 20	8.6
Middle 20	14.6
Next highest 20	23.2
Highest 20	50.2

In 2009, the poorest 20 percent of households received 3.4 percent of total income; the second poorest 20 percent received 8.6 percent; the middle 20 percent received 14.6 percent; the next highest 20 percent received 23.2 percent; and the highest 20 percent received 50.2 percent.

Source of data: See Fig. 19.1.

myeconlab animation

The Income Lorenz Curve

The income **Lorenz curve** graphs the cumulative percentage of income against the cumulative percentage of households. Figure 19.3 shows the income Lorenz curve using the quintile shares from Fig. 19.2. The table shows the percentage of income of each quintile group. For example, row *A* tells us that the lowest quintile of households receives 3.4 percent of total income. The table also shows the *cumulative* percentages of households and income. For example, row *B* tells us that the lowest two quintiles (lowest 40 percent) of households receive 12.0 percent of total income (3.4 percent for the lowest quintile plus 8.6 percent for the next lowest).

FIGURE 19.3   The Income Lorenz Curve in 2009

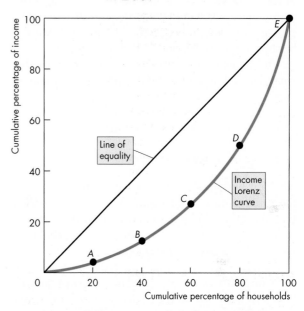

	Households		Income	
	Percentage	Cumulative percentage	Percentage	Cumulative percentage
A	Lowest 20	20	3.4	3.4
B	Second 20	40	8.6	12.0
C	Middle 20	60	14.6	26.6
D	Next highest 20	80	23.2	49.8
E	Highest 20	100	50.2	100.0

The cumulative percentage of income is graphed against the cumulative percentage of households. Points *A* through *E* on the Lorenz curve correspond to the rows of the table. If incomes were distributed equally, each 20 percent of households would receive 20 percent of total income and the Lorenz curve would fall along the line of equality. The Lorenz curve shows that income is unequally distributed.

Source of data: See Fig. 19.1.

 myeconlab animation

The Lorenz curve provides a direct visual clue about the degree of income inequality by comparing it with the line of equality. This line, identified in Fig. 19.3, shows what the Lorenz curve would be if everyone had the same level of income.

If income were distributed equally across all the households, each quintile would receive 20 percent of total income and the cumulative percentages of income received would equal the cumulative percentages of households, so the Lorenz curve would be the straight line labeled "Line of equality."

The actual distribution of income shown by the curve labeled "Income Lorenz curve" can be compared with the Line of equality. The closer the Lorenz curve is to the line of equality, the more equal is the distribution of income.

The Distribution of Wealth

The distribution of wealth provides another way of measuring economic inequality. A household's **wealth** is the value of the things that it owns at a *point in time*. In contrast, income is the amount that the household receives over a given *period of time*.

Figure 19.4 shows the Lorenz curve for wealth in the United States in 1998 (the most recent year for which we have wealth distribution data). The median household wealth in 1998 was $60,700. Wealth is extremely unequally distributed, and for this reason, the data are grouped by seven unequal groups of households. The poorest 40 percent of households own only 0.2 percent of total wealth (row *A'* in the table in Fig. 19.4). The richest 20 percent of households own 83.4 percent of total wealth. Because this group owns almost all the wealth, we need to break the group into smaller parts. That is what rows *D'* through *G'* do. The richest 1 percent of households in row *G'* own 38.1 percent of total wealth.

Figure 19.4 shows the income Lorenz curve (from Fig. 19.3) alongside the wealth Lorenz curve. You can see that the Lorenz curve for wealth is much farther away from the line of equality than is the Lorenz curve for income, which means that the distribution of wealth is much more unequal than the distribution of income.

Wealth or Income?

We've seen that wealth is much more unequally distributed than is income. Which distribution provides the better description of the degree of inequality? To answer this question, we need to think about the connection between wealth and income.

Wealth is a stock of assets, and income is the flow of earnings that results from the stock of wealth. Suppose that a person owns assets worth

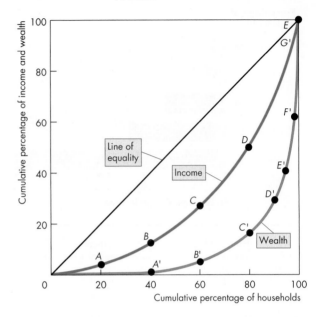

FIGURE 19.4   Lorenz Curves for Income and Wealth

Households			Wealth		
	Percentage	Cumulative percentage		Percentage	Cumulative percentage
A'	Lowest 40	40		0.2	0.2
B'	Next 20	60		4.5	4.7
C'	Next 20	80		11.9	16.6
D'	Next 10	90		12.5	29.1
E'	Next 5	95		11.5	40.6
F'	Next 4	99		21.3	61.9
G'	Highest 1	100		38.1	100.0

The cumulative percentage of wealth is graphed against the cumulative percentage of households. Points *A'* through *G'* on the Lorenz curve for wealth correspond to the rows of the table. By comparing the Lorenz curves for income and wealth, we can see that wealth is distributed much more unequally than is income.

Sources of data: For the income distribution data, see Fig. 19.1. The Wealth distribution data are from Edward N. Wolff, "Recent Trends in Wealth Ownership, 1938–1998," Jerome Levy Economics Institute Working Paper No. 300, April 2000.

myeconlab   animation

$1 million—has a wealth of $1 million. If the rate of return on assets is 5 percent a year, then this person receives an income of $50,000 a year from those assets. We can describe this person's economic condition by using either the wealth of $1 million or the income of $50,000. When the rate of return is 5 percent a year, $1 million of wealth equals $50,000 of income in perpetuity. Wealth and income are just different ways of looking at the same thing.

But in Fig. 19.4, the distribution of wealth is more unequal than the distribution of income. Why? It is because the wealth data do not include the value of human capital, while the income data measure income from all wealth, including human capital.

Think about Lee and Peter, two people with equal income and equal wealth. Lee's wealth is human capital and his entire income is from employment. Peter's wealth is in the form of investments in stocks and bonds and his entire income is from these investments.

When a Census Bureau agent interviews Lee and Peter in a national income and wealth survey, their incomes are recorded as being equal, but Lee's wealth is recorded as zero, while Peter's wealth is recorded as the value of his investments. Peter looks vastly more wealthy than Lee in the survey data.

Because the national survey of wealth excludes human capital, the income distribution is a more accurate measure of economic inequality than the wealth distribution.

Annual or Lifetime Income and Wealth?

A typical household's income changes over its life cycle. Income starts out low, grows to a peak when the household's workers reach retirement age, and then falls after retirement. Also, a typical household's wealth changes over time. Like income, it starts out low, grows to a peak at the point of retirement, and falls after retirement.

Think about three households with identical lifetime incomes, one young, one middle-aged, and one retired. The middle-aged household has the highest income and wealth, the retired household has the lowest, and the young household falls in the middle. The distributions of annual income and wealth in a given year are unequal, but the distributions of lifetime income and wealth are equal.

The data on inequality share the bias that you've just seen. Inequality in annual income and wealth data overstates lifetime inequality because households are at different stages in their life cycles.

Trends in Inequality

To see trends in the income distribution, we need a measure that enables us to rank distributions on the scale of more equal and less equal. No perfect scale exists, but one that is much used is called the Gini ratio. The **Gini ratio** is based on the Lorenz curve and equals the ratio of the area between the line of equality and the Lorenz curve to the entire area beneath the line of equality. The larger the Gini ratio, the greater is the degree of income inequality. If income is equally distributed, the Lorenz curve is the same as the line of equality, so the Gini ratio is zero. If one person has all the income and everyone else has none, the Gini ratio is 1.

Figure 19.5 shows the U.S. Gini ratio from 1970 to 2009. The figure shows breaks in the data in 1992 and 2000 because in those years, the Census

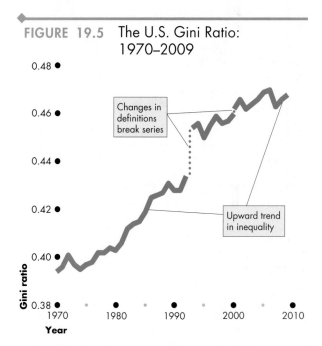

FIGURE 19.5   The U.S. Gini Ratio: 1970–2009

Measured by the Gini ratio, the distribution of income in the United States became more unequal from 1970 to 2009. The percentage of income earned by the richest households increased through these years. Changes in definitions make the numbers before and after 1992 and before and after 2000 not comparable. Despite the breaks in the data, the trends are still visible.

Source of data: See Fig. 19.1.

Economics in Action

The Rich Get Richer, but School Still Pays

The percentage of Americans who tell the Gallup poll that wealth should be distributed more evenly has been rising. In 2008, it reached 70 percent. A reason might be the trend in the incomes of the super rich. Emmanuel Saez, an economics professor at the University of California, Berkeley, used tax returns data to get the numbers graphed in Fig. 1.

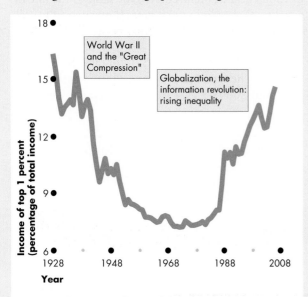

Figure 1 The Income Shares of the Top One Percent

Source of data: Adapted from Table II, "Income Inequality in the United States, 1913–1998" by Thomas Piketty and Emmanuel Saez. *Quarterly Journal of Economics,* February 2003, Vol. 118, Issue 1. © The President and Fellows of the Harvard College an MIT.

After decades of a falling share, starting in 1981, the share of income received by the richest one percent began a steady climb. By 2006 (the latest year in Professor Saez's database), the richest one percent were earning 14.6 percent of the nation's income.

Movie stars, sports stars, and the CEOs of large corporations are among the super rich. People who scratch out a living doing seasonal work on farms earn the lowest incomes. Aside from these extremes, what are the characteristics of people who earn high incomes and people who earn low incomes? Figure 2 answers this question. (The data are for 2009 but the patterns are persistent).

Education A postgraduate education is the main source of a high income. A person with a professional degree (such as a medical or law degree), earns (on average) $124,000—more than double the median income. Just completing high school raises a person's income by more than $14,000 a year; and getting a bachelor's degree adds another $36,000 a year. The average income of people who have not completed 9th grade is $22,000—less than half the median income.

Type of Household Married couples earn more, on the average, than people who live alone. A married couple earns about $72,000. In contrast, men who live alone earn about $48,000, and women who live alone earn only $33,000.

Age of Householder Households with the oldest and youngest householders have lower incomes than do those with middle-aged householders. When the householder is aged between 45 and 54, household income

Bureau changed its method of collecting the data and definitions, so the numbers before and after the breaks can't be compared. Despite the breaks in the series, the Gini ratio has clearly increased, which means that on this measure, incomes have become less equal.

The major change is that the share of income received by the richest households has increased. You can see in *Economics in Action* above how the income of the richest one percent has increased. No one knows for sure *why* this trend has occurred, but a possibility that we'll explore in the next section is that technological change has increased the value of marginal product of high-skilled workers and decreased the value of marginal product of low-skilled workers.

Poverty

Households at the low end of the income distribution are so poor that they are considered to be living in poverty. **Poverty** is a situation in which a household's income is too low to be able to buy the quantities of food, shelter, and clothing that are deemed necessary. Poverty is a relative concept. Millions of people living in Africa and Asia survive on incomes of less than $400 a year. In the United States, the poverty level is calculated each year by the Social Security Administration. In 2009, the poverty level for a four-person household was an income of $21,756. In that year, 44 million Americans—14 percent of the population— lived in households that had incomes below the

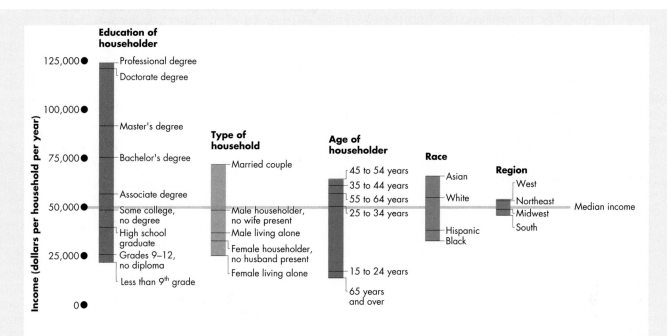

Figure 2 The Distribution of Income by Selected Household Characteristics

Source of data: See Fig. 19.1.

averages $64,000. And when the householder is aged between 35 and 44, household income averages $61,000. When the householder is aged between 15 and 24, average household income is $31,000. And for householders over 65, the average household income is also $31,000.

Race and Ethnicity White Americans have an average income of $54,000, while black Americans have an average income of $33,000. People of Hispanic origin

are a bit better off, with an average income of $38,000. Asians are best off with an average income of $65,000.

Region People who live in the West and Northeast earn more, on average, than people who live in the Midwest and the South. While the region does make a difference, its magnitude is small compared to the dominating effect of education.

The bottom line: School pays and so does marriage.

poverty level. Many of these households benefited from Medicare and Medicaid, two government programs that aid the poorest households and lift some of them above the poverty level.

The distribution of poverty by race is unequal: 9.4 percent of white Americans live in poor households compared to 25 percent of Hispanic-origin Americans and 26 percent of black Americans. Poverty is also influenced by household status. More than 28 percent of households in which the householder is a female with no husband present had incomes below the poverty level.

Despite the widening of the income distribution, poverty rates are falling.

REVIEW QUIZ

1 Which is distributed more unequally, income or wealth? Why? Which is the better measure?

2 From 1970 to 2009 did the distribution of income become more equal or more unequal? How did the richest quintile's share change?

3 What are the main characteristics of people who earn large incomes and who earn small incomes?

4 What is poverty and how does its incidence vary across the races?

You can work these questions in Study Plan 19.1 and get instant feedback.

◆ Inequality in the World Economy

Which countries have the greatest economic inequality and which have the least and the greatest equality? Where does the United States rank? Is it one of the most equal or most unequal or somewhere in the middle? And how much inequality is there in the world as a whole when we consider the entire world as a single global economy?

We'll answer these questions by first looking at the income distribution in a selection of countries and then by examining features of the global distribution of income.

Income Distributions in Selected Countries

By inspecting the income distribution data for every country, we can compare the degree of income inequality and identify the countries with the most inequality and those with the least inequality.

Figure 19.6 summarizes some extremes and shows where the United States lies in the range of degrees of income inequality.

Look first at the numbers in the table. They tell us that in Brazil and South Africa, the poorest 20 percent of households receive only 2 percent of total income while the highest 20 percent receive 65 percent of total income. An average person in the highest quintile receives 32.5 times the income of an average person in the lowest quintile.

Contrast these numbers with those for Finland and Sweden. In these countries, the poorest 20 percent receive 8 percent of total income and the highest 20 percent receive 35 percent. So an average person in the highest quintile receives 4.4 times the income of an average person in the lowest quintile.

The numbers for the United States lie between these extremes with an average person in the highest quintile receiving just under 10 times the amount received by an average person in the lowest quintile.

Brazil and South Africa are extremes not matched in any other major country or region. Inequality is large in these countries because they have a relatively small but rich European population and a large and relatively poor indigenous population.

Finland and Sweden are extremes, but they are not unusual. Income distributions similar to these are found in many European countries in which governments pursue aggressive income redistribution policies.

We look next at the global income distribution.

FIGURE 19.6   Lorenz Curves Compared

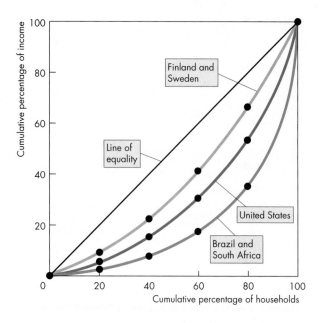

The table shows the percentages of total income received by each quintile. The figure shows the cumulative percentage of income graphed against the cumulative percentage of households. The data and the Lorenz curves show that income is distributed most unequally in Brazil and South Africa and least unequally in Finland and Sweden. The degree of income inequality in the United States lies between these extremes.

	Percentage of total income[1]		
Households	**Brazil and South Africa**	**United States**	**Finland and Sweden**
Lowest 20 percent	2	5	8
Second 20 percent	5	10	14
Middle 20 percent	10	16	20
Next highest 20 percent	18	22	23
Highest 20 percent	65	47	35

Sources of data: Brazil, South Africa, Finland, and Sweden, Klaus W. Deininger and Lyn Squire, Measuring Income Inequality Database, World Bank, http://go.worldbank.org/. United States, See Fig. 19.1.

[1]The data are based on income *after* redistribution. See pp. 455–457 for an account of income redistribution in the United States.

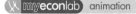 animation

Global Inequality and Its Trends

The global distribution of income is much more unequal than the distribution within any one country. The reason is that many countries, especially in Africa and Asia, are in a pre-industrial stage of economic development and are poor, while industrial countries such as the United States are rich. When we look at the distribution of income across the entire world population that goes from the low income of the poorest African to the high income of the richest American, we observe a very large degree of inequality.

To put some raw numbers on this inequality, start with the poorest. Measured in the value of the U.S. dollar in 2005, a total of 3 billion people or 50 percent of the world population live on $2.50 a day or less. Another 2 billion people or 30 percent of the world population live on more than $2.50 but less than $10 a day. So 5 billion people or 80 percent of the world population live on $10 a day or less.

In contrast, in the rich United States, the *average* person has an income of $115 per day and an average person in the highest income quintile has an income of $460 a day.

So the average American earns 46 times the income of one of the world's 3 billion poorest people and more than 11.5 times the income of 80 percent of the people who live in developing economies. An American with the average income in the highest quintile earns 184 times that of the world's poorest people but only 15 times that of an average bottom quintile American.

World Gini Ratio We can compare world inequality with U.S. inequality by comparing Gini ratios. You saw that the U.S. Gini ratio in 2009 was about 0.47. The world Gini ratio is about 0.64. Recalling the interpretation of the Gini ratio in terms of the Lorenz curve, the world Lorenz curve lies much farther from the line of equality than the U.S. Lorenz curve.

World Trend You saw (in Fig. 19.5 on p. 445) that incomes have become more unequal in the United States—the Gini ratio has increased. The same trends are found in most economies. Increased income inequality is a big issue in two of the world's largest and poorer nations, China and India. In these two economies, urban middle classes are getting richer at a faster pace than the rural farmers.

Despite greater inequality within countries, the world is becoming *less* unequal. Figure 19.7 shows

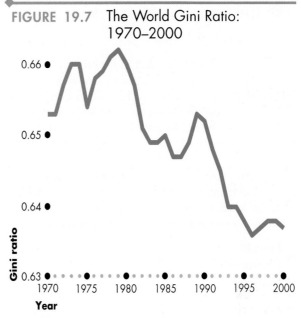

FIGURE 19.7   The World Gini Ratio: 1970–2000

Measured by the Gini ratio, the distribution of income in the entire world became more equal between 1970 and 2000.

Source of data: From "The World Distribution of Income: Falling Poverty and ... Convergence, Period" by Xavier Sala-i-Martin, *Quarterly Journal of Economics*, Vol. 121, No. 2, pp. 351-397, May 2006. Reprinted by permission of MIT Press Journals.

 animation

this trend toward less inequality as measured by the world Gini ratio. How can the world income distribution become less unequal while individual countries become more unequal? The answer is that average incomes in poorer countries are rising much faster than average incomes in rich countries. While the gap between rich and poor is widening within countries, it is narrowing across countries.

◼ REVIEW QUIZ

1 In which countries are incomes distributed most unequally and least unequally?
2 Which income distribution is more unequal and why: the income distribution in the United States or in the entire world?
3 How can incomes become *more* unequally distributed within countries and *less* unequally distributed across countries?

You can work these questions in Study Plan 19.2 and get instant feedback.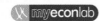

The Sources of Economic Inequality

We've described some key facts about economic inequality and its trends and our task now is to explain those facts. We began this task in Chapter 18 by learning about the forces that influence demand and supply in the markets for labor, capital, and land. We're now going to deepen our understanding of these forces.

Inequality arises from unequal labor market outcomes and from unequal ownership of capital. We'll begin by looking at labor markets and three features of them that contribute to differences in income:

■ Human capital
■ Discrimination
■ Contests among superstars

Human Capital

A clerk in a law firm earns less than a tenth of the amount earned by the attorney he assists. An operating room assistant earns less than a tenth of the amount earned by the surgeon with whom she works. A bank teller earns less than a tenth of the amount earned by the bank's CEO. Some of the differences in these earnings arise from differences in human capital.

To see the influence of human capital on labor incomes, consider the example of a law clerk and the attorney he assists. (The same reasoning can be applied to an operating room assistant and surgeon, or a bank teller and bank CEO.)

Demand, Supply, and Wage Rates An attorney performs many tasks that a law clerk cannot perform. Imagine an untrained law clerk cross-examining a witness in a complicated trial. The tasks that the attorney performs are valued highly by her clients who willingly pay for her services. Using a term that you learned in Chapter 18, an attorney has a *high value of marginal product*, and a higher value of marginal product than her law clerk. But you also learned in Chapter 18 that the value of marginal product of labor determines (is the same as) the demand for labor. So, because an attorney has a high value of marginal product, there is also has a high demand for her services.

To become an attorney, a person must acquire human capital. But human capital is costly to acquire. This cost—an opportunity cost—includes expenditures on tuition and textbooks. It also includes forgone earnings during the years spent in college and law school. It might also include low earnings doing on-the-job training in a law office during the summer.

Because the human capital needed to supply attorney services is costly to acquire, a person's willingness to supply these services reflects this cost. The supply of attorney services is smaller than the supply of law-clerk services.

The demand for and supply of each type of labor determine the wage rates that each type earns. Attorneys earn a higher wage rate than law clerks because the demand for attorneys is greater and the supply of attorneys is smaller. The gap between the wage rates reflects the higher value of marginal product of an attorney (demand) and the cost of acquiring human capital (supply).

Do Education and Training Pay? You know that an attorney earns much more than a law clerk, but does human capital add more to earning power generally and on average? The answer is that it does. Rates of return on high school and college education have been estimated to be in the range of 5 percent to 10 percent a year after allowing for inflation, which suggests that a college degree is a better investment than almost any other that a person can undertake

Human capital differences help to explain much of the inequality that we observe. High-income households tend to be better educated, middle-aged, Asian or white, and married couples (see the figure on p. 447). Human capital differences are correlated with these household characteristics. Education contributes directly to human capital. Age contributes indirectly to human capital because older workers have more experience than younger workers. Human capital differences can also explain a small part of the inequality associated with sex and race. A larger proportion of men (25 percent) than women (20 percent) have completed four years of college, and a larger proportion of whites (24 percent) than blacks (13 percent) have completed a bachelor's degree or higher. These differences in education levels among the sexes and the races are becoming smaller, but they have not been eliminated.

Career interruptions can decrease human capital. A person (most often a woman) who interrupts a career to raise young children usually returns to the labor force with a lower earning capacity than a similar person who has kept working. Likewise, a person who has suffered a spell of unemployment often finds a new job at a lower wage rate than that of a similar person who has not been unemployed.

Trends in Inequality Explained by Technological Change and Globalization

You've seen that high-income households have earned an increasing share of total income while low-income households have earned a decreasing share: The distribution of income in the United States has become more unequal. Technological change and globalization are two possible sources of this increased inequality.

Technological Change Information technologies such as computers and laser scanners are *substitutes* for low-skilled labor: They perform tasks that previously were performed by low-skilled labor. The introduction of these technologies has lowered the marginal product and the demand for low-skilled labor. These same technologies require high-skilled labor to design, program, and run them. High-skilled labor and the information technologies are *complements*. So the introduction of these technologies has increased the marginal product and demand for high-skilled labor.

Figure 19.8 illustrates the effects on wages and employment. The supply of low-skilled labor (part a) and that of high-skilled labor (part b) are S, and initially, the demand in each market is D_0. The low-skill wage rate is \$5 an hour, and the high-skill wage rate is \$10 an hour. The demand for low-skilled labor decreases to D_1 in part (a) and the demand for high-skilled labor increases to D_1 in part (b). The low-skill wage rate falls to \$4 an hour and the high-skill wage rate rises to \$15 an hour.

Globalization The entry of China and other developing countries into the global economy has lowered the prices of many manufactured goods. Lower prices for the firm's output lowers the value of marginal product of the firm's workers and decreases the demand for their labor. A situation like that in Fig. 19.8(a) occurs. The wage rate falls, and employment shrinks.

At the same time, the growing global economy increases the demand for services that employ high-skilled workers, and the value of marginal product and the demand for high-skilled labor increases. A situation like that in Fig. 19.8(b) occurs. The wage rate rises, and employment opportunities for high-skilled workers expand.

FIGURE 19.8   Explaining the Trend in Income Distribution

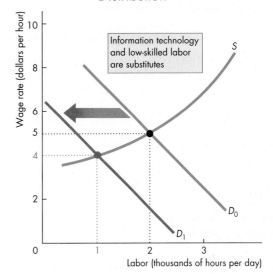

(a) A decrease in demand for low-skilled labor

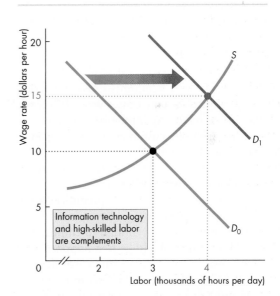

(b) An increase in demand for high-skilled labor

Low-skilled labor in part (a) and information technologies are substitutes. Advances in information technology decrease the demand for low-skilled labor and lower its wage rate. High-skilled labor in part (b) and information technologies are complements. Advances in information technology increase the demand for high-skilled labor and raise its wage rate.

myeconlab   animation

Discrimination

Human capital differences can explain some of the economic inequality that we observe. Discrimination is another possible source of inequality.

Suppose that black females and white males have identical abilities as investment advisors. Figure 19.9 shows the supply curves of black females, S_{BF} (in part a), and of white males, S_{WM} (in part b). The value of marginal product of investment advisors, shown by the two curves labeled *VMP* in parts (a) and (b), is the same for both groups.

If everyone is free of race and sex prejudice, the market determines a wage rate of $40,000 a year for investment advisors. But if the customers are prejudiced against women and minorities, this prejudice is reflected in the wage rate and employment.

Suppose that the perceived value of marginal product of the black females, when discriminated against, is VMP_{DA}. Suppose that the perceived value of marginal product for white males, the group discriminated in favor of, is VMP_{DF}. With these *VMP* curves, black females earn $20,000 a year and only 1,000 black females work as investment advisors. White males earn $60,000 a year, and 3,000 of them work as investment advisors.

Counteracting Forces Economists disagree about whether prejudice actually causes wage differentials, and one line of reasoning implies that it does not. In the above example, customers who buy from white men pay a higher service charge for investment advice than do the customers who buy from black women. This price difference acts as an incentive to encourage people who are prejudiced to buy from the people against whom they are prejudiced. This force could be strong enough to eliminate the effects of discrimination altogether. Suppose, as is true in manufacturing, that a firm's customers never meet its workers. If such a firm discriminates against women or minorities, it can't compete with firms who hire these groups because its costs are higher than those of the nonprejudiced firms. Only firms that do not discriminate survive in a competitive industry.

Whether because of discrimination or from some other source, women and visible minorities do earn lower incomes than white males. Another possible source of lower wage rates of women arises from differences in the relative degree of specialization of women and men.

FIGURE 19.9 Discrimination

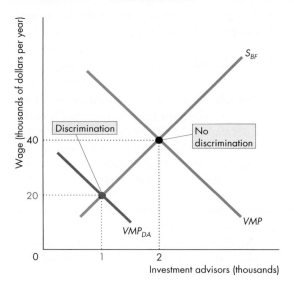

(a) Black females

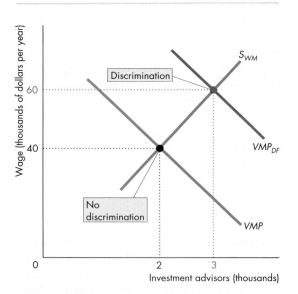

(b) White males

With no discrimination, the wage rate is $40,000 a year and 2,000 of each group are hired. With discrimination against blacks and women, the value of marginal product curve in part (a) is VMP_{DA} and that in part (b) is VMP_{DF}. The wage rate for black women falls to $20,000 a year, and only 1,000 are employed. The wage rate for white men rises to $60,000 a year, and 3,000 are employed.

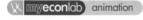

Differences in the Degree of Specialization Couples must choose how to allocate their time between working for a wage and doing jobs in the home, such as cooking, cleaning, shopping, organizing vacations, and, most important, bearing and raising children. Let's look at the choices of Bob and Sue.

Bob might specialize in earning an income and Sue in taking care of the home. Or Sue might specialize in earning an income and Bob in taking care of the home. Or both of them might earn an income and share home production jobs.

The allocation they choose depends on their preferences and on their earning potential. The choice of an increasing number of households is for each person to diversify between earning an income and doing some household chores. But in most households, Bob will specialize in earning an income and Sue will both earn an income and bear a larger share of the task of running the home. With this allocation, Bob will probably earn more than Sue. If Sue devotes time and effort to ensuring Bob's mental and physical well-being, the quality of Bob's market labor will be higher than it would be if he were diversified. If the roles were reversed, Sue would be able to supply market labor that earns more than Bob's.

To test whether the degree of specialization accounts for earnings differences between the sexes, economists have compared the incomes of never-married men and women. They have found that, on the average, with equal amounts of human capital, the wages of these two groups are the same.

Contests Among Superstars

The differences in income that arise from differences in human capital are important and affect a large proportion of the population. But human capital differences can't account for some of the really large income differences.

The super rich—those in the top one percent of the income distribution whose income share has been rising—earn vastly more than can be explained by human capital differences. What makes a person super rich?

A clue to the answer is provided by thinking about the super rich in tennis and golf. What makes tennis players and golfers special is that their earnings depend on where they finish in a tournament. When Serena Williams won the Wimbledon Championship in 2010, she received £1,000,000 or $1,540,000. The runner-up in this event, Russian Vera Zvonareva,

received £500,000. So Serena earned double the amount earned by Vera. And she earned 88 times the amount received by the players who lost in the first round of the tournament.

It is true that Serena Williams has a lot of human capital. She practices hard and long and is a remarkable athlete. But anyone who is good enough to get into a tennis Grand Slam tournament is similarly well equipped with human capital and has spent a similar number of long hours in training and practice. It isn't human capital that explains the differences in earnings. It is the tournament and the prize differences that accounts for the large differences in earnings.

But three questions jump out: First, why do we reward superstar tennis players (and golfers) with prizes for winning a contest? Second, why are the prizes so different? And third, do the principles that apply on the tennis court (and golf course) apply more generally?

Why Prizes for a Contest? The answer to this question (which was noted in Chapter 5, see p. 106) is that contests with prizes do a good job of allocating scarce resources efficiently when the efforts of the participants are hard to monitor and reward directly. There is only one winner, but many people work hard in an attempt to be that person. So a great deal of diligent effort is induced by a contest.

Why Are Prizes So Different? The prizes need to be substantially different to induce enough effort. If the winner received 10 percent more than the runner up, the gain from being the winner would be insufficient to encourage anyone to work hard enough. Someone would win but no one would put in much effort. Tennis matches would be boring, golf scores would be high, and no one would be willing to pay to see these sports. Big differences are necessary to induce a big enough effort to generate the quality of performance that people are willing to pay to see.

Does the Principle Apply More Generally? Winner-takes-all isn't confined to tennis and golf. Movie stars, superstars in baseball, basketball, football, and ice hockey, and top corporate executives can all be viewed as participants in contests that decide the winners. The prize for the winner is an income at least double that of the runner up and many multiples of the incomes of those who drop out earlier in the tournament.

Do Contests Among Superstars Explain the Trend?
Contests among superstars can explain large differences in incomes. But can contests explain the trend toward greater inequality with an increasing share of total income going to the super rich as shown on p. 445?

An idea first suggested by University of Chicago economist Sherwin Rosen suggests that a winner-takes-all contest can explain the trend. The key is that globalization has increased the market reach of the winner and increased the spread between the winner and the runners-up.

Global television audiences now watch all the world's major sporting events and the total revenue generated by advertising spots during these events has increased. Competition among networks and cable and satellite television distributors has increased the fees that event organizers receive. And to attract the top star performers, prize money has increased and the winner gets the biggest share of the prize pot.

So the prizes in sports have become bigger and the share of income going to the "winner" has increased.

A similar story can be told about superstars and the super rich in business. As the cost of doing business on a global scale has fallen, more and more businesses have become global in their reach. Not only are large multinational corporations sourcing their inputs from far afield and selling in every country, they are also recruiting their top executives from a global talent pool. With a larger source of talent, and a larger total revenue, firms must make the "prize"—the reward for the top job—more attractive to compete for the best managers.

We've examined some sources of inequality in the labor market. Let's now look at the way inequality arises from unequal ownership of capital.

Unequal Wealth

You've seen that wealth inequality—excluding human capital—is much greater than income inequality. This greater wealth inequality arises from two sources: life-cycle saving patterns and transfers of wealth from one generation to the next.

Life-Cycle Saving Patterns Over a family's life cycle, wealth starts out at zero or perhaps less than zero. A student who has financed education all the way through graduate school might have lots of human capital and an outstanding student loan of $60,000. This person has negative wealth. Gradually loans get paid off and a retirement fund is accumulated. At the point of retiring from full-time work, the family has maximum wealth. Then, during its retirement years, the family spends its wealth. This life-cycle pattern means that much of the wealth is owned by people in their sixties.

Intergenerational Transfers Some households inherit wealth from the previous generation. Some save more than enough on which to live during retirement and transfer wealth to the next generation. But these intergenerational transfers of wealth do not always increase wealth inequality. If a generation that has a high income saves a large part of that income and leaves wealth to a succeeding generation that has a lower income, this transfer decreases the degree of inequality. But one feature of intergenerational transfers of wealth leads to increased inequality: wealth concentration through marriage.

Marriage and Wealth Concentration People tend to marry within their own socioeconomic class—a phenomenon called *assortative mating*. In everyday language, "like attracts like." Although there is a good deal of folklore that "opposites attract," perhaps such Cinderella tales appeal to us because they are so rare in reality. Wealthy people seek wealthy partners.

Because of assortative mating, wealth becomes more concentrated in a small number of families and the distribution of wealth becomes more unequal.

REVIEW QUIZ

1 What role does human capital play in accounting for income inequality?
2 What role might discrimination play in accounting for income inequality?
3 What role might contests among superstars play in accounting for income inequality?
4 How might technological change and globalization explain trends in the distribution of income?
5 Does inherited wealth make the distribution of income less equal or more equal?

You can work these questions in Study Plan 19.3 and get instant feedback.

Next, we're going to see how taxes and government programs redistribute income and decrease the degree of economic inequality.

Income Redistribution

The three main ways in which governments in the United States redistribute income are

- Income taxes
- Income maintenance programs
- Subsidized services

Income Taxes

Income taxes may be progressive, regressive, or proportional. A **progressive income tax** is one that taxes income at an average rate that increases as income increases. A **regressive income tax** is one that taxes income at an average rate that decreases as income increases. A **proportional income tax** (also called a *flat-rate income tax*) is one that taxes income at a constant average rate, regardless of the level of income.

The income tax rates that apply in the United States are composed of two parts: federal and state taxes. Some cities, such as New York City, also have an income tax. There is variety in the detailed tax arrangements in the individual states, but the tax system, at both the federal and state levels, is progressive. The poorest working households receive money from the government through an earned income tax credit. Successively higher-income households pay 10 percent, 15 percent, 25 percent, 28 percent, 33 percent, and 35 percent of each additional dollar earned.

Income Maintenance Programs

Three main types of programs redistribute income by making direct payments (in cash, services, or vouchers) to people in the lower part of the income distribution. They are

- Social Security programs
- Unemployment compensation
- Welfare programs

Social Security Programs The main Social Security program is OASDHI—Old Age, Survivors, Disability, and Health Insurance. Monthly cash payments to retired or disabled workers or their surviving spouses and children are paid for by compulsory payroll taxes on both employers and employees. In 2010, total Social Security expenditure was budgeted at $736 billion, and the standard monthly Social Security check for a married couple was a bit more than $1,892 in 2010.

The other component of Social Security is Medicare, which provides hospital and health insurance for the elderly and disabled.

Unemployment Compensation To provide an income to unemployed workers, every state has established an unemployment compensation program. Under these programs, a tax is paid that is based on the income of each covered worker and such a worker receives a benefit when he or she becomes unemployed. The details of the benefits vary from state to state.

Welfare Programs The purpose of welfare is to provide incomes for people who do not qualify for Social Security or unemployment compensation. They are

1. Supplementary Security Income (SSI) program, designed to help the neediest elderly, disabled, and blind people

2. Temporary Assistance for Needy Households (TANF) program, designed to help households that have inadequate financial resources

3. Food Stamp program, designed to help the poorest households obtain a basic diet

4. Medicaid, designed to cover the costs of medical care for households receiving help under the SSI and TANF programs

Subsidized Services

A great deal of redistribution takes place in the United States through the provision of subsidized services—services provided by the government at prices below the cost of production. The taxpayers who consume these goods and services receive a transfer in kind from the taxpayers who do not consume them. The two most important areas in which this form of redistribution takes place are health care and education—both kindergarten through grade 12 and college and university.

In 2010–2011, students enrolled in the University of California system paid annual tuition fees of $10,781. The cost of providing a year's education at the University of California was probably about $22,000. So households with a member enrolled in one of these institutions received a benefit from the government of more than $11,000 a year.

Economics in Action

Income Redistribution: Only the Richest Pay

A household's *market income* tells us what a household earns in the absence of government redistribution. You've seen that market income is *not* the official basis for measuring the distribution of income that we've used in this chapter. The Census Bureau's measure is *money income* (market income plus cash transfers from the government). But market income is the correct starting point for measuring the scale of income redistribution.

We begin with market income and then subtract taxes and add the amounts received in benefits. The result is the distribution of income after taxes and benefits. The data available on benefits exclude the value of subsidized services such as college, so the resulting distribution might understate the total amount of redistribution from the rich to the poor.

The figures show the scale of redistribution in 2001, the most recent year for which the Census Bureau has provided these data. In Fig. 1, the blue Lorenz curve describes the market distribution of income and the green Lorenz curve shows the distribution of income after all taxes and benefits, including Medicaid and Medicare benefits. (The Lorenz curve based on money income in Fig. 19.3 lies between these two curves.)

The distribution after taxes and benefits is less unequal than is the market distribution. The lowest 20 percent of households received only 0.9 percent of market income but 4.6 percent of income after taxes and benefits. The highest 20 percent of households received 55.6 percent of market income, but only 46.7 percent of income after taxes and benefits.

Figure 2 highlights the percentage of total income redistributed among the five groups. The share of total income received by the lowest 60 percent of households increased. The share received by the fourth quintile barely changed. And the share received by the highest quintile fell by 8.9 percent.

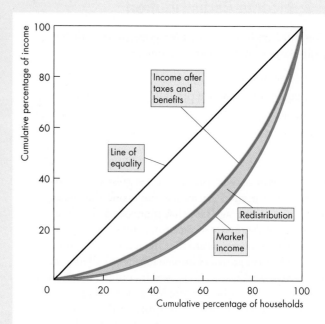

Figure 1 Income Distribution Before and After Redistribution

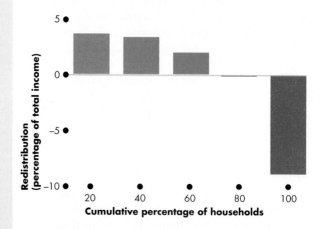

Figure 2 The Scale of Redistribution

Source of data: U.S. Bureau of the Census, "Income Poverty, and Health Insurance Coverage in the United States: 2007," *Current Population Reports*, P-60-235 (Washington, DC: U.S. Government Printing Office, 2008).

Government provision of health-care services has grown to the scale of private provision. Programs such as Medicaid and Medicare bring high-quality and high-cost health care to millions of people who earn too little to buy such services themselves.

The Big Tradeoff

The redistribution of income creates what has been called the **big tradeoff**, a tradeoff between equity and efficiency. The big tradeoff arises because redistribution uses scarce resources and weakens incentives.

A dollar collected from a rich person does not translate into a dollar received by a poor person. Some of it gets used up in the process of redistribution. Tax-collecting agencies such as the Internal Revenue Service and welfare-administering agencies (as well as tax accountants and lawyers) use skilled labor, computers, and other scarce resources to do their work. The bigger the scale of redistribution, the greater is the opportunity cost of administering it.

But the cost of collecting taxes and making welfare payments is a small part of the total cost of redistribution. A bigger cost arises from the inefficiency (deadweight loss) of taxes and benefits. Greater equality can be achieved only by taxing productive activities such as work and saving. Taxing people's income from their work and saving lowers the after-tax income they receive. This lower after-tax income makes them work and save less, which in turn results in smaller output and less consumption not only for the rich who pay the taxes but also for the poor who receive the benefits.

It is not only taxpayers who face weaker incentives to work. Benefit recipients also face weaker incentives. In fact, under the welfare arrangements that prevailed before the 1996 reforms, the weakest incentives to work were those faced by households that benefited from welfare. When a welfare recipient got a job, benefits were withdrawn and eligibility for programs such as Medicaid ended, so the household in effect paid a tax of more than 100 percent on its earnings. This arrangement locked poor households in a welfare trap.

So the agencies that determine the scale and methods of income redistribution must pay close attention to the incentive effects of taxes and benefits. Let's close this chapter by looking at one way in which lawmakers are tackling the big tradeoff today.

A Major Welfare Challenge Young women who have not completed high school, have a child (or children), live without a partner, and more likely are black or Hispanic are among the poorest people in the United States today. They and their children present a major welfare challenge.

First, their numbers are large. In 2009, there were 14 million single-mother families. This number is 12 percent of families. In 1997 (the most recent year with census data), single mothers were owed $26 billion in child support. Of this amount, $10 billion was

not paid and 30 percent of the women received no support from their children's fathers.

The long-term solution to the problem these women face is education and job training—acquiring human capital. The short-term solutions are enforcing child support payments by absent fathers and former spouses and providing welfare.

Welfare must be designed to minimize the disincentive to pursue the long-term goal of becoming self-supporting. The current welfare program in the United States tries to walk this fine line.

Passed in 1996, the Personal Responsibility and Work Opportunities Reconciliation Act strengthened the Office of Child Support Enforcement and increased the penalties for nonpayment of support. The act also created the Temporary Assistance for Needy Households (TANF) program. TANF is a block grant paid to the states, which administer payments to individuals. It is not an open-ended entitlement program. An adult member of a household that is receiving assistance must either work or perform community service, and there is a five-year limit for assistance.

REVIEW QUIZ

1 How do governments in the United States redistribute income?
2 Describe the scale of redistribution in the United States.
3 What is one of the major welfare challenges today and how is it being tackled in the United States?

You can work these questions in Study Plan 19.4 and get instant feedback.

◆ We've examined economic inequality in the United States. We've seen how inequality arises and that inequality has been increasing. *Reading Between the Lines* on pp. 458–459 looks at the increasing inequality that began during the early 1980s and continues today.

The next chapter focuses on some problems for the market economy that arise from uncertainty and incomplete information. But unlike the cases we studied in Chapters 16 and 17, this time the market does a good job of coping with the problems.

Trends in Incomes of the Super Rich

What Happened to All That Anger Over CEO Pay?

http://www.csmonitor.com
July 12, 2010

With last month's sweeping financial reform bill, Congress has finally moved to tame runaway executive pay. Sort of.

It says shareholders must vote on a CEO's pay package, though the vote is nonbinding. Has Congress thereby put an end to sky-high salaries in the executive suite?

"Totally ridiculous," says Sam Pizzigati, an editor of a newsletter on income inequality put out by the liberal Institute for Policy Studies. Shareholder votes only rarely alter corporate decisions.

Given the political anger last year over the pay and bonuses of corporate officials, especially those on Wall Street and at American International Group, such tepid reform is surprising. President Obama expressed outrage in March 2009. His administration capped executive pay at firms receiving bailout money.

That move and the recession had a small impact. In 2008, the CEOs of major U.S. firms were paid more than 300 times the wage of the average American worker. Last year, they were paid just under 300 times average pay, according to new research by Mr. Pizzigati. Now that most of those firms have paid back the government, they're setting their own compensation levels again.

Those levels would astonish the bosses of top corporations in the late 1960s. Those CEOs got about 30 times the average wage of U.S. workers.

Are today's bosses 10 times more capable? Is there a shortage of able managers? Nope and nope, says Pizzigati. "There is more management talent today than ever before." ...

ESSENCE OF THE STORY

- Congress says shareholders must hold a nonbinding vote on a CEO's pay package.

- Sam Pizzigati, editor of a liberal newsletter on income inequality, says shareholder votes rarely have force.

- The Obama Administration capped executive pay at firms receiving government bailout money.

- The Administration cap and the recession had a small impact on CEO pay.

- The CEOs of major U.S. firms were paid more than 300 times the wage of the average American worker in 2008 and just under 300 times in 2009.

- During the 1960s, CEOs got about 30 times the average wage of U.S. workers.

- Sam Pizzigati says that today's bosses are not 10 times more capable than those of the 1960s and that there is more management talent available today than ever before.

ECONOMIC ANALYSIS

- The news article says that the incomes of top CEOs have increased from 30 times the average wage in the 1960s to 300 times in 2008.

- The facts about top CEO pay are correct and they are in line with broader changes in the incomes of the super rich.

- Economists Thomas Piketty (of l'Ecole d'économie de Paris—Paris School of Economics) and Emmanuel Saez (of U.C. Berkely) examined the tax returns of the super rich and found the trend shown in Fig. 1.

- Figure 1 shows the income share (percentage of total income) received by the top 0.01 percent of the population.

- The top 0.01 includes the top CEOs and in 2008 was made up of 15,246 families with incomes that exceeded $9,141,000.

- The average family in the top 0.01 percent received 296 times the income of the average family in the bottom quintile. This ratio was 27 in 1965. These ratios are in line with the trend reported in the news article.

- Sam Pizzigati is reported as saying that CEOs are paid too much today and, with an abundance of talent around, could and should be paid much less.

- He is right that there is an abundance of talent. Globalization has made the entire world the talent pool that large corporations tap for their CEO spot.

- But it is because of the abundance of talent that CEO pay has become so high.

- You saw on p. 453 that we can view top CEOs as the winners of a contest among potential superstars.

- Contests induce high effort and productivity from managers at all levels as they compete for the top job.

- How hard people compete (how productive they are) depends on the size of the prize and the probability of winning it.

- You can think of the contest in terms of the pyramids in Fig. 2. The talent pool is the base of the pyramid and the contest delivers a winner who gets to the top.

- When the talent pool is small, as it was in 1965, the chance of being the winner is large enough for a moderate prize to induce enough effort.

- When the talent pool gets large, as it is today, the chance of being the winner is very small, so to induce the same amount of effort, the prize is very large.

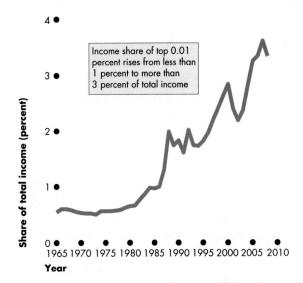

Figure 1 Income share of the top 0.01 percent

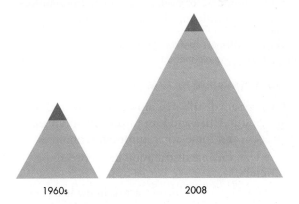

Figure 2 Bigger pyramid means bigger prizes for getting to top

Source of data: Figure 1, Emmanuel Saez, "Striking it Richer: The Evolution of Top Incomes in the United States" *Pathways*, Winter 2008 issue.

- This superstar contest idea explains the direction of change—why top CEOs' earnings have increased relative to the average wage.

- It also answers the question: Are today's managers 10 times as productive as their 1960s predecessors? The answer is no, they are not, but they are paid 10 times as much (relative to the average) to maximize the productivity of the pool of potential CEOs.

SUMMARY

Key Points

Economic Inequality in the United States (pp. 442–447)

- In 2007, the mode money income was $13,000 a year, the median money income was $50,233, and the mean money income was $67,609.
- The income distribution is positively skewed.
- In 2007, the poorest 20 percent of households received 3.4 percent of total income and the wealthiest 20 percent received 49.7 percent of total income.
- Wealth is distributed more unequally than income because the wealth data exclude the value of human capital.
- Since 1970, the distribution of income has become more unequal.
- Education, type of household, age of householder, and race all influence household income.

Working Problems 1 to 7 will give you a better understanding of economic inequality in the United States.

Inequality in the World Economy (pp. 448–449)

- Incomes are distributed most unequally in Brazil and South Africa and least unequally in Finland, Sweden, and some other European economies.
- The U.S. income distribution lies between the extremes.
- The distribution of income across individuals in the global economy is much more unequal than in the United States.
- The global income distribution has been getting less unequal as rapid income growth in China and India has lifted millions from poverty.

Working Problems 8 to 11 will give you a better understanding of economic inequality in the world economy.

The Sources of Economic Inequality (pp. 450–454)

- Inequality arises from differences in human capital and from contests among superstars.
- Trends in the distribution of human capital and in the rewards to superstars that arise from technological change and globalization can explain some of the trend in increased inequality.
- Inequality might arise from discrimination.
- Inequality between men and women might arise from differences in the degree of specialization.
- Intergenerational transfers of wealth lead to increased inequality because people can't inherit debts and assortative mating tends to concentrate wealth.

Working Problems 12 to 15 will give you a better understanding of the sources of economic inequality.

Income Redistribution (pp. 455–457)

- Governments redistribute income through progressive income taxes, income maintenance programs, and subsidized services.
- Redistribution increases the share of total income received by the lowest 60 percent of households and decreases the share of total income received by the highest quintile. The share of the fourth quintile barely changes.
- Because the redistribution of income weakens incentives, it creates a tradeoff between equity and efficiency.
- Effective redistribution seeks to support the long-term solution to low income, which is education and job training—acquiring human capital.

Working Problems 16 to 17 will give you a better understanding of income redistribution.

Key Terms

Big tradeoff, 456
Gini ratio, 445
Lorenz curve, 443
Market income, 442

Money income, 442
Poverty, 446
Progressive income tax, 455
Proportional income tax, 455

Regressive income tax, 455
Wealth, 444

STUDY PLAN PROBLEMS AND APPLICATIONS

 You can work Problems 1 to 17 in MyEconLab Chapter 19 Study Plan and get instant feedback.

Economic Inequality in the United States

(Study Plan19.1)

1. What is money income? Describe the distribution of money income in the United States in 2009.

2. The table shows money income shares in the United States in 1967.

Households	Money income (percent of total)
Lowest 20 percent	4.0
Second 20 percent	10.8
Middle 20 percent	17.3
Next highest 20 percent	24.2
Highest 20 percent	43.7

   a. Draw a Lorenz curve for the United States in 1967 and compare it with the Lorenz curve in 2007 shown in Fig. 19.3 on p. 443.

   b. Was U.S. money income distributed more equally or less equally in 2007 than it was in 1967?

Use the following news clip to work Problems 3 to 6.

Household Incomes Rise but …

As household income crept higher last year, more people in each household had to work because median earnings for those working full-time year-round actually fell. As the poverty rate edged lower, the percent of Americans living below the poverty line slipped to 12.3 percent in 2006.

The poverty threshold is based on personal data and not on the local cost of living, so the poverty threshold is the same in rural towns and large cities. Also it does not reflect the value of household subsidies such as food stamps, tax credits, and Medicaid, which are intended to alleviate the effects of poverty. Over the years, the gap between high-income and low-income households has grown, but income inequality remained unchanged between 2005 and 2006.

Source: CNN, August 28, 2007

3. Why is the recent increase in median household income a misleading statistic when attempting to measure the change in economic inequality?

4. How does using set poverty thresholds that apply to the entire United States complicate the attempt to measure poverty?

5. Why does excluding household subsidies lead to a misleading measurement of the percentage of people actually living in poverty?

6. Why has the gap between high-income and low-income households grown in recent decades?

7. **Census: Income Fell Sharply Last Year**

   The U.S. Census Bureau reported that in 2008 the median household income fell 3.6%. The share of people living in poverty rose to 13.2% in 2008 from 12.5% in 2007. Only households led by people aged 65 or older enjoyed income gains—a 1.2% increase.

   Source: *USA Today,* September 11, 2009

   a. What does the information in this news report tell you about changes in the distribution of income in 2008?

   b. What additional information would you need to know how the changes described changed the U.S. Lorenz curve?

Inequality in the World Economy (Study Plan19.2)

8. Incomes in China and India are a small fraction of incomes in the United States. But incomes in China and India are growing at more than twice the rate of those in the United States.

   a. Explain how economic inequality in China and India is changing relative to that in the United States.

   b. How is the world Lorenz curve and world Gini ratio changing?

Use the following table to work Problems 9 to 11.

The table shows the money income shares in Canada and the United Kingdom.

Households	Canadian money income (percent of total)	U.K. money income (percent of total)
Lowest 20 percent	7	3
Second 20 percent	13	5
Middle 20 percent	18	14
Next highest 20 percent	25	25
Highest 20 percent	37	53

9. Create a table that shows the cumulative distribution of Canadian and U.K. incomes. Is the distribution of income more unequal in Canada or in the United Kingdom?

10. Draw a Lorenz curve for Canada and compare it with the Lorenz curve in Fig. 19.3 on p. 443. In which country is income less equally distributed?

11. Draw a Lorenz curve for the United Kingdom and compare it with the Lorenz curve in Fig. 19.3 on p. 443. In which country is income less equally distributed?

The Sources of Economic Inequality (Study Plan19.3)

12. The following figure shows the market for low-skilled labor.

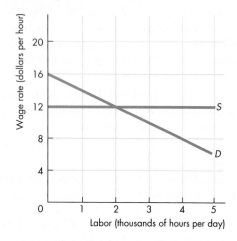

The value of marginal product of high-skilled workers is $16 an hour greater than that of low-skilled workers at each quantity of labor. The cost of acquiring human capital adds $12 an hour to the wage that must be offered to attract high-skilled labor.

Compare the equilibrium wage rates of low-skilled labor and high-skilled labor. Explain why the difference between these wage rates equals the cost of acquiring human capital.

Use the following information to work Problems 13 and 14.

In 2000, 30 million Americans had full-time professional jobs that paid about $800 a week while 10 million Americans had full-time sales jobs that paid about $530 a week.

13. Explain why professionals are paid more than salespeople and why, despite the higher weekly wage, more people are employed as professionals than as salespeople.

14. If the online shopping trend continues, how do you think the market for salespeople will change in coming years?

15. The figure shows the market for a group of workers who are discriminated against. Suppose that others workers in the same industry are not discriminated against and their value of marginal product is perceived to be twice that of the workers who are discriminated against. Suppose also that the supply of these other workers is 2,000 hours per day less at each wage rate.

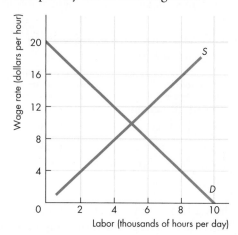

a. What is the wage rate of the workers who are discriminated against?

b. What is the quantity of workers employed who are discriminated against?

c. What is the wage rate of the workers who do not face discrimination?

d. What is the quantity of workers employed who do not face discrimination?

Income Redistribution (Study Plan19.4)

Use the following table to work Problems 16 and 17. The table shows three redistribution schemes.

Before-tax income (dollars)	Plan A tax (dollars)	Plan B tax (dollars)	Plan C tax (dollars)
10,000	1,000	1,000	2,000
20,000	2,000	4,000	2,000
30,000	3,000	9,000	2,000

16. Which scheme has a proportional tax? Which scheme has a regressive tax? Which scheme has a progressive tax?

17. Which scheme will increase economic inequality? Which scheme will reduce economic inequality? Which scheme will have no effect on economic inequality?

ADDITIONAL PROBLEMS AND APPLICATIONS

myeconlab You can work these problems in MyEconLab if assigned by your instructor.

Economic Inequality in the United States

Use the following table to work Problems 18 and 19. The table shows the distribution of market income in the United States in 2007.

Households	Market income (percentage of total)
Lowest 20 percent	1.1
Second 20 percent	7.1
Middle 20 percent	13.9
Next highest 20 percent	22.8
Highest 20 percent	55.1

18. a. What is the definition of market income?
   b. Draw the Lorenz curve for the distribution of market income.

19. Compare the distribution of market income with the distribution of money income shown in Fig. 19.3 on p. 443. Which distribution is more unequal and why?

Inequality in the World Economy

Use the following table to work Problems 20 to 22. The table shows shares of income in Australia.

Households	Income share (percentage of total)
Lowest 20 percent	7
Second 20 percent	13
Middle 20 percent	18
Next highest 20 percent	24
Highest 20 percent	38

20. Draw the Lorenz curve for the income distribution in Australia and in Brazil and South Africa (use the data in Fig. 19.6 on p. 448). Is income distributed more equally or less equally in Brazil and South Africa than in Australia?

21. Is the Gini ratio for Australia larger or smaller than that for Brazil and South Africa? Explain your answer.

22. What are some reasons for the differences in the distribution of income in Australia and in Brazil and South Africa?

The Sources of Economic Inequality

Use the following news clip to work Problems 23 to 26.

Bernanke Links Education and Equality

Ben Bernanke, the chairman of the Federal Reserve, said that increased education opportunities would help reduce the increased economic inequality that has occurred over the last 30 years. He also said that globalization and the advent of new technologies, the two main causes of income inequality, will lead to economic growth, but inhibiting them will do far more harm than good in the long run.

Instead, the Fed chief said the best method to improve economic opportunities is to focus on raising the level of and access to education. Workers will become more skilful, and firms will undertake more innovation.

It is time to recognize that education should be lifelong and can come in many forms: early childhood education, community colleges, vocational schools, on-the-job training, online courses, adult education. With increased skills, lifetime earning power will increase.

Source: *International Herald Tribune*, June 5, 2008

23. Explain how the two main causes of increased income inequality in the United States identified by Mr. Bernanke work.

24. Draw a graph to illustrate how the two main causes of increased income inequality generate this outcome.

25. What are the short-term costs and long-term benefits associated with these two causes of inequality?

26. Explain Bernanke's solutions to help address growing income inequality.

27. **Where Women's Pay Trumps Men's**
   Men work more than women on the job, at least in terms of overall hours. That's just one reason why in most fields, men's earnings exceed women's earnings. But Warren Farrell found 39 occupations in which women's median earnings exceeded men's earnings by at least 5 percent and

in some cases by as much as 43 percent. In fields like engineering, a company may get one woman and seven men applying for a job. If the company wants to hire the woman, it might have to pay a premium to get her. Also, where women can combine technical expertise with people skills—such as those required in sales and where customers prefer dealing with a woman—that's likely to contribute to a premium in pay.

Source: CNN, March 2, 2006

a. Draw a graph to illustrate why discrimination could result in female workers getting paid more than male workers for some jobs.

b. Explain how market competition could potentially eliminate this wage differential.

c. If customers "prefer dealing with a woman" in some markets, how might that lead to a persistent wage differential between men and women?

Income Redistribution

28. Use the information provided in Problem 16 and in Fig. 19.3 on p. 443.

a. What is the percentage of total income that is redistributed from the highest income group?

b. What percentages of total income are redistributed to the lower income groups?

29. Describe the effects of increasing the amount of income redistribution in the United States to the point at which the lowest income group receives 15 percent of total income and the highest income group receives 30 percent of total income.

Use the following news clip to work Problems 30 and 31.

The Tax Debate We Should be Having

A shrinking number of Americans are bearing an even bigger share of the nation's income tax burden. In 2005, the bottom 40 percent of Americans by income had, in the aggregate, an effective tax rate that's negative: Their households received more money through the income tax system, largely from the earned income tax credit, than they paid. The top 50% of taxpayers pay 97% of total income tax and the top 10% of taxpayers pay 70%. The top 1% paid almost 40% of all income tax, a proportion that has jumped dramatically since 1986.

Given the U.S. tax system, any tax cut must benefit the rich, but in terms of the change in effective tax rates: The bottom 50% got a much bigger tax cut under the Bush tax cut than the top 1%. Did the dollar value of Bush's tax cuts go mostly to the wealthy? Absolutely.

Source: Fortune, April 14, 2008

30. Explain why tax cuts in a progressive income tax system are consistently criticized for favoring the wealthy.

31. How might the benefits of tax cuts "trickle down" to others whose taxes are not cut?

Economics in the News

32. After you have studied Reading Between the Lines on pp. 458–459 answer the following questions.

a. What are the broad facts reported in the news article about the gap in the incomes of CEOs and the average wage rate during the 1960s and in 2008?

b. What does Sam Pizzigati say should happen to top CEO pay?

c. How can the idea of a contest among potential CEOs explain the trend in CEO pay?

d. If the contest among potential CEOs is the correct explanation for the trend in CEO pay, what would be the effects of a cap on CEO pay?

33. **The Best and Worst College Degrees by Salary**

Business administration is always a strong contender for honors as the most popular college major. This is no surprise since students think business is the way to make big bucks. But is business administration really as lucrative as students and their parents believe? Nope.

In a new survey by PayScale, Inc. of salaries by college degree, business administration didn't even break into the list of the top 10 or 20 most lucrative college degrees. A variety of engineering majors claim eight of the top 10 salary spots with chemical engineering ($65,700) winning best for starting salaries. Out of 75 undergrad college majors, business administration ($42,900) came in 35th, behind such degrees as occupational therapy ($61,300), information technology ($49,400), and economics ($48,800).

Source: moneywatch.com, July 21, 2009

a. Why do college graduates with different majors have drastically different starting salaries?

b. Draw a graph of the labor markets for economics majors and business administration majors to illustrate your explanation of the differences in the starting salaries of these two groups.

20

UNCERTAINTY AND
INFORMATION

After studying this chapter,
you will be able to:

◆ Explain how people make decisions when they are
  uncertain about the consequences
◆ Explain how markets enable people to buy and sell risk
◆ Explain how markets cope when buyers and sellers
  have private information
◆ Explain how the presence of uncertainty and incomplete
  information influences the ability of markets to achieve
  an efficient allocation of resources

Life is like a lottery. You set up a summer business and work hard at it. But
will you make enough income to keep you in school next year or will you get
wiped out? How do people make a decision when they don't know what its
consequences will be?

As you drive across an intersection on a green light, you see a car on your left
that's still moving. Will it stop or will it run the red light? You buy insurance against
such a risk, and insurance companies gain from your business. Why are we
willing to buy insurance at prices that leave insurance companies with a gain?

Buying a new car—or a used car—is fun, but it's also scary. You could get
stuck with a lemon. Just about every complicated product you buy
could be defective. How do car dealers and retailers induce us to
buy goods that might turn out to be lemons?

Although markets do a good job in helping people to use scarce resources
efficiently, there are impediments to efficiency. Can markets lead to an efficient
outcome when there is uncertainty and incomplete information? In this chapter, we
answer questions such as these. And in *Reading Between the Lines* at the end of
the chapter, you will see how accurate grading by high schools, colleges, and
universities helps students get the right jobs **and the problem** that arises in job
markets if grades are inflated.

◆ Decisions in the Face of Uncertainty

Tania, a student, is trying to decide which of two summer jobs to take. She can work as a house painter and earn enough for her to save $2,000 by the end of the summer. There is no uncertainty about the income from this job. If Tania takes it, she will definitely have $2,000 in her bank account at the end of the summer. The other job, working as a telemarketer selling subscriptions to a magazine, is risky. If Tania takes this job, her bank balance at the end of the summer will depend on her success at selling. She will earn enough to save $5,000 if she is successful but only $1,000 if she turns out to be a poor salesperson. Tania has never tried selling, so she doesn't know how successful she'll be. But some of her friends have done this job, and 50 percent of them do well and 50 percent do poorly. Basing her expectations on this experience, Tania thinks there is a 50 percent chance that she will earn $5,000 and a 50 percent chance that she will earn $1,000.

Tania is equally as happy to paint as she is to make phone calls. She cares only about the money. Which job does she prefer: the one that provides her with $2,000 for sure or the one that offers her a 50 percent chance of making $5,000 but a 50 percent risk of making only $1,000?

To answer this question, we need a way of comparing the two outcomes. One comparison is the expected wealth that each job creates.

Expected Wealth

Expected wealth is the money value of what a person expects to own at a given point in time. An expectation is an average calculated by using a formula that weights each possible outcome with the probability (chance) that it will occur.

For Tania, the probability that she will have $5,000 is 0.5 (a 50 percent chance). The probability that she will have $1,000 is also 0.5. Notice that the probabilities sum to 1. Using these numbers, we can calculate Tania's expected wealth, EW, which is

$$EW = (\$5,000 \times 0.5) + (\$1,000 \times 0.5) = \$3,000.$$

Notice that expected wealth decreases if the risk of a poor outcome increases. For example, if Tania has a

20 percent chance of success (and 80 percent chance of failure), her expected wealth falls to $1,800—

$$(\$5,000 \times 0.2) + (\$1,000 \times 0.8) = \$1,800.$$

Tania can now compare the expected wealth from each job—$3,000 for the risky job and $2,000 for the non-risky job.

So does Tania prefer the risky job because it gives her a greater expected wealth? The answer is we don't know because we don't know how much Tania dislikes risk.

Risk Aversion

Risk aversion is the dislike of risk. Almost everyone is risk averse but some more than others. In football, running is less risky than passing. Coach John Harbaugh of the Baltimore Ravens, who favors a cautious running game, is risk averse. Indianapolis quarterback Peyton Manning, who favors a risky passing game, is less risk averse. But almost everyone is risk averse to some degree.

We can measure the degree of risk aversion by the compensation needed to make a given amount of risk acceptable. Returning to Tania: If she needs to be paid more than $1,000 to take on the risk arising from the telemarketing job, she will choose the safe painting job and take the $2,000 non-risky income. But if she thinks that the extra $1,000 of expected income is enough to compensate her for the risk, she will take the risky job.

To make this idea concrete, we need a way of thinking about how a person values different levels of wealth. The concept that we use is *utility*. We apply the same idea that explains how people make expenditure decisions (see Chapter 8) to explain risk aversion and decisions in the face of risk.

Utility of Wealth

Wealth (money in the bank and other assets of value) is like all good things. It yields utility. The more wealth a person has, the greater is that person's total utility. But each additional dollar of wealth brings a diminishing increment in total utility—the marginal utility of wealth diminishes as wealth increases.

Diminishing marginal utility of wealth means that the gain in utility from an increase in wealth is smaller than the loss in utility from an equal decrease in wealth. Stated differently, *the pain from a loss is greater than the pleasure from a gain of equal size.*

Figure 20.1 illustrates Tania's utility of wealth. Each point *A* through *F* on Tania's utility of wealth curve corresponds to the value identified by the same letter in the table. For example, at point *C*, Tania's wealth is $2,000, and her total utility is 70 units. As Tania's wealth increases, her total utility increases and her marginal utility decreases. Her marginal utility is 25 units when wealth increases from $1,000 to $2,000, but only 13 units when wealth increases from $2,000 to $3,000.

We can use a person's utility of wealth curve to calculate expected utility and the cost of risk.

Expected Utility

Expected utility is the utility value of what a person expects to own at a given point in time. Like expected wealth, it is calculated by using a formula that weights each possible outcome with the probability that it will occur. But it is the utility outcome, not the money outcome, that is used to calculate expected utility.

Figure 20.2 illustrates the calculation for Tania. Wealth of $5,000 gives 95 units of utility and wealth of $1,000 gives 45 units of utility. Each outcome has a probability of 0.5 (a 50 percent chance). Using these numbers, we can calculate Tania's expected utility, *EU*, which is

$$EU = (95 \times 0.5) + (45 \times 0.5) = 70.$$

FIGURE 20.1   The Utility of Wealth

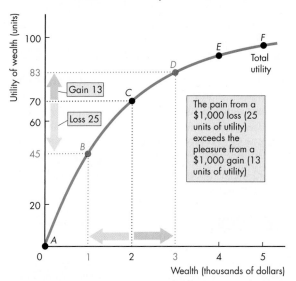

	Wealth (dollars)	Total utility (units)	Marginal utility (units)
A	0	0	
			45
B	1,000	45	
			25
C	**2,000**	**70**	
			13
D	3,000	83	
			8
E	4,000	91	
			4
F	5,000	95	

The table shows Tania's utility of wealth schedule, and the figure shows her utility of wealth curve. Utility increases as wealth increases, but the marginal utility of wealth diminishes.

myeconlab animation

FIGURE 20.2   Expected Utility

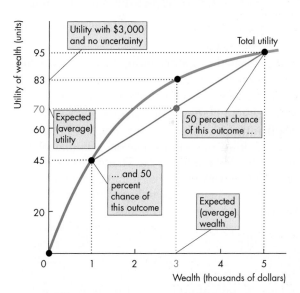

Tania has a 50 percent chance of having $5,000 of wealth and a total utility of 95 units. She also has a 50 percent chance of having $1,000 of wealth and a total utility of 45 units. Tania's expected wealth is $3,000 (the average of $5,000 and $1,000) and her expected utility is 70 units (the average of 95 and 45). With a wealth of $3,000 and no uncertainty, Tania's total utility is 83 units. For a given expected wealth, the greater the range of uncertainty, the smaller is expected utility.

myeconlab animation

Expected utility decreases if the risk of a poor outcome increases. For example, if Tania has a 20 percent chance of success (and an 80 percent chance of failure), her expected utility is 55 units—

$$(95 \times 0.2) + (45 \times 0.8) = 55.$$

Notice how the range of uncertainty affects expected utility. Figure 20.2 shows that with $3,000 of wealth and no uncertainty, total utility is 83 units. But with the same expected wealth and Tania's uncertainty—a 50 percent chance of having $5,000 and a 50 percent chance of having $1,000—expected utility is only 70 units. Tania's uncertainty lowers her expected utility by 13 units.

Expected utility combines expected wealth and risk into a single index.

Making a Choice with Uncertainty

Faced with uncertainty, a person chooses the action that maximizes expected utility. To select the job that gives her the maximum expected utility, Tania must:

1. Calculate the expected utility from the risky telemarketing job
2. Calculate the expected utility from the safe painting job
3. Compare the two expected utilities

Figure 20.3 illustrates the calculations. You've just seen that the risky telemarketing job gives Tania an expected utility of 70 units. The safe painting job also gives Tania a utility of 70. That is, the total utility of $2,000 with no risk is 70 units. So with either job, Tania has an expected utility of 70 units. She is indifferent between these two jobs.

If Tania had only a 20 percent chance of success and an 80 percent chance of failure in the telemarketing job, her expected utility would be 55 (calculated above). In this case, she would take the painting job and get 70 units of utility. But if the probabilities were reversed and she had an 80 percent chance of success and only a 20 percent chance of failure in the telemarketing job, her expected utility would be 85 units—$(95 \times 0.8) + (45 \times 0.2) = 85$. In this case, she would take the risky telemarketing job.

We can calculate the cost of risk by comparing the expected wealth in a given risky situation with the wealth that gives the same total utility but no risk. Using this principle, we can find Tania's cost of bearing the risk that arises from the telemarketing job. That cost, highlighted in Figure 20.3, is $1,000.

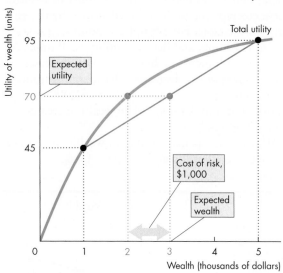

FIGURE 20.3   Choice Under Uncertainty

With a 50 percent chance of having $5,000 of wealth and a 50 percent chance of having $1,000 of wealth, Tania's expected wealth is $3,000 and her expected utility is 70 units. Tania would have the same 70 units of total utility with wealth of $2,000 and no risk, so Tania's cost of bearing this risk is $1,000. Tania is indifferent between the job that pays $2,000 with no risk and the job that offers an equal chance of $5,000 and $1,000.

 animation

REVIEW QUIZ

1 What is the distinction between expected wealth and expected utility?
2 How does the concept of utility of wealth capture the idea that pain of loss exceeds the pleasure of gain?
3 What do people try to achieve when they make a decision under uncertainty?
4 How is the cost of the risk calculated when making a decision with an uncertain outcome?

You can work these questions in Study Plan 20.1 and get instant feedback.

You've now seen how a person makes a risky decision. In the next section, we'll see how markets enable people to reduce the risks they face.

◆ Buying and Selling Risk

You've seen at many points in your study of markets how both buyers and sellers gain from trade. Buyers gain because they value what they buy more highly than the price they must pay—they receive a *consumer surplus*. And sellers gain because they face costs that are less than the price at which they can sell—they receive a *producer surplus*.

Just as buyers and sellers gain from trading goods and services, so they can also gain by trading risk. But risk is a bad, not a good. The good that is traded is risk avoidance. A buyer of risk avoidance can gain because the value of avoiding risk is greater than the price that must be paid to someone else to get them to bear the risk. The seller of risk avoidance faces a lower cost of risk than the price that people are willing to pay to avoid the risk.

We're going to put some flesh on the bare bones of this brief account of how people can gain from trading risk by looking at insurance markets.

Insurance Markets

Insurance plays a huge role in our economic lives. We'll explain

- How insurance reduces risk
- Why people buy insurance
- How insurance companies earn a profit

How Insurance Reduces Risk Insurance reduces the risk that people face by sharing or pooling the risks. When people buy insurance against the risk of an unwanted event, they pay an insurance company a *premium*. If the unwanted event occurs, the insurance company pays out the amount of the insured loss.

Think about auto collision insurance. The probability that any one person will have a serious auto accident is small. But a person who does have an auto accident incurs a large loss. For a large population, the probability of one person having an accident is the proportion of the population that has an accident. But this proportion is known, so the probability of an accident occurring and the total cost of accidents can be predicted. An insurance company can pool the risks of a large population and enable everyone to share the costs. It does so by collecting premiums from everyone and paying out benefits to

those who suffer a loss. An insurance company that remains in business collects at least as much in premiums as it pays out in benefits.

Why People Buy Insurance People buy insurance and insurance companies earn a profit by selling insurance because people are risk averse. To see why people buy insurance and why it is profitable, let's consider an example. Dan owns a car worth $10,000, and that is his only wealth. There is a 10 percent chance that Dan will have a serious accident that makes his car worth nothing. So there is a 90 percent chance that Dan's wealth will remain at $10,000 and a 10 percent chance that his wealth will be zero. Dan's expected wealth is $9,000—($10,000 × 0.9) + ($0 × 0.1).

Dan is risk averse (just like Tania in the previous example). Because Dan is risk averse, he will be better off by buying insurance to avoid the risk that he faces, if the insurance premium isn't too high.

Without knowing some details about just how risk averse Dan is, we don't know the most that he would be willing to pay to avoid this risk. But we do know that he would pay more than $1,000. If Dan did pay $1,000 to avoid the risk, he would have $9,000 of wealth and face no uncertainty about his wealth. If he does not have an accident, his wealth is the $10,000 value of his car minus the $1,000 he pays the insurance company. If he does lose his car, the insurance company pays him $10,000, so he still has $9,000. Being risk averse, Dan's expected utility from $9,000 with no risk is greater than his expected utility from an expected $9,000 with risk. So Dan would be willing to pay more than $1,000 to avoid this risk.

How Insurance Companies Earn a Profit For the insurance company, $1,000 is the minimum amount at which it would be willing to insure Dan and other people like him. With say 50,000 customers all like Dan, 5,000 customers (50,000 × 0.1) lose their cars and 45,000 don't. Premiums of $1,000 give the insurance company a total revenue of $50,000,000. With 5,000 claims of $10,000, the insurance company pays out $50,000,000. So a premium of $1,000 enables the insurance company to break even (make zero economic profit) on this business.

But Dan (and everyone else) is willing to pay more than $1,000, so insurance is a profitable business and there is a gain from trading risk.

The gain from trading risk is shared by Dan (and the other people who buy insurance) and the insurance company. The exact share of the gain depends on the state of competition in the market for insurance.

If the insurance market is a monopoly, the insurance company can take all the gains from trading risk. But if the insurance market is competitive, economic profit will induce entry and profits will be competed away. In this case, Dan (and the other buyers of insurance) get the gain.

A Graphical Analysis of Insurance

We can illustrate the gains from insurance by using a graph of Dan's utility of wealth curve. We begin, in Figure 20.4, with the situation if Dan doesn't buy insurance and decides to bear the risk he faces.

Risk-Taking Without Insurance With no accident, Dan's wealth is $10,000 and his total utility is 100 units. If Dan has an accident, his car is worthless, he has no wealth and no utility. Because the chance of an accident is 10 percent (or 0.1), the chance of not having an accident is 90 percent (or 0.9). Dan's expected wealth is $9,000—($10,000 × 0.9) + ($0 × 0.1)—and his expected utility is 90 units—(100 × 0.9) + (0 × 0.1).

You've just seen that without insurance, Dan gets 90 units of utility. But Dan also gets 90 units of utility if he faces no uncertainty with a smaller amount of wealth.

We're now going to see how much Dan will pay to avoid uncertainty.

The Value and Cost of Insurance Figure 20.5 shows the situation when Dan buys insurance. You can see that for Dan, having $7,000 with no risk is just as good as facing a 90 percent chance of having $10,000 and a 10 percent chance of having no wealth. So if Dan pays $3,000 for insurance, he has $7,000 of wealth, faces no uncertainty, and gets 90 units of utility. The amount of $3,000 is the maximum that Dan is willing to pay for insurance. It is the value of insurance to Dan.

Figure 20.5 also shows the cost of insurance. With a large number of customers each of whom has a 10 percent chance of making a $10,000 claim for the loss of a vehicle, the insurance company can provide insurance at a cost of $1,000 (10 percent of $10,000). If Dan pays only $1,000 for insurance, his

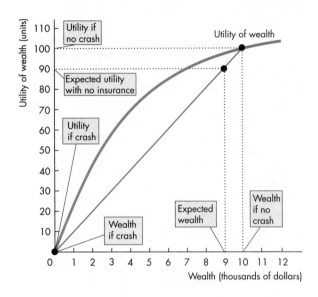

FIGURE 20.4   Taking a Risk Without Insurance

Dan's wealth (the value of his car) is $10,000, which gives him 100 units of utility.

With no insurance, if Dan has a crash, he has no wealth and no utility.

With a 10 percent chance of a crash, Dan's expected wealth is $9,000 and his expected utility is 90 units.

myeconlab   animation

wealth is $9,000 (the $10,000 value of his car minus the $1,000 he pays for insurance), and his utility from $9,000 of wealth with no uncertainty is about 98 units.

Gains from Trade Because Dan is willing to pay up to $3,000 for insurance that costs the insurance company $1,000, there is a gain from trading risk of $2,000 per insured person. How the gains are shared depends on the nature of the market. If the insurance market is competitive, entry will increase supply and lower the price to $1,000 (plus normal profit and operating costs). Dan (and the other buyers of insurance) enjoy a consumer surplus. If the insurance market is a monopoly, the insurance company takes the $2,000 per insured person as economic profit.

FIGURE 20.5   The Gains from Insurance

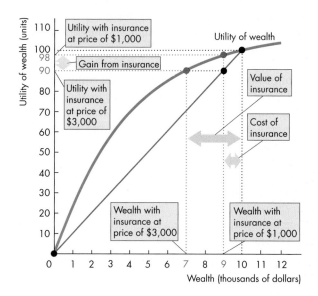

If Dan pays $3,000 for insurance, his wealth is $7,000 and his utility is 90 units—the same utility as with no insurance—so $3,000 is the value of insurance for Dan.

If Dan pays $1,000 for insurance, which is the insurance company's cost of providing insurance, his wealth is $9,000 and his utility is about 98 units.

Dan and the insurance company share the gain from insurance.

 animation

Risk That Can't Be Insured

The gains from auto collision insurance that we've studied here apply to all types of insurance. Examples are property and casualty insurance, life insurance, and health-care insurance. One person's risks associated with driving, life, and health are independent of other persons'. That's why insurance is possible. The risks are spread across a population.

But not all risks can be insured. To be insurable, risks must be independent. If an event causes everyone to be a loser, it isn't possible to spread and pool the risks. For example, flood insurance is often not available for people who live on a floodplain because if one person incurs a loss, most likely all do.

Also, to be insurable, a risky event must be observable to both the buyer and seller of insurance. But much of the uncertainty that we face arises

Economics in Action
Insurance in the United States

We spend 7 percent of our income on private insurance. That's more than we spend on cars or food. In addition, we buy Social Security and unemployment insurance through our taxes. The figure shows the relative sizes of the four main types of private insurance. More than 80 percent of Americans have life insurance, and after 2010, most have health insurance. The United States only recently made health insurance compulsory.

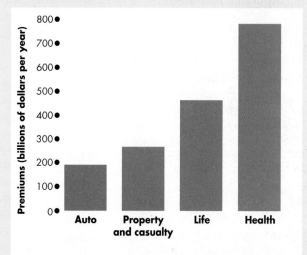

The U.S. Insurance Industry

Source of data: U.S. Bureau of the Census, *Statistical Abstract of the United States 2010*, Tables 128, 1184, and 1185.

REVIEW QUIZ

1 How does insurance reduce risk?

2 How do we determine the value (willingness to pay) for insurance?

3 How can an insurance company offer people a deal worth taking? Why do both the buyers and the sellers of insurance gain?

4 What kinds of risks can't be insured?

You can work these questions in Study Plan 20.2 and get instant feedback.   myeconlab

because we know less (or more) than others with whom we do business. In the next section, we look at the way markets cope when buyers and sellers have different information.

◆ Private Information

In all the markets that you've studied so far, the buyers and the sellers are well informed about the good, service, or factor of production being traded. But in some markets, either the buyers or the sellers—usually the sellers—are better informed about the value of the item being traded than the person on the other side of the market. Information about the value of the item being traded that is possessed by only buyers or sellers is called **private information**. And a market in which the buyers or sellers have private information has **asymmetric information**.

Asymmetric Information: Examples and Problems

Asymmetric information affects many of your own economic transactions. One example is your knowledge about your driving skills and temperament. You know much more than your auto insurance company does about how carefully and defensively you drive—about your personal risk of having an accident that would cause the insurance company to pay a claim. Another example is your knowledge about your work effort. You know more than your employer about how hard you are willing to work. Yet another example is your knowledge about the quality of your car. You know whether it's a lemon, but the person to whom you are about to sell it does not know and can't find out until after he or she has bought it.

Asymmetric information creates two problems:

- Adverse selection
- Moral hazard

Adverse Selection **Adverse selection** is the tendency for people to *enter into agreements* in which they can use their private information to their own advantage and to the disadvantage of the uninformed party.

For example, if Jackie offers her salespeople a fixed wage, she will attract lazy salespeople. Hardworking salespeople will prefer not to work for Jackie because they can earn more by working for someone who pays by results. The fixed-wage contract adversely selects those with private information (knowledge about their work habits) who can use that knowledge to their own advantage and to the disadvantage of the other party.

Moral Hazard **Moral hazard** is the tendency for people with private information, *after entering into an agreement*, to use that information for their own benefit and at the cost of the less-informed party. For example, Jackie hires Mitch as a salesperson and pays him a fixed wage regardless of how much he sells. Mitch faces a moral hazard. He has an incentive to put in the least possible effort, benefiting himself and lowering Jackie's profits. For this reason, salespeople are usually paid by a formula that makes their income higher, the greater is the volume (or value) of their sales.

A variety of devices have evolved that enable markets to function in the face of moral hazard and adverse selection. We've just seen one, the use of incentive payments for salespeople. We're going to look at how three markets cope with adverse selection and moral hazard. They are

- The market for used cars
- The market for loans
- The market for insurance

The Market for Used Cars

When a person buys a car, it might turn out to be a lemon. If the car is a lemon, it is worth less to the buyer than if it has no defects. Does the used car market have two prices reflecting these two values—a low price for lemons and a higher price for cars without defects? It turns out that it does. But it needs some help to do so and to overcome what is called the **lemon problem**—the problem that in a market in which it is not possible to distinguish reliable products from lemons, there are too many lemons and too few reliable products traded.

To see how the used car market overcomes the lemon problem, we'll first look at a used car market that has a lemon problem.

The Lemon Problem in a Used Car Market

To explain the lemon problem as clearly as possible, we'll assume that there are only two kinds of cars: defective cars—lemons—and cars without defects that we'll call good cars. Whether or not a car is a lemon is private information that is available only to the current owner. The buyer of a used car can't tell whether he is buying a lemon until after he has bought the car and learned as much about it as its current owner knows.

Some people with low incomes and the time and ability to fix cars are willing to buy lemons as long as they know what they're buying and pay an appropriately low price. Suppose that a lemon is worth $5,000 to a buyer. More people want to buy a good car and we'll assume that a good car is worth $25,000 to a buyer.

But the buyer can't tell the difference between a lemon and a good car. Only the seller has this information. And telling the buyer that a car is not a lemon does not help. The seller has no incentive to tell the truth.

So the most that the buyer knows is the probability of buying a lemon. If half of the used cars sold turn out to be lemons, the buyer knows that he has a 50 percent chance of getting a good car and a 50 percent chance of getting a lemon.

The price that a buyer is willing to pay for a car of unknown quality is more than the value of a lemon because the car might be a good one. But the price is less than the value of a good car because it might turn out to be a lemon.

Now think about the sellers of used cars, who know the quality of their cars. Someone who owns a good car is going to be offered a price that is less than the value of that car to the buyer. Many owners will be reluctant to sell for such a low price. So the quantity of good used cars supplied will not be as large as it would be if people paid the price they are worth.

In contrast, someone who owns a lemon is going to be offered a price that is greater than the value of that car to the buyer. So owners of lemons will be eager to sell and the quantity of lemons supplied will be greater than it would be if people paid the price that a lemon is worth.

Figure 20.6 illustrates the used car market that we've just described. Part (a) shows the demand for used cars, D, and the supply of used cars, S. Equilibrium occurs at a price of $10,000 per car with 400 cars traded each month.

Some cars are good ones and some are lemons, but buyers can't tell the difference until it is too late to influence their decision to buy. But buyers do know what a good car and a lemon are worth to them, and sellers know the quality of the cars they are offering for sale. Figure 20.6(b) shows the demand curve for good cars, D_G, and the supply curve of good cars, S_G. Figure 20.6(c) shows the demand curve for lemons, D_L, and the supply curve of lemons, S_L.

At the market price of $10,000, owners of good cars supply 200 cars a month for sale. Owners of lemons also supply 200 cars a month for sale. The used car market is inefficient because there are too

FIGURE 20.6   The Lemon Problem

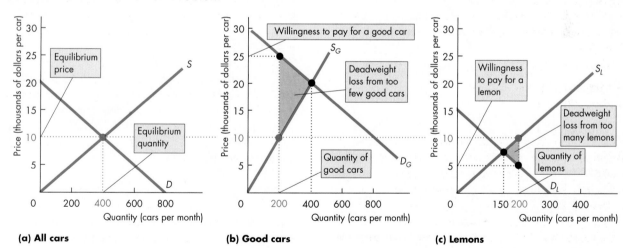

(a) All cars   **(b) Good cars**   **(c) Lemons**

Buyers can't tell a good used car from a lemon. Demand and supply determine the price and quantity of used cars traded in part (a). In part (b), D_G is the demand curve for good used cars and S_G is the supply curve. At the market price, too few

good cars are available, which brings a deadweight loss. In part (c), D_L is the demand curve for lemons and S_L is the supply curve. At the market price, too many lemons are available, which brings a deadweight loss.

myeconlab animation

many lemons and not enough good cars. Figure 20.6 makes this inefficiency clear by using the concept of deadweight loss (see Chapter 5, pp. 115–116).

At the quantity of good cars supplied, buyers are willing to pay $25,000 for a good car. They are willing to pay more than a good car is worth to its current owner for all good cars up to 400 cars a month. The gray triangle shows the deadweight loss that results from there being too few good used cars.

At the quantity of lemons supplied, buyers are willing to pay $5,000 for a lemon. They are willing to pay less than a lemon is worth to its current owner for all lemons above 150 cars a month. The gray triangle shows the deadweight loss that results from there being too many lemons.

You can see *adverse selection* in this used car market because there is a greater incentive to offer a lemon for sale. You can also see *moral hazard* because the owner of a lemon has little incentive to take good care of the car, so it is likely to become an even worse lemon. The market for used cars is not working well. Too many lemons and too few good used cars are traded.

A Used Car Market with Dealers' Warranties

How can used car dealers convince buyers that a car isn't a lemon? The answer is by giving a guarantee in the form of a warranty. By providing warranties only on good cars, dealers signal which cars are good ones and which are lemons.

Signaling occurs when an informed person takes actions that send information to uninformed persons. The grades and degrees that a university awards students are signals. They inform potential (uninformed) employers about the ability of the people they are considering hiring.

In the market for used cars, dealers send signals by giving warranties on the used cars they offer for sale. The message in the signal is that the dealer agrees to pay the costs of repairing the car if it turns out to have a defect.

Buyers believe the signal because the cost of sending a false signal is high. A dealer who gives a warranty on a lemon ends up bearing a high cost of repairs—and gains a bad reputation. A dealer who gives a warranty only on good cars has no repair costs and a reputation that gets better and better. It pays

---

FIGURE 20.7   Warranties Make the Used Car Market Efficient

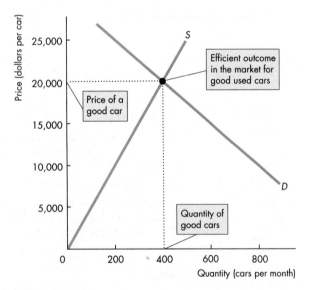

(a) Good cars

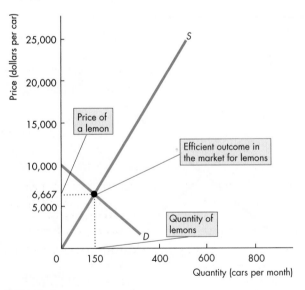

(b) Lemons

With dealers' warranties as signals, the equilibrium price of a good used car is $20,000 and 400 cars are traded. The market for good used cars is efficient. Because the signal

enables buyers to spot a lemon, the price of a lemon is $6,667 and 150 lemons are traded. The market for lemons is efficient.

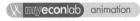

dealers to send an accurate signal, and it is rational for buyers to believe the signal.

So a car with a warranty is a good car; a car without a warranty is a lemon. Warranties solve the lemon problem and enable the used car market to function efficiently with two prices: one for lemons and one for good cars.

Figure 20.7 illustrates this outcome. In part (a) the demand for and supply of good cars determine the price of a good car. In part (b), the demand for and supply of lemons determine the price of a lemon. Both markets are efficient.

Pooling Equilibrium and Separating Equilibrium

You've seen two outcomes in the market for used cars. Without warranties, there is only one message visible to the buyer: All cars look the same. So there is one price regardless of whether the car is a good car or a lemon. We call the equilibrium in a market when only one message is available and an uninformed person cannot determine quality a **pooling equilibrium**.

But in a used car market with warranties, there are two messages. Good cars have warranties and lemons don't. So there are two car prices for the two types of cars. We call the equilibrium in a market when signaling provides full information to a previously uninformed person a **separating equilibrium**.

The Market for Loans

When you buy a tank of gasoline and swipe your credit card, you are taking a loan from the bank that issued your card. You demand and your bank supplies a loan. Have you noticed the interest rate on an unpaid credit card balance? In 2007, it ranged between 7 percent a year and 36 percent a year. Why are these interest rates so high? And why is there such a huge range?

The answer is that when banks make loans, they face the risk that the loan will not be repaid. The risk that a borrower, also known as a creditor, might not repay a loan is called **credit risk** or **default risk**. For credit card borrowing, the credit risk is high and it varies among borrowers. The highest-risk borrowers pay the highest interest rate.

Interest rates and the price of credit risk are determined in the market for loans. The lower the interest rate, the greater is the quantity of loans demanded and for a given level of credit risk, the higher the interest rate, the greater is the quantity of loans supplied. Demand and supply determine the interest rate and the price of credit risk.

If lenders were unable to charge different interest rates to reflect different degrees of credit risk, there would be a pooling equilibrium and an inefficient loans market.

Inefficient Pooling Equilibrium To see why a pooling equilibrium would be inefficient, suppose that banks can't identify the individual credit risk of their borrowers: they have no way of knowing how likely it is that a given loan will be repaid. In this situation, every borrower pays the same interest rate and the market is in a pooling equilibrium.

If all borrowers pay the same interest rate, the market for loans has the same problem as the used car market. Low-risk customers borrow less than they would if they were offered the low interest rate appropriate for their low credit risk. High-risk customers borrow more than they would if they faced the high interest rate appropriate for their high credit risk. So banks face an *adverse selection* problem. Too many borrowers are high risk and too few are low risk.

Signaling and Screening in the Market for Loans

Lenders don't know how likely it is that a given loan will be repaid, but the borrower does know. Low-risk borrowers have an incentive to signal their risk by providing lenders with relevant information. Signals might include information about the length of time a person has been in the current job or has lived at the current address, home ownership, marital status, age, and business record.

High-risk borrowers might be identified simply as those who have failed to signal low risk. These borrowers have an incentive to mislead lenders; and lenders have an incentive to induce high-risk borrowers to reveal their risk level. Inducing an informed party to reveal private information is called **screening**.

By not lending to people who refuse to reveal relevant information, banks are able to screen as well as receive signals that help them to separate their borrowers into a number of credit-risk categories. If lenders succeed, the market for loans comes to a separating equilibrium with a high interest rate for high-risk borrowers and a low interest rate for low-risk borrowers. Signaling and screening in the market for loans works like warranties in the used car market and avoids the deadweight loss of a pooling equilibrium.

Economics in Action
The Sub-Prime Credit Crisis

A sub-prime mortgage is a loan to a homebuyer who has a high risk of default. Figure 1 shows that between 2001 and 2005, the price of risk was low. Figure 2 shows why: The supply of credit, S_0, was large and so was the amount of risk taking. In 2007, the supply of credit decreased to S_1. The price of risk jumped and, faced with a higher interest rate, many sub-prime borrowers defaulted. Defaults in the sub-prime mortgage market spread to other markets that supplied the funds that financed mortgages.

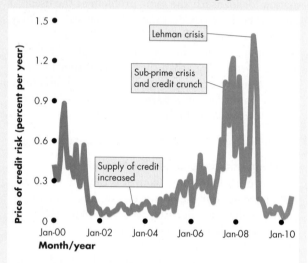

Figure 1   The Price of Commercial Credit Risk

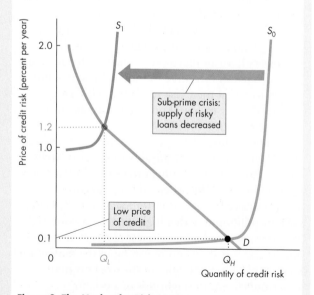

Figure 2   The Market for Risky Loans

The Market for Insurance

People who buy insurance face moral hazard, and insurance companies face adverse selection. Moral hazard arises because a person with insurance against a loss has less incentive than an uninsured person to avoid the loss. For example, a business with fire insurance has less incentive to install a fire alarm or sprinkler system than a business with no fire insurance does. Adverse selection arises because people who create greater risks are more likely to buy insurance. For example, a person with a family history of serious illness is more likely to buy health insurance than is a person with a family history of good health. Insurance companies have an incentive to find ways around the moral hazard and adverse selection problems. By doing so, they can lower premiums for low-risk people and raise premiums for high-risk people. One way in which auto insurance companies separate high-risk and low-risk customers is with a "no-claim" bonus. A driver accumulates a no-claim bonus by driving safely and avoiding accidents. The greater the bonus, the greater is the incentive to drive carefully. Insurance companies also use a deductible. A deductible is the amount of a loss that the insured person agrees to bear. The premium is smaller, the larger is the deductible, and the decrease in the premium is more than proportionate to the increase in the deductible. By offering insurance with full coverage—no deductible—on terms that are attractive only to the high-risk people and by offering coverage with a deductible on more favorable terms that are attractive to low-risk people, insurance companies can do profitable business with everyone. High-risk people choose policies with a low deductible and a high premium; low-risk people choose policies with a high deductible and a low premium.

◆ REVIEW QUIZ

1   How does private information create adverse selection and moral hazard?
2   How do markets for cars use warranties to cope with private information?
3   How do markets for loans use signaling and screening to cope with private information?
4   How do markets for insurance use no-claim bonuses to cope with private information?

You can work these questions in Study Plan 20.3 and get instant feedback.

Uncertainty, Information, and the Invisible Hand

A recurring theme throughout microeconomics is the big question: When do choices made in the pursuit of *self-interest* also promote the *social interest?* When does the invisible hand work well and when does it fail us? You've learned about the concept of efficiency, a major component of what we mean by the social interest. And you've seen that while competitive markets generally do a good job in helping to achieve efficiency, impediments such as monopoly and the absence of well-defined property rights can prevent the attainment of an efficient use of resources.

How do uncertainty and incomplete information affect the ability of self-interested choices to lead to a social interest outcome? Are these features of economic life another reason why markets fail and why some type of government intervention is required to achieve efficiency?

These are hard questions, and there are no definitive answers. But there are some useful things that we can say about the effects of uncertainty and a lack of complete information on the efficiency of resource use. We'll begin our brief review of this issue by thinking about information as just another good.

Information as a Good

More information is generally useful, and less uncertainty about the future is generally useful. Think about information as one of the goods that we want more of.

The most basic lesson about efficiency that you learned in Chapter 2 can be applied to information. Along our production possibilities frontier, we face a tradeoff between information and all other goods and services. Information, like everything else, can be produced at an increasing opportunity cost—an increasing marginal cost. For example, we could get more accurate weather forecasts, but only at increasing marginal cost, as we increased the amount of information that we gather from the atmosphere and the amount of money that we spend on supercomputers to process the data.

The principle of decreasing marginal benefit also applies to information. More information is valuable, but the more you know, the less you value another increment of information. For example, knowing that it will rain tomorrow is valuable information.

Knowing the amount of rain to within an inch is even more useful. But knowing the amount of rain to within a millimeter probably isn't worth much more.

Because the marginal cost of information is increasing and the marginal benefit is decreasing, there is an efficient amount of information. It would be inefficient to be overinformed.

In principle, competitive markets in information might deliver this efficient quantity. Whether they actually do so is hard to determine.

Monopoly in Markets that Cope with Uncertainty

There are probably large economies of scale in providing services that cope with uncertainty and incomplete information. The insurance industry, for example, is highly concentrated. Where monopoly elements exist, exactly the same inefficiency issues arise as occur in markets where uncertainty and incomplete information are not big issues. So it is likely that in some information markets, including insurance markets, there is underproduction arising from the attempt to maximize monopoly profit.

REVIEW QUIZ

1 Thinking about information as a good, what determines the information that people are willing to pay for?
2 Why is it inefficient to be overinformed?
3 Why are some of the markets that provide information likely to be dominated by monopolies?

You can work these questions in Study Plan 20.4 and get instant feedback.

You've seen how people make decisions when faced with uncertainty and how markets work when there is asymmetric information. *Reading Between the Lines* on pp. 478–479 looks at the way markets in human capital and labor use grades as signals that sort students by ability so that employers can hire the type of labor they seek. You'll see why grade deflation can be efficient and grade inflation is inefficient. Discriminating grades are in the social interest and in the self-interest of universities and students.

Grades as Signals

Princeton Leads in Grade Deflation

http://www.usatoday.com

March 28, 2007

Jennifer Mickel, a Princeton University senior, can't help but look around a class of 10 students and think, "Just three of us can get A's."

Since Princeton took the lead among Ivy League schools to formally adopt a grade-deflation policy three years ago—limiting A's to an average 35% across departments—students say the pressure to score the scarcer A has intensified. Students say they now eye competitive class-mates warily and shy away from classes perceived as difficult. …

There is no quota in individual courses, despite what students think, says Dean of the College Nancy Malkiel. …

Though a typical Princeton overachiever might blanch at the mere mention of a B, the university is sticking by its policy, Malkiel says. Students' employment and graduate school placements actually have improved the past two years, she says.

Grade inflation, well documented at many schools, is most pronounced in the Ivy League, according to an American Academy of Arts and Sciences 2002 study. For example, in 1966, 22% of all grades given to Harvard undergraduates were A's. That grew to 46% in 1996, the study found.

Princeton's grade spike became alarming in the last decade, Malkiel says. The policy, supported by a faculty vote, returns grades to early 1990s levels. "By grading in a more discriminating fashion, faculty members are able to give clearer signals about whether a student's work is inadequate, ordinary, good or excellent," Malkiel says. …

Princeton undergrads may take heart from Merrill Lynch's director of campus recruiting, Connie Thana-soulis. "I'm not in the least bit concerned about the chances for those at Princeton in comparison with any other Ivy League student," she says.

"I have never seen the quality of students that I've seen this year," she says. "I'm impressed."

From *USA Today*, a division of Gannett Co., Inc. Reprinted with permission.

ESSENCE OF THE STORY

- Princeton was the first Ivy League school to formally adopt a grade-deflation policy.

- The school limits A's to an average 35 percent across departments but has no quota in individual courses.

- Graduate school placements have improved since the policy was adopted.

- At Harvard, A's increased from 22 percent in 1966 to 46 percent in 1996.

- Princeton's grade inflation became alarming in the 1990s.

- More discriminating grades give clearer signals about students, says Dean Malkiel.

- Merrill Lynch's director of campus recruiting is impressed with the high quality of Princeton students.

ECONOMIC ANALYSIS

- Accurate grades provide valuable information to students and potential employers about a student's ability.

- Princeton University wants to provide accurate information and avoid grade inflation—awarding a high grade to most students—because this practice fails to provide information about a student's true ability.

- The labor market for new college graduates works badly with grade inflation and works well with accurate grading.

- Figure 1 shows a labor market for new college graduates when there is grade inflation.

- Students with high ability are not distinguished from other students, and the supply curve represents the supply of students of all ability levels.

- The demand curve shows the employers' willingness to hire new workers without knowledge of their true ability.

- Students get hired for a low wage rate. Eventually, they get sorted by ability as employers discover the true ability of their workers from on-the-job performance.

- Figures 2 and 3 show the outcome with accurate grading.

- In Fig. 2, students with high grades get high-wage jobs and in Fig. 3, students with low grades get low-wage jobs.

- The outcomes in Figs. 2 and 3 that arise immediately with accurate grading occur eventually with grade inflation as information about ability accumulates.

- But the cost to the student and the employer of discovering true ability is greater with grade inflation than with accurate grading.

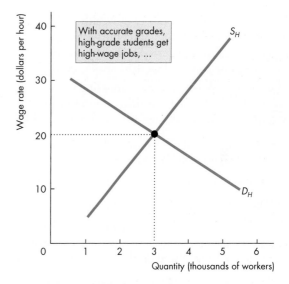

Figure 2 The market for A students

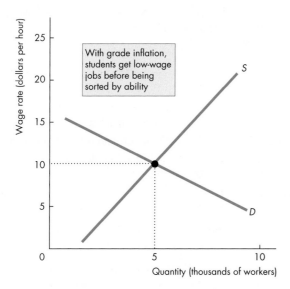

Figure 1 Market with grade inflation

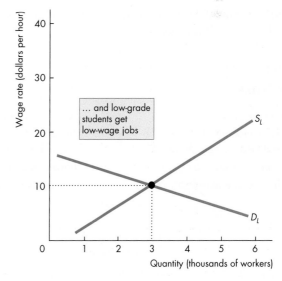

Figure 3 The market for D students

479

SUMMARY

Key Points

Decisions in the Face of Uncertainty (pp. 466–468)

- To make a rational choice under uncertainty, people choose the action that maximizes the expected utility of wealth.
- A decreasing marginal utility of wealth makes people risk averse. A sure outcome with a given expected wealth is preferred to a risky outcome with the same expected wealth—risk is costly.
- The cost of risk is found by comparing the expected wealth in a given risky situation with the wealth that gives the same utility but with no risk.

Working Problems 1 to 3 will give you a better understanding of decisions in the face of uncertainty.

Buying and Selling Risk (pp. 469–471)

- People trade risk in markets for insurance.
- By pooling risks, insurance companies can reduce the risks people face (from insured activities) at a lower cost than the value placed on the lower risk.

Working Problems 4 to 6 will give you a better understanding of buying and selling risk.

Private Information (pp. 472–476)

- Asymmetric information creates adverse selection and moral hazard problems.

- When it is not possible to distinguish good-quality products from lemons, too many lemons and too few good-quality products are traded in a pooling equilibrium.
- Signaling can overcome the lemon problem.
- In the market for used cars, warranties signal good cars and enable an efficient separating equilibrium.
- Private information about credit risk is overcome by using signals and screening based on personal characteristics.
- Private information about risk in insurance markets is overcome by using the no-claim bonus and deductibles.

Working Problems 7 to 11 will give you a better understanding of private information.

Uncertainty, Information, and the Invisible Hand (p. 477)

- Less uncertainty and more information can be viewed as a good that has increasing marginal cost and decreasing marginal benefit.
- Competitive information markets might be efficient, but economies of scale might bring inefficient underproduction of information and insurance.

Working Problems 12 and 13 will give you a better understanding of uncertainty, information, and the invisible hand.

Key Terms

Adverse selection, 472
Asymmetric information, 472
Credit risk or default risk, 475
Expected utility, 467
Expected wealth, 466

Lemon problem, 472
Moral hazard, 472
Pooling equilibrium, 475
Private information, 472
Risk aversion, 466

Screening, 475
Separating equilibrium, 475
Signaling, 474

STUDY PLAN PROBLEMS AND APPLICATIONS

 myeconlab You can work Problems 1 to 14 in MyEconLab Chapter 20 Study Plan and get instant feedback.

Decisions in the Face of Uncertainty (Study Plan 20.1)

1. The figure shows Lee's utility of wealth curve.

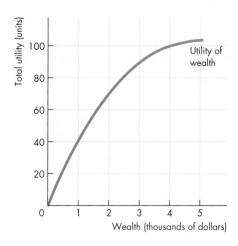

Lee is offered a job as a salesperson in which there is a 50 percent chance that she will make $4,000 a month and a 50 percent chance that she will make nothing.

a. What is Lee's expected income from taking this job?

b. What is Lee's expected utility from taking this job?

c. How much would another firm have to offer Lee with certainty to persuade her not to take the risky sales job?

d. What is Lee's cost of risk?

Use the following news clip to work Problems 2 and 3.

Larry Page on How to Change the World

As president of Google, Larry Page said that the risks that Google has taken have led to hot new applications like Gmail and Google Maps. In 2004, Page set out Google's risk strategy: Google would do some things that would have only a 10 percent chance of making $1 billion over the long term, but not many people will work on those things; 90 percent work on everything else. So that's not a big risk. Many of Google's new features come from the riskier investments. Before we began, we thought that Google might fail and we almost didn't do it. The reason we started Google was probably Stanford's decision that

we could go back and finish our Ph.D.s if we didn't succeed.

Source: *Fortune*, May 12, 2008

2. If much of Google's success has come from "riskier investments," then why doesn't Google dedicate all of their resources toward these riskier innovations?

3. In spite of the many risks that Larry Page has taken with Google, what evidence does this news clip provide that he is risk averse?

Buying and Selling Risk (Study Plan 20.2)

4. Lee in Problem 1 has built a small weekend shack on a steep, unstable hillside. She spent all her wealth, which is $5,000, on this project. There is a 75 percent chance that the house will be washed down the hill and be worthless. How much is Lee willing to pay for an insurance policy that pays her $5,000 if the house is washed away?

Use the following information to work Problems 5 and 6.

Larry lives in a neighborhood in which 20 percent of the cars are stolen every year. Larry's car, which he parks on the street overnight, is worth $20,000. (This is Larry's only wealth). The table shows Larry's utility of wealth schedule.

Wealth (dollars)	Utility (units)
20,000	400
16,000	350
12,000	280
8,000	200
4,000	110
0	0

5. If Larry cannot buy auto theft insurance, what is his expected wealth and his expected utility?

6. High-Crime Auto Theft, an insurance company, offers to sell Larry insurance at $8,000 a year and promises to provide Larry with a replacement car worth $20,000 if his car is stolen. Is Larry willing to buy this insurance? If not, is he willing to pay $4,000 a year for such insurance?

Private Information (Study Plan 20.3)

Use the following information to work Problems 7 and 8.

Zaneb is a high-school teacher and is well known in her community for her honesty and integrity. She is shopping for a used car and plans to borrow the money from her local bank to pay for the car.

7. a. Does Zaneb create any moral hazard or adverse selection problems for either the bank or the car dealer? Explain your answer.

   b. Does either the bank or the car dealer create any moral hazard or adverse selection problems for Zaneb? Explain your answer.

8. What arrangements is Zaneb likely to encounter that are designed to help her cope with the moral hazard and adverse selection problems she encounters in her car buying and bank loan transactions?

9. Suppose that there are three national football leagues: Time League, Goal Difference League, and Bonus for Win League. The leagues are of equal quality, but the players are paid differently. In the Time League, they are paid by the hour for time spent practicing and time spent playing. In the Goal Difference league, they are paid an amount that depends on the points that the team scores minus the points scored against it. In the Bonus for Win League, the players are paid one wage for a loss, a higher wage for a tie, and the highest wage of all for a win.

   a. Briefly describe the predicted differences in the quality of the games played by each of the leagues.

   b. Which league is the most attractive to players?

   c. Which league will generate the largest profits?

10. **We All Pay for the Uninsured**

    When buying health care, most of us don't behave like regular consumers: Seven out of the eight dollars we spend is somebody else's money, and we don't have very good information about doctors or hospitals. You can go online and find out your physician's fee before you make an appointment. That's helpful for a routine service, but when you have a serious condition, you really want to know about the physician's quality. Now, with the collaboration of physicians, to agree on quality standards and all health plans

willing to pool their data, consumers can look at a set of performance indicators that physicians think are appropriate, and be able to judge the quality of their physicians.

Source: *Fortune*, May 12, 2008

   a. Explain how the adverse selection problem applies to health care.

   b. How does the moral hazard problem apply to health insurance?

11. You can't buy insurance against the risk of being sold a lemon. Why isn't there a market in insurance against being sold a lemon? How does the market provide a buyer with some protection against being sold a lemon? What are the main ways in which markets overcome the lemon problem?

Uncertainty, Information, and the Invisible Hand

(Study Plan 20.4)

12. In Problem 10, what role can better information play in the health care market? Is it possible for there to be too much information in this market?

13. **Show Us Our Money**

    I have no clue what my colleagues make and I consider my salary my own business. It turns out that could be a huge mistake. What if employers made all employee salaries known? If you think about it, who is served by all the secrecy? Knowing what other workers make might be more ammunition to gun for a raise.

Source: *Time*, May 12, 2008

    Explain why a worker might be willing to pay for the salary information of other workers.

Economics in the News (Study Plan 20.N)

14. **Making the Grade**

    Grade inflation is unfair to students who truly deserve exceptional marks. It also is unfair to graduate applicants who come from schools that don't inflate grades.

Source: NJ.com, September 25, 2007

    What economic role do accurate grades play? Who benefits from grade inflation: students, professors, universities, or future employers? Who bears the cost of grade inflation? How do you think grade inflation might be controlled? Is grade inflation efficient?

ADDITIONAL PROBLEMS AND APPLICATIONS

 You can work these problems in MyEconLab if assigned by your instructor.

Decisions in the Face of Uncertainty

Use the following table, which shows Jimmy's and Zenda's utility of wealth schedules, to work Problems 15 to 17.

Wealth	Jimmy's utility	Zenda's utility
0	0	0
100	200	512
200	300	640
300	350	672
400	375	678
500	387	681
600	393	683
700	396	684

15. What are Jimmy's and Zenda's expected utilities from a bet that gives them a 50 percent chance of having a wealth of $600 and a 50 percent chance of having nothing?

16. a. Calculate Jimmy's and Zenda's marginal utility of wealth schedules.
    b. Who is more risk averse, Jimmy or Zenda? How do you know?

17. Suppose that Jimmy and Zenda each have $400 and are offered a business investment opportunity that involves committing the entire $400 to the project. The project could return $600 (a profit of $200) with a probability of 0.85 or $200 (a loss of $200) with a probability of 0.15. Who goes for the project and who hangs on to the initial $400?

Use the following information to work Problems 18 to 20.

Two students, Jim and Kim, are offered summer jobs managing a student house-painting business. There is a 50 percent chance that either of them will be successful and end up with $21,000 of wealth to get them through the next school year. But there is also a 50 percent chance that either will end up with only $3,000 of wealth. Each could take a completely safe but back-breaking job picking fruit that would leave them with a guaranteed $9,000 at the end of the summer. The table in the next column shows Jim's and Kim's utility of wealth schedules.

Wealth	Jim's utility	Kim's utility
0	0	0
3,000	100	200
6,000	200	350
9,000	298	475
12,000	391	560
15,000	491	620
18,000	586	660
21,000	680	680

18. Does anyone take the painting job? If so, who takes it and why? Does anyone take the job picking fruit? If so, who takes it and why?

19. In Problem 18, what is each student's maximized expected utility? Who has the larger expected wealth? Who ends up with the larger wealth at the end of the summer?

20. In Problem 18, if one of the students takes the risky job, how much more would the fruit-picking job have needed to pay to attract that student?

Buying and Selling Risk

Use the following table, which shows Chris's utility of wealth schedule, to work Problems 21 and 22.

Chris's wealth is $5,000 and it consists entirely of her share in a risky ice cream business. If the summer is cold, the business will fail, and she will have no wealth. Where Chris lives there is a 50 percent chance each year that the summer will be cold.

Wealth (dollars)	Utility (units)
5,000	150
4,000	140
3,000	120
2,000	90
1,000	50
0	0

21. If Chris cannot buy cold summer insurance, what is her expected wealth and what is her expected utility?

22. Business Loss Recovery, an insurance company, is willing to sell Chris cold summer insurance at a price of $3,000 a year and promises to pay her

$5,000 if the summer is cold and the business fails. Is Chris willing to buy this loss insurance? If she is, is she willing to pay $4,000 a year for it?

Private Information

Use the following information to work Problems 23 to 25.

Larry has a good car that he wants to sell; Harry has a lemon that he wants to sell. Each knows what type of car he is selling. You are looking at used cars and plan to buy one.

23. If both Larry and Harry are offering their cars for sale at the same price, from whom would you most want to buy, Larry or Harry, and why?

24. If you made an offer of the same price to Larry and Harry, who would sell to you and why? Describe the adverse selection problem that arises if you offer the same price to Larry and Harry.

25. How can Larry signal that he is selling a good car so that you are willing to pay Larry the price that he knows his car is worth, and a higher price than what you are willing to offer Harry?

26. Pam is a safe driver and Fran is a reckless driver. Each knows what type of driver she is, but no one else knows. What might an automobile insurance company do to get Pam to signal that she is a safe driver so that it can offer her insurance at a lower premium than it offers to Fran?

27. Why do you think it is not possible to buy insurance against having to put up with a low-paying, miserable job? Explain why a market in insurance of this type would be valuable to workers but unprofitable for an insurance provider and so would not work.

Uncertainty, Information, and the Invisible Hand

Use the following news clip to work Problems 28 and 29.

Why We Worry About the Things We Shouldn't … and Ignore the Things We Should

We pride ourselves on being the only species that understands the concept of risk, yet we have a confounding habit of worrying about mere possibilities while ignoring probabilities, building barricades against perceived dangers while leaving ourselves exposed to real ones: 20% of all adults still smoke; nearly 20% of drivers and more than 30% of backseat passengers don't use seat belts; two thirds of us are overweight or obese. We dash across the street against the light and build our homes in hurricane-prone areas—and when they're demolished by a storm, we rebuild in the same spot.

Source: *Time*, December 4, 2006

28. Explain how "worrying about mere possibilities while ignoring probabilities" can result in people making decisions that not only fail to satisfy social interest, but also fail to satisfy self-interest.

29. How can information be used to improve people's decision making?

Economics in the News

30. After you have studied *Reading Between the Lines* on pp. 478–479 answer the following questions.
    a. What information do accurate grades provide that grade inflation hides?
    b. If grade inflation became widespread in high schools, colleges, and universities, what new arrangements do you predict would emerge to provide better information about student ability?
    c. Do you think grade inflation is in anyone's self-interest? Explain who benefits and how they benefit from grade inflation.
    d. How do you think grade inflation might be controlled?

31. **Are You Paid What You're Worth?**

    How do you know if your pay adequately reflects your contributions to your employer's profits? In many instances, you don't. Your employer has more and better information than you do about how your salary and bonus compare to others in your field, to others in your office, and relative to the company's profits in any given year. You can narrow the information gap a bit if you're willing to buy salary reports from compensation sources. For example, at $200, a quick-call salary report from Economic Research Institute will offer you compensation data for your position based on your years of experience, your industry and the place where your company is located.

    Source: CNN, April 3, 2006

    a. Explain the role that asymmetric information can play in worker wages.
    b. What adverse selection problem exists if a firm offers lower wages to existing workers?
    c. What will determine how much a worker should actually pay for a detailed salary report?

For Whom?

During the past 35 years, the gap between the richest and the poorest in America has widened. But millions in Asia have been lifted from poverty and are now enjoying a high and rapidly rising standard of living. What are the forces that generate these trends? The answer to this question is the forces of demand and supply in factor markets. These forces determine wages, interest rates, rents, and the prices of natural resources. These forces also determine people's incomes.

In America, human capital and entrepreneurship are the most prized resources, and their incomes have grown most rapidly. In Asia, labor has seen its wage rates transformed. And in all regions rich in oil, incomes have risen on the back of high and fast-rising energy prices.

Many outstanding economists have advanced our understanding of factor markets and the role they play in helping to resolve the conflict between the demands of humans and the resources available. One of them is Thomas Robert Malthus.

Another is Harold Hotelling whose prediction of an ever-rising price of nonrenewable natural resources implies an ever-falling rate of their use and an intensifying search for substitutes.

Yet another is Julian Simon, who challenged both the Malthusian gloom and the Hotelling Principle. He believed that people are the "ultimate resource" and predicted that a rising population lessens the pressure on natural resources. A bigger population provides a larger number of resourceful people who can discover more efficient ways of using scarce resources.

Thomas Robert Malthus *(1766–1834), an English clergyman and economist, was an extremely influential social scientist. In his best-selling* Essay on the Principle of Population, *published in 1798, he predicted that population growth would outstrip food production and said that wars, famine, and disease were inevitable unless population growth was held in check by marrying at a late age and living a celibate life. (He married at 38 a wife of 27, marriage ages that he recommended for others.)*

Malthus had a profound influence on Charles Darwin, who got the key idea that led him to the theory of natural selection from the Essay on the Principle of Population. *But it was also Malthus's gloomy predictions that made economics the "dismal science."*

"The passion between the sexes has appeared in every age to be so nearly the same, that it may always be considered, in algebraic language, as a given quantity."

THOMAS ROBERT MALTHUS

An Essay on the Principle of Population

Professor Card, what attracted you to economics?

When I went to university I had no intention of studying economics: I was planning to be a physics major. I was helping a friend with her problem set and started reading the supply and demand section of the textbook. I was impressed with how well the model seemed to describe the paradox that a bumper crop can be bad for farmers. I read most of the book over the next few days. The next year, I signed up as an economics major.

Almost all your work is grounded in data. You are an empirical economist. How do you go about your work, where do your data come from, and how do you use data?

The data I use come from many different sources. I have collected my own data from surveys; transcribed data from historical sources and government publications; and used computerized data files based on records from Censuses and surveys in the United States, Canada, Britain, and other countries.

An economist can do three things with data. The first is to develop simple statistics on basic questions such as "What fraction of families live in poverty?" For this, one needs to understand how the data were collected and processed and how the questions were asked. For example, the poverty rate depends on how you define a "family." If a single mother and her child live with the mother's parents, the income of the mother and the grandparents is counted as "family income."

The second thing economists do with data is develop descriptive comparisons. For example, I have compared the wage differences between male and female workers. Again, the details are important. For example, the male-female wage differential is much bigger if you look at annual earnings than at earnings per hour, because women work fewer hours per year.

Once you've established some simple facts, you start to get ideas for possible explanations. You can also rule out a lot of other ideas.

The third and most difficult thing that empirical economists try to do is infer a causal relationship. In rare instances, we have a true experiment in which a random subgroup of volunteers is enrolled in a "treatment group" and the remainder become the "control group." The Self Sufficiency Program (SSP)—an experimental welfare reform demonstration in Canada—was conducted this way. Because of random assignment, we know that the treatment and control groups would have looked very similar in the absence of the treatment. Thus when we see a difference in behavior, such as the higher level of work activity by

single parents in the treatment group of SSP, we can infer that the financial incentives of SSP caused people to work more.

Most often, we don't have an experiment. We see a group of people who are subject to some "treatment" (such as a higher minimum wage) and we try to construct a comparison group by finding some other group similar to the treatment group who tell us what the treatment group would have looked like in the absence of treatment. If we can't find a compelling comparison group, we have to be cautious.

In your book on the minimum wage with Alan Krueger, you reported that an increase in the minimum wage increased employment—the opposite of the conventional wisdom. How did you reach that conclusion?

DAVID CARD is Class of 1950 Professor of Economics and Director of the Center for Labor Economics at the University of California, Berkeley, and Faculty Research Associate at the National Bureau of Economic Research.

Born in Canada, Professor Card obtained his B.A. at Queen's University, Kingston, Ontario, in 1977 and his Ph.D. at Princeton University in 1983. He has received many honors, the most notable of which is the American Economic Association's John Bates Clark Prize, awarded to the best economist under 40.

Professor Card's research on labor markets and the effects of public policies on earnings, jobs, and the distribution of income has produced around 150 articles and several books. His most recent book (co-edited with Alan Auerbach and John Quigley) is *Poverty, the Distribution of Income, and Public Policy* (New York: Russell Sage Foundation, 2006). An earlier book (co-authored with Alan B. Krueger), *Myth and Measurement: The New Economics of the Minimum Wage* (Princeton, NJ: Princeton University Press, 1995), made a big splash and upset one of the most fundamental beliefs about the effects of minimum wages.

Michael Parkin talked with David Card about his work and the progress that economists have made in understanding how public policies can influence the distribution of income and economic well-being.

We studied several instances where minimum wages were raised in one place but not in another. For example, when we found out that the New Jersey legislature had recently voted to raise the minimum wage, we set up a survey of fast-food restaurants in New Jersey and in nearby parts of Pennsylvania. We surveyed the stores a few months before the New Jersey minimum went up and then again one year later, after the minimum had been raised. The first-round survey found that conditions were very similar in the two states. In the second round, we found that although wages were now higher in New Jersey, employment was also slightly higher. It was very

> The most difficult thing that empirical economists try to do is infer a causal relationship.

important to have the first-round survey to benchmark any differences that existed prior to the rise in the minimum. Thus, we argued that any differential changes in New Jersey relative to Pennsylvania from the first round to the second round were most plausibly due to the minimum wage.

How did you explain what you found?

We argued that many employers in New Jersey before the rise in the minimum were operating with vacancies and would have liked to hire more workers but could not do so without raising their wages. In this situation, an increase in the minimum wage can cause some employers to hire more and others to hire less. On average, the net effect on employment can be small. What we saw was a rise in wages and a reduction in vacancies in New Jersey, coupled with a small gain in employment.

You've examined just about every labor market policy. Let's talk about welfare payments to single mothers: How do they influence labor market decisions?

The Self Sufficiency Program welfare demonstration in Canada tested an earnings subsidy as an alternative to conventional welfare payments. The problem with conventional welfare is that recipients have no incentive to work: If they earn $1, their payments are reduced by $1. That led Milton Friedman in the early 1950s to advocate an alternative "negative income tax" program, such as SSP, in which recipients who earn more only lose a fraction of their benefits (in the case of SSP, 50 cents per dollar earned). The results showed that this alternative system encourages single parents to work more.

Immigration has been big news in recent years. Can you describe your work on this issue and your findings?

My research has tried to understand whether the arrival of low-skilled immigrants hurts the labor market opportunities for less-skilled natives. One of my papers studies the effect of the Mariel Boatlift, which occurred in 1980 following a political uprising that led Fidel Castro to declare that people who wanted to leave Cuba were free to exit from the port of Mariel. Within days, a flotilla of small boats from the United States began transporting people to Miami, and 150,000 people eventually left. Over one half stayed in Miami, creating a huge "shock" to the supply of low-skilled labor. I studied the effect by looking at wages and unemployment rates for various groups in Miami and in a set of comparison cities that had very similar wage and employment trends in the previous decade. I found that the influx of the boatlift had no discernible effect on wages or unemployment of other workers in Miami. My later work has confirmed that the Miami story seems to hold in most other cities. Cities can absorb big inflows of low-skilled immigrants with remarkably little negative impact on natives.

> ... find out what life is like for other people. ... The best economists are observant and thoughtful social scientists.

The distribution of income has become increasingly unequal. Do we know why?

There are many sources. Family incomes have become more unequal in part because of a rise in families with two very high-wage earners. These families have pulled away from the rest, creating a widening distribution. The very richest families, whose incomes are above the 95th or 99th percentile of the income distribution, earn an increasingly large share of national income. The trends in income for this group account for most of the rise in inequality we have seen in the last 10 years.

Unfortunately, it is very hard to study this group because they represent such a small fraction of families, and they are often under-reported on surveys. The best available data, from tax returns, don't tell us much about the sources of this group's success, though it seems to be due to labor market earnings rather than to previous investments or family wealth.

There is a large literature on wage inequality among the larger "middle" of the population: people who earn up to $150,000 per year, for example. Wage inequality for men in this group rose very sharply in the early 1980s in the United States, rose a little more between 1985 and 1990, and was fairly stable (or even decreasing) in the 1990s. Some of the rise in the 1980s was due to decreases in unionization, and some was due to the changing effects of the minimum wage, which fell in real terms in the early 1980s, and then gained in the early to mid-1990s.

Some researchers ascribe the rest of the trend in wage inequality to the spread of computers and increasing demands for highly skilled workers. Others blame international trade and, most recently, immigration. Those explanations are hard to evaluate because we don't really see the forces of new technology or trade that affect any particular worker. One thing we do know is that wage inequality trends were quite different in many other countries. Canada, for instance, had relatively modest rises in inequality in the 1980s.

What advice do you have for someone who is just beginning to study economics? What other subjects do you think work well alongside economics? Do you have some reading suggestions?

The part of economics that most interests me is the behavior of people in their everyday life. People constantly have to answer questions such as: Should I get more education? How much should I save? Should I send my children to the local public school? It's extremely important to see how these questions are answered by different people: people from poorer families or other countries or who had to make very different choices. Take any opportunity to find out what life is like for other people. You can learn a lot from reading novels, spending a year abroad, or taking classes in sociology or history. The best economists are observant and thoughtful social scientists. My other piece of advice is study mathematics. The more mathematics training you have, the more easily you can understand what economists are doing. Newton invented calculus to study the motion of planets, but economics benefits from the same tools.

After studying this chapter,
you will be able to:

◆ Define GDP and use the circular flow model to explain why GDP equals aggregate expenditure and aggregate income

◆ Explain how the Bureau of Economic Analysis measures U.S. GDP and real GDP

◆ Describe how real GDP is used to measure economic growth and fluctuations and explain the limitations of real GDP as a measure of economic well-being

21

MEASURING GDP AND ECONOMIC GROWTH

Will our economy expand more rapidly in 2011 or will it sink into another recession—a "double-dip"? Many U.S. corporations wanted to know the answers to these questions at the beginning of 2011. Google wanted to know whether to expand its server network and introduce new services or hold off on any new launches. Amazon.com wanted to know whether to increase its warehousing facilities. To assess the state of the economy and to make big decisions about business expansion, firms such as Google and Amazon use forecasts of GDP. What exactly is GDP and what does it tell us about the state of the economy?

Some countries are rich while others are poor. How do we compare economic well-being in one country with that in another? How can we make international comparisons of production?

In this chapter, you will find out how economic statisticians at the Bureau of Economic Analysis measure GDP and the economic growth rate. You will also learn about the uses and the limitations of these measures. In *Reading Between the Lines* at the end of the chapter, we'll look at some future scenarios for the U.S. economy.

◆ Gross Domestic Product

What exactly is GDP, how is it calculated, what does it mean, and why do we care about it? You are going to discover the answers to these questions in this chapter. First, what *is* GDP?

GDP Defined

GDP, or **gross domestic product**, is the market value of the final goods and services produced within a country in a given time period. This definition has four parts:

- Market value
- Final goods and services
- Produced within a country
- In a given time period

We'll examine each in turn.

Market Value To measure total production, we must add together the production of apples and oranges, computers and popcorn. Just counting the items doesn't get us very far. For example, which is the greater total production: 100 apples and 50 oranges or 50 apples and 100 oranges?

GDP answers this question by valuing items at their *market values*—the prices at which items are traded in markets. If the price of an apple is 10 cents, then the market value of 50 apples is $5. If the price of an orange is 20 cents, then the market value of 100 oranges is $20. By using market prices to value production, we can add the apples and oranges together. The market value of 50 apples and 100 oranges is $5 plus $20, or $25.

Final Goods and Services To calculate GDP, we value the *final goods and services* produced. A **final good** (or service) is an item that is bought by its final user during a specified time period. It contrasts with an **intermediate good** (or service), which is an item that is produced by one firm, bought by another firm, and used as a component of a final good or service.

For example, a Ford truck is a final good, but a Firestone tire on the truck is an intermediate good. A Dell computer is a final good, but an Intel Pentium chip inside it is an intermediate good.

If we were to add the value of intermediate goods and services produced to the value of final goods and services, we would count the same thing many times—a problem called *double counting*. The value of a truck already includes the value of the tires, and the value of a Dell PC already includes the value of the Pentium chip inside it.

Some goods can be an intermediate good in some situations and a final good in other situations. For example, the ice cream that you buy on a hot summer day is a final good, but the ice cream that a restaurant buys and uses to make sundaes is an intermediate good. The sundae is the final good. So whether a good is an intermediate good or a final good depends on what it is used for, not what it is.

Some items that people buy are neither final goods nor intermediate goods and they are not part of GDP. Examples of such items include financial assets—stocks and bonds—and secondhand goods—used cars or existing homes. A secondhand good was part of GDP in the year in which it was produced, but not in GDP this year.

Produced Within a Country Only goods and services that are produced *within a country* count as part of that country's GDP. Nike Corporation, a U.S. firm, produces sneakers in Vietnam, and the market value of those shoes is part of Vietnam's GDP, not part of U.S. GDP. Toyota, a Japanese firm, produces automobiles in Georgetown, Kentucky, and the value of this production is part of U.S. GDP, not part of Japan's GDP.

In a Given Time Period GDP measures the value of production *in a given time period*—normally either a quarter of a year—called the quarterly GDP data—or a year—called the annual GDP data.

GDP measures not only the value of total production but also total income and total expenditure. The equality between the value of total production and total income is important because it shows the direct link between productivity and living standards. Our standard of living rises when our incomes rise and we can afford to buy more goods and services. But we must produce more goods and services if we are to be able to buy more goods and services.

Rising incomes and a rising value of production go together. They are two aspects of the same phenomenon: increasing productivity. To see why, we study the circular flow of expenditure and income.

GDP and the Circular Flow of Expenditure and Income

Figure 21.1 illustrates the circular flow of expenditure and income. The economy consists of households, firms, governments, and the rest of the world (the rectangles), which trade in factor markets and goods (and services) markets. We focus first on households and firms.

Households and Firms Households sell and firms buy the services of labor, capital, and land in factor markets. For these factor services, firms pay income to households: wages for labor services, interest for the use of capital, and rent for the use of land. A fourth factor of production, entrepreneurship, receives profit.

Firms' retained earnings—profits that are not distributed to households—are part of the household sector's income. You can think of retained earnings as

being income that households save and lend back to firms. Figure 21.1 shows the total income—*aggregate income*—received by households, including retained earnings, as the blue flow labeled *Y*.

Firms sell and households buy consumer goods and services—such as inline skates and haircuts—in the goods market. The total payment for these goods and services is **consumption expenditure**, shown by the red flow labeled *C*.

Firms buy and sell new capital equipment—such as computer systems, airplanes, trucks, and assembly line equipment—in the goods market. Some of what firms produce is not sold but is added to inventory. For example, if GM produces 1,000 cars and sells 950 of them, the other 50 cars remain in GM's inventory of unsold cars, which increases by 50 cars. When a firm adds unsold output to inventory, we can think of the firm as buying goods from itself. The

---

FIGURE 21.1 The Circular Flow of Expenditure and Income

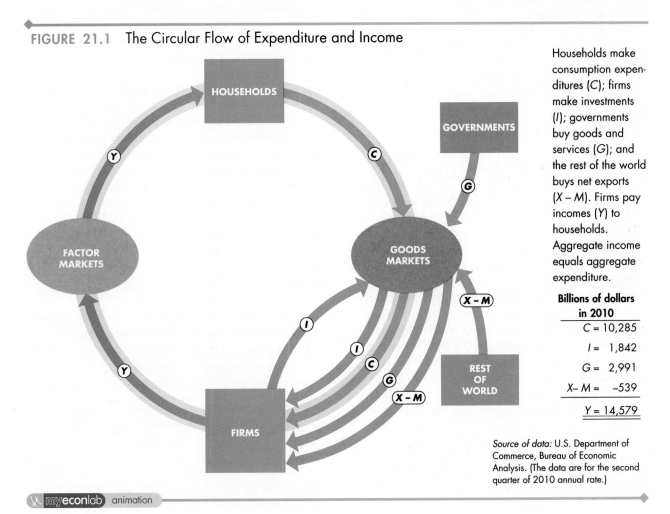

Households make consumption expenditures (*C*); firms make investments (*I*); governments buy goods and services (*G*); and the rest of the world buys net exports (*X – M*). Firms pay incomes (*Y*) to households. Aggregate income equals aggregate expenditure.

Billions of dollars in 2010	
C =	10,285
I =	1,842
G =	2,991
X– M =	–539
Y =	14,579

Source of data: U.S. Department of Commerce, Bureau of Economic Analysis. (The data are for the second quarter of 2010 annual rate.)

purchase of new plant, equipment, and buildings and the additions to inventories are **investment**, shown by the red flow labeled *I*.

Governments Governments buy goods and services from firms and their expenditure on goods and services is called **government expenditure**. In Fig. 21.1, government expenditure is shown as the red flow *G*.

Governments finance their expenditure with taxes. But taxes are not part of the circular flow of expenditure and income. Governments also make financial transfers to households, such as Social Security benefits and unemployment benefits, and pay subsidies to firms. These financial transfers, like taxes, are not part of the circular flow of expenditure and income.

Rest of the World Firms in the United States sell goods and services to the rest of the world—**exports**—and buy goods and services from the rest of the world—**imports**. The value of exports (*X*) minus the value of imports (*M*) is called **net exports**, the red flow *X* − *M* in Fig 21.1. If net exports are positive, the net flow of goods and services is from U.S. firms to the rest of the world. If net exports are negative, the net flow of goods and services is from the rest of the world to U.S. firms.

GDP Equals Expenditure Equals Income Gross domestic product can be measured in two ways: By the total expenditure on goods and services or by the total income earned producing goods and services.

The total expenditure—*aggregate expenditure*—is the sum of the red flows in Fig. 21.1. Aggregate expenditure equals consumption expenditure plus investment plus government expenditure plus net exports.

Aggregate income is equal to the total amount paid for the services of the factors of production used to produce final goods and services—wages, interest, rent, and profit. The blue flow in Fig. 21.1 shows aggregate income. Because firms pay out as incomes (including retained profits) everything they receive from the sale of their output, aggregate income (the blue flow) equals aggregate expenditure (the sum of the red flows). That is,

$$Y = C + I + G + X - M.$$

The table in Fig. 21.1 shows the values of the expenditures for 2010 and that their sum is $14,579 billion, which also equals aggregate income.

Because aggregate expenditure equals aggregate income, the two methods of measuring GDP give the same answer. So

GDP equals aggregate expenditure and equals aggregate income.

The circular flow model is the foundation on which the national economic accounts are built.

Why Is Domestic Product "Gross"?

"Gross" means before subtracting the depreciation of capital. The opposite of "gross" is "net," which means after subtracting the depreciation of capital.

Depreciation is the decrease in the value of a firm's capital that results from wear and tear and obsolescence. The total amount spent both buying new capital and replacing depreciated capital is called **gross investment**. The amount by which the value of capital increases is called **net investment**. Net investment equals gross investment minus depreciation.

For example, if an airline buys 5 new airplanes and retires 2 old airplanes from service, its gross investment is the value of the 5 new airplanes, depreciation is the value of the 2 old airplanes retired, and net investment is the value of 3 new airplanes.

Gross investment is one of the expenditures included in the expenditure approach to measuring GDP. So the resulting value of total product is a gross measure.

Gross profit, which is a firm's profit before subtracting depreciation, is one of the incomes included in the income approach to measuring GDP. So again, the resulting value of total product is a gross measure.

REVIEW QUIZ

1   Define GDP and distinguish between a final good and an intermediate good. Provide examples.
2   Why does GDP equal aggregate income and also equal aggregate expenditure?
3   What is the distinction between gross and net?

You can work these questions in Study Plan 21.1 and get instant feedback.

Let's now see how the ideas that you've just studied are used in practice. We'll see how GDP and its components are measured in the United States today.

Measuring U.S. GDP

The Bureau of Economic Analysis (BEA) uses the concepts in the circular flow model to measure GDP and its components in the *National Income and Product Accounts*. Because the value of aggregate production equals aggregate expenditure and aggregate income, there are two approaches available for measuring GDP, and both are used. They are

- The expenditure approach
- The income approach

The Expenditure Approach

The *expenditure approach* measures GDP as the sum of consumption expenditure (C), investment (I), government expenditure on goods and services (G), and net exports of goods and services ($X - M$). These expenditures correspond to the red flows through the goods markets in the circular flow model in Fig. 21.1. Table 21.1 shows these expenditures and GDP for 2010. The table uses the terms in the *National Income and Product Accounts*.

Personal consumption expenditures are the expenditures by U.S. households on goods and services produced in the United States and in the rest of the world. They include goods such as soda and books and services such as banking and legal advice. They also include the purchase of consumer durable goods, such as TVs and microwave ovens. But they do *not* include the purchase of new homes, which the BEA counts as part of investment.

Gross private domestic investment is expenditure on capital equipment and buildings by firms and the additions to business inventories. It also includes expenditure on new homes by households.

Government expenditure on goods and services is the expenditure by all levels of government on goods and services, such as national defense and garbage collection. It does *not* include *transfer payments*, such as unemployment benefits, because they are not expenditures on goods and services.

Net exports of goods and services are the value of exports minus the value of imports. This item includes airplanes that Boeing sells to British Airways (a U.S. export), and Japanese DVD players that Circuit City buys from Sony (a U.S. import).

Table 21.1 shows the relative magnitudes of the four items of aggregate expenditure.

TABLE 21.1   GDP: The Expenditure Approach

Item	Symbol	Amount in 2010 (billions of dollars)	Percentage of GDP
Personal consumption expenditures	C	10,285	70.5
Gross private domestic investment	I	1,842	12.6
Government expenditure on goods and services	G	2,991	20.5
Net exports of goods and services	X – M	–539	–3.7
Gross domestic product	Y	**14,579**	**100.0**

The expenditure approach measures GDP as the sum of personal consumption expenditures (*C*), gross private domestic investment (*I*), government expenditure on goods and services (*G*), and net exports (*X – M*). In 2010, GDP measured by the expenditure approach was $14,579 billion. More than two thirds of aggregate expenditure is on personal consumption goods and services.

Source of data: U.S. Department of Commerce, Bureau of Economic Analysis.

The Income Approach

The *income approach* measures GDP by summing the incomes that firms pay households for the services of the factors of production they hire—wages for labor, interest for capital, rent for land, and profit for entrepreneurship. These incomes correspond to the blue flow through the factor markets in the circular flow model in Fig. 21.1.

The *National Income and Product Accounts* divide incomes into two big categories:

1. Compensation of employees
2. Net operating surplus

Compensation of employees is the payment for labor services. It includes net wages and salaries (called "take-home pay") that workers receive plus taxes withheld on earnings plus fringe benefits such as Social Security and pension fund contributions.

Net operating surplus is the sum of all other factor incomes. It has four components: *net interest, rental income*, *corporate profits*, and *proprietors' income*.

Net interest is the interest households receive on loans they make minus the interest households pay on their own borrowing.

Rental income is the payment for the use of land and other rented resources.

Corporate profits are the profits of corporations, some of which are paid to households in the form of dividends and some of which are retained by corporations as undistributed profits. They are all income.

Proprietors' income is the income earned by the owner-operator of a business, which includes compensation for the owner's labor, the use of the owner's capital, and profit.

Table 21.2 shows the two big categories of factor incomes and their relative magnitudes. You can see that compensation of employees—labor income—is approximately twice the magnitude of the other factor incomes that make up the net operating surplus.

The factor incomes sum to *net domestic income at factor cost*. The term "factor cost" is used because it is the cost of the factors of production used to produce final goods. When we sum the expenditures on final goods, we arrive at a total called *domestic product at market prices*. Market prices and factor cost diverge because of indirect taxes and subsidies.

An *indirect tax* is a tax paid by consumers when they buy goods and services. (In contrast, a *direct tax* is a tax on income.) State sales taxes and taxes on alcohol, gasoline, and tobacco products are indirect taxes. Because of indirect taxes, consumers pay more for some goods and services than producers receive. Market price exceeds factor cost. For example, if the sales tax is 7 percent, you pay $1.07 when you buy a $1 chocolate bar. The factor cost of the chocolate bar including profit is $1. The market price is $1.07.

A *subsidy* is a payment by the government to a producer. Payments made to grain growers and dairy farmers are subsidies. Because of subsidies, consumers pay less for some goods and services than producers receive. Factor cost exceeds market price.

To get from factor cost to market price, we add indirect taxes and subtract subsidies. Making this adjustment brings us to *net domestic income at market prices*. We still must get from a *net* to a *gross* measure.

Total expenditure is a *gross* number because it includes *gross* investment. Net domestic income at market prices is a net income measure because corporate profits are measured *after deducting depreciation*. They are a *net* income measure. To get from net income to gross income, we must *add depreciation*.

TABLE 21.2   GDP: The Income Approach

Item	Amount in 2010 (billions of dollars)	Percentage of GDP
Compensation of employees	7,929	54.4
Net interest	924	6.3
Rental income	299	2.1
Corporate profits	1,210	8.3
Proprietors' income	1,050	7.2
Net domestic income at factor cost	11,412	78.3
Indirect taxes *less* subsidies	1,127	7.7
Net domestic income at market prices	12,539	86.0
Depreciation	1,860	12.8
GDP (income approach)	**14,399**	**98.8**
Statistical discrepancy	180	1.2
GDP (expenditure approach)	**14,579**	**100.0**

The sum of factor incomes equals *net domestic income at factor cost*. GDP equals net domestic income at factor cost plus indirect taxes less subsidies plus depreciation.

In 2010, GDP measured by the income approach was $14,399 billion. This amount is $180 billion less than GDP measured by the expenditure approach—a statistical discrepancy of $151 billion or 1.2 percent of GDP.

Compensation of employees—labor income—is by far the largest part of aggregate income.

Source of data: U.S. Department of Commerce, Bureau of Economic Analysis.

We've now arrived at GDP using the income approach. This number is not exactly the same as GDP using the expenditure approach. For example, if a waiter doesn't report all his tips when he fills out his income tax return, they get missed in the income approach but they show up in the expenditure approach when he spends his income. So the sum of expenditures might exceed the sum of incomes. Also the sum of expenditures might exceed the sum of incomes because some expenditure items are estimated rather than directly measured.

The gap between the expenditure approach and the income approach is called the *statistical discrepancy* and it is calculated as the GDP expenditure total minus the GDP income total. The discrepancy is never large. In 2010, it was 1.2 percent of GDP.

Nominal GDP and Real GDP

Often, we want to *compare* GDP in two periods, say 2000 and 2010. In 2000, GDP was $9,952 billion and in 2010, it was $14,579 billion—46 percent higher than in 2000. This increase in GDP is a combination of an increase in production and a rise in prices. To isolate the increase in production from the rise in prices, we distinguish between *real* GDP and *nominal* GDP.

Real GDP is the value of final goods and services produced in a given year when *valued at the prices of a reference base year*. By comparing the value of production in the two years at the same prices, we reveal the change in production.

Currently, the reference base year is 2005 and we describe real GDP as measured in 2005 dollars—in terms of what the dollar would buy in 2005.

Nominal GDP is the value of final goods and services produced in a given year when valued at the prices of that year. Nominal GDP is just a more precise name for GDP.

Economists at the Bureau of Economic Analysis calculate real GDP using the method described in the Mathematical Note on pp. 506–507. Here, we'll explain the basic idea but not the technical details.

Calculating Real GDP

We'll calculate real GDP for an economy that produces one consumption good, one capital good, and one government service. Net exports are zero.

Table 21.3 shows the quantities produced and the prices in 2005 (the base year) and in 2010. In part (a), we calculate nominal GDP in 2005. For each item, we multiply the quantity produced in 2005 by its price in 2005 to find the total expenditure on the item. We sum the expenditures to find nominal GDP, which in 2005 is $100 million. Because 2005 is the base year, both real GDP and nominal GDP equal $100 million.

In Table 21.3(b), we calculate nominal GDP in 2010, which is $300 million. Nominal GDP in 2010 is three times its value in 2005. But by how much has production increased? Real GDP will tell us.

In Table 21.3(c), we calculate real GDP in 2010. The quantities of the goods and services produced are those of 2010, as in part (b). The prices are those in the reference base year—2005, as in part (a).

For each item, we multiply the quantity produced in 2010 by its price in 2005. We then sum these expenditures to find real GDP in 2010, which is $160 million. This number is what total expenditure

TABLE 21.3 Calculating Nominal GDP and Real GDP

	Item	Quantity (millions)	Price (dollars)	Expenditure (millions of dollars)
(a) In 2005				
C	T-shirts	10	5	50
I	Computer chips	3	10	30
G	Security services	1	20	20
Y	Real and Nominal GDP in 2005			100
(b) In 2010				
C	T-shirts	4	5	20
I	Computer chips	2	20	40
G	Security services	6	40	240
Y	Nominal GDP in 2010			300
(c) Quantities of 2010 valued at prices of 2005				
C	T-shirts	4	5	20
I	Computer chips	2	10	20
G	Security services	6	20	120
Y	Real GDP in 2010			160

In 2005, the reference base year, real GDP equals nominal GDP and was $100 million. In 2010, nominal GDP increased to $300 million. But real GDP in 2010 in part (c), which is calculated by using the quantities of 2010 in part (b) and the prices of 2005 in part (a), was only $160 million—a 60 percent increase from 2005.

would have been in 2010 if prices had remained the same as they were in 2005.

Nominal GDP in 2010 is three times its value in 2005, but real GDP in 2010 is only 1.6 times its 2005 value—a 60 percent increase in production.

REVIEW QUIZ

1 What is the expenditure approach to measuring GDP?
2 What is the income approach to measuring GDP?
3 What adjustments must be made to total income to make it equal GDP?
4 What is the distinction between nominal GDP and real GDP?
5 How is real GDP calculated?

You can work these questions in Study Plan 21.2 and get instant feedback.

The Uses and Limitations of Real GDP

Economists use estimates of real GDP for two main purposes:

- To compare the standard of living over time
- To compare the standard of living across countries

The Standard of Living Over Time

One method of comparing the standard of living over time is to calculate real GDP per person in different years. **Real GDP per person** is real GDP divided by the population. Real GDP per person tells us the value of goods and services that the average person can enjoy. By using *real* GDP, we remove any influence that rising prices and a rising cost of living might have had on our comparison.

We're interested in both the long-term trends and the shorter-term cycles in the standard of living.

Long-Term Trend A handy way of comparing real GDP per person over time is to express it as a ratio of some reference year. For example, in 1960, real GDP per person was $15,850 and in 2010, it was $42,800. So real GDP per person in 2010 was 2.7 times its 1960 level—that is, $42,800 ÷ $15,850 = 2.7. To the extent that real GDP per person measures the standard of living, people were 2.7 times as well off in 2010 as their grandparents had been in 1960.

Figure 21.2 shows the path of U.S. real GDP per person for the 50 years from 1960 to 2010 and highlights two features of our expanding living standard:

- The growth of potential GDP per person
- Fluctuations of real GDP per person

The Growth of Potential GDP **Potential GDP** is the maximum level of real GDP that can be produced while avoiding shortages of labor, capital, land, and entrepreneurial ability that would bring rising inflation. Potential GDP per person, the smoother black line in Fig. 21.2, grows at a steady pace because the quantities of the factors of production and their productivities grow at a steady pace.

But potential GDP per person doesn't grow at a *constant* pace. During the 1960s, it grew at 2.8 percent per year but slowed to only 2.3 percent per year during the 1970s. This slowdown might seem small, but it had big consequences, as you'll soon see.

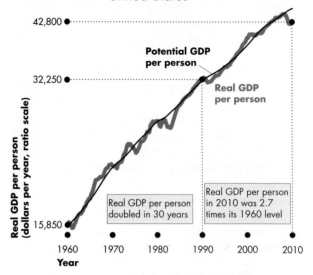

FIGURE 21.2 Rising Standard of Living in the United States

Real GDP per person in the United States doubled between 1960 and 1990. In 2010, real GDP per person was 2.7 times its 1960 level. Real GDP per person, the red line, fluctuates around potential GDP per person, the black line. (The y-axis is a ratio scale—see the Appendix, pp, 504–505.)

Sources of data: U.S. Department of Commerce, Bureau of Economic Analysis and Congressional Budget Office.

myeconlab   animation

Fluctuations of Real GDP You can see that real GDP shown by the red line in Fig. 21.2 fluctuates around potential GDP, and sometimes real GDP shrinks.

Let's take a closer look at the two features of our expanding living standard that we've just outlined.

Productivity Growth Slowdown How costly was the slowdown in productivity growth after 1970? The answer is provided by the *Lucas wedge*, which is the dollar value of the accumulated gap between what real GDP per person would have been if the 1960s growth rate had persisted and what real GDP per person turned out to be. (Nobel Laureate Robert E. Lucas Jr. drew attention to this gap.)

Figure 21.3 illustrates the Lucas wedge. The wedge started out small during the 1970s, but by 2010 real GDP per person was $28,400 per year lower than it would have been with no growth slowdown, and the accumulated gap was an astonishing $380,000 per person.

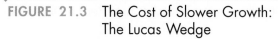

FIGURE 21.3   The Cost of Slower Growth: The Lucas Wedge

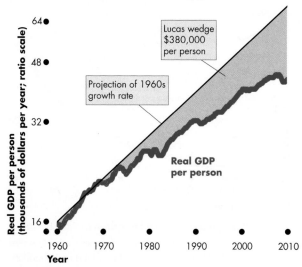

The black line projects the 1960s growth rate of real GDP per person to 2010. The Lucas wedge arises from the slow-down of productivity growth that began during the 1970s. The cost of the slowdown is $380,000 per person.

Sources of data: U.S. Department of Commerce Bureau of Economic Analysis, Congressional Budget Office, and author's calculations.

 animation

Real GDP Fluctuations—The Business Cycle

We call the fluctuations in the pace of expansion of real GDP the business cycle. The **business cycle** is a periodic but irregular up-and-down movement of total production and other measures of economic activity. The business cycle isn't a regular predictable cycle like the phases of the moon, but every cycle has two phases:

1. Expansion
2. Recession

and two turning points:

1. Peak
2. Trough

Figure 21.4 shows these features of the most recent U.S. business cycle.

An **expansion** is a period during which real GDP increases. In the early stage of an expansion real GDP returns to potential GDP and as the expansion progresses, potential GDP grows and real GDP eventually exceeds potential GDP.

A common definition of **recession** is a period during which real GDP decreases—its growth rate is negative—for at least two successive quarters. The definition used by the National Bureau of Economic Research, which dates the U.S. business cycle phases and turning points, is "a period of significant decline in total output, income, employment, and trade, usually lasting from six months to a year, and marked by contractions in many sectors of the economy."

An expansion ends and recession begins at a business cycle *peak*, which is the highest level that real GDP has attained up to that time. A recession ends at a *trough*, when real GDP reaches a temporary low point and from which the next expansion begins.

In 2008, the U.S. economy went into an unusually severe recession. Starting from a long way below potential GDP, a new expansion began in mid-2009. But the outlook for the expansion in 2011 and beyond was very uncertain (see *Reading Between the Lines* on pp. 502–503).

FIGURE 21.4   The Most Recent U.S. Business Cycle

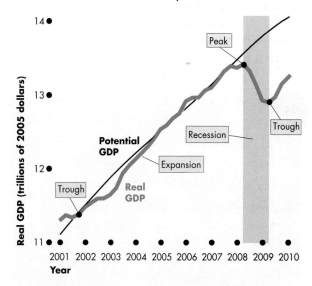

A business cycle expansion began from a trough in the fourth quarter of 2001 and ended at a peak in the second quarter of 2008. A deep and long recession followed the 2008 peak.

Sources of data: U.S. Department of Commerce Bureau of Economic Analysis, Congressional Budget Office, and National Bureau of Economic Research.

 animation

The Standard of Living Across Countries

Two problems arise in using real GDP to compare living standards across countries. First, the real GDP of one country must be converted into the same currency units as the real GDP of the other country. Second, the goods and services in both countries must be valued at the same prices. Comparing the United States and China provides a striking example of these two problems.

China and the United States in U.S. Dollars In 2010, real GDP per person in the United States was $42,800 and in China it was 23,400 yuan. The yuan is the currency of China and the price at which the dollar and the yuan exchanged, the *market exchange rate*, was 8.2 yuan per $1 U.S. Using this exchange rate, 23,400 yuan converts to $2,850. On these numbers, real GDP per person in the United States was 15 times that in China.

The red line in Fig. 21.5 shows real GDP per person in China from 1980 to 2010 when the market exchange rate is used to convert yuan to U.S. dollars.

China and the United States at PPP Figure 21.5 shows a second estimate of China's real GDP per person that values China's production on the same terms as U.S. production. It uses *purchasing power parity* or *PPP* prices, which are the *same prices* for both countries.

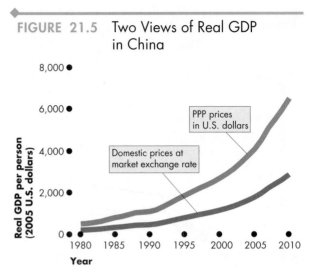

FIGURE 21.5   Two Views of Real GDP in China

Real GDP per person in China has grown rapidly. But how rapidly it has grown and to what level depends on how real GDP is valued. When GDP in 2010 is valued at the market exchange rate, U.S. income per person is 15 times that in China. China looks like a poor developing country. But the comparison is misleading. When GDP is valued at purchasing power parity prices, U.S. income per person is only 6.5 times that in China.

Source of data: International Monetary Fund, *World Economic Outlook database*, April 2010 .

myeconlab   animation

A Big Mac costs $3.75 in Chicago and 13.25 yuan or $1.62 in Shanghai. To compare real GDP in China and the United States, we must value China's Big Macs at the $3.75 U.S. price—the PPP price.

The prices of some goods are higher in the United States than in China, so these items get a smaller weight in China's real GDP than they get in U.S. real GDP. An example is a Big Mac that costs $3.75 in Chicago. In Shanghai, a Big Mac costs 13.25 yuan which is the equivalent of $1.62. So in China's real GDP, a Big Mac gets less than half the weight that it gets in U.S. real GDP.

Some prices in China are higher than in the United States but more prices are lower, so Chinese prices put a lower value on China's production than do U.S. prices.

According to the PPP comparisons, real GDP per person in the United States in 2010 was 6.5 times that of China, not 15 times.

You've seen how real GDP is used to make standard of living comparisons over time and across countries. But real GDP isn't a perfect measure of the standard of living and we'll now examine its limitations.

Limitations of Real GDP

Real GDP measures the value of goods and services that are bought in markets. Some of the factors that influence the standard of living and that are not part of GDP are

- Household production
- Underground economic activity
- Health and life expectancy
- Leisure time
- Environmental quality
- Political freedom and social justice

Household Production An enormous amount of production takes place every day in our homes. Preparing meals, cleaning the kitchen, changing a light bulb, cutting grass, washing a car, and caring for a child are all examples of household production. Because these productive activities are not traded in markets, they are not included in GDP.

The omission of household production from GDP means that GDP *underestimates* total production. But it also means that the growth rate of GDP *overestimates* the growth rate of total production. The reason is that some of the growth rate of market production (included in GDP) is a replacement for home production. So part of the increase in GDP arises from a decrease in home production.

Two trends point in this direction. One is the number of women who have jobs, which increased from 38 percent in 1960 to 58 percent in 2010. The other is the trend in the market purchase of traditionally home-produced goods and services. For example, more

and more families now eat in restaurants—one of the fastest-growing industries in the United States—and use day-care services. This trend means that an increasing proportion of food preparation and child care that were part of household production are now measured as part of GDP. So real GDP grows more rapidly than does real GDP plus home production.

Underground Economic Activity The *underground economy* is the part of the economy that is purposely hidden from the view of the government to avoid taxes and regulations or because the goods and services being produced are illegal. Because underground economic activity is unreported, it is omitted from GDP.

The underground economy is easy to describe, even if it is hard to measure. It includes the production and distribution of illegal drugs, production that uses illegal labor that is paid less than the minimum wage, and jobs done for cash to avoid paying income taxes. This last category might be quite large and includes tips earned by cab drivers, hairdressers, and hotel and restaurant workers.

Estimates of the scale of the underground economy in the United States range between 9 and 30 percent of GDP ($1,300 billion to $4,333 billion).

Provided that the underground economy is a stable proportion of the total economy, the growth rate of real GDP still gives a useful estimate of changes in economic well-being and the standard of living. But sometimes production shifts from the underground economy to the rest of the economy, and sometimes it shifts the other way. The underground economy expands relative to the rest of the economy if taxes

Whose production is more valuable: the chef's whose work gets counted in GDP ...

... or the busy mother's whose dinner preparation and child minding don't get counted?

become especially high or if regulations become especially restrictive. And the underground economy shrinks relative to the rest of the economy if the burdens of taxes and regulations are eased. During the 1980s, when tax rates were cut, there was an increase in the reporting of previously hidden income and tax revenues increased. So some part (but probably a very small part) of the expansion of real GDP during the 1980s represented a shift from the underground economy rather than an increase in production.

Health and Life Expectancy Good health and a long life—the hopes of everyone—do not show up in real GDP, at least not directly. A higher real GDP enables us to spend more on medical research, health care, a good diet, and exercise equipment. And as real GDP has increased, our life expectancy has lengthened—from 70 years at the end of World War II to approaching 80 years today.

But we face new health and life expectancy problems every year. AIDS and drug abuse are taking young lives at a rate that causes serious concern. When we take these negative influences into account, we see that real GDP growth overstates the improvements in the standard of living.

Leisure Time Leisure time is an economic good that adds to our economic well-being and the standard of living. Other things remaining the same, the more leisure we have, the better off we are. Our working time is valued as part of GDP, but our leisure time is not. Yet that leisure time must be at least as valuable to us as the wage that we earn for the last hour worked. If it were not, we would work instead of taking leisure. Over the years, leisure time has steadily increased. The workweek has become shorter, more people take early retirement, and the number of vacation days has increased. These improvements in economic well-being are not reflected in real GDP.

Environmental Quality Economic activity directly influences the quality of the environment. The burning of hydrocarbon fuels is the most visible activity that damages our environment. But it is not the only example. The depletion of nonrenewable natural resources, the mass clearing of forests, and the pollution of lakes and rivers are other major environmental consequences of industrial production.

Resources that are used to protect the environment are valued as part of GDP. For example, the value of catalytic converters that help to protect the atmosphere from automobile emissions is part of GDP. But if we did not use such pieces of equipment and instead polluted the atmosphere, we would not count the deteriorating air that we were breathing as a negative part of GDP.

An industrial society possibly produces more atmospheric pollution than an agricultural society does. But pollution does not always increase as we become wealthier. Wealthy people value a clean environment and are willing to pay for one. Compare the pollution in China today with pollution in the United States. China, a poor country, pollutes its rivers, lakes, and atmosphere in a way that is unimaginable in the United States.

Political Freedom and Social Justice Most people in the Western world value political freedoms such as those provided by the U.S. Constitution. And they value social justice—equality of opportunity and of access to social security safety nets that protect people from the extremes of misfortune.

A country might have a very large real GDP per person but have limited political freedom and social justice. For example, a small elite might enjoy political liberty and extreme wealth while the vast majority are effectively enslaved and live in abject poverty. Such an economy would generally be regarded as having a lower standard of living than one that had the same amount of real GDP but in which political freedoms were enjoyed by everyone. Today, China has rapid real GDP growth but limited political freedoms, while Poland and Ukraine have moderate real GDP growth but democratic political systems. Economists have no easy way to determine which of these countries is better off.

The Bottom Line Do we get the wrong message about the level and growth in economic well-being and the standard of living by looking at the growth of real GDP? The influences that are omitted from real GDP are probably important and could be large. Developing countries have a larger amount of household production and a larger underground economy than do developed countries so the gap between their living standards is exaggerated. Also, as real GDP grows, part of the measured growth might reflect a switch from home production to market production and underground to regular production. This measurement error overstates the growth in economic well-being and the improvement in the standard of living.

Economics in Action
A Broader Indicator of Economic Well-Being

The limitations of real GDP reviewed in this chapter affect the standard of living and general well-being of every country. So to make international comparisons of the general state of economic well-being, we must look at real GDP and other indicators.

The United Nations has constructed a broader measure called the Human Development Index (HDI), which combines real GDP, life expectancy and health, and education. Real GDP per person (measured on the PPP basis) is a major component of the HDI.

The dots in the figure show the relationship between real GDP per person and the HDI. The United States (along with a few other countries) has the highest real GDP per person, but the United States has the thirteenth highest HDI. (Norway has the highest HDI, and Australia, Canada, and Japan have a higher HDI than the United States.)

The HDI of the United States is lower than that of 12 other countries because the people of those countries live longer and have better access to health care and education than do Americans.

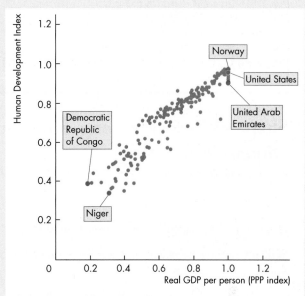

The Human Development Index

Source of data: United nations hdr.undp.org/en/statistics/data

African nations have the lowest levels of economic well-being. The Democratic Republic of Congo has the lowest real GDP per person and Niger has the lowest HDI.

Other influences on the standard of living include the amount of leisure time available, the quality of the environment, the security of jobs and homes, and the safety of city streets.

It is possible to construct broader measures that combine the many influences that contribute to human happiness. Real GDP will be one element in those broader measures, but it will by no means be the whole of those measures. The United Nation's Human Development Index (HDI) is one example of attempts to provide broader measures of economic well-being and the standard of living. This measure places a good deal of weight on real GDP.

Dozens of other measures have been proposed. One includes resource depletion and emissions in a Green GDP measure. Another emphasizes the enjoyment of life rather than the production of goods in a "genuine progress index" or GPI.

Despite all the alternatives, real GDP per person remains the most widely used indicator of economic well-being.

 REVIEW QUIZ

1 Distinguish between real GDP and potential GDP and describe how each grows over time.
2 How does the growth rate of real GDP contribute to an improved standard of living?
3 What is a business cycle and what are its phases and turning points?
4 What is PPP and how does it help us to make valid international comparisons of real GDP?
5 Explain why real GDP might be an unreliable indicator of the standard of living.

You can work these questions in Study Plan 21.3 and get instant feedback.

◆ You now know how economists measure GDP and what the GDP data tell us. *Reading Between the Lines* on pp. 502–503 uses GDP to describe some possible future paths as we emerge from recession.

Real GDP Forecasts in the Uncertain Economy of 2010

Shape of Recovery Long, Slow Growth … a "Square Root" Slog

http://www.denverpost.com
July 26, 2010

Hopes for a "V-shaped" recovery have shifted to fears of a "W-shaped" double dip.

William Greiner, president of Scout Investment Advisors, wants to add another symbol to the mix—the square root.

The square root represents a rebound, a smaller version of the V, followed by an extended period of below-average growth. No double dip, just a long, hard slog.

Greiner … predicts [a fall in] inflation-adjusted economic growth from 3.3 percent, the average in the post-war period, to about 2 percent, hence the square root.

No big deal? Think again.

"Potentially, the economic implications as to slow growth are monumental," Greiner said. "It is hard to overstate this issue."

Two percent real GDP growth will keep pace with U.S. population growth of 0.89 percent a year. But it won't leave much to form capital, fund research and development, and improve living standards.

Since World War II, the country has grown fast enough to double living standards every 29 years—translating into bigger homes, more cars and consumer goods, and more trips and meals out than previous generations enjoyed.

But at a 2 percent growth rate, living standards double every 64 years. Americans could be forced to shift their hopes for greater prosperity from their children to their grandchildren. …

What will make the slower growth feel even worse is that nominal economic growth, or GDP unadjusted for inflation, will run closer to 4 percent in the near term, far below its 7 percent average in recent decades. …

The Denver Post and Aldo Svaldi, July 26, 2010.

ESSENCE OF THE STORY

- Investment advisor William Greiner says the recovery will be neither a V nor a W but the shape of the square root symbol.

- Greiner predicts real GDP growth of 2 percent a year, down from a 3.3 percent post-war average.

- A growth rate of 3.3 percent per year doubles the standard of living every 29 years, but at 2 percent a year the standard of living doubles every 64 years.

- The news article says that growth will feel even worse because nominal GDP will grow at only 4 percent a year, down from 7 percent a year in recent decades.

ECONOMIC ANALYSIS

- The 2008 recession was an unusually deep one and even by the middle of 2010, recovery was weak.

- Figure 1 illustrates the severity of the 2008 recession using the concepts of potential GDP and real GDP that you learned about in this chapter.

- At the *trough* in the second quarter of 2009, real GDP was almost $1 trillion below potential GDP.

- When real GDP is below potential GDP, the economy is operating *inside* the *PPF* (Chapter 2, pp. 30–31) and production is lost.

- To put the magnitude of the gap between potential GDP and real GDP into perspective, each person's share (*your* share) of the lost production in 2009 was about $3,250.

- The severity of the recession and the slow recovery led economists to speculate about the shape of the future recovery—about whether it will be V-shaped or W-shaped.

- A V-shaped recovery, illustrated in Fig. 2, would mean the resumption of rapid real GDP growth.

- A W-shaped recovery, also illustrated in Fig. 2, would be bad news. It means a "double-dip" recession. That is, there will be another downturn and recession before a recovery finally gets going.

- The news article speculates about a third shape—a "square-root" recovery. Figure 2 illustrates this possibility. A square root symbol has a flat top, which means zero real GDP growth. The real GDP path predicted in the news article is almost flat.

- The news article is correct to emphasize that a growth slowdown is a big deal. The Lucas wedge (p. 497) occurred because of a similar slowdown during the 1970s.

- But if real GDP growth does slow to 2 percent a year, the Lucas wedge will become extremely large.

- The news article is *not* correct that slow growth will feel even worse because nominal GDP will grow at only 4 percent a year, down from 7 percent a year in recent decades.

- The numbers are correct, but the reasoning is wrong. Growth will feel slow because (if the forecast is correct) it really will be slow.

- The point of calculating *real* GDP is to isolate the change in the quantity of goods and services

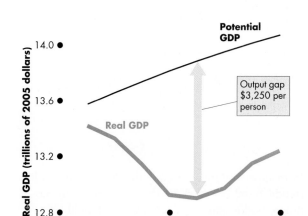

Figure 1 The deep 2008 recession

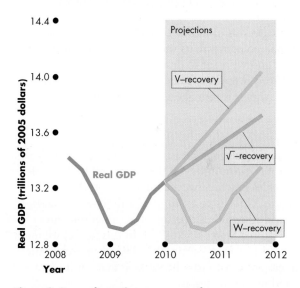

Figure 2 Some alternative recovery paths

produced—the real things on which the standard of living depends.

- A slowdown in *nominal* GDP growth combines the slowdown in real GDP growth and a slowdown in the inflation rate and obscures what is *really* happening to the standard of living.

APPENDIX

Graphs in Macroeconomics

After studying this appendix, you will be able to:

◆ Make and interpret a time-series graph

◆ Make and interpret a graph that uses a ratio scale

The Time-Series Graph

In macroeconomics we study the fluctuations and trends in the key variables that describe macroeconomic performance and policy. These variables include GDP and its expenditure and income components that you've learned about in this chapter. They also include variables that describe the labor market and consumer prices that you study in Chapter 22.

Regardless of the variable of interest, we want to be able to compare its value today with that in the past; and we want to describe how the variable has changed over time. The most effective way to do these things is to make a time-series graph.

Making a Time-Series Graph

A **time-series graph** measures time (for example, years, quarters, or months) on the *x*-axis and the variable or variables in which we are interested on the *y*-axis. Figure A21.1 is an example of a time-series graph. It provides some information about unemployment in the United States since 1980. In this figure, we measure time in years starting in 1980. We measure the unemployment rate (the variable that we are interested in) on the *y*-axis.

A time-series graph enables us to visualize how a variable has changed over time and how its value in one period relates to its value in another period. It conveys an enormous amount of information quickly and easily.

Let's see how to "read" a time-series graph.

Reading a Time-Series Graph

To practice reading a time-series graph, take a close look at Fig. A21.1. The graph shows the level, change and speed of change of the variable.

FIGURE A21.1   A Time-Series Graph

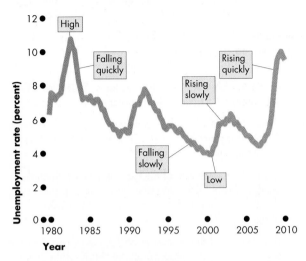

A time-series graph plots the level of a variable on the *y*-axis against time (here measured in years) on the *x*-axis. This graph shows the unemployment rate each year from 1980 to 2010. Its shows when unemployment was high, when it was low, when it increased, when it decreased and when it changed quickly and slowly.

myeconlab   animation

■ The *level* of the variable: It tells us when unemployment is *high* and *low*. When the line is a long distance above the *x*-axis, the unemployment rate is high, as it was, for example, in 1983 and again in 2009. When the line is close to the *x*-axis, the unemployment rate is low, as it was, for example, in 2001.

■ The *change* in the variable: It tells us how unemployment *changes*—whether it *increases* or *decreases*. When the line slopes upward, as it did in 2008 and 2009, the unemployment rate is rising. When the line slopes downward, as it did in 1984 and 1997, the unemployment rate is falling.

■ The *speed of change* in the variable: It tells us whether the unemployment rate is rising or falling *quickly* or *slowly*. If the line is very steep, then the unemployment rate increases or decreases quickly. If the line is not steep, the unemployment rate increases or decreases slowly. For example, the unemployment rate rose quickly in 2008 and slowly in 2003 and it fell quickly in 1984 and slowly in 1997.

Ratio Scale Reveals Trend

A time-series graph also reveals whether a variable has a **cycle**, which is a tendency for a variable to alternate between upward and downward movements, or a **trend**, which is a tendency for a variable to move in one general direction.

The unemployment rate in Fig. A21.1 has a cycle but no trend. When a trend is present, a special kind of time-series graph, one that uses a ratio scale on the *y*-axis, reveals the trend.

A Time-Series with a Trend

Many macroeconomics variables, among them GDP and the average level of prices, have an upward trend. Figure A21.2 shows an example of such a variable: the average prices paid by consumers.

In Fig. A21.2(a), consumer prices since 1970 are graphed on a normal scale. In 1970 the level is 100. In other years, the average level of prices is measured as a percentage of the 1970 level.

The graph clearly shows the upward trend of prices. But it doesn't tell us when prices were rising fastest or whether there was any change in the trend. Just looking at the upward-sloping line in Fig. A21.2(a) gives the impression that the pace of growth of consumer prices was constant.

Using a Ratio Scale

On a graph axis with a normal scale, the gap between 1 and 2 is the same as that between 3 and 4. On a graph axis with a ratio scale, the gap between 1 and 2 is the same as that between 2 and 4. The ratio 2 to 1 equals the ratio 4 to 2. By using a ratio scale, we can "see" when the growth rate (the percentage change per unit of time) changes.

Figure A21.2(b) shows an example of a ratio scale. Notice that the values on the *y*-axis get closer together but the gap between 400 and 200 equals the gap between 200 and 100: The ratio gaps are equal.

Graphing the data on a ratio scale reveals the trends. In the case of consumer prices, the trend is much steeper during the 1970s and early 1980s than in the later years. The steeper the line in the ratio-scale graph in part (b), the faster are prices rising. Prices rose rapidly during the 1970s and early 1980s and more slowly in the later 1980s and 1990s. The ratio-scale graph reveals this fact. We use ratio-scale graphs extensively in macroeconomics.

FIGURE A21.2   Ratio Scale Reveals Trend

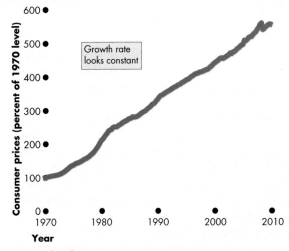

(a) Normal scale

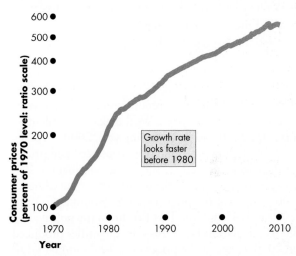

(b) Ratio scale

The graph shows the average of consumer prices from 1970 to 2010. The level is 100 in 1970 and the value for other years are percentages of the 1970 level. Consumer prices normally rise each year so the line slopes upward. In part (a), where the *y*-axis scale is normal, the rate of increase appears to be constant.

In part (b), where the y-axis is a ratio scale (the ratio of 400 to 200 equals the ratio 200 to 100), prices rose faster in the 1970s and early 1980s and slower in the later years. The ratio scale reveals this trend.

MATHEMATICAL NOTE
Chained-Dollar Real GDP

In the real GDP calculation on p. 495, real GDP in 2010 is 1.6 times its value in 2005. But suppose that we use 2010 as the reference base year and value real GDP in 2005 at 2010 prices. If you do the math, you will see that real GDP in 2005 is $150 million at 2010 prices. GDP in 2010 is $300 million (in 2010 prices), so now the numbers say that real GDP has doubled. Which is correct: Did real GDP increase 1.6 times or double? Should we use the prices of 2005 or 2010? The answer is that we need to use *both* sets of prices.

The Bureau of Economic Analysis uses a measure of real GDP called **chained-dollar real GDP**. Three steps are needed to calculate this measure:

- Value production in the prices of adjacent years
- Find the average of two percentage changes
- Link (chain) back to the reference base year

Value Production in Prices of Adjacent Years

The first step is to value production in *adjacent* years at the prices of *both* years. We'll make these calculations for 2010 and its preceding year, 2009.

Table 1 shows the quantities produced and prices in the two years. Part (a) shows the nominal GDP calculation for 2009—the quantities produced in 2009 valued at the prices of 2009. Nominal GDP in 2009 is $145 million. Part (b) shows the nominal GDP calculation for 2010—the quantities produced in 2010 valued at the prices of 2010. Nominal GDP in 2010 is $300 million. Part (c) shows the value of the quantities produced in 2010 at the prices of 2009. This total is $160 million. Finally, part (d) shows the value of the quantities produced in 2009 at the prices of 2010. This total is $275 million.

Find the Average of Two Percentage Changes

The second step is to find the percentage change in the value of production based on the prices in the two adjacent years. Table 2 summarizes these calculations.

Part (a) shows that, valued at the prices of 2009, production increased from $145 million in 2009 to $160 million in 2010, an increase of 10.3 percent.

TABLE 1   Real GDP Calculation Step 1: Value Production in Adjacent Years at Prices of Both Years

Item		Quantity (millions)	Price (dollars)	Expenditure (millions of dollars)
(a) In 2009				
C	T-shirts	3	5	15
I	Computer chips	3	10	30
G	Security services	5	20	100
Y	Real and Nominal GDP in 2009			**145**
(b) In 2010				
C	T-shirts	4	5	20
I	Computer chips	2	20	40
G	Security services	6	40	240
Y	Nominal GDP in 2010			**300**
(c) Quantities of 2010 valued at prices of 2009				
C	T-shirts	4	5	20
I	Computer chips	2	10	20
G	Security services	6	20	120
Y	2010 production at 2009 prices			**160**
(d) Quantities of 2009 valued at prices of 2010				
C	T-shirts	3	5	15
I	Computer chips	3	20	60
G	Security services	5	40	200
Y	2009 production at 2010 prices			**275**

Step 1 is to value the production of adjacent years at the prices of both years. Here, we value the production of 2009 and 2010 at the prices of both 2009 and 2010. The value of 2009 production at 2009 prices, in part (a), is nominal GDP in 2009. The value of 2010 production at 2010 prices, in part (b), is nominal GDP in 2010. Part (c) calculates the value of 2010 production at 2009 prices, and part (d) calculates the value of 2009 production at 2010 prices. We use these numbers in Step 2.

Part (b) shows that, valued at the prices of 2010, production increased from $275 million in 2009 to $300 million in 2010, an increase of 9.1 percent. Part (c) shows that the average of these two percentage changes in the value of production is 9.7. That is, $(10.3 + 9.1) \div 2 = 9.7$.

By applying this average percentage change to real GDP, we can find the value of real GDP in 2010. Real GDP in 2009 is $145 million, so a 9.7 percent increase is $14 million. Then real GDP in 2010 is

TABLE 2 Real GDP Calculation Step 2:
Find Average of Two Percentage
Changes

Value of Production	Millions of dollars	
(a) At 2009 prices		
Nominal GDP in 2009	145	
2010 production at 2009 prices	160	
Percentage change in production at 2009 prices		10.3
(b) At 2010 prices		
2009 production at 2010 prices	275	
Nominal GDP in 2010	300	
Percentage change in production at 2010 prices		9.1
(c) Average percentage change in 2010		**9.7**

Using the numbers calculated in Step 1, the percentage
change in production from 2009 to 2010 valued at
2009 prices is 10.3 percent, in part (a). The percentage
change in production from 2009 to 2010 valued at
2010 prices is 9.1 percent, in part (b). The average of
these two percentage changes is 9.7 percent, in part (c).

$145 million plus $14 million, which equals $159
million. Because real GDP in 2009 is in 2009 dollars,
real GDP in 2010 is also in 2009 dollars.

Although the real GDP of $159 million is
expressed in 2009 dollars, the calculation uses the
average of the prices of the final goods and services
that make up GDP in 2009 and 2010.

Link (Chain) to the Base Year

The third step is to express GDP in the prices of the
reference base year. To do this, the BEA performs calculations like the ones that you've just worked
through to find the percentage change in real GDP
in *each* pair of years. It then selects a base year (currently 2005) in which, by definition, real GDP
equals nominal GDP. Finally, it uses the percentage
changes to calculate real GDP in 2005 prices starting
from real GDP in 2005.

To illustrate this third step, we'll assume that the
BEA has calculated the growth rates since 2004
shown in Table 3. The 2010 growth rate that we've
just calculated is highlighted in the table. The other
(assumed) growth rates are calculated in exactly the
same way as that for 2010.

TABLE 3 Real GDP Calculation Step 3:
Repeat Growth Rate Calculations

Year	2005	2006	2007	2008	2009	**2010**
Growth rate	7.0	8.0	6.0	7.0	8.0	**9.7**

Figure 1 illustrates the chain link calculations. In
the reference base year, 2005, real GDP equals nominal GDP, which we'll assume is $125 million. Table 3
tells us that the growth rate in 2005 was 7 percent, so
real GDP in 2005 is 7 percent higher than it was in
2004, which means that real GDP in 2004 is $117
million (117 × 1.07 = 125).

Table 3 also tells us that the growth rate in 2006
was 8 percent, so real GDP in 2006 is 8 percent
higher than it was in 2005, which means that real
GDP in 2006 is $135 million (125 × 1.08 = 135).

By repeating these calculations for each year, we
obtain *chained-dollar real GDP* in 2005 dollars for
each year. In 2009, *chained-dollar real GDP* in 2005
dollars is $165 million. So the 9.7 percent growth
rate in 2010 that we calculated in Table 2 means that
real GDP in 2010 is $181 million.

Notice that the growth rates are independent of
the reference base year, so changing the reference base
year does not change the growth rates.

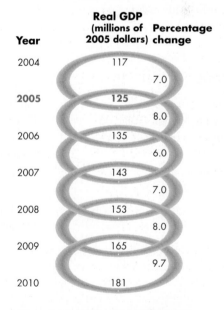

**Figure 1 Real GDP calculation step 3:
link (chain) back to base year**

SUMMARY

Key Points

Gross Domestic Product (pp. 490–492)

- GDP, or gross domestic product, is the market value of all the final goods and services produced in a country during a given period.
- A final good is an item that is bought by its final user, and it contrasts with an intermediate good, which is a component of a final good.
- GDP is calculated by using either the expenditure or income totals in the circular flow model.
- Aggregate expenditure on goods and services equals aggregate income and GDP.

Working Problems 1 to 7 will give you a better understanding of gross domestic product.

Measuring U.S. GDP (pp. 493–495)

- Because aggregate expenditure, aggregate income, and the value of aggregate production are equal, we can measure GDP by using the expenditure approach or the income approach.
- The expenditure approach sums consumption expenditure, investment, government expenditure on goods and services, and net exports.
- The income approach sums wages, interest, rent, and profit (plus indirect taxes less subsidies plus depreciation).

- Real GDP is measured using a common set of prices to remove the effects of inflation from GDP.

Working Problems 8 to 15 will give you a better understanding of measuring U.S. GDP.

The Uses and Limitations of Real GDP (pp. 496–501)

- Real GDP is used to compare the standard of living over time and across countries.
- Real GDP per person grows and fluctuates around the more smoothly growing potential GDP.
- A slowing of the growth rate of real GDP per person during the 1970s has lowered incomes by a large amount.
- International real GDP comparisons use PPP prices.
- Real GDP is not a perfect measure of the standard of living because it excludes household production, the underground economy, health and life expectancy, leisure time, environmental quality, and political freedom and social justice.

Working Problem 16 will give you a better understanding of the uses and limitations of real GDP.

Key Terms

Business cycle, 497
Chained-dollar real GDP, 506
Consumption expenditure, 491
Cycle, 505
Depreciation, 492
Expansion, 497
Exports, 492
Final good, 490

Government expenditure, 492
Gross domestic product (GDP), 490
Gross investment, 492
Imports, 492
Intermediate good, 490
Investment, 492
Net exports, 492
Net investment, 492

Nominal GDP, 495
Potential GDP, 496
Real GDP, 495
Real GDP per person, 496
Recession, 497
Time-series graph, 504
Trend, 505

STUDY PLAN PROBLEMS AND APPLICATIONS

 myeconlab You can work Problems 1 to 17 in MyEconLab Chapter 21 Study Plan and get instant feedback.

Gross Domestic Product (Study Plan 21.1)

1. Classify each of the following items as a final good or service or an intermediate good or service and identify which is a component of consumption expenditure, investment, or government expenditure on goods and services:
   - Banking services bought by a student.
   - New cars bought by Hertz, the car rental firm.
   - Newsprint bought by *USA Today*.
   - The purchase of a new limo for the president.
   - New house bought by Al Gore.

2. The firm that printed this textbook bought the paper from XYZ Paper Mills. Was this purchase of paper part of GDP? If not, how does the value of the paper get counted in GDP?

Use the following figure, which illustrates the circular flow model, to work Problems 3 and 4.

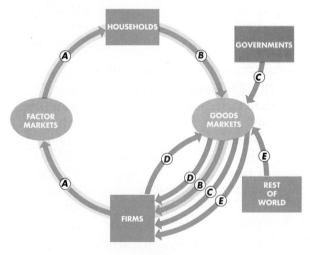

3. During 2008, in an economy:
   - Flow *B* was $9 trillion.
   - Flow *C* was $2 trillion.
   - Flow *D* was $3 trillion.
   - Flow *E* was –$0.7 trillion.

   Name the flows and calculate the value of
   a. Aggregate income.
   b. GDP.

4. During 2009, flow *A* was $13.0 trillion, flow *B* was $9.1 trillion, flow *D* was $3.3 trillion, and flow *E* was –$0.8 trillion.

Calculate the 2009 values of
a. GDP.
b. Government expenditure.

5. Use the following data to calculate aggregate expenditure and imports of goods and services.
   - Government expenditure: $20 billion
   - Aggregate income: $100 billion
   - Consumption expenditure: $67 billion
   - Investment: $21 billion
   - Exports of goods and services: $30 billion

6. **U.S. Economy Shrinks Modestly**
   GDP fell 1 percent as businesses cut investment by 8.9 percent, consumers cut spending by 1.2 percent, purchases of new houses fell 38 percent, and exports fell 29.9 percent.
   Source: Reuters, July 31, 2009
   Use the letters on the figure in Problem 3 to indicate the flow in which each item in the news clip occurs. How can GDP have fallen by only 1.0 percent with the big expenditure cuts reported?

7. A U.S. market research firm deconstructed an Apple iPod and studied the manufacturers, costs, and profits of each of the parts and components. The final results are
   - An Apple iPod sells in the United States for $299.
   - A Japanese firm, Toshiba, makes the hard disk and display screen, which cost $93.
   - Other components produced in South Korea cost $25.
   - Other components produced in the United States cost $21.
   - The iPod is assembled in China at a cost of $5.
   - The costs and profits of retailers, advertisers, and transportation firms in the United States are $75.
   a. What is Apple's profit?
   b. Where in the national income and product accounts of the United States, Japan, South Korea, and China are these transactions recorded.
   c. What contribution does one iPod make to world GDP?

Measuring U.S. GDP (Study Plan 21.2)

Use the following data to work Problems 8 and 9.
The table lists some macroeconomic data for the United States in 2008.

Item	Billions of dollars
Wages paid to labor	8,000
Consumption expenditure	10,000
Net operating surplus	3,200
Investment	2,000
Government expenditure	2,800
Net exports	–700
Depreciation	1,800

8. Calculate U.S. GDP in 2008.

9. Explain the approach (expenditure or income) that you used to calculate GDP.

Use the following data to work Problems 10 and 11.

The national accounts of Parchment Paradise are kept on (you guessed it) parchment. A fire destroys the statistics office. The accounts are now incomplete but they contain the following data:

- GDP (income approach): $2,900
- Consumption expenditure: $2,000
- Indirect taxes less subsidies: $100
- Net operating surplus: $500
- Investment: $800
- Government expenditure: $400
- Wages: $2,000
- Net exports: –$200

10. Calculate GDP (expenditure approach) and depreciation.

11. Calculate net domestic income at factor cost and the statistical discrepancy.

Use the following data to work Problems 12 and 13.
Tropical Republic produces only bananas and coconuts. The base year is 2008, and the table gives the quantities produced and the prices.

Quantities	2008	2009
Bananas	800 bunches	900 bunches
Coconuts	400 bunches	500 bunches

Prices	2008	2009
Bananas	$2 a bunch	$4 a bunch
Coconuts	$10 a bunch	$5 a bunch

12. Calculate nominal GDP in 2008 and 2009.

13. Calculate real GDP in 2009 expressed in base-year prices.

Use the following news clip to work Problems 14 and 15.

Toyota to Shift U.S. Manufacturing Efforts

Toyota announced it planned to adjust its U.S. manufacturing operations to meet customer demands for smaller, more fuel-efficient vehicles. In 2008, Toyota started building a plant to produce the 2010 Prius for the U.S. market in Blue Springs, Mississippi. Earlier models of the Prius were produced in Asia.

Source: CNN, July 10, 2008

14. Explain how this change by Toyota will influence U.S. GDP and the components of aggregate expenditure.

15. Explain how this change by Toyota will influence the factor incomes that make up U.S. GDP.

The Uses and Limitations of Real GDP (Study Plan 21.3)

16. Use the following table to work out in which year the U.S. standard of living (i) increases and (ii) decreases? Explain your answer.

Year	Real GDP	Population
2006	$13.0 trillion	300 million
2007	$13.2 trillion	302 million
2008	$13.2 trillion	304 million
2009	$12.8 trillion	307 million

Mathematical Note (Study Plan 21.MN)

17. The table provides data on the economy of Maritime Republic that produces only fish and crabs.

Quantities	2009	2010
Fish	1,000 tons	1,100 tons
Crabs	500 tons	525 tons

Prices	2009	2010
Fish	$20 a ton	$30 a ton
Crabs	$10 a ton	$8 a ton

a. Calculate Maritime Republic's nominal GDP in 2009 and 2010.

b. Calculate Maritime Republic's chained-dollar real GDP in 2010 expressed in 2009 dollars.

Data Graphing

Use the *Data Grapher* in MyEconLab to work Problems 18 and 19.

18. In which country in 2009 was the growth rate of real GDP per person highest: Canada, Japan, or the United States?

19. In which country in 2009 was the growth rate of real GDP per person lowest: France, China, or the United States?

ADDITIONAL PROBLEMS AND APPLICATIONS

 You can work these problems in MyEconLab if assigned by your instructor.

Gross Domestic Product

20. Classify each of the following items as a final good or service or an intermediate good or service and identify which is a component of consumption expenditure, investment, or government expenditure on goods and services:

  - Banking services bought by Google.
  - Security system bought by the New York Stock Exchange.
  - Coffee beans bought by Starbucks.
  - New coffee grinders bought by Starbucks.
  - Starbuck's grande mocha frappuccino bought by a student.
  - New battle ship bought by the U.S. Navy.

Use the figure in Problem 3 to work Problems 21 and 22.

21. In 2009, flow *A* was $1,000 billion, flow *C* was $250 billion, flow *B* was $650 billion, and flow *E* was $50 billion. Calculate investment.

22. In 2010, flow *D* was $2 trillion, flow *E* was –$1 trillion, flow *A* was $10 trillion, and flow *C* was $4 trillion. Calculate consumption expenditure.

Use the following information to work Problems 23 and 24.

Mitsubishi Heavy Industries makes the wings of the new Boeing 787 Dreamliner in Japan. Toyota assembles cars for the U.S. market in Kentucky.

23. Explain where these activities appear in the U.S. National Income and Product Accounts.

24. Explain where these activities appear in Japan's National Income and Product Accounts.

Use the following news clip to work Problems 25 and 26, and use the circular flow model to illustrate your answers.

Boeing Bets the House

Boeing is producing some components of its new 787 Dreamliner in Japan and is assembling it in the United States. Much of the first year's production will be sold to ANA (All Nippon Airways), a Japanese airline.

Source: *The New York Times*, May 7, 2006

25. Explain how Boeing's activities and its transactions affect U.S. and Japanese GDP.

26. Explain how ANA's activities and its transactions affect U.S. and Japanese GDP.

Measuring U.S. GDP

Use the following data to work Problems 27 and 28. The table lists some macroeconomic data for the United States in 2009.

Item	Billions of dollars
Wages paid to labor	8,000
Consumption expenditure	10,000
Net operating surplus	3,400
Investment	1,500
Government expenditure	2,900
Net exports	–340

27. Calculate U.S. GDP in 2009.

28. Explain the approach (expenditure or income) that you used to calculate GDP.

Use the following data to work Problems 29 to 31. An economy produces only apples and oranges. The base year is 2009, and the table gives the quantities produced and the prices.

Quantities	2009	2010
Apples	60	160
Oranges	80	220

Prices	2009	2010
Apples	$0.50	$1.00
Oranges	$0.25	$2.00

29. Calculate nominal GDP in 2009 and 2010.

30. Calculate real GDP in 2009 and 2010 expressed in base-year prices.

31. **GDP Expands 11.4 Percent, Fastest in 13 Years**

China's gross domestic product grew 11.4 percent last year and marked a fifth year of double-digit growth. The increase was especially remarkable given that the United States is experiencing a slowdown due to the sub-prime crisis and housing slump. Citigroup estimates that each 1 percent drop in the U.S. economy will shave 1.3 percent off China's growth, because Americans are heavy users of Chinese products. In spite of the uncertainties, China is expected to post its sixth year of double-digit growth next year.

Source: *The China Daily*, January 24, 2008

Use the expenditure approach for calculating China's GDP to explain why "each 1 percent drop in the U.S. economy will shave 1.3 percent off China's growth."

The Uses and Limitations of Real GDP

32. The United Nations' Human Development Index (HDI) is based on real GDP per person, life expectancy at birth, and indicators of the quality and quantity of education.

    a. Explain why the HDI might be better than real GDP as a measure of economic welfare.

    b. Which items in the HDI are part of real GDP and which items are not in real GDP?

    c. Do you think the HDI should be expanded to include items such as pollution, resource depletion, and political freedom? Explain.

    d. What other influences on economic welfare should be included in a comprehensive measure?

33. **U.K. Living Standards Outstrip U.S.**

    Oxford analysts report that living standards in Britain are set to rise above those in America for the first time since the nineteenth century. Real GDP per person in Britain will be £23,500 this year, compared with £23,250 in America, reflecting not only the strength of the pound against the dollar but also the UK economy's record run of growth since 2001. But the Oxford analysts also point out that Americans benefit from lower prices than those in Britain.

    Source: *The Sunday Times*, January 6, 2008

    If real GDP per person is more in the United Kingdom than in the United States but Americans benefit from lower prices, does this comparison of real GDP per person really tell us which country has the higher standard of living?

34. Use the news clip in Problem 31.

    a. Why might China's recent GDP growth rates overstate the actual increase in the level of production taking place in China?

    b. Explain the complications involved with attempting to compare the economic welfare in China and the United States by using the GDP for each country.

35. **Poor India Makes Millionaires at Fastest Pace**

    India, with the world's largest population of poor people created millionaires at the fastest pace in the world in 2007. India added another 23,000 more millionaires in 2007 to its 2006 tally of 100,000 millionaires measured in dollars. That is 1 millionaire for about 7,000 people living on less than $2 a day.

    Source: *The Times of India*, June 25, 2008

    a. Why might real GDP per person misrepresent the standard of living of the average Indian?

    b. Why might $2 a day underestimate the standard of living of the poorest Indians?

Economics in the News

36. After you have studied *Reading Between the Lines* on pp. 502–503 answer the following questions.

    a. Which measure of GDP would you use to describe the shape of the recovery from recession: real GDP or nominal GDP? Explain your answer.

    b. Which measure of GDP would you use to describe the rate of growth of the standard of living: real GDP or nominal GDP? Explain your answer.

    c. If the recovery was a precise "square-root" shape, what would the growth rate of real GDP be?

    d. Why is the news article wrong about the effect of a slowdown in nominal GDP growth on how slow the growth rate will "feel"?

37. **Totally Gross**

    GDP has proved useful in tracking both short-term fluctuations and long-run growth. Which isn't to say GDP doesn't miss some things. Amartya Sen, at Harvard, helped create the United Nations' Human Development Index, which combines health and education data with per capita GDP to give a better measure of the wealth of nations. Joseph Stiglitz, at Columbia, advocates a "green net national product" that takes into account the depletion of natural resources. Others want to include happiness in the measure. These alternative benchmarks have merit but can they be measured with anything like the frequency, reliability and impartiality of GDP?

    Source: *Time*, April 21, 2008

    a. Explain the factors that the news clip identifies as limiting the usefulness of GDP as a measure of economic welfare.

    b. What are the challenges involved in trying to incorporate measurements of those factors in an effort to better measure economic welfare?

    c. What does the ranking of the United States in the Human Development Index imply about the levels of health and education relative to other nations?

Mathematical Note

38. Use the information in Problem 29 to calculate the chained-dollar real GDP in 2010 expressed in 2009 dollars.

After studying this chapter, you will be able to:

◆ Explain why unemployment is a problem, define the unemployment rate, the employment-to-population ratio, and the labor force participation rate, and describe the trends and cycles in these labor market indicators

◆ Explain why unemployment is an imperfect measure of underutilized labor, why it is present even at full employment, and how unemployment and real GDP fluctuate together over a business cycle

◆ Explain why inflation is a problem, how we measure the price level and the inflation rate, and why the CPI measure of inflation might be biased

Each month, we chart the course of employment and unemployment as measures of U.S. economic health. How do we count the number of people working and the number unemployed? What do the level of employment and the unemployment rate tell us? Are they reliable vital signs for the economy?

Having a good job that pays a decent wage is only half of the equation that translates into a good standard of living. The other half is the cost of living. We track the cost of the items that we buy with another number that is published every month, the Consumer Price Index, or CPI. What is the CPI? How is it calculated? And does it provide a reliable guide to the changes in our cost of living?

As the U.S. economy expanded after a recession in 2001, job growth was weak and questions about the health of the labor market became of vital importance to millions of American families. *Reading Between the Lines*, at the end of this chapter, puts the spotlight on the labor market during the expansion of the past few years and the slowdown of 2008.

We begin by looking at unemployment: What it is, why it matters, and how we measure it.

◆ Employment and Unemployment

What kind of job market will you enter when you graduate? Will there be plenty of good jobs to choose among, or will jobs be so hard to find that you end up taking one that doesn't use your education and pays a low wage? The answer depends, to a large degree, on the total number of jobs available and on the number of people competing for them.

The class of 2009 had an unusually tough time in the jobs market. At the depth of recession in October 2009, 16.5 million American's wanted a job but couldn't find one. In a normal year, unemployment is less than half that level. And the U.S. economy is an incredible job-creating machine. Even in 2009 at the depths of recession, 139 million people had jobs—4 million more than in 1999 and 22 million more than in 1989. But in recent years, population growth has outstripped jobs growth, so unemployment is a serious problem.

Why Unemployment Is a Problem

Unemployment is a serious personal and social economic problem for two main reasons. It results in

- Lost incomes and production
- Lost human capital

Lost Incomes and Production The loss of a job brings a loss of income and lost production. These losses are devastating for the people who bear them and they make unemployment a frightening prospect for everyone. Unemployment benefits create a safety net, but they don't fully replace lost earnings.

Lost production means lower consumption and a lower investment in capital, which lowers the living standard in both the present and the future.

Lost Human Capital Prolonged unemployment permanently damages a person's job prospects by destroying human capital.

Economics in Action
What Keeps Ben Bernanke Awake at Night

The Great Depression began in October 1929, when the U.S. stock market crashed. It reached its deepest point in 1933, when 25 percent of the labor force was unemployed, and lasted until 1941, when the United States entered World War II. The depression quickly spread globally to envelop most nations.

The 1930s were and remain the longest and worst period of high unemployment in history. Failed banks, shops, farms, and factories left millions of Americans without jobs, homes, and food. Without the support of government and charities, millions would have starved.

The Great Depression was an enormous political event: It fostered the rise of the German and Japanese militarism that were to bring the most devastating war humans have ever fought. It also led to President Franklin D. Roosevelt's "New Deal," which enhanced the role of government in economic life and made government intervention in markets popular and the market economy unpopular.

The Great Depression also brought a revolution in economics. British economist John Maynard Keynes published his *General Theory of Employment, Interest, and Money* and created what we now call macroeconomics.

Many economists have studied the Great Depression and tried to determine why what started out as an ordinary recession became so devastating. Among them is Ben Bernanke, the Chairman of the Federal Reserve.

One of the reasons the Fed was so aggressive in cutting interest rates, saving Bear Stearns, and propping up Fannie Mae and Freddie Mac is because Ben Bernanke is so vividly aware of the horrors of total economic collapse and determined to avoid any risk of a repeat of the Great Depression.

Think about a manager who loses his job when his employer downsizes. The only work he can find is driving a taxi. After a year in this work, he discovers that he can't compete with new MBA graduates. Eventually, he gets hired as a manager but in a small firm and at a lower wage than before. He has lost some of his human capital.

The cost of unemployment is spread unequally, which makes it a highly charged political problem as well as a serious economic problem.

Governments make strenuous efforts to measure unemployment accurately and to adopt policies to moderate its level and ease its pain. Here, we'll learn how the U.S. government monitors unemployment.

Current Population Survey

Every month, the U.S. Census Bureau surveys 60,000 households and asks a series of questions about the age and job market status of the members of each household. This survey is called the Current Population Survey. The Census Bureau uses the answers to describe the anatomy of the labor force.

Figure 22.1 shows the population categories used by the Census Bureau and the relationships among the categories.

The population divides into two broad groups: the working-age population and others who are too young to work or who live in institutions and are unable to work. The **working-age population** is the total number of people aged 16 years and over who are not in jail, hospital, or some other form of institutional care.

The Census Bureau divides the working-age population into two groups: those in the labor force and those not in the labor force. It also divides the labor force into two groups: the employed and the unemployed. So the **labor force** is the sum of the employed and the unemployed.

To be counted as employed in the Current Population Survey, a person must have either a full-time job or a part-time job. To be counted as *un*employed, a person must be available for work and must be in one of three categories:

1. Without work but has made specific efforts to find a job within the previous four weeks

2. Waiting to be called back to a job from which he or she has been laid off

3. Waiting to start a new job within 30 days

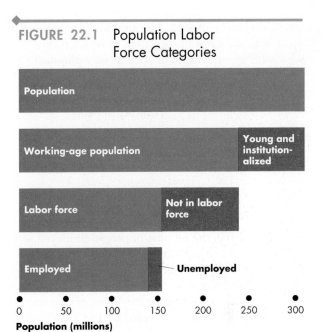

FIGURE 22.1   Population Labor Force Categories

The total population is divided into the working-age population and the young and institutionalized. The working-age population is divided into those in the labor force and those not in the labor force. The labor force is divided into the employed and the unemployed.

Source of data: Bureau of Labor Statistics.

Anyone surveyed who satisfies one of these three criteria is counted as unemployed. People in the working-age population who are neither employed nor unemployed are classified as not in the labor force.

In June 2010, the population of the United States was 309.6 million; the working-age population was 237.7 million. Of this number, 84 million were not in the labor force. Most of these people were in school full time or had retired from work. The remaining 153.7 million people made up the U.S. labor force. Of these, 139.1 million were employed and 14.6 million were unemployed.

Three Labor Market Indicators

The Census Bureau calculates three indicators of the state of the labor market. They are

- The unemployment rate
- The employment-to-population ratio
- The labor force participation rate

The Unemployment Rate The amount of unemployment is an indicator of the extent to which people who want jobs can't find them. The **unemployment rate** is the percentage of the people in the labor force who are unemployed. That is,

$$\text{Unemployment rate} = \frac{\text{Number of people unemployed}}{\text{Labor force}} \times 100$$

and

$$\text{Labor force} = \frac{\text{Number of people employed} +}{\text{Number of people unemployed.}}$$

In June 2010, the number of people employed was 139.1 million and the number unemployed was 14.6 million. By using the above equations, you can verify that the labor force was 153.7 million (139.1 million plus 14.6 million) and the unemployment rate was 9.5 percent (14.6 million divided by 153.7 million, multiplied by 100).

Figure 22.2 shows the unemployment rate from 1980 to 2010. The average unemployment rate during this period is 6.2 percent—equivalent to 9.5 million people being unemployed in 2010.

The unemployment rate fluctuates over the business cycle and reaches a peak value after a recession ends.

Each peak unemployment rate in the recessions of 1982, 1990–1991, and 2001 was lower than the previous one. But the recession of 2008–2009 ended the downward trend.

The Employment-to-Population Ratio The number of people of working age who have jobs is an indicator of both the availability of jobs and the degree of match between people's skills and jobs. The **employment-to-population ratio** is the percentage of people of working age who have jobs. That is,

$$\text{Employment-to-population ratio} = \frac{\text{Number of people employed}}{\text{Working-age population}} \times 100.$$

In June 2010, the number of people employed was 139.1 million and the working-age population was 237.7 million. By using the above equation, you can verify that the employment-to-population ratio was 58.5 percent (139.1 million divided by 237.7 million, multiplied by 100).

Figure 22.3 shows the employment-to-population ratio. This indicator followed an upward trend before 2000 and then a downward trend. The increase before 2000 means that the U.S. economy created

FIGURE 22.2   The Unemployment Rate: 1980–2010

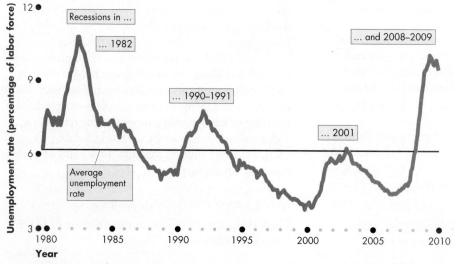

The average unemployment rate from 1980 to 2010 was 6.2 percent. The unemployment rate increases in a recession, peaks after the recession ends, and decreases in an expansion. The peak unemployment rate during a recession was on a downward trend before the 2008–2009 recession, with each successive recession having a lower unemployment rate. The severe recession of 2008–2009 broke this trend.

Source of data: Bureau of Labor Statistics.

FIGURE 22.3   Labor Force Participation and Employment: 1980–2010

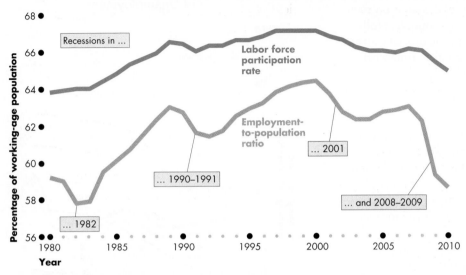

Source of data: Bureau of Labor Statistics.

The trend in the labor force participation rate and the employment-to-population ratio is upward before 2000 and downward after 2000.

The employment-to-population ratio fluctuates more than the labor force participation rate over the business cycle and reflects cyclical fluctuations in the unemployment rate.

myeconlab animation

jobs at a faster rate than the working-age population grew. This indicator also fluctuates: It falls during a recession and increases during an expansion.

The Labor Force Participation Rate The number of people in the labor force is an indicator of the willingness of people of working age to take jobs. The **labor force participation rate** is the percentage of the working-age population who are members of the labor force. That is,

$$\text{Labor force participation rate} = \frac{\text{Labor force}}{\text{Working-age population}} \times 100.$$

In June 2010, the labor force was 153.7 million and the working-age population was 237.7 million. By using the above equation, you can verify that the labor force participation rate was 64.7 percent (153.7 million divided by 237.7 million, multiplied by 100).

Figure 22.3 shows the labor force participation rate. Like the employment-to-population ratio, this indicator has an upward trend before 2000 and then a downward trend. It also has mild fluctuations around the trend. These fluctuations result from unsuccessful job seekers leaving the labor force during a recession and reentering during an expansion.

Other Definitions of Unemployment

Do fluctuations in the labor force participation rate over the business cycle mean that people who leave the labor force during a recession should be counted as unemployed? Or are they correctly counted as not-in-the-labor force?

The Bureau of Labor Statistics (BLS) believes that the official unemployment definition gives the correct measure of the unemployment rate. But the BLS provides data on two types of underutilized labor excluded from the official measure. They are

- Marginally attached workers
- Part-time workers who want full-time jobs

Marginally Attached Workers A **marginally attached worker** is a person who currently is neither working nor looking for work but has indicated that he or she wants and is available for a job and has looked for work sometime in the recent past. A marginally attached worker who has stopped looking for a job because of repeated failure to find one is called a **discouraged worker**.

The official unemployment measure excludes marginally attached workers because they haven't made specific efforts to find a job within the past four weeks. In all other respects, they are unemployed.

Part-Time Workers Who Want Full-Time Jobs Many part-time workers want to work part time. This arrangement fits in with the other demands on their time. But some part-time workers would like full-time jobs and can't find them. In the official statistics, these workers are called economic part-time workers and they are partly unemployed.

Most Costly Unemployment

All unemployment is costly, but the most costly is long-term unemployment that results from job loss.

People who are unemployed for a few weeks and then find another job bear some costs of unemployment. But these costs are low compared to the costs borne by people who remain unemployed for many weeks.

Also, people who are unemployed because they voluntarily quit their jobs to find better ones or because they have just entered or reentered the labor market bear some costs of unemployment. But these costs are lower than those borne by people who lose their job and are forced back into the job market.

The unemployment rate doesn't distinguish among these different categories of unemployment. If most of the unemployed are long-term job losers, the situation is much worse than if most are short-term voluntary job searchers.

Alternative Measures of Unemployment

To provide information about the aspects of unemployment that we've just discussed, the Bureau of Labor Statistics reports six alternative measures of the unemployment rate: two narrower than the official measure and three broader ones. The narrower measures focus on the personal cost of unemployment and the broader measures focus on assessing the full amount of unused labor resources.

Figure 22.4 shows these measures from 1994 (the first year for which they are available) to 2010. U–3 is the official unemployment rate. Long-term unemployment (U–1) and unemployed job losers (U–2) are about 40 percent of the unemployed on average but 60 percent in a deep recession. Adding discouraged workers (U–4) makes very little difference to the unemployment rate, but adding all marginally attached workers (U–5) adds one percentage point. A big difference is made by adding the economic part-time workers (U–6). In June 2010, after adding these workers the unemployment rate was 16 percent.

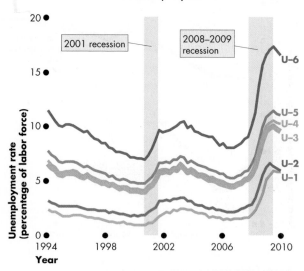

FIGURE 22.4 Six Alternative Measures of Unemployment

U–1 are those unemployed for 15 weeks or more, and U–2 are job losers. U–3 is the official unemployment rate. U–4 adds discouraged workers, and U–5 adds all marginally attached workers. The broadest measure, U–6, adds part-time workers who want full-time jobs. Fluctuations in all the alternative measures are similar to those in the official measure, U–3.

Source of data: Bureau of Labor Statistics.

 animation

REVIEW QUIZ

1 What determines if a person is in the labor force?
2 What distinguishes an unemployed person from one who is not in the labor force?
3 Describe the trends and fluctuations in the U.S. unemployment rate from 1980 to 2010.
4 Describe the trends and fluctuations in the U.S. employment-to-population ratio and labor force participation rate from 1980 to 2010.
5 Describe the alternative measures of unemployment.

You can work these questions in Study Plan 22.1 and get instant feedback.   myeconlab

You've seen how we measure employment and unemployment. Your next task is to see what we mean by full employment and how unemployment and real GDP fluctuate over the business cycle.

Unemployment and Full Employment

There is always someone without a job who is searching for one, so there is always some unemployment. The key reason is that the economy is a complex mechanism that is always changing—it experiences frictions, structural change, and cycles.

Frictional Unemployment

There is an unending flow of people into and out of the labor force as people move through the stages of life—from being in school to finding a job, to working, perhaps to becoming unhappy with a job and looking for a new one, and finally, to retiring from full-time work.

There is also an unending process of job creation and job destruction as new firms are born, firms expand or contract, and some firms fail and go out of business.

The flows into and out of the labor force and the processes of job creation and job destruction create the need for people to search for jobs and for businesses to search for workers. Businesses don't usually hire the first person who applies for a job, and unemployed people don't usually take the first job that comes their way. Instead, both firms and workers spend time searching for what they believe will be the best available match. By this process of search, people can match their own skills and interests with the available jobs and find a satisfying job and a good income.

The unemployment that arises from the normal labor turnover we've just described—from people entering and leaving the labor force and from the ongoing creation and destruction of jobs—is called **frictional unemployment**. Frictional unemployment is a permanent and healthy phenomenon in a dynamic, growing economy.

Structural Unemployment

The unemployment that arises when changes in technology or international competition change the skills needed to perform jobs or change the locations of jobs is called **structural unemployment**. Structural unemployment usually lasts longer than frictional unemployment because workers must retrain and possibly relocate to find a job. When a steel plant in Gary, Indiana, is automated, some jobs in that city disappear. Meanwhile, new jobs for security guards, retail clerks, and life-insurance salespeople are created in Chicago and Indianapolis. The unemployed former steelworkers remain unemployed for several months until they move, retrain, and get one of these jobs. Structural unemployment is painful, especially for older workers for whom the best available option might be to retire early or take a lower-skilled, lower-paying job.

Cyclical Unemployment

The higher than normal unemployment at a business cycle trough and the lower than normal unemployment at a business cycle peak is called **cyclical unemployment**. A worker who is laid off because the economy is in a recession and who gets rehired some months later when the expansion begins has experienced cyclical unemployment.

"Natural" Unemployment

Natural unemployment is the unemployment that arises from frictions and structural change when there is no cyclical unemployment—when all the unemployment is frictional and structural. Natural unemployment as a percentage of the labor force is called the **natural unemployment rate**.

Full employment is defined as a situation in which the unemployment rate equals the natural unemployment rate.

What determines the natural unemployment rate? Is it constant or does it change over time?

The natural unemployment rate is influenced by many factors but the most important ones are

- The age distribution of the population
- The scale of structural change
- The real wage rate
- Unemployment benefits

The Age Distribution of the Population An economy with a young population has a large number of new job seekers every year and has a high level of frictional unemployment. An economy with an aging population has fewer new job seekers and a low level of frictional unemployment.

The Scale of Structural Change The scale of structural change is sometimes small. The same jobs using the same machines remain in place for many years. But sometimes there is a technological upheaval. The old ways are swept aside and millions of jobs are lost and the skill to perform them loses value. The amount of structural unemployment fluctuates with the pace and volume of technological change and the change driven by fierce international competition, especially from fast-changing Asian economies. A high level of structural unemployment is present in many parts of the United States today (as you can see in *Economics in Action* below).

The Real Wage Rate The natural unemployment rate is influenced by the level of the real wage rate. Real wage rates that bring unemployment are a *minimum wage* and an *efficiency wage*. Chapter 6 (see pp. 131–133) explains how the minimum wage creates unemployment. An *efficiency wage* is a wage set above the going market wage to enables firms to attract the most productive workers, get them to work hard, and discourage them from quitting.

Unemployment Benefits Unemployment benefits increase the natural unemployment rate by lowering the opportunity cost of job search. European coun-tries have more generous unemployment benefits and higher natural unemployment rates than the United States. Extending unemployment benefits increases the natural unemployment rate.

There is no controversy about the existence of a natural unemployment rate. Nor is there disagree-ment that the natural unemployment rate changes. But economists don't know its exact size or the extent to which it fluctuates. The Congressional Budget Office estimates the natural unemployment rate and its estimate for 2010 was 4.8 percent—about a half of the unemployment in that year.

Real GDP and Unemployment Over the Cycle

The quantity of real GDP at full employment is *potential GDP* (p. 496). Over the business cycle, real GDP fluctuates around potential GDP. The gap between real GDP and potential GDP is called the **output gap**. As the output gap fluctuates over the busi-ness cycle, the unemployment rate fluctuates around the natural unemployment rate.

Economics in Action
Structural Unemployment and Labor Reallocation in Michigan

At 13.6 percent, Michigan had the nation's highest official unemployment rate in 2010. The long-term unemployment rate was 8.4 percent and when marginally attached workers and part-time workers who want full time jobs are added, almost 22 per-cent of the state's labor force was unemployed or underemployed.

Michigan's main problem is structural—a collapse of manufacturing jobs centered on the auto industry. These jobs had been disappearing steadily as robot technologies spread to do ever more of the tasks in the assembly of automobiles. The 2008–2009 reces-sion accelerated this rate of job loss.

But the story is not all negative, and the outlook is not all bleak. Around 11,000 businesses in Michigan produce high-tech scientific instruments and compo-nents for defense equipment, energy plants, and medical equipment. These businesses employ almost 400,000 people, which is more than 10 percent of the state's labor force and two thirds of all manufac-turing jobs. Workers in high-tech manufacturing enjoy incomes almost 60 percent higher than the state's average income. Although the recession hit these firms, they cut employment by only 10 percent, compared with a 24 percent cut in manufacturing jobs in the rest of the Michigan economy.

The structural unemployment rate remains high because job gains in new advanced-manufacturing firms are not yet enough to offset the job losses in the shrinking parts of manufacturing.

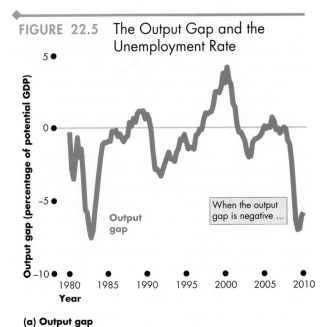

FIGURE 22.5   The Output Gap and the Unemployment Rate

(a) Output gap

Output gap

When the output gap is negative ...

(b) Unemployment rate

Unemployment rate

... the unemployment rate exceeds the natural unemployment rate

Natural unemployment rate

As real GDP fluctuates around potential GDP in part (a), the unemployment rate fluctuates around the natural unemployment rate in part (b). In recessions, cyclical unemployment peaks and the output gap becomes negative. At business cycle peaks, the unemployment rate falls below the natural rate and the output gap becomes positive. The natural unemployment rate decreased during the 1980s and 1990s.

Sources of data: Bureau of Economic Analysis, Bureau of Labor Statistics, and Congressional Budget Office.

myeconlab animation

Figure 22.5 illustrates these fluctuations in the United States between 1980 and 2010—the output gap in part (a) and the unemployment rate and natural unemployment rate in part (b).

When the economy is at full employment, the unemployment rate equals the natural unemployment rate and real GDP equals potential GDP so the output gap is zero. When the unemployment rate is less than the natural unemployment rate, real GDP is greater than potential GDP and the output gap is positive. And when the unemployment rate is greater than the natural unemployment rate, real GDP is less than potential GDP and the output gap is negative.

Figure 22.5(b) shows the natural unemployment rate estimated by the Congressional Budget Office. This estimate puts the natural unemployment rate at 6.2 percent in 1980 and falling steadily through the 1980s and 1990s to 4.8 percent by 2000. This estimate of the natural unemployment rate in the United States is one that many, but not all, economists agree with.

REVIEW QUIZ

1 Why does unemployment arise and what makes some unemployment unavoidable?
2 Define frictional unemployment, structural unemployment, and cyclical unemployment. Give examples of each type of unemployment.
3 What is the natural unemployment rate?
4 How does the natural unemployment rate change and what factors might make it change?
5 Why is the unemployment rate never zero, even at full employment?
6 What is the output gap? How does it change when the economy goes into recession?
7 How does the unemployment rate fluctuate over the business cycle?

You can work these questions in Study Plan 22.2 and get instant feedback.    **myeconlab**

Your next task is to see how we monitor the price level and the inflation rate. You will learn about the Consumer Price Index (CPI), which is monitored every month. You will also learn about other measures of the price level and the inflation rate.

◆ The Price Level, Inflation, and Deflation

What will it *really* cost you to pay off your student loan? What will your parent's life savings buy when they retire? The answers depend on what happens to the **price level**, the average level of prices, and the value of money. A persistently rising price level is called **inflation;** a persistently falling price level is called **deflation**.

We are interested in the price level, inflation, and deflation for two main reasons. First, we want to measure the annual percentage change of the price level—the inflation rate or deflation rate. Second, we want to distinguish between the money values and real values of economic variables such as your student loan and your parent's savings.

We begin by explaining why inflation and deflation are problems. Then we'll look at how we measure the price level and the inflation rate. Finally, we'll return to the task of distinguishing real values from money values.

Why Inflation and Deflation are Problems

Low, steady, and anticipated inflation or deflation isn't a problem, but an unexpected burst of inflation or period of deflation brings big problems and costs. An unexpected inflation or deflation:

- Redistributes income
- Redistributes wealth
- Lowers real GDP and employment
- Diverts resources from production

Redistribution of Income Workers and employers sign wage contracts that last for a year or more. An unexpected burst of inflation raises prices but doesn't immediately raise the wages. Workers are worse off because their wages buy less than they bargained for and employers are better off because their profits rise.

An unexpected period of deflation has the opposite effect. Wage rates don't fall but the prices fall. Workers are better off because their fixed wages buy more than they bargained for and employers are worse off with lower profits.

Redistribution of Wealth People enter into loan contracts that are fixed in money terms and that pay an interest rate agreed as a percentage of the money borrowed and lent. With an unexpected burst of infla-

tion, the money that the borrower repays to the lender buys less than the money originally loaned. The borrower wins and the lender loses. The interest paid on the loan doesn't compensate the lender for the loss in the value of the money loaned. With an unexpected deflation, the money that the borrower repays to the lender buys *more* than the money originally loaned. The borrower loses and the lender wins.

Lowers Real GDP and Employment Unexpected inflation that raises firms' profits brings a rise in investment and a boom in production and employment. Real GDP rises above potential GDP and the unemployment rate falls below the natural rate. But this situation is *temporary*. Profitable investment dries up, spending falls, real GDP falls below potential GDP and the unemployment rate rises. Avoiding these swings in production and jobs means avoiding unexpected swings in the inflation rate.

An unexpected deflation has even greater consequences for real GDP and jobs. Businesses and households that are in debt (borrowers) are worse off and they cut their spending. A fall in total spending brings a recession and rising unemployment.

Diverts Resources from Production Unpredictable inflation or deflation turns the economy into a casino and diverts resources from productive activities to forecasting inflation. It can become more profitable to forecast the inflation rate or deflation rate correctly than to invent a new product. Doctors, lawyers, accountants, farmers—just about everyone—can make themselves better off, not by specializing in the profession for which they have been trained but by spending more of their time dabbling as amateur economists and inflation forecasters and managing their investments.

From a social perspective, the diversion of talent that results from unpredictable inflation is like throwing scarce resources onto a pile of garbage. This waste of resources is a cost of inflation.

At its worst, inflation becomes **hyperinflation**—an inflation rate of 50 percent a month or higher that grinds the economy to a halt and causes a society to collapse. Hyperinflation is rare, but Zimbabwe in recent years and several European and Latin American countries have experienced it.

We pay close attention to the inflation rate, even when its rate is low, to avoid its consequences. We monitor the price level every month and devote considerable resources to measuring it accurately. You're now going to see how we do this.

The Consumer Price Index

Every month, the Bureau of Labor Statistics (BLS) measures the price level by calculating the **Consumer Price Index (CPI)**, which is a measure of the average of the prices paid by urban consumers for a fixed basket of consumer goods and services. What you learn here will help you to make sense of the CPI and relate it to your own economic life. The CPI tells you about the *value* of the money in your pocket.

Reading the CPI Numbers

The CPI is defined to equal 100 for a period called the *reference base period*. Currently, the reference base period is 1982–1984. That is, for the average of the 36 months from January 1982 through December 1984, the CPI equals 100.

In June 2010, the CPI was 218. This number tells us that the average of the prices paid by urban consumers for a fixed market basket of consumer goods and services was 118 percent higher in 2010 than it was on the average during 1982–1984.

Constructing the CPI

Constructing the CPI involves three stages:

- Selecting the CPI basket
- Conducting the monthly price survey
- Calculating the CPI

The CPI Basket The first stage in constructing the CPI is to select what is called the *CPI basket*. This basket contains the goods and services represented in the index, each weighted by its relative importance. The idea is to make the relative importance of the items in the CPI basket the same as that in the budget of an average urban household. For example, because people spend more on housing than on bus rides, the CPI places more weight on the price of housing than on the price of a bus ride.

To determine the CPI basket, the BLS conducts a Consumer Expenditure Survey. Today's CPI basket is based on data gathered in the Consumer Expenditure Survey of 2008.

Figure 22.6 shows the CPI basket in June 2010. As you look at the relative importance of the items in the CPI basket, remember that it applies to the *average* household. *Individual* household's baskets are spread around the average. Think about what you buy and compare your basket with the CPI basket.

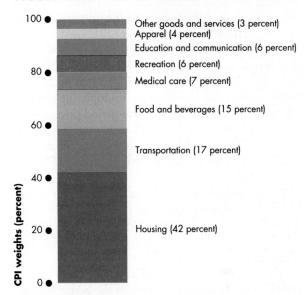

FIGURE 22.6 The CPI Basket

The CPI basket consists of the items that an average urban household buys. It consists mainly of housing (42 percent), transportation (17 percent), and food and beverages (15 percent). All other items add up to 26 percent of the total.

Sources of data: United States Census Bureau and Bureau of Labor Statistics.

myeconlab animation

The Monthly Price Survey Each month, BLS employees check the prices of the 80,000 goods and services in the CPI basket in 30 metropolitan areas. Because the CPI aims to measure price *changes*, it is important that the prices recorded each month refer to exactly the same item. For example, suppose the price of a box of jelly beans has increased but a box now contains more beans. Has the price of jelly beans increased? The BLS employee must record the details of changes in quality or packaging so that price changes can be isolated from other changes.

Once the raw price data are in hand, the next task is to calculate the CPI.

Calculating the CPI To calculate the CPI, we

1. Find the cost of the CPI basket at base-period prices.
2. Find the cost of the CPI basket at current-period prices.
3. Calculate the CPI for the base period and the current period.

We'll work through these three steps for the simple artificial economy in Table 22.1, which shows the quantities in the CPI basket and the prices in the base period (2010) and current period (2011).

Part (a) contains the data for the base period. In that period, consumers bought 10 oranges at $1 each and 5 haircuts at $8 each. To find the cost of the CPI basket in the base-period prices, multiply the quantities in the CPI basket by the base-period prices. The cost of oranges is $10 (10 at $1 each), and the cost of haircuts is $40 (5 at $8 each). So total cost of the CPI basket in the base period of the CPI basket is $50 ($10 + $40).

Part (b) contains the price data for the current period. The price of an orange increased from $1 to $2, which is a 100 percent increase—($1 ÷ $1) × 100 = 100. The price of a haircut increased from $8 to $10, which is a 25 percent increase—($2 ÷ $8) × 100 = 25.

The CPI provides a way of averaging these price increases by comparing the cost of the basket rather than the price of each item. To find the cost of the CPI basket in the current period, 2011, multiply the quantities in the basket by their 2011 prices. The cost of

oranges is $20 (10 at $2 each), and the cost of haircuts is $50 (5 at $10 each). So total cost of the fixed CPI basket at current-period prices is $70 ($20 + $50).

You've now taken the first two steps toward calculating the CPI: calculating the cost of the CPI basket in the base period and the current period. The third step uses the numbers you've just calculated to find the CPI for 2010 and 2011.

The formula for the CPI is

$$\text{CPI} = \frac{\text{Cost of CPI basket at current prices}}{\text{Cost of CPI basket at base-period prices}} \times 100.$$

In Table 22.1, you established that in 2010 (the base period), the cost of the CPI basket was $50 and in 2011, it was $70. If we use these numbers in the CPI formula, we can find the CPI for 2010 and 2011. For 2010, the CPI is

$$\text{CPI in 2010} = \frac{\$50}{\$50} \times 100 = 100.$$

For 2011, the CPI is

$$\text{CPI in 2011} = \frac{\$70}{\$50} \times 100 = 140.$$

The principles that you've applied in this simplified CPI calculation apply to the more complex calculations performed every month by the BLS.

Measuring the Inflation Rate

A major purpose of the CPI is to measure changes in the cost of living and in the value of money. To measure these changes, we calculate the *inflation rate* as the annual percentage change in the CPI. To calculate the inflation rate, we use the formula:

$$\text{Inflation rate} = \frac{\text{CPI this year} - \text{CPI last year}}{\text{CPI last year}} \times 100.$$

We can use this formula to calculate the inflation rate in 2010. The CPI in June 2010 was 218.0, and the CPI in June 2009 was 215.7. So the inflation rate during the twelve months to June 2010 was

$$\text{Inflation rate} = \frac{(218.0 - 215.7)}{215.7} \times 100 = 1.1\%.$$

TABLE 22.1 The CPI: A Simplified Calculation

(a) The cost of the CPI basket at base-period prices: 2010

	CPI basket		Cost of CPI Basket
Item	Quantity	Price	
Oranges	10	$1.00	$10
Haircuts	5	$8.00	$40
Cost of CPI basket at base-period prices			$50

(b) The cost of the CPI basket at current-period prices: 2011

	CPI basket		Cost of CPI Basket
Item	Quantity	Price	
Oranges	10	$2.00	$20
Haircuts	5	$10.00	$50
Cost of CPI basket at current-period prices			$70

Distinguishing High Inflation from a High Price Level

Figure 22.7 shows the CPI and the inflation rate in the United States between 1970 and 2010. The two parts of the figure are related and emphasize the distinction between high inflation and high prices.

When the price level in part (a) *rises rapidly*, (1970 through 1982), the inflation rate in part (b) is *high*. When the price level in part (a) *rises slowly*, (after 1982), the inflation rate in part (b) is *low*.

A high inflation rate means that the price level is rising rapidly. A high price level means that there has been a sustained period of rising prices.

When the price level in part (a) *falls* (2009), the inflation rate in part (b) is negative—deflation.

The CPI is not a perfect measure of the price level and changes in the CPI probably overstate the inflation rate. Let's look at the sources of bias.

The Biased CPI

The main sources of bias in the CPI are

- New goods bias
- Quality change bias
- Commodity substitution bias
- Outlet substitution bias

New Goods Bias If you want to compare the price level in 2009 with that in 1969, you must somehow compare the price of a computer today with that of a typewriter in 1969. Because a PC is more expensive than a typewriter was, the arrival of the PC puts an upward bias into the CPI and its inflation rate.

Quality Change Bias Cars, CD players, and many other items get better every year. Part of the rise in the prices of these items is a payment for improved quality and is not inflation. But the CPI counts the entire price rise as inflation and so overstates inflation.

Commodity Substitution Bias Changes in relative prices lead consumers to change the items they buy. For example, if the price of beef rises and the price of chicken remains unchanged, people buy more chicken and less beef. This switch from beef to chicken might provide the same amount of protein and the same enjoyment as before and expenditure is the same as before. The price of protein has not changed. But because the CPI ignores the substitution of chicken for beef, it says the price of protein has increased.

FIGURE 22.7   The CPI and the Inflation Rate

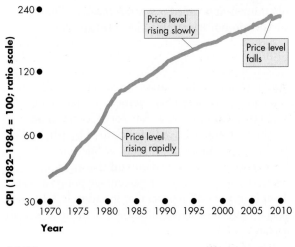

(a) CPI

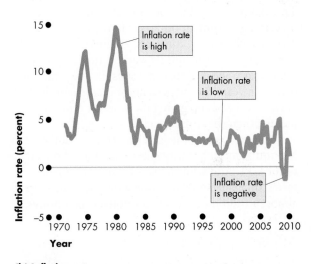

(b) Inflation rate

When the price level rises rapidly, the inflation rate is high, and when the price level rises slowly, the inflation rate is low. When the price level falls, the inflation rate is negative.

From 1970 through 1982, the price level increased rapidly in part (a) and the inflation rate was high in part (b). After 1982, the price level rose slowly in part (a) and the inflation rate was low in part (b). In 2009, the price level fell and the inflation rate was negative—there was deflation.

Source of data: Bureau of Labor Statistics.

myeconlab   animation

Outlet Substitution Bias When confronted with higher prices, people use discount stores more frequently and convenience stores less frequently. This phenomenon is called *outlet substitution*. The CPI surveys do not monitor outlet substitutions.

The Magnitude of the Bias

You've reviewed the sources of bias in the CPI. But how big is the bias? This question was tackled in 1996 by a Congressional Advisory Commission on the Consumer Price Index chaired by Michael Boskin, an economics professor at Stanford University. This commission said that the CPI overstates inflation by 1.1 percentage points a year. That is, if the CPI reports that inflation is 3.1 percent a year, most likely inflation is actually 2 percent a year.

Some Consequences of the Bias

The bias in the CPI distorts private contracts and increases government outlays. Many private agreements, such as wage contracts, are linked to the CPI. For example, a firm and its workers might agree to a three-year wage deal that increases the wage rate by 2 percent a year *plus* the percentage increase in the CPI. Such a deal ends up giving the workers more real income than the firm intended.

Close to a third of federal government outlays, including Social Security checks, are linked directly to the CPI. And while a bias of 1 percent a year seems small, accumulated over a decade it adds up to almost a trillion dollars of additional expenditures.

Alternative Price Indexes

The CPI is just one of many alternative price level index numbers and because of the bias in the CPI, other measures are used for some purposes. We'll describe three alternatives to the CPI and explain when and why they might be preferred to the CPI. The alternatives are

- Chained CPI
- Personal consumption expenditure deflator
- GDP deflator

Chained CPI The *chained CPI* is a price index that is calculated using a similar method to that used to calculate *chained-dollar real GDP* described in Chapter 21 (see pp. 504–505).

The *chained* CPI overcomes the sources of bias in the CPI. It incorporates substitutions and new goods bias by using current and previous period quantities rather than fixed quantities from an earlier period.

The practical difference made by the chained CPI is small. This index has been calculated since 2000 and the average inflation rate since then as measured by the chained CPI is only 0.3 percentage points lower than the standard CPI—2.5 percent versus 2.8 percent per year.

Personal Consumption Expenditure Deflator The *personal consumption expenditure deflator* (or *PCE deflator*) is calculated from data in the national income accounts that you studied in Chapter 21. When the Bureau of Economic Analysis calculates *real GDP*, it also calculates the real values of its expenditure components: real consumption expenditure, real investment, real government expenditure, and real net exports. These calculations are done in the same way as that for real GDP described in simplified terms on p. 495 and more technically on pp. 504–505 in Chapter 21.

To calculate the PCE deflator, we use the formula:

$$\text{PCE deflator} = (\text{Nominal } C \div \text{Real } C) \times 100,$$

where C is personal consumption expenditure.

The basket of goods and services included in the PCE deflator is broader than that in the CPI because it includes all consumption expenditure, not only the items bought by a typical urban family.

The difference between the PCE deflator and the CPI is small. Since 2000, the inflation rate measured by the PCE deflator is 2.4 percent per year, 0.4 percentage points lower than the CPI inflation rate.

GDP Deflator The *GDP deflator* is a bit like the PCE deflator except that it includes all the goods and services that are counted as part of GDP. So it is an index of the prices of the items in consumption, investment, government expenditure, and net exports.

$$\frac{\text{GDP}}{\text{deflator}} = (\text{Nominal GDP} \div \text{Real GDP}) \times 100.$$

This broader price index is appropriate for macroeconomics because it is a comprehensive measure of the cost of the real GDP basket of goods and services.

Since 2000, the GDP deflator has increased at an average rate of 2.6 percent per year, only 0.2 percentage points below the CPI inflation rate.

Core CPI Inflation

No matter whether we calculate the inflation rate using the CPI, the chained CPI, the personal consumption expenditure deflator, or the GDP deflator, the number bounces around a good deal from month to month or quarter to quarter. To determine the trend in the inflation rate, we need to strip the raw numbers of their volatility. The **core CPI inflation rate**, which is the CPI inflation rate excluding volatile elements, attempts to do just that and reveal the underlying inflation trend.

As a practical matter, the core CPI inflation rate is calculated as the percentage change in the CPI (or other price index) excluding food and fuel. The prices of these two items are among the most volatile.

While the core CPI inflation rate removes the volatile elements in inflation, it can give a misleading view of the true underlying inflation rate. If the relative prices of the excluded items are changing, the core CPI inflation rate will give a biased measure of the true underlying inflation rate.

Such a misleading account was given during the years between 2003 and 2008 when the relative prices of food and fuel were rising. The result was a core CPI inflation rate that was systematically below the CPI inflation rate. Figure 22.8 shows the two series since 2000. More refined measures of core inflation have been suggested that eliminate the bias.

The Real Variables in Macroeconomics

You saw in Chapter 21 how we measure real GDP. And you've seen in this chapter how we can use nominal GDP and real GDP to provide another measure of the price level—the GDP deflator. But viewing real GDP as nominal GDP deflated, opens up the idea of other real variables. By using the GDP deflator, we can deflate other nominal variables to find their real values. For example, the *real wage rate* is the nominal wage rate divided by the GDP deflator.

We can adjust any nominal quantity or price variable for inflation by deflating it—by dividing it by the price level.

There is one variable that is a bit different—an interest rate. A real interest rate is *not* a nominal interest rate divided by the price level. You'll learn how to adjust the nominal interest rate for inflation to find the real interest rate in Chapter 24. But all the other real variables of macroeconomics are calculated by dividing a nominal variable by the price level.

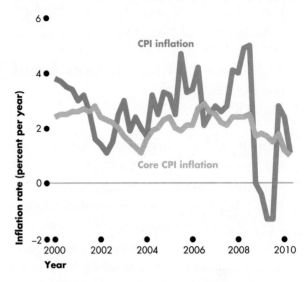

FIGURE 22.8   Core Inflation

The core CPI inflation rate excludes volatile price changes of food and fuel. Since 2003, the core CPI inflation rate has mostly been below the CPI inflation rate because the relative prices of food and fuel have been rising.

Source of data: Bureau of Labor Statistics.

myeconlab   animation

REVIEW QUIZ

1 What is the price level?
2 What is the CPI and how is it calculated?
3 How do we calculate the inflation rate and what is its relationship with the CPI?
4 What are the four main ways in which the CPI is an upward-biased measure of the price level?
5 What problems arise from the CPI bias?
6 What are the alternative measures of the price level and how do they address the problem of bias in the CPI?

You can work these questions in Study Plan 22.3 and get instant feedback.    myeconlab

You've now completed your study of the measurement of macroeconomic performance. Your next task is to learn what determines that performance and how policy actions might improve it. But first, take a close-up look at the labor market in 2009 and 2010 in *Reading Between the Lines* on pp. 528–529.

Jobs Growth Lags Recovery

U.S. Labor Force Shrinks Amid Jobs Market Woes

http://www.ft.com
August 8, 2010

When the U.S. unemployment rate moved up from 9.7 percent to 9.9 percent in April, economists cheered it as an oddly encouraging sign.

The increase was largely the result of a massive influx of 805,000 workers into the labor force—Americans who were not even looking for a job during the recession and finally felt they had better chances to find employment.

However, over the past three months, that hope seems to have vanished. Since May, the size of the U.S. labor force has shrunk by 1.15m people, with 188,000 of those dropping out last month, according to data released by the U.S. government on Friday.

Although labor force participation data are notoriously volatile, the underlying trend is unmistakable: the majority of the 1.65m people who jumped back into the labor force in the first four months of the year are back on the sidelines, cowed by the sudden slowdown in the U.S. economy and the tepid pace of private-sector job creation. …

Additionally, downward pressure on the size of the labor force could be exacerbated as Americans exhaust their unemployment benefits, which in some states last as long as 99 weeks. To receive jobless checks, workers have to prove that they are searching for a post, keeping them inside the labor force.

Indeed, in the latest government data, there were already signs of long-term unemployed Americans exiting the workforce in desperation after running out of benefits. In July, 179,000 people who had been unemployed for 27 weeks or longer left the labor force, accounting for most of the overall decline. …

ESSENCE OF THE STORY

- The U.S. unemployment rate increased from 9.7 percent to 9.9 percent in April 2010 mainly because 805,000 workers entered the labor force.

- In May, June, and July 2010, the U.S. labor force decreased by 1.15 million people.

- Monthly labor force participation data are volatile, but the underlying trend is downward and is being driven by slow economic growth and a slow pace of job creation in the private sector.

- To receive unemployment benefits, workers must search for work so that they are counted as unemployed and in the labor force.

- As benefits run out, a worker might stop looking for work and leave the labor force, which distorts the true change in unemployment.

- In July 2010, 179,000 people who had been unemployed for 27 weeks or longer left the labor force, accounting for most of the overall decline.

- This news article reports and comments on some labor market data for April through July 2010.

- During 2010, the economy was expanding following a deep recession. Figure 1 shows real GDP bottomed in mid-2009.

- Despite the expanding economy, the labor force participation rate continued on a downward trend (as reported in the news article) and the unemployment rate continued to rise.

- Figure 2 shows that the unemployment rate continued to rise until October 2009 when it reached a peak.

- The tendency for the turning point in the unemployment rate to lag the turning point in real GDP by a few months is a normal feature of the business cycle.

- The unemployment path looks the same regardless of whether we use the official measure, U–3, or add in discouraged workers (U–4) or other marginally attached workers (U–5).

- Because all the unemployment rates move up and down together, we can conclude that the falling labor force participation rate is not being driven by a fall in the number of marginally attached workers.

- Rather, as the news article says, it is long-term unemployed who are withdrawing from the labor force.

- But as Fig. 3 shows, the percentage of the unemployed who are long-term unemployed (15 weeks or longer) continued to rise through mid-2010.

- The news article identifies one link between unemployment benefits and the unemployment rate—for those whose benefits run out, the incentive to remain unemployed weakens so these people are more likely to withdraw from the labor force.

- There is a second link between unemployment benefits and the unemployment rate: When benefits are extended (to 99 weeks in some states), for those who qualify, the incentive to remain unemployed and take longer to find a suitable job strengthens.

- The increase in the percentage of the unemployed who remain unemployed for 15 weeks or longer shown in Fig. 3 might be influenced by this effect.

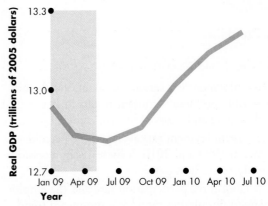

Figure 1 Real GDP

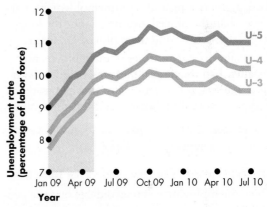

Figure 2 Unemployment

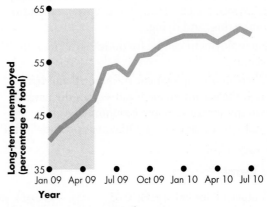

Figure 3 Long-term unemployment

SUMMARY

Key Points

Employment and Unemployment (pp. 514–518)

- Unemployment is a serious personal, social, and economic problem because it results in lost output and income and a loss of human capital.
- The unemployment rate averaged 6.2 percent between 1980 and 2010. It increases in recessions and decreases in expansions.
- The labor force participation rate and the employment-to-population ratio have an upward trend and fluctuate with the business cycle.
- Two alternative measures of unemployment, narrower than the official measure, count the long-term unemployed and unemployed job losers.
- Three alternative measures of unemployment, broader than the official measure, count discouraged workers, other marginally attached workers, and part-time workers who want full-time jobs.

Working Problems 1 to 5 will give you a better understanding of employment and unemployment.

Unemployment and Full Employment (pp. 519–521)

- Some unemployment is unavoidable because people are constantly entering and leaving the labor force and losing or quitting jobs; also firms that create jobs are constantly being borne, expanding, contracting, and dying.
- Unemployment can be frictional, structural, or cyclical.
- When all unemployment is frictional and structural, the unemployment rate equals the natural unemployment rate, the economy is at full employment, and real GDP equals potential GDP.

- Over the business cycle, real GDP fluctuates around potential GDP and the unemployment rate fluctuates around the natural unemployment rate.

Working Problems 6 to 11 will give you a better understanding of unemployment and full employment.

The Price Level, Inflation, and Deflation (pp. 522–527)

- Inflation and deflation that are unexpected redistribute income and wealth and divert resources from production.
- The Consumer Price Index (CPI) is a measure of the average of the prices paid by urban consumers for a fixed basket of consumer goods and services.
- The CPI is defined to equal 100 for a reference base period—currently 1982–1984.
- The inflation rate is the percentage change in the CPI from one period to the next.
- Changes in the CPI probably overstate the inflation rate because of the bias that arises from new goods, quality changes, commodity substitution, and outlet substitution.
- The bias in the CPI distorts private contracts and increases government outlays.
- Alternative price level measures such as the PCE deflator and GDP deflator avoid the bias of the CPI but do not make a large difference to the measured inflation rate.
- Real economic variables are calculated by dividing nominal variables by the price level.

Working Problems 12 to 20 will give you a better understanding of the price level, inflation, and deflation.

Key Terms

Consumer Price Index (CPI), 523
Core CPI inflation rate, 527
Cyclical unemployment, 519
Deflation, 522
Discouraged worker, 517
Employment-to-population ratio, 516
Frictional unemployment, 519

Full employment, 519
Hyperinflation, 522
Inflation, 522
Labor force, 515
Labor force participation rate, 517
Marginally attached worker, 517
Natural unemployment rate, 519

Output gap, 520
Price level, 522
Structural unemployment, 519
Unemployment rate, 516
Working-age population, 515

STUDY PLAN PROBLEMS AND APPLICATIONS

myeconlab You can work Problems 1 to 20 in MyEconLab Chapter 22 Study Plan and get instant feedback.

Employment and Unemployment (Study Plan 22.1)

1. The Bureau of Labor Statistics reported the following data for 2008:

   Labor force: 154,287,000
   Employment: 145,362,000
   Working-age population: 233,788,000
   Calculate the

   a. Unemployment rate.

   b. Labor force participation rate.

   c. Employment-to-population ratio.

2. In July 2009, in the economy of Sandy Island, 10,000 people were employed, 1,000 were unemployed, and 5,000 were not in the labor force. During August 2009, 80 people lost their jobs and didn't look for new ones, 20 people quit their jobs and retired, 150 unemployed people were hired, 50 people quit the labor force, and 40 people entered the labor force to look for work. Calculate for July 2009

   a. The unemployment rate.

   b. The employment-to-population ratio.

   And calculate for the end of August 2009

   c. The number of people unemployed.

   d. The number of people employed.

   e. The unemployment rate.

Use the following information to work Problems 3 and 4.

In March 2007, the U.S. unemployment rate was 4.4 percent. In August 2008, the unemployment rate was 6.1 percent. Predict what happened to

3. Unemployment between March 2007 and August 2008, assuming that the labor force was constant.

4. The labor force between March 2007 and August 2008, assuming that unemployment was constant.

5. **Shrinking U.S. Labor Force Keeps Unemployment Rate From Rising**

   An exodus of discouraged workers from the job market kept the unemployment rate from climbing above 10 percent. Had the labor force not decreased by 661,000, the unemployment rate would have been 10.4 percent. The number of discouraged workers rose to 929,000 last month.

   Source: Bloomberg, January 9, 2010

What is a discouraged worker? Explain how an increase in discouraged workers influences the official unemployment rate and U–4.

Unemployment and Full Employment (Study Plan 22.2)

Use the following news clip to work Problems 6 to 8.

Nation's Economic Pain Deepens

A spike in the unemployment rate—the biggest in more than two decades—raised new concerns that the economy is heading into a recession. The U.S. unemployment rate soared to 5.5% in May from 5% in April—much higher than forecasted. The surge marked the biggest one-month jump in unemployment since February 1986, and the 5.5% rate is the highest seen since October 2004.

Source: CNN, June 6, 2008

6. How does the unemployment rate in May compare to the unemployment rate during the earlier recessions?

7. Why might the unemployment rate tend to actually underestimate the unemployment problem, especially during a recession?

8. How does the unemployment rate in May compare to the estimated natural unemployment rate? What does this imply about the relationship between real GDP and potential GDP at this time?

Use the following information to work Problems 9 and 10.

Some Firms Struggle to Hire Despite High Unemployment

Matching people with available jobs is always difficult after a recession as the economy remakes itself. But Labor Department data suggest the disconnect is particularly acute this time. Since the recovery began in mid-2009, the number of job openings has risen more than twice as fast as actual hires. If the job market were working normally, openings would be getting filled as they appear. Some five million more would be employed and the unemployment rate would be 6.8%, instead of 9.5%.

Source: *The Wall Street Journal*, August 9, 2010

9. If the labor market is working properly, why would there be any unemployment at all?

10. Are the 5 million workers who cannot find jobs because of mismatching in the labor market

counted as part of the economy's structural unemployment or part of its cyclical unemployment?

11. Which of the following people are unemployed because of labor market mismatching?
    - Michael has unemployment benefits of $450 a week and he turned down a full-time job paying $7.75 an hour.
    - Tory used to earn $60,000 a year and he turned down a low-paid job to search for one that pays at least $50,000 a year.
    - David turned down a temporary full-time job paying $15 an hour because it was an hour's drive away and the gas cost would be high.

The Price Level, Inflation, and Deflation

(Study Plan 22.3)

Use the following information to work Problems 12 and 13.

The people on Coral Island buy only juice and cloth. The CPI basket contains the quantities bought in 2009. The average household spent $60 on juice and $30 on cloth in 2009 when the price of juice was $2 a bottle and the price of cloth was $5 a yard. In the current year, 2010, juice is $4 a bottle and cloth is $6 a yard.

12. Calculate the CPI basket and the percentage of the household's budget spent on juice in 2009.

13. Calculate the CPI and the inflation rate in 2010.

Use the following data to work Problems 14 to 16.
The BLS reported the following CPI data:

June 2006	201.9
June 2007	207.2
June 2008	217.4

14. Calculate the inflation rates for the years ended June 2007 and June 2008. How did the inflation rate change in 2008?

15. Why might these CPI numbers be biased?

16. How do alternative price indexes help to avoid the bias in the CPI numbers?

17. **Inflation Can Act as a Safety Valve**
    Workers will more readily accept a real wage cut that arises from an increase in the price level than a cut in their nominal wage rate.
    Source: FT.com, May 28, 2009
    Explain why inflation influences a worker's real wage rate. Why might this observation be true?

18. The IMF *World Economic Outlook* reported the following price level data (2000 = 100):

Region	2006	2007	2008
United States	117.1	120.4	124.0
Euro area	113.6	117.1	119.6
Japan	98.1	98.1	98.8

   a. In which region was the inflation rate highest in 2007 and in 2008?

   b. Describe the path of the price level in Japan.

19. **Inflation Getting "Uglier and Uglier"**
    The Labor Department reported that the CPI rose 4.2% through the 12 months ending in May and 0.6% in May. Energy costs rose 4.4% in May, and surged 17.4% over the 12 months ending in May; transportation costs increased 2% in May, and jumped 8.1% over the 12 months ending in May. The price of food increased 0.3% in May, and jumped 5.1% during the 12 months ending in May. The price of milk increased 10.2% over the 12 months. The price of clothing fell 0.2% in May, and decreased 0.4% over the 12 months. The core CPI rose 0.2% in May and 2.3% during the 12 months ending in May.
    Source: CNN, June 13, 2008

    a. Which components of the CPI basket experienced price increases (i) faster than the average and (ii) slower than the average?

    b. Distinguish between the CPI and the core CPI. Why might the core CPI be a useful measurement and why might it be misleading?

20. **Dress for Less**
    Since 1998, the price of the Louis Vuitton "Speedy" handbag has more than doubled, to $685, while the price of Joe Boxer's "licky face" underwear has dropped by nearly half, to $8.99. As luxury fashion has become more expensive, mainstream apparel has become markedly less so. Clothing is one of the few categories in the CPI in which overall prices have declined—about 10 percent—since 1998.
    Source: *The New York Times*, May 29, 2008

    a. What percentage of the CPI basket does apparel comprise?

    b. If luxury clothing prices have increased dramatically since the late 1990s, why has the clothing category of the CPI actually declined by about 10 percent?

ADDITIONAL PROBLEMS AND APPLICATIONS

myeconlab You can work these problems in MyEconLab if assigned by your instructor.

Employment and Unemployment

21. What is the unemployment rate supposed to measure and why is it an imperfect measure?

22. The Bureau of Labor Statistics reported the following data for 2005:

    Labor force participation rate: 66 percent
    Working-age population: 226 million
    Employment-to-population ratio: 62.7
    Calculate the
    a. Labor force.
    b. Employment.
    c. Unemployment rate.

23. In the New Orleans metropolitan area in August 2005, the labor force was 634,512 and 35,222 people were unemployed. In September 2005 following Hurricane Katrina, the labor force fell by 156,518 and the number employed fell by 206,024. Calculate the unemployment rate in August 2005 and in September 2005.

24. The BLS reported the following data: In July 2010, employment declined by 131,000 but the unemployment rate was unchanged at 9.5 percent. About 2.6 million persons were marginally attached to the labor force and among the marginally attached, 1.2 million workers were discouraged.
    a. Calculate the change in unemployment in July 2010.
    b. With 2.6 million marginally attached workers and 1.2 million of them discouraged workers, what are the characteristics of the other 1.4 million marginally attached workers?

25. A high unemployment rate tells us a large percentage of the labor force is unemployed, but it doesn't tell us why the unemployment rate is high. What measure of unemployment tells us if (i) people are taking longer than usual to find a job, (ii) more people are economic part-time workers, or (iii) more unemployed people are job losers?

26. **Some Firms Struggle to Hire Despite High Unemployment**
    With about 15 million Americans looking for work, some employers are swamped with job applicants, but many employers can't hire enough workers. What has changed in the jobs market? During the recession, millions of middle-skill, middle-wage jobs disappeared. Now with the recovery, these people can't find the skilled jobs that they seek and have a hard time adjusting to lower-skilled work with less pay.
    Source: *The Wall Street Journal*, August 9, 2010
    How will extending the period over which the government is willing to pay unemployment benefits to 99 weeks influence the cost of unemployment?

27. Why might the unemployment rate underestimate the underutilization of labor resources?

Unemployment and Full Employment

Use the following data to work Problems 28 and 29.
The IMF *World Economic Outlook* reports the following unemployment rates:

Region	2007	2008
United States	4.6	5.4
Euro area	7.4	7.3
Japan	3.9	3.9

28. What do these numbers tell you about the phase of the business cycle in the United States, Euro area, and Japan in 2008?

29. What do these numbers tell us about the relative size of the natural unemployment rates in the United States, the Euro area, and Japan?

30. Do these numbers tell us anything about the relative size of the labor force participation rates and employment-to-population ratios in the three regions?

31. **A Half-Year of Job Losses**
    Employers trimmed jobs in June for the sixth straight month, with the total for the first six months at 438,000 jobs lost by the U.S. economy. The job losses in June were concentrated in manufacturing and construction, two sectors that have been badly battered in the recession.
    Source: CNN, July 3, 2008
    a. Based on the news clip, what might be the main source of increased unemployment?
    b. Based on the news clip, what might be the main type of increased unemployment?

32. **Governor Plans to Boost Economy with Eco-friendly Jobs**

    Oregon's 5.6 percent unemployment rate hovers close to the national average of 5.5 percent. A few years ago, Oregon had one of the highest unemployment rates in the nation. To avoid rising unemployment, Oregon Governor Kulongoski introduced a plan that provides public schools and universities with enough state funds to meet growing demand for skilled workers. Also Kulongoski wants to use state and federal money for bridges, roads, and buildings to stimulate more construction jobs.

    Source: *The Oregonian*, July 8, 2008

    a. What is the main type of unemployment that Governor Kulongoski is using policies to avoid? Explain.

    b. How might these policies impact Oregon's natural unemployment rate? Explain.

The Price Level, Inflation, and Deflation

33. A typical family on Sandy Island consumes only juice and cloth. Last year, which was the base year, the family spent $40 on juice and $25 on cloth. In the base year, juice was $4 a bottle and cloth was $5 a length. This year, juice is $4 a bottle and cloth is $6 a length. Calculate

    a. The CPI basket.

    b. The CPI in the current year.

    c. The inflation rate in the current year.

34. Amazon.com agreed to pay its workers $20 an hour in 1999 and $22 an hour in 2001. The price level for these years was 166 in 1999 and 180 in 2001. Calculate the real wage rate in each year. Did these workers really get a pay raise between 1999 and 2001?

35. **News release**

    In June 2010, real personal consumption expenditure (PCE) was $9,283.4 billion and the PCE deflator was 110.8. In July 2010, real personal consumption expenditure was $9,301.3 billion and personal consumption expenditure was $10,325.5 billion.

    Source: Bureau of Economic Analysis, August 30, 2010

    Calculate personal consumption expenditure in June 2010 and the PCE deflator in July 2010. Was the percentage increase in real personal consumption expenditure greater or smaller than that in personal consumption expenditure?

Economics in the News

36. After you have studied *Reading Between the Lines* on pp. 528–529 answer the following questions.

    a. When did the unemployment rate peak after the 2008–2009 recession?

    b. What might we conclude from the three unemployment measures in Fig. 2 (p. 529)?

    c. Why might unemployment benefits influence the unemployment rate?

    d. Do unemployment benefits influence cyclical unemployment or natural unemployment? Explain.

    e. Is the rise in unemployment after mid-2009 most likely cyclical, structural, or frictional? Explain.

    f. Suggest some actions that the U.S. government might take to create more jobs.

37. **Out of a Job and Out of Luck at 54**

    Too young to retire, too old to get a new job. That's how many older workers feel after getting the pink slip and spending time on the unemployment line. Many lack the skills to craft resumes and search online, experts say. Older workers took an average of 21.1 weeks to land a new job in 2007, about 5 weeks longer than younger people. "Older workers will be more adversely affected because of the time it takes to transition into another job," said Deborah Russell, AARP's director of workforce issues.

    Source: CNN, May 21, 2008

    a. What type of unemployment might older workers be more prone to experience?

    b. Explain how the unemployment rate of older workers is influenced by the business cycle.

    c. Why might older unemployed workers become marginally attached or discouraged workers during a recession?

Data Graphing

Use the *Data Grapher* in MyEconLab to work Problems 38 to 40.

38. In which country in 2009 was the unemployment rate highest and in which was it lowest: Canada, Japan, France, or the United States?

39. In which country in 2009 was the inflation rate highest and in which was it lowest: Australia, United Kingdom, France, or the United States?

40. Make a scatter diagram of U.S. inflation and unemployment. Describe the relationship.

The Big Picture

Macroeconomics is a large and controversial subject that is interlaced with political ideological disputes. And it is a field in which charlatans as well as serious thinkers have much to say.

You have just learned in Chapters 21 and 22 how we monitor and measure the main macroeconomic variables. We use real GDP to calculate the rate of economic growth and business cycle fluctuations. And we use the CPI and other measures of the price level to calculate the inflation rate and to "deflate" nominal values to find *real* values.

In the chapters that lie ahead, you will learn the theories that economists have developed to explain economic growth, fluctuations, and inflation.

First, in Chapters 23 through 26, you will study the long-term trends. This material is central to the oldest question in macroeconomics that Adam Smith tried to answer: What are the causes of the wealth of nations? You will also study three other old questions that Adam Smith's contemporary and friend David Hume first addressed: What causes inflation? What causes international deficits and surpluses? And why do exchange rates fluctuate?

In Chapters 27 through 29, you will study macroeconomic fluctuations.

Finally, in Chapters 30 and 31, you will study the policies that the federal government and Federal Reserve might adopt to make the economy perform well.

David Hume, *a Scot who lived from 1711 to 1776, did not call himself an economist. "Philosophy and general learning" is how he described the subject of his life's work. Hume was an extraordinary thinker and writer. Published in 1742, his* Essays, Moral and Political, *range across economics, political science, moral philosophy, history, literature, ethics, and religion and explore such topics as love, marriage, divorce, suicide, death, and the immortality of the soul!*

His economic essays provide astonishing insights into the forces that cause inflation, business cycle fluctuations, balance of payments deficits, and interest rate fluctuations; and they explain the effects of taxes and government deficits and debts.

Data were scarce in Hume's day, so he was not able to draw on detailed evidence to support his analysis. But he was empirical. He repeatedly appealed to experience and evidence as the ultimate judge of the validity of an argument. Hume's fundamentally empirical approach dominates macroeconomics today.

"... in every kingdom into which money begins to flow in greater abundance than formerly, everything takes a new face: labor and industry gain life; the merchant becomes more enterprising, the manufacturer more diligent and skillful, and even the farmer follows his plow with greater alacrity and attention."

DAVID HUME
Essays, Moral and Political

Professor Clarida, why did you decide to become an economist and what drew you to macroeconomics?

I had the great fortune to have some excellent, inspiring economics professors in college (Fred Gotheil and Matt Canzoneri) and decided by my sophomore year to put myself on a path that would take me to Ph.D. work in economics. To me, there was (and still is!) enormous appeal and satisfaction from being able to distill the complexities of the economy, really the global economy, into the major fundamental forces that are driving the interactions that are of interest to people. I'm by nature a 'big picture' guy but require and respect rigor and robustness of analysis. In college and grad school, the rational expectations revolution was just emerging and so it was quite an exciting time to be jumping into macro.

> To me, there was (and still is!) enormous appeal and satisfaction from being able to distill the complexities of the economy, really the global economy, into the major fundamental forces that are driving the interactions that are of interest to people.

When you consider the United States and global economies today, there are many topics that have made headlines, most notably, the state of our economy and the rise in power of developing countries. Let's start with the state of the U.S. economy. What brought the recession from which we're now slowly recovering?

The U.S. economy was hit in 2007 and 2008 by four significant, negative shocks: The bursting of the housing bubble, a major global dislocation in financial markets, a credit crunch as banks suffered losses and tightened lending standards, and record oil and gasoline prices.

The collapse of the housing market was a significant shock to aggregate demand. The dislocation in financial markets and the credit crunch were also negative shocks to aggregate demand. This is because tighter lending standards and higher credit spreads made it more expensive for firms and households to borrow for any given level of the interest rate set by the Fed. These three shocks shifted the aggregate demand curve to the left.

Higher oil and commodity prices were a negative supply shock,which shifted the aggregate supply curve to the left.

The combination of these shocks brought an unusually large decrease in real GDP and increase in unemployment. These shocks also severely disrupted international trade and financial markets and triggered the largest ever fiscal and monetary stimulus measures.

When did the recession begin and end and why is the recovery so painfully slow?

The National Bureau of Economic Research (with whom I am affiliated as a Research Associate) is the arbiter of when a recession begins and ends and the Bureau declared the recession began in December 2007 and ended in June 2009. So the U.S. economy is now in the second year of recovery from the worst recession in 75 years. But the recovery to date has been sluggish. Unemployment remains high and eco-

RICHARD H. CLARIDA is the C. Lowell Harriss Professor of Economics at Columbia University, where he has taught since 1988. He graduated with highest honors from the University of Illinois at Urbana in 1979 and received his masters and Ph.D. in Economics from Harvard University in 1983, writing his dissertation under the supervision of Benjamin Friedman.

Professor Clarida has taught at Yale University and held public service positions as Senior Staff Economist with the President's Council of Economic Advisers in President Ronald Reagan's Administration and most recently as Assistant Secretary of the Treasury for Economic Policy in the Administration of President George W. Bush. He has also been a visiting scholar at the International Monetary Fund and at many central banks around the world, including the Federal Reserve, the European Central Bank, the Bank of Canada, the Deutsche Bundesbank, the Bank of Italy, and the Bank of England.

Professor Clarida has published a large number of important articles in leading academic journals and books on monetary policy, exchange rates, interest rates, and international capital flows.

Michael Parkin talked with Richard Clarida about his research and some of the macroeconomic policy challenges facing the United States and the world today.

nomic growth, while positive, has been much slower than in a typical recovery. This is because the U.S. economy continues to suffer the consequences of the significant negative shocks that caused the recession. The bursting of the housing bubble, the financial crisis, and the credit crunch continue to hamper bank lending.

The collapse of the housing market and the financial crisis have forced U.S. households to reduce borrowing and increase savings, which has brought a further negative shock to aggregate demand that fiscal and monetary policy have been unable to fully offset.

Research by the International Monetary Fund has found that recoveries from recessions associated with financial crises are usually sluggish, with slower growth and higher unemployment than recoveries

that are not associated with financial crises. In this case—I hope my forecast is wrong—it would seem that the United States runs the risk of going through a sustained period of slow growth.

As the recovery gains momentum, do you think we might have a period of stagflation like the 1970s?

Because of the recession, inflation in the United States was well below two percent, the level that the Fed and most central banks strive for. This is mostly due to the large output gap that opened up during the recession as well as surprisingly strong productivity growth. Despite these trends, measures of expected inflation remain well anchored at around 2 percent. Stagflation is not a near-term risk.

The Fed has an implicit target for inflation over a horizon of three years. It realizes that monetary policy operates

> ... measures of expected inflation remain well anchored at 2 percent.

with long lags, so it seeks to set a path for policy that it expects will bring inflation to two percent over several years.

If inflation expectations start to drift up, I am confident that the Fed will eventually do what it takes to keep inflation around the two percent level.

Is the current account deficit sustainable? Do you see it correcting?

The U.S. current account deficit has been shrinking as a share of GDP for almost two years. In a growing global economy, with the dollar as reserve currency, the United States can run a sustainable current account deficit of two to three percent of GDP forever. Over time, as budget deficits fall and a more competitive dollar boosts exports, the current account deficit should stabilize at the high end of this range.

In the past, the dollar has been relatively strong when compared to the euro, the pound and the yen, but now we are experiencing a weaker dollar with drastically unfavorable exchange rates. Is the dollar going to continue to go down? Does it matter?

The dollar has been trending down for some time and I expect this to continue. The United States is now lagging, not leading global growth, and the share of dollars in global portfolios will continue to trend down. I don't see a free fall or crash landing in the dollar, if only because the euro, at this time, is not a viable alternative.

Why isn't the euro a viable alternative to the dollar?

At this time there isn't an integrated financial market in Europe. There is a collection of a dozen markets. Also, with the privileges of being a global reserve currency come obligations. Global growth drives growing global demand for currency of the reserve country and this implies that the reserve currency country on average, runs a balance of payments deficit as Britain did until World War I and as the United States has since the 1960s.

Many central banks around the world, including those at which you've been a visiting scholar, have an explicit inflation target. Should the Fed target inflation like these other central banks do?

The Fed has a dual mandate to keep prices stable and the economy at full employment. I do not foresee the Fed changing this mandate. But through its communication strategy, the Fed has moved pretty close to an inflation forecast target.

With the deep and sustained recession and the record low interest rates, has fiscal policy been reinstated as a stabilization tool?

Given the huge impact that falling house prices had on wealth and the balance sheets of financial institutions, fiscal policy is proving to be a necessary tool in the cycle to complement monetary policy. However, the 'bang per buck', or multiplier from fiscal policy, was less than many expected. This was because the impairment of credit markets and a desire to rebuild savings offset much of the impact of fiscal policy.

The world economy has been getting much attention in the press, as many Asian countries are growing in global market share in emerging and established industries. Are China and India going to keep nudging double digit growth rates for the foreseeable future?

I am bullish on global growth prospects for the next five years for China, India, and the many other "emerging" economies that are benefiting from a combination of favorable fundamentals and globalization.

Is China's exchange rate policy a problem for the United States?

China is allowing its currency to appreciate versus the dollar and will continue to do so. This is in China's interest as much as it is in the United States' interest.

China in recent years has seen a sharp rise in inflation and a surge in capital inflows in anticipation that its currency will strengthen. China has and will continue to allow its currency to strengthen in order to reduce inflation and short term capital inflows.

What is your advice to a student who is just starting to study economics? Is it a good subject in which to major? What other subjects work well with it?

It won't surprise you to learn that I think economics is an excellent subject in which to major. In many colleges, including Columbia, it is among the most popular majors. My advice would be to take a broad range of electives and to avoid the temptation to specialize in one narrow area of economics. Also, do as much data, statistics, and presentation work as you can. You will learn the most when you have to explain yourself to others.

After studying this chapter,
you will be able to:

◆ Define and calculate the economic growth rate and explain the implications of sustained growth

◆ Describe the economic growth trends in the United States and other countries and regions

◆ Explain how population growth and labor productivity growth make potential GDP grow

◆ Explain the sources of labor productivity growth

◆ Explain the theories of economic growth, the empirical evidence on its causes, and policies to increase its rate

23

ECONOMIC GROWTH

Real GDP *per person* in the United States tripled between 1960 and 2010. If you live in a dorm that was built during the 1960s, it is likely to have just two power outlets: one for a desk lamp and one for a bedside lamp. Today, with the help of a power bar (or two), your room bulges with a personal computer, television and DVD player, microwave, refrigerator, coffeemaker, and toaster— and the list goes on. Economic growth has brought about this improvement in living standards.

We see even greater economic growth in modern Asia. At the mouth of the Yangtze River in one of the world's great cities, Shanghai, people are creating businesses, investing in new technologies, developing local and global markets, and transforming their lives. Incomes have tripled not in 50 years but in the 13 years since 1997. In the summer of 2010, China overtook Japan as the world's second largest economy. Why are incomes in China growing so rapidly?

In this chapter, we study the forces that make real GDP grow. In *Reading Between the Lines* at the end of the chapter, we return to the economic growth of China and see how it compares with that of Japan and the United States.

◆ The Basics of Economic Growth

Economic growth is a sustained expansion of production possibilities measured as the increase in real GDP over a given period. Rapid economic growth maintained over a number of years can transform a poor nation into a rich one. Such have been the stories of Hong Kong, South Korea, and some other Asian economies. Slow economic growth or the absence of growth can condemn a nation to devastating poverty. Such has been the fate of Sierra Leone, Somalia, Zambia, and much of the rest of Africa.

The goal of this chapter is to help you to understand why some economies expand rapidly and others stagnate. We'll begin by learning how to calculate the economic growth rate and by discovering the magic of sustained growth.

Calculating Growth Rates

We express the **economic growth rate** as the annual percentage change of real GDP. To calculate this growth rate, we use the formula:

$$\text{Real GDP growth rate} = \frac{\text{Real GDP in current year} - \text{Real GDP in previous year}}{\text{Real GDP in previous year}} \times 100.$$

For example, if real GDP in the current year is $11 trillion and if real GDP in the previous year was $10 trillion, then the economic growth rate is 10 percent.

The growth rate of real GDP tells us how rapidly the *total* economy is expanding. This measure is useful for telling us about potential changes in the balance of economic power among nations. But it does not tell us about changes in the standard of living.

The standard of living depends on **real GDP per person** (also called *per capita* real GDP), which is real GDP divided by the population. So the contribution of real GDP growth to the change in the standard of living depends on the growth rate of real GDP per person. We use the above formula to calculate this growth rate, replacing real GDP with real GDP per person.

Suppose, for example, that in the current year, when real GDP is $11 trillion, the population is 202 million. Then real GDP per person is $11 trillion divided by 202 million, which equals $54,455. And suppose that in the previous year, when real GDP was $10 trillion, the population was 200 million. Then real GDP per person in that year was $10 trillion divided by 200 million, which equals $50,000.

Use these two values of real GDP per person with the growth formula above to calculate the growth rate of real GDP per person. That is,

$$\text{Real GDP per person growth rate} = \frac{\$54,455 - \$50,000}{\$50,000} \times 100 = 8.9 \text{ percent.}$$

The growth rate of real GDP per person can also be calculated (approximately) by subtracting the population growth rate from the real GDP growth rate. In the example you've just worked through, the growth rate of real GDP is 10 percent. The population changes from 200 million to 202 million, so the population growth rate is 1 percent. The growth rate of real GDP per person is approximately equal to 10 percent minus 1 percent, which equals 9 percent.

Real GDP per person grows only if real GDP grows faster than the population grows. If the growth rate of the population exceeds the growth of real GDP, then real GDP per person falls.

The Magic of Sustained Growth

Sustained growth of real GDP per person can transform a poor society into a wealthy one. The reason is that economic growth is like compound interest.

Compound Interest Suppose that you put $100 in the bank and earn 5 percent a year interest on it. After one year, you have $105. If you leave that $105 in the bank for another year, you earn 5 percent interest on the original $100 *and on the $5 interest that you earned last year*. You are now earning interest on interest! The next year, things get even better. Then you earn 5 percent on the original $100 and on the interest earned in the first year and the second year. You are even earning interest on the interest that you earned on the interest of the first year.

Your money in the bank is growing at a rate of 5 percent a year. Before too many years have passed, your initial deposit of $100 will have grown to $200. But after how many years?

The answer is provided by a formula called the **Rule of 70**, which states that the number of years it takes for the level of any variable to double is approx-

FIGURE 23.1   The Rule of 70

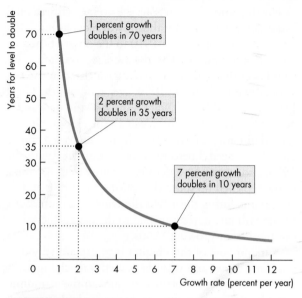

Growth rate (percent per year)	Years for level to double
1	70.0
2	35.0
3	23.3
4	17.5
5	14.0
6	11.7
7	10.0
8	8.8
9	7.8
10	7.0
11	6.4
12	5.8

The number of years it takes for the level of a variable to double is approximately 70 divided by the annual percentage growth rate of the variable.

myeconlab   animation

imately 70 divided by the annual percentage growth rate of the variable. Using the Rule of 70, you can now calculate how many years it takes your $100 to become $200. It is 70 divided by 5, which is 14 years.

Applying the Rule of 70

The Rule of 70 applies to any variable, so it applies to real GDP per person. Figure 23.1 shows the doubling time for growth rates of 1 percent per year to 12 percent per year.

You can see that real GDP per person doubles in 70 years (70 divided by 1)—an average human life span—if the growth rate is 1 percent a year. It doubles in 35 years if the growth rate is 2 percent a year and in just 10 years if the growth rate is 7 percent a year.

We can use the Rule of 70 to answer other questions about economic growth. For example, in 2010, U.S. real GDP per person was approximately 4 times that of China. China's recent growth rate of real GDP per person was 10 percent a year. If this growth rate were maintained, how long would it take China's real GDP per person to reach that of the United States in 2010? The answer, provided by the Rule of 70, is 14 years. China's real GDP per person doubles in 7 years

(70 divided by 10). It doubles again to 4 times its current level in another 7 years. So after 14 years of growth at 10 percent a year, China's real GDP per person is 4 times its current level and equals that of the United States in 2010. Of course, after 14 years, U.S. real GDP per person would have increased, so China would still not have caught up to the United States. But at the current growth rates, China's real GDP per person will equal that of the United States by 2026.

REVIEW QUIZ

1 What is economic growth and how do we calculate its rate?
2 What is the relationship between the growth rate of real GDP and the growth rate of real GDP per person?
3 Use the Rule of 70 to calculate the growth rate that leads to a doubling of real GDP per person in 20 years.

You can work these questions in Study Plan 23.1 and get instant feedback.

Economic Growth Trends

You have just seen the power of economic growth to increase incomes. At a 1 percent growth rate, it takes a human life span to double the standard of living. But at a 7 percent growth rate, the standard of living doubles every decade. How fast is our economy growing? How fast are other economies growing? Are poor countries catching up to rich ones, or do the gaps between the rich and poor persist or even widen? Let's answer these questions.

Growth in the U.S. Economy

Figure 23.2 shows real GDP per person in the United States for the hundred years from 1910 to 2010. The red line is actual real GDP and the black line (that starts in 1949) is potential GDP. The trend in potential GDP tells us about economic growth. Fluctuations around potential GDP tell us about the business cycle.

Two extraordinary events dominate the graph: the Great Depression of the 1930s, when growth stopped for a decade, and World War II of the 1940s, when growth briefly exploded.

For the century as a whole, the average growth rate was 2 percent a year. But the growth rate has not remained constant. From 1910 to the onset of the Great Depression in 1929, the average growth rate was a bit lower than the century average at 1.8 percent a year. Between 1930 and 1950, averaging out the Great Depression and World War II, the growth rate was 2.4 percent a year. After World War II, the growth rate started out at 2 percent a year. It then increased and growth averaged 3 percent a year during the 1960s. In 1973, and lasting for a decade, the growth rate slowed. Growth picked up somewhat during the 1980s and even more during the 1990s dot.com expansion. But the growth rate never returned to the pace achieved during the fast-growing 1960s.

A major goal of this chapter is to explain why our economy grows and why the growth rate changes. Another goal is to explain variations in the economic growth rate across countries. Let's now look at some of these growth rates.

FIGURE 23.2   A Hundred Years of Economic Growth in the United States

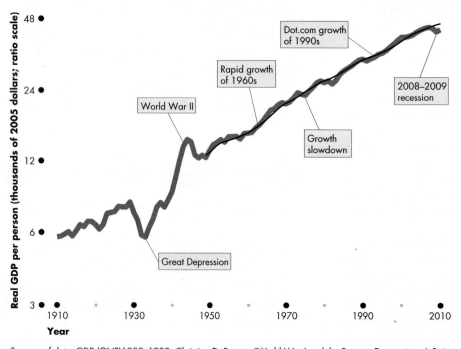

During the 100 years from 1910 to 2010, real GDP per person in the United States grew by 2 percent a year, on average. The growth rate was greater after World War II than it was before the Great Depression. Growth was most rapid during the 1960s. It slowed during the 1970s and speeded up again during the 1980s and 1990s, but it never returned to its 1960s' rate.

Sources of data: GDP (GNP) 1908–1928, Christina D. Romer, "World War I and the Postwar Depression: A Reinterpretation Based on Alternative Estimates of GNP," *Journal of Monetary Economics*, 22, 1988; 1929–2008, Bureau of Economic Analysis. Population Census Bureau.

Real GDP Growth in the World Economy

Figure 23.3 shows real GDP per person in the United States and in other countries between 1960 and 2010. Part (a) looks at the seven richest countries—known as the G7 nations. Among these nations, the United States has the highest real GDP per person. In 2010, Canada had the second-highest real GDP per person, ahead of Japan and France, Germany, Italy, and the United Kingdom (collectively the Europe Big 4).

During the fifty years shown here, the gaps between the United States, Canada, and the Europe Big 4 have been almost constant. But starting from a long way below, Japan grew fastest. It caught up to Europe in 1970 and to Canada in 1990. But during the 1990s, Japan's economy stagnated.

Many other countries are growing more slowly than, and falling farther behind, the United States. Figure 23.3(b) looks at some of these countries.

Real GDP per person in Central and South America was 28 percent of the U.S. level in 1960. It grew more quickly than the United States and reached 30 percent of the U.S. level by 1980, but then growth slowed and by 2010, real GDP per person in these countries was 23 percent of the U.S. level.

In Eastern Europe, real GDP per person has grown more slowly than anywhere except Africa, and fell from 32 percent of the U.S. level in 1980 to 19 percent in 2003 and then increased again to 22 percent in 2010.

Real GDP per person in Africa, the world's poorest continent, fell from 10 percent of the U.S. level in 1960 to 5 percent in 2007 and then increased slightly to 6 percent in 2010.

FIGURE 23.3   Economic Growth Around the World: Catch-Up or Not?

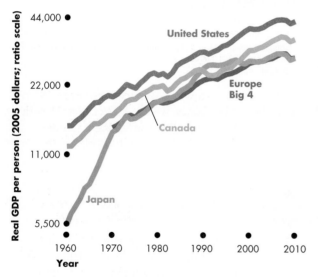

(a) Catch-up?

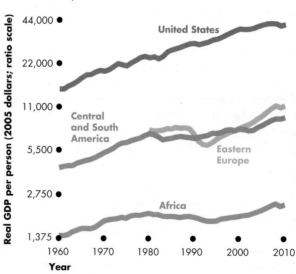

(b) No catch-up?

Real GDP per person has grown throughout the world. Among the rich industrial countries in part (a), real GDP per person has grown slightly faster in the United States than in Canada and the four big countries of Europe (France, Germany, Italy, and the United Kingdom). Japan had the fastest growth rate before 1973 but then growth slowed and Japan's economy stagnated during the 1990s.

Among a wider range of countries shown in part (b), growth rates have been lower than that of the United States. The gaps between the real GDP per person in the United States and in these countries have widened. The gap between the real GDP per person in the United States and Africa has widened by a large amount.

Sources of data: (1960–2007) Alan Heston, Robert Summers, and Bettina Aten, Penn World Table Version 6.3, Center for International Comparisons of the University of Pennsylvania (CICUP), August 2009; and (2008–2010) International Monetary Fund, *World Economic Outlook*, April 2010.

myeconlab   animation

Economics in Action
Fast Trains on the Same Track

Four Asian economies, Hong Kong, Korea, Singapore, and China, have experienced spectacular growth, which you can see in the figure. During the 1960s, real GDP per person in these economies ranged from 3 to 28 percent of that in the United States. But by 2010, real GDP per person in Singapore and Hong Kong had surpassed that of the United States.

The figure also shows that China is catching up rapidly but from a long way behind. China's real GDP per person increased from 3 percent of the U.S. level in 1960 to 26 percent in 2010.

The Asian economies shown here are like fast trains running on the same track at similar speeds and with a roughly constant gap between them. Singapore and Hong Kong are hooked together as the lead train, which runs about 20 years in front of Korea and about 40 years in front of China.

Real GDP per person in Korea in 2010 was similar to that in Hong Kong in 1988, and real GDP in China in 2010 was similar to that of Hong Kong in 1976. Between 1976 and 2010, Hong Kong transformed itself from a poor developing economy into one of the richest economies in the world.

The rest of China is now doing what Hong Kong has done. China has a population 200 times that of Hong Kong and more than 4 times that of the United States. So if China continues its rapid growth, the world economy will change dramatically.

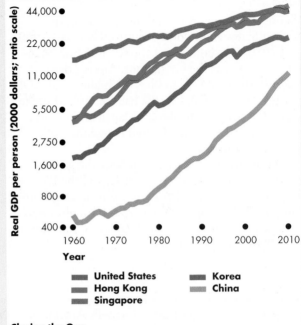

Closing the Gap

Sources of data: (1960–2007) Alan Heston, Robert Summers, and Bettina Aten, Penn World Table Version 6.3, Center for International Comparisons of the University of Pennsylvania (CICUP), August 2009; and (2008–2010) International Monetary Fund, *World Economic Outlook*, April 2010.

As these fast-growing Asian economies catch up with the United States, we can expect their growth rates to slow. But it will be surprising if China's growth rate slows much before it has closed the gap on the United States.

Even modest differences in economic growth rates sustained over a number of years bring enormous differences in the standard of living. And some of the differences that you've just seen are enormous. So the facts about economic growth in the United States and around the world raise some big questions.

What are the preconditions for economic growth? What sustains economic growth once it gets going? How can we identify the sources of economic growth and measure the contribution that each source makes? What can we do to increase the sustainable rate of economic growth?

We're now going to address these questions and discover the causes of economic growth. We start by seeing how potential GDP is determined and what makes it grow. You will see that labor productivity growth is the key to rising living standards and go on to explore the sources of this growth.

REVIEW QUIZ

1 What has been the average growth rate of U.S. real GDP per person over the past 100 years? In which periods was growth most rapid and in which periods was it slowest?

2 Describe the gaps between real GDP per person in the United States and in other countries. For which countries is the gap narrowing? For which is it widening? For which is it the same?

3 Compare real GDP per person and its growth rate in Hong Kong, Korea, Singapore, China, and the United States. In terms of real GDP per person, how far is China behind these others?

You can work these questions in Study Plan 23.2 and get instant feedback.

How Potential GDP Grows

Economic growth occurs when real GDP increases. But a one-shot rise in real GDP or a recovery from recession isn't economic growth. Economic growth is a sustained, year-after-year increase in *potential GDP*.

So what determines potential GDP and what are the forces that make it grow?

What Determines Potential GDP?

Labor, capital, land, and entrepreneurship produce real GDP, and the productivity of the factors of production determines the quantity of real GDP that can be produced.

The quantity of land is fixed and on any given day, the quantities of entrepreneurial ability and capital are also fixed and their productivities are given. The quantity of labor employed is the only *variable* factor of production. Potential GDP is the level of real GDP when the quantity of labor employed is the full-employment quantity.

To determine potential GDP, we use a model with two components:

- An aggregate production function
- An aggregate labor market

Aggregate Production Function When you studied the limits to production in Chapter 2 (see p. 30), you learned that the *production possibilities frontier* is the boundary between the combinations of goods and services that can be produced and those that cannot. We're now going to think about the production possibilities frontier for two special "goods": real GDP and the quantity of leisure time.

Think of real GDP as a number of big shopping carts. Each cart contains some of each kind of different goods and services produced, and one cartload of items costs $1 trillion. To say that real GDP is $13 trillion means that it is 13 very big shopping carts of goods and services.

The quantity of leisure time is the number of hours spent not working. Each leisure hour could be spent working. If we spent all our time taking leisure, we would do no work and produce nothing. Real GDP would be zero. The more leisure we forgo, the greater is the quantity of labor we supply and the greater is the quantity of real GDP produced.

But labor hours are not all equally productive. We use our most productive hours first and as more hours are worked less and less productive hours are used. So for each additional hour of leisure forgone (each additional hour of labor), real GDP increases but by successively smaller amounts.

The **aggregate production function** is the relationship that tells us how real GDP changes as the quantity of labor changes when all other influences on production remain the same. Figure 23.4 shows this relationship—the curve labeled *PF*. An increase in the quantity of labor (and a corresponding decrease in leisure hours) brings a movement along the production function and an increase in real GDP.

Aggregate Labor Market In macroeconomics, we pretend that there is one large labor market that determines the quantity of labor employed and the quantity of real GDP produced. To see how this aggregate labor market works, we study the demand for labor, the supply of labor, and labor market equilibrium.

The Demand for Labor The *demand for labor* is the relationship between the quantity of labor demanded and the real wage rate. The quantity of labor demanded is the number of labor hours hired by all the firms in the economy during a given period. This

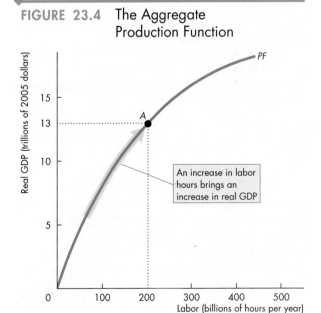

FIGURE 23.4   The Aggregate Production Function

At point A on the aggregate production function PF, 200 billion hours of labor produce $13 trillion of real GDP.

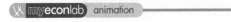

quantity depends on the price of labor, which is the real wage rate.

The **real wage rate** is the money wage rate divided by the price level. The real wage rate is the quantity of goods and services that an hour of labor earns. It contrasts with the money wage rate, which is the number of dollars that an hour of labor earns.

The *real* wage rate influences the quantity of labor demanded because what matters to firms is not the number of dollars they pay (money wage rate) but how much output they must sell to earn those dollars.

The quantity of labor demanded *increases* as the real wage rate *decreases*—the demand for labor curve slopes downward. Why? The answer lies in the shape of the production function.

You've seen that along the production function, each additional hour of labor increases real GDP by successively smaller amounts. This tendency has a name: the *law of diminishing returns*. Because of diminishing returns, firms will hire more labor only if the real wage rate falls to match the fall in the extra output produced by that labor.

The Supply of Labor The *supply of labor* is the relationship between the quantity of labor supplied and the real wage rate. The quantity of labor supplied is the number of labor hours that all the households in the economy plan to work during a given period. This quantity depends on the real wage rate.

The *real* wage rate influences the quantity of labor supplied because what matters to households is not the number of dollars they earn (money wage rate) but what they can buy with those dollars.

The quantity of labor supplied *increases* as the real wage rate *increases*—the supply of labor curve slopes upward. At a higher real wage rate, more people choose to work and more people choose to work longer hours if they can earn more per hour.

Labor Market Equilibrium The price of labor is the real wage rate. The forces of supply and demand operate in labor markets just as they do in the markets for goods and services to eliminate a shortage or a surplus. But a shortage or a surplus of labor brings only a gradual change in the real wage rate. If there is a shortage of labor, the real wage rate rises to eliminate it; and if there is a surplus of labor, the real wage rate eventually falls to eliminate it. When there is neither a shortage nor a surplus, the labor market is in equilibrium—a full-employment equilibrium.

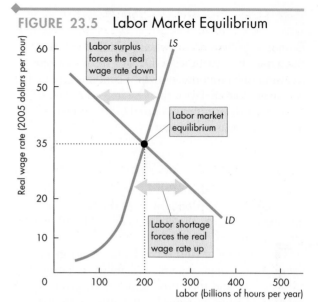

FIGURE 23.5 Labor Market Equilibrium

Labor market equilibrium occurs when the quantity of labor demanded equals the quantity of labor supplied. The equilibrium real wage rate is $35 an hour, and equilibrium employment is 200 billion hours per year.

At a wage rate above $35 an hour, there is a surplus of labor and the real wage rate falls to eliminate the surplus. At a wage rate below $35 an hour, there is a shortage of labor and the real wage rate rises to eliminate the shortage.

Figure 23.5 illustrates labor market equilibrium. The demand for labor curve is *LD* and the supply of labor curve is *LS*. This labor market is in equilibrium at a real wage rate of $35 an hour and 200 billion hours a year are employed.

If the real wage rate exceeds $35 an hour, the quantity of labor supplied exceeds the quantity demanded and there is a surplus of labor. When there is a surplus of labor, the real wage rate falls toward the equilibrium real wage rate where the surplus is eliminated.

If the real wage rate is less than $35 an hour, the quantity of labor demanded exceeds the quantity supplied and there is a shortage of labor. When there is a shortage of labor, the real wage rate rises toward the equilibrium real wage rate where the shortage is eliminated.

If the real wage rate is $35 an hour, the quantity of labor demanded equals the quantity supplied and there is neither a shortage nor a surplus of labor. In this situation, there is no pressure in either direction on the real wage rate. So the real wage rate remains constant and the market is in equilibrium. At this equilibrium real wage rate and level of employment, the economy is at *full employment*.

Potential GDP You've seen that the production function tells us the quantity of real GDP that a given amount of labor can produce—see Fig. 23.4. The quantity of real GDP produced increases as the quantity of labor increases. At the equilibrium quantity of labor, the economy is at full employment, and the quantity of real GDP at full employment is potential GDP. So the full-employment quantity of labor produces potential GDP.

Figure 23.6 illustrates the determination of potential GDP. Part (a) shows labor market equilibrium. At the equilibrium real wage rate, equilibrium employment is 200 billion hours. Part (b) shows the production function. With 200 billion hours of labor, the economy can produce a real GDP of $13 trillion. This amount is potential GDP.

What Makes Potential GDP Grow?

We can divide all the forces that make potential GDP grow into two categories:

- Growth of the supply of labor
- Growth of labor productivity

Growth of the Supply of Labor When the supply of labor grows, the supply of labor curve shifts rightward. The quantity of labor at a given real wage rate increases.

The quantity of labor is the number of workers employed multiplied by average hours per worker; and the number employed equals the employment-to-population ratio multiplied by the working-age population (see Chapter 22, p. 516). So the quantity of labor changes as a result of changes in

1. Average hours per worker
2. The employment-to-population ratio
3. The working-age population

Average hours per worker have decreased as the workweek has become shorter, and the employment-to-population ratio has increased as more women have entered the labor force. The combined effect of

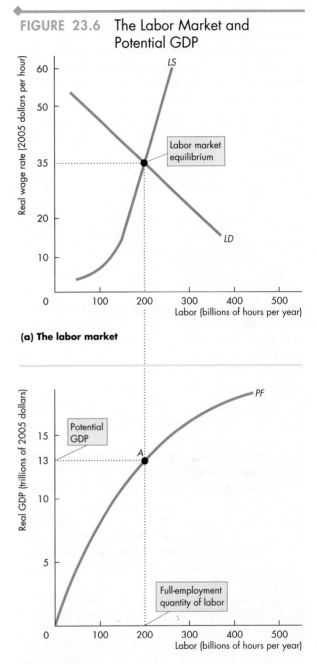

FIGURE 23.6   The Labor Market and Potential GDP

(a) The labor market

(b) Potential GDP

The economy is at full employment when the quantity of labor demanded equals the quantity of labor supplied, in part (a). The real wage rate is $35 an hour, and employment is 200 billion hours a year. Part (b) shows potential GDP. It is the quantity of real GDP determined by the production function at the full-employment quantity of labor.

 animation

these two factors has kept the average hours per working-age person (approximately) constant.

Growth in the supply of labor has come from growth in the working-age population. In the long run, the working-age population grows at the same rate as the total population.

The Effects of Population Growth Population growth brings growth in the supply of labor, but it does not change the demand for labor or the production function. The economy can produce more output by using more labor, but there is no change in the quantity of real GDP that a given quantity of labor can produce.

With an increase in the supply of labor and no change in the demand for labor, the real wage rate falls and the equilibrium quantity of labor increases. The increased quantity of labor produces more output and potential GDP increases.

Illustrating the Effects of Population Growth Figure 23.7 illustrates the effects of an increase in the population. In Fig. 23.7(a), the demand for labor curve is *LD* and initially the supply of labor curve is LS_0. The equilibrium real wage rate is $35 an hour and the quantity of labor is 200 billion hours a year. In Fig. 23.7(b), the production function (*PF*) shows that with 200 billion hours of labor employed, potential GDP is $13 trillion at point *A*.

An increase in the population increases the supply of labor and the supply of labor curve shifts rightward to LS_1. At a real wage rate of $35 an hour, there is now a surplus of labor. So the real wage rate falls. In this example, the real wage rate will fall until it reaches $25 an hour. At $25 an hour, the quantity of labor demanded equals the quantity of labor supplied. The equilibrium quantity of labor increases to 300 billion a year.

Figure 23.7(b) shows the effect on real GDP. As the equilibrium quantity of labor increases from 200 billion to 300 billion hours, potential GDP increases along the production function from $13 trillion to $16 trillion at point *B*.

So an increase in the population increases the full-employment quantity of labor, increases potential GDP, and lowers the real wage rate. But the population increase *decreases* potential GDP per hour of labor. Initially, it was $65 ($13 trillion divided by 200 billion). With the population increase, potential GDP per hour of labor is $53.33 ($16 trillion divided by 300 billion). Diminishing returns are the source of the decrease in potential GDP per hour of labor.

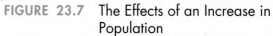

FIGURE 23.7   The Effects of an Increase in Population

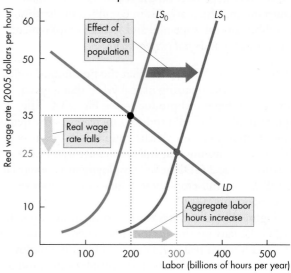

(a) The labor market

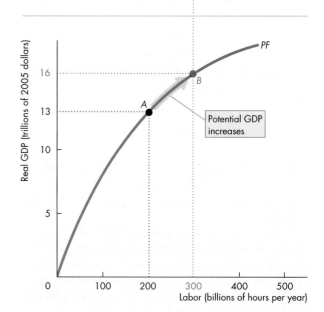

(b) Potential GDP

An increase in the population increases the supply of labor. In part (a), the supply of labor curve shifts rightward. The real wage rate falls and aggregate labor hours increase. In part (b), the increase in aggregate labor hours brings an increase in potential GDP. But diminishing returns bring a decrease in potential GDP per hour of labor.

myeconlab   animation

Growth of Labor Productivity **Labor productivity** is the quantity of real GDP produced by an hour of labor. It is calculated by dividing real GDP by aggregate labor hours. For example, if real GDP is $13 trillion and aggregate hours are 200 billion, labor productivity is $65 per hour.

When labor productivity grows, real GDP per person grows and brings a rising standard of living. Let's see how an increase in labor productivity changes potential GDP.

Effects of an Increase in Labor Productivity If labor productivity increases, production possibilities expand. The quantity of real GDP that any given quantity of labor can produce increases. If labor is more productive, firms are willing to pay more for a given number of hours of labor so the demand for labor also increases.

With an increase in the demand for labor and *no change in the supply of labor*, the real wage rate rises and the quantity of labor supplied increases. The equilibrium quantity of labor also increases.

So an increase in labor productivity increases potential GDP for two reasons: Labor is more productive and more labor is employed.

Illustrating the Effects of an Increase in Labor Productivity Figure 23.8 illustrates the effects of an increase in labor productivity.

In part (a), the production function initially is PF_0. With 200 billion hours of labor employed, potential GDP is $13 trillion at point A.

In part (b), the demand for labor curve is LD_0 and the supply of labor curve is LS. The real wage rate is $35 an hour, and the equilibrium quantity of labor is 200 billion hours a year.

Now labor productivity increases. In Fig. 23.8(a), the increase in labor productivity shifts the production function upward to PF_1. At each quantity of labor, more real GDP can be produced. For example, at 200 billion hours, the economy can now produce $18 trillion of real GDP at point B.

In Fig. 23.8(b), the increase in labor productivity increases the demand for labor and the demand for labor curve shifts rightward to LD_1. At the initial real wage rate of $35 an hour, there is now a shortage of labor. The real wage rate rises. In this example, the real wage rate will rise until it reaches $45 an hour. At $45 an hour, the quantity of labor demanded equals the quantity of labor supplied and the equilibrium quantity of labor is 225 billion hours a year.

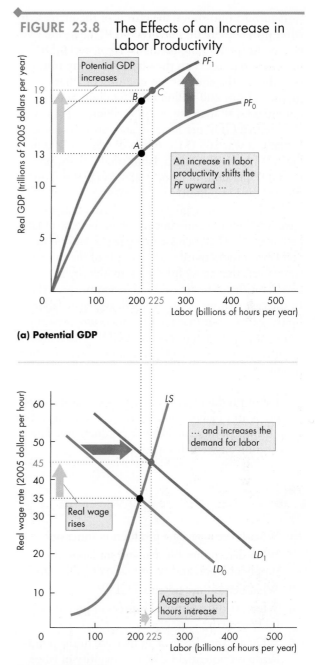

FIGURE 23.8 The Effects of an Increase in Labor Productivity

(a) Potential GDP

(b) The labor market

An increase in labor productivity shifts the production function upward from PF_0 to PF_1 in part (a) and shifts the demand for labor curve rightward from LD_0 to LD_1 in part (b). The real wage rate rises to $45 an hour, and aggregate labor hours increase from 200 billion to 225 billion. Potential GDP increases from $13 trillion to $19 trillion.

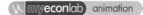 animation

Figure 23.8(a) shows the effects of the increase in labor productivity on potential GDP. There are two effects. At the initial quantity of labor, real GDP increases to point *B* on the new production function. But as the equilibrium quantity of labor increases from 200 billion to 225 billion hours, potential GDP increases to $19 trillion at point *C*.

Potential GDP per hour of labor also increases. Initially, it was $65 ($13 trillion divided by 200 billion). With the increase in labor productivity, potential GDP per hour of labor is $84.44 ($19 trillion divided by 225 billion).

The increase in aggregate labor hours that you have just seen is a consequence of an increase in labor productivity. This increase in aggregate labor hours and labor productivity is an example of the interaction effects that economists seek to identify in their search for the ultimate *causes* of economic growth. In the case that we've just studied, aggregate labor hours increase but that increase is a *consequence*, not a cause, of the growth of potential GDP. The source of the increase in potential GDP is an increase in labor productivity.

Labor productivity is the key to increasing output per hour of labor and rising living standards. But what brings an increase in labor productivity? The next section answers this question.

REVIEW QUIZ

1 What is the aggregate production function?
2 What determines the demand for labor, the supply of labor, and labor market equilibrium?
3 What determines potential GDP?
4 What are the two broad sources of potential GDP growth?
5 What are the effects of an increase in the population on potential GDP, the quantity of labor, the real wage rate, and potential GDP per hour of labor?
6 What are the effects of an increase in labor productivity on potential GDP, the quantity of labor, the real wage rate, and potential GDP per hour of labor?

You can work these questions in Study Plan 23.3 and get instant feedback.

◆ Why Labor Productivity Grows

You've seen that labor productivity growth makes potential GDP grow; and you've seen that labor productivity growth is essential if real GDP per person and the standard of living are to grow. But *why* does labor productivity grow? What are the preconditions that make labor productivity growth possible and what are the forces that make it grow? Why does labor productivity grow faster at some times and in some places than others?

Preconditions for Labor Productivity Growth

The fundamental precondition for labor productivity growth is the *incentive* system created by firms, markets, property rights, and money. These four social institutions are the same as those described in Chapter 2 (see pp. 41–42) that enable people to gain by specializing and trading.

Economics in Action
Intellectual Property Rights Propel Growth

In 1760, when the states that 16 years later would become the United States of America were developing agricultural economies, England was on the cusp of an economic revolution, the *Industrial Revolution*.

For 70 dazzling years, technological advances in the use of steam power, the manufacture of cotton, wool, iron, and steel, and in transportation, accompanied by massive capital investment associated with these technologies, transformed the economy of England. Incomes rose and brought an explosion in an increasingly urbanized population.

By 1825, advances in steam technology had reached a level of sophistication that enabled Robert Stevenson to build the world's first steam-powered rail engine (the Rocket pictured here) and the birth of the world's first railroad.

Why did the Industrial Revolution happen? Why did it start in 1760? And why in England?

Economic historians say that intellectual property rights—England's patent system—provides the answer.

England's patent system began with the Statute of Monopolies of 1624, which gave inventors a monopoly to use their idea for a term of 14 years. For about 100 years, the system was used to reward friends of the

It was the presence of secure property rights in Britain in the middle 1700s that got the Industrial Revolution going (see Economics in Action below). And it is their absence in some parts of Africa today that is keeping labor productivity stagnant.

With the preconditions for labor productivity growth in place, three things influence its pace:

- Physical capital growth
- Human capital growth
- Technological advances

Physical Capital Growth

As the amount of capital per worker increases, labor productivity also increases. Production processes that use hand tools can create beautiful objects, but production methods that use large amounts of capital per worker are much more productive. The accumulation of capital on farms, in textile factories, in iron

royal court rather than true inventors. But from around 1720 onward, the system started to work well. To be granted a 14-year monopoly, an inventor only had to pay the required £100 fee (about $22,000 in today's money) and register his or her invention. The inventor was not required to describe the invention in too much detail, so registering and getting a patent didn't mean sharing the invention with competitors.

This patent system, which is in all essentials the same as today's, aligned the self-interest of entrepreneurial inventors with the social interest and unleashed a flood of inventions, the most transformative of which was steam power and, by 1825, the steam locomotive.

foundries and steel mills, in coal mines, on building sites, in chemical plants, in auto plants, in banks and insurance companies, and in shopping malls has added incredibly to the labor productivity of our economy. The next time you see a movie that is set in the Old West or colonial times, look carefully at the small amount of capital around. Try to imagine how productive you would be in such circumstances compared with your productivity today.

Human Capital Growth

Human capital—the accumulated skill and knowledge of human beings—is the fundamental source of labor productivity growth. Human capital grows when a new discovery is made and it grows as more and more people learn how to use past discoveries.

The development of one of the most basic human skills—writing—was the source of some of the earliest major gains in productivity. The ability to keep written records made it possible to reap ever-larger gains from specialization and trade. Imagine how hard it would be to do any kind of business if all the accounts, invoices, and agreements existed only in people's memories.

Later, the development of mathematics laid the foundation for the eventual extension of knowledge about physical forces and chemical and biological processes. This base of scientific knowledge was the foundation for the technological advances of the Industrial Revolution and of today's information revolution.

But a lot of human capital that is extremely productive is much more humble. It takes the form of millions of individuals learning and becoming remarkably more productive by repetitively doing simple production tasks. One much-studied example of this type of human capital growth occurred in World War II. With no change in physical capital, thousands of workers and managers in U.S. shipyards learned from experience and accumulated human capital that more than doubled their productivity in less than two years.

Technological Advances

The accumulation of physical capital and human capital have made a large contribution to labor productivity growth. But technological change—the discovery and the application of new technologies—has made an even greater contribution.

FIGURE 23.9   The Sources of Economic Growth

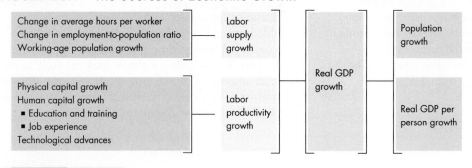

Labor supply growth and labor productivity growth combine to determine real GDP growth. Real GDP per person growth depends on real GDP growth and population growth.

 animation

Economics in Action

Women Are the Better Borrowers

Economic growth is driven by the decisions made by billions of individuals to save and invest, and borrow and lend. But most people are poor, have no credit history, and can't borrow from a bank.

These people—many of whom are women—can, however, start a business, employ a few people, and earn an income with the help of a *microloan*.

Microloans originated in Bangladesh but have spread throughout the developing world. Kiva.org and MicroPlace.com (owned by eBay) are Web sites that enable people to lend money that is used to make microloans in developing economies.

Throughout the developing world, microloans are helping women to feed and clothe their families and to grow their small businesses, often in agriculture. As the incomes of microloan borrowers rise, they pay off their loans and accumulate capital. A billion microloans pack a macro punch.

Labor is many times more productive today than it was a hundred years ago but not because we have more steam engines and more horse-drawn carriages per person. Rather, it is because we have transportation equipment that uses technologies that were unknown a hundred years ago and that are more productive than the old technologies were.

Technological advance arises from formal research and development programs and from informal trial and error, and it involves discovering new ways of getting more out of our resources.

To reap the benefits of technological change, capital must increase. Some of the most powerful and far-reaching fundamental technologies are embodied in human capital—for example, language, writing, and mathematics. But most technologies are embodied in physical capital. For example, to reap the benefits of the internal combustion engine, millions of horse-drawn carriages had to be replaced with automobiles; and to reap the benefits of digital music, millions of Discmans had to be replaced by iPods.

Figure 23.9 summarizes the sources of labor productivity growth and more broadly of real GDP growth. The figure also emphasizes that for real GDP per person to grow, real GDP must grow faster than the population.

REVIEW QUIZ

1   What are the preconditions for labor productivity growth?
2   Explain the influences on the pace of labor productivity growth.

You can work these questions in Study Plan 23.4 and get instant feedback.

◆ Growth Theories, Evidence, and Policies

You've seen how population growth and labor productivity growth make potential GDP grow. You've also seen that the growth of physical capital and human capital and technological advances make labor productivity grow. How do all these factors interact? What is cause and what is effect? Growth theories address these questions.

Alternative theories of economic growth provide insights into the process of economic growth, but none provides a complete and definite answer to the basic questions: What causes economic growth and why do growth rates vary? Economics has some way to go before it can provide definite answers to these questions. We look at the current state of the empirical evidence. Finally, we'll look at the policies that might achieve faster growth.

Let's start by studying the three main theories of economic growth:

- Classical growth theory
- Neoclassical growth theory
- New growth theory

Classical Growth Theory

Classical growth theory is the view that the growth of real GDP per person is temporary and that when it rises above the subsistence level, a population explosion eventually brings it back to the subsistence level. Adam Smith, Thomas Robert Malthus, and David Ricardo—the leading economists of the late eighteenth century and early nineteenth century—proposed this theory, but the view is most closely associated with the name of Malthus and is sometimes called the *Malthusian theory*. Charles Darwin's ideas about evolution by natural selection were inspired by the insights of Malthus.

Modern-Day Malthusians Many people today are Malthusians. They say that if today's global population of 6.9 billion explodes to 11 billion by 2050 and perhaps 35 billion by 2300, we will run out of resources, real GDP per person will decline, and we will return to a primitive standard of living. We must, say Malthusians, contain population growth.

Modern-day Malthusians also point to global warming and climate change as reasons to believe that eventually, real GDP per person will decrease.

Neoclassical Growth Theory

Neoclassical growth theory is the proposition that real GDP per person grows because technological change induces saving and investment that make capital per hour of labor grow. Growth ends if technological change stops because of diminishing marginal returns to both labor and capital. Robert Solow of MIT suggested the most popular version of this growth theory in the 1950s.

Neoclassical growth theory's big break with its classical predecessor is its view about population growth.

The Neoclassical Theory of Population Growth The population explosion of eighteenth century Europe that created the classical theory of population eventually ended. The birth rate fell, and while the population continued to increase, its rate of increase moderated.

The key economic influence that slowed the population growth rate is the opportunity cost of a woman's time. As women's wage rates increase and their job opportunities expand, the opportunity cost of having children increases. Faced with a higher opportunity cost, families choose to have fewer children and the birth rate falls.

Technological advances that bring higher incomes also brings advances in health care that extends lives. So as incomes increase, both the birth rate and the death rate decrease. These opposing forces offset each other and result in a slowly rising population.

This modern view of population growth and the historical trends that support it contradict the views of the classical economists. They also call into question the modern doomsday view that the planet will be swamped with more people than it can support.

Technological Change and Diminishing Returns In neoclassical growth theory, the pace of technological change influences the economic growth rate but economic growth does not influence the pace of technological change. It is assumed that technological change results from chance. When we're lucky, we have rapid technological change, and when bad luck strikes, the pace of technological advance slows.

To understand neoclassical growth theory, imagine the world of the mid-1950s, when Robert Solow is explaining his idea. Income per person is around $12,000 a year in today's money. The population is growing at about 1 percent a year. Saving and investment are about 20 percent of GDP, enough to keep the quantity of capital per hour of labor constant. Income per person is growing but not very fast.

Then technology begins to advance at a more rapid pace across a range of activities. The transistor revolutionizes an emerging electronics industry. New plastics revolutionize the manufacture of household appliances. The interstate highway system revolutionizes road transportation. Jet airliners start to replace piston-engine airplanes and speed air transportation.

These technological advances bring new profit opportunities. Businesses expand, and new businesses are created to exploit the newly available profitable technologies. Investment and saving increase. The economy enjoys new levels of prosperity and growth. But will the prosperity last? And will the growth last? Neoclassical growth theory says that the *prosperity* will last but the *growth* will not last unless technology keeps advancing.

According to neoclassical growth theory, the prosperity will persist because there is no classical population growth to induce the wage rate to fall. So the gains in income per person are permanent.

But growth will eventually stop if technology stops advancing because of diminishing marginal returns to capital. The high profit rates that result from technological change bring increased saving and capital accumulation. But as more capital is accumulated, more and more projects are undertaken that have lower rates of return—diminishing marginal returns. As the return on capital falls, the incentive to keep investing weakens. With weaker incentives to save and invest, saving decreases and the rate of capital accumulation slows. Eventually, the pace of capital accumulation slows so that it is only keeping up with population growth. Capital per worker remains constant.

A Problem with Neoclassical Growth Theory

All economies have access to the same technologies, and capital is free to roam the globe, seeking the highest available real interest rate. Capital will flow until rates of return are equal, and rates of return will be equal when capital per hour of labor are equal. Real GDP growth rates and income levels per person around the world will converge. Figure 23.3 on p. 543 shows that while there is some sign of convergence among the rich countries in part (a), convergence is slow, and part (b) shows that it does not appear to be imminent for all countries. New growth theory overcomes this shortcoming of neoclassical growth theory. It also explains what determines the pace of technological change.

New Growth Theory

New growth theory holds that real GDP per person grows because of the choices people make in the pursuit of profit and that growth will persist indefinitely. Paul Romer of Stanford University developed this theory during the 1980s, based on ideas of Joseph Schumpeter during the 1930s and 1940s.

According to the new growth theory, the pace at which new discoveries are made—and at which technology advances—is not determined by chance. It depends on how many people are looking for a new technology and how intensively they are looking. The search for new technologies is driven by incentives.

Profit is the spur to technological change. The forces of competition squeeze profits, so to increase profit, people constantly seek either lower-cost methods of production or new and better products for which people are willing to pay a higher price. Inventors can maintain a profit for several years by taking out a patent or a copyright, but eventually, a new discovery is copied, and profits disappear. So more research and development is undertaken in the hope of creating a new burst of profitable investment and growth.

Two facts about discoveries and technological knowledge play a key role in the new growth theory: Discoveries are (at least eventually) a public capital good; and knowledge is capital that is not subject to diminishing marginal returns.

Economists call a good a *public good* when no one can be excluded from using it and when one person's use does not prevent others from using it. National defense is the classic example of a public good. The programming language used to write apps for the iPhone is another.

Because knowledge is a public good, as the benefits of a new discovery spread, free resources become available. Nothing is given up when they are used: They have a zero opportunity cost. When a student in Austin writes a new iPhone app, his use of the programming language doesn't prevent another student in Seattle from using it.

Knowledge is even more special because it is *not* subject to diminishing returns. But increasing the stock of knowledge makes both labor and machines more productive. Knowledge capital does not bring diminishing returns. Biotech knowledge illustrates this idea well. Biologists have spent a lot of time developing DNA sequencing technology. As more has been discovered, the productivity of this knowledge capital has relentlessly increased. In 1990, it cost about $50 to sequence one DNA base pair. That cost had fallen to $1 by 2000 and to 1/10,000th of a penny by 2010.

The implication of this simple and appealing observation is astonishing. Unlike the other two theories, new growth theory has no growth-stopping mechanism. As physical capital accumulates, the return to capital—the real interest rate—falls. But the incentive to innovate and earn a higher profit becomes stronger. So innovation occurs, capital becomes more productive, the demand for capital increases, and the real interest rate rises again.

Labor productivity grows indefinitely as people discover new technologies that yield a higher real interest rate. The growth rate depends only on people's incentives and ability to innovate.

A Perpetual Motion Economy New growth theory sees the economy as a perpetual motion machine, which Fig. 23.10 illustrates.

No matter how rich we become, our wants exceed our ability to satisfy them. We always want a higher standard of living. In the pursuit of a higher standard of living, human societies have developed incentive systems—markets, property rights, and money—that enable people to profit from innovation. Innovation leads to the development of new and better techniques of production and new and better products. To take advantage of new techniques and to produce new products, new firms start up and old firms go out of business—firms are born and die. As old firms die and new firms are born, some jobs are destroyed and others are created. The new jobs created are better than the old ones and they pay higher real wage rates. Also, with higher wage rates and more productive techniques, leisure increases. New and better jobs and new and better products lead to more consumption goods and services and, combined with increased leisure, bring a higher standard of living.

But our insatiable wants are still there, so the process continues: Wants and incentives create innovation, new and better products, and a yet higher standard of living.

FIGURE 23.10   A Perpetual Motion Machine

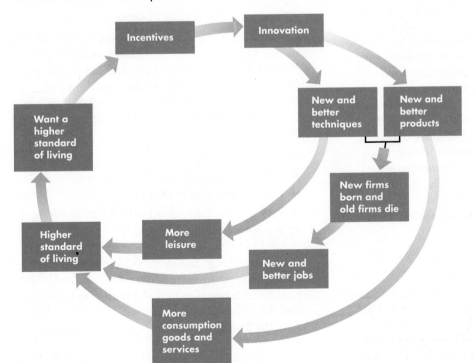

People want a higher standard of living and are spurred by profit incentives to make the innovations that lead to new and better techniques and new and better products.

These new and better techniques and products, in turn, lead to the birth of new firms and the death of some old firms, new and better jobs, and more leisure and more consumption goods and services.

The result is a higher standard of living, but people want a still higher standard of living, and the growth process continues.

Source: Based on a similar figure in These Are the Good Old Days: A Report on U.S. Living Standards, Federal Reserve Bank of Dallas 1993 Annual Report.

myeconlab animation

New Growth Theory Versus Malthusian Theory

The contrast between the Malthusian theory and new growth theory couldn't be more sharp. Malthusians see the end of prosperity as we know it today and new growth theorists see unending plenty. The contrast becomes clearest by thinking about the differing views about population growth.

To a Malthusian, population growth is part of the problem. To a new growth theorist, population growth is part of the solution. People are the ultimate economic resource. A larger population brings forth more wants, but it also brings a greater amount of scientific discovery and technological advance. So rather than being the source of falling real GDP per person, population growth generates faster labor productivity growth and rising real GDP per person. Resources are limited, but the human imagination and ability to increase productivity are unlimited.

Sorting Out the Theories

Which theory is correct? None of them tells us the whole story, but each teaches us something of value.

Classical growth theory reminds us that our physical resources are limited and that without advances in technology, we must eventually hit diminishing returns.

Neoclassical growth theory reaches the same conclusion but not because of a population explosion. Instead, it emphasizes diminishing returns to capital and reminds us that we cannot keep growth going just by accumulating physical capital. We must also advance technology and accumulate human capital. We must become more creative in our use of scarce resources.

New growth theory emphasizes the capacity of human resources to innovate at a pace that offsets diminishing returns. New growth theory fits the facts of today's world more closely than do either of the other two theories. But that doesn't make it correct.

The Empirical Evidence on the Causes of Economic Growth

Economics makes progress by the interplay between theory and empirical evidence. A theory makes predictions about what we will observe if the theory is correct. Empirical evidence, the data generated by history and the natural experiments that it performs, provide the data for testing the theory.

Economists have done an enormous amount of research confronting theories of growth with the empirical evidence. The way in which this research has been conducted has changed over the years.

In 1776, when Adam Smith wrote about "the nature and causes of the Wealth of Nations" in his celebrated book, empirical evidence took the form of carefully selected facts described in words and stories. Today, large databases, sophisticated statistical methods, and fast computers provide numerical measurements of the causes of economic growth.

Economists have looked at the growth rate data for more than 100 countries for the period since 1960 and explored the correlations between the growth rate and more than 60 possible influences on it. The conclusion of this data crunching is that most of these possible influences have variable and unpredictable effects, but a few of them have strong and clear effects. Table 23.1 summarizes these more robust influences. They are arranged in order of difficulty (or in the case of region, impossiblity) of changing. Political and economic systems are hard to change, but market distortions, investment, and openness to international trade are features of a nation's economy that can be influenced by policy.

Let's now look at growth policies.

Policies for Achieving Faster Growth

Growth theory supported by empirical evidence tells us that to achieve faster economic growth, we must increase the growth rate of physical capital, the pace of technological advance, or the growth rate of human capital and openness to international trade.

The main suggestions for achieving these objectives are

- Stimulate saving
- Stimulate research and development
- Improve the quality of education
- Provide international aid to developing nations
- Encourage international trade

Stimulate Saving Saving finances investment so stimulating saving increases economic growth. The East Asian economies have the highest growth rates and the highest saving rates. Some African economies have the lowest growth rates and the lowest saving rates.

Tax incentives can increase saving. Individual Retirement Accounts (IRAs) are a tax incentive to save. Economists claim that a tax on consumption rather than income provides the best saving incentive.

TABLE 23.1   The Influences on Economic Growth

Influence	Good for Economic Growth	Bad for Economic Growth
Region	■ Far from equator	■ Sub-Sahara Africa
Politics	■ Rule of law	■ Revolutions
	■ Civil liberties	■ Military coups
		■ Wars
Economic system	■ Capitalist	
Market distortions		■ Exchange rate distortions
		■ Price controls and black markets
Investment	■ Human capital	
	■ Physical capital	
International trade	■ Open to trade	

Source of data: Xavier Sala-i-Martin, "I Just Ran Two Million Regressions," *The American Economic Review*, Vol. 87, No 2, (May 1997), pp. 178–183.

Stimulate Research and Development Everyone can use the fruits of *basic* research and development efforts. For example, all biotechnology firms can use advances in gene-splicing technology. Because basic inventions can be copied, the inventor's profit is limited and the market allocates too few resources to this activity. Governments can direct public funds toward financing basic research, but this solution is not foolproof. It requires a mechanism for allocating the public funds to their highest-valued use.

Improve the Quality of Education The free market produces too little education because it brings benefits beyond those valued by the people who receive the education. By funding basic education and by ensuring high standards in basic skills such as language, mathematics, and science, governments can contribute to a nation's growth potential. Education can also be stimulated and improved by using tax incentives to encourage improved private provision.

Provide International Aid to Developing Nations It seems obvious that if rich countries give financial aid to developing countries, investment and growth will increase in the recipient countries. Unfortunately, the obvious does not routinely happen. A large amount of data-driven research on the effects of aid on growth has turned up a zero and even negative effect. Aid often gets diverted and spent on consumption.

Encourage International Trade Trade, not aid, stimulates economic growth. It works by extracting the available gains from specialization and trade. The fastest-growing nations are those most open to trade. If the rich nations truly want to aid economic development, they will lower their trade barriers against developing nations, especially in farm products. The World Trade Organization's efforts to achieve more open trade are being resisted by the richer nations.

 REVIEW QUIZ

1 What is the key idea of classical growth theory that leads to the dismal outcome?

2 What, according to neoclassical growth theory, is the fundamental cause of economic growth?

3 What is the key proposition of new growth theory that makes economic growth persist?

You can work these questions in Study Plan 23.5 and get instant feedback.

◆ To complete your study of economic growth, take a look at *Reading Between the Lines* on pp. 558–559 and see how economic growth is changing the GDP rankings of nations.

Economic Growth in China

China Pips Japan but "Still a Developing Nation"

http://www.afp.com
August 17, 2010

China insisted Tuesday it was still a developing nation despite overtaking Japan as the world's second largest economy, in the face of pressure to take on a greater role in global affairs. ...

Thirty years after opening its doors to the outside world, China has enjoyed spectacular economic growth and already claimed the titles of world's top exporter, auto market, and steelmaker.

After outpacing its neighbor in the second quarter, China is on course this year to officially confirm its position as world number two—a title Japan held for 40 years—underscoring its emergence as a global economic and political force.

While some analysts are predicting that China could take on the top spot from the United States within a few decades, commentators insisted it remained a developing nation with tens of millions living in poverty.

Commerce ministry spokesman Yao Jian said China still lagged far behind its rivals in per capita terms and has a long way to go to becoming a world-class power.

"The quality of China's economic growth still needs to be improved, no matter whether it is in terms of people's quality of life or in terms of science, technology, and environmental protection," the spokesman said.

"We still have an enormous gap to make up."

He said China's per capita GDP was 3,800 dollars—putting it around 105th in the world—and that 150 million of its 1.3 billion people live below the poverty line, according to UN standards.

"China's economy will continue to develop because China has a large population and its economy lagged behind," he said. ...

ESSENCE OF THE STORY

- China is a large developing nation that ranks at 105 in the world on per capita income with 150 million of its 1.3 billion people living below the UN poverty line.

- After opening to global trade and investment 30 years ago, China has experienced rapid economic growth.

- In mid-2010, China displaced Japan as the world's number 2 economy. Japan held this spot for 40 years.

- Some analysts predict that China will take the top spot from the United States within a few decades.

- A commerce ministry spokesman says people's quality of life, and science, technology, and environmental protection need to be improved.

ECONOMIC ANALYSIS

- The news that China overtook Japan in mid-2010 to become the world's second largest economy is based on GDP data.

- When the GDP of China measured in yuan and the GDP of Japan measured in yen are converted to U.S. dollars at the current exchange rate, China's GDP became slightly larger than Japan's in the second quarter of 2010.

- Figure 1 shows the data on GDP in China, Japan, and the United States. You can see that Japan has stagnated since 1995 while China has streaked upward.

- You learned in Chapter 21 that PPP prices provide a more useful international comparison of GDP. You also learned that real GDP measures economic growth and nominal GDP (in Fig. 1) measures a combination of economic growth and inflation (or deflation).

- Comparing China and Japan using real GDP in PPP prices (in Fig. 2), China became the number 2 economy as long ago as 1995, and in 2010 it became not the number 2 economy but the number 1, overtaking the United States.

- In 2010, China had 4 times as many people as the United States and they earned, on average, 1/4 the income of Americans. So total income and GDP in China roughly equaled that in the United States.

- China remains a poor country in three respects: Income per person is low; income inequality is large so many people live in poverty; and most of the country's advanced technology is imported from the United States and Europe.

- How poor China appears depends on the numbers used. At the current exchange rate and in China's prices, income per person was $3,800 in 2010, but in PPP prices, it was $11,000. Figure 3 shows how far China is behind Japan and the United States when measured by income per person valued in PPP prices.

- The growth of physical capital and human capital and technological change are proceeding at a rapid pace in China and bringing rapid growth in real GDP per person.

- But China lags a long way behind the United States in science, technology, and environmental protection.

- As China's economy continues to expand, it will devote more resources to narrowing the gap in these areas as well as narrowing the income gap.

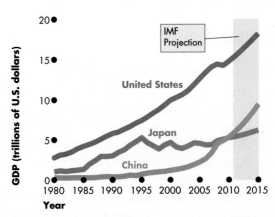

Figure 1 GDP in U.S. dollars

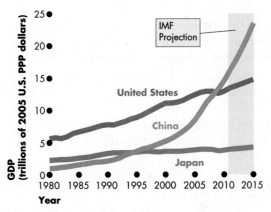

Figure 2 Real GDP in PPP prices

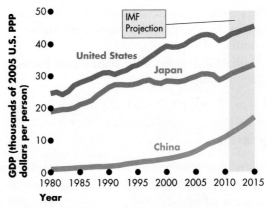

Figure 3 Real GDP per person in PPP prices

SUMMARY

Key Points

The Basics of Economic Growth (pp. 540–541)

- Economic growth is the sustained expansion of production possibilities and is measured as the annual percentage rate of change of real GDP.
- The Rule of 70 tells us the number of years in which real GDP doubles—70 divided by the annual percentage growth rate.

Working Problems 1 to 5 will give you a better understanding the basics of economic growth.

Economic Growth Trends (pp. 542–544)

- Real GDP per person in the United States grows at an average rate of 2 percent a year. Growth was most rapid during the 1960s and the 1990s.
- The gap in real GDP per person between the United States and Central and South America has persisted. The gaps between the United States and Hong Kong, Korea, and China have narrowed. The gaps between the United States and Africa and Central Europe have widened.

Working Problem 6 will give you a better understanding of economic growth trends.

How Potential GDP Grows (pp. 545–550)

- The aggregate production function and equilibrium in the aggregate labor market determine potential GDP.
- Potential GDP grows if the labor supply grows or if labor productivity grows.

- Only labor productivity growth makes real GDP per person and the standard of living grow.

Working Problems 7 to 14 will give you a better understanding of how potential GDP grows.

Why Labor Productivity Grows (pp. 550–552)

- Labor productivity growth requires an incentive system created by firms, markets, property rights, and money.
- The sources of labor productivity growth are growth of physical capital and human capital and advances in technology.

Working Problems 15 and 16 will give you a better understanding of why labor productivity grows.

Growth Theories, Evidence, and Policies (pp. 553–557)

- In classical theory, real GDP per person keeps returning to the subsistence level.
- In neoclassical growth theory, diminishing returns to capital limit economic growth.
- In new growth theory, economic growth persists indefinitely at a rate determined by decisions that lead to innovation and technological change.
- Policies for achieving faster growth include stimulating saving and research and development, encouraging international trade, and improving the quality of education.

Working Problems 17 and 18 will give you a better understanding of growth theories, evidence, and policies.

Key Terms

Aggregate production function, 545
Classical growth theory, 553
Economic growth rate, 540

Labor productivity, 549
Neoclassical growth theory, 553
New growth theory, 554

Real GDP per person, 540
Real wage rate, 546
Rule of 70, 540

STUDY PLAN PROBLEMS AND APPLICATIONS

myeconlab You can work Problems 1 to 18 in MyEconLab Chapter 23 Study Plan and get instant feedback.

The Basics of Economic Growth (Study Plan 23.1)

1. Brazil's real GDP was 1,360 trillion reais in 2009 and 1,434 trillion reais in 2010. Brazil's population was 191.5 million in 2009 and 193.3 million in 2010. Calculate
   a. The economic growth rate.
   b. The growth rate of real GDP per person.
   c. The approximate number of years it takes for real GDP per person in Brazil to double if the 2010 economic growth rate and population growth rate are maintained.

2. Japan's real GDP was 525 trillion yen in 2009 and 535 trillion yen in 2010. Japan's population was 127.6 million in 2009 and 127.5 million in 2010. Calculate
   a. The economic growth rate.
   b. The growth rate of real GDP per person.
   c. The approximate number of years it takes for real GDP per person in Japan to double if the real GDP economic growth rate returns to 3 percent a year and the population growth rate is maintained.

Use the following data to work Problems 3 and 4.
China's real GDP per person was 9,280 yuan in 2009 and 10,110 yuan in 2010. India's real GDP per person was 30,880 rupees in 2009 and 32,160 rupees in 2010.

3. By maintaining their current growth rates, which country will double its 2010 standard of living first?

4. The population of China is growing at 1 percent a year and the population of India is growing at 1.4 percent a year. Calculate the growth rate of real GDP in each country.

5. **China's Economy Picks Up Speed**
   China's trend growth rate of real GDP per person was 2.2 percent a year before 1980 and 8.7 percent a year after 1980. In the year to August 2009, China's output increased by 11.3 percent.
   Source: World Economic Outlook and FT.com, September 14, 2009
   Distinguish between a rise in China's economic growth rate and a temporary cyclical expansion.

How long, at the current growth rate, will it take for China to double its real GDP per person?

Economic Growth Trends (Study Plan 23.2)

6. China was the largest economy for centuries because everyone had the same type of economy— subsistence—and so the country with the most people would be economically biggest. Then the Industrial Revolution sent the West on a more prosperous path. Now the world is returning to a common economy, this time technology- and information-based, so once again population triumphs.
   a. Why was China the world's largest economy until 1890?
   b. Why did the United States surpass China in 1890 to become the world's largest economy?

How Potential GDP Grows (Study Plan 23.3)

Use the following information to work Problems 7 and 8.
Suppose that the United States cracks down on illegal immigrants and returns millions of workers to their home countries.

7. Explain what will happen to U.S. potential GDP, employment, and the real wage rate.

8. Explain what will happen in the countries to which the immigrants return to potential GDP, employment, and the real wage rate.

Use the following news clip to work Problems 9 to 11.
U.S. Workers World's Most Productive
Americans work longer hours than those in other rich nations. Americans also produce more per person but only part of the U.S. productivity growth can be explained by the longer hours they work. Americans also create more wealth per hour of work. U.S. employees worked an average of 1,804 hours in 2006, compared to 1,564.4 for the French, but far less than the 2,200 hours that Asians worked. But in Asian countries the average labor productivity is lower.
Source: CBS News, September 3, 2007

9. What is the difference between productivity in this news clip and real GDP per person?

10. Identify and correct a confusion between levels and growth rates of productivity in the news clip.

11. If workers in developing Asian economies work more hours than Americans, why are they not the world's most productive?

Use the following tables to work Problems 12 to 14. The tables describe an economy's labor market and its production function in 2010.

Real wage rate (dollars per hour)	Labor hours supplied	Labor hours demanded
80	45	5
70	40	10
60	35	15
50	30	20
40	25	25
30	20	30
20	15	35

Labor (hours)	Real GDP (2005 dollars)
5	425
10	800
15	1,125
20	1,400
25	1,625
30	1,800
35	1,925
40	2,000

12. What are the equilibrium real wage rate, the quantity of labor employed in 2010, labor productivity, and potential GDP in 2010?

13. In 2011, the population increases and labor hours supplied increase by 10 at each real wage rate. What are the equilibrium real wage rate, labor productivity, and potential GDP in 2011?

14. In 2011, the population increases and labor hours supplied increase by 10 at each real wage rate. Does the standard of living in this economy increase in 2011? Explain why or why not.

Why Labor Productivity Grows (Study Plan 23.4)

15. **Labor Productivity on the Rise**
    The Bureau of Labor Statistics reported the following data for the year ended June 2009: In the nonfarm sector, output fell 5.5 percent as labor productivity increased 1.9 percent—the largest increase since 2003—but in the manufacturing sector, output fell 9.8 percent as labor productivity increased by 4.9 percent—the largest increase since the first quarter of 2005.
    Source: bls.gov/news.release, August 11, 2009

In both sectors, output fell while labor productivity increased. Did the quantity of labor (aggregate hours) increase or decrease? In which sector was the change in the quantity of labor larger?

16. For three years, there was no technological change in Longland but capital per hour of labor increased from $10 to $20 to $30 and real GDP per hour of labor increased from $3.80 to $5.70 to $7.13. Then, in the fourth year, capital per hour of labor remained constant but real GDP per hour of labor increased to $10. Does Longland experience diminishing returns? Explain why or why not.

Growth Theories, Evidence, and Policies

(Study Plan 23.5)

17. Explain the processes that will bring the growth of real GDP per person to a stop according to
    a. Classical growth theory.
    b. Neoclassical growth theory.
    c. New growth theory.

18. In the economy of Cape Despair, the subsistence real wage rate is $15 an hour. Whenever real GDP per hour rises above $15, the population grows, and whenever real GDP per hour of labor falls below this level, the population falls. The table shows Cape Despair's production function:

Labor (billions of hours per year)	Real GDP (billions of 2000 dollars)
0.5	8
1.0	15
1.5	21
2.0	26
2.5	30
3.0	33
3.5	35

Initially, the population of Cape Despair is constant and real GDP per hour of labor is at the subsistence level of $15. Then a technological advance shifts the production function upward by 50 percent at each level of labor.

a. What are the initial levels of real GDP and labor productivity?

b. What happens to labor productivity immediately following the technological advance?

c. What happens to the population growth rate following the technological advance?

d. What are the eventual levels of real GDP and real GDP per hour of labor?

ADDITIONAL PROBLEMS AND APPLICATIONS

 myeconlab You can work these problems in MyEconLab if assigned by your instructor.

The Basics of Economic Growth

19. If in 2010 China's real GDP is growing at 9 percent a year, its population is growing at 1 percent a year, and these growth rates continue, in what year will China's real GDP per person be twice what it is in 2010?

20. Mexico's real GDP was 8,600 trillion pesos in 2009 and 8,688 trillion pesos in 2010. Mexico's population was 107 million in 2009 and 108 million in 2010. Calculate
    a. The economic growth rate.
    b. The growth rate of real GDP per person.
    c. The approximate number of years it takes for real GDP per person in Mexico to double if the 2010 economic growth rate and population growth rate are maintained.

21. Venezuela's real GDP was 57,049 trillion bolivares in 2009 and 56,764 trillion bolivares in 2010. Venezuela's population was 28.6 million in 2009 and 29.2 million in 2010. Calculate
    a. The economic growth rate.
    b. The growth rate of real GDP per person.
    c. The approximate number of years it takes for real GDP per person in Venezuela to double if economic growth returns to its average since 2009 of 3.6 percent a year and is maintained.

Economic Growth Trends

22. **The New World Order**

    While gross domestic product growth is cooling a bit in emerging market economies, the results are still tremendous compared with the United States and much of Western Europe. The emerging market economies posted a 6.7% jump in real GDP in 2008, down from 7.5% in 2007. The advanced economies grew an estimated 1.6% in 2008. The difference in growth rates represents the largest spread between emerging market economies and advanced economies in the 37-year history of the survey.

    Source: *Fortune*, July 14, 2008

    Do growth rates over the past few decades indicate that gaps in real GDP per person around the world are shrinking, growing, or staying the same? Explain.

How Potential GDP Grows

23. If a large increase in investment increases labor productivity, explain what happens to
    a. Potential GDP.
    b. Employment.
    c. The real wage rate.

24. If a severe drought decreases labor productivity, explain what happens to
    a. Potential GDP.
    b. Employment.
    c. The real wage rate.

Use the following tables to work Problems 25 to 27. The first table describes an economy's labor market in 2010 and the second table describes its production function in 2010.

Real wage rate (dollars per hour)	Labor hours supplied	Labor hours demanded
80	55	15
70	50	20
60	45	25
50	40	30
40	35	35
30	30	40
20	25	45

Labor (hours)	Real GDP (2005 dollars)
15	1,425
20	1,800
25	2,125
30	2,400
35	2,625
40	2,800
45	2,925
50	3,000

25. What are the equilibrium real wage rate and the quantity of labor employed in 2010 ?

26. What are labor productivity and potential GDP in 2010?

27. Suppose that labor productivity increases in 2010. What effect does the increased labor productivity have on the demand for labor, the supply of labor, potential GDP, and real GDP per person?

Why Labor Productivity Grows

28. India's Economy Hits the Wall

Just six months ago, India was looking good. Annual growth was 9%, consumer demand was huge, and foreign investment was growing. But now most economic forecasts expect growth to slow to 7%—a big drop for a country that needs to accelerate growth. India needs urgently to upgrade its infrastructure and education and health-care facilities. Agriculture is unproductive and needs better technology. The legal system needs to be strengthened with more judges and courtrooms.

Source: *BusinessWeek*, July 1, 2008

Explain five potential sources for faster economic growth in India suggested in this news clip.

Growth Theories, Evidence, and Policies

29. The Productivity Watch

According to former Federal Reserve chairman Alan Greenspan, IT investments in the 1990s boosted productivity, which boosted corporate profits, which led to more IT investments, and so on, leading to a nirvana of high growth.

Source: *Fortune*, September 4, 2006

Which of the growth theories that you've studied in this chapter best corresponds to the explanation given by Mr. Greenspan?

30.

Is faster economic growth always a good thing? Argue the case for faster growth and the case for slower growth. Then reach a conclusion on whether growth should be increased or slowed.

31. Makani Power: A Mighty Wind

Makani Power aims to generate energy from what are known as high-altitude wind-extraction technologies. And that's about all its 34-year-old Aussie founder, Saul Griffith, wants to say about it. But Makani can't hide entirely, not when its marquee investor is Google.org, the tech company's philanthropic arm. Makani's plan is to capture that high-altitude wind with a very old tool: kites. Harnessing higher-altitude wind, at least in theory, has greater potential than the existing wind industry because at a thousand feet above the ground, the wind is stronger and more consistent.

Source: *Fortune*, April 28, 2008

Explain which growth theory best describes the news clip.

Economics in the News

32.

After you have studied *Reading Between the Lines* on pp. 558–559 answer the following questions.

a. On what criterion is China the second largest economy in the world?

b. What is the distinction between the size of an economy and the standard of living of its people?

c. Where does China rank on a standard of living comparison? How is that rank changing and why?

d. What is the distinction between market prices and PPP prices?

e. Using PPP prices, where does China's economy rank in size and standard of living?

f. For what might the size of an economy matter?

33. Make Way for India—The Next China

China grows at around 9 percent a year, but its one-child policy will start to reduce the size of China's working-age population within the next 10 years. India, by contrast, will have an increasing working-age population for another generation at least.

Source: *The Independent*, March 1, 2006

a. Given the expected population changes, do you think China or India will have the greater economic growth rate? Why?

b. Would China's growth rate remain at 9 percent a year without the restriction on its population growth rate?

c. India's population growth rate is 1.6 percent a year, and in 2005 its economic growth rate was 8 percent a year. China's population growth rate is 0.6 percent a year, and in 2005 its economic growth rate was 9 percent a year. In what year will real GDP per person double in each country?

Data Graphing

34.

Use the *Data Grapher* to create a graph of the growth rate of real GDP per person in the United States, Canada, Germany, and the United Kingdom.

a. Which country had the fastest growth of real GDP per person since 1980 and which had the slowest?

b. In which country has real GDP per person fluctuated most?

After studying this chapter,
you will be able to:

◆ Describe and define the flows of funds through financial markets and the financial institutions

◆ Explain how investment and saving along with borrowing and lending decisions are made and how these decisions interact in the loanable funds market

◆ Explain how a government deficit (or surplus) influences the real interest rate, saving, and investment in the loanable funds market

◆ Explain how international borrowing or lending influences the real interest rate, saving, and investment in the global loanable funds market

24

FINANCE, SAVING, AND INVESTMENT

During September 2008, Wall Street put on a spectacular show. To prevent the collapse of Fannie Mae and Freddie Mac, the two largest lenders to home buyers, the U.S. government took over their risky debts. When Lehman Brothers, a venerable Wall Street investment bank, was on the verge of bankruptcy, secure phone lines and limousines worked overtime as the Federal Reserve Bank of New York, the U.S. Treasury, and senior officials of Bank of America and Barclays Bank (a British bank) tried to find ways to save the bank. The effort failed. On the same weekend, Bank of America bought Merrill Lynch, another big Wall Street investment bank. And a few days later, the U.S. government bought insurance giant AIG and tried to get Congress to provide $700 billion to buy just about every risky debt that anyone wanted to unload.

Behind such drama, Wall Street plays a crucial unseen role funneling funds from savers and lenders to investors and borrowers. This chapter explains how financial markets work and their place in the economy.

In *Reading Between the Lines* at the end of the chapter, we'll look at the effects of government budget deficits and apply what you've learned to better understand what is happening in U.S. and global financial markets today.

◆ Financial Institutions and Financial Markets

The financial institutions and markets that we study in this chapter play a crucial role in the economy. They provide the channels through which saving flows to finance the investment in new capital that makes the economy grow.

In studying the economics of financial institutions and markets, we distinguish between:

- Finance and money
- Physical capital and financial capital

Finance and Money

In economics, we use the term *finance* to describe the activity of providing the funds that finance expenditures on capital. The study of finance looks at how households and firms obtain and use financial resources and how they cope with the risks that arise in this activity.

Money is what we use to pay for goods and services and factors of production and to make financial transactions. The study of money looks at how households and firms use it, how much of it they hold, how banks create and manage it, and how its quantity influences the economy.

In the economic lives of individuals and businesses, finance and money are closely interrelated. And some of the main financial institutions, such as banks, provide both financial services and monetary services. Nevertheless, by distinguishing between *finance* and *money* and studying them separately, we will better understand our financial and monetary markets and institutions.

For the rest of this chapter, we study finance. Money is the topic of the next chapter.

Physical Capital and Financial Capital

Economists distinguish between physical capital and financial capital. *Physical capital* is the tools, instruments, machines, buildings, and other items that have been produced in the past and that are used today to produce goods and services. Inventories of raw materials, semifinished goods, and components are part of physical capital. When economists use the term capital, they mean *physical* capital. The funds that firms use to buy physical capital are called **financial capital**.

Along the *aggregate production function* in Chapter 23 (see p. 545), the quantity of capital is fixed. An increase in the quantity of capital increases production possibilities and shifts the aggregate production function upward. You're going to see, in this chapter, how investment, saving, borrowing, and lending decisions influence the quantity of capital and make it grow, and as a consequence, make real GDP grow.

We begin by describing the links between capital and investment and between wealth and saving.

Capital and Investment

The quantity of capital changes because of investment and depreciation. *Investment* increases the quantity of capital and *depreciation* decreases it (see Chapter 21, p. 492). The total amount spent on new capital is called **gross investment**. The change in the value of capital is called **net investment**. Net investment equals gross investment minus depreciation.

Figure 24.1 illustrates these terms. On January 1, 2010, Ace Bottling Inc. had machines worth $30,000—Ace's initial capital. During 2010, the market value of Ace's machines fell by 67 percent—$20,000. After this depreciation, Ace's machines were valued at $10,000. During 2010, Ace spent $30,000 on new machines. This amount is Ace's gross investment. By December 31, 2010, Ace Bottling had capital valued at $40,000, so its capital had increased by $10,000. This amount is Ace's net investment. Ace's net investment equals its gross investment of $30,000 minus depreciation of its initial capital of $20,000.

Wealth and Saving

Wealth is the value of all the things that people own. What people own is related to what they earn, but it is not the same thing. People earn an *income*, which is the amount they receive during a given time period from supplying the services of the resources they own. **Saving** is the amount of income that is not paid in taxes or spent on consumption goods and services. Saving increases wealth. Wealth also increases when the market value of assets rises—called *capital gains*—and decreases when the market value of assets falls—called *capital losses*.

For example, at the end of the school year you have $250 in the bank and a coin collection worth $300, so your wealth is $550. During the summer,

FIGURE 24.1   Capital and Investment

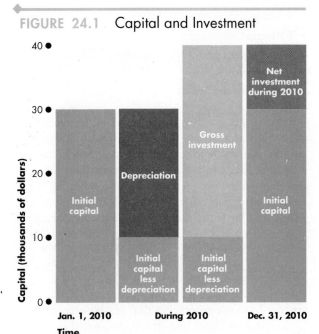

On January 1, 2010, Ace Bottling had capital worth $30,000. During the year, the value of Ace's capital fell by $20,000—depreciation—and it spent $30,000 on new capital—gross investment. Ace's net investment was $10,000 ($30,000 gross investment minus $20,000 depreciation) so that at the end of 2010, Ace had capital worth $40,000.

myeconlab   animation

you earn $5,000 (net of taxes) and spend $1,000 on consumption goods and services so your saving is $4,000. Your bank account increases to $4,250 and your wealth becomes $4,550. The $4,000 increase in wealth equals saving. If coins rise in value and your coin collection is now worth $500, you have a capital gain of $200, which is also added to your wealth.

National wealth and national saving work like this personal example. The wealth of a nation at the end of a year equals its wealth at the start of the year plus its saving during the year, which equals income minus consumption expenditure.

To make real GDP grow, saving and wealth must be transformed into investment and capital. This transformation takes place in the markets for financial capital and through the activities of financial institutions. We're now going to describe these markets and institutions.

Financial Capital Markets

Saving is the source of the funds that are used to finance investment, and these funds are supplied and demanded in three types of financial markets:

- Loan markets
- Bond markets
- Stock markets

Loan Markets Businesses often want short-term finance to buy inventories or to extend credit to their customers. Sometimes they get this finance in the form of a loan from a bank. Households often want finance to purchase big ticket items, such as automobiles or household furnishings and appliances. They get this finance as bank loans, often in the form of outstanding credit card balances.

Households also get finance to buy new homes. (Expenditure on new homes is counted as part of investment.) These funds are usually obtained as a loan that is secured by a **mortgage**—a legal contract that gives ownership of a home to the lender in the event that the borrower fails to meet the agreed loan payments (repayments and interest). Mortgage loans were at the center of the U.S. credit crisis of 2007–2008.

All of these types of financing take place in loan markets.

Bond Markets When Wal-Mart expands its business and opens new stores, it gets the finance it needs by selling bonds. Governments—federal, state, and municipal—also raise finance by issuing bonds.

A **bond** is a promise to make specified payments on specified dates. For example, you can buy a Wal-Mart bond that promises to pay $5.00 every year until 2024 and then to make a final payment of $100 in 2025.

The buyer of a bond from Wal-Mart makes a loan to the company and is entitled to the payments promised by the bond. When a person buys a newly issued bond, he or she may hold the bond until the borrower has repaid the amount borrowed or sell it to someone else. Bonds issued by firms and governments are traded in the **bond market**.

The term of a bond might be long (decades) or short (just a month or two). Firms often issue very short-term bonds as a way of getting paid for their sales before the buyer is able to pay. For example, when GM sells $100 million of railway locomotives to Union Pacific, GM wants to be paid when the items are shipped. But Union Pacific doesn't want to pay until the locomotives are earning an income. In this situation, Union Pacific might promise to pay GM $101 million three months in the future. A bank would be willing to buy this promise for (say) $100 million. GM gets $100 million immediately and the bank gets $101 million in three months when Union Pacific honors its promise. The U.S. Treasury issues promises of this type, called Treasury bills.

Another type of bond is a **mortgage-backed security**, which entitles its holder to the income from a package of mortgages. Mortgage lenders create mortgage-backed securities. They make mortgage loans to homebuyers and then create securities that they sell to obtain more funds to make more mortgage loans. The holder of a mortgage-backed security is entitled to receive payments that derive from the payments received by the mortgage lender from the home-buyer–borrower.

Mortgage-backed securities were at the center of the storm in the financial markets in 2007–2008.

Stock Markets When Boeing wants finance to expand its airplane building business, it issues stock. A **stock** is a certificate of ownership and claim to the firm's profits. Boeing has issued about 900 million shares of its stock. So if you owned 900 Boeing shares, you would own one millionth of Boeing and be entitled to receive one millionth of its profits.

Unlike a stockholder, a bondholder does not own part of the firm that issued the bond.

A **stock market** is a financial market in which shares of stocks of corporations are traded. The New York Stock Exchange, the London Stock Exchange (in England), the Tokyo Stock Exchange (in Japan), and the Frankfurt Stock Exchange (in Germany) are all examples of stock markets.

Financial Institutions

Financial markets are highly competitive because of the role played by financial institutions in those markets. A **financial institution** is a firm that operates on both sides of the markets for financial capital. The financial institution is a borrower in one market and a lender in another.

Financial institutions also stand ready to trade so that households with funds to lend and firms or households seeking funds can always find someone on the other side of the market with whom to trade.

The key financial institutions are

- Commercial banks
- Government-sponsored mortgage lenders
- Pension funds
- Insurance companies

Commercial Banks Commercial banks are financial institutions that accept deposits, provide payment services, and make loans to firms and households. The bank that you use for your own banking services and that issues your credit card is a commercial bank. These institutions play a central role in the monetary system and we study them in detail in Chapter 25.

Government-Sponsored Mortgage Lenders Two large financial institutions, the Federal National Mortgage Association, or Fannie Mae, and the Federal Home Loan Mortgage Corporation, or Freddie Mac, are enterprises that buy mortgages from banks, package them into mortgage-backed securities, and sell them. In September 2008, Fannie and Freddie owned or guaranteed $6 trillion worth of mortgages (half of the U.S. $12 trillion of mortgages) and were taken over by the federal government.

Economics in Action
The Financial Crisis and the Fix

Bear Stearns: absorbed by JPMorgan Chase with help from the Federal Reserve. Lehman Brothers: gone. Fannie Mae and Freddie Mac: taken into government oversight. Merrill Lynch: absorbed by Bank of America. AIG: given an $85 billion lifeline by the Federal Reserve and sold off in parcels to financial institutions around the world. Wachovia: taken over by Wells Fargo. Washington Mutual: taken over by JPMorgan Chase. Morgan Stanley: 20 percent bought by Mitsubishi, a large Japanese bank. These are some of the events in the financial crisis of 2008. What was going on and how can a replay be avoided?

Between 2002 and 2005, mortgage lending exploded and home prices rocketed. Mortgage lenders bundled their loans into *mortgage-backed securities* and sold them to eager buyers around the world.

When interest rates began to rise in 2006 and asset prices fell, financial institutions took big losses. Some losses were too big to bear and big-name institutions failed.

Pension Funds Pension funds are financial institutions that use the pension contributions of firms and workers to buy bonds and stocks. The mortgage-backed securities of Fannie Mae and Freddie Mac are among the assets of pension funds. Some pension funds are very large and play an active role in the firms whose stock they hold.

Insurance Companies Insurance companies enable households and firms to cope with risks such as accident, theft, fire, ill-health, and a host of other misfortunes. They receive premiums from their customers and pay claims. Insurance companies use the funds they have received but not paid out as claims to buy bonds and stocks on which they earn interest income.

In normal times, insurance companies have a steady flow of funds coming in from premiums and interest on the financial assets they hold and a steady, but smaller, flow of funds paying claims. Their profit is the gap between the two flows. But in unusual times, when large and widespread losses are being incurred, insurance companies can run into difficulty in meeting their obligations. Such a situation arose in 2008 for one of the biggest insurers, AIG, and the firm was taken into public ownership.

Insolvency and Illiquidity

A financial institution's **net worth** is the market value of what it has lent minus the market value of what it has borrowed. If net worth is positive, the institution is *solvent*. But if net worth is negative, the institution is *insolvent* and must go out of business. The owners of an insolvent financial institution—usually its stockholders—bear the loss.

A financial institution both borrows and lends, so it is exposed to the risk that its net worth might become negative. To limit that risk, financial institutions are regulated and a minimum amount of their lending must be backed by their net worth.

Sometimes, a financial institution is solvent but illiquid. A firm is *illiquid* if it has made long-term loans with borrowed funds and is faced with a sudden demand to repay more of what it has borrowed than its available cash. In normal times, a financial institution that is illiquid can borrow from another institution. But if all the financial institutions are short of cash, the market for loans among financial institutions dries up.

Insolvency and illiquidity were at the core of the financial meltdown of 2007–2008.

In the hope of avoiding a replay, Congress has enacted the *Restoring American Financial Stability Act of 2010*. The main points of the Act are

- A Consumer Financial Protection Agency to enforce consumer-oriented regulation, ensure that the fine print on financial services contracts is clear and accurate, and maintain a toll-free hotline for consumers to report alleged deception.
- A Financial Services Oversight Council to anticipate financial market weakness.
- Authority for the Federal Deposit Insurance Corporation to seize, liquidate, and reconstruct troubled financial firms.
- Tight restrictions to stop banks gambling for their own profits and limit their risky investments.
- Mortgage reforms that require lenders to review the income and credit histories of applicants and ensure they can afford payments.
- Require firms that create mortgage-backed securities to keep at least 5 percent of them.

The 2010 Act does nothing to solve the problem that Fannie and Freddie remain under government oversight. Many people believe that the measures are too timid and leave the financial system fragile.

Interest Rates and Asset Prices

Stocks, bonds, short-term securities, and loans are collectively called *financial assets*. The interest rate on a financial asset is the interest received expressed as a percentage of the price of the asset.

Because the interest rate is a percentage of the price of an asset, if the asset price rises, other things remaining the same, the interest rate falls. Conversely, if the asset price falls, other things remaining the same, the interest rate rises.

To see this inverse relationship between an asset price and the interest rate, let's look at an example. We'll consider a bond that promises to pay its holder $5 a year forever. What is the rate of return—the interest rate—on this bond? The answer depends on the price of the bond. If you could buy this bond for $50, the interest rate would be 10 percent per year:

Interest rate = ($5 ÷ $50) × 100 = 10 percent.

But if the price of this bond increased to $200, its rate of return or interest rate would be only 2.5 percent per year. That is,

Interest rate = ($5 ÷ $200) × 100 = 2.5 percent.

This relationship means that the price of an asset and the interest rate on that asset are determined simultaneously—one implies the other.

This relationship also means that if the interest rate on the asset rises, the price of the asset falls, debts become harder to pay, and the net worth of the financial institution falls. Insolvency can arise from a previously unexpected large rise in the interest rate.

In the next part of this chapter, we learn how interest rates and asset prices are determined in the financial markets.

REVIEW QUIZ

1 Distinguish between physical capital and financial capital and give two examples of each.
2 What is the distinction between gross investment and net investment?
3 What are the three main types of markets for financial capital?
4 Explain the connection between the price of a financial asset and its interest rate.

You can work these questions in Study Plan 24.1 and get instant feedback.

◆ The Loanable Funds Market

In macroeconomics, we group all the financial markets that we described in the previous section into a single loanable funds market. The **loanable funds market** is the aggregate of all the individual financial markets.

The circular flow model of Chapter 21 (see p. 491) can be extended to include flows in the loanable funds market that finance investment.

Funds that Finance Investment

Figure 24.2 shows the flows of funds that finance investment. They come from three sources:

1. Household saving
2. Government budget surplus
3. Borrowing from the rest of the world

Households' income, Y, is spent on consumption goods and services, C, saved, S, or paid in net taxes, T. **Net taxes** are the taxes paid to governments minus the cash transfers received from governments (such as Social Security and unemployment benefits). So income is equal to the sum of consumption expenditure, saving, and net taxes:

$$Y = C + S + T.$$

You saw in Chapter 21 (p. 492) that Y also equals the sum of the items of aggregate expenditure: consumption expenditure, C, investment, I, government expenditure, G, and exports, X, minus imports, M. That is:

$$Y = C + I + G + X - M.$$

By using these two equations, you can see that

$$I + G + X = M + S + T.$$

Subtract G and X from both sides of the last equation to obtain

$$I = S + (T - G) + (M - X).$$

This equation tells us that investment, I, is financed by household saving, S, the government budget surplus, $(T - G)$, and borrowing from the rest of the world, $(M - X)$.

A government budget surplus $(T > G)$ contributes funds to finance investment, but a government budget deficit $(T < G)$ competes with investment for funds.

FIGURE 24.2   Financial Flows and the Circular Flow of Expenditure and Income

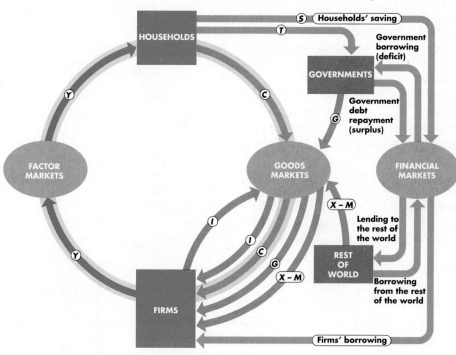

Households use their income for consumption expenditure (C), saving (S), and net taxes (T). Firms borrow to finance their investment expenditure. Governments borrow to finance a budget deficit or repay debt if they have a budget surplus. The rest of the world borrows to finance its deficit or lends its surplus.

If we export less than we import, we borrow $(M - X)$ from the rest of the world to finance some of our investment. If we export more than we import, we lend $(X - M)$ to the rest of the world and part of U.S. saving finances investment in other countries.

The sum of private saving, S, and government saving, $(T - G)$, is called **national saving**. National saving and foreign borrowing finance investment.

In 2010, U.S. investment was $1.8 trillion. Governments (federal, state, and local combined) had a deficit of $1.5 trillion. This total of $3.3 trillion was financed by private saving of $2.8 trillion and borrowing from the rest of the world (negative net exports) of $0.5 trillion.

You're going to see how investment and saving and the flows of loanable funds—all measured in constant 2005 dollars—are determined. The price in the loanable funds market that achieves equilibrium is an interest rate, which we also measure in real terms as the *real* interest rate. In the loanable funds market, there is just one interest rate, which is an average of the interest rates on all the different types of financial securities that we described earlier. Let's see what we mean by the real interest rate.

The Real Interest Rate

The **nominal interest rate** is the number of dollars that a borrower pays and a lender receives in interest in a year expressed as a percentage of the number of dollars borrowed and lent. For example, if the annual interest paid on a $500 loan is $25, the nominal interest rate is 5 percent per year: $25 ÷ $500 × 100 or 5 percent.

The **real interest rate** is the nominal interest rate adjusted to remove the effects of inflation on the buying power of money. The real interest rate is approximately equal to the nominal interest rate minus the inflation rate.

You can see why if you suppose that you have put $500 in a savings account that earns 5 percent a year. At the end of a year, you have $525 in your savings account. Suppose that the inflation rate is 2 percent per year—during the year, all prices increased by 2 percent. Now, at the end of the year, it costs $510 to buy what $500 would have bought one year ago. Your money in the bank has really only increased by $15, from $510 to $525. That $15 is equivalent to a real interest rate of 3 percent a year on your original

$500. So the real interest rate is the 5 percent nominal interest rate minus the 2 percent inflation rate[1].

The real interest rate is the opportunity cost of loanable funds. The real interest *paid* on borrowed funds is the opportunity cost of borrowing. And the real interest rate *forgone* when funds are used either to buy consumption goods and services or to invest in new capital goods is the opportunity cost of not saving or not lending those funds.

We're now going to see how the loanable funds market determines the real interest rate, the quantity of funds loaned, saving, and investment. In the rest of this section, we will ignore the government and the rest of the world and focus on households and firms in the loanable funds market. We will study

- The demand for loanable funds
- The supply of loanable funds
- Equilibrium in the loanable funds market

The Demand for Loanable Funds

The *quantity of loanable funds demanded* is the total quantity of funds demanded to finance investment, the government budget deficit, and international investment or lending during a given period. Our focus here is on investment. We'll bring the other two items into the picture in later sections of this chapter.

What determines investment and the demand for loanable funds to finance it? Many details influence this decision, but we can summarize them in two factors:

1. The real interest rate
2. Expected profit

Firms invest in capital only if they expect to earn a profit and fewer projects are profitable at a high real interest rate than at a low real interest rate, so

Other things remaining the same, the higher the real interest rate, the smaller is the quantity of loanable funds demanded; and the lower the real interest rate, the greater the quantity of loanable funds demanded.

---

[1]The *exact* real interest rate formula, which allows for the change in the purchasing power of both the interest and the loan is: Real interest rate = (Nominal interest rate − Inflation rate) ÷ (1 + Inflation rate/100). If the nominal interest rate is 5 percent a year and the inflation rate is 2 percent a year, the real interest rate is (5 − 2) ÷ (1 + 0.02) = 2.94 percent a year.

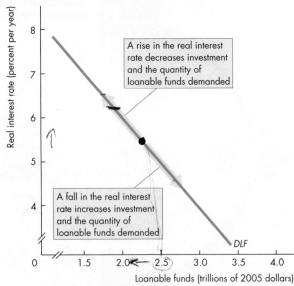

FIGURE 24.3 The Demand for Loanable Funds

A change in the real interest rate changes the quantity of loanable funds demanded and brings a movement along the demand for loanable funds curve.

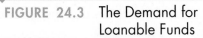

Demand for Loanable Funds Curve The **demand for loanable funds** is the relationship between the quantity of loanable funds demanded and the real interest rate, when all other influences on borrowing plans remain the same. The demand curve *DLF* in Fig. 24.3 is a demand for loanable funds curve.

To understand the demand for loanable funds, think about Amazon.com's decision to borrow $100 million to build some new warehouses. If Amazon expects to get a return of $5 million a year from this investment before paying interest costs and the interest rate is less than 5 percent a year, Amazon would make a profit, so it builds the warehouses. But if the interest rate is more than 5 percent a year, Amazon would incur a loss, so it doesn't build the warehouses. The quantity of loanable funds demanded is greater the lower is the real interest rate.

Changes in the Demand for Loanable Funds When the expected profit changes, the demand for loanable funds changes. Other things remaining the same, the greater the expected profit from new capital, the greater is the amount of investment and the greater the demand for loanable funds.

Expected profit rises during a business cycle expansion and falls during a recession; rises when technological change creates profitable new products; rises as a growing population brings increased demand for goods and services; and fluctuates with contagious swings of optimism and pessimism, called "animal spirits" by Keynes and "irrational exuberance" by Alan Greenspan.

When expected profit changes, the demand for loanable funds curve shifts.

The Supply of Loanable Funds

The *quantity of loanable funds supplied* is the total funds available from private saving, the government budget surplus, and international borrowing during a given period. Our focus here is on saving. We'll bring the other two items into the picture later.

How do you decide how much of your income to save and supply in the loanable funds market? Your decision is influenced by many factors, but chief among them are

1. The real interest rate
2. Disposable income
3. Expected future income
4. Wealth
5. Default risk

We begin by focusing on the real interest rate.

Other things remaining the same, the higher the real interest rate, the greater is the quantity of loanable funds supplied; and the lower the real interest rate, the smaller is the quantity of loanable funds supplied.

The Supply of Loanable Funds Curve The **supply of loanable funds** is the relationship between the quantity of loanable funds supplied and the real interest rate when all other influences on lending plans remain the same. The curve *SLF* in Fig. 24.4 is a supply of loanable funds curve.

Think about a student's decision to save some of what she earns from her summer job. With a real interest rate of 2 percent a year, she decides that it is not worth saving much—better to spend the income and take a student loan if funds run out during the semester. But if the real interest rate jumped to 10 percent a year, the payoff from saving would be high enough to encourage her to cut back on spending and increase the amount she saves.

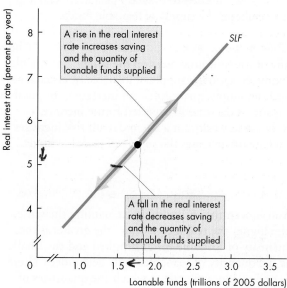

A change in the real interest rate changes the quantity of loanable funds supplied and brings a movement along the supply of loanable funds curve.

Changes in the Supply of Loanable Funds A change in disposable income, expected future income, wealth, or default risk changes the supply of loanable funds.

Disposable Income A household's *disposable income* is the income earned minus net taxes. When disposable income increases, other things remaining the same, consumption expenditure increases but by less than the increase in income. Some of the increase in income is saved. So the greater a household's disposable income, other things remaining the same, the greater is its saving.

Expected Future Income The higher a household's expected future income, other things remaining the same, the smaller is its saving today.

Wealth The higher a household's wealth, other things remaining the same, the smaller is its saving. If a person's wealth increases because of a capital gain, the person sees less need to save. For example, from 2002 through 2006, when house prices were rising rapidly, wealth increased despite the fact that personal saving dropped close to zero.

Default Risk Default risk is the risk that a loan will not be repaid. The greater that risk, the higher is the interest rate needed to induce a person to lend and the smaller is the supply of loanable funds.

Shifts of the Supply of Loanable Funds Curve When any of the four influences on the supply of loanable funds changes, the supply of loanable funds changes and the supply curve shifts. An increase in disposable income, a decrease in expected future income, a decrease in wealth, or a fall in default risk increases saving and increases the supply of loanable funds.

Equilibrium in the Loanable Funds Market

You've seen that other things remaining the same, the higher the real interest rate, the greater is the quantity of loanable funds supplied and the smaller is the quantity of loanable funds demanded. There is one real interest rate at which the quantities of loanable funds demanded and supplied are equal, and that interest rate is the equilibrium real interest rate.

Figure 24.5 shows how the demand for and supply of loanable funds determine the real interest rate. The *DLF* curve is the demand curve and the *SLF* curve is the supply curve. If the real interest rate exceeds 6 percent a year, the quantity of loanable funds supplied exceeds the quantity demanded—a surplus of funds. Borrowers find it easy to get funds, but lenders are unable to lend all the funds they have available. The real interest rate falls and continues to fall until the quantity of funds supplied equals the quantity of funds demanded.

If the real interest rate is less than 6 percent a year, the quantity of loanable funds supplied is less than the quantity demanded—a shortage of funds. Borrowers can't get the funds they want, but lenders are able to lend all the funds they have. So the real interest rate rises and continues to rise until the quantity of funds supplied equals the quantity demanded.

Regardless of whether there is a surplus or a shortage of loanable funds, the real interest rate changes and is pulled toward an equilibrium level. In Fig. 24.5, the equilibrium real interest rate is 6 percent a year. At this interest rate, there is neither a surplus nor a shortage of loanable funds. Borrowers can get the funds they want, and lenders can lend all the funds they have available. The investment plans of borrowers and the saving plans of lenders are consistent with each other.

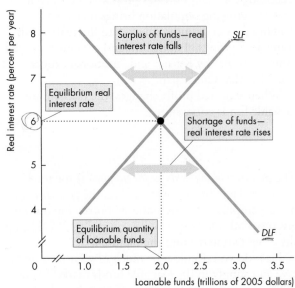

FIGURE 24.5 Equilibrium in the Loanable Funds Market

A surplus of funds lowers the real interest rate and a shortage of funds raises it. At an interest rate of 6 percent a year, the quantity of funds demanded equals the quantity supplied and the market is in equilibrium.

myeconlab animation

Changes in Demand and Supply

Financial markets are highly volatile in the short run but remarkably stable in the long run. Volatility in the market comes from fluctuations in either the demand for loanable funds or the supply of loanable funds. These fluctuations bring fluctuations in the real interest rate and in the equilibrium quantity of funds lent and borrowed. They also bring fluctuations in asset prices.

Here we'll illustrate the effects of *increases* in demand and supply in the loanable funds market.

An Increase in Demand If the profits that firms expect to earn increase, they increase their planned investment and increase their demand for loanable funds to finance that investment. With an increase in the demand for loanable funds, but no change in the supply of loanable funds, there is a shortage of funds. As borrowers compete for funds, the interest rate rises and lenders increase the quantity of funds supplied.

Figure 24.6(a) illustrates these changes. An increase in the demand for loanable funds shifts the demand curve rightward from DLF_0 to DLF_1. With

FIGURE 24.6   Changes in Demand and Supply

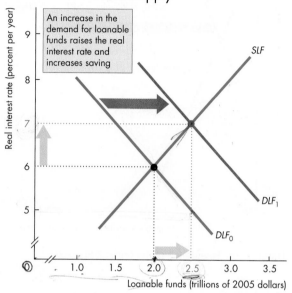

An increase in the demand for loanable funds raises the real interest rate and increases saving

(a) An increase in demand

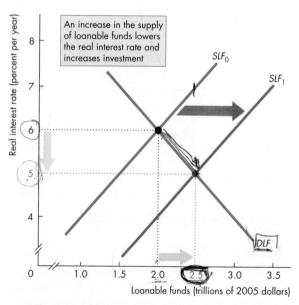

An increase in the supply of loanable funds lowers the real interest rate and increases investment

(b) An increase in supply

In part (a), the demand for loanable funds increases and supply doesn't change. The real interest rate rises (financial asset prices fall) and the quantity of funds increases.
In part (b), the supply of loanable funds increases and demand doesn't change. The real interest rate falls (financial asset prices rise) and the quantity of funds increases.

 animation

no change in the supply of loanable funds, there is a shortage of funds at a real interest rate of 6 percent a year. The real interest rate rises until it is 7 percent a year. Equilibrium is restored and the equilibrium quantity of funds has increased.

An Increase in Supply   If one of the influences on saving plans changes and increases saving, the supply of loanable funds increases. With no change in the demand for loanable funds, the market is flush with loanable funds. Borrowers find bargains and lenders find themselves accepting a lower interest rate. At the lower interest rate, borrowers find additional investment projects profitable and increase the quantity of loanable funds that they borrow.

Figure 24.6(b) illustrates these changes. An increase in supply shifts the supply curve rightward from SLF_0 to SLF_1. With no change in demand, there is a surplus of funds at a real interest rate of 6 percent a year. The real interest rate falls until it is 5 percent a year. Equilibrium is restored and the equilibrium quantity of funds has increased.

Long-Run Growth of Demand and Supply   Over time, both demand and supply in the loanable funds market fluctuate and the real interest rate rises and falls. Both the supply of loanable funds and the demand for loanable funds tend to increase over time. On the average, they increase at a similar pace, so although demand and supply trend upward, the real interest rate has no trend. It fluctuates around a constant average level.

REVIEW QUIZ

1 What is the loanable funds market?
2 Why is the real interest rate the opportunity cost of loanable funds?
3 How do firms make investment decisions?
4 What determines the demand for loanable funds and what makes it change?
5 How do households make saving decisions?
6 What determines the supply of loanable funds and what makes it change?
7 How do changes in the demand for and supply of loanable funds change the real interest rate and quantity of loanable funds?

You can work these questions in Study Plan 24.2 and get instant feedback.   myeconlab

Economics in Actions

Loanable Funds Fuel Home Price Bubble

The financial crisis that gripped the U.S. and global economies in 2007 and cascaded through the financial markets in 2008 had its origins much earlier in events taking place in the loanable funds market.

Between 2001 and 2005, a massive injection of loanable funds occurred. Some funds came from the rest of the world, but that source of supply has been stable. The Federal Reserve provided funds to keep interest rates low and that was a major source of the increase in the supply of funds. (The next chapter explains how the Fed does this.)

Figure 1 illustrates the loanable funds market starting in 2001. In that year, the demand for loanable funds was DLF_{01} and the supply of loanable funds was SLF_{01}. The equilibrium real interest rate was 4 percent a year and the equilibrium quantity of loanable funds was $29 trillion (in 2005 dollars).

During the ensuing four years, a massive increase in the supply of loanable funds shifted the supply curve rightward to SLF_{05}. A smaller increase in demand shifted the demand for loanable funds curve to DLF_{05}. The real interest rate fell to 1 percent a year and the quantity of loanable funds increased to $36 trillion—a 24 percent increase in just four years.

With this large increase in available funds, much of it in the form of mortgage loans to home buyers, the demand for homes increased by more than the increase in the supply of homes. Home prices rose and the expectation of further increases fueled the demand for loanable funds.

By 2006, the expectation of continued rapidly rising home prices brought a very large increase in the demand for loanable funds. At the same time, the Federal Reserve began to tighten credit. (Again, you'll learn how this is done in the next chapter). The result of the Fed's tighter credit policy was a slowdown in the pace of increase in the supply of loanable funds.

Figure 2 illustrates these events. In 2006, the demand for loanable funds increased from DLF_{05} to DLF_{06} and the supply of loanable funds increased by a smaller amount from SLF_{05} to SLF_{06}. The real interest rate increased to 3 percent a year.

The rise in the real interest rate (and a much higher rise in the nominal interest rate) put many homeowners in financial difficulty. Mortgage payments increased and some borrowers stopped repaying their loans.

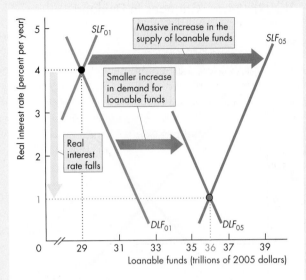

Figure 1 The Foundation of the Crisis: 2001–2005

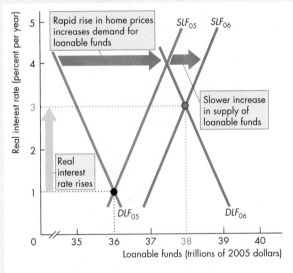

Figure 2 The Start of the Crisis: 2005–2006

By August 2007, the damage from mortgage default and foreclosure was so large that the credit market began to dry up. A large decrease in both demand and supply kept interest rates roughly constant but decreased the quantity of new business.

The total quantity of loanable funds didn't decrease, but the rate of increase slowed to a snail's pace and financial institutions most exposed to the bad mortgage debts and the securities that they backed (described on p. 568) began to fail.

These events illustrate the crucial role played by the loanable funds market in our economy.

Government in the Loanable Funds Market

Government enters the loanable funds market when it has a budget surplus or budget deficit. A government budget surplus increases the supply of loanable funds and contributes to financing investment; a government budget deficit increases the demand for loanable funds and competes with businesses for funds. Let's study the effects of government on the loanable funds market.

A Government Budget Surplus

A government budget surplus increases the supply of loanable funds. The real interest rate falls, which decreases household saving and decreases the quantity of private funds supplied. The lower real interest rate increases the quantity of loanable funds demanded, and increases investment.

FIGURE 24.7   A Government Budget Surplus

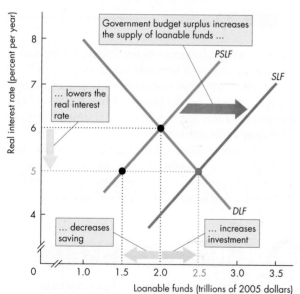

A government budget surplus of $1 trillion is added to private saving and the private supply of loanable funds (*PSLF*) to determine the supply of loanable funds, *SLF*. The real interest rate falls to 5 percent a year, private saving decreases, but investment increases to $2.5 trillion.

myeconlab   animation

Figure 24.7 shows these effects of a government budget surplus. The private supply of loanable funds curve is *PSLF*. The supply of loanable funds curve, *SLF*, shows the sum of private supply and the government budget surplus. Here, the government budget surplus is $1 trillion, so at each real interest rate the *SLF* curve lies $1 trillion to the right of the *PSLF* curve. That is, the horizontal distance between the *PSLF* curve and the *SLF* curve equals the government budget surplus.

With no government surplus, the real interest rate is 6 percent a year, the quantity of loanable funds is $2 trillion a year, and investment is $2 trillion a year. But with the government surplus of $1 trillion a year, the equilibrium real interest rate falls to 5 percent a year and the equilibrium quantity of loanable funds increases to $2.5 trillion a year.

The fall in the interest rate decreases private saving to $1.5 trillion, but investment increases to $2.5 trillion, which is financed by private saving plus the government budget surplus (government saving).

A Government Budget Deficit

A government budget deficit increases the demand for loanable funds. The real interest rate rises, which increases household saving and increases the quantity of private funds supplied. But the higher real interest rate decreases investment and the quantity of loanable funds demanded by firms to finance investment.

Figure 24.8 shows these effects of a government budget deficit. The private demand for loanable funds curve is *PDLF*. The demand for loanable funds curve, *DLF*, shows the sum of private demand and the government budget deficit. Here, the government budget deficit is $1 trillion, so at each real interest rate the *DLF* curve lies $1 trillion to the right of the *PDLF* curve. That is, the horizontal distance between the *PDLF* curve and the *DLF* curve equals the government budget deficit.

With no government deficit, the real interest rate is 6 percent a year, the quantity of loanable funds is $2 trillion a year and investment is $2 trillion a year. But with the government budget deficit of $1 trillion a year, the equilibrium real interest rate rises to 7 percent a year and the equilibrium quantity of loanable funds increases to $2.5 trillion a year.

The rise in the real interest rate increases private saving to $2.5 trillion, but investment decreases to $1.5 trillion because $1 trillion of private saving must finance the government budget deficit.

FIGURE 24.8   A Government Budget Deficit

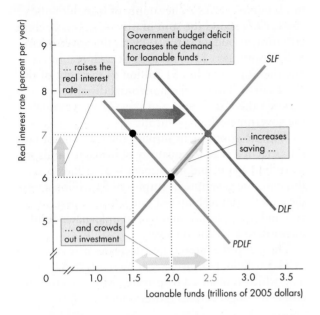

A government budget deficit adds to the private demand for loanable funds curve (*PDLF*) to determine the demand for loanable funds curve, *DLF*. The real interest rate rises, saving increases, but investment decreases—a crowding-out effect.

myeconlab animation

FIGURE 24.9   The Ricardo-Barro Effect

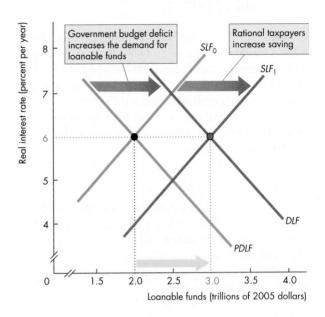

A budget deficit increases the demand for loanable funds. Rational taxpayers increase saving, which increases the supply of loanable funds curve from SLF_0 to SLF_1. Crowding out is avoided: Increased saving finances the budget deficit.

myeconlab animation

The Crowding-Out Effect The tendency for a government budget deficit to raise the real interest rate and decrease investment is called the **crowding-out effect**. The budget deficit crowds out investment by competing with businesses for scarce financial capital.

The crowding-out effect does not decrease investment by the full amount of the government budget deficit because the higher real interest rate induces an increase in private saving that partly contributes toward financing the deficit.

The Ricardo-Barro Effect First suggested by the English economist David Ricardo in the eighteenth century and refined by Robert J. Barro of Harvard University, the Ricardo-Barro effect holds that both of the effects we've just shown are wrong and the government budget, whether in surplus or deficit, has no effect on either the real interest rate or investment.

Barro says that taxpayers are rational. They can see that a budget deficit today means that future taxes will be higher and future disposable incomes will be smaller. With smaller expected future disposable

incomes, saving increases today. Private saving and the private supply of loanable funds increase to match the quantity of loanable funds demanded by the government. So the budget deficit has no effect on either the real interest rate or investment. Figure 24.9 shows this outcome.

Most economists regard the Ricardo-Barro view as extreme. But there might be some change in private saving that goes in the direction suggested by the Ricardo-Barro effect that lessens the crowding-out effect.

REVIEW QUIZ

1 How does a government budget surplus or deficit influence the loanable funds market?
2 What is the crowding-out effect and how does it work?
3 What is the Ricardo-Barro effect and how does it modify the crowding-out effect?

You can work these questions in Study Plan 24.3 and get instant feedback.

The Global Loanable Funds Market

The loanable funds market is global, not national. Lenders on the supply side of the market want to earn the highest possible real interest rate and they will seek it by looking everywhere in the world. Borrowers on the demand side of the market want to pay the lowest possible real interest rate and they will seek it by looking everywhere in the world. Financial capital is mobile: It moves to the best advantage of lenders and borrowers.

International Capital Mobility

If a U.S. supplier of loanable funds can earn a higher interest rate in Tokyo than in New York, funds supplied in Japan will increase and funds supplied in the United States will decrease—funds will flow from the United States to Japan.

If a U.S. demander of loanable funds can pay a lower interest rate in Paris than in New York, the demand for funds in France will increase and the demand for funds in the United States will decrease —funds will flow from France to the United States.

Because lenders are free to seek the highest real interest rate and borrowers are free to seek the lowest real interest rate, the loanable funds market is a single, integrated, global market. Funds flow into the country in which the interest rate is highest and out of the country in which the interest rate is lowest.

When funds leave the country with the lowest interest rate, a shortage of funds raises the real interest rate. When funds move into the country with the highest interest rate, a surplus of funds lowers the real interest rate. The free international mobility of financial capital pulls real interest rates around the world toward equality.

Only when the real interest rates in New York, Tokyo, and Paris are equal does the incentive to move funds from one country to another stop.

Equality of real interest rates does not mean that if you calculate the average real interest rate in New York, Tokyo, and Paris, you'll get the same number. To compare real interest rates, we must compare financial assets of equal risk.

Lending is risky. A loan might not be repaid. Or the price of a stock or bond might fall. Interest rates include a risk premium—the riskier the loan, other things remaining the same, the higher is the interest rate. The interest rate on a risky loan minus that on a safe loan is called the *risk premium*.

International capital mobility brings *real* interest rates in all parts of the world to equality except for differences that reflect differences in risk—differences in the risk premium.

International Borrowing and Lending

A country's loanable funds market connects with the global market through net exports. If a country's net exports are negative $(X < M)$, the rest of the world supplies funds to that country and the quantity of loanable funds in that country is greater than national saving. If a country's net exports are positive $(X > M)$, the country is a net supplier of funds to the rest of the world and the quantity of loanable funds in that country is less than national saving.

Demand and Supply in the Global and National Markets

The demand for and supply of funds in the global loanable funds market determines the world equilibrium real interest rate. This interest rate makes the quantity of loanable funds demanded equal the quantity supplied in the world economy. But it does not make the quantity of funds demanded and supplied equal in each national economy. The demand for and supply of funds in a national economy determine whether the country is a lender to or a borrower from the rest of the world.

The Global Loanable Funds Market Figure 24.10(a) illustrates the global market. The demand for loanable funds, DLF_W is the sum of the demands in all countries. Similarly, the supply of loanable funds, SLF_W is the sum of the supplies in all countries. The world equilibrium real interest rate makes the quantity of funds supplied in the world as a whole equal to the quantity demanded. In this example, the equilibrium real interest rate is 5 percent a year and the quantity of funds is $10 trillion.

An International Borrower Figure 24.10(b) shows the loanable funds market in a country that borrows from the rest of the world. The country's demand for loanable funds, DLF, is part of the world demand in Fig. 24.10(a). The country's supply of loanable funds, SLF_D, is part of the world supply.

FIGURE 24.10   Borrowing and Lending in the Global Loanable Funds Market

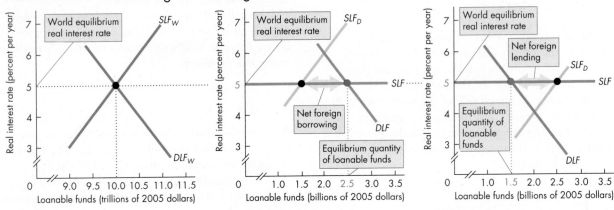

(a) The global market   **(b) An international borrower**   **(c) An international lender**

In the global loanable funds market in part (a), the demand for loanable funds, DLF_W, and the supply of funds, SLF_W, determine the world real interest rate. Each country can get funds at the world real interest rate and faces the (horizontal) supply curve SLF in parts (b) and (c).

At the world real interest rate, borrowers in part (b)

want more funds than the quantity supplied by domestic lenders (SLF_D). The shortage is made up by international borrowing.

Domestic suppliers of funds in part (c) want to lend more than domestic borrowers demand. The excess quantity supplied goes to foreign borrowers.

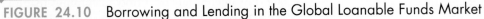

myeconlab   animation

If this country were isolated from the global market, the real interest rate would be 6 percent a year (where the DLF and SLF_D curves intersect). But if the country is integrated into the global economy, with an interest rate of 6 percent a year, funds would *flood into* it. With a real interest rate of 5 percent a year in the rest of the world, suppliers of loanable funds would seek the higher return in this country. In effect, the country faces the supply of loanable funds curve SLF, which is horizontal at the world equilibrium real interest rate.

The country's demand for loanable funds and the world interest rate determine the equilibrium quantity of loanable funds—$2.5 billion in Fig. 24.10(b).

An International Lender Figure 24.10(c) shows the situation in a country that lends to the rest of the world. As before, the country's demand for loanable funds, DLF, is part of the world demand and the country's supply of loanable funds, SLF_D, is part of the world supply in Fig. 24.10(a).

If this country were isolated from the global economy, the real interest rate would be 4 percent a year (where the DLF and SLF_D curves intersect). But if this country is integrated into the global economy, with an interest rate of 4 percent a year, funds would

quickly *flow out* of it. With a real interest rate of 5 percent a year in the rest of the world, domestic suppliers of loanable funds would seek the higher return in other countries. Again, the country faces the supply of loanable funds curve SLF, which is horizontal at the world equilibrium real interest rate.

The country's demand for loanable funds and the world interest rate determine the equilibrium quantity of loanable funds—$1.5 billion in Fig. 24.10(c).

Changes in Demand and Supply A change in the demand or supply in the global loanable funds market changes the real interest rate in the way shown in Fig. 24.6 (see p. 575). The effect of a change in demand or supply in a national market depends on the size of the country. A change in demand or supply in a small country has no significant effect on global demand or supply, so it leaves the world real interest rate unchanged and changes only the country's net exports and international borrowing or lending. A change in demand or supply in a large country has a significant effect on global demand or supply, so it changes the world real interest rate as well as the country's net exports and international borrowing or lending. Every country feels some of the effect of a large country's change in demand or supply.

Economics in Action
Greenspan's Interest Rate Puzzle

The real interest rate paid by big corporations in the United States fell from 5.5 percent a year in 2001 to 2.5 percent a year in 2005. Alan Greenspan, then the Chairman of the Federal Reserve, said he was puzzled that the real interest rate was falling at a time when the U.S. government budget deficit was increasing.

Why did the real interest rate fall?

The answer lies in the global loanable funds market. Rapid economic growth in Asia and Europe brought a large increase in global saving, which in turn increased the global supply of loanable funds. The supply of loanable funds increased because Asian and European saving increased strongly.

The U.S. government budget deficit increased the U.S. and global demand for loanable funds. But this increase was very small compared to the increase in the global supply of loanable funds.

The result of a large increase in supply and a small increase in demand was a fall in the world equilibrium real interest rate and an increase in the equilibrium quantity of loanable funds.

The figure illustrates these events. The supply of loanable funds increased from SLF_{01} in 2001 to SLF_{05} in 2005. (In the figure, we ignore the change in the global demand for loanable funds because it was small relative to the increase in supply.)

With the increase in supply, the real interest rate fell from 5.5 percent to 2.5 percent a year and the

quantity of loanable funds increased.

In the United States, borrowing from the rest of the world increased to finance the increased government budget deficit.

The interest rate puzzle illustrates the important fact that the loanable funds market is a global market, not a national market.

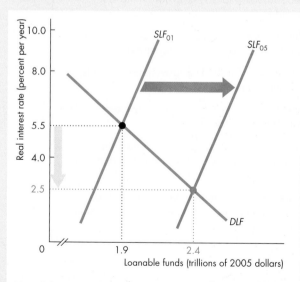

The Global Loanable Funds Market

REVIEW QUIZ

1 Why do loanable funds flow among countries?
2 What determines the demand for and supply of loanable funds in an individual economy?
3 What happens if a country has a shortage of loanable funds at the world real interest rate?
4 What happens if a country has a surplus of loanable funds at the world real interest rate?
5 How is a government budget deficit financed in an open economy?

You can work these questions in Study Plan 24.4 and get instant feedback.

◆ To complete your study of financial markets, take a look at *Reading Between the Lines* on pp. 582–583 and see how you can use the model of the loanable funds market to understand the events in the financial market crisis of 2008.

Crowding Out in the Global Recession

"Borrowing to Live" Weighs on Families, Firms, Nation

http://www.dallasmorningnews.com
June 13, 2010

... In the last decade, American household, business, and government debts doubled to $39.2 trillion. We did not double the size of the economy. And that's the problem. ...

The average Dallas consumer owed $26,599 in March [2010] on credit cards and loans covering cars, tuition, and other personal needs. (The amount doesn't include mortgages.) Dallas County delinquency rates for student, auto, and credit card loans are above the national average.

Now the U.S. government is on a borrowing spree. For every dollar it spends, it is borrowing 40 cents. ...

Some politicians and policy wonks say we have 10 years. Gold bugs and debt Jeremiahs say the day [of reckoning] is at hand.

In April, Federal Reserve Chairman Ben Bernanke told a Dallas audience that we should plan now to cut spending, raise taxes, or both. That seems to be the middle ground—it's time we have a plan. ...

It would be easier if we owed the money to ourselves. More than $4 trillion of our federal debt of $8.572 trillion (not counting loans the government owes itself) was borrowed from foreigners.

China is our top creditor. It holds roughly $1.2 trillion in U.S. government debt. ...

Reprinted with permission of the *Dallas Morning News*.

ESSENCE OF THE STORY

- U.S. household, business, and government debts doubled to $39.2 trillion in the last decade.

- The average Dallas consumer owed $26,599 in March 2010, not counting mortgages.

- For every dollar the U.S. government spends, it borrows 40 cents.

- Some people think the government's deficit will bring financial collapse.

- Most people, including Fed chairman Ben Bernanke, think that taxes should rise and government spending be cut.

- More than $4 trillion of the federal debt of $8.6 trillion is owed to foreigners, $1.2 trillion to China alone.

- This news article says that the growth of both U.S. government debt and U.S. international debt are unsustainable and must be stopped.

- The article speculates about impending doom at an unknown future date, perhaps in 10 years.

- Government debt grows when the government runs a budget deficit. The news article correctly points out that the U.S. government is running a whopping deficit.

- In 2009, of every dollar the government spent, it borrowed 40 cents.

- The U.S. government is not alone. Governments in Europe, Japan, China, and many other countries are running large budget deficits.

- These deficits might bring a "day of reckoning" as the article states, but they bring a more immediate problem: crowding out investment and slowing the pace of economic growth.

- In 2009, the increase in government borrowing in the loanable funds market sent the real interest rate on long-term corporate bonds to 6 percent per year, up from 2 percent per year in 2008.

- Figure 1, which is like Fig. 24.10(a) on p. 580, illustrates what happened in the global loanable funds market, and Fig. 2, which is like Fig. 24.10(b), illustrates the U.S. loanable funds market.

- In both figures, the supply of loanable funds curve is SLF and the private (non-government) demand for loanable funds curve is $PDLF$. These supply and demand curves are (assumed to be) the same in 2008 and 2009.

- In 2008, the demand for loanable funds curve was DLF_{08} in both figures. The real interest rate, determined in the global market, was 2 percent per year.

- Fiscal stimulus packages increased government budget deficits and increased the demand for loanable funds. The demand curves (both figures) shifted to DLF_{09}. The real interest rate increased in the global market to 6 percent per year.

- In the global market in Fig. 1, the higher real interest rate crowded out (lowered) investment by 25 percent.

- In the U.S. market in Fig. 2, the higher real interest rate crowded out (lowered) investment by almost 25 percent.

- The higher real interest rate had a second effect in the U.S. market: It increased saving and the quantity of loanable funds supplied.

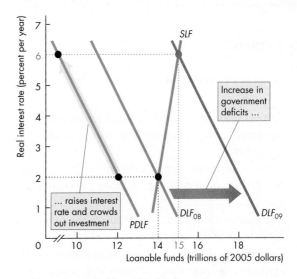

Figure 1 The global loanable funds market

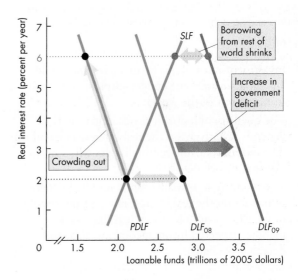

Figure 2 The U.S. loanable funds market

- The increase in the quantity of loanable funds supplied from U.S. sources decreased the amount borrowed from the rest of the world.

- So, although the long-term problems correctly identified in the news article are a concern, crowding out brings an immediate problem.

- But the drop in borrowing from the rest of the world is a move in the direction hoped for in the article.

SUMMARY

Key Points

Financial Institutions and Financial Markets

(pp. 566–570)

- Capital (*physical capital*) is a real productive resource; financial capital is the funds used to buy capital.
- Gross investment increases the quantity of capital and depreciation decreases it. Saving increases wealth.
- The markets for financial capital are the markets for loans, bonds, and stocks.
- Financial institutions ensure that borrowers and lenders can always find someone with whom to trade.

Working Study Plan Problems 1 to 5 will give you a better understanding of financial institutions and markets.

The Loanable Funds Market (pp. 570–576)

- Investment in capital is financed by household saving, a government budget surplus, and funds from the rest of the world.
- The quantity of loanable funds demanded depends negatively on the real interest rate and the demand for loanable funds changes when profit expectations change.
- The quantity of loanable funds supplied depends positively on the real interest rate and the supply of loanable funds changes when disposable income, expected future income, wealth, and default risk change.

- Equilibrium in the loanable funds market determines the real interest rate and quantity of funds.

Working Study Plan Problems 6 to 9 will give you a better understanding of the loanable funds market.

Government in the Loanable Funds Market

(pp. 577–578)

- A government budget surplus increases the supply of loanable funds, lowers the real interest rate, and increases investment and the equilibrium quantity of loanable funds.
- A government budget deficit increases the demand for loanable funds, raises the real interest rate, and increases the equilibrium quantity of loanable funds, but decreases investment in a crowding-out effect.
- The Ricardo-Barro effect is the response of rational taxpayers to a budget deficit: private saving increases to finance the budget deficit. The real interest rate remains constant and the crowding-out effect is avoided.

Working Study Plan Problems 10 to 15 will give you a better understanding of government in the loanable funds market.

The Global Loanable Funds Market (pp. 579–581)

- The loanable funds market is a global market.
- The equilibrium real interest rate is determined in the global loanable funds market and national demand and supply determine the quantity of international borrowing or lending.

Working Study Plan Problems 16 to 18 will give you a better understanding of the global loanable funds market.

Key Terms

Bond, 567
Bond market, 567
Crowding-out effect, 578
Demand for loanable funds, 572
Financial capital, 566
Financial institution, 568
Gross investment, 566

Loanable funds market, 570
Mortgage, 567
Mortgage-backed security, 568
National saving, 571
Net investment, 566
Net taxes, 570
Net worth, 569

Nominal interest rate, 571
Real interest rate, 571
Saving, 566
Stock, 568
Stock market, 568
Supply of loanable funds, 573
Wealth, 566

STUDY PLAN PROBLEMS AND APPLICATIONS

 myeconlab You can work Problems 1 to 18 in MyEconLab Chapter 24 Study Plan and get instant feedback.

Financial Institutions and Financial Markets

(Study Plan 24.1)

Use the following information to work Problems 1 and 2.

Michael is an Internet service provider. On December 31, 2009, he bought an existing business with servers and a building worth $400,000. During his first year of operation, his business grew and he bought new servers for $500,000. The market value of some of his older servers fell by $100,000.

1. What was Michael's gross investment, depreciation, and net investment during 2010?

2. What is the value of Michael's capital at the end of 2010?

3. Lori is a student who teaches golf on the weekend and in a year earns $20,000 after paying her taxes. At the beginning of 2010, Lori owned $1,000 worth of books, CDs, and golf clubs and she had $5,000 in a savings account at the bank. During 2010, the interest on her savings account was $300 and she spent a total of $15,300 on consumption goods and services. There was no change in the market values of her books, CDs, and golf clubs.

   a. How much did Lori save in 2010?

   b. What was her wealth at the end of 2010?

4. In a speech at the CFA Society of Nebraska in February 2007, William Poole, former Chairman of the St. Louis Federal Reserve Bank said:

   Over most of the post–World War II period, the personal saving rate averaged about 6 percent, with some higher years from the mid-1970s to mid-1980s. The negative trend in the saving rate started in the mid-1990s, about the same time the stock market boom started. Thus it is hard to dismiss the hypothesis that the decline in the measured saving rate in the late 1990s reflected the response of consumption to large capital gains from corporate equity [stock]. Evidence from panel data of households also supports the conclusion that the decline in the personal saving rate since 1984 is largely a consequence of capital gains on corporate equities.

   a. Is the purchase of corporate equities part of household consumption or saving? Explain your answer.

   b. Equities reap a capital gain in the same way that houses reap a capital gain. Does this mean that the purchase of equities is investment? If not, explain why it is not.

5. **G-20 Leaders Look to Shake off Lingering Economic Troubles**

   The G-20 aims to take stock of the economic recovery. One achievement of the G-20 in Pittsburgh could be a deal to require that financial institutions hold more capital.

   Source: *USA Today*, September 24, 2009

   What are the financial institutions that the G-20 might require to hold more capital? What exactly is the "capital" referred to in the news clip? How might the requirement to hold more capital make financial institutions safer?

The Loanable Funds Market (Study Plan 24.2)

Use the following information to work Problems 6 and 7.

First Call, Inc., is a cellular phone company. It plans to build an assembly plant that costs $10 million if the real interest rate is 6 percent a year. If the real interest rate is 5 percent a year, First Call will build a larger plant that costs $12 million. And if the real interest rate is 7 percent a year, First Call will build a smaller plant that costs $8 million.

6. Draw a graph of First Call's demand for loanable funds curve.

7. First Call expects its profit from the sale of cellular phones to double next year. If other things remain the same, explain how this increase in expected profit influences First Call's demand for loanable funds.

8. Draw a graph to illustrate how an increase in the supply of loanable funds and a decrease in the demand for loanable funds can lower the real interest rate and leave the equilibrium quantity of loanable funds unchanged.

9. Use the information in Problem 4.

a. U.S. household income has grown considerably since 1984. Has U.S. saving been on a downward trend because Americans feel wealthier?

b. Explain why households preferred to buy corporate equities rather than bonds.

Government in the Loanable Funds Market

(Study Plan 24.3)

Use the following table to work Problems 10 to 12. The table shows an economy's demand for loanable funds and the supply of loanable funds schedules, when the government's budget is balanced.

Real interest rate (percent per year)	Loanable funds demanded	Loanable funds supplied
	(trillions of 2005 dollars)	
4	8.5	5.5
5	8.0	6.0
6	7.5	6.5
7	7.0	7.0
8	6.5	7.5
9	6.0	8.0
10	5.5	8.5

10. Suppose that the government has a budget surplus of $1 trillion. What are the real interest rate, the quantity of investment, and the quantity of private saving? Is there any crowding out in this situation?

11. Suppose that the government has a budget deficit of $1 trillion. What are the real interest rate, the quantity of investment, and the quantity of private saving? Is there any crowding out in this situation?

12. Suppose that the government has a budget deficit of $1 trillion and the Ricardo-Barro effect occurs. What are the real interest rate and the quantity of investment?

Use the table in Problem 10 to work Problems 13 to 15.

Suppose that the quantity of loanable funds demanded increases by $1 trillion at each real interest rate and the quantity of loanable funds supplied increases by $2 trillion at each interest rate.

13. If the government budget is balanced, what are the real interest rate, the quantity of loanable funds, investment, and private saving? Does any crowding out occur?

14. If the government budget becomes a deficit of $1 trillion, what are the real interest rate, the quantity

of loanable funds, investment, and private saving? Does any crowding out occur?

15. If the government wants to stimulate investment and increase it to $9 trillion, what must it do?

The Global Loanable Funds Market (Study Plan 24.4)

Use the following information to work Problems 16 and 17.

Global Saving Glut and U.S. Current Account, remarks by Ben Bernanke (when a governor of the Federal Reserve) on March 10, 2005:

The U.S. economy appears to be performing well: Output growth has returned to healthy levels, the labor market is firming, and inflation appears to be under control. But, one aspect of U.S. economic performance still evokes concern: the nation's large and growing current account deficit (negative net exports). Most forecasters expect the nation's current account imbalance to decline slowly at best, implying a continued need for foreign credit and a concomitant decline in the U.S. net foreign asset position.

16. Why is the United States, with the world's largest economy, borrowing heavily on international capital markets—rather than lending, as would seem more natural?

17. a. What implications do the U.S. current account deficit (negative net exports) and our reliance on foreign credit have for economic performance in the United States?

b. What policies, if any, should be used to address this situation?

18. **IMF Says It Battled Crisis Well**

The International Monetary Fund (IMF) reported that it acted effectively in combating the global recession. Since September 2008, the IMF made $163 billion available to developing countries. While the IMF urged developed countries and China to run deficits to stimulate their economies, the IMF required developing countries with large deficits to cut spending and not increase spending.

Source: *The Wall Street Journal*, September 29, 2009

a. Explain how increased government budget deficits change the loanable funds market.

b. Would the global recession have been less severe had the IMF made larger loans to developing countries?

ADDITIONAL PROBLEMS AND APPLICATIONS

Financial Institutions and Financial Markets

19. On January 1, 2009, Terry's Towing Service owned 4 tow trucks valued at $300,000. During 2009, Terry's bought 2 new trucks for a total of $180,000. At the end of 2009, the market value of all of the firm's trucks was $400,000. What was Terry's gross investment? Calculate Terry's depreciation and net investment.

Use the following information to work Problems 20 and 21.

The Bureau of Economic Analysis reported that the U.S. capital stock was $40.4 trillion at the end of 2007, $41.1 trillion at the end of 2008, and $41.4 trillion at the end of 2009. Depreciation in 2008 was $1.3 trillion, and gross investment during 2009 was $1.5 trillion (all in 2005 dollars).

20. Calculate U. S. net investment and gross investment during 2008.

21. Calculate U.S. depreciation and net investment during 2009.

22. Annie runs a fitness center. On December 31, 2009, she bought an existing business with exercise equipment and a building worth $300,000. During 2010, business improved and she bought some new equipment for $50,000. At the end of 2010, her equipment and buildings were worth $325,000. Calculate Annie's gross investment, depreciation, and net investment during 2010.

23. Karrie is a golf pro, and after she paid taxes, her income from golf and interest from financial assets was $1,500,000 in 2010. At the beginning of 2010, she owned $900,000 worth of financial assets. At the end of 2010, Karrie's financial assets were worth $1,900,000.
    a. How much did Karrie save during 2010?
    b. How much did she spend on consumption goods and services?

The Loanable Funds Market

Use the following information to work Problems 24 and 25.

In 2010, the Lee family had disposable income of $80,000, wealth of $140,000, and an expected future income of $80,000 a year. At a real interest rate of 4 percent a year, the Lee family saves $15,000 a year; at a real interest rate of 6 percent a year, they save $20,000 a year; and at a real interest rate of 8 percent, they save $25,000 a year.

24. Draw a graph of the Lee family's supply of loanable funds curve.

25. In 2011, suppose that the stock market crashes and the default risk increases. Explain how this increase in default risk influences the Lee family's supply of loanable funds curve.

26. Draw a graph to illustrate the effect of an increase in the demand for loanable funds and an even larger increase in the supply of loanable funds on the real interest rate and the equilibrium quantity of loanable funds.

27. **Greenspan's Conundrum Spells Confusion for Us All**

    In January 2005, the interest rate on bonds was 4% a year and it was expected to rise to 5% a year by the end of 2005. As the rate rose to 4.3% during February, most commentators focused, not on why the interest rate rose, but on why it was so low before. Explanations of this "conundrum" included that unusual buying and expectations for an economic slowdown were keeping the interest rate low.

    Source: *Financial Times*, February 26, 2005
    a. Explain how "unusual buying" might lead to a low real interest rate.
    b. Explain how investors' "expectations for an economic slowdown" might lead to a lower real interest rate.

Government in the Loanable Funds Market

Use the following information to work Problems 28 and 29.

India's Economy Hits the Wall

At the start of 2008, India had an annual growth of 9%, huge consumer demand, and increasing foreign investment. But by July 2008, India had 11.4% inflation, large government deficits, and rising interest rates. Economic growth is expected to fall to 7% by the end of 2008. A Goldman Sachs report suggests that India needs to lower the government's deficit, raise educational achievement, control inflation, and liberalize its financial markets.

Source: *Business Week*, July 1, 2008

28. If the Indian government reduces its deficit and returns to a balanced budget, how will the demand for or supply of loanable funds in India change?

29. With economic growth forecasted to slow, future incomes are expected to fall. If other things remain the same, how will the demand or supply of loanable funds in India change?

30. **Federal Deficit Surges to $1.38 trillion through August**

House Republican Leader John Boehner of Ohio asks: When will the White House tackle these jaw-dropping deficits that pile more and more debt on future generations while it massively increases federal spending?

Source: *USA Today*, September 11, 2009

Explain the effect of the federal deficit and the mounting debt on U.S. economic growth.

The Global Loanable Funds Market

31. **The Global Savings Glut and Its Consequences**

Several developing countries are running large current account surpluses (representing an excess of savings over investment) and rapid growth has led to high saving rates as people save a large fraction of additional income. In India, the saving rate has risen from 23% a decade ago to 33% today. China's saving rate is 55%. The glut of saving in Asia is being put into U.S. bonds. When a poor country buys U.S. bonds, it is in effect lending to the United States.

Source: *The Cato Institute*, June 8, 2007

a. Graphically illustrate and explain the impact of the "glut of savings" on the real interest rate and the quantity of loanable funds.

b. How do the high saving rates in Asia impact investment in the United States?

Use the following information to work Problems 32 to 35.

Most economists agree that the problems we are witnessing today developed over a long period of time. For more than a decade, a massive amount of money flowed into the United States from investors abroad, because our country is an attractive and secure place to do business. This large influx of money to U.S.

financial institutions—along with low interest rates—made it easier for Americans to get credit. These developments allowed more families to borrow money for cars and homes and college tuition—some for the first time. They allowed more entrepreneurs to get loans to start new businesses and create jobs.

President George W. Bush, *Address to the Nation*, September 24, 2008

32. Explain why, for more than a decade, a massive amount of money flowed into the United States. Compare and contrast your explanation with that of the President.

33. Provide a graphical analysis of the reasons why the interest rate was low.

34. Funds have been flowing into the United States since the early 1980s. Why might they have created problems in 2008 but not earlier?

35. Could the United States stop funds from flowing in from other countries? How?

Economics in the News

36. After you have studied *Reading Between the Lines* on pp. 582–583 answer the following questions.

a. What are the long-term problems to which the news article draws attention?

b. What was the major event in the global and U.S. loanable funds markets in 2009?

c. How did the event identified in part (b) influence the world real interest rate and the global supply of and demand for loanable funds?

d. How did the event identified in part (b) influence the U.S. supply of and demand for loanable funds and the amount that the United States borrowed from the rest of the world?

e. If governments in other countries were to lower their budget deficits but the U.S. government did not lower its deficit, what would happen to the world real interest rate, the supply of and demand for loanable funds in the United States, and the amount that the United States borrows from the rest of the world?

f. If the U.S. government lowered its budget deficit but the governments in other countries did not lower their deficits, what would happen to the world real interest rate, the supply of and demand for loanable funds in the United States, and the amount that the United States borrows from the rest of the world?

After studying this chapter,
you will be able to:

◆ Define money and describe its functions

◆ Explain the economic functions of banks and other depository institutions

◆ Describe the structure and functions of the Federal Reserve System (the Fed)

◆ Explain how the banking system creates money

◆ Explain what determines the demand for money, the supply of money, and the nominal interest rate

◆ Explain how the quantity of money influences the price level and the inflation rate in the long run

25

MONEY, THE PRICE LEVEL, AND INFLATION

Money, like fire and the wheel, has been around for a long time, and it has taken many forms. Money was wampum (beads made from shells) for North American Indians, whale's teeth for Fijians, and tobacco for early American colonists. Cakes of salt served as money in Ethiopia and Tibet. Today, when we want to buy something, we use coins or dollar bills, write a check, or swipe a debit card or a credit card. Soon, we'll be using a "smart card" or even a cell phone to make payments. Are all these things money?

The quantity of money in our economy is regulated by the Federal Reserve—the Fed. How does the Fed influence the quantity of money? And what happens if the Fed creates too much money or too little money?

In this chapter, we study the functions of money, the banks that create it, the Federal Reserve and its influence on the quantity of money, and the long-run consequences of changes in the quantity of money. In *Reading Between the Lines* at the end of the chapter, we look at the extraordinary actions taken by the Fed during the recent financial crisis.

What Is Money?

What do wampum, tobacco, and nickels and dimes have in common? They are all examples of **money**, which is defined as any commodity or token that is generally acceptable as a means of payment. A **means of payment** is a method of settling a debt. When a payment has been made, there is no remaining obligation between the parties to a transaction. So what wampum, tobacco, and nickels and dimes have in common is that they have served (or still do serve) as the means of payment. Money serves three other functions:

- Medium of exchange
- Unit of account
- Store of value

Medium of Exchange

A *medium of exchange* is any object that is generally accepted in exchange for goods and services. Without a medium of exchange, goods and services must be exchanged directly for other goods and services—an exchange called *barter*. Barter requires a *double coincidence of wants*, a situation that rarely occurs. For example, if you want a hamburger, you might offer a CD in exchange for it. But you must find someone who is selling hamburgers and wants your CD.

A medium of exchange overcomes the need for a double coincidence of wants. Money acts as a medium of exchange because people with something to sell will always accept money in exchange for it. But money isn't the only medium of exchange. You can buy with a credit card, but a credit card isn't money. It doesn't make a final payment, and the debt it creates must eventually be settled by using money.

Unit of Account

A *unit of account* is an agreed measure for stating the prices of goods and services. To get the most out of your budget, you have to figure out whether seeing one more movie is worth its opportunity cost. But that cost is not dollars and cents. It is the number of ice-cream cones, sodas, or cups of coffee that you must give up. It's easy to do such calculations when all these goods have prices in terms of dollars and cents (see Table 25.1). If the price of a movie is $8 and the price of a cappuccino is $4, you know right away that seeing one movie costs you 2 cappuc-

TABLE 25.1 The Unit of Account Function of Money Simplifies Price Comparisons

Good	Price in money units	Price in units of another good
Movie	$8.00 each	2 cappuccinos
Cappuccino	$4.00 each	2 ice-cream cones
Ice cream	$2 per cone	2 packs of jelly beans
Jelly beans	$1 per pack	2 sticks of gum
Gum	$0.50 per stick	

Money as a unit of account: The price of a movie is $8 and the price of a stick of gum is 50¢, so the opportunity cost of a movie is 16 sticks of gum ($8.00 ÷ 50¢ = 16).

No unit of account: You go to a movie theater and learn that the cost of seeing a movie is 2 cappuccinos. You go to a grocery store and learn that a pack of jelly beans costs 2 sticks of gum. But how many sticks of gum does seeing a movie cost you? To answer that question, you go to the coffee shop and find that a cappuccino costs 2 ice-cream cones. Now you head for the ice-cream shop, where an ice-cream cone costs 2 packs of jelly beans. Now you get out your pocket calculator: 1 movie costs 2 cappuccinos, or 4 ice-cream cones, or 8 packs of jelly beans, or 16 sticks of gum!

cinos. If jelly beans are $1 a pack, one movie costs 8 packs of jelly beans. You need only one calculation to figure out the opportunity cost of any pair of goods and services.

Imagine how troublesome it would be if your local movie theater posted its price as 2 cappuccinos, the coffee shop posted the price of a cappuccino as 2 ice-cream cones, the ice-cream shop posted the price of an ice-cream cone as 2 packs of jelly beans, and the grocery store priced a pack of jelly beans as 2 sticks of gum! Now how much running around and calculating will you have to do to find out how much that movie is going to cost you in terms of the cappuccinos, ice cream cones, jelly beans, or gum that you must give up to see it? You get the answer for cappuccinos right away from the sign posted on the movie theater. But for all the other goods, you're going to have to visit many different stores to establish the price of each good in terms of another and then calculate the prices in units that are relevant for your own decision. The hassle of doing all this research might be enough to make a person swear off movies! You can see how much simpler it is if all the prices are expressed in dollars and cents.

Store of Value

Money is a *store of value* in the sense that it can be held and exchanged later for goods and services. If money were not a store of value, it could not serve as a means of payment.

Money is not alone in acting as a store of value. A house, a car, and a work of art are other examples.

The more stable the value of a commodity or token, the better it can act as a store of value and the more useful it is as money. No store of value has a completely stable value. The value of a house, a car, or a work of art fluctuates over time. The value of the commodities and tokens that are used as money also fluctuate over time.

Inflation lowers the value of money and the values of other commodities and tokens that are used as money. To make money as useful as possible as a store of value, a low inflation rate is needed.

Money in the United States Today

In the United States today, money consists of

- Currency
- Deposits at banks and other depository institutions

Currency The notes and coins held by individuals and businesses are known as **currency**. Notes are money because the government declares them so with the words "This note is legal tender for all debts, public and private." You can see these words on every dollar bill. Notes and coins *inside* banks are not counted as currency because they are not held by individuals and businesses.

Deposits Deposits of individuals and businesses at banks and other depository institutions, such as savings and loan associations, are also counted as money. Deposits are money because the owners of the deposits can use them to make payments.

Official Measures of Money Two official measures of money in the United States today are known as M1

and M2. **M1** consists of currency and traveler's checks plus checking deposits owned by individuals and businesses. M1 does *not* include currency held by banks, and it does not include currency and checking deposits owned by the U.S. government. **M2** consists of M1 plus time deposits, savings deposits, and money market mutual funds and other deposits.

Economics in Action
Official Measures of U.S. Money

The figure shows the relative magnitudes of the items that make up M1 and M2. Notice that M2 is almost five times as large as M1 and that currency is a small part of our money.

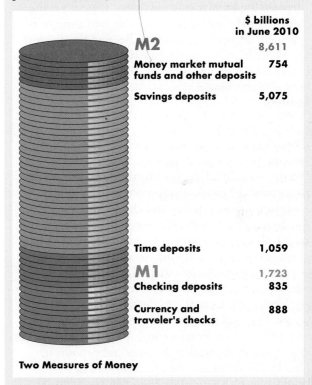

	$ billions in June 2010
M2	8,611
Money market mutual funds and other deposits	754
Savings deposits	5,075
Time deposits	1,059
M1	1,723
Checking deposits	835
Currency and traveler's checks	888

Two Measures of Money

M1	- Currency and traveler's checks
	- Checking deposits at commercial banks, savings and loan associations, savings banks, and credit unions
M2	- M1
	- Time deposits
	- Savings deposits
	- Money market mutual funds and other deposits

Source of data: The Federal Reserve Board. The data are for June 2010.

Are M1 and M2 Really Money? Money is the means of payment. So the test of whether an asset is money is whether it serves as a means of payment. Currency passes the test. But what about deposits? Checking deposits are money because they can be transferred from one person to another by writing a check or using a debit card. Such a transfer of ownership is equivalent to handing over currency. Because M1 consists of currency plus checking deposits and each of these is a means of payment, *M1 is money*.

But what about M2? Some of the savings deposits in M2 are just as much a means of payment as the checking deposits in M1. You can use an ATM to get funds from your savings account to pay for your purchase at the grocery store or the gas station. But some savings deposits are not means of payment. These deposits are known as liquid assets. *Liquidity* is the property of being easily convertible into a means of payment without loss in value. Because the deposits in M2 that are not means of payment are quickly and easily converted into a means of payment—into currency or checking deposits—they are counted as money.

Deposits Are Money but Checks Are Not In defining money, we include, along with currency, deposits at banks and other depository institutions. But we do not count the checks that people write as money. Why are deposits money and checks not?

To see why deposits are money but checks are not, think about what happens when Colleen buys some roller-blades for $100 from Rocky's Rollers. When Colleen goes to Rocky's shop, she has $500 in her deposit account at the Laser Bank. Rocky has $1,000 in his deposit account—at the same bank, as it happens. The total deposits of these two people are $1,500. Colleen writes a check for $100. Rocky takes the check to the bank right away and deposits it. Rocky's bank balance rises from $1,000 to $1,100, and Colleen's balance falls from $500 to $400. The total deposits of Colleen and Rocky are still the same as before: $1,500. Rocky now has $100 more than before, and Colleen has $100 less.

This transaction has transferred money from Colleen to Rocky, but the check itself was never money. There wasn't an extra $100 of money while the check was in circulation. The check instructs the bank to transfer money from Colleen to Rocky.

If Colleen and Rocky use different banks, there is an extra step. Rocky's bank credits $100 to Rocky's

account and then takes the check to a check-clearing center. The check is then sent to Colleen's bank, which pays Rocky's bank $100 and then debits Colleen's account $100. This process can take a few days, but the principles are the same as when two people use the same bank.

Credit Cards Are Not Money You've just seen that checks are not money. What about credit cards? Isn't having a credit card in your wallet and presenting the card to pay for your roller-blades the same thing as using money? Why aren't credit cards somehow valued and counted as part of the quantity of money?

When you pay by check, you are frequently asked to prove your identity by showing your driver's license. It would never occur to you to think of your driver's license as money. It's just an ID card. A credit card is also an ID card, but one that lets you take out a loan at the instant you buy something. When you sign a credit card sales slip, you are saying, "I agree to pay for these goods when the credit card company bills me." Once you get your statement from the credit card company, you must make at least the minimum payment due. To make that payment, you need money—you need to have currency or a checking deposit to pay the credit card company. So although you use a credit card when you buy something, the credit card is not the *means of payment* and it is not money.

REVIEW QUIZ

1 What makes something money? What functions does money perform? Why do you think packs of chewing gum don't serve as money?
2 What are the problems that arise when a commodity is used as money?
3 What are the main components of money in the United States today?
4 What are the official measures of money? Are all the measures really money?
5 Why are checks and credit cards not money?

You can work these questions in Study Plan 25.1 and get instant feedback.

We've seen that the main component of money in the United States is deposits at banks and other depository institutions. Let's take a closer look at these institutions.

Depository Institutions

A **depository institution** is a financial firm that takes deposits from households and firms. These deposits are components of M1 and M2. You will learn what these institutions are, what they do, the economic benefits they bring, how they are regulated, and how they have innovated to create new financial products.

Types of Depository Institutions

The deposits of three types of financial firms make up the nation's money. They are

- Commercial banks
- Thrift institutions
- Money market mutual funds

Commercial Banks A *commercial bank* is a firm that is licensed to receive deposits and make loans. In 2010, about 7,000 commercial banks operated in the United States but mergers make this number fall each year as small banks disappear and big banks expand.

A few very large commercial banks offer a wide range of banking services and have extensive international operations. The largest of these banks are Bank of America, Wells Fargo, JPMorgan Chase, and Citigroup. Most commercial banks are small and serve their regional and local communities.

The deposits of commercial banks represent 40 percent of M1 and 65 percent of M2.

Thrift Institutions Savings and loan associations, savings banks, and credit unions are *thrift institutions*.

Savings and Loan Association A *savings and loan association* (S&L) is a depository institution that receives deposits and makes personal, commercial, and home-purchase loans.

Savings Bank A *savings bank* is a depository institution that accepts savings deposits and makes mostly home-purchase loans.

Credit Union A *credit union* is a depository institution owned by a social or economic group, such as a firm's employees, that accepts savings deposits and makes mostly personal loans.

The deposits of the thrift institutions represent 9 percent of M1 and 16 percent of M2.

Money Market Mutual Funds A *money market mutual fund* is a fund operated by a financial institution that sells shares in the fund and holds assets such as U.S. Treasury bills and short-term commercial bills.

Money market mutual fund shares act like bank deposits. Shareholders can write checks on their money market mutual fund accounts, but there are restrictions on most of these accounts. For example, the minimum deposit accepted might be $2,500, and the smallest check a depositor is permitted to write might be $500.

Money market mutual funds do not feature in M1 and represent 9 percent of M2.

What Depository Institutions Do

Depository institutions provide services such as check clearing, account management, credit cards, and Internet banking, all of which provide an income from service fees.

But depository institutions earn most of their income by using the funds they receive from depositors to make loans and to buy securities that earn a higher interest rate than that paid to depositors. In this activity, a depository institution must perform a balancing act weighing return against risk. To see this balancing act, we'll focus on the commercial banks.

A commercial bank puts the funds it receives from depositors and other funds that it borrows into four types of assets:

1. A bank's **reserves** are notes and coins in the bank's vault or in a deposit account at the Federal Reserve. (We'll study the Federal Reserve later in this chapter.) These funds are used to meet depositors' currency withdrawals and to make payments to other banks. In normal times, a bank keeps about a half of one percent of deposits as reserves. (You'll see in Table 25.2 on the next page that 2010 is not a normal time.)

2. *Liquid assets* are overnight loans to other banks, U.S. government Treasury bills, and commercial bills. These assets are the banks' first line of defense if they need reserves. Liquid assets can be sold and instantly converted into reserves with virtually no risk of loss. Because they have a low risk, they earn a low interest rate.

   The interest rate on overnight loans to other banks, called the **federal funds rate**, is targeted by the Fed. We explain how and why on pp. 756–757.

3. *Securities* are U.S. government bonds and other bonds such as mortgage-backed securities. These assets can be sold and converted into reserves but at prices that fluctuate, so they are riskier than liquid assets and have a higher interest rate.

4. *Loans* are funds committed for an agreed-upon period of time to corporations to finance investment and to households to finance the purchase of homes, cars, and other durable goods. The outstanding balances on credit card accounts are also bank loans. Loans are a bank's riskiest and highest-earning assets: They can't be converted into reserves until they are due to be repaid, and some borrowers default and never repay.

Table 25.2 provides a snapshot of the sources and uses of funds of all the commercial banks in June 2010 that serves as a summary of the above account.

Economic Benefits Provided by Depository Institutions

You've seen that a depository institution earns part of its profit because it pays a lower interest rate on deposits than what it earns on loans. What benefits do these institutions provide that make depositors willing to put up with a low interest rate and borrowers willing to pay a higher one?

TABLE 25.2 Commercial Banks: Sources and Uses of Funds

	Funds (billions of dollars)	Percentage of deposits
Total funds	11,096	144.3
Sources		
Deposits	7,694	100.0
Borrowing	1,997	26.0
Own capital and other sources	1,405	18.3
Uses		
Reserves	1,097	14.3
Liquid assets	98	1.3
Securities and other assets	3,040	39.5
Loans	6,861	89.2

Commercial banks get most of their funds from depositors and use most of them to make loans. In normal times banks hold about 0.5 percent of deposits as reserves. But in 2010, at a time of great financial uncertainty, they held an unusually large 14.3 percent as reserves.

Source of data: The Federal Reserve Board. The data are for June, 2010.

Depository institutions provide four benefits:
- Create liquidity
- Pool risk
- Lower the cost of borrowing
- Lower the cost of monitoring borrowers

Create Liquidity Depository institutions create liquidity by *borrowing short and lending long*—taking deposits and standing ready to repay them on short notice or on demand and making loan commitments that run for terms of many years.

Pool Risk A loan might not be repaid—a default. If you lend to one person who defaults, you lose the entire amount loaned. If you lend to 1,000 people (through a bank) and one person defaults, you lose almost nothing. Depository institutions pool risk.

Lower the Cost of Borrowing Imagine there are no depository institutions and a firm is looking for $1 million to buy a new factory. It hunts around for several dozen people from whom to borrow the funds. Depository institutions lower the cost of this search. The firm gets its $1 million from a single institution that gets deposits from a large number of people but spreads the cost of this activity over many borrowers.

Lower the Cost of Monitoring Borrowers By monitoring borrowers, a lender can encourage good decisions that prevent defaults. But this activity is costly. Imagine how costly it would be if each household that lent money to a firm incurred the costs of monitoring that firm directly. Depository institutions can perform this task at a much lower cost.

How Depository Institutions Are Regulated

Depository institutions are engaged in a risky business, and a failure, especially of a large bank, would have damaging effects on the entire financial system and economy. To make the risk of failure small, depository institutions are required to hold levels of reserves and owners' capital that equal or surpass ratios laid down by regulation. If a depository institution fails, its deposits are guaranteed up to $250,000 per depositor per bank by the *Federal Deposit Insurance Corporation* or FDIC. The FDIC can take over management of a bank that appears to be heading toward failure.

Economics in Action
Commercial Banks Flush with Reserves

When Lehman Brothers (a New York investment bank) failed in October 2008, panic spread through financial markets. Banks that are normally happy to lend to each other overnight for an interest rate barely above the rate they can earn on safe Treasury bills lost confidence and the interest rate in this market shot up to 3 percentage points above the Treasury bill rate. Banks wanted to be safe and to hold cash. The Fed created and the banks willingly held reserves at the unheard of level of $1 trillion or 14 percent of deposits.

Throughout 2009 and 2010, bank reserves remained at this extraordinary level. And despite having plenty of funds to lend, the level of bank loans barely changed over 2009 and 2010.

The figure compares the commercial banks' sources and uses of funds (sources are liabilities and uses are assets) in 2008 with those in 2010.

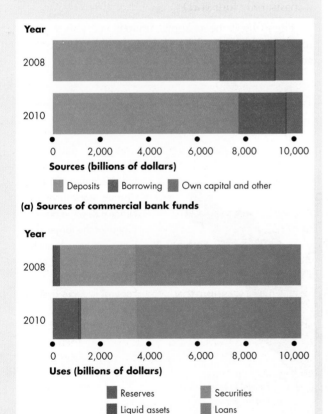

(a) Sources of commercial bank funds

(b) Uses of commercial bank funds

Changes in the Sources and Uses of Commercial Bank Funds
Source of data: The Federal Reserve Board.

Financial Innovation

In the pursuit of larger profit, depository institutions are constantly seeking ways to improve their products in a process called *financial innovation.*

During the late 1970s, a high inflation rate sent the interest rate on home-purchase loans to 15 percent a year. Traditional fixed interest rate mortgages became unprofitable and variable interest rate mortgages were introduced.

During the 2000s, when interest rates were low and depository institutions were flush with funds, sub-prime mortgages were developed. To avoid the risk of carrying these mortgages, mortgage-backed securities were developed. The original lending institution sold these securities, lowered their own exposure to risk, and obtained funds to make more loans.

The development of low-cost computing and communication brought financial innovations such as credit cards and daily interest deposit accounts.

Financial innovation has brought changes in the composition of money. Checking deposits at thrift institutions have become an increasing percentage of M1 while checking deposits at commercial banks have become a decreasing percentage. Savings deposits have decreased as a percentage of M2, while time deposits and money market mutual funds have expanded. Surprisingly, the use of currency has not fallen much.

 REVIEW QUIZ

1 What are depository institutions?
2 What are the functions of depository institutions?
3 How do depository institutions balance risk and return?
4 How do depository institutions create liquidity, pool risks, and lower the cost of borrowing?
5 How have depository institutions made innovations that have influenced the composition of money?

You can work these questions in Study Plan 25.2 and get instant feedback.

You now know what money is. Your next task is to learn about the Federal Reserve System and the ways in which it can influence the quantity of money.

◆ The Federal Reserve System

The **Federal Reserve System** (usually called the **Fed**) is the central bank of the United States. A **central bank** is a bank's bank and a public authority that regulates a nation's depository institutions and conducts *monetary policy*, which means that it adjusts the quantity of money in circulation and influences interest rates.

We begin by describing the structure of the Fed.

The Structure of the Fed

Three key elements of the Fed's structure are

- The Board of Governors
- The regional Federal Reserve banks
- The Federal Open Market Committee

The Board of Governors A seven-member board appointed by the President of the United States and confirmed by the Senate governs the Fed. Members have 14-year (staggered) terms and one seat on the board becomes vacant every two years. The President appoints one board member as chairman for a 4-year renewable term—currently Ben Bernanke, a former economics professor at Princeton University.

The Federal Reserve Banks The nation is divided into 12 Federal Reserve districts (shown in Fig. 25.1). Each district has a Federal Reserve Bank that provides check-clearing services to commercial banks and issues bank notes.

The Federal Reserve Bank of New York (known as the New York Fed), occupies a special place in the Federal Reserve System because it implements the Fed's policy decisions in the financial markets.

The Federal Open Market Committee The **Federal Open Market Committee** (FOMC) is the main policy-making organ of the Federal Reserve System. The FOMC consists of the following voting members:

- The chairman and the other six members of the Board of Governors

- The president of the Federal Reserve Bank of New York

- The presidents of the other regional Federal Reserve banks (of whom, on a yearly rotating basis, only four vote)

The FOMC meets approximately every six weeks to review the state of the economy and to decide the actions to be carried out by the New York Fed.

FIGURE 25.1   The Federal Reserve System

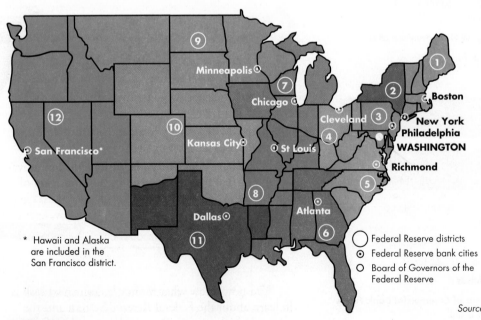

The nation is divided into 12 Federal Reserve districts, each having a Federal Reserve bank. (Some of the larger districts also have branch banks.) The Board of Governors of the Federal Reserve System is located in Washington, D.C.

* Hawaii and Alaska are included in the San Francisco district.

○ Federal Reserve districts
◉ Federal Reserve bank cities
○ Board of Governors of the Federal Reserve

Source: Federal Reserve Bulletin.

myeconlab animation

The Fed's Balance Sheet

The Fed influences the economy through the size and composition of its balance sheet—the assets that the Fed owns and the liabilities that it owes.

The Fed's Assets The Fed has two main assets:

1. U.S. government securities
2. Loans to depository institutions

The Fed holds U.S. securities—Treasury bills and Treasury bonds—that it buys in the bond market. When the Fed buys or sells bonds, it participates in the *loanable funds market* (see pp. 570–576).

The Fed makes loans to depository institutions. When these institutions in aggregate are short of reserves, they can borrow from the Fed. In normal times this item is small, but during 2007 and 2008, it grew as the Fed provided increasing amounts of relief from the financial crisis. By October 2008, loans to depository institutions exceeded government securities in the Fed's balance sheet.

The Fed's Liabilities The Fed has two liabilities:

1. Federal Reserve notes
2. Depository institution deposits

Federal Reserve notes are the dollar bills that we use in our daily transactions. Some of these notes are held by individuals and businesses; others are in the tills and vaults of banks and other depository institutions.

Depository institution deposits at the Fed are part of the reserves of these institutions (see p. 593).

The Monetary Base The Fed's liabilities together with coins issued by the Treasury (coins are not liabilities of the Fed) make up the monetary base. That is, the **monetary base** is the sum of currency (Federal Reserve notes and coins) and depository institution deposits at the Fed.

The Fed's assets are the sources of the monetary base. They are also called the backing for the monetary base. The Fed's liabilities are the uses of the monetary base as currency and bank reserves. Table 25.3 provides a snapshot of the sources and uses of the monetary base in June 2010.

When the Fed changes the monetary base, the quantity of money and interest rate change. You're going to see how these changes come about later in this chapter. First, we'll look at the Fed's tools that enable it to influence money and interest rates.

TABLE 25.3 The Sources and Uses of the Monetary Base

Sources (billions of dollars)		Uses (billions of dollars)	
U.S. government securities	777	Currency	900
Loans to depository institutions	70	Reserves of depository institutions	1,099
Other items (net)	1,152		
Monetary base	1,999	Monetary base	1,999

Source of data: Federal Reserve Board. The data are for June, 2010.

The Fed's Policy Tools

The Fed influences the quantity of money and interest rates by adjusting the quantity of reserves available to the banks and the reserves the banks must hold. To do this, the Fed manipulates three tools:

- Open market operations
- Last resort loans
- Required reserve ratio

Open Market Operations An **open market operation** is the purchase or sale of securities by the Fed in the *loanable funds market*. When the Fed buys securities, it pays for them with newly created bank reserves. When the Fed sells securities, the Fed is paid with reserves held by banks. So open market operations directly influence the reserves of banks. By changing the quantity of bank reserves, the Fed changes the quantity of monetary base, which influences the quantity of money.

An Open Market Purchase To see how an open market operation changes bank reserves, suppose the Fed buys $100 million of government securities from the Bank of America. When the Fed makes this transaction, two things happen:

1. The Bank of America has $100 million less securities, and the Fed has $100 million more securities.
2. The Fed pays for the securities by placing $100 million in the Bank of America's deposit account at the Fed.

Figure 25.2 shows the effects of these actions on the balance sheets of the Fed and the Bank of America. Ownership of the securities passes from the

FIGURE 25.2   The Fed Buys Securities in the Open Market

Federal Reserve Bank of New York

Assets (millions)		Liabilities (millions)	
Securities	+$100	Reserves of Bank of America	+$100

The Federal Reserve Bank of New York buys securities from a bank ...

... and pays for the securities by increasing the reserves of the bank

Bank of America

Assets (millions)		Liabilities (millions)	
Securities	–$100		
Reserves	+$100		

When the Fed buys securities in the open market, it creates bank reserves. The Fed's assets and liabilities increase, and the Bank of America exchanges securities for reserves.

 myeconlab animation

Bank of America to the Fed, so the Bank of America's assets decrease by $100 million and the Fed's assets increase by $100 million, as shown by the blue arrow running from the Bank of America to the Fed.

The Fed pays for the securities by placing $100 million in the Bank of America's reserve account at the Fed, as shown by the green arrow running from the Fed to the Bank of America.

The Fed's assets and liabilities increase by $100 million. The Bank of America's total assets are unchanged: It sold securities to increase its reserves.

An Open Market Sale If the Fed sells $100 million of government securities to the Bank of America in the open market:

1. The Bank of America has $100 million more securities, and the Fed has $100 million less securities.

2. The Bank of America pays for the securities by using $100 million of its reserve deposit at the Fed.

You can follow the effects of these actions on the balance sheets of the Fed and the Bank of America by reversing the arrows and the plus and minus signs in Fig. 25.2. Ownership of the securities passes from the Fed to the Bank of America, so the Fed's assets decrease by $100 million and the Bank of America's assets increase by $100 million.

Economics in Action
The Fed's Balance Sheet Explodes

The Fed's balance sheet underwent some remarkable changes during the financial crisis of 2007–2008 and the recession that the crisis triggered. The figure shows the effects of these changes on the size and composition of the monetary base by comparing the situation in 2010 with that before the financial crisis began in late 2007.

In a normal year, 2007, the Fed's holding of U.S. government securities is almost as large as the monetary base and the monetary base is composed of almost all currency.

But between 2007 and 2010 the Fed made huge loans to banks and other financial institutions that more than doubled the monetary base. Almost all of this increase was composed of bank reserves.

When, and how quickly, to unwind the large increase in the monetary base and bank reserves was a source of disagreement at the Fed in 2010.

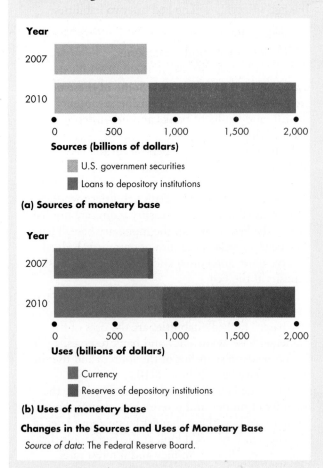

(a) Sources of monetary base

- U.S. government securities
- Loans to depository institutions

(b) Uses of monetary base

- Currency
- Reserves of depository institutions

Changes in the Sources and Uses of Monetary Base

Source of data: The Federal Reserve Board.

The Bank of America uses $100 million of its reserves to pay for the securities.

Both the Fed's assets and liabilities decrease by $100 million. The Bank of America's total assets are unchanged: It has used reserves to buy securities.

The New York Fed conducts these open-market transactions on directions from the FOMC.

Last Resort Loans The Fed is the **lender of last resort**, which means that if a bank is short of reserves, it can borrow from the Fed. But the Fed sets the interest rate on last resort loans and this interest rate is called the *discount rate*.

During the period since August 2007 when the first effects of the financial crisis started to be felt, the Fed has been especially active as lender of last resort and, with the U.S. Treasury, has created a number of new lending facilities and initiatives to prevent banks from failing.

Required Reserve Ratio The **required reserve ratio** is the minimum percentage of deposits that depository institutions are required to hold as reserves. In 2010, required reserves were 3 percent of checking deposits between $10.7 million and $55.2 million and 10 percent of checking deposits in excess of $55.2 million. If the Fed requires the banks to hold more reserves, they must cut their lending.

REVIEW QUIZ

1 What is the central bank of the United States and what functions does it perform?

2 What is the monetary base and how does it relate to the Fed's balance sheet?

3 What are the Fed's three policy tools?

4 What is the Federal Open Market Committee and what are its main functions?

5 How does an open market operation change the monetary base?

You can work these questions in Study Plan 25.3 and get instant feedback.

Next, we're going to see how the banking system—the banks and the Fed—creates money and how the quantity of money changes when the Fed changes the monetary base.

◆ How Banks Create Money

Banks create money. But this doesn't mean that they have smoke-filled back rooms in which counterfeiters are busily working. Remember, money is both currency and bank deposits. What banks create is deposits, and they do so by making loans.

Creating Deposits by Making Loans

The easiest way to see that banks create deposits is to think about what happens when Andy, who has a Visa card issued by Citibank, uses his card to buy a tank of gas from Chevron. When Andy signs the card sales slip, he takes a loan from Citibank and obligates himself to repay the loan at a later date. At the end of the business day, a Chevron clerk takes a pile of signed credit card sales slips, including Andy's, to Chevron's bank. For now, let's assume that Chevron also banks at Citibank. The bank immediately credits Chevron's account with the value of the slips (minus the bank's commission).

You can see that these transactions have created a bank deposit and a loan. Andy has increased the size of his loan (his credit card balance), and Chevron has increased the size of its bank deposit. Because bank deposits are money, Citibank has created money.

If, as we've just assumed, Andy and Chevron use the same bank, no further transactions take place. But the outcome is essentially the same when two banks are involved. If Chevron's bank is Bank of America, then Citibank uses its reserves to pay Bank of America. Citibank has an increase in loans and a decrease in reserves; Bank of America has an increase in reserves and an increase in deposits. The banking system as a whole has an increase in loans and deposits but no change in reserves.

If Andy had swiped his card at an automatic payment pump, all these transactions would have occurred at the time he filled his tank, and the quantity of money would have increased by the amount of his purchase (minus the bank's commission for conducting the transactions).

Three factors limit the quantity of loans and deposits that the banking system can create through transactions like Andy's. They are:

- The monetary base
- Desired reserves
- Desired currency holding

The Monetary Base You've seen that the *monetary base* is the sum of Federal Reserve notes, coins, and banks' deposits at the Fed. The size of the monetary base limits the total quantity of money that the banking system can create. The reason is that banks have a desired level of reserves, households and firms have a desired holding of currency, and both of these desired holdings of the monetary base depend on the quantity of deposits.

Desired Reserves A bank's *desired reserves* are the reserves that it *plans* to hold. They contrast with a bank's *required reserves*, which is the minimum quantity of reserves that a bank *must* hold.

The quantity of desired reserves depends on the level of deposits and is determined by the **desired reserve ratio**—the ratio of reserves to deposits that the banks *plan* to hold. The *desired* reserve ratio exceeds the *required* reserve ratio by an amount that the banks determine to be prudent on the basis of their daily business requirements and in the light of the current outlook in financial markets.

Desired Currency Holding The proportions of money held as currency and bank deposits—the ratio of currency to deposits— depend on how households and firms choose to make payments: Whether they plan to use currency or debit cards and checks.

Choices about how to make payments change slowly so the ratio of desired currency to deposits also changes slowly, and at any given time this ratio is fixed. If bank deposits increase, desired currency holding also increases. For this reason, when banks make loans that increase deposits, some currency leaves the banks—the banking system leaks reserves. We call the leakage of bank reserves into currency the *currency drain*, and we call the ratio of currency to deposits the **currency drain ratio**.

We've sketched the way that a loan creates a deposit and described the three factors that limit the amount of loans and deposits that can be created. We're now going to examine the money creation process more closely and discover a money multiplier.

The Money Creation Process

The money creation process begins with an increase in the monetary base, which occurs if the Fed conducts an open market operation in which it buys securities from banks and other institutions. The Fed pays for the securities it buys with newly created bank reserves.

When the Fed buys securities from a bank, the bank's reserves increase but its deposits don't change. So the bank has excess reserves. A bank's **excess reserves** are its actual reserves minus its desired reserves.

When a bank has excess reserves, it makes loans and creates deposits. When the entire banking system has excess reserves, total loans and deposits increase and the quantity of money increases.

One bank can make a loan and get rid of excess reserves. But the banking system as a whole can't get rid of excess reserves so easily. When the banks make loans and create deposits, the extra deposits lower excess reserves for two reasons. First, the increase in deposits increases desired reserves. Second, a currency drain decreases total reserves. But excess reserves don't completely disappear. So the banks lend some more and the process repeats.

As the process of making loans and increasing deposits repeats, desired reserves increase, total reserves decrease through the currency drain, and eventually enough new deposits have been created to use all the new monetary base.

Figure 25.3 summarizes one round in the process we've just described. The sequence has the following eight steps:

1. Banks have excess reserves.

2. Banks lend excess reserves.

3. The quantity of money increases.

4. New money is used to make payments.

5. Some of the new money remains on deposit.

6. Some of the new money is a *currency drain*.

7. Desired reserves increase because deposits have increased.

8. Excess reserves decrease.

If the Fed *sells* securities in an open market operation, then banks have negative excess reserves— they are short of reserves. When the banks are short of reserves, loans and deposits decrease and the process we've described above works in a downward direction until desired reserves plus desired currency holding has decreased by an amount equal to the decrease in monetary base.

A money multiplier determines the change in the quantity of money that results from a change in the monetary base.

FIGURE 25.3   How the Banking System Creates Money by Making Loans

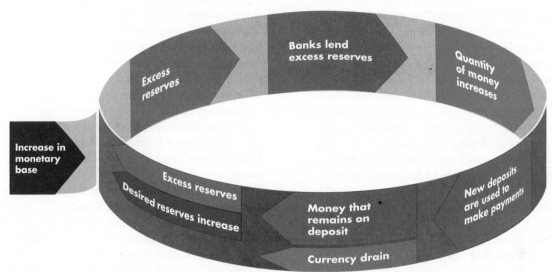

The Federal Reserve increases the monetary base, which increases bank reserves and creates excess reserves. Banks lend the excess reserves, which creates new deposits. The quantity of money increases. New deposits are used to make payments. Some of the new money remains on deposit at banks and some leaves the banks in a currency drain. The increase in bank deposits increases banks' desired reserves. But the banks still have excess reserves, though less than before. The process repeats until excess reserves have been eliminated.

 myeconlab animation

The Money Multiplier

The **money multiplier** is the ratio of the change in the quantity of money to the change in monetary base. For example, if a $1 million increase in the monetary base increases the quantity of money by $2.5 million, then the money multiplier is 2.5.

The smaller the banks' desired reserve ratio and the smaller the currency drain ratio, the larger is the money multiplier. (See the Mathematical Note on pp. 610–611 for details on the money multiplier).

◆ REVIEW QUIZ

1 How do banks create money?
2 What limits the quantity of money that the banking system can create?
3 A bank manager tells you that she doesn't create money. She just lends the money that people deposit. Explain why she's wrong.

You can work these questions in Study Plan 25.4 and get instant feedback. myeconlab

Economics in Action
The Variable Money Multipliers

We can measure the money multiplier, other things remaining the same, as the ratio of the quantity of money (M1 or M2) to the monetary base. In normal times, these ratios (and the money multipliers) change slowly.

In the early 1990s, the M1 multiplier—the ratio of M1 to the monetary base—was about 3 and the M2 multiplier—the ratio of M2 to the monetary base—was about 12. Through the 1990s and 2000s, the currency drain ratio gradually increased and the money multipliers decreased. By 2007 the M1 multiplier was 2 and the M2 multiplier was 9.

Then, in 2008 and 2009 when the Fed increased the monetary base by an unprecedented $1 trillion, almost all of the newly created reserves were willingly held by the banks. In an environment of enormous uncertainty, desired reserves increased by an amount similar to the increase in actual reserves. The quantity of money barely changed.

The Money Market

There is no limit to the amount of money we would like to *receive* in payment for our labor or as interest on our savings. But there *is* a limit to how big an inventory of money we would like to *hold* and neither spend nor use to buy assets that generate an income. The *quantity of money demanded* is the inventory of money that people plan to hold on any given day. It is the quantity of money in our wallets and in our deposit accounts at banks. The quantity of money held must equal the quantity supplied, and the forces that bring about this equality in the money market have powerful effects on the economy, as you will see in the rest of this chapter.

But first, we need to explain what determines the amount of money that people plan to hold.

The Influences on Money Holding

The quantity of money that people plan to hold depends on four main factors:

- The price level
- The *nominal* interest rate
- Real GDP
- Financial innovation

The Price Level The quantity of money measured in dollars is *nominal money*. The quantity of nominal money demanded is proportional to the price level, other things remaining the same. If the price level rises by 10 percent, people hold 10 percent more nominal money than before, other things remaining the same. If you hold $20 to buy your weekly movies and soda, you will increase your money holding to $22 if the prices of movies and soda—and your wage rate—increase by 10 percent.

The quantity of money measured in constant dollars (for example, in 2005 dollars) is real money. *Real money* is equal to nominal money divided by the price level and is the quantity of money measured in terms of what it will buy. In the above example, when the price level rises by 10 percent and you increase your money holding by 10 percent, your *real* money holding is constant. Your $22 at the new price level buys the same quantity of goods and is the same quantity of *real money* as your $20 at the original price level. The quantity of real money demanded is independent of the price level.

The *Nominal* Interest Rate A fundamental principle of economics is that as the opportunity cost of something increases, people try to find substitutes for it. Money is no exception. The higher the opportunity cost of holding money, other things remaining the same, the smaller is the quantity of real money demanded. The nominal interest rate on other assets minus the nominal interest rate on money is the opportunity cost of holding money.

The interest rate that you earn on currency and checking deposits is zero. So the opportunity cost of holding these items is the nominal interest rate on other assets such as a savings bond or Treasury bill. By holding money instead, you forgo the interest that you otherwise would have received.

Money loses value because of inflation, so why isn't the inflation rate part of the cost of holding money? It is. Other things remaining the same, the higher the expected inflation rate, the higher is the nominal interest rate.

Real GDP The quantity of money that households and firms plan to hold depends on the amount they are spending. The quantity of money demanded in the economy as a whole depends on aggregate expenditure—real GDP.

Again, suppose that you hold an average of $20 to finance your weekly purchases of movies and soda. Now imagine that the prices of these goods and of all other goods remain constant but that your income increases. As a consequence, you now buy more goods and services and you also keep a larger amount of money on hand to finance your higher volume of expenditure.

Financial Innovation Technological change and the arrival of new financial products influence the quantity of money held. Financial innovations include

1. Daily interest checking deposits
2. Automatic transfers between checking and saving deposits
3. Automatic teller machines
4. Credit cards and debit cards
5. Internet banking and bill paying

These innovations have occurred because of the development of computing power that has lowered the cost of calculations and record keeping.

We summarize the effects of the influences on money holding by using a demand for money curve.

The Demand for Money

The **demand for money** is the relationship between the quantity of real money demanded and the nominal interest rate when all other influences on the amount of money that people wish to hold remain the same.

Figure 25.4 shows a demand for money curve, *MD*. When the interest rate rises, other things remaining the same, the opportunity cost of holding money rises and the quantity of real money demanded decreases—there is a movement up along the demand for money curve. Similarly, when the interest rate falls, the opportunity cost of holding money falls, and the quantity of real money demanded increases—there is a movement down along the demand for money curve.

When any influence on money holding other than the interest rate changes, there is a change in the demand for money and the demand for money curve shifts. Let's study these shifts.

Shifts in the Demand for Money Curve

A change in real GDP or financial innovation changes the demand for money and shifts the demand for money curve.

Figure 25.5 illustrates the change in the demand for money. A decrease in real GDP decreases the demand for money and shifts the demand for money curve leftward from MD_0 to MD_1. An increase in real GDP has the opposite effect: It increases the demand for money and shifts the demand for money curve rightward from MD_0 to MD_2.

The influence of financial innovation on the demand for money curve is more complicated. It decreases the demand for currency and might increase the demand for some types of deposits and decrease the demand for others. But generally, financial innovation decreases the demand for money.

Changes in real GDP and financial innovation have brought large shifts in the demand for money in the United States.

FIGURE 25.4   The Demand for Money

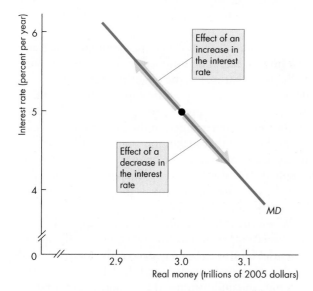

The demand for money curve, *MD*, shows the relationship between the quantity of real money that people plan to hold and the nominal interest rate, other things remaining the same. The interest rate is the opportunity cost of holding money. A change in the interest rate brings a movement along the demand for money curve.

myeconlab animation

FIGURE 25.5   Changes in the Demand for Money

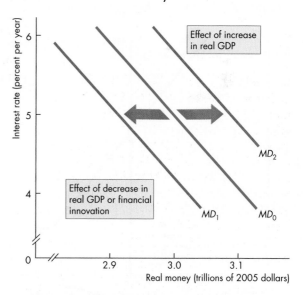

A decrease in real GDP decreases the demand for money. The demand for money curve shifts leftward from MD_0 to MD_1. An increase in real GDP increases the demand for money. The demand for money curve shifts rightward from MD_0 to MD_2. Financial innovation generally decreases the demand for money.

myeconlab animation

Money Market Equilibrium

You now know what determines the demand for money, and you've seen how the banking system creates money. Let's now see how the money market reaches an equilibrium.

Money market equilibrium occurs when the quantity of money demanded equals the quantity of money supplied. The adjustments that occur to bring money market equilibrium are fundamentally different in the short run and the long run.

Short-Run Equilibrium The quantity of money supplied is determined by the actions of the banks and the Fed. As the Fed adjusts the quantity of money, the interest rate changes.

In Fig. 25.6, the Fed uses open market operations to make the quantity of real money supplied $3.0 trillion and the supply of money curve *MS*. With demand for money curve *MD*, the equilibrium interest rate is 5 percent a year.

If the interest rate were 4 percent a year, people would want to hold more money than is available.

FIGURE 25.6   Money Market Equilibrium

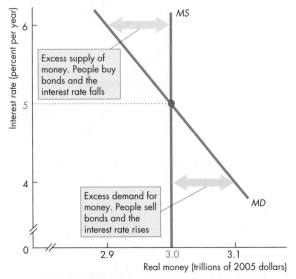

Money market equilibrium occurs when the quantity of money demanded equals the quantity supplied. In the short run, real GDP determines the demand for money curve, *MD*, and the Fed determines the quantity of real money supplied and the supply of money curve, *MS*. The interest rate adjusts to achieve equilibrium, here 5 percent a year.

myeconlab animation

They would sell bonds, bid down their price, and the interest rate would rise. If the interest rate were 6 percent a year, people would want to hold less money than is available. They would buy bonds, bid up their price, and the interest rate would fall.

The Short-Run Effect of a Change in the Supply of Money Starting from a short-run equilibrium, if the Fed increases the quantity of money, people find themselves holding more money than the quantity demanded. With a surplus of money holding, people enter the loanable funds market and buy bonds. The increase in demand for bonds raises the price of a bond and lowers the interest rate (refresh your memory by looking at Chapter 24, p. 570).

If the Fed decreases the quantity of money, people find themselves holding less money than the quantity demanded. They now enter the loanable funds market to sell bonds. The decrease in the demand for bonds lowers their price and raises the interest rate.

Figure 25.7 illustrates the effects of the changes in the quantity of money that we've just described. When the supply of money curve shifts rightward from MS_0 to MS_1, the interest rate falls to 4 percent a year; when the supply of money curve shifts leftward to MS_2, the interest rate rises to 6 percent a year.

Long-Run Equilibrium You've just seen how the nominal interest rate is determined in the money market at the level that makes the quantity of money demanded equal the quantity supplied by the Fed. You learned in Chapter 24 (on p. 574) that the real interest rate is determined in the loanable funds market at the level that makes the quantity of loanable funds demanded equal the quantity of loanable funds supplied. You also learned in Chapter 24 (on p. 571) that the real interest rate equals the nominal interest rate minus the inflation rate.

When the inflation rate equals the expected (or forecasted) inflation rate and when real GDP equals potential GDP, the money market, the loanable funds market, the goods market, and the labor market are in long-run equilibrium—the economy is in long-run equilibrium.

If in long-run equilibrium, the Fed increases the quantity of money, eventually a new long-run equilibrium is reached in which nothing real has changed. Real GDP, employment, the real quantity of money, and the real interest rate all return to their original levels. But something does change: the price level. The price level rises by the same percentage as the rise

FIGURE 25.7 A Change in the Supply of Money

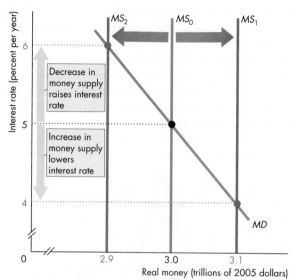

An increase in the supply of money shifts the supply of money curve from MS_0 to MS_1 and the interest rate falls. A decrease in the supply of money shifts the supply of money curve from MS_0 to MS_2 and the interest rate rises.

myeconlab animation

in the quantity of money. Why does this outcome occur in the long run?

The reason is that real GDP and employment are determined by the demand for labor, the supply of labor, and the production function—the real forces described in Chapter 23 (pp. 545–547); and the real interest rate is determined by the demand for and supply of (real) loanable funds—the real forces described in Chapter 24 (pp. 572–574). The only variable that is free to respond to a change in the supply of money in the long run is the price level. The price level adjusts to make the quantity of real money supplied equal to the quantity demanded.

So when the Fed changes the nominal quantity of money, in the long run the price level changes by a percentage equal to the percentage change in the quantity of nominal money. In the long run, the change in the price level is proportional to the change in the quantity of money.

The Transition from the Short Run to the Long Run

How does the economy move from the first short-run response to an increase in the quantity of money to the long-run response?

The adjustment process is lengthy and complex. Here, we'll only provide a sketch of the process. A more thorough account must wait until you've studied Chapter 26.

We start out in long-run equilibrium and the Fed increases the quantity of money by 10 percent. Here are the steps in what happens next.

First, the nominal interest rate falls (just like you saw on p. 604 and in Fig. 25.6). The real interest rate falls too, as people try to get rid of their excess money holdings and buy bonds.

With a lower real interest rate, people want to borrow and spend more. Firms want to borrow to invest and households want to borrow to invest in bigger homes or to buy more consumer goods.

The increase in the demand for goods cannot be met by an increase in supply because the economy is already at full employment. So there is a general shortage of all kinds of goods and services.

The shortage of goods and services forces the price level to rise.

As the price level rises, the real quantity of money decreases. The decrease in the quantity of real money raises the nominal interest rate and the real interest rate. As the interest rate rises, spending plans are cut back, and eventually the original full-employment equilibrium is restored. At the new long-run equilibrium, the price level has risen by 10 percent and nothing real has changed.

REVIEW QUIZ

1 What are the main influences on the quantity of real money that people and businesses plan to hold?

2 Show the effects of a change in the nominal interest rate and a change in real GDP using the demand for money curve.

3 How is money market equilibrium determined in the short run?

4 How does a change in the supply of money change the interest rate in the short run?

5 How does a change in the supply of money change the interest rate in the long run?

You can work these questions in Study Plan 25.5 and get instant feedback.  myeconlab

Let's explore the long-run link between money and the price level a bit further.

The Quantity Theory of Money

In the long run, the price level adjusts to make the quantity of real money demanded equal the quantity supplied. A special theory of the price level and inflation—the quantity theory of money—explains this long-run adjustment of the price level.

The **quantity theory of money** is the proposition that in the long run, an increase in the quantity of money brings an equal percentage increase in the price level. To explain the quantity theory of money, we first need to define *the velocity of circulation*.

The **velocity of circulation** is the average number of times a dollar of money is used annually to buy the goods and services that make up GDP. But GDP equals the price level (P) multiplied by *real* GDP (Y). That is,

$$GDP = PY.$$

Call the quantity of money M. The velocity of circulation, V, is determined by the equation

$$V = PY/M.$$

For example, if GDP is $1,000 billion ($PY$ = $1,000 billion) and the quantity of money is $250 billion, then the velocity of circulation is 4.

From the definition of the velocity of circulation, the *equation of exchange* tells us how M, V, P, and Y are connected. This equation is

$$MV = PY.$$

Given the definition of the velocity of circulation, the equation of exchange is always true—it is true by definition. It becomes the quantity theory of money if the quantity of money does not influence the velocity of circulation or real GDP. In this case, the equation of exchange tells us that in the long run, the price level is determined by the quantity of money. That is,

$$P = M(V/Y),$$

where (V/Y) is independent of M. So a change in M brings a proportional change in P.

We can also express the equation of exchange in growth rates,[1] in which form it states that

$$\begin{array}{c}\text{Money} \\ \text{growth rate}\end{array} + \begin{array}{c}\text{Rate of} \\ \text{velocity} \\ \text{change}\end{array} = \begin{array}{c}\text{Inflation} \\ \text{rate}\end{array} + \begin{array}{c}\text{Real GDP} \\ \text{growth rate}\end{array}$$

Economics in Action

Does the Quantity Theory Work?

On average, as predicted by the quantity theory of money, the inflation rate fluctuates in line with fluctuations in the money growth rate minus the real GDP growth rate. Figure 1 shows the relationship between money growth (M2 definition) and inflation in the United States. You can see a clear relationship between the two variables.

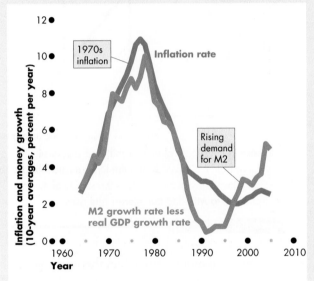

Figure 1 U.S. Money Growth and Inflation

Sources of data: Federal Reserve and Bureau of Labor Statistics.

Solving this equation for the inflation rate gives

$$\begin{array}{c}\text{Inflation} \\ \text{rate}\end{array} = \begin{array}{c}\text{Money} \\ \text{growth rate}\end{array} + \begin{array}{c}\text{Rate of} \\ \text{velocity} \\ \text{change}\end{array} - \begin{array}{c}\text{Real GDP} \\ \text{growth rate}\end{array}$$

In the long run, the rate of velocity change is not influenced by the money growth rate. More strongly, in the long run, the rate of velocity change is approxi-

---

[1] To obtain this equation, begin with
$$MV = PY.$$
Then changes in these variables are related by the equation
$$\Delta MV + M\Delta V = \Delta PY + P\Delta Y.$$
Divide this equation by the equation of exchange to obtain
$$\Delta M/M + \Delta V/V = \Delta P/P + \Delta Y/Y.$$
The term $\Delta M/M$ is the money growth rate, $\Delta V/V$ is the rate of velocity change, $\Delta P/P$ is the inflation rate, and $\Delta Y/Y$ is the real GDP growth rate.

International data also support the quantity theory. Figure 2 shows a scatter diagram of the inflation rate and the money growth rate in 134 countries and Fig. 3 shows the inflation rate and money growth rate in countries with inflation rates below 20 percent a year. You can see a general tendency for money growth and inflation to be correlated, but the quantity theory (the red line) does not predict inflation precisely.

The correlation between money growth and inflation isn't perfect, and the correlation does not tell us that money growth *causes* inflation. Money growth might cause inflation; inflation might cause money growth; or some third variable might cause both inflation and money growth. Other evidence does confirm, though, that causation runs from money growth to inflation.

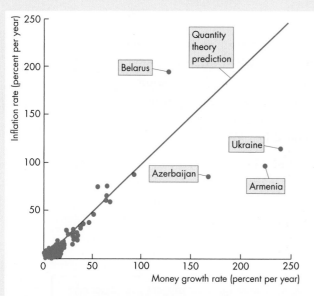

Figure 2   134 Countries: 1990–2005

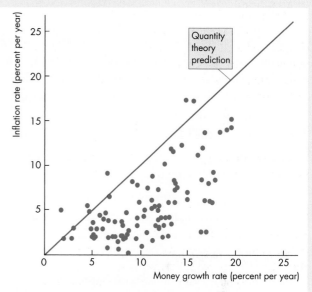

Figure 3   Lower-Inflation Countries: 1990–2005

Sources of data: International Financial Statistics Yearbook, 2008 and International Monetary Fund, *World Economic Outlook*, October, 2008.

mately zero. With this assumption, the inflation rate in the long run is determined as

$$\text{Inflation rate} = \text{Money growth rate} - \text{Real GDP growth rate}.$$

In the long run, fluctuations in the money growth rate minus the real GDP growth rate bring equal fluctuations in the inflation rate.

Also, in the long run, with the economy at full employment, real GDP equals potential GDP, so the real GDP growth rate equals the potential GDP growth rate. This growth rate might be influenced by inflation, but the influence is most likely small and the quantity theory assumes that it is zero. So the real GDP growth rate is given and doesn't change when the money growth rate changes—inflation is correlated with money growth.

REVIEW QUIZ

1   What is the quantity theory of money?
2   How is the velocity of circulation calculated?
3   What is the equation of exchange?
4   Does the quantity theory correctly predict the effects of money growth on inflation?

You can work these questions in Study Plan 25.6 and get instant feedback.

◆ You now know what money is, how the banks create it, and how the quantity of money influences the nominal interest rate in the short run and the price level in the long run. *Reading Between the Lines* on pp. 608–609 looks at the Fed's incredible actions in the recent financial crisis.

Can More Money Keep the Recovery Going?

It Falls to the Fed to Fuel Recovery

The Financial Times
August 30, 2010

The U.S. recovery is stalling. ... The recovery is in danger of petering out altogether. Recent numbers have been dismal. Second-quarter growth was marked down to 1.6 percent on Friday. Earlier, signs of a new crunch in the housing market gave the stock market another pummelling. Already low expectations were disappointed nonetheless: Sales of existing single-family homes in July fell by nearly 30 percent, to their lowest for 15 years. Sales of new homes were at their lowest since the series began to be reported in 1963. ...

At the end of last week, speaking at the Jackson Hole conference, Ben Bernanke, Fed chief, acknowledged the faltering recovery, and reminded his audience that the central bank has untapped capacity for stimulus. The benchmark interest rate is effectively zero, but that leaves quantitative easing (QE) and other unconventional measures. So far as QE goes, the Fed has already pumped trillions of dollars into the economy by buying debt. If it chose, it could pump in trillions more. ...

As the monetary economist Scott Sumner has pointed out, Milton Friedman—name me a less reconstructed monetarist—talked of "the fallacy of identifying tight money with high interest rates and easy money with low interest rates." When long-term nominal interest rates are very low, and inflation expectations are therefore also very low, money is tight in the sense that matters. When money is loose, inflation expectations rise, and so do long-term interest rates. ... Under current circumstances, better to print money and be damned. ...

ESSENCE OF THE STORY

- The 2010 second-quarter real GDP growth rate was a low 1.6 percent a year and home sales were at their lowest since measurement started in 1963.

- Fed Chairman Ben Bernanke agrees the recovery is weak but says the Fed has weapons to fight recession.

- Interest rates are close to zero but the Fed has pumped trillions of dollars into the economy by buying debt (quantitative easing) and the Fed can pump in trillions more.

- Economist Scott Sumner, citing Milton Friedman, says the interest rate that influences spending decisions is the real interest rate and that isn't low when inflation is expected to be low.

- With the U.S. recovery stalling and possibly ending, the Fed should pump in more money.

- Between October 2007 and October 2008, to counter a global financial crisis, the Fed cut the federal funds interest rate to almost zero.

- Between October 2008 and October 2009, the Fed increased the monetary base by an unprecedented $900 billion.

- Between October 2009 and March 2010, the Fed added a further $300 billion to the monetary base—a total increase of $1.2 trillion over 18 months.

- Figure 1 shows these extraordinary increases in the monetary base.

- As you've seen in this chapter, most of the increase in monetary base was willingly held by the banks. They increased their desired reserves.

- These monetary actions by the Fed lowered the interest rates that firms and households pay on very short-term loans, as you can see in Fig. 2.

- But the interest rate on long-term loans that finance business investment barely changed.

- You can see in Fig. 2 that the long-term corporate bond rate (the rate paid by the safest big firms) hovered around 5.5 percent.

- For the Fed's injection of monetary base to lower the long-term corporate bond rate, the banks would have to get into the loanable funds market and start to lend their large volume of reserves.

- As the news article notes, it is the real interest rate, not the nominal interest rate, that influences expenditure. And because for a few months, deflation was expected (a falling price level), the real interest rate spiked upward.

- Figure 3 shows the real interest rate on long-term corporate borrowing.

- Despite massive injections of monetary base (quantitative easing) and powerful effects on the short-term interest rate, it is hard to see the effects of the Fed's actions on the long-term real interest rate.

- Increasing the monetary base further, as advocated in the news article, might lower the long-term real interest rate, but it might alternatively merely add to bank reserves and leave the long-term interest rate unchanged.

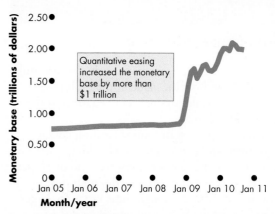

Figure 1 Monetary base

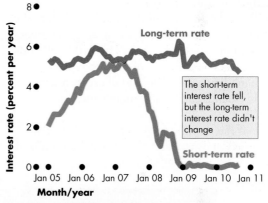

Figure 2 Nominal interest rates

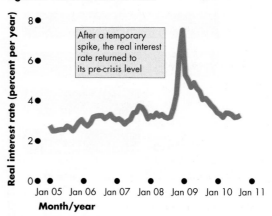

Figure 3 The long-term real interest rate

◆ MATHEMATICAL NOTE

The Money Multiplier

This note explains the basic math of the money multiplier and shows how the value of the multiplier depends on the banks' desired reserve ratio and the currency drain ratio.

To make the process of money creation concrete, we work through an example for a banking system in which each bank has a desired reserve ratio of 10 percent of deposits and the currency drain ratio is 50 percent of deposits. (Although these ratios are larger than the ones in the U.S. economy, they make the process end more quickly and enable you to see more clearly the principles at work.)

The figure keeps track of the numbers. Before the process begins, all the banks have no excess reserves. Then the monetary base increases by $100,000 and one bank has excess reserves of this amount.

The bank lends the $100,000 of excess reserves. When this loan is made, new money increases by $100,000.

Some of the new money will be held as currency and some as deposits. With a currency drain ratio of 50 percent of deposits, one third of the new money will be held as currency and two thirds will be held as deposits. That is, $33,333 drains out of the banks as currency and $66,667 remains in the banks as deposits. The increase in the quantity of money of $100,000 equals the increase in deposits plus the increase in currency holdings.

The increased bank deposits of $66,667 generate an increase in desired reserves of 10 percent of that amount, which is $6,667. Actual reserves have increased by the same amount as the increase in deposits: $66,667. So the banks now have excess reserves of $60,000.

The process we've just described repeats but begins with excess reserves of $60,000. The figure shows the next two rounds. At the end of the process, the quantity of money has increased by a multiple of the increase in the monetary base. In this case, the increase is $250,000, which is 2.5 times the increase in the monetary base.

The sequence in the figure shows the first stages of the process that finally reaches the total shown in the final row of the "money" column.

To calculate what happens at the later stages in the process and the final increase in the quantity of

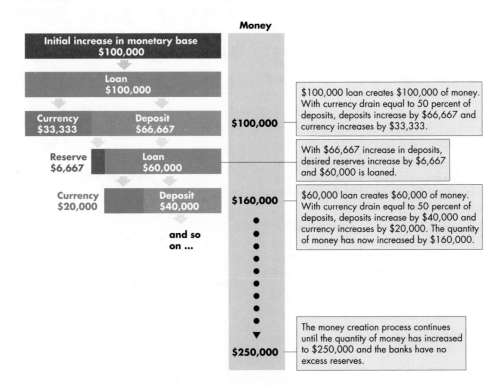

Figure 1 The money creation process

money, look closely at the numbers in the figure. The initial increase in reserves is $100,000 (call it A). At each stage, the loan is 60 percent (0.6) of the previous loan and the quantity of money increases by 0.6 of the previous increase. Call that proportion L ($L = 0.6$). We can write down the complete sequence for the increase in the quantity of money as

$$A + AL + AL^2 + AL^3 + AL^4 + AL^5 + \dots \,.$$

Remember, L is a fraction, so at each stage in this sequence, the amount of new loans and new money gets smaller. The total value of loans made and money created at the end of the process is the sum of the sequence, which is[1]

$$A/(1 - L).$$

If we use the numbers from the example, the total increase in the quantity of money is

$100,000 + 60,000 + 36,000 + \dots$

$= \$100,000 \, (1 + 0.6 + 0.36 + \dots)$

$= \$100,000 \, (1 + 0.6 + 0.6^2 + \dots)$

$= \$100,000 \times 1/(1 - 0.6)$

$= \$100,000 \times 1/(0.4)$

$= \$100,000 \times 2.5$

$= \$250,000.$

The magnitude of the money multiplier depends on the desired reserve ratio and the currency drain ratio. Let's explore this relationship

The money multiplier is the ratio of money to the monetary base. Call the money multiplier mm, the quantity of money M, and the monetary base MB.

---

[1] The sequence of values is called a convergent geometric series. To find the sum of a series such as this, begin by calling the sum S. Then write the sum as

$$S = A + AL + AL^2 + AL^3 + AL^4 + AL^5 + \dots \,.$$

Multiply by L to get

$$LS = AL + AL^2 + AL^3 + AL^4 + AL^5 + \dots$$

and then subtract the second equation from the first to get

$$S(1 - L) = A$$

or

$$S = A/(1 - L).$$

Then

$$mm = M/MB.$$

Next recall that money, M, is the sum of deposits and currency. Call deposits D and currency C. Then

$$M = D + C.$$

Finally, recall that the monetary base, MB, is the sum of banks' reserves and currency. Call banks' reserves R. Then

$$MB = R + C.$$

Use the equations for M and MB in the mm equation to give:

$$mm = M/MB = (D + C)/(R + C).$$

Now divide all the variables on the right side of the equation by D to give:

$$mm = M/MB = (1 + C/D)/(R/D + C/D).$$

In this equation, C/D is the currency drain ratio and R/D is the banks' reserve ratio. If we use the values in the example on the previous page, C/D is 0.5 and R/D is 0.1, and

$$mm = (1 + 0.5)/(0.1 + 0.5).$$

$$= 1.5/0.6 = 2.5.$$

The U.S. Money Multiplier

The money multiplier in the United States can be found by using the formula above along with the values of C/D and R/D in the U.S. economy.

Because we have two definitions of money, M1 and M2, we have two money multipliers. Call the M1 deposits $D1$ and call the M2 deposits $D2$.

The numbers for M1 in 2010 are $C/D1 = 1.06$ and $R/D1 = 1.32$. So

M1 multiplier $= (1 + 1.06)/(1.32 + 1.06) = 0.87.$

For M2 in 2010, $C/D2 = 0.11$ and $R/D2 = 0.14$, so

M2 multiplier $= (1 + 0.11)/(0.14 + 0.11) = 4.44.$

SUMMARY

Key Points

What Is Money? (pp. 590–592)

- Money is the means of payment. It functions as a medium of exchange, a unit of account, and a store of value.
- Today, money consists of currency and deposits.

Working Problems 1 to 4 will give you a better understanding of what money is.

Depository Institutions (pp. 593–595)

- Commercial banks, S&Ls, savings banks, credit unions, and money market mutual funds are depository institutions whose deposits are money.
- Depository institutions provide four main economic services: They create liquidity, minimize the cost of obtaining funds, minimize the cost of monitoring borrowers, and pool risks.

Working Problems 5 and 6 will give you a better understanding of depository institutions.

The Federal Reserve System (pp. 596–599)

- The Federal Reserve System is the central bank of the United States.
- The Fed influences the quantity of money by setting the required reserve ratio, making last resort loans, and by conducting open market operations.
- When the Fed buys securities in an open market operation, the monetary base increases; when the Fed sells securities, the monetary base decreases.

Working Problems 7 to 9 will give you a better understanding of the Federal Reserve System

How Banks Create Money (pp. 599–601)

- Banks create money by making loans.
- The total quantity of money that can be created depends on the monetary base, the desired reserve ratio, and the currency drain ratio.

Working Problems 10 to 14 will give you a better understanding of how banks create money.

The Money Market (pp. 602–605)

- The quantity of money demanded is the amount of money that people plan to hold.
- The quantity of real money equals the quantity of nominal money divided by the price level.
- The quantity of real money demanded depends on the nominal interest rate, real GDP, and financial innovation.
- The nominal interest rate makes the quantity of money demanded equal the quantity supplied.
- When the Fed increases the supply of money, the nominal interest rate falls (the short-run effect).
- In the long run, when the Fed increases the supply of money, the price level rises and the nominal interest rate returns to its initial level.

Working Problems 15 and 16 will give you a better understanding of the money market.

The Quantity Theory of Money (pp. 606–607)

- The quantity theory of money is the proposition that money growth and inflation move up and down together in the long run.

Working Problem 17 will give you a better understanding of the quantity theory of money.

Key Terms

Central bank, 596
Currency, 591
Currency drain ratio, 600
Demand for money, 603
Depository institution, 593
Desired reserve ratio, 600
Excess reserves, 600
Federal funds rate, 593

Federal Open Market
    Committee, 596
Federal Reserve System
    (the Fed), 596
Lender of last resort, 599
M1, 591
M2, 591
Means of payment, 590

Monetary base, 597
Money, 590
Money multiplier, 601
Open market operation, 597
Quantity theory of money, 606
Required reserve ratio, 599
Reserves, 593
Velocity of circulation, 606

STUDY PLAN PROBLEMS AND APPLICATIONS

myeconlab You can work Problems 1 to 19 in MyEconLab Chapter 25 Study Plan and get instant feedback.

What Is Money? (Study Plan 25.1)

1. In the United States today, money includes which of the following items?
   a. Federal Reserve bank notes in Citibank's cash machines
   b. Your Visa card
   c. Coins inside a vending machine
   d. U.S. dollar bills in your wallet
   e. The check you have just written to pay for your rent
   f. The loan you took out last August to pay for your school fees

2. In June 2009, currency held by individuals and businesses was $853 billion; traveler's checks were $5 billion; checkable deposits owned by individuals and businesses were $792 billion; savings deposits were $4,472 billion; time deposits were $1281 billion; and money market funds and other deposits were $968 billion. Calculate M1 and M2 in June 2009.

3. In June 2008, M1 was $1,394 billion; M2 was $7,681 billion; checkable deposits owned by individuals and businesses were $619 billion; time deposits were $1,209 billion; and money market funds and other deposits were $1,057 billion. Calculate currency and traveler's checks held by individuals and businesses and calculate savings deposits.

4. **One More Thing Cell Phones Could Do: Replace Wallets**
   Soon you'll be able to pull out your cell phone and wave it over a scanner to make a payment. The convenience of whipping out your phone as a payment mechanism is driving the transition.
   Source: *USA Today*, November 21, 2007
   If people can use their cell phones to make payments, will currency disappear? How will the components of M1 change?

Depository Institutions (Study Plan 25.2)

Use the following news clip to work Problems 5 and 6.

Regulators Give Bleak Forecast for Banks
Regulators said that they were bracing for an uptick in the number of bank failures. The Fed declined to comment on the health of specific companies but said that Wall Street firms have learned a great deal from Bear Stearns and have reduced leverage and built up their liquidity. Today, investment banks are stronger than they were a month-and-a-half ago.
Source: CNN, June 5, 2008

5. Explain a bank's "balancing act" and how the over-pursuit of profit or underestimation of risk can lead to a bank failure.

6. During a time of uncertainty, why might it be necessary for a bank to build up its liquidity?

The Federal Reserve System (Study Plan 25.3)

7. Suppose that at the end of December 2009, the monetary base in the United States was $700 billion, Federal Reserve notes were $650 billion, and banks' reserves at the Fed were $20 billion. Calculate the quantity of coins.

8. **Risky Assets: Counting to a Trillion**
   Prior to the financial crisis, the Fed held less than $1 trillion in assets and most were in safe U.S. government securities. By mid-December 2008, the Fed's balance sheet had increased to over $2.3 trillion. The massive expansion began when the Fed rolled out its lending program: sending banks cash in exchange for risky assets.
   Source: CNNMoney, September 29, 2009
   What are the Fed's policy tools and which policy tool did the Fed use to increase its assets to $2.3 trillion in 2008?

9. The FOMC sells $20 million of securities to Wells Fargo. Enter the transactions that take place to show the changes in the following balance sheets.

Federal Reserve Bank of New York

Assets (millions)	Liabilities (millions)

Wells Fargo

Assets (millions)	Liabilities (millions)

How Banks Create Money (Study Plan 25.4)

10. The commercial banks in Zap have

Reserves	$250 million
Loans	$1,000 million
Deposits	$2,000 million
Total assets	$2,500 million

    If the banks hold no excess reserves, calculate their desired reserve ratio.

Use the following information to work Problems 11 and 12.

In the economy of Nocoin, banks have deposits of $300 billion. Their reserves are $15 billion, two thirds of which is in deposits with the central bank. Households and firms hold $30 billion in bank notes. There are no coins!

11. Calculate the monetary base and the quantity of money.

12. Calculate the banks' desired reserve ratio and the currency drain ratio (as percentages).

Use the following news clip to work Problems 13 and 14.

Banks Drop on Higher Reserve Requirement

China's central bank will raise its reserve ratio requirement by a percentage point to a record 17.5 percent, stepping up a battle to contain lending growth. Banks' ratio of excess reserves to deposits was 2 percent. Every half-point increase in the required reserve ratio cuts banks' profits by 1.5 percent.

Source: *People's Daily Online*, June 11, 2008

13. Explain how increasing the required reserve ratio impacts banks' money creation process.

14. Why might a higher required reserve ratio decrease bank profits?

The Money Market (Study Plan 25.5)

15. The spreadsheet provides information about the demand for money in Minland. Column A is the nominal interest rate, r. Columns B and C show

	A	B	C
1	r	Y_0	Y_1
2	7	1.0	1.5
3	6	1.5	2.0
4	5	2.0	2.5
5	4	2.5	3.0
6	3	3.0	3.5
7	2	3.5	4.0
8	1	4.0	4.5

the quantity of money demanded at two values of real GDP: Y_0 is $10 billion and Y_1 is $20 billion. The quantity of money supplied is $3 billion. Initially, real GDP is $20 billion. What happens in Minland if the interest rate (i) exceeds 4 percent a year and (ii) is less than 4 percent a year?

16. The figure shows the demand for money curve.

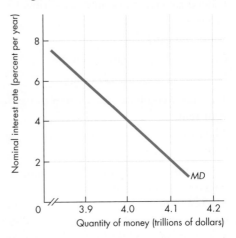

If the Fed decreases the quantity of real money supplied from $4 trillion to $3.9 trillion, explain how the price of a bond will change.

The Quantity Theory of Money (Study Plan 25.6)

17. Quantecon is a country in which the quantity theory of money operates. In year 1, the economy is at full employment and real GDP is $400 million, the price level is 200, and the velocity of circulation is 20. In year 2, the quantity of money increases by 20 percent. Calculate the quantity of money, the price level, real GDP, and the velocity of circulation in year 2.

Mathematical Note (Study Plan 25.MN)

18. In Problem 11, the banks have no excess reserves. Suppose that the Bank of Nocoin, the central bank, increases bank reserves by $0.5 billion.
    a. What happens to the quantity of money?
    b. Explain why the change in the quantity of money is not equal to the change in the monetary base.
    c. Calculate the money multiplier.

19. In Problem 11, the banks have no excess reserves. Suppose that the Bank of Nocoin, the central bank, decreases bank reserves by $0.5 billion.
    a. Calculate the money multiplier.
    b. What happens to the quantity of money, deposits, and currency?

ADDITIONAL PROBLEMS AND APPLICATIONS

What Is Money?

20. Sara withdraws $1,000 from her savings account at the Lucky S&L, keeps $50 in cash, and deposits the balance in her checking account at the Bank of Illinois. What is the immediate change in M1 and M2?

21. Rapid inflation in Brazil in the early 1990s caused the cruzeiro to lose its ability to function as money. Which of the following commodities would most likely have taken the place of the cruzeiro in the Brazilian economy? Explain why.
    a. Tractor parts
    b. Packs of cigarettes
    c. Loaves of bread
    d. Impressionist paintings
    e. Baseball trading cards

22. **From Paper-Clip to House, in 14 Trades**

    A 26-year-old Montreal man appears to have succeeded in his quest to barter a single, red paper-clip all the way up to a house. It took almost a year and 14 trades. ...

    Source: *CBC News*, 7 July 2006

    Is barter a means of payment? Is it just as efficient as money when trading on e-Bay? Explain.

Depository Institutions

Use the following news clip to work Problems 23 and 24.

What Bad Banking Means to You

Bad news about the banking industry makes you wonder about the safety of your cash in the bank. Regulators expect 100–200 bank failures over the next 12–24 months. Expected loan losses, the deteriorating housing market, and the credit squeeze are blamed for the drop in bank profits. The number of institutions classed as "problem" institutions was at 76 at the end of 2007, but, to put that number in perspective, at the end of the banking crisis in 1992 1,063 banks were on that "trouble" list. One thing that will save your money if your bank goes under is FDIC insurance. The FDIC insures deposits in banks and thrift institutions and it maintains that not one depositor has lost a single cent of insured funds as a result of a bank failure since it was created in 1934.

Source: CNN, February 28, 2008

23. Explain how attempts by banks to maximize profits can sometimes lead to bank failures.

24. How does FDIC insurance help minimize bank failures and bring more stability to the banking system?

The Federal Reserve System

25. Explain the distinction between a central bank and a commercial bank.

26. If the Fed makes an open market sale of $1 million of securities to a bank, what initial changes occur in the economy?

27. Set out the transactions that the Fed undertakes to increase the quantity of money.

28. Describe the Fed's assets and liabilities. What is the monetary base and how does it relate to the Fed's balance sheet?

29. **Banks Using Fewer Emergency Loans**

    In a sign of some improvement in the financial crisis, during the week ending July 9 investment banks didn't borrow from the Federal Reserve's emergency lending program and commercial banks also scaled back. In March the Fed scrambled to avert the crisis by giving investment banks a place to go for emergency overnight loans. In exchange for short-term loans of Treasury securities, companies can put up as collateral more risky investments.

    Source: *Time*, July 11, 2008

    What is the rationale behind allowing the Federal Reserve to make loans to banks?

How Banks Create Money

30. Banks in New Transylvania have a desired reserve ratio of 10 percent and no excess reserves. The currency drain ratio is 50 percent. Then the central bank increases the monetary base by $1,200 billion.
    a. How much do the banks lend in the first round of the money creation process?
    b. How much of the initial amount lent flows back to the banking system as new deposits?
    c. How much of the initial amount lent does not return to the banks but is held as currency?
    d. Why does a second round of lending occur?

The Money Market

31. Explain the change in the nominal interest rate in the short run if
    a. Real GDP increases.
    b. The money supply increases.
    c. The price level rises.

32. In Minland in Problem 15, the interest rate is 4 percent a year. Suppose that real GDP decreases to $10 billion and the quantity of money supplied remains unchanged. Do people buy bonds or sell bonds? Explain how the interest rate changes.

The Quantity Theory of Money

33. The table provides some data for the United States in the first decade following the Civil War.

	1869	1879
Quantity of money	$1.3 billion	$1.7 billion
Real GDP (1929 dollars)	$7.4 billion	Z
Price level (1929 = 100)	X	54
Velocity of circulation	4.50	4.61

Source of data: Milton Friedman and Anna J. Schwartz, A Monetary History of the United States 1867–1960

    a. Calculate the value of X in 1869.
    b. Calculate the value of Z in 1879.
    c. Are the data consistent with the quantity theory of money? Explain your answer.

Mathematical Note

34. In the United Kingdom, the currency drain ratio is 0.38 of deposits and the reserve ratio is 0.002. In Australia, the quantity of money is $150 billion, the currency drain ratio is 33 percent of deposits, and the reserve ratio is 8 percent.
    a. Calculate the U.K. money multiplier.
    b. Calculate the monetary base in Australia.

Economics in the News

35. After you have studied *Reading Between the Lines* on pp. 608–609 answer the following questions.
    a. What changes in the monetary base have occurred since October 2008?
    b. How does the Fed bring about an increase in the monetary base?
    c. How did the increase in the monetary base change the quantities of M1 and M2? Why?
    d. How did the change in monetary base influence short-term nominal interest rates? Why?
    e. How did the change in monetary base influence long-term nominal interest rates? Why?
    f. How did the change in monetary base influence long-term real interest rates? Why?

36. **Fed at Odds with ECB over Value of Policy Tool**

    Financial innovation and the spread of U.S. currency throughout the world has broken down relationships between money, inflation, and growth, making monetary gauges a less useful tool for policy makers, the U.S. Federal Reserve chairman, Ben Bernanke, said. Many other central banks use monetary aggregates as a guide to policy decision, but Bernanke believes reliance on monetary aggregates would be unwise because empirical relationship between U.S. money growth, inflation, and output growth is unstable. Bernanke said that the Fed had "philosophical" and economic differences with the European Central Bank and the Bank of England regarding the role of money and that debate between institutions was healthy. "Unfortunately, forecast errors for money growth are often significant," reducing their effectiveness as a tool for policy, Bernanke said. "There are differences between the U.S. and Europe in terms of the stability of money demand," Bernanke said. Ultimately, the risk of bad policy arising from a devoted following of money growth led the Fed to downgrade the importance of money measures.

    Source: *International Herald Tribune*, November 10, 2006

    a. Explain how the debate surrounding the quantity theory of money could make "monetary gauges a less useful tool for policy makers."
    b. What do Bernanke's statements reveal about his stance on the accuracy of the quantity theory of money?

After studying this chapter,
you will be able to:

◆ Describe the foreign exchange market and explain how the exchange rate is determined day by day

◆ Explain the trends and fluctuations in the exchange rate and explain interest rate parity and purchasing power parity

◆ Describe the alternative exchange rate policies and explain their effects

◆ Describe the balance of payments accounts and explain what causes an international deficit

26

THE EXCHANGE RATE AND THE BALANCE OF PAYMENTS

The dollar ($), the euro (€), and the yen (¥) are three of the world's monies and most international payments are made using one of them. But the world has more than 100 different monies.

In October 2000, one U.S. dollar bought 1.17 euros, but from 2000 through 2008, the dollar sank against the euro and by July 2008 one U.S. dollar bought only 63 euro cents. Why did the dollar fall against the euro? Can or should the United States do anything to stabilize the value of the dollar?

Every year since 1988, foreign entrepreneurs have roamed the United States with giant virtual shopping carts and loaded them up with Gerber, Firestone, Columbia Pictures, Ben & Jerry's, and Anheuser-Busch, all of which are now controlled by Japanese or European companies. Why have foreigners been buying U.S. businesses?

In this chapter, you're going to discover the answers to these questions. In *Reading Between the Lines* at the end of the chapter, we'll look at a risky investment strategy that exploits interest rate differences and the foreign exchange market.

617

◆ The Foreign Exchange Market

When Wal-Mart imports DVD players from Japan, it pays for them using Japanese yen. And when Japan Airlines buys an airplane from Boeing, it pays using U.S. dollars. Whenever people buy things from another country, they use the currency of that country to make the transaction. It doesn't make any difference what the item is that is being traded internationally. It might be a DVD player, an airplane, insurance or banking services, real estate, the stocks and bonds of a government or corporation, or even an entire business.

Foreign money is just like U.S. money. It consists of notes and coins issued by a central bank and mint and deposits in banks and other depository institutions. When we described U.S. money in Chapter 25, we distinguished between currency (notes and coins) and deposits. But when we talk about foreign money, we refer to it as foreign currency. **Foreign currency** is the money of other countries regardless of whether that money is in the form of notes, coins, or bank deposits.

We buy these foreign currencies and foreigners buy U.S. dollars in the foreign exchange market.

Trading Currencies

The currency of one country is exchanged for the currency of another in the **foreign exchange market.** The foreign exchange market is not a place like a downtown flea market or a fruit and vegetable market. The foreign exchange market is made up of thousands of people—importers and exporters, banks, international investors and speculators, international travelers, and specialist traders called *foreign exchange brokers.*

The foreign exchange market opens on Monday morning in Sydney, Australia, and Hong Kong, which is still Sunday evening in New York. As the day advances, markets open in Singapore, Tokyo, Bahrain, Frankfurt, London, New York, Chicago, and San Francisco. As the West Coast markets close, Sydney is only an hour away from opening for the next day of business. The sun barely sets in the foreign exchange market. Dealers around the world are in continual contact by telephone and computer, and on a typical day in 2010, around $3 trillion (of all currencies) were traded in the foreign exchange market—or more than $600 trillion in a year.

Exchange Rates

An **exchange rate** is the price at which one currency exchanges for another currency in the foreign exchange market. For example, on September 1, 2010, $1 would buy 84 Japanese yen or 79 euro cents. So the exchange rate was 84 yen per dollar or, equivalently, 79 euro cents per dollar.

The exchange rate fluctuates. Sometimes it rises and sometimes it falls. A rise in the exchange rate is called an *appreciation* of the dollar, and a fall in the exchange rate is called a *depreciation* of the dollar. For example, when the exchange rate rises from 84 yen to 100 yen per dollar, the dollar appreciates, and when the exchange rate falls from 100 yen to 84 yen per dollar, the dollar depreciates.

Economics in Action on the next page shows the fluctuations in the U.S. dollar against three currencies since 2000.

Questions About the U.S. Dollar Exchange Rate

The performance of the U.S. dollar in the foreign exchange market raises a number of questions that we address in this chapter.

First, how is the exchange rate determined? Why did the U.S. dollar appreciate from 2000 to 2002 and then begin to depreciate?

Second, how do the Fed and other central banks operate in the foreign exchange market? In particular, how was the exchange rate between the U.S. dollar and the Chinese yuan fixed and why did it remain constant for many years?

Third, how do exchange rate fluctuations influence our international trade and international payments? In particular, could we eliminate, or at least decrease, our international deficit by changing the exchange rate? Would an appreciation of the yuan change the balance of trade and payments between the United States and China?

We begin by learning how trading in the foreign exchange market determines the exchange rate.

An Exchange Rate Is a Price

An exchange rate is a price—the price of one currency in terms of another. And like all prices, an exchange rate is determined in a market—the *foreign exchange market.*

The U.S. dollar trades in the foreign exchange market and is supplied and demanded by tens of

Economics in Action

The U.S. Dollar: More Down than Up

The figure shows the U.S. dollar exchange rate against the three currencies that feature prominently in U.S. imports—the Chinese yuan, the European euro, and the Japanese yen—between 2000 and 2010.

Against the Chinese yuan, the dollar was constant before 2005 and then started to depreciate. Against the European euro and the Japanese yen, the dollar appreciated before 2002 and then mainly depreciated but staged a brief appreciation against the yen in 2005–2007.

Notice the high-frequency fluctuations (rapid brief up and down movements) of the dollar against the euro and the yen compared to the smooth changes against the yuan. Think about why that might be, and we'll check your answer later in this chapter.

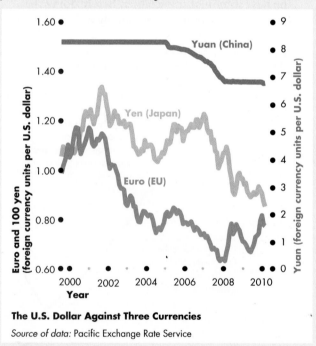

The U.S. Dollar Against Three Currencies

Source of data: Pacific Exchange Rate Service

thousands of traders every hour of every business day. Because it has many traders and no restrictions on who may trade, the foreign exchange market is a *competitive market.*

In a competitive market, demand and supply determine the price. So to understand the forces that determine the exchange rate, we need to study the factors that influence demand and supply in the foreign exchange market. But there is a feature of the foreign exchange market that makes it special.

The Demand for One Money Is the Supply of Another Money

When people who are holding the money of some other country want to exchange it for U.S. dollars, they demand U.S. dollars and supply that other country's money. And when people who are holding U.S. dollars want to exchange them for the money of some other country, they supply U.S. dollars and demand that other country's money.

So the factors that influence the demand for U.S. dollars also influence the supply of European Union euros, or Japanese yen, or Chinese yuan. And the factors that influence the demand for that other country's money also influence the supply of U.S. dollars.

We'll first look at the influences on the demand for U.S. dollars in the foreign exchange market.

Demand in the Foreign Exchange Market

People buy U.S. dollars in the foreign exchange market so that they can buy U.S.-produced goods and services—U.S. exports. They also buy U.S. dollars so that they can buy U.S. assets such as bonds, stocks, businesses, and real estate or so that they can keep part of their money holding in a U.S. dollar bank account.

The quantity of U.S. dollars demanded in the foreign exchange market is the amount that traders plan to buy during a given time period at a given exchange rate. This quantity depends on many factors, but the main ones are

1. The exchange rate
2. World demand for U.S. exports
3. Interest rates in the United States and other countries
4. The expected future exchange rate

We look first at the relationship between the quantity of U.S. dollars demanded in the foreign exchange market and the exchange rate when the other three influences remain the same.

The Law of Demand for Foreign Exchange The law of demand applies to U.S. dollars just as it does to anything else that people value. Other things remaining the same, the higher the exchange rate, the smaller is the quantity of U.S. dollars demanded in the foreign exchange market. For example, if the price of the U.S. dollar rises from 100 yen to 120 yen but nothing else changes, the quantity of U.S. dollars that people plan to buy in the foreign exchange market decreases. The exchange rate influences the quantity of U.S. dollars demanded for two reasons:

■ Exports effect
■ Expected profit effect

Exports Effect The larger the value of U.S. exports, the larger is the quantity of U.S. dollars demanded in the foreign exchange market. But the value of U.S. exports depends on the prices of U.S.-produced goods and services *expressed in the currency of the foreign buyer*. And these prices depend on the exchange rate. The lower the exchange rate, other things remaining the same, the lower are the prices of U.S.-produced goods and services to foreigners and the greater is the volume of U.S. exports. So if the exchange rate falls (and other influences remain the same), the quantity of U.S. dollars demanded in the foreign exchange market increases.

To see the exports effect at work, think about orders for Boeing's new 787 airplane. If the price of a 787 is $100 million and the exchange rate is 90 euro cents per U.S. dollar, the price of this airplane to KLM, a European airline, is €90 million. KLM decides that this price is too high, so it doesn't buy a new 787. If the exchange rate falls to 80 euro cents per U.S. dollar and other things remain the same, the price of a 787 falls to €80 million. KLM now decides to buy a 787 and buys U.S. dollars in the foreign exchange market.

Expected Profit Effect The larger the expected profit from holding U.S. dollars, the greater is the quantity of U.S. dollars demanded in the foreign exchange market. But expected profit depends on the exchange rate. For a given expected future exchange rate, the lower the exchange rate today, the larger is the expected profit from buying U.S. dollars today and holding them, so the greater is the quantity of U.S. dollars demanded in the foreign exchange market today. Let's look at an example.

Suppose that Mizuho Bank, a Japanese bank, expects the exchange rate to be 120 yen per U.S. dollar at the end of the year. If today's exchange rate is also 120 yen per U.S. dollar, Mizuho Bank expects no profit from buying U.S. dollars and holding them until the end of the year. But if today's exchange rate is 100 yen per U.S. dollar and Mizuho Bank buys

U.S. dollars, it expects to sell those dollars at the end of the year for 120 yen per dollar and make a profit of 20 yen per U.S. dollar.

The lower the exchange rate today, other things remaining the same, the greater is the expected profit from holding U.S. dollars and the greater is the quantity of U.S. dollars demanded in the foreign exchange market today.

Demand Curve for U.S. Dollars

Figure 26.1 shows the demand curve for U.S. dollars in the foreign exchange market. A change in the exchange rate, other things remaining the same, brings a change in the quantity of U.S. dollars demanded and a movement along the demand curve. The arrows show such movements.

We will look at the factors that *change* demand in the next section of this chapter. Before doing that, let's see what determines the supply of U.S. dollars.

FIGURE 26.1   The Demand for U.S. Dollars

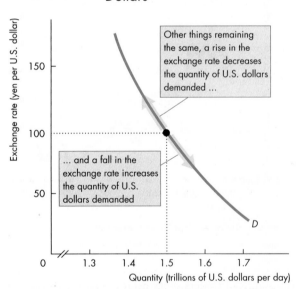

The quantity of U.S. dollars demanded depends on the exchange rate. Other things remaining the same, if the exchange rate rises, the quantity of U.S. dollars demanded decreases and there is a movement up along the demand curve for U.S. dollars. If the exchange rate falls, the quantity of U.S. dollars demanded increases and there is a movement down along the demand curve for U.S. dollars.

myeconlab animation

Supply in the Foreign Exchange Market

People sell U.S. dollars and buy other currencies so that they can buy foreign-produced goods and services—U.S. imports. People also sell U.S. dollars and buy foreign currencies so that they can buy foreign assets such as bonds, stocks, businesses, and real estate or so that they can hold part of their money in bank deposits denominated in a foreign currency.

The quantity of U.S. dollars supplied in the foreign exchange market is the amount that traders plan to sell during a given time period at a given exchange rate. This quantity depends on many factors, but the main ones are

1. The exchange rate
2. U.S. demand for imports
3. Interest rates in the United States and other countries
4. The expected future exchange rate

Let's look at the law of supply in the foreign exchange market—the relationship between the quantity of U.S. dollars supplied in the foreign exchange market and the exchange rate when the other three influences remain the same.

The Law of Supply of Foreign Exchange Other things remaining the same, the higher the exchange rate, the greater is the quantity of U.S. dollars supplied in the foreign exchange market. For example, if the exchange rate rises from 100 yen to 120 yen per U.S. dollar and other things remain the same, the quantity of U.S. dollars that people plan to sell in the foreign exchange market increases.

The exchange rate influences the quantity of dollars supplied for two reasons:

- Imports effect
- Expected profit effect

Imports Effect The larger the value of U.S. imports, the larger is the quantity of U.S. dollars supplied in the foreign exchange market. But the value of U.S. imports depends on the prices of foreign-produced goods and services *expressed in U.S. dollars*. These prices depend on the exchange rate. The higher the exchange rate, other things remaining the same, the lower are the prices of foreign-produced goods and services to Americans and the greater is the volume of U.S. imports. So if the exchange rate rises (and other influences remain the same), the quantity of

U.S. dollars supplied in the foreign exchange market increases.

Expected Profit Effect This effect works just like that on the demand for the U.S. dollar but in the opposite direction. The higher the exchange rate today, other things remaining the same, the larger is the expected profit from selling U.S. dollars today and holding foreign currencies, so the greater is the quantity of U.S. dollars supplied.

Supply Curve for U.S. Dollars

Figure 26.2 shows the supply curve of U.S. dollars in the foreign exchange market. A change in the exchange rate, other things remaining the same, brings a change in the quantity of U.S. dollars supplied and a movement along the supply curve. The arrows show such movements.

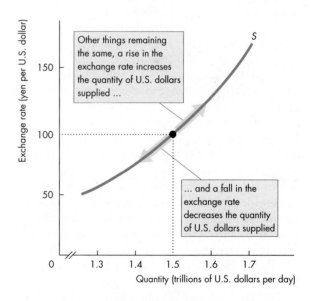

FIGURE 26.2   The Supply of U.S. Dollars

The quantity of U.S. dollars supplied depends on the exchange rate. Other things remaining the same, if the exchange rate rises, the quantity of U.S. dollars supplied increases and there is a movement up along the supply curve of U.S. dollars. If the exchange rate falls, the quantity of U.S. dollars supplied decreases and there is a movement down along the supply curve of U.S. dollars.

myeconlab animation

Market Equilibrium

Equilibrium in the foreign exchange market depends on how the Federal Reserve and other central banks operate. Here, we will study equilibrium when central banks keep out of this market. In a later section (on pp. 628–630), we examine the effects of alternative actions that the Fed or another central bank might take in the foreign exchange market.

Figure 26.3 shows the demand curve for U.S. dollars, D, from Fig. 26.1 and the supply curve of U.S. dollars, S, from Fig. 26.2, and the equilibrium exchange rate.

The exchange rate acts as a regulator of the quantities demanded and supplied. If the exchange rate is too high, there is a surplus—the quantity supplied exceeds the quantity demanded. For example, in Fig. 26.3, if the exchange rate is 150 yen per U.S. dollar, there is a surplus of U.S. dollars. If the exchange rate is too low, there is a shortage—the quantity supplied is less than the quantity demanded. For example, if the exchange rate is 50 yen per U.S. dollar, there is a shortage of U.S. dollars.

At the equilibrium exchange rate, there is neither a shortage nor a surplus—the quantity supplied equals the quantity demanded. In Fig. 26.3, the equilibrium exchange rate is 100 yen per U.S. dollar. At this exchange rate, the quantity demanded and the quantity supplied are each $1.5 trillion a day.

The foreign exchange market is constantly pulled to its equilibrium by the forces of supply and demand. Foreign exchange traders are constantly looking for the best price they can get. If they are selling, they want the highest price available. If they are buying, they want the lowest price available. Information flows from trader to trader through the worldwide computer network, and the price adjusts minute by minute to keep buying plans and selling plans in balance. That is, the price adjusts minute by minute to keep the exchange rate at its equilibrium.

Figure 26.3 shows how the exchange rate between the U.S. dollar and the Japanese yen is determined. The exchange rates between the U.S. dollar and all other currencies are determined in a similar way. So are the exchange rates among the other currencies. But the exchange rates are tied together so that no profit can be made by buying one currency, selling it for a second one, and then buying back the first one. If such a profit were available, traders would spot it, demand and supply would change, and the exchange rates would snap into alignment.

FIGURE 26.3   Equilibrium Exchange Rate

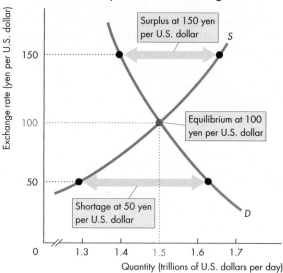

The demand curve for U.S. dollars is D, and the supply curve of U.S. dollars is S. If the exchange rate is 150 yen per U.S. dollar, there is a surplus of U.S. dollars and the exchange rate falls. If the exchange rate is 50 yen per U.S. dollar, there is a shortage of U.S. dollars and the exchange rate rises. If the exchange rate is 100 yen per U.S. dollar, there is neither a shortage nor a surplus of U.S. dollars and the exchange rate remains constant. The foreign exchange market is in equilibrium.

myeconlab   animation

REVIEW QUIZ

1 What are the influences on the demand for U.S. dollars in the foreign exchange market?
2 Provide an example of the exports effect on the demand for U.S. dollars.
3 What are the influences on the supply of U.S. dollars in the foreign exchange market?
4 Provide an example of the imports effect on the supply of U.S. dollars.
5 How is the equilibrium exchange rate determined?
6 What happens if there is a shortage or a surplus of U.S. dollars in the foreign exchange market?

You can work these questions in Study Plan 26.1 and get instant feedback.

◆ Exchange Rate Fluctuations

You've seen (in the box on p. 619) that the U.S. dollar fluctuates a lot against the yen and the euro. Changes in the demand for U.S. dollars or the supply of U.S. dollars bring these exchange rate fluctuations. We'll now look at the factors that make demand and supply change, starting with the demand side of the market.

Changes in the Demand for U.S. Dollars

The demand for U.S. dollars in the foreign exchange market changes when there is a change in

- World demand for U.S. exports
- U.S. interest rate relative to the foreign interest rate
- The expected future exchange rate

World Demand for U.S. Exports An increase in world demand for U.S. exports increases the demand for U.S. dollars. To see this effect, think about Boeing's airplane sales. An increase in demand for air travel in Australia sends that country's airlines on a global shopping spree. They decide that the 787 is the ideal product, so they order 50 airplanes from Boeing. The demand for U.S. dollars now increases.

U.S. Interest Rate Relative to the Foreign Interest Rate People and businesses buy financial assets to make a return. The higher the interest rate that people can make on U.S. assets compared with foreign assets, the more U.S. assets they buy.

What matters is not the *level* of the U.S. interest rate, but the U.S. interest rate minus the foreign interest rate—a gap that is called the **U.S. interest rate differential**. If the U.S. interest rate rises and the foreign interest rate remains constant, the U.S. interest rate differential increases. The larger the U.S. interest rate differential, the greater is the demand for U.S. assets and the greater is the demand for U.S. dollars in the foreign exchange market.

The Expected Future Exchange Rate For a given current exchange rate, other things remaining the same, a rise in the expected future exchange rate increases the profit that people expect to make by holding U.S. dollars and the demand for U.S. dollars increases today.

Figure 26.4 summarizes the influences on the demand for U.S. dollars. An increase in the demand for U.S. exports, a rise in the U.S. interest rate differential, or a rise in the expected future exchange rate increases the demand for U.S. dollars today and shifts the demand curve rightward from D_0 to D_1. A decrease in the demand for U.S. exports, a fall in the U.S. interest rate differential, or a fall in the expected future exchange rate decreases the demand for U.S. dollars today and shifts the demand curve leftward from D_0 to D_2.

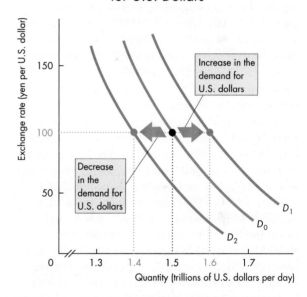

FIGURE 26.4   Changes in the Demand for U.S. Dollars

A change in any influence on the quantity of U.S. dollars that people plan to buy, other than the exchange rate, brings a change in the demand for U.S. dollars.

The demand for U.S. dollars

Increases if:	*Decreases if:*
■ World demand for U.S. exports increases	■ World demand for U.S. exports decreases
■ The U.S. interest rate differential rises	■ The U.S. interest rate differential falls
■ The expected future exchange rate rises	■ The expected future exchange rate falls

myeconlab animation

Changes in the Supply of U.S. Dollars

The supply of U.S. dollars in the foreign exchange market changes when there is a change in

- U.S. demand for imports
- U.S. interest rate relative to the foreign interest rate
- The expected future exchange rate

U.S. Demand for Imports An increase in the U.S. demand for imports increases the supply of U.S. dollars in the foreign exchange market. To see why, think about Wal-Mart's purchase of DVD players. An increase in the demand for DVD players sends Wal-Mart out on a global shopping spree. Wal-Mart decides that Panasonic DVD players produced in Japan are the best buy, so Wal-Mart increases its purchases of these players. The supply of U.S. dollars now increases as Wal-Mart goes to the foreign exchange market for Japanese yen to pay Panasonic.

U.S. Interest Rate Relative to the Foreign Interest Rate The effect of the U.S. interest rate differential on the supply of U.S. dollars is the opposite of its effect on the demand for U.S. dollars. The larger the U.S. interest rate differential, the *smaller* is the supply of U.S. dollars in the foreign exchange market.

With a higher U.S. interest rate differential, people decide to keep more of their funds in U.S. dollar assets and less in foreign currency assets. They buy a smaller quantity of foreign currency and sell a smaller quantity of dollars in the foreign exchange market.

So, a rise in the U.S. interest rate, other things remaining the same, decreases the supply of U.S. dollars in the foreign exchange market.

The Expected Future Exchange Rate For a given current exchange rate, other things remaining the same, a fall in the expected future exchange rate decreases the profit that can be made by holding U.S. dollars and decreases the quantity of U.S. dollars that people want to hold. To reduce their holdings of U.S. dollar assets, people must sell U.S. dollars. When they do so, the supply of U.S. dollars in the foreign exchange market increases.

Figure 26.5 summarizes the influences on the supply of U.S. dollars. If the supply of U.S. dollars decreases, the supply curve shifts leftward from S_0 to S_1. And if the supply of U.S. dollars increases, the supply curve shifts rightward from S_0 to S_2.

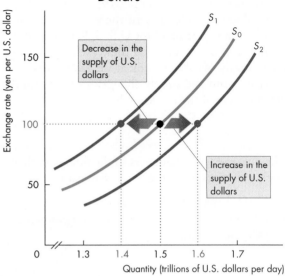

FIGURE 26.5 Changes in the Supply of U.S. Dollars

A change in any influence on the quantity of U.S. dollars that people plan to sell, other than the exchange rate, brings a change in the supply of dollars.

The supply of U.S. dollars

Increases if:	*Decreases if:*
■ U.S. import demand increases	■ U.S. import demand decreases
■ The U.S. interest rate differential falls	■ The U.S. interest rate differential rises
■ The expected future exchange rate falls	■ The expected future exchange rate rises

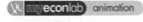

Changes in the Exchange Rate

If the demand for U.S. dollars increases and the supply does not change, the exchange rate rises. If the demand for U.S. dollars decreases and the supply does not change, the exchange rate falls. Similarly, if the supply of U.S. dollars decreases and the demand does not change, the exchange rate rises. If the supply of U.S. dollars increases and the demand does not change, the exchange rate falls.

These predictions are exactly the same as those for any other market. Two episodes in the life of the U.S. dollar (next page) illustrate these predictions.

Economics in Action

The Dollar on a Roller Coaster

The foreign exchange market is a striking example of a competitive market. The expectations of thousands of traders around the world influence this market minute-by-minute throughout the 24-hour global trading day.

Demand and supply rarely stand still and their fluctuations bring a fluctuating exchange rate. Two episodes in the life of the dollar illustrate these fluctuations: 2005–2007, when the dollar appreciated and 2007–2008, when the dollar depreciated.

An Appreciating U.S. Dollar: 2005–2007 Between January 2005 and July 2007, the U.S. dollar appreciated against the yen. It rose from 103 yen to 123 yen per U.S. dollar. Part (a) of the figure provides an explanation for this appreciation.

In 2005, the demand and supply curves were those labeled D_{05} and S_{05}. The exchange rate was 103 yen per U.S. dollar.

During 2005 and 2006, the Federal Reserve raised the interest rate, but the interest rate in Japan barely changed. With an increase in the U.S. interest rate differential, funds flowed into the United States. Also, currency traders, anticipating this increased flow of funds into the United States, expected the dollar to appreciate against the yen. The demand for U.S. dol-

lars increased, and the supply of U.S. dollars decreased.

In the figure, the demand curve shifted rightward from D_{05} to D_{07} and the supply curve shifted leftward from S_{05} to S_{07}. The exchange rate rose to 123 yen per U.S. dollar. In the figure, the equilibrium quantity remained unchanged—an assumption.

A Depreciating U.S. Dollar: 2007–2008 Between July 2007 and September 2008, the U.S. dollar depreciated against the yen. It fell from 123 yen to 107 yen per U.S. dollar. Part (b) of the figure provides a possible explanation for this depreciation. The demand and supply curves labeled D_{07} and S_{07} are the same as in part (a).

During the last quarter of 2007 and the first three quarters of 2008, the U.S. economy entered a severe credit crisis and the Federal Reserve cut the interest rate in the United States. But the Bank of Japan kept the interest rate unchanged in Japan. With a narrowing of the U.S. interest rate differential, funds flowed out of the United States. Also, currency traders expected the U.S. dollar to depreciate against the yen. The demand for U.S. dollars decreased and the supply of U.S. dollars increased.

In part (b) of the figure, the demand curve shifted leftward from D_{07} to D_{08}, the supply curve shifted rightward from S_{07} to S_{08}, and the exchange rate fell to 107 yen per U.S. dollar.

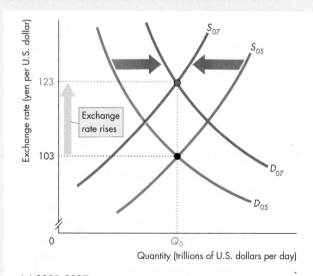

(a) 2005–2007

The Rising and Falling U.S. Dollar

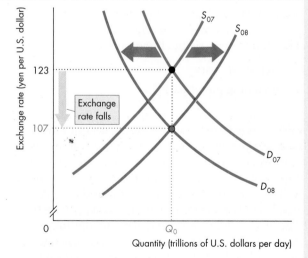

(b) 2007–2008

Fundamentals, Expectations, and Arbitrage

Changes in the *expected* exchange rate change the *actual* exchange rate. But what makes the expected exchange rate change? The answer is new information about the *fundamental influences* on the exchange rate—the world demand for U.S. exports, U.S. demand for imports, and the U.S. interest rate relative to the foreign interest rate. Expectations about these variables change the exchange rate through their influence on the expected exchange rate, and the effect is instant.

To see why, suppose news breaks that the Fed will raise the interest rate next week. Traders now expect the demand for dollars to increase and the dollar to appreciate: They expect to profit by buying dollars today and selling them next week for a higher price than they paid. The rise in the expected future value of the dollar increases the demand for dollars today, decreases the supply of dollars today, and raises the exchange rate. The exchange rate changes as soon as the news about a fundamental influence is received.

Profiting by trading in the foreign exchange market often involves *arbitrage*: The practice of buying in one market and selling for a higher price in another related market. Arbitrage ensures that the exchange rate is the same in New York, London, and all other trading centers. It isn't possible to buy at a low price in London and sell for a higher price in New York. If it were possible, demand would increase in London and decrease in New York to make the prices equal.

Arbitrage also removes profit from borrowing in one currency and lending in another and buying goods in one currency and selling them in another. These arbitrage activities bring about

- Interest rate parity
- Purchasing power parity

Interest Rate Parity Suppose a bank deposit earns 1 percent a year in Tokyo and 3 percent a year in New York. Why wouldn't people move their funds to New York, and even borrow in Japan to do so? The answer is that some would, in an activity called the "carry trade" (see *Reading Between the Lines* on pp. 636–637). The New York deposit is in dollars and the Tokyo deposit is in yen. So a change in the exchange rate brings risk to borrowing in one currency and lending in another. If investors *expect* the yen to appreciate by 2 percent a year and they buy and hold yen for a year they will earn 1 percent interest and *expect* a 2 percent

return from the higher yen. The total *expected* return is 3 percent, the same as on U.S. dollars in New York.

This situation is called **interest rate parity**, which means equal rates of return. Adjusted for risk, interest rate parity always prevails. Funds move to get the highest *expected* return available. If for a few seconds a higher return is available in New York than in Tokyo, the demand for U.S. dollars increases and the exchange rate rises until the expected rates of return are equal.

Purchasing Power Parity Suppose a memory stick costs 5,000 yen in Tokyo and $50 in New York. If the exchange rate is 100 yen per dollar, the two monies have the same value. You can buy a memory stick in either Tokyo or New York for the same price. You can express that price as either 5,000 yen or $50, but the price is the same in the two currencies.

The situation we've just described is called **purchasing power parity**, which means *equal value of money*. If purchasing power parity does not prevail, powerful arbitrage forces go to work. To see these forces, suppose that the price of a memory stick in New York rises to $60, but in Tokyo it remains at 5,000 yen. Further, suppose the exchange rate remains at 100 yen per dollar. In this case, a memory stick in Tokyo still costs 5,000 yen or $50, but in New York, it costs $60 or 6,000 yen. Money buys more in Japan than in the United States. Money is not of equal value in the two countries.

If all (or most) prices have increased in the United States and not increased in Japan, then people will generally expect that the value of the U.S. dollar in the foreign exchange market must fall. In this situation, the exchange rate is expected to fall. The demand for U.S. dollars decreases, and the supply of U.S. dollars increases. The exchange rate falls, as expected. If the exchange rate falls to 83.33 yen per dollar and there are no further price changes, purchasing power parity is restored. A memory stick that costs $60 in New York also costs the equivalent of $60 (60 × 83.33 = 5,000) in Tokyo.

If prices rise in Japan and other countries but remain constant in the United States, then people will expect the U.S. dollar to appreciate. The demand for U.S. dollars increases, and the supply of U.S. dollars decreases. The exchange rate rises, as expected.

So far we've been looking at the forces that determine the *nominal* exchange rate—the amount of one money that another money buys. We're now going to study the *real* exchange rate.

The Real Exchange Rate

The **real exchange rate** is the relative price of U.S.-produced goods and services to foreign-produced goods and services. It is a measure of the quantity of the real GDP of other countries that a unit of U.S. real GDP buys.

The real Japanese yen exchange rate, *RER*, is

$$RER = (E \times P)/P^*,$$

where E is the exchange rate (yen per U.S. dollar), P is the U.S. price level, and P^* is the Japanese price level.

To understand the real exchange rate, suppose that each country produces only one good and that the exchange rate E is 100 yen per dollar. The United States produces only computer chips priced at $150 each, so P equals $150 and $E \times P$ equals 15,000 yen. Japan produces only iPods priced at 5,000 yen each, so P^* equals 5,000 yen. Then the real Japanese yen exchange rate is

$$RER = (100 \times 150)/5,000 = 3 \text{ iPods per chip.}$$

The Short Run In the short run, if the nominal exchange rate changes, the real exchange rate also changes. The reason is that prices and the price levels in the United States and Japan don't change every time the exchange rate changes. Sticking with the chips and iPods example, if the dollar appreciates to 200 yen per dollar and prices don't change, the real exchange rate rises to 6 iPods per chip. The price of an iPod in the United States falls to $25 (5,000 yen ÷ 200 yen per dollar = $25).

Changes in the real exchange rate bring short-run changes in the quantity of imports demanded and the quantity of exports supplied.

The Long Run But in the long run, the situation is radically different: In the long run, the nominal exchange rate and the price level are determined together and the real exchange rate does *not* change when the nominal exchange rate changes.

In the long run, demand and supply in the markets for goods and services determine prices. In the chips and iPod example, the world markets for chips and iPods determine their *relative* price. In our example the relative price is 3 iPods per chip. The same forces determine all relative prices and so determine nations' relative price levels.

In the long run, if the dollar appreciates prices *do* change. To see why, recall the quantity theory of money that you met in Chapter 25 (pp. 606–607).

In the long run, the quantity of money determines the price level. But the quantity theory of money applies to all countries, so the quantity of money in Japan determines the price level in Japan, and the quantity of money in the United States determines the price level in the United States.

For a given real exchange rate, a change in the quantity of money brings a change in the price level *and* a change in the exchange rate.

Suppose that the quantity of money doubles in Japan. The dollar appreciates (the yen depreciatates) from 100 yen per dollar to 200 yen per dollar and all prices double, so the price of an iPod rises from 5,000 yen to 10,000 yen.

At the new price in Japan and the new exchange rate, an iPod still costs $50 (10,000 yen ÷ 200 yen per dollar = $50). The real exchange rate remains at 3 iPods per chip.

If Japan and the United States produced identical goods (if GDP in both countries consisted only of computer chips), the real exchange rate in the long run would equal 1.

In reality, although there is overlap in what each country produces, U.S. real GDP is a different bundle of goods and services from Japanese real GDP. So the relative price of Japanese and U.S. real GDP—the real exchange rate—is not 1, and it changes over time. The forces of demand and supply in the markets for the millions of goods and services that make up real GDP determine the relative price of Japanese and U.S. real GDP, and changes in these forces change the real exchange rate.

 REVIEW QUIZ

1 Why does the demand for U.S. dollars change?
2 Why does the supply of U.S. dollars change?
3 What makes the U.S. dollar exchange rate fluctuate?
4 What is interest rate parity and what happens when this condition doesn't hold?
5 What is purchasing power parity and what happens when this condition doesn't hold?
6 What determines the real exchange rate and the nominal exchange rate in the short run?
7 What determines the real exchange rate and the nominal exchange rate in the long run?

You can work these questions in Study Plan 26.2 and get instant feedback.

◆ Exchange Rate Policy

Because the exchange rate is the price of a country's money in terms of another country's money, governments and central banks must have a policy toward the exchange rate. Three possible exchange rate policies are

- Flexible exchange rate
- Fixed exchange rate
- Crawling peg

Flexible Exchange Rate

A **flexible exchange rate** is an exchange rate that is determined by demand and supply in the foreign exchange market with no direct intervention by the central bank.

Most countries, including the United States, operate a flexible exchange rate, and the foreign exchange market that we have studied so far in this chapter is an example of a flexible exchange rate regime.

But even a flexible exchange rate is influenced by central bank actions. If the Fed raises the U.S. interest rate and other countries keep their interest rates unchanged, the demand for U.S. dollars increases, the supply of U.S. dollars decreases, and the exchange rate rises. (Similarly, if the Fed lowers the U.S. interest rate, the demand for U.S. dollars decreases, the supply increases, and the exchange rate falls.)

In a flexible exchange rate regime, when the central bank changes the interest rate, its purpose is not usually to influence the exchange rate, but to achieve some other monetary policy objective. (We return to this topic at length in Chapter 31.)

Fixed Exchange Rate

A **fixed exchange rate** is an exchange rate that is determined by a decision of the government or the central bank and is achieved by central bank intervention in the foreign exchange market to block the unregulated forces of demand and supply.

The world economy operated a fixed exchange rate regime from the end of World War II to the early 1970s. China had a fixed exchange rate until recently. Hong Kong has had a fixed exchange rate for many years and continues with that policy today.

Active intervention in the foreign exchange market is required to achieve a fixed exchange rate.

If the Fed wanted to fix the U.S. dollar exchange rate against the Japanese yen, the Fed would have to sell U.S. dollars to prevent the exchange rate from rising above the target value and buy U.S. dollars to prevent the exchange rate from falling below the target value.

There is no limit to the quantity of U.S. dollars that the Fed can *sell*. The Fed creates U.S. dollars and can create any quantity it chooses. But there is a limit to the quantity of U.S. dollars the Fed can *buy*. That limit is set by U.S. official foreign currency reserves because to buy U.S. dollars the Fed must sell foreign currency. Intervention to buy U.S. dollars stops when U.S. official foreign currency reserves run out.

Let's look at the foreign exchange interventions that the Fed can make.

Suppose the Fed wants the exchange rate to be steady at 100 yen per U.S. dollar. If the exchange rate rises above 100 yen, the Fed sells dollars. If the exchange rate falls below 100 yen, the Fed buys dollars. By these actions, the Fed keeps the exchange rate close to its target rate of 100 yen per U.S. dollar.

Figure 26.6 shows the Fed's intervention in the foreign exchange market. The supply of dollars is S and initially the demand for dollars is D_0. The equilibrium exchange rate is 100 yen per dollar. This exchange rate is also the Fed's target exchange rate, shown by the horizontal red line.

When the demand for U.S. dollars increases and the demand curve shifts rightward to D_1, the Fed sells $100 billion. This action prevents the exchange rate from rising. When the demand for U.S. dollars decreases and the demand curve shifts leftward to D_2, the Fed buys $100 billion. This action prevents the exchange rate from falling.

If the demand for U.S. dollars fluctuates between D_1 and D_2 and on average is D_0, the Fed can repeatedly intervene in the way we've just seen. Sometimes the Fed buys and sometimes it sells but, on average, it neither buys nor sells.

But suppose the demand for U.S. dollars *increases permanently* from D_0 to D_1. To maintain the exchange rate at 100 yen per U.S. dollar, the Fed must sell dollars and buy foreign currency, so U.S. official foreign currency reserves would be increasing. At some point, the Fed would abandon the exchange rate of 100 yen per U.S. dollar and stop piling up foreign currency reserves.

Now suppose the demand for U.S. dollars *decreases permanently* from D_0 to D_2. In this situation, the Fed

FIGURE 26.6   Foreign Exchange Market Intervention

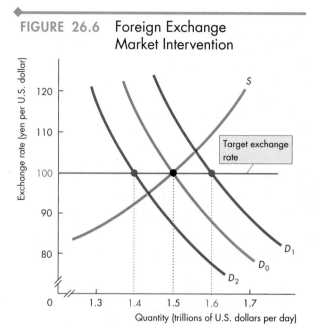

Initially, the demand for U.S. dollars is D_0, the supply of U.S. dollars is S, and the exchange rate is 100 yen per U.S. dollar. The Fed can intervene in the foreign exchange market to keep the exchange rate close to its target rate (100 yen in this example). If the demand for U.S. dollars increases and the demand curve shifts from D_0 to D_1, the Fed sells dollars. If the demand for U.S. dollars decreases and the demand curve shifts from D_0 to D_2, the Fed buys dollars. Persistent intervention on one side of the market cannot be sustained.

cannot maintain the exchange rate at 100 yen per U.S. dollar indefinitely. To hold the exchange rate at 100 yen, the Fed must *buy* U.S. dollars. When the Fed buys U.S. dollars in the foreign exchange market, it uses U.S. official foreign currency reserves. So the Fed's action decreases its foreign currency reserves. Eventually, the Fed would run out of foreign currency and would then have to abandon the target exchange rate of 100 yen per U.S. dollar.

Crawling Peg

A **crawling peg** is an exchange rate that follows a path determined by a decision of the government or the central bank and is achieved in a similar way to a fixed exchange rate by central bank intervention in the foreign exchange market. A crawling peg works like a fixed exchange rate except that the target value

changes. The target might change at fixed intervals (daily, weekly, monthly) or at random intervals.

The Fed has never operated a crawling peg, but some prominent countries do use this system. When China abandoned its fixed exchange rate, it replaced it with a crawling peg. Developing countries might use a crawling peg as a method of trying to control inflation—of keeping the inflation rate close to target.

The ideal crawling peg sets a target for the exchange rate equal to the equilibrium exchange rate

Economics in Action
The People's Bank of China in the Foreign Exchange Market

You saw in the figure on p. 619 that the exchange rate between the U.S. dollar and the Chinese yuan was constant for several years. The reason for this near constant exchange rate is that China's central bank, the People's Bank of China, intervened to operate a *fixed exchange rate policy*. From 1997 until 2005, the yuan was pegged at 8.28 yuan per U.S. dollar. Since 2005, the yuan has appreciated slightly but it has not been permitted to fluctuate freely. Since 2005, the yuan has been on a crawling peg.

Why Does China Manage Its Exchange Rate? The popular story is that China manages its exchange rate to keep its export prices low and to make it easier to compete in world markets. You've seen that this story is correct *only in the short run*. With prices in China unchanged, a lower yuan–U.S. dollar exchange rate brings lower U.S. dollar prices for China's exports. But the yuan–U.S. dollar exchange rate was fixed for almost 10 years and has been managed for five more years. This long period of a fixed exchange rate has long-run, not short-run, effects. In the long run, the exchange rate has no effect on competitiveness. The reason is that prices adjust to reflect the exchange rate and the real exchange rate is unaffected by the nominal exchange rate.

So why does China fix its exchange rate? The most convincing answer is that China sees a fixed exchange rate as a way of controlling its inflation rate. By making the yuan crawl against the U.S. dollar, China's inflation rate is anchored to the U.S. inflation rate and will depart from U.S. inflation by an amount determined by the speed of the crawl.

The bottom line is that in the long run, exchange rate policy is monetary policy, not foreign trade policy. To change its exports and imports, a country must change its comparative advantage (Chapter 2).

How Does China Manage Its Exchange Rate? The People's Bank pegs the yuan at 7 yuan per U.S. dollar by intervening in the foreign exchange market and buying U.S. dollars. But to do so, it must pile up U.S. dollars.

Part (a) of the figure shows the scale of China's increase in official foreign currency reserves, some of which are euros and yen but most of which are U.S. dollars. You can see that China's reserves increased by more than $400 billion in 2007, 2008, and 2009.

The demand and supply curves in part (b) of the figure illustrate what is happening in the market for U.S. dollars priced in terms of the yuan and explains why China's reserves have increased. The demand curve *D* and supply curve *S* intersect at 5 yuan per U.S. dollar. If the People's Bank of China takes no actions in the market, this exchange rate is the equilibrium rate (an assumed value).

The consequence of the fixed (and crawling peg) yuan exchange rate is that China has piled up U.S. dollar reserves on a huge scale. By mid-2006, China's official foreign currency reserves approached $1 trillion and by the end of 2009, they exceeded $2 trillion!

If the People's Bank stopped buying U.S. dollars, the U.S. dollar would depreciate and the yuan would appreciate—the yuan–U.S. dollar exchange rate would fall—and China would stop piling up U.S. dollar reserves.

In the example in the figure, the dollar would depreciate to 5 yuan per dollar.

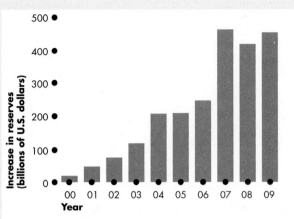

(a) Increase in U.S. dollar reserves

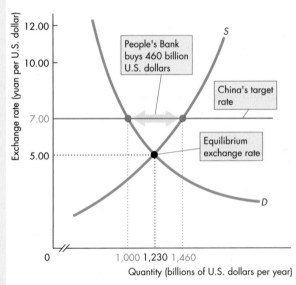

(b) Pegging the yuan

China's Foreign Exchange Market Intervention

on average. The peg seeks only to prevent large swings in the expected future exchange rate that change demand and supply and make the exchange rate fluctuate too wildly.

A crawling peg departs from the ideal if, as often happens with a fixed exchange rate, the target rate departs from the equilibrium exchange rate for too long. When this happens, the country either runs out of reserves or piles up reserves.

In the final part of this chapter, we explain how the balance of international payments is determined.

REVIEW QUIZ

1 What is a flexible exchange rate and how does it work?
2 What is a fixed exchange rate and how is its value fixed?
3 What is a crawling peg and how does it work?
4 How has China operated in the foreign exchange market, why, and with what effect?

You can work these questions in Study Plan 26.3 and get instant feedback.

Financing International Trade

You now know how the exchange rate is determined, but what is the effect of the exchange rate? How does currency depreciation or currency appreciation influence our international trade and payments? We're going to lay the foundation for addressing these questions by looking at the scale of international trading, borrowing, and lending and at the way in which we keep our records of international transactions. These records are called the *balance of payments accounts*.

Balance of Payments Accounts

A country's **balance of payments accounts** records its international trading, borrowing, and lending in three accounts:

1. Current account
2. Capital and financial account
3. Official settlements account

The **current account** records receipts from exports of goods and services sold abroad, payments for imports of goods and services from abroad, net interest income paid abroad, and net transfers abroad (such as foreign aid payments). The *current account balance* equals the sum of exports minus imports, net interest income, and net transfers.

The **capital and financial account** records foreign investment in the United States minus U.S. investment abroad. (This account also has a statistical discrepancy that arises from errors and omissions in measuring international capital transactions.)

The **official settlements account** records the change in **U.S. official reserves**, which are the government's holdings of foreign currency. If U.S. official reserves *increase*, the official settlements account balance is *negative*. The reason is that holding foreign money is like investing abroad. U.S. investment abroad is a minus item in the capital and financial account and in the official settlements account.

The sum of the balances on the three accounts *always* equals zero. That is, to pay for our current account deficit, we must either borrow more from abroad than we lend abroad or use our official reserves to cover the shortfall.

Table 26.1 shows the U.S. balance of payments accounts in 2010. Items in the current account and the capital and financial account that provide foreign currency to the United States have a plus sign; items that cost the United States foreign currency have a minus sign. The table shows that in 2010, U.S. imports exceeded U.S. exports and the current account had a deficit of $436 billion. How do we pay for imports that exceed the value of our exports? That is, how do we pay for our current account deficit?

We pay by borrowing from the rest of the world. The capital account tells us by how much. We borrowed $1,408 billion (foreign investment in the United States) but made loans of $1,200 billion (U.S. investment abroad). Our *net* foreign borrowing was $1,408 billion minus $1,200 billion, which equals $208 billion. There is almost always a statistical discrepancy between our capital account and current account transactions, and in 2010, the discrepancy was $231 billion. Combining the discrepancy with the measured net foreign borrowing gives a capital and financial account balance of $439 billion.

TABLE 26.1   U.S. Balance of Payments Accounts in 2010

Current account	Billions of dollars
Exports of goods and services	+1,754
Imports of goods and services	−2,215
Net interest income	+167
Net transfers	−142
Current account balance	−436

Capital and financial account	
Foreign investment in the United States	+1,408
U.S. investment abroad	−1,200
Statistical discrepancy	231
Capital and financial account balance	+439

Official settlements account	
Official settlements account balance	−3

Source of data: Bureau of Economic Analysis (based on first quarter).

The capital and financial account balance plus the current account balance equals the change in U.S. official reserves. In 2010, the capital and financial account balance of $439 billion plus the current account balance of –$436 billion equaled $3 billion. Official reserves *increased* in 2010 by $3 billion. Holding more foreign reserves is like lending to the rest of the world, so this amount appears in the official settlements account in Table 26.1 as –$3 billion. The sum of the balances on the three balance of payments accounts equals zero.

To see more clearly what the nation's balance of payments accounts mean, think about your own balance of payments accounts. They are similar to the nation's accounts.

An Individual's Balance of Payments Accounts An individual's current account records the income from supplying the services of factors of production and the expenditure on goods and services. Consider Jackie, for example. She worked in 2010 and earned an income of $25,000. Jackie has $10,000 worth of investments that earned her an interest income of $1,000. Jackie's current account shows an income of $26,000. Jackie spent $18,000 buying consumption goods and services. She also bought a new house, which cost her $60,000. So Jackie's total expenditure was $78,000. Jackie's expenditure minus her income is $52,000 ($78,000 minus $26,000). This amount is Jackie's current account deficit.

Economics in Action
Three Decades of Deficits

The numbers that you reviewed in Table 26.1 give a snapshot of the balance of payments accounts in 2010. The figure below puts that snapshot into perspective by showing the balance of payments between 1980 and 2010.

Because the economy grows and the price level rises, changes in the dollar value of the balance of payments do not convey much information. To remove the influences of economic growth and inflation, the fig-

ure shows the balance of payments expressed as a percentage of nominal GDP.

As you can see, a large current account deficit emerged during the 1980s but declined from 1987 to 1991. The current account deficit then increased through 2000, decreased slightly in 2001, and then increased through 2006 after which it decreased again but increased slightly in 2010. The capital and financial account balance is almost a mirror image of the current account balance. The official settlements balance is very small in comparison with the balances on the other two accounts.

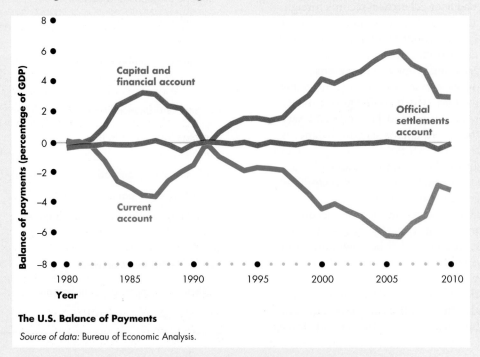

The U.S. Balance of Payments

Source of data: Bureau of Economic Analysis.

To pay for expenditure of $52,000 in excess of her income, Jackie must either use the money that she has in the bank or take out a loan. Suppose that Jackie took out a loan of $50,000 to help buy her house and that this loan was the only borrowing that she did. Borrowing is an *inflow* in the capital account, so Jackie's capital account *surplus* was $50,000. With a current account deficit of $52,000 and a capital account surplus of $50,000, Jackie was still $2,000 short. She got that $2,000 from her own bank account. Her cash holdings decreased by $2,000.

Jackie's income from her work is like a country's income from its exports. Her income from her investments is like a country's interest income from foreigners. Her purchases of goods and services, including her purchase of a house, are like a country's imports. Jackie's loan—borrowing from someone else—is like a country's borrowing from the rest of the world. The change in Jackie's bank account is like the change in the country's official reserves.

Borrowers and Lenders

A country that is borrowing more from the rest of the world than it is lending to the rest of the world is called a **net borrower**. Similarly, a **net lender** is a country that is lending more to the rest of the world than it is borrowing from the rest of the world.

The United States is a net borrower, but it has not always been in this situation. Throughout the 1960s and most of the 1970s, the United States was a net lender to the rest of the world—the United States had a current account surplus and a capital account deficit. But from the early 1980s, with the exception of only a single year, 1991, the United States has been a net borrower from the rest of the world. And during the years since 1992, the scale of U.S. borrowing has mushroomed.

Most countries are net borrowers like the United States. But a few countries, including China, Japan, and oil-rich Saudi Arabia, are net lenders. In 2010, when the United States borrowed more than $400 billion from the rest of the world, most of it came from China.

Debtors and Creditors

A net borrower might be decreasing its net assets held in the rest of the world, or it might be going deeper into debt. A nation's total stock of foreign investment determines whether it is a debtor or a creditor. A **debtor nation** is a country that during its entire history has borrowed more from the rest of the world than it has lent to it. It has a stock of outstanding debt to the rest of the world that exceeds the stock of its own claims on the rest of the world. A **creditor nation** is a country that during its entire history has invested more in the rest of the world than other countries have invested in it.

The United States was a debtor nation through the nineteenth century as we borrowed from Europe to finance our westward expansion, railroads, and industrialization. We paid off our debt and became a creditor nation for most of the twentieth century. But following a string of current account deficits, we became a debtor nation again in 1986.

Since 1986, the total stock of U.S. borrowing from the rest of the world has exceeded U.S. lending to the rest of the world. The largest debtor nations are the capital-hungry developing countries (such as the United States was during the nineteenth century). The international debt of these countries grew from less than a third to more than a half of their gross domestic product during the 1980s and created what was called the "Third World debt crisis."

Should we be concerned that the United States is a net borrower and a debtor? The answer to this question depends mainly on what the net borrower is doing with the borrowed money. If borrowing is financing investment that in turn is generating economic growth and higher income, borrowing is not a problem. It earns a return that more than pays the interest. But if borrowed money is used to finance consumption, to pay the interest and repay the loan, consumption will eventually have to be reduced. In this case, the greater the borrowing and the longer it goes on, the greater is the reduction in consumption that will eventually be necessary.

Is U.S. Borrowing for Consumption?

In 2010, we borrowed $439 billion from abroad. In that year, private investment in buildings, plant, and equipment was $1,840 billion and government investment in defense equipment and social projects was $500 billion. All this investment added to the nation's capital, and increased productivity. Government also spends on education and health care services, which increase *human capital*. Our international borrowing is financing private and public investment, not consumption.

Current Account Balance

What determines a country's current account balance and net foreign borrowing? You've seen that net exports (*NX*) is the main item in the current account. We can define the current account balance (*CAB*) as

CAB = *NX* + Net interest income + Net transfers.

We can study the current account balance by looking at what determines net exports because the other two items are small and do not fluctuate much.

Net Exports

Net exports are determined by the government budget and private saving and investment. To see how net exports are determined, we need to recall some of the things that we learned in Chapter 24 about the flows of funds that finance investment. Table 26.2 refreshes your memory and summarizes some calculations.

Part (a) lists the national income variables that are needed, with their symbols. Part (b) defines three balances: net exports, the government sector balance, and the private sector balance.

Net exports is exports of goods and services minus imports of goods and services.

The **government sector balance** is equal to net taxes minus government expenditures on goods and services. If that number is positive, a government sector surplus is lent to other sectors; if that number is negative, a government deficit must be financed by borrowing from other sectors. The government sector deficit is the sum of the deficits of the federal, state, and local governments.

The **private sector balance** is saving minus investment. If saving exceeds investment, a private sector surplus is lent to other sectors. If investment exceeds saving, a private sector deficit is financed by borrowing from other sectors.

Part (b) also shows the values of these balances for the United States in 2010. As you can see, net exports were –$536 billion, a deficit of $536 billion. The government sector's revenue from *net* taxes was $1,698 billion and its expenditure was $2,993 billion, so the government sector balance was –$1,295 billion—a deficit of $1,295 billion. The private sector saved $2,598 billion and invested $1,839 billion, so its balance was $759 billion—a surplus of $759 billion.

Part (c) shows the relationship among the three balances. From the *National Income and Product*

TABLE 26.2   Net Exports, the Government Budget, Saving, and Investment

	Symbols and equations	United States in 2010 (billions of dollars)
(a) Variables		
Exports*	X	1,818
Imports*	M	2,354
Government expenditures	G	2,993
Net taxes	T	1,698
Investment	I	1,839
Saving	S	2,598

(b) Balances		
Net exports	$X - M$	1,818 – 2,354 = –536
Government sector	$T - G$	1,698 – 2,993 = –1,295
Private sector	$S - I$	2,598 – 1,839 = 759

(c) Relationship among balances

National accounts	$Y = C + I + G + X - M$	
	$= C + S + T$	
Rearranging:	$X - M = S - I + T - G$	
Net exports	$X - M$	–536
equals:		
Government sector	$T - G$	–1,295
plus		
Private sector	$S - I$	759

Source of data: Bureau of Economic Analysis. The data are for 2010, average of first two quarters, seasonally adjusted at annual rate.

* The *National Income and Product Accounts* measures of exports and imports are slightly different from the balance of payments accounts measures in Table 26.1 on p. 631.

Accounts, we know that real GDP, *Y*, is the sum of consumption expenditure (*C*), investment, government expenditure, and net exports. Real GDP also equals the sum of consumption expenditure, saving, and net taxes. Rearranging these equations tells us that net exports is the sum of the government sector balance and the private sector balance. In the United States in 2010, the government sector balance was

Economics in Action
The Three Sector Balances

You've seen that net exports equal the sum of the government sector balance and the private sector balance. How do these three sector balances fluctuate over time?

The figure answers this question. It shows the government sector balance (the red line), net exports (the blue line), and the private sector balance (the green line).

The private sector balance and the government sector balance move in opposite directions. When the government sector deficit increased during the late 1980s and early 1990s, the private sector surplus increased. And when the government sector deficit decreased and became a surplus during the 1990s and early 2000s, the private sector's surplus decreased and became a deficit. And when the government deficit increased yet again from 2007 to 2009, the private sector deficit shrank and became a surplus.

Sometimes, when the government sector deficit increases, as it did during the first half of the 1980s, net exports become more negative. But after the early 1990s, net exports did not follow the government sector balance closely. Rather, net exports respond to the *sum* of the government sector and private sector

balances. When both the private sector and the government sector have a deficit, net exports are negative and the combined private and government deficit is financed by borrowing from the rest of the world. But the dominant trend in net exports is negative.

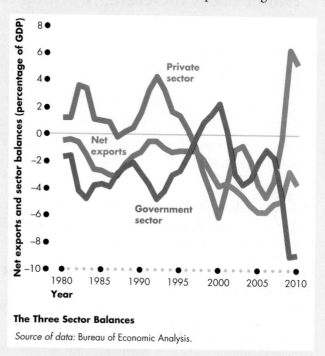

The Three Sector Balances

Source of data: Bureau of Economic Analysis.

–$1,295 billion and the private sector balance was $759 billion. The government sector balance plus the private sector balance equaled net exports of –$536 billion.

Where Is the Exchange Rate?

We haven't mentioned the exchange rate while discussing the balance of payments. Doesn't it play a role? The answer is that in the short run it does but in the long run it doesn't.

In the short run, a fall in the dollar lowers the real exchange rate, which makes U.S. imports more costly and U.S. exports more competitive. A higher price of imported consumption goods and services might induce a decrease in consumption expenditure and an increase in saving. A higher price of imported capital goods might induce a decrease in investment. Other things remaining the same, an increase in saving or a decrease in investment decreases the private sector deficit and decreases the current account deficit.

But in the long run, a change in the nominal exchange rate leaves the real exchange rate unchanged and plays no role in influencing the current account balance.

 REVIEW QUIZ

1 What are the transactions that the balance of payments accounts record?
2 Is the United States a net borrower or a net lender? Is it a debtor or a creditor nation?
3 How are net exports and the government sector balance linked?

You can work these questions in Study Plan 26.4 and get instant feedback.

◆ *Reading Between the Lines* on pp. 636–637 looks at risky trading that exploits the U.S. interest rate differential in the foreign exchange market.

The Dollar and "Carry Trade"

Dollar Faces Increasingly Strong Set of Headwinds

http://www.financialtimes.com
August 5, 2010

Only a few weeks ago, the dollar was powering toward its highest levels in four years, the beneficiary of widespread gloom about Europe's debt crisis and rising optimism about the U.S. recovery.

Since then, investors have soured on the world's largest economy. The dollar has tumbled 9 percent on a trade-weighted basis in two months, and yesterday fell to ¥85.29, within a whisker of a 15-year low. ...

A wave of weak economic data, including disappointing jobs figures, and expectations of further monetary easing by the U.S. Federal Reserve to head off the risk of a double-dip recession have been the main drivers of the dollar's fall. ...

As they pull money out of the greenback, investors are betting the recovery in other parts of the world will outpace that of the United States. Asian countries, expected to enjoy stronger growth than the debt-burdened west, have enjoyed strong inflows of funds. ...

The conditions are building, too, for a return of the dollar "carry trade", in which investors take advantage of low U.S. borrowing costs to invest in higher-yielding assets elsewhere. ...

One dollar "carry trade" has involved buying Indonesian bonds. Foreign ownership of Indonesian bonds has risen to a record, while bond yields—which move inversely to prices—have fallen to record lows. Tim Lee at Pi Economics, a consultancy, says the dollar carry trade may now be worth more than $750 billion. ...

In the longer term, the success of the dollar "carry trade" will depend on the U.S. economy remaining weak—but not too weak. ...

ESSENCE OF THE STORY

- Concern about Europe's debt crisis and optimism about U.S. real GDP growth brought an appreciation of the U.S. dollar.

- Disappointing jobs figures and expectations of further monetary easing by the Fed changed the outlook, ended the rise in the dollar, and lowered its value by 9 percent on average and close to a 15-year low against the Japanese yen (¥).

- Investors are pulling funds out of the U.S. dollar and moving them to the Asian currencies.

- The dollar "carry trade" is expanding and one estimate puts it at more than $750 billion.

- The longer term success of the dollar "carry trade" will depend on the U.S. economy remaining weak so that interest rates remain low.

- The news article says the dollar will keep depreciating and U.S. interest rates will remain low, so the "carry trade" will be profitable.

- The *carry trade* is borrowing at a low interest rate in one currency, converting the funds to another currency to earn a higher interest rate, then converting the funds back to the original currency.

- Carry trade is profitable provided the interest rate difference doesn't get wiped out by a fall in the value of the currency with the higher interest rate.

- If the carry trade was persistently profitable, it would mean that *interest rate parity* did not hold.

- *Interest rate parity* (explained on p. 626) is a situation in which, adjusted for risk, expected rates of return are equal in all currencies.

- The "carry trade" was profitable in 2009 and 2010.

- Figure 1 shows that the Indonesian rupiah has *appreciated* against the U.S. dollar (the dollar has depreciated).

- Figure 2 shows the interest rates in Indonesia and the United States. Large investors can borrow at the U.S. commercial bill rate (almost zero) and small investors can borrow at an interest rate of about 2 percentage points above the prime lending rate.

- Large investors can buy and sell rupiah for a small percentage transaction fee. Small investors pay a large percentage transaction fee.

- Figure 3 shows the profit (and loss) from borrowing $100 and using the carry trade to earn the Indonesian interest rate.

- Because the Indonesian interest rate exceeds the U.S. interest rate *and the rupiah has appreciated*, the carry trade has been profitable.

- But the percentage rate of return has fallen, and it turned negative for small investors.

- Does the profitable carry trade mean that interest rate parity doesn't hold?

- It does not. Investing in Indonesian rupiah is risky. The rupiah might depreciate and wipe out the interest rate difference.

- The economic rear-view mirror is much clearer than the windshield.

- Expected returns are equal, but actual past returns are unequal. As people have increased investments in Indonesia, the "carry trade" profit has shrunk.

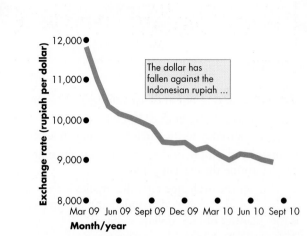

Figure 1 The falling dollar and rising Indonesian rupiah

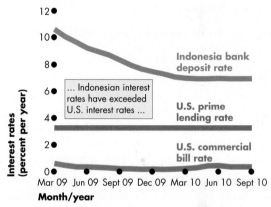

Figure 2 U.S. and Indonesian interest rates

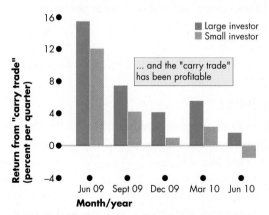

Figure 3 Profit from U.S.–Indonesian "carry trade"

637

SUMMARY

Key Points

The Foreign Exchange Market (pp. 618–622)

- Foreign currency is obtained in exchange for domestic currency in the foreign exchange market.
- Demand and supply in the foreign exchange market determine the exchange rate.
- The higher the exchange rate, the smaller is the quantity of U.S. dollars demanded and the greater is the quantity of U.S. dollars supplied.
- The equilibrium exchange rate makes the quantity of U.S. dollars demanded equal the quantity of U.S. dollars supplied.

Working Problems 1 to 6 will give you a better understanding of the foreign exchange market.

Exchange Rate Fluctuations (pp. 623–627)

- Changes in the world demand for U.S. exports, the U.S. interest rate differential, or the expected future exchange rate change the demand for U.S. dollars.
- Changes in U.S. demand for imports, the U.S. interest rate differential, or the expected future exchange rate change the supply of U.S. dollars.
- Exchange rate expectations are influenced by purchasing power parity and interest rate parity.

- In the long run, the nominal exchange rate is a monetary phenomenon and the real exchange rate is independent of the nominal exchange rate.

Working Problems 7 to 15 will give you a better understanding of exchange rate fluctuations.

Exchange Rate Policy (pp. 628–630)

- An exchange rate can be flexible, fixed, or a crawling peg.
- To achieve a fixed or a crawling exchange rate, a central bank must intervene in the foreign exchange market and either buy or sell foreign currency.

Working Problems 16 and 17 will give you a better understanding of exchange rate policy.

Financing International Trade (pp. 631–635)

- International trade, borrowing, and lending are financed by using foreign currency.
- A country's international transactions are recorded in its current account, capital account, and official settlements account.
- The current account balance is similar to net exports and is determined by the government sector balance plus the private sector balance.

Working Problems 18 and 19 will give you a better understanding of financing international trade.

Key Terms

Balance of payments accounts, 631
Capital and financial account, 631
Crawling peg, 629
Creditor nation, 633
Current account, 631
Debtor nation, 633
Exchange rate, 618
Fixed exchange rate, 628

Flexible exchange rate, 628
Foreign currency, 618
Foreign exchange market, 618
Government sector balance, 634
Interest rate parity, 626
Net borrower, 633
Net exports, 634
Net lender, 633

Official settlements account, 631
Private sector balance, 634
Purchasing power parity, 626
Real exchange rate, 627
U.S. interest rate differential, 623
U.S. official reserves, 631

STUDY PLAN PROBLEMS AND APPLICATIONS

myeconlab You can work Problems 1 to 19 in MyEconLab Chapter 26 Study Plan and get instant feedback.

The Foreign Exchange Market (Study Plan 26.1)

Use the following data to work Problems 1 to 3.
The U.S. dollar exchange rate increased from $0.89 Canadian in June 2009 to $0.96 Canadian in June 2010, and it decreased from 83.8 euro cents in January 2009 to 76.9 euro cents in January 2010.

1. Did the U.S. dollar appreciate or depreciate against the Canadian dollar? Did the U.S. dollar appreciate or depreciate against the euro?

2. What was the value of the Canadian dollar in terms of U.S. dollars in June 2009 and June 2010? Did the Canadian dollar appreciate or depreciate against the U.S. dollar over the year June 2009 to June 2010?

3. What was the value of one euro (100 euro cents) in terms of U.S. dollars in January 2009 and January 2010? Did the euro appreciate or depreciate against the U.S. dollar in 2009?

Use the following data to work Problems 4 to 6.

In January 2010, the exchange rate was 91 yen per U.S. dollar. By September 2010, the exchange rate had fallen to 84 yen per U.S. dollar.

4. Explain the exports effect of this change in the exchange rate.

5. Explain the imports effect of this change in the exchange rate.

6. Explain the expected profit effect of this change in the exchange rate.

Exchange Rate Fluctuations (Study Plan 26.2)

7. On August 3, 2010, the U.S. dollar was trading at 86 yen per U.S. dollar on the foreign exchange market. On September 13, 2010, the U.S. dollar was trading at 83 yen per U.S. dollar.
   a. What events in the foreign exchange market might have brought this fall in the value of the U.S. dollar?
   b. Did the events change the demand for U.S. dollars, the supply of U.S. dollars, or both demand and supply in the foreign exchange market?

8. Colombia is the world's biggest producer of roses. The global demand for roses increases and at the same time, the central bank in Colombia increases the interest rate. In the foreign exchange market for Colombian pesos, what happens to
   a. The demand for pesos?
   b. The supply of pesos?
   c. The quantity of pesos demanded?
   d. The quantity of pesos supplied?
   e. The exchange rate of the peso against the U.S. dollar?

9. If a euro deposit in a bank in Paris, France, earns interest of 4 percent a year and a yen deposit in Tokyo, Japan, earns 0.5 percent a year, everything else remaining the same and adjusted for risk, what is the exchange rate expectation of the Japanese yen?

10. The U.K. pound is trading at 1.54 U.S. dollars per U.K. pound. There is purchasing power parity at this exchange rate. The interest rate in the United States is 2 percent a year and the interest rate in the United Kingdom is 4 percent a year.
    a. Calculate the U.S. interest rate differential.
    b. What is the U.K. pound expected to be worth in terms of U.S. dollars one year from now?
    c. Which country more likely has the lower inflation rate? How can you tell?

11. You can purchase a laptop in Mexico City for 12,960 Mexican pesos. If the exchange rate is 10.8 Mexican pesos per U.S. dollar and if purchasing power parity prevails, at what price can you buy an identical computer in Dallas, Texas?

12. **When the Chips Are Down**
    The *Economist* magazine uses the price of a Big Mac to determine whether a currency is undervalued or overvalued. In July 2010, the price of a Big Mac was $3.73 in New York, 13.2 yuan in Beijing, and 6.50 Swiss francs in Geneva. The exchanges rates were 6.78 yuan per U.S. dollar and 1.05 Swiss francs per U.S. dollar.
                    Source: *The Economist*, July 22, 2010
    a. Was the yuan undervalued or overvalued relative to purchasing power parity?
    b. Was the Swiss franc undervalued or overvalued relative to purchasing power parity?
    c. Do you think the price of a Big Mac in different countries provides a valid test of purchasing power parity?

13. The price level in the Eurozone is 112.4, the price level in the United States is 109.1, and the nominal exchange rate was 80 euro cents per U.S. dollar. What is the real exchange rate expressed as Eurozone real GDP per unit of U.S. real GDP?

14. The U.S. price level is 106.3, the Japanese price level is 95.4, and the real exchange rate is 103.6 Japanese real GDP per unit of U.S. real GDP. What is the nominal exchange rate?

15. **Dollar Hits 15-Year Low vs Yen**

Today in Tokyo a dollar bought only 84.71 yen, the lowest since 1995. The dollar's weakness against the yen is making Japanese exports more expensive. Investors stepped up selling of U.S. dollars after the Federal Reserve announced yesterday only small steps aimed at shoring up the flagging U.S. economy. "Investors were unnerved by the Fed's statement. It just confirmed that the U.S. economic recovery is slowing," said a dealer at a Japanese bank in Tokyo.

Source: *USA Today*, August 11, 2010

On a graph of the foreign exchange market show the effects of

a. Japanese exports becoming more expensive.

b. Investors stepping up the sale of dollars.

Exchange Rate Policy (Study Plan 26.3)

16. With the strengthening of the yen against the U.S. dollar in 2010, Japan's central bank did not take any action. A leading Japanese politician has called on the central bank to take actions to weaken the yen, saying it will help exporters in the short run and have no long-run effects.

a. What is Japan's current exchange rate policy?

b. What does the politician want the exchange rate policy to be in the short run? Why would such a policy have no effect on the exchange rate in the long run?

17. **Double-Talking the Dollar**

In the 1970s and 1980s, the United States was constantly buying and selling foreign currencies to change the value of the dollar, but since 1995 it has made only a few transactions and since 2000 none at all. The foreign exchange market is so huge, trying to manipulate the dollar is largely futile. A currency's value reflects an economy's fundamentals: How well a country allocates resources, how productive its workers are, how it contains inflation, etc., but for years on end, currencies can move in directions that seem to have little to do with fundamentals. They overshoot their correct values, in part because nobody is ever sure exactly what those correct values are.

Source: *Time*, May 5, 2008

a. How has U.S. exchange rate policy evolved since the early 1970s?

b. Explain why "trying to manipulate the dollar is largely futile," especially in the long run.

c. Explain why a currency can experience short-run fluctuations "that seem to have little to do with fundamentals." Illustrate with a graph.

Financing International Trade (Study Plan 26.4)

18. The table gives some information about the U.S. international transactions in 2008.

Item	Billions of U.S. dollars
Imports of goods and services	2,561
Foreign investment in the United States	955
Exports of goods and services	1,853
U.S. investment abroad	300
Net interest income	121
Net transfers	−123
Statistical discrepancy	66

a. Calculate the current account balance.

b. Calculate the capital and financial account balance.

c. Did U.S. official reserves increase or decrease?

d. Was the United States a net borrower or a net lender in 2008? Explain your answer.

19. **The United States, Debtor Nation**

The United States is a debtor nation, and for most of the past 30 years it has been piling up large trade deficits. The current account has now reached a deficit of 6 percent of GDP, and must be financed by capital inflows. Foreigners must purchase large amounts of U.S. assets, or the current account deficit cannot be financed.

Source: *Asia Times*, September 28, 2006

a. Explain why a current account deficit "must be financed by capital inflows."

b. Under what circumstances should the debtor nation status of the United States be a concern?

ADDITIONAL PROBLEMS AND APPLICATIONS

myeconlab You can work these problems in MyEconLab if assigned by your instructor.

The Foreign Exchange Market

20. Suppose that yesterday, the U.S. dollar was trading on the foreign exchange market at 0.75 euros per U.S. dollar and today the U.S. dollar is trading at 0.78 euros per U.S. dollar. Which of the two currencies (the U.S. dollar or the euro) has appreciated and which has depreciated today?

21. Suppose that the exchange rate fell from 84 yen per U.S. dollar to 71 yen per U.S. dollar. What is the effect of this change on the quantity of U.S. dollars that people plan to buy in the foreign exchange market?

22. Suppose that the exchange rate rose from 71 yen per U.S. dollar to 100 yen per U.S. dollar. What is the effect of this change on the quantity of U.S. dollars that people plan to sell in the foreign exchange market?

23. Today's exchange rate between the yuan and the U.S. dollar is 6.78 yuan per dollar and the central bank of China is buying U.S. dollars in the foreign exchange market. If the central bank of China did not purchase U.S. dollars would there be excess demand or excess supply of U.S. dollars in the foreign exchange market? Would the exchange rate remain at 6.78 yuan per U.S. dollar? If not, which currency would appreciate?

Exchange Rate Fluctuations

24. Yesterday, the current exchange rate was $1.05 Canadian per U.S. dollar and traders expected the exchange rate to remain unchanged for the next month. Today, with new information, traders now expect the exchange rate next month to fall to $1 Canadian per U.S. dollar. Explain how the revised expected future exchange rate influences the demand for U.S. dollars, or the supply of U.S. dollars, or both in the foreign exchange market.

25. On January 1, 2010, the exchange rate was 91 yen per U.S. dollar. Over the year, the supply of U.S. dollars increased and by January, 2011, the exchange rate fell to 84 yen per U.S. dollar. What happened to the quantity of U.S. dollars that people planned to buy in the foreign exchange market?

26. On August 1, 2010, the exchange rate was 84 yen per U.S. dollar. Over the year, the demand for U.S. dollars increased and by August 1, 2011, the exchange rate was 100 yen per U.S. dollar. What happened to the quantity of U.S. dollars that people planned to sell in the foreign exchange market?

Use the following news clip to work Problems 27 and 28.

Top U.S. Real Estate Markets for Investment

Rahul Reddy has been investing in Australian real estate for the last two years. Now, with the Australian dollar growing in strength and the American housing market strained, he's got his eye on real estate in Florida and California. Encouraged by a weak dollar and a belief in the resiliency of the U.S. economy, investors are seeking investment properties and development opportunities in the United States. "The United States is good for speculative higher-risk investments from our perspective because the strong Australian dollar will enable us to gain hold of real estate at prices we will probably not see for a long time," says Reddy. "The United States is an economic powerhouse that I think will recover, and if the exchange rate goes back to what it was a few years ago, we will benefit."

Source: *Forbes*, July 10, 2008

27. Explain why foreigners are "seeking investment properties and development opportunities in the United States."

28. Explain what would happen if the speculation made by Reddy became widespread. Would expectations become self-fulfilling?

Use the following information to work Problems 29 and 30.

Brazil's Overvalued Real

The Brazilian real has appreciated 33 percent against the U.S. dollar and has pushed up the price of a Big Mac in Sao Paulo to $4.60, higher than the New York price of $3.99. Despite Brazil's interest rate being at 8.75 percent a year compared to the U.S. interest rate at near zero, foreign funds flowing into Brazil surged in October.

Source: Bloomberg News, October 27, 2009

29. Does purchasing power parity hold? If not, does PPP predict that the Brazilian real will appreciate or depreciate against the U.S. dollar? Explain.

30. Does interest rate parity hold? If not, why not? Will the Brazilian real appreciate further or depreciate against the U.S. dollar if the Fed raises the interest rate while the Brazilian interest rate remains at 8.75 percent a year?

Exchange Rate Policy

Use the following news clip to work Problems 31 to 34.

U.S. Declines to Cite China as Currency Manipulator

The Bush administration has declined to cite China for manipulating its currency to gain unfair trade advantages against the United States. America's growing trade deficit with China, which last year hit an all-time high of $256.3 billion, is the largest deficit ever recorded with a single country. Chinese currency, the yuan, has risen in value by 18.4 percent against the U.S. dollar since the Chinese government loosened its currency system in July 2005. However, American manufacturers contend the yuan is still undervalued by as much as 40 percent, making Chinese products more competitive in this country and U.S. goods more expensive in China. China buys U.S. dollar-denominated securities to maintain the value of the yuan in terms of the U.S. dollar.

Source: MSN, May 15, 2008

31. What was the exchange rate policy adopted by China until July 2005? Explain how it worked. Draw a graph to illustrate your answer.

32. What was the exchange rate policy adopted by China after July 2005? Explain how it works.

33. Explain how fixed and crawling peg exchange rates can be used to manipulate trade balances in the short run, but not the long run.

34. Explain the long-run effect of China's current exchange rate policy.

35. **Aussie Dollar Hit by Interest Rate Talk**

The Australian dollar fell against the U.S. dollar to its lowest value in the past two weeks. The CPI inflation rate was reported to be generally as expected but not high enough to justify previous expectations for an aggressive interest rate rise by Australia's central bank next week.

Source: Reuters, October 28, 2009

a. What is Australia's exchange rate policy? Explain why expectations about the Australian interest rate lowered the value of the Australian dollar against the U.S. dollar.

b. To avoid the fall in the value of the Australian dollar against the U.S. dollar, what action could the central bank of Australia have taken? Would such an action signal a change in Australia's exchange rate policy?

Financing International Trade

Use the following table to work Problems 36 to 38.

The table gives some data about the U.K. economy:

Item	Billions of U.K. pounds
Consumption expenditure	721
Exports of goods and services	277
Government expenditures	230
Net taxes	217
Investment	181
Saving	162

36. Calculate the private sector balance.

37. Calculate the government sector balance.

38. Calculate net exports and show the relationship between the government sector balance and net exports.

Economics in the News

39. After you have studied *Reading Between the Lines* on pp. 636–637 answer the following questions.

a. What is the "carry trade" and between what types of countries and currencies is it likely to take place?

b. What are the risks in the "carry trade"?

c. Is it possible to earn a profit in the "carry trade" in the long run? Explain why or why not.

d. Explain how participating in the "carry trade" reduces the profit available to other traders.

e. Define interest rate parity and explain its connection with the "carry trade."

f. Define purchasing power parity and explain how this concept might be used in the "carry trade."

Expanding the Frontier

Economics is about how we cope with scarcity. We cope as individuals by making choices that balance marginal benefits and marginal costs so that we use our scarce resources efficiently. We cope as societies by creating incentive systems and social institutions that encourage specialization and exchange.

These choices and the incentive systems that guide them determine what we specialize in; how much work we do; how hard we work at school to learn the mental skills that form our human capital and that determine the kinds of jobs we get and the incomes we earn; how much we save for future big-ticket expenditures; how much businesses and governments spend on new capital—on auto assembly lines, computers and fiber cables for improved Internet services, shopping malls, highways, bridges, and tunnels; how intensively existing capital and natural resources are used and how quickly they wear out or are used up; and the problems that scientists, engineers, and other inventors work on to develop new technologies.

All the choices we've just described combine to determine the standard of living and the rate at which it improves—the economic growth rate.

Money that makes specialization and exchange in markets possible is a huge contributor to economic growth. But too much money brings a rising cost of living with no improvement in the standard of living.

Joseph Schumpeter, *the son of a textile factory owner, was born in Austria in 1883. He moved from Austria to Germany during the tumultuous 1920s when those two countries experienced hyperinflation. In 1932, in the depths of the Great Depression, he came to the United States and became a professor of economics at Harvard University.*

This creative economic thinker wrote about economic growth and development, business cycles, political systems, and economic biography. He was a person of strong opinions who expressed them forcefully and delighted in verbal battles.

Schumpeter saw the development and diffusion of new technologies by profit-seeking entrepreneurs as the source of economic progress. But he saw economic progress as a process of creative destruction—the creation of new profit opportunities and the destruction of currently profitable businesses. For Schumpeter, economic growth and the business cycle were a single phenomenon.

"Economic progress, in capitalist society, means turmoil."

JOSEPH SCHUMPETER
Capitalism, Socialism, and Democracy

What attracted you to economics?

It was a random event. I wanted to be rich, so I asked my mom, "In my family, who is the richest guy?" She said, "Your uncle John." And I asked, "What did he study?" And she said, "Economics." So I went into economics!

In Spain, there are no liberal arts colleges where you can study lots of things. At age 18, you must decide what career you will follow. If you choose economics, you go to economics school and take economics five years in a row. So you have to make a decision in a crazy way, like I did.

How did economic growth become your major field of research?

I studied economics. I liked it. I studied mathematical economics. I liked it too, and I went to graduate school. In my second year at Harvard, Jeffrey Sachs hired me to go to Bolivia. I saw poor people for the first time in my life. I was shocked. I decided I should try to answer the question "Why are these people so poor and why are we so rich, and what can we do to turn their state into our state?" We live in a bubble world in the United States and Europe, and we don't realize how poor people really are. When you see poverty at first hand, it is very hard to think about something else. So I decided to study economic growth. Coincidentally, when I returned from Bolivia, I was assigned to be Robert Barro's teaching assistant. He was teaching economic growth, so I studied with him and eventually wrote books and articles with him.

In your first research on economic growth, you tested the neoclassical growth model using data for a number of countries and for the states of the United States. What did you discover?

Neoclassical theory was criticized on two grounds. First, its source of growth, technological change, is exogenous—not explained. Second, its assumption of diminishing marginal returns to capital seems to imply that income per person should converge to the same level in every country. If you are poor, your marginal product should be high. Every cookie that you save should generate huge growth. If you are rich, your marginal product should be low. Every cookie you save should generate very little growth. Therefore poor countries should grow faster than rich countries, and convergence of income levels should occur. Convergence doesn't occur, so, said its critics, neoclassical theory must be wrong.

It turned out that it was this criticism that was wrong. Growth depends on the productivity of your cookies and on how many cookies you save. If you don't save any cookies, you don't grow, even if your marginal product is large.

Conditional convergence is the idea that income per person will converge only if countries have similar savings rates, similar technologies, and similar everything. That's what I tested. To hold every relevant factor equal, I tested the hypothesis using regions:

> Growth through capital accumulation is very, very hard. Growth has to come from other things, such as technological change.

states within the United States or countries that are similar. And once you're careful to hold other things equal, you see a perfect negative relationship between growth rates and income levels.

XAVIER SALA-I-MARTIN is Professor of Economics at Columbia University. He is also a Research Associate at the National Bureau of Economic Research, Senior Economic Advisor to the World Economic Forum, Associate Editor of the *Journal of Economic Growth,* founder and CEO of Umbele Foundation: A Future for Africa, and President of the Economic Commission of the Barcelona Football Club.

Professor Sala-i-Martin was an undergraduate at Universitat Autonoma de Barcelona and a graduate student at Harvard University, where he obtained his Ph.D. in 1990.

In 2004, he was awarded the Premio Juan Carlos I de Economía, a biannual prize given by the Bank of Spain to the best economist in Spain and Latin America. With Robert Barro, he is the author of *Economic Growth* Second Edition (MIT Press, 2003), the definitive graduate level text on this topic.

Michael Parkin talked with Xavier Sala-i-Martin about his work and the progress that economists have made in understanding economic growth.

As predicted by neoclassical theory, poor countries grow faster than rich countries if they are similar. So my research shows that it is not so easy to reject neoclassical theory. The law of diminishing returns that comes from Adam Smith and Malthus and Ricardo is very powerful. Growth through capital accumulation is very, very hard. Growth has to come from other things, such as technological change.

What do we know today about the nature and causes of the wealth of nations that Adam Smith didn't know?

Actually, even though over the last two hundred years some of the best minds have looked at the question, we know surprisingly little. We have some general principles that are not very easy to apply in practice. We know, for example, that markets are good. We know that for the economy to work, we need property rights to be guaranteed. If there are thieves—government or private thieves—that can steal the proceeds of the investment, there's no investment and there's no growth. We know that the incentives are very important.

These are general principles. Because we know these principles we should ask: How come Africa is still poor? The answer is, it is very hard to translate "Markets are good" and "Property rights work" into practical actions. We know that Zimbabwe has to guarantee property rights. With the government it has, that's not going to work. The U.S. constitution works in the United States. If you try to copy the constitution and impose the system in Zimbabwe, it's not going to work.

You've done a lot of work on distribution of income, and you say we've made a lot of progress. What is the evidence to support this conclusion?

There are two issues: poverty and inequality. When in 2001 I said poverty is going down, everyone said I was crazy. The United Nations Development Report, which uses World Bank data, was saying the exact opposite. I said the World Bank methodology was flawed. After a big public argument that you can see in *The Economist,* the World Bank revised their poverty numbers and they now agree with me that poverty rates are falling.

Now why is poverty falling? In 1970, 80 percent of the world's poor were in Asia—in China, India, Bangladesh, and Indonesia. China's "Great Leap Forward" was a great leap backward. People were starving to death. Now, the growth of these countries has been spectacular and the global poverty rate has fallen. Yes, if you look at Africa, Africa is going backwards. But Africa has 700 million people. China has 1.3 billion. India has 1.1 billion. Indonesia has 300 million. Asia has 4 billion of the world's 6 billion people. These big guys are growing. It's impossible that global poverty is not going down.

But what we care about is poverty in different regions of the world. Asia has been doing very well, but Africa has not. Unfortunately, Africa is still going in the wrong direction.

You've made a big personal commitment to Africa. What is the Africa problem? Why does this continent lag behind Asia? Why, as you've just put it, is Africa going in the wrong direction?

Number one, Africa is a very violent continent. There are twenty-two wars in Africa as we speak. Two, nobody will invest in Africa. Three, we in the rich world—the United States, Europe, and Japan—won't let them trade. Because we have agricultural subsidies, trade barriers, and tariffs for their products, they can't sell to us.

Africans should globalize themselves. They should open, and we should let them open. They should introduce markets. But to get markets, you need legal systems, police, transparency, less red tape. You need a lot of the things we have now. They have corrupt economies, very bureaucratic, with no property rights, the judiciary is corrupt. All of that has to change.

They need female education. One of the biggest rates of return that we have is educating girls. To educate girls, they'll need to build schools, they need to pay teachers, they need to buy uniforms, they need to provide the incentives for girls to go to school, which usually is like a string. You pull it, you don't push it. Pushing education doesn't work. What you need is: Let the girls know that the rate of return on education is very high by providing jobs after they leave school. So you need to change the incentives of the girls to go to school and educate themselves. That's going to increase the national product, but it will also increase health, and it will also reduce fertility.

Returning to the problems of poverty and inequality, how can inequality be increasing within countries but decreasing globally—across countries?

Because most inequality comes from the fact that some people live in rich countries and some people live in poor countries. The big difference across people is not that there are rich Americans and poor Americans. Americans are very close to each other relative to the difference between Americans and people from Senegal. What is closing today is the gap *across* countries—and for the first time in history. Before the Industrial Revolution, everybody was equal. Equal and poor. Equally poor. People were living at subsistence levels, which means you eat, you're clothed, you have a house, you die. No movies, no travel, no music, no toothbrush. Just subsist. And if the weather is not good, one third of the population dies. That was the history of the world between 10,000 B.C. and today.

Yes, there was a king, there was Caesar, but the majority of the population were peasants.

All of a sudden, the Industrial Revolution means that one small country, England, takes off and there is 2 percent growth every year. The living standard of the workers of England goes up and up and up. Then the United States, then France, then the rest of Europe, then Canada all begin to grow.

In terms of today's population, one billion people become rich and five billion remain poor. Now for the first time in history, the majority of these five billion people are growing more rapidly than the rich guys. They're catching up quickly. The incomes of the majority of poor citizens of the world are growing faster than those of Americans.

What advice do you have for someone who is just beginning to study economics?

Question! Question everything! Take some courses in history and math. And read my latest favorite book, Bill Easterly's *White Man's Burden.*[*] It shows why we have not been doing the right thing in the aid business. I'm a little bit less dramatic than he is. He says that nothing has worked. I think some things have worked, and we have to take advantage of what has worked to build on it. But I agree with the general principle that being nice, being good, doesn't necessarily mean doing good. Lots of people with good intentions do harm. Economic science teaches us that incentives are the key.

> Question!
> Question everything!

---

[*]William Easterly, *The White Man's Burden: Why the West's Efforts to Aid the Rest Have Done So Much Ill and So Little Good.* New York, Penguin Books, 2006.

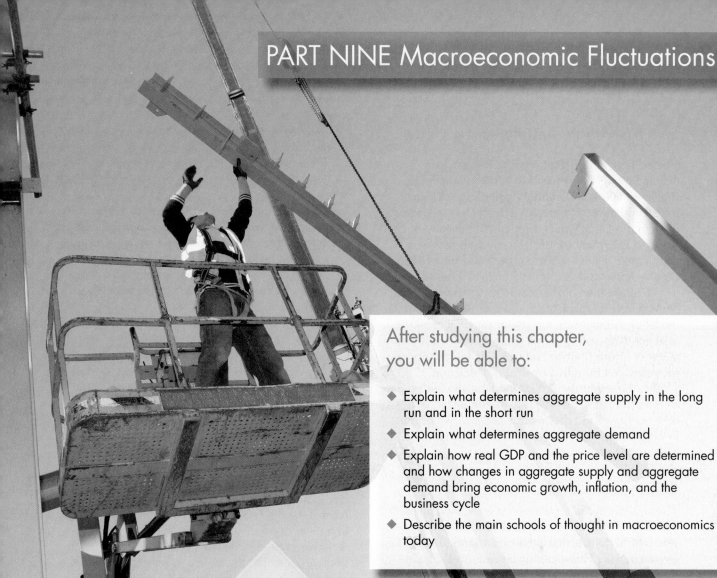

After studying this chapter,
you will be able to:

◆ Explain what determines aggregate supply in the long
  run and in the short run

◆ Explain what determines aggregate demand

◆ Explain how real GDP and the price level are determined
  and how changes in aggregate supply and aggregate
  demand bring economic growth, inflation, and the
  business cycle

◆ Describe the main schools of thought in macroeconomics
  today

27

AGGREGATE SUPPLY AND AGGREGATE DEMAND

The pace at which production grows and prices rise is uneven. In 2004, real
GDP grew by 3.6 percent, but 2008 had zero growth and 2009 saw real
GDP shrink by more than 2 percent.

Similarly, during recent years, prices have increased at rates ranging from
more than 3 percent in 2005 to a barely perceptible less than 1 percent in 2009.

The uneven pace of economic growth and inflation—the business cycle—is
the subject of this chapter and the two that follow it.

This chapter explains a model of real GDP and the price level—the *aggregate
supply–aggregate demand model* or *AS-AD model*. This model represents the
consensus view of macroeconomists on how real GDP and the price
level are determined. The model provides a framework for
understanding the forces that make our economy expand, that bring
inflation, and that cause business cycle fluctuations. The *AS-AD* model
also provides a framework within which we can see the range of views
of macroeconomists in different schools of thought.

In *Reading Between the Lines* at the end of the chapter, we use the *AS-AD*
model to interpret the course of U.S. real GDP and the price level in 2010.

647

◆ Aggregate Supply

The purpose of the aggregate supply–aggregate demand model that you study in this chapter is to explain how real GDP and the price level are determined and how they interact. The model uses similar ideas to those that you encountered in Chapter 3 when you learned how the quantity and price in a competitive market are determined. But the *aggregate supply–aggregate* demand model (*AS-AD* model) isn't just an application of the competitive market model. Some differences arise because the *AS-AD* model is a model of an imaginary market for the total of all the final goods and services that make up real GDP. The quantity in this "market" is real GDP and the price is the price level measured by the GDP deflator.

One thing that the *AS-AD* model shares with the competitive market model is that both distinguish between *supply* and the *quantity supplied*. We begin by explaining what we mean by the quantity of real GDP supplied.

Quantity Supplied and Supply

The *quantity of real GDP supplied* is the total quantity of goods and services, valued in constant base-year (2005) dollars, that firms plan to produce during a given period. This quantity depends on the quantity of labor employed, the quantity of physical and human capital, and the state of technology.

At any given time, the quantity of capital and the state of technology are fixed. They depend on decisions that were made in the past. The population is also fixed. But the quantity of labor is not fixed. It depends on decisions made by households and firms about the supply of and demand for labor.

The labor market can be in any one of three states: at full employment, above full employment, or below full employment. At full employment, the quantity of real GDP supplied is *potential GDP*, which depends on the full-employment quantity of labor (see Chapter 23, pp. 545–547). Over the business cycle, employment fluctuates around full employment and the quantity of real GDP supplied fluctuates around potential GDP.

Aggregate supply is the relationship between the quantity of real GDP supplied and the price level. This relationship is different in the long run than in the short run and to study aggregate supply, we distinguish between two time frames:

- Long-run aggregate supply
- Short-run aggregate supply

Long-Run Aggregate Supply

Long-run aggregate supply is the relationship between the quantity of real GDP supplied and the price level when the money wage rate changes in step with the price level to maintain full employment. The quantity of real GDP supplied at full employment equals potential GDP and this quantity is the same regardless of the price level.

The long-run aggregate supply curve in Fig. 27.1 illustrates long-run aggregate supply as the vertical line at potential GDP labeled *LAS*. Along the long-run aggregate supply curve, as the price level changes, the money wage rate also changes so the real wage rate remains at the full-employment equilibrium level and real GDP remains at potential GDP. The long-run aggregate supply curve is always vertical and is always located at potential GDP.

The long-run aggregate supply curve is vertical because potential GDP is independent of the price level. The reason for this independence is that a movement along the *LAS* curve is accompanied by a change in *two* sets of prices: the prices of goods and services—the price level—and the prices of the factors of production, most notably, the money wage rate. A 10 percent increase in the prices of goods and services is matched by a 10 percent increase in the money wage rate. Because the price level and the money wage rate change by the same percentage, the *real wage rate* remains unchanged at its full-employment equilibrium level. So when the price level changes and the real wage rate remains constant, employment remains constant and real GDP remains constant at potential GDP.

Production at a Pepsi Plant You can see more clearly why real GDP is unchanged when all prices change by the same percentage by thinking about production decisions at a Pepsi bottling plant. How does the quantity of Pepsi supplied change if the price of Pepsi changes and the wage rate of the workers and prices of all the other resources used vary by the same percentage? The answer is that the quantity supplied doesn't change. The firm produces the quantity that maximizes profit. That quantity depends on the price of Pepsi relative to the cost of producing it. With no change in price *relative to cost*, production doesn't change.

Short-Run Aggregate Supply

Short-run aggregate supply is the relationship between the quantity of real GDP supplied and the price level *when the money wage rate, the prices of other resources, and potential GDP remain constant.* Figure 27.1 illustrates this relationship as the short-run aggregate supply curve *SAS* and the short-run aggregate supply schedule. Each point on the *SAS* curve corresponds to a row of the short-run aggregate supply schedule. For example, point *A* on the *SAS* curve and row *A* of the schedule tell us that if the price level is 100, the quantity of real GDP supplied is $12 trillion. In the short run, a rise in the price level brings an increase in the quantity of real GDP supplied. The short-run aggregate supply curve slopes upward.

With a given money wage rate, there is one price level at which the real wage rate is at its full-employment equilibrium level. At this price level, the quantity of real GDP supplied equals potential GDP and the *SAS* curve intersects the *LAS* curve. In this example, that price level is 110. If the price level rises above 110, the quantity of real GDP supplied increases along the *SAS* curve and exceeds potential GDP; if the price level falls below 110, the quantity of real GDP supplied decreases along the *SAS* curve and is less than potential GDP.

Back at the Pepsi Plant You can see why the short-run aggregate supply curve slopes upward by returning to the Pepsi bottling plant. If production increases, marginal cost rises and if production decreases, marginal cost falls (see Chapter 2, p. 33).

If the price of Pepsi rises with no change in the money wage rate and other costs, Pepsi can increase profit by increasing production. Pepsi is in business to maximize its profit, so it increases production.

Similarly, if the price of Pepsi falls while the money wage rate and other costs remain constant, Pepsi can avoid a loss by decreasing production. The lower price weakens the incentive to produce, so Pepsi decreases production.

What's true for Pepsi bottlers is true for the producers of all goods and services. When all prices rise, the *price level rises.* If the price level rises and the money wage rate and other factor prices remain constant, all firms increase production and the quantity of real GDP supplied increases. A fall in the price level has the opposite effect and decreases the quantity of real GDP supplied.

FIGURE 27.1   Long-Run and Short-Run Aggregate Supply

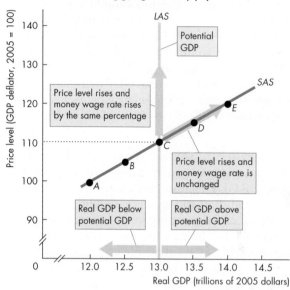

	Price level (GDP deflator)	Real GDP supplied (trillions of 2005 dollars)
A	100	12.0
B	105	12.5
C	**110**	**13.0**
D	115	13.5
E	120	14.0

In the long run, the quantity of real GDP supplied is potential GDP and the *LAS* curve is vertical at potential GDP. In the short-run, the quantity of real GDP supplied increases if the price level rises, while all other influences on supply plans remain the same.

The short-run aggregate supply curve, *SAS*, slopes upward. The short-run aggregate supply curve is based on the aggregate supply schedule in the table. Each point *A* through *E* on the curve corresponds to the row in the table identified by the same letter.

When the price level is 110, the quantity of real GDP supplied is $13 trillion, which is potential GDP. If the price level rises above 110, the quantity of real GDP supplied increases and exceeds potential GDP; if the price level falls below 110, the quantity of real GDP supplied decreases below potential GDP.

myeconlab   animation

Changes in Aggregate Supply

A change in the price level changes the quantity of real GDP supplied, which is illustrated by a movement along the short-run aggregate supply curve. It does not change aggregate supply. Aggregate supply changes when an influence on production plans other than the price level changes. These other influences include changes in potential GDP and changes in the money wage rate. Let's begin by looking at a change in potential GDP.

Changes in Potential GDP When potential GDP changes, aggregate supply changes. An increase in potential GDP increases both long-run aggregate supply and short-run aggregate supply.

Figure 27.2 shows the effects of an increase in potential GDP. Initially, the long-run aggregate supply curve is LAS_0 and the short-run aggregate supply curve is SAS_0. If potential GDP increases to $14 trillion, long-run aggregate supply increases and the long-run aggregate supply curve shifts rightward to LAS_1. Short-run aggregate supply also increases, and the short-run aggregate supply curve shifts rightward to SAS_1. The two supply curves shift by the same amount only if the full-employment price level remains constant, which we will assume to be the case.

Potential GDP can increase for any of three reasons:

- An increase in the full-employment quantity of labor
- An increase in the quantity of capital
- An advance in technology

Let's look at these influences on potential GDP and the aggregate supply curves.

An Increase in the Full-Employment Quantity of Labor A Pepsi bottling plant that employs 100 workers bottles more Pepsi than does an otherwise identical plant that employs 10 workers. The same is true for the economy as a whole. The larger the quantity of labor employed, the greater is real GDP.

Over time, potential GDP increases because the labor force increases. But (with constant capital and technology) *potential* GDP increases only if the full-employment quantity of labor increases. Fluctuations in employment over the business cycle bring fluctuations in real GDP. But these changes in real GDP are fluctuations around potential GDP. They are not changes in potential GDP and long-run aggregate supply.

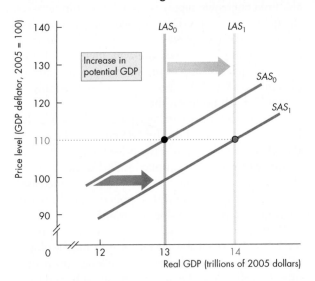

FIGURE 27.2   A Change in Potential GDP

An increase in potential GDP increases both long-run aggregate supply and short-run aggregate supply. The long-run aggregate supply curve shifts rightward from LAS_0 to LAS_1 and the short-run aggregate supply curve shifts from SAS_0 to SAS_1.

myeconlab   animation

An Increase in the Quantity of Capital A Pepsi bottling plant with two production lines bottles more Pepsi than does an otherwise identical plant that has only one production line. For the economy, the larger the quantity of capital, the more productive is the labor force and the greater is its potential GDP. Potential GDP per person in the capital-rich United States is vastly greater than that in capital-poor China or Russia.

Capital includes *human capital*. One Pepsi plant is managed by an economics major with an MBA and has a labor force with an average of 10 years of experience. This plant produces a larger output than does an otherwise identical plant that is managed by someone with no business training or experience and that has a young labor force that is new to bottling. The first plant has a greater amount of human capital than the second. For the economy as a whole, the larger the quantity of *human capital*—the skills that people have acquired in school and through on-the-job training—the greater is potential GDP.

An Advance in Technology A Pepsi plant that has pre-computer age machines produces less than one that uses the latest robot technology. Technological change enables firms to produce more from any given amount of factors of production. So even with fixed quantities of labor and capital, improvements in technology increase potential GDP.

Technological advances are by far the most important source of increased production over the past two centuries. As a result of technological advances, one farmer in the United States today can feed 100 people and in a year one autoworker can produce almost 14 cars and trucks.

Let's now look at the effects of changes in the money wage rate.

Changes in the Money Wage Rate When the money wage rate (or the money price of any other factor of production such as oil) changes, short-run aggregate supply changes but long-run aggregate supply does not change.

Figure 27.3 shows the effect of an increase in the money wage rate. Initially, the short-run aggregate supply curve is SAS_0. A rise in the money wage rate *decreases* short-run aggregate supply and shifts the short-run aggregate supply curve leftward to SAS_2.

A rise in the money wage rate decreases short-run aggregate supply because it increases firms' costs. With increased costs, the quantity that firms are willing to supply at each price level decreases, which is shown by a leftward shift of the *SAS* curve.

A change in the money wage rate does not change long-run aggregate supply because on the *LAS* curve, the change in the money wage rate is accompanied by an equal percentage change in the price level. With no change in *relative* prices, firms have no incentive to change production and real GDP remains constant at potential GDP. With no change in potential GDP, the long-run aggregate supply curve *LAS* does not shift.

What Makes the Money Wage Rate Change? The money wage rate can change for two reasons: departures from full employment and expectations about inflation. Unemployment above the natural rate puts downward pressure on the money wage rate, and unemployment below the natural rate puts upward pressure on it. An expected rise in the inflation rate makes the money wage rate rise faster, and an expected fall in the inflation rate slows the rate at which the money wage rate rises.

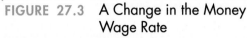

FIGURE 27.3 A Change in the Money Wage Rate

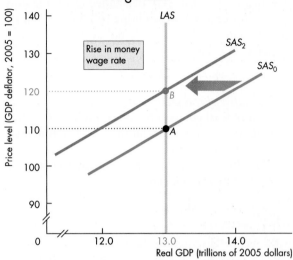

A rise in the money wage rate decreases short-run aggregate supply and shifts the short-run aggregate supply curve leftward from SAS_0 to SAS_2. A rise in the money wage rate does not change potential GDP, so the long-run aggregate supply curve does not shift.

myeconlab animation

REVIEW QUIZ

1 If the price level and the money wage rate rise by the same percentage, what happens to the quantity of real GDP supplied? Along which aggregate supply curve does the economy move?

2 If the price level rises and the money wage rate remains constant, what happens to the quantity of real GDP supplied? Along which aggregate supply curve does the economy move?

3 If potential GDP increases, what happens to aggregate supply? Does the *LAS* curve shift or is there a movement along the *LAS* curve? Does the *SAS* curve shift or is there a movement along the *SAS* curve?

4 If the money wage rate rises and potential GDP remains the same, does the *LAS* curve or the *SAS* curve shift or is there a movement along the *LAS* curve or the *SAS* curve?

You can work these questions in Study Plan 27.1 and get instant feedback.

◆ Aggregate Demand

The quantity of real GDP demanded (Y) is the sum of real consumption expenditure (C), investment (I), government expenditure (G), and exports (X) minus imports (M). That is,

$$Y = C + I + G + X - M.$$

The *quantity of real GDP demanded* is the total amount of final goods and services produced in the United States that people, businesses, governments, and foreigners plan to buy.

These buying plans depend on many factors. Some of the main ones are

1. The price level
2. Expectations
3. Fiscal policy and monetary policy
4. The world economy

We first focus on the relationship between the quantity of real GDP demanded and the price level. To study this relationship, we keep all other influences on buying plans the same and ask: How does the quantity of real GDP demanded vary as the price level varies?

The Aggregate Demand Curve

Other things remaining the same, the higher the price level, the smaller is the quantity of real GDP demanded. This relationship between the quantity of real GDP demanded and the price level is called **aggregate demand**. Aggregate demand is described by an *aggregate demand schedule* and an *aggregate demand curve*.

Figure 27.4 shows an aggregate demand curve (AD) and an aggregate demand schedule. Each point on the AD curve corresponds to a row of the schedule. For example, point C' on the AD curve and row C' of the schedule tell us that if the price level is 110, the quantity of real GDP demanded is $13 trillion.

The aggregate demand curve slopes downward for two reasons:

- Wealth effect
- Substitution effects

Wealth Effect When the price level rises but other things remain the same, *real* wealth decreases. Real

FIGURE 27.4   Aggregate Demand

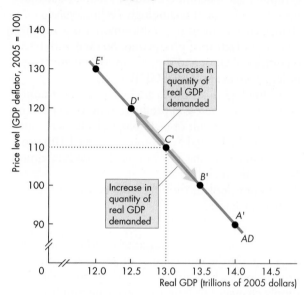

	Price level (GDP deflator)	Real GDP demanded (trillions of 2005 dollars)
A'	90	14.0
B'	100	13.5
C'	**110**	**13.0**
D'	120	12.5
E'	130	12.0

The aggregate demand curve (*AD*) shows the relationship between the quantity of real GDP demanded and the price level. The aggregate demand curve is based on the aggregate demand schedule in the table. Each point A' through E' on the curve corresponds to the row in the table identified by the same letter. When the price level is 110, the quantity of real GDP demanded is $13 trillion, as shown by point C' in the figure. A change in the price level, when all other influences on aggregate buying plans remain the same, brings a change in the quantity of real GDP demanded and a movement along the *AD* curve.

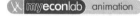
myeconlab   animation

wealth is the amount of money in the bank, bonds, stocks, and other assets that people own, measured not in dollars but in terms of the goods and services that the money, bonds, and stocks will buy.

People save and hold money, bonds, and stocks for many reasons. One reason is to build up funds for education expenses. Another reason is to build up enough funds to meet possible medical expenses or other big bills. But the biggest reason is to build up enough funds to provide a retirement income.

If the price level rises, real wealth decreases. People then try to restore their wealth. To do so, they must increase saving and, equivalently, decrease current consumption. Such a decrease in consumption is a decrease in aggregate demand.

Maria's Wealth Effect You can see how the wealth effect works by thinking about Maria's buying plans. Maria lives in Moscow, Russia. She has worked hard all summer and saved 20,000 rubles (the ruble is the currency of Russia), which she plans to spend attending graduate school when she has finished her economics degree. So Maria's wealth is 20,000 rubles. Maria has a part-time job, and her income from this job pays her current expenses. The price level in Russia rises by 100 percent, and now Maria needs 40,000 rubles to buy what 20,000 once bought. To try to make up some of the fall in value of her savings, Maria saves even more and cuts her current spending to the bare minimum.

Substitution Effects When the price level rises and other things remain the same, interest rates rise. The reason is related to the wealth effect that you've just studied. A rise in the price level decreases the real value of the money in people's pockets and bank accounts. With a smaller amount of real money around, banks and other lenders can get a higher interest rate on loans. But faced with a higher interest rate, people and businesses delay plans to buy new capital and consumer durable goods and cut back on spending.

This substitution effect involves changing the timing of purchases of capital and consumer durable goods and is called an *intertemporal* substitution effect—a substitution across time. Saving increases to increase future consumption.

To see this intertemporal substitution effect more clearly, think about your own plan to buy a new computer. At an interest rate of 5 percent a year, you might borrow $1,000 and buy the new computer. But at an interest rate of 10 percent a year, you might decide that the payments would be too high. You don't abandon your plan to buy the computer, but you decide to delay your purchase.

A second substitution effect works through international prices. When the U.S. price level rises and other things remain the same, U.S.-made goods and services become more expensive relative to foreign-made goods and services. This change in *relative prices* encourages people to spend less on U.S.-made items and more on foreign-made items. For example, if the U.S. price level rises relative to the Japanese price level, Japanese buy fewer U.S.-made cars (U.S. exports decrease) and Americans buy more Japanese-made cars (U.S. imports increase). U.S. GDP decreases.

Maria's Substitution Effects In Moscow, Russia, Maria makes some substitutions. She was planning to trade in her old motor scooter and get a new one. But with a higher price level and a higher interest rate, she decides to make her old scooter last one more year. Also, with the prices of Russian goods sharply increasing, Maria substitutes a low-cost dress made in Malaysia for the Russian-made dress she had originally planned to buy.

Changes in the Quantity of Real GDP Demanded

When the price level rises and other things remain the same, the quantity of real GDP demanded decreases— a movement up along the *AD* curve as shown by the arrow in Fig. 27.4. When the price level falls and other things remain the same, the quantity of real GDP demanded increases—a movement down along the *AD* curve.

We've now seen how the quantity of real GDP demanded changes when the price level changes. How do other influences on buying plans affect aggregate demand?

Changes in Aggregate Demand

A change in any factor that influences buying plans other than the price level brings a change in aggregate demand. The main factors are

- Expectations
- Fiscal policy and monetary policy
- The world economy

Expectations An increase in expected future income increases the amount of consumption goods (especially big-ticket items such as cars) that people plan to buy today and increases aggregate demand.

An increase in the expected future inflation rate increases aggregate demand today because people decide to buy more goods and services at today's relatively lower prices.

An increase in expected future profits increases the investment that firms plan to undertake today and increases aggregate demand.

Fiscal Policy and Monetary Policy The government's attempt to influence the economy by setting and changing taxes, making transfer payments, and purchasing goods and services is called **fiscal policy**. A tax cut or an increase in transfer payments—for example, unemployment benefits or welfare payments—increases aggregate demand. Both of these influences operate by increasing households' *disposable* income. **Disposable income** is aggregate income minus taxes plus transfer payments. The greater the disposable income, the greater is the quantity of consumption goods and services that households plan to buy and the greater is aggregate demand.

Government expenditure on goods and services is one component of aggregate demand. So if the government spends more on spy satellites, schools, and highways, aggregate demand increases.

The Federal Reserve's (Fed's) attempt to influence the economy by changing interest rates and the quantity of money is called **monetary policy**. The Fed influences the quantity of money and interest rates by using the tools and methods described in Chapter 25.

An increase in the quantity of money increases aggregate demand through two main channels: It lowers interest rates and makes it easier to get a loan.

With lower interest rates, businesses plan a greater level of investment in new capital and households plan greater expenditure on new homes, on home improvements, on automobiles, and a host of other consumer durable goods. Banks and others eager to lend lower their standards for making loans and more people are able to get home loans and other consumer loans.

A decrease in the quantity of money has the opposite effects and lowers aggregate demand.

The World Economy Two main influences that the world economy has on aggregate demand are the exchange rate and foreign income. The *exchange rate* is the amount of a foreign currency that you can buy with a U.S. dollar. Other things remaining the same, a rise in the exchange rate decreases aggregate

Economics in Action
Fiscal Policy to Fight Recession

In February 2008, Congress passed legislation that gave $168 billion to businesses and low- and middle-income Americans—$600 to a single person and $1,200 to a couple with an additional $300 for each child. The benefit was scaled back for individuals with incomes above $75,000 a year and for families with incomes greater than $150,000 a year.

The idea of the package was to stimulate business investment and consumption expenditure and increase aggregate demand.

Monetary Policy to Fight Recession

In October 2008 and the months that followed, the Federal Reserve, in concert with the European Central Bank, the Bank of Canada, and the Bank of England, cut the interest rate and took other measures to ease credit and encourage banks and other financial institutions to increase their lending. The U.S. interest rate was the lowest (see below).

Like the earlier fiscal stimulus package, the idea of these interest rate cuts and easier credit was to stimulate business investment and consumption expenditure and increase aggregate demand.

Deal makers Senators Harry Reid and Mitch McConnell

FIGURE 27.5   Changes in Aggregate Demand

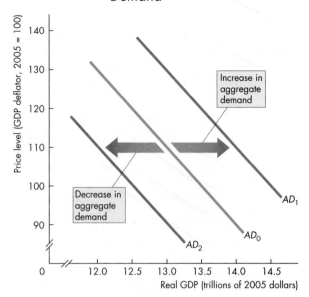

Aggregate demand

Decreases if:

- Expected future income, inflation, or profit decreases
- Fiscal policy decreases government expenditure, increases taxes, or decreases transfer payments
- Monetary policy decreases the quantity of money and increases interest rates
- The exchange rate increases or foreign income decreases

Increases if:

- Expected future income, inflation, or profit increases
- Fiscal policy increases government expenditure, decreases taxes, or increases transfer payments
- Monetary policy increases the quantity of money and decreases interest rates
- The exchange rate decreases or foreign income increases

 animation

demand. To see how the exchange rate influences aggregate demand, suppose that the exchange rate is 1.20 euros per U.S. dollar. A Nokia cell phone made in Finland costs 120 euros, and an equivalent Motorola phone made in the United States costs $110. In U.S. dollars, the Nokia phone costs $100,

so people around the world buy the cheaper phone from Finland. Now suppose the exchange rate falls to 1 euro per U.S. dollar. The Nokia phone now costs $120 and is more expensive than the Motorola phone. People will switch from the Nokia phone to the Motorola phone. U.S. exports will increase and U.S. imports will decrease, so U.S. aggregate demand will increase.

An increase in foreign income increases U.S. exports and increases U.S. aggregate demand. For example, an increase in income in Japan and Germany increases Japanese and German consumers' and producers' planned expenditures on U.S.-produced goods and services.

Shifts of the Aggregate Demand Curve When aggregate demand changes, the aggregate demand curve shifts. Figure 27.5 shows two changes in aggregate demand and summarizes the factors that bring about such changes.

Aggregate demand increases and the AD curve shifts rightward from AD_0 to AD_1 when expected future income, inflation, or profit increases; government expenditure on goods and services increases; taxes are cut; transfer payments increase; the quantity of money increases and the interest rate falls; the exchange rate falls; or foreign income increases.

Aggregate demand decreases and the AD curve shifts leftward from AD_0 to AD_2 when expected future income, inflation, or profit decreases; government expenditure on goods and services decreases; taxes increase; transfer payments decrease; the quantity of money decreases and the interest rate rises; the exchange rate rises; or foreign income decreases.

◤ REVIEW QUIZ

1 What does the aggregate demand curve show? What factors change and what factors remain the same when there is a movement along the aggregate demand curve?
2 Why does the aggregate demand curve slope downward?
3 How do changes in expectations, fiscal policy and monetary policy, and the world economy change aggregate demand and the aggregate demand curve?

You can work these questions in Study Plan 27.2 and get instant feedback.

Explaining Macroeconomic Trends and Fluctuations

The purpose of the *AS-AD* model is to explain changes in real GDP and the price level. The model's main purpose is to explain business cycle fluctuations in these variables. But the model also aids our understanding of economic growth and inflation trends. We begin by combining aggregate supply and aggregate demand to determine real GDP and the price level in equilibrium. Just as there are two time frames for aggregate supply, there are two time frames for macroeconomic equilibrium: a long-run equilibrium and a short-run equilibrium. We'll first look at short-run equilibrium.

Short-Run Macroeconomic Equilibrium

The aggregate demand curve tells us the quantity of real GDP demanded at each price level, and the short-run aggregate supply curve tells us the quantity of real GDP supplied at each price level. **Short-run macroeconomic equilibrium** occurs when the quantity of real GDP demanded equals the quantity of real GDP supplied. That is, short-run macroeconomic equilibrium occurs at the point of intersection of the *AD* curve and the *SAS* curve.

Figure 27.6 shows such an equilibrium at a price level of 110 and real GDP of $13 trillion (points *C* and *C'*).

To see why this position is the equilibrium, think about what happens if the price level is something other than 110. Suppose, for example, that the price level is 120 and that real GDP is $14 trillion (at point *E* on the *SAS* curve). The quantity of real GDP demanded is less than $14 trillion, so firms are unable to sell all their output. Unwanted inventories pile up, and firms cut both production and prices. Production and prices are cut until firms can sell all their output. This situation occurs only when real GDP is $13 trillion and the price level is 110.

Now suppose the price level is 100 and real GDP is $12 trillion (at point *A* on the *SAS* curve). The quantity of real GDP demanded exceeds $12 trillion, so firms are unable to meet the demand for their output. Inventories decrease, and customers clamor for goods and services, so firms increase production and raise prices. Production and prices increase until firms can meet the demand for their

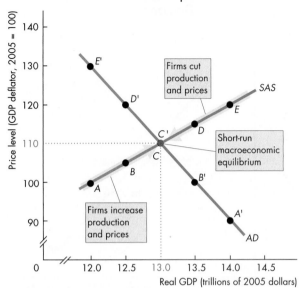

FIGURE 27.6   Short-Run Equilibrium

Short-run macroeconomic equilibrium occurs when real GDP demanded equals real GDP supplied—at the intersection of the aggregate demand curve (*AD*) and the short-run aggregate supply curve (*SAS*).

 animation

output. This situation occurs only when real GDP is $13 trillion and the price level is 110.

In the short run, the money wage rate is fixed. It does not adjust to move the economy to full employment. So in the short run, real GDP can be greater than or less than potential GDP. But in the long run, the money wage rate does adjust and real GDP moves toward potential GDP. Let's look at long-run equilibrium and see how we get there.

Long-Run Macroeconomic Equilibrium

Long-run macroeconomic equilibrium occurs when real GDP equals potential GDP—equivalently, when the economy is on its *LAS* curve.

When the economy is a away from long-run equilibrium, the money wage rate adjusts. If the money wage rate is too high, short-run equilibrium is below potential GDP and the unemployment rate is above the natural rate. With an excess supply of labor, the money wage rate falls. If the money wage rate is too low, short-run equilibrium is above potential GDP and the unemployment rate is below the natural rate.

With an excess demand for labor, the money wage rate rises.

Figure 27.7 shows the long-run equilibrium and how it comes about. If short-run aggregate supply curve is SAS_1, the money wage rate is too high to achieve full employment. A fall in the money wage rate shifts the SAS curve to SAS^* and brings full employment. If short-run aggregate supply curve is SAS_2, the money wage rate is too low to achieve full employment. Now, a rise in the money wage rate shifts the SAS curve to SAS^* and brings full employment.

In long-run equilibrium, potential GDP determines real GDP and potential GDP and aggregate demand together determine the price level. The money wage rate adjusts until the SAS curve passes through the long-run equilibrium point.

Let's now see how the *AS-AD* model helps us to understand economic growth and inflation.

Economic Growth and Inflation in the *AS-AD* Model

Economic growth results from a growing labor force and increasing labor productivity, which together make potential GDP grow (Chapter 23, pp. 547–550). Inflation results from a growing quantity of money that outpaces the growth of potential GDP (Chapter 25, pp. 606–607).

The *AS-AD* model explains and illustrates economic growth and inflation. It explains economic growth as increasing long-run aggregate supply and it explains inflation as a persistent increase in aggregate demand at a faster pace than that of the increase in potential GDP.

Economics in Action
U.S. Economic Growth and Inflation

The figure is a *scatter diagram* of U.S. real GDP and the price level. The graph has the same axes as those of the *AS-AD* model. Each dot represents a year between 1960 and 2010. The red dots are recession years. The pattern formed by the dots shows the combination of economic growth and inflation. Economic growth was fastest during the 1960s; inflation was fastest during the 1970s.

The *AS-AD* model interprets each dot as being at the intersection of the *SAS* and *AD* curves.

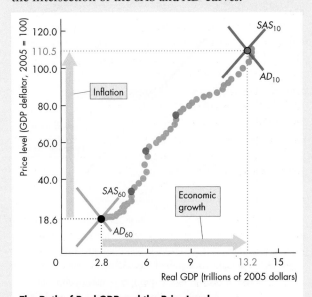

The Path of Real GDP and the Price Level
Source of data: Bureau of Economic Analysis.

FIGURE 27.7   Long-Run Equilibrium

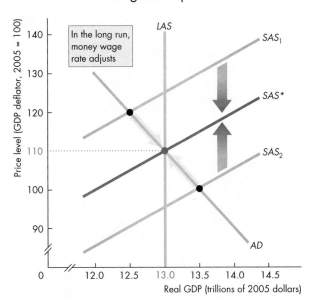

In long-run macroeconomic equilibrium, real GDP equals potential GDP. So long-run equilibrium occurs where the aggregate demand curve, *AD*, intersects the long-run aggregate supply curve, *LAS*. In the long run, aggregate demand determines the price level and has no effect on real GDP. The money wage rate adjusts in the long run, so that the *SAS* curve intersects the *LAS* curve at the long-run equilibrium price level.

myeconlab animation

Figure 27.8 illustrates this explanation in terms of the shifting *LAS* and *AD* curves.

When the *LAS* curve shifts rightward from LAS_0 to LAS_1, potential GDP grows from $13 trillion to $14 trillion and in long-run equilibrium, real GDP also grows to $14 trillion.

Whan the *AD* curve shifts rightward from AD_0 to AD_1, which is a growth of aggregate demand that outpaces the growth of potential GDP, the price level rises from 110 to 120.

If aggregate demand were to increase at the same pace as long-run aggregate supply, real GDP would grow with no inflation.

Our economy experiences periods of growth and inflation, like those shown in Fig. 27.8, but it does not experience *steady* growth and *steady* inflation. Real GDP fluctuates around potential GDP in a business cycle. When we study the business cycle, we ignore economic growth and focus on the fluctuations around the trend. By doing so, we see the business cycle more clearly. Let's now see how the *AS-AD* model explains the business cycle.

FIGURE 27.8   Economic Growth and Inflation

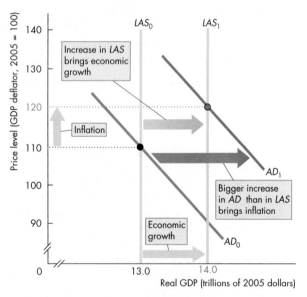

Economic growth results from a persistent increase in potential GDP—a rightward shift of the *LAS* curve. Inflation results from persistent growth in the quantity of money that shifts the *AD* curve rightward at a faster pace than the real GDP growth rate.

myeconlab   animation

The Business Cycle in the *AS-AD* Model

The business cycle occurs because aggregate demand and short-run aggregate supply fluctuate but the money wage rate does not adjust quickly enough to keep real GDP at potential GDP. Figure 27.9 shows three types of short-run equilibrium.

Figure 27.9(a) shows an above full-employment equilibrium. An **above full-employment equilibrium** is an equilibrium in which real GDP exceeds potential GDP. The gap between real GDP and potential GDP is the **output gap.** When real GDP exceeds potential GDP, the output gap is called an **inflationary gap**.

The above full-employment equilibrium shown in Fig. 27.9(a) occurs where the aggregate demand curve AD_0 intersects the short-run aggregate supply curve SAS_0 at a real GDP of $13.2 trillion. There is an inflationary gap of $0.2 trillion.

Economics in Action
The U.S. Business Cycle

The U.S. economy had an inflationary gap in 2006 (at *A* in the figure), full employment in 2006 (at *B*), and a recessionary gap in 2009 (at *C*). The fluctuating output gap in the figure is the real-world version of Fig. 27.9(d) and is generated by fluctuations in aggregate demand and short-run aggregate supply.

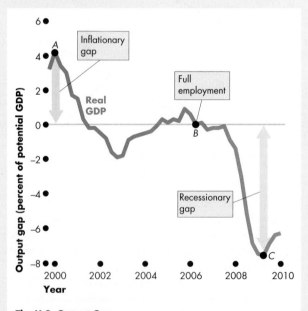

The U.S. Output Gap

Sources of data: Bureau of Economic Analysis and Congressional Budget Office.

Figure 27.9(b) is an example of **full-employment equilibrium,** in which real GDP equals potential GDP. In this example, the equilibrium occurs where the aggregate demand curve AD_1 intersects the short-run aggregate supply curve SAS_1 at an actual and potential GDP of $13 trillion.

In part (c), there is a below full-employment equilibrium. A **below full-employment equilibrium** is an equilibrium in which potential GDP exceeds real GDP. When potential GDP exceeds real GDP, the output gap is called a **recessionary gap.**

The below full-employment equilibrium shown in

Fig. 27.9(c) occurs where the aggregate demand curve AD_2 intersects the short-run aggregate supply curve SAS_2 at a real GDP of $12.8 trillion. Potential GDP is $13 trillion, so the recessionary gap is $0.2 trillion.

The economy moves from one type of macroeconomic equilibrium to another as a result of fluctuations in aggregate demand and in short-run aggregate supply. These fluctuations produce fluctuations in real GDP. Figure 27.9(d) shows how real GDP fluctuates around potential GDP.

Let's now look at some of the sources of these fluctuations around potential GDP.

FIGURE 27.9   The Business Cycle

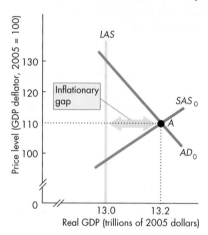

(a) Above full-employment equilibrium

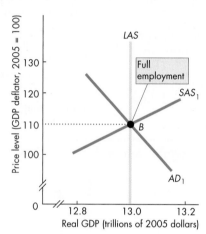

(b) Full-employment equilibrium

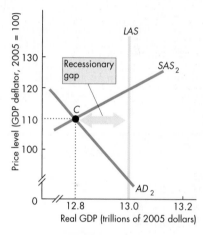

(c) Below full-employment equilibrium

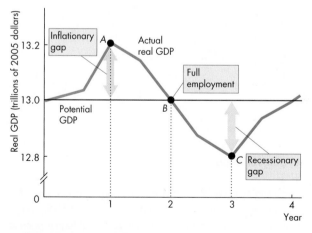

(d) Fluctuations in real GDP

Part (a) shows an above full-employment equilibrium in year 1; part (b) shows a full-employment equilibrium in year 2; and part (c) shows a below full-employment equilibrium in year 3. Part (d) shows how real GDP fluctuates around potential GDP in a business cycle.

In year 1, an inflationary gap exists and the economy is at point A in parts (a) and (d). In year 2, the economy is at full employment and the economy is at point B in parts (b) and (d). In year 3, a recessionary gap exists and the economy is at point C in parts (c) and (d).

Fluctuations in Aggregate Demand

One reason real GDP fluctuates around potential GDP is that aggregate demand fluctuates. Let's see what happens when aggregate demand increases.

Figure 27.10(a) shows an economy at full employment. The aggregate demand curve is AD_0, the short-run aggregate supply curve is SAS_0, and the long-run aggregate supply curve is LAS. Real GDP equals potential GDP at $13 trillion, and the price level is 110.

Now suppose that the world economy expands and that the demand for U.S.-produced goods increases in Asia and Europe. The increase in U.S. exports increases aggregate demand in the United States, and the aggregate demand curve shifts rightward from AD_0 to AD_1 in Fig. 27.10(a).

Faced with an increase in demand, firms increase production and raise prices. Real GDP increases to $13.5 trillion, and the price level rises to 115. The economy is now in an above full-employment equilibrium. Real GDP exceeds potential GDP, and there is an inflationary gap.

The increase in aggregate demand has increased the prices of all goods and services. Faced with higher prices, firms increased their output rates. At this stage, prices of goods and services have increased but the money wage rate has not changed. (Recall that as we move along the SAS curve, the money wage rate is constant.)

The economy cannot produce in excess of potential GDP forever. Why not? What are the forces at work that bring real GDP back to potential GDP?

Because the price level has increased and the money wage rate is unchanged, workers have experienced a fall in the buying power of their wages and firms' profits have increased. Under these circumstances, workers demand higher wages and firms, anxious to maintain their employment and output levels, meet those demands. If firms do not raise the money wage rate, they will either lose workers or have to hire less productive ones.

As the money wage rate rises, the short-run aggregate supply begins to decrease. In Fig. 27.10(b), the short-run aggregate supply curve begins to shift from

---

FIGURE 27.10   An Increase in Aggregate Demand

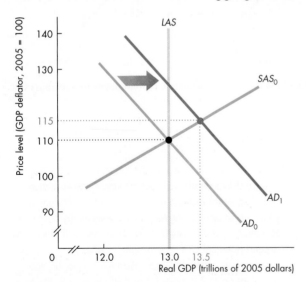

(a) Short-run effect

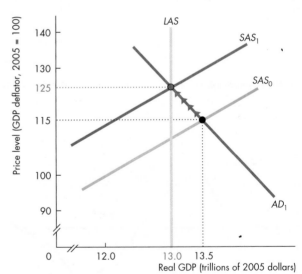

(b) Long-run effect

An increase in aggregate demand shifts the aggregate demand curve from AD_0 to AD_1. In short-run equilibrium, real GDP increases to $13.5 trillion and the price level rises to 115. In this situation, an inflationary gap exists. In the long run in part (b), the money wage rate rises and the short-run aggre-

gate supply curve shifts leftward. As short-run aggregate supply decreases, the SAS curve shifts from SAS_0 to SAS_1 and intersects the aggregate demand curve AD_1 at higher price levels and real GDP decreases. Eventually, the price level rises to 125 and real GDP decreases to $13 trillion—potential GDP.

SAS_0 toward SAS_1. The rise in the money wage rate and the shift in the SAS curve produce a sequence of new equilibrium positions. Along the adjustment path, real GDP decreases and the price level rises. The economy moves up along its aggregate demand curve as shown by the arrows in the figure.

Eventually, the money wage rate rises by the same percentage as the price level. At this time, the aggregate demand curve AD_1 intersects SAS_1 at a new full-employment equilibrium. The price level has risen to 125, and real GDP is back where it started, at potential GDP.

A decrease in aggregate demand has effects similar but opposite to those of an increase in aggregate demand. That is, a decrease in aggregate demand shifts the aggregate demand curve leftward. Real GDP decreases to less than potential GDP, and a recessionary gap emerges. Firms cut prices. The lower price level increases the purchasing power of wages and increases firms' costs relative to their output prices because the money wage rate is unchanged. Eventually, the money wage rate falls and the short-run aggregate supply increases.

Let's now work out how real GDP and the price level change when aggregate supply changes.

Fluctuations in Aggregate Supply

Fluctuations in short-run aggregate supply can bring fluctuations in real GDP around potential GDP. Suppose that initially real GDP equals potential GDP. Then there is a large but temporary rise in the price of oil. What happens to real GDP and the price level?

Figure 27.11 answers this question. The aggregate demand curve is AD_0, the short-run aggregate supply curve is SAS_0, and the long-run aggregate supply curve is LAS. Real GDP is $13 trillion, which equals potential GDP, and the price level is 110. Then the price of oil rises. Faced with higher energy and transportation costs, firms decrease production. Short-run aggregate supply decreases, and the short-run aggregate supply curve shifts leftward to SAS_1. The price level rises to 120, and real GDP decreases to $12.5 trillion. Because real GDP decreases, the economy experiences recession. Because the price level increases, the economy experiences inflation. A combination of recession and inflation, called **stagflation**, actually occurred in the United States in the mid-1970s and early 1980s, but events like this are not common.

When the price of oil returns to its original level, the economy returns to full employment.

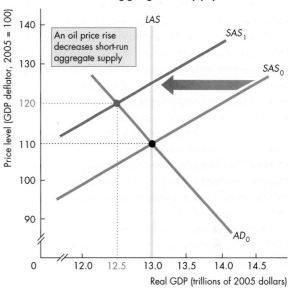

FIGURE 27.11 A Decrease in Aggregate Supply

An increase in the price of oil decreases short-run aggregate supply and shifts the short-run aggregate supply curve from SAS_0 to SAS_1. Real GDP falls from $13 trillion to $12.5 trillion, and the price level rises from 110 to 120. The economy experiences stagflation.

REVIEW QUIZ

1 Does economic growth result from increases in aggregate demand, short-run aggregate supply, or long-run aggregate supply?
2 Does inflation result from increases in aggregate demand, short-run aggregate supply, or long-run aggregate supply?
3 Describe three types of short-run macroeconomic equilibrium.
4 How do fluctuations in aggregate demand and short-run aggregate supply bring fluctuations in real GDP around potential GDP?

You can work these questions in Study Plan 27.3 and get instant feedback.

We can use the *AS-AD* model to explain and illustrate the views of the alternative schools of thought in macroeconomics. That is your next task.

◆ Macroeconomic Schools of Thought

Macroeconomics is an active field of research, and much remains to be learned about the forces that make our economy grow and fluctuate. There is a greater degree of consensus and certainty about economic growth and inflation—the longer-term trends in real GDP and the price level—than there is about the business cycle—the short-term fluctuations in these variables. Here, we'll look only at differences of view about short-term fluctuations.

The *AS-AD* model that you've studied in this chapter provides a good foundation for understanding the range of views that macroeconomists hold about this topic. But what you will learn here is just a first glimpse at the scientific controversy and debate. We'll return to these issues at various points later in the text and deepen your appreciation of the alternative views.

Classification usually requires simplification, and classifying macroeconomists is no exception to this general rule. The classification that we'll use here is simple, but it is not misleading. We're going to divide macroeconomists into three broad schools of thought and examine the views of each group in turn. The groups are

- Classical
- Keynesian
- Monetarist

The Classical View

A **classical** macroeconomist believes that the economy is self-regulating and always at full employment. The term "classical" derives from the name of the founding school of economics that includes Adam Smith, David Ricardo, and John Stuart Mill.

A **new classical** view is that business cycle fluctuations are the efficient responses of a well-functioning market economy that is bombarded by shocks that arise from the uneven pace of technological change.

The classical view can be understood in terms of beliefs about aggregate demand and aggregate supply.

Aggregate Demand Fluctuations In the classical view, technological change is the most significant influence on both aggregate demand and aggregate supply. For this reason, classical macroeconomists don't use the *AS-AD* framework. But their views can be interpreted in this framework. A technological change that increases the productivity of capital brings an increase in aggregate demand because firms increase their expenditure on new plant and equipment. A technological change that lengthens the useful life of existing capital decreases the demand for new capital, which decreases aggregate demand.

Aggregate Supply Response In the classical view, the money wage rate that lies behind the short-run aggregate supply curve is instantly and completely flexible. The money wage rate adjusts so quickly to maintain equilibrium in the labor market that real GDP always adjusts to equal potential GDP.

Potential GDP itself fluctuates for the same reasons that aggregate demand fluctuates: technological change. When the pace of technological change is rapid, potential GDP increases quickly and so does real GDP. And when the pace of technological change slows, so does the growth rate of potential GDP.

Classical Policy The classical view of policy emphasizes the potential for taxes to stunt incentives and create inefficiency. By minimizing the disincentive effects of taxes, employment, investment, and technological advance are at their efficient levels and the economy expands at an appropriate and rapid pace.

The Keynesian View

A **Keynesian** macroeconomist believes that left alone, the economy would rarely operate at full employment and that to achieve and maintain full employment, active help from fiscal policy and monetary policy is required.

The term "Keynesian" derives from the name of one of the twentieth century's most famous economists, John Maynard Keynes (see p. 723).

The Keynesian view is based on beliefs about the forces that determine aggregate demand and short-run aggregate supply.

Aggregate Demand Fluctuations In the Keynesian view, *expectations* are the most significant influence on aggregate demand. Those expectations are based on herd instinct, or what Keynes himself called "animal spirits." A wave of pessimism about future profit prospects can lead to a fall in aggregate demand and plunge the economy into recession.

Aggregate Supply Response In the Keynesian view, the money wage rate that lies behind the short-run aggregate supply curve is extremely sticky in the downward direction. Basically, the money wage rate doesn't fall. So if there is a recessionary gap, there is no automatic mechanism for getting rid of it. If it were to happen, a fall in the money wage rate would increase short-run aggregate supply and restore full employment. But the money wage rate doesn't fall, so the economy remains stuck in recession.

A modern version of the Keynesian view, known as the **new Keynesian** view, holds not only that the money wage rate is sticky but also that prices of goods and services are sticky. With a sticky price level, the short-run aggregate supply curve is horizontal at a fixed price level.

Policy Response Needed The Keynesian view calls for fiscal policy and monetary policy to actively offset changes in aggregate demand that bring recession.

By stimulating aggregate demand in a recession, full employment can be restored.

The Monetarist View

A **monetarist** is a macroeconomist who believes that the economy is self-regulating and that it will normally operate at full employment, provided that monetary policy is not erratic and that the pace of money growth is kept steady.

The term "monetarist" was coined by an outstanding twentieth-century economist, Karl Brunner, to describe his own views and those of Milton Friedman (see p. 781).

The monetarist view can be interpreted in terms of beliefs about the forces that determine aggregate demand and short-run aggregate supply.

Aggregate Demand Fluctuations In the monetarist view, *the quantity of money* is the most significant influence on aggregate demand. The quantity of money is determined by the Federal Reserve (the Fed). If the Fed keeps money growing at a steady pace, aggregate demand fluctuations will be minimized and the economy will operate close to full employment. But if the Fed decreases the quantity of money or even just slows its growth rate too abruptly, the economy will go into recession. In the monetarist view, all recessions result from inappropriate monetary policy.

Aggregate Supply Response The monetarist view of short-run aggregate supply is the same as the Keynesian view: the money wage rate is sticky. If the economy is in recession, it will take an unnecessarily long time for it to return unaided to full employment.

Monetarist Policy The monetarist view of policy is the same as the classical view on fiscal policy. Taxes should be kept low to avoid disincentive effects that decrease potential GDP. Provided that the quantity of money is kept on a steady growth path, no active stabilization is needed to offset changes in aggregate demand.

The Way Ahead

In the chapters that follow, you're going to encounter Keynesian, classical, and monetarist views again. In the next chapter, we study the original Keynesian model of aggregate demand. This model remains useful today because it explains how expenditure fluctuations are magnified and bring changes in aggregate demand that are larger than the changes in expenditure. We then go on to apply the *AS-AD* model to a deeper look at U.S. inflation and business cycles.

Our attention then turns to short-run macroeconomic policy—the fiscal policy of the Administration and Congress and the monetary policy of the Fed.

REVIEW QUIZ

1   What are the defining features of classical macroeconomics and what policies do classical macroeconomists recommend?
2   What are the defining features of Keynesian macroeconomics and what policies do Keynesian macroeconomists recommend?
3   What are the defining features of monetarist macroeconomics and what policies do monetarist macroeconomists recommend?

You can work these questions in Study Plan 27.4 and get instant feedback.

◆ To complete your study of the *AS-AD* model, *Reading Between the Lines* on pp. 664–665 looks at the U.S. economy in 2010 through the eyes of this model.

Aggregate Supply and Aggregate Demand in Action

GDP Figures Revised Downward

Associated Press
August 27, 2010

The economy grew at a much slower pace this spring than previously estimated, mostly because of the largest surge in imports in 26 years and a slower buildup in inventories.

The nation's gross domestic product—the broadest measure of the economy's output—grew at a 1.6 percent annual rate in the April-to-June period, the Commerce Department said Friday. That's down from an initial estimate of 2.4 percent last month and much slower than the first quarter's 3.7 percent pace. Many economists had expected a sharper drop.

Shortly after the revision was announced, Federal Reserve Chairman Ben Bernanke ... described the economic outlook as "inherently uncertain" and said the economy "remains vulnerable to unexpected developments." The lower estimate for economic growth and Bernanke's comments follow a week of disappointing economic reports. The housing sector is slumping badly after the expiration of a government home buyer tax credit. And business spending on big-ticket manufactured items such as machinery and software, an important source of growth earlier this year, is also tapering off.

Most analysts expect the economy will grow at a similarly weak pace for the rest of this year.

"We seem to be in the early stages of what might be called a 'growth recession'," said Ethan Harris, an economist at Bank of America-Merrill Lynch. The economy is likely to keep expanding, but at a snail's pace and without creating many more jobs. Harris expects the nation's output will grow at about a 2 percent pace in the second half of this year. As a result, the jobless rate could rise from its current level of 9.5 percent.

ESSENCE OF THE STORY

- Real GDP grew at a 1.6 percent annual rate in the second quarter of 2010, down from a previously estimated 2.4 percent and down from 3.7 percent in the first quarter.

- Imports increased at their fastest pace in 26 years and inventories increased at a slow pace.

- Fed Chairman Ben Bernanke says the economic outlook is uncertain.

- Other bad news included a slump in home construction and lower investment expenditure.

- Most forecasters expect slow 2 percent growth for the rest of 2010 and a rise in the unemployment rate.

- U.S. real GDP grew at a 1.6 percent annual rate during the second quarter of 2010—a slower than average growth rate and slower than the original estimate a month earlier.

- In the second quarter of 2010, real GDP was estimated to be $13.2 trillion, up from $12.8 trillion in the second quarter of 2009. The price level was 110 (up 10 percent since 2005).

- Figure 1 illustrates the situation in the second quarter of 2009. The aggregate demand curve was AD_{09} and the short-run aggregate supply curve was SAS_{09}. Real GDP ($12.8 trillion) and the price level (110) are at the intersection of these curves.

- The Congressional Budget Office (CBO) estimated that potential GDP in the second quarter of 2009 was $13.9 trillion, so the long-run aggregate supply curve in 2009 was LAS_{09} in Fig. 1.

- Figure 1 shows the output gap in 2009, which was a recessionary gap of $1.1 trillion or 8 percent of potential GDP.

- During the year from June 2009 to June 2010, the labor force increased, the capital stock increased, and labor productivity increased. Potential GDP increased to an estimated $14.1 trillion.

- In Fig. 2, the LAS curve shifted rightward to LAS_{10}.

- Also during the year from June 2009 to June 2010, a combination of fiscal and monetary policy stimulus and an increase in demand from an expanding world economy increased aggregate demand.

- The increase in aggregate demand exceeded the increase in long-run aggregate supply and the AD curve shifted rightward to AD_{10}. Short-run aggregate supply increased by a similar amount to the increase in AD and the SAS shifted rightward to SAS_{10}.

- Real GDP increased to $13.2 trillion and the price level remained constant at 110.

- The output gap narrowed slightly to $0.9 trillion or 6.4 percent of potential GDP.

- With real GDP forecast to grow at only 2 percent a year for the rest of 2010, the output gap would remain very large.

- Real GDP would need to grow faster than potential GDP for some time for the output gap to close.

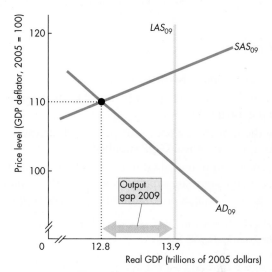

Figure 1 *AS-AD* **in second quarter of 2009**

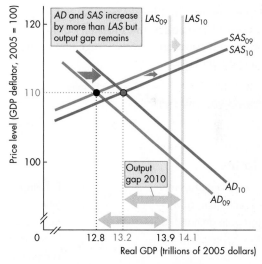

Figure 2 *AS-AD* **in second quarter of 2010**

SUMMARY

Key Points

Aggregate Supply (pp. 648–651)

- In the long run, the quantity of real GDP supplied is potential GDP.
- In the short run, a rise in the price level increases the quantity of real GDP supplied.
- A change in potential GDP changes long-run and short-run aggregate supply. A change in the money wage rate changes only short-run aggregate supply.

Working Problems 1 to 3 will give you a better understanding of aggregate supply.

Aggregate Demand (pp. 652–655)

- A rise in the price level decreases the quantity of real GDP demanded.
- Changes in expected future income, inflation, and profits; in fiscal policy and monetary policy; and in foreign income and the exchange rate change aggregate demand.

Working Problems 4 to 7 will give you a better understanding of aggregate demand.

Explaining Macroeconomic Trends and Fluctuations (pp. 656–661)

- Aggregate demand and short-run aggregate supply determine real GDP and the price level.
- In the long run, real GDP equals potential GDP and aggregate demand determines the price level.
- The business cycle occurs because aggregate demand and aggregate supply fluctuate.

Working Problems 8 to 16 will give you a better understanding of macroeconomic trends and fluctuations.

Macroeconomic Schools of Thought (pp. 662–663)

- Classical economists believe that the economy is self-regulating and always at full employment.
- Keynesian economists believe that full employment can be achieved only with active policy.
- Monetarist economists believe that recessions result from inappropriate monetary policy.

Working Problems 17 to 19 will give you a better understanding of the macroeconomic schools of thought.

Key Terms

Above full-employment equilibrium, 658
Aggregate demand, 652
Below full-employment equilibrium, 659
Classical, 662
Disposable income, 654
Fiscal policy, 654

Full-employment equilibrium, 659
Inflationary gap, 658
Keynesian, 662
Long-run aggregate supply, 648
Long-run macroeconomic equilibrium, 656
Monetarist, 663
Monetary policy, 654

New classical, 662
New Keynesian, 663
Output gap, 658
Recessionary gap, 659
Short-run aggregate supply, 649
Short-run macroeconomic equilibrium, 656
Stagflation, 661

STUDY PLAN PROBLEMS AND APPLICATIONS

myeconlab You can work Problems 1 to 19 in MyEconLab Chapter 27 Study Plan and get instant feedback.

Aggregate Supply (Study Plan 27.1)

1. Explain the influence of each of the following events on the quantity of real GDP supplied and aggregate supply in India and use a graph to illustrate.
   - U.S. firms move their call handling, IT, and data functions to India.
   - Fuel prices rise.
   - Wal-Mart and Starbucks open in India.
   - Universities in India increased the number of engineering graduates.
   - The money wage rate rises.
   - The price level in India increases.

2. **Wages Could Hit Steepest Plunge in 18 Years**

   A bad economy is starting to drag down wages for millions of workers. The average weekly wage has fallen 1.4% this year through September. Colorado will become the first state to lower its minimum wage since the federal minimum wage law was passed in 1938, when the state cuts its rate by 4 cents an hour.

   Source: *USA Today*, October 16, 2009

   Explain how the fall in the average weekly wage and the minimum wage will influence aggregate supply.

3. Chinese Premier Wen Jiabao has warned Japan that its companies operating in China should raise pay for their workers. Explain how a rise in wages in China will influence the quantity of real GDP supplied and aggregate supply in China.

Aggregate Demand (Study Plan 27.2)

4. Canada trades with the United States. Explain the effect of each of the following events on Canada's aggregate demand.
   - The government of Canada cuts income taxes.
   - The United States experiences strong economic growth.
   - Canada sets new environmental standards that require power utilities to upgrade their production facilities.

5. The Fed cuts the quantity of money and all other things remain the same. Explain the effect of the cut in the quantity of money on aggregate demand in the short run.

6. Mexico trades with the United States. Explain the effect of each of the following events on the quantity of real GDP demanded and aggregate demand in Mexico.
   - The United States goes into a recession.
   - The price level in Mexico rises.
   - Mexico increases the quantity of money.

7. **Durable Goods Orders Surge in May, New-Homes Sales Dip**

   The Commerce Department announced that demand for durable goods rose 1.8 percent, while new-home sales dropped 0.6 percent in May. U.S. companies suffered a sharp drop in exports as other countries struggle with recession.

   Source: *USA Today*, June 24, 2009

   Explain how the items in the news clip influence U.S. aggregate demand.

Explaining Macroeconomic Trends and Fluctuations

(Study Plan 27.3)

Use the following graph to work Problems 8 to 10. Initially, the short-run aggregate supply curve is SAS_0 and the aggregate demand curve is AD_0.

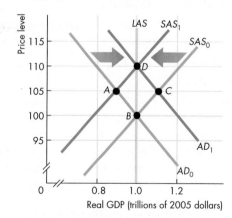

8. Some events change aggregate demand from AD_0 to AD_1. Describe two events that could have created this change in aggregate demand. What is the equilibrium after aggregate demand changed? If potential GDP is $1 trillion, the economy is at what type of macroeconomic equilibrium?

9. Some events change aggregate supply from SAS_0 to SAS_1. Describe two events that could have created this change in aggregate supply. What is the

equilibrium after aggregate supply changed? If potential GDP is $1 trillion, does the economy have an inflationary gap, a recessionary gap, or no output gap?

10. Some events change aggregate demand from AD_0 to AD_1 and aggregate supply from SAS_0 to SAS_1. What is the new macroeconomic equilibrium?

Use the following data to work Problems 11 to 13.

The following events have occurred in the history of the United States:

- A deep recession hits the world economy.
- The world oil price rises sharply.
- U.S. businesses expect future profits to fall.

11. Explain for each event whether it changes short-run aggregate supply, long-run aggregate supply, aggregate demand, or some combination of them.

12. Explain the separate effects of each event on U.S. real GDP and the price level, starting from a position of long-run equilibrium.

13. Explain the combined effects of these events on U.S. real GDP and the price level, starting from a position of long-run equilibrium.

Use the following data to work Problems 14 and 15.

The table shows the aggregate demand and short-run aggregate supply schedules of a country in which potential GDP is $1,050 billion.

Price level	Real GDP demanded	Real GDP supplied in the short run
	(billions of 2005 dollars)	
100	1,150	1,050
110	1,100	1,100
120	1,050	1,150
130	1,000	1,200
140	950	1,250
150	900	1,300
160	850	1,350

14. What is the short-run equilibrium real GDP and price level?

15. Does the country have an inflationary gap or a recessionary gap and what is its magnitude?

16. **Geithner Urges Action on Economy**
Treasury Secretary Timothy Geithner is reported as having said that the United States can no longer rely on consumer spending to be the growth engine of recovery from recession.

Washington needs to plant the seeds for business investment and exports. "We can't go back to a situation where we're depending on a near short-term boost in consumption to carry us forward," he said.

Source: *The Wall Street Journal*, September 12, 2010

a. Explain the effects of an increase in consumer spending on the short-run macroeconomic equilibrium.

b. Explain the effects of an increase in business investment on the short-run macroeconomic equilibrium.

c. Explain the effects of an increase in exports on the short-run macroeconomic equilibrium.

Macroeconomic Schools of Thought (Study Plan 27.4)

17. Describe what a classical macroeconomist, a Keynesian, and a monetarist would want to do in response to each of the events listed in Problem 11.

18. **Adding Up the Cost of Obama's Agenda**
When campaigning, Barack Obama has made a long list of promises for new federal programs costing tens of billions of dollars. Obama has said he would strengthen the nation's bridges and dams ($6 billion a year), extend health insurance to more people (part of a $65-billion-a-year health plan), develop cleaner energy sources ($15 billion a year), curb home foreclosures ($10 billion in one-time spending) and add $18 billion a year to education spending. In total a $50-billion plan to stimulate the economy through increased government spending. A different blueprint offered by McCain proposes relatively little new spending and tax cuts as a more effective means of solving problems.

Source: *Los Angeles Times*, July 8, 2008

a. Based upon this news clip, explain what macroeconomic school of thought Barack Obama most likely follows.

b. Based upon this news clip, explain what macroeconomic school of thought John McCain most likely follows.

19. Based upon the news clip in Problem 16, explain what macroeconomics school of thought Treasury Secretary Timothy Geithner most likely follows?

ADDITIONAL PROBLEMS AND APPLICATIONS

myeconlab You can work these problems in MyEconLab if assigned by your instructor.

Aggregate Supply

20. Explain for each event whether it changes the quantity of real GDP supplied, short-run aggregate supply, long-run aggregate supply, or a combination of them.
    - Automotive firms in the United States switch to a new technology that raises productivity.
    - Toyota and Honda build additional plants in the United States.
    - The prices of auto parts imported from China rise.
    - Autoworkers agree to a cut in the nominal wage rate.
    - The U.S. price level rises.

Aggregate Demand

21. Explain for each event whether it changes the quantity of real GDP demanded or aggregate demand.
    - Automotive firms in the United States switch to a new technology that raises productivity.
    - Toyota and Honda build new plants in the United States.
    - Autoworkers agree to a lower money wage rate.
    - The U.S. price level rises.

22. **Inventories Surge**

    The Commerce Department reported that wholesale inventories rose 1.3 percent in July, the best performance since July 2008. A major driver of the economy since late last year has been the restocking of depleted store shelves.

    Source: *Associated Press*, September 13, 2010

    Explain how a surge in inventories influences current aggregate demand.

23. **Low Spending Is Taking Toll on Economy**

    The Commerce Department reported that the economy continued to stagnate during the first three months of the year, with a sharp pullback in consumer spending the primary factor at play. Consumer spending fell for a broad range of goods and services, including cars, auto parts, furniture, food and recreation, reflecting a growing inclination toward thrift.

    Source: *The New York Times*, May 1, 2008

    Explain how a fall in consumer expenditure influences the quantity of real GDP demanded and aggregate demand.

Explaining Macroeconomic Trends and Fluctuations

Use the following information to work Problems 24 to 26.

The following events have occurred at times in the history of the United States:
- The world economy goes into an expansion.
- U.S. businesses expect future profits to rise.
- The government increases its expenditure on goods and services in a time of war or increased international tension.

24. Explain for each event whether it changes short-run aggregate supply, long-run aggregate supply, aggregate demand, or some combination of them.

25. Explain the separate effects of each event on U.S. real GDP and the price level, starting from a position of long-run equilibrium.

26. Explain the combined effects of these events on U.S. real GDP and the price level, starting from a position of long-run equilibrium.

Use the following information to work Problems 27 and 28.

In Japan, potential GDP is 600 trillion yen and the table shows the aggregate demand and short-run aggregate supply schedules.

Price level	Real GDP demanded	Real GDP supplied in the short run
	(trillions of 2005 yen)	
75	600	400
85	550	450
95	500	500
105	450	550
115	400	600
125	350	650
135	300	700

27. a. Draw a graph of the aggregate demand curve and the short-run aggregate supply curve.
    b. What is the short-run equilibrium real GDP and price level?

28. Does Japan have an inflationary gap or a recessionary gap and what is its magnitude?

Use the following information to work Problems 29 and 30.

Spending by Women Jumps

The magazine *Women of China* reported that Chinese women in big cities spent 63% of their income on consumer goods last year, up from a meager 26% in 2007. Clothing accounted for the biggest chunk of that spending, at nearly 30%, followed by digital products such as cellphones and cameras (11%) and travel (10%). Chinese consumption as a whole grew faster than the overall economy in the first half of the year and is expected to reach 42% of GDP by 2020, up from the current 36%.

Source: *The Wall Street Journal*,
August 27, 2010

29. Explain the effect of a rise in consumption expenditure on real GDP and the price level in the short run.

30. If the economy had been operating at a full-employment equilibrium,
    a. Describe the macroeconomic equilibrium after the rise in consumer spending.
    b. Explain and draw a graph to illustrate how the economy can adjust in the long run to restore a full-employment equilibrium.

31. Why do changes in consumer spending play a large role in the business cycle?

32. **It's Pinching Everyone**

    The current inflationary process is a global phenomenon, but emerging and developing countries have been growing significantly faster than the rest of the world. Because there is no reason to believe that world production will rise miraculously at least in the immediate future, many people expect that prices will keep on rising. These expectations in turn exacerbate the inflationary process. Households buy more of non-perishable goods than they need for their immediate consumption because they expect prices to go up even further. What is worse is that traders withhold stocks from the market in the hope of being able to sell these at higher prices later on. In other words, expectations of higher prices become self-fulfilling.

    Source: *The Times of India*, June 24, 2008

    Explain and draw a graph to illustrate how inflation and inflation expectations "become self-fulfilling."

Macroeconomic Schools of Thought

33. **Should Congress Pass a New Stimulus Bill? No, Cut Taxes and Curb Spending Instead**

    The first stimulus was not too meager, but it was the wrong policy prescription. Anybody who studies economic history would know that government spending doesn't produce long-term, sustainable growth, and jobs. The only sure way to perk up the job market is to cut taxes permanently and rein in public spending and excessive regulation.

    Source: sgvtribune.com, September 11, 2010

    Economists from which macroeconomic school of thought would recommend a second spending stimulus and which a permanent tax cut?

Economics in the News

34. After you have studied *Reading Between the Lines* on pp. 664–665 answer the following questions.
    a. What are the main features of the U.S. economy in the second quarter of 2010?
    b. Did the United States have a recessionary gap or an inflationary gap in 2010? How do you know?
    c. Use the *AS-AD* model to show the changes in aggregate demand and aggregate supply that occurred in 2009 and 2010 that brought the economy to its situation in mid-2010.
    d. Use the *AS-AD* model to show the changes in aggregate demand and aggregate supply that would occur if monetary policy cut the interest rate and increased the quantity of money by enough to restore full employment.
    e. Use the *AS-AD* model to show the changes in aggregate demand and aggregate supply that would occur if the federal government increased its expenditure on goods and services or cut taxes further by enough to restore full employment.
    f. Use the *AS-AD* model to show the changes in aggregate demand and aggregate supply that would occur if monetary and fiscal policy stimulus turned out to be too much and took the economy into an inflationary gap. Show the short-run and the long-run effects.

28

EXPENDITURE MULTIPLIERS: THE KEYNESIAN MODEL

After studying this chapter, you will be able to:

◆ Explain how expenditure plans are determined when the price level is fixed

◆ Explain how real GDP is determined when the price level is fixed

◆ Explain the expenditure multiplier when the price level is fixed

◆ Explain the relationship between aggregate expenditure and aggregate demand and explain the multiplier when the price level changes

Alicia Keys sings into a microphone in a barely audible whisper and through the magic of electronic amplification, her voice fills Central Park.

Michael Bloomberg, the mayor of New York, and an assistant are being driven to a business meeting along one of the cobblestone streets of downtown Manhattan. The car's wheels bounce and vibrate over the uneven surface, but the assistant's notes are tapped into a BlackBerry without missing a keystroke, thanks to the car's efficient shock absorbers.

Investment and exports fluctuate like the volume of Alicia Keys' voice and the uneven surface of a New York City street. How does the economy react to those fluctuations? Does it behave like an amplifier, blowing up the fluctuations and spreading them out to affect the many millions of participants in an economic rock concert? Or does it react like a limousine, absorbing the shocks and providing a smooth ride for the economy's passengers?

You will explore these questions in this chapter and in *Reading Between the Lines* at the end of the chapter you will see the role played by inventory investment during 2010 as the economy expanded.

◆ Fixed Prices and Expenditure Plans

In the Keynesian model that we study in this chapter, all the firms are like your grocery store: They set their prices and sell the quantities their customers are willing to buy. If they persistently sell a greater quantity than they plan to and are constantly running out of inventory, they eventually raise their prices. And if they persistently sell a smaller quantity than they plan to and have inventories piling up, they eventually cut their prices. But on any given day, their prices are fixed and the quantities they sell depend on demand, not supply.

Because each firm's prices are fixed, for the economy as a whole:

1. The *price level* is fixed, and
2. *Aggregate demand* determines real GDP.

The Keynesian model explains fluctuations in aggregate demand at a fixed price level by identifying the forces that determine expenditure plans.

Expenditure Plans

Aggregate expenditure has four components: consumption expenditure, investment, government expenditure on goods and services, and net exports (exports *minus* imports). These four components of aggregate expenditure sum to real GDP (see Chapter 21, pp. 491–492).

Aggregate planned expenditure is equal to the sum of the *planned* levels of consumption expenditure, investment, government expenditure on goods and services, and exports minus imports. Two of these components of planned expenditure, consumption expenditure and imports, change when income changes and so they depend on real GDP.

A Two-Way Link Between Aggregate Expenditure and Real GDP
There is a two-way link between aggregate expenditure and real GDP. Other things remaining the same,

■ An increase in real GDP increases aggregate expenditure, and

■ An increase in aggregate expenditure increases real GDP.

You are now going to study this two-way link.

Consumption and Saving Plans

Several factors influence consumption expenditure and saving plans. The more important ones are

1. Disposable income
2. Real interest rate
3. Wealth
4. Expected future income

Disposable income is aggregate income minus taxes plus transfer payments. Aggregate income equals real GDP, so disposable income depends on real GDP. To explore the two-way link between real GDP and planned consumption expenditure, we focus on the relationship between consumption expenditure and disposable income when the other three factors listed above are constant.

Consumption Expenditure and Saving The table in Fig. 28.1 lists the consumption expenditure and the saving that people plan at each level of disposable income. Households can only spend their disposable income on consumption or save it, so planned consumption expenditure plus planned saving *always* equals disposable income.

The relationship between consumption expenditure and disposable income, other things remaining the same, is called the **consumption function.** The relationship between saving and disposable income, other things remaining the same, is called the **saving function.**

Consumption Function Figure 28.1(a) shows a consumption function. The *y*-axis measures consumption expenditure, and the *x*-axis measures disposable income. Along the consumption function, the points labeled *A* through *F* correspond to the rows of the table. For example, point *E* shows that when disposable income is $8 trillion, consumption expenditure is $7.5 trillion. As disposable income increases, consumption expenditure also increases.

At point *A* on the consumption function, consumption expenditure is $1.5 trillion even though disposable income is zero. This consumption expenditure is called *autonomous consumption*, and it is the amount of consumption expenditure that would take place in the short run even if people had no current income. Consumption expenditure in excess of this amount is called *induced consumption*, which is the consumption expenditure that is induced by an increase in disposable income.

45° Line Figure 28.1(a) also contains a 45° line, the height of which measures disposable income. At each point on this line, consumption expenditure equals disposable income. Between *A* and *D*, consumption expenditure exceeds disposable income, between *D* and *F* consumption expenditure is less than disposable income, and at point *D*, consumption expenditure equals disposable income.

Saving Function Figure 28.1(b) shows a saving function. Again, the points *A* through *F* correspond to the rows of the table. For example, point *E* shows that when disposable income is $8 trillion, saving is $0.5 trillion. As disposable income increases, saving increases. Notice that when consumption expenditure exceeds disposable income in part (a), saving is negative, called *dissaving*, in part (b).

FIGURE 28.1   Consumption Function and Saving Function

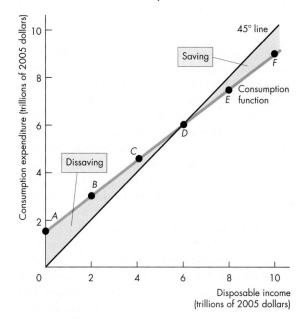

(a) Consumption function

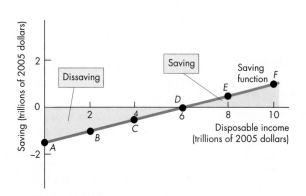

(b) Saving function

	Disposable income	Planned consumption expenditure	Planned saving
		(trillions of 2005 dollars)	
A	0	1.5	−1.5
B	2	3.0	−1.0
C	4	4.5	−0.5
D	6	6.0	0
E	8	7.5	0.5
F	10	9.0	1.0

The table shows consumption expenditure and saving plans at various levels of disposable income. Part (a) of the figure shows the relationship between consumption expenditure and disposable income (the consumption function). The height of the consumption function measures consumption expenditure at each level of disposable income. Part (b) shows the relationship between saving and disposable income (the saving function). The height of the saving function measures saving at each level of disposable income. Points *A* through *F* on the consumption and saving functions correspond to the rows in the table.

The height of the 45° line in part (a) measures disposable income. So along the 45° line, consumption expenditure equals disposable income. Consumption expenditure plus saving equals disposable income. When the consumption function is above the 45° line, saving is negative (dissaving occurs). When the consumption function is below the 45° line, saving is positive. At the point where the consumption function intersects the 45° line, all disposable income is spent on consumption and saving is zero.

Marginal Propensities to Consume and Save

The **marginal propensity to consume** (*MPC*) is the fraction of a *change* in disposable income that is spent on consumption. It is calculated as the *change* in consumption expenditure (ΔC) divided by the *change* in disposable income (ΔYD). The formula is

$$MPC = \frac{\Delta C}{\Delta YD}.$$

In the table in Fig. 28.1, when disposable income increases by $2 trillion, consumption expenditure increases by $1.5 trillion. The *MPC* is $1.5 trillion divided by $2 trillion, which equals 0.75.

The **marginal propensity to save** (*MPS*) is the fraction of a *change* in disposable income that is saved. It is calculated as the *change* in saving (ΔS) divided by the *change* in disposable income (ΔYD). The formula is

$$MPS = \frac{\Delta S}{\Delta YD}.$$

In the table in Fig. 28.1, when disposable income increases by $2 trillion, saving increases by $0.5 trillion. The *MPS* is $0.5 trillion divided by $2 trillion, which equals 0.25.

Because an increase in disposable income is either spent on consumption or saved, the marginal propensity to consume plus the marginal propensity to save equals 1. You can see why by using the equation:

$$\Delta C + \Delta S = \Delta YD.$$

Divide both sides of the equation by the change in disposable income to obtain

$$\frac{\Delta C}{\Delta YD} + \frac{\Delta S}{\Delta YD} = 1.$$

$\Delta C/\Delta YD$ is the marginal propensity to consume (*MPC*), and $\Delta S/\Delta YD$ is the marginal propensity to save (*MPS*), so

$$MPC + MPS = 1.$$

Slopes and Marginal Propensities

The slope of the consumption function is the marginal propensity to consume, and the slope of the saving function is the marginal propensity to save.

Figure 28.2(a) shows the *MPC* as the slope of the consumption function. An increase in disposable income of $2 trillion is the base of the red triangle. The increase in consumption expenditure that results from this increase in disposable income is $1.5 trillion and is the height of the triangle. The slope of the consumption function is given by the formula "slope equals rise over run" and is $1.5 trillion divided by $2 trillion, which equals 0.75—the *MPC*.

Figure 28.2(b) shows the *MPS* as the slope of the saving function. An increase in disposable income of $2 trillion (the base of the red triangle) increases saving by $0.5 trillion (the height of the triangle). The slope of the saving function is $0.5 trillion divided by $2 trillion, which equals 0.25—the *MPS*.

FIGURE 28.2   The Marginal Propensities to Consume and Save

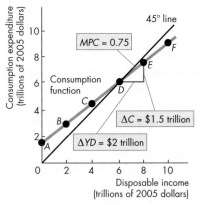

(a) Consumption function

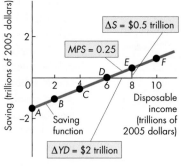

(b) Saving function

The marginal propensity to consume, *MPC*, is equal to the change in consumption expenditure divided by the change in disposable income, other things remaining the same. It is measured by the slope of the consumption function. In part (a), the *MPC* is 0.75.

The marginal propensity to save, *MPS*, is equal to the change in saving divided by the change in disposable income, other things remaining the same. It is measured by the slope of the saving function. In part (b), the *MPS* is 0.25.

myeconlab   animation

Economics in Action
The U.S. Consumption Function

The figure shows the U.S. consumption function. Each point identified by a blue dot represents consumption expenditure and disposable income for a particular year. (The dots are for the years 1970 to 2010, and the dots for five of those years are identified in the figure.)

The U.S. consumption function is CF_0 in 1970 and CF_1 in 2010.

The slope of the consumption function in the figure is 0.9, which means that a $1 increase in disposable income increases consumption expenditure by 90 cents. This slope, which is an estimate of the marginal propensity to consume, is an assumption that is at the upper end of the range of values that economists have estimated for the marginal propensity to consume.

The consumption function shifts upward over time as other influences on consumption expenditure change. Of these other influences, the real interest rate and wealth fluctuate and so bring upward and downward shifts in the consumption function.

But rising wealth and rising expected future income bring a steady upward shift in the consumption function. As the consumption function shifts upward, autonomous consumption increases.

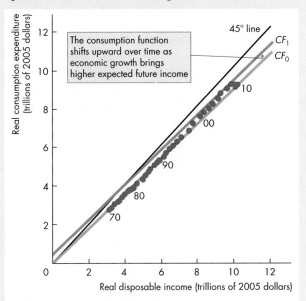

The U.S. Consumption Function

Source of data: Bureau of Economic Analysis.

Consumption as a Function of Real GDP

Consumption expenditure changes when disposable income changes and disposable income changes when real GDP changes. So consumption expenditure depends not only on disposable income but also on real GDP. We use this link between consumption expenditure and real GDP to determine equilibrium expenditure. But before we do so, we need to look at one further component of aggregate expenditure: imports. Like consumption expenditure, imports are influenced by real GDP.

Import Function

Of the many influences on U.S. imports in the short run, U.S. real GDP is the main influence. Other things remaining the same, an increase in U.S. real GDP increases the quantity of U.S. imports.

The relationship between imports and real GDP is determined by the **marginal propensity to import**, which is the fraction of an increase in real GDP that is spent on imports. It is calculated as the change in imports divided by the change in real GDP, other things remaining the same. For example, if an increase in real GDP of $1 trillion increases imports by $0.25 trillion, the marginal propensity to import is 0.25.

REVIEW QUIZ

1 Which components of aggregate expenditure are influenced by real GDP?
2 Define and explain how we calculate the marginal propensity to consume and the marginal propensity to save.
3 How do we calculate the effects of real GDP on consumption expenditure and imports by using the marginal propensity to consume and the marginal propensity to import?

You can work these questions in Study Plan 28.1 and get instant feedback.

Real GDP influences consumption expenditure and imports, which in turn influence real GDP. Your next task is to study this second piece of the two-way link between aggregate expenditure and real GDP and see how all the components of aggregate planned expenditure interact to determine real GDP.

◆ Real GDP with a Fixed Price Level

You are now going to see how, at a given price level, aggregate expenditure plans determine real GDP. We start by looking at the relationship between aggregate planned expenditure and real GDP. This relationship can be described by an aggregate expenditure schedule or an aggregate expenditure curve. The *aggregate expenditure schedule* lists aggregate planned expenditure generated at each level of real GDP. The *aggregate expenditure curve* is a graph of the aggregate expenditure schedule.

Aggregate Planned Expenditure

The table in Fig. 28.3 sets out an aggregate expenditure schedule. To calculate aggregate planned expenditure at a given real GDP, we add the expenditure components together. The first column of the table shows real GDP, and the second column shows the planned consumption at each level of real GDP. A $1 trillion increase in real GDP increases consumption expenditure by $0.7 trillion—the *MPC* is 0.7.

The next two columns show investment and government expenditure on goods and services, both of which are independent of the level of real GDP. Investment depends on the real interest rate and the expected profit (see Chapter 24, p. 572). At a given point in time, these factors generate a given level of investment. Suppose this level of investment is $2.0 trillion. Also, suppose that government expenditure is $2.5 trillion.

The next two columns show exports and imports. Exports are influenced by events in the rest of the world, prices of foreign-produced goods and services relative to the prices of similar U.S.-produced goods and services, and exchange rates. But they are not directly affected by U.S. real GDP. Exports are a constant $2.0 trillion. Imports increase as U.S. real GDP increases. A $1 trillion increase in U.S. real GDP generates a $0.2 trillion increase in imports—the marginal propensity to import is 0.2.

The final column shows aggregate planned expenditure—the sum of planned consumption expenditure, investment, government expenditure on goods and services, and exports minus imports.

Figure 28.3 plots an aggregate expenditure curve. Real GDP is shown on the *x*-axis, and aggregate planned expenditure is shown on the *y*-axis. The aggregate expenditure curve is the red line *AE*. Points

A through *F* on that curve correspond to the rows of the table. The *AE* curve is a graph of aggregate planned expenditure (the last column) plotted against real GDP (the first column).

Figure 28.3 also shows the components of aggregate expenditure. The constant components—investment (I), government expenditure on goods and services (G), and exports (X)—are shown by the horizontal lines in the figure. Consumption expenditure (C) is the vertical gap between the lines labeled $I + G + X$ and $I + G + X + C$.

To construct the *AE* curve, subtract imports (M) from the $I + G + X + C$ line. Aggregate expenditure is expenditure on U.S.-produced goods and services. But the components of aggregate expenditure—C, I, and G—include expenditure on imported goods and services. For example, if you buy a new cell phone, your expenditure is part of consumption expenditure. But if the cell phone is a Nokia made in Finland, your expenditure on it must be subtracted from consumption expenditure to find out how much is spent on goods and services produced in the United States—on U.S. real GDP. Money paid to Nokia for cell phone imports from Finland does not add to aggregate expenditure in the United States.

Because imports are only a part of aggregate expenditure, when we subtract imports from the other components of aggregate expenditure, aggregate planned expenditure still increases as real GDP increases, as you can see in Fig. 28.3.

Consumption expenditure minus imports, which varies with real GDP, is called **induced expenditure**. The sum of investment, government expenditure, and exports, which does not vary with real GDP, is called **autonomous expenditure**. Consumption expenditure and imports can also have an autonomous component—a component that does not vary with real GDP. Another way of thinking about autonomous expenditure is that it would be the level of aggregate planned expenditure if real GDP were zero.

In Fig. 28.3, autonomous expenditure is $6.5 trillion—aggregate planned expenditure when real GDP is zero (point *A*). For each $1 trillion increase in real GDP, induced expenditure increases by $0.5 trillion.

The aggregate expenditure curve summarizes the relationship between aggregate *planned* expenditure and real GDP. But what determines the point on the aggregate expenditure curve at which the economy operates? What determines *actual* aggregate expenditure?

FIGURE 28.3   Aggregate Planned Expenditure: The *AE* Curve

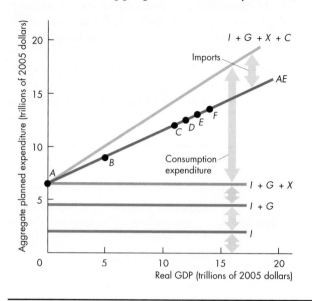

Aggregate planned expenditure is the sum of planned consumption expenditure, investment, government expenditure on goods and services, and exports minus imports. For example, in row *C* of the table, when real GDP is $11 trillion, planned consumption expenditure is $7.7 trillion, planned investment is $2.0 trillion, planned government expenditure is $2.5 trillion, planned exports are $2.0 trillion, and planned imports are $2.2 trillion. So when real GDP is $11 trillion, aggregate planned expenditure is $12 trillion ($7.7 + $2.0 + $2.5 + $2.0 − $2.2). The schedule shows that aggregate planned expenditure increases as real GDP increases. This relationship is graphed as the aggregate expenditure curve *AE*. The components of aggregate expenditure that increase with real GDP are consumption expenditure and imports. The other components—investment, government expenditure, and exports—do not vary with real GDP.

		Planned expenditure					
	Real GDP (Y)	Consumption expenditure (C)	Investment (I)	Government expenditure (G)	Exports (X)	Imports (M)	Aggregate planned expenditure (AE = C + I + G + X − M)
				(trillions of 2005 dollars)			
A	0	0	2.0	2.5	2.0	0.0	6.5
B	5	3.5	2.0	2.5	2.0	1.0	9.0
C	11	7.7	2.0	2.5	2.0	2.2	12.0
D	12	8.4	2.0	2.5	2.0	2.4	12.5
E	13	9.1	2.0	2.5	2.0	2.6	13.0
F	14	9.8	2.0	2.5	2.0	2.8	13.5

 myeconlab   animation

Actual Expenditure, Planned Expenditure, and Real GDP

Actual aggregate expenditure is always equal to real GDP, as we saw in Chapter 21 (p. 492). But aggregate *planned* expenditure is not always equal to actual aggregate expenditure and therefore is not always equal to real GDP. How can actual expenditure and planned expenditure differ? The answer is that firms can end up with inventories that are greater or smaller than planned. People carry out their consumption

expenditure plans, the government implements its planned expenditure on goods and services, and net exports are as planned. Firms carry out their plans to purchase new buildings, plant, and equipment. But one component of investment is the change in firms' inventories. If aggregate planned expenditure is less than real GDP, firms sell less than they planned to sell and end up with unplanned inventories. If aggregate planned expenditure exceeds real GDP, firms sell more than they planned to sell and end up with inventories being too low.

Equilibrium Expenditure

Equilibrium expenditure is the level of aggregate expenditure that occurs when aggregate *planned* expenditure equals real GDP. Equilibrium expenditure is a level of aggregate expenditure and real GDP at which spending plans are fulfilled. At a given price level, equilibrium expenditure determines real GDP. When aggregate planned expenditure and actual aggregate expenditure are unequal, a process of convergence toward equilibrium expenditure occurs. Throughout this process, real GDP adjusts. Let's examine equilibrium expenditure and the process that brings it about.

Figure 28.4(a) illustrates equilibrium expenditure. The table sets out aggregate planned expenditure at various levels of real GDP. These values are plotted as

FIGURE 28.4   Equilibrium Expenditure

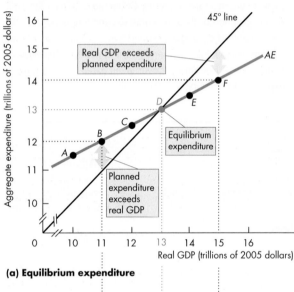

(a) Equilibrium expenditure

(b) Unplanned inventory changes

	Real GDP (Y)	Aggregate planned expenditure (AE)	Unplanned inventory change (Y − AE)
		(trillions of 2005 dollars)	
A	10	11.5	−1.5
B	11	12.0	−1.0
C	12	12.5	−0.5
D	13	13.0	0
E	14	13.5	0.5
F	15	14.0	1.0

The table shows expenditure plans at different levels of real GDP. When real GDP is $13 trillion, aggregate planned expenditure equals real GDP.

Part (a) of the figure illustrates equilibrium expenditure, which occurs when aggregate planned expenditure equals real GDP at the intersection of the 45° line and the AE curve. Part (b) of the figure shows the forces that bring about equilibrium expenditure. When aggregate planned expenditure exceeds real GDP, inventories decrease—for example, at point B in both parts of the figure. Firms increase production, and real GDP increases.

When aggregate planned expenditure is less than real GDP, inventories increase—for example, at point F in both parts of the figure. Firms decrease production, and real GDP decreases. When aggregate planned expenditure equals real GDP, there are no unplanned inventory changes and real GDP remains constant at equilibrium expenditure.

points *A* through *F* along the *AE* curve. The 45° line shows all the points at which aggregate planned expenditure equals real GDP. So where the *AE* curve lies above the 45° line, aggregate planned expenditure exceeds real GDP; where the *AE* curve lies below the 45° line, aggregate planned expenditure is less than real GDP; and where the *AE* curve intersects the 45° line, aggregate planned expenditure equals real GDP. Point *D* illustrates equilibrium expenditure. At this point, real GDP is $13 trillion.

Convergence to Equilibrium

What are the forces that move aggregate expenditure toward its equilibrium level? To answer this question, we must look at a situation in which aggregate expenditure is away from its equilibrium level.

From Below Equilibrium Suppose that in Fig. 28.4, real GDP is $11 trillion. With real GDP at $11 trillion, actual aggregate expenditure is also $11 trillion. But aggregate *planned* expenditure is $12 trillion, point *B* in Fig. 28.4(a). Aggregate planned expenditure exceeds *actual* expenditure. When people spend $12 trillion and firms produce goods and services worth $11 trillion, firms' inventories fall by $1 trillion, point *B* in Fig. 28.4(b). Because the change in inventories is part of investment, *actual* investment is $1 trillion less than *planned* investment.

Real GDP doesn't remain at $11 trillion for very long. Firms have inventory targets based on their sales. When inventories fall below target, firms increase production to restore inventories to the target level. To increase inventories, firms hire additional labor and increase production. Suppose that they increase production in the next period by $1 trillion. Real GDP increases by $1.0 trillion to $12.0 trillion. But again, aggregate planned expenditure exceeds real GDP. When real GDP is $12.0 trillion, aggregate planned expenditure is $12.5 trillion, point *C* in Fig. 28.4(a). Again, inventories decrease, but this time by less than before. With real GDP of $12.0 trillion and aggregate planned expenditure of $12.5 trillion, inventories decrease by $0.5 trillion, point *C* in Fig. 28.4(b). Again, firms hire additional labor and production increases; real GDP increases yet further.

The process that we've just described—planned expenditure exceeds real GDP, inventories decrease, and production increases to restore inventories—ends when real GDP has reached $13 trillion. At this real

GDP, there is equilibrium. Unplanned inventory changes are zero. Firms do not change their production.

From Above Equilibrium If in Fig. 28.4, real GDP is $15 trillion, the process that we've just described works in reverse. With real GDP at $15 trillion, actual aggregate expenditure is also $15 trillion. But aggregate planned expenditure is $14 trillion, point *F* in Fig. 28.4(a). Actual expenditure exceeds planned expenditure. When people spend $14 trillion and firms produce goods and services worth $15 trillion, firms' inventories rise by $1 trillion, point *F* in Fig. 28.4(b). Now, real GDP begins to fall. As long as actual expenditure exceeds planned expenditure, inventories rise, and production decreases. Again, the process ends when real GDP has reached $13 trillion, the equilibrium at which unplanned inventory changes are zero and firms do not change their production.

REVIEW QUIZ

1 What is the relationship between aggregate planned expenditure and real GDP at equilibrium expenditure?
2 How does equilibrium expenditure come about? What adjusts to achieve equilibrium?
3 If real GDP and aggregate expenditure are less than equilibrium expenditure, what happens to firms' inventories? How do firms change their production? And what happens to real GDP?
4 If real GDP and aggregate expenditure are greater than equilibrium expenditure, what happens to firms' inventories? How do firms change their production? And what happens to real GDP?

You can work these questions in Study Plan 28.2 and get instant feedback.

We've learned that when the price level is fixed, real GDP is determined by equilibrium expenditure. And we have seen how unplanned changes in inventories and the production response they generate bring a convergence toward equilibrium expenditure. We're now going to study *changes* in equilibrium expenditure and discover an economic amplifier called the *multiplier*.

◆ The Multiplier

Investment and exports can change for many reasons. A fall in the real interest rate might induce firms to increase their planned investment. A wave of innovation, such as occurred with the spread of multimedia computers in the 1990s, might increase expected future profits and lead firms to increase their planned investment. An economic boom in Western Europe and Japan might lead to a large increase in their expenditure on U.S.-produced goods and services—on U.S. exports. These are all examples of increases in autonomous expenditure.

When autonomous expenditure increases, aggregate expenditure increases and so does equilibrium expenditure and real GDP. But the increase in real GDP is *larger* than the change in autonomous expenditure. The **multiplier** is the amount by which a change in autonomous expenditure is magnified or multiplied to determine the change in equilibrium expenditure and real GDP.

To get the basic idea of the multiplier, we'll work with an example economy in which there are no income taxes and no imports. So we'll first assume that these factors are absent. Then, when you understand the basic idea, we'll bring these factors back into play and see what difference they make to the multiplier.

The Basic Idea of the Multiplier

Suppose that investment increases. The additional expenditure by businesses means that aggregate expenditure and real GDP increase. The increase in real GDP increases disposable income, and with no income taxes, real GDP and disposable income increase by the same amount. The increase in disposable income brings an increase in consumption expenditure. And the increased consumption expenditure adds even more to aggregate expenditure. Real GDP and disposable income increase further, and so does consumption expenditure. The initial increase in investment brings an even bigger increase in aggregate expenditure because it induces an increase in consumption expenditure. The magnitude of the increase in aggregate expenditure that results from an increase in autonomous expenditure is determined by the *multiplier*.

The table in Fig. 28.5 sets out an aggregate planned expenditure schedule. Initially, when real GDP is $12 trillion, aggregate planned expenditure is $12.25 trillion. For each $1 trillion increase in real

GDP, aggregate planned expenditure increases by $0.75 trillion. This aggregate expenditure schedule is shown in the figure as the aggregate expenditure curve AE_0. Initially, equilibrium expenditure is $13 trillion. You can see this equilibrium in row B of the table and in the figure where the curve AE_0 intersects the 45° line at the point marked B.

Now suppose that autonomous expenditure increases by $0.5 trillion. What happens to equilibrium expenditure? You can see the answer in Fig. 28.5. When this increase in autonomous expenditure is added to the original aggregate planned expenditure, aggregate planned expenditure increases by $0.5 trillion at each level of real GDP. The new aggregate expenditure curve is AE_1. The new equilibrium expenditure, highlighted in the table (row D'), occurs where AE_1 intersects the 45° line and is $15 trillion (point D'). At this real GDP, aggregate planned expenditure equals real GDP.

The Multiplier Effect

In Fig. 28.5, the increase in autonomous expenditure of $0.5 trillion increases equilibrium expenditure by $2 trillion. That is, the change in autonomous expenditure leads, like Alicia Keys' electronic equipment, to an amplified change in equilibrium expenditure. This amplified change is the *multiplier effect*—equilibrium expenditure increases by *more than* the increase in autonomous expenditure. The multiplier is greater than 1.

Initially, when autonomous expenditure increases, aggregate planned expenditure exceeds real GDP. As a result, inventories decrease. Firms respond by increasing production so as to restore their inventories to the target level. As production increases, so does real GDP. With a higher level of real GDP, *induced expenditure* increases. Equilibrium expenditure increases by the sum of the initial increase in autonomous expenditure and the increase in induced expenditure. In this example, equilibrium expenditure increases by $2 trillion following the increase in autonomous expenditure of $0.5 trillion, so induced expenditure increases by $1.5 trillion.

Although we have just analyzed the effects of an *increase* in autonomous expenditure, this analysis also applies to a decrease in autonomous expenditure. If initially the aggregate expenditure curve is AE_1, equilibrium expenditure and real GDP are $15 trillion. A decrease in autonomous expenditure of $0.5 trillion shifts the aggregate expenditure curve downward by

FIGURE 28.5   The Multiplier

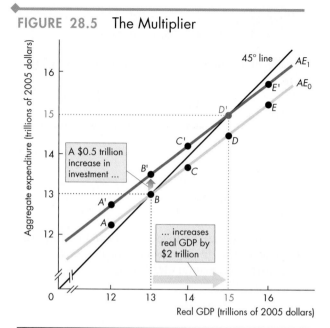

Real GDP (Y)	Aggregate planned expenditure			
	Original (AE₀)		New (AE₁)	
	(trillions of 2005 dollars)			
12	A	12.25	A'	12.75
13	**B**	**13.00**	B'	13.50
14	C	13.75	C'	14.25
15	D	14.50	D'	15.00
16	E	15.25	E'	15.75

A \$0.5 trillion increase in autonomous expenditure shifts the AE curve upward by \$0.5 trillion from AE_0 to AE_1. Equilibrium expenditure increases by \$2 trillion from \$13 trillion to \$15 trillion. The increase in equilibrium expenditure is 4 times the increase in autonomous expenditure, so the multiplier is 4.

\$0.5 trillion to AE_0. Equilibrium expenditure decreases from \$15 trillion to \$13 trillion. The decrease in equilibrium expenditure (\$2 trillion) is larger than the decrease in autonomous expenditure that brought it about (\$0.5 trillion).

Why Is the Multiplier Greater Than 1?

We've seen that equilibrium expenditure increases by more than the increase in autonomous expenditure. This makes the multiplier greater than 1. How come? Why does equilibrium expenditure increase by more than the increase in autonomous expenditure?

The multiplier is greater than 1 because induced expenditure increases—an increase in autonomous expenditure *induces* further increases in expenditure. The NASA space shuttle program costs about \$5 billion a year. This expenditure adds \$5 billion a year directly to real GDP. But that is not the end of the story. Astronauts and engineers now have more income, and they spend part of the extra income on goods and services. Real GDP now rises by the initial \$5 billion plus the extra consumption expenditure induced by the \$5 billion increase in income. The producers of cars, flat-screen TVs, vacations, and other goods and services now have increased incomes, and they, in turn, spend part of the increase in their incomes on consumption goods and services. Additional income induces additional expenditure, which creates additional income.

How big is the multiplier effect?

The Size of the Multiplier

Suppose that the economy is in a recession. Profit prospects start to look better, and firms are planning a large increase in investment. The world economy is also heading toward expansion. The question on everyone's lips is: How strong will the expansion be? This is a hard question to answer, but an important ingredient in the answer is the size of the multiplier.

The *multiplier* is the amount by which a change in autonomous expenditure is multiplied to determine the change in equilibrium expenditure that it generates. To calculate the multiplier, we divide the change in equilibrium expenditure by the change in autonomous expenditure.

Let's calculate the multiplier for the example in Fig. 28.5. Initially, equilibrium expenditure is \$13 trillion. Then autonomous expenditure increases by \$0.5 trillion, and equilibrium expenditure increases by \$2 trillion, to \$15 trillion. Then

$$\text{Multiplier} = \frac{\text{Change in equilibrium expenditure}}{\text{Change in autonomous expenditure}}$$

$$\text{Multiplier} = \frac{\$2 \text{ trillion}}{\$0.5 \text{ trillion}} = 4.$$

The Multiplier and the Slope of the *AE* Curve

The magnitude of the multiplier depends on the slope of the *AE* curve. In Fig. 28.6, the *AE* curve in part (a) is steeper than the *AE* curve in part (b), and the multiplier is larger in part (a) than in part (b). To see why, let's do a calculation.

Aggregate expenditure and real GDP change because induced expenditure and autonomous expenditure change. The change in real GDP (ΔY) equals the change in induced expenditure (ΔN) plus the change in autonomous expenditure (ΔA). That is,

$$\Delta Y = \Delta N + \Delta A.$$

But the change in induced expenditure is determined by the change in real GDP and the slope of the *AE* curve. To see why, begin with the fact that the slope of the *AE* curve equals the "rise," ΔN, divided by the "run," ΔY. That is,

$$\text{Slope of } AE \text{ curve } = \Delta N \div \Delta Y.$$

So

$$\Delta N = \text{Slope of } AE \text{ curve} \times \Delta Y.$$

Now, use this equation to replace ΔN in the first equation above to give

$$\Delta Y = \text{Slope of } AE \text{ curve} \times \Delta Y + \Delta A.$$

Now, solve for ΔY as

$$(1 - \text{Slope of } AE \text{ curve}) \times \Delta Y = \Delta A$$

and rearrange to give

$$\Delta Y = \frac{\Delta A}{1 - \text{Slope of } AE \text{ curve}}.$$

Finally, divide both sides of this equation by ΔA to give

$$\text{Multiplier} = \frac{\Delta Y}{\Delta A} = \frac{1}{1 - \text{Slope of } AE \text{ curve}}.$$

If we use the example in Fig. 28.5, the slope of the *AE* curve is 0.75, so

$$\text{Multiplier} = \frac{1}{1 - 0.75} = \frac{1}{0.25} = 4.$$

Where there are no income taxes and no imports, the slope of the *AE* curve equals the marginal propensity to consume (*MPC*). So

$$\text{Multiplier} = \frac{1}{1 - MPC}.$$

But $(1 - MPC)$ equals *MPS*. So another formula is

$$\text{Multiplier} = \frac{1}{MPS}.$$

Again using the numbers in Fig. 28.5, we have

$$\text{Multiplier} = \frac{1}{0.25} = 4.$$

Because the marginal propensity to save (*MPS*) is a fraction—a number between 0 and 1—the multiplier is greater than 1.

FIGURE 28.6   The Multiplier and the Slope of the *AE* Curve

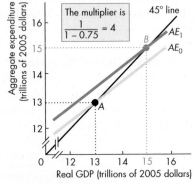

(a) Multiplier is 4

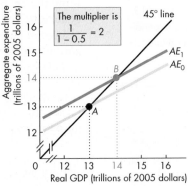

(b) Multiplier is 2

Imports and income taxes make the *AE* curve less steep and reduce the value of the multiplier. In part (a), with no imports and no income taxes, the slope of the *AE* curve is 0.75 (the marginal propensity to consume) and the multiplier is 4. But with imports and income taxes, the slope of the *AE* curve is less than the marginal propensity to consume. In part (b), the slope of the *AE* curve is 0.5. In this case, the multiplier is 2.

myeconlab animation

Imports and Income Taxes

Imports and income taxes influence the size of the multiplier and make it smaller than it otherwise would be.

To see why imports make the multiplier smaller, think about what happens following an increase in investment. The increase in investment increases real GDP, which in turn increases consumption expenditure. But part of the increase in expenditure is on imported goods and services. Only expenditure on U.S.-produced goods and services increases U.S. real GDP. The larger the marginal propensity to import, the smaller is the change in U.S. real GDP. The Mathematical Note on pp. 692–695 shows the effects of imports and income taxes on the multiplier.

Income taxes also make the multiplier smaller than it otherwise would be. Again, think about what happens following an increase in investment. The increase in investment increases real GDP. Income tax payments increase so disposable income increases by less than the increase in real GDP and consumption expenditure increases by less than it would if taxes had not changed. The larger the income tax rate, the smaller is the change in real GDP.

The marginal propensity to import and the income tax rate together with the marginal propensity to consume determine the multiplier. And their combined influence determines the slope of the *AE* curve.

Over time, the value of the multiplier changes as tax rates change and as the marginal propensity to consume and the marginal propensity to import change. These ongoing changes make the multiplier hard to predict. But they do not change the fundamental fact that an initial change in autonomous expenditure leads to a magnified change in aggregate expenditure and real GDP.

The Multiplier Process

The multiplier effect isn't a one-shot event. It is a process that plays out over a few months. Figure 28.7 illustrates the multiplier process. Autonomous expenditure increases by $0.5 trillion and real GDP increases by $0.5 trillion (the green bar in round 1). This increase in real GDP increases induced expenditure in round 2. With the slope of the *AE* curve equal to 0.75, induced expenditure increases by 0.75 times the increase in real GDP, so the increase in real GDP of $0.5 trillion induces a further increase in expenditure of $0.375 trillion. This

change in induced expenditure (the green bar in round 2) when added to the previous increase in expenditure (the blue bar in round 2) increases real GDP by $0.875 trillion. The round 2 increase in real GDP induces a round 3 increase in induced expenditure. The process repeats through successive rounds. Each increase in real GDP is 0.75 times the previous increase and eventually real GDP increases by $2 trillion.

FIGURE 28.7 The Multiplier Process

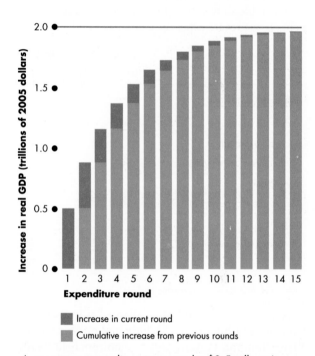

Autonomous expenditure increases by $0.5 trillion. In round 1, real GDP increases by the same amount. With the slope of the *AE* curve equal to 0.75, each additional dollar of real GDP induces an additional 0.75 of a dollar of induced expenditure. The round 1 increase in real GDP brings an increase in induced expenditure of $0.375 trillion in round 2. At the end of round 2, real GDP has increased by $0.875 trillion. The extra $0.375 trillion of real GDP in round 2 brings a further increase in induced expenditure of $0.281 trillion in round 3. At the end of round 3, real GDP has increased by $1.156 trillion. This process continues with real GDP increasing by ever-smaller amounts. When the process comes to an end, real GDP has increased by a total of $2 trillion.

myeconlab animation

Economics in Action
The Multiplier in the Great Depression

The aggregate expenditure model and its multiplier were developed during the 1930s by John Maynard Keynes to understand the most traumatic event in economic history, the *Great Depression*.

In 1929, the U.S. and global economies were booming. U.S. real GDP and real GDP per person had never been higher. By 1933, real GDP had fallen to 73 percent of its 1929 level and more than a quarter of the labor force was unemployed.

The table shows the GDP numbers and components of aggregate expenditure in 1929 and 1933.

	1929	1933
	(billions of 1929 dollars)	
Induced consumption	47	34
Induced imports	–6	–4
Induced expenditure	41	30
Autonomous consumption	30	30
Investment	17	3
Government expenditure	10	10
Exports	6	3
Autonomous expenditure	63	46
GDP	**104**	**76**

Source of data: Bureau of Economic Analysis.

Autonomous expenditure collapsed as investment fell from $17 billion to $3 billion and exports fell by a large amount. Government expenditure held steady.

The figure uses the *AE* model to illustrate the Great Depression. In 1929, with autonomous expenditure of $63 billion, the *AE* curve was AE_{29}. Equilibrium expenditure and real GDP were $104 billion.

By 1933, autonomous expenditure had fallen by $17 billion to $46 billion and the *AE* curve had shifted downward to AE_{33}. Equilibrium expenditure and real GDP had fallen to $76 billion.

The decrease in autonomous expenditure of $17 billion brought a decrease in real GDP of $28 billion. The multiplier was $28/$17 = 1.6. The slope of the *AE* curve is 0.39—the fall in induced expenditure, $11 billion, divided by the fall in real GDP, $28 billion. The multiplier formula, $1/(1 - $ Slope of *AE* curve$)$, delivers a multiplier equal to 1.6.

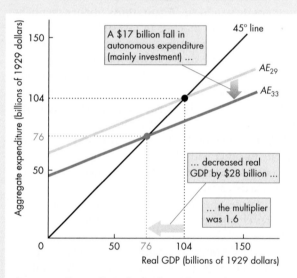

Aggregate Expenditure in the Great Depression

Business Cycle Turning Points

At business cycle turning points, the economy moves from expansion to recession or from recession to expansion. Economists understand these turning points as seismologists understand earthquakes. They know quite a lot about the forces and mechanisms that produce them, but they can't predict them. The forces that bring business cycle turning points are the swings in autonomous expenditure, such as investment and exports. The multiplier that you've just studied is the mechanism that gives momentum to the economy's new direction.

 REVIEW QUIZ

1 What is the multiplier? What does it determine? Why does it matter?

2 How do the marginal propensity to consume, the marginal propensity to import, and the income tax rate influence the multiplier?

3 How do fluctuations in autonomous expenditure influence real GDP?

You can work these questions in Study Plan 28.3 and get instant feedback.

The Multiplier and the Price Level

We have just considered adjustments in spending that occur in the very short run when the price level is fixed. In this time frame, the economy's cobblestones, which are changes in investment and exports, are not smoothed by shock absorbers like those on Michael Bloomberg's car. Instead, they are amplified like Alicia Keys' voice. But these outcomes occur only when the price level is fixed. We now investigate what happens after a long enough time lapse for the price level to change.

Adjusting Quantities and Prices

When firms can't keep up with sales and their inventories fall below target, they increase production, but at some point, they raise their prices. Similarly, when firms find unwanted inventories piling up, they decrease production, but eventually they cut their prices. So far, we've studied the macroeconomic consequences of firms changing their production levels when their sales change, but we haven't looked at the effects of price changes. When individual firms change their prices, the economy's price level changes.

To study the simultaneous determination of real GDP and the price level, we use the *AS-AD model*, which is explained in Chapter 27. But to understand how aggregate demand adjusts, we need to work out the connection between the *AS-AD* model and the aggregate expenditure model that we've used in this chapter. The key to understanding the relationship between these two models is the distinction between the aggregate *expenditure* and aggregate *demand* and the related distinction between the aggregate *expenditure curve* and the aggregate *demand curve*.

Aggregate Expenditure and Aggregate Demand

The aggregate expenditure curve is the relationship between the aggregate planned expenditure and real GDP, all other influences on aggregate planned expenditure remaining the same. The aggregate demand curve is the relationship between the aggregate quantity of goods and services demanded and the price level, all other influences on aggregate demand remaining the same. Let's explore the links between these two relationships.

Deriving the Aggregate Demand Curve

When the price level changes, aggregate planned expenditure changes and the quantity of real GDP demanded changes. The aggregate demand curve slopes downward. Why? There are two main reasons:

- Wealth effect
- Substitution effects

Wealth Effect Other things remaining the same, the higher the price level, the smaller is the purchasing power of wealth. For example, suppose you have $100 in the bank and the price level is 105. If the price level rises to 125, your $100 buys fewer goods and services. You are less wealthy. With less wealth, you will probably want to try to spend a bit less and save a bit more. The higher the price level, other things remaining the same, the lower is aggregate planned expenditure.

Substitution Effects For a given expected future price level, a rise in the price level today makes current goods and services more expensive relative to future goods and services and results in a delay in purchases—an *intertemporal substitution*. A rise in the U.S. price level, other things remaining the same, makes U.S.-produced goods and services more expensive relative to foreign-produced goods and services. As a result, U.S. imports increase and U.S. exports decrease—an *international substitution*.

When the price level rises, each of these effects reduces aggregate planned expenditure at each level of real GDP. As a result, when the price level *rises*, the aggregate expenditure curve shifts *downward*. A fall in the price level has the opposite effect. When the price level *falls*, the aggregate expenditure curve shifts *upward*.

Figure 28.8(a) shows the shifts of the *AE* curve. When the price level is 110, the aggregate expenditure curve is AE_0, which intersects the 45° line at point *B*. Equilibrium expenditure is $13 trillion. If the price level increases to 130, the aggregate expenditure curve shifts downward to AE_1, which intersects the 45° line at point *A*. Equilibrium expenditure decreases to $12 trillion. If the price level decreases to 90, the aggregate expenditure curve shifts upward to AE_2, which intersects the 45° line at point C. Equilibrium expenditure increases to $14 trillion.

We've just seen that when the price level changes, other things remaining the same, the aggregate expenditure curve shifts and the equilibrium expenditure changes. But when the price level changes, other things remaining the same, there is a movement along the aggregate demand curve.

Figure 28.8(b) shows the movements along the aggregate demand curve. At a price level of 110, the aggregate quantity of goods and services demanded is $13 trillion—point B on the AD curve. If the price level rises to 130, the aggregate quantity of goods and services demanded decreases to $12 trillion. There is a movement up along the aggregate demand curve to point A. If the price level falls to 90, the aggregate quantity of goods and services demanded increases to $14 trillion. There is a movement down along the aggregate demand curve to point C.

Each point on the aggregate demand curve corresponds to a point of equilibrium expenditure. The equilibrium expenditure points A, B, and C in Fig. 28.8(a) correspond to the points A, B, and C on the aggregate demand curve in Fig. 28.8(b).

Changes in Aggregate Expenditure and Aggregate Demand

When any influence on aggregate planned expenditure other than the price level changes, both the aggregate expenditure curve and the aggregate demand curve shift. For example, an increase in investment or exports increases both aggregate planned expenditure and aggregate demand and shifts both the AE curve and the AD curve. Figure 28.9 illustrates the effect of such an increase.

Initially, the aggregate expenditure curve is AE_0 in part (a) and the aggregate demand curve is AD_0 in part (b). The price level is 110, real GDP is $13 trillion, and the economy is at point A in both parts of Fig. 28.9. Now suppose that investment increases by $1 trillion. At a constant price level of 110, the aggregate expenditure curve shifts upward to AE_1. This curve intersects the 45° line at an equilibrium expenditure of $15 trillion (point B). This equilibrium expenditure of $15 trillion is the aggregate quantity of goods and services demanded at a price level of 110, as shown by point B in part (b). Point B lies on

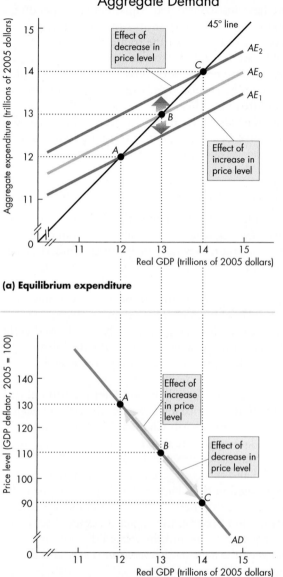

FIGURE 28.8   Equilibrium Expenditure and Aggregate Demand

(a) Equilibrium expenditure

(b) Aggregate demand

A change in the price level *shifts* the *AE* curve and results in a *movement along* the *AD* curve. When the price level is 110, the *AE* curve is AE_0 and equilibrium expenditure is $13 trillion at point *B*. When the price level rises to 130, the *AE* curve is AE_1 and equilibrium expenditure is $12 trillion at point *A*. When the price level falls to 90, the *AE* curve is AE_2 and equilibrium expenditure is $14 trillion at point *C*. Points *A*, *B*, and *C* on the *AD* curve in part (b) correspond to the equilibrium expenditure points *A*, *B*, and *C* in part (a).

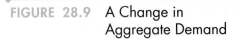

FIGURE 28.9 A Change in Aggregate Demand

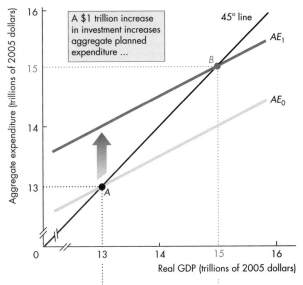

(a) Aggregate expenditure

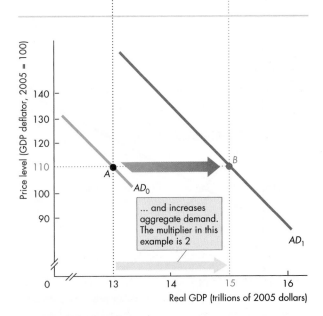

(b) Aggregate demand

The price level is 110. When the aggregate expenditure curve is AE_0 in part (a), the aggregate demand curve is AD_0 in part (b). An increase in autonomous expenditure shifts the AE curve upward to AE_1. In the new equilibrium, real GDP is $15 trillion (at point B). Because the quantity of real GDP demanded at a price level of 110 increases to $15 trillion, the AD curve shifts rightward to AD_1.

a new aggregate demand curve. The aggregate demand curve has shifted rightward to AD_1.

But how do we know by how much the AD curve shifts? The multiplier determines the answer. The larger the multiplier, the larger is the shift in the aggregate demand curve that results from a given change in autonomous expenditure. In this example, the multiplier is 2. A $1 trillion increase in investment produces a $2 trillion increase in the aggregate quantity of goods and services demanded at each price level. That is, a $1 trillion increase in autonomous expenditure shifts the aggregate demand curve rightward by $2 trillion.

A decrease in autonomous expenditure shifts the aggregate expenditure curve downward and shifts the aggregate demand curve leftward. You can see these effects by reversing the change that we've just described. If the economy is initially at point B on the aggregate expenditure curve AE_1 and on the aggregate demand curve AD_1, a decrease in autonomous expenditure shifts the aggregate expenditure curve downward to AE_0. The aggregate quantity of goods and services demanded decreases from $15 trillion to $13 trillion, and the aggregate demand curve shifts leftward to AD_0.

Let's summarize what we have just discovered:

If some factor other than a change in the price level increases autonomous expenditure, the AE curve shifts upward and the AD curve shifts rightward. The size of the AD curve shift equals the change in autonomous expenditure multiplied by the multiplier.

Equilibrium Real GDP and the Price Level

In Chapter 27, we learned that aggregate demand and short-run aggregate supply determine equilibrium real GDP and the price level. We've now put aggregate demand under a more powerful microscope and have discovered that a change in investment (or in any component of autonomous expenditure) changes aggregate demand and shifts the aggregate demand curve. The magnitude of the shift depends on the multiplier. But whether a change in autonomous expenditure results ultimately in a change in real GDP, a change in the price level, or a combination of the two depends on aggregate supply. There are two time frames to consider: the short run and the long run. First we'll see what happens in the short run.

An Increase in Aggregate Demand in the Short Run
Figure 28.10 describes the economy. Initially, in part
(a), the aggregate expenditure curve is AE_0 and equilibrium expenditure is $13 trillion—point A. In part
(b), aggregate demand is AD_0 and the short-run
aggregate supply curve is SAS. (Chapter 27,
pp. 649–651, explains the SAS curve.) Equilibrium
is at point A in part (b), where the aggregate demand
and short-run aggregate supply curves intersect. The
price level is 110, and real GDP is $13 trillion.

Now suppose that investment increases by $1 tril-
lion. With the price level fixed at 110, the aggregate
expenditure curve shifts upward to AE_1. Equilibrium
expenditure increases to $15 trillion—point B in part
(a). In part (b), the aggregate demand curve shifts
rightward by $2 trillion, from AD_0 to AD_1. How far
the aggregate demand curve shifts is determined by the
multiplier when the price level is fixed.

But with this new aggregate demand curve, the
price level does not remain fixed. The price level rises,
and as it does, the aggregate expenditure curve shifts
downward. The short-run equilibrium occurs when
the aggregate expenditure curve has shifted downward to AE_2 and the new aggregate demand curve,
AD_1, intersects the short-run aggregate supply curve
at point C in both part (a) and part (b). Real GDP is
$14.3 trillion, and the price level is 123.

When price level effects are taken into account,
the increase in investment still has a multiplier effect
on real GDP, but the multiplier is smaller than it
would be if the price level were fixed. The steeper the
slope of the short-run aggregate supply curve, the
larger is the increase in the price level and the smaller
is the multiplier effect on real GDP.

An Increase in Aggregate Demand in the Long Run
Figure 28.11 illustrates the long-run effect of an
increase in aggregate demand. In the long run, real
GDP equals potential GDP and there is full employment. Potential GDP is $13 trillion, and the long-
run aggregate supply curve is LAS. Initially, the
economy is at point A in parts (a) and (b).

Investment increases by $1 trillion. In Fig. 28.11,
the aggregate expenditure curve shifts to AE_1 and the
aggregate demand curve shifts to AD_1. With no
change in the price level, the economy would move to
point B and real GDP would increase to $15 trillion.
But in the short run, the price level rises to 123 and
real GDP increases to only $14.3 trillion. With the
higher price level, the AE curve shifts from AE_1 to

FIGURE 28.10   The Multiplier in the Short Run

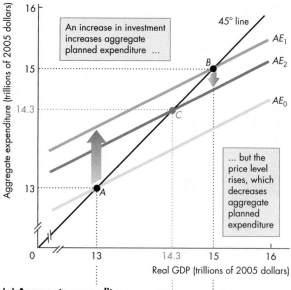

(a) Aggregate expenditure

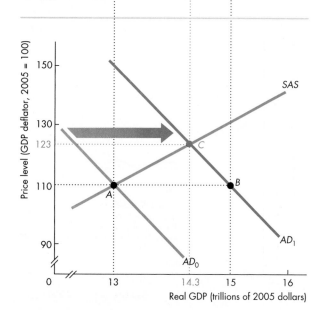

(b) Aggregate demand

An increase in investment shifts the AE curve from AE_0 to
AE_1 and the AD curve from AD_0 to AD_1. The price level
rises, and the higher price level shifts the AE curve downward from AE_1 to AE_2. The economy moves to point C in
both parts. In the short run, when prices are flexible, the multiplier effect is smaller than when the price level is fixed.

myeconlab   animation

FIGURE 28.11   The Multiplier in the Long Run

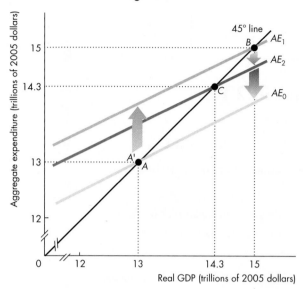

(a) Aggregate expenditure

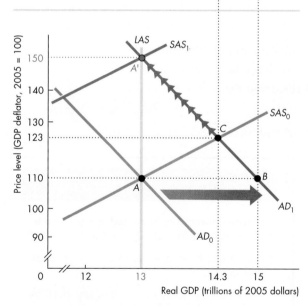

(b) Aggregate demand

Starting from point *A*, an increase in investment shifts the *AE* curve to AE_1 and the *AD* curve to AD_1. In the short run, the economy moves to point *C*. In the long run, the money wage rate rises and the *SAS* curve shifts to SAS_1. As the price level rises, the *AE* curve shifts back to AE_0 and the economy moves to point *A'*. In the long run, the multiplier is zero.

 animation

AE_2. The economy is now in a short-run equilibrium at point *C* in both part (a) and part (b).

Real GDP now exceeds potential GDP. The labor force is more than fully employed, and in the long run, shortages of labor increase the money wage rate. The higher money wage rate increases firms' costs, which decreases short-run aggregate supply and shifts the *SAS* curve leftward to SAS_1. The price level rises further, and real GDP decreases. There is a movement along AD_1, and the *AE* curve shifts downward from AE_2 toward AE_0. When the money wage rate and the price level have increased by the same percentage, real GDP is again equal to potential GDP and the economy is at point *A'*. In the long run, the multiplier is zero.

REVIEW QUIZ

1 How does a change in the price level influence the *AE* curve and the *AD* curve?

2 If autonomous expenditure increases with no change in the price level, what happens to the *AE* curve and the *AD* curve? Which curve shifts by an amount that is determined by the multiplier and why?

3 How does an increase in autonomous expenditure change real GDP in the short run? Does real GDP change by the same amount as the change in aggregate demand? Why or why not?

4 How does real GDP change in the long run when autonomous expenditure increases? Does real GDP change by the same amount as the change in aggregate demand? Why or why not?

You can work these questions in Study Plan 28.4 and get instant feedback.   myeconlab

◆ You are now ready to build on what you've learned about aggregate expenditure fluctuations. We'll study the business cycle and the roles of fiscal policy and monetary policy in smoothing the cycle while achieving price stability and sustained economic growth. In Chapter 29 we study the U.S. business cycle and inflation, and in Chapters 30 and 31 we study fiscal policy and monetary policy, respectively. But before you leave the current topic, look at *Reading Between the Lines* on pp. 690–691 and see the aggregate expenditure model in action in the U.S. economy during 2009 and 2010.

Inventory Investment in the 2010 Expansion

Business Inventories Post Biggest Gain in 2 Years

http://www.seattletimes.com
September 14, 2010

Inventories held by businesses jumped in July by the largest amount in two years while sales rebounded after two months of declines.

Business inventories rose 1 percent in July, the biggest monthly gain since a similar increase in July 2008, the Commerce Department reported Tuesday. Inventories have grown for seven consecutive months.

Total business sales were up 0.7 percent in July after falling 0.5 percent in June and 1.2 percent in May.

The rebound in sales was an encouraging sign that consumer demand is rising after the two weak months. Businesses build up their stocks when they anticipate stronger retail demand.

Inventory growth helped drive economic expansion in the final quarter of 2009 and early this year. Many businesses replenished their stockpiles after slashing them during the recession. That led to rising orders at American factories and helped lead the early stages of the modest economic recovery.

For July, sales were up 1.1 percent at the manufacturing level with smaller gains at the wholesale and retail levels. A separate report Tuesday showed that retail sales increased in August by the largest amount since March, another encouraging sign that consumers are beginning to spend again.

The big jump in inventories in July might not have been voluntary. Businesses may have been caught with some unwanted stockpiles with the unexpected slowdown in sales in the previous two months. However, the hope is that sales will keep growing in coming months and this will spur businesses to continue stocking their shelves in anticipation of further gains in demand. ...

ESSENCE OF THE STORY

- Business inventories increased in July 2010 by 1 percent, the largest increase since July 2008.

- Inventories have increased for seven consecutive months.

- Total business sales increased in July 2010 by 0.7 percent after falling in May and June.

- The increase in business inventories contributed to the increase in real GDP in the final quarter of 2009 and early 2010.

- Businesses replenished inventories after cutting them during the recession.

- The large increase in inventories in July might not have been voluntary.

ECONOMIC ANALYSIS

- The news article reports that inventories decreased during the recession of 2009 and were increasing in 2010 but not all of the increase was voluntary.

- Table 1 shows the real GDP and aggregate expenditure numbers for the second quarters of 2009 and 2010 along with the change over the year.

- The increase in investment and exports increased aggregate planned expenditure, which induced the increases in consumption expenditure and imports.

- Figure 1 shows how the change in inventories lags the change in real GDP. When real GDP starts to expand, inventories are still falling.

- Figure 2 uses the aggregate expenditure model to explain the behavior of inventories.

- In 2009 Q2, the AE curve was AE_0 and real GDP was $12.8 trillion, which we're assuming to be an expenditure equilibrium.

- The increase in investment and exports increased aggregate planned expenditure and shifted the AE curve upward to AE_1. Part of the increase in investment was a planned increase in inventories.

- When investment and exports increased, aggregate planned expenditure temporarily exceeded real GDP and an unplanned decrease in inventories occurred.

- In contrast to what the news article says, the planned increase in inventories in 2010 most likely *exceeded* the actual increase as the economy expanded.

Table 1 The Components of Aggregate Expenditure

Item	2009 Q2	2010 Q2	Change
	(billions of 2005 dollars)		
Consumption expenditure	9,117	9,270	153
Investment	1,453	1,787	334
Government expenditure	2,549	2,567	18
Exports	1,448	1,652	204
Imports	1,790	2,097	307
Residual*	33	13	–20
Real GDP	**12,810**	**13,192**	**382**
Change in inventories	–162	–39	123

*The residual arises because chain-dollar real variables are calculated for each expenditure component independently of chain-dollar real GDP and the components don't exactly sum to real GDP.

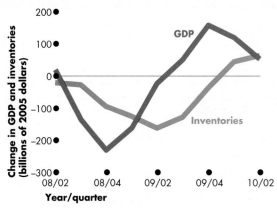

Figure 1 Real GDP and inventories

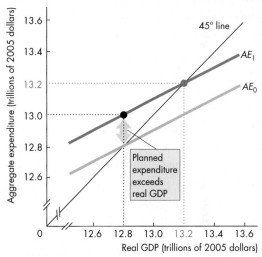

(a) Convergence to equilibrium expenditure in 2010

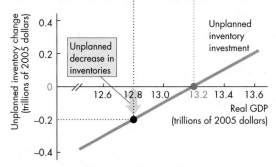

(b) Unplanned inventory change in 2010

Figure 2 Equilibrium expenditure in 2010

691

MATHEMATICAL NOTE

The Algebra of the Keynesian Model

This mathematical note derives formulas for equilibrium expenditure and the multipliers when the price level is fixed. The variables are

- Aggregate planned expenditure, AE
- Real GDP, Y
- Consumption expenditure, C
- Disposable income, YD
- Investment, I
- Government expenditure, G
- Exports, X
- Imports, M
- Net taxes, T
- Autonomous consumption expenditure, a
- Autonomous taxes, T_a
- Marginal propensity to consume, b
- Marginal propensity to import, m
- Marginal tax rate, t
- Autonomous expenditure, A

Aggregate Expenditure

Aggregate planned expenditure (AE) is the sum of the planned amounts of consumption expenditure (C), investment (I), government expenditure (G), and exports (X) minus the planned amount of imports (M).

$$AE = C + I + G + X - M.$$

Consumption Function Consumption expenditure (C) depends on disposable income (YD), and we write the consumption function as

$$C = a + bYD.$$

Disposable income (YD) equals real GDP minus net taxes ($Y - T$). So if we replace YD with ($Y - T$), the consumption function becomes

$$C = a + b(Y - T).$$

Net taxes, T, equal autonomous taxes (that are independent of income), T_a, plus induced taxes (that vary with income), tY.

So we can write net taxes as

$$T = T_a + tY.$$

Use this last equation to replace T in the consumption function. The consumption function becomes

$$C = a - bT_a + b(1 - t)Y.$$

This equation describes consumption expenditure as a function of real GDP.

Import Function Imports depend on real GDP, and the import function is

$$M = mY.$$

Aggregate Expenditure Curve Use the consumption function and the import function to replace C and M in the AE equation. That is,

$$AE = a - bT_a + b(1 - t)Y + I + G + X - mY.$$

Collect the terms that involve Y on the right side of the equation to obtain

$$AE = (a - bT_a + I + G + X) + [b(1 - t) - m]Y.$$

Autonomous expenditure (A) is $(a - bT_a + I + G + X)$, and the slope of the AE curve is $[b(1 - t) - m]$. So the equation for the AE curve, which is shown in Fig. 1, is

$$AE = A + [b(1 - t) - m]Y.$$

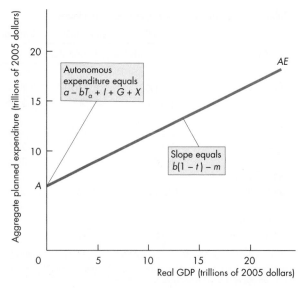

Figure 1   The AE curve

Equilibrium Expenditure

Equilibrium expenditure occurs when aggregate planned expenditure (AE) equals real GDP (Y). That is,

$$AE = Y.$$

In Fig. 2, the scales of the x-axis (real GDP) and the y-axis (aggregate planned expenditure) are identical, so the 45° line shows the points at which aggregate planned expenditure equals real GDP.

Figure 2 shows the point of equilibrium expenditure at the intersection of the AE curve and the 45° line.

To calculate equilibrium expenditure, solve the equations for the AE curve and the 45° line for the two unknown quantities AE and Y. So starting with

$$AE = A + [b(1 - t) - m]Y$$

$$AE = Y,$$

replace AE with Y in the AE equation to obtain

$$Y = A + [b(1 - t) - m]Y.$$

The solution for Y is

$$Y = \frac{1}{1 - [b(1 - t) - m]}A.$$

The Multiplier

The *multiplier* equals the change in equilibrium expenditure and real GDP (Y) that results from a change in autonomous expenditure (A) divided by the change in autonomous expenditure.

A change in autonomous expenditure (ΔA) changes equilibrium expenditure and real GDP by

$$\Delta Y = \frac{1}{1 - [b(1 - t) - m]}\Delta A.$$

$$\text{Multiplier} = \frac{1}{1 - [b(1 - t) - m]}.$$

The size of the multiplier depends on the slope of the AE curve, $b(1 - t) - m$. The larger the slope, the larger is the multiplier. So the multiplier is larger,

- The greater the marginal propensity to consume (b)
- The smaller the marginal tax rate (t)
- The smaller the marginal propensity to import (m)

An economy with no imports and no income taxes has $m = 0$ and $t = 0$. In this special case, the multiplier equals $1/(1 - b)$. If b is 0.75, then the multiplier is 4, as shown in Fig. 3.

In an economy with imports and income taxes, if $b = 0.75$, $t = 0.2$, and $m = 0.1$, the multiplier equals 1 divided by $[1 - 0.75(1 - 0.2) - 0.1]$, which equals 2. Make up some more examples to show the effects of b, t, and m on the multiplier.

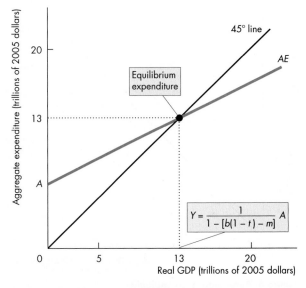

Figure 2 Equilibrium expenditure

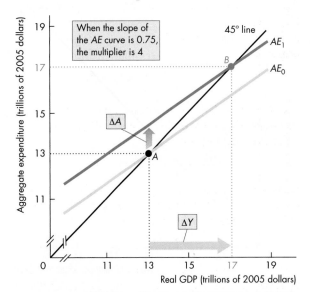

Figure 3 The multiplier

Government Expenditure Multiplier

The **government expenditure multiplier** equals the change in equilibrium expenditure and real GDP (Y) that results from a change in government expenditure (G) divided by the change in government expenditure. Because autonomous expenditure is equal to

$$A = a - bT_a + I + G + X,$$

the change in autonomous expenditure equals the change in government expenditure. That is,

$$\Delta A = \Delta G.$$

You can see from the solution for equilibrium expenditure Y that

$$\Delta Y = \frac{1}{1 - [b(1 - t) - m]}\Delta G.$$

The government expenditure multiplier equals

$$\frac{1}{1 - [b(1 - t) - m]}.$$

In an economy in which $t = 0$ and $m = 0$, the government expenditure multiplier is $1/(1 - b)$. With $b = 0.75$, the government expenditure multiplier is 4, as Fig. 4 shows. Make up some examples and use the above formula to show how b, m, and t influence the government expenditure multiplier.

Autonomous Tax Multiplier

The **autonomous tax multiplier** equals the change in equilibrium expenditure and real GDP (Y) that results from a change in autonomous taxes (T_a) divided by the change in autonomous taxes. Because autonomous expenditure is equal to

$$A = a - bT_a + I + G + X,$$

the change in autonomous expenditure equals *minus* b multiplied by the change in autonomous taxes. That is,

$$\Delta A = -b\Delta T_a.$$

You can see from the solution for equilibrium expenditure Y that

$$\Delta Y = \frac{-b}{1 - [b(1 - t) - m]}\Delta T_a.$$

The autonomous tax multiplier equals

$$\frac{-b}{1 - [b(1 - t) - m]}.$$

In an economy in which $t = 0$ and $m = 0$, the autonomous tax multiplier is $-b/(1 - b)$. In this special case, with $b = 0.75$, the autonomous tax multiplier equals -3, as Fig. 5 shows. Make up some examples and use the above formula to show how b, m, and t influence the autonomous tax multiplier.

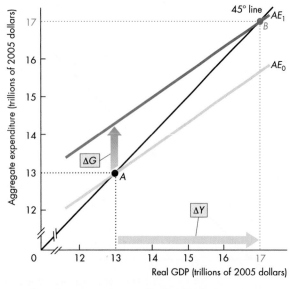

Figure 4 Government expenditure multiplier

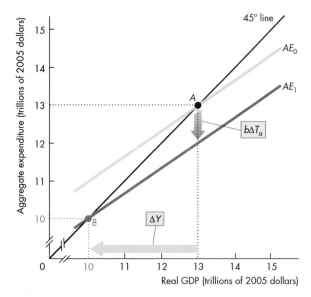

Figure 5 Autonomous tax multiplier

Balanced Budget Multiplier

The **balanced budget multiplier** equals the change in equilibrium expenditure and real GDP (Y) that results from equal changes in government expenditure and lump-sum taxes divided by the change in government expenditure. Because government expenditure and autono-mous taxes change by the same amount, the budget balance does not change.

The change in equilibrium expenditure that results from the change in government expenditure is

$$\Delta Y = \frac{1}{1 - [b(1 - t) - m]}\Delta G.$$

And the change in equilibrium expenditure that results from the change in autonomous taxes is

$$\Delta Y = \frac{-b}{1 - [b(1 - t) - m]}\Delta T_a.$$

So the change in equilibrium expenditure resulting from the changes in government expenditure and autonomous taxes is

$$\Delta Y = \frac{1}{1 - [b(1 - t) - m]}\Delta G +$$

$$\frac{-b}{1-[b(1 - t)-m]}\Delta T_a.$$

Notice that

$$\frac{1}{1-[b(1 - t)-m]}$$

is common to both terms on the right side. So we can rewrite the equation as

$$\Delta Y = \frac{1}{1 - [b(1 - t) - m]}(\Delta G - b\Delta T_a)$$

The AE curve shifts upward by $\Delta G - b\Delta T_a$ as shown in Fig. 6.

But the change in government expenditure equals the change in autonomous taxes. That is,

$$\Delta G = \Delta T_a.$$

So we can write the equation as

$$\Delta Y = \frac{1 - b}{1 - [b(1 - t) - m]}\Delta G.$$

The balanced budget multiplier equals

$$\frac{1 - b}{1 - [b(1 - t) - m]}.$$

In an economy in which $t = 0$ and $m = 0$, the balanced budget multiplier is $(1 - b)/(1 - b)$, which equals 1, as Fig. 6 shows. Make up some examples and use the above formula to show how b, m, and t influence the balanced budget multiplier.

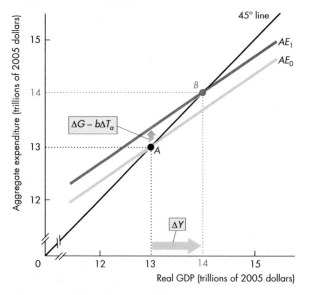

Figure 6 Balanced budget multiplier

SUMMARY

Key Points

Fixed Prices and Expenditure Plans (pp. 672–675)

- When the price level is fixed, expenditure plans determine real GDP.
- Consumption expenditure is determined by disposable income, and the marginal propensity to consume (*MPC*) determines the change in consumption expenditure brought about by a change in disposable income. Real GDP determines disposable income.
- Imports are determined by real GDP, and the marginal propensity to import determines the change in imports brought about by a change in real GDP.

Working Problems 1 to 3 will give you a better understanding of fixed prices and expenditure plans.

Real GDP with a Fixed Price Level (pp. 676–679)

- Aggregate *planned* expenditure depends on real GDP.
- Equilibrium expenditure occurs when aggregate planned expenditure equals actual expenditure and real GDP.

Working Problems 4 to 7 will give you a better understanding of real GDP with a fixed price level.

The Multiplier (pp. 680–684)

- The multiplier is the magnified effect of a change in autonomous expenditure on equilibrium expenditure and real GDP.

- The multiplier is determined by the slope of the *AE* curve.
- The slope of the *AE* curve is influenced by the marginal propensity to consume, the marginal propensity to import, and the income tax rate.

Working Problems 8 to 11 will give you a better understanding of the multiplier.

The Multiplier and the Price Level (pp. 685–689)

- The *AD* curve is the relationship between the quantity of real GDP demanded and the price level, other things remaining the same.
- The *AE* curve is the relationship between aggregate planned expenditure and real GDP, other things remaining the same.
- At a given price level, there is a given *AE* curve. A change in the price level changes aggregate planned expenditure and shifts the *AE* curve. A change in the price level also creates a movement along the *AD* curve.
- A change in autonomous expenditure that is not caused by a change in the price level shifts the *AE* curve and shifts the *AD* curve. The magnitude of the shift of the *AD* curve depends on the multiplier and on the change in autonomous expenditure.
- The multiplier decreases as the price level changes, and the long-run multiplier is zero.

Working Problems 12 to 21 will give you a better understanding of the multiplier and the price level.

Key Terms

Aggregate planned expenditure, 672

Autonomous expenditure, 676

Autonomous tax multiplier, 694

Balanced budget multiplier, 695

Consumption function, 672

Disposable income, 672

Equilibrium expenditure, 678

Government expenditure multiplier, 694

Induced expenditure, 676

Marginal propensity to consume, 674

Marginal propensity to import, 675

Marginal propensity to save, 674

Multiplier, 680

Saving function, 672

STUDY PLAN PROBLEMS AND APPLICATIONS

myeconlab You can work Problems 1 to 22 in MyEconLab Chapter 28 Study Plan and get instant feedback.

Fixed Prices and Expenditure Plans (Study Plan 28.1)

Use the following data to work Problems 1 and 2. You are given the following information about the economy of the United Kingdom.

Disposable income	Consumption expenditure
(billions of pounds per year)	
300	340
400	420
500	500
600	580
700	660

1. Calculate the marginal propensity to consume.
2. Calculate saving at each level of disposable income and calculate the marginal propensity to save.
3. **The U.S. and China's Savings Problems**
   Last year China saved about half of its gross domestic product while the United States saved only 13 percent of its national income. The contrast is even starker at the household level—a personal saving rate in China of about 30 percent of household income, compared with a U.S. rate that dipped into negative territory last year (–0.4% of after-tax household income). Similar extremes show up in the consumption shares of the two economies.

   Source: *Fortune*, March 8, 2006
   Compare the *MPC* and *MPS* in the United States and China. Why might they differ?

Real GDP with a Fixed Price Level (Study Plan 28.2)

Use the following figure to work Problems 4 and 5. The figure illustrates the components of aggregate planned expenditure on Turtle Island. Turtle Island has no imports or exports, no incomes taxes, and the price level is fixed.

4. Calculate autonomous expenditure and the marginal propensity to consume.
5. a. What is aggregate planned expenditure when real GDP is $6 billion?
   b. If real GDP is $4 billion, what is happening to inventories?

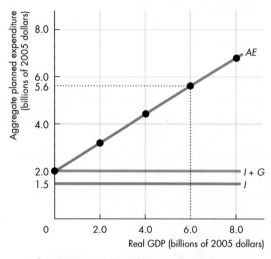

c. If real GDP is $6 billion, what is happening to inventories?

6. Explain the difference between induced consumption expenditure and autonomous consumption expenditure. Why isn't all consumption expenditure induced expenditure?

7. **Recovery?**
   In the second quarter, businesses increased spending on equipment and software by 21.9%, while a category that includes home building grew amid a rush by consumers to take advantage of tax credits for homes.

   Source: *The Wall Street Journal*, July 31, 2010
   Explain how an increase in business investment at a constant price level changes equilibrium expenditure.

The Multiplier (Study Plan 28.3)

Use the following data to work Problems 8 and 9. An economy has a fixed price level, no imports, and no income taxes. *MPC* is 0.80, and real GDP is $150 billion. Businesses increase investment by $5 billion.

8. Calculate the multiplier and the change in real GDP.
9. Calculate the new real GDP and explain why real GDP increases by more than $5 billion.

Use the following data to work Problems 10 and 11. An economy has a fixed price level, no imports, and no income taxes. An increase in autonomous expenditure of $2 trillion increases equilibrium expenditure by $8 trillion.

10. Calculate the multiplier and the marginal propensity to consume.

11. What happens to the multiplier if an income tax is introduced?

The Multiplier and the Price Level (Study Plan 28.4)

Use the following data to work Problems 12 to 16. Suppose that the economy is at full employment, the price level is 100, and the multiplier is 2. Investment increases by $100 billion.

12. What is the change in equilibrium expenditure if the price level remains at 100?

13. a. What is the immediate change in the quantity of real GDP demanded?

    b. In the short run, does real GDP increase by more than, less than, or the same amount as the immediate change in the quantity of real GDP demanded?

14. In the short run, does the price level remain at 100? Explain why or why not.

15. a. In the long run, does real GDP increase by more than, less than, or the same amount as the immediate increase in the quantity of real GDP demanded?

    b. Explain how the price level changes in the long run.

16. Are the values of the multipliers in the short run and the long run larger or smaller than 2?

Use the following news clip to work Problems 17 and 18.

Understimulated

A stimulus package would send more than $100 billion to American taxpayers before the end of 2008. The theory behind the rebates is that American taxpayers will take the cash and spend it—thus providing a jolt of stimulus to the economy. But will they? In 2001, Washington sought to jolt the economy back into life with tax rebates. In all, 90 million households received some $38 billion in cash. Months later, economists discovered that households spent 20 to 40 percent of their rebates during the first three months and about another third during the following three months. People with low incomes spent more.

Source: *Newsweek*, February 7, 2008

17. Will $100 billion of tax rebates to American consumers increase aggregate expenditure by more

than, less than, or exactly $100 billion? Explain.

18. Explain and draw a graph to illustrate how this fiscal stimulus will influence aggregate expenditure and aggregate demand in both the short run and the long run.

Use the following news clip to work Problems 19 to 21.

Working Poor More Pinched as Rich Cut Back

Cutbacks by the wealthy have a ripple effect across all consumer spending, said Michael P. Niemira, chief economist at the International Council of Shopping Centers. The top 20 percent of households spend about $94,000 annually, almost five times what the bottom 20 percent spend and more than what the bottom sixty percent combined spend. Then there's also the multiplier effect: When shoppers splurge on $1,000 dinners and $300 limousine rides, that means fatter tips for the waiter and the driver. Sales clerks at upscale stores, who typically earn sales commissions, also depend on spending sprees of mink coats and jewelry. But the trickling down is starting to dry up, threatening to hurt a broad base of low-paid workers.

Source: MSNBC, January 28, 2008

19. Explain and draw a graph to illustrate the process by which "cutbacks by the wealthy have a ripple effect."

20. Explain and draw a graph to illustrate how real GDP will be driven back to potential GDP in the long run.

21. Why is the multiplier only a short-run influence on real GDP?

Mathematical Note (Study Plan 28.MN)

22. In the Canadian economy, autonomous consumption expenditure is $50 billion, investment is $200 billion, and government expenditure is $250 billion. The marginal propensity to consume is 0.7 and net taxes are $250 billion. Exports are $500 billion and imports are $450 billion. Assume that net taxes and imports are autonomous and the price level is fixed.

    a. What is the consumption function?

    b. What is the equation of the *AE* curve?

    c. Calculate equilibrium expenditure.

    d. Calculate the multiplier.

    e. If investment decreases to $150 billion, what is the change in equilibrium expenditure?

    f. Describe the process in part (e) that moves the economy to its new equilibrium expenditure.

ADDITIONAL PROBLEMS AND APPLICATIONS

 myeconlab You can work these problems in MyEconLab if assigned by your instructor.

Fixed Prices and Expenditure Plans

Use the following data to work Problems 23 and 24. You are given the following information about the economy of Australia.

Disposable income	Saving
(billions of dollars per year)	
0	−5
100	20
200	45
300	70
400	95

23. Calculate the marginal propensity to save.

24. Calculate consumption at each level of disposable income. Calculate the marginal propensity to consume.

Use the following news clip to work Problems 25 to 27.

Americans $1.7 trillion Poorer

Americans saw their net worth decline by $1.7 trillion in the first quarter of 2008. Until then, net worth had been rising steadily since 2003. "The recent declines, however, may not affect consumer spending," said Michael Englund, senior economist with Action Economics. Americans have actually spent more in recent months—spending everything in their wallet and borrowing more. Household debt grew by 3.5 percent with consumer credit rising at an annual rate of 5.75 percent.

Source: CNN, June 5, 2008

25. Explain and draw a graph to illustrate how a decrease in household wealth theoretically impacts the consumption function and saving function.

26. According to the news clip, how did consumption expenditure respond in the first quarter of 2008? What factors might explain why consumers' actual response differs from what the consumption function model predicts?

27. Draw a graph of a consumption function and show at what point consumers were actually operating in the first quarter. Explain your answer.

Real GDP with a Fixed Price Level

Use the following spreadsheet, which lists real GDP (Y) and the components of aggregate planned expenditure in billions of dollars, to work Problems 28 and 29.

	A	B	C	D	E	F	G
1		Y	C	I	G	X	M
2	A	100	110	50	60	60	15
3	B	200	170	50	60	60	30
4	C	300	230	50	60	60	45
5	D	400	290	50	60	60	60
6	E	500	350	50	60	60	75
7	F	600	410	50	60	60	90

28. Calculate autonomous expenditure. Calculate the marginal propensity to consume.

29. a. What is aggregate planned expenditure when real GDP is $200 billion?

  b. If real GDP is $200 billion, explain the process that moves the economy toward equilibrium expenditure.

  c. If real GDP is $500 billion, explain the process that moves the economy toward equilibrium expenditure.

30. **Wholesale Inventories Decline, Sales Rise**

The Commerce Department reported that wholesale inventories fell 1.3 percent in August for a record 12th consecutive month, evidence that companies are trimming orders to factories, which helped depress economic output during the recession. Economists hope that the rising sales will encourage businesses to begin restocking their inventories, which would boost factory production and help bolster broad economic growth in coming months.

Source: The New York Times, October 8, 2009

Explain why a fall in inventories is associated with recession and a restocking of inventories might bolster economic growth.

The Multiplier

31. Obama's New Stimulus

The Obama recovery plan announced on Monday includes proposed spending of $50 billion to rebuild 150,000 miles of roads, construct and maintain 4,000 miles of rail, and fix or rebuild 150 miles of runways.

Source: *USA Today*, September 10, 2010

If the slope of the *AE* curve is 0.7, calculate the immediate change in aggregate planned expenditure and the change in real GDP in the short run if the price level remains unchanged.

32. Obama's Economic Recovery Plan

President Obama's proposal to jolt a listless recovery with $180 billion worth of tax breaks and transportation projects left economists largely unimpressed Tuesday.

Source: *USA Today*, September 10, 2010

If taxes fall by $90 billion and the spending on transport projects increase by $90 billion, which component of Obama's recovery plan would have the larger effect on equilibrium expenditure, other things remaining the same?

The Multiplier and the Price Level

33. Price Jump Worst Since '91

The biggest annual jump in the CPI since 1991 has fanned fears about growing pressures on consumers. The Labor Department report confirms what every consumer in America has known for months: Inflation is soaring and it's having an adverse impact on the economy.

Source: CNN, July 16, 2008

Explain and draw a graph to illustrate the effect of a rise in the price level on equilibrium expenditure.

Use the following news clip to work Problems 34 to 36.

Where Americans Will (and Won't) Cut Back

Consumer confidence has tumbled but even as consumers cut back on spending, there are some things they refuse to give up. Market research reports that Americans are demonstrating a strong reluctance to give up everyday pleasures, but many are forced to prioritize and scale back some of their spending. Spending on dining out, out-of-the-home entertainment, clothes, vacations, and buying lunch tend to be the first to be cut and many Americans are driving less and staying at home more. A whopping 50 percent of Americans plan to buy an HD or flat-panel TV in the next year. Cable and satellite TV subscriptions are also way down the list on cutbacks. Despite the expense, another thing consumers refuse to go without completely is travel. Even in these tough times, 59 percent of Americans plan to take a trip in the next six months.

Source: CNN, July 16, 2008

34. Which of the expenditures listed in the news clip are part of induced consumption expenditure and which is part of autonomous consumption expenditure? Explain why all consumption expenditure is not induced expenditure.

35. Explain and draw a graph to illustrate how declining consumer confidence influences aggregate expenditure and aggregate demand in the short run.

36. Explain and draw a graph to illustrate the long-run effect on aggregate expenditure and aggregate demand of the decline in consumer confidence.

Economics in the News

37. After you have studied *Reading Between the Lines* on pp. 690–691 answer the following questions.

   a. If the 2010 changes in inventories were mainly *planned* changes, what role did they play in shifting the *AE* curve and changing equilibrium expenditure? Use a two-part figure (similar to that on p. 678) to answer this question.

   b. Could the news article report that some of the rise in inventories in 2010 was unplanned be consistent with the *AE* model? Draw an appropriate graph to illustrate your answer.

   c. What do you think will happen to unplanned inventory changes when real GDP returns to potential GDP?

Mathematical Note

38. In an economy autonomous spending is $20 trillion and the slope of the *AE* curve is 0.6.

   a. What is the equation of the *AE* curve?

   b. Calculate equilibrium expenditure.

   c. Calculate the multiplier if the price level is unchanged.

After studying this chapter, you will be able to:

◆ Explain how demand-pull and cost-push forces bring cycles in inflation and output

◆ Explain the short-run and long-run tradeoff between inflation and unemployment

◆ Explain how the mainstream business cycle theory and real business cycle theory account for fluctuations in output and employment

29

U.S. INFLATION, UNEMPLOYMENT, AND BUSINESS CYCLE

B ack in the 1970s, when inflation was raging at a double-digit rate, economist Arthur M. Okun proposed what he called the "misery index." Misery, he suggested, could be measured as the sum of the inflation rate and the unemployment rate. At its peak, in 1980, the misery index hit 22. At its lowest, in 1953, the misery index was 3.

Inflation and unemployment make us miserable for good reasons. We care about inflation because it raises our cost of living. And we care about unemployment because either it hits us directly and takes our jobs or it scares us into thinking that we might lose our jobs.

We want rapid income growth, low unemployment, and low inflation. But can we have all these things at the same time? Or do we face a tradeoff among them? As this chapter explains, we face a tradeoff in the short run but not in the long run.

At the end of the chapter, in *Reading Between the Lines*, we examine the state of unemployment and inflation and the "misery index" in 2010 compared with some earlier episodes.

◆ Inflation Cycles

In the long run, inflation is a monetary phenomenon. It occurs if the quantity of money grows faster
than potential GDP. But in the short run, many factors can start an inflation, and real GDP and the
price level interact. To study these interactions, we
distinguish between two sources of inflation:

- Demand-pull inflation
- Cost-push inflation

Demand-Pull Inflation

An inflation that starts because aggregate demand
increases is called **demand-pull inflation**. Demand-
pull inflation can be kicked off by *any* of the factors
that change aggregate demand. Examples are a cut
in the interest rate, an increase in the quantity of
money, an increase in government expenditure, a
tax cut, an increase in exports, or an increase in
investment stimulated by an increase in expected
future profits.

Initial Effect of an Increase in Aggregate Demand

Suppose that last year the price level was 110 and real
GDP was $13 trillion. Potential GDP was also $13
trillion. Figure 29.1(a) illustrates this situation. The
aggregate demand curve is AD_0, the short-run aggregate supply curve is SAS_0, and the long-run aggregate
supply curve is LAS.

Now suppose that the Fed cuts the interest rate.
The quantity of money increases and the aggregate
demand curve shifts from AD_0 to AD_1. With no
change in potential GDP and no change in the money
wage rate, the long-run aggregate supply curve and the
short-run aggregate supply curve remain at LAS and
SAS_0, respectively.

The price level and real GDP are determined at
the point where the aggregate demand curve AD_1
intersects the short-run aggregate supply curve. The
price level rises to 113, and real GDP increases above
potential GDP to $13.5 trillion. Unemployment falls
below its natural rate. The economy is at an above
full-employment equilibrium and there is an inflationary gap. The next step in the unfolding story is a
rise in the money wage rate.

FIGURE 29.1   A Demand-Pull Rise in the Price Level

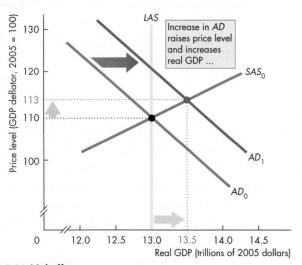

(a) Initial effect

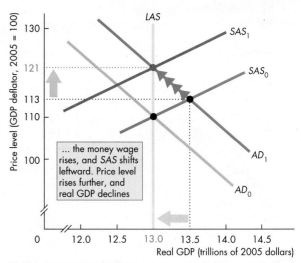

(b) The money wage adjusts

In part (a), the aggregate demand curve is AD_0, the short-run
aggregate supply curve is SAS_0, and the long-run aggregate
supply curve is LAS. The price level is 110, and real GDP is
$13 trillion, which equals potential GDP. Aggregate demand
increases to AD_1. The price level rises to 113, and real GDP
increases to $13.5 trillion.

In part (b), starting from the above full-employment equilibrium, the money wage rate begins to rise and the short-run
aggregate supply curve shifts leftward toward SAS_1. The
price level rises further, and real GDP returns to potential
GDP.

Money Wage Rate Response Real GDP cannot remain above potential GDP forever. With unemployment below its natural rate, there is a shortage of labor. In this situation, the money wage rate begins to rise. As it does so, short-run aggregate supply decreases and the *SAS* curve starts to shift leftward. The price level rises further, and real GDP begins to decrease.

With no further change in aggregate demand—that is, the aggregate demand curve remains at AD_1—this process ends when the short-run aggregate supply curve has shifted to SAS_1 in Fig. 29.1(b). At this time, the price level has increased to 121 and real GDP has returned to potential GDP of $13 trillion, the level at which it started.

A Demand-Pull Inflation Process The events that we've just described bring a *one-time rise in the price level*, not an inflation. For inflation to proceed, aggregate demand must *persistently* increase.

The only way in which aggregate demand can persistently increase is if the quantity of money persistently increases. Suppose the government has a budget deficit that it finances by selling bonds. Also suppose that the Fed buys some of these bonds. When the Fed buys bonds, it creates more money. In this situation, aggregate demand increases year after year. The aggregate demand curve keeps shifting rightward. This persistent increase in aggregate demand puts continual upward pressure on the price level. The economy now experiences demand-pull inflation.

Figure 29.2 illustrates the process of demand-pull inflation. The starting point is the same as that shown in Fig. 29.1. The aggregate demand curve is AD_0, the short-run aggregate supply curve is SAS_0, and the long-run aggregate supply curve is *LAS*. Real GDP is $13 trillion, and the price level is 110. Aggregate demand increases, shifting the aggregate demand curve to AD_1. Real GDP increases to $13.5 trillion, and the price level rises to 113. The economy is at an above full-employment equilibrium. There is a shortage of labor, and the money wage rate rises. The short-run aggregate supply curve shifts to SAS_1. The price level rises to 121, and real GDP returns to potential GDP.

But the Fed increases the quantity of money again, and aggregate demand continues to increase. The aggregate demand curve shifts rightward to AD_2. The price level rises further to 125, and real GDP again exceeds potential GDP at $13.5 trillion. Yet again,

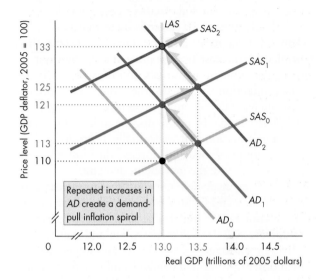

FIGURE 29.2   A Demand-Pull Inflation Spiral

Each time the quantity of money increases, aggregate demand increases and the aggregate demand curve shifts rightward from AD_0 to AD_1 to AD_2, and so on. Each time real GDP increases above potential GDP, the money wage rate rises and the short-run aggregate supply curve shifts leftward from SAS_0 to SAS_1 to SAS_2, and so on. The price level rises from 110 to 113, 121, 125, 133, and so on. There is a demand-pull inflation spiral. Real GDP fluctuates between $13 trillion and $13.5 trillion.

myeconlab animation

the money wage rate rises and decreases short-run aggregate supply. The *SAS* curve shifts to SAS_2, and the price level rises further, to 133. As the quantity of money continues to grow, aggregate demand increases and the price level rises in an ongoing demand-pull inflation process.

The process you have just studied generates inflation—an ongoing process of a rising price level.

Demand-Pull Inflation in Kalamazoo You may better understand the inflation process that we've just described by considering what is going on in an individual part of the economy, such as a Kalamazoo soda-bottling plant. Initially, when aggregate demand increases, the demand for soda increases and the price of soda rises. Faced with a higher price, the soda plant works overtime and increases production. Conditions are good for workers in Kalamazoo, and the soda factory finds it hard to hang on to its best people. To do so, it offers a higher money wage rate. As the wage rate rises, so do the soda factory's costs.

What happens next depends on aggregate demand. If aggregate demand remains constant, the firm's costs increase but the price of soda does not increase as quickly as its costs. In this case, the firm cuts production. Eventually, the money wage rate and costs increase by the same percentage as the rise in the price of soda. In real terms, the soda factory is in the same situation as it was initially. It produces the same amount of soda and employs the same amount of labor as before the increase in demand.

But if aggregate demand continues to increase, so does the demand for soda and the price of soda rises at the same rate as wages. The soda factory continues to operate at above full employment and there is a persistent shortage of labor. Prices and wages chase each other upward in a demand-pull inflation spiral.

Demand-Pull Inflation in the United States A

demand-pull inflation like the one you've just studied occurred in the United States during the late 1960s. In 1960, inflation was a moderate 2 percent a year, but its rate increased slowly to 3 percent by 1966. Then, in 1967, a large increase in government expenditure on the Vietnam War and an increase in spending on social programs, together with an increase in the growth rate of the quantity of money, increased aggregate demand more quickly. Consequently, the rightward shift of the aggregate demand curve accelerated and the price level increased more quickly. Real GDP moved above potential GDP, and the unemployment rate fell below its natural rate.

With unemployment below its natural rate, the money wage rate started to rise more quickly and the short-run aggregate supply curve shifted leftward. The Fed responded with a further increase in the money growth rate, and a demand-pull inflation spiral unfolded. By 1970, the inflation rate had reached 5 percent a year.

For the next few years, aggregate demand grew even more quickly and the inflation rate kept rising. By 1974, the inflation rate had reached 11 percent a year.

Next, let's see how shocks to aggregate supply can create cost-push inflation.

Cost-Push Inflation

An inflation that is kicked off by an increase in costs is called **cost-push inflation**. The two main sources of cost increases are

1. An increase in the money wage rate
2. An increase in the money prices of raw materials

At a given price level, the higher the cost of production, the smaller is the amount that firms are willing to produce. So if the money wage rate rises or if the prices of raw materials (for example, oil) rise, firms decrease their supply of goods and services. Aggregate supply decreases, and the short-run aggregate supply curve shifts leftward.[1] Let's trace the effects of such a decrease in short-run aggregate supply on the price level and real GDP.

Initial Effect of a Decrease in Aggregate Supply

Suppose that last year the price level was 110 and real GDP was $13 trillion. Potential real GDP was also $13 trillion. Figure 29.3(a) illustrates this situation. The aggregate demand curve was AD_0, the short-run aggregate supply curve was SAS_0, and the long-run aggregate supply curve was LAS. In the current year, the world's oil producers form a price-fixing organization that strengthens their market power and increases the relative price of oil. They raise the price of oil, and this action decreases short-run aggregate supply. The short-run aggregate supply curve shifts leftward to SAS_1. The price level rises to 117, and real GDP decreases to $12.5 trillion. The economy is at a below full-employment equilibrium and there is a recessionary gap.

This event is a *one-time rise in the price level*. It is not inflation. In fact, a supply shock on its own cannot cause inflation. Something more must happen to enable a one-time supply shock, which causes a one-time rise in the price level, to be converted into a process of ongoing inflation. The quantity of money must persistently increase. Sometimes it does increase, as you will now see.

---

[1] Some cost-push forces, such as an increase in the price of oil accompanied by a decrease in the availability of oil, can also decrease long-run aggregate supply. We'll ignore such effects here and examine cost-push factors that change only short-run aggregate supply. Later in the chapter, we study the effects of shocks to long-run aggregate supply.

FIGURE 29.3   A Cost-Push Rise in the Price Level

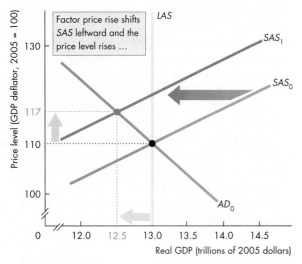

(a) Initial cost push

Initially, the aggregate demand curve is AD_0, the short-run aggregate supply curve is SAS_0, and the long-run aggregate supply curve is LAS. A decrease in aggregate supply (for example, resulting from a rise in the world price of oil) shifts the short-run aggregate supply curve to SAS_1. The economy moves to the point where the short-run aggregate supply curve SAS_1 intersects the aggregate demand curve

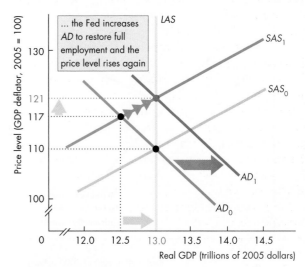

(b) The Fed responds

AD_0. The price level rises to 117, and real GDP decreases to $12.5 trillion.

In part (b), if the Fed responds by increasing aggregate demand to restore full employment, the aggregate demand curve shifts rightward to AD_1. The economy returns to full employment, but the price level rises further to 121.

myeconlab   animation

Aggregate Demand Response When real GDP decreases, unemployment rises above its natural rate. In such a situation, there is often an outcry of concern and a call for action to restore full employment. Suppose that the Fed cuts the interest rate and increases the quantity of money. Aggregate demand increases. In Fig. 29.3(b), the aggregate demand curve shifts rightward to AD_1 and full employment is restored. But the price level rises further to 121.

A Cost-Push Inflation Process The oil producers now see the prices of everything they buy increasing, so oil producers increase the price of oil again to restore its new high relative price. Figure 29.4 continues the story. The short-run aggregate supply curve now shifts to SAS_2. The price level rises and real GDP decreases.

The price level rises further, to 129, and real GDP decreases to $12.5 trillion. Unemployment

increases above its natural rate. If the Fed responds yet again with an increase in the quantity of money, aggregate demand increases and the aggregate demand curve shifts to AD_2. The price level rises even higher—to 133—and full employment is again restored. A cost-push inflation spiral results. The combination of a rising price level and decreasing real GDP is called **stagflation.**

You can see that the Fed has a dilemma. If it does not respond when producers raise the oil price, the economy remains below full employment. If the Fed increases the quantity of money to restore full employment, it invites another oil price hike that will call forth yet a further increase in the quantity of money.

If the Fed responds to each oil price hike by increasing the quantity of money, inflation will rage along at a rate decided by oil producers. But if the Fed keeps the lid on money growth, the economy remains below full employment.

FIGURE 29.4   A Cost-Push Inflation Spiral

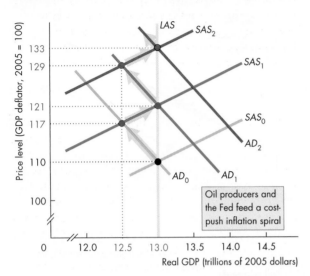

Each time a cost increase occurs, the short-run aggregate supply curve shifts leftward from SAS_0 to SAS_1 to SAS_2, and so on. Each time real GDP decreases below potential GDP, the Fed increases the quantity of money and the aggregate demand curve shifts rightward from AD_0 to AD_1 to AD_2, and so on. The price level rises from 110 to 117, 121, 129, 133, and so on. There is a cost-push inflation spiral. Real GDP fluctuates between $13 trillion and $12.5 trillion.

myeconlab   animation

Cost-Push Inflation in Kalamazoo What is going on in the Kalamazoo soda-bottling plant when the economy is experiencing cost-push inflation?

When the oil price increases, so do the costs of bottling soda. These higher costs decrease the supply of soda, increasing its price and decreasing the quantity produced. The soda plant lays off some workers.

This situation persists until either the Fed increases aggregate demand or the price of oil falls. If the Fed increases aggregate demand, the demand for soda increases and so does its price. The higher price of soda brings higher profits, and the bottling plant increases its production. The soda factory rehires the laid-off workers.

Cost-Push Inflation in the United States A cost-push inflation like the one you've just studied occurred in the United States during the 1970s. It began in 1974

when the Organization of the Petroleum Exporting Countries (OPEC) raised the price of oil fourfold. The higher oil price decreased aggregate supply, which caused the price level to rise more quickly and real GDP to shrink. The Fed then faced a dilemma: Would it increase the quantity of money and accommodate the cost-push forces, or would it keep aggregate demand growth in check by limiting money growth? In 1975, 1976, and 1977, the Fed repeatedly allowed the quantity of money to grow quickly and inflation proceeded at a rapid rate. In 1979 and 1980, OPEC was again able to push oil prices higher. On that occasion, the Fed decided not to respond to the oil price hike with an increase in the quantity of money. The result was a recession but also, eventually, a fall in inflation.

Expected Inflation

If inflation is expected, the fluctuations in real GDP that accompany demand-pull and cost-push inflation that you've just studied don't occur. Instead, inflation proceeds as it does in the long run, with real GDP equal to potential GDP and unemployment at its natural rate. Figure 29.5 explains why.

Suppose that last year the aggregate demand curve was AD_0, the aggregate supply curve was SAS_0, and the long-run aggregate supply curve was LAS. The price level was 110, and real GDP was $13 trillion, which is also potential GDP.

To keep things as simple as possible, suppose that potential GDP does not change, so the LAS curve doesn't shift. Also suppose that aggregate demand is *expected to increase* to AD_1.

In anticipation of this increase in aggregate demand, the money wage rate rises and the short-run aggregate supply curve shifts leftward. If the money wage rate rises by the same percentage as the price level is expected to rise, the short-run aggregate supply curve for next year is SAS_1.

If aggregate demand turns out to be the same as expected, the aggregate demand curve is AD_1. The short-run aggregate supply curve, SAS_1, and AD_1 determine the actual price level at 121. Between last year and this year, the price level increased from 110 to 121 and the economy experienced an inflation rate equal to that expected. If this inflation is ongoing, aggregate demand increases (as expected) in the following year and the aggregate demand curve shifts to AD_2. The money wage rate rises to reflect the expected inflation, and the short-run aggregate sup-

FIGURE 29.5   Expected Inflation

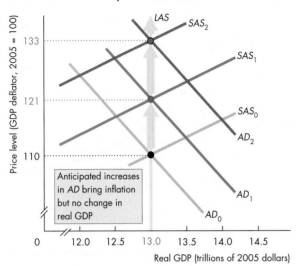

Anticipated increases in AD bring inflation but no change in real GDP

 myeconlab animation

Potential real GDP is $13 trillion. Last year, aggregate demand was AD_0 and the short-run aggregate supply curve was SAS_0. The actual price level was the same as the expected price level: 110. This year, aggregate demand is expected to increase to AD_1 and the price level is expected to rise from 110 to 121. As a result, the money wage rate rises and the short-run aggregate supply curve shifts to SAS_1. If aggregate demand actually increases as expected, the actual aggregate demand curve AD_1 is the same as the expected aggregate demand curve. Real GDP is $13 trillion, and the actual price level rises to 121. The inflation is expected. Next year, the process continues with aggregate demand increasing as expected to AD_2 and the money wage rate rising to shift the short-run aggregate supply curve to SAS_2. Again, real GDP remains at $13 trillion, and the price level rises, as expected, to 133.

ply curve shifts to SAS_2. The price level rises, as expected, to 133.

What caused this inflation? The immediate answer is that because people expected inflation, the money wage rate increased and the price level increased. But the expectation was correct. Aggregate demand was expected to increase, and it did increase. It is the actual and expected increase in aggregate demand that caused the inflation.

An expected inflation at full employment is exactly the process that the quantity theory of money predicts. To review the quantity theory of money, see Chapter 25, pp. 606–607.

This broader account of the inflation process and its short-run effects show why the quantity theory of money doesn't explain the *fluctuations* in inflation. The economy follows the course described in Fig. 29.5, but as predicted by the quantity theory, only if aggregate demand growth is forecasted correctly.

Forecasting Inflation

To anticipate inflation, people must forecast it. Some economists who work for macroeconomic forecasting agencies, banks, insurance companies, labor unions, and large corporations specialize in inflation forecasting. The best forecast available is one that is based on all the relevant information and is called a **rational expectation**. A rational expectation is not necessarily a correct forecast. It is simply the best forecast with the information available. It will often turn out to be wrong, but no other forecast that could have been made with the information available could do better.

Inflation and the Business Cycle

When the inflation forecast is correct, the economy operates at full employment. If aggregate demand grows faster than expected, real GDP rises above potential GDP, the inflation rate exceeds its expected rate, and the economy behaves like it does in a demand-pull inflation. If aggregate demand grows more slowly than expected, real GDP falls below potential GDP and the inflation rate slows.

REVIEW QUIZ

1 How does demand-pull inflation begin?
2 What must happen to create a demand-pull inflation spiral?
3 How does cost-push inflation begin?
4 What must happen to create a cost-push inflation spiral?
5 What is stagflation and why does cost-push inflation cause stagflation?
6 How does expected inflation occur?
7 How do real GDP and the price level change if the forecast of inflation is incorrect?

You can work these questions in Study Plan 29.1 and get instant feedback.

Inflation and Unemployment: The Phillips Curve

Another way of studying inflation cycles focuses on the relationship and the short-run tradeoff between inflation and unemployment, a relationship called the **Phillips curve**—so named because it was first suggested by New Zealand economist A.W. Phillips.

Why do we need another way of studying inflation? What is wrong with the *AS-AD* explanation of the fluctuations in inflation and real GDP? The first answer to both questions is that we often want to study changes in both the expected and actual inflation rates and for this purpose, the Phillips curve provides a simpler tool and clearer insights than the *AS-AD* model provides. The second answer to both questions is that we often want to study changes in the short-run tradeoff between inflation and real economic activity (real GDP and unemployment) and again, the Phillips curve serves this purpose well.

To begin our explanation of the Phillips curve, we distinguish between two time frames (similar to the two aggregate supply time frames). We study

- The short-run Phillips curve
- The long-run Phillips curve

The Short-Run Phillips Curve

The **short-run Phillips curve** shows the relationship between inflation and unemployment, holding constant:

1. The expected inflation rate
2. The natural unemployment rate

You've just seen what determines the expected inflation rate. The natural unemployment rate and the factors that influence it are explained in Chapter 22, pp. 519–520.

Figure 29.6 shows a short-run Phillips curve, *SRPC*. Suppose that the expected inflation rate is 10 percent a year and the natural unemployment rate is 6 percent, point *A* in the figure. A short-run Phillips curve passes through this point. If inflation rises above its expected rate, unemployment falls below its natural rate. This joint movement in the inflation rate and the unemployment rate is illustrated as a movement up along the short-run Phillips curve from point *A* to point *B*. Similarly, if inflation falls below its expected rate, unemploy-

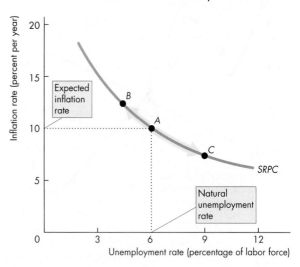

FIGURE 29.6   A Short-Run Phillips Curve

The short-run Phillips curve (*SRPC*) shows the relationship between inflation and unemployment at a given expected inflation rate and a given natural unemployment rate. With an expected inflation rate of 10 percent a year and a natural unemployment rate of 6 percent, the short-run Phillips curve passes through point *A*.

An unexpected increase in aggregate demand lowers unemployment and increases the inflation rate—a movement up along the short-run Phillips curve to point *B*. An unexpected decrease in aggregate demand increases unemployment and lowers the inflation rate—a movement down along the short-run Phillips curve to point *C*.

myeconlab   animation

ment rises above its natural rate. In this case, there is movement down along the short-run Phillips curve from point *A* to point *C*.

The short-run Phillips curve is like the short-run aggregate supply curve. A movement along the *SAS* curve that brings a higher price level and an increase in real GDP is equivalent to a movement along the short-run Phillips curve from *A* to *B* that brings an increase in the inflation rate and a decrease in the unemployment rate.

Similarly, a movement along the *SAS* curve that brings a lower price level and a decrease in real GDP is equivalent to a movement along the short-run Phillips curve from *A* to *C* that brings a decrease in the inflation rate and an increase in the unemployment rate.

The Long-Run Phillips Curve

The **long-run Phillips curve** shows the relationship between inflation and unemployment when the actual inflation rate equals the expected inflation rate. The long-run Phillips curve is vertical at the natural unemployment rate. In Fig. 29.7, it is the vertical line *LRPC*.

The long-run Phillips curve tells us that any expected inflation rate is possible at the natural unemployment rate. This proposition is consistent with the *AS-AD* model, which predicts (and which Fig. 29.5 illustrates) that when inflation is expected, real GDP equals potential GDP and unemployment is at its natural rate.

The short-run Phillips curve intersects the long-run Phillips curve at the expected inflation rate. A change in the expected inflation rate shifts the short-run Phillips curve but it does not shift the long-run Phillips curve.

In Fig. 29.7, if the expected inflation rate is 10 percent a year, the short-run Phillips curve is $SRPC_0$.

If the expected inflation rate falls to 6 percent a year, the short-run Phillips curve shifts downward to $SRPC_1$. The vertical distance by which the short-run Phillips curve shifts from point *A* to point *D* is equal to the change in the expected inflation rate. If the actual inflation rate also falls from 10 percent to 6 percent, there is a movement down the long-run Phillips curve from *A* to *D*. An increase in the expected inflation rate has the opposite effect to that shown in Fig. 29.7.

The other source of a shift in the Phillips curve is a change in the natural unemployment rate.

Changes in the Natural Unemployment Rate

The natural unemployment rate changes for many reasons (see Chapter 22, pp. 519–520). A change in the natural unemployment rate shifts both the short-run and long-run Phillips curves. Figure 29.8 illustrates such shifts.

FIGURE 29.7   Short-Run and Long-Run Phillips Curves

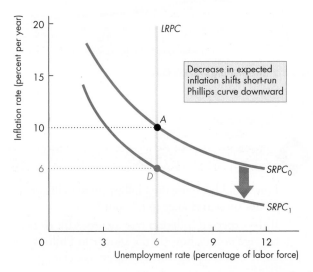

The long-run Phillips curve is *LRPC*. A fall in expected inflation from 10 percent a year to 6 percent a year shifts the short-run Phillips curve downward from $SRPC_0$ to $SRPC_1$. The long-run Phillips curve does not shift. The new short-run Phillips curve intersects the long-run Phillips curve at the new expected inflation rate—point *D*.

FIGURE 29.8   A Change in the Natural Unemployment Rate

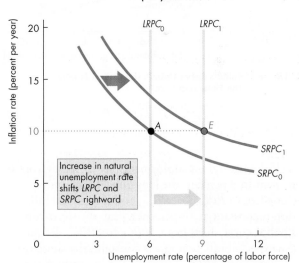

A change in the natural unemployment rate shifts both the short-run and long-run Phillips curves. An increase in the natural unemployment rate from 6 percent to 9 percent shifts the Phillips curves rightward to $SRPC_1$ and $LRPC_1$. The new long-run Phillips curve intersects the new short-run Phillips curve at the expected inflation rate—point *E*.

Economics in Action

The Shifting Short-Run Tradeoff

Figure 1 is a scatter diagram of the U.S. inflation rate (measured by the GDP deflator) and the unemployment rate since 1961. We can interpret the data in terms of the shifting short-run Phillips curve in Fig. 2.

During the 1960s, the short-run Phillips curve was $SRPC_0$, with a natural unemployment rate of 4.5 percent and an expected inflation rate of 2 percent a year (point A).

During the early 1970s, the short-run Phillips curve was $SRPC_1$, with a natural unemployment rate of 5 percent and an expected inflation rate of 6 percent a year (point B).

During the late 1970s, the natural unemployment rate increased to 8 percent (point C) and the short-run Phillips curve shifted to $SRPC_2$. Briefly in 1975 and again in 1981, the expected inflation rate surged to 9 percent a year (point D) and the short-run Phillips curve shifted to $SRPC_3$.

During the 1980s and 1990s, the expected inflation rate and the natural unemployment rate decreased and the short-run Phillips curve shifted leftward back to $SRPC_1$ and, by the mid-1990s, back to $SRPC_0$, where it remained into the 2000s.

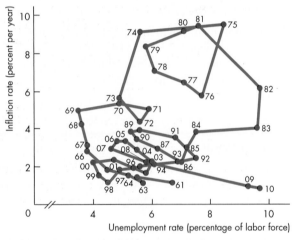

Figure 1 Phillips Curve Data in the United States: The Time Sequence

Source of data: Bureau of Labor Statistics.

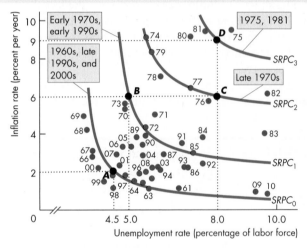

Figure 2 The Shifting Phillips Curves

If the natural unemployment rate increases from 6 percent to 9 percent, the long-run Phillips curve shifts from $LRPC_0$ to $LRPC_1$, and if expected inflation is constant at 10 percent a year, the short-run Phillips curve shifts from $SRPC_0$ to $SRPC_1$. Because the expected inflation rate is constant, the short-run Phillips curve $SRPC_1$ intersects the long-run curve $LRPC_1$ (point E) at the same inflation rate at which the short-run Phillips curve $SRPC_0$ intersects the long-run curve $LRPC_0$ (point A).

Changes in both the expected inflation rate and the natural unemployment rate have shifted the U.S. Phillips curve but the expected inflation rate has had the greater effect.

 REVIEW QUIZ

1 How would you use the Phillips curve to illustrate an unexpected change in inflation?

2 If the expected inflation rate increases by 10 percentage points, how do the short-run Phillips curve and the long-run Phillips curve change?

3 If the natural unemployment rate increases, what happens to the short-run Phillips curve and the long-run Phillips curve?

4 Does the United States have a stable short-run Phillips curve? Explain why or why not.

You can work these questions in Study Plan 29.2 and get instant feedback.

The Business Cycle

The business cycle is easy to describe but hard to explain and business cycle theory remains unsettled and a source of controversy. We'll look at two approaches to understanding the business cycle:

- Mainstream business cycle theory
- Real business cycle theory

Mainstream Business Cycle Theory

The mainstream business cycle theory is that potential GDP grows at a steady rate while aggregate demand grows at a fluctuating rate. Because the money wage rate is sticky, if aggregate demand grows faster than potential GDP, real GDP moves above potential GDP and an inflationary gap emerges. And if aggregate demand grows slower than potential GDP, real GDP moves below potential GDP and a recessionary gap emerges. If aggregate demand decreases, real GDP also decreases in a recession.

Figure 29.9 illustrates this business cycle theory. Initially, actual and potential GDP are $10 trillion. The long-run aggregate supply curve is LAS_0, the aggregate demand curve is AD_0, and the price level is 100. The economy is at full employment at point A.

An expansion occurs when potential GDP increases and the LAS curve shifts rightward to LAS_1. During an expansion, aggregate demand also increases, and usually by more than potential GDP, so the price level rises. Assume that in the current expansion, the price level is expected to rise to 110 and the money wage rate has been set based on that expectation. The short-run aggregate supply curve is SAS_1.

If aggregate demand increases to AD_1, real GDP increases to $13 trillion, the new level of potential GDP, and the price level rises, as expected, to 110. The economy remains at full employment but now at point B.

If aggregate demand increases more slowly to AD_2, real GDP grows by less than potential GDP and the economy moves to point C, with real GDP at $12.5 trillion and the price level at 107. Real GDP growth is slower and inflation is lower than expected.

If aggregate demand increases more quickly to AD_3, real GDP grows by more than potential GDP and the economy moves to point D, with real GDP at $13.5 trillion and the price level at 113. Real GDP growth is faster and inflation is higher than expected.

Growth, inflation, and the business cycle arise from the relentless increases in potential GDP, faster (on average) increases in aggregate demand, and fluctuations in the pace of aggregate demand growth.

FIGURE 29.9   The Mainstream Business Cycle Theory

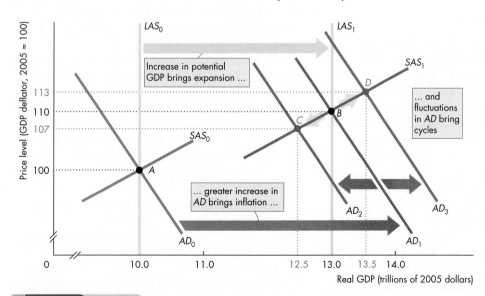

In a business cycle expansion, potential GDP increases and the LAS curve shifts rightward from LAS_0 to LAS_1. A greater than expected increase in aggregate demand brings inflation.

If the aggregate demand curve shifts to AD_1, the economy remains at full employment. If the aggregate demand curve shifts to AD_2, a recessionary gap arises. If the aggregate demand curve shifts to AD_3, an inflationary gap arises.

myeconlab   animation

This mainstream theory comes in a number of special forms that differ regarding the source of fluctuations in aggregate demand growth and the source of money wage stickiness.

Keynesian Cycle Theory In **Keynesian cycle theory**, fluctuations in investment driven by fluctuations in business confidence—summarized by the phrase "animal spirits"—are the main source of fluctuations in aggregate demand.

Monetarist Cycle Theory In **monetarist cycle theory**, fluctuations in both investment and consumption expenditure, driven by fluctuations in the growth rate of the quantity of money, are the main source of fluctuations in aggregate demand.

Both the Keynesian and monetarist cycle theories simply assume that the money wage rate is rigid and don't explain that rigidity.

Two newer theories seek to explain money wage rate rigidity and to be more careful about working out its consequences.

New Classical Cycle Theory In **new classical cycle theory**, the rational expectation of the price level, which is determined by potential GDP and *expected* aggregate demand, determines the money wage rate and the position of the *SAS* curve. In this theory, only *unexpected* fluctuations in aggregate demand bring fluctuations in real GDP around potential GDP.

New Keynesian Cycle Theory The **new Keynesian cycle theory** emphasizes the fact that today's money wage rates were negotiated at many past dates, which means that *past* rational expectations of the current price level influence the money wage rate and the position of the *SAS* curve. In this theory, both unexpected and currently expected fluctuations in aggregate demand bring fluctuations in real GDP around potential GDP.

The mainstream cycle theories don't rule out the possibility that occasionally an aggregate supply shock might occur. An oil price rise, a widespread drought, a major hurricane, or another natural disaster, could, for example, bring a recession. But supply shocks are not the normal source of fluctuations in the mainstream theories. In contrast, real business cycle theory puts supply shocks at center stage.

Real Business Cycle Theory

The newest theory of the business cycle, known as **real business cycle theory** (or RBC theory), regards random fluctuations in productivity as the main source of economic fluctuations. These productivity fluctuations are assumed to result mainly from fluctuations in the pace of technological change, but they might also have other sources, such as international disturbances, climate fluctuations, or natural disasters. The origins of RBC theory can be traced to the rational expectations revolution set off by Robert E. Lucas, Jr., but the first demonstrations of the power of this theory were given by Edward Prescott and Finn Kydland and by John Long and Charles Plosser. Today, RBC theory is part of a broad research agenda called dynamic general equilibrium analysis, and hundreds of young macroeconomists do research on this topic.

We'll explore RBC theory by looking first at its impulse and then at the mechanism that converts that impulse into a cycle in real GDP.

The RBC Impulse The impulse in RBC theory is the growth rate of productivity that results from technological change. RBC theorists believe this impulse to be generated mainly by the process of research and development that leads to the creation and use of new technologies.

To isolate the RBC theory impulse, economists measure the change in the combined productivity of capital and labor. Figure 29.10 shows the RBC impulse for the United States from 1964 through 2009. You can see that fluctuations in productivity growth are correlated with real GDP fluctuations.

The pace of technological change and productivity growth is not constant. Sometimes productivity growth speeds up, sometimes it slows, and occasionally it even *falls*—labor and capital become less productive, on average. A period of rapid productivity growth brings a business cycle expansion, and a slowdown or fall in productivity triggers a recession.

It is easy to understand why technological change brings productivity growth. But how does it *decrease* productivity? All technological change eventually increases productivity. But if initially, technological change makes a sufficient amount of existing capital—especially human capital—obsolete, productivity can temporarily fall. At such a time, more jobs are destroyed than created and more businesses fail than start up.

FIGURE 29.10   The Real Business Cycle Impulse

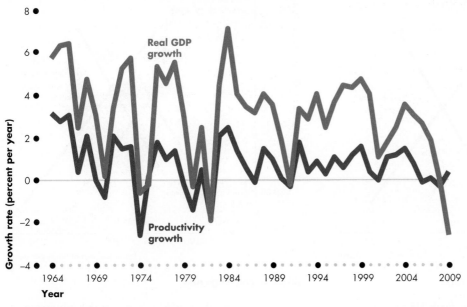

The real business cycle is caused by changes in technology that bring fluctuations in the growth rate of productivity*. Productivity fluctuations are correlated with real GDP fluctuations and most recessions are associated with a slowdown in productivity growth. The 2008-2009 recession is an exception and occurred at a time when productivity growth increased.

*Productivity growth calculations are based on assumptions about the aggregate production function.

Source of data: Bureau of Economic Analysis.

myeconlab animation

The RBC Mechanism Two effects follow from a change in productivity that sparks an expansion or a contraction:

1. Investment demand changes.
2. The demand for labor changes.

We'll study these effects and their consequences during a recession. In an expansion, they work in the direction opposite to what is described here.

Technological change makes some existing capital obsolete and temporarily decreases productivity. Firms expect the future profits to fall and see their labor productivity falling. With lower profit expectations, they cut back their purchases of new capital, and with lower labor productivity, they plan to lay off some workers. So the initial effect of a temporary fall in productivity is a decrease in investment demand and a decrease in the demand for labor.

Figure 29.11 illustrates these two initial effects of a decrease in productivity. Part (a) shows the effects of a decrease in investment demand in the loanable funds market. The demand for loanable funds curve is *DLF* and the supply of loanable funds curve is *SLF* (both of which are explained in Chapter 24, pp.

572–574). Initially, the demand for loanable funds curve is DLF_0 and the equilibrium quantity of funds is $2 trillion at a real interest rate of 6 percent a year. A decrease in productivity decreases investment demand, and the demand for loanable funds curve shifts leftward from DLF to DLF_1. The real interest rate falls to 4 percent a year, and the equilibrium quantity of loanable funds decreases to $1.7 trillion.

Figure 29.11(b) shows the demand for labor and supply of labor (which are explained in Chapter 23, pp. 545–546). Initially, the demand for labor curve is LD_0, the supply of labor curve LS_0, and equilibrium employment is 200 billion hours a year at a real wage rate of $35 an hour. The decrease in productivity decreases the demand for labor, and the demand for labor curve shifts leftward from LD_0 to LD_1.

Before we can determine the new level of employment and real wage rate, we need to take a ripple effect into account—the key effect in RBC theory.

The Key Decision: When to Work? According to RBC theory, people decide *when* to work by doing a cost-benefit calculation. They compare the return

FIGURE 29.11   Loanable Funds and Labor Markets in a Real Business Cycle

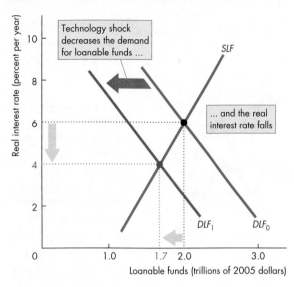

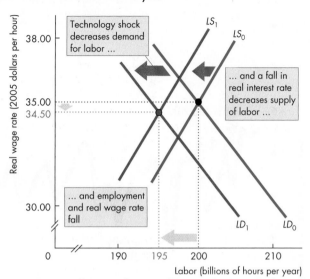

(a) Loanable funds and interest rate

(b) Labor and wage rate

In part (a), the supply of loanable funds *SLF* and initial demand for loanable funds *DLF₀* determine the real interest rate at 6 percent a year. In part (b), the initial demand for labor *LD₀* and supply of labor, *LS₀*, determine the real wage rate at $35 an hour and employment at 200 billion hours. A technological change temporarily decreases productivity, and both the demand for loanable funds and the demand for

labor decrease. The two demand curves shift leftward to *DLF₁* and *LD₁*. In part (a), the real interest rate falls to 4 percent a year. In part (b), the fall in the real interest rate decreases the supply of labor (the when-to-work decision) and the supply of labor curve shifts leftward to *LS₁*. Employment decreases to 195 billion hours, and the real wage rate falls to $34.50 an hour. A recession is under way.

myeconlab   animation

from working in the current period with the *expected* return from working in a later period. You make such a comparison every day in school. Suppose your goal in this course is to get an A. To achieve this goal, you work hard most of the time. But during the few days before the midterm and final exams, you work especially hard. Why? Because you believe that the return from studying close to the exam is greater than the return from studying when the exam is a long time away. So during the term, you take time off for the movies and other leisure pursuits, but at exam time, you study every evening and weekend.

RBC theory says that workers behave like you. They work fewer hours, sometimes zero hours, when the real wage rate is temporarily low, and they work more hours when the real wage rate is temporarily high. But to properly compare the current wage rate with the expected future wage rate, workers must use

the real interest rate. If the real interest rate is 6 percent a year, a real wage of $1 an hour earned this week will become $1.06 a year from now. If the real wage rate is expected to be $1.05 an hour next year, today's real wage of $1 looks good. By working longer hours now and shorter hours a year from now, a person can get a 1 percent higher real wage. But suppose the real interest rate is 4 percent a year. In this case, $1 earned now is worth $1.04 next year. Working fewer hours now and more next year is the way to get a 1 percent higher real wage.

So the when-to-work decision depends on the real interest rate. The lower the real interest rate, other things remaining the same, the smaller is the supply of labor today. Many economists believe this *intertemporal substitution* effect to be of negligible size. RBC theorists believe that the effect is large, and it is the key feature of the RBC mechanism.

You saw in Fig. 29.11(a) that the decrease in the demand for loanable funds lowers the real interest rate. This fall in the real interest rate lowers the return to current work and decreases the supply of labor.

In Fig. 29.11(b), the labor supply curve shifts leftward to LS_1. The effect of the decrease in productivity on the demand for labor is larger than the effect of the fall in the real interest rate on the supply of labor. That is, the demand curve shifts farther leftward than does the supply curve. As a result, the real wage rate falls to $34.50 an hour and employment decreases to 195 billion hours. A recession has begun and is intensifying.

What Happened to Money? The name *real* business cycle theory is no accident. It reflects the central prediction of the theory. Real things, not nominal or monetary things, cause the business cycle. If the quantity of money changes, aggregate demand changes. But if there is no real change—with no change in the use of resources and no change in potential GDP—the change in the quantity of money changes only the price level. In RBC theory, this outcome occurs because the aggregate supply curve is the *LAS* curve, which pins real GDP down at potential GDP, so when aggregate demand changes, only the price level changes.

Cycles and Growth The shock that drives the business cycle of RBC theory is the same as the force that generates economic growth: technological change. On average, as technology advances, productivity grows; but as you saw in Fig. 29.10, it grows at an uneven pace. Economic growth arises from the upward trend in productivity growth and, according to RBC theory, the mostly positive but occasionally negative higher frequency shocks to productivity bring the business cycle.

Criticisms and Defenses of RBC Theory The three main criticisms of RBC theory are that (1) the money wage rate *is* sticky, and to assume otherwise is at odds with a clear fact; (2) intertemporal substitution is too weak a force to account for large fluctuations in labor supply and employment with small real wage rate changes; and (3) productivity shocks are as likely to be caused by *changes in aggregate demand* as by technological change.

If aggregate demand fluctuations cause the fluctuations in productivity, then the traditional aggregate demand theories are needed to explain them. Fluctuations in productivity do not cause the business cycle but are caused by it!

Building on this theme, the critics point out that the so-called productivity fluctuations that growth accounting measures are correlated with changes in the growth rate of money and other indicators of changes in aggregate demand.

The defenders of RBC theory claim that the theory explains the macroeconomic facts about the business cycle and is consistent with the facts about economic growth. In effect, a single theory explains *both growth and the business cycle*. The growth accounting exercise that explains slowly changing trends also explains the more frequent business cycle swings. Its defenders also claim that RBC theory is consistent with a wide range of *micro*economic evidence about labor supply decisions, labor demand and investment demand decisions, and information on the distribution of income between labor and capital.

REVIEW QUIZ

1 Explain the mainstream theory of the business cycle.
2 What are the four special forms of the mainstream theory of the business cycle and how do they differ?
3 According to RBC theory, what is the source of the business cycle? What is the role of fluctuations in the rate of technological change?
4 According to RBC theory, how does a fall in productivity growth influence investment demand, the market for loanable funds, the real interest rate, the demand for labor, the supply of labor, employment, and the real wage rate?
5 What are the main criticisms of RBC theory and how do its supporters defend it?

You can work these questions in Study Plan 29.3 and get instant feedback.

⬥ You can complete your study of economic fluctuations in *Reading Between the Lines* on pp. 716–717, which looks at the shifting inflation–unemployment tradeoff and misery index in the United States.

The Shifting Inflation–Unemployment Tradeoff

Evidence and Denial; Obama Advisers Refuse to Believe They're Failing

The Washington Times

August 4, 2010

... President Obama likes to say that he inherited the "worst" economy since the Great Depression, but the fact is that the economic "Misery Index" (inflation plus unemployment) ... was twice as high when President Reagan took office [in 1981]. (By the time President Reagan left the presidency, the Misery Index had dropped to less than half of what it had been when he assumed office.) ...

Reagan's policy was to sharply cut individual and corporate tax rates, and to restrain the growth in government spending and regulation. The Democrats, who were in control of the House of Representatives, resisted and delayed the Reagan tax cuts, so they were not fully implemented until 1983. Mr. Obama had the luxury of having his party in control of both houses of Congress, so he was able to get his proposed, massive government spending increases enacted almost immediately. ...

Keynesian economics, practiced during the late 1960s and 1970s, became thoroughly discredited with the stagflation of the 1970s ... and the subsequent Reagan supply-side boom. The Clinton administration ... partially reverted to Reaganomics in its second term; with a capital-gains rate cut and reductions in spending as a percentage of GDP. The result was very strong economic growth and budget surpluses.

Given the above facts ... would you follow the Reagan/Clinton II economic policies or the Obama ones? Where is the evidence ... that Obamanomics will work, particularly since it is not now working as advertised? Will the Misery Index be cut by more than half during the Obama administration, as it was during Reagan's terms, or will it rise?...

Excerpted from "Evidence and Denial; Obama Advisers Refuse to Believe They're Failing" by Richard W. Rahn. *The Washington Times*, August 4, 2010. Reported with permission from the Foster Printing Service.

ESSENCE OF THE STORY

- The misery index, which is the inflation rate plus the unemployment rate, was twice as high in 1981 when President Reagan took office as it was in 2009 when President Obama's term began.

- President Reagan lowered the misery index to less than half its 1981 level by cutting taxes and restraining the growth in government spending and regulation.

- President Obama is trying to lower the misery index by increasing government spending.

- This approach is the Keynesian policy of the late 1960s and 1970s that brought stagflation and a rising misery index.

- When President Obama assumed office in January 2009, the CPI inflation rate was zero and the unemployment rate was 7.7 percent, so the misery index was 7.7.

- When President Reagan assumed office in January 1981, the CPI inflation rate was 11.8 percent and the unemployment rate was 7.5 percent, so the misery index was 19.3.

- When President Reagan left office in January 1989, the CPI inflation rate was 4.7 percent and the unemployment rate was 5.4 percent, so the misery index was 10.1 (approximately half its 1981 level, as stated in the news article).

- In the year to August 2010, the CPI inflation rate was 1.1 percent and the unemployment rate was 9.6 percent. Combining these numbers generates a misery index of 10.7.

- Figure 1 puts these snapshots of the misery index in a longer perspective.

- The index was trending upward before 1980 and downward after its peak in June1980 when it reached 22 (the sum of an unemployment rate of 7.6 percent and an inflation rate of 14.4 percent a year).

- The misery index increases when the expected inflation rate rises, which shifts the short-run Phillips curve upward, and the natural unemployment rate rises, which shifts the short-run Phillips curve rightward.

- Figure 2 shows the paths followed by inflation and unemployment.

- In 1976, on the eve of Jimmy Carter's term as president, the economy was at point A. The unemployment rate was 7.5 percent and the inflation rate was 5.2 percent a year.

- By 1980, when Jimmy Carter left office and Ronald Reagan came into office, the economy was at point B.

- When Ronald Reagan left office, the economy had moved to point C.

- In January 2009, when President Obama entered office, the economy was at point D and by August 2010, the economy had moved to point E.

- Figure 2 contrasts the current and previous rises in the misery index. The rise of the index during the 1970s was the result of rising inflation and the rise of the index during 2009 and 2010 was the result of rising unemployment.

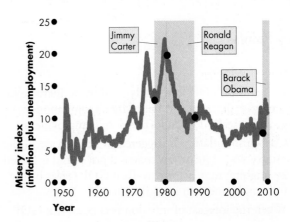

Figure 1 The U.S. misery index

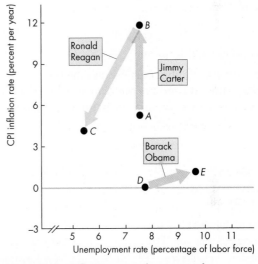

Figure 2 The inflation–unemployment paths

- Ronald Reagan's term in office saw a lower unemployment rate *and* a lower inflation rate.

- To lower the 2010 misery index, the Obama Administration must lower the unemployment rate while avoiding inflation.

- Economists were divided on the policies most likely to succeed. The author of the article (Richard W. Rahn) says that Reagan "supply-side" policies are needed. The Administration economists say more fiscal and monetary stimulus is needed.

- You can enter this debate in Chapters 30 and 31.

SUMMARY

Key Points

Inflation Cycles (pp. 702–707)

- Demand-pull inflation is triggered by an increase in aggregate demand and fueled by ongoing money growth. Real GDP cycles above full employment.
- Cost-push inflation is triggered by an increase in the money wage rate or raw material prices and is fueled by ongoing money growth. Real GDP cycles below full employment in a stagflation.
- When the forecast of inflation is correct, real GDP remains at potential GDP.

Working Problems 1 to 11 will give you a better understanding of inflation cycles.

Inflation and Unemployment:

The Phillips Curve (pp. 708–710)

- The short-run Phillips curve shows the tradeoff between inflation and unemployment when the expected inflation rate and the natural unemployment rate are constant.

- The long-run Phillips curve, which is vertical, shows that when the actual inflation rate equals the expected inflation rate, the unemployment rate equals the natural unemployment rate.

Working Problems 12 to 14 will give you a better understanding of inflation and unemployment: the Phillips curve.

The Business Cycle (pp. 711–715)

- The mainstream business cycle theory explains the business cycle as fluctuations of real GDP around potential GDP and as arising from a steady expansion of potential GDP combined with an expansion of aggregate demand at a fluctuating rate.
- Real business cycle theory explains the business cycle as fluctuations of potential GDP, which arise from fluctuations in the influence of technological change on productivity growth.

Working Problem 15 will give you a better understanding of the business cycle.

Key Terms

Cost-push inflation, 704
Demand-pull inflation, 702
Keynesian cycle theory, 712
Long-run Phillips curve, 709

Monetarist cycle theory, 712
New classical cycle theory, 712
New Keynesian cycle theory, 712
Phillips curve, 708

Rational expectation, 707
Real business cycle theory, 712
Short-run Phillips curve, 708
Stagflation, 705

STUDY PLAN PROBLEMS AND APPLICATIONS

 myeconlab   You can work Problems 1 to 15 in MyEconLab Chapter 29 Study Plan and get instant feedback.

Inflation Cycles (Study Plan 29.1)

1. **Pakistan: Is It Cost-Push Inflation?**

   With CPI already spiking 11.8 percent for the first ten months of the fiscal year, the average CPI inflation for the same period last year stood at 22.35 percent. Some economists insist the current bout of inflationary pressures is spawned by increasing prices of fuel, food, raw materials, transportation, construction materials, elimination of energy subsidies, etc. as indicated by the spike in the wholesale price index (WPI), which rose 21.99 percent in April from a year earlier.

   Source: *Daily the Pak Banker,* May 22, 2010

   Explain what type of inflation Pakistan is experiencing.

Use the following figure to answer Problems 2, 3, 4, and 5. In each question, the economy starts out on the curves labeled AD_0 and SAS_0.

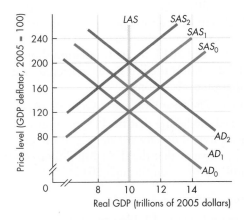

2. Some events occur and the economy experiences a demand-pull inflation.
   a. List the events that might cause a demand-pull inflation.
   b. Describe the initial effects of a demand-pull inflation.
   c. Describe what happens as a demand-pull inflation spiral proceeds.

3. Some events occur and the economy experiences a cost-push inflation.
   a. List the events that might cause a cost-push inflation.

   b. Describe the initial effects of a cost-push inflation.
   c. Describe what happens as a cost-push inflation spiral proceeds.

4. Some events occur and the economy is expected to experience inflation.
   a. List the events that might cause an expected inflation.
   b. Describe the initial effects of an expected inflation.
   c. Describe what happens as an expected inflation proceeds.

5. Suppose that people expect deflation (a falling price level), but aggregate demand remains at AD_0.
   a. What happens to the short-run and long-run aggregate supply curves? (Draw some new curves if you need to.)
   b. Describe the initial effects of an expected deflation.
   c. Describe what happens as it becomes obvious to everyone that the expected deflation is not going to occur.

Use the following news clip to work Problems 6 to 8.

The Right Way to Beat Chinese Inflation

High inflation is threatening social stability in China, soaring from 3.3 percent in March 2007 to 8.3 percent in March 2008. China's accelerating inflation reflects a similar climb in its GDP growth rate, from 11 percent in 2006 to 11.5 percent in 2007. The proximate cause of price growth since mid-2007 is the appearance of production bottlenecks as domestic demand exceeds supply in an increasing number of sectors, such as power generation, transportation, and intermediate-goods industries. The prolonged rapid increase in Chinese aggregate demand has been fueled by an investment boom, as well as a growing trade surplus.

Source: Brookings Institution, July 2, 2008

6. Is China experiencing demand-pull or cost-push inflation? Explain.

7. Draw a graph to illustrate the initial rise in the price level and the money wage rate response to a one-time rise in the price level.

8. Draw a graph to illustrate and explain how China might experience an inflation spiral.

Use the following news clip to work Problems 9 to 11.

Tight Money Won't Slay Food, Energy Inflation

It's important to differentiate between a general increase in prices—a situation in which aggregate demand exceeds their aggregate supply—and a relative price shock. For example, a specific shock to energy prices can become generalized if producers are able to pass on the higher costs. So far, global competition has made that difficult for companies, while higher input costs have largely been neutralized by rising labor productivity. Since 2003, core inflation has averaged less than 2 percent a year in the 30 major economies. History also suggests the Fed's gamble that slowing growth will shackle core inflation is a winning wager. The risk is that if U.S. consumers don't believe price increases will slow, growing inflation expectations may become self-fulfilling.

Source: *Bloomberg*, May 9, 2008

9. a. Explain the two types of inflation described in this news clip.

   b. Explain why "rising labor productivity" can neutralize the effect on inflation of "higher input costs."

10. Explain how "slowing growth" can reduce inflationary pressure.

11. Draw a graph to illustrate and explain how "growing inflation expectations may become self-fulfilling."

Inflation and Unemployment: The Phillips Curve

(Study Plan 29.2)

12. **Iran Postpones Cutting Gasoline Subsidies**

    Inflation is about 10 percent and the unemployment rate is about 14 percent. Earlier this month Iran's main audit body slammed the government's plan to scrap gasoline subsidies, warning that implementing such a reform might result in unrest. The government also intends to scrap subsidies on natural gas, which most Iranians use for cooking and heating, as well as electricity, but the new prices are still not known. However, in recent weeks some households have received electricity bills with nearly sevenfold price increases.

    Source: AFP, September 15, 2010

    a. If Iran removes the subsidies and consumers don't know what the higher prices will be, draw a graph to show the most likely path of inflation and unemployment.

    b. If Iran removes the subsidies and announces the new prices so that consumers know what they are, draw a graph to show the most likely path of inflation and unemployment.

13. **Recession? Maybe. Depression? Get Real.**

    The unemployment rate during the Great Depression peaked at nearly 25 percent in 1933, after an initial spike from 3 percent in 1929 to nearly 8.7 percent in 1930. The unemployment rate is just 5 percent, only up from 4.5 percent a year ago. Also during the Great Depression there was deflation, which is not happening today.

    Source: CNN, May 28, 2008

    a. Can the inflation and unemployment trends during the Great Depression be explained by a movement along a short-run Phillips curve?

    b. Can the inflation and unemployment trends during 2008 be explained by a movement along a short-run Phillips curve?

14. **From the Fed's Minutes**

    The Fed expects the unemployment rate will drop from 9.8 percent today to 9.25 percent by the end of 2010 and to 8 percent by the end of 2011. Private economists predict that the unemployment rate won't drop to a more normal 5 or 6 percent until 2013 or 2014. Inflation should stay subdued, but the Fed needs to keep its eye on inflation expectations.

    Source: *The New York Times*, October 14, 2009

    Is the Fed predicting that the U.S. economy will move rightward or leftward along a short-run Phillips curve or that the short-run Phillips curve will shift up or down through 2011?

The Business Cycle (Study Plan 29.3)

15. **Debate on Causes of Joblessness Grows**

    What is the cause of the high unemployment rate? One side says more government spending can reduce it. The other says its a structural problem—people who can't move to take new jobs because they are tied down to burdensome mortgages or firms that can't find workers with the requisite skills to fill job openings.

    Source: *The Wall Street Journal*, September 4, 2010

    Which business cycle theory would say that the rise in unemployment is cyclical? Which would say it is an increase in the natural rate? Why?

ADDITIONAL PROBLEMS AND APPLICATIONS

myeconlab You can work these problems in MyEconLab if assigned by your instructor.

Inflation Cycles

Use the following news clip to work Problems 16 and 17.

Bernanke Sees No Repeat of '70s-Style Inflation

There is little indication today of the beginnings of a 1970s-style wage-price spiral. Then, as now, a serious oil price shock occurred, but today's economy is more flexible in responding to difficulties and the country is more energy efficient than a generation ago, Bernanke said. Also, today the Fed monitors "inflation expectations." If people believe inflation will keep going up, they will change their behavior in ways that aggravate inflation—thus, a self-fulfilling prophecy. In the 1970s, people were demanding— and getting —higher wages in anticipation of rapidly rising prices; hence, the "wage-price" spiral Bernanke cited. The inflation rate has averaged about 3.5 percent over the past four quarters. That is "significantly higher" than the Fed would like but much less than the double-digit inflation rates of the mid-1970s and 1980, Bernanke said.

Source: *USA Today*, June 4, 2008

16. Draw a graph to illustrate and explain the inflation spiral that the U.S. experienced in the 1970s.

17. a. Explain the role that inflation expectations play in creating a self-fulfilling prophecy.

   b. Explain Bernanke's predictions about the impact of the 2008 oil price shock as compared to the 1970s shock.

Inflation and Unemployment: The Phillips Curve

Use the following information to work Problems 18 and 19.

The Reserve Bank of New Zealand signed an agreement with the New Zealand government in which the Bank agreed to maintain inflation inside a low target range. Failure to achieve the target would result in the governor of the Bank (the equivalent of the chairman of the Fed) losing his job.

18. Explain how this arrangement might have influenced New Zealand's short-run Phillips curve.

19. Explain how this arrangement might have influenced New Zealand's long-run Phillips curve.

Use the following information to work Problems 20 and 21.

An economy has an unemployment rate of 4 percent and an inflation rate of 5 percent a year at point A in the figure.

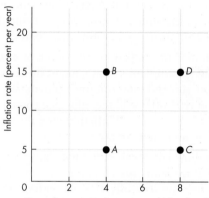

Some events occur that move the economy in a clockwise loop from A to B to D to C and back to A.

20. Describe the events that could create this sequence. Has the economy experienced demand-pull inflation, cost-push inflation, expected inflation, or none of these?

21. Draw in the figure the sequence of the economy's short-run and long-run Phillips curves.

Use the following news clip to work Problems 22 and 23.

Fed Pause Promises Financial Disaster

The indication is that inflationary expectations have become entrenched and strongly rooted in world markets. As a result, the risk of global stagflation has become significant. A drawn-out inflationary process always precedes stagflation, anathema to the so-called Phillips Curve. Following the attritional effect of inflation, the economy starts to grow below its potential. It experiences a persistent output gap, rising unemployment, and increasingly entrenched inflationary expectations.

Source: *Asia Times Online*, May 20, 2008

22. Evaluate the claim that stagflation is anathema to the Phillips curve.

23. Evaluate the claim made in this article that if "inflationary expectations" become strongly

"entrenched" an economy will experience "a persistent output gap."

Use the following information to work Problems 24 and 25.

Because the Fed doubled the monetary base in 2008 and the government spent billions of dollars bailing out troubled banks, insurance companies, and auto producers, some people are concerned that a serious upturn in the inflation rate will occur, not immediately but in a few years' time. At the same time, massive changes in the global economy might bring the need for structural change in the United States.

24. Explain how the Fed's doubling of the monetary base and government bailouts might influence the short-run and long-run unemployment–inflation tradeoffs. Will the influence come from changes in the expected inflation rate, the natural unemployment rate, or both?

25. Explain how large-scale structural change might influence the short-run and long-run unemployment–inflation tradeoffs. Will the influence come from changes in the expected inflation rate, the natural unemployment rate, or both?

The Business Cycle

Use the following information to work Problems 26 to 28.

Suppose that the business cycle in the United States is best described by RBC theory and that a new technology increases productivity.

26. Draw a graph to show the effect of the new technology in the market for loanable funds.

27. Draw a graph to show the effect of the new technology in the labor market.

28. Explain the when-to-work decision when technology advances.

29. **Real Wages Fail to Match a Rise in Productivity**

For most of the last century, wages and productivity—the key measure of the economy's efficiency—have risen together, increasing rapidly through the 1950s and '60s and far more slowly in the 1970s and '80s. But in recent years, the productivity gains have continued while the pay increases have not kept up.

Source: *The New York Times*, August 28, 2006

Explain the relationship between wages and productivity in this news clip in terms of real business cycle theory.

Economics in the News

30. After you have studied *Reading Between the Lines* on pp. 716–717 answer the following questions.

a. What are the main features of U.S. inflation and unemployment since 1950 that brought fluctuations in the misery index?

b. When the misery index was at its peak in 1980, did inflation or unemployment contribute most to the high index?

c. Do you think the U.S. economy had a recessionary gap or an inflationary gap or no gap in 1980? How might you be able to tell?

d. Use the *AS-AD* model to show the changes in aggregate demand and aggregate supply that are consistent with the rise of the misery index to its peak in June 1980.

e. Use the *AS-AD* model to show the changes in aggregate demand and aggregate supply that are consistent with the rise of the misery index since President Obama assumed office.

31. **Germany Leads Slowdown in Eurozone**

The pace of German economic growth has weakened "markedly," but the reason is the weaker global prospects. Although German policymakers worry about the country's exposure to a fall in demand for its export goods, evidence is growing that the recovery is broadening with real wage rates rising and unemployment falling, which will lead into stronger consumer spending.

Source: *The Financial Times*, September 23, 2010

a. How does "exposure to a fall in demand for its export goods" influence Germany's aggregate demand, aggregate supply, unemployment, and inflation?

b. Use the *AS-AD* model to illustrate your answer to part (a).

c. Use the Phillips curve model to illustrate your answer to part (a).

d. What do you think the news clip means by "the recovery is broadening with real wage rates rising and unemployment falling, which will lead into stronger consumer spending"?

e. Use the *AS-AD* model to illustrate your answer to part (d).

f. Use the Phillips curve model to illustrate your answer to part (d).

Boom and Bust

PART NINE

To cure a disease, doctors must first understand how the disease responds to different treatments. It helps to understand the mechanisms that operate to cause the disease, but sometimes a workable cure can be found even before the full story of the causes has been told.

Curing economic ills is similar to curing our medical ills. We need to understand how the economy responds to the treatments we might prescribe for it. And sometimes, we want to try a cure even though we don't fully understand the reasons for the problem we're trying to control.

You've seen how the pace of capital accumulation and technological change determine the long-term growth trend. You've learned how fluctuations around the long-term trend can be generated by changes in aggregate demand and aggregate supply. And you've learned about the key sources of fluctuations in aggregate demand and aggregate supply.

The *AS-AD* model explains the forces that determine real GDP and the price level in the short run. The model also enables us to see the big picture or grand vision of the different schools of macroeconomic thought concerning the sources of aggregate fluctuations. The Keynesian aggregate expenditure model provides an account of the factors that determine aggregate demand and make it fluctuate.

An alternative real business cycle theory puts all the emphasis on fluctuations in long-run aggregate supply. According to this theory, money changes aggregate demand and the price level but leaves the real economy untouched. The events of 2008 and 2009 will provide a powerful test of this theory.

John Maynard Keynes, *born in England in 1883, was one of the outstanding minds of the twentieth century. He represented Britain at the Versailles peace conference at the end of World War I, was a master speculator on international financial markets (an activity he conducted from bed every morning and which made and lost him several fortunes), and played a prominent role in creating the International Monetary Fund.*

He was a member of the Bloomsbury Group, a circle of outstanding artists and writers that included E. M. Forster, Bertrand Russell, and Virginia Woolf.

Keynes was a controversial and quick-witted figure. A critic once complained that Keynes had changed his opinion on some matter, to which Keynes retorted: "When I discover I am wrong, I change my mind. What do you do?"

Keynes' book, The General Theory of Employment, Interest and Money, *written during the Great Depression and published in 1936, revolutionanized macroeconomics.*

"The ideas of economists and political philosophers, both when they are right and when they are wrong, are more powerful than is commonly understood. Indeed the world is ruled by little else."

JOHN MAYNARD KEYNES
The General Theory of Employment, Interest and Money

Professor Caballero, why did you decide to become an economist?

Did I decide? I'm convinced that one is either born an economist or not. I began studying business, but as soon as I took the first course in economics, I was captivated by the simple but elegant logic of (good) economic reasoning. Given the complexity of the real world, economic analysis is necessarily abstract. But at the same time, economics is mostly about concrete and important issues that affect the lives of millions of people. Abstraction and relevance—this is a wonderful but strange combination. Not everybody feels comfortable with it, but if you do, economics is for you.

Most of your work has been on business cycles and other high-frequency phenomena. Can we begin by reviewing the costs of recessions? Robert Lucas says that postwar U.S. recessions have cost very little. Do you agree?

No . . . but I'm not sure Robert Lucas was really trying to say that. My sense is that he was trying to push the profession to focus a bit more on long-run growth issues. Putting down the costs of recessions was a useful debating device to make his important point.

I believe that the statement that recessions are not costly is incorrect. First, I think his calculation of this magnitude reflects some fundamental flaw in the way the workhorse models we use in economics fail to account for the costs of risk and volatility. This flaw shows up in many different puzzles in economics, including the well-known equity premium puzzle. Economic models underestimate, by an order of magnitude, how unhappy agents are about facing uncertainty. Second, it is highly unlikely that recessions and medium-term growth are completely separable. In particular, the ongoing process of restructuring, which is central to productivity growth, is severely hampered by deep recessions.

Recessions are costly because they waste enormous resources, affect physical and human investment decisions, have large negative distributional consequences, influence political outcomes, and so on.

What about the costs of recessions in other parts of the world, especially Latin America?

The cost of recessions grows exponentially with their size and the country's inability to soften the impact on the most affected. Less developed economies suffer much larger shocks because their economies are not

well diversified, and they experience capital outflows that exacerbate the impact of recessionary shocks. Their domestic financial sectors are small and often become strained during recessions, making it difficult to reallocate scarce resources toward those who need them the most. To make matters worse, the government's ability to use fiscal policy becomes impaired by the capital outflows, and monetary policy is also out of the question when the currency is in free fall and liabilities are dollarized. There are many things that we take for granted in the United States that simply are not feasible for emerging markets in distress. One has to be careful with extrapolating too directly the countercyclical recipes used for developed economies to these countries.

> Recessions are costly because they waste enormous resources [and] affect physical and human investment decisions.

Your first work, in your M.A. dissertation, was to build a macroeconomic model of the economy of Chile. What do we learn by comparing economies? Does the Chilean economy behave essentially like the U.S. economy or are there fundamental differences?

RICARDO J. CABALLERO is Ford Professor of International Economics at MIT. He has received many honors, the most notable of which are the Frisch Medal of the Econometric Society (2002) and being named Chile's Economist of the Year (2001). A highly regarded teacher, he is much sought as a special lecturer and in 2005 gave the prestigious Yrjo Jahnsson Lecture at the University of Helsinki.

Professor Caballero earned his B.S. degree in 1982 and M.A. in 1983 at Pontificia Universidad Católica de Chile. He then moved to the United States and obtained his Ph.D. at MIT in 1988.

Michael Parkin talked with Ricardo Caballero about his work and the progress that economists have made in understanding economic fluctuations.

Chile is a special economy among emerging markets. It began pro-market reforms many years before the rest and has had very prudent macroeconomic management for several decades by now. For that reason, it is a bit more "like the U.S. economy" than most other emerging market economies. However, there are still important differences, of the sort described in my answer to the previous question.

Beyond the specifics of Chile, at some deep level, macroeconomic principles, and economic principles more generally, are the same everywhere. It is all about incentives, tradeoffs, effort, commitment, discipline, transparency, insurance, and so on. But different economies hurt in different places, and hence the practice of economics has plenty of diversity.

You've studied situations in which capital suddenly stops flowing into an economy from abroad. What are the lessons you've learned from this research?

First things first. I think we need to get used to the presence of speculative bubbles. The reason is that the world today has a massive shortage of financial assets that savers can use to store value. Because of this shortage, "artificial" assets are ready to emerge at all times. Specific bubbles come and go—from the NASDAQ, to real estate, to commodities—but the total is much more stable.

I do not think the distinction between bubbles and fundamentals is as clear-cut as people describe. Probably outside periods of liquidity crises, all assets have some bubble component in them. The question is how much.

You've studied situations in which capital suddenly stops flowing into an economy from abroad. What are the lessons you've learned from this research?

The most basic lesson for emerging markets is that capital flows are volatile. Sometimes they simply magnify domestic problems, but in many other cases, they are the direct source of volatility. However, the conclusion from this observation is not that capital flows should be limited, just as we do not close the banks in the United States to eliminate the possibility of bank runs. On the contrary, much of the volatility comes from insufficient integration with international capital markets, which makes emerging markets illiquid and the target of specialists and speculators. For the short and medium run, the main policy lesson is that sudden stops to the inflow of capital must be put at the center of macroeconomic policy design in emerging markets. This has deep implications for the design of monetary and fiscal policy, as well as for international reserves management practices and domestic financial markets regulation.

> **The most basic lesson for emerging markets is that capital flows are volatile.**

The U.S. current account deficit has been large and increasing for many years, and dollar debt levels around the world have increased. Do you see any danger in this process for either the United States or the rest of the world?

I believe the persistent current account deficits in the United States are not the result of an anomaly that, as such, must go away in a sudden crash, as the attractive to international private and public investors.

Absent major shocks, this process may still last for quite some time. But of course shocks do happen, and in that sense, leverage is dangerous. However, there isn't much we can or should do, short of implementing structural reforms around the world aimed at improving growth potential in some cases and domestic financial development in others.

You've suggested that an insatiable appetite for safe securities is the root cause of the global financial crisis and that governments must accept a larger responsibility for bearing risk arising from the financial system. Would you explain this idea?

Foreign central banks and investors and U.S. financial institutions have an insatiable demand for safe securities, which puts enormous pressure on the U.S. financial system. The global financial crisis was the result of an interaction between the initial tremors caused by the rise in subprime mortgage defaults and securities created from these mortgages to feed the demand for safe-assets.

By 2001, the demand for safe assets began to exceed their supply, and financial institutions searched for ways to create safe assets from previously untapped and riskier ones. Subprime mortgage borrowers were a source of raw material. To convert risky mortgages (and other risky assets, ranging from auto loans to student loans) into safe assets, "banks" created complex securities made from large numbers of risky mortgages broken into tiers of increasing risk.

> By 2001, the demand for safe assets began to exceed their supply . . .

How did these new complex securities get out of control and lead to the real estate bubble and financial crisis?

A positive feedback loop was created: Supplied with safe assets, funds flowed into banks to finance real estate purchases financed by mortgages. Real estate prices rose rapidly, which reinforced the belief that the securities created from mortgages were indeed safe. But for the banking system and economy, the new-found source of "safe" assets was not safe at all. Combining a large number of risky mortgages to create a safe security works if the risk of default by the initial borrower is uncorrelated with that of others. But in the environment of 2007, the risks were highly correlated. There was one source of default—generally falling home prices.

The triggering event was the crash in the real estate "bubble" and the rise in subprime mortgage defaults that followed it. But this cannot be all of it.

The global financial system went into cardiac arrest in response to a relatively small shock which was well within the range of possible scenarios. The real damage came from the unexpected and sudden freezing of the entire securitization industry. Almost instantaneously, confidence vanished and the complexity which made possible the "multiplication of bread" during the boom, turned into a source of counterparty risk, both real and imaginary. Fear fed into more fear, causing reluctance to engage in financial transactions, even among the prime financial institutions. Safe interest rates plummeted to record low levels.

Addressing these issues requires governments to explicitly bear a greater share of systemic risk. There are two prongs within this approach. The first prong is for the countries that demand safe financial assets to rebalance their portfolios toward riskier assets. The second prong is for governments in countries that produce safe assets to provide a greater share of risk-bearing. There are many detailed ways in which this might be done.

What advice do you have for someone who is just beginning to study economics but who wants to become an economist? If they are not in the United States, should they come here for graduate work as you did?

There is no other place in the world like the United States to pursue a Ph.D. and do research in economics. However, this is only the last stage in the process of becoming an economist. There are many superb economists, especially applied ones, all around the world.

> Almost everything in life has an economic angle to it—look for it . . .

I believe the most important step is to learn to think like an economist. I heard Milton Friedman say that he knows many economists who have never gone through a Ph.D. program, and equally many who have completed their Ph.D. but are not really economists. I agree with him on this one. A good undergraduate program and talking about economics is a great first step. Almost everything in life has an economic angle to it—look for it and discuss it with your friends. It will not improve your social life, but it will make you a better economist.

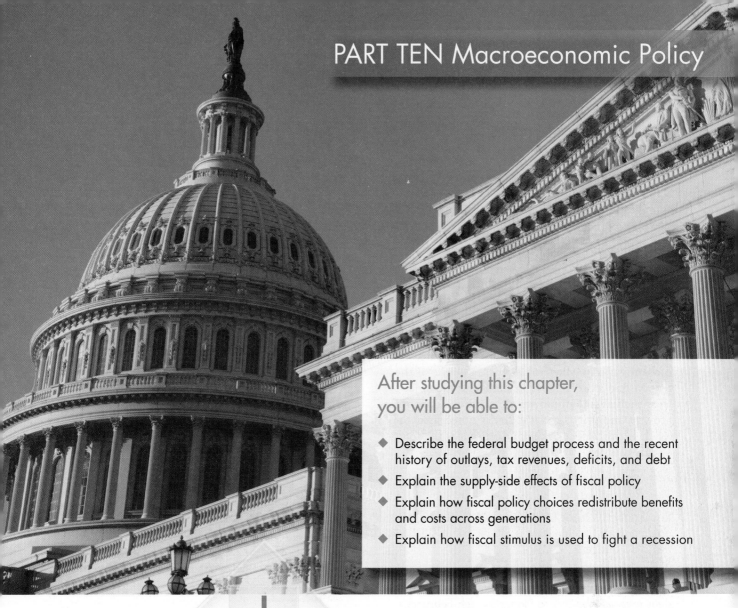

After studying this chapter,
you will be able to:

◆ Describe the federal budget process and the recent history of outlays, tax revenues, deficits, and debt

◆ Explain the supply-side effects of fiscal policy

◆ Explain how fiscal policy choices redistribute benefits and costs across generations

◆ Explain how fiscal stimulus is used to fight a recession

30

FISCAL POLICY

In 2010, the federal government spent 28 cents of every dollar that Americans earned. It raised 16 of those cents in taxes and borrowed the other 12. The government had a deficit of 12 cents on every dollar earned and a total deficit of $1.5 trillion. The 2010 deficit was exceptionally large, but federal government deficits are not new. Aside from the four years 1998–2001, the government's budget has been in deficit every year since 1970. Deficits bring debts, and your share of the federal government's debt is around $40,000.

Does it matter if the government doesn't balance its books? What are the effects of an ongoing government deficit and accumulating debt? Do they slow economic growth? Do they impose a burden on future generations—on you and your children?

What are the effects of taxes and government spending on the economy? Does a dollar spent by the government on goods and services have the same effect as a dollar spent by someone else? Does it create jobs, or does it destroy them?

These are the fiscal policy issues that you will study in this chapter. In *Reading Between the Lines* at the end of the chapter, we look at fiscal policy ideas to create jobs and boost real GDP in 2010.

◆ The Federal Budget

The **federal budget** is an annual statement of the outlays and receipts of the government of the United States together with the laws and regulations that approve and support them. The federal budget has two purposes:

1. To finance federal government programs and activities, and
2. To achieve macroeconomic objectives

The first purpose of the federal budget was its only purpose before the Great Depression of the 1930s. The second purpose arose as a reaction to the Great Depression and the rise of the ideas of economist John Maynard Keynes. The use of the federal budget to achieve macroeconomic objectives such as full employment, sustained economic growth, and price level stability is called **fiscal policy**. It is this aspect of the budget that is the focus of this chapter.

The Institutions and Laws

Fiscal policy is made by the president and Congress on an annual timeline that is shown in Fig. 30.1 for the 2011 budget.

The Roles of the President and Congress The president *proposes* a budget to Congress each February. Congress debates the proposed budget and passes the budget acts in September. The president either signs those acts into law or vetoes the *entire* budget bill. The president does not have the veto power to eliminate specific items in a budget bill and approve others—known as a *line-item veto*. Many state governors have long had line-item veto authority. Congress attempted to grant these powers to the president of the United States in 1996, but in a 1998 Supreme Court ruling, the line-item veto for the president was declared unconstitutional. Although the president proposes and ultimately approves the budget, the task of making the tough decisions on spending and taxes rests with Congress.

Congress begins its work on the budget with the president's proposal. The House of Representatives and the Senate develop their own budget ideas in their respective House and Senate Budget Committees. Formal conferences between the two houses eventually resolve differences of view, and a series of spend-

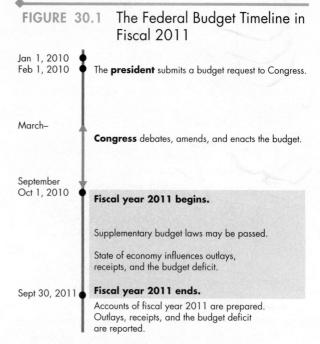

FIGURE 30.1   The Federal Budget Timeline in Fiscal 2011

Jan 1, 2010 / Feb 1, 2010 — The **president** submits a budget request to Congress.

March– — **Congress** debates, amends, and enacts the budget.

September / Oct 1, 2010 — **Fiscal year 2011 begins.**

Supplementary budget laws may be passed.

State of economy influences outlays, receipts, and the budget deficit.

Sept 30, 2011 — **Fiscal year 2011 ends.**

Accounts of fiscal year 2011 are prepared. Outlays, receipts, and the budget deficit are reported.

The federal budget process begins with the president's request in February. Congress debates and amends the request and enacts a budget before the start of the fiscal year on October 1. The president signs the budget acts into law or vetoes the entire budget bill. Throughout the fiscal year, Congress might pass supplementary budget laws. The budget outcome is calculated after the end of the fiscal year.

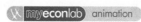
myeconlab   animation

ing acts and an overall budget act are usually passed by both houses before the start of the fiscal year. A *fiscal year* is a year that runs from October 1 to September 30 in the next calendar year. *Fiscal* 2011 is the fiscal year that *begins* on October 1, 2010.

During a fiscal year, Congress often passes supplementary budget laws, and the budget outcome is influenced by the evolving state of the economy. For example, if a recession begins, tax revenues fall and welfare payments increase.

The Employment Act of 1946 Fiscal policy operates within the framework of the landmark **Employment Act of 1946** in which Congress declared that

> . . . it is the continuing policy and responsibility of the Federal Government to use all practicable means . . . to coordinate and utilize all its plans, functions, and resources . . . to promote maximum employment, production, and purchasing power.

This act recognized a role for government actions to keep unemployment low, the economy expanding, and inflation in check. The *Full Employment and Balanced Growth Act of 1978*, more commonly known as the *Humphrey-Hawkins Act*, went farther than the Employment Act of 1946 and set a specific target of 4 percent for the unemployment rate. But this target has never been treated as an unwavering policy goal. Under the 1946 act, the president must describe the current economic situation and the policies he believes are needed in the annual *Economic Report of the President*, which the Council of Economic Advisers writes.

The Council of Economic Advisers The president's Council of Economic Advisers was established in the Employment Act of 1946. The Council consists of a chairperson and two other members, all of whom are economists on a one- or two-year leave from their regular university or public service jobs. In 2010, the chair of President Obama's Council of Economic Advisers was Austan Goolsbee of the University of Chicago. The **Council of Economic Advisers** monitors the economy and keeps the President and the public well informed about the current state of the economy and the best available forecasts of where it is heading. This economic intelligence activity is one source of data that informs the budget-making process.

Let's look at the most recent federal budget.

Highlights of the 2011 Budget

Table 30.1 shows the main items in the federal budget proposed by President Obama for 2011. The numbers are projected amounts for the fiscal year beginning on October 1, 2010—fiscal 2011. Notice the three main parts of the table: *Receipts* are the government's tax revenues, *outlays* are the government's payments, and the *deficit* is the amount by which the government's outlays exceed its receipts.

Receipts Receipts were projected to be $2,807 billion in fiscal 2011. These receipts come from four sources:

1. Personal income taxes
2. Social Security taxes
3. Corporate income taxes
4. Indirect taxes and other receipts

The largest source of receipts is *personal income taxes*, which in 2011 are expected to be $1,076 bil-

lion. These taxes are paid by individuals on their incomes. The second largest source is *Social Security taxes*. These taxes are paid by workers and their employers to finance the government's Social Security programs. Third in size are *corporate income taxes*. These taxes are paid by companies on their profits. Finally, the smallest source of federal receipts is what are called *indirect taxes*. These taxes are on the sale of gasoline, alcoholic beverages, and a few other items.

Outlays Outlays are classified into three categories:

1. Transfer payments
2. Expenditure on goods and services
3. Debt interest

The largest item of outlays, *transfer payments*, is the payment to individuals, businesses, other levels of government, and the rest of the world. In 2011, this item is expected to be $2,588 billion. It includes Social Security benefits, Medicare and Medicaid, unemployment checks, welfare payments, farm subsidies, grants to state and local governments, and payments to international agencies. It also includes capital transfers to bail out failing financial institutions. Transfer payments, especially those for Medicare and Medicaid, are sources of persistent growth in

TABLE 30.1   Federal Budget in Fiscal 2011

Item	Projections (billions of dollars)
Receipts	**2,807**
Personal income taxes	1,076
Social Security taxes	1,054
Corporate income taxes	432
Indirect taxes and other receipts	245
Outlays	**4,129**
Transfer payments	2,588
Expenditure on goods and services	1,181
Debt interest	360
Deficit	**1,322**

Source of data: Budget of the United States Government, Fiscal Year 2011, Table 14.1.

government expenditures and are a major source of concern and political debate.

Expenditure on goods and services is the expenditure on final goods and services, and in 2011, it is expected to total $1,181 billion. This expenditure, which includes that on national defense, homeland security, research on cures for AIDS, computers for the Internal Revenue Service, government cars and trucks, and federal highways, has decreased in recent years. This component of the federal budget is the *government expenditure on goods and services* that appears in the circular flow of expenditure and income and in the National Income and Product Accounts (see Chapter 21, pp. 491–492).

Debt interest is the interest on the government debt. In 2011, this item is expected to be $360 billion—about 9 percent of total expenditure. This interest payment is large because the government has a debt of more than $6 trillion, which has arisen from many years of budget deficits during the 1970s, 1980s, 1990s, and 2000s.

Surplus or Deficit　The government's budget balance is equal to receipts minus outlays.

$$\text{Budget balance} = \text{Receipts} - \text{Outlays}.$$

If receipts exceed outlays, the government has a **budget surplus**. If outlays exceed receipts, the government has a **budget deficit**. If receipts equal outlays, the government has a **balanced budget**. For fiscal 2011, with projected outlays of $4,129 billion and receipts of $2,807 billion, the government projected a budget deficit of $1,322 billion.

Big numbers like these are hard to visualize and hard to compare over time. To get a better sense of the magnitude of receipts, outlays, and the deficit, we often express them as percentages of GDP. Expressing them in this way lets us see how large government is relative to the size of the economy and also helps us to study *changes* in the scale of government over time.

How typical is the federal budget of 2011? Let's look at the recent history of the budget.

The Budget in Historical Perspective

Figure 30.2 shows the government's receipts, outlays, and budget surplus or deficit since 1980. You can see that except for the four years around 2000, the budget has been in persistent deficit.

You can also see that after 2008, the deficit was extraordinarily large, peaking in 2010 at almost 12 percent of GDP. The next highest deficit had been in 1983 at 6 percent of GDP.

The large deficit of the 1980s gradually shrank through 1990s expansion and in 1998 the first budget

---

FIGURE 30.2　The Budget Surplus and Deficit

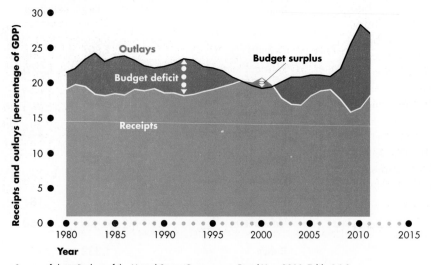

The figure records the federal government's outlays, receipts, and budget balance from 1980 to 2011. Except for the four years 1998 through 2001, the budget has been in deficit. The deficit after 2008 reached a new all-time high and occurred because outlays increased. Receipts have fluctuated but have displayed no trend (as a percentage of GDP).

Source of data: Budget of the United States Government, Fiscal Year 2011, Table 14.2.

myeconlab　animation

surplus since 1969 emerged. But by 2002, the budget was again in deficit and during the 2008–2009 recession, the deficit reached a new all-time high.

Why did the budget deficit grow during the 1980s, vanish in the late 1990s, and re-emerge in the 2000s? Did outlays increase, or did receipts shrink, and which components of outlays and receipts changed most to swell and then shrink the deficit? Let's look at receipts and outlays in a bit more detail.

Receipts Figure 30.3(a) shows the components of government receipts as percentages of GDP from 1980 to 2011. Total receipts fluctuate because personal income taxes and corporate income taxes fluctuate. Other receipts (Social Security taxes and indirect taxes) are a near constant percentage of GDP.

Income tax receipts trended downward during the early 1980s and 2000s, upward during the 1990s, and slightly downward over the 30 years to 2010.

FIGURE 30.3   Federal Government Receipts and Outlays

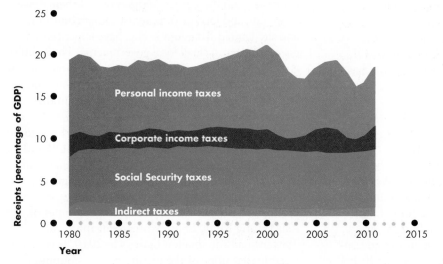

(a) Receipts

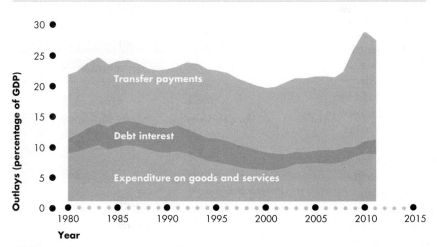

(b) Outlays

In part (a), receipts from personal and corporate income taxes (as a percentage of GDP) fell during the early1980s, increased during the 1990s, and fluctuated wildly during the 2000s. The other components of receipts remained steady. Over the entire period, receipts fell slightly.

In part (b), expenditure on goods and services as a percentage of GDP decreased through 2001 but then increased because expenditure on security-related goods and services increased sharply after 2001. Transfer payments increased over the entire period and exploded to a new all-time high percentage of GDP after 2008. Debt interest held steady during the 1980s and decreased during the 1990s and 2000s, helped by a shrinking budget deficit during the 1990s and low interest rates after 2008.

Source of data: Budget of the United States Government, Fiscal Year 2011, Table 14.2.

Outlays Figure 30.3(b) shows the components of government outlays as percentages of GDP from 1980 to 2011. Two features of government outlays stand out. First, expenditure on goods and services decreased from 1983 through 2000 and then increased. The increase after 2000 was mainly on security-related goods and services in the wake of the attacks that occurred on September 11, 2001, and defense expenditure. Second, transfer payments increased over the entire period and exploded after 2008 when the government tried to stimulate economic activity.

You've seen that the U.S. government budget deficit is large. But how does it compare to the deficits of other countries? The answer is that it is one of the largest, as *Economics in Action* shows. Of the major economies, only the United Kingdom has a larger deficit as a percentage of GDP.

Deficits bring debts, as you will now see.

Budget Balance and Debt

When the government has a budget deficit it borrows, and when it has a budget surplus it makes loan repayments. **Government debt** is the total amount that the government has borrowed. It is the sum of past budget deficits minus the sum of past budget surpluses. A government budget deficit increases government debt. A persistent budget deficit feeds itself: It leads to increased borrowing, which leads to larger interest payments, which in turn lead to a larger deficit. That is the story of the increasing budget deficit during the 1970s and 1980s.

Figure 30.4 shows two measures of government debt since 1940. Gross debt includes the amounts that the government owes to future generations in Social Security payments. Net debt is the debt held by the public, and it excludes Social Security obligations.

Government debt (as a percentage of GDP) was at an all-time high at the end of World War II. Budget surpluses and rapid economic growth lowered the debt-to-GDP ratio through 1974. Small budget deficits increased the debt-to-GDP ratio slightly through the 1970s, and large budget deficits increased it dramatically during the 1980s and the 1990–1991 recession. The growth rate of the debt-to-GDP ratio slowed as the economy expanded during the mid-1990s, fell when the budget went into surplus in the late 1990s and early 2000s, and began to rise again as the budget returned to deficit.

Economics in Action

The U.S. Government Budget in Global Perspective

The U.S. government budget deficit in Fiscal 2010 was projected to be 11.8 percent of GDP. You've seen that this deficit is historically high but how does it compare with the deficits of other countries?

To compare the deficits of governments across countries, we must take into account the differences in local and regional government arrangements. Some countries, and the United States is one of them, have large state and local governments. Other countries, and the United Kingdom is one, have larger central government and small local governments. These differences make the international comparison more valid at the level of total government. The figure shows the budget balances of all levels of government in the United States and other countries.

Of the countries shown here, the United Kingdom has the largest deficit, as a percentage of GDP, and the United States has the second largest. Japan and some European countries also have large deficits.

Italy, Canada, other advanced economies as a group, and the newly industrialized economies of Asia (Hong Kong, South Korea, Singapore, and Taiwan) had the smallest deficits in 2010. It is notable that none of the world's major economies had a budget surplus in 2010. Fiscal stimulus to fight recession resulted in deficits everywhere.

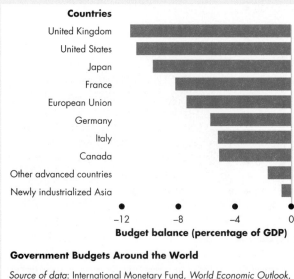

Government Budgets Around the World

Source of data: International Monetary Fund, *World Economic Outlook*, April 2010.

FIGURE 30.4   The Federal Government Debt

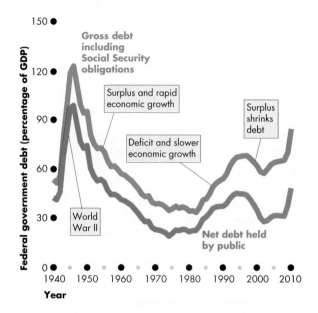

Gross and net government debt (the accumulation of past budget deficits less past budget surpluses) was at its highest at the end of World War II. Debt as a percentage of GDP fell through 1974 but then started to increase. After a further brief decline during the late 1970s, it exploded during the 1980s and continued to increase through 1995, after which it fell. After 2002, it began to rise again.

Source of data: Budget of the United States Government, Fiscal Year 2011, Table 7.1.

 myeconlab animation

Debt and Capital

Businesses and individuals incur debts to buy capital—assets that yield a return. In fact, the main point of debt is to enable people to buy assets that will earn a return that exceeds the interest paid on the debt. The government is similar to individuals and businesses in this regard. Much government expenditure is on public assets that yield a return. Highways, public schools and universities, and the stock of national defense capital all yield a social rate of return that probably far exceeds the interest rate the government pays on its debt.

But total government debt, which exceeds $4 trillion, is four times the value of the government's capital stock. So some government debt has been incurred to finance public consumption expenditure and transfer payments, which do not have a social return. Future generations bear the cost of this debt.

State and Local Budgets

The *total government* sector of the United States includes state and local governments as well as the federal government. In 2010, when federal government outlays were $4,129 billion, state and local outlays were a further $2,000 billion. Most of these expenditures were on public schools, colleges, and universities ($550 billion); local police and fire services; and roads.

It is the combination of federal, state, and local government receipts, outlays, and budget deficits that influences the economy. But state and local budgets are not designed to stabilize the aggregate economy. So sometimes, when the federal government cuts taxes or outlays, state and local governments do the reverse and, to a degree, cancel out the effects of the federal actions. For example, since 2000, federal taxes decreased as a percentage of GDP, but state and local taxes and total government taxes increased.

REVIEW QUIZ

1 What is fiscal policy, who makes it, and what is it designed to influence?
2 What special role does the president play in creating fiscal policy?
3 What special roles do the Budget Committees of the House of Representatives and the Senate play in creating fiscal policy?
4 What is the timeline for the U.S. federal budget each year? When does a fiscal year begin and end?
5 Is the federal government budget today in surplus or deficit?

You can work these questions in Study Plan 30.1 and get instant feedback.    myeconlab

Now that you know what the federal budget is and what the main components of receipts and outlays are, it is time to study the *effects* of fiscal policy. We'll begin by learning about the effects of taxes on employment, aggregate supply, and potential GDP. Then we'll study the effects of budget deficits and see how fiscal policy brings redistribution across generations. Finally, we'll look at fiscal stimulus and see how it might be used to speed recovery from recession and stabilize the business cycle.

Supply-Side Effects of Fiscal Policy

How do taxes on personal and corporate income affect real GDP and employment? The answer to these questions is controversial. Some economists, known as *supply-siders*, believe these effects to be large and an accumulating body of evidence suggests that they are correct. To see why these effects might be large, we'll begin with a refresher on how full employment and potential GDP are determined in the absence of taxes. Then we'll introduce an income tax and see how it changes the economic outcome.

Full Employment and Potential GDP

You learned in Chapter 23 (pp. 545–547) how the full-employment quantity of labor and potential GDP are determined. At full employment, the real wage rate adjusts to make the quantity of labor demanded equal the quantity of labor supplied. Potential GDP is the real GDP that the full-employment quantity of labor produces.

Figure 30.5 illustrates a full-employment situation. In part (a), the demand for labor curve is *LD*, and the supply of labor curve is *LS*. At a real wage rate of $30 an hour and 250 billion hours of labor a year employed, the economy is at full employment.

In Fig. 30.5(b), the production function is *PF*. When 250 billion hours of labor are employed, real GDP—which is also potential GDP—is $13 trillion.

Let's now see how an income tax changes potential GDP.

The Effects of the Income Tax

The tax on labor income influences potential GDP and aggregate supply by changing the full-employment quantity of labor. The income tax weakens the incentive to work and drives a wedge between the take-home wage of workers and the cost of labor to firms. The result is a smaller quantity of labor and a lower potential GDP.

Figure 30.5 shows this outcome. In the labor market, the income tax has no effect on the demand for labor, which remains at *LD*. The reason is that the quantity of labor that firms plan to hire depends only on how productive labor is and what it costs—its real wage rate.

FIGURE 30.5   The Effects of the Income Tax on Aggregate Supply

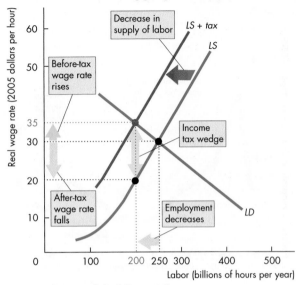

(a) Income tax and the labor market

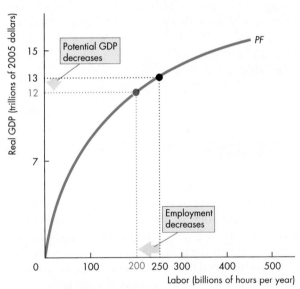

(b) Income tax and potential GDP

In part (a), with no income tax, the real wage rate is $30 an hour and employment is 250 billion hours. In part (b), potential GDP is $13 trillion. An income tax shifts the supply of labor curve leftward to *LS + tax*. The before-tax wage rate rises to $35 an hour, the after-tax wage rate falls to $20 an hour, and the quantity of labor employed decreases to 200 billion hours. With less labor, potential GDP decreases.

myeconlab   animation

But the supply of labor *does* change. With no income tax, the real wage rate is $30 an hour and 250 billion hours of labor a year are employed. An income tax weakens the incentive to work and decreases the supply of labor. The reason is that for each dollar of before-tax earnings, workers must pay the government an amount determined by the income tax code. So workers look at the after-tax wage rate when they decide how much labor to supply. An income tax shifts the supply curve leftward to *LS + tax*. The vertical distance between the *LS* curve and the *LS + tax* curve measures the amount of income tax. With the smaller supply of labor, the *before-tax* wage rate rises to $35 an hour but the *after-tax* wage rate falls to $20 an hour. The gap created between the before-tax and after-tax wage rates is called the **tax wedge**.

The new equilibrium quantity of labor employed is 200 billion hours a year—less than in the no-tax case. Because the full-employment quantity of labor decreases, so does potential GDP. And a decrease in potential GDP decreases aggregate supply.

In this example, the tax rate is high—$15 tax on a $35 wage rate is a tax rate of about 43 percent. A lower tax rate would have a smaller effect on employment and potential GDP.

An increase in the tax rate to above 43 percent would decrease the supply of labor by more than the decrease shown in Fig. 30.5. Equilibrium employment and potential GDP would also decrease still further. A tax cut would increase the supply of labor, increase equilibrium employment, and increase potential GDP.

Taxes on Expenditure and the Tax Wedge

The tax wedge that we've just considered is only a part of the wedge that affects labor-supply decisions. Taxes on consumption expenditure add to the wedge. The reason is that a tax on consumption raises the prices paid for consumption goods and services and is equivalent to a cut in the real wage rate.

The incentive to supply labor depends on the goods and services that an hour of labor can buy. The higher the taxes on goods and services and the lower the after-tax wage rate, the less is the incentive to supply labor. If the income tax rate is 25 percent and the tax rate on consumption expenditure is 10 percent, a dollar earned buys only 65 cents worth of goods and services. The tax wedge is 35 percent.

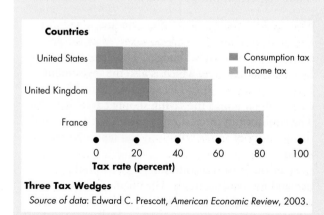

Taxes and the Incentive to Save and Invest

A tax on interest income weakens the incentive to save and drives a wedge between the after-tax interest rate earned by savers and the interest rate paid by firms. These effects are analogous to those of a tax on labor income. But they are more serious for two reasons.

First, a tax on labor income lowers the quantity of labor employed and lowers potential GDP, while a tax on capital income lowers the quantity of saving and investment and *slows the growth rate of real GDP*.

Second, the true tax rate on interest income is much higher than that on labor income because of the way in which inflation and taxes on interest income interact. Let's examine this interaction.

Effect of Tax Rate on Real Interest Rate

The interest rate that influences investment and saving plans is the *real after-tax interest rate*. The real *after-tax* interest rate subtracts the income tax rate paid on interest income from the real interest rate. But the taxes depend on the nominal interest rate, not the real interest rate. So the higher the inflation rate, the higher is the true tax rate on interest income. Here is an example. Suppose the real interest rate is 4 percent a year and the tax rate is 40 percent.

If there is no inflation, the nominal interest rate equals the real interest rate. The tax on 4 percent interest is 1.6 percent (40 percent of 4 percent), so the real after-tax interest rate is 4 percent minus 1.6 percent, which equals 2.4 percent.

If the inflation rate is 6 percent a year, the nominal interest rate is 10 percent. The tax on 10 percent interest is 4 percent (40 percent of 10 percent), so the real after-tax interest rate is 4 percent minus 4 percent, which equals zero. The true tax rate in this case is not 40 percent but 100 percent!

Effect of Income Tax on Saving and Investment

In Fig. 30.6, initially there are no taxes. Also, the government has a balanced budget. The demand for loanable funds curve, which is also the investment demand curve, is *DLF*. The supply of loanable funds curve, which is also the saving supply curve, is *SLF*. The equilibrium interest rate is 3 percent a year, and the quantity of funds borrowed and lent is $2 trillion a year.

A tax on interest income has no effect on the demand for loanable funds. The quantity of investment and borrowing that firms plan to undertake depends only on how productive capital is and what it costs—its

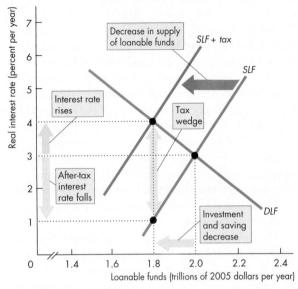

FIGURE 30.6   The Effects of a Tax on Capital Income

The demand for loanable funds and investment demand curve is *DLF*, and the supply of loanable funds and saving supply curve is *SLF*. With no income tax, the real interest rate is 3 percent a year and investment is $2 trillion. An income tax shifts the supply curve leftward to *SLF + tax*. The interest rate rises to 4 percent a year, the after-tax interest rate falls to 1 percent a year, and investment decreases to $1.8 trillion. With less investment, the real GDP growth rate decreases.

myeconlab   animation

real interest rate. But a tax on interest income weakens the incentive to save and lend and decreases the supply of loanable funds. For each dollar of before-tax interest, savers must pay the government an amount determined by the tax code. So savers look at the after-tax real interest rate when they decide how much to save.

When a tax is imposed, saving decreases and the supply of loanable funds curve shifts leftward to *SLF + tax*. The amount of tax payable is measured by the vertical distance between the *SLF* curve and the *SLF + tax* curve. With this smaller supply of loanable funds, the interest rate rises to 4 percent a year but the *after-tax* interest rate falls to 1 percent a year. A tax wedge is driven between the interest rate and the after-tax interest rate, and the equilibrium quantity of loanable funds decreases. Saving and investment also decrease.

Tax Revenues and the Laffer Curve

An interesting consequence of the effect of taxes on employment and saving is that a higher tax *rate* does not always bring greater tax *revenue*. A higher tax rate brings in more revenue per dollar earned. But because a higher tax rate decreases the number of dollars earned, two forces operate in opposite directions on the tax revenue collected.

The relationship between the tax rate and the amount of tax revenue collected is called the **Laffer curve**. The curve is so named because Arthur B. Laffer, a member of President Reagan's Economic Policy Advisory Board, drew such a curve on a table napkin and launched the idea that tax *cuts* could *increase* tax revenue.

Figure 30.7 shows a Laffer curve. The tax *rate* is on the *x*-axis, and total tax *revenue* is on the *y*-axis. For tax rates below T^*, an increase in the tax rate increases tax revenue; at T^*, tax revenue is maximized; and a tax rate increase above T^* decreases tax revenue.

Most people think that the United States is on the upward-sloping part of the Laffer curve; so is the United Kingdom. But France might be close to the maximum point or perhaps even beyond it.

The Supply-Side Debate

Before 1980, few economists paid attention to the supply-side effects of taxes on employment and potential GDP. Then, when Ronald Reagan took office as president, a group of supply-siders began to argue the virtues of cutting taxes. Arthur Laffer was one of them. Laffer and his supporters were not held in high esteem among mainstream economists, but they were influential for a period. They correctly argued that tax cuts would increase employment and increase output. But they incorrectly argued that tax cuts would increase tax revenues and decrease the budget deficit. For this prediction to be correct, the United States would have had to be on the "wrong" side of the Laffer curve. Given that U.S. tax rates are among the lowest in the industrial world, it is unlikely that this condition was met. And when the Reagan administration did cut taxes, the budget deficit increased, a fact that reinforces this view.

Supply-side economics became tarnished because of its association with Laffer and came to be called "voodoo economics." But mainstream economists, including Martin Feldstein, a Harvard professor who was Reagan's chief economic adviser, recognized the

FIGURE 30.7   A Laffer Curve

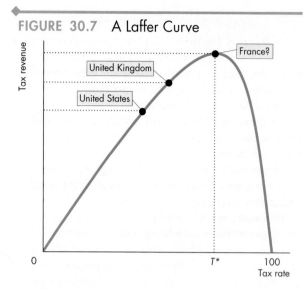

A Laffer curve shows the relationship between the tax rate and tax revenues. For tax rates below T^*, an increase in the tax rate increases tax revenue. At the tax rate T^*, tax revenue is maximized. For tax rates above T^*, an increase in the tax rate decreases tax revenue.

 animation

power of tax cuts as incentives but took the standard view that tax cuts without spending cuts would swell the budget deficit and bring serious further problems. This view is now widely accepted by economists of all political persuasions.

◢ REVIEW QUIZ

1 How does a tax on labor income influence the equilibrium quantity of employment?
2 How does the tax wedge influence potential GDP?
3 Why are consumption taxes relevant for measuring the tax wedge?
4 Why are income taxes on capital income more powerful than those on labor income?
5 What is the Laffer curve and why is it unlikely that the United States is on the "wrong" side of it?

You can work these questions in Study Plan 30.2 and get instant feedback.   myeconlab

You now know how taxes influence potential GDP and saving and investment. Next we look at the intergenerational effects of fiscal policy.

◆ Generational Effects of Fiscal Policy

Is a budget deficit a burden on future generations? If it is, how will the burden be borne? And is the budget deficit the only burden on future generations? What about the deficit in the Social Security fund? Does it matter who owns the bonds that the government sells to finance its deficit? What about the bonds owned by foreigners? Won't repaying those bonds impose a bigger burden than repaying bonds owned by Americans?

To answer questions like these, we use a tool called **generational accounting**—an accounting system that measures the lifetime tax burden and benefits of each generation. This accounting system was developed by Alan Auerbach of the University of Pennsylvania and Laurence Kotlikoff of Boston University. Generational accounts for the United States have been prepared by Jagadeesh Gokhale of the Cato Institute and Kent Smetters of the Wharton School at the University of Pennsylvania.

Generational Accounting and Present Value

Income taxes and Social Security taxes are paid by people who have jobs. Social Security benefits are paid to people after they retire. So to compare taxes and benefits, we must compare the value of taxes paid by people during their working years with the benefits received in their retirement years. To compare the value of an amount of money at one date with that at a later date, we use the concept of present value. A **present value** is an amount of money that, if invested today, will grow to equal a given future amount when the interest that it earns is taken into account. We can compare dollars today with dollars in 2030 or any other future year by using present values.

For example, if the interest rate is 5 percent a year, $1,000 invested today will grow, with interest, to $11,467 after 50 years. So the present value (in 2010) of $11,467 in 2060 is $1,000.

By using present values, we can assess the magnitude of the government's debts to older Americans in the form of pensions and medical benefits.

But the assumed interest rate and growth rate of taxes and benefits critically influence the answers we get. For example, at an interest rate of 3 percent a year, the present value (in 2010) of $11,467 in 2060

is $2,616. The lower the interest rate, the greater is the present value of a given future amount.

Because there is uncertainty about the proper interest rate to use to calculate present values, plausible alternative numbers are used to estimate a range of present values.

Using generational accounting and present values, economists have studied the situation facing the federal government arising from its Social Security obligations, and they have found a time bomb!

The Social Security Time Bomb

When Social Security was introduced in the New Deal of the 1930s, today's demographic situation was not foreseen. The age distribution of the U.S. population today is dominated by the surge in the birth rate after World War II that created what is called the "baby boom generation." There are 77 million "baby boomers."

The first of the baby boomers start collecting Social Security pensions in 2008 and in 2011 they became eligible for Medicare benefits. By 2030, all the baby boomers will have reached retirement age and the population supported by Social Security and Medicare benefits will have doubled.

Under the existing laws, the federal government has an obligation to this increasing number of citizens to pay pensions and Medicare benefits on an already declared scale. These obligations are a debt owed by the government and are just as real as the bonds that the government issues to finance its current budget deficit.

To assess the full extent of the government's obligations, economists use the concept of fiscal imbalance. **Fiscal imbalance** is the present value of the government's commitments to pay benefits minus the present value of its tax revenues. Fiscal imbalance is an attempt to measure the scale of the government's true liabilities.

Gokhale and Smetters estimated that the fiscal imbalance was $79 trillion in 2010. To put the $79 trillion in perspective, note that U.S. GDP in 2010 was $13.6 trillion. So the fiscal imbalance was 5.8 times the value of one year's production. And the fiscal imbalance grows every year by an amount that in 2010 was approaching $2 trillion.

These are enormous numbers and point to a catastrophic future. How can the federal government meet its Social Security obligations? Gokhale and Smetters consider four alternatives:

- Raise income taxes
- Raise Social Security taxes
- Cut Social Security benefits
- Cut federal government discretionary spending

They estimated that if we had started in 2003 and made only one of these changes, income taxes would need to be raised by 69 percent, or Social Security taxes raised by 95 percent, or Social Security benefits cut by 56 percent. Even if the government stopped all its discretionary spending, including that on national defense, it would not be able to pay its bills. By combining the four measures, the pain from each could be lessened, but the pain would still be severe.

A further way of meeting these obligations is to pay by printing money. As you learned in Chapter 25 (see pp. 606–607), the consequence of this solution would be a seriously high inflation rate.

Generational Imbalance

A fiscal imbalance must eventually be corrected and when it is, people either pay higher taxes or receive lower benefits. The concept of generational imbalance tells us who will pay. **Generational imbalance** is the division of the fiscal imbalance between the current and future generations, assuming that the current generation will enjoy the existing levels of taxes and benefits.

Figure 30.8 shows an estimate of how the fiscal imbalance is distributed across the current (born before 1988) and future (born in or after 1988) generations. It also shows that the major source of the imbalances is Medicare. Social Security pension benefits create a fiscal imbalance, but these benefits will be more than fully paid for by the current generation. But the current generation will pay less than 50 percent of its Medicare costs, and the balance will fall on future generations. If we sum all the items, the current generation will pay 43 percent and future generations will pay 57 percent of the fiscal imbalance.

Because the estimated fiscal imbalance is so large, it is not possible to predict how it will be resolved. But we can predict that the outcome will involve both lower benefits and higher taxes or paying bills with new money and creating inflation.

The Fed would have to cooperate if inflation were to be used to deal with the imbalance, and this cooperation might be hard to obtain.

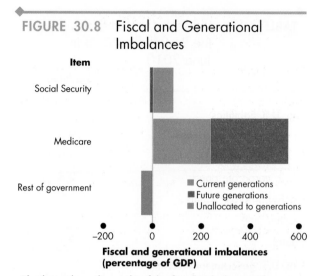

FIGURE 30.8   Fiscal and Generational Imbalances

The bars show the scale of the fiscal imbalance. The largest component at almost 600 percent of GDP is Medicare benefits. These benefits are also the main component of the generational imbalance. Social Security pensions are paid for entirely by the current generation.

Source of data: Jagadeesh Gokhale and Kent Smetters, "Fiscal and Generational Imbalances: An Update" *Tax Policy and the Economy*, Vol. 20, pp. 193-223, University of Chicago Press, 2006.

International Debt

So far in our discussion of government deficits and debts, we've ignored the role played by the rest of the world. We'll conclude this discussion by considering the role and magnitude of international debt.

You've seen that borrowing from the rest of the world is one source of loanable funds. And you've also seen that this source of funds became larger during the late 1990s and 2000s.

How large is the contribution of the rest of the world? How much business investment have we paid for by borrowing from the rest of the world? And how much U.S. government debt is held abroad?

Table 30.2 answers these questions. In June 2010, the United States had a net debt to the rest of the world of $9.5 trillion. Of that debt, $4.0 trillion was U.S. government debt. U.S. corporations had used $4.7 trillion of foreign funds ($2.4 trillion in bonds and $2.3 trillion in equities). About two thirds of U.S. government debt is held by foreigners.

The international debt of the United States is important because, when that debt is repaid, the United States will transfer real resources to the rest of

TABLE 30.2   What the United States Owed the Rest of the World in June 2010

	$ trillions
(a) U.S. liabilities	
Deposits in U.S. banks	0.6
U.S. government securities	4.0
U.S. corporate bonds	2.4
U.S. corporate equities	2.3
Other (net)	0.2
Total	**9.5**
(b) U.S. government securities	
Held by rest of world	4.0
Held in the United States	2.0
Total	**6.0**

Source of data: Federal Reserve Board.

the world. Instead of running a large net exports deficit, the United States will need a surplus of exports over imports. To make a surplus possible, U.S. saving must increase and consumption must decrease. Some tough choices lie ahead.

REVIEW QUIZ

1   What is a present value?
2   Distinguish between fiscal imbalance and generational imbalance.
3   How large was the estimated U.S. fiscal imbalance in 2010 and how did it divide between current and future generations?
4   What is the source of the U.S. fiscal imbalance and what are the painful choices that we face?
5   How much of U.S. government debt is held by the rest of the world?

You can work these questions in Study Plan 30.3 and get instant feedback.

You now know how the supply-side effects of fiscal policy work and you've seen the shocking scale of fiscal imbalance. We conclude this chapter by looking at fiscal policy as a tool for fighting a recession.

Fiscal Stimulus

The 2008–2009 recession brought Keynesian macroeconomic ideas (see p. 662) back into fashion and put a spotlight on **fiscal stimulus**—the use of fiscal policy to increase production and employment. But whether fiscal policy is truly stimulating, and if so, how stimulating, are questions that generate much discussion and disagreement. You're now going to explore these questions.

Fiscal stimulus can be either *automatic* or *discretionary*. A fiscal policy action that is triggered by the state of the economy with no action by government is called **automatic fiscal policy**. The increase in total unemployment benefits triggered by the massive rise in the unemployment rate through 2009 is an example of automatic fiscal policy.

A fiscal policy action initiated by an act of Congress is called **discretionary fiscal policy**. It requires a change in a spending program or in a tax law. A fiscal stimulus act passed by Congress in 2009 (see *Economics in Action* on p. 742) is an example of discretionary fiscal policy.

Whether automatic or discretionary, an increase in government outlays or a decrease in government receipts can stimulate production and jobs. An increase in expenditure on goods and services directly increases aggregate expenditure. And an increase in transfer payments (such as unemployment benefits) or a decrease in tax revenues increases disposable income, which enables people to increase consumption expenditure. Lower taxes also strengthen the incentives to work and invest.

We'll begin by looking at automatic fiscal policy and the interaction between the business cycle and the budget balance.

Automatic Fiscal Policy and Cyclical and Structural Budget Balances

Two items in the government budget change automatically in response to the state of the economy. They are *tax revenues* and *needs-tested spending*.

Automatic Changes in Tax Revenues   The tax laws that Congress enacts don't legislate the number of tax *dollars* the government will raise. Rather they define the tax *rates* that people must pay. Tax dollars paid depend on tax rates and incomes. But incomes vary with real GDP, so tax revenues depend on real GDP. When real GDP increases in a business cycle expansion, wages and profits rise, so tax revenues from these incomes rise. When real GDP decreases in a recession, wages and profits fall, so tax revenues fall.

Needs-Tested Spending The government creates programs that pay benefits to qualified people and businesses. The spending on these programs results in transfer payments that depend on the economic state of individual citizens and businesses. When the economy expands, unemployment falls, the number of people experiencing economic hardship decreases, so needs-tested spending decreases. When the economy is in a recession, unemployment is high and the number of people experiencing economic hardship increases, so needs-tested spending on unemployment benefits and food stamps increases.

Automatic Stimulus Because government receipts fall and outlays increase in a recession, the budget provides automatic stimulus that helps to shrink the recessionary gap. Similarly, because receipts rise and outlays decrease in a boom, the budget provides automatic restraint to shrink an inflationary gap.

Cyclical and Structural Budget Balances To identify the government budget deficit that arises from the business cycle, we distinguish between the **structural surplus or deficit**, which is the budget balance that would occur if the economy were at full employment, and the **cyclical surplus or deficit**, which is the actual surplus or deficit *minus* the structural surplus or deficit.

Figure 30.9 illustrates these concepts. Outlays *decrease* as real GDP *increases*, so the outlays curve slopes downward; and receipts *increase* as real GDP *increases*, so the receipts curve slopes upward.

In Fig. 30.9(a), potential GDP is $14 trillion and if real GDP equals potential GDP, the government has a *balanced budget*. There is no structural surplus or deficit. But there might be a cyclical surplus or deficit. If real GDP is less than potential GDP at $13 trillion, outlays exceed receipts and there is a *cyclical deficit*. If real GDP is greater than potential GDP at $15 trillion, outlays are less than receipts and there is a *cyclical surplus*.

In Fig. 30.9(b), if potential GDP equals $14 trillion (line *B*), the *structural balance is zero*. But if potential GDP is $13 trillion (line *A*), the government budget has a *structural deficit*. And if potential GDP is $15 trillion (line *C*), the government budget has a *structural surplus*.

FIGURE 30.9 Cyclical and Structural Surpluses and Deficits

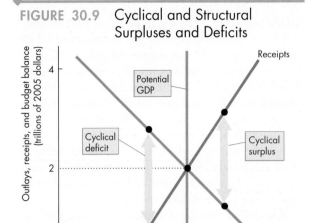

(a) Cyclical deficit and cyclical surplus

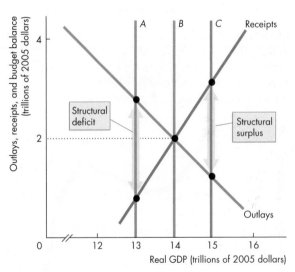

(b) Structural deficit and structural surplus

In part (a), potential GDP is $14 trillion. When real GDP is less than potential GDP, the budget is in a *cyclical deficit*. When real GDP exceeds potential GDP, the budget is in a *cyclical surplus*. The government has a *balanced budget* when real GDP equals potential GDP.

In part (b), if potential GDP is $13 trillion, there is a *structural deficit* and if potential GDP is $15 trillion, there is a *structural surplus*. If potential GDP is $14 trillion, the budget is in structural balance.

myeconlab animation

U.S. Structural Budget Balance in 2010 The U.S. federal budget in 2010 was in deficit at $1.4 trillion and the recessionary gap (the gap between real GDP and potential GDP) was close to $1 trillion. With a large recessionary gap, you would expect some of the deficit to be cyclical. But how much of the 2010 deficit was cyclical and how much was structural?

The Congressional Budget Office (CBO) answers this question by analyzing the detailed items in the budget. According to the CBO, the cyclical deficit in 2010 was $0.4 trillion and the structural deficit was $1 trillion. Figure 30.10 shows the cyclical and structural deficit between 2000 and 2010.

You can see that the structural deficit was small in 2007, increased in 2008, and exploded in 2009. The 2009 fiscal stimulus package (see *Economics in Action*) created most of this structural deficit.

When full employment returns, which the CBO says will be in 2014, the cyclical deficit will vanish. But the structural deficit must be addressed by further acts of Congress. No one knows the discretionary measures that will be taken to reduce the structural deficit and this awkward fact creates enormous uncertainty.

FIGURE 30.10   U.S. Cyclical and Structural Budget Balance

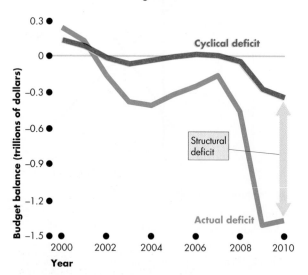

As real GDP shrank in the 2008–2009 recession, receipts fell, outlays increased, and the budget deficit increased. The cyclical deficit was small compared to the actual deficit; most of the 2010 deficit was structural.

Source of data: Congressional Budget Office.

Economics in Action
The 2009 Fiscal Stimulus Package

Congress passed the *American Recovery and Reinvestment Act of 2009* (the 2009 Fiscal Stimulus Act) in February 2009, and President Obama signed it into law at an economic forum he hosted in Denver. This act was the third and most ambitious in a series of stimulus packages and its purpose was to increase investment and consumer expenditure and lead to the creation of jobs.

The total package added $862 billion to the federal government's budget deficit: $288 billion from tax cuts and the rest from increased spending. The spending increases included payments to state and local governments ($144 billion), spending on infrastructure and science projects ($111 billion), programs in health care ($59 billion), education and training ($53 billion), and energy ($43 billion).

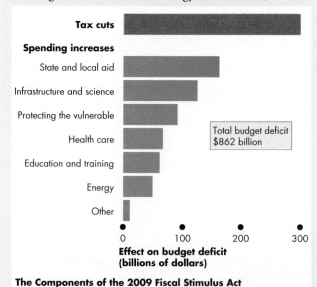

The Components of the 2009 Fiscal Stimulus Act

The president signs the 2009 fiscal stimulus act.

Discretionary Fiscal Stimulus

Most discussion of *discretionary* fiscal stimulus focuses on its effects on aggregate demand. But you've seen (on pp. 734–737) that taxes influence aggregate supply and that the balance of taxes and spending—the government budget deficit—can crowd out investment and slow the pace of economic growth. So discretionary fiscal stimulus has both supply-side and demand-side effects that end up determining its overall effectiveness.

We're going to begin our examination of discretionary fiscal stimulus by looking at its effects on aggregate demand.

Fiscal Stimulus and Aggregate Demand Changes in government expenditure and changes in taxes change aggregate demand by their influence on spending plans, and they also have multiplier effects.

Let's look at the two main fiscal policy multipliers: the government expenditure and tax multipliers.

The **government expenditure multiplier** is the quantitative effect of a change in government expenditure on real GDP. Because government expenditure is a component of aggregate expenditure, an increase in government spending increases aggregate expenditure and real GDP. But does a $1 billion increase in government expenditure increase real GDP by $1 billion, or more than $1 billion, or less than $1 billion?

When an increase in government expenditure increases real GDP, incomes rise and the higher incomes bring an increase in consumption expenditure. If this were the only consequence of increased government expenditure, the government expenditure multiplier would be greater than 1.

But an increase in government expenditure increases government borrowing (or decreases government lending if there is a budget surplus) and raises the real interest rate. With a higher cost of borrowing, investment decreases, which partly offsets the increase in government spending. If this were the only consequence of increased government expenditure, the multiplier would be less than 1.

The actual multiplier depends on which of the above effects is stronger and the consensus is that the crowding-out effect is strong enough to make the government expenditure multiplier less than 1.

The **tax multiplier** is the quantitative effect of a change in taxes on real GDP. The demand-side effects of a tax cut are likely to be smaller than an equivalent increase in government expenditure. The reason is that a tax cut influences aggregate demand by increasing

disposable income, only part of which gets spent. So the initial injection of expenditure from a $1 billion tax cut is less than $1 billion.

A tax cut has similar crowding-out consequences to a spending increase. It increases government borrowing (or decreases government lending), raises the real interest rate, and cuts investment.

The tax multiplier effect on aggregate demand depends on these two opposing effects and is probably quite small.

Graphical Illustration of Fiscal Stimulus Figure 30.11 shows how fiscal stimulus is supposed to work if it is perfectly executed and has its desired effects.

Potential GDP is $14 trillion and real GDP is below potential at $13 trillion so the economy has a recessionary gap of $1 trillion.

To restore full employment, the government passes a fiscal stimulus package. An increase in

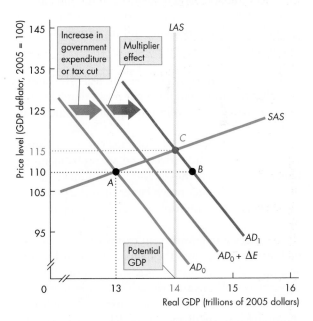

FIGURE 30.11 Expansionary Fiscal Policy

Potential GDP is $14 trillion, real GDP is $13 trillion, and there is a $1 trillion recessionary gap. An increase in government expenditure and a tax cut increase aggregate expenditure by ΔE. The multiplier increases consumption expenditure. The AD curve shifts rightward to AD₁, the price level rises to 115, real GDP increases to $14 trillion, and the recessionary gap is eliminated.

myeconlab animation

government expenditure and a tax cut increase aggregate expenditure by ΔE. If this were the only change in spending plans, the AD curve would shift rightward to become the curve labeled $AD_0 + \Delta E$ in Fig. 30.11. But if fiscal stimulus sets off a multiplier process that increases consumption expenditure, and does not crowd out much investment expenditure, aggregate demand increases further and the AD curve shifts to AD_1.

With no change in the price level, the economy would move from point A to point B on AD_1. But the increase in aggregate demand brings a rise in the price level along the upward-sloping SAS curve and the economy moves to point C.

At point C, the economy returns to full employment and the recessionary gap is eliminated.

Fiscal Stimulus and Aggregate Supply You've seen earlier in this chapter that taxes influence aggregate supply. A tax on labor income (on wages) drives a wedge between the cost of labor and the take-home pay of workers and lowers employment and output (p. 734). A tax on capital income (on interest) drives a wedge between the cost of borrowing and the return to lending and lowers saving and investment (p. 736). With less saving and investment, the real GDP growth rate slows.

These negative effects of taxes on real GDP and its growth rate and on employment mean that a tax *cut* increases real GDP and its growth rate and increases employment.

These supply-side effects of a tax cut occur along with the demand-side effects and are probably much larger than the demand-side effects and make the overall tax multiplier much larger than the government expenditure multiplier—see *Economics in Action*.

An increase in government expenditure financed by borrowing increases the demand for loanable funds and raises the real interest rate, which in turn lowers investment and private saving. This cut in investment is the main reason why the government expenditure multiplier is so small and why a deficit-financed increase in government spending ends up making only a small contribution to job creation. And because government expenditure crowds out investment, it lowers future real GDP.

So a fiscal stimulus package that is heavy on tax cuts and light on government spending works. But an increase in government expenditure alone is not an effective way to stimulate production and create jobs.

The description of the effects of discretionary fiscal stimulus and its graphical illustration in Fig. 30.11 make it look easy: Calculate the recessionary gap and the multipliers, change government expenditure and taxes, and eliminate the gap. In reality, things are not that easy.

Getting the magnitude and the timing right is difficult, and we'll now examine this challenge.

Magnitude of Stimulus Economists have diverging views about the size of the government spending and tax multipliers because there is insufficient empirical evidence on which to pin their size with accuracy. This fact makes it impossible for Congress to determine the amount of stimulus needed to close a given

Economics in Action
How Big Are the Fiscal Stimulus Multipliers?

When the 2009 fiscal stimulus package cut taxes by $300 billion and increased government spending by almost $500 billion, by how much did aggregate expenditure and real GDP change? How big were the fiscal policy multipliers? Was the government expenditure multiplier larger than the tax multiplier? These questions are about the multiplier effects on *equilibrium real GDP*, not just on aggregate demand.

President Obama's chief economic adviser in 2009, Christina Romer, a University of California, Berkeley, professor, expected the government expenditure multiplier to be about 1.5. So she was expecting the spending increase of $500 billion to go a long way toward closing the $1 trillion output gap by some time in 2010.

Robert Barro, a professor at Harvard University, says this multiplier number is not in line with previous experience. Based on his calculations, an additional $500 billion of government spending would increase aggregate expenditure by only $250 billion because it would lower private spending in a crowding-out effect by $250 billion—the multiplier is 0.5.

Harald Uhlig, a professor at the University of Chicago, says that the government expenditure multiplier on real GDP is even smaller and lies between 0.3 and 0.4, so that a $500 billion increase in government spending increases aggregate expenditure by between $150 billion and $200 billion.

output gap. Further, the actual output gap is not known and can only be estimated with error. For these two reasons, discretionary fiscal policy is risky.

Time Lags Discretionary fiscal stimulus actions are also seriously hampered by three time lags:

- Recognition lag
- Law-making lag
- Impact lag

Recognition Lag The recognition lag is the time it takes to figure out that fiscal policy actions are needed. This process involves assessing the current state of the economy and forecasting its future state.

There is greater agreement about tax multipliers. Because tax cuts strengthen the incentive to work and to invest, they increase aggregate supply as well as aggregate demand.

These multipliers get bigger as more time elapses. Harald Uhlig says that after one year, the tax multiplier is 0.5 so that the $300 billion tax cut would increase real GDP by about $150 billion by early 2010. But with two years of time to respond, real GDP would be $600 billion higher—a multiplier of 2. And after three years, the tax multiplier builds up to more than 6.

The implications of the work of Barro and Uhlig are that tax cuts are a powerful way to stimulate real GDP and employment but spending increases are not effective.

Christina Romer agrees that the economy hasn't performed in line with a multiplier of 1.5 but says other factors deteriorated and without the fiscal stimulus, the outcome would have been even worse.

Christina Romer: 1.5

Robert Barro: 0.5

Harald Uhlig: 0.4

Law-Making Lag The *law-making lag* is the time it takes Congress to pass the laws needed to change taxes or spending. This process takes time because each member of Congress has a different idea about what is the best tax or spending program to change, so long debates and committee meetings are needed to reconcile conflicting views. The economy might benefit from fiscal stimulation today, but by the time Congress acts, a different fiscal medicine might be needed.

Impact Lag The *impact lag* is the time it takes from passing a tax or spending change to its effects on real GDP being felt. This lag depends partly on the speed with which government agencies can act and partly on the timing of changes in spending plans by households and businesses. These changes are spread out over a number of quarters and possibly a number of years.

Economic forecasting is steadily improving, but it remains inexact and subject to error. The range of uncertainty about the magnitudes of the spending and tax mulitpliers make discretionary fiscal stimulus an imprecise tool for boosting production and jobs and the crowding out consequences raise serious questions about its effects on long-term economic growth.

◢■ REVIEW QUIZ

1 What is the distinction between automatic and discretionary fiscal policy?
2 How do taxes and needs-tested spending programs work as automatic fiscal policy to dampen the business cycle?
3 How do we tell whether a budget deficit needs discretionary action to remove it?
4 How can the federal government use discretionary fiscal policy to stimulate the economy?
5 Why might fiscal stimulus crowd out investment?

You can work these questions in Study Plan 30.4 and get instant feedback.

◆ You've now seen the effects of fiscal policy, and *Reading Between the Lines* on pp. 746–747 applies what you've learned to U.S. fiscal policy.

Obama Fiscal Policy

Republicans' Two-Point Plan to Create Jobs: Can It Work?

http://www.csmonitor.com
September 21, 2010

Republicans in Congress are urging two simple steps they say will help put Americans back to work: Freeze all tax rates at current levels and reduce federal spending. ... Cut government spending when the private sector is in slow gear? That's not what the textbooks typically offer as a way to rev up growth. ... So how viable is that "two-point plan," espoused recently by House Republican leader John Boehner? Would it work?

Economists are divided on these questions, but fairly broad agreement exists on a few points. One is that it would be beneficial to provide clarity on tax rates—which the first part of the Republican plan seeks to achieve and critics say President Obama has failed to do. Another is that spending cuts hold less promise than tax-rate policy as a lever for job creation.

Supporters and critics of these GOP proposals concur on one more thing: Voters shouldn't expect a quick fix. Good policies can help the job market heal faster, but the process will still take several years, forecasters predict. ...

Spending cuts could help signal that Washington policymakers are starting to get serious about tackling America's long-term fiscal challenge— a persistent gap between federal spending and revenues. ...

The case for spending cuts is partly an expression of doubt about the effectiveness of traditional stimulus via deficit spending. Researchers, including Harvard University's Robert Barro, have published studies suggesting that increased spending serves mainly to shift money around within the economy, while doing relatively little to expand the gross domestic product. ...

Foes of spending cuts say the move would harm a still-fragile economy that remains at risk of falling back into recession. When the economy is weak, economists in this camp argue, government spending acts to fuel demand for goods and services, rather than "crowding out" private-sector activity. ...

By Mark Trumball. Reproduced with permission from the September 21, 2010 issue of the Christian Science Monitor (www.CSMonitor.com).
© 2010 The Christian Science Monitor.

ESSENCE OF THE STORY

- Republicans in Congress say freezing all tax rates at current levels and cutting government spending will help put Americans back to work.

- Economists are divided on whether the plan would work.

- Economists agree that clarity on tax rates would be beneficial, that tax policy holds more promise than spending, and that there is no quick fix.

- Republicans say spending cuts signal that policymakers are serious about tackling the long-term fiscal deficit.

- Research by Robert Barro and others suggests that increased spending does little to expand GDP.

- Others say government spending does not crowd out private spending and cuts in government spending would create a risk of a fall back into recession.

ECONOMIC ANALYSIS

- The policies proposed in the news article are designed to tackle a daunting problem.

- In mid-2010, after more than $800 billion of fiscal stimulus, the U.S. economy remained in a deep and stubborn recessionary gap.

- Cyclical unemployment—the excess of unemployment above the natural unemployment rate—was running at about 8 million workers.

- The output gap—the shortfall of real GDP below potential GDP—was $1 trillion.

- Figure 1 illustrates the situation in the labor market. The demand for labor is *LD* and the supply of labor is *LS*. The real wage rate is $25 per hour (an assumed level) and at the market real wage rate, 139 million workers are demanded but 147 million are supplied, so 8 million are unemployed.

- A very large increase in the demand for labor is needed to shift the demand for labor curve to *LD** and restore full employment.

- Figure 2 illustrates the situation in the market for real GDP. The aggregate demand curve is *AD* and the short-run aggregate supply curve is *SAS*. Equilibrium real GDP is $13 trillion and the price level is 115. Potential GDP, and long-run aggregate supply (*LAS*), is $14 trillion so the recessionary gap is $1 trillion.

- A very large fiscal stimulus is needed to shift the aggregate demand curve to *AD** to close the recessionary gap.

- Which components of aggregate demand are the source of the problem? What type of expenditure needs to be stimulated?

- The answer is investment. Consumption, government expenditure, and net exports were all greater both in dollars and as a percentage of real GDP than they had been at full employment in 2006.

- But investment was lower by $400 billion and had slipped from 17.2 percent of GDP to 13.6 percent.

- The proposed fiscal stimulus policy must be judged by its likely effect on investment.

- Two influences on investment need to be considered: the real interest rate, which is the opportunity cost of the funds used to finance investment, and the expected future return from investment including the degree of uncertainty about that future return.

- More government spending has an adverse effect on both of these influences on investment.

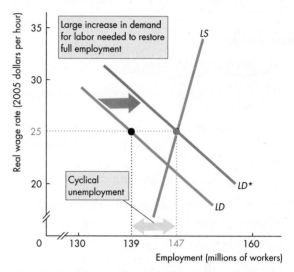

Figure 1 The labor market and cyclical unemployment

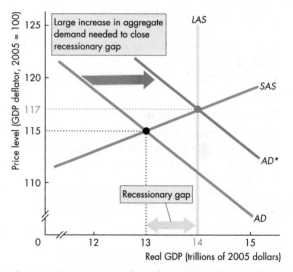

Figure 2 Aggregate supply and aggregate demand in 2010

- A larger budget deficit puts upward pressure on the real interest rate and crowds out some investment.

- A larger budget deficit also brings uncertainty about what future tax and expenditure changes will be made to eventually bring the deficit under control.

SUMMARY

Key Points

The Federal Budget (pp. 728–733)

- The federal budget is used to achieve macroeconomic objectives.
- Tax revenues can exceed, equal, or fall short of outlays—the budget can be in surplus, balanced, or in deficit.
- Budget deficits create government debt.

Working Problems 1 to 3 will give you a better understanding of the federal budget.

Supply-Side Effects of Fiscal Policy

(pp. 734–737)

- Fiscal policy has supply-side effects because taxes weaken the incentive to work and decrease employment and potential GDP.
- The U.S. labor market tax wedge is large, but it is small compared to those of other industrialized countries.
- Fiscal policy has supply-side effects because taxes weaken the incentive to save and invest, which lowers the growth rate of real GDP.
- The Laffer curve shows the relationship between the tax rate and the amount of tax revenue collected.

Working Problems 4 to 7 will give you a better understanding of the supply-side effects of fiscal policy.

Generational Effects of Fiscal Policy (pp. 738–740)

- Generational accounting measures the lifetime tax burden and benefits of each generation.
- A major study estimated the U.S. fiscal imbalance to be $79 trillion—5.8 times the value of one year's production.
- Future generations will pay for 57 percent of the benefits of the current generation.
- About two thirds of U.S. government debt is held by the rest of the world.

Working Problems 8 and 9 will give you a better understanding of the generational effects of fiscal policy.

Fiscal Stimulus (pp. 740–745)

- Fiscal policy can be automatic or discretionary.
- Automatic fiscal policy might moderate the business cycle by stimulating demand in recession and restraining demand in a boom.
- Discretionary fiscal stimulus influences aggregate demand *and* aggregate supply.
- Discretionary changes in government expenditure or taxes have multiplier effects of uncertain magnitude but the tax multiplier is likely the larger one.
- Fiscal stimulus policies are hampered by uncertainty about the multipliers and by time lags (law-making lags and the difficulty of correctly diagnosing and forecasting the state of the economy).

Working Problems 10 to 21 will give you a better understanding of fiscal stimulus.

Key Terms

Automatic fiscal policy, 740
Balanced budget, 730
Budget deficit, 730
Budget surplus, 730
Council of Economic Advisers, 729
Cyclical surplus or deficit, 741
Discretionary fiscal policy, 740

Employment Act of 1946, 728
Federal budget, 728
Fiscal imbalance, 738
Fiscal policy, 728
Fiscal stimulus, 740
Generational accounting, 738
Generational imbalance, 739
Government debt, 732

Government expenditure multiplier, 743
Laffer curve, 737
Present value, 738
Structural surplus or deficit, 741
Tax multiplier, 743
Tax wedge, 735

STUDY PLAN PROBLEMS AND APPLICATIONS

myeconlab You can work Problems 1 to 21 in MyEconLab Chapter 30 Study Plan and get instant feedback.

The Federal Budget (Study Plan 30.1)

Use the following news clip to work Problems 1 and 2.

Economy Needs Treatment

It's the debt, stupid! Only when the government sets out a credible business plan will confidence and hiring rebound.

Source: *The Wall Street Journal*, October 7, 2010

1. How has the U.S. government debt changed since 2006? What are the sources of the change in U.S. government debt?

2. What would be a "credible business plan" for the government to adopt?

3. At the end of 2008, the government of China's debt was ¥4,700 billion. (¥ is yuan, the currency of China). In 2009, the government spent ¥6,000 billion and ended the year with a debt of ¥5,300 billion. How much did the government receive in tax revenue in 2009? How can you tell?

Supply-Side Effects of Fiscal Policy (Study Plan 30.2)

4. The government is considering raising the tax rate on labor income and asks you to report on the supply-side effects of such an action. Answer the following questions using appropriate graphs. You are being asked about *directions* of change, not exact magnitudes. What will happen to

   a. The supply of labor and why?

   b. The demand for labor and why?

   c. The equilibrium level of employment and why?

   d. The equilibrium before-tax wage rate and why?

   e. The equilibrium after-tax wage rate and why?

   f. Potential GDP?

5. What fiscal policy action might increase investment and speed economic growth? Explain how the policy action would work.

6. Suppose that instead of taxing *nominal* capital income, the government taxed *real* capital income. Use appropriate graphs to explain and illustrate the effect that this change would have on

   a. The tax rate on capital income.

   b. The supply of and demand for loanable funds.

   c. Investment and the real interest rate.

7. **What Obama Means for Business**

   The core of Obama's economic plan is (a) more government spending: $65 billion a year for universal health insurance, $15 billion a year on alternative energy, $20 billion to help homeowners, $60 billion to bolster the nation's infrastructure, $10 billion annually to give students college tuition in exchange for public service, and on and on; and (b) ending the Bush tax cuts on families making more than $250,000 and raising payroll taxes on those same higher-income earners. He would increase the 15 percent capital gains tax rate—probably to 25 percent—raise the tax on dividends, and close $1.3 trillion in "corporate tax loopholes."

   Source: *Fortune*, June 23, 2008

   Explain the potential supply-side effects of the various components of Obama's economic plan. How might these policies change potential GDP and its growth rate?

Generational Effects of Fiscal Policy (Study Plan 30.3)

8. The Congressional Budget Office projects that, under current policies, U.S. public debt will reach 233 percent of GDP in 30 years and nearly 500 percent in 50 years.

   a. What is a fiscal imbalance? How might the U.S. government reduce the fiscal imbalance?

   b. How would your answer to part (a) influence the generational imbalance?

9. **Increase in Payroll Taxes Needed for Social Security**

   Social Security faces a $5.3 trillion shortfall over the next 75 years, but a congressional report says the massive gap could be erased by increasing payroll taxes paid by both employees and employers from 6.2 percent to 7.3 percent and by raising the retirement age to 70.

   Source: *USA Today*, May 21, 2010

   a. Why is Social Security facing a $5.3 trillion shortfall over the next 75 years?

   b. Explain how the suggestions in the news clip would reduce the shortfall.

   c. Would the suggestions in the news clip change the generational imbalance?

Fiscal Stimulus (Study Plan 30.4)

10. The economy is in a recession, and the recessionary gap is large.

    a. Describe the discretionary and automatic fiscal policy actions that might occur.

    b. Describe a discretionary fiscal stimulus package that could be used that would *not* bring an increase in the budget deficit.

    c. Explain the risks of discretionary fiscal policy in this situation.

Use the following news clip to work Problems 11 to 13.

Obama's Economic Recovery Plan

If the president is serious about focusing on jobs, a good start would be to freeze all tax rates and cut federal spending back to where it was before all the recent bailouts and stimulus spending.

Source: *USA Today*, September 9, 2010

11. What would be the effect on the budget deficit and real GDP of freezing tax rates and cutting government spending?

12. What would be the effect on jobs of freezing tax rates and cutting government spending?

13. If the government froze its current spending and instead cut taxes, what would be the effect on investment and jobs?

14. The economy is in a recession, the recessionary gap is large, and there is a budget deficit.

    a. Do we know whether the budget deficit is structural or cyclical? Explain your answer.

    b. Do we know whether automatic fiscal policy is increasing or decreasing the output gap? Explain your answer.

    c. If a discretionary increase in government expenditure occurs, what happens to the structural deficit or surplus? Explain.

15. **Comprehensive Tax Code Overhaul Is Overdue**

    Some right-wingers in Congress claim that tax cuts pay for themselves. Despite their insistence, there is ample evidence and general expert agreement that they do not.

    Source: *The Washington Post*, April 24, 2006

    a. Explain what is meant by tax cuts paying for themselves. What does this statement imply about the tax multiplier?

    b. Why would tax cuts not pay for themselves?

Use the following news clip to work Problems 16 and 17.

Summers Calls for Infrastructure Spending

Larry Summers, the outgoing director of the White House National Economic Council, said the United States must ramp up spending on domestic infrastructure to drive the economic recovery. He said that a combination of low borrowing costs, cheap building costs, and high unemployment in the construction industry make this the ideal time to rebuild roads, bridges, and airports.

Source: Ft.com, October 7, 2010

16. Is this infrastructure spending a fiscal stimulus? Would such spending be a discretionary or an automatic fiscal policy?

17. Explain how the rebuilding of roads, bridges, and airports would drive the economic recovery.

Use the following news clip to work Problems 18 to 20.

Stimulus Debate Turns on Rebates

As pressure built up on Washington to juice the economy, a one-time consumer rebate emerged as the likely centerpiece of a $150-billion stimulus program. But who should actually get rebates? Everyone who pays income taxes? Or only lower- and middle-income households because they are more likely to spend more of their rebate than are higher-income households, spend it quickly, and every dollar spent on stimulus could generate a dollar in GDP?

Source: *CNN*, January 22, 2008

18. a. Explain the intended effect of the $150 billion fiscal stimulus package. Draw a graph to illustrate the effect.

    b. Explain why the effect of this fiscal policy depends on who receives the tax rebates.

19. What would have a larger effect on aggregate demand: $150 billion worth of tax rebates or $150 billion worth of government spending?

20. Explain whether a stimulus package centered around a one-time consumer tax rebate is likely to have a small or a large supply-side effect.

21. Compare the impact on equilibrium real GDP of a same-sized decrease in taxes and increase in government expenditure.

ADDITIONAL PROBLEMS AND APPLICATIONS

myeconlab You can work these problems in MyEconLab if assigned by your instructor.

The Federal Budget

22. **U.S. Budget Deficit to Hit $1.3 trillion**

The Congressional Budget Office said this year's budget gap would be $71 billion less than last year's. The U.S. budget deficit of $1.3 trillion makes it the second largest deficit ever in dollars, trailing only last year's $1.4 trillion. To put those numbers in perspective, the shortfalls for 2009 and 2010 are each three times as big as the government's annual deficit had ever been previously.

Source: *The Associated Press*, August 19, 2010

Of the components of government outlays and receipts, which have changed most to contribute to these huge budget gaps in 2009 and 2010?

Supply-Side Effects of Fiscal Policy

Use the following information to work Problems 23 and 24.

Suppose that in the United States, investment is $1,600 billion, saving is $1,400 billion, government expenditure on goods and services is $1,500 billion, exports are $2,000 billion, and imports are $2,500 billion.

23. What is the amount of tax revenue? What is the government budget balance?

24. a. Is the government's budget exerting a positive or negative impact on investment?

 b. What fiscal policy action might increase investment and speed economic growth? Explain how the policy action would work.

25. Suppose that capital income taxes are based (as they are in the United States and most countries) on nominal interest rates. And suppose that the inflation rate increases by 5 percent. Use appropriate diagrams to explain and illustrate the effect that this change would have on

 a. The tax rate on capital income.

 b. The supply of loanable funds.

 c. The demand for loanable funds.

 d. Equilibrium investment.

 e. The equilibrium real interest rate.

Use the following information to work Problems 26 and 27.

Obama: Give Economy $50 Billion Boost

Barack Obama said that lawmakers should inject another $50 billion immediately into the sluggish

U.S. economy. "Such relief can't wait until the next president takes office." Obama supports the expansion and extension of unemployment benefits and calls for an additional 13 weeks of benefits to be added to what is typically a 26-week cap on federal payments. At the same time, Obama criticized John McCain for proposing to extend all of President Bush's 2001 and 2003 tax cuts.

Source: CNN, June 9, 2008

26. a. Explain the potential demand-side effect of extending unemployment benefits.

 b. Explain the potential supply-side effect of extending unemployment benefits.

 c. Draw a graph to illustrate the combined demand-side and supply-side effect of extending unemployment benefits.

27. Compare the supply-side effect of Obama's proposal to extend unemployment benefits with McCain's policy to extend Bush's 2001 and 2003 tax cuts.

Use the following news clip to work Problems 28 and 29.

John McCain's Tax Policy

McCain wants to make the Bush tax cuts permanent; then cut taxes further. He would slash the corporate tax, double the child-care tax credit, and allow businesses to write off the full cost of capital investments in one year. Despite these cuts, McCain insists that he can balance the budget within four years with promised savings from running a tighter ship and increased tax revenues as the economy expands.

Source: *Fortune*, July 7, 2008

28. Explain the potential supply-side effects of the various components of McCain's economic plan.

29. Where on the Laffer curve do you think McCain believes the U.S. economy lies? Explain your answer.

Generational Effects of Fiscal Policy

30. **Push to Cut Deficit Collides With Politics as Usual**

So it goes in Campaign 2010, where cutting the deficit is a big issue, but where support for doing some of the hard things to achieve that is running into politics as usual. Nowhere is that more apparent than in the debate—or lack thereof—on the nation's spending on big entitlement

programs. According to the latest projections from the Congressional Budget Office, spending on the big three entitlement programs—Social Security, Medicare, and Medicaid—is to rise by 70 percent, 79 percent, and 99 percent, respectively, over the next 10 years.
Source: *The Wall Street Journal*, October 5, 2010

If politicians continue to avoid debating the projected increases in these three entitlement programs, how do you think the fiscal imbalance will change? If Congress holds the budget deficit at $3.1 trillion, who will pay for the projected increases in expenditure?

Fiscal Stimulus

31. The economy is in a boom and the inflationary gap is large.
    a. Describe the discretionary and automatic fiscal policy actions that might occur.
    b. Describe a discretionary fiscal restraint package that could be used that would not produce serious negative supply-side effects.
    c. Explain the risks of discretionary fiscal policy in this situation.

32. The economy is growing slowly, the inflationary gap is large, and there is a budget deficit.
    a. Do we know whether the budget deficit is structural or cyclical? Explain your answer.
    b. Do we know whether automatic stabilizers are increasing or decreasing aggregate demand? Explain your answer.
    c. If a discretionary decrease in government expenditure occurs, what happens to the structural budget balance? Explain your answer.

Use the following news clip to work Problems 33 to 35.

Juicing the Economy Will Come at a Cost
The $150-billion stimulus plan will bump up the deficit, but not necessarily dollar for dollar. Here's why: If the stimulus works, the increased economic activity will generate federal tax revenue. But it isn't clear what the cost to the economy will be if a stimulus package comes too late—a real concern since legislation could get bogged down by politics.
Source: CNN, January 23, 2008

33. Explain why $150 billion of stimulus won't increase the budget deficit by $150 billion.
34. Is the budget deficit arising from the action described in the news clip structural or cyclical or a combination of the two? Explain.
35. Why might the stimulus package come "too late?" What are the potential consequences of the stimulus package coming "too late?"

Economics in the News

36. After you have studied *Reading Between the Lines* on pp. 746–747 answer the following questions.
    a. What were the key proposals of Republicans in Congress for restoring the U.S. economy to full employment. Describe them.
    b. Explain why holding the line on taxes and cutting government spending might be more effective than increasing government spending. Draw a graph to illustrate your answer.
    c. Explain why an increase in government expenditure could be counterproductive in the economic climate of 2010 and 2011. Draw a graph to illustrate your answer.

37. **U.S. Financial Crisis Over? Not Really**
    Economist Deepak Lal says the U.S. financial crisis is not solved and contains the seeds of a more serious future crisis. For India and China, with no structural deficit, a temporary budget deficit above that resulting from automatic fiscal policy makes sense. But it doesn't make sense for the United States with its large structural deficit.
    Source: rediff.com, October 18, 2010

    More Fiscal Stimulus Needed
    Economist Laura Tyson says there is a strong argument for more fiscal stimulus combined with a multi-year deficit reduction plan.
    Source: marketwatch.com, October 15, 2010
    a. How has the business cycle influenced the U.S. federal budget in the 2008–2009 recession?
    b. With which news clip opinion do you agree and why?
    c. Why might Laura Tyson favor a multi-year deficit reduction plan and would that address the concerns of Deepak Lal?

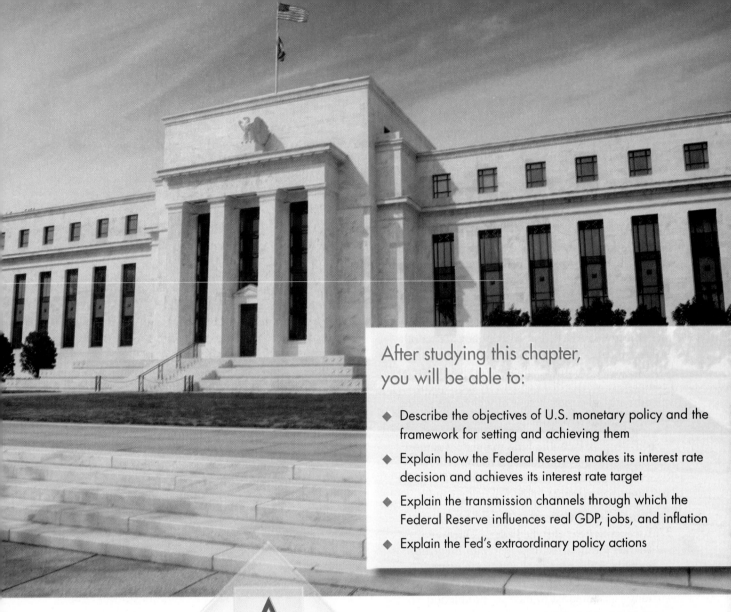

After studying this chapter, you will be able to:

◆ Describe the objectives of U.S. monetary policy and the framework for setting and achieving them

◆ Explain how the Federal Reserve makes its interest rate decision and achieves its interest rate target

◆ Explain the transmission channels through which the Federal Reserve influences real GDP, jobs, and inflation

◆ Explain the Fed's extraordinary policy actions

31

MONETARY POLICY

A t eight regularly scheduled meetings a year, and in an emergency between regular meetings, the Federal Reserve decides whether to change its interest rate target. And every business day, the Federal Reserve Bank of New York operates in financial markets to implement the Fed's decision and ensure that its target interest rate is achieved. Financial market traders, journalists, and pundits watch the economy for clues about what the Fed will decide at its next meeting.

How does the Fed make its interest rate decision? Can the Fed speed up economic growth and lower unemployment by lowering the interest rate and keep inflation in check by raising the interest rate?

What special measures can the Fed take in a financial crisis like the one that engulfed the U.S. and global economies in 2008?

This chapter combines what you learned about the functions of the Fed in Chapter 25 and about aggregate demand and aggregate supply in Chapter 27. You will learn how the Fed influences the interest rate and how the interest rate influences the economy. You will also review the extraordinary challenge faced by the Fed today. In *Reading Between the Lines* at the end of the chapter, you will see the Fed's dilemma in the face of stubborn recession and massive monetary stimulus.

◆ Monetary Policy Objectives and Framework

A nation's monetary policy objectives and the framework for setting and achieving those objectives stem from the relationship between the central bank and the government.

We'll describe the objectives of U.S. monetary policy and the framework and assignment of responsibility for achieving those objectives.

Monetary Policy Objectives

The objectives of U.S. monetary policy are set out in the mandate of the Board of Governors of the Federal Reserve System, which is defined by the Federal Reserve Act of 1913 and its subsequent amendments, the most recent of which was passed in 2000.

Federal Reserve Act The Fed's mandate was most recently clarified in amendments to the Federal Reserve Act passed by Congress in 2000. The 2000 law states that mandate in the following words:

> The Board of Governors of the Federal Reserve System and the Federal Open Market Committee shall maintain long-run growth of the monetary and credit aggregates commensurate with the economy's long-run potential to increase production, so as to promote effectively the goals of maximum employment, stable prices, and moderate long-term interest rates.

Goals and Means This description of the Fed's monetary policy objectives has two distinct parts: a statement of the goals, or ultimate objectives, and a prescription of the means by which the Fed should pursue its goals.

Goals of Monetary Policy The goals are "maximum employment, stable prices, and moderate long-term interest rates." In the long run, these goals are in harmony and reinforce each other. But in the short run, these goals might come into conflict. Let's examine these goals a bit more closely.

Achieving the goal of "maximum employment" means attaining the maximum sustainable growth rate of potential GDP and keeping real GDP close to potential GDP. It also means keeping the unemployment rate close to the natural unemployment rate.

Achieving the goal of "stable prices" means keeping the inflation rate low (and perhaps close to zero).

Achieving the goal of "moderate long-term interest rates" means keeping long-term *nominal* interest rates close to (or even equal to) long-term *real* interest rates.

Price stability is the key goal. It is the source of maximum employment and moderate long-term interest rates. Price stability provides the best available environment for households and firms to make the saving and investment decisions that bring economic growth. So price stability encourages the maximum sustainable growth rate of potential GDP.

Price stability delivers moderate long-term interest rates because the nominal interest rate reflects the inflation rate. The nominal interest rate equals the real interest rate plus the inflation rate. With stable prices, the nominal interest rate is close to the real interest rate, and most of the time, this rate is likely to be moderate.

In the short run, the Fed faces a tradeoff between inflation and interest rates and between inflation and real GDP, employment, and unemployment. Taking an action that is designed to lower the inflation rate and achieve stable prices might mean raising interest rates, which lowers employment and real GDP and increases the unemployment rate in the short run.

Means for Achieving the Goals The 2000 law instructs the Fed to pursue its goals by "maintain[ing] long-run growth of the monetary and credit aggregates commensurate with the economy's long-run potential to increase production." You perhaps recognize this statement as being consistent with the quantity theory of money that you studied in Chapter 25 (see pp. 606–607). The "economy's long-run potential to increase production" is the growth rate of potential GDP. The "monetary and credit aggregates" are the quantities of money and loans. By keeping the growth rate of the quantity of money in line with the growth rate of potential GDP, the Fed is expected to be able to maintain full employment and keep the price level stable.

To pursue the goals of monetary policy, the Fed must make the general concepts of price stability and maximum employment precise and operational.

Operational "Stable Prices" Goal

The Fed pays attention to two measures of inflation: the Consumer Price Index (CPI) and the personal consumption expenditure (PCE) deflator. But the *core PCE deflator,* which excludes food and fuel prices, is the Fed's operational guide and the Fed defines the rate of increase in the core PCE deflator as the **core inflation rate.**

The Fed focuses on the core inflation rate because it is less volatile than the total CPI inflation rate and the Fed believes that it provides a better indication of whether price stability is being achieved.

Figure 31.1 shows the core inflation rate alongside the total CPI inflation rate since 2000. You can see why the Fed says that the core inflation rate is a better indicator. Its fluctuations are smoother and represent a sort of trend through the wider fluctuations in total CPI inflation.

The Fed has not defined price stability, but it almost certainly doesn't regard price stability as meaning a core inflation rate equal to zero. Former Fed Chairman Alan Greenspan suggests that "price stability is best thought of as an environment in which inflation is so low and stable over time that it does not materially enter into the decisions of households and firms." He also believes that a "specific numerical inflation target would represent an unhelpful and false precision."[1]

Ben Bernanke, Alan Greenspan's successor, has been more precise and suggested that a core inflation rate of between 1 and 2 percent a year is the equivalent of price stability. This inflation range might be thought of as the Fed's "comfort zone" for the inflation rate.

Operational "Maximum Employment" Goal

The Fed regards stable prices (a core inflation rate of 1 to 2 percent a year) as the primary goal of monetary policy and as a means to achieving the other two goals. But the Fed also pays attention to the business cycle and tries to steer a steady course between inflation and recession. To gauge the state of output and employment relative to full employment, the Fed looks at a large number of indicators that include the labor force participation rate, the unemployment rate, measures of capacity utilization, activity in the

---

[1] Alan Greenspan, "Transparency in Monetary Policy," *Federal Reserve of St. Louis Review,* 84(4), 5–6, July/August 2002.

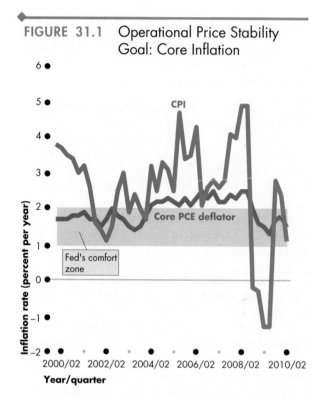

FIGURE 31.1   Operational Price Stability Goal: Core Inflation

The CPI inflation rate fluctuates more than the core inflation rate. The core inflation rate was inside the Fed's comfort zone between 2000 and 2004 and after 2008 but above the comfort zone upper limit between 2004 and 2008.

Sources of data: Bureau of Labor Statistics and Bureau of Economic Analysis.

myeconlab   animation

---

housing market, the stock market, and regional information gathered by the regional Federal Reserve Banks. All these data that describe the current state of the economy are summarized in the Fed's **Beige Book.**

While the Fed considers a vast range of data, one number stands out as a summary of the overall state of aggregate demand relative to potential GDP. That number is the *output gap*—the percentage deviation of real GDP from potential GDP.

When the output gap is positive, it is an inflationary gap that brings an increase in the inflation rate. And when the output gap is negative, it is a recessionary gap that results in lost output and in employment being below its full-employment equilibrium level. So the Fed tries to minimize the output gap.

Responsibility for Monetary Policy

Who is responsible for monetary policy in the United States? What are the roles of the Fed, Congress, and the president?

The Role of the Fed The Federal Reserve Act makes the Board of Governors of the Federal Reserve System and the Federal Open Market Committee (FOMC) responsible for the conduct of monetary policy. We described the composition of the FOMC in Chapter 25 (see p. 596). The FOMC makes a monetary policy decision at eight scheduled meetings each year and communicates its decision with a brief explanation. Three weeks after an FOMC meeting, the full minutes are published.

The Role of Congress Congress plays no role in making monetary policy decisions but the Federal Reserve Act requires the Board of Governors to report on monetary policy to Congress. The Fed makes two reports each year, one in February and another in July. These reports and the Fed chairman's testimony before Congress along with the minutes of the FOMC communicate the Fed's thinking on monetary policy to lawmakers and the public.

The Role of the President The formal role of the president of the United States is limited to appointing the members and the chairman of the Board of Governors. But some presidents—Richard Nixon was one—have tried to influence Fed decisions.

You now know the objectives of monetary policy and can describe the framework and assignment of responsibility for achieving those objectives. Your next task is to see how the Federal Reserve conducts its monetary policy.

REVIEW QUIZ

1 What are the objectives of monetary policy?
2 Are the goals of monetary policy in harmony or in conflict (a) in the long run and (b) in the short run?
3 What is the core inflation rate and how does it differ from the overall CPI inflation rate?
4 Who is responsible for U.S. monetary policy?

You can work these questions in Study Plan 31.1 and get instant feedback.

The Conduct of Monetary Policy

How does the Fed conduct its monetary policy? This question has two parts:

- What is the monetary policy instrument?
- How does the Fed make its policy decisions?

The Monetary Policy Instrument

A **monetary policy instrument** is a variable that the Fed can directly control or at least very closely target. The Fed has two possible instruments: the monetary base or the interest rate at which banks borrow and lend monetary base overnight.

The Fed's choice of monetary policy instrument is the interest rate at which the banks make overnight loans to each other. The market in which the banks borrow and lend overnight is called the *federal funds market* and the interest rate in that market is called the **federal funds rate**.

Figure 31.2 shows the federal funds rate since 2000. You can see that the federal funds rate ranges between a high of 6.5 percent a year and a low of 0.2 percent a year. In 2000 and 2006, when the federal funds rate was high, the Fed's actions were aimed at lowering the inflation rate.

Between 2002 and 2004 and again in and since 2008, the federal funds rate was set at historically low levels. During these years, inflation was well anchored at close to or below 2 percent a year, and the Fed was less concerned about inflation than it was about recession and high unemployment. So the Fed set a low interest rate to fight recession.

Although the Fed can change the federal funds rate by any (reasonable) amount that it chooses, it normally changes the federal funds rate by only a quarter of a percentage point.[2]

Having decided the appropriate level for the federal funds rate, how does the Fed move the rate to its target level? The answer is by using open-market operations (see pp. 597–599) to adjust the quantity of monetary base.

To see how an open market operation changes the federal funds rate, we need to examine the federal funds market and the market for bank reserves.

In the federal funds market, the higher the federal funds rate, the greater is the quantity of overnight

---

[2] A quarter of a percentage point is also called 25 *basis points*. A basis point is one hundredth of one percentage point.

FIGURE 31.2   The Federal Funds Rate

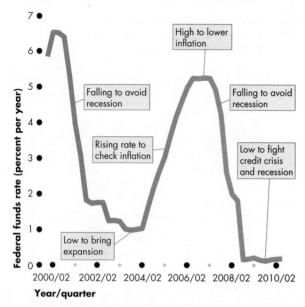

The Fed sets a target for the federal funds rate and then takes actions to keep the rate close to its target. When the Fed wants to slow inflation, it takes actions that raise the federal funds rate. When inflation is low and the Fed wants to avoid recession, it takes actions that lower the federal funds rate.

Source of data: Board of Governors of the Federal Reserve System.

myeconlab animation

loans supplied and the smaller is the quantity of overnight loans demanded. The equilibrium federal funds rate balances the quantities demanded and supplied.

An equivalent way of looking at the forces that determine the federal funds rate is to consider the demand for and supply of bank reserves. Banks hold reserves to meet the required reserve ratio and so that they can make payments. But reserves are costly to hold because they can be loaned in the federal funds market and earn the federal funds rate. So the higher the federal funds rate, the smaller is the quantity of reserves demanded.

Figure 31.3 illustrates the demand for bank reserves. The *x*-axis measures the quantity of reserves that banks hold on deposit at the Fed, and the *y*-axis measures the federal funds rate. The demand for reserves is the curve labeled *RD*.

The Fed's open market operations determine the supply of reserves, which is shown by the supply

FIGURE 31.3   The Market for Reserves

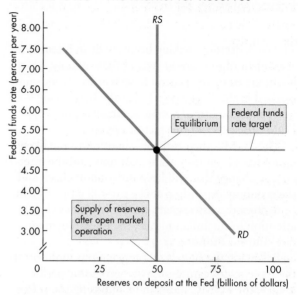

The demand curve for reserves is *RD*. The quantity of reserves demanded decreases as the federal funds rate rises because the federal funds rate is the opportunity cost of holding reserves. The supply curve of reserves is *RS*. The Fed uses open market operations to make the quantity of reserves supplied equal the quantity of reserves demanded ($50 billion in this case) at the federal funds rate target (5 percent a year in this case).

myeconlab animation

curve *RS*. Equilibrium in the market for bank reserves determines the federal funds rate where the quantity of reserves demanded by the banks equals the quantity of reserves supplied by the Fed. By using open market operations, the Fed adjusts the supply of reserves to keep the federal funds rate on target.

Next, we see how the Fed makes it policy decisions.

The Fed's Decision-Making Strategy

The Fed's decision making begins with the *Beige Book* exercise described in *Economics in Action* on the next page. The Fed then turns to forecasting three key variables: the inflation rate, the unemployment rate, and the output gap.

Inflation Rate The Fed's forecasts of the inflation rate are a crucial ingredient in its interest rate decision. If inflation is above or is expected to move above the top of the comfort zone, the Fed considers raising the

Economics in Action
FOMC Decision Making

The Fed's decision making begins with an intensive assessment of the current state of the economy, which is conducted by the Federal Reserve districts and summarized in the *Beige Book*. Today, the Beige Book is a web posting at http://www.federalreserve.gov/FOMC/BeigeBook/ (see picture opposite).

The FOMC then turns its attention to the likely near-future evolution of the economy and the interest rate change that will keep inflation in check and the economy expanding at close to full employment. In making this assessment, the FOMC pays close attention to the inflation rate, the unemployment rate, and the output gap.

Balancing the signals that it gets from monitoring the three main features of macroeconomic performance, the FOMC meets in its imposing room (see photo opposite) and makes a decision on whether to change is federal funds rate target and if so, what the new target should be.

Having decided on the appropriate target for the federal funds rate, the FOMC instructs the New York Fed to conduct open market operations aimed at hitting the federal funds rate target.

If the goal is to raise the federal funds rate, the New York Fed sells securities in the open market. If the goal is to lower the federal funds rate, the New York Fed buys securities in the open market.

2010

Summary of Commentary on
Current Economic Conditions
by Federal Reserve District

Commonly known as the Beige Book, this report is published eight times per year. Each Federal Reserve Bank gathers anecdotal information on current economic conditions in its District through reports from Bank and Branch directors and interviews with key business contacts, economists, market experts, and other sources. The Beige Book summarizes this information by District and sector. An overall summary of the twelve district reports is prepared by a designated Federal Reserve Bank on a rotating basis.

2010					
January	February	March	April	May	June
13		3	14		9
HTML		HTML	HTML		HTML
273 KB PDF		925 KB PDF	683 KB PDF		225 KB PDF
July	August	September	October	November	December
28		8	20		1
HTML		HTML	HTML		
297 KB PDF		135 KB PDF	187 KB PDF		

federal funds rate target; and if inflation is below or is expected to move below the bottom of the comfort zone, it considers lowering the interest rate.

Unemployment Rate The Fed monitors and forecasts the unemployment rate and its relation to the natural unemployment rate (see pp. 519–521). If the unemployment rate is below the natural rate, a labor shortage might put upward pressure on wage rates, which might feed through to increase the inflation rate. So a higher interest rate might be called for. If the unemployment rate is above the natural rate, a lower inflation rate is expected, which indicates the need for a lower interest rate.

Output Gap The Fed monitors and forecasts real GDP and potential GDP and the gap between them, the *output gap* (see pp. 658–659). If the output gap is positive, an *inflationary gap*, the inflation rate will

most likely accelerate, so a higher interest rate might be required. If the output gap is negative, a *recessionary gap*, inflation might ease, which indicates room to lower the interest rate.

We next look at the transmission of monetary policy and see how it achieves its goals.

 REVIEW QUIZ

1 What is the Fed's monetary policy instrument?
2 How is the federal funds rate determined in the market for reserves?
3 What are the main influences on the FOMC federal funds rate decision?

You can work these questions in Study Plan 31.2 and get instant feedback.

◆ Monetary Policy Transmission

You've seen that the Fed's goal is to keep the price level stable (keep the inflation rate around 2 percent a year) and to achieve maximum employment (keep the output gap close to zero). And you've seen how the Fed can use its power to set the federal funds rate at its desired level. We're now going to trace the events that follow a change in the federal funds rate and see how those events lead to the ultimate policy goal. We'll begin with a quick overview of the transmission process and then look at each step a bit more closely.

Quick Overview

When the Fed lowers the federal funds rate, other short-term interest rates and the exchange rate also fall. The quantity of money and the supply of loanable funds increase. The long-term real interest rate falls. The lower real interest rate increases consumption expenditure and investment. And the lower exchange rate makes U.S. exports cheaper and imports more costly, so net exports increase. Easier bank loans reinforce the effect of lower interest rates on aggregate expenditure. Aggregate demand increases, which increases real GDP and the price level relative to what they would have been. Real GDP growth and inflation speed up.

When the Fed raises the federal funds rate, as the sequence of events that we've just reviewed plays out, the effects are in the opposite directions.

Figure 31.4 provides a schematic summary of these ripple effects for both a cut and a rise in the federal funds rate.

These ripple effects stretch out over a period of between one and two years. The interest rate and exchange rate effects are immediate. The effects on money and bank loans follow in a few weeks and run for a few months. Real long-term interest rates change quickly and often in anticipation of the short-term interest rate changes. Spending plans change and real GDP growth changes after about one year. The inflation rate changes between one year and two years after the change in the federal funds rate. But these time lags are not entirely predictable and can be longer or shorter.

We're going to look at each stage in the transmission process, starting with the interest rate effects.

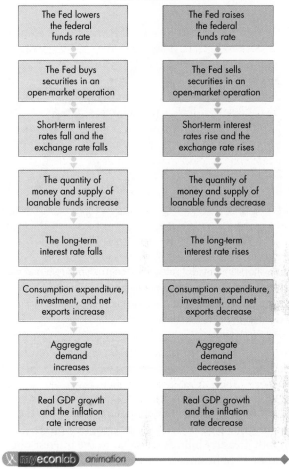

FIGURE 31.4 The Ripple Effects of a Change in the Federal Funds Rate

The Fed lowers the federal funds rate	The Fed raises the federal funds rate
The Fed buys securities in an open-market operation	The Fed sells securities in an open-market operation
Short-term interest rates fall and the exchange rate falls	Short-term interest rates rise and the exchange rate rises
The quantity of money and supply of loanable funds increase	The quantity of money and supply of loanable funds decrease
The long-term interest rate falls	The long-term interest rate rises
Consumption expenditure, investment, and net exports increase	Consumption expenditure, investment, and net exports decrease
Aggregate demand increases	Aggregate demand decreases
Real GDP growth and the inflation rate increase	Real GDP growth and the inflation rate decrease

myeconlab animation

Interest Rate Changes

The first effect of a monetary policy decision by the FOMC is a change in the federal funds rate. Other interest rates then change. These interest rate effects occur quickly and relatively predictably.

Figure 31.5 shows the fluctuations in three interest rates: the federal funds rate, the short-term bill rate, and the long-term bond rate.

Federal Funds Rate As soon as the FOMC announces a new setting for the federal funds rate, the New York Fed undertakes the necessary open market operations to hit the target. There is no doubt about where the interest rate changes shown in Fig. 31.5 are generated. They are driven by the Fed's monetary policy.

FIGURE 31.5   Three Interest Rates

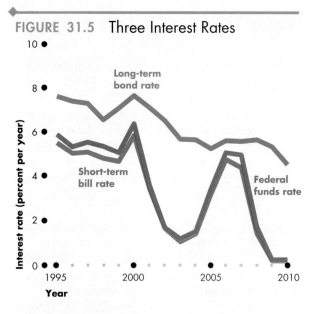

The short-term interest rates—the federal funds rate and the short-term bill rate—move closely together. The long-term bond rate is higher than the short-term rates, and it fluctuates less than the short-term rates.

Source of data: Board of Governors of the Federal Reserve System.

Short-Term Bill Rate The short-term bill rate is the interest rate paid by the U.S. government on 3-month Treasury bills. It is similar to the interest rate paid by U.S. businesses on short-term loans. Notice how closely the short-term bill rate follows the federal funds rate. The two rates are almost identical.

A powerful substitution effect keeps these two interest rates close. Commercial banks have a choice about how to hold their short-term liquid assets, and an overnight loan to another bank is a close substitute for short-term securities such as Treasury bills. If the interest rate on Treasury bills is higher than the federal funds rate, the quantity of overnight loans supplied decreases and the demand for Treasury bills increases. The price of Treasury bills rises and the interest rate falls.

Similarly, if the interest rate on Treasury bills is lower than the federal funds rate, the quantity of overnight loans supplied increases and the demand for Treasury bills decreases. The price of Treasury bills falls, and the interest rate rises.

When the interest rate on Treasury bills is close to the federal funds rate, there is no incentive for a bank to switch between making an overnight loan and buying Treasury bills. Both the Treasury bill market and the federal funds market are in equilibrium.

The Long-Term Bond Rate The long-term bond rate is the interest rate paid on bonds issued by large corporations. It is this interest rate that businesses pay on the loans that finance their purchase of new capital and that influences their investment decisions.

Two features of the long-term bond rate stand out: It is higher than the short-term rates, and it fluctuates less than the short-term rates.

The long-term interest rate is higher than the two short-term rates because long-term loans are riskier than short-term loans. To provide the incentive that brings forth a supply of long-term loans, lenders must be compensated for the additional risk. Without compensation for the additional risk, only short-term loans would be supplied.

The long-term interest rate fluctuates less than the short-term rates because it is influenced by expectations about future short-term interest rates as well as current short-term interest rates. The alternative to borrowing or lending long term is to borrow or lend using a sequence of short-term securities. If the long-term interest rate exceeds the expected average of future short-term interest rates, people will lend long term and borrow short term. The long-term interest rate will fall. And if the long-term interest rate is below the expected average of future short-term interest rates, people will borrow long term and lend short term. The long-term interest rate will rise.

These market forces keep the long-term interest rate close to the expected average of future short-term interest rates (plus a premium for the extra risk associated with long-term loans). The expected average future short-term interest rate fluctuates less than the current short-term interest rate.

Exchange Rate Fluctuations

The exchange rate responds to changes in the interest rate in the United States relative to the interest rates in other countries—*the U.S. interest rate differential*. We explain this influence in Chapter 26 (see p. 623).

When the Fed raises the federal funds rate, the U.S. interest rate differential rises and, other things remaining the same, the U.S. dollar appreciates, and when the Fed lowers the federal funds rate, the U.S. interest rate differential falls and, other things remaining the same, the U.S. dollar depreciates.

Many factors other than the U.S. interest rate differential influence the exchange rate, so when the Fed changes the federal funds rate, the exchange rate does not usually change in exactly the way it would with other things remaining the same. So while monetary policy influences the exchange rate, many other factors also make the exchange rate change.

Money and Bank Loans

The quantity of money and bank loans change when the Fed changes the federal funds rate target. A rise in the federal funds rate decreases the quantity of money and bank loans, and a fall in the federal funds rate increases the quantity of money and bank loans. These changes occur for two reasons: The quantity of deposits and loans created by the banking system changes and the quantity of money demanded changes.

You've seen that to change the federal funds rate, the Fed must change the quantity of bank reserves. A change in the quantity of bank reserves changes the monetary base, which in turn changes the quantity of deposits and loans that the banking system can create. A rise in the federal funds rate decreases reserves and decreases the quantity of deposits and bank loans created; and a fall in the federal funds rate increases reserves and increases the quantity of deposits and bank loans created.

The quantity of money created by the banking system must be held by households and firms. The change in the interest rate changes the quantity of money demanded. A fall in the interest rate increases the quantity of money demanded, and a rise in the interest rate decreases the quantity of money demanded.

A change in the quantity of money and the supply of bank loans directly affects consumption and investment plans. With more money and easier access to loans, consumers and firms spend more. With less money and loans harder to get, consumers and firms spend less.

The Long-Term Real Interest Rate

Demand and supply in the market for loanable funds determine the long-term *real interest rate*, which

equals the long-term *nominal* interest rate minus the expected inflation rate. The long-term real interest rate influences expenditure decisions.

In the long run, demand and supply in the loanable funds market depend only on real forces—on saving and investment decisions. But in the short run, when the price level is not fully flexible, the supply of loanable funds is influenced by the supply of bank loans. Changes in the federal funds rate change the supply of bank loans, which changes the supply of loanable funds and changes the interest rate in the loanable funds market.

A fall in the federal funds rate that increases the supply of bank loans increases the supply of loanable funds and lowers the equilibrium real interest rate. A rise in the federal funds rate that decreases the supply of bank loans decreases the supply of loanable funds and raises the equilibrium real interest rate.

These changes in the real interest rate, along with the other factors we've just described, change expenditure plans.

Expenditure Plans

The ripple effects that follow a change in the federal funds rate change three components of aggregate expenditure:

- Consumption expenditure
- Investment
- Net exports

Consumption Expenditure Other things remaining the same, the lower the real interest rate, the greater is the amount of consumption expenditure and the smaller is the amount of saving.

Investment Other things remaining the same, the lower the real interest rate, the greater is the amount of investment.

Net Exports Other things remaining the same, the lower the interest rate, the lower is the exchange rate and the greater are exports and the smaller are imports.

So eventually, a cut in the federal funds rate increases aggregate expenditure and a rise in the federal funds rate curtails aggregate expenditure. These changes in aggregate expenditure plans change aggregate demand, real GDP, and the price level.

The Change in Aggregate Demand, Real GDP, and the Price Level

The final link in the transmission chain is a change in aggregate demand and a resulting change in real GDP and the price level. By changing real GDP and the price level relative to what they would have been without a change in the federal funds rate, the Fed influences its ultimate goals: the inflation rate and the output gap.

The Fed Fights Recession

If inflation is low and real GDP is below potential GDP, the Fed takes actions that are designed to restore full employment. Figure 31.6 shows the effects of the Fed's actions, starting in the market for bank reserves and ending in the market for real GDP.

Market for Bank Reserves In Fig. 31.6(a), which shows the market for bank reserves, the FOMC lowers the target federal funds rate from 5 percent to 4

percent a year. To achieve the new target, the New York Fed buys securities and increases the supply of reserves of the banking system from RS_0 to RS_1.

Money Market With increased reserves, the banks create deposits by making loans and the supply of money increases. The short-term interest rate falls and the quantity of money demanded increases. In Fig. 31.6(b), the supply of money increases from MS_0 to MS_1, the interest rate falls from 5 percent to 4 percent a year, and the quantity of money increases from $3 trillion to $3.1 trillion. The interest rate in the money market and the federal funds rate are kept close to each other by the powerful substitution effect described on p. 760.

Loanable Funds Market Banks create money by making loans. In the long run, an increase in the supply of bank loans is matched by a rise in the price level and the quantity of *real* loans is unchanged. But in the short run, with a sticky price level, an increase in the supply of bank loans increases the supply of (real) loanable funds.

FIGURE 31.6   The Fed Fights Recession

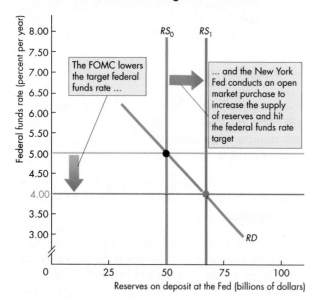

(a) The market for bank reserves

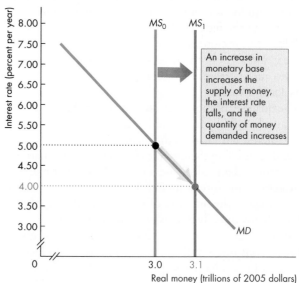

(b) Money market

In part (a), the FOMC lowers the federal funds rate target from 5 percent to 4 percent. The New York Fed buys securities in an open market operation and increases the supply of reserves from RS_0 to RS_1 to hit the new federal funds rate target.

In part (b), the supply of money increases from MS_0 to MS_1, the short-term interest rate falls, and the quantity of money demanded increases. The short-term interest rate and the federal funds rate change by similar amounts.

myeconlab   animation

In Fig. 31.6(c), the supply of loanable funds curve shifts rightward from SLF_0 to SLF_1. With the demand for loanable funds at DLF, the real interest rate falls from 6 percent to 5.5 percent a year. (We're assuming a zero inflation rate so that the real interest rate equals the nominal interest rate.) The long-term interest rate changes by a smaller amount than the change in the short-term interest rate for the reason explained on p. 760.

The Market for Real GDP Figure 31.6(d) shows aggregate demand and aggregate supply—the demand for and supply of real GDP. Potential GDP is $13 trillion, where LAS is located. The short-run aggregate supply curve is SAS, and initially, the aggregate demand curve is AD_0. Real GDP is $12.8 trillion, which is less than potential GDP, so there is a recessionary gap. The Fed is reacting to this recessionary gap.

The increase in the supply of loans and the decrease in the real interest rate increase aggregate planned expenditure. (Not shown in the figure, a fall

in the interest rate lowers the exchange rate, which increases net exports and aggregate planned expenditure.) The increase in aggregate expenditure, ΔE, increases aggregate demand and shifts the aggregate demand curve rightward to $AD_0 + \Delta E$. A multiplier process begins. The increase in expenditure increases income, which induces an increase in consumption expenditure. Aggregate demand increases further, and the aggregate demand curve eventually shifts rightward to AD_1.

The new equilibrium is at full employment. Real GDP is equal to potential GDP. The price level rises to 120 and then becomes stable at that level. So after a one-time adjustment, there is price stability.

In this example, we have given the Fed a perfect hit at achieving full employment and keeping the price level stable. It is unlikely that the Fed would be able to achieve the precision of this example. If the Fed stimulated demand by too little and too late, the economy would experience a recession. And if the Fed hit the gas pedal too hard, it would push the economy from recession to inflation.

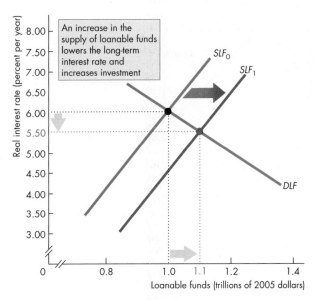

(c) The market for loanable funds

In part (c), an increase in the supply of bank loans increases the supply of loanable funds and shifts the supply curve from SLF_0 to SLF_1. The real interest rate falls and investment increases.

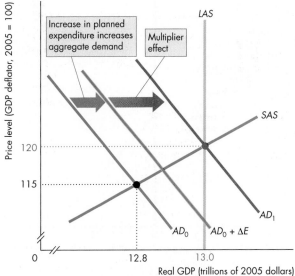

(d) Real GDP and the price level

In part (d), the increase in investment increases aggregate planned expenditure. The aggregate demand curve shifts to $AD_0 + \Delta E$ and eventually it shifts rightward to AD_1. Real GDP increases to potential GDP, and the price level rises.

The Fed Fights Inflation

If the inflation rate is too high and real GDP is above potential GDP, the Fed takes actions that are designed to lower the inflation rate and restore price stability. Figure 31.7 shows the effects of the Fed's actions starting in the market for reserves and ending in the market for real GDP.

Market for Bank Reserves In Fig. 31.7(a), which shows the market for bank reserves, the FOMC raises the target federal funds rate from 5 percent to 6 percent a year. To achieve the new target, the New York Fed sells securities and decreases the supply of reserves of the banking system from RS_0 to RS_1.

Money Market With decreased reserves, the banks shrink deposits by decreasing loans and the supply of money decreases. The short-term interest rate rises and the quantity of money demanded decreases. In Fig. 31.7(b), the supply of money decreases from MS_0 to MS_1, the interest rate rises from 5 percent to

6 percent a year, and the quantity of money decreases from $3 trillion to $2.9 trillion.

Loanable Funds Market With a decrease in reserves, banks must decrease the supply of loans. The supply of (real) loanable funds decreases, and the supply of loanable funds curve shifts leftward in Fig. 31.7(c) from SLF_0 to SLF_1. With the demand for loanable funds at DLF, the real interest rate rises from 6 percent to 6.5 percent a year. (Again, we're assuming a zero inflation rate so that the real interest rate equals the nominal interest rate.)

The Market for Real GDP Figure 31.7(d) shows aggregate demand and aggregate supply in the market for real GDP. Potential GDP is $13 trillion where LAS is located. The short-run aggregate supply curve is SAS and initially the aggregate demand is AD_0. Now, real GDP is $13.2 trillion, which is greater than potential GDP, so there is an inflationary gap. The Fed is reacting to this inflationary gap.

FIGURE 31.7 The Fed Fights Inflation

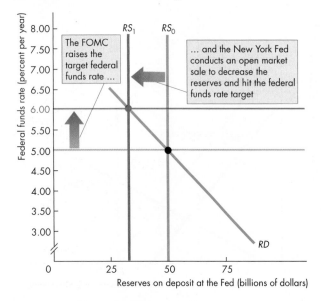

(a) The market for bank reserves

In part (a), the FOMC raises the federal funds rate from 5 percent to 6 percent. The New York Fed sells securities in an open market operation to decrease the supply of reserves from RS_0 to RS_1 and hit the new federal funds rate target.

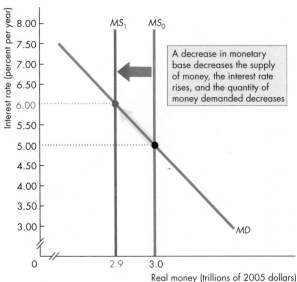

(b) Money market

In part (b), the supply of money decreases from MS_0 to MS_1, the short-term interest rate rises, and the quantity of money demanded decreases. The short-term interest rate and the federal funds rate change by similar amounts.

The increase in the short-term interest rate, the decrease in the supply of bank loans, and the increase in the real interest rate decrease aggregate planned expenditure. (Not shown in the figures, a rise in the interest rate raises the exchange rate, which decreases net exports and aggregate planned expenditure.)

The decrease in aggregate expenditure, ΔE, decreases aggregate demand and shifts the aggregate demand curve to $AD_0 - \Delta E$. A multiplier process begins. The decrease in expenditure decreases income, which induces a decrease in consumption expenditure. Aggregate demand decreases further, and the aggregate demand curve eventually shifts leftward to AD_1.

The economy returns to full employment. Real GDP is equal to potential GDP. The price level falls to 120 and then becomes stable at that level. So after a one-time adjustment, there is price stability.

Again, in this example, we have given the Fed a perfect hit at achieving full employment and keeping the price level stable. If the Fed decreased aggregate demand by too little and too late, the economy would

have remained with an inflationary gap and the inflation rate would have moved above the rate that is consistent with price stability. And if the Fed hit the brakes too hard, it would push the economy from inflation to recession.

Loose Links and Long and Variable Lags

The ripple effects of monetary policy that we've just analyzed with the precision of an economic model are, in reality, very hard to predict and anticipate.

To achieve price stability and full employment, the Fed needs a combination of good judgment and good luck. Too large an interest rate cut in an underemployed economy can bring inflation, as it did during the 1970s. And too large an interest rate rise in an inflationary economy can create unemployment, as it did in 1981 and 1991. Loose links between the federal funds rate and the ultimate policy goals make unwanted outcomes inevitable and long and variable time lags add to the Fed's challenges.

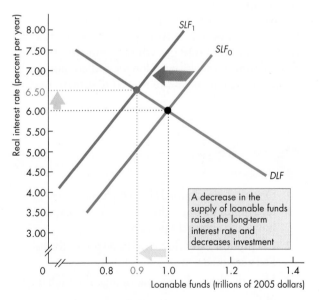

(c) The market for loanable funds

In part (c), a decrease in the supply of bank loans decreases the supply of loanable funds and the supply curve shifts from SLF_0 to SLF_1. The real interest rate rises and investment decreases.

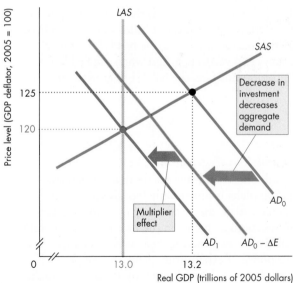

(d) Real GDP and the price level

In part (d), the decrease in investment decreases aggregate planned expenditure. Aggregate demand decreases and the AD curve shifts leftward from AD_0 to AD_1. Real GDP decreases to potential GDP, and the price level falls.

Economics in Action

A View of the Long and Variable Lag

You've studied the theory of monetary policy. Does it really work in the way we've described? It does, and the figure opposite provides some evidence to support this claim.

The blue line in the figure is the federal funds rate that the Fed targets *minus* the long-term bond rate. (When the long-term bond rate exceeds the federal funds rate, this gap is negative.)

We can view the gap between the federal funds rate and the long-term bond rate as a measure of how hard the Fed is trying to steer a change in course.

When the Fed is more concerned about recession than inflation and is trying to stimulate real GDP growth, it cuts the federal funds rate target and the gap between the long-term bond rate and the federal funds rate widens.

When the Fed is more concerned about inflation than recession and is trying to restrain real GDP growth, it raises the federal funds rate target and the gap between the long-term bond rate and the federal funds rate narrows.

The red line in the figure is the real GDP growth rate *two years later*. You can see that when the FOMC raises the federal funds rate, the real GDP growth rate slows two years later. And when the Fed lowers the federal funds rate, the real GDP growth rate

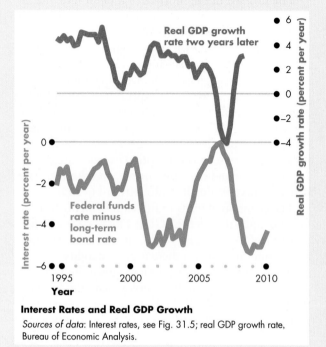

Interest Rates and Real GDP Growth

Sources of data: Interest rates, see Fig. 31.5; real GDP growth rate, Bureau of Economic Analysis.

speeds up two years later.

Not shown in the figure, the inflation rate increases and decreases corresponding to the fluctuations in the real GDP growth rate. But the effects on the inflation rate take even longer and are not as strong as the effects on the real GDP growth rate.

Loose Link from Federal Funds Rate to Spending

The real long-term interest rate that influences spending plans is linked only loosely to the federal funds rate. Also, the response of the *real* long-term interest rate to a change in the nominal interest rate depends on how inflation expectations change. And the response of expenditure plans to changes in the real interest rate depend on many factors that make the response hard to predict.

Time Lags in the Adjustment Process
The Fed is especially handicapped by the fact that the monetary policy transmission process is long and drawn out. Also, the economy does not always respond in exactly the same way to a policy change. Further, many factors other than policy are constantly changing and bringing new situations to which policy must respond.

REVIEW QUIZ

1   Describe the channels by which monetary policy ripples through the economy and explain how each channel operates.
2   Do interest rates fluctuate in response to the Fed's actions?
3   How do the Fed's actions change the exchange rate?
4   How do the Fed's actions influence real GDP and how long does it take for real GDP to respond to the Fed's policy changes?
5   How do the Fed's actions influence the inflation rate and how long does it take for inflation to respond to the Fed's policy changes?

You can work these questions in Study
Plan 31.3 and get instant feedback.

◆ Extraordinary Monetary Stimulus

During the financial crisis and recession of 2008–2009, the Fed lowered the federal funds rate target to the floor. The rate can't go below zero, so what can the Fed do to stimulate the economy when it can't lower the interest rate any further?

The Fed has answered this question with some extraordinary policy actions. To understand those actions, we need to dig a bit into the anatomy of the financial crisis to which the Fed is responding. That's what we'll now do. We'll look at the key elements in the financial crisis and then look at the Fed's response.

The Key Elements of the Crisis

We can describe the crisis by identifying the events that changed the values of the assets and liabilities of banks and other financial institutions.

Figure 31.8 shows the stylized balance sheet of a bank: deposits plus equity equals reserves plus loans and securities (see Chapter 25, p. 594). Deposits and own capital —equity—are the bank's sources of funds (other borrowing by banks is ignored here). Deposits are the funds loaned to the bank by households and firms. Equity is the capital provided by the bank's stockholders and includes the bank's undistributed profits (and losses). The bank's reserves are currency and its deposit at the Fed. The bank's loans and securities are the loans made by the bank and government bonds, private bonds, asset-backed bonds, and other securities that the bank holds.

Three main events can put a bank under stress:

1. Widespread fall in asset prices
2. A significant currency drain
3. A run on the bank

Figure 31.8 summarizes the problems that each event presents to a bank. A widespread fall in asset

prices means that the bank suffers a *capital loss*. It must write down the value of its assets and the value of the bank's equity decreases by the same amount as the fall in the value of its securities. If the fall in asset prices is large enough, the bank's equity might fall to zero, in which case the bank is insolvent. It fails.

A significant currency drain means that depositors withdraw funds and the bank loses reserves. This event puts the bank in a liquidity crisis. It is short of cash reserves.

A run on the bank occurs when depositors lose confidence in the bank and massive withdrawals of deposits occur. The bank loses reserves and must call in loans and sell off securities at unfavorable prices. Its equity shrinks.

The red arrows in Fig. 31.8 summarize the effects of these events and the problems they brought in the 2007–2008 financial crisis. A widespread fall in asset prices was triggered by the bursting of a house-price bubble that saw house prices switch from rapidly rising to falling. With falling house prices, sub-prime mortgage defaults occurred and the prices of mortgage-backed securities and derivatives whose values are based on these securities began to fall.

People with money market mutual fund deposits began to withdraw them, which created a fear of a massive withdrawal of these funds analagous to a run on a bank. In the United Kingdom, one bank, Northern Rock, experienced a bank run.

With low reserves and even lower equity, banks turned their attention to securing their balance sheets and called in loans. The loanable funds market and money market dried up.

Because the loanable funds market is global, the same problems quickly spread to other economies, and foreign exchange markets became highly volatile.

Hard-to-get loans, market volatility, and increased uncertainty transmitted the financial and monetary crisis to real expenditure decisions.

FIGURE 31.8   The Ingredients of a Financial and Banking Crisis

Event	Deposits	+	Equity	=	Reserves	+	Loans and securities	Problem
Widespread fall in asset prices			▼				▼	Solvency
Currency drain	▼				▼			Liquidity
Run on bank	▼		▼		▼		▼	Liquidity and solvency

The Policy Actions

Policy actions in response to the financial crisis dribbled out over a period of more than a year. But by November 2008, eight groups of policies designed to contain the crisis and minimize its impact on the real economy were in place. Figure 31.9 summarizes them, describes their effects on a bank's balance sheet (red and blue arrows), and identifies the problem that each action sought to address.

An open market operation is the classic policy (see pp. 597–598) for providing liquidity and enabling the Fed to hit its interest rate target. With substantial interest rate cuts, open market operations were used on a massive scale to keep the banks well supplied with reserves. This action lowered bank holdings of securities and increased their reserves.

By extending deposit insurance (see p. 594), the FDIC gave depositors greater security and less incentive to withdraw their bank deposits. This action increased both deposits and reserves.

Three actions by the Fed provided additional liquidity in exchange for troubled assets. Term auction credit, primary dealer and broker credit, and the asset-backed commercial paper money market mutual fund liquidity facility enabled institutions to swap troubled assets for reserves or safer assets. All of these actions decreased bank holdings of securities and increased reserves.

The Troubled Asset Relief Program (TARP) was an action by the U.S. Treasury, so technically it isn't a monetary policy action, but it has a direct impact on banks and other financial institutions. The program was funded by $700 billion of national debt.

The original intent (we'll call it TARP 1) was for the U.S. Treasury to buy troubled assets from banks and other holders and replace them with U.S. government securities. Implementing this program proved more difficult than initially anticipated and the benefits of the action came to be questioned.

So instead of buying troubled assets, the Treasury decided to buy equity stakes in troubled institutions (we'll call it TARP 2). This action directly increased the institutions reserves and equity.

The final action was neither monetary policy nor fiscal policy but a change in accounting standards. It relaxed the requirement for institutions to value their assets at current market value—called "mark-to-market"—and permitted them, in rare conditions, to use a model to assess "fair market value."

Taken as a whole, a huge amount of relief was thrown at the financial crisis but the economy continued to perform poorly through 2009 and 2010.

Persistently Slow Recovery

Despite extraordinary monetary (and fiscal) stimulus, at the end of 2010, the U.S. economy remained stuck with slow real GDP growth and an unemployment rate close to 10 percent. Why?

No one knows for sure, but the Fed's critics say that the Fed itself contributed to the problem more than to the solution. That problem is extreme uncertainty about the future that is keeping business investment low. Critics emphasize the need for greater clarity about monetary policy *strategy*. We'll conclude this review of monetary policy by looking at two suggested policy strategies.

FIGURE 31.9   Policy Actions in a Financial and Banking Crisis

Action	Deposits	+ Equity	= Reserves	+ Loans and securities	Problem addressed
Open market operation			▲	▼	Liquidity
Extension of deposit insurance	▲		▲		Liquidity
Term auction credit			▲	▼	Liquidity
Primary dealer and other broker credit			▲	▼	Liquidity
Asset-backed commercial paper money market mutual fund liquidity facility			▲	▼	Liquidity
Troubled Asset Relief Program (TARP 1)			▲	▼	Liquidity
Troubled Asset Relief Program (TARP 2)		▲	▲		Solvency
Fair value accounting		▲		▲	Solvency

myeconlab animation

Policy Strategies and Clarity

Two alternative approaches to monetary policy have been suggested and one of them has been used in other countries. They are

- Inflation rate targeting
- Taylor rule

Inflation Rate Targeting A monetary policy strategy in which the central bank makes a public commitment to achieve an explicit inflation target and explain how its policy actions will achieve it is called **inflation rate targeting**. Australia, Canada, New Zealand, Sweden, the United Kingdom, and the European Union have been targeting inflation since the 1990s.

Inflation targeting focuses the public debate on what monetary policy can achieve and the best contribution it can make to attaining full employment and sustained growth. The central fact is that monetary policy is about managing inflation expectations. An explicit inflation target that is taken seriously and toward which policy actions are aimed and explained is a sensible way to manage those expectations.

It is when the going gets tough that inflation targeting has the greatest benefit. It is difficult to imagine a serious inflation-targeting central bank permitting inflation to take off in the way that it did during the 1970s. And it is difficult to imagine deflation and ongoing recession such as Japan has endured for the past 10 years if monetary policy is guided by an explicit inflation target.

Taylor Rule One way to pursue an inflation target is to set the policy interest rate (for the Fed, the federal funds rate) by using a rule or formula. The most famous and most studied interest rate rule is the *Taylor rule* described in *Economics in Action*.

Supporters of the Taylor rule argue that in computer simulations, the rule works well and limits fluctuations in inflation and output. By using such a rule, monetary policy contributes toward lessening uncertainty—the opposite of current monetary policy. In financial markets, labor markets, and markets for goods and services, people make long-term commitments. So markets work best when plans are based on correctly anticipated inflation. A well-understood monetary policy helps to create an environment in which inflation is easier to forecast and manage.

The debates on inflation targeting and the Taylor rule will continue!

Economics in Action
The Taylor Rule

The *Taylor rule* is a formula for setting the federal funds rate. Calling the federal funds rate *FFR*, the inflation rate *INF*, and the output gap *GAP* (all percentages), the Taylor rule formula is

$$FFR = 2 + INF + 0.5(INF - 2) + 0.5GAP.$$

In words, the Taylor rule sets the federal funds rate at 2 percent plus the inflation rate plus one half of the deviation of inflation from 2 percent, plus one half of the output gap.

Stanford University economist John B. Taylor, who devised this rule, says inflation and real GDP would fluctuate much less if the FOMC were to use it—the Taylor rule beats the FOMC's historical performance.

The Taylor rule implies that the Fed caused the boom and bust of the past decade. The federal funds rate was 1.5 percentage points (on average) too low from 2001 through 2005, which fuelled the boom; and the rate was 0.5 percentage points (on average) too high in 2006 and 2007, which triggered the bust.

In the conditions of 2009, the Taylor rule delivered a negative interest rate, a situation that wouldn't have arisen if the rule had been followed.

 REVIEW QUIZ

1 What are the three ingredients of a financial and banking crisis?
2 What are the policy actions taken by the Fed and the U.S. Treasury in response to the financial crisis?
3 Why was the recovery from the 2008–2009 recession so slow?
4 How might inflation targeting improve the Fed's monetary policy?
5 How might using the Taylor rule improve the Fed's monetary policy?

You can work these questions in Study Plan 31.4 and get instant feedback.

◆ To complete your study of monetary policy, take a look at *Reading Between the Lines* on pages 770–771, which examines the Fed's aggressive monetary stimulus in 2010.

The Fed's Monetary Policy Dilemma

Poor U.S. Jobs Data Open Way for Stimulus

http://www.ft.com
October 8, 2010

Worse-than-expected September jobs figures underlining the U.S. economy's chronic weakness has removed the last major hurdle to a new stimulus program by the Federal Reserve. ...

A number of Fed officials have said that the U.S. central bank should act soon unless the economic data improve. The September jobs report represented the last opportunity for the data to get better before the Fed's next rate-setting meeting at the start of November.

If the Fed does act, it is likely to buy hundreds of billions of dollars in Treasury bonds—the strategy known as quantitative easing—in an effort to drive down long-term interest rates. Lower interest rates on U.S. assets relative to other countries tend to weaken the dollar.

Stephen Wood, a senior market strategist at Russell Investments, said Friday's jobs data "at a minimum take away the ammunition from the hawks and reinforce the argument of advocates of quantitative easing" on the Federal Open Market Committee.

The main surprise in the report was a 76,000 fall in local government jobs. It suggests that the effects of last year's $787bn fiscal stimulus are starting to fade.

The private sector created a modest 64,000 jobs, most of them in services, well below the 300,000 to 400,000 a month needed to keep up with population growth and tackle rapidly the 9.6 percent unemployment rate.

ESSENCE OF THE STORY

- An increase of 64,000 in private-sector jobs and a fall of 76,000 in local government jobs left the unemployment rate at 9.6 percent.

- Between 300,000 and 400,000 new jobs a month are needed to keep up with population growth.

- The poor jobs figure signals a possible new stimulus by the Fed.

- The Fed would undertake quantitative easing—buy hundreds of billions of dollars of Treasury bonds in an effort to drive down the long-term interest rate.

- Lower U.S. interest rates relative to those in other countries would weaken the dollar.

- Fed "hawks" don't want more quantitative easing.

- Some FOMC members want to use quantitative easing (QE) in a further attempt to boost real GDP and employment.

- Other FOMC members (the "hawks" refered to in the news article) fear inflation and believe that too much QE has already been undertaken.

- The Fed's dilemma is that with unemployment remaining stubbornly high and with inflation subdued, more monetary stimulus seems to be needed, but enormous stimulus is already in place and monetary policy does operate with a long and variable time lag.

- Further, if the dollar starts to depreciate in the foreign exchange market, inflation might take off (the fear of the hawks).

- The figures illustrate the economy in 2010, the possible effects of more stimulus, and the fear of the hawks.

- In Fig. 1, the banks' demand for reserves is RD. At a federal funds rate of 0.2 percent a year, the banks are willing to hold any quantity of reserves.

- The Fed's supply of reserves is $2 trillion on the supply curve RS_0. If the Fed undertakes QE and boosts the monetary base by a $0.5 trillion, the supply of reserves increases and the supply curve shifts to RS_1 in Fig. 1, but the interest rate doesn't fall.

- In Fig. 2, the economy real interest rate is 3 percent a year at the intersection of the supply of loanable funds curve SLF_0 and the demand for loanable funds curve DLF.

- When the Fed buys government securities to increase reserves, the supply of loanable funds increases and the supply curve in Fig. 2 shifts to SLF_1. But if the dollar is expected to depreciate, speculators move their funds into other currencies. The supply of loanable funds curve reverts to SLF_0, so the interest rate doesn't fall.

- In Fig. 3, real GDP is $13 trillion and the price level is 115 at the intersection of AD_0 and SAS_0. Potential GDP is $14 trillion, so there is a recessionary gap.

- If QE stimulates aggregate demand, the AD curve shifts rightward, like the shift to AD_1.

- If the expected depreciation of the dollar brings expected inflation and a higher expected price level, money wage rates rise and the short-run aggregate supply curve shifts to SAS_1. The price level rises and real GDP is stuck at $13 trillion with no change in the output gap. This is the fear of the hawks.

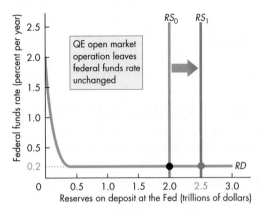

Figure 1 The market for bank reserves

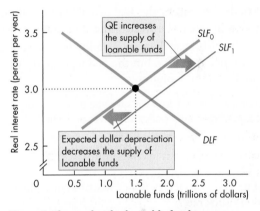

Figure 2 The market for loanable funds

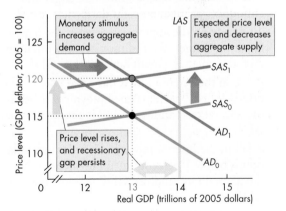

Figure 3 The risk of inflation

771

SUMMARY

Key Points

Monetary Policy Objectives and Framework

(pp. 754–756)

- The Federal Reserve Act requires the Fed to use monetary policy to achieve maximum employment, stable prices, and moderate long-term interest rates.
- The goal of stable prices delivers maximum employment and low interest rates in the long run but can conflict with the other goals in the short run.
- The Fed translates the goal of stable prices as an inflation rate of between 1 and 2 percent per year.
- The FOMC has the responsibility for the conduct of monetary policy, but the Fed reports to the public and to Congress.

Working Problems 1 to 5 will give you a better understanding of monetary policy objectives and framework.

The Conduct of Monetary Policy

(pp. 756–758)

- The Fed's monetary policy instrument is the federal funds rate.
- The Fed sets the federal funds rate target and announces changes on eight dates each year.
- To decide on the appropriate level of the federal funds rate target, the Fed monitors the inflation rate, the unemployment rate, and real GDP.
- A rise in the interest rate is indicated when inflation is above 2 percent, unemployment is below the natural rate, and real GDP is above potential GDP.
- A fall in the interest rate is indicated when inflation is below 1 percent, unemployment is above the natural rate, and real GDP is below potential GDP.

- The Fed hits its federal funds rate target by using open market operations.
- By buying or selling government securities in the open market, the Fed is able to change bank reserves and change the federal funds rate.

Working Problems 6 to 10 will give you a better understanding of the conduct of monetary policy.

Monetary Policy Transmission

(pp. 759–766)

- A change in the federal funds rate changes other interest rates, the exchange rate, the quantity of money and loans, aggregate demand, and eventually real GDP and the price level.
- Changes in the federal funds rate change real GDP about one year later and change the inflation rate with an even longer time lag.

Working Problems 11 to 20 will give you a better understanding of monetary policy transmission.

Extraordinary Monetary Stimulus

(pp. 767–769)

- A financial crisis has three ingredients: a widespread fall in asset prices, a currency drain, and a run on banks.
- The Fed and U.S. Treasury responded to financial crisis with classic open market operations on a massive scale and by several other unconventional measures.
- Inflation targeting and the Taylor rule are monetary policy strategies designed to enable the central bank to manage inflation expectations and reduce uncertainty.

Working Problems 21 to 26 will give you a better understanding of extraordinary monetary stimulus.

Key Terms

Beige Book, 755
Core inflation rate, 755
Federal funds rate, 756

Inflation rate targeting, 769
Monetary policy instrument, 756

STUDY PLAN PROBLEMS AND APPLICATIONS

myeconlab You can work Problems 1 to 26 in MyEconLab Chapter 31 Study Plan and get instant feedback.

Monetary Policy Objectives and Framework

(Study Plan 31.1)

1. "Unemployment is a more serious economic problem than inflation and it should be the focus of the Fed's monetary policy." Evaluate this statement and explain why the Fed's primary policy goal is price stability.

2. "Because the core inflation rate excludes the prices of food and fuel, the Fed should pay no attention to it and should instead be concerned about the CPI inflation rate." Explain why the Fed regards the core inflation rate as a good measure on which to focus.

3. "Monetary policy is too important to be left to the Fed. The President should be responsible for it." How is responsibility for monetary policy allocated among the Fed, the Congress, and the President?

4. **Bernanke Warns of High Budget Deficits**

   The government must rein in budget deficits in the years ahead, Federal Reserve Chairman Ben S. Bernanke told Congress.

   The Washington Post, October 5, 2010

   a. Does the Fed Chairman have either authority or responsibility for federal budget deficits?

   b. How might a federal budget deficit complicate the Fed's monetary policy? (Hint: Think about the effects of a deficit on interest rates.)

   c. How might the Fed's monetary policy complicate Congress's deficit cutting? (Hint: Think about the effects of monetary policy on interest rates.)

5. **Fed's $2 trillion May Buy Little Improvement in Jobs**

   The Fed has boosted bank reserves and the monetary base by $2 trillion but this action might not have much effect on jobs.

   Source: *Bloomberg*, October 7, 2010

   a. What does the Federal Reserve Act of 2000 say about the Fed's control of the quantity of money?

   b. How can the $2 trillion be reconciled with the Federal Reserve Act of 2000?

The Conduct of Monetary Policy (Study Plan 31.2)

6. What are the two possible monetary policy instruments, which one does the Fed use, and how has its value behaved since 2000?

7. How does the Fed hit its federal funds rate target? Illustrate your answer with an appropriate graph.

8. What does the Fed do to determine whether the federal funds rate should be raised, lowered, or left unchanged?

Use the following news clip to work Problems 9 and 10.

Fed Sees Unemployment and Inflation Rising

It is May 2008 and the Fed is confronted with a rising unemployment rate and rising inflation.

Source: CNN, May 21, 2008

9. Explain the dilemma faced by the Fed in May 2008.

10. a. Why might the Fed decide to cut the interest rate in the months after May 2008?

    b. Why might the Fed have decided to raise the interest rate in the months after May 2008?

Monetary Policy Transmission (Study Plan 31.3)

Use the following news clip to work Problems 11 and 12.

Sorry Ben, You Don't Control Long-Term Rates

Perhaps Ben Bernanke didn't learn in school that long-term interest rates are set by the market, but he is about to learn this lesson. Long-term interest rates cannot be manipulated lower by the central bank for a great length of time.

Source: safehaven.com, May 5, 2009

11. What is the role of the long-term interest rate in the monetary policy transmission process?

12. a. Is it the long-term nominal interest rate or the long-term real interest rate that influences spending decisions? Explain why.

    b. How does the market determine the long-term nominal interest rate and why doesn't it move as much as the short-term interest rates?

Use the following news clip to work Problems 13 and 14.

Dollar Down Slightly on Unabated Fed Concern

Worse-than-expected U.S. employment numbers created an expectation of further easing by the Fed and a fall in the exchange rate.

Source: *The Wall Street Journal*, October 11, 2010

13. How does further easing lower the exchange rate? How does a fall in the exchange rate influence monetary policy transmission?

14. Would a fall in the exchange rate mainly influence unemployment or inflation?

Use the following news clip to work Problems 15 to 17.

Economists' Growth Forecasts Through 2011

Economists surveyed boosted their forecasts for business investment in 2011.

Source: *Bloomberg*, October 11, 2010

15. Explain the effects of the Fed's low interest rates on business investment. Draw a graph to illustrate your explanation.

16. Explain the effects of business investment on aggregate demand. Would you expect it to have a multiplier effect? Why or why not?

17. What actions might the Fed take to stimulate business investment further?

Use the following news clip to work Problems 18 to 20.

IMF Forecasts a Slowdown in U.S. Growth

For the year 2010 the IMF reduced its U.S. real GDP growth forecast from 3.3 percent down to 2.6 percent. The IMF also lowered its growth forecast for 2011 from 2.9 percent to 2.3 percent.

Source: bloggingstocks.com, October 5, 2010

18. If the IMF forecasts turn out to be correct, what would most likely happen to the output gap and unemployment in 2011?

19. a. What actions that the Fed had taken in 2009 and 2010 would you expect to influence U.S. real GDP growth in 2011? Explain how those policy actions would transmit to real GDP.

    b. Draw a graph of aggregate demand and aggregate supply to illustrate your answer to part (a).

20. What further actions might the Fed take in 2011 to influence the real GDP growth rate in 2011? (Remember the time lags in the operation of monetary policy.)

Extraordinary Monetary Stimulus (Study Plan 31.4)

Use the following news clip to work Problems 21 to 23.

Dollar Under Pressure Amid QE2 Speculation

Persistent speculation that the Federal Reserve would soon embark on a fresh program of long-term asset purchases—a second round of quantitative easing or QE2—kept the dollar under pressure in the foreign exchange market ahead of crucial U.S. employment data.

Source: ft.com, October 7, 2010

21. What is the connection between actions that the Fed might take and U.S. employment data?

22. What does the news clip mean by "the dollar under pressure"?

23. Why was the Fed contemplating QE2? What were the arguments for and against further quantitative easing in the fall of 2010?

24. **Prospects Rise for Fed Easing Policy**

    William Dudley, president of the New York Fed, raised the prospect of the Fed becoming more explicit about its inflation goal to "help anchor inflation expectations at the desired rate."

    Source: ft.com, October 1, 2010

    a. What monetary policy strategy is Mr Dudley raising?

    b. How does inflation rate targeting work and why might it "help anchor inflation expectations at the desired rate"?

25. Suppose that the Bank of England decides to follow the Taylor rule. In 2005, the United Kingdom has an inflation rate of 2.1 percent a year and its output gap is −0.3 percent. At what level does the Bank of England set the repo rate (the U.K. equivalent of the federal funds rate)?

26. Suppose that the FOMC had followed the Taylor rule starting in 2000.

    a. How would the federal funds rate have differed from its actual path?

    b. How would real GDP and the inflation rate have been different?

ADDITIONAL PROBLEMS AND APPLICATIONS

myeconlab You can work these problems in MyEconLab if assigned by your instructor.

Monetary Policy Objectives and Framework

Use the following information to work Problems 27 to 29.

The Fed's mandated policy goals are "maximum employment, stable prices, and moderate long-term interest rates."

27. Explain the harmony among these goals in the long run.

28. Explain the conflict among these goals in the short run.

29. Based on the performance of U.S. inflation and unemployment, which of the Fed's goals appears to have taken priority since 2000?

30. What is the core inflation rate and why does the Fed regard it as a better measure than the CPI on which to focus?

31. Suppose Congress decided to strip the Fed of its monetary policy independence and legislate interest rate changes. How would you expect the policy choices to change? Which arrangement would most likely provide price stability?

Use the following news clip to work Problems 32 to 34.

Fiscal 2010 Deficit Seen Slightly Below $1.3 trillion

The federal government recorded a budget deficit of just slightly less than $1.3 trillion in fiscal 2010, the second-worst mark since 1945, the Congressional Budget Office said Thursday.

Source: *The Wall Street Journal*, October 7, 2010

32. How does the federal government get funds to cover its budget deficit? How does financing the budget deficit affect the Fed's monetary policy?

33. How was the budget deficit of 2010 influenced by the Fed's low interest rate policy?

34. a. How would the budget deficit change in 2011 and 2012 if the Fed moved interest rates up?

    b. How would the budget deficit change in 2011 and 2012 if the Fed's monetary policy led to a rapid depreciation of the dollar?

35. The Federal Reserve Act of 2000 instructs the Fed to pursue its goals by "maintain[ing] long-run growth of the monetary and credit aggregates commensurate with the economy's long-run potential to increase production."

    a. Has the Fed followed this instruction?

    b. Why might the Fed increase money by more than the potential to increase production?

The Conduct of Monetary Policy

36. Looking at the federal funds rate since 2000, identify periods during which, with the benefit of hindsight, the rate might have been kept too low. Identify periods during which it might have been too high.

37. Now that the Fed has created $2 trillion of bank reserves, how would you expect a further open market purchase of securities to influence the federal funds rate? Why? Illustrate your answer with an appropriate graph.

38. What is the Beige Book and what role does it play in the Fed's monetary policy decision-making process?

Use the information that during 2009 and 2010 both the inflation rate and the unemployment rate increased to work Problems 39 to 41.

39. Explain the dilemma that rising inflation and rising unemployment poses for the Fed.

40. Why might the Fed decide to try to lower interest rates in this situation?

41. Why might the Fed decide to raise interest rates in this situation?

Monetary Policy Transmission

Use the following information to work Problems 42 to 44.

From 2001 through 2005, the long-term *real* interest rate paid by the safest U.S. corporations fell from 5.5 percent to 2.5 percent. During that same period, the federal funds rate fell from 5.25 percent to 2.5 percent a year.

42. What role does the long-term real interest rate play in the monetary policy transmission process?

43. How does the federal funds rate influence the long-term real interest rate?

44. What do you think happened to inflation expectations between 2001 and 2005 and why?

45. **Dollar Tumbles to 15-year Low Against Yen**

    The dollar tumbled to a fresh 15-year low on persistent fears over the U.S. economic outlook.

    Source: yahoo.com, October 7, 2010

    a. How do "fears over the U.S. economic outlook" influence the exchange rate?

    b. How does monetary policy influence the exchange rate?

Use the following news clip to work Problems 46 and 47.

Top Economist says America Could Plunge into Recession

Robert Shiller, Professor of Economics at Yale University, predicted that there was a very real possibility that the United States would be plunged into a Japan-style slump, with house prices declining for years.

Source: timesonline.co.uk, December 31, 2007

46. If the Fed had agreed with Robert Shiller in December 2007, what actions might it have taken differently from those it did take? How could monetary policy prevent house prices from falling?

47. Describe the time lags in the response of output and inflation to the policy actions you have prescribed.

Use the following news clip to work Problems 48 and 49.

Greenspan Says Economy Strong

The central bank chairman said inflation was low, consumer spending had held up well through the downturn, housing-market strength was likely to continue, and businesses appeared to have unloaded their glut of inventories, setting the stage for a rebound in production.

Source: cnn.com, July 16, 2002

48. What monetary policy actions had the Fed taken in the year before Alan Greenspan's optimistic assessment?

49. What monetary policy actions would you expect the Fed to take in the situation described by Alan Greenspan?

Extraordinary Monetary Stimulus

50. **Fed's Plosser: Doesn't Currently Support Further Asset Buying**

    Further Federal Reserve asset purchases will not speed up the labor market recovery and could damage the Fed's credibility, said Federal Reserve Bank of Philadelphia President Charles Plosser, who is opposed to further asset buying of any size at this time.

    Source: nasdaq.com, October 12, 2010

    a. Describe the asset purchases that are causing Charles Plosser concern.

    b. How might asset purchases damage the Fed's credibility?

51. Suppose that the Reserve Bank of New Zealand is following the Taylor rule. In 2009, it sets the official cash rate (its equivalent of the federal funds rate) at 4 percent a year. If the inflation rate in New Zealand is 2.0 percent a year, what is its output gap?

Economics in the News

52. After you have studied *Reading Between the Lines* on pp. 770–771 answer the following questions.

    a. What was particularly unusual about the state of the economy in 2010?

    b. What was the Fed's expectation about future employment, real GDP growth, and inflation at the time of the news article?

    c. How would quantitative easing influence the market for bank reserves, the market for loanable funds, and aggregate demand and aggregate supply?

    d. How would you expect the exchange rate to feature in the transmission of monetary policy to real GDP and the price level?

53. **Fed Official Issues Call for Aggressive Action**

    Charles Evans, president of the Federal Reserve Bank of Chicago, wants the Fed to do much more to stimulate the economy. He wants the Fed to buy U.S. Treasury bonds and commit to raising the inflation rate above its informal 2 percent target.

    Source: *The Wall Street Journal*, October 5, 2010

    a. Why, in the economic conditions of October 2010, did Charles Evans want to see the Fed stimulating more?

    b. What would be the effects of the Fed buying U.S. Treasury bonds? Explain the immediate effects and the ripple effects.

    c. What would be the effects of the Fed committing to an inflation rate greater than 2 percent?

    d. What are the risks arising from greater monetary stimulus?

Tradeoffs and Free Lunches

A policy tradeoff arises if, in taking an action to achieve one goal, some other goal must be forgone. The Fed wants to avoid a rise in the inflation rate and a rise in the unemployment rate. But if the Fed raises the interest rate to curb inflation, it might lower expenditure and increase unemployment. The Fed faces a short-run tradeoff between inflation and unemployment.

A policy free lunch arises if in taking actions to pursue one goal, some other (intended or unintended) goal is also achieved. The Fed wants to keep inflation in check and, at the same time, to boost the economic growth rate. If lower inflation brings greater certainty about the future and stimulates saving and investment, the Fed gets both lower inflation and faster real GDP growth. It enjoys a free lunch.

The two chapters in this part have described the institutional framework in which fiscal policy (Chapter 30) and monetary policy (Chapter 31) are made, described the instruments of policy, and analyzed the effects of policy. This exploration of economic policy draws on almost everything that you learned in previous chapters.

These policy chapters serve as a capstone on your knowledge of macroeconomics and draw together all the strands in your study of the previous chapters.

Milton Friedman, whom you meet below, has profoundly influenced our understanding of macroeconomic policy, especially monetary policy.

Milton Friedman *was born into a poor immigrant family in New York City in 1912. He was an undergraduate at Rutgers and a graduate student at Columbia University during the Great Depression. From 1977 until his death in 2006, Professor Friedman was a Senior Fellow at the Hoover Institution at Stanford University. But his reputation was built between 1946 and 1983, when he was a leading member of the "Chicago School," an approach to economics developed at the University of Chicago and based on the views that free markets allocate resources efficiently and that stable and low money supply growth delivers macroeconomic stability.*

Friedman has advanced our understanding of the forces that determine macroeconomic performance and clarified the effects of the quantity of money. For this work, he was awarded the 1977 Nobel Prize for Economic Science.

By reasoning from basic economic principles, Friedman (along with Edmund S. Phelps, the 2006 Economics

"Inflation is always and everywhere a monetary phenomenon."

MILTON FRIEDMAN
The Counter-Revolution in Monetary Theory

Nobel Laureate) predicted that persistent demand stimulation would not increase output but would cause inflation.

When output growth slowed and inflation broke out in the 1970s, Friedman seemed like a prophet, and for a time, his policy prescription, known as monetarism, *was embraced around the world.*

What attracted you to economics?

When I graduated from high school, I was interested in both chemistry and economics but I wasn't sure which I wanted to study, so I enrolled in both programs. Within the first year of study, I realized that I wanted to pursue a career in economics. I took a class in which we learned how fiat money can have value and how the central bank can control the inflation rate. This seemed very important to me at the time—and still does after so many years.

What led you to focus your research on monetary and fiscal stabilization policy?

I always was very interested in economic policy and both monetary and fiscal stabilization policy have large and clear effects on a society's well-being. The same is certainly true for other areas of economics, but the benefits of macroeconomic stabilization policy are particularly easy to see; and it isn't difficult to find historical examples where bad monetary and fiscal policies unnecessarily lowered the standard of living.

What was your first job as a professional economist? How did you get started?

My first job out of graduate school was at the Board of Governors of the Federal Reserve System in Washington. This was a fabulous experience. Watching the policy-making process, I became motivated to work on having a more consistent and compelling theoretical framework on which to base monetary policy advice, and in particular, learning to develop tools to perform evaluation of alternative monetary policy proposals.

Only a few years out of graduate school, you and your economist husband Martin Uribe accepted a challenge to contribute to an assessment of "dollarization" for Mexico. First, would you explain what dollarization is?

When a country dollarizes, the U.S. dollar becomes legal tender, replacing the domestic currency. Ecuador, for example, is dollarized. In the case of Mexico in 1999, there were proposals, mainly coming from the business community, to replace the peso with the U.S. dollar.

Why might dollarization be a good idea?

Such proposals are typically motivated by the desire to avoid excessive inflation and excessive exchange

rate volatility. Dollarization also makes inflationary finance of the Treasury Department impossible.

And what are the costs of dollarization?

One cost is that the country loses the revenues it gains from issuing money. A second cost is that the country loses the ability to conduct monetary stabilization policy. In effect, the domestic central bank can no longer influence the business cycle through interest rate or exchange rate policy. The question that Martin and I wanted to answer was "how costly is it for a country to give up the ability to conduct monetary stabilization policy?" We quickly realized that we didn't have the tools to answer this question in a way that we regarded as satisfying.

Briefly, what did you have to do to enable you to say whether dollarization is a good or bad idea?

STEPHANIE SCHMITT-GROHÉ is Professor of Economics at Columbia University. Born in Germany, she received her first economics degree at Westfälische Wilhelms-Universität Münster in 1987, her M.B.A in Finance at Baruch College, City University of New York in 1989, and her Ph.D. in economics at the University of Chicago in 1994.

Professor Schmitt-Grohé's research covers a wide range of fiscal policy and monetary policy issues that are especially relevant in today's economy as the consequences of the 2007 mortgage crisis play out.

Working with her husband, Martin Uribe, also a Professor of Economics at Columbia University, she has published papers in leading economics journals on how best to conduct monetary policy and fiscal policy and how to avoid problems that might arise from the inappropriate use of a simple policy rule for setting the federal funds rate. She has also contributed to the debate on inflation targeting.

In 2004, Professor Schmitt-Grohé was awarded the Bernácer Prize, awarded annually to a European economist under the age of 40 who has made outstanding contributions in the fields of macroeconomics and finance.

Michael Parkin talked with Stephanie Schmitt-Grohé about her work and the challenges of conducting stabilization policy.

We wanted to be able to quantify the loss in economic welfare that comes from not being able to target monetary policy at stabilizing the domestic economy. To do this, we needed to compute two measures of economic welfare, one arising from Mexican monetary policy and another under dollarization. But we wanted our measures to be based on an empirically compelling and sufficiently detailed model of the Mexican business cycle.

At that time there were no measurement techniques available that allowed us to perform this task. So over the course of the next five years we developed the tools that we needed. One tool is an algorithm that computes (approximately but with sufficient accuracy) economic welfare under any given monetary policy, including the two of interest

> . . . if the central bank responds to the output gap, economic welfare suffers.

to us: Mexican dollarization and actual Mexican monetary policy. A second tool that we developed is another algorithm to compute optimal monetary policy—the best available monetary policy.

Knowing the highest level of economic welfare that can be achieved allows us to judge how close practical policy proposals come to optimal policy.

And what was your biggest surprise?

I think our biggest surprise in this research program was how small the welfare costs of some very simple policy rules are vis-à-vis the optimal policy. Martin and I have shown in a number of papers that simple interest rate rules are very close to the best that can be achieved.

How would you describe the best stabilization policy for smoothing the business cycle and keeping inflation in check?

Good stabilization policy is not necessarily a policy that smoothes the business cycle, in the sense that it minimizes output fluctuations. On the contrary, it might be that try-

> Good stabilization policy is not necessarily a policy that smoothes the business cycle

ing to avoid cyclical fluctuations lowers economic welfare. Suppose, for example, that business-cycle fluctuations arise from fluctuations in the growth rate of productivity—as real business cycle theory suggests. Then economic welfare decreases if we limit the cyclical increase in output that comes from the increase in productivity.

The findings of my work with Martin suggest that a simple and highly effective monetary policy is one whereby the central bank raises the short-term interest rate by more than one-for-one when inflation exceeds the targeted level of inflation. Interest rate feedback rules of this type are similar to the Taylor rule, but contrary to Taylor's rule, our results suggest that the central bank should not respond to output variations in setting the short-term nominal interest rate. We find that if the central bank responds to the output gap, economic welfare suffers.

Regarding fiscal policies, the results of several of our papers strongly suggest smoothing out distortionary tax rates and using variations in the level of government debt to address cyclical budget shortfalls.

You've done some recent research with Martin on the optimal or best inflation rate. What is the optimal rate?

Many central banks have an inflation target. In developed economies it is about 2 percent per year and in emerging market economies it is about 4 percent per year. Martin and I are trying to answer the seemingly simple and innocent question: Which level of the inflation rate should a central bank target? Is it the observed values of 2 percent and 4 percent? Or should it be zero, or 6 percent, or why not aim for a negative inflation rate—a falling price level?

Three costs of inflation are relevant for determining the best inflation rate. The first is the burden of inflation as a tax—a tax on money holdings that decreases the quantity of money that people want to hold and increases transactions costs. To avoid the inflation tax and minimize transactions costs, it would be best if money had the same rate of return as a bond. This outcome is achieved if the nominal interest rate is zero and the inflation rate is negative and equal to minus the real of interest. This result regarding the best level of inflation is known as the Friedman rule.

The second is the cost of changing nominal prices. If inflation is, say 5 percent per year and firms cannot freely adjust their prices, then the firms which for some reason have not adjusted their prices in a long time will be charging an inefficient price. So with sluggish price adjustment, inflation distorts relative prices and thus leads to inefficient resource allocations in the economy. The best way to avoid such inefficiencies is to target zero inflation.

Avoiding these two costs require different inflation rates, one negative and one zero, but neither is close to the positive inflation targets that we observe almost every central pursuing.

The third cost is one that arises if the nominal prices of goods and the nominal wages of workers are rigid downward, meaning that nominal prices and nominal wages can only go up but never down. If this is a valid description of the world, then any relative price change between two goods or any fall in the real wage can only be brought about by a rise in the price level. So in principle, nominal downward rigidities

> ... the optimal inflation rate is well below the two percent or more that we observe.

can explain why we see positive inflation targets. However, in a realistic model of the economy that incorporates this idea, the best inflation rate is at most half a percent per year. So the optimal inflation rate is well below the two percent or more that we observe.

What are the implications of your work for avoiding and living with the credit market conditions that emerged in August 2007 and dominated the economy through 2008?

Over the past decade, financial institutions that act like banks have developed. They are not, however, required by law to be under the regulations and supervision of the government in the same way as regular banks are. Going forward, I believe that it is desirable to have an overhaul of the existing regulatory system in order to ensure equal regulation and supervision for all financial institutions.

What advice do you have for a student who is just starting to study economics? Is it a good choice of major? What subjects go well with it?

If you are just starting studying economics, be patient. Economics can be more formal than other social sciences, and because of this, it may take a little while before you can apply what you learn in your economics classes to enhance your understanding of the economy around you. Subjects that are nice complements with economics are statistics and applied math.

Do you have any special advice for young women who might be contemplating a career in economics?

About one third of newly minted economics Ph.Ds are women, but only about 8 percent of full professors in a Ph.D.-granting economics department are women. Looking at statistics like this can be discouraging. However, from my fifteen years of experience of working in this field, I don't see any reason why young women who are about to start a career in economics will not be able to change these statistics.

Above full-employment equilibrium A macroeconomic equilibrium in which real GDP exceeds potential GDP. (p. 658)

Absolute advantage A person has an absolute advantage if that person is more productive than another person. (p. 38)

Adverse selection The tendency for people to *enter into agreements* in which that can use their private information to their own advantage and to the disadvantage of the uninformed party. (p. 472)

Aggregate demand The relationship between the quantity of real GDP demanded and the price level. (p. 652)

Aggregate planned expenditure The sum of planned consumption expenditure, planned investment, planned government expenditure on goods and services, and planned exports minus planned imports. (p. 672)

Aggregate production function The relationship between real GDP and the quantity of labor when all other influences on production remain the same. (p. 545)

Allocative efficiency A situation in which goods and services are produced at the lowest possible cost and in the quantities that provide the greatest possible benefit. We cannot produce more of any good without giving up some of another good that we *value more highly*. (p. 33)

Antitrust law A law that regulates oligopolies and prevents them from becoming monopolies or behaving like monopolies. (p. 356)

Asymmetric information A market in which buyers and sellers have private information. (p. 472)

Automatic fiscal policy A fiscal policy action that is triggered by the state of the economy with no action by the government. (p. 740)

Autonomous expenditure The sum of those components of aggregate planned expenditure that are not influenced by real GDP. Autonomous expenditure equals the sum of investment, government expenditure, exports, and the autonomous parts of consumption expenditure and imports. (p. 676)

Autonomous tax multiplier The change in equilibrium expenditure and real GDP that results from a change in autonomous taxes divided by the change in autonomous taxes. (p. 694)

Average cost pricing rule A rule that sets price to cover cost including normal profit, which means setting the price equal to average total cost. (p. 314)

Average fixed cost Total fixed cost per unit of output. (p. 258)

Average product The average product of a factor of production. It equals total product divided by the quantity of the factor employed. (p. 253)

Average total cost Total cost per unit of output. (p. 258)

Average variable cost Total variable cost per unit of output. (p. 258)

Balanced budget A government budget in which receipts and outlays are equal. (p. 730)

Balanced budget multiplier The change in equilibrium expenditure and real GDP that results from equal changes in government expenditure and lump-sum taxes divided by the change in government expenditure. (p. 695)

Balance of payments accounts A country's record of international trading, borrowing, and lending. (p. 631)

Barrier to entry A natural or legal constraint that protects a firm from potential competitors. (p. 300)

Behavioral economics A study of the ways in which limits on the human brain's ability to compute and implement rational decisions influences economic behavior—both the decisions that people make and the consequences of those decisions for the way markets work. (p. 194)

Beige book The Fed's publication that summarizes all the data that it gathers and that describes the current state of the economy. (p. 755)

Below full-employment equilibrium A macroeconomic equilibrium in which potential GDP exceeds real GDP. (p. 659)

Benefit The benefit of something is the gain or pleasure that it brings and is determined by preferences. (p. 8)

Big tradeoff The tradeoff between equality and efficiency. (pp. 117, 456)

Bilateral monopoly A situation in which a monopoly seller faces a monopsony buyer. (p. 425)

Black market An illegal market in which the price exceeds the legally imposed price ceiling. (p. 128)

Bond A promise to make specified payments on specified dates. (p. 567)

Bond market The market in which bonds issued by firms and governments are traded. (p. 567)

Budget deficit A government's budget balance that is negative—outlays exceed receipts. (p. 730)

Budget line The limit to a household's consumption choices. It marks the boundary between those combinations of goods and services that a household can afford to buy and those that it cannot afford. (pp. 180, 204)

Budget surplus A government's budget balance that is positive—receipts exceed outlays. (p. 730)

Business cycle The periodic but irregular up-and-down movement of total production and other measures of economic activity. (p. 497)

Capital The tools, equipment, buildings, and other constructions that businesses use to produce goods and services. (p. 4)

Capital and financial account A record of foreign investment in a country minus its investment abroad. (p. 631)

Capital accumulation The growth of capital resources, including *human capital*. (p. 36)

Capture theory A theory that regulation serves the self-interest of the producer, who captures the regulator and maximizes economic profit. (p. 313)

Cartel A group of firms acting together—colluding—to limit output, raise the price, and increase economic profit. (p. 343)

Central bank A bank's bank and a public authority that regulates the nation's depository institutions and conducts monetary policy, which means it adjusts the quantity of money in circulation and influences interest rates. (p. 596)

Ceteris paribus Other things being equal—all other relevant things remaining the same. (p. 22)

Chained-dollar real GDP A measure of real GDP derived by valuing production at the prices of both the current year and previous year and linking (chaining) those prices back to the prices of the reference base year. (p. 506)

Change in demand A change in buyers' plans that occurs when some influence on those plans other than the price of the good changes. It is illustrated by a shift of the demand curve. (p. 58)

Change in supply A change in sellers' plans that occurs when some influence on those plans other than the price of the good changes. It is illustrated by a shift of the supply curve. (p. 63)

Change in the quantity demanded A change in buyers' plans that occurs when the price of a good changes but all other influences on buyers' plans remain unchanged. It is illustrated by a movement along the demand curve. (p. 61)

Change in the quantity supplied A change in sellers' plans that occurs when the price of a good changes but all other influences on sellers' plans remain unchanged. It is illustrated by a movement along the supply curve. (p. 64)

Classical A macroeconomist who believes that the economy is self-regulating and always at full employment. (p. 662)

Classical growth theory A theory of economic growth based on the view that the growth of real GDP per person is temporary and that when it rises above subsistence level, a population explosion eventually brings it back to subsistence level. (p. 553)

Coase theorem The proposition that if property rights exist, if only a small number of parties are involved, and transactions costs are low, then private transactions are efficient. (p. 397)

Collusive agreement An agreement between two (or more) producers to form a cartel to restrict output, raise

the price, and increase profits. (p. 346)

Command system A method of allocating resources by the order (command) of someone in authority. In a firm a managerial hierarchy organizes production. (pp. 106, 233)

Common resource A resource that is rival and nonexcludable. (p. 374)

Comparative advantage A person or country has a comparative advantage in an activity if that person or country can perform the activity at a lower opportunity cost than anyone else or any other country. (p. 38)

Competitive market A market that has many buyers and many sellers, so no single buyer or seller can influence the price. (p. 56)

Complement A good that is used in conjunction with another good. (p. 59)

Compound interest The interest on an initial investment plus the interest on the interest that the investment has previously earned. (p. 434)

Constant returns to scale Features of a firm's technology that lead to constant long-run average cost as output increases. When constant returns to scale are present, the *LRAC* curve is horizontal. (p. 264)

Consumer equilibrium A situation in which a consumer has allocated all his or her available income in the way that, given the prices of goods and services, maximizes his or her total utility. (p. 183)

Consumer Price Index (CPI) An index that measures the average of the prices paid by urban consumers for a fixed basket of consumer goods and services. (p. 523)

Consumer surplus The excess of the benefit received from a good over the amount paid for it. It is calculated as the marginal benefit (or value) of a good minus its price, summed over the quantity bought. (p. 109)

Consumption expenditure The total payment for consumer goods and services. (p. 491)

Consumption function The relationship between consumption expenditure and disposable income, other things remaining the same. (p. 672)

Contestable market A market in which firms can enter and leave so easily that firms in the market face competition from *potential* entrants. (p. 354)

Cooperative equilibrium The outcome of a game in which the players make and share the monopoly profit. (p. 353)

Core inflation rate The Fed's operational guide is the rate of increase in the core PCE deflator, which is the PCE deflator excluding food and fuel prices. (p. 755)

Core CPI inflation rate The CPI inflation rate excluding volatile elements (food and fuel). (p. 527)

Cost-push inflation An inflation that results from an initial increase in costs. (p. 704)

Council of Economic Advisers The President's council whose main work is to monitor the economy and keep the President and the public well informed about the current state of the economy and the best available forecasts of where it is heading. (p. 729)

Crawling peg An exchange rate that follows a path determined by a decision of the government or the central bank and is achieved in a similar way to a fixed exchange rate. (p. 629)

Creditor nation A country that during its entire history has invested more in the rest of the world than other countries have invested in it. (p. 633)

Credit risk The risk that a borrower, also known as a creditor, might not repay a loan. (p. 475)

Cross elasticity of demand The responsiveness of the demand for a good to a change in the price of a substitute or complement, other things remaining the same. It is calculated as the percentage change in the quantity demanded of the good divided by the percentage change in the price of the substitute or complement. (p. 91)

Crowding-out effect The tendency for a government budget deficit to raise the real interest rate and decrease investment. (p. 578)

Currency The notes and coins held by individuals and businesses. (p. 591)

Currency drain ratio The ratio of currency to deposits. (p. 600)

Current account A record of receipts from exports of goods and services, payments for imports of goods and services, net interest income paid abroad and net transfers received from abroad. (p. 631)

Cycle The tendency for a variable to alternate between upward and downward movements. (p. 505)

Cyclical surplus or deficit The actual surplus or deficit minus the structural surplus or deficit. (p. 741)

Cyclical unemployment The higher than normal unemployment at a business cycle trough and the lower than normal unemployment at a business cycle peak. (p. 519)

Deadweight loss A measure of inefficiency. It is equal to the decrease in total surplus that results from an inefficient level of production. (p. 113)

Debtor nation A country that during its entire history has borrowed more from the rest of the world than other countries have lent it. (p. 633)

Default risk The risk that a borrower, also known as a creditor, might not repay a loan. (p. 475)

Deflation A persistently falling price level. (p. 522)

Demand The entire relationship between the price of the good and the quantity demanded of it when all other influences on buyers' plans remain the same. It is illustrated by a demand curve and described by a demand schedule. (p. 57)

Demand curve A curve that shows the relationship between the quantity demanded of a good and its price when all other influences on consumers' planned purchases remain the same. (p. 58)

Demand for loanable funds The relationship between the quantity of loanable funds demanded and the real interest rate when all other influences on borrowing plans remain the same. (p. 572)

Demand for money The relationship between the quantity of real money demanded and the nominal interest rate when all other influences on the amount of money that people wish to hold remain the same. (p. 603)

Demand-pull inflation An inflation that starts because aggregate demand increases. (p. 702)

Depository institution A financial firm that takes deposits from households and firms. (p. 593)

Depreciation The decrease in the value of a firm's capital that results from wear and tear and obsolescence. (p. 492)

Deregulation The process of removing regulation of prices, quantities, entry, and other aspects of economic activity in a firm or industry. (p. 313)

Derived demand Demand for a factor of production—it is derived from the demand for the goods and services produced by that factor. (p. 419)

Desired reserve ratio The ratio of reserves to deposits that banks *plan* to hold. (p. 600)

Diminishing marginal rate of substitution The general tendency for a person to be willing to give up less of good *y* to get one more unit of good *x*, while at the same time remaining indifferent as the quantity of good *x* increases. (p. 208)

Diminishing marginal returns The tendency for the marginal product of an additional unit of a factor of production to be less than the marginal product of the previous unit of the factor. (p. 255)

Diminishing marginal utility The tendency for marginal utility to decrease as the quantity consumed of a good increases. (p. 182)

Direct relationship A relationship between two variables that move in the same direction. (p. 16)

Discounting The calculation we use to convert a future amount of money to its present value. (p. 434)

Discouraged worker A marginally attached worker who has stopped looking for a job because of repeated failure to find one. (p. 517)

Discretionary fiscal policy A fiscal action that is initiated by an act of Congress. (p. 740)

Diseconomies of scale Features of a firm's technology that make average total cost rise as output increases—the *LRAC* curve slopes upward.(p. 264)

Disposable income Aggregate income minus taxes plus transfer payments. (pp. 654, 672)

Doha Development Agenda (Doha Round) Negotiations held in Doha, Qatar, to lower tariff barriers and quotas that restrict international trade in farm products and services. (p. 162)

Dominant strategy equilibrium An equilibrium in which the best strategy for each player is to cheat *regardless of the strategy of the other player*. (p. 345)

Dumping The sale by a foreign firm of exports at a lower price than the cost of production. (p. 163)

Duopoly A market structure in which two producers of a good or service compete. (p. 342)

Economic depreciation The *fall* in the market value of a firm's capital over a given period. (p. 229)

Economic efficiency A situation that occurs when the firm produces a given output at the least cost. (p. 231)

Economic growth The expansion of production possibilities. (p. 36)

Economic growth rate The annual percentage change in real GDP. (p. 540)

Economic model A description of some aspect of the economic world that includes only those features of the world that are needed for the purpose at hand. (p. 10)

Economic profit A firm's total revenue minus its total cost, with total cost measured as the opportunity cost of production. (p. 228)

Economic rent Any surplus—consumer surplus, producer surplus or economic profit. (p. 308)

Economics The social science that studies the *choices* that individuals, businesses, governments, and entire societies make as they cope with *scarcity* and the *incentives* that influence and reconcile those choices. (p. 2)

Economies of scale Features of a firm's technology that make average total cost fall as output increases—the *LRAC* curve slopes downward. (pp. 242, 264)

Economies of scope Decreases in average total cost that occur when a firm uses specialized resources to produce a range of goods and services. (p. 243)

Efficiency A situation in which the available resources are used to produce goods and services at the lowest possible cost and in quantities that give the greatest value or benefit. (p. 5)

Efficient scale The quantity at which average total cost is a minimum—the quantity at the bottom of the U-shaped *ATC* curve. (p. 328)

Elastic demand Demand with a price elasticity greater than 1; other things remaining the same, the percentage change in the quantity demanded exceeds the percentage change in price. (p. 87)

Elasticity of supply The responsiveness of the quantity supplied of a good to a change in its price, other things remaining the same. (p. 94)

Employment Act of 1946 A landmark Congressional act that recognizes a role for government actions to keep unemployment low, the economy expanding, and inflation in check. (p. 728)

Employment-to-population ratio The percentage of people of working age who have jobs. (p. 516)

Entrepreneurship The human resource that organizes the other three factors of production: labor, land, and capital. (p. 4)

Equilibrium expenditure The level of aggregate expenditure that occurs when aggregate *planned* expenditure equals real GDP. (p. 678)

Equilibrium price The price at which the quantity demanded equals the quantity supplied. (p. 66)

Equilibrium quantity The quantity bought and sold at the equilibrium price. (p. 66)

Excess capacity A firm has excess capacity if it produces below its efficient scale. (p. 328)

Excess reserves A bank's actual reserves minus its desired reserves. (p. 600)

Exchange rate The price at which one currency exchanges for another in the foreign exchange market. (p. 618)

Excludable A good or service or a resource is excludable if it is possible to prevent someone from enjoying the benefit of it. (p. 374)

Expansion A business cycle phase between a trough and a peak—a period in which real GDP increases. (p. 497)

Expected utility The utility value of what a person expects to own at a given point in time. (p. 467)

Expected wealth The money value of what a person expects to own at a given point in time. (p. 466)

Exports The goods and services that we sell to people in other countries. (pp. 152, 492)

External diseconomies Factors outside the control of a firm that raise the firm's costs as the market output increases. (p. 287)

External economies Factors beyond the control of a firm that lower the firm's costs as the market output increases. (p. 287)

Externality A cost (external cost) or a benefit (external benefit) that arises from production or consumption of a private good and that falls on someone other than its producer or consumer. (p. 374)

Factors of production The productive resources used to produce goods and services. (p. 3)

Federal budget The annual statement of the outlays and receipts of the government of the United States, together with the laws and regulations that approve and support those outlays and taxes. (p. 728)

Federal funds rate The interest rate that the banks charge each other on overnight loans. (pp. 593, 756)

Federal Open Market Committee The main policy-making organ of the Federal Reserve System. (p. 596)

Federal Reserve System (the Fed) The central bank of the United States. (p. 596)

Final good An item that is bought by its final user during the specified time period. (p. 490)

Financial capital The funds that firms use to buy physical capital. (p. 566)

Financial institution A firm that operates on both sides of the market for financial capital. It borrows in one market and lends in another. (p. 568)

Firm An economic unit that hires factors of production and organizes those factors to produce and sell goods and services. (pp. 41, 228)

Fiscal imbalance The present value of the government's commitments to pay benefits minus the present value of its tax revenues. (p. 738)

Fiscal policy The use of the federal budget, by setting and changing tax rates, making transfer payments, and purchasing goods and services, to achieve macroeconomic objectives such as full employment, sustained economic growth, and price level stability. (pp. 654, 728)

Fiscal stimulus The use of fiscal policy to increase production and employment. (p. 740)

Fixed exchange rate An exchange rate the value of which is determined by a decision of the government or the central bank and is achieved by central bank intervention in the foreign exchange market to block the unregulated forces of demand and supply. (p. 628)

Flexible exchange rate An exchange rate that is determined by demand and supply in the foreign exchange market with no direct intervention by the central bank. (p. 628)

Foreign currency The money of other countries regardless of whether that money is in the form of notes, coins, or bank deposits. (p. 618)

Foreign exchange market The market in which the currency of one country is exchanged for the currency of another. (p. 618)

Four-firm concentration ratio A measure of market power that is calculated as the percentage of the value of sales accounted for by the four largest firms in an industry. (p. 238)

Free-rider problem The problem that the market would provide an inefficiently small quantity of a public good. (p. 377)

Frictional unemployment The unemployment that arises from normal labor turnover—from people entering and leaving the labor force and from the ongoing creation and destruction of jobs. (p. 519)

Full employment A situation in which the unemployment rate equals the natural unemployment rate. At full employment, there is no cyclical unemployment—all unemployment is frictional and structural. (p. 519)

Full-employment equilibrium A macroeconomic equilibrium in which real GDP equals potential GDP. (p. 659)

Game theory A set of tools for studying strategic behavior—behavior that takes into account the expected behavior of others and the recognition of mutual interdependence. (p. 344)

General Agreement on Tariffs and Trade (GATT) An international agreement signed in 1947 to reduce tariffs on international trade. (p. 159)

Generational accounting An accounting system that measures the lifetime tax burden and benefits of each generation. (p. 738)

Generational imbalance The division of the fiscal imbalance between the current and future generations, assuming that the current generation will enjoy the existing levels of taxes and benefits. (p. 739)

Gini ratio The ratio of the area between the line of equality and the Lorenz curve to the entire area beneath the line of equality. (p. 445)

Goods and services The objects that people value and produce to satisfy human wants. (p. 3)

Government debt The total amount that the government has borrowed. It equals the sum of past budget deficits minus the sum of past budget surpluses. (p. 732)

Government expenditure Goods and services bought by government. (p. 492)

Government expenditure multiplier the quantitative effect of a change in government expenditure on real GDP. It is calculated as the change in real GDP that results from a change in government expenditure divided by the change in government expenditure. (pp. 694, 743)

Government failure A situation in which government actions lead to inefficiency—to either underprovision or overprovision. (p. 372)

Government sector balance An amount equal to net taxes minus government expenditure on goods and services. (p. 634)

Gross domestic product (GDP) The market value of all final goods and services produced within a country during a given time period. (p. 490)

Gross investment The total amount spent on purchases of new capital and on replacing depreciated capital. (pp. 492, 566)

Herfindahl–Hirschman Index A measure of market power that is calculated as the square of the market share of each firm (as a percentage) summed over the largest 50 firms (or over all firms if there are fewer than 50) in a market. (p. 238)

Hotelling Principle The idea that traders expect the price of a nonrenewable natural resource to rise at a rate equal to the interest rate. (p. 430)

Human capital The knowledge and skill that people obtain from education, on-the-job training, and work experience. (p. 3)

Hyperinflation An inflation rate of 50 percent a month or higher that grinds the economy to a halt and causes a society to collapse. (p. 522)

Implicit rental rate The firm's opportunity cost of using its own capital. (p. 228)

Import quota A restriction that limits the maximum quantity of a good that may be imported in a given period. (p. 160)

Imports The goods and services that we buy from people in other countries. (pp. 152, 492)

Incentive A reward that encourages an action or a penalty that discourages one. (p. 2)

Incentive system A method of organizing production that uses a market-like mechanism inside the firm. (p. 233)

Income effect The effect of a change in income on buying plans, other things remaining the same. (p. 213)

Income elasticity of demand The responsiveness of demand to a change in income, other things remaining the same. It is calculated as the percentage change in the quantity demanded divided by the percentage change in income. (p. 92)

Indifference curve A line that shows combinations of goods among which a consumer is *indifferent*. (p. 207)

Individual transferable quota (ITQ) A production limit that is assigned to an individual who is free to transfer (sell) the quota to someone else. (p. 404)

Induced expenditure The sum of the components of aggregate planned expenditure that vary with real GDP. Induced expenditure equals consumption expenditure minus imports. (p. 676)

Inelastic demand A demand with a price elasticity between 0 and 1; the percentage change in the quantity demanded is less than the percentage change in price. (p. 86)

Infant-industry argument The argument that it is necessary to protect a new industry to enable it to grow into a mature industry that can compete in world markets. (p. 163)

Inferior good A good for which demand decreases as income increases. (p. 60)

Inflation A persistently rising price level. (p. 522)

Inflationary gap An output gap in which real GDP exceeds potential GDP. (p. 658)

Inflation rate targeting A monetary policy strategy in which the central bank makes a public commitment to achieve an explicit inflation rate and to explain how its policy actions will achieve that target. (p. 769)

Interest The income that capital earns. (p. 4)

Interest rate parity A situation in which the rates of return on assets in different currencies are equal. (p. 626)

Intermediate good An item that is produced by one firm, bought by another firm, and used as a component of a final good or service. (p. 490)

Inverse relationship A relationship between variables that move in opposite directions. (p. 17)

Investment The purchase of new plant, equipment, and buildings, and additions to inventories. (p. 492)

Job A contract for the trade of labor services. (p. 418)

Keynesian A macroeconomist who believes that left alone, the economy would rarely operate at full employment and that to achieve full employment, active help from fiscal policy and monetary policy is required. (p. 662)

Keynesian cycle theory A theory that fluctuations in investment driven by fluctuations in business confidence—summarized by the phrase "animal spirits"—are the main source of fluctuations in aggregate demand. (p. 712)

Labor The work time and work effort that people devote to producing goods and services. (p. 3)

Labor force The sum of the people who are employed and who are unemployed. (p. 515)

Labor force participation rate The percentage of the working-age population who are members of the labor force. (p. 517)

Labor productivity The quantity of real GDP produced by an hour of labor. (p. 549)

Labor union An organized group of workers that aims to increase the wage rate and influence other job conditions. (p. 424)

Laffer curve The relationship between the tax rate and the amount of tax revenue collected. (p. 737)

Land The "gifts of nature" that we use to produce goods and services. (p. 3)

Law of demand Other things remaining the same, the higher the price of a good, the smaller is the quantity demanded of it; the lower the price of a good, the larger is the quantity demanded of it. (p. 57)

Law of diminishing returns As a firm uses more of a variable factor of production with a given quantity of the fixed factor of production, the

marginal product of the variable factor of production eventually diminishes. (p. 255)

Law of supply Other things remaining the same, the higher the price of a good, the greater is the quantity supplied of it. (p. 62)

Legal monopoly A market in which competition and entry are restricted by the granting of a public franchise, government license, patent, or copyright. (p. 300)

Lemon problem The problem that in a market in which it is not possible to distinguish reliable products from lemons, there are too many lemons and too few reliable products traded. (p. 472)

Lender of last resort The Fed is the lender of last resort—depository institutions that are short of reserves can borrow from the Fed. (p. 599)

Limit pricing The practice of setting the price at the highest level that inflicts a loss on an entrant. (p. 355)

Linear relationship A relationship between two variables that is illustrated by a straight line. (p. 16)

Loanable funds market The aggregate of all the individual markets in which households, firms, governments, banks, and other financial institutions borrow and lend. (p. 570)

Long run The time frame in which the quantities of *all* factors of production can be varied. (p. 252)

Long-run aggregate supply The relationship between the quantity of real GDP supplied and the price level when the money wage rate changes in step with the price level to maintain full employment. (p. 648)

Long-run average cost curve The relationship between the lowest attainable average total cost and output when the firm can change both the plant it uses and the quantity of labor it employs. (p. 263)

Long-run macroeconomic equilibrium A situation that occurs when real GDP equals potential GDP—the economy is on its long-run aggregate supply curve. (p. 656)

Long-run market supply curve A curve that shows how the quantity

supplied in a market varies as the market price varies after all the possible adjustments have been made, including changes in each firm's plant and the number of firms in the market. (p. 287)

Long-run Phillips curve A curve that shows the relationship between inflation and unemployment when the actual inflation rate equals the expected inflation rate. (p. 709)

Lorenz curve A curve that graphs the cumulative percentage of income or wealth against the cumulative percentage of households. (p. 443)

M1 A measure of money that consists of currency and traveler's checks plus checking deposits owned by individuals and businesses. (p. 591)

M2 A measure of money that consists of M1 plus time deposits, savings deposits, money market mutual funds, and other deposits. (p. 591)

Macroeconomics The study of the performance of the national economy and the global economy. (p. 2)

Margin When a choice is made by comparing a little more of something with its cost, the choice is made at the margin. (p. 9)

Marginal benefit The benefit that a person receives from consuming one more unit of a good or service. It is measured as the maximum amount that a person is willing to pay for one more unit of the good or service. (pp. 9, 34)

Marginal benefit curve A curve that shows the relationship between the marginal benefit of a good and the quantity of that good consumed. (p. 34)

Marginal cost The *opportunity cost* of producing *one* more unit of a good or service. It is the best alternative forgone. It is calculated as the increase in total cost divided by the increase in output. (pp. 9, 33, 258)

Marginal cost pricing rule A rule that sets the price of a good or service equal to the marginal cost of producing it. (p. 313)

Marginal external benefit The benefit from an additional unit of a good or service that people other than the consumer enjoy. (p. 381)

Marginal external cost The cost of producing an additional unit of a good or service that falls on people other than the producer. (p. 395)

Marginal private benefit The benefit from an additional unit of a good or service that the consumer of that good or service receives. (p. 381)

Marginal private cost The cost of producing an additional unit of a good or service that is borne by the producer of that good or service. (p. 395)

Marginal product The increase in total product that results from a one-unit increase in the variable input, with all other inputs remaining the same. It is calculated as the increase in total product divided by the increase in the variable input employed, when the quantities of all other inputs remain the same. (p. 253)

Marginal propensity to consume The fraction of a *change* in disposable income that is spent on consumption. It is calculated as the *change* in consumption expenditure divided by the *change* in disposable income. (p. 674)

Marginal propensity to import The fraction of an increase in real GDP that is spent on imports. It is calculated as the *change* in imports divided by the *change* in real GDP, other things remaining the same. (p. 675)

Marginal propensity to save The fraction of a *change* in disposable income that is saved. It is calculated as the *change* in saving divided by the *change* in disposable income. (p. 674)

Marginal rate of substitution The rate at which a person will give up good *y* (the good measured on the *y*-axis) to get an additional unit of good *x* (the good measured on the *x*-axis) while at the same time remaining indifferent (remaining on the same indifference curve) as the quantity of *x* increases. (p. 208)

Marginal revenue The change in total revenue that results from a one-unit increase in the quantity sold. It is calculated as the change in total revenue divided by the change in quantity sold. (p. 274)

Marginal social benefit The marginal benefit enjoyed by society—by the consumer of a good or service (marginal private benefit) plus the marginal benefit enjoyed by others (marginal external benefit). (p. 381)

Marginal social cost The marginal cost incurred by the producer and by everyone else on whom the cost falls—by society. It is the sum of marginal private cost and marginal external cost. (p. 395)

Marginal utility The *change* in total utility resulting from a one-unit increase in the quantity of a good consumed. (p. 181)

Marginal utility per dollar The marginal utility from a good that results from spending one more dollar on it. It is calculated as the marginal utility from the good divided by its price. (p. 184)

Marginally attached worker A person who currently is neither working nor looking for work but has indicated that he or she wants and is available for a job and has looked for work some time in the recent past. (p. 517)

Market Any arrangement that enables buyers and sellers to get information and to do business with each other. (p. 42)

Market failure A situation in which a market delivers an inefficient outcome. (p. 113)

Market income The wages, interest, rent, and profit earned in factor markets and before paying income taxes. (p. 442)

Markup The amount by which the firm's price exceeds its marginal cost. (p. 329)

Means of payment A method of settling a debt. (p. 590)

Microeconomics The study of the choices that individuals and businesses make, the way these choices interact in markets, and the influence of governments. (p. 2)

Minimum efficient scale The *smallest* quantity of output at which the long-run average cost reaches its lowest level. (p. 265)

Minimum wage A regulation that makes the hiring of labor below a specified wage rate illegal. The lowest wage at which a firm may legally hire labor. (p. 131)

Mixed good A private good the production or consumption of which creates an externality. (p. 374)

Monetarist A macroeconomist who believes that the economy is self-regulating and that it will normally operate at full employment, provided that monetary policy is not erratic and that the pace of money growth is kept steady. (p. 663)

Monetarist cycle theory A theory that fluctuations in both investment and consumption expenditure, driven by fluctuations in the growth rate of the quantity of money, are the main source of fluctuations in aggregate demand. (p. 712)

Monetary base The sum of Federal Reserve notes, coins and depository institution deposits at the Fed. (p. 597)

Monetary policy The Fed conducts the nation's monetary policy by changing interest rates and adjusting the quantity of money. (p. 654)

Monetary policy instrument A variable that the Fed can directly control or at least very closely target. (p. 756)

Money Any commodity or token that is generally acceptable as a means of payment. (pp. 42, 590)

Money income Market income plus cash payments to households by the government. (p. 442)

Money multiplier The ratio of the change in the quantity of money to the change in the monetary base. (p. 601)

Money price The number of dollars that must be given up in exchange for a good or service. (p. 56)

Monopolistic competition A market structure in which a large number of firms make similar but slightly different products and compete on product quality, price, and marketing, and firms are free to enter or exit the market. (pp. 237, 324)

Monopoly A market structure in which there is one firm, which produces a good or service that has no close substitutes and in which the firm is protected from competition by a barrier preventing the entry of new firms. (pp. 237, 300)

Monopsony A market in which there is a single buyer. (p. 425)

Moral hazard A tendency for people with private information, *after entering into an agreement*, to use that information for their own benefit and at the cost of the less-informed party. (p. 472)

Mortgage A legal contract that gives ownership of a home to the lender in the event that the borrower fails to meet the agreed loan payments (repayments and interest). (p. 567)

Mortgage-backed security A type of bond that entitles its holder to the income from a package of mortgages. (p. 568)

Multiplier The amount by which a change in autonomous expenditure is magnified or multiplied to determine the change in equilibrium expenditure and real GDP. (p. 680)

Nash equilibrium The outcome of a game that occurs when player A takes the best possible action given the action of player B and player B takes the best possible action given the action of player A. (p. 345)

National saving The sum of private saving (saving by households and businesses) and government saving. (p. 571)

Natural monopoly A market in which economies of scale enable one firm to supply the entire market at the lowest possible cost. (p. 300)

Natural monopoly good A good that is nonrival and excludable. When buyers can be excluded if they don't pay but the good is nonrival, marginal cost is zero. (p. 374)

Natural unemployment rate The unemployment rate when the economy is at full employment—natural unemployment as a percentage of the labor force. (p. 519)

Negative externality An externality that arises from either production or consumption and that imposes an external cost. (p. 374)

Negative relationship A relationship between variables that move in opposite directions. (p. 17)

Neoclassical growth theory A theory of economic growth that proposes that real GDP per person grows because technological change induces an amount of saving and investment that makes capital per hour of labor grow. (p. 553)

Net borrower A country that is borrowing more from the rest of the world than it is lending to it. (p. 633)

Net exports The value of exports of goods and services minus the value of imports of goods and services. (pp. 492, 634)

Net investment The amount by which the value of capital increases—gross investment minus depreciation. (pp. 492, 566)

Net lender A country that is lending more to the rest of the world than it is borrowing from it. (p. 633)

Net taxes Taxes paid to governments minus cash transfers received from governments. (p. 570)

Net worth The market value of what a financial institution has lent minus the market value of what it has borrowed. (p. 569)

Neuroeconomics The study of the activity of the human brain when a person makes an economic decision. (p. 195)

New classical A macroeconomist who holds the view that business cycle fluctuations are the efficient responses of a well-functioning market economy bombarded by shocks that arise from the uneven pace of technological change. (p. 662)

New classical cycle theory A rational expectations theory of the business cycle in which the rational expectation of the price level, which is determined by potential GDP and *expected* aggregate demand, determines the money wage rate and the position of the *SAS* curve. (p. 712)

New growth theory A theory of economic growth based on the idea that real GDP per person grows because of the choices that people make in the pursuit of profit and that growth will persist indefinitely. (p. 554)

New Keynesian A macroeconomist who holds the view that not only is the money wage rate sticky but also

that the prices of goods and services are sticky. (p. 663)

New Keynesian cycle theory A rational expectations theory of the business cycle that emphasizes the fact that today's money wage rates were negotiated at many past dates, which means that *past* rational expectations of the current price level influence the money wage rate and the position of the *SAS* curve. (p. 712)

Nominal GDP The value of the final goods and services produced in a given year valued at the prices that prevailed in that same year. It is a more precise name for GDP. (p. 495)

Nominal interest rate The number of dollars that a borrower pays and a lender receives in interest in a year expressed as a percentage of the number of dollars borrowed and lent. (p. 571)

Nonexcludable A good or service or a resource is nonexcludable if it is impossible (or extremely costly) to prevent someone from enjoying its benefits. (p. 374)

Nonrenewable natural resources Natural resources that can be used only once. (p. 418)

Nonrival A good or service or a resource is nonrival if its use by one person does not decrease the quantity available for someone else. (p. 374)

Normal good A good for which demand increases as income increases. (p. 60)

Normal profit The return to entrepreneurship is normal profit and it is the profit that an entrepreneur earns *on average*. (p. 229)

Official settlements account A record of the change in official reserves, which are the government's holdings of foreign currency. (p. 631)

Offshore outsourcing A U.S. firm buys finished goods, components, or services from other firms in other countries. (p. 165)

Offshoring A U.S. firm hires foreign labor and produces in a foreign country or a U.S. firm buys finished goods, components, or services from firms in other countries. (p. 165)

Oligopoly A market structure in which a small number of firms compete. (pp. 237, 342)

Open market operation The purchase or sale of government securities—U.S. Treasury bills and bonds—by the Federal Reserve in the loanable funds market. (p. 597)

Opportunity cost The highest-valued alternative that we must give up to get something. (pp. 8, 31)

Output gap The gap between real GDP and potential GDP. (pp. 520, 658)

Outsourcing A U.S. firm buys finished goods, components, or services from other firms in the United States or from firms in other countries. (p. 165)

Payoff matrix A table that shows the payoffs for every possible action by each player for every possible action by each other player. (p. 344)

Perfect competition A market in which there are many firms each selling an identical product; there are many buyers; there are no restrictions on entry into the industry; firms in the industry have no advantage over potential new entrants; and firms and buyers are well informed about the price of each firm's product. (pp. 237, 274)

Perfectly elastic demand Demand with an infinite price elasticity; the quantity demanded changes by an infinitely large percentage in response to a tiny price change. (p. 87)

Perfectly inelastic demand Demand with a price elasticity of zero; the quantity demanded remains constant when the price changes. (p. 86)

Perfect price discrimination Price discrimination that occurs when a firm sells each unit of output for the highest price that anyone is willing to pay for it. The firm extracts the entire consumer surplus. (p. 311)

Phillips curve A curve that shows a relationship between inflation and unemployment. (p. 708)

Pigovian taxes Taxes that are used as an incentive for producers to cut back on an activity that creates an external cost. (p. 398)

Political equilibrium The situation in which the choices of voters, firms, politicians, and bureaucrats are all compatible and no group can see a way of improving its position by making a different choice. (p. 373)

Pooling equilibrium The equilibrium in a market when only one message is available and an uninformed person cannot determine quality. (p. 475)

Positive externality An externality that arises from either production or consumption and that creates an external benefit. (p. 374)

Positive relationship A relationship between two variables that move in the same direction. (p. 16)

Potential GDP The value of production when all the economy's labor, capital, land, and entrepreneurial ability are fully employed; the quantity of real GDP at full employment. (p. 496)

Poverty A state in which a household's income is too low to be able to buy the quantities of food, shelter, and clothing that are deemed necessary. (p. 446)

Predatory pricing Setting a low price to drive competitors out of business with the intention of setting a monopoly price when the competition has gone. (p. 358)

Preferences A description of a person's likes and dislikes and the intensity of those feelings. (pp. 8, 34, 181)

Present value The amount of money that, if invested today, will grow to be as large as a given future amount when the interest that it will earn is taken into account. (pp. 434, 738)

Price cap A regulation that makes it illegal to charge a price higher than a specified level. (p. 128)

Price cap regulation A rule that specifies the highest price that the firm is permitted to set—a price ceiling. (p. 315)

Price ceiling A regulation that makes it illegal to charge a price higher than a specified level. (p. 128)

Price discrimination The practice of selling different units of a good or service for different prices. (p. 301)

Price effect The effect of a change in the price of a good on the quantity of the good consumed, other things remaining the same. (p. 211)

Price elasticity of demand A units-free measure of the responsiveness of the quantity demanded of a good to a change in its price, when all other influences on buyers' plans remain the same. (p. 84)

Price floor A regulation that makes it illegal to trade at a price lower than a specified level. (p. 131)

Price level The average level of prices. (p. 522)

Price taker A firm that cannot influence the price of the good or service it produces. (p. 274)

Principal–agent problem The problem of devising compensation rules that induce an *agent* to act in the best interest of a *principal*. (p. 234)

Principle of minimum differentiation The tendency for competitors to make themselves similar to appeal to the maximum number of clients or voters. (p. 379)

Private good A good or service that is both rival and excludable. (p. 374)

Private information Information about the value of an item being traded that is possessed by only buyers or sellers. (p. 472)

Private sector balance An amount equal to saving minus investment. (p. 634)

Producer surplus The excess of the amount received from the sale of a good or service over the cost of producing it. It is calculated as the price of a good minus the marginal cost (or minimum supply-price), summed over the quantity sold. (p. 111)

Product differentiation Making a product slightly different from the product of a competing firm. (pp. 237, 324)

Production efficiency A situation in which goods and services are produced at the lowest possible cost. (p. 31)

Production possibilities frontier The boundary between the combinations of goods and services that can be produced and the combinations that cannot. (p. 30)

Production quota An upper limit to the quantity of a good that may be produced in a specified period. (p. 139)

Profit The income earned by entrepreneurship. (p. 4)

Progressive income tax A tax on income at an average rate that increases as income increases. (p. 455)

Property rights The social arrangements that govern the ownership, use, and disposal of anything that people value. Property rights are enforceable in the courts. (pp. 42, 396)

Proportional income tax A tax on income at a constant average rate, regardless of the level of income. (p. 455)

Public choice A decision that has consequences for many people and perhaps for the entire society. (p. 372)

Public good A good or service that is both nonrival and nonexcludable. It can be consumed simultaneously by everyone and from which no one can be excluded from enjoying its benefits. (p. 374)

Public production The production of a good or service by a public authority that receives its revenue from the government. (p. 383)

Purchasing power parity A situation in which the prices in two countries are equal when converted at the exchange rate. (p. 626)

Quantity demanded The amount of a good or service that consumers plan to buy during a given time period at a particular price. (p. 57)

Quantity supplied The amount of a good or service that producers plan to sell during a given time period at a particular price. (p. 62)

Quantity theory of money The proposition that in the long run, an increase in the quantity of money brings an equal percentage increase in the price level. (p. 606)

Rate of return regulation A regulation that requires the firm to justify its price by showing that its return on capital doesn't exceed a specified target rate. (p. 314)

Rational choice A choice that compares costs and benefits and achieves the greatest benefit over cost for the person making the choice. (p. 8)

Rational expectation The best forecast possible, a forecast that uses all the available information. (p. 707)

Real business cycle theory A theory of the business cycle that regards random fluctuations in productivity as the main source of economic fluctuations. (p. 712)

Real exchange rate The relative price of U.S.-produced goods and services to foreign-produced goods and services. (p. 627)

Real GDP The value of final goods and services produced in a given year when valued at the prices of a reference base year. (p. 495)

Real GDP per person Real GDP divided by the population. (pp. 496, 540)

Real income A household's income expressed as a quantity of goods that the household can afford to buy. (p. 205)

Real interest rate The nominal interest rate adjusted to remove the effects of inflation on the buying power of money. It is approximately equal to the nominal interest rate minus the inflation rate. (p. 571)

Real wage rate The money (or nominal) wage rate divided by the price level. The real wage rate is the quantity of goods and services that an hour of labor earns. (p. 546)

Recession A business cycle phase in which real GDP decreases for at least two successive quarters. (p. 497)

Recessionary gap An output gap in which potential GDP exceeds real GDP. (p. 659)

Regressive income tax A tax on income at an average rate that decreases as income increases. (p. 455)

Regulation Rules administered by a government agency to influence prices, quantities, entry, and other aspects of economic activity in a firm or industry. (p. 313)

Relative price The ratio of the price of one good or service to the price of another good or service. A relative price is an opportunity cost. (pp. 56, 205)

Rent The income that land earns. (p. 4)

Rent ceiling A regulation that makes it illegal to charge a rent higher than a specified level. (p. 128)

Rent seeking The lobbying for special treatment by the government to create economic profit or to divert consumer surplus or producer surplus away from others. The pursuit of wealth by capturing economic rent. (pp. 167, 308)

Required reserve ratio The minimum percentage of deposits that depository institutions are required to hold as reserves. (p. 599)

Resale price maintenance A distributor's agreement with a manufacturer to resell a product *at or above a specified minimum price*. (p. 357)

Reserves A bank's reserves consist of notes and coins in its vaults plus its deposit at the Federal Reserve. (p. 593)

Risk aversion The dislike of risk. (p. 466)

Rival A good, service, or a resource is rival if its use by one person decreases the quantity available for someone else. (p. 374)

Rule of 70 A rule that states that the number of years it takes for the level of any variable to double is approximately 70 divided by the annual percentage growth rate of the variable. (p. 540)

Saving The amount of income that is not paid in taxes or spent on consumption goods and services. (p. 566)

Saving function The relationship between saving and disposable income, other things remaining the same. (p. 672)

Scarcity Our inability to satisfy all our wants. (p. 2)

Scatter diagram A graph that plots the value of one variable against the value of another variable for a number of different values of each variable. (p. 14)

Screening Inducing an informed party to reveal private information. (p. 475)

Search activity The time spent looking for someone with whom to do business. (p. 128)

Self-interest The choices that you think are the best ones available for you are choices made in your self-interest. (p. 5)

Separating equilibrium The equilibrium in a market when signaling provides full information to a previously uninformed person. (p. 475)

Short run The time frame in which the quantity of at least one factor of production is fixed and the quantities of the other factors can be varied. The fixed factor is usually capital—that is, the firm uses a given plant. (p. 252)

Short-run aggregate supply The relationship between the quantity of real GDP supplied and the price level when the money wage rate, the prices of other resources, and potential GDP remain constant. (p. 649)

Short-run market supply curve A curve that shows the quantity supplied in a market at each price when each firm's plant and the number of firms remain the same. (p. 280)

Short-run macroeconomic equilibrium A situation that occurs when the quantity of real GDP demanded equals the quantity of real GDP supplied—at the point of intersection of the *AD* curve and the *SAS* curve. (p. 656)

Short-run Phillips curve A curve that shows the tradeoff between inflation and unemployment, when the expected inflation rate and the natural unemployment rate are held constant. (p. 708)

Shutdown point The price and quantity at which the firm is indifferent between producing the profit-maximizing output and shutting down temporarily. The shutdown point occurs at the price and the quantity at which average variable cost is a minimum. (p. 278)

Signal An action taken by an informed person (or firm) to send a message to uninformed people. (p. 332)

Signaling A situation in which an informed person takes actions that send information to uninformed persons. (p. 474)

Single-price monopoly A monopoly that must sell each unit of its output for the same price to all its customers. (p. 301)

Slope The change in the value of the variable measured on the y-axis divided by the change in the value of the variable measured on the x-axis. (p. 20)

Social interest Choices that are the best ones for society as a whole. (p. 5)

Social interest theory A theory that the political and regulatory process relentlessly seeks out inefficiency and introduces regulation that eliminates deadweight loss and allocates resources efficiently. (p. 313)

Stagflation The combination of inflation and recession. (pp. 661, 705)

Stock A certificate of ownership and claim to the firm's profits. (p. 568)

Stock market A financial market in which shares of stocks of corporations are traded. (p. 568)

Strategies All the possible actions of each player in a game. (p. 344)

Structural surplus or deficit The budget balance that would occur if the economy were at full employment and real GDP were equal to potential GDP. (p. 741)

Structural unemployment The unemployment that arises when changes in technology or international competition change the skills needed to perform jobs or change the locations of jobs. (p. 519)

Subsidy A payment made by the government to a producer. (pp. 140, 383)

Substitute A good that can be used in place of another good. (p. 59)

Substitution effect The effect of a change in price of a good or service on the quantity bought when the consumer (hypothetically) remains indifferent between the original and the new consumption situations—that is, the consumer remains on the same indifference curve. (p. 214)

Sunk cost The past expenditure on a plant that has no resale value. (p. 252)

Supply The entire relationship between the price of a good and the quantity supplied of it when all other

influences on producers' planned sales remain the same. It is described by a supply schedule and illustrated by a supply curve. (p. 62)

Supply curve A curve that shows the relationship between the quantity supplied of a good and its price when all other influences on producers' planned sales remain the same. (p. 62)

Supply of loanable funds The relationship between the quantity of loanable funds supplied and the real interest rate when all other influences on lending plans remain the same. (p. 573)

Symmetry principle A requirement that people in similar situations be treated similarly. (p. 118)

Tariff A tax that is imposed by the importing country when an imported good crosses its international boundary. (p. 157)

Tax incidence The division of the burden of the tax between the buyer and the seller. (p. 133)

Tax multiplier The quantitative effect of a change in taxes on real GDP. It is calculated as the change in real GDP that results from a change in taxes divided by the change in taxes. (p. 743)

Tax wedge The gap between the before-tax and after-tax wage rates. (p. 735)

Technological change The development of new goods and of better ways of producing goods and services. (p. 36)

Technological efficiency A situation that occurs when the firm produces a given output by using the least amount of inputs. (p. 231)

Technology Any method of producing a good or service. (p. 230)

Time-series graph A graph that measures time (for example, years, quarter, or months) on the *x*-axis and the variable or variables in which we are interested on the *y*-axis. (p. 504)

Total cost The cost of all the productive resources that a firm uses. (p. 257)

Total fixed cost The cost of the firm's fixed inputs. (p. 257)

Total product The maximum output that a given quantity of labor can produce. (p. 253)

Total revenue The value of a firm's sales. It is calculated as the price of the good multiplied by the quantity sold. (pp. 88, 274)

Total revenue test A method of estimating the price elasticity of demand by observing the change in total revenue that results from a change in the price, when all other influences on the quantity sold remain the same. (p. 88)

Total surplus The sum of consumer surplus and producer surplus. (p. 112)

Total utility The total benefit that a person gets from the consumption of all the different goods and services. (p. 181)

Total variable cost The cost of all the firm's variable inputs. (p. 257)

Tradeoff A constraint that involves giving up one thing to get something else. (p. 8)

Tragedy of the commons The absence of incentives to prevent the overuse and depletion of a commonly owned resource. (p. 400)

Transactions costs The opportunity costs of making trades in a market. The costs that arise from finding someone with whom to do business, of reaching an agreement about the price and other aspects of the exchange, and of ensuring that the terms of the agreement are fulfilled. (pp. 115, 242, 397)

Trend The tendency for a variable to move in one general direction. (p. 505)

Tying arrangement An agreement to sell one product only if the buyer agrees to buy another, different product. (p. 357)

Unemployment rate The percentage of the people in the labor force who are unemployed. (p. 516)

Unit elastic demand Demand with a price elasticity of 1; the percentage change in the quantity demanded equals the percentage change in price. (p. 86)

U.S. interest rate differential The U.S. interest rate minus the foreign interest rate. (p. 623)

U.S. official reserves The government's holding of foreign currency. (p. 631)

Utilitarianism A principle that states that we should strive to achieve "the greatest happiness for the greatest number of people." (p. 116)

Utility The benefit or satisfaction that a person gets from the consumption of goods and services. (p. 181)

Value of marginal product The value to the firm of hiring one more unit of a factor of production. It is calculated as the price of a unit of output multiplied by the marginal product of the factor of production. (p. 419)

Velocity of circulation The average number of times a dollar of money is used annually to buy the goods and services that make up GDP. (p. 606)

Voucher A token that the government provides to households, which they can use to buy specified goods and services. (p. 383)

Wages The income that labor earns. (p. 4)

Wealth The value of all the things that people own—the market value of their assets—at a point in time. (pp. 444, 566)

Working-age population The total number of people aged 16 years and over who are not in jail, hospital, or some other form of institutional care. (p. 515)

World Trade Organization (WTO) An international organization that places greater obligations on its member countries to observe the GATT rules. (p. 162)

Ability-to-pay principle, 138
Abortion, 225–226
Above full-employment equilibrium, 658
Absolute advantage, 38
Accounting
    economic, 228
    generational, 738
    profit for firms, 228
Acid rain, 393
Acquisitions, 359
Actual aggregate expenditure, 677
Adidas, 324
Advanced Micro Devices, 341
Adverse selection, 472, 475
Advertising
    brand names, 333
    efficiency of, 333
    Internet market battles (Reading Between the Lines), 244–245
    in monopolistic competition, 330, 332–333
    quality signaled by, 332–333
    signaling with, 332–333, 474, 475
Affordable Care Act of 2010, 371, 384–385
Africa, 141, 162, 446, 448–449, 645–646
After-tax interest rate, 736
Aggregate demand, 652, 652–655
    changes in, 686–687
    in classical view, 662
    cost-push inflation and, 705
    demand-pull inflation and, 702
    equilibrium expenditure and, 678–679
    expectations in changes, 654–655
    fiscal and monetary policy related to, 655
    fiscal stimulus and, 743
    fluctuations in, 660–661
    global markets related to, 654–655
    in Keynesian view, 663
    in long run, 688–689
    in monetarist view, 663
    monetary policy and, 663
    price level and, 685
    in short run, 688
    substitution effects and, 653
    wealth and, 652–653
Aggregate demand curve, 652–653
    real GDP explained in, 653
    shifts in, 655
    substitution effects, 685–686
    wealth effect, 685
Aggregate expenditure, 682
    actual, 677
    changes in, 686–687
    curve, 676, 692
    in Keynesian economics, 663, 692
    price level and, 685
    real GDP and, 672
    schedule, 676
Aggregate labor market, 545–546
Aggregate planned expenditure, 672, 676, 677, 681
Aggregate production function, 545, 566

Aggregate supply, 648–651. *See also* Aggregate supply-aggregate demand model
    changes in, 650
    in classical view, 662
    cost-push inflation and, 704
    fiscal stimulus and, 744
    fluctuations in, 661
    in Keynesian view, 663
    long-run, 648
    in monetarist view, 663
    potential GDP changes and, 545, 566
    quantity of real GDP supplied, 648
    short-run, 649, 650
Aggregate supply-aggregate demand model (AS-AD model), 647, 648, 723
    business cycle in, 658–659
    economic growth in, 657–658
    inflation in, 657–658
    Reading Between the Lines, 664
Agricultural revolution, 51
Agriculture
    Farm Bill, 140
    production, 3
AIG. See American International Group
Airbus, 341
Airline industry, 154, 554
Airplanes, 154
Air pollution, 394
Allocative efficiency, 33, 35, 290–291
Alternative price indexes, 526
Amazon.com, 216–217, 489
American Academy of Arts and Sciences, 478
American International Group (AIG), 458, 568, 569
American Recovery and Reinvestment Act of 2009 (2009 Fiscal Stimulus Act), 742
Anarchy, State, and Utopia (Nozick), 118
Android, 334
Anheuser-Busch InBev, 359
Antitrust Division, U.S. Department of Justice, 356, 358
Antitrust law, 356, 356–359
    Clayton Act, 356
    Sherman Act, of 1890, 356, 357, 358
AOL, 326
Apple, 6, 165, 227, 243, 321, 334–335, 352, 358, 367
Arbitrage, 626
AS-AD model. See Aggregate supply-aggregate demand model
The Ascent of Man (Bronowski), 367
Asia. *See also* specific country
    economies in, 544
Asic, 324
Asset prices, 570
Assets
    financial, 570
    liquid, 593
Asymmetric information, 472
Athey, Susan, 176–178
Atlantic cod, 401
Auerback, Alan, 487, 738
Automatic fiscal policy, 740
Automatic stabilizers, 740–742

Automatic stimulus, 741
Autonomous consumption, 672
Autonomous expenditure, 676, 680, 683
Autonomous tax multiplier, 683, 694
Average cost, 258
Average cost pricing rule, 314
Average fixed cost (AFC), 258
Average price and quantity, 85–86
Average product, 253
Average product curve, 256
Average total cost (ATC), 258
Average total cost curve, 258–259
Average variable cost (AVC), 258

Balanced budget, 730, 741. *See also* Budget deficit; Budget surplus; Federal budget
Balanced budget multiplier, 695
Balance of payments accounts, 631, 631–632
Baltimore Ravens, 466
Banana Republic, 329
Bangladesh, 552
Bank of America, 165, 565, 568, 597–598, 664
Bank of Canada, 654
Bank of England, 654
Bank of Japan, 625
Banks. *See also* Commercial banks; specific banks
    capital loss in, 767
    central, 368
    financial crisis of 2008-2009 and, 767–768
    monetary policy and loans from, 761
    money created by, 599–601
    savings, 593
Barclays Bank, 565
Barriers to entry, 240, 300, 301, 342
Barro, Robert J., 578, 644, 645, 744, 745
Barter, 590
BEA. See Bureau of Economic Analysis
Bear Stearns, 568
A Beautiful Mind (film), 345, 351
Behavioral economics, 194
Beige Book, 755, **758**
Below full-employment equilibrium, 659
Benefit, 8, 108
Benefits principle, 138
Benhabib, Jess, 780
Bentham, Jeremy, 116, 223
Bernanke, Ben, 514, 582, 608, 654, 664, 755
Berners-Lee, Tim, 227
Best affordable choice, 210–211
Best affordable point, 210–211
Bhagwati, Jagdish, 10, 52–54
Biased CPI, 525–526
Big tradeoff, 117, 456, 456–457
Bilateral monopoly, 425, 425–426
Biotech, 554
BlackBerry, 334
Black market, 128, 128–129
Bloomberg, Michael, 133, 671, 685
BLS. See Bureau of Labor Statistics
Boehner, John, 746

Boeing, 341, 493
Bond, 567
    government, 538, 594, 767
    long term rate, 760
    market, 567–568
Bond markets, 567, 567–568
Books, paper v. e-books (*Reading Between the Lines*), 216–217
Boorstin, Daniel J., 175
Borenstein, Severin, 406
Borrowing, 633
    international, 579, 580
    lowering cost of, 594
    U.S., for consumption, 633
    women, 552
Bounded rationality, 194
Bounded self-interest, 194–195
Bounded willpower, 194
Brand names, 333
British Airways, 493
Bronowski, Jacob, 367
Brunner, Karl, 663
BSE. *See* Mad cow disease
Budget deficit, 730. *See also* Federal budget
    government, 577–578
Budget equation, 205–206
Budget line, 180, 204, 211
Budget surplus, 730
Bureaucratic inefficiency, 383–384
Bureaucrats, 373, 380
Bureau of Economic Analysis (BEA), 493, 526
Bureau of Labor Statistics (BLS), 432, 523
Bush, George W., 537, 588
Business cycle, 497, 647, 724
    in AS-AD model, 658–659
    automatic stabilizers in, 740–742
    inflation and, 707
    mainstream theory, 711–712
    multiplier and, 684
    RBC theory, 712–715
    turning points, 684
    in U.S., 497, 658
Business organization, 234–235

Caballero, Ricardo J., 724–726
Cable television, 313, 314
California's underground economy (*Reading Between the Lines*), 144–145
Canada, 542, 654. *See also* North American Free Trade Agreement
Canzoneri, Matt, 536
Cap-and-trade, 399, 406–407
Capital, 3–4, **4,** 262, 418. *See also* Financial capital; Human capital
Capital, aggregate supply related to increase of, 650
Capital accumulation, 36
Capital and financial account, 631
Capital gains, 566
    capital losses, 566, 767
Capital rental markets, 428
Capital services, 418
Capture theory, 313
Carbon emissions, 6, 394, 398, 399
Card, David, 132–133, 486–488

Carry trade, 636–637
Cartel, 343, 357
Carter, Jimmy, 717
Castro, Fidel, 487
Casual labor, 418
Causal relationships, 486
Causation, 26
Cause and effect, 10, 132–133
CBO. *See* Congressional Budget Office
CBS, 426
Celler-Kefauver Act, 356
Cell phones, 313, 334–335
Central bank, 596
CEO pay (*Reading Between the Lines*), 458–459
Ceteris paribus, 22
Chained CPI, 526
Chained-dollar Real GDP, 504–505
Change in demand, 58, 58–59, 68
    permanent, 286–287
    quantity demanded change v., 60–61
Change in price, 90, 205–206
Change in quantity demanded, 60–61, **61**
Change in quantity supplied, 64
Change in supply, 63, 63–64
Cheating, 140, 224
Checks, 592
Chevron, 599
Chew, Lindell, 360
Chicago School, 777
China, 498, 539
    currency in, 498, 618
    economic growth (*Reading Between the Lines*), 558–559
    economic inequality and, 451
    exchange rate and, 618, 629–630
    standard of living in, 498
    tire trade penalties (*Reading Between the Lines*), 168–169
    as top U.S. creditor, 582
    trade with, 41, 151, 152
China Airlines, 5
Choices, 3–4
    best affordable, 210–211
    competition, efficiency and, 290
    consumer, 194–195
    fuel (*Reading Between the Lines*), 44–45
    at margin, 9
    predicting consumer, 210–211, 213–215
    public, 371, 372–373, 376
    public choice, 376
    public choice theory, 372, 405
    rational, 8
    with uncertainty, 468
Chomsky, Noam, 53
Chrysler, 359
Circular flow
    of expenditure and income, 491–492
    through markets, 42, 43
Citibank, 165, 599
Citicorp, 234
CK, 329
Clarida, Richard, 536–538
Classical growth theory, 553
Classical macroeconomics, 653, 662
Clayton Act, 356
Clean Air Act, 394

Climate change, 6
Close substitute, 89, 209, 300
Coase, Ronald, 369, 375, 397, 413
Coase theorem, 397
Coca-Cola, 332–333, 359
Cod fishing, 401
College Choices (Hoxby), 415
Collusion, 346–348. *See also* Price fixing
Collusive agreement, 346, 348
Columbia University, 10, 52–53
Command system, 106, 233
Commercial banks
    credit crisis of 2008, 476, 767
    flush with reserves, 568, 593, 595
Commodity markets, 418
Commodity prices, 418
Commodity substitution bias, 525
Common resources, 115, 374
    conserving, 376
    efficient use of, 403–405
    overfishing equilibrium, 402–403
    overuse of, 402–403
    sustainable production, 400–401
    tragedy of the commons, 376, 400, 401–405
Comparative advantage, 38, 38–39, 152–153, 164
    in international trade, 152
    national, 152
Compensation
    of employees, 493
    unemployment, 455
Competition. *See also* Monopolistic competition; Perfect competition
    compared to single-price monopoly, 306–309
    efficiency and, 290–291, 307
    efficient use of resources and, 289
    markets and, 237–241
    between schools, 414–415
    single-price monopoly compared to, 306–309
Competitive equilibrium, 112
Competitive market, 56, 241
    efficiency, 112–115
    fairness, 116–119
Complement, 59, 209–210
Compound interest, 434
Concentration measures, 238, 240–241, 454
Congress, U.S., 728, 756
Congressional Budget Office (CBO), 742
Constant returns to scale, 264
Constraints, 230. *See also* Short-run technology constraints
Consumer choices, 194–195
    predicting, 210–211, 213–215
Consumer equilibrium, 183
Consumer Financial Protection Bureau, 569
Consumer Price Index (CPI), 513, 521, 523. *See also* Alternative price indexes; Core CPI inflation rate
    biased, 525–526
    calculating, 524
    chained, 526
    constructing, 523
    inflation measured by, 524–525, 755
    reading numbers of, 523

Consumer surplus, 109, 191, 307, 469, 470
  capturing, 309–310
Consumer Watchdog, 299, 316–317
Consumption, 180–182
  autonomous, 672
  borrowing for, in U.S., 633
  induced, 672
  PCE deflator, 526, 755
  as real GDP function, 675
  saving plans and, 672
  U.S., 675
Consumption expenditure, 491, 526, 672, 755, 761
Consumption function, 672, 675, 692
Contest, 106
Contestable market, 354, 355
Contests among superstars, 453–454
Contracts, long-term, 234
Convergence, to equilibrium, 679
Cooperative equilibrium, 353
Coordinating decisions, 42
Copyright, 301
Core CPI inflation rate, 527
Core inflation rate, 755
Corn, 271, 292–293
Corney, Mark, 654
Corporate income taxes, 729
Corporate profit, 494
Corporation, 235
Correlation, 26
Correspondence, markets and industry, 240–241
Cost curves, 276
  average total, 258–259
  long-run average, 263, 264, 300
  prices of factors of production, 261
  technology factor, 260–261
Cost-push inflation, 704, 704–706
Costs, 108. *See also* specific cost
  long-run, 262–265
  minimum efficient, 383
  output and, 395
  private, 395
  selling, and demand, 331–332
  short-run, 257–261
  sunk, 252
  total, 257, 331
  transaction, 115, 242, 397
Council of Economic Advisors, 729
Countervailing duties, 163
Cox Communications, 313
CPI. *See* Consumer Price Index
CPI basket, 523
Crawling peg, 629
Credit
  crunch, 7
  expected future, 60
  sub-prime crisis, 476, 767
Credit cards, 592
Credit crisis, of 2007-2008, 476, 767
Creditor nation, 633
Creditors, 582, 633
Credit risk, 475
Credit unions, 593
Criminal activity, and economics, 224–226
Cross elasticity of demand, 91, 91–92, 97

Crowding-out effect, 578, 582–583
Crude oil, 69, 429–430
Currency, 591, 600. *See also* Dollars, U.S.
  in China, 498, 618
  Euro, 537, 618
  of Japan, 617
  trading, 618
Currency drain ratio, 600
Current account, 631
Current account balance, 634
Current account deficit, 725–726
Cyclical surplus or deficit, 741, 742
Cyclical unemployment, 519

DaimlerChrysler, 359
Darwin, Charles, 485, 553
Data, 486
Deadweight loss, 113
  efficiency comparison and, 307
  monopoly and, 307
  from overfishing, 403
  redistribution of income and, 457
  rent ceiling and, 129
  tariffs and, 158
  in underproduction, 113–114
Debt
  government, 732
  interest, 729, 730
  international, 739–740
  third world, 633
Debtor nation, 633
Debtors, 633
Decisions
  coordinating, 42
  in face of uncertainty, 466–468
  Fed strategies in making, 757–758
  output, 276–279, 302–305
  rent-v.-buy, 428
  shutdown, 278
  temporary shutdown, 278, 283
  time frames for, 252
Decreasing marginal benefit, 34, 477
Default risk, 475, 574
Deficits, 729, 730
  budget, 730
  cyclical, 741, 742
  government budget, 577–578
  structural, 741
  structural surplus or, 741
  three decades of, 632
  of U.S. current account, 725–726
Deflation, 522
Dell, 242, 285, 324
Demand, 57, 108. *See also* Law of demand; specific types
  all possible changes in, 72–73
  behavioral economics, 194
  change in, 58–59, 68
  consumer choices, 194–195
  controversy, 195
  costs, 331–332
  cross elasticity of, 91–92, 97
  decrease in, 68
  derived, 419
  elastic, 86–87, 89, 303
  for factors of production, 419–422
  increase in, 59, 68, 574–575
  individual, 108–109

  labor, 419–421, 424, 545–546
  markets and prices, 108–109
  neuroeconomics, 195
  for oil, 429
  in perfect competition, 328–329
  permanent changes in, 286–287
  prices of related goods, 59
  selling costs and, 332
  speculative influence on, 429
  stimulus, 777
  unit elastic, 86, 303
  willingness to pay and value, 58
Demand curve, 57–58, 58, 76, 213
  elasticity along linear, 87
  income effect and, 213
  for labor, 420
  movement along, 61
  shift of, 61
Demand for labor, 419–420
  in aggregate labor market, 545–546
  changes in, 421
  population and, 60
Demand for loanable funds, 572, 572–573
Demand for money, 603, 619
Demand-pull inflation, 702, 703–704
Demand schedule, 57–58
Department of Commerce, U.S., 239, 690
Department of Energy, U.S., 266
Depository institutions, 593
  economic benefits from, 594
  financial innovation of, 595, 602
  regulation of, 594
Deposits, 591, 592
  loan making creating, 599
Depreciation, 228, 229, **492,** 625
Deregulation, 313
Derived demand, 419
Desired currency holding, 600
Desired reserve ratio, 600
Diadora, 324
Diesel, 329
Diminishing marginal rate of substitution, 208
Diminishing marginal returns, 255
Diminishing marginal utility, 181–182, 182
Direct relationships, 16, 17
Discounting, 434
Discouraged worker, 517
The Discoverers (Boorstin), 175
Discretionary fiscal policy, 740
Discretionary fiscal stimulus, 743–745
Discrimination
  economic inequality resulting from, 452–453
  among groups of buyers, 309–310
  perfect price, 311, 312
  among units of a good, 310
Diseconomies of scale, 264
Disney, 312
Disposable income, 573, 655, 672, 673
Dissaving, 673
Divisible goods, 204
DKNY, 329
Doha, Qatar, 162
Doha Development Agenda, 162
Doha Round, 162

Dollarization, 778–779
Dollars, U.S., 184
    appreciating, 625
    carry trade (*Reading Between the Lines*),
        636–637
    chained-, 504–505
    demand curve for, 620–621
    depreciating, 625
    exchange rate questions, 618
    on roller coaster, 625
    supply curve, 621
    supply of, 624
Dominant-strategy equilibrium, 345
Domino's, 32
Dopamine, 195
dot.com, 227
Double counting, 490
Dr Pepper, 359
Drugs. *See also* Food and Drug
        Administration
    illegal, 142–143
    legalizing and taxing, 143
Dubner, Stephen J., 225
Dumping argument, 163
Duopoly, 342
    price-fixing game explaining, 346–350
    razors (*Reading Between the Lines*),
        360–361
    repeated game for, 353–354

Earl Jackets, 329
Earnings sharing regulation, 315
Easterly, Bill, 646
East Point Seafood, 374
eBay, 177–178, 299, 301
Economics, 2, 8, 10. *See also* Keynesian
        economics; Macroeconomics;
        Microeconomics
    behavioral, 194
    choices in, 3–4
    criminal activity and, 224–226
    definition, 2
    of education, 414
    graphs in, 13–24
    scope of, 8
    as social science, 10
    studying, 416, 726
    supply-side, 734–737
    voodoo, 737
    way of thinking, 6–9
Economic accounting, 228
Economic activity, underground,
        144–145, 499–500
Economic coordination, 41–43
Economic depreciation, 229
Economic efficiency, 231, 231–232
Economic growth, 36–37. *See also* Gross
        domestic product
    in *AS-AD* model, 657–658
    basics of, 540–541
    calculating, 540
    causes of, 556
    in China (*Reading Between the Lines*),
        558–559
    classical growth theory, 553
    international trade stimulating, 557
    neoclassical growth theory, 553–554
    new growth theory, 554–556

perpetual motion, 555–556
policies for achieving faster,
        556–557
R&D to stimulate, 557
rule of 70, 540–541
savings to stimulate, 556
sources of, 552
sustained, 540–541
trends in, 542–544
in U.S., 37, 542, 657
Economic Growth (Salai-i-Martin, Barro),
        645
Economic growth rate, 540
Economic inequality
    CEO pay (*Reading Between the Lines*),
        458–459
    contest among superstars concept,
        453–454
    discrimination, 452–453
    distribution of income, 442, 443,
        445–448, 449, 488
    distribution of wealth, 444
    education/training and, 450–451
    global, 448–449
    globalization and, 451
    human capital contributing to,
        450–451
    income Lorenz curve, 443–444
    income or wealth, 444–445
    income redistribution, 455–457, 522
    life cycle of income and wealth, 454
    poverty, 446–447
    sources of, 450–454
    technology and, 451
    trends, 445–446, 449
    unequal wealth, 454
    wealth and, 444–445
    in world economy, 448–449
Economic instability, 7
Economic loss, 282
Economic model, 10, 16–19
Economic Policy Advisory Board, 737
Economic profit, 228
    in long run, 327–328
    maximizing, 274, 304
    perfect competition and, 274–275
    in short run, 282, 326–327
Economic rent, 308
Economic Report of the President (Council
        of Economic Advisors), 729
Economic revolution, 51–54
The Economics of School Choice (Hoxby),
        415
Economies of scale, 242, 242–243, **264,**
        265
Economies of scope, 243
Economies of team production, 243
Economy
    in Asia, 544
    perpetual motion, 555–556
    real GDP and world, 543–544
    underground, 144–145, 499–500
Education
    competition between schools, 414–415
    economic inequality and, 450–451
    economics of, 414
    efficiency v. equity in, 416
    fast food v., 414

financing of, 415–416
as mixed good, 381–384
public v. private schools, 415
to stimulate economic growth, 557
subsidies and, 383
wealth relating to, 446
Efficiency, 5, 105, 118. *See also*
        Bureaucratic inefficiency; Economic
        efficiency
    of advertising/brand names, 333
    allocative, 33, 35, 290–291
    in common resources, 403–405
    competition and, 290–291, 307
    of competitive equilibrium, 112
    of competitive market, 112–115
    equilibrium and, 290
    equity v., in education, 416
    of health care delivery, 384
    of monopolistic competition, 329
    of political outcome, 378–380
    with price discrimination, 312
    of private provision, 378
    product innovation and, 330
    production, 31
    of public provision, 378–380
    of resource allocation methods, 106
    of resources, 33–35
    rose market (*Reading Between the
        Lines*), 120–121
    taxes and, 137–138
    technological, 231, 254
Efficient scale, 265, 328
E Ink, 216
Elastic demand, 86–87, 87, 89, 303
Elasticities of demand and supply for
        tomatoes (*Reading Between the
        Lines*), 98–100
Elasticity, 83. *See also* Elasticity of
        demand; Elasticity of supply;
        Income elasticity of demand
    compact glossary of, 97
    of demand and supply for tomatoes,
        98–99
    expenditures and, 89
    along linear demand curve, 87
    marginal revenue and, 303
    minus sign and, 86
    total revenue and, 88
Elasticity of demand
    cross, 91–92, 97
    factors influencing, 89
    income, 92, 97
    in monopoly, 303
    price, 84–90, 97
    taxes and, 135–136
Elasticity of supply, 94, 94–96, 97
    taxes and, 136–137
Electrical production, 266–267
Electronic book readers, 216
Emission charges, 394, 398, 399
Employment, 514–517, 755. *See also* Full
        employment; Unemployment
    aggregate supply related to, 650
    full, 519
    job growth lagging (*Reading Between
        the Lines*), 528–529
    minimum wage increasing, 486–487
    -population ratio in labor markets, 516

Employment Act of 1946, 728, 729
Employment-to-population ratio, 516
Endowment effect, 195
Energizer, 360
Entrepreneurship, 4, 229, 418, 485
Environment. *See also* Pollution
　acid rain, 393
　air pollution, 394
　carbon emissions, 394, 398, 399
　climate change, 6
　competitive, 237–241
　fossil fuels, 6, 435
　global warming, 393
　greenhouse gas, 6
　Mexico's policy on, 164
　natural disaster water shortage study,
　　118–119
　quality of, 500
　sustainable production, 400–401
　water pollution, 394
Environmental standards, 164–165
Equality of opportunity, 118
Equations
　budget, 205–206
　linear, 24
　of straight lines, 24–25
Equilibrium, 66
　below full-employment, 659
　competitive, 112
　consumer, 183
　convergence to, 679
　cooperative, 353
　dominant strategy, 345
　efficiency and, 290
　in foreign exchange market, 622
　full-employment, 659
　above full-employment, 658
　in labor markets, 423, 424, 546–547
　for loanable funds, 574
　long run, 285, 604
　long-run macroeconomic, 656–657
　market, 66–67, 77
　money market, 604–605
　Nash, 345, 349–352
　overfishing, 402–403
　political, 373, 405
　pooling, 475
　price, 430
　price of oil, 430
　prices, 430
　quantity, 66
　real GDP, 687–689
　rent-seeking, 308, 309
　separating, 475
　short-run, 281
　short-run macroeconomic, 656
Equilibrium expenditure, 678, 679,
　693
Equilibrium price, 66
Equilibrium quantity, 66
Equity, 105
Essay on the Principle of Population
　(Malthus), 485
Essays, Moral and Political (Hume), 535
Etonic, 324
Euro, 537, 618
Excess capacity, 328
Excess reserves, 600

Exchange rate, 618. *See also* Foreign
　exchange market
　changes in, 624–625
　in China, 618, 629–630
　crawling peg, 629
　expectations of, 626
　expected future, 623, 624
　on exports, 620
　fixed, 628–629
　flexible, 628
　fluctuations, 623–627, 760–761
　fundamental influences on, 626
　nominal, 626–627
　policy, 628–630
　as price, 618–619
　real, 627
　role of, 635
Excite@Home, 326–327
Excludable, 374, 375
Expansion, 497
Expansionary fiscal policy, 743
Expectations, 662–663
　aggregate demand changes, 654–655
　on exchange rate, 626
　future prices, 59–60
　rational, 707
Expected future income, 573
Expected inflation, 706–707
Expected utility, 467–468
Expected wealth, 466
Expenditures, 89. *See also* Aggregate
　　expenditure
　actual aggregate, 677
　aggregate planned, 672, 676, 677, 681
　autonomous, 676, 680, 683
　circular flow of, 491–492
　consumption, 491, 526, 672, 755, 761
　elasticity and, 89
　equilibrium, 678, 679, 693
　fixed prices and, 672–675
　government, 492, 493
　induced, 676, 680
　measuring GDP, 493
　multiplier, 694, 743
　taxes on, 735
　total, 494
Expenditure approach, 493
Expenditure plans
　fixed prices and, 672–675
　monetary policy and, 761
　real GDP and, 672, 676, 677, 681
Exploitation, of developing countries, 165
Exports, 152, 492. *See also* Net exports
　airplanes, from U.S., 154
　exchange rate related to, 620
　gains and losses from, 156
　net, 492, 634–635, 761
　subsidy, 162
　trade gains and losses, 156
　voluntary restraint on, 162
　world demand for U.S., 623
External benefit, 374–375, 381–385
External cost
　government action and, 398–399
　inefficiency with, 396
　marginal, 395, 402
　mixed good with, 375–376
　output and, 395

　pollution, 394–399
　valuing, 395
External diseconomies, 287, 287–289
External economies, 287, 287–289
Externalities, 114, 374
　benefits, private/social, 381–382
　Coase theorem, 397
　copyright, 301
　government actions regarding,
　　398–399
　negative production, 300, 394, 398
　patents, 301
　Pigovian taxes, 398
　pollution, 394–399
　property rights, 396, 397, 403–404
　public provision, 378–380
　subsidies, 114, 139, 140–141, 162,
　　314, 383, 384
　vouchers, 383, 384, 415–416

Facebook, 227, 244–245
Factor markets
　anatomy of, 418
　for capital services, 418
　entrepreneurship, 418
　for land services and natural resources,
　　418
　uncertainty, inequality, and, 485
Factors of production, 3, 63, 261, 418
　cost curves and, 261
　demand for, 419–422
　prices of, 63
Fair Labor Standards Act, 132
Fairness, 105, 118
　competitive market, 116–119
　of minimum wage, 132
　taxes and, 138
Fair trade, 53
Fannie Mae. *See* Federal National
　　Mortgage Association
Farm Bill, 140
Farmer subsidies, 140–141
Farm machines, 285
FDA. *See* Food and Drug Administration
FDIC. *See* Federal Deposit Insurance
　　Corporation
Fed, 596. *See also* Federal Reserve System
Federal budget, 728
　global perspective, 733
　historical perspective, 730–733
　institutions and laws, 728–729
　2011 highlights, 729–730
Federal Deposit Insurance Corporation
　　(FDIC), 569, 594–595, 768
Federal funds rate (FFR), 593, 593–594,
　756, 757, 766
　exchange rate fluctuations and,
　　760–761
　expenditure plans and, 761
　money and bank loan changes relating
　　to, 761
　target, 759
Federal Government debt, 732
Federal Home Loan Mortgage
　　Corporation (Freddie Mac), 514,
　　565, 568, 569
Federal National Mortgage Association
　　(Fannie Mae), 514, 565, 568, 569

Federal Open Market Committee (FOMC), 596, 756, 758
Federal Reserve Act, of 2000, 754
Federal Reserve Bank of New York (New York Fed), 753, 759, 762
Federal Reserve Banks, 596, 755
Federal Reserve System (Fed), 568, 576, 581, 582, 589, **596,** 596–599, 625, 753
  balance sheet of, 597, 598
  Beige Book, 755, 758
  Board of Governors, 756
  decision-making strategy of, 757–758
  exchange rate and, 760–761
  fighting, 763–764
  financial crisis of 2008-2009 and, 568, 576, 598, 767–768
  inflation challenges, 764–765
  Inflation rate decision making of, 757–758
  liabilities of, 597
  loose links and time lags, 765–766
  open market operations of, 597
  policy tools of, 597–598
  recession challenges, 762–763
  stimulus policies (*Reading Between the Lines*), 770–771
  structure of, 596
  targeting rule of, 769
  Taylor rule of, 769, 779, 780
Federal Trade Commission (FTC), 356, 359
FedEx, 301
Feldstein, Martin, 737
Fertilizers, 292
FFR. *See* Federal funds rate
Fila, 324
Final good, 490
Financial Accounting Standards Board, 228
Financial assets, 570
Financial capital, 566
  physical capital distinguished from, 551
Financial capital markets, 567–568
Financial crisis, of 2008-2009, 568, 576, 598, 767–768
Financial innovation, 595, 602
Financial institutions, 568, 568–569. *See also* Market for loanable funds
  capital and investment, 566–577
  commercial banks, 568, 593, 595
  finance and money, 566
  insolvency and illiquidity, 569
  insurance companies, 469–470, 569
  physical and financial capital, 566
  physical capital, 551
  stock markets, 568
  wealth and saving, 566
Financial international trade, 631–635
Financial Services Oversight Council, 569
Financial Times, 370
Firestorm Wildfire Suppression, 378, 379
Firms, 41–42, **228**
  accounting profit, 228
  constraints, 230
  coordination, 242
  decisions of, 275

economic profit, 228
information constraints of, 230
labor demand of, 419–421
market constraints of, 230
monopolistic competition in, 324
output decisions of, 276–279
principal-agent problem, 234
short-run technology constraint of, 252–256
supply curve of, 279
technological change and, 289
technological constraints of, 230
time frames for decisions, 252
turnover, 240
First-come, first-served, resource allocation by, 106–107
Fiscal imbalance, 738
Fiscal policy, 655, 728
  aggregate demand related to, 655
  automatic, 740
  discretionary, 740
  expansionary, 743
  federal budget, 728–733
  full employment and supply-side, 734
  generational effects of, 738–740
  income taxes related to, 734–735
  of Obama (*Reading Between the Lines*), 746–747
  recession fought by, 654
  Social Security and, 738–739
  supply-side effects of, 734–737
Fiscal stimulus, 740, 741–745
  aggregate demand and, 743
  aggregate supply and, 744
  automatic, 741
  discretionary, 743–745
  magnitude of, 744–745
  time lags, 745
Fiscal year, 728
Fixed exchange rate, 628, 628–629
Fixed prices
  expenditure plans and, 672–675
  real GDP with, 676–679
Flexible exchange rate, 628
Flu vaccination, 375
FOMC. *See* Federal Open Market Committee
Food, 90, 414
Food and Drug Administration (FDA), 414
Food Stamps, 455
Force, 107
Ford, 265
Foreign currency, 618
Foreign exchange brokers, 618
Foreign exchange market, 618, 618–622
  demand in, 619
  dollar on roller coaster, 625
  equilibrium in, 622
  exchange rate as price, 618–619
  exchange rates, 618
  exports effect, 620
  imports effect, 621
  intervention, 629
  law of demand, 619–620
  law of supply in, 621
  market equilibrium in, 622
  money demand and supply, 619
  money demand in, 619–620

People's Bank of China, 629–630
  profits expected, 620, 621
  supply in, 621
  trading currencies, 618
  U.S. dollar demand curve, 620–621
  U.S. dollar questions, 618
  U.S. dollar supply curve, 621
Foreign labor, 164
Forgone interest, 229
Forster, E. M., 723
Fossil fuels, 6, 435
Four-firm concentration ratio, 238
France, 542
Freakonomics (Levitt and Dubner), 225
Freddie Mac. *See* Federal Home Loan Mortgage Corporation
Free lunches, 777
Free market, for drugs, 142
Free-rider problem, 377
Free trade, 53
Fresh flower market, 120–121
Frictional unemployment, 519
Friedman, Milton, 487, 608, 726, 777
FTC. *See* Federal Trade Commission
Full employment, 519–521
  supply-side fiscal policy and, 734
  unemployment and, 519–521
Full employment, 519
Full Employment and Balanced Growth Act of 1978, 729
Full-employment equilibrium, 659
Future amounts
  discounting, 434–435
  present value of sequence of, 435
Future prices, expectation, 59–60

Gains, capital, 566
Games
  chicken, 352
  price-fixing, 346–350
  price wars and, 354
  prisoner's dilemma, 344–345
  R&D, 350–351
  repeated, 353–354
  sequential entry, 354–355
Game theory, 344, 367
Gap, 327, 329
Gasoline prices (*Reading Between the Lines*), 74–75
Gates, Bill, 6
Gateway, 285
GATT. *See* General Agreement on Tariffs and Trade
GDP. *See* Gross domestic product
GDP deflator, 526
General Agreement on Tariffs and Trade (GATT), 53, 159
General Motors (GM), 41, 62, 251, 265, 567–569
General Theory of Employment, Interest, and Money (Keynes), 514, 723
Generational accounting, 738
Generational imbalance, 739
Gerik, Ronnie, 32
Gibbs, Robert, 168
Gillette, 341, 360–361
Gini Ratio, 445, 446, 449
Given time period, GDP in, 490

Globalization, 5–6, 41
    economic inequality and, 451
Global loanable funds market, 579–580,
    581
Global markets, 151–178. *See also*
    International trade
    aggregate demand related to,
        654–655
    borrowing in, 579, 580
    for crude oil, 69
    dumping argument, 163
    economic inequality, 448–449, 451
    exploitation in, 165
    foreign labor, 164
    net gain from trade, 155–156
    oil, 431
Global recession (*Reading Between the
    Lines*), 582–583
Global warming, 393
GM. *See* General Motors
Gokhale, Jagadeesh, 738
Goods and resources. *See also* Common
    resources
    classification of, 374
    excludable, 374
    information as, 477
    natural monopolies, 374
    private goods, 374
    public goods, 374–380
    rival/nonrival, 374
Goods and services, 3
    government expenditure on,
        492, 493
Google, 227, 244–245, 299, 316–317,
    334, 489
Google (*Reading Between the Lines*),
    316–317
Goolsbee, Austan, 729
Gotheil, Fred, 536
Government. *See also* Taxes
    action in labor markets (*Reading
        Between the Lines*), 144–145
    actions in markets, 127
    bonds, 538, 594, 767
    budget deficit, 577–578
    budget surplus, 577
    debt, 732
    expenditure multiplier, 694, 743
    expenditures, 493
    external costs and, 398–399
    illegal goods markets, 142–143
    license, 300–301
    in loanable funds market, 577–578
    mixed goods and, 381–385
    production quotas, 404
    reasons for existence, 372
    rent ceilings, 128–130
    sponsored mortgage lenders, 568
    subsidy, 314
    surplus budget, 577
Government debt, 732
Government expenditure, 492, 493
**Government expenditure multiplier,
    694, 743**
Government failure, 371, 380, 383–384
Government sector balance, 634
Grades, as Signals (*Reading Between the
    Lines*), 478–479

Graphs
    economic, 13–24
    of economic data, 14
    in economic models, 16–19
    equations of straight lines, 24–25
    making, 13–14
    misleading, 16
    more than two variables, 22–23
    Scatter diagrams, 14–15
Great Depression, 7, 514, 542, 684, 723,
    728
Great Moderation, 7
Greenhouse gas, 6
Greenspan, Alan, 581, 755
Greiner, William, 502–503
Gross domestic product (GDP). *See also*
    Potential GDP; Real GDP
    aggregate supply and changes in,
        650–651
    circular flow of expenditure and
        income, 491–492
    defined, 490
    equals expenditure equals income,
        492
    expenditure approach, 493
    final goods and services, 490
    in given time period, 490
    "gross" defined, 492
    income approach, 493–494
    market value, 490
    measuring U.S., 493–495
    nominal and real, 489, **490,** 495
    produced within country, 490
    in U.S., 493–495
Gross investment, 492, 566
Gross private domestic investment, 493
Growth theories, 553–557

Hamermesh, Daniel, 133
Harbaugh, Jim, 466
Harley-Davidson, 283
Harris, Ethan, 664
Harvard University, 177, 478
HDI. *See* Human Development Index
Health, 500
Health care, 455
    efficient delivery of, 384
    as mixed good, 384–385
    reforming, 386–387
Health Care Financing Administration,
    117
Heilbronner, Robert L., 370
**Herfindahl-Hirschman Index (HHI),
    238,** 239
    mergers, 359
    in monopolistic competition, 325
    oligopolies, 343
HHI. *See* Herfindahl-Hirschman Index
Holiday Inn, 333
Hong Kong, 37
Hotelling, Harold, 485
Hotelling Principle, 430, 431, 485
Households, production, 499
Housing market, 128–130
Housing shortage, 128
Hoxby, Caroline M., 414–416
HTC, 334–335
Hubbard, Tom, 368–370

Human capital, 3, 3–4, 36, 485, 650
    demand/supply/wage rates, 450
    economic inequality explained by,
        450–451
    education/training and, 450–451
    globalization and, 451
    growth, 551
    technological change and, 451
Human Development Index (HDI), 501
Human nature, incentive, 9
Hume, David, 535
Humphrey-Hawkins Act, 729
Hyperinflation, 522

IBM, 285, 354, 367
Ignorance, rational, 380
Illegal goods markets, 142–143
Illiquidity, 569
Immediate good, 490
Immigration, 487–488
Impact lag, 745
Implicit rental rate, 228
Imports, 152, 492
    barriers, 162
    foreign exchange market and, 621
    function of U.S., 675
    gains and losses from, 155–156
    multiplier size and, 683
    t-shirts, 152, 153
    U.S. demand for, 624
Import function, 675, 692
Import quota, 109, 160, 160–161, 191,
    307, 309–310, 469, 470
InBev, 359
Incentive, 2, 9
    to cheating, 140, 224
    human nature, institutions and, 9
    to overproduction, 140
    pay, 234
Incentive system, 140, 233
Income, 60. *See also* Poverty; Real income;
    Wealth
    change in, 206
    circular flow of, 491–492
    corporate, taxes, 720
    disposable, 573, 655, 672, 673
    distribution of, 442, 443, 445–448,
        449, 488
    economic inequality, 444–445
    elastic demand, 92
    expected future, 60
    inelastic demand, 92
    maintenance programs, 455
    market, 422, 456
    measuring GDP, 493–494
    money, 442, 456
    proportion spent on good, 89
    real, 205
    redistribution, 455–457, 522
    rental, 493–494
    rise in, 190
    taxes and proportional, 455
    U.S. distribution of, 442, 443,
        446–447
    wealth v., 444–445
Income approach, 493–494
Income effect, 57, 210, 213, 423
Income elasticity of demand, 92, 97

Income Lorenz curve, 443–444
Income tax
    corporate, 729
    fiscal policy supply-side influenced by,
        734–735
    investment influenced by, 736
    multiplier size and, 683
    personal, 729
    progressive, 455
    proportional, 455
    regressive, 455
    savings influenced by, 736
Indifference curves, 207, 207–210
Individual demand, 108–109
Individual supply, 110
Individual transferable quotas (ITQs),
    404–405
Indivisible goods, 204
Induced consumption, 672
Induced expenditure, 676, 680
Inefficiency
    bureaucratic, 383–384
    with external cost, 396
    of minimum wage, 131–132
    of monopoly, 307
    overproduction, 141
    of pooling equilibrium, 475
    of private provision, 378
    production, 31
    public choice requiring, 376
    of public overprovision, 380
Inelastic demand, 86, 86–87, 89, 303
Inequality. *See also* Economic inequality
    in income distribution, 442, 443,
        445–448, 449, 488
    uncertainty, factor markets and,
        485
    wage, 488
Infant-industry argument, 163
Inferior goods, 60, 92, 215
Inflation, 522
    in AS-AD model, 657–658
    business cycle and, 707
    cost-push, 704–706
    CPI, 524–525, 755
    cycles, 702–707
    demand-pull, 702–704
    demand stimulation and, 777
    expected, 706–707
    Fed fighting, 764–765
    forecasting, 707
    money growth and, 606–607
    real GDP and, 522
    unemployment and, 708–710
    unemployment tradeoff with (*Reading
        Between the Lines*), 716–717
Inflationary gap, 658, 758
Inflation rate. *See also* Core CPI inflation
        rate; Core inflation rate
    Fed decision making and, 757–758
    misery index and, 701, 716–717
Inflation rate targeting, 769, 780
Information. *See also* Private information
    constraints, 230
    as good, 477
    technology, 6, 301, 451
    uncertainty and, 477
Information-age economy, 6

Information-age monopoly, 301
Information Revolution, 6, 51
Innovation
    financial, 595, 602
    in monopolistic competition, 330
    patents and, 301
Inside Google, 316
Insolvency, 569
Institute for Policy Studies, 458
Insurance
    companies, 469–470, 569
    FDIC, 569, 594–595, 768
    markets, 476
    OASDHI, 455
    Pre-Existing Condition Insurance Plan,
        385
    reducing risk with, 469
    SSI, 455
Intel, 6, 227, 341, 354
Intellectual property rights, 550–551
Interest, 4. *See also* Bounded self-interest;
        Social-interest; Social interest theory
    compound, 434
    debt, 729, 730
    forgone, 229
Interest rate, 570. *See also* Real interest
        rate
    after-tax, 736
    credit risk and, 475
    long-term bond rate, 760
    long-term real, 761
    monetary policy and changes in,
        759–760
    nominal, 571, 602
    short-term bill rate, 760
    U.S. differential, 623
    U.S. relative to foreign, 624
Interest rate parity, 626
Intergenerational transfers, 454
Internal Revenue Service (IRS), 228, 457,
    730
International aid, 557
International borrowing and lending, 579,
    580
International capital mobility, 579
International debts, 739–740
International Harvester, 285
International lending, 579, 580, 581
International markets, 579–580
International Monetary Fund, 723
International substitution, 685
International trade, 41, 152
    balance of payments accounts,
        631–632
    comparative advantage in, 152
    driving force of, 152
    financial, 631–635
    protection in, 163–167
    restrictions, 157–162, 166
    to stimulate economic growth, 557
    U.S. airplane export, 154
International Trade Commission (ITC), 164
Internet advertising market battles
    (*Reading Between the Lines*),
    244–245
Intertemporal substitution, 685
Invention, 301
Inventory investment, 678-679

Inventories in Expansion (*Reading Between
    the Lines*), 690–691
Inverse relationships, 17–18
Investment, 492
    federal funds rate change and, 761
    financial institutions, 566–577
    funds that finance, 570–571
    gross, 492, 566
    gross private domestic, 493
    income tax influencing, 736
    net, 492, 566
Invisible hand, 113, 351, 477
iPhone, 243, 321, 334–335
IRS. *See* Internal Revenue Service
ITC. *See* International Trade Commission
ITQs. *See* Individual transferable quotas
iTunes, 14, 374
Ivy League, 478

Japan, 539, 542, 558–559, 617, 618, 625,
    630
Jefferson, Thomas, 413
Jevons, William Stanley, 194
Jobs, 164, **418**
Jobs, Steve, 334
Johnson, Harry, 52
Jolie, Angelina, 4
Jones, Damon, 360
JP Morgan Chase, 568
Justice Department, Antitrust Division,
    356, 358

Kalamazoo
    cost-push inflation in, 706
    demand-pull inflation in, 703–704
Kay's Kloset, 357
Ke$ha, 179
Keynes, John Maynard, 514, 684, 723,
    728
Keynesian cycle theory, 712
Keynesian economics
    aggregate expenditure, 663, 692
    algebra of, 692–695
    autonomous tax multiplier, 683, 694
    fixed prices and expenditure plans,
        672–675
    inflation-unemployment tradeoff and,
        716
    multiplier, 680–684
    multiplier and price level, 685–689
    real GDP with fixed price level,
        676–679
Keynesian macroeconomics, 2, 653,
    662–663
Keys, Alicia, 671, 680, 685
Kimberly-Clark, 350–351
Kindle (electronic book reader), 216
King, Marvyn, 654
Kotlikoff, Laurence, 385, 738
Krueger, Alan, 132–133, 486, 487
Kutcher, Ashton, 332

Labor, 3, 485
    casual, 418
    demand, 419–421, 424, 545–546
    foreign, 164
    services, 229, 418

supply influences, 424
supply of, 546, 547–548, 734–735
underutilized, 517
Labor force, 515, 528–529, 548
Labor force participation rate, 517
Labor markets, 144–145
    aggregate, 545–546
    competitive, 422–423
    employment-population ratio, 516
    equilibrium, 423, 424, 546–547
    government action in (*Reading Between
        the Lines*), 144–145
    indicators of state of, 515–517
    labor force participation rate, 517
    minimum wage, 131–133
    monopsony in, 425–426
    potential GDP and, 547
    supply curve for, 423
    with union, 424–426
    union-nonunion wage gap, 426
    wage rates trends in, 427
Labor productivity, 549
    growth of, 550–552
    human capital growth, 551
    increase in, 549–550
    physical capital growth, 551
    technological advances and, 551–552
Labor union, 424
Laffer, Arthur, 737
Laffer curve, 737
Land, 3, 418, 428–429
Landes, David S., 370
Land rental markets, 428–429
Land services, 418
LAPD, 374
Last resort loans, 599
Law-making lag, 745
Law of demand, 57
Law of diminishing returns, 255, 258
Law of supply, 62
Learning-by-doing, 163
Lee, Tim, 636
Legal barrier to entry, 300–301
Legal monopoly, 300–301
"The Legend of Zelda; Twilight Princess,"
    330
Lehman Brothers, 568, 595
Leisure time, 500
Lemon problem, 472–474
Lender, net, 633
Lender of last resort, 599
Lending, 579, 580, 581, 633
Levi's, 329
Levitt, Steven, 224–226
Liabilities
    of Fed, 597
    unlimited, 234–236
Life-cycle saving patterns, 454
Life expectancy, 500
Lighthouses, 375
Limit pricing, 355
Linear equations, 24
Linear relationships, 16
Line-item veto, 728
Liquid assets, 593
Liquidity
    creating, 594
    traps, 779–780

Loanable funds, 570
    changes in demand for, 572–573
    changes in supply for, 573–574
    curve, 573, 574
    demand for, 572–573
    equilibrium in market for, 574
    government in market for, 577–578
    home price bubble fueled by, 576
    market, 597, 762–763, 764, 767
    supply of, 573–574
Loanable funds market, 76, 570,
    570–575, 597, 762–763, 764, 767
    global, 579–580, 581
    government in, 577–578
Loan markets, 475, 476, 567
Loans, 594. *See also* Microloans
    creating money through, 599–601
    last resort, 599
    monetary policy transmission and
        bank, 761
Long run, 252, 283–285
Long-run aggregate supply, 648
Long-run average cost curve, 263, 264,
    300
Long-run cost, 262–265
Long-run equilibrium, 285, 604
**Long-run macroeconomic equilibrium,
    656,** 656–657
**Long-run market supply curve,
    287–288**
Long-run Phillips curve, 709
Long-run supply, 96
Long-term bond rate, 760
Long-term contracts, 234
Long-term real interest rate, 761
Lorenz curve, 442, **443–444,** 445, 448,
    456
Losses, 155–156
    capital, 566, 767
    comparisons of, 278
    economic, 282
    minimizing, 326–327
    short-run, 281–282
Lottery, resource allocation by, 107
Lucas, Robert E., Jr., 724
Lucas wedge, 496, 497, 503
Luna, Demetrio, 417
Luxuries, 93

M1, 591, 591–592, 595, 601
M2, 591, 591–592, 595, 601
Macroeconomics, 2
    classical view, 653, 662
    fluctuations in, 535, 656–661, 723
    Keynesian view, 2, 653, 662–663
    Monetarist view of, 663
    new classical, 653
    real variables in, 527
    schools of thought, 662–663
    short-run, equilibrium, 656
    trends in, 535, 656–661
Mad cow disease (BSE), 162
Mainstream business cycle theory,
    711–712
Majority rule, resource allocation by, 106
Malkeil, Nancy, 478
Malthus, Thomas Robert, 485, 553, 645
Malthusian theory, 485, 553, 554–555, 556

Manning, Peyton, 466
Manufacturing production, 3
Margin, 9, 184
Marginal analysis, 186, 277
Marginal benefit, 9, 381
    decreasing, 34, 477
    demand and, 58
    preferences and, 34–35
Marginal cost, 109–110, 139, 140, **258**
    increase, 62
    PPF and, 33
    supply and, 63
Marginal cost of labor curve (MCL), 425
Marginal cost pricing rule, 313
Marginal external benefit, 381
Marginal external cost, 395, 402
Marginally attached worker, 517,
    517–518
Marginal private benefit (MB), 381
Marginal private cost (MC), 395, 402
Marginal product, 253, 419, 433
Marginal product curve, 254–255
Marginal product of capital, 262
**Marginal propensity to consume
    (MPC), 674**
Marginal propensity to import, 675
Marginal propensity to save (MPS), 674
**Marginal rate of substitution (MRS),
    208,** 211
Marginal revenue, 274
    elasticity and, 303
    price and, 302
Marginal social benefit (MSB), 381
    common resources and, 402–403
    of innovation, 330
    of public good, 377
Marginal social cost (MSC), 110, 378,
    395, 402
Marginal utility, 181
Marginal utility per dollar, 184
Marginal utility theory, 187–192
Mariel Boatlift, 487
Markets, 42. *See also* Factor markets;
        Global markets; Labor markets;
        Money market
    alternatives, 115
    black, 128–129
    bond, 567–568
    capital rental, 428
    circular flows through, 42, 43
    commodity, 418
    competitive, 56, 237–241
    constraints, 230
    contestable, 354, 355
    coordination, 242
    efficiency of competitive, 112–115
    entry/exit from, 283–285
    financial capital, 567–568
    geographical scope of, 240
    housing, 128–130
    illegal goods, 142–143
    insurance, 476
    international, 579–580
    land rental, 428–429
    loan, 475, 476, 567
    loanable funds, 767
    money, 602–605, 762, 764, 767
    for oil, 431

Markets (*continued*)
  political, 372–373
  prices and, 56, 106, 108–109
  for real GDP, 763, 764–765
  rental, 418, 428–429
  risk insurance, 476
  stock, 568
  understanding, 175
Marketable permits, 399
Market demand, 108–109
Market equilibrium, 66–67, 77
  in foreign exchange market, 622
  money, 604–605
Market failure, 113, 113–114, 372, 398, 413
Market for loanable funds, 570, 570–575, 597, 762–763, 764, 767
Market income, 442, 456
Marketing, in monopolistic competition, 324–325, 330–333
Market power, 367
Market price, resource allocation by, 106
Market supply, 110
Market supply curve, 423
  long-run, 287–288
  short-run, 280
Market value, 490
Markup, 329
Marriage, wealth concentration and, 454
Marshall, Alfred, 175
Marshall, Bob, 176
Marshall, Mary Paley, 175
Massachusetts Institute of Technology (MIT), 52–53, 216
MB. *See* Marginal private benefit
MC. *See* Marginal private cost
McConnell, Mitch, 654
McDonald's, 4, 369, 498
MCL. *See* Marginal cost of labor curve
Means of payment, 590
Measures of concentration, 238–241
Medicaid, 384, 386–387, 455, 456
Medicare, 384, 385, 386–387, 455, 456, 738, 739
Medicare Part C for all (Kotlikoff), 385
Medium of exchange, 590
Mergers and acquisitions, 359
Merrill Lynch, 478, 568, 664
Mexico, 164. *See also* North American Free Trade Agreement
MGM, 426
Michigan, 521
Mickel, Jennifer, 478
Microeconomics, 2
Microloans, 552
Microsoft, 6, 227, 244, 299, 301, 358, 367
Mill, John Stuart, 116, 375
Minimum differentiation, 378–379
Minimum efficient cost, 383
Minimum efficient scale, 265
Minimum wage, 131, 131–133
  cause and effect of, 132–133
  employment increased by, 486–487
  fairness of, 132
  inefficiency of, 131–132
  monopsony and, 426
  unemployment brought by, 131

Minus sign and elasticity, 86
Misery index, 701, 716–717
MIT. *See* Massachusetts Institute of Technology
Mitsubishi, 568
Mixed good, 374
  with external benefits, 374–375, 381–385
  with external costs, 375–376
  government and, 381–385
  providing, 376, 381–385
Mizuho Bank, 630
Modern-day Malthusians, 553
Momentary supply, 96
Monetarism, 777
Monetarist cycle theory, 712
Monetarist macroeconomics, 663
Monetary base, 597, 600
Monetary policy, 655
  aggregate demand and, 663
  aggregate demand related to, 655
  conduct of, 756–758
  exchange rate fluctuations, 760–761
  expenditure plans, 761
  federal funds rate, 759
  Federal Reserve Act, 754
  to fight recession, 654
  interest rate changes, 759–760
  money and bank loans, 761
  objectives, 754
  operational 'maximum employment' goal, 755
  operational 'stable prices' goal, 755
  responsibility for, 756
  strategies for, 769
  transmission of, 759–766
Monetary policy instrument, **756,** 757
Monetary stimulus, 767–769
Money, 42, 590
  aggregate supply related to change in wage rate, 651
  appreciating U.S. dollar, 625
  banks creating, 599–601
  demand for, 603, 619
  depreciating U.S. dollar, 625
  FFR and changes in, 761
  finance and, 566
  growth and inflation, 606–607
  holding, 602
  income, 442, 456
  measures of, 591–592
  nominal interest rate, 602
  price level, 602
  prices, 56
  quantity theory of, 606–607
  recovery and (*Reading Between the Lines*), 608–609
  as store of value, 591
  supply and demand of, 604–605, 619–621
  in U.S. today, 591–592
Money income, 442, 456
Money market, 602–605, 762, 764, 767
Money market equilibrium, 604–605
Money market mutual funds, 593
Money multiplier, 601, 610–611
Money price, 56
Money wage rate, 703

Monitoring, lowering cost of borrower, 594
Monopolistic competition, 237, 240, **324,** 367
  advertising in, 330, 332–333
  efficiency of, 329
  entry and exit in, 325
  examples of, 325
  firms in, 324
  HHI in, 325
  innovation in, 330
  marketing in, 324–325, 330–333
  output in, 326–329
  perfect competition compared with, 328–329
  price and output in, 306
  price in, 306, 324, 326–329
  product development, 330–333
  product differentiation, 324
  product quality in, 324
Monopoly, 115, **237,** 237–238, 240, **300,** 550–551. *See also* Natural monopoly; Oligopoly; Single-price monopoly
  antitrust law and, 356–359
  bilateral, 425–426
  buying a, 308
  creating, 308
  deadweight loss and, 307
  elasticity of demand in, 303
  inefficiency of, 307
  information-age, 301
  legal, 300–301
  natural, 300, 313–315, 342, 374, 376
  output and price decision, 302–305
  price and output comparison, 306
  price discrimination, 309–312
  price-setting strategies, 301
  reasons for, 300–301
  regulation, 313–315, 376
  single-price, 301–309
  uncertainty and, 477
Monopsony, 425, 425–426
Monthly price survey, 523
Moore, Gordon, 6
Moral hazard, 472
Morgan, J. P., 356
Morgan Stanley, 568
Morgenstern, Oskar, 344
Mortgage, 567, 767. *See also* Federal Home Loan Mortgage Corporation; Federal National Mortgage Association
Mortgage-backed securities, 568
Motorola, 334, 655
Movies, and DVDs, 212
MPC. *See* Marginal propensity to consume
MPS. *See* Marginal propensity to save
MRS. *See* Marginal rate of substitution
MSB. *See* Marginal social benefit
MSC. *See* Marginal social cost
MSN, 326
Multifiber Arrangement, 164
Multiplier, 679, **680,** 693
  aggregate expenditure slope of curve, 682
  autonomous expenditure, 683, 694

autonomous tax, 694
balanced budget, 695
business cycle turning points, 684
effect, 680–681
government expenditure, 694, 743
in Great Depression, 684
greater than 1, 681
imports and, 683
income taxes and, 683
money, 610–611
price level and, 685–689
process, 683
size of, 681
tax, 743, 745
variable money, 601
Murdoch, Rupert, 359
Murphy, Kevin, 133
Music industry, 192–193
Mutual funds, 593
MySpace, 359

NAFTA. *See* North American Free Trade
    Agreement
Nash, John, 345, 351
Nash equilibrium, 345, 349–350, 351,
    352
National Bureau of Economic Research,
    645
National comparative advantage, 152
National Income and Product Accounts, 493
National saving, 571
Natural barrier to entry, 300
Natural disaster water shortage study,
    118–119
Natural experiment, 24–25
Natural monopoly, 300, 342
    goods and resources in, 374
    regulation of, 313, 314–315, 376
Natural monopoly good, 374
Natural oligopoly, 342
Natural resources
    nonrenewable, 418
    renewable, 400–401
Natural unemployment, 519–520
Natural unemployment rate, 519,
    709–710
Nautica, 326–329
Navistar International, 285
NBC, 426
NEC, 285
Necessities, 93
Needs-tested spending, 740, 741
Negative production externalities, 300,
    394, 398
Negative relationships, 17, 17–18, 25
Neoclassical growth theory, 553,
    553–554
Nestlé, 70
Net borrower, 633
Net exports, 492, 493, **634,** 634–635,
    761
Net interest, 493, 494
Net investment, 492, 566
Net lender, 633
Net operating surplus, 493–494
Netscape, 358
Net taxes, 570
Net worth, 569

Neuroeconomics, 195
New Balance, 324
New classical cycle theory, 712
New classical macroeconomics, 653
New Deal, 738
New growth theory, 554, 554–555, 556
New Keynesian cycle theory, 712
News Corp, 359
Newsom, Darin, 74–75
New York Fed. *See* Federal Reserve Bank
    of New York
New York Yankees, 4
Nexus One, 334
Nike, 5, 165, 324
Nikon, 332
Nokia, 352, 655
Nominal exchange rate, 626–627
Nominal GDP, 495
Nominal interest rate, 571, 602
Nonexcludable, 374, 375
Nonrenewable natural resources, 418,
    429–430
Nonrival, 374
Normal good, 60
Normal profit, 229
Normative statements, 10
North, Douglas, 370
North American Free Trade Agreement
    (NAFTA), 53, 162, 167
Northern Rock, 767
Nozick, Robert, 118
Nursing, 432–433

OASDHI. *See* Old-Age Survivors
    Disability and Health Insurance
Obama, Barack, 10, 151, 168, 458, 729,
    742, 744
    fiscal policy of (*Reading Between the
    Lines*), 746–747
    inflation-unemployment tradeoff and
    (*Reading Between the Lines*),
    716–717
Office of Child Support Enforcement,
    457
Official settlements account, 631
Offshore outsourcing, 165
Offshoring, 165, 165–166
Oil
    crude, 69, 429–430
    demand, 429
    equilibrium price of, 430
    supply, 429–430
    trade and, 152
    world and U.S. markets for, 431
Okun, Arthur M., 701
Old-Age Survivors Disability and Health
    Insurance(OASDHI), 455
Oligopoly, 237, 240, **342**
    antitrust law, 356
    examples of, 343
    game theory, 344–352
    Nash equilibrium, 345, 349–350, 351,
    352
    price-fixing game, 346–350
    repeated games, 353–354
    sequential games, 354–355
OPEC. *See* Organization of Petroleum
    Exporting Countries

Open market operation, 597
Open market purchase, 597–598
Open market sale, 598–599
Operational price stability goal, 755
Opportunity cost, 8, 8–9, 31, 128, 228
    increasing, 32
    of production, 228–229
    production possibilities and, 30–32
    as ratio, 31–32
    relative price as, 56, 205
    wage rate and, 423
Organization of Petroleum Exporting
    Countries (OPEC), 69
Origin, 13
Outlays, 729
Outlet substitution bias, 526
Output
    costs and, 395
    decisions, 276–279, 302–305
    external cost and, 395
    firms and price of, 276–279
    firms decisions, 276–279
    in monopolistic competition, 306,
    326–329
    perfect competition and, 276–279,
    280–285, 306
    price compared to, 306, 326–328
    profit-maximizing, 326–327
    short-run technology constraint,
    280–282
    time frame decisions, 252
Output decisions, supply curve, 279
Output gap, 520, 521, **658,** 755, 758
Outsourcing, 165
Overfishing, 401, 402–403
Overgrazing, 400
Overproduction, 114
    incentive to, 140
    inefficient, 141
Overprovision, 380, 383, 384
Overuse of common resource, 402–403
Ownership
    as barrier to entry, 300
    principal-agent problem relating to, 234
Oyier, Daniel, 120

Paperbooks v. e-books (*Reading Between
    the Lines*), 216–217
Paramedics and hockey players (*Reading
    Between the Lines*), 196–197
Partnership, 234–236
Patents, 301, 550–551
Patient Protection and Affordable Care
    Act. *See* Affordable Care Act of
    2010
Pay. *See also* Ability-to-pay principle
CEO (*Reading Between the Lines*),
    458–459
    incentive, 234
    willingness and ability to, 58
Payoff matrix, 344, 345, 349–350
Payroll taxes, 386
PCE deflator. *See* Personal consumption
    expenditure deflator
Pell Grant, 383
PennPower, 251
Pension funds, 569
People's Bank of China, 629–630

PepsiCo, 359, 648, 649, 650, 651
Percentages and proportions, 86
Perfect competition, 237, 240, **274**
　advancing technology and changing
　　tastes, 286–289
　of corn (*Reading Between the Lines*),
　　292–293
　economic profit and revenue in,
　　274–275
　efficiency of, 290–291, 307
　marginal analysis, 277
　monopolistic competition compared
　　with, 328–329
　output, price, and profit in long run,
　　283–285
　output decisions of firm, 276–279
　price and output comparison, 306
　price takers in, 274
　short run output, price and profit,
　　280–282
　temporary shutdown decision, 278
Perfect competition of corn (*Reading
　　Between the Lines*), 292–293
Perfectly elastic demand, 87, 136
Perfectly elastic supply, 136–137
Perfectly inelastic demand, 86, 135
Perfectly inelastic supply, 136
Perfect price discrimination, 311, 312
Permits, marketable, 399
Perry, Corey, 196–197
Personal characteristics, resource allocation
　　by, 107
Personal consumption expenditure defla-
　　tor (PCE deflator), 526, 755
Personal income taxes, 729
Personal Responsibility and Work
　　Opportunities Reconciliation Act,
　　457
Phelps, Edmund S., 777
Phillips, A.W., 708
Phillips curve, 701, 708, 709–710
Physical capital growth, 551
Pigou, Arthur Cecil, 398
Pigovian taxes, 398
Pizzigati, Sam, 458, 459
Policy free lunch, 777
Policy tradeoff, 777
Political equilibrium, 373, 405
Political freedom, 500
Political marketplace, 372–373
Political outcomes, efficient, 378–380
Pollution
　air, 394
　effects of, 394
　as external cost, 394–399
　as negative production externalities,
　　300, 394, 398
　production and, 396
　sources of, 394
　tax, 398–399
　trading permits for, 399
　trends in, 394
　water, 394
Pooling equilibrium, 475
Pool risk, 594
Population, 60, 485, 516
　demand for labor and, 60
　growth theory, 553

labor force and growth of, 548
　working-age, 515
Position of line, 25
Positive marginal utility, 181
Positive relationships, 16, 17, 25
Positive statements, 10
Postal Service, U.S., 300, 301
Potential entry, 240
Potential GDP, 496, 520–521
　aggregate production function, 545,
　　566
　determining, 545–547
　fluctuations around, 496
　growth of, 496, 545–550
　labor market and, 547
Poverty, 446–447
PowerBar, 70
PPF. *See* Production possibilities frontier
PPP. *See* Purchasing power parity
Predatory pricing, 358
Pre-Existing Condition Insurance Plan,
　　385
Preferences, 8, 60, 181, 186
　indifference curves and, 207–210
　marginal benefits and, 34–35
Premium, 469
Prescott, Edward, 735
Present value, 434, 738
　rent-v.-buy decision and, 428
　of sequence of future amounts, 435
Prices. *See also* Single-price monopoly
　adjustments, 67
　alternative, indexes, 526
　asset, 570
　average, quantity and, 85–86
　best deal available, 67
　change in, 90, 205–206
　commodity, 418
　demand and, 59, 108–109
　elasticity of demand and, 84–90, 97
　equilibrium, 66, 430
　exchange rate as, 618–619
　expectation of future, 59–60
　of factors of production, cost curves
　　and, 63, 261
　firms' output decision and, 276–279
　of gasoline (*Reading Between the Lines*),
　　74–75
　limit, 355
　long run and, 283–285
　maintaining resale, 357
　marginal revenue and, 302
　markets and, 56, 106, 108–109
　money, 56
　in monopolistic competition, 306,
　　324, 326–329
　monopoly output decision and,
　　302–306
　monopoly strategies for, 301
　of oil, 430
　output compared to, 306, 326–328
　perfect competition and, 280–285,
　　306
　predatory, 358
　predicting changes in, 68, 70, 72
　as regulator, 66–67
　relative, 56, 205
　resource allocation by, 56, 106

short run and, 280–282
　single-price monopoly decisions for,
　　302–305
　supply and, 63, 64, 110
　time since change in, 90
Price cap regulation, 128, 315
Price discrimination, 301
　consumer surplus capture, 309–310
　efficiency and rent seeking with, 312
　monopoly and, 309–312
　perfect, 311, 312
　profiting by, 310
Price effect, 211
Price elasticity of demand, 84, 84–90,
　　97
　calculating, 85–86
　for food, 90
Price fixing, 346–350, 357
Price floor, 131
Price level, 522, 602
　aggregate demand and, 685
　equilibrium real GDP and, 687–689
　fixed, 672
　Keynesian economics related to,
　　676–679, 685–689
　money, 602
　multiplier and, 685–689
　real GDP and fixed, 676–679
　unemployment and, 522–527
Price regulations, 114
Price takers, 274
Price wars, 354
Princeton University, 132, 478–479
Principal-agent problem, 234
Principle of decreasing marginal benefit,
　　34, 477
**Principle of minimum differentiation,
　　379–380**
The Principles of Economics (Marshall, A.),
　　175
Prisoner's dilemma, 344–345
Private benefits, 381–382
Private cost, 395
Private good, 374
Private information, 472
　asymmetric information, 472
　insurance market, 476
　loan market, 475
　used car market, 472–475
Private property, 403–404
Private provision, 378
Private schools, public schools v., 415
Private sector balance, 624–635, 634
Private subsidy, 384
Proctor & Gamble, 350–351, 360
Producer surplus, 111, 307, 469
Product curves, 252–256, 260
Product development, 330–333
Product differentiation, 237, 324,
　　334–335
Production. *See also* Factors of production
　under, 113–114
　agriculture, 3
　efficiency of, 31
　electrical, 266–267
　factors of, 418, 419–422
　government quotas, 404
　incentive systems, 140

inefficient, 31
manufacturing, 3
opportunity cost of, 228–229
over, 114, 140, 141
pollution and, 396
possibilities for, opportunity cost and, 30–32
principal-agent problem, 234
public, 383
quotas, 139–140, 404
sustainable, 400–401
team, 243
technological change and, 289
technological efficiency and, 231, 254
Production cutbacks, 283
Production efficiency, 31
Production possibilities, opportunity cost and, 30–32
Production possibilities frontier (PPF), 30, 254, 545
marginal cost and, 33
tradeoffs, 30–31
Production quotas, 139, 139–140, 404
Product schedules, 253
Profits, 4. *See also* Economic profit; Normal profit
accounting, 228
colluding to maximize, 347
of corporation, 494
from holding U.S. dollars, 620
long run, 327–328
loss minimizing and, 326–327
normal, 229
output for maximizing, 326–327
perfect competition and, 274–275, 280–285
price discrimination influencing, 310
product innovation and maximizing, 330
short-run, 281–282
Progressive income tax, 455
Prohibition, 143
Property, private, 403–404
Property rights, 42, 396, 397, 403–404
intellectual, 550–551
Proportional income tax, 455
Proprietorship, 234–236
Proprietors' income, 494
Protection, argument against, 163–167
Public choice, 371
inefficiencies that require, 376
political marketplace and, 372–373
theory, 372, 405
Public franchise, 300
Public goods, 115, 374, 554
efficient quantity of, 378
excludable, 375
lighthouses as, 375
marginal social benefit from, 377
marginal social cost of, 378
providing, 376, 377–380
rival, 374
Public overprovision, 380
Public production, 383
Public provision, 378–380
Public schools
competition between, 414–415
private schools v., 415

Puma, 324
Purchasing power parity (PPP), 498, **626**

Qatar, 162
QE. *See* Quantitative easing
Quality change bias, 525
Quantitative easing (QE), 608
Quantity
average, price and, 85–86
efficient, of public good, 378
equilibrium, 66
regulations, 114
Quantity demanded, 57, 60–61
Quantity supplied, 62, 64
Quantity theory of money, 606, 606–607
Quigley, John, 487
Quotas
import, 109, 160–161, 191, 307, 309–310, 469, 470
ITQs, 404–405
production, 139–140, 404

Ralph Lauren, 329
Rate of return regulation, 314
Rational choice, 8
Rational expectation, 707
Rational ignorance, 380
Rawls, John, 117
Razors (*Reading Between the Lines*), 360–361
RBC. *See* Real business cycle theory
R&D. *See* Research and development
Reading Between the Lines
AS-AD model, 664
California's underground economy, 144–145
CEO pay, 458–459
China's economic growth, 558–559
China tire trade penalties, 168–169
crowding out in global recession, 582–583
dollar and carry trade, 636–637
elasticities of demand and supply for tomatoes, 98–100
Facebook, 244–245
Federal Reserve stimulus policies, 770–771
fuel choices, food crises, and finger-pointing, 44–45
gasoline prices, 74–75
Google, 316–317
government action in labor markets, 144–145
Internet advertising market battles, 244–245
inventories in expansion, 690–691
jobs growth lags recovery, 528–529
money and recovery, 608–609
Obama fiscal policy, 746–747
paperbooks v. e-books, 216–217
paramedics and hockey players, 196–197
perfect competition of corn, 292–293
product differentiation, 334–335
razors, 360–361
real GDP in 2010, 502–503
rose market efficiency, 120–121

shifting inflation-unemployment trade-off, 716–717
smart meters, 266–267
Web Ads, 244–245
Reagan, Ronald, 716, 737
Real business cycle (RBC) theory, 712, 713–715
criticisms and defenses of, 715
mechanism of, 713
Real exchange rate, 627
Real GDP, 495
actual and planned expenditure and, 677
aggregate demand curve related to, 653
aggregate expenditure two-way link with, 672
aggregate planned expenditure and, 672, 676, 677, 681
aggregate supply and, 648
business cycle, 497
chained-dollar, 504–505
change in quantity demanded, 60–61
consumption as function of, 675
equilibrium, 687–689
fixed price level and, 676–679
growth in world economy, 543–544
HDI, 501
health and life expectancy, 500
inflation and deflation relating to, 522
Keynesian economics and, 676–679
leisure time, 500
limitations of, 499–501
market for, 763, 764–765
money holding and, 602
productivity growth slowdown, 496–497
standard of living, 496, 498
in 2010 forecasts (*Reading Between the Lines*), 502–503
unemployment over the cycle, 520–521
in U.S., 542, 543, 657
uses and limitations of, 496–497
Real GDP per person, 496, 540
Real income, 205
Real interest rate, 571, 571–572, 761
Real wage rate, 520, **546**
Recession, 497
challenges of Fed, 762–763
costs of, 724
crowding out in global (*Reading Between the Lines*), 582–583
Fed fighting, 763–764
fiscal policy to fight, 654
monetary policy to fight, 654
Recessionary gap, 659, 758
Recognition lag, 745
Redistribution
income, 455–457, 522
of surplus, 308
of wealth, 522
Reebok, 324
Reference base period, 523
Regressive income tax, 455
Regulation, 313. *See also* Deregulation
earnings sharing, 315
monopoly, 313–315, 376
of natural monopoly, 313, 314–315, 376

Regulation (*continued*)
  price cap, 128, 315
  rate of return, 314
Reid, Harry, 654
Relative price, 56, **205**
Renewable natural resources,
    400–401
Rent, 4
  capital, 428
  economic, 308
  land, 428–429
Rental income, 493–494
Rental markets, 418, 428–429
Rental rate, 228, 418
Rent ceiling, 128, 128–130
Rent seeking, 167, **308**
  equilibrium, 308, 309
  with price discrimination, 312
Rent-v.-buy decision, 428, 434
Repeated duopoly game, 353–354
Required reserve ratio, 599
Resale price maintenance, 357
Research and development (R&D)
    games, 350–351
  to stimulate economic growth, 557
Research in Motion, 334–335
Reservation wage, 422
Reserves, 593
  desired, 600
  excess, 600
Reserve ratio
  desired, 600
  required, 599
Resources, 228. *See also* Common
    resources; Goods and resources;
    Natural resources; Renewable
    natural resources
  allocation methods, 106–107
  competition and efficient use of, 289
  efficient use of, 33–35
Resource allocation, 56, 106, 107, 522
Restoring American Financial Stability Act
    of 2010, 569
Ricardo, David, 553, 578, 645
Ricardo-Barro effect, 578
Risk
  buying and selling, 469–471
  credit, 475
  decisions in face of, 466–468
  default, 475, 574
  insurance markets, 476
  pool, 594
  trading, 470
Risk aversion, 466
Rival, 374
Robinson, Joan, 52
Robinson-Patman Act, 356
Rockefeller, John D., 356, 358
Rodriguez, Alex, 4
Roe v. Wade, 225
Romer, Christina, 10, 744, 745
Romer, Paul, 554
Roosevelt, Franklin D., 514
Rose market efficiency (*Reading Between
    the Lines*), 120–121
Rosen, Sherwin, 454
Rule of 70, 540, 540–541

Runge, C. Ford, 44
Russell, Bertrand, 723

Saez, Emmanuel, 446, 459
Salai-i-Martin, Xavier, 644–646
Samuelson, Paul, 53
Savings, 566, 571
  bank, 593
  consumption and, 672
  income tax influencing, 736
  MPS, 674
  National, 571
  to stimulate economic growth, 556
  taxes influencing, 736
  wealth and, 566
Saving function, 672, 673
Savings and loan associations (S&L), 593
Scarcity, 2
Scatter diagrams, 14, 14–15
Schick, 341, 360–361
Schmitt-Grohé, Stephanie, 778–780
Schumpeter, Joseph, 643
Screening, 475
Search activity, 128
Securities, 568, 594
Self-interest, 5, 5–7, 194–195, 477
Self-interested actions, 9
Self Sufficiency Program (SSP), 486, 487
Selling costs, 331–332
Separating equilibrium, 475
Sequential entry games, 354–355
7-Up, 359
Seymour, Richard, 417
Shephard, William G., 241
Sherman Act, of 1890, 356, 357, 358
Shoebuy.com, 321
Shoes, 321, 324, 331
Shortages, 67
  housing, 128
  Water, case study, 118–119
Short run, 252
  aggregate demand in, 688
  costs, 257–261
  economic profit, 282, 326–327
  equilibrium, 281, 604, 605
  output, price, and profit, 280–282
  possible outcomes, 282
  profits and losses in, 281–282
  supply, 96
Short-run aggregate supply, 649, 650
**Short-run macroeconomic equilibrium,
    656**
Short-run market supply curve, 280
Short-run Phillips curve, 708
Short-run technology constraints,
    253–256
  average product curve, 255
  marginal product curve, 253–254
  product curves, 252
  product schedules, 252
  total product curve, 253
Short-term bill rate, 760
Shutdown decision, 278, 283
Shutdown point, 278
Signal, 332, 478–479
Signaling, with advertising, 332–333,
    474, 475

Simon, Julian, 485
Single-price monopoly, 301
competition compared to, 306–309
output and price decision, 302–305
S&L. *See* Savings and loan associations
Slope, 20
  aggregate expenditure, 682
  across arc, 21–22
  of curved line, 21–22
  of line, 24–24
  marginal propensities and, 674
  at point, 21
  of relationship, 20
  of straight line, 20–21
Smart meters (*Reading Between the Lines*),
    266–267
Smart phones. *See* Cell phones; specific
    phone
Smetters, Kent, 738
Smith, Adam, 51, 113, 223, 351, 414,
    535, 553, 556, 645
Smoot-Hawley Act, 159
Social benefits, 381–382. *See also*
    Marginal Social benefit
Social-interest, 5, 5–7, 477
Social interest theory, 313
Social justice, 500
Social networking, 244–245
Social Security, 455, 471, 729, 738–739
Social Security tax, 133, 135, 729, 735
Solow, Robert, 553
Sony, 493
Sony Reader, 216
Specialization, 453
Spending, 740, 741
SSI. *See* Supplementary Security Insurance
SSP. *See* Self Sufficiency Program
Stabilization policy, 779
Stagflation, 661, 705, 716
Standard of living
  globally, 498
  over time, 496
Standard Oil, 358
Starbucks, 343
Stark, Pete, 406
State of nature, 64
Statistical discrepancy, 494
Statute of Monopolies, of 1624,
    550–551
Stern, Nicholas, 398
*Stern Review on the Economics of Climate
    Change* (Stern), 398
Stimulus. *See also* Fiscal stimulus
  automatic, 741
  demand, 777
  discretionary fiscal, 743–745
  Federal Reserve policies (*Reading
    Between the Lines*), 770–771
  monetary, 767–769
  package, 2009, 742
Stock, 568
Stock markets, 568
Store of value, 591
Straight line equations, 24–25
Strategic interdependence, 367
Strategies, 301, **344,** 345
Strawberries, 71

Structural surplus or deficit, 741
Structural unemployment, 519,
    519–521
Sub-prime credit crisis, 476, 767
Subsidies, 114, 139, 140–141, **141,** 162,
    383
    education and, 383
    exports, 162
    to farmers, 140–141
    government, 314
    private, 384
Subsidized services, 455–456
Substitutability, degree of, 209–210
Substitute, 59, 89, 209, 300
Substitution bias
    commodity, 525
    outlet, 526
Substitution effect, 57, 210, **214,** 423,
    653, 685–686
Sumner, Scott, 608
Sunk cost, 252
Supplementary Security Insurance (SSI),
    455
Supply, 62. *See also* Law of supply
    all possible changes in, 72–73
    change in, 64–65, 70
    decision time-frame, 252
    decrease in, 70, 139–140
    expected future prices, 64
    foreign exchange market and, 619, 621
    increase in, 64, 70, 140, 575
    of labor, 546, 547–548, 734–735
    of land, 429
    law of, 62
    marginal analysis and, decision for, 277
    marginal cost and, 109–110
    minimum price and cost, 110
    of money, 604–605, 621
    number of suppliers, 64
    of oil, 429–430
    perfectly elastic, 136
    perfectly inelastic, 136
    prices of factors of production, 63
    prices of related goods produced, 63
    schedule, 62
    short-run, 96
    state of nature, 64
    technology, 64
    U.S. dollar changes in, 624
Supply curve, 62, 63, 76
    for labor markets, 423
    in output decisions, 279
    short-run market, 280
Supply of loanable funds, 573, 573–574
Supply-side effects, 734–737
Surplus, 67, 108, 730
    budget, 730
    consumer, 109, 191, 307, 309–310,
    469, 470
    cyclical, 741, 742
    government budget, 577
    net operating, 493–494
    producer, 111, 307, 469
    redistribution of, 308
    structural, 741
    total, 112
Sustainable Fishing Act, 405

Sustainable production, 400–401
Symmetry principle, 118
Talking with
    Caroline M. Hoxby, 414–416
    David Card, 486–488
    Jagdish Bhagwati, 10, 52–54
    Ricardo J. Caballero, 724–726
    Richard Clarida, 536–538
    Stephanie Schmitt-Grohé, 778–780
    Steven D. Levitt, 224–226
    Susan Athey, 176–178
    Tom Hubbard, 368–370
    Xavier Salai-i-Martin, 644–646
TANF. *See* Temporary Assistance for
    Needy Households
Tariffs, 157
    deadweight loss, 158
    effects of, 158
    revenue, 166
    social loss from, 159
    t-shirt, 157–158
    two-part, 313
TARP. *See* Troubled Asset Relief Program
Taxes, 114, 133–138. *See also* Tax multi-
    plier
    on buyers, 134, 135
    cap-and-trade v., 406–407
    corporate income, 729
    on drugs, 143
    efficiency and, 137–138
    elasticity of demand and, 135–136
    elasticity of supply and, 136–137
    equivalence of, on buyers and sellers,
    134–135
    on expenditure, 735
    fairness and, 138
    Laffer curve and, 737
    net, 570
    payroll, 386
    with perfectly elastic demand, 136
    with perfectly inelastic demand, 135
    personal income, 729
    Pigovian, 398
    pollution and, 398–399
    progressive income, 455
    prohibition v., 143
    proportional income, 455
    regressive income, 455
    on sellers, 133–134
    Social Security, 133, 135, 729, 735
    tax incidence, 133
    workers and consumers paying most,
    138
Tax incidence, 133
Tax multiplier, 694, **743,** 745
Tax revenues, 737, 740–741
Tax wedge, 735
Taylor, John B., 769
Taylor rule, 769, 779, 780
Team production, economies of, 243
Technology, 64, **230**
    advancing, 286–289
    aggregate supply related to, 651
    change in, 289
    constraints, 230, 280–282
    cost curves and, 260–261, 451

    diminishing returns and change in,
    553–554
    economic inequality and, 451
    efficiency, 231
    in firms, 230, 252–256, 289
    human capital and change in, 451
    information-age, 6, 301, 451
    labor demand and, 421
    labor productivity and advances in,
    551–552
    short-run constraint of, 253–256
Technological change, 36
Technological efficiency, 231, 254
Telvent DTN, 74
Temperature analogy, 192
Temporary Assistance for Needy
    Households (TANF), 455, 457
Temporary shutdown decision, 278, 283
Term Auction Credit, 768
Terrorism, 226
Texas A&M University, 133
Thanasoulis, Connie, 478
A Theory of Justice (Rawls), 117
Third World debt crisis, 633
Three sector balances, 635
Thrift institutions, 593
Time elapsed since price change, 90
Tire trade penalties, 168–169
Tomatoes, 98–99
Total cost (TC), 257, 331
Total expenditure, 494
Total fixed cost (TFC), 257
Total product, 253
Total product curve, 254
Total revenue, 88, **274,** 302
Total surplus, 112
Total utility, 181
Total variable cost (TVC), 257
Trade. *See also* Cap-and-trade; Fair trade;
    International trade
    carry, 636–637
    with China, 41, 151, 152
    financial international, 631–635
    gains and losses from exports, 156
    gains and losses from imports,
    155–156
    gains from, 38, 39–40
    net gain from, 155–156
    protection in, 163–167
    in risk, 470
    of services for oil, 152
    in U.S., 41
Tradeoff, 8, 777
    big, 117, 456–457
    along PPF, 30–31
Trade wars, avoiding, 166
Tragedy of the commons, 376, 400,
    401–405
Transaction costs, 115, **242, 397**
Transfer payments, 729
Trichet, Jean-Claude, 654
Troubled Asset Relief Program (TARP),
    768
Trump, Donald, 441
T-shirts, 152, 153, 157–158, 165
Twitter, 227
2009 fiscal stimulus package, 654, 742

Two-part tariff, 313
Tying arrangement, 357–358

U2, 374
UC Energy Institute, 406
Uhlig, Harald, 744, 745
Umbele Foundation, 645
Uncertainty
    buying and selling risk, 469–471
    choice with, 468
    decisions in face of, 466–468
    expected utility, 467–468
    expected wealth, 466
    factor markets, inequality, and, 485
    information, invisible hand, and, 477
    insurance markets, 476
    monopoly and, 477
    risk aversion, 466
    utility of wealth, 466–467
Underground economy, 144–145,
    499–500
Underproduction, 113–114
Underprovision, 383, 384
Underutilized labor, 517
Unemployment
    alternative measures of, 518
    benefits, 520
    compensation, 455
    current population survey, 515
    cyclical, 519
    employment and, 514–518
    frictional, 519
    full employment and, 519–521
    inflation and, 708–710
    inflation tradeoff with (*Reading
        Between the Lines*), 716–717
    labor market indicators, 515–517
    marginally attached workers, 517–518
    minimum wage bringing, 131
    misery index and rate of, 701,
        716–717
    most costly, 518
    Phillips curve, 701, 708–710
    price level and, 522–527
    problem of, 514–515
    real GDP and, 520–521
    structural, 519–521
Unemployment rate, 516, 758
    natural, 519, 709–710
Unequal wealth, 454
Union-nonunion wage gap, 426
Union Pacific, 567–569
Unions, 424–426
United Kingdom, 767
United Nations Development Index
    (HDI), 501
United States (U.S.). *See also* Dollars,
    U.S.; Great Depression
    airplane exports in, 154
    air pollution trends in, 394
    balance of payments accounts, 631
    borrowing for consumption, 633
    budget in historical perspective,
        730–733
    business cycle in, 497, 658
    China as top creditor to, 582

China tire trade penalties, 168–169
Congress, 728, 756
consumption function, 675
credit crisis, of 2007-2008, 476, 767
current account deficit of, 725–726
demand-pull inflation in, 704
Department of Commerce, 239, 690
Department of Energy, 266
differential interest rate, 623
distribution of Income, 442, 443,
    446–447
economic growth in, 37, 542, 657
financial crisis, of 2008-2009, 568,
    576, 598, 767–768
flexible exchange rate in, 628
foreigners buying businesses in, 617
foreign interest rates relative to, 624
GDP measured in, 493–495
government bonds, 538, 594, 767
import demand in, 624
import function, 675
inflation in, 657
international debts, 739–740
Justice Department, 356, 358
labor force shrinking (*Reading Between
    the Lines*), 528–529
money in, 591–592
money multiplier, 610–611
natural unemployment rate in,
    519–520, 709–710
oil markets in, 431
output gap in, 658
Phillips curve data in, 710
Postal Service, 300, 301
real GDP in, 542, 543, 657
rich getting richer in, 441
standard of living in, 498
structural budget balance in, 742
tax wedge in, 735
trade in, 41
t-shirt import in, 152, 153
t-shirt tariffs in, 157–158
2009 fiscal stimulus package, 742
underground economy in, 144–145,
    499–500
world demand for exports, 623
United States v. Microsoft, 358
Unit elastic demand, 86, 303
Unit of account, 590–591
Units-free measure, 86
University of California, Berkeley, 10,
    132
University of Chicago, 133, 223, 225, 241
University of Texas, Austin, 133
Unlimited liability, 234–236
UPS, 301
Uribe, Martin, 778–780
U.S. *See* United States
U.S. Department of Agriculture (USDA),
    292
U.S. interest rate differential, 623
U.S. interstate highways, 370
U.S. official reserves, 631
U.S. Treasury, 768
Used car market, 472–475
Utilitarianism, 116, 116–117

Utility, 181, 466
    choosing at margin, 184
    expected, 467–468
    marginal, 181, 184, 187–192
    maximizing, 183–186
    risk aversion and, 466
    temperature analogy, 192
    total, 181
    of wealth, 466–467

Vaccinations, 375
Value, 108. *See also* Present value
    of demand, 58
    GDP market, 490
    paradox of, 191
    store of, 591
Value of marginal product, 419, 433
Vanderbilt, W. H., 356
Variable money multipliers, 601
Variables
    having maximum and minimum
        points, 18–19
    more than two, 22–23
    moving in opposite direction, 17
    moving in same direction, 16–17
    unrelated, 19
Velocity of circulation, 606
Verizon, 313
VF Corporation, 326
Voluntary export restraint, 162
von Neumann, John, 344, 367
Voodoo economics, 737
Voucher, 383, 384, 415–416

Wachovia, 568
Wage rate
    aggregate supply related to change in,
        651
    human capital and, 450
    money, 703
    opportunity cost and, 423
    real, 520, 546
    trends in labor markets, 427
Wages, 4, 450. *See also* Minimum wage;
        Real wage rate
    demand-pull inflation and, 703
    efficiency, 520
    inequality in, 488
    rates, 423, 427, 485, 735
    reservation, 422
    union-nonunion gap in, 426
Wall Street firms, 565
Wal-Mart, 41, 165
Warranties, 474–475
Washington Mutual, 568
Water pollution, 394
Water shortage, case study, 118–119
Wealth, 444, 466, **566,** 573–574
    aggregate demand curve and, 685
    aggregate demand related to effect of,
        652–653, 685
    distribution of, 444
    economic inequality, 444–445
    education relating to, 446
    expected, 466
    income v., 444–445

intergenerational transfers of, 454
marriage and, 454
redistribution of, 522
saving and, 566
unequal, 454
utility of, 466–467
Wealth of Nations (Smith), **51,** 113, 414, 556
Web Ads (*Reading Between the Lines*), 244–245
Web browsers, 358
Welch, Finis, 133
Welfare, 455, 457
Wells Fargo, 568

Wendy's, 98
Westinghouse, 240
White Man's Burden (Easterly), 646
Williams, Serena, 453
William Wrigley Jr. Company, 239
Wimbledon, 453
Women, as better borrowers, 552
Wood, Stephen, 770
Woolf, Virginia, 723
Working-age population, 515
World Economic Forum, 645
The Worldly Philosophers (Heilbronner), 370
World Trade Organization (WTO), 54, **162**

World Wide Web, 227
Wright, Sanders, 32
Writers Guild of America, 425–426
WTO. *See* World Trade Organization

Yahoo!, 227, 244
Yen, 617, 618
YouTube, 316
Yuan, 498, 618

Zimbabwe, 522
Zvonareva, Vera, 453

Michael Parkin (page iv) John Tamblyn

College campus (page 1) Image Source/Getty Images

Parrot cartoon (page 2) Copyright © 1985 The New Yorker Collection/Frank Modell from cartoonbank.com. All Rights Reserved.

Sneaker factory (page 5) Adek Berry/Getty Images

Intel Chip (page 6) Imagebroker/Alamy

Pollution (page 6) Digital Vision

Lehman Brothers (page 7) Kurt Brady/Alamy

Corn (page 29) MNPhoto/Alamy

Ethanol gasoline pump (page 29) Alex Farnsworth/The Image Works

Boeing (page 41) Randy Duchaine/Alamy

Clothing factory (page 41) INSADCO Photography/Alamy

Smith (page 51) Bettmann/Corbis

Bhagwati (page 52) Michael Parkin

Gas prices (page 55) Justin Sullivan/Staff/Getty Images

Oil drill (page 69) Alberto Incrocci/Getty Images

Strawberry picking (page 71) Chris O'Meara/AP Images

Rotting tomato plants (page 83) Chris O'Meara/AP Images

Rose (page 105) Corbis Super RF/Alamy

Hot dog stand cartoon (page 113) Copyright © 1988 The New Yorker Collection/Mike Twohy from cartoonbank.com. All Rights Reserved.

Flower traders (page 121) Picture Contact/Alamy

Ted Kennedy (page 127) Win McNamee/Staff/Getty Images

FedEx planes (page 151) Oliver Berg/DPA/Corbis

Marshall (page 175) Stock Montage

Athey (page 176) Photo courtesy of Susan Athey

Ke$ha album (page 179) Photo courtesy of Deepa Chungi

e-reader (page 203) Chris Hackett/Getty Images

Wine cartoon (page 210) Copyright © 1988 The New Yorker Collection/Robert Weber from cartoonbank.com. All Rights Reserved.

Redbox (page 212) Justin Sullivan/Getty Images

Theater foyer (page 212) Corbis

Sony reader (page 216) Newscom

Bentham (page 223) Bettmann/Corbis

Levitt (page 224) Photo courtesy of Steven D. Levitt

Computer server room (page 227) Jetta Productions/Dana Neely/Blend Images/Corbis

Pizza (page 237) Michael Newman/PhotoEdit Inc.

Corn fields (page 237) Robert Glusic/Getty Images

Comcast (page 237) George Widman/AP Images

Boeing (page 237) Alastair Miller/Bloomberg News/Landov

iPhone (page 243) Oliver Leedham/Alamy

Electric plant (page 251) Jonutis/Shutterstock

Auto plant (page 265) Glowimages/Getty Images

Smart meter (page 267) Pat Sullivan/AP Images

Corn harvest (page 273) Woudew/Shutterstock

Motorcycle (page 283) Rena Schild/Shutterstock

Woman on Computer (page 285) Digital Vision/Getty Images

Tractor (page 285) Elena Elisseeva/Shutterstock

Google campus (page 299) Paul Sakuma/AP Images

Airline cartoon (page 312) William Hamilton

Sneaker display (page 323) Vario Images GmbH & Co. KG/Alamy

Computer store display (page 341) Paul Sakuma/AP Images

von Neumann (page 367) Topham/The Image Works

Hubbard (page 368) Photo Courtesy of Evanston Photographic Studios Inc.

Firefighters (page 371) Patti McConville/Getty Images

Lighthouse (page 275) Kenneth C. Zirkel/Getty Images\

Forest fire (page 379) Code Red/Getty Images

Kotlikoff (page 385) Kalman Zabarsky/ Boston University

The Healthcare Fox (page 385) The Healthcare Fix: Universal Insurance for All Americans by Laurence J. Kotlikoff, published by The MIT Press.

Pollution (page 393) Charlie Waite/Getty Images

Tragedy of the Commons (page 400) *River Valley with Swineherd; Hamlet Beyond* (ca 1600), Marten Ryckaert. Oil on panel. Private collection/Christie's Images/Bridgeman Art Library

Cod (page 401) Jeff Rotman/Getty Images

Coase (page 413) David Joel Photography

Hoxby (page 414) Caroline M. Hoxby/E.S. Lee

Nurse (page 417) Dana Neely/Getty Images

Homeless man (page 441) Getty Images, Inc.—Agence France Presse

Lemon car (page 465) iStockphoto

Malthus (page 485) Bettmann/Corbis

Card (page 486) David Card/Photo courtesy of Stuart Schwartz

Man at Computer (page 489) OJO Images Ltd/Alamy

American McDonalds (page 498) Scott Olson/Staff/ Getty Images

Asian McDonalds (page 498) Bloomberg via Getty Images

Chefs (page 499) AFP/Getty Images

Mother (page 499) AFP/Getty Images

Interview (page 513) Alexander Raths/Shutterstock

Great Depression (page 514) Library of Congress Prints and Photographs Division [LC-USZ62-63966]

Workers at Machine (page 520) Bloomberg/Getty Images

Hume (page 535) Print Collector/HIP/The Image Works

Clarida (page 536) Courtesy of author

Shangai (page 539) Image Source/Getty Images

The Rocket (page 551) National Railway Museum/SSPL/The Image Works

Outdoor market (page 552) Jose Silva Pinto/AP Images

Stock exchange (page 565) Richard Drew/AP Images

Fannie Mae (page 569) Frontpage/Shutterstock

Freddie Mac (page 569) Frontpage/Shutterstock

Greenspan (page 581) Scott J. Ferrell/Congressional Quarterly/Getty Image

Credit card (page 589) VladKol/Shutterstock

Exchange desk (page 617) Greg Balfour Evans/Alamy

Schumpeter (page 643) Bettmann/Corbis

Sala-i-Martin (page 644) Courtesy of author

Construction worker (page 647) Joe Gough/Shutterstock

Harry Reid, et all (page 654) Evan Vucci/AP Images

Bernanke (page 654) Susan Walsh/AP Images

Trichet (page 654) Bernd Kammerer/AP Images

King (page 654) Martin Rickett/AP Images

Carney (page 654) Adrian Wyld/The Canadian Press/AP Images

Seattle port (page 671) Gabe Palmer/Alamy

Couple paying bills (page 701) Jose Luis Pelaez Inc/Getty Images

Maynard Keyes (page 723) Stock Montage

Caballero (page 724) Courtesy of author

Capitol Building (page 727) Jonathan Larsen/Shutterstock

Obama signing Fiscal Act (page 742) Pete Souza/The White House

Romer (page 745) Photo by Peg Skorpinski

Barro (page 745) Courtesy of Robert J. Barro, Harvard University

Uhlig (page 745) Courtesy of Harlad Uhlig

Federal Reserve (page 753) Jonathan Larsen/Shutterstock

Beige Book (page 758) US Federal Reserve

Fed board meeting (page 758) Courtesy of the Federal Reserve Bank of Philadelphia

Freidman (page 777) Marshall Heinrichs/Addison Wesley

Schmitt Grohe (page 778) Courtesy of author

Quincy Market in Boston, Massachusetts, USA (cover) Medioimages/Photodisc

The Pearson Series in Economics

Abel/Bernanke/Croushore
Macroeconomics*

Bade/Parkin
Foundations of Economics*

Berck/Helfand
The Economics of the Environment

Bierman/Fernandez
Game Theory with Economic Applications

Blanchard
Macroeconomics*

Blau/Ferber/Winkler
The Economics of Women, Men and Work

Boardman/Greenberg/ Vining/ Weimer
Cost-Benefit Analysis

Boyer
Principles of Transportation Economics

Branson
Macroeconomic Theory and Policy

Brock/Adams
The Structure of American Industry

Bruce
Public Finance and the American Economy

Carlton/Perloff
Modern Industrial Organization

Case/Fair/Oster
Principles of Economics*

Caves/Frankel/Jones
World Trade and Payments: An Introduction

Chapman
Environmental Economics: Theory, Application, and Policy

Cooter/Ulen
Law & Economics

Downs
An Economic Theory of Democracy

Ehrenberg/Smith
Modern Labor Economics

Ekelund/Ressler/Tollison
Economics*

Farnham
Economics for Managers

Folland/Goodman/Stano
The Economics of Health and Health Care

Fort
Sports Economics

Froyen
Macroeconomics

Fusfeld
The Age of the Economist

Gerber
International Economics*

Gordon
Macroeconomics*

Greene
Econometric Analysis

Gregory
Essentials of Economics

Gregory/Stuart
Russian and Soviet Economic Performance and Structure

Hartwick/Olewiler
The Economics of Natural Resource Use

Heilbroner/Milberg
The Making of the Economic Society

Heyne/Boettke/Prychitko
The Economic Way of Thinking

Hoffman/Averett
Women and the Economy: Family, Work, and Pay

Holt
Markets, Games and Strategic Behavior

Hubbard/O'Brien
Economics*
Money and Banking*

Hughes/Cain
American Economic History

Husted/Melvin
International Economics

Jehle/Reny
Advanced Microeconomic Theory

Johnson-Lans
A Health Economics Primer

Keat/Young
Managerial Economics

Klein
Mathematical Methods for Economics

Krugman/Obstfeld/Melitz
International Economics: Theory & Policy*

Laidler
The Demand for Money

Leeds/von Allmen
The Economics of Sports

Leeds/von Allmen/Schiming
Economics*

Lipsey/Ragan/Storer
Economics*

Lynn
Economic Development: Theory and Practice for a Divided World

Miller
Economics Today*
Understanding Modern Economics

Miller/Benjamin
The Economics of Macro Issues

Miller/Benjamin/North
The Economics of Public Issues

Mills/Hamilton
Urban Economics

Mishkin
The Economics of Money, Banking, and Financial Markets*
The Economics of Money, Banking, and Financial Markets, Business School Edition*
Macroeconomics: Policy and Practice*

Murray
Econometrics: A ModernIntroduction

Nafziger
The Economics of Developing Countries

O'Sullivan/Sheffrin/Perez
Economics: Principles, Applications and Tools*

Parkin
Economics*

Perloff
Microeconomics*
Microeconomics: Theory and Applications with Calculus*

Perman/Common/ McGilvray/Ma
Natural Resources and Environmental Economics

Phelps
Health Economics

Pindyck/Rubinfeld
Microeconomics*

Riddell/Shackelford/Stamos/ Schneider
Economics: A Tool for Critically Understanding Society

Ritter/Silber/Udell
Principles of Money, Banking & Financial Markets*

Roberts
The Choice: A Fable of Free Trade and Protection

Rohlf
Introduction to Economic Reasoning

Ruffin/Gregory
Principles of Economics

Sargent
Rational Expectations and Inflation

Sawyer/Sprinkle
International Economics

Scherer
Industry Structure, Strategy, and Public Policy

Schiller
The Economics of Poverty and Discrimination

Sherman
Market Regulation

Silberberg
Principles of Microeconomics

Stock/Watson
Introduction to Econometrics
Introduction to Econometrics, Brief Edition

Studenmund
Using Econometrics: A Practical Guide

Tietenberg/Lewis
Environmental and Natural Resource Economics
Environmental Economics and Policy

Todaro/Smith
Economic Development

Waldman
Microeconomics

Waldman/Jensen
Industrial Organization: Theory and Practice

Weil
Economic Growth

Williamson
Macroeconomics

Macroeconomic Data

These macroeconomic data series show some of the trends in GDP and its components, the price level, and other variables that provide information about changes in the standard of living and the cost of living—the central questions of macroeconomics. You will find these data in a spreadsheet that you can download from your MyEconLab Web site.

NATIONAL INCOME AND PRODUCT ACCOUNTS			1964	1965	1966	1967	1968	1969	1970	1971	1972	1973
		EXPENDITURE APPROACH										
the sum of	1	Personal consumption expenditures	411.5	443.8	480.9	507.8	558.0	605.1	648.3	701.6	770.2	852.0
	2	Gross private domestic investment	102.1	118.2	131.3	128.6	141.2	156.4	152.4	178.2	207.6	244.5
	3	Government expenditure	143.2	151.4	171.6	192.5	209.3	221.4	233.7	246.4	263.4	281.7
	4	Exports	35.0	37.1	40.9	43.5	47.9	51.9	59.7	63.0	70.8	95.3
less	5	Imports	28.1	31.5	37.1	39.9	46.6	50.5	55.8	62.3	74.2	91.2
equals	6	Gross domestic product	663.6	719.1	787.7	832.4	909.8	984.4	1,038.3	1,126.8	1,237.9	1,382.3
		INCOME APPROACH										
	7	Compensation of employees	370.7	399.5	442.6	475.1	524.3	577.6	617.2	658.9	725.1	811.2
plus	8	Net operating surplus	171.2	189.7	203.2	205.8	218.6	225.5	219.3	243.3	275.4	310.2
equals	9	Net domestic income at factor cost	541.9	589.2	645.8	680.9	742.9	803.1	836.5	902.2	1,000.5	1,121.4
	10	Indirect taxes less subsidies	54.6	57.7	59.3	64.1	72.2	79.4	86.6	95.8	101.3	112.0
plus	11	Depreciation (capital consumption)	66.4	70.7	76.5	82.9	90.4	99.2	108.3	117.8	127.2	140.8
	12	GDP (income approach)	662.9	717.6	781.6	827.9	905.5	981.7	1,031.4	1,115.8	1,229.0	1,374.2
	13	Statistical discrepancy	0.8	1.5	6.2	4.5	4.3	2.9	6.9	11.0	8.9	8.0
equals	14	GDP (expenditure approach)	663.7	719.1	787.8	832.4	909.8	984.6	1,038.3	1,126.8	1,237.9	1,382.2
	15	Real GDP (billions of 2005 dollars)	3,392.3	3,610.1	3,845.3	3,942.5	4,133.4	4,261.8	4,269.9	4,413.3	4,647.7	4,917.0
	16	Real GDP growth rate (percent per year)	5.8	6.4	6.5	2.5	4.8	3.1	0.2	3.4	5.3	5.8
OTHER DATA												
	17	Population (millions)	191.9	194.3	196.6	198.8	200.7	202.7	205.1	207.7	209.9	211.9
	18	Labor force (millions)	73.1	74.4	75.7	77.3	78.7	80.7	82.8	84.4	87.0	89.4
	19	Employment (millions)	69.3	71.1	72.9	74.4	75.9	77.9	78.7	79.4	82.1	85.1
	20	Unemployment (millions)	3.8	3.4	2.9	3.0	2.8	2.8	4.1	5.0	4.9	4.4
	21	Labor force participation rate (percent of working-age population)	58.7	58.9	59.2	59.6	59.6	60.1	60.4	60.2	60.4	60.8
	22	Unemployment rate (percent of labor force)	5.2	4.5	3.8	3.8	3.5	3.5	5.0	6.0	5.6	4.9
	23	Real GDP per person (2005 dollars per year)	17,675	18,576	19,559	19,836	20,590	21,021	20,820	21,249	22,140	23,200
	24	Growth rate of real GDP per person (percent per year)	4.3	5.1	5.3	1.4	3.8	2.1	–1.0	2.1	4.2	4.8
	25	Quantity of money (M2, billions of dollars)	424.7	459.2	480.2	524.8	566.8	587.9	626.5	710.3	802.3	855.5
	26	GDP deflator (2005 = 100)	19.6	19.9	20.5	21.1	22.0	23.1	24.3	25.5	26.6	28.1
	27	GDP deflator inflation rate (percent per year)	1.6	1.8	2.9	3.1	4.3	5.0	5.3	5.0	4.3	5.5
	28	Price index (1982–1984 = 100)	31.0	31.5	32.4	33.4	34.8	36.7	38.8	40.5	41.8	44.4
	29	CPI inflation rate (percent per year)	1.3	1.6	2.9	3.1	4.2	5.5	5.7	4.4	3.2	6.2
	30	Current account balance (billions of dollars)	6.8	5.4	3.0	2.6	0.6	0.4	2.3	–1.4	–5.8	7.1

1974	1975	1976	1977	1978	1979	1980	1981	1982	1983	1984	1985	1986
932.9	1,033.8	1,151.3	1,277.8	1,427.6	1,591.2	1,755.8	1,939.5	2,075.5	2,288.6	2,501.1	2,717.6	2,896.7
249.4	230.2	292.0	361.3	438.0	492.9	479.3	572.4	517.2	564.3	735.6	736.2	746.5
317.9	357.7	383.0	414.1	453.6	500.7	566.1	627.5	680.4	733.4	796.9	878.9	949.3
126.7	138.7	149.5	159.4	186.9	230.1	280.8	305.2	283.2	277.0	302.4	302.0	320.3
127.5	122.7	151.1	182.4	212.3	252.7	293.8	317.8	303.2	328.6	405.1	417.2	452.9
1,499.5	1,637.7	1,824.6	2,030.1	2,293.8	2,562.2	2,788.1	3,126.8	3,253.2	3,534.6	3,930.9	4,217.5	4,460.1
890.3	949.2	1,059.4	1,180.6	1,335.6	1,498.4	1,647.7	1,819.8	1,919.8	2,035.7	2,245.7	2,412.0	2,559.4
314.1	351.0	392.3	444.0	508.8	546.4	560.6	652.9	669.2	756.1	910.6	971.0	995.9
1,204.4	1,300.2	1,451.7	1,624.6	1,844.4	2,044.8	2,208.3	2,472.7	2,589.0	2,791.8	3,156.3	3,383.0	3,555.3
121.6	130.8	141.3	152.6	162.0	171.6	190.5	224.1	225.9	242.0	268.7	286.7	298.5
163.7	190.4	208.2	231.8	261.4	298.9	344.1	393.3	433.5	451.1	474.3	505.4	538.5
1,489.7	1,621.4	1,801.2	2,009.0	2,267.8	2,515.3	2,742.9	3,090.1	3,248.4	3,484.9	3,899.3	4,175.1	4,392.3
9.8	16.3	23.5	21.2	26.1	47.0	45.3	36.6	4.8	49.7	31.5	42.3	67.7
1,499.5	1,637.7	1,824.7	2,030.2	2,293.9	2,562.3	2,788.2	3,126.7	3,253.2	3,534.6	3,930.8	4,217.4	4,460.0
4,889.9	4,879.5	5,141.3	5,377.7	5,677.6	5,855.0	5,839.0	5,987.2	5,870.9	6,136.2	6,577.1	6,849.3	7,086.5
–0.6	–0.2	5.4	4.6	5.6	3.1	–0.3	2.5	–1.9	4.5	7.2	4.1	3.5
213.9	216.0	218.1	220.3	222.6	225.1	227.7	230.0	232.2	234.3	236.4	238.5	240.7
92.0	93.8	96.2	99.0	102.2	105.0	107.0	108.7	110.2	111.5	113.5	115.5	117.8
86.8	85.8	88.8	92.0	96.0	98.8	99.3	100.4	99.5	100.8	105.0	107.2	109.6
5.2	7.9	7.4	7.0	6.2	6.1	7.7	8.3	10.7	10.7	8.5	8.3	8.2
61.3	61.2	61.6	62.2	63.2	63.7	63.8	63.9	64.0	64.0	64.4	64.8	65.3
5.6	8.5	7.7	7.0	6.1	5.9	7.2	7.6	9.7	9.6	7.5	7.2	7.0
22,861	22,592	23,575	24,412	25,503	26,010	25,640	26,030	25,282	26,186	27,823	28,718	29,443
–1.5	–1.2	4.3	3.6	4.5	2.0	–1.4	1.5	–2.9	3.6	6.3	3.2	2.5
902.1	1,016.2	1,152.0	1,270.3	1,366.0	1,473.7	1,599.8	1,755.5	1,909.3	2,125.7	2,308.8	2,494.6	2,731.4
30.7	33.6	35.5	37.8	40.4	43.8	47.8	52.2	55.4	57.6	59.8	61.6	62.9
9.1	9.4	5.7	6.4	7.0	8.3	9.1	9.4	6.1	4.0	3.8	3.0	2.2
49.3	53.8	56.9	60.6	65.2	72.6	82.4	90.9	96.5	99.6	103.9	107.6	109.6
11.0	9.1	5.8	6.5	7.6	11.3	13.5	10.3	6.2	3.2	4.3	3.6	1.9
2.0	18.1	4.3	–14.3	–15.1	–0.3	2.3	5.0	–5.5	–38.7	–94.3	–118.2	–147.2

Macroeconomic Data

These macroeconomic data series show some of the trends in GDP and its components, the price level, and other variables that provide information about changes in the standard of living and the cost of living—the central questions of macroeconomics. You will find these data in a spreadsheet that you can download from your MyEconLab Web site.

	NATIONAL INCOME AND PRODUCT ACCOUNTS	1987	1988	1989	1990	1991	1992	1993	1994	1995	1996
	EXPENDITURE APPROACH										
the sum of	1 Personal consumption expenditures	3,097.0	3,350.1	3,594.5	3,835.5	3,980.1	4,236.9	4,483.6	4,750.8	4,987.3	5,273.6
	2 Gross private domestic investment	785.0	821.6	874.9	861.0	802.9	864.8	953.3	1,097.3	1,144.0	1,240.2
	3 Government expenditure	999.4	1,038.9	1,100.6	1,181.7	1,236.1	1,273.5	1,294.8	1,329.8	1,374.0	1,421.0
	4 Exports	363.8	443.9	503.1	552.1	596.6	635.0	655.6	720.7	811.9	867.7
less	5 Imports	508.7	554.0	591.0	629.7	623.5	667.8	720.0	813.4	902.6	964.0
equals	6 Gross domestic product	4,736.4	5,100.4	5,482.1	5,800.5	5,992.1	6,342.3	6,667.4	7,085.2	7,414.7	7,838.5
	INCOME APPROACH										
	7 Compensation of employees	2,737.0	2,955.0	3,132.6	3,328.6	3,441.1	3,634.4	3,800.4	4,002.5	4,199.3	4,395.5
plus	8 Net operating surplus	1,078.1	1,199.0	1,270.6	1,298.6	1,317.3	1,400.3	1,486.7	1,641.9	1,770.3	1,959.0
equals	9 Net domestic income at factor cost	3,815.1	4,154.0	4,403.2	4,627.2	4,758.4	5,034.7	5,287.1	5,644.4	5,969.6	6,354.5
	10 Indirect taxes less subsidies	317.2	345.0	371.5	398.0	429.6	453.3	466.4	512.7	523.1	545.6
plus	11 Depreciation (capital consumption)	571.1	611.0	651.5	691.2	724.4	744.4	778.0	819.2	869.5	912.5
	12 GDP (income approach)	4,703.4	5,110.0	5,426.2	5,716.4	5,912.4	6,232.4	6,531.5	6,976.3	7,362.2	7,812.6
	13 Statistical discrepancy	32.9	−9.5	56.1	84.2	79.7	110.0	135.8	108.8	52.5	25.9
equals	14 GDP (expenditure approach)	4,736.3	5,100.5	5,482.3	5,800.6	5,992.1	6,342.4	6,667.3	7,085.1	7,414.7	7,838.5
	15 Real GDP (billions of 2005 dollars)	7,313.3	7,613.9	7,885.9	8,033.9	8,015.1	8,287.1	8,523.4	8,870.7	9,093.7	9,433.9
	16 Real GDP growth rate (percent per year)	3.2	4.1	3.6	1.9	−0.2	3.4	2.9	4.1	2.5	3.7
	OTHER DATA										
	17 Population (millions)	242.8	245.1	247.4	250.2	253.5	256.9	260.3	263.5	266.6	269.7
	18 Labor force (millions)	119.9	121.7	123.9	125.9	126.4	128.1	129.2	131.0	132.3	134.0
	19 Employment (millions)	112.4	115.0	117.3	118.8	117.7	118.5	120.3	123.1	124.9	126.7
	20 Unemployment (millions)	7.4	6.7	6.5	7.1	8.6	9.6	8.9	8.0	7.4	7.2
	21 Labor force participation rate (percent of working-age population)	65.6	65.9	66.4	66.5	66.2	66.5	66.3	66.6	66.6	66.8
	22 Unemployment rate (percent of labor force)	6.2	5.5	5.3	5.6	6.9	7.5	6.9	6.1	5.6	5.4
	23 Real GDP per person (2005 dollars per year)	30,115	31,069	31,877	32,112	31,614	32,255	32,747	33,671	34,111	34,977
	24 Growth rate of real GDP per person (percent per year)	2.3	3.2	2.6	0.7	−1.6	2.0	1.5	2.8	1.3	2.5
	25 Quantity of money (M2, billions of dollars)	2,830.8	2,993.9	3,158.4	3,276.8	3,377.0	3,430.2	3,480.7	3,496.5	3,640.3	3,819.6
	26 GDP deflator (2005 = 100)	64.8	67.0	69.5	72.2	74.8	76.5	78.2	79.9	81.5	83.1
	27 GDP deflator inflation rate (percent per year)	2.9	3.4	3.8	3.9	3.5	2.4	2.2	2.1	2.1	1.9
	28 Price index (1982–1984 = 100)	113.6	118.3	124.0	130.7	136.2	140.3	144.5	148.2	152.4	156.9
	29 CPI inflation rate (percent per year)	3.6	4.1	4.8	5.4	4.2	3.0	3.0	2.6	2.8	3.0
	30 Current account balance (billions of dollars)	−160.7	−121.2	−99.5	−79.0	2.9	−51.6	−84.8	−121.6	−113.6	−124.8

1997	1998	1999	2000	2001	2002	2003	2004	2005	2006	2007	2008	2009
5,570.6	5,918.5	6,342.8	6,830.4	7,148.8	7,439.2	7,804.0	8,285.1	8,819.0	9,322.7	9,806.3	10,104.5	10,001.3
1,388.7	1,510.8	1,641.5	1,772.2	1,661.9	1,647.0	1,729.7	1,968.6	2,172.2	2,327.2	2,295.2	2,096.7	1,589.2
1,474.4	1,526.1	1,631.3	1,731.0	1,846.4	1,983.3	2,112.6	2,232.8	2,369.9	2,518.4	2,674.2	2,878.3	2,914.9
954.4	953.9	989.3	1,093.2	1,027.7	1,003.0	1,041.0	1,180.2	1,305.1	1,471.0	1,661.7	1,843.4	1,578.4
1,055.8	1,115.7	1,251.4	1,475.3	1,398.7	1,430.2	1,545.1	1,798.9	2,027.8	2,240.3	2,375.7	2,553.8	1,964.7
8,332.4	8,793.5	9,353.5	9,951.5	10,286.2	10,642.3	11,142.1	11,867.8	12,638.4	13,398.9	14,061.8	14,369.1	14,119.0
4,670.0	5,027.8	5,359.2	5,793.5	5,984.5	6,116.4	6,388.3	6,699.6	7,071.5	7,483.6	7,863.0	8,068.1	7,819.5
2,134.7	2,227.4	2,342.6	2,444.9	2,479.8	2,521.6	2,625.4	2,926.3	3,236.0	3,539.7	3,437.5	3,322.8	3,294.9
6,804.7	7,255.2	7,701.8	8,238.4	8,464.3	8,638.0	9,013.7	9,625.9	10,307.5	11,023.3	11,300.5	11,390.9	11,114.4
577.8	603.1	628.4	662.8	669.0	721.4	757.7	817.0	869.3	935.4	972.6	992.3	964.4
963.8	1,020.5	1,094.4	1,184.3	1,256.2	1,305.0	1,354.1	1,432.8	1,541.4	1,660.7	1,767.5	1,849.2	1,861.1
8,346.3	8,878.8	9,424.6	10,085.5	10,389.5	10,664.4	11,125.5	11,875.7	12,718.2	13,619.4	14,040.6	14,232.4	13,939.9
−14.0	−85.3	−71.1	−134.0	−103.4	−22.1	16.6	−7.8	−79.7	−220.6	21.1	136.6	179.1
8,332.3	8,793.5	9,353.5	9,951.5	10,286.1	10,642.3	11,142.1	11,867.9	12,638.5	13,398.8	14,061.7	14,369.0	14,119.0
9,854.3	10,283.5	10,779.8	11,226.0	11,347.2	11,553.0	11,840.7	12,263.8	12,638.4	12,976.2	13,228.9	13,228.8	12,880.6
4.5	4.4	4.8	4.1	1.1	1.8	2.5	3.6	3.1	2.7	1.9	0.0	−2.6
273.0	276.2	279.3	282.4	285.3	288.1	290.8	293.5	296.2	299.1	302.0	304.8	307.5
136.3	137.7	139.4	142.6	143.8	144.9	146.5	147.4	149.3	151.4	153.1	154.3	154.2
129.6	131.5	133.5	136.9	136.9	136.5	137.7	139.2	141.7	144.4	146.0	145.4	139.9
6.7	6.2	5.9	5.7	6.8	8.4	8.8	8.1	7.6	7.0	7.1	9.0	14.3
67.1	67.1	67.1	67.1	66.9	66.6	66.2	66.0	66.0	66.2	66.0	66.0	65.4
5.0	4.5	4.2	4.0	4.7	5.8	6.0	5.5	5.1	4.6	4.6	5.8	9.3
36,102	37,238	38,592	39,750	39,768	40,096	40,711	41,784	42,664	43,391	43,801	43,397	41,890
3.2	3.1	3.6	3.0	0.0	0.8	1.5	2.6	2.1	1.7	0.9	−0.9	−3.5
4,033.0	4,376.3	4,634.6	4,917.9	5,434.1	5,785.9	6,073.7	6,415.2	6,679.2	7,079.5	7,509.4	8,241.6	8,524.3
84.6	85.5	86.8	88.6	90.6	92.1	94.1	96.8	100.0	103.3	106.3	108.6	109.6
1.8	1.1	1.5	2.2	2.3	1.6	2.2	2.8	3.3	3.3	2.9	2.2	0.9
160.5	163	166.6	172.2	177.1	179.9	184.0	188.9	195.3	201.6	207.3	215.3	214.5
2.3	1.6	2.2	3.4	2.8	1.6	2.3	2.7	3.4	3.2	2.8	3.8	−0.4
−140.7	−215.1	−300.8	−416.4	−397.2	−458.1	−520.7	−630.5	−747.6	−802.6	−718.1	−668.9	−378.4

READING BETWEEN THE LINES

Reading Between the Lines, which appears at the end of each chapter, helps students think like economists by connecting chapter tools and concepts to the world around them.

2   Fuel Choices, Food Crises, and Finger-Pointing   44

3   Coffee Surges on Poor Colombian Harvests   74

4   Frigid Florida Winter Is Bad News for Tomato Lovers   98

5   More Ash Fallout: 10 Million Roses Ruined   120

6   Bipartisan Plan to Crack Down on California's Underground Economy   144

7   China: Tire Trade Penalties Will Hurt Relations with U.S.   168

8   Salaries, Strong Recruitment Ease Area Paramedic Shortage   196

      Ducks Give Perry $26.6 Million Deal   196

9   Amazon.com E-Book Sales Exceed Hardcovers for First Time   216

10   Facebook Makes Gains in Web Ads   244

11   Here Come the "Smart" Meters   266

12   Bumper Harvests Bring Stability   292

13   Data Show Google Abuses Search Role, Group Contends   316

14   Apple Sues Rival HTC as Phone Competition Rises   334

15   Battle for Beards Heats Up   360

16   Protective Net for All Residents; Q&A Legislation Details   386

17   Oil Spill Pushes Carbon Tax Back into Spotlight   406

18   Outlook for Job Market Is Grim; When Jobs Do Return, Many Won't Pay Well   432

19   What Happened to All That Anger Over CEO Pay?   458

20   Princeton Leads in Grade Deflation   478

21   Shape of Recovery Long, Slow Growth … a "Square Root" Slog   502

22   U.S. Labor Force Shrinks Amid Jobs Market Woes   528

23   China Pips Japan but "Still a Developing Nation"   558

24   "Borrowing to Live" Weighs on Families, Firms, Nation   582

25   It Falls to the Fed to Fuel Recovery   608

26   Dollar Faces Increasingly Strong Set of Headwinds   636

27   GDP Figures Revised Downward   664

28   Business Inventories Post Biggest Gain in 2 Years   690

29   Evidence and Denial; Obama Advisers Refuse to Believe They're Failing   716

30   Republicans' Two-Point Plan to Create Jobs: Can It Work?   746

31   Poor U.S. Jobs Data Open Way for Stimulus   770